THE
ANALYTICAL LEXICON
TO THE
SEPTUAGINT

A COMPLETE PARSING GUIDE

BERNARD A. TAYLOR

ZondervanPublishingHouse
Grand Rapids, Michigan

A Division of HarperCollinsPublishers

Dedication

Dedicated to the memory of my father

Fred L. Taylor

whose love of learning was contagious

Analytical Lexicon to the Septuagint
Copyright ©1994 by Bernard Taylor

Requests for information should be addressed to:
Zondervan Publishing House
Grand Rapids, MI 49530

Library of Congress Cataloging in Publication Data

Taylor, Bernard A. (Bernard Alwyn), 1944-
    Analytical lexicon to the Septuagint: a complete parsing guide / Bernard A. Taylor
      p.   cm.
    ISBN 0-310-53540-9
    1. Bible. O.T. Greek—Versions—Septuagint—Language, style. 2. Greek language, Biblical—
Parsing. 3. Greek language, Biblical—Dictionaries. I. Title.
    BS744.T38   1994
    221.4'8'03—dc20   94-11720
                                                            CIP

Cover design by Dennis Hill

Printed in the United States of America

94 95 96 97 98 99 /DC/ 10 9 8 7 6 5 4 3 2 1

This edition is printed on acid-free paper and meets the American National Standards Institute Z39.48
standard.

Contents

Preface

In this lexicon all the words of the Rahlfs text of the Septuagint are fully parsed, and the dictionary form for each word is listed. This simple statement belies the complex history that has brought the work to this point.

In 1969-70, the International Organization for Septuagint and Cognate Studies (IOSCS) proposed that work begin on a project to create a modern lexicon for the Septuagint (LXX), and appointed Emanuel Tov of Hebrew University (Jerusalem) editor-designate. In 1974 he became editor. When linked to the resources being developed by Robert Kraft at the University of Pennsylvania, the project was under way. Known still by its original name, Computer Assisted Tools for Septuagint studies (CATSS) became co-directed by Kraft and Tov, and was from the outset dedicated to utilizing computer technology.

Of the various activities begun under the project it was the morphological analysis that was the direct ancestor of this analytical lexicon. By the early 1980s the LXX was in machine-readable form, having been encoded by the Thesaurus Linguae Graecae (TLG) project, based at University of California, Irvine, under the direction of Theodore Brunner. David Packard had written a morphological analysis program for classical Greek, and he adapted this program to *koine* Greek for the CATSS project, and it was run on the TLG text. As the CATSS programmers gained experience, they added some items to the program's routines to make it more accurate with the LXX materials. Even so, it never did analyze all of the forms.

Once the program had run, the analysis was checked and rechecked over a period of years by a cadre of University of Pennsylvania graduate students, under the successive leadership of Bill Adler, Ben Wright, and Ted Bergren.

Under the Penn-Israel exchange program, Emanuel Tov spent the 1980-81 academic year at the University of Pennsylvania. I met him that winter for the first time when he came to present a paper at Hebrew Union College in Cincinnati (Ohio) where I was a graduate student. Some two or three months later he called to invite me to become an adjunct member of the CATSS project. In the summer of 1981 I traveled to Philadelphia to meet with him, and in turn he introduced me to Kraft and the CATSS preliminary work already under way.

Based upon my frustrating attempts to read the LXX on my own back in Australia, I had brought with me to the United States in 1978 a dream of preparing a LXX analytical lexicon, though at the time I knew nothing of computers. When I saw their potential, I expressed an interest to Kraft, both in person and in writing, in publishing a lexicon in "hard copy" based on the CATSS database.

In the meantime, the CATSS project received its first major funding in 1982, a two-year grant from the National Endowment for the Humanities (later to be extended by renewals through 1994), after four years of planning and preparation. The morphological analysis was completed in 1987 and released on the first Packard Humanities Institute CD-ROM late that year. Two years later I completed my graduate studies and was able to begin preliminary work on the analytical lexicon. Discussions were initiated with Zondervan that year, and in January 1990 the contract was signed.

Following the initial release of the morphological analysis in 1987 it became clear that it was in need of further work, and so the analysis was revised under the leadership of Ted Bergren. I received a copy of this second edition, and my work began in earnest. As it turned out, considerably more work remained than originally estimated, since errors, inconsistencies, and lacunae were still present in the database.

The first step was to create a new database consisting of one each of all the different entries. Any variation whatsoever in the three categories in each record—lemma (in this context the word from the Rahlfs text), morphological analysis, and dictionary form—warranted a separate entry at this point. Next, this database was sorted by dictionary form. Packard's program separated verbal prepositional prefixes from the root for verbs in this category. One of the more challenging aspects was to recombine these, since not all follow the standard crasis patterns. Next, all of the dictionary forms were checked against Hatch and Redpath's Concordance, and inconsistencies and errors were corrected. After this, the database was sorted by lemma, and on two successive passes over the last four years each entry has been checked. Beyond that, numerous words and word-types have been searched and corrected in the interests of overall consistency.

One could wish that all errors have thereby been eliminated, but reality indicates this is unlikely, even though there are far fewer now. The next phase involves the scholars and students who use the lexicon. The author can be contacted through the publisher, and errors found will be corrected in subsequent editions.

My thanks go, then, to all of those named above for their vision and hard work, but also to the larger group that toiled in the project, most of whom are unknown to me.

Second, I would like to thank Ed van der Maas, the Zondervan editor with whom I have been privileged to work, for his initial and ongoing enthusiasm for this Lexicon, as well as his personal friendship.

Finally, my heartfelt thanks to my family: Alyna, Clynton, Danelle. For over five years they have shared the dream while enduring the delay.

Bernard Taylor
Loma Linda, CA
September 15, 1994

Introduction

I. Overview

The classical scholar cannot but be shocked when first reading the Septuagint (LXX). Like the experience of Isaac when being deceived into granting the birthright to his younger son Jacob: the words are Greek, but the syntax is Hebrew. For the most part, the Greek is not classical, but *koine*. The enticing conclusion to be drawn from this is that a vast gulf must exist between the two. In fact this is not the case. For the most part one may use either classical or New Testament (NT) paradigms to study the LXX, since they share so much in common.

Although far from complete, several LXX grammars exist. The primary focus of much of this work is upon the differences between classical and *koine* Greek. When this is the focus of attention, the differences are numerous. Yet they easily belie the commonality that exists. Once this was fully understood, the process of checking the data was simplified, since many apparent exceptions could be recognized as errors.

a. The Rahlfs Text

In retrospect, the publication of the Rahlfs text[1] in 1935 was a watershed in Septuagintal studies. Its immediate predecessor, the three volume Swete text[2], which formed the running text for the Larger Cambridge Septuagint,[3] was based on Codex Vaticanus, supplemented from other uncial manuscripts. In contrast, the Rahlfs text is a (semi-)critical edition based on the three uncial manuscripts Alexandrinus (A), Vaticanus (B), and Sinaiticus (ℵ), but also citing the evidence of other sources such as Origen's *Hexapla*, the Complutensian Polyglot, and the Lucianic text. Like the Swete text, the Rahlfs text is complete, and to this date is still the only complete critical text.[4] This *Lexicon* is based on the Rahlfs text, not including the variants listed in the critical apparatus.

---

[1] A. Rahlfs, *Septuaginta, id est Vetus Testmentum Graece iuxta LXX Interpretes*. 2 vols., Stuttgart, 1935.

[2] H. B. Swete, *The Old Testament in Greek according to the Septuagint*. 3 vols., Cambridge 1887-1912.

[3] A. E. Brooke, and N. McLean, with H. St J. Thackeray, *The Old Testament in Greek According to the Text of Codex Vaticanus, Supplemented from Other Uncial Manuscripts, with a Critical Apparatus containing the Variants of the Chief Ancient Authorities for the Text of the Septuagint*. 3 vols. 1906-1940.

[4] The Rahlfs text is being superseded book-by-book by the volumes of the Göttingen Septuagint as they become available. This is a full critical edition.

For the most part, manuscripts did not have any accents, breathing marks, or punctuation. Rather, these are supplied by the editors of the modern texts. While in the main the meaning is crystal clear, inevitably some readings are open to alternative interpretations.[5] In this *Lexicon*, all words and forms, including those of proper nouns, are parsed, and parsed in the context of the Rahlfs text.

As is perhaps inevitable, the Rahlfs text is not without typographical errors. Their existence is established by first of all checking to see whether Rahlfs has a note in the apparatus to account for the particular form. Where they are included, these notes are a mine of information since at times they go beyond simply recording the manuscript evidence to citing page numbers in works such as Thackeray's Grammar.[6] Where there is no such note, or the evidence is inconclusive, the other relevant and available texts[7] were compared for the word in question. On the basis of these it was possible to determine which words are errors.

Errors are noted in the lexicon according to the formula "xxx *see* yyy":

ἐπελειώθη *see* ἐπελιώθη
αὐτός *see* αὐτός.

In addition to citing errors, this formula is also used to list the full word for elided forms, such as:

ἀλλ᾽ see ἀλλά.

In the case of crasis, forms are listed in the text in the following manner:

τἀνδρός = τοῦ + ἀνδρός.

The parsing of all such words is found at the appropriate place in the alphabetical listings.

b. Dictionary Forms

For each entry, the root form is listed so that the user is able to locate the word and its meanings in a lexicon. At the present time, however, no standard LXX lexicon exists, though two are currently in production.[8]

---

[5]An example of this is found in 1 Rgn 24:17:

     Rahlfs: ἡ φωνή σου
     Cambridge: ἡ φωνή σου.

The same expression is also found in 1 Rgn 26:17.

[6]Henry St. John Thackeray, *A Grammar of the Old Testament in Greek*. Cambridge, 1909.

[7]Göttingen, The Larger Cambridge Septuagint, the portions of text included in Hatch and Redpath, and Bagster. The last, *The Septuagint Version of the Old Testament, with an English Translation; and with various readings and critical notes*, Samuel Bagster & Sons, 1851, includes the translation by Sir Lancelot C. L. Brenton, and was republished by Zondervan in 1970.

[8]*A Greek-English Lexicon of the Septuagint*, Part I [of three], compiled by J. Lust, E. Eynikel and K. Haupsie, Stuttgart, 1992; and T. Muraoka, *A Greek-English Lexicon of the Septuagint*, Louvain, 1993 (Twelve Prophets).

While it was in print and available, the work of Schleusner[9] helped in this regard, though it was not without its problems. In the final analysis, its *forte* was in the area of Greek-Hebrew parallels, rather than precise meanings of the words. Were it still in print, it would be of little practical use for most, since it was in Latin.

Some progress can be made using the standard NT lexicons, but according to Abbot-Smith, whose *Manual Lexicon*[10] was a pioneer in sensitivity to the importance of the LXX in understanding NT vocabulary, these cover only 40% of the LXX words.[11]

In the meantime, then, the only available work has been the standard classical Greek lexicon of Liddell and Scott.[12] While this volume does not ignore *koine* Greek, it does not do it justice. Consequently, LXX forms are listed under the classical forms, even though the LXX forms are often clearly different.

Coupled with this is the penchant of Hatch and Redpath to typically list classical forms ahead of *koine* forms in their *Concordance*.[13] For instance, they list νεομηνία under νουμηνία. While ever classical (Attic) forms are perceived as the norm, this approach can be defended. The problem is that LXX lexicography is thereby easily subsumed under the classical rubrics, as some sort of illegitimate step-child. What to LSJ are "later forms," are for the LXX often normative. Contrariwise, the manifest classicism of the 1-4 Maccabees, and especially 4 Maccabees, is a reversion. It is not normative. LXX Greek is first and foremost *koine* Greek.

In the *Lexicon*, then, words are listed in the form in which they occur, not a mythical lexical entry. The form ἐπανιστανόμενοι, for instance, derives from ἐπανιστάνω, not the earlier—and classical—ἐπανίστημι.

c. Entries

In the *Lexicon* there is only one part of speech (noun, verb, etc.) per lemma. If more than one part of speech shares a particular form, then the form—along with its parsing—is listed as many times as necessary.[14] Conversely, when there are two different forms of the same part of

[9]J. F. Schleusner, *Novus Thesaurus philologico-criticus, sive Lexicon in LXX et reliquos Interpretes Graecos ac Scriptores Apocryphos Veteris Testamenti. Post Bielium, et alios viros doctos congessit et edidit Joh. Fried. Schleusner.* 3 vols., Leipzig, 1820-1.

[10]G. Abbott-Smith, *A Manual Greek Lexicon of the New Testament.* Edinburgh, 1937³.

[11]Ibid, p. xvi.

[12]H. G. Liddell, and R. Scott. *A Greek-English Lexicon.* New (9th) ed. revised and augmented by Henry Stuart Jones and Roderick McKenzie. Oxford, 1925-40 (hereinafter, LSJ).

[13]Edwin Hatch, and H. A. Redpath, *A Concordance to the Septuagint, and the other Greek Versions of the Old Testament (Including the Apocryphal Books).* Oxford, 1897; reprinted, Graz, 1975.

[14]   ὑπάρξει   noun fem dat sg . . . .   ὕπαρξις
       ὑπάρξει   vb fut act ind 3rd pers sg . . . .   ὑπάρχω

speech, the lemma is listed only once.[15] Thus when an adjective is used adverbially it is listed separately from the adjective entry. The one exception to this are words with multiple one-word parsings. In this case only one line is used to list the appropriate parts of speech.[16]

Where two essentially identical forms exist, only the more complete one is retained.[17] Where two forms are the same, except for a movable *nu*, then the *nu* is enclosed in parentheses. Where only one or the other form occurs, that form is listed with or without the *nu* as it occurs.

Sequencing within the parsing itself varies from lexicon to lexicon. For this lexicon, a top-down approach was adopted since this is the sequence one follows when looking up a word in a paradigm or on a verb chart.[18] Although there is a definite move towards computer-oriented forms for the parsing itself where letter—and even number—codes are used, simple English abbreviations are used since they are much more intuitive.

II. Nouns

In most instances the vocative is the same as the nominative. This is always the case with plurals. When singular vocatives are different from the nominative they are listed separately.

In those instances where it is not possible to ascertain the gender of a word from the context, the gender is assumed to be that found elsewhere.[19]

Some ambiguous forms occur, such as ζυγός, which also has a neuter form ζυγόν. In the accusative, genitive, and dative cases these two forms cannot be distinguished one from the other, whether or not the definite article or an adjective is present, so both genders are supplied in the analysis.[20]

One of the most neglected areas of LXX study is that of names, and the CATSS database is no exception. Most lexicons exclude names, or at best treat them separately. However, it was decided to include them in this study to maximize its usefulness.

In the *Lexicon*, where only proper nouns are capitalized, it is easy to distinguish them from common nouns. However, the standard texts include syntactical capitalization, and this can

---

[15] καλεῖτε vb pres act impv 2nd pers pl,
        pres act ind 2nd pers pl . . . . καλέω

[16] ἔμπροσθεν adverb and preposition

[17]In the following examples only the former is retained each time:

        ῥοΐσκους - ῥοΐσκους
        ῥοΐσκων - ῥοΐσκων.

[18]For nouns, pronouns and adjectives: part of speech, gender, case, and number; for verbs: part of speech, tense, voice, mood, person, and number; or for participles: part of speech, tense, voice, mood, gender, case, and number.

[19]For the most part this occurs with proper nouns.

[20]For nouns, where at times two genders are in use, both are listed using "or" as in: "masc or fem." This is in contrast to adjectives, where ambiguous forms are listed, for instance, as "masc and fem."

make it difficult for the beginning student to separate these two types of nouns. The intermediate to advanced student/scholar will seldom use them, the beginner will use them often.

For the most part, the lemma form for names in the database does not have any accentuation, though the dictionary form often does. It was decided to limit the use of accents in the dictionary form to that of the lemma—present when the lemma has it, absent when it does not. As work was progressing, it was found that the lemma forms for proper nouns in the database do not necessarily correspond to the Rahlfs text. Somehow, the text has suffered in transmission. Along the way, most breathing marks and accents have been removed from proper nouns. The decision to limit to the Rahlfs form turned out to be a standardization to a mythical norm.

One of the biggest problems with proper nouns in any language is the wide variation in spelling, and the LXX is no exception. However, Rahlfs strove to standardize such variants as between -ει- and -ι-, etc. In accord with this, the dictionary forms of names were brought into accord with the lemma form, or underlying lemma form for cases other than the nominative singular.[21]

However, there are other problems as well. Rahlfs at times partially inflected a proper noun in an oblique case, and in the process generated a hybrid form. For instance, Χελκια (2 Chr 34:20) is clearly dative singular in its context, but Rahlfs omitted the *iota* subscript under the *alpha*. Thus it is a declinable noun partially declined. For such nouns the analysis is listed, even though it appears anomalous.

In apparent contradistinction to this, indeclinable proper nouns are not parsed, even when the parsing is clear from the context. For instance, in Tobit 5:6 (א text) Ραγα is feminine accusative singular, but it is an indeclinable noun, so it is simply listed as a proper noun.

III. Transliterations

Though not part of the original CATSS plan, by manipulating the information in the database, it was possible to isolate and identify the category of transliteration.[22] However, except for the transliteration of the letters of the Hebrew alephbet,[23] no Hebrew equivalents are supplied.

---

[21]For instance, in the context of the Rahlfs text, Χελκιου is the genitive singular of Χελκιας not Χελκειας, even though the latter is the preferred form in Hatch and Redpath. Similarly, Σουσοις, an indeclinable noun, is thereby not a form of Σουσα, whether or not they refer to the same geographical location.

[22]In common with both proper nouns and common nouns, the first letter of the database parsing is "N" for noun. In common with some proper nouns, but *only* proper nouns, the parsing is only one letter: <N>. In contrast to those names parsed in this way, transliterations never begin with a capital letter. Thus they were able to be isolated and identified.

[23]These occur as headings in Psalm 118 (Heb. 119).

IV. Adjectives

For the most part, the parsing of adjectives is straightforward. The dictionary form is the masculine nominative singular. However, one parsing in particular invites explanation: the rather terse "adj acc sg, neut nom sg". This occurs in connection with two-termination adjectives where the feminine form is always the same as the corresponding masculine form. In this case the masculine, feminine, and neuter forms are all the same in the accusative singular, and the neuter nominative singular also shares this form. The above parsing is shorter than writing "masc and fem acc sg, neut nom and acc sg". Similarly, for these adjectives the genitive and dative singular and plural have shared forms through all three genders. In these cases no gender is listed, as in "dat sg", "gen pl".

In general, adjectives used as substantives, such as τρισαλιτήριος (2 Mac 15:3), are parsed as adjectives. However, when the noun form has a life of its own, this has been recognized as much as possible. The adjective ἐπίπεμτος only occurs in Leviticus and once in Numbers, and only as the neuter substantive ἐπίπεμτον as the translation of חֲמִישִׁי: ʻthe fifth part,ʼ so it is parsed as a (neuter) noun.

V. Verbs

a. Dictionary Forms

Where they existed, prefixes were separated from the root verb in the database. These have been recombined into the standard format for the lexicon. In accord with most Greek lexica (but not H-R), the dictionary form for verbs is the present indicative first person singular, rather than the present infinitive.

b. Ambiguity of Form

One set of ambiguous forms that illustrates this well is the verbs that share the ending -σαι: first aorist active optative third person singular, first aorist active infinitive, first aorist middle imperative second person singular. Not every verb can have all of these permutations, since one must also take into account differences in accentuation. For instance, in the first aorist paradigm for λύω, the infinitive active and the imperative middle are λῦσαι, while the optative active is λύσαι. However, with some verbs the vowels do not take the circumflex accent. Also, when the verb has enough syllables, the accent is recessive for the imperative, but not for the other two.

In time, LXX Greek moved towards removing some of the ambiguities. One of these addressed the problem of identical forms in imperfect and second aorist active first person singular, and third person plural: -ov. To distinguish, the plural is at times -oσαv.[24] Another way to make the same distinction was to use first aorist endings on second aorist verbs, such as εἶπα, ἦλθαν, etc.

---

[24]At first glance, the aorist ending -σαv looks like the typical first aorist active indicative 3rd person plural ending. In fact it is the -o that is determinative, and it is second aorist.

Two of the long-standing confusions in LXX analysis are that of the first aorist active subjunctive first person singular and the future indicative active first person singular, and the first aorist active subjunctive 3rd person singular and the future indicative middle 2nd person singular. In the database these were often mis-parsed as per their context, and so were corrected. However, this at times created a problem since it was not possible to know if there was another instance where this was the correct form. Nevertheless this risk was deemed preferable to creating endless multiple entries.[25]

A significant number of verbs, such as ἐκτείνω, use the same root for the present/imperfect and the aorist forms. Thus while some of the forms are unambiguous, others are ambiguous, so that absolute parsing would be arbitrary at best. In cases like this, the forms are parsed as both present/imperfect and aorist as appropriate.

c. Optative

Students of NT Greek will be surprised by the number of optative forms in the LXX, while students of classical Greek will be surprised by their paucity. Since the accent on these forms is not recessive, and the final syllable in the 3rd person singular is considered long, they are easy to distinguish in the first aorist active from the infinitive which, while also not being recessive, has a short final syllable and so is able to take a long accent on the penultimate if the verbal stem permits. If this is not the case, then context is determinative.

d. Dictionary Forms

Contra Hatch and Redpath, the verbs are listed according to their present indicative active or deponent 1st person singular form, not the present infinitive. Though a good case can be made for the latter, the former is the more traditional and common.

As with nouns, verbs are listed here in their *koine* form when this differs from classical (Attic) forms. Accordingly, the form is γίνομαι not γίγνομαι, and γινώσκω not γιγνώσκω, etc.

Similarly, H-R listed ῥήσσω under ῥήγνυμι, but clearly it is not the same word, even if related. Part of the problem is knowing—or not knowing—how these will be listed in the LXX lexica. However, some indication of what is likely to happen can be seen from the listing of ἐξολλύει under ἐξόλλυμι by Lust, *et al*, with no indication of any alternative forms.

How precise should the lexicographer aim to be? The LXX uses ἔσθετε (etc.), which is obviously not a form of ἐσθίω, but rather from the poetic form ἔσθω. It is easy to be imprecise for the sake of fitting into conventional canons. By doing so, though, it is easy to miss the distinctive flavor of LXX Greek *vis-à-vis* both classical and *koine* (including NT) Greek.

---

[25]Where the length of entry in Hatch and Redpath was of manageable proportions, the entire entry was searched for other uses of the form under consideration.

e. Deponent Verbs

In general, in those tenses that have no forms distinguishing middle from passive,[26] such verbs are listed as "m/p". In the case of deponent verbs in these tenses the abbreviation "dep" is used. Verbs in this category are distinguished by the -ομαι ending in the dictionary form. If a verb occurs both as an active and as a deponent, the two forms may not be distinguished. In this case a deponent may be listed as "m/p", since a conscious effort was made not to list as deponent a verb that has an active form listed. One such example is κοιτάζομαι (H-R and CATSS), which has an active form κοιτάζεις (Cant 1:7), so the dictionary form was changed to κοιτάζω (LSJ), and covered elsewhere by "m/p" when appropriate.

Since aorist and future verbs have forms that distinguish between middle and passive, no attempt was made to distinguish between deponents and "middles." If the root ends in -ομαι, then the verb is known to be deponent.

A good example of the difference of opinion in this connection is the verb ἐπισπάω. LSJ list as -άω, while Lust, *et al*, list as -άομαι. H-R list 12 references, and all are middle/passive or deponent. Does this necessitate a listing as a deponent? Another example is ἐξισόω (LSJ, CATSS, H-R), but ἐξισόομαι in Lust, *et al*.

f. Verbal Adjectives

The student of NT Greek is not prepared for the form of verbal adjectives in -τέον/-τέα, since only one occurs in the NT.[27] CATSS did not make separate provision for these, choosing to parse them as adjectives. However, this does not do them justice since they do not decline in the usual way, and can be used as the main verb in a sentence. On the other hand, LSJ simply list them separately in the frozen form without analysis and uniformly translate as "one must ...." Lust, *et al*, sometimes have them listed as part of the verb (ἐλευστέον under ἔρχομαι as ἐλευστέος), and other times they are listed separately (γνωστέος, -α,-ον).[28] In the parsing they are listed as "verbal adj sg" or "verbal adj pl" as appropriate.

---

[26]Present, imperfect, perfect, pluperfect and future perfect.

[27]Luke 5:38 βλητέον.

[28]Muraoka is not quoted in this connection since no verbal adjectives occur in the Twelve Prophets.

Using the Lexicon

For too long students have been deprived of access to the vast body of *koine* literature contained in the LXX because of the lack of the necessary tools. Yet one of the fears of many teachers is that students will learn of the existence of analytical lexicons. They are often referred to as a crutch that keeps the student from walking, or similar derogatory analogies. Not surprisingly, it is not the existence of the lexicon that is the problem. Rather, it is the use to which it is put. There are four main areas of use for this *Lexicon*.

First of all, the *Analytical Lexicon* is a boon to the student with limited Greek ability who is confronted with a portion of the Septuagint to study. As those of us who in our study approached the Septuagint on our own armed only with NT Greek, this can be an intimidating experience. The first step is to be able to confidently identify the forms and know where to look in a dictionary for definitions. While this is not the ideal approach to the text, it is often reality under a variety of circumstances. One must first know what the text says before one can determine what it means. Again, while morphology does not teach syntax and exegesis, it is a necessary prelude to such study. Or, in the context of the crutch analogy, limited mobility is better than no mobility. To maximize assistance to these students in particular, all the words in the Rahlfs text are parsed, including the proper nouns, and all parts of speech such as noun, verb, adjective, etc., are clearly identified.

Second is the student of NT Greek who has the opportunity to read the Septuagint. The purist demands that this not be attempted until the grammar and syntax have been studied and understood. If time for such a luxury existed in the past, it is scarce today. Rather, a quarter or semester is set aside for reading the Septuagint, with the various elements of the language being addressed as they happen to arise. In this circumstance the student cannot prepare for class without assistance since forms arise before they are addressed in class, but class preparation in advance is a *sine qua non*.

Third is the all-too-rare student of Septuagintal Greek. Especially in this case, the best progress will be made by not consulting the *Analytical Lexicon* until an independent parsing has been made, and preferably committed to writing. While this approach is recommended for the other types of students already mentioned, it is vital for the serious student. Otherwise the *Analytical Lexicon* becomes a crutch that keeps the student from walking—and running—with the language.

Though time-consuming, it has been found helpful to attempt to read through the assigned passage, all the while writing down, one word per line, all of the words not readily recognized and/or understood. These words are then studied both on their own and in context to ascertain their form and meaning. Those words still not understood are then looked up in the *Analytical Lexicon*.

Finally, there is the Greek scholar who needs to refresh his or her memory on a particular form from time to time, or identify an unusual form.

For each this *Lexicon* has its place, but it must be borne in mind that it takes students only so far. It enables one to establish the form of any word and to know where to look in a dictionary to find the meaning and use of the word in context. Once in command of this information, however, one has only begun to understand the meaning of the sentence, since one knows nothing, or virtually nothing, of its syntax based on this minimal information; it tells the "what" but not the "why." For the latter, one must turn to the grammars, etc.

Abbreviations

1st	first	interr	interrogative
2nd	second	m/p	middle/passive
3rd	third	masc	masculine
Dan	Daniel	mid	middle
Heb	Hebrew	neut	neut
OG	Old Greek	nom	nominative
acc	accusative	opt	optative
act	active	part	participle
adj	adjective	pass	passive
aor	aorist	perf	perfect
art	article	pers	personal
comp	comparative	pl	plural
conj	conjunction	plpf	pluperfect
dat	dative	poss	possessive
dem	demonstrative	pr	proper
dep	deponent	pres	present
fem	feminine	pron	pronoun
fut	future	recipr	reciprocal
gen	genitive	refl	reflexive
id.	*idem* ("the same")	rel	relative
impf	imperfect	sg	singular
impv	imperative	subj	subjunctive
ind	indicative	superl	superlative
indecl	indeclinable	translit	transliteration
indef	indefinite	vb	verb
inf	infinitive		

A α

α΄ indecl number

ἅ rel pron neut nom and acc pl . . . . ὅς

ἇ interjection

Ααλαφ pr noun

Ααρα pr noun

Ααρων pr noun

Ααρωνιδης pr noun

Αβαδια pr noun

Αβαδιας pr noun masc nom sg

Αβαδων pr noun

Αβαιαν pr noun

Αβαισαν pr noun

αβακ translit

Αβαλ pr noun

Αβαμα pr noun

Αβανα pr noun

Αβαρ pr noun

Αβαραν pr noun

Αβαριμ pr noun

Αβαριν pr noun

αβαρκηνιν translit

ἀβασίλευτον adj masc acc sg,

       neut nom and acc sg . . . . ἀβασίλευτος

Αβαταζα pr noun

ἀβάτοις adj masc and neut dat pl . . . . ὀβατος

ἄβατον adj acc sg, neut nom sg   id.

ἄβατος adj masc and fem nom sg   id.

ἀβάτους adj masc and fem acc pl   id.

ἀβάτῳ adj dat sg   id.

ἀβατωθῇ vb 1st aor pass subj 3rd pers sg . . . . ἀβατόω

Αββα pr noun

Αβδεδομ pr noun

Αβδεμελεχ pr noun

Αβδεναγω pr noun

Αβδησελμα pr noun

Αβδι pr noun

Αβδια pr noun

Αβδιαν pr noun masc acc sg . . . . Αβδια

Αβδιας pr noun

Αβδιηλ pr noun

Αβδιου pr noun

Αβδιου pr noun masc gen sg . . . . Αβδιας

Αβδων pr noun

Αβεδ pr noun

Αβεδδαρα pr noun

Αβεδδαραμ

αβεδηριν translit

Αβελ pr noun

Αβελβαιθαμααχα pr noun

Αβελμαα pr noun

Αβελμαιν pr noun

Αβελμαουλα pr noun

Αβελμεουλα pr noun

Αβενεζερ pr noun

Αβεννεζερ pr noun

Αβεννερ pr noun

Αβεννηρ pr noun

Αβερ pr noun

Αβεσσα pr noun

Αβεσσαλωμ pr noun

Αβι pr noun

Αβια pr noun

Αβιαθαρ pr noun

Αβιασαφ pr noun

Αβιγαια pr noun

Αβιγαιαν pr noun fem acc sg . . . . Αβιγαια

Αβιγαιας pr noun fem gen sg   id.

Αβιδα pr noun

Αβιδαν pr noun

Αβιεζεκ pr noun

Αβιεζερ pr noun

Αβιεζρι pr noun

Αβιεσδρι pr noun

Αβιηλ pr noun

Αβιμεηλ pr noun

Αβιμελεχ pr noun

Αβινεεμ pr noun

Αβιου pr noun

Αβιουδ pr noun

αβιρα translit

Αβιρα pr noun

Αβιρων pr noun

Αβισακ pr noun	ἀγαγόντα vb 2nd aor act part masc acc sg,
Αβισου pr noun	neut nom and acc pl . . . . ἄγω
Αβισουε pr noun	ἀγαγόντας vb 2nd aor act part masc acc pl id.
Αβισουρ pr noun	ἀγαγόντος vb 2nd aor act part masc and neut gen sg id.
Αβιταλ pr noun	ἀγαγοῦσαν vb 2nd aor act part fem acc sg id.
Αβιτωβ pr noun	ἀγάγω vb 2nd aor act subj 1st pers sg id.
Αβιχαιλ pr noun	ἀγάγωμεν vb 2nd aor act subj 1st pers pl id.
ἀβλαβεῖς adj masc and fem nom and acc pl . . . . . . ἀβλαβής	ἀγαγών vb 2nd aor act part masc nom sg id.
ἀβλαβῆ adj masc and fem acc sg id.	ἀγαθά adj neut nom and acc pl . . . . ἀγαθός
ἀβοηθησίας noun fem gen sg . . . . ἀβοηθησία	ἀγαθαί adj fem nom pl id.
ἀβοήθητον adj acc sg, neut nom sg . . . . ἀβοήθητος	ἀγαθάς adj fem acc pl id.
ἀβοήθητος adj masc and fem nom sg id.	ἀγαθέ adj masc voc sg id.
ἀβοηθήτων adj gen pl id.	ἀγαθή adj fem nom sg id.
Αβου pr noun	ἀγαθῇ adj fem dat sg id.
᾿Αβουβου pr noun masc gen sg . . . . ᾿Αβουβος	ἀγαθήν adj fem acc sg id.
ἀβουλεύτως adverb	ἀγαθῆς adj fem gen sg id.
ἀβουλίαν noun fem acc sg . . . . ἀβουλία	ἀγαθοί adj masc nom pl id.
ἀβουλίας noun fem gen sg id.	ἀγαθοῖς adj masc and neut dat pl id.
ἄβρᾳ noun fem dat sg . . . . ἄβρα	ἀγαθόν adj masc acc sg, neut nom and acc sg id.
Αβρααμ pr noun	ἀγαθόν adv id.
Αβρααμιτιδος pr noun fem gen sg . . . . Αβρααμιτις	ἀγαθοποιήσαι vb 1st aor act opt 3rd pers sg . . ἀγαθοποιέω
ἄβραι noun fem nom pl . . . . ἄβρα	ἀγαθοποιήσῃ vb 1st aor act subj 3rd pers sg id.
ἄβραις noun fem dat pl id.	ἀγαθοποιός adj masc and fem nom sg
Αβραμ pr noun	ἀγαθοποιῶν vb pres act part masc nom sg . . . . ἀγαθοποιέω
Αβραμιαῖοι adj masc nom pl . . . . Αβραμιαῖος	ἀγαθός adj masc nom sg
Αβραμιαῖος adj masc nom sg id.	ἀγαθότητα noun fem acc sg . . . . ἀγαθότης
Αβραμιαιων adj masc gen pl id.	ἀγαθότητι noun fem dat sg id.
ἄβραν noun fem acc sg . . . . ἄβρα	ἀγαθότητος noun fem gen sg id.
ἄβρας noun fem gen sg and acc pl id.	ἀγαθοῦ adj masc and neut gen sg . . . . ἀγαθός
ἀβροχίας noun fem gen sg . . . . ἀβροχία	ἀγαθούς adj masc acc pl id.
Αβρωνα pr noun	ἀγαθύναι vb 1st aor act opt 3rd pers sg . . . . ἀγαθύνω
ἄβρωτα adj neut nom and acc pl . . . . ἄβρωτος	ἀγαθῦναι vb 1st aor act inf id.
ἄβυσσοι noun fem nom pl . . . . ἄβυσσος	ἀγαθυνάτω vb 1st aor act impv 3rd pers sg id.
ἀβύσσοις noun fem dat pl id.	ἀγαθυνεῖ vb fut act ind 3rd pers sg id.
ἄβυσσον noun fem acc sg id.	ἀγαθύνῃς vb 1st aor act subj 2nd pers sg id.
ἄβυσσος noun fem nom sg id.	ἀγαθυνθέντων vb 1st aor pass part masc and neut gen pl id.
ἀβύσσου noun fem gen sg id.	ἀγαθυνθῇ vb 1st aor pass subj 3rd pers sg id.
ἀβύσσους noun fem acc pl id.	ἀγαθυνθήσεται vb fut pass ind 3rd pers sg id.
ἀβύσσῳ noun fem dat sg id.	ἀγαθυνθήτω vb 1st aor pass impv 3rd pers sg id.
ἀβύσσων noun fem gen pl id.	ἀγάθυνον vb 1st aor act impv 2nd pers sg id.
Αβωμεουλα pr noun	ἀγαθύνοντες vb pres act part masc nom pl id.
Αβωρ pr noun	ἀγαθῷ adj masc and neut dat sg . . . . ἀγαθός
Αγαβ pr noun	ἀγαθῶν adj gen pl id.
Αγαβα pr noun	ἀγαθῶς adverb
Αγαγ pr noun	ἀγαθῶσαι vb 1st aor act inf . . . . ἀγαθόω
ἄγαγε vb 2nd aor act impv 2nd pers sg . . . . ἄγω	ἀγαθώσει vb fut act ind 3rd pers sg id.
ἀγαγεῖν vb 2nd aor act inf id.	ἀγαθωσύνῃ noun fem dat sg . . . . ἀγαθωσύνη
ἀγαγέσθαι vb 2nd aor mid inf id.	ἀγαθωσύνην noun fem acc sg id.
ἀγάγετε vb 2nd aor act impv 2nd pers pl id.	ἀγαθωσύνης noun fem gen sg id.
ἀγαγέτωσαν vb 2nd aor act impv 3rd pers pl id.	ἀγαθωτέρα comp adj neut nom and acc pl . . . . ἀγαθός
ἀγάγῃς vb 2nd aor act subj 2nd pers sg id.	ἀγαθώτερος comp adj masc nom sg id.
ἀγάγοις vb 2nd aor act opt 2nd pers sg id.	ἀγαλλίαμα noun neut nom and acc sg

ἀγαλλιάματι   noun neut dat sg . . . . ἀγαλλίαμα
ἀγαλλιάματος   noun neut gen sg   id.
ἀγαλλιάσαι   vb 1st aor mid impv
       2nd pers sg . . . . ἀγαλλιάομαι
ἀγαλλιάσαιντο   vb 1st aor mid opt 3rd pers pl
ἀγαλλιάσει   noun fem dat sg . . . . ἀγαλλίασις
ἀγαλλιάσει   vb fut act ind 3rd pers sg . . . . . ἀγαλλιάομαι
ἀγαλλιάσεται   vb fut mid ind 3rd pers sg   id.
ἀγαλλιάσεως   noun fem gen sg . . . . ἀγαλλίασις
ἀγαλλιάσῃ   vb fut mid ind 2nd pers sg,
       1st aor mid subj 2nd pers sg . . . . ἀγαλλιάομαι
ἀγαλλιᾶσθε   vb pres dep impv 2nd pers pl,
       pres dep ind 2nd pers pl,
       1st aor mid impv 2nd pers pl   id.
ἀγαλλιάσθω   vb pres dep impv 3rd pers sg,
       1st aor mid impv 3rd pers sg   id.
ἀγαλλιάσθωσαν   vb pres dep impv 3rd pers pl   id.
ἀγαλλίασιν   noun fem acc sg . . . . ἀγαλλίασις
ἀγαλλίασις   noun fem nom sg   id.
ἀγαλλιάσομαι   vb fut mid ind 1st pers sg . . . ἀγαλλιάομαι
ἀγαλλιασόμεθα   vb fut mid ind 1st pers pl   id.
ἀγαλλιάσονται   vb fut mid ind 3rd pers pl   id.
ἀγαλλιασώμεθα   vb 1st aor mid subj 1st pers pl   id.
ἀγαλλιάσωνται   vb 1st aor mid subj 3rd pers pl   id.
Αγαλλιμ   pr noun
ἀγάλματα   noun neut nom and acc pl . . . . ἄγαλμα
ἄγαμοι   adj masc nom pl . . . . ἄγαμος
ἄγαν   adverb
ἀγανακτήσασα   vb 1st aor act part fem nom sg . ἀγανακτέω
ἀγανακτήσει   vb fut act ind 3rd pers sg   id.
ἀγάπα   vb pres act impv 2nd pers sg . . . . ἀγαπάω
ἀγαπᾷ   vb pres act ind 3rd pers sg   id.
ἀγαπᾶν   vb pres act inf   id.
ἀγαπᾷς   vb pres act ind 2nd pers sg   id.
ἀγαπᾶτε   vb pres act ind 2nd pers pl   id.
ἀγαπάτω   vb pres act impv 3rd pers sg   id.
ἀγάπη   noun fem nom sg
ἀγάπῃ   noun fem dat sg . . . . ἀγάπη
ἀγαπηθήσεται   vb fut pass ind 3rd pers sg . . . . . ἀγαπάω
ἀγαπηθήσῃ   vb fut pass ind 2nd pers sg   id.
ἀγάπην   noun fem acc sg . . . . ἀγάπη
ἀγάπης   noun fem gen sg   id.
ἀγαπῆσαι   vb 1st aor act opt 3rd pers sg . . . . ἀγαπάω
ἀγαπῆσαι   vb 1st aor act inf   id.
ἀγαπήσαντος   vb 1st aor act part masc and neut gen sg   id.
ἀγαπήσασα   vb 1st aor act part fem nom sg   id.
ἀγαπήσατε   vb 1st aor act impv 2nd pers pl   id.
ἀγαπήσει   noun fem dat sg . . . . ἀγάπησις
ἀγαπήσει   vb fut act ind 3rd pers sg . . . . ἀγαπάω
ἀγαπήσεις   vb fut act ind 2nd pers sg   id.
ἀγαπήσετε   vb fut act ind 2nd pers pl   id.
ἀγαπήσεως   noun fem gen sg . . . . ἀγάπησις

ἀγαπήσῃς   vb 1st aor act subj 2nd pers sg . . . . ἀγαπάω
ἀγάπησιν   noun fem acc sg . . . . ἀγάπησις
ἀγάπησις   noun fem nom sg   id.
ἀγαπήσομεν   vb fut act ind 1st pers pl . . . . ἀγαπάω
ἀγάπησον   vb 1st aor act impv 2nd pers sg   id.
ἀγαπήσω   vb fut act ind 1st pers sg   id.
ἀγαπητά   adj neut nom and acc pl . . . . ἀγαπητός
ἀγαπητέ   adj masc voc sg   id.
ἀγαπητή   adj fem nom sg   id.
ἀγαπητοί   adj masc nom pl   id.
ἀγαπητοῖς   adj masc and neut dat pl   id.
ἀγαπητόν   adj masc acc sg, neut nom and acc sg   id.
ἀγαπητός   adj masc nom sg   id.
ἀγαπητοῦ   adj masc and neut gen sg   id.
ἀγαπητούς   adj masc acc pl   id.
ἀγαπητῷ   adj masc and neut dat sg   id.
ἀγαπῶ   vb pres act ind 1st pers sg . . . . ἀγαπάω
ἀγαπώμεναι   vb pres m/p part fem nom pl   id.
ἀγαπώμενος   vb pres m/p part masc nom sg   id.
ἀγαπῶν   vb pres act part masc nom sg   id.
ἀγαπῶντας   vb pres act part masc acc pl   id.
ἀγαπῶντες   vb pres act part masc nom pl   id.
ἀγαπῶντος   vb pres act part masc and neut gen sg   id.
ἀγαπώντων   vb pres act part masc and neut gen pl   id.
ἀγαπῶσαν   vb pres act part fem acc sg   id.
ἀγαπῶσι(ν)   vb pres act ind 3rd pers pl,
       pres act part masc and neut dat pl   id.
Αγαρ   pr noun
Αγαραῖοι   pr noun masc nom pl . . . . Αγαραῖος
Αγαρηνοι   pr noun masc nom pl . . . . Αγαρηνος
Αγαρηνῶν   pr noun masc gen pl   id.
Αγαρι   pr noun
Αγαριτης   pr noun masc nom sg
Αγαρμι   pr noun
ἀγαυρίαμα   noun neut nom and acc sg
Αγγαβα   pr noun
Αγγαι   pr noun
Αγγαιον   pr noun masc acc sg . . . . Αγγαιος
Αγγαιος   pr noun masc nom sg   id.
Αγγαιου   pr noun masc gen sg   id.
ἀγγεῖα   noun neut nom and acc pl . . . . ἀγγεῖον
ἀγγείοις   noun neut dat pl   id.
ἀγγεῖον   noun neut nom and acc sg   id.
ἀγγείου   noun neut gen sg   id.
ἀγγείῳ   noun neut dat sg   id.
ἀγγείων   noun neut gen pl   id.
ἀγγελία   noun fem nom sg
ἀγγελίᾳ   noun fem dat sg . . . . ἀγγελία
ἀγγελίαν   noun fem acc sg   id.
ἄγγελοι   noun masc nom pl . . . . ἄγγελος
ἀγγέλοις   noun masc dat pl   id.
ἄγγελον   noun masc acc sg   id.

ἄγγελος noun masc nom sg
ἀγγέλου noun masc gen sg .... ἄγγελος
ἀγγέλους noun masc acc pl — id.
ἀγγέλῳ noun masc dat sg — id.
ἀγγέλων noun masc gen pl — id.
Αγγι pr noun
Αγγια pr noun
Αγγιθ pr noun
Αγγις pr noun
ἄγγος noun neut nom and acc sg
ἄγε vb pres act impv 2nd pers sg .... ἄγω
Αγεαδδαϊρ pr noun
ἄγει vb pres act ind 3rd pers sg .... ἄγω
ἄγειν vb pres act inf — id.
ἀγειόχασιν vb perf act ind 3rd pers pl — id.
ἀγείοχεν vb perf act ind 3rd pers sg — id.
ἀγειοχέναι vb perf act inf — id.
ἀγειοχώς vb perf act part masc nom sg — id.
ἀγέλαι noun fem nom pl .... ἀγέλη
ἀγελαίους adj masc acc pl .... ἀγελαῖος
ἀγέλαις noun fem dat pl .... ἀγέλη
ἀγέλας noun fem acc pl — id.
ἀγεληδόν adverb
ἀγέλης noun fem gen sg .... ἀγέλη
ἀγερωχία noun fem dat sg .... ἀγερωχία
ἀγερωχίας noun fem gen sg — id.
ἀγέρωχον adj masc acc sg, neut nom and acc sg .. ἀγέρωχος
ἄγεται vb pres m/p ind 3rd pers sg .... ἄγω
ἄγετε vb pres act ind 2nd pers pl — id.
ἄγητε vb pres act subj 2nd pers pl — id.
Αγια pr noun
ἅγια adj neut nom and acc pl .... ἅγιος
ἁγία adj fem nom sg — id.
ἁγίᾳ adj fem dat sg — id.
ἁγιάζειν vb pres act inf .... ἁγιάζω
ἁγιάζετε vb pres act impv 2nd pers pl — id.
ἁγιαζόμενα vb pres m/p part neut nom and acc pl — id.
ἁγιαζομένη vb pres m/p part fem nom sg — id.
ἁγιαζόμενον vb pres m/p part masc acc sg,
  neut nom and acc sg — id.
ἁγιάζοντες vb pres act part masc nom pl — id.
ἁγιάζουσα vb pres act part fem nom sg — id.
ἁγιάζουσιν vb pres act ind 3rd pers pl — id.
ἁγιάζων vb pres act part masc nom sg — id.
ἁγιάζωσιν vb pres act subj 3rd pers pl — id.
ἅγιαι adj fem nom pl .... ἅγιος
ἁγίαις adj fem dat pl — id.
ἁγίαν adj fem acc sg — id.
ἁγίας adj fem gen sg and acc pl — id.
ἁγιάσαι vb 1st aor mid impv 2nd pers sg .... ἁγιάζω
ἁγιάσαι vb 1st aor act inf,
  1st aor act opt 3rd pers sg — id.

ἁγιάσαντες vb 1st aor act part masc nom pl .... ἁγιάζω
ἁγιάσας vb 1st aor act part masc nom sg — id.
ἁγιάσατε vb 1st aor act impv 2nd pers pl — id.
ἁγιάσει vb fut act ind 3rd pers sg — id.
ἁγιάσεις vb fut act ind 2nd pers sg — id.
ἁγιάσετε vb fut act ind 2nd pers pl — id.
ἁγιάσῃ vb 1st aor act subj 3rd pers sg — id.
ἁγιασθέντες vb 1st aor pass part masc nom pl — id.
ἁγιασθῇ vb 1st aor pass subj 3rd pers sg — id.
ἁγιασθῆναι vb 1st aor pass inf — id.
ἁγιασθήσεσθε vb fut pass ind 2nd pers pl — id.
ἁγιασθήσεται vb fut pass ind 3rd pers sg — id.
ἁγιασθήσομαι vb fut pass ind 1st pers sg — id.
ἁγιάσθητε vb 1st aor pass subj 2nd pers pl — id.
ἁγιασθήτωσαν vb 1st aor pass impv 3rd pers pl — id.
ἁγιασθῶσι vb 1st aor pass subj 3rd pers pl — id.
ἁγίασμα noun neut nom and acc sg
ἁγιάσμασι noun neut dat pl .... ἁγίασμα
ἁγιάσματι noun neut dat sg — id.
ἁγιάσματος noun neut gen sg — id.
ἁγιασμόν noun masc acc sg .... ἁγιασμός
ἁγιασμοῦ noun masc gen sg — id.
ἁγιασμῷ noun masc dat sg — id.
ἁγίασον vb 1st aor act impv 2nd pers sg .... ἁγιάζω
ἁγιάσουσιν vb fut act ind 3rd pers pl — id.
ἁγιαστήριον noun neut nom and acc sg
ἁγιαστίαν noun fem acc sg .... ἁγιαστία
ἁγιάσω vb fut act ind 1st pers sg .... ἁγιάζω
ἁγιάσωσιν vb 1st aor act subj 3rd pers pl — id.
ἅγιε adj masc voc sg .... ἅγιος
Αγιν pr noun
ἅγιοι adj masc nom pl .... ἅγιος
ἁγίοις adj masc and neut dat pl — id.
ἅγιον adj masc acc sg, neut nom and acc sg — id.
ἅγιος adj masc nom sg
ἁγιότητος noun fem gen sg .... ἁγιότης
ἁγίου adj masc and neut gen sg .... ἅγιος
ἁγίους adj masc acc pl — id.
ἁγίῳ adj masc and neut dat sg — id.
ἁγίων adj gen pl — id.
ἁγιωσύνη noun fem nom sg
ἁγιωσύνῃ noun fem dat sg .... ἁγιωσύνη
ἁγιωσύνης noun fem gen sg — id.
ἁγιώτατον superl adj masc acc sg,
  neut nom and acc sg .... ἅγιος
ἀγκάλαις noun fem dat pl .... ἀγκάλη
ἀγκάλας noun fem acc pl — id.
ἀγκαλίδα noun fem acc sg .... ἀγκαλίς
ἀγκαλῶν noun fem gen pl .... ἀγκάλη
ἄγκιστρα noun neut nom and acc pl .... ἄγκιστρον
ἄγκιστρον noun neut nom and acc sg — id.
ἀγκίστρῳ noun neut dat sg — id.

ἀγκύλαι	noun fem nom pl	ἀγκύλη
ἀγκύλας	noun fem acc pl	id.
ἀγκυλῶν	noun fem gen pl	id.
ἀγκῶνα	noun masc acc sg	ἀγκών
ἀγκῶνας	noun masc acc pl	id.
ἀγκῶνες	noun masc nom pl	id.
ἀγκωνίσκους	noun masc acc pl	αγκωνίσκος
ἀγκῶνος	noun masc gen sg	ἀγκών
Αγλα	pr noun	
Αγλαθ-σαλισια	pr noun	
Αγλων	pr noun	
ἀγνά	adj neut nom and acc pl	ἀγνός
ἀγναί	adj fem nom pl	id.
ἀγνάς	adj fem acc pl	id.
ἀγνείᾳ	noun fem dat sg	ἀγνεία
ἀγνείαν	noun fem acc sg	id.
ἀγνείας	noun fem gen sg and acc pl	id.
ἀγνή	adj fem nom sg	ἀγνός
ἀγνήν	adj fem acc sg	id.
ἀγνιζόμενοι	vb pres m/p part masc nom pl	ἁγνίζω
ἁγνίσαι	vb 1st aor act inf	id.
ἁγνίσασθε	vb 1st aor mid impv 2nd pers pl	id.
ἁγνίσατε	vb 1st aor act impv 2nd pers pl	id.
ἁγνισθέντες	vb 1st aor pass part masc nom pl	id.
ἁγνισθῆναι	vb 1st aor pass inf	id.
ἁγνισθήσεται	vb fut pass ind 3rd pers sg	id.
ἁγνίσθητε	vb 1st aor pass impv 2nd pers pl	id.
ἅγνισμα	noun neut nom and acc sg	
ἁγνισμόν	noun masc acc sg	ἁγνισμός
ἁγνισμοῦ	noun masc gen sg	id.
ἅγνισον	vb 1st aor act impv 2nd pers sg	ἁγνίζω
ἀγνόει	vb pres act impv 2nd pers sg	ἀγνοέω
ἀγνοεῖτε	vb pres act ind 2nd pers pl	id.
ἀγνόημα	noun neut nom and acc sg	
ἀγνοήμασι	noun neut dat pl	ἀγνόημα
ἀγνοήματα	noun neut nom and acc pl	id.
ἀγνοῆσαι	vb 1st aor act inf	ἀγνοέω
ἀγνοήσῃ	vb 1st aor act subj 3rd pers sg	id.
ἄγνοια	noun fem nom sg	
ἀγνοίᾳ	noun fem dat sg	ἄγνοια
ἄγνοιαι	noun fem nom pl	id.
ἀγνοίαις	noun fem dat pl	id.
ἄγνοιαν	noun fem acc sg	id.
ἀγνοίας	noun fem gen sg and acc pl	id.
ἀγνοιῶν	noun fem gen pl	id.
ἁγνόν	adj masc acc sg, neut nom and acc sg	ἀγνός
ἀγνοοῦν	vb pres act part neut nom and acc sg	ἀγνοέω
ἀγνοοῦντας	vb pres act part masc acc pl	id.
ἀγνοοῦντες	vb pres act part masc nom pl	id.
ἀγνός	adj masc nom sg	
ἄγνου	noun fem gen sg	ἄγνος
ἀγνοῶν	vb pres act part masc nom sg	ἀγνοέω
ἁγνῶν	adj gen pl	ἀγνός
ἀγνωσία	noun fem nom sg	
ἀγνωσίᾳ	noun fem dat sg	ἀγνωσία
ἄγνωστον	adj acc sg	ἄγνωστος
ἄγνωστος	adj masc and fem nom sg	id.
ἀγνώστου	adj gen sg	id.
ἀγνώστους	adj masc and fem acc pl	id.
ἄγξαι	vb 1st aor act inf	ἄγχω
ἀγόμεναι	vb pres m/p part fem nom pl	ἄγω
ἀγομένη	vb pres m/p part fem nom sg	id.
ἀγομένην	vb pres m/p part fem acc sg	id.
ἀγόμενοι	vb pres m/p part masc nom pl	id.
ἀγόμενον	vb pres m/p part neut nom and acc sg	id.
ἀγομένου	vb pres m/p part masc and neut gen sg	id.
ἀγομένους	vb pres m/p part masc acc pl	id.
ἄγονος	adj masc and fem nom sg	
ἄγοντες	vb pres act part masc nom pl	ἄγω
ἄγοντος	vb pres act part masc and neut gen sg	id.
ἀγόντων	vb pres act part masc and neut gen pl	id.
ἀγορᾷ	noun fem dat sg	ἀγορά
ἀγοράζειν	vb pres act inf	ἀγοράζω
ἀγοράζοντος	vb pres act part masc and neut gen sg	id.
ἀγοράζω	vb pres act ind 1st pers sg	id.
ἀγοράζων	vb pres act part masc nom sg	id.
ἀγοράζωσιν	vb pres act subj 3rd pers pl	id.
ἀγοραῖς	noun fem dat pl	ἀγορά
ἀγοράν	noun fem acc sg	id.
ἀγορανομίας	noun fem gen sg	ἀγορανομία
ἀγοράς	noun fem acc pl	ἀγορά
ἀγοράσαι	vb 1st aor act inf	ἀγοράζω
ἀγοράσατε	vb 1st aor act impv 2nd pers pl	id.
ἀγορασμοῖς	noun masc dat pl	ἀγορασμός
ἀγορασμόν	noun masc acc sg	id.
ἀγορασμοῦ	noun masc gen sg	id.
ἀγορασμούς	noun masc acc pl	id.
ἀγοραστής	noun masc nom sg	
ἀγοράσωμεν	vb 1st aor act subj 1st pers pl	ἀγοράζω
ἀγορῶμεν	vb fut act ind 1st pers pl	id.
ἄγουσιν	vb pres act ind 3rd pers pl	ἄγω
ἀγρεύει	vb pres act ind 3rd pers sg	ἀγρεύω
ἀγρευθῇς	vb 1st aor pass subj 2nd pers sg	id.
ἀγρεύομαι	vb pres m/p ind 1st pers sg	id.
ἀγρεύοντες	vb pres act part masc nom pl	id.
ἀγρεύουσιν	vb pres act ind 3rd pers pl	id.
ἄγρια	adj neut nom and acc pl	ἄγριος
ἀγρία	adj fem nom sg	id.
ἀγρίᾳ	adj fem dat sg	id.
ἀγρίαν	adj fem acc sg	id.
ἀγριανθήσεται	vb fut pass ind 3rd pers sg	ἀγριαίνω
ἄγριοι	adj masc nom pl	ἄγριος
ἀγρίοις	adj masc and neut dat pl	id.
ἀγριομυρίκη	noun fem nom sg	

ἄγριον adj masc acc sg, neut nom and acc sg ...... ἄγριος
ἄγριος adj masc nom sg   id.
ἀγριότητα noun fem acc sg .... ἀγριότης
ἀγριωθέντας vb 1st aor pass part masc acc pl ..... ἀγριόω
ἀγρίων adj gen pl .... ἄγριος
ἀγρίως adverb
ἀγριωτάτους superl adj masc acc pl .... ἄγριος
ἀγριωτέραν comp adj fem acc sg   id.
ἀγροί noun masc nom pl .... ἀγρός
ἄγροικος adj masc and fem nom sg
ἀγροικότερον comp adj masc acc sg,
          neut nom and acc sg .... ἄγροικος
ἀγροῖς noun masc dat pl .... ἀγρός
ἀγρόν noun masc acc sg   id.
ἀγρός noun masc nom sg   id.
ἀγροῦ noun masc gen sg   id.
ἀγρούς noun masc acc pl   id.
ἀγρυπνεῖ vb pres act ind 3rd pers sg .... ἀγρυπνέω
ἀγρυπνεῖτε vb pres act impv 2nd pers pl   id.
ἀγρυπνήσας vb 1st aor act part masc nom sg   id.
ἀγρυπνία noun fem nom sg
ἀγρυπνίαν noun fem acc sg .... ἀγρυπνία
ἀγρυπνίας noun fem gen sg   id.
ἀγρυπνῶν vb pres act part masc nom sg .... ἀγρυπνέω
ἀγρῷ noun masc dat sg .... ἀγρός
ἀγρῶν noun masc gen pl   id.
ἄγρωστιν noun fem acc sg .... ἄγρωστις
ἄγρωστις noun fem nom sg   id.
ἀγυιαί noun fem nom pl .... ἀγυιά
ἀγυιάς noun fem acc pl   id.
Αγχις pr noun
ἀγχιστέα noun masc acc sg .... ἀγχιστεύς
ἀγχιστεῖ noun masc dat sg   id.
ἀγχιστεία noun fem dat sg .... ἀγχιστεία
ἀγχιστείαν noun fem acc sg   id.
ἀγχίστευε vb pres act impv 2nd pers sg .... ἀγχιστεύω
ἀγχιστεύεις vb pres act ind 2nd pers sg   id.
ἀγχιστευέτω vb pres act impv 3rd pers sg   id.
ἀγχιστεύοντι vb pres act part masc and neut dat sg id.
ἀγχιστεύοντος vb pres act part masc and neut gen sg id.
ἀγχιστευόντων vb pres act part masc and neut gen pl id.
ἀγχιστεύουσα vb pres act part fem nom sg   id.
ἀγχιστεύς noun masc nom sg
ἀγχιστεῦσαι vb 1st aor act inf .... ἀγχιστεύω
ἀγχιστεύσῃ vb 1st aor act subj 3rd pers sg   id.
ἀγχίστευσον vb 1st aor act impv 2nd pers sg   id.
ἀγχιστεύσω vb fut act ind 1st pers sg   id.
ἀγχιστεύσωσιν vb 1st aor act subj 3rd pers pl   id.
ἀγχιστευτής noun masc nom sg
ἀγχιστεύων vb pres act part masc nom sg ..... ἀγχιστεύω
ἀγχόμενος vb pres m/p part masc nom sg .... ἄγχω
Αγχους pr noun

Αγχωχ pr noun
ἄγω vb pres act ind 1st pers sg
ἀγωγάς noun fem acc pl .... ἀγωγή
ἀγωγήν noun fem acc sg   id.
ἄγων vb pres act part masc nom sg .... ἄγω
ἀγών noun masc nom sg
ἀγῶνα noun masc acc sg .... ἀγών
ἀγῶνας noun masc acc pl   id.
ἀγῶνι noun masc dat sg   id.
ἀγωνία noun fem nom sg
ἀγωνίαν noun fem acc sg .... ἀγωνία
ἀγωνιάσας vb 1st aor act part masc nom sg ...... ἀγωνιάω
ἀγωνιζόμενοι vb pres dep part masc nom pl .. ἀγωνίζομαι
ἀγωνιζόμενος vb pres dep part masc nom sg   id.
ἀγώνισαι vb 1st aor mid impv 2nd pers sg   id.
ἀγωνίσασθαι vb 1st aor mid inf   id.
ἀγωνιστάς noun masc acc pl .... ἀγωνιστής
ἀγωνιῶ vb pres act ind 1st pers sg .... ἀγωνιάω
ἀγωνιῶντος vb pres act part masc and neut gen sg id.
ἀγῶνος noun masc gen sg .... ἀγών
ἄγωνται vb pres m/p subj 3rd pers pl .... ἄγω
ἀγώνων noun masc gen pl .... ἀγών
ἀγῶσι noun masc dat pl   id.
Αδα pr noun
Αδαδ pr noun
Αδαδα pr noun
Αδαι pr noun
Αδαια pr noun
Αδαιας pr noun
Αδαμ pr noun
Αδαμα pr noun
ἀδάμαντα noun masc acc sg .... ἀδάμας
ἀδαμάντινον adj masc acc sg,
          neut nom and acc sg .... ἀδαμάντινος
ἀδαμαντίνου adj masc and neut gen sg   id.
ἀδάμας noun masc nom sg
ἀδάμαστα adj neut nom and acc pl .... ἀδάμαστος
ἀδάμαστος adj masc and fem nom sg   id.
Αδαμι pr noun
Αδαν pr noun
Αδαρ pr noun
Αδαρι pr noun
Αδας pr noun gen sg .... Αδα
Αδασα pr noun
Αδασαι pr noun
Αδασαν pr noun
Αδδαι pr noun
Αδδαιον pr noun
Αδδαιω pr noun
Αδδαμιν pr noun
Αδδαρα pr noun
Αδδι pr noun

Αδδους pr noun
Αδδω pr noun
ἄδειαν noun fem acc sg . . . . ἄδεια
ἀδείας noun fem gen sg   id.
ᾄδειν vb pres act inf . . . . ᾄδω
ἄδειπνος adj masc and fem nom sg
ἀδελφαί noun fem nom pl . . . . ἀδελφή
ἀδελφάς noun fem acc pl   id.
ἄδελφε noun masc voc sg . . . . ἀδελφός
ἀδελφή noun fem nom sg
ἀδελφῇ noun fem dat sg . . . . ἀδελφή
ἀδελφήν noun fem acc sg   id.
ἀδελφῆς noun fem gen sg   id.
ἀδελφιδέ noun masc voc sg . . . . ἀδελφιδός
ἀδελφιδόν noun masc acc sg   id.
ἀδελφιδός noun masc nom sg   id.
ἀδελφιδοῦ noun masc gen sg   id.
ἀδελφιδῷ noun masc dat sg   id.
ἀδελφικῶς adverb
ἀδελφοί noun masc nom pl . . . . ἀδελφός
ἀδελφοῖς noun masc dat pl   id.
ἀδελφοκτόνοις adj masc and neut dat pl . . . ἀδελφοκτόνος
ἀδελφόν noun masc acc sg . . . . ἀδελφός
ἀδελφοπρεπῶς adverb
ἀδελφός noun masc nom sg
ἀδελφότητα noun fem acc sg . . . . ἀδελφότης
ἀδελφότητος noun fem gen sg   id.
ἀδελφοῦ noun masc gen sg . . . . ἀδελφός
ἀδελφούς noun masc acc pl   id.
ἀδελφῷ noun masc dat sg   id.
ἀδελφῶν noun masc gen pl   id.
Αδενικαμ pr noun
Αδερ pr noun
ἀδεῶς adverb
ᾄδη noun masc voc sg . . . . ᾄδης
ᾄδη noun masc dat sg   id.
ἄδηλα adj neut nom and acc pl . . . . ἄδηλος
ἀδήλοις adj dat pl   id.
ἄδηλον adj acc sg, neut nom sg   id.
ᾄδην noun masc acc sg . . . . ᾄδης
ᾄδης noun masc nom sg   id.
Αδι pr noun
Αδια pr noun
Αδιαθαϊμ pr noun
ἀδιάκριτοι adj masc and fem nom pl . . . . ἀδιάκριτος
ἀδιαλείπτως adverb
ἀδιάλυτον adj acc sg, neut nom sg . . . . ἀδιάλυτος
ἀδιάπτωτος adj masc and fem nom sg
ἀδιάστροφον adj acc sg, neut nom sg . . . . . . ἀδιάστροφος
ἀδιατρέπτῳ adj dat sg . . . . ἀδιάτρεπτος
Αδιδ pr noun
Αδιδα pr noun

Αδιδοις pr noun fem dat pl . . . . Αδιδα
ἀδιεξέταστοι adj masc nom pl . . . . ἀδιεξέταστος
Αδιηλ pr noun
ἄδικα adj neut nom and acc pl . . . . ἄδικος
ἀδικεῖ vb pres act ind 3rd pers sg . . . . ἀδικέω
ἀδικεῖν vb pres act inf   id.
ἀδικεῖτε vb pres act ind 2nd pers pl   id.
ἀδικηθῆναι vb 1st aor pass inf   id.
ἀδίκημα noun neut nom and acc sg
ἀδικήματα noun neut nom and acc pl . . . . ἀδίκημα
ἀδικήματι noun neut dat sg   id.
ἀδικημάτων noun neut gen pl   id.
ἀδικῆσαι vb 1st aor act inf . . . . ἀδικέω
ἀδικήσαντας vb 1st aor act part masc acc pl   id.
ἀδικησάντων vb 1st aor act part masc and neut gen pl id.
ἀδικήσει vb fut act ind 3rd pers sg   id.
ἀδικήσειν vb fut act inf   id.
ἀδικήσεις vb fut act ind 2nd pers sg   id.
ἀδικήσῃ vb 1st aor act subj 3rd pers sg   id.
ἀδικήσητε vb 1st aor act subj 2nd pers pl   id.
ἀδικήσουσιν vb fut act ind 3rd pers pl   id.
ἀδικήσω vb 1st aor act subj 1st pers sg   id.
ἀδικία noun fem nom sg
ἀδικίᾳ noun fem dat sg . . . . ἀδικία
ἀδικίαι noun fem nom pl   id.
ἀδικίαις noun fem dat pl   id.
ἀδικίαν noun fem acc sg   id.
ἀδικίας noun fem gen sg and acc pl   id.
ἀδικιῶν noun fem gen pl   id.
ἄδικοι adj masc and fem nom pl . . . . ἄδικος
ἀδίκοις adj dat pl   id.
ἄδικον adj acc sg, neut nom sg   id.
ἄδικος adj masc and fem nom sg   id.
ἀδίκου adj gen sg   id.
ἀδικοῦμαι vb pres m/p ind 1st pers sg . . . . ἀδικέω
ἀδικουμένοις vb pres m/p part masc and neut dat pl   id.
ἀδικούμενον vb pres m/p part masc acc sg,
          neut nom and acc sg   id.
ἀδικούμενος vb pres m/p part masc nom sg   id.
ἀδικουμένων vb pres m/p part gen pl   id.
ἀδικοῦντας vb pres act part masc acc pl   id.
ἀδικοῦντι vb pres act part masc and neut dat sg   id.
ἀδικοῦντος vb pres act part masc and neut gen sg   id.
ἀδίκους adj masc and fem acc pl . . . . ἄδικος
ἀδικοῦσιν vb pres act ind 3rd pers pl . . . . ἀδικέω
ἀδίκῳ adj dat sg . . . . ἄδικος
ἀδίκων adj gen pl   id.
ἀδικῶν vb pres act part masc nom sg . . . . ἀδικέω
ἀδίκως adverb
Αδιν pr noun
Αδινα pr noun
Αδινου pr noun

Αδινων pr noun

Αδλι pr noun

Αδνας pr noun

ἀδόκητοι adj masc and fem nom pl . . . . ἀδόκητος

ἀδόκιμον adj acc sg, neut nom sg . . . . ἀδόκιμος

ἀδολέσχει vb pres act impv 2nd pers sg . . . . . . ἀδολεσχέω

ἀδολεσχῆσαι vb 1st aor act inf   id.

ἀδολεσχήσω vb 1st aor act subj 1st pers sg,
      fut act ind 1st pers sg   id.

ἀδολεσχία noun fem nom sg

ἀδολεσχίᾳ noun fem dat sg . . . . ἀδολεσχία

ἀδολεσχίαν noun fem acc sg   id.

ἀδολεσχίας noun fem gen sg and acc pl   id.

ἀδόλως adverb

ᾄδοντας vb pres act part masc acc pl . . . . ᾄδω

ᾄδοντες vb pres act part masc nom pl   id.

ᾀδόντων vb pres act part masc and neut gen pl   id.

ἀδοξήσει vb fut act ind 3rd pers sg . . . . ἀδοξέω

ἀδοξίᾳ noun fem dat sg . . . . ἀδοξία

ἄδοξος adj masc and fem nom sg

ᾅδου noun masc gen sg . . . . ᾅδης

Αδουηλ pr noun

ᾄδουσαι vb pres act part fem nom pl . . . . ᾄδω

ᾀδούσας vb pres act part fem acc pl   id.

ᾄδουσι vb pres act part masc and neut dat pl   id.

ᾀδουσῶν vb pres act part fem gen pl   id.

Αδρααζαρ pr noun

Αδραζαρ pr noun

Αδραμελεχ pr noun

ἀδρανέστατον superl adj masc acc sg,
      neut nom and acc sg . . . . ἀδρανής

ἀδροί adj masc nom pl . . . . ἀδρός

ἀδροῖς adj masc and neut dat pl   id.

ἀδρούς adj masc acc pl   id.

ἀδρυνθέντος vb 1st aor pass part
      masc and neut gen sg . . . . ἀδρύνω

ἀδρυνθῆναι vb 1st aor pass inf   id.

ἀδρυνθῶσιν vb 1st aor pass subj 3rd pers pl   id.

ἀδυναμεῖν vb pres act inf . . . . ἀδυναμέω

ἀδυναμίᾳ noun fem dat sg . . . . ἀδυναμία

ἀδυναμίαις noun fem dat pl   id.

ἀδύνατα adj neut nom and acc pl . . . . ἀδύνατος

ἀδυνατεῖ vb pres act ind 3rd pers sg . . . . ἀδυνατέω

ἀδυνατήσει vb fut act ind 3rd pers sg   id.

ἀδυνατήσῃ vb 1st aor act subj 3rd pers sg   id.

ἀδυνατήσουσιν vb fut act ind 3rd pers pl   id.

ἀδύνατοι adj masc and fem nom pl . . . . ἀδύνατος

ἀδύνατον adj acc sg, neut nom sg   id.

ἀδύνατος adj masc and fem nom sg   id.

ἀδυνάτου adj gen sg   id.

ἀδυνάτους adj masc and fem acc pl   id.

ἀδυνατοῦσι vb pres act part masc and neut dat pl   ἀδυνατέω

ἀδυνάτῳ adj dat sg . . . . ἀδύνατος

ἀδυνάτων adj gen pl   id.

ἀδυνατῶν vb pres act part masc nom sg . . . . ἀδυνατέω

αδων translit

Αδωναι pr noun

Αδωναιε pr noun

Αδωνια pr noun

Αδωνια pr noun masc dat sg . . . . Αδωνιας

Αδωνιας pr noun masc nom sg   id.

Αδωνιβεζεκ pr noun

Αδωνικαμ pr noun

Αδωνιου pr noun masc gen sg . . . . Αδωνιας

Αδωνιραμ pr noun

Αδωρα pr noun

Αδωραιμ pr noun

αδωρηεμ translit

ἀεί adverb

Αεμε pr noun

ἀέναος adj masc and fem nom sg

ἀενάου adj gen sg . . . . ἀέναος

ἀενάους adj masc and fem acc pl   id.

ἀενάων adj gen pl   id.

Αενδωρ pr noun

Αερ pr noun

ἀέρα noun masc acc sg . . . . ἀήρ

ἀεργός adj masc and fem nom sg

ἀεργοῦ adj gen sg . . . . ἀεργός

ἀεργῶν adj gen pl   id.

Αερμων pr noun

ἀέρος noun masc gen sg . . . . ἀήρ

ἀέρων noun masc gen pl   id.

ἀετοί noun masc nom pl . . . . ἀετός

ἀετόν noun masc acc sg   id.

ἀετός noun masc nom sg   id.

ἀετοῦ noun masc gen sg   id.

ἀετούς noun masc acc pl   id.

ἀετῶν noun masc gen pl   id.

Αζαβουχ pr noun

Αζαηλ pr noun

Αζαηλος pr noun

Αζαηλου pr noun gen sg . . . . Ἀζαηλος

Αζαια pr noun

Αζακι pr noun

Αζανια pr noun

Αζανωθ pr noun

Αζαραηλ pr noun

Αζαρια pr noun masc

Αζαρια pr noun masc voc sg and dat sg . . . . Αζαριας

Αζαριαν pr noun masc acc sg   id.

Αζαριας pr noun masc nom sg

Αζαριον pr noun

Αζαριου pr noun

Αζαριου pr noun masc gen sg . . . . Αζαριας	ἀθέσμου adj masc and fem gen sg . . . . ἄθεσμος
Αζαυ pr noun	ἀθέσμως adverb
Αζενι pr noun	ἀθετεῖ vb pres act ind 3rd pers sg . . . . ἀθετέω
Αζερ pr noun	ἀθετεῖν vb pres act inf id.
Αζηκα pr noun	ἀθετηθῇ vb 1st aor pass subj 3rd pers sg id.
Αζηρ pr noun	ἀθετηθήσεται vb fut pass ind 3rd pers sg id.
Αζητας pr noun	ἀθετήματα noun neut nom and acc pl . . . . ἀθέτημα
Αζιηλ pr noun	ἀθετῆσαι vb 1st aor act inf . . . . ἀθετέω
Αζιν pr noun	ἀθετήσει vb fut act ind 3rd pers sg id.
Αζιφ pr noun	ἀθετήσεις vb fut act ind 2nd pers sg id.
Αζμωθ pr noun	ἀθετήσῃ vb 1st aor act subj 3rd pers sg id.
Αζοβ pr noun	ἀθέτησις noun fem nom sg
Αζουβα pr noun	ἀθετήσω vb 1st aor act subj 1st pers sg,
Αζουρ pr noun	fut act ind 1st pers sg . . . . ἀθετέω
Αζουρου pr noun	ἀθετήσωσιν vb 1st aor act subj 3rd pers pl id.
ἄζυμα adj neut nom and acc pl . . . . ἄζυμος	ἀθετοῦντες vb pres act part masc nom pl id.
ἄζυμον adj acc sg, neut nom sg id.	ἀθετούντων vb pres act part masc and neut gen pl id.
ἀζύμους adj masc and fem acc pl id.	ἀθετοῦσιν vb pres act ind 3rd pers pl id.
ἀζύμων adj gen pl id.	ἀθετῶν vb pres act part masc nom sg id.
Αζωβαι pr noun	ἀθεώρητος adj masc and fem nom sg
Αζωρ pr noun	Ἀθηναιοις pr noun masc dat pl . . . . Ἀθηναῖος
Ἀζωτιας pr noun gen sg . . . . Ἀζωτια	Ἀθηναῖον pr noun masc acc sg id.
Ἀζωτιοι pr noun masc nom pl . . . . Ἀζωτιος	Ἀθηνοβιον pr noun masc acc sg . . . . Ἀθηνοβιος
Ἀζωτιους pr noun masc acc pl id.	Ἀθηνοβιος pr noun masc nom sg id.
Ἀζωτιστι pr noun	Αθιν pr noun
Ἀζωτιῳ pr noun fem dat sg . . . . Ἀζωτιος	ἄθλα noun neut nom and acc pl . . . . ἆθλον
Ἀζωτον pr noun fem acc sg . . . . Ἀζωτος	ἀθλητάς noun masc acc pl . . . . ἀθλητής
Ἀζωτος pr noun fem nom sg id.	ἀθλητής noun masc nom sg id.
Ἀζωτου pr noun fem gen sg id.	ἀθλιώτατε superl adj masc voc sg . . . . ἄθλιος
Ἀζωτῳ pr noun fem dat sg id.	ἀθλιωτάτης superl adj fem gen sg id.
ἀηδιαι noun fem nom pl . . . . ἀηδία	ἀθλοφόρε adj masc and fem voc sg . . . . ἀθλοφόρος
Αηδις pr noun	ἀθλοφόρῳ adj dat sg id.
ἀήρ noun masc nom sg	ἄθλων noun neut gen pl . . . . ἆθλον
Αθαθ pr noun	αθουκιιν translit
Αθαια pr noun	Αθουρ pr noun
ἀθανασία noun fem nom sg	Αθουριας pr noun masc nom sg
ἀθανασίαν noun fem acc sg . . . . ἀθανασία	ἀθροίσατε vb 1st aor act impv 2nd pers pl . . . . ἀθροίζω
ἀθανασίας noun fem gen sg id.	ἀθροίσθητε vb 1st aor pass impv 2nd pers pl id.
ἀθάνατος adj masc and fem nom sg	ἄθροισμα noun neut nom and acc sg
ἀθανάτου adj gen sg . . . . ἀθάνατος	ἀθροισον vb 1st aor act impv 2nd pers sg . . . . ἀθροίζω
ἀθανάτους adj masc and fem acc pl id.	ἀθροίσω vb fut act ind 1st pers sg id.
Αθανι pr noun	ἀθρόους adj masc acc pl . . . . ἀθρόος
Αθανιν pr noun	ἀθυμήσασι vb 1st aor act part masc and neut dat pl . ἀθυμέω
Αθαριν pr noun	ἀθυμία noun fem nom sg
Αθελια pr noun	ἀθυμίαν noun fem acc sg . . . . ἀθυμία
ἀθεμίτοις adj dat pl . . . . ἀθέμιτος	ἀθυμοῦσαν vb pres act part fem acc sg . . . . ἀθυμέω
ἀθεμίτους adj masc and fem acc pl id.	ἄθυτον adj acc sg, neut nom sg . . . . ἄθυτος
ἀθεμίτων adj gen pl id.	ἀθῴα adj fem nom sg . . . . ἀθῷος
Αθερ pr noun	ἀθῷοι adj masc and fem nom pl id.
Αθερσαθα pr noun	ἀθῴοις adj dat pl id.
ἀθεσία noun fem dat sg . . . . ἀθεσία	ἀθῷον adj acc sg, neut nom sg id.
ἀθεσίαν noun fem acc sg id.	ἀθῷος adj masc and fem nom sg

ἀθῴου adj gen sg . . . . ἀθῷος	αἰδοῦμαι vb pres dep ind 1st pers sg . . . . αἰδέομαι
ἀθῴους adj masc and fem acc pl id.	αἰδοῦς noun fem gen sg . . . . αἰδώς
ἀθῴῳ adj dat sg id.	αἰδώ noun fem acc sg id.
ἀθῳωθῇς vb 1st aor pass subj 2nd pers sg . . . . ἀθῳόω	Αιε pr noun
ἀθῳωθήσεται vb fut pass ind 3rd pers sg id.	αἰεί adverb . . . . ἀεί
ἀθῳωθήσῃ vb fut mid ind 2nd pers sg id.	Αιζηλ pr noun
ἀθῳωμένη vb pres m/p part fem nom sg id.	αἰθάλην noun fem acc sg . . . . αἰθάλη
ἀθῴων adj gen pl . . . . ἀθῷος	αἰθάλης noun fem gen sg id.
ἀθῳῶν vb pres act part masc nom sg . . . . ἀθῳόω	Αιθαλιμ pr noun
ἀθῳώσει vb fut act ind 3rd pers sg id.	Αιθαμ pr noun
ἀθῳώσῃς vb 1st aor act subj 2nd pers sg id.	Αιθαμιν pr noun
ἀθῳώσον vb 1st aor act impv 2nd pers sg id.	Αιθαν pr noun
ἀθῳώσω vb fut act ind 1st pers sg id.	Αιθι pr noun
αἱ art fem nom pl . . . . ὁ	Αιθιηλ pr noun
αἵ rel pron fem nom pl . . . . ὅς	Αἰθιοπα pr noun masc acc sg . . . . Αἰθιοψ
Αια pr noun	Αἰθιοπας pr noun masc acc pl id.
Αϊα pr noun	Αἰθιοπες pr noun masc nom pl id.
Αιαλων pr noun	Αἰθιοπια pr noun fem nom sg
αἶγα noun fem or masc acc sg . . . . αἴξ	Αἰθιοπια pr noun fem dat sg . . . . Αἰθιοπια
αἶγας noun fem or masc acc pl id.	Αἰθιοπιαν pr noun fem acc sg id.
Αιγγαδοις pr noun	Αἰθιοπιας pr noun fem gen sg id.
αἰγείας adj fem gen sg and acc pl . . . . αἴγειος	Αἰθιοπισσαν pr noun fem acc sg . . . . Αἰθιοπισσα
αἶγες noun fem or masc nom pl . . . . αἴξ	Αἰθιοπισσης pr noun fem gen sg id.
αἰγιαλόν noun masc acc sg . . . . αἰγιαλός	Αἰθιοπων pr noun gen pl . . . . Αἰθιοψ
αἰγίδια noun neut nom and acc pl . . . . αἰγίδιον	Αἰθιοψ pr noun masc nom sg id.
Αιγλα pr noun	Αἰθιοψι(ν) pr noun masc dat pl id.
Αἰγυπτια adj fem nom sg . . . . Αἰγυπτιος	αἴθριοι adj masc and fem nom pl . . . . αἴθριος
Αἰγυπτιαν adj fem acc sg id.	αἴθριον adj acc sg, neut nom sg id.
Αἰγυπτιας adj fem gen sg id.	αἴθριος adj masc and fem nom sg id.
Αἰγυπτιοι adj masc nom pl id.	αἰθρίου adj gen sg id.
Αἰγυπτιοις adj masc dat pl id.	Αιιν pr noun
Αἰγυπτιον adj masc acc sg id.	Αικαρεν pr noun
Αἰγυπτιος adj masc nom sg id.	αἰκίαις noun fem dat pl . . . . αἰκία
Αἰγυπτιου adj masc gen sg id.	αἰκίας noun fem acc pl id.
Αἰγυπτιους adj masc acc pl id.	αἰκιζόμενοι vb pres dep part masc nom pl . . . . . . αἰκίζομαι
Αἰγυπτιῳ adj masc dat sg id.	αἰκιζομένους vb pres dep part masc acc pl id.
Αἰγυπτιων adj gen pl id.	αἰκισαμένων vb 1st aor mid part gen pl id.
Αἰγυπτον pr noun fem acc sg . . . . Αἰγυπτος	αἰκισθείς vb 1st aor pass part masc nom sg id.
Αἰγυπτος pr noun fem nom sg id.	αἰκισμοῖς noun masc dat pl . . . . αἰκισμός
Αἰγυπτου pr noun fem gen sg id.	αἰκισμόν noun masc acc sg id.
Αἰγυπτῳ pr noun fem dat sg id.	αἰκισμούς noun masc acc pl id.
αἰγῶν noun fem or masc gen pl . . . . αἴξ	αιλ translit
αιδαδ translit	Αιλαθ pr noun
Αιδαν pr noun	αιλαμ translit
αἰδεῖσθαι vb pres dep inf . . . . αἰδέομαι	Αιλαμ pr noun
αἰδεσθείς vb 1st aor pass part masc nom sg id.	Αιλαμῖται pr noun masc nom pl . . . . Αιλαμιτης
αἰδήμονα adj masc and fem acc sg . . . . αἰδήμων	Αιλαμιτῶν pr noun masc gen pl id.
αἰδήμονες adj masc and fem nom pl id.	αιλαμμιν translit
ἀΐδιον adj acc sg, neut nom sg . . . . ἀΐδιος	αιλαμμω translit
ἀϊδιότητος noun fem gen sg . . . . ἀϊδιότης	αιλευ translit
ἀϊδίου adj gen sg . . . . ἀΐδιος	Αιλιμ pr noun
αἰδοῖα adj neut nom and acc pl . . . . αἰδοῖος	αἴλουροι noun masc nom pl . . . . αἴλουρος

Αιλους pr noun

Αιλωθ pr noun

Αιλωμ pr noun

Αιλων pr noun

αἷμα noun neut nom and acc sg

Αιμαθ pr noun

Αιμαν pr noun

Αιμανι pr noun

αἱμάξαι vb 1st aor act inf . . . . αἱμάσσω

Αιμαρεκ pr noun

αἵμασι noun neut dat pl . . . . αἷμα

αἵματα noun neut nom and acc pl   id.

αἵματι noun neut dat sg   id.

αἵματος noun neut gen sg   id.

αἱμάτων noun neut gen pl   id.

αἱμοβόρος adj masc and fem nom sg

αἱμορροούσῃ vb pres act part fem dat sg . . . . . αἱμορροέω

αἱμωδιάσουσιν vb fut act ind 3rd pers pl . . . . . . αἱμωδιάω

αιν translit (Heb. letter: ע)

Αιν pr noun

Αιναγαλιμ pr noun

Αινακιμ pr noun

Αιναν pr noun

Αινγαδιν pr noun

αἴνει vb pres act impv 2nd pers sg . . . . αἰνέω

αἰνεῖν vb pres act inf   id.

αἰνείσθω vb pres m/p impv 3rd pers sg   id.

αἰνεῖτε vb pres act impv 2nd pers pl,
       pres act ind 2nd pers pl   id.

αἰνείτω vb pres act impv 3rd pers sg   id.

αἰνέσαι vb 1st aor act inf   id.

αἰνέσαισαν vb 1st aor act opt 3rd pers pl   id.

αἰνέσατε vb 1st aor act impv 2nd pers pl   id.

αἰνεσάτω vb 1st aor act impv 3rd pers sg   id.

αἰνεσάτωσαν vb 1st aor act impv 3rd pers pl   id.

αἰνέσει noun fem dat sg . . . . αἴνεσις

αἰνέσει vb fut act ind 3rd pers sg . . . . αἰνέω

αἰνέσεις noun fem acc pl . . . . αἴνεσις

αἰνέσεσιν noun fem dat pl   id.

αἰνέσετε vb fut act ind 2nd pers pl . . . . αἰνέω

αἰνέσεως noun fem gen sg . . . . αἴνεσις

αἰνέσῃς vb 1st aor act subj 2nd pers sg . . . . αἰνέω

αἴνεσιν noun fem acc sg . . . . αἴνεσις

αἴνεσις noun fem nom sg   id.

αἰνέσομεν vb fut act ind 1st pers pl . . . . αἰνέω

αἰνέσουσιν vb fut act ind 3rd pers pl   id.

αἰνέσω vb 1st aor act subj 1st pers sg,
       fut act ind 1st pers sg   id.

αἰνέσωμεν vb 1st aor act subj 1st pers pl   id.

αἰνετόν adj masc acc sg, neut nom and acc sg . . . . . αἰνετός

αἰνετός adj masc nom sg   id.

αἰνετῷ adj masc and neut dat sg   id.

αἰνῇ vb pres act subj 3rd pers sg . . . . αἰνέω

αἰνίγμασι noun neut dat pl . . . . αἴνιγμα

αἰνίγματα noun neut nom and acc pl   id.

αἰνίγματι noun neut dat sg   id.

αἰνιγματισταί noun masc nom pl . . . . αἰνιγματιστής

αἰνιγμάτων noun neut gen pl . . . . αἴνιγμα

αἴνοις noun masc dat pl . . . . αἶνος

αἶνον noun masc acc sg   id.

αἶνος noun masc nom sg   id.

αἰνοῦμεν vb pres act ind 1st pers pl . . . . αἰνέω

αἰνοῦντας vb pres act part masc acc pl   id.

αἰνοῦντες vb pres act part masc nom pl   id.

αἰνούντων vb pres act part masc and neut gen pl   id.

αἴνους noun masc acc pl . . . . αἶνος

αἰνῶ vb pres act ind 1st pers sg . . . . αἰνέω

αἴνῳ noun masc dat sg . . . . αἶνος

Αινων pr noun

αἰνῶν vb pres act part masc nom sg . . . . αἰνέω

αἰξί noun fem or masc dat pl . . . . αἴξ

αἰπολίου noun neut gen sg . . . . αἰπόλιον

αἰπόλος noun masc nom sg

αἴρειν vb pres act inf . . . . αἴρω

αἱρεῖται vb pres m/p ind 3rd pers sg . . . . αἱρέω

Αιρεμ pr noun

αἱρέσεως noun fem gen sg . . . . αἵρεσις

αἵρεσιν noun fem acc sg   id.

αἴρεται vb pres m/p ind 3rd pers sg . . . . αἴρω

αἴρετε vb pres act impv 2nd pers pl,
       pres act ind 2nd pers pl   id.

αἱρετιεῖ vb fut act ind 3rd pers sg . . . . αἱρετίζω

αἱρετίζει vb pres act ind 3rd pers sg   id.

αἱρετίζοντας vb pres act part masc acc pl   id.

αἱρετίζουσιν vb pres act ind 3rd pers pl   id.

αἱρετίς noun fem nom sg

αἱρετιῶ vb fut act ind 1st pers sg . . . . αἱρετίζω

αἱρετοῖς adj masc and neut dat pl . . . . αἱρετός

αἱρετόν adj masc acc sg, neut nom and acc sg   id.

αἱρετώτεραι comp adj fem nom pl   id.

αἱρετώτερον comp adj masc acc sg, neut nom and acc sg   id.

αἱρόμενα vb pres m/p part neut nom and acc pl . . . . . . αἴρω

αἱρόμενοι vb pres m/p part masc nom pl   id.

αἱρομένους vb pres m/p part masc acc pl   id.

αἱρομένων vb pres m/p part gen pl   id.

αἶρον vb pres act part neut nom and acc sg   id.

αἴροντα vb pres act part masc acc sg,
       neut nom and acc pl   id.

αἴρονται vb pres m/p ind 3rd pers pl   id.

αἴροντας vb pres act part masc acc pl   id.

αἴροντες vb pres act part masc nom pl   id.

αἴροντι vb pres act part masc and neut dat sg   id.

αἴροντος vb pres act part masc and neut gen sg   id.

αἰρόντων vb pres act part masc and neut gen pl   id.

αἱρούμενοι vb pres m/p part masc nom pl . . . . αἱρέω

αἴρουσα vb pres act part fem nom sg . . . . αἴρω

αἴρουσαι vb pres act part fem nom pl   id.

αἱρούσας vb pres act part fem acc pl   id.

αἴρουσι(ν) vb pres act ind 3rd pers pl,

         pres act part masc and neut dat pl   id.

αἴρω vb pres act ind 1st pers sg   id.

αἴρων vb pres act part masc nom sg   id.

αἷς rel pron fem dat pl . . . . ὅς

Αισαμ pr noun

Αισαν pr noun

αἰσθάνεται vb pres dep ind 3rd pers sg . . . . . . αἰσθάνομαι

αἰσθανθήσεται vb fut pass ind 3rd pers sg   id.

αἰσθάνονται vb pres dep ind 3rd pers pl   id.

αἰσθέσθαι vb 2nd aor mid inf   id.

αἰσθηθῇ vb 1st aor pass subj 3rd pers sg   id.

αἰσθηθήσεσθε vb fut pass ind 2nd pers pl   id.

αἰσθήσει noun fem dat sg . . . . αἴσθησις

αἰσθήσεως noun fem gen sg   id.

αἰσθήσῃ vb fut pass ind 2nd pers sg . . . . αἰσθάνομαι

αἴσθησιν noun fem acc sg . . . . αἴσθησις

αἴσθησις noun fem nom sg   id.

αἰσθητήρια noun neut nom and acc pl . . . . . αἰσθητήριον

αἰσθητηρίων noun neut gen pl   id.

αἰσθητική adj fem nom sg . . . . αἰσθητικός

αἰσθοίμην vb 2nd aor mid opt 1st pers sg . . . . αἰσθάνομαι

Αισιμωθ pr noun

αἰσχίσταις superl adj fem dat pl . . . . αἰσχρός

αἰσχραί adj fem nom pl   id.

αἰσχρόν adj masc acc sg, neut nom and acc sg   id.

αἰσχροτέρας comp adj fem acc pl   id.

αἰσχρῶν adj gen pl   id.

αἰσχρῶς adverb

αἰσχύνει vb pres act ind 3rd pers sg . . . . αἰσχύνω

αἰσχυνεῖ vb fut act ind 3rd pers sg   id.

αἰσχύνεσθε vb pres m/p impv 2nd pers pl   id.

αἰσχύνεται vb pres m/p ind 3rd pers sg   id.

αἰσχύνη noun fem nom sg

αἰσχύνῃ noun fem dat sg . . . . αἰσχύνη

αἰσχύνην noun fem acc sg   id.

αἰσχύνης noun fem gen sg   id.

αἰσχυνθείησαν vb 1st aor pass opt 3rd pers pl . . . αἰσχύνω

αἰσχυνθείητε vb 1st aor pass opt 2nd pers pl   id.

αἰσχυνθέντες vb 1st aor pass part masc nom pl   id.

αἰσχυνθῇς vb 1st aor pass subj 2nd pers sg   id.

αἰσχυνθήσεσθε vb fut pass ind 2nd pers pl   id.

αἰσχυνθήσεται vb fut pass ind 3rd pers sg   id.

αἰσχυνθήσῃ vb fut pass ind 2nd pers sg   id.

αἰσχυνθήσομαι vb fut pass ind 1st pers sg   id.

αἰσχυνθήσονται vb fut pass ind 3rd pers pl   id.

αἰσχύνθητε vb 1st aor pass impv 2nd pers pl   id.

αἰσχύνθητι vb 1st aor pass impv 2nd pers sg   id.

αἰσχυνθήτωσαν vb 1st aor pass impv 3rd pers pl . αἰσχύνω

αἰσχυνθῶ vb 1st aor pass subj 1st pers sg   id.

αἰσχυνθῶσιν vb 1st aor pass subj 3rd pers pl   id.

αἰσχυνόμεθα vb pres m/p ind 1st pers pl   id.

αἰσχυνόμενοι vb pres m/p part masc nom pl   id.

αἰσχυνόμενος vb pres m/p part masc nom sg   id.

αἰσχύνονται vb pres m/p ind 3rd pers pl   id.

αἰσχυντηρά adj fem nom sg . . . . αἰσχυντηρός

αἰσχυντηρός adj masc nom sg   id.

αἰσχυντηροῦ adj masc and neut gen sg   id.

Αισωρα pr noun

Αιταμ pr noun

Αιταν pr noun

αἰτεῖ vb pres act ind 3rd pers sg . . . . αἰτέω

αἰτεῖς vb pres act ind 2nd pers sg   id.

αἰτεῖσθε vb pres m/p impv 2nd pers pl   id.

αἰτεῖται vb pres m/p ind 3rd pers sg   id.

αἰτηθείς vb 1st aor pass part masc nom sg   id.

αἴτημα noun neut nom and acc sg

αἰτήματα noun neut nom and acc pl . . . . αἴτημα

αἰτήματι noun neut dat sg   id.

αἴτησαι vb 1st aor mid impv 2nd pers sg . . . . αἰτέω

αἰτῆσαι vb 1st aor act inf   id.

αἰτησάμενος vb 1st aor mid part masc nom sg   id.

αἰτήσαντες vb 1st aor act part masc nom pl   id.

αἰτήσασθαι vb 1st aor mid inf   id.

αἰτησάτω vb 1st aor act impv 3rd pers sg   id.

αἰτήσει vb fut act ind 3rd pers sg   id.

αἰτήσῃ vb 1st aor act subj 3rd pers sg   id.

αἴτησιν noun fem acc sg . . . . αἴτησις

αἴτησις noun fem nom sg   id.

αἰτήσομαι vb fut mid ind 1st pers sg . . . . αἰτέω

αἴτησον vb 1st aor act impv 2nd pers sg   id.

αἰτήσω vb fut act ind 1st pers sg   id.

αἰτήσωσιν vb 1st aor act subj 3rd pers pl   id.

αἰτία noun fem nom sg

αἰτίᾳ noun fem dat sg . . . . αἰτία

αἰτίαν noun fem acc sg   id.

αἰτίας noun fem gen sg and acc pl   id.

αἰτιάσεται vb fut mid ind 3rd pers sg . . . . αἰτιάομαι

αἰτιᾶται vb pres dep ind 3rd pers sg   id.

αἵτινες rel pron fem nom pl . . . . ὅστις

αἴτιοι adj masc nom pl . . . . αἴτιος

αἴτιον adj masc acc sg, neut nom and acc sg   id.

αἴτιος adj masc nom sg   id.

αἰτίους adj masc acc pl   id.

αἰτιῶν noun fem gen pl . . . . αἰτία

αἰτοῦμαι vb pres m/p ind 1st pers sg . . . . αἰτέω

αἰτούμενοι vb pres m/p part masc nom pl   id.

αἰτοῦντας vb pres act part masc acc pl   id.

αἰτοῦσιν vb pres act ind 3rd pers pl   id.

Αἶτωβ pr noun

αἰφνίδιον adj acc sg, neut nom sg . . . . αἰφνίδιος
αἰφνίδιος adj masc and fem nom sg id.
αἰφνιδίου adj gen sg id.
αἰφνιδίως adverb
Αιχιοζα pr noun
αἰχμαλωσία noun fem nom sg
αἰχμαλωσίᾳ noun fem dat sg . . . . αἰχμαλωσία
αἰχμαλωσίαν noun fem acc sg id.
αἰχμαλωσίας noun fem gen sg id.
αἰχμαλωσιῶν noun fem gen pl id.
αἰχμάλωτα adj neut nom and acc pl . . . . αἰχμάλωτος
αἰχμαλωτευθήσεται vb fut pass ind
    3rd pers sg . . . . αἰχμαλωτεύω
αἰχμαλωτευθήσῃ vb fut pass ind 2nd pers sg id.
αἰχμαλωτευομένη vb pres m/p part fem nom sg id.
αἰχμαλωτεύοντες vb pres act part masc nom pl id.
αἰχμαλωτευόντων vb pres act part masc and neut gen pl id.
αἰχμαλωτεῦσαι vb 1st aor act inf id.
αἰχμαλωτεύσαντες vb 1st aor act part masc nom pl id.
αἰχμαλωτευσάντων vb 1st aor act part
    masc and neut gen pl id.
αἰχμαλωτεύσῃ vb 1st aor act subj 3rd pers sg id.
αἰχμαλωτεύσουσιν vb fut act ind 3rd pers pl id.
αἰχμαλώτιδας noun fem acc pl . . . . αἰχμαλωτίς
αἰχμαλωτίδος noun fem gen sg id.
αἰχμαλώτιζε vb pres act impv 2nd pers sg . . . αἰχμαλωτίζω
αἰχμαλωτίζειν vb pres act inf id.
αἰχμαλωτίζοντες vb pres act part masc nom pl id.
αἰχμαλωτιοῦσιν vb fut act ind 3rd pers pl id.
αἰχμαλωτισάντων vb 1st aor act part
    masc and neut gen pl id.
αἰχμαλωτίσας vb 1st aor act part masc nom sg id.
αἰχμαλωτισθεῖσαν vb 1st aor pass part fem acc sg id.
αἰχμαλωτισθέντων vb 1st aor pass part
    masc and neut gen pl id.
αἰχμαλωτισθῆναι vb 1st aor pass inf id.
αἰχμαλωτισθήσονται vb fut pass ind 3rd pers pl id.
αἰχμαλώτισον vb 1st aor act impv 2nd pers sg id.
αἰχμάλωτοι adj masc and fem nom pl . . . . αἰχμάλωτος
αἰχμαλώτοις adj dat pl id.
αἰχμάλωτον adj acc sg, neut nom sg id.
αἰχμάλωτος adj masc and fem nom sg id.
αἰχμαλώτους adj masc and fem acc pl id.
αἰχμαλώτων adj gen pl id.
αἰών noun masc nom sg
αἰῶνα noun masc acc sg . . . . αἰών
αἰῶνας noun masc acc pl id.
αἰῶνι noun masc dat sg id.
αἰώνια adj neut nom and acc pl . . . . αἰώνιος
αἰωνία adj fem nom sg id.
αἰωνίᾳ adj fem dat sg id.
αἰωνίαν adj fem acc sg id.

αἰωνίας adj fem gen sg and acc pl . . . . αἰώνιος
αἰώνιε adj masc voc sg id.
αἰώνιοι adj masc nom pl id.
αἰωνίοις adj masc and neut dat pl id.
αἰώνιον adj masc acc sg, neut nom and acc sg id.
αἰώνιος adj masc nom sg id.
αἰωνίου adj masc and neut gen sg id.
αἰωνίους adj masc acc pl id.
αἰωνίῳ adj masc and neut dat sg id.
αἰωνίων adj gen pl id.
αἰῶνος noun masc gen sg . . . . αἰών
αἰώνων noun masc gen pl id.
αἰῶσι noun masc dat pl id.
Ακαβωθ pr noun
ἀκαθαρσία noun fem nom sg
ἀκαθαρσίᾳ noun fem dat sg . . . . ἀκαθαρσία
ἀκαθαρσίαις noun fem dat pl id.
ἀκαθαρσίαν noun fem acc sg id.
ἀκαθαρσίας noun fem gen sg and acc pl id.
ἀκαθαρσιῶν noun fem gen pl id.
ἀκάθαρτα adj neut nom and acc pl . . . . ἀκάθαρτος
ἀκάθαρτοι adj masc and fem nom pl id.
ἀκάθαρτον adj acc sg, neut nom sg id.
ἀκάθαρτος adj masc and fem nom sg id.
ἀκαθάρτου adj gen sg id.
ἀκαθάρτῳ adj dat sg id.
ἀκαθάρτων adj gen pl id.
ἄκαιρος adj masc and fem nom sg
ἀκαίρως adverb
ἀκακία noun fem nom sg
ἀκακίᾳ noun fem dat sg . . . . ἀκακία
ἀκακίαν noun fem acc sg id.
ἀκακίας noun fem gen sg id.
ἄκακοι adj masc and fem nom pl . . . . ἄκακος
ἀκάκοις adj dat pl id.
ἄκακον adj acc sg, neut nom sg id.
ἄκακος adj masc and fem nom sg id.
ἀκάκου adj gen sg id.
ἀκάκους adj masc and fem acc pl id.
ἀκάκων adj gen pl id.
ἀκάλυπτοι adj masc and fem nom pl . . . . ἀκάλυπτος
ἀκάλυπτον adj acc sg, neut nom sg id.
ἀκαλύπτως adverb
ακαν translit
ακανα translit
ἄκανθα noun fem nom sg
ἄκανθαι noun fem nom pl . . . . ἄκανθα
ἀκάνθαις noun fem dat pl id.
ἄκανθαν noun fem acc sg id.
ἀκάνθας noun fem acc pl id.
ἀκάνθης noun fem gen sg id.
ἀκάνθινα adj neut nom and acc pl . . . . ἀκάνθινος

ἀκανθῶν noun fem gen pl . . . . ἄκανθα
ἀκάρδιον adj acc sg, neut nom sg . . . . ἀκάρδιος
ἀκάρδιος adj masc and fem nom sg   id.
ἀκαριαῖον adj masc acc sg, neut nom and acc sg   ἀκαριαῖος
ἀκαρπίαν noun fem acc sg . . . . ἀκαρπία
ἄκαρποι adj masc and fem nom pl . . . . ἄκαρπος
ἄκαρπος adj masc and fem nom sg   id.
ἀκάρπῳ adj dat sg   id.
ἀκατάγνωστοι adj masc and fem nom pl . . . ἀκατάγνωστος
ἀκατακάλυπτος adj masc and fem nom sg
ἀκαταλύτους adj masc and fem acc pl . . . . . . ἀκατάλυτος
ἀκαταμάχητον adj acc sg, neut nom sg . . . ἀκαταμάχητος
Ακαταν pr noun
ἀκατάποτος adj masc nom sg
ἀκατασκεύαστος adj masc and fem nom sg
ἀκαταστασία noun fem nom sg
ἀκαταστασίας noun fem acc pl . . . . ἀκαταστασία
ἀκατάστατος adj masc and fem nom sg
ἀκατάσχετον adj acc sg, neut nom sg . . . . . ἀκατάσχετος
ἀκατάσχετος adj masc and fem nom sg   id.
ἀκατέργαστον adj acc sg, neut nom sg . . . . ἀκατέργαστος
ἄκαυστον adj acc sg, neut nom sg . . . . ἄκαυστος
ἀκέραιον adj acc sg, neut nom sg . . . . ἀκέραιος
ἀκηδίας noun fem gen sg and acc pl . . . . ἀκηδία
ἀκηδιάσαι vb 1st aor act inf . . . . ἀκηδιάω
ἀκηδιάσας vb 1st aor act part masc nom sg   id.
ἀκηδιάσῃ vb 1st aor act subj 3rd pers sg   id.
ἀκηδιάσῃς vb 1st aor act subj 2nd pers sg   id.
ἀκηδιῶν noun fem gen pl . . . . ἀκηδία
ἀκήκοα vb perf act ind 1st pers sg . . . . ἀκούω
ἀκηκόαμεν vb perf act ind 1st pers pl   id.
ἀκήκοας vb perf act ind 2nd pers sg   id.
ἀκηκόασιν vb perf act ind 3rd pers pl   id.
ἀκηκόατε vb perf act ind 2nd pers pl   id.
ἀκηκόει vb plpf act ind 3rd pers sg   id.
ἀκήκοεν vb perf act ind 3rd pers sg   id.
ἀκηκοότες vb perf act part masc nom pl   id.
ἀκηλίδωτον adj acc sg, neut nom sg . . . . ἀκηλίδωτος
ἀκηλίδωτος adj masc and fem nom sg   id.
ἀκιδωτόν noun neut nom and acc sg
Ακιεζι pr noun
Ακιμ pr noun
ἀκινάκην noun masc acc sg . . . . ἀκινάκης
ἀκινάκης noun masc nom sg   id.
ἀκίνητοι adj masc and fem nom pl . . . . ἀκίνητος
ἀκινήτοις adj dat pl   id.
ἀκίνητος adj masc and fem nom sg   id.
ἀκίσιν noun fem dat pl . . . . ἀκίς
Ακιφα pr noun
Ακκαριωθ pr noun
Ακκαρων pr noun
Ακκαρωνιτῃ pr noun masc dat sg . . . . Ακκαρωνιτης

Ακκως pr noun
ἀκλεῆ adj masc and fem acc sg . . . . ἀκλεής
ἀκλεῶς adverb
ἀκληρεῖ vb pres act ind 3rd pers sg . . . . ἀκληρέω
ἄκλητος adj masc and fem nom sg
ἀκλινῆ adj masc and fem acc sg . . . . ἀκλινής
ἀκλινής adj masc and fem nom sg   id.
ἀκμάζων vb pres act part masc nom sg . . . . ἀκμάζω
ἀκμαίας adj fem gen sg . . . . ἀκμαῖος
ἀκμαῖς noun fem dat pl . . . . ἀκμή
ἀκμή noun fem nom sg   id.
ἀκμῇ noun fem dat sg   id.
ἀκμῆς noun fem gen sg   id.
ἄκμονος noun masc gen sg . . . . ἄκμων
ἄκμων noun masc nom sg   id.
ἀκοαί noun fem nom pl . . . . ἀκοή
ἀκοαῖς noun fem dat pl   id.
ἀκοάς noun fem acc pl   id.
ἀκοή noun fem nom sg   id.
ἀκοῇ noun fem dat sg   id.
ἀκοήν noun fem acc sg   id.
ἀκοῆς noun fem gen sg   id.
ἀκοίμητον adj acc sg, neut nom sg . . . . ἀκοίμητος
ἀκοινώνητον adj acc sg, neut nom sg . . . . . . ἀκοινώνητος
ἀκολασίαν noun fem acc sg . . . . ἀκολασία
ἀκολάστοις adj dat pl . . . . ἀκόλαστος
ἀκόλαστον adj acc sg, neut nom sg   id.
ἀκολάστου adj gen sg   id.
ἀκόλουθα adj neut nom and acc pl . . . . ἀκόλουθος
ἀκολουθεῖν vb pres act inf . . . . ἀκολουθέω
ἀκολουθῆσαι vb 1st aor act inf   id.
ἀκολούθησον vb 1st aor act impv 2nd pers sg   id.
ἀκολουθήσουσιν vb fut act ind 3rd pers pl   id.
ἀκολουθήσω vb fut act ind 1st pers sg   id.
ἀκολουθίαι noun fem nom pl . . . . ἀκολουθία
ἀκόλουθος adj masc and fem nom sg
ἀκολούθως adverb
ἀκοντίζω vb pres act ind 1st pers sg
ἀκοντίζων vb pres act part masc nom sg . . . . ἀκοντίζω
ἀκοντισταί noun masc nom pl . . . . ἀκοντιστής
ἀκοπιάτως adverb . . . . ἀκοπιάστως
Ακορ pr noun
ἄκοσμον adj acc sg, neut nom sg . . . . ἄκοσμος
ἀκόσμως adverb
Ακουβ pr noun
Ακουδ pr noun
ἄκουε vb pres act impv 2nd pers sg . . . . ἀκούω
ἀκούει vb pres act ind 3rd pers sg   id.
ἀκούειν vb pres act inf   id.
ἀκούεις vb pres act ind 2nd pers sg   id.
ἀκούεσθαι vb pres m/p inf   id.
ἀκούεται vb pres m/p ind 3rd pers sg   id.

ἀκούετε vb pres act impv 2nd pers pl,

    pres act ind 2nd pers pl . . . . ἀκούω

ἀκουέτω vb pres act impv 3rd pers sg   id.

ἀκούηται vb pres m/p subj 3rd pers sg   id.

Ακουν pr noun

ἀκούομεν vb pres act ind 1st pers pl . . . . ἀκούω

ἀκουόμενοι vb pres m/p part masc nom pl   id.

ἀκούοντα vb pres act part masc acc sg,

    neut nom and acc pl   id.

ἀκούονται vb pres m/p ind 3rd pers pl   id.

ἀκούοντας vb pres act part masc acc pl   id.

ἀκούοντες vb pres act part masc nom pl   id.

ἀκούοντι vb pres act part masc and neut dat sg   id.

ἀκούοντος vb pres act part masc and neut gen sg   id.

ἀκουόντων vb pres act part masc and neut gen pl   id.

ἀκούουσιν vb pres act ind 3rd pers pl   id.

Ακους pr noun

ἀκούσαι vb 1st aor act opt 3rd pers sg . . . . ἀκούω

ἀκοῦσαι vb 1st aor act inf   id.

ἀκούσαιμι vb 1st aor act opt 1st pers sg   id.

ἀκούσαντα vb 1st aor act part masc acc sg   id.

ἀκούσαντες vb 1st aor act part masc nom pl   id.

ἀκούσας vb 1st aor act part masc nom sg   id.

ἀκούσασα vb 1st aor act part fem nom sg   id.

ἀκούσασαι vb 1st aor act part fem nom pl   id.

ἀκούσατε vb 1st aor act impv 2nd pers pl   id.

ἀκουσάτω vb 1st aor act impv 3rd pers sg   id.

ἀκουσάτωσαν vb 1st aor act impv 3rd pers pl   id.

ἀκούσει vb fut act ind 3rd pers sg   id.

ἀκούσεσθε vb fut mid ind 2nd pers pl   id.

ἀκούσεται vb fut mid ind 3rd pers sg   id.

ἀκούσετε vb fut act ind 2nd pers pl   id.

ἀκούση vb 1st aor act subj 3rd pers sg,

    fut mid ind 2nd pers sg   .   id.

ἀκούσης vb 1st aor act subj 2nd pers sg   id.

ἀκούσητε vb 1st aor act subj 2nd pers pl   id.

ἀκουσθῇ vb 1st aor pass subj 3rd pers sg   id.

ἀκουσθῆναι vb 1st aor pass inf   id.

ἀκουσθήσεται vb fut pass ind 3rd pers sg   id.

ἀκουσθήσῃ vb fut pass ind 2nd pers sg   id.

ἀκουσθήτω vb 1st aor pass impv 3rd pers sg   id.

ἀκουσιασθείσης vb 1st aor pass part

    fem gen sg . . . . ἀκουσιάζω

ἀκούσιον adj acc sg, neut nom sg . . . . ἀκούσιος

ἀκουσίων adj gen pl   id.

ἀκουσίως adverb

ἀκούσομαι vb fut mid ind 1st pers sg . . . . ἀκούω

ἀκουσόμεθα vb fut mid ind 1st pers pl   id.

ἀκούσομεν vb fut act ind 1st pers pl   id.

ἄκουσον vb 1st aor act impv 2nd pers sg   id.

ἀκούσονται vb fut mid ind 3rd pers pl   id.

ἀκουστά adj neut nom and acc pl . . . . ἀκουστός

ἀκουστάς adj fem acc pl   id.

ἀκουστή adj fem nom sg   id.

ἀκουστήν adj fem acc sg   id.

ἀκουστῆς adj fem gen sg   id.

ἀκουστόν adj masc acc sg, neut nom and acc sg   id.

ἀκούσω vb 1st aor act subj 1st pers sg . . . . ἀκούω

ἀκούσωμεν vb 1st aor act subj 1st pers pl   id.

ἀκούσωσιν vb 1st aor act subj 3rd pers pl   id.

ἀκουτιεῖς vb fut act ind 2nd pers sg . . . . ἀκουτίζω

ἀκουτίσασθε vb 1st aor mid impv 2nd pers pl   id.

ἀκούτισον vb 1st aor act impv 2nd pers sg   id.

ἀκουτιῶ vb fut act ind 1st pers sg   id.

Ακουφ pr noun

ἀκούω vb pres act ind 1st pers sg

ἀκούων vb pres act part masc nom sg . . . . ἀκούω

ἄκρα adj neut nom and acc pl . . . . ἄκρος

ἄκρᾳ adj fem dat sg   id.

ἄκρα noun fem dat sg . . . . ἄκρα

ἄκρᾳ noun fem dat sg . . . . ἄκρα

Ακραβαττηνην pr noun fem acc sg . . . . . . Ακραβαττηνη

Ακραβιν pr noun

ἄκραις adj fem dat pl . . . . ἄκρος

ἄκραν adj fem acc sg   id.

ἄκραν noun fem acc sg . . . . ἄκρα

ἄκρας adj fem gen sg . . . . ἄκρος

ἄκρας noun fem gen sg and acc pl . . . . ἄκρα

ἀκρασίαις noun fem dat pl . . . . ἀκρασία

ἀκρατεῖς adj masc and fem nom and acc pl . . . . . . ἀκρατής

ἀκράτου adj gen sg . . . . ἄκρατος

ἀκράτῳ adj dat sg   id.

ἀκριβασμοί noun masc nom pl . . . . ἀκριβασμός

ἀκριβεῖ adj fem dat sg . . . . ἀκριβής

ἀκριβείᾳ noun fem dat sg . . . . ἀκρίβεια

ἀκρίβειαν noun fem acc sg   id.

ἀκριβείας noun fem gen sg   id.

ἀκριβεῖς adj masc and fem nom and acc acc pl . . . . ἀκριβής

ἀκριβές adj neut nom and acc sg   id.

ἀκριβής adj masc and fem nom sg   id.

ἀκριβῶς adverb

ἀκρίδα noun fem acc sg . . . . ἀκρίς

ἀκρίδας noun fem acc pl   id.

ἀκρίδες noun fem nom pl   id.

ἀκρίδι noun fem dat sg   id.

ἀκρίδος noun fem gen sg   id.

ἀκρίδων noun fem gen pl   id.

ἀκρίς noun fem nom sg

ἀκρίτως adverb

ἀκρόαμα noun neut nom and acc sg

ἀκρόασαι vb 1st aor mid impv 2nd pers sg . . . ἀκροάομαι

ἀκροάσει noun fem dat sg . . . . ἀκρόασις

ἀκροάσεται vb fut mid ind 3rd pers sg . . . . . . ἀκροάομαι

ἀκροάσεως noun fem gen sg . . . . ἀκρόασις

ἀκροᾶσθαι vb pres dep inf . . . . ἀκροάομαι	ἀλαζονεύεται vb pres dep ind 3rd pers sg . . ἀλαζονεύομαι
ἀκρόασιν noun fem acc sg . . . . ἀκρόασις	ἀλαζονεύου vb pres dep impv 2nd pers sg id.
ἀκρόασις noun fem nom sg id.	ἀλαζόνων noun masc gen pl . . . . ἀλαζών
ἀκροᾶται vb pres dep ind 3rd pers sg . . . . ἀκροάομαι	ἀλαζών noun masc nom sg id.
ἀκροατήν noun masc acc sg . . . . ἀκροατής	ἀλαιμωθ translit
ἀκροατοῦ noun masc gen sg id.	ἄλαλα adj neut nom and acc pl . . . . ἄλαλος
ἀκροβυστίαις noun fem dat pl . . . . ἀκροβυστία	ἀλαλαγμόν noun masc acc sg . . . . ἀλαλαγμός
ἀκροβυστίαν noun fem acc sg id.	ἀλαλαγμός noun masc nom sg id.
ἀκροβυστίας noun fem gen sg and acc pl id.	ἀλαλαγμοῦ noun masc gen sg id.
ἀκροβυστιῶν noun fem gen pl id.	ἀλαλαγμῷ noun masc dat sg id.
ἀκρογωνιαῖον adj masc acc sg,	ἀλαλαγμῶν noun masc gen pl id.
neut nom and acc sg . . . . ἀκρογωνιαῖος	ἀλαλάξατε vb 1st aor act impv 2nd pers pl . . . . . ἀλαλάζω
ἀκρόδρυα noun neut nom and acc pl	ἀλάλαξον vb 1st aor act impv 2nd pers sg id.
ἀκροδρύων noun neut gen pl . . . . ἀκρόδρυα	ἀλαλάξουσιν vb fut act ind 3rd pers pl id.
ἄκρον adj masc acc sg, neut nom and acc sg . . . . ἄκρος	ἀλαλάξωμεν vb 1st aor act subj 1st pers pl id.
ἀκροπόλεως noun fem gen sg . . . . ἀκρόπολις	ἄλαλος adj masc and fem nom sg
ἀκρόπολιν noun fem acc sg id.	ἅλας noun masc acc pl . . . . ἅλς
ἀκροτόμοις adj dat pl . . . . ἀκρότομος	ἀλάστορα noun masc acc sg . . . . ἀλάστωρ
ἀκρότομον adj acc sg, neut nom sg id.	ἀλάστωρ noun masc nom sg id.
ἀκροτόμου adj gen sg id.	Αλαωθ pr noun
ἀκροτόμους adj masc and fem acc pl id.	ἀλγεῖν vb pres act inf . . . . ἀλγέω
ἀκροτόμῳ adj dat sg id.	ἀλγηδόνα noun fem acc sg . . . . ἀλγηδών
ἄκρου adj masc and neut gen sg . . . . ἄκρος	ἀλγηδόνας noun fem acc pl id.
ἀκροφύλακας noun masc acc pl . . . . ἀκροφύλαξ	ἀλγηδόνων noun fem gen pl id.
ἄκρῳ adj masc and neut dat sg . . . . ἄκρος	ἀλγηδόσιν noun fem dat pl id.
ἄκρων adj gen pl id.	ἀλγηδών noun fem nom sg id.
ἀκρωτηριάζειν vb pres act inf . . . . ἀκρωτηριάζω	ἄλγημα noun neut nom and acc sg
ἀκρωτηριαζόμεθα vb pres m/p ind 1st pers pl id.	ἀλγημάτων noun neut gen pl . . . . ἄλγημα
ἀκρωτηρίοις noun neut dat pl . . . . ἀκρωτήριον	ἀλγηρά adj fem nom sg . . . . ἀλγηρός
ἀκρωτήριον noun neut nom and acc sg id.	ἀλγηρόν adj masc acc sg, neut nom and acc sg id.
ἀκρωτηρίων noun neut gen pl id.	ἀλγήσω vb fut act ind 1st pers sg . . . . ἀλγέω
ἀκτῖνας noun fem acc pl . . . . ἀκτίς	ἄλγος noun neut nom and acc sg
ἀκτῖνος noun fem gen sg id.	ἀλγοῦντα vb pres act part neut nom and acc pl . . . . . . ἀλγέω
ἀκτίνων noun fem gen pl id.	ἀλγῶ vb pres act ind 1st pers sg id.
ἀκυμάτους adj masc and fem acc pl . . . . ἀκύματος	ἀλγῶν vb pres act part masc nom sg id.
ἀκυροῦνται vb pres m/p ind 3rd pers pl . . . . ἀκυρόω	ἁλεεῖς noun masc nom and acc pl . . . . ἁλιεύς
ἀκύρους adj masc and fem acc pl . . . . ἄκυρος	ἄλειμμα noun neut nom and acc sg
ἀκυρῶσαι vb 1st aor act inf . . . . ἀκυρόω	ἁλεῖται vb fut act ind 3rd pers sg . . . . ἅλλομαι
ἀκυρώσασα vb 1st aor act part fem nom sg id.	ἀλειφόμεναι vb pres m/p part fem nom pl . . . . ἀλείφω
ἀκυρώσωσιν vb 1st aor act subj 3rd pers pl id.	ἀλείφοντας vb pres act part masc acc pl id.
Ακχοβωρ pr noun	ἀλείφοντες vb pres act part masc nom pl id.
Ακχω pr noun	ἀλείφουσιν vb pres act ind 3rd pers pl id.
ἀκώλυτον adj acc sg, neut nom sg . . . . ἀκώλυτος	ἀλείψασθαι vb 1st aor act mid inf id.
ἄκων adj masc nom sg	ἀλείψεις vb fut act ind 2nd pers sg id.
Ακως pr noun	ἀλείψῃ vb 1st aor act subj 3rd pers sg,
Αλα pr noun	1st aor mid subj 2nd pers sg,
ἅλα noun masc acc sg . . . . ἅλς	fut mid ind 2nd pers sg id.
ἀλάβαστρος noun masc nom sg	ἀλείψομαι vb fut mid ind 1st pers sg id.
Αλαε pr noun	ἀλεκτρυών noun masc nom sg
ἀλαζονεία noun fem nom sg	ἀλέκτωρ noun masc nom sg
ἀλαζονείαν noun fem acc sg . . . . ἀλαζονεία	Αλεμα pr noun
ἀλαζονείας noun fem gen sg and acc pl id.	Αλεμοις pr noun dat pl . . . . Αλεμοι

Αλεμωνι pr noun

Ἀλεξάνδρειαν pr noun fem acc sg . . . . ᾽Αλεξάνδρεια

᾽Αλεξανδρεῦσι pr noun masc dat pl . . . . ᾽Αλεξανδρεύς

᾽Αλεξάνδρεων pr noun masc gen pl   id.

᾽Αλέξανδρον pr noun masc acc sg . . . . ᾽Αλέξανδρος

᾽Αλέξανδρος pr noun masc nom sg   id.

᾽Αλεξάνδρου pr noun masc gen sg   id.

᾽Αλεξάνδρῳ pr noun masc dat sg   id.

ἄλεσον vb 1st aor act impv 2nd pers sg . . . . ἀλέω

ἄλευρα noun neut nom and acc pl . . . . ἄλευρον

ἄλευρον noun neut nom and acc sg   id.

ἀλεύρου noun neut gen sg   id.

Αλεφ pr noun

ἀλήθεια noun fem nom sg

ἀληθείᾳ noun fem dat sg . . . . ἀλήθεια

ἀλήθειαι noun fem nom pl   id.

ἀληθείαις noun fem dat pl   id.

ἀλήθειαν noun fem acc sg   id.

ἀληθείας noun fem gen sg   id.

ἀληθεῖς adj masc and fem nom and acc pl . . . . ἀληθής

ἀληθές adj neut nom and acc sg   id.

ἀληθεστάτη superl adj fem nom sg   id.

ἀληθεύειν vb pres act inf . . . . ἀληθεύω

ἀληθεύετε vb pres act ind 2nd pers pl   id.

ἀληθεύσει vb fut act ind 3rd pers sg   id.

ἀλήθευσον vb 1st aor act impv 2nd pers sg   id.

ἀληθεύων vb pres act part masc nom sg   id.

ἀληθῆ adj masc and fem acc sg,

         neut nom and acc pl . . . . ἀληθής

ἀληθής adj masc and fem nom sg   id.

ἀληθινά adj neut nom and acc pl . . . . ἀληθινός

ἀληθιναί adj fem nom pl   id.

ἀληθινή adj fem nom sg   id.

ἀληθινῇ adj fem dat sg   id.

ἀληθινήν adj fem acc sg   id.

ἀληθινοί adj masc nom pl   id.

ἀληθινόν adj masc acc sg, neut nom and acc sg   id.

ἀληθινός adj masc nom sg   id.

ἀληθινοῦ adj masc and neut gen sg   id.

ἀληθινούς adj masc acc pl   id.

ἀληθινῷ adj masc and neut dat sg   id.

ἀληθινῶν adj gen pl   id.

ἀληθινῶς adverb

ἀλήθουσαι vb pres act part fem nom pl . . . . ἀλήθω

ἀληθούσης vb pres act part fem gen sg   id.

ἀλήθων vb pres act part masc nom sg   id.

ἀληθῶς adverb

ἄληκτον adj acc sg, neut nom sg . . . . ἄληκτος

ἁλί noun masc dat sg . . . . ἅλς

ἁλιαίετον noun masc acc sg . . . . ἁλιάετος

ἁλιεύσουσιν vb fut act ind 3rd pers pl . . . . ἁλιεύω

ἁλιέων noun masc gen pl . . . . ἁλιεύς

Αλιηλ pr noun

Ἁλικαρνασσον pr noun acc sg . . . . Ἁλικαρνασσος

ἅλιμα adj neut nom and acc pl . . . . ἅλιμον

Αλιμαζονεῖς pr noun

ἅλιμοις adj fem dat pl . . . . ἅλιμος

ἁλισγηθῇ vb 1st aor pass subj 3rd pers sg . . . . . ἁλισγέω

ἁλισγήσει vb fut act ind 3rd pers sg   id.

ἁλισθήσεται vb fut pass ind 3rd pers sg . . . . ἁλίζω

ἁλίσκεται vb pres m/p ind 3rd pers sg . . . . ἁλίσκω

ἁλίσκονται vb pres m/p ind 3rd pers pl   id.

ἀλιτηρίοις noun masc dat pl . . . . ἀλιτήριος

ἀλιτήριον adj acc sg, neut nom sg   id.

ἀλιτηρίους adj masc and fem acc pl   id.

ἀλιτηρίων adj gen pl   id.

Αλιφαλατ pr noun

Αλιφαλεθ pr noun

Αλκαθα pr noun

ἀλκάς noun fem acc pl . . . . ἀλκή

ἀλκήν noun fem acc sg   id.

ἀλκῆς noun fem gen sg   id.

᾽Αλκιμον pr noun masc acc sg . . . . ᾽Αλκιμος

᾽Αλκιμος pr noun masc nom sg   id.

᾽Αλκιμῳ pr noun masc dat sg   id.

ἀλλ᾽ see ἀλλά

ἄλλα adj neut nom and acc pl . . . . ἄλλος

ἀλλά conjunction

ἀλλαγάς noun fem acc pl . . . . ἀλλαγή

ἀλλαγῇ vb 2nd aor pass subj 3rd pers sg . . . . ἀλλάσσω

ἀλλαγήσονται vb fut pass ind 3rd pers pl   id.

ἄλλαγμα noun neut nom and acc sg

ἀλλάγμασι noun neut dat pl . . . . ἄλλαγμα

ἀλλάγματα noun neut nom and acc pl   id.

ἀλλάγματι noun neut dat sg   id.

ἀλλάγματος noun neut gen sg   id.

ἄλλαι adj fem nom pl . . . . ἄλλος

ἀλλάξαι vb 1st aor act inf . . . . ἀλλάσσω

ἀλλάξατε vb 1st aor act impv 2nd pers pl   id.

ἀλλάξει vb fut act ind 3rd pers sg   id.

ἀλλάξεις vb fut act ind 2nd pers sg   id.

ἀλλάξεται vb fut mid ind 3rd pers sg   id.

ἀλλάξῃ vb 1st aor act subj 3rd pers sg   id.

ἀλλάξῃς vb 1st aor act subj 2nd pers sg   id.

ἀλλάξομεν vb fut act ind 1st pers pl   id.

ἀλλάξονται vb fut mid ind 3rd pers pl   id.

ἀλλάξουσιν vb fut act ind 3rd pers pl   id.

ἄλλας adj fem acc pl . . . . ἄλλος

ἀλλασσομένας vb pres m/p part fem acc pl . . . . . ἀλλάσσω

ἀλλασσόμενοι vb pres m/p part masc nom pl   id.

ἀλλασσομένων vb pres m/p part gen pl   id.

ἀλλάσσων vb pres act part masc nom sg   id.

ἀλλαχῇ adverb . . . . ἀλλαχῇ

ἀλλαχόθεν adverb

ἄλλη   adj fem nom sg .... ἄλλος
ἄλλη   adj fem dat sg   id.
Αλληλ   pr noun
ἄλληλα   recipr pron neut nom and acc pl .... ἀλλήλους
ἀλλήλαις   recipr pron fem dat pl   id.
ἀλλήλας   recipr pron fem acc pl   id.
Αλληλι   pr noun
ἀλλήλοις   recipr pron masc and neut dat pl ...... ἀλλήλους
αλληλουια   translit, interjection
ἀλλήλους   recipr pron masc acc pl .... ἀλλήλους
ἀλλήλων   recipr pron gen pl   id.
ἄλλην   adj fem acc sg .... ἄλλος
ἄλλης   adj fem gen sg   id.
ἄλλο   adj neut nom and acc sg   id.
ἀλλογενεῖ   adj dat sg .... ἀλλογενής
ἀλλογενεῖς   adj masc and fem nom and acc pl   id.
ἀλλογενέσι   adj dat pl   id.
ἀλλογενῆ   adj neut nom and acc pl   id.
ἀλλογενής   adj masc and fem nom sg   id.
ἀλλογενοῦς   adj gen sg   id.
ἀλλογενῶν   adj gen pl   id.
ἀλλόγλωσσον   adj acc sg, neut nom sg ..... ἀλλόγλωσσος
ἀλλογλώσσους   adj masc and fem acc pl   id.
ἀλλοεθνέσι   adj dat pl .... ἀλλοεθνής
ἄλλοθεν   adverb
ἄλλοι   adj masc nom pl .... ἄλλος
ἀλλοιοῖ   vb pres act ind 3rd pers sg .... ἀλλοιόω
ἀλλοιούσθω   vb pres m/p impv 3rd pers sg .... ἀλλοιόω
ἀλλοιοῦται   vb pres m/p ind 3rd pers sg   id.
ἄλλοις   adj masc and neut dat pl .... ἄλλος
ἀλλοιωθείσης   vb 1st aor pass part fem gen sg .... ἀλλοιόω
ἀλλοιωθῇ   vb 1st aor pass subj 3rd pers sg   id.
ἀλλοιωθήσεται   vb fut pass ind 3rd pers sg   id.
ἀλλοιωθησομένοις   vb fut pass part
        masc and neut dat pl   id.
ἀλλοιωθησομένων   vb fut pass part masc gen pl   id.
ἀλλοιωθῶσιν   vb 1st aor pass subj 3rd pers pl   id.
ἀλλοιῶσαι   vb 1st aor act inf   id.
ἀλλοιώσει   noun fem dat sg .... ἀλλοίωσις
ἀλλοιώσει   vb fut act ind 3rd pers sg .... ἀλλοιόω
ἀλλοιώσεως   noun fem gen sg .... ἀλλοίωσις
ἀλλοιώσῃ   vb 1st aor act subj 3rd pers sg .... ἀλλοιόω
ἀλλοιώσῃς   vb 1st aor act subj 2nd pers sg   id.
ἀλλοίωσις   noun fem nom sg
ἀλλοίωσον   vb 1st aor act impv 2nd pers sg ...... ἀλλοιόω
ἀλλομένοις   vb pres dep part
        masc and neut dat pl .... ἄλλομαι
ἀλλομένους   vb pres dep part masc acc pl   id.
ἄλλον   adj masc acc sg .... ἄλλος
ἄλλος   adj masc nom sg   id.
ἄλλοτε   adverb
ἀλλότρια   adj neut nom and acc pl .... ἀλλότριος

ἀλλοτρία   adj fem nom sg .... ἀλλότριος
ἀλλοτρίᾳ   adj fem dat sg   id.
ἀλλότριαι   adj fem nom pl   id.
ἀλλοτρίαις   adj fem dat pl   id.
ἀλλοτρίαν   adj fem acc sg   id.
ἀλλοτρίας   adj fem gen sg and acc pl   id.
ἀλλότριοι   adj masc nom pl   id.
ἀλλοτρίοις   adj masc and neut dat pl   id.
ἀλλότριον   adj masc acc sg, neut nom and acc sg   id.
ἀλλότριος   adj masc nom sg   id.
ἀλλοτριότητι   noun fem dat sg .... ἀλλοτριότης
ἀλλοτρίου   adj masc and neut gen sg .... ἀλλότριος
ἀλλοτρίους   adj masc acc pl   id.
ἀλλοτρίῳ   adj masc and neut dat sg   id.
ἀλλοτριωθήσεται   vb fut pass ind 3rd pers sg .. ἀλλοτριόω
ἀλλοτρίων   adj gen pl .... ἀλλότριος
ἀλλοτρίως   adverb
ἀλλοτριώσεως   noun fem gen sg .... ἀλλοτρίωσις
ἀλλοτρίωσιν   noun fem acc sg   id.
ἄλλου   adj masc and neut gen sg .... ἄλλος
ἄλλους   adj masc acc pl   id.
ἀλλόφυλα   adj neut nom and acc pl .... ἀλλόφυλος
ἀλλοφυλῆσαι   vb 1st aor act inf .... ἀλλοφυλέω
ἀλλοφυλισμόν   noun masc acc sg .... ἀλλοφυλισμός
ἀλλοφυλισμοῦ   noun masc gen sg   id.
ἀλλόφυλοι   adj masc nom pl .... ἀλλόφυλος
ἀλλοφύλοις   adj masc and neut dat pl   id.
ἀλλόφυλον   adj masc acc sg   id.
ἀλλόφυλος   adj masc nom sg   id.
ἀλλοφύλου   adj masc gen sg   id.
ἀλλοφύλους   adj masc acc pl   id.
ἀλλοφύλῳ   adj masc dat sg   id.
ἀλλοφύλων   adj gen pl   id.
ἀλλοφώνους   adj masc acc pl .... ἀλλόφωνος
ἄλλῳ   adj masc and neut dat sg .... ἄλλος
Αλλως   pr noun
Αλλων   pr noun
ἄλλων   adj gen pl .... ἄλλος
Αλλωνι   pr noun
ἄλλως   adverb
ἅλματι   noun neut dat sg .... ἅλμα
ἅλμην   noun fem acc sg .... ἅλμη
ἁλμυρᾷ   adj fem dat sg .... ἁλμυρός
ἁλμυρίδα   noun neut nom and acc pl .... ἁλμυρίς
ἁλόα   vb pres act impv 2nd pers sg .... ἁλοάω
ἄλογα   adj neut nom and acc pl .... ἄλογος
ἀλογηθῆναι   vb 1st aor pass inf .... ἀλογέω
ἀλογιστία   noun fem dat sg .... ἀλογιστία
ἀλογιστίας   noun fem gen sg   id.
ἀλογίστοις   adj dat pl .... ἀλόγιστος
ἀλόγιστον   adj acc sg, neut nom sg   id.
ἀλόγιστος   adj masc nom sg

ἀλογίστως adverb

ἄλογοι adj masc and fem nom pl . . . . ἄλογος

ἄλογον adj acc sg, neut nom sg   id.

ἄλογος adj masc and fem nom sg   id.

ἀλόγους adj masc and fem acc pl   id.

ἀλόγων adj gen pl   id.

ἀλόγως adverb

ἀλοηθήσονται vb fut pass ind 3rd pers pl . . . . ἀλοάω

Αλοηλ pr noun

ἀλοήσεις vb fut act ind 2nd pers sg . . . . ἀλοάω

ἀλοήσουσιν vb fut act ind 3rd pers pl   id.

ἀλοήσω vb fut act ind 1st pers sg   id.

ἀλοητός noun masc nom sg

ἀλοιφή noun fem nom sg

ἀλοιφῇ noun fem dat sg . . . . ἀλοιφή

ἀλοιφήν noun fem acc sg   id.

ἀλοιφῆς noun fem gen sg   id.

ἀλόντες vb 2nd aor act part masc nom pl . . . . ἀλίσκω

ἀλός noun masc gen sg . . . . ἅλς

Αλουα pr noun

Αλουλ pr noun

ἀλοῦνται vb fut mid ind 3rd pers pl . . . . ἄλλομαι

ἀλούς vb 2nd aor act part masc nom sg . . . . ἀλίσκω

ἀλοῶν vb pres act part masc nom sg . . . . ἀλοάω

ἀλοῶντα vb pres act part masc acc sg   id.

ἀλοῶντας vb pres act part masc acc pl   id.

ἄλσει noun neut dat sg . . . . ἄλσος

ἄλσεσι noun neut dat pl   id.

ἄλσεων noun neut gen pl   id.

ἄλση noun neut nom and acc pl   id.

ἄλσος noun neut nom and acc sg   id.

ἄλσους noun neut gen sg   id.

ἀλσώδεις adj masc and fem nom and acc pl . . . . . . ἀλσώδης

ἀλσώδη adj neut nom and acc pl   id.

ἀλσώδους adj gen sg   id.

ἀλσῶν noun neut gen pl . . . . ἄλσος

Αλσωρηχ pr noun

ἀλυκή adj fem nom sg . . . . ἀλυκός

ἀλυκῇ adj fem dat sg   id.

ἀλυκήν adj fem acc sg   id.

ἀλυκῆς adj fem gen sg   id.

ἀλύσει noun fem dat sg . . . . ἄλυσις

ἀλυσιδωτά adj neut nom and acc pl . . . . ἀλυσιδωτός

ἀλυσιδωτοῖς adj masc dat pl   id.

ἀλυσιδωτόν adj masc acc sg, neut nom and acc sg   id.

αλφ translit (Heb letter: א)

Αλφααλ pr noun

ἄλφιτον noun neut nom and acc sg

ἀλφίτου noun neut gen sg . . . . ἄλφιτον

ἀλφίτων noun neut gen pl   id.

ἀλφός noun masc nom sg

ἅλω noun fem acc, gen and dat sg, acc pl . . . . ἅλων

ἅλῷ vb 2nd aor act subj 3rd pers sg . . . . ἁλίσκω

Αλωης pr noun

αλωθ translit

ἅλων noun fem nom sg

ἁλῶν noun masc gen pl . . . . ἅλς

ἅλωνα noun fem acc sg . . . . ἅλων

ἁλῶναι vb 2nd aor act inf . . . . ἁλίσκω

Αλωναμ pr noun

ἅλωνες noun fem nom pl . . . . ἅλων

ἅλωνι noun fem dat sg   id.

ἅλωνος noun fem gen sg   id.

ἀλώπεκας noun fem acc pl . . . . ἀλώπηξ

ἀλώπεκες noun fem nom pl   id.

ἀλωπέκων noun fem gen pl   id.

ἀλώπεξιν noun fem dat pl   id.

ἀλώπηξ noun fem nom sg   id.

ἁλῷς vb 2nd aor act subj 2nd pers sg . . . . ἁλίσκω

ἁλώσεσθε vb fut mid ind 2nd pers pl   id.

ἁλώσεται vb fut mid ind 3rd pers sg   id.

ἁλώσεως noun fem gen sg . . . . ἅλωσις

ἁλώσῃ vb fut mid ind 2nd pers sg . . . . ἁλίσκω

ἁλώσονται vb fut mid ind 3rd pers pl   id.

ἅμα adverb and preposition

Αμαδ pr noun

Αμαδα pr noun

Αμαδαθου pr noun masc gen sg . . . . Αμαδαθος

αμαδαρωθ translit

Αμαδια pr noun

Αμαζονεῖς pr noun masc acc pl . . . . Αμαζονὶς

Αμαθ pr noun

Αμαθαρ pr noun

Αμαθι pr noun

ἀμαθίας noun fem gen sg and acc pl . . . . ἀμαθία

Αμαθῖτιν pr noun fem acc sg . . . . 'Αμαθῖτις

Αμαλ pr noun

Αμαληκ pr noun

Αμαληκῖται pr noun masc nom pl . . . . Αμαληκίτης

Αμαληκιτου pr noun masc gen sg   id.

'Αμαλθειας pr noun fem gen sg . . . . 'Αμαλθεια

Αμαμ pr noun

Αμαν pr noun

ἅμαξα noun fem nom sg

ἁμάξαις noun fem dat pl . . . . ἅμαξα

ἅμαξαν noun fem acc sg   id.

ἁμάξας noun fem acc pl   id.

ἁμάξῃ noun fem dat sg   id.

ἁμάξης noun fem gen sg   id.

Αμαρ pr noun

ἀμάραντος adj masc and fem nom sg

Αμαρι pr noun

Αμαρια pr noun

ἀμαρία noun fem nom sg

Αμαριας pr noun masc nom sg
Αμαριου pr noun masc gen sg . . . . Αμαριας
ἁμάρτανε vb pres act impv 2nd pers sg . . . . . . ἁμαρτάνω
ἁμαρτάνει vb pres act ind 3rd pers sg   id.
ἁμαρτάνειν vb pres act inf   id.
ἁμαρτάνεις vb pres act ind 2nd pers sg   id.
ἁμαρτάνετε vb pres act impv 2nd pers pl   id.
ἁμαρτάνητε vb pres act subj 2nd pers pl   id.
ἁμαρτάνοντα vb pres act part masc acc sg   id.
ἁμαρτάνοντας vb pres act part masc acc pl   id.
ἁμαρτάνοντες vb pres act part masc nom pl   id.
ἁμαρτάνοντι vb pres act part masc and neut dat sg   id.
ἁμαρτανόντων vb pres act part masc and neut gen pl id.
ἁμαρτάνουσα vb pres act part fem nom sg   id.
ἁμαρτάνουσι(ν) vb pres act ind 3rd pers pl,
          pres act part masc and neut dat pl   id.
ἁμαρτάνων vb pres act part masc nom sg   id.
ἁμαρτεῖν vb 2nd aor act inf   id.
ἁμάρτῃ vb 2nd aor act subj 3rd pers sg   id.
ἁμάρτημα noun neut nom and acc sg
ἁμαρτήμασι noun neut dat pl . . . . ἁμάρτημα
ἁμαρτήματα noun neut nom and acc pl   id.
ἁμαρτήματος noun neut gen sg   id.
ἁμαρτημάτων noun neut gen pl   id.
ἁμάρτης vb 2nd aor act subj 2nd pers sg . . . . . . ἁμαρτάνω
ἁμαρτησάτω vb 1st aor act impv 3rd pers sg   id.
ἁμαρτήσεις vb fut act ind 2nd pers sg   id.
ἁμαρτήσεσθε vb fut mid ind 2nd pers pl   id.
ἁμαρτήσεται vb fut mid ind 3rd pers sg   id.
ἁμαρτήσομαι vb fut mid ind 1st pers sg   id.
ἁμαρτησόμεθα vb fut mid ind 1st pers pl   id.
ἁμαρτήσονται vb fut mid ind 3rd pers pl   id.
ἁμαρτήσουσιν vb fut act ind 3rd pers pl   id.
ἁμαρτήσω vb fut act ind 1st pers sg   id.
ἁμάρτητε vb 2nd aor act subj 2nd pers pl   id.
ἁμαρτία noun fem nom sg
ἁμαρτία noun fem dat sg . . . . ἁμαρτία
ἁμαρτίαι noun fem nom pl   id.
ἁμαρτίαις noun fem dat pl   id.
ἁμαρτίαν noun fem acc sg   id.
ἁμαρτίας noun fem gen sg and acc pl   id.
ἁμαρτιῶν noun fem gen pl   id.
ἁμαρτόντες vb 2nd aor act part masc nom pl . . . ἁμαρτάνω
ἁμαρτόντι vb 2nd aor act part
          masc and neut dat sg   id.
ἁμαρτόντων vb 2nd aor act part masc and neut gen pl id.
ἁμαρτούσης vb 2nd aor act part fem gen sg   id.
ἁμάρτω vb 2nd aor act subj 1st pers sg   id.
ἁμαρτωλέ adj masc and fem voc sg . . . . ἁμαρτωλός
ἁμαρτωλοί adj masc and fem nom pl   id.
ἁμαρτωλοῖς adj dat pl   id.
ἁμαρτωλόν adj acc sg, neut nom sg   id.

ἁμαρτωλός adj masc and fem nom sg
ἁμαρτωλοῦ adj gen sg . . . . ἁμαρτωλός
ἁμαρτωλούς adj masc and fem acc pl   id.
ἁμαρτωλῷ adj dat sg   id.
ἁμαρτωλῶν adj gen pl   id.
ἁμάρτωμεν vb 2nd aor act subj 1st pers pl . . . . . ἁμαρτάνω
ἁμαρτών vb 2nd aor act part masc nom sg   id.
ἁμάρτωσιν vb 2nd aor act subj 3rd pers pl   id.
Αμαρφαλ pr noun
Αμασαι pr noun
αμασενιθ translit
ἁμάσητος adj masc and fem nom sg
Αμασι pr noun
Αμασια pr noun
Αμασιαν pr noun masc acc sg . . . . Αμασιας
Αμασιας pr noun masc nom sg   id.
Αμασιου pr noun masc gen sg   id.
αματταρι translit
ἀμαυρά adj fem nom sg . . . . ἀμαυρός
ἀμαυροῖ adj masc nom pl   id.
ἀμαυροῖ vb pres act ind 3rd pers sg . . . . ἀμαυρόω
ἀμαυρόν adj masc acc sg, neut nom and acc sg . . . . ἀμαυρός
ἀμαυρωθήσεται vb fut pass ind 3rd pers sg . . . . ἀμαυρόω
αμαφεθ translit
Αμβακουμ pr noun
ἀμβλάκημα noun neut nom and acc sg
ἀμβλακίας noun fem acc pl . . . . ἀμπλακία
Αμβραμ pr noun
Αμβρι pr noun
ἀμβροσίας adj fem gen sg . . . . ἀμβρόσιος
ἀμέθυστον noun fem acc sg . . . . ἀμέθυστος
ἀμέθυστος noun fem nom sg   id.
ἀμειδήτοις adj dat pl . . . . ἀμείδητος
ἀμειξίας noun fem gen sg . . . . ἀμιξία
Αμεκασις pr noun
Αμεκκασις pr noun
ἄμελγε vb pres act impv 2nd pers sg . . . . ἀμέλγω
ἀμελήσαντες vb 1st aor act part masc nom pl . . . . . ἀμελέω
ἄμελξιν noun fem acc sg . . . . ἄμελξις
ἀμελοῦντες vb pres act part masc nom pl . . . . ἀμελέω
Αμελσαδ pr noun
ἀμελῶς adverb
ἄμεμπτον adj acc sg, neut nom sg . . . . ἄμεμπτος
ἄμεμπτος adj masc and fem nom sg   id.
ἀμέμπτως adverb
ἀμερεῖ adj dat sg . . . . ἀμερής
ἀμερῆ adj masc and fem acc sg   id.
ἀμέριμνον adj acc sg, neut nom sg . . . . ἀμέριμνος
ἀμέριμνος adj masc and fem nom sg   id.
Αμεσσα pr noun
Αμεσσαι pr noun
Αμεσσαϊ pr noun

Αμεσσια	pr noun	
Αμεσσιαν	pr noun masc acc sg	Αμεσσιας
Αμεσσιας	pr noun masc nom sg	id.
Αμεσσιου	pr noun masc gen sg	id.
ἀμετάθετος	adj masc and fem nom sg	ἀμετάθετος
ἀμεταθέτου	adj gen sg	id.
ἀμέτρητον	adj acc sg, neut nom sg	ἀμέτρητος
ἀμέτρητος	adj masc and fem nom sg	id.
ἀμετρήτῳ	adj dat sg	id.
Αμηαχι	pr noun	
αμην	translit, interjection	
ἀμήσατε	vb 1st aor act impv 2nd pers pl	ἀμάω
ἀμήσετε	vb fut act ind 2nd pers pl	id.
ἀμήσῃ	vb 1st aor act subj 3rd pers sg	id.
ἀμήσῃς	vb 1st aor act subj 2nd pers sg	id.
ἀμητόν	noun masc acc sg	ἀμητός
ἄμητος	noun masc nom sg	
ἀμητός	noun masc nom sg	
ἀμήτου	noun masc gen sg	ἄμητος
ἀμητοῦ	noun masc gen sg	ἀμητός
ἀμητούς	noun masc acc pl	id.
ἀμήτῳ	noun masc dat sg	ἄμητος
ἀμήχανον	adj acc sg, neut nom sg	ἀμήχανος
ἀμίαντον	adj acc sg, neut nom sg	ἀμίαντος
ἀμίαντος	adj masc and fem nom sg	id.
ἀμιάντων	adj gen pl	id.
Αμιζαβαθ	pr noun	
Αμιτλ	pr noun	
Αμιναδαβ	pr noun	
Αμισυδ	pr noun	
Αμισαδαι	pr noun	
ἀμισθί	adverb	
Αμιτααλ	pr noun	
Αμιταλ	pr noun	
Αμμε	pr noun	
Αμμαδι	pr noun	
Αμμαθαριμ	pr noun	
Αμμαν	pr noun	
Αμμανιθ	pr noun	
Αμμανιται	pr noun masc nom pl	Αμμανιτης
Αμμανιτην	pr noun masc acc sg	id.
Αμμανιτης	pr noun masc nom sg	id.
Αμμανιτιδας	pr noun fem acc pl	Αμμανῖτις
Αμμανῖτιν	pr noun fem acc sg	id.
Αμμανῖτις	pr noun fem nom sg	
Αμμανιτῶν	pr noun masc gen pl	Αμμανιτης
Αμμαους	pr noun	
Αμμαχ	pr noun	
Αμμιἕιοι	pr noun	
Αμμιουδ	pr noun	
ἄμμον	noun fem acc sg	ἄμμος
ἄμμος	noun fem nom sg	
ἄμμου	noun fem gen sg	ἄμμος
ἄμμῳ	noun fem dat sg	id.
ἀμμώδης	adj masc and fem nom sg	
Αμμων	pr noun	
Αμμωνι	pr noun	
ἀμνάδα	noun fem acc sg	ἀμνάς
ἀμνάδας	noun fem acc pl	id.
ἀμνάδες	noun fem nom pl	id.
ἀμνάδων	noun fem gen pl	id.
ἀμνάς	noun fem nom sg	id.
ἀμνάσιν	noun fem dat pl	id.
ἀμνημονήσῃς	vb 1st aor act subj 2nd pers sg . . .	ἀμνημονέω
ἀμνησία	noun fem nom sg	
ἀμνησικακίαν	noun fem acc sg	ἀμνησικακία
ἀμνήστευτον	adj fem acc sg	ἀμνήστευτος
ἀμνηστία	noun fem nom sg	
ἀμνηστίαν	noun fem acc sg	ἀμνηστία
ἀμνοί	noun masc nom pl	ἀμνός
ἀμνοῖς	noun masc dat pl	id.
ἀμνόν	noun masc acc sg	id.
ἀμνός	noun masc nom sg	id.
ἀμνούς	noun masc acc pl	id.
ἀμνῷ	noun masc dat sg	id.
Αμνων	pr noun	
ἀμνῶν	noun masc gen pl	ἀμνός
ἄμοιρος	adj masc and fem nom sg	
ἀμόλυντον	adj acc sg, neut nom sg	ἀμόλυντος
ἀμόραις	adj fem dat pl	ἄμορος
Αμορι	pr noun	
Αμορια	pr noun	
Αμορις	pr noun	
ἀμορίτην	noun fem acc sg	ἀμορίτης
Αμορραιας	pr noun fem gen sg and acc pl	Αμορραια
Αμορραιοι	pr noun masc nom pl	Αμορραιος
Αμορραιον	pr noun masc acc sg	id.
Αμορραιος	pr noun masc nom sg	id.
Αμορραιου	pr noun masc gen sg	id.
Αμορραιους	pr noun masc acc pl	id.
Αμορραιῳ	pr noun masc dat sg	id.
Αμορραιων	pr noun masc gen pl	id.
Αμορρι	pr noun	
ἀμόρφου	adj gen sg	ἄμορφος
Αμουηλ	pr noun	
Αμουκ	pr noun	
ἄμπελοι	noun fem nom pl	ἄμπελος
ἀμπέλοις	noun fem dat pl	id.
ἄμπελον	noun fem acc sg	id.
ἄμπελος	noun fem nom sg	id.
ἀμπέλου	noun fem gen sg	id.
ἀμπελουργοί	noun masc nom pl	ἀμπελουργός
ἀμπελουργούς	noun masc acc pl	id.
ἀμπέλους	noun fem acc pl	ἄμπελος

ἀμπέλῳ noun fem dat sg . . . . ἄμπελος

ἀμπέλων noun fem gen pl   id.

ἀμπελών noun masc nom sg

ἀμπελῶνα noun masc acc sg . . . . ἀμπελών

ἀμπελῶνας noun masc acc pl   id.

ἀμπελῶνες noun masc nom pl   id.

ἀμπελῶνι noun masc dat sg   id.

ἀμπελῶνος noun masc gen sg   id.

ἀμπελώνων noun masc gen pl   id.

ἀμπελῶσι noun masc dat pl   id.

Αμραμ pr noun

Αμραμις pr noun

Αμρι pr noun

ἀμύγδαλον noun neut nom and acc sg

ἀμύθητα adj neut nom and acc pl . . . . ἀμύθητος

ἀμύθητος adj masc and fem nom sg   id.

ἀμυθήτους adj masc and fem acc pl   id.

ἀμυθήτων adj gen pl   id.

ἄμυναν noun fem acc sg . . . . ἄμυνα

ἀμύνασθαι vb 1st aor mid inf . . . . ἀμύνω

ἀμύνωνται vb pres m/p subj 3rd pers pl   id.

ἀμφίασιν noun masc acc sg . . . . ἀμφίασις

ἀμφιβαλεῖ vb fut act ind 3rd pers sg . . . . . . ἀμφιβάλλω

ἀμφίβληστρον noun neut nom and acc sg

ἀμφιβλήστρῳ noun neut dat sg . . . . ἀμφίβληστρον

ἀμφιβολεῖς noun masc nom pl . . . . ἀμφιβολεύς

ἀμφίεσαι vb 1st aor mid impv 2nd pers sg . . . . . ἀμφιέννυμι

ἀμφιλαφεῖς adj masc and fem nom and acc pl . . ἀμφιλαφής

Αμφιν pr noun

ἀμφιτάποις noun masc dat pl . . . . ἀμφίταπος

ἀμφιτάπους noun masc acc pl   id.

ἄμφοδα noun neut nom and acc pl . . . . ἄμφοδον

ἀμφότερα adj neut nom and acc pl . . . . ἀμφότεροι

ἀμφότεραι adj fem nom pl   id.

ἀμφοτέραις adj fem dat pl   id.

ἀμφοτέρας adj fem acc pl   id.

ἀμφοτεροδέξιοι adj masc and fem

        nom pl . . . . ἀμφοτεροδέξιος

ἀμφοτεροδέξιον adj acc sg, neut nom sg   id.

ἀμφότεροι adj masc nom pl

ἀμφοτέροις adj masc and neut dat pl . . . . ἀμφότεροι

ἀμφοτέρους adj masc acc pl   id.

ἀμφοτέρων adj gen pl   id.

Αμωθ pr noun

Αμωκη pr noun

ἄμωμα adj neut nom and acc pl . . . . ἄμωμος

ἄμωμοι adj masc and fem nom pl   id.

ἄμωμον adj acc sg, neut nom sg   id.

ἄμωμος adj masc and fem nom sg   id.

ἀμώμους adj masc and fem acc pl   id.

ἀμώμῳ adj dat sg   id.

ἀμώμων adj gen pl   id.

Αμων pr noun

Αμωρα pr noun

Αμως pr noun

Αμωσα pr noun

ἄν particle

Ανα pr noun

ἀνά preposition

ἀναβαθμίσιν noun fem dat pl . . . . ἀναβαθμίς

ἀναβαθμοί noun masc nom pl . . . . ἀναβαθμός

ἀναβαθμοῖς noun masc dat pl   id.

ἀναβαθμούς noun masc acc pl   id.

ἀναβαθμῶν noun masc gen pl   id.

ἀνάβαινε vb pres act impv 2nd pers sg . . . . ἀναβαίνω

ἀναβαίνει vb pres act ind 3rd pers sg   id.

ἀναβαίνειν vb pres act inf   id.

ἀναβαίνεις vb pres act ind 2nd pers sg   id.

ἀναβαίνετε vb pres act impv 2nd pers pl,

        pres act ind 2nd pers pl   id.

ἀναβαινέτωσαν vb pres act impv 3rd pers pl   id.

ἀναβαίνῃς vb pres act subj 2nd pers sg   id.

ἀναβαίνομεν vb pres act ind 1st pers pl   id.

ἀναβαίνοντα vb pres act part masc acc sg,

        neut nom and acc pl   id.

ἀναβαίνοντας vb pres act part masc acc pl   id.

ἀναβαίνοντες vb pres act part masc nom pl   id.

ἀναβαίνοντος vb pres act part masc and neut gen sg   id.

ἀναβαινόντων vb pres act part masc and neut gen pl   id.

ἀναβαίνουσα vb pres act part fem nom sg   id.

ἀναβαίνουσαι vb pres act part fem nom pl   id.

ἀναβαινούσῃ vb pres act part fem dat sg   id.

ἀναβαινούσης vb pres act part fem gen sg   id.

ἀναβαίνουσι(ν) vb pres act ind 3rd pers pl,

        pres act part masc and neut dat pl   id.

ἀναβαίνω vb pres act ind 1st pers sg   id.

ἀναβαίνων vb pres act part masc nom sg   id.

ἀναβαίνωσιν vb pres act subj 3rd pers pl   id.

ἀναβαλλόμενος vb pres m/p part

        masc nom sg . . . . ἀναβάλλω

ἀναβάντα vb 2nd aor act part

        neut nom and acc pl . . . . ἀναβαίνω

ἀναβάντες vb 2nd aor act part masc nom pl   id.

ἀναβάντι vb 2nd aor act part masc and neut dat sg   id.

ἀναβάντος vb 2nd aor act part masc and neut gen sg   id.

ἀναβάς vb 2nd aor act part masc nom sg   id.

ἀναβάσα vb 2nd aor act part fem nom sg   id.

ἀναβάσει noun fem dat sg . . . . ἀνάβασις

ἀναβάσεις noun fem nom and acc pl   id.

ἀναβάσεων noun fem gen pl   id.

ἀναβάσεως noun fem gen sg   id.

ἀνάβασιν noun fem acc sg   id.

ἀνάβασις noun fem nom sg   id.

ἀναβάται noun masc nom pl . . . . ἀναβάτης

ἀναβάταις noun masc dat pl . . . . ἀναβάτης	ἀναβολῇ noun fem dat sg . . . . ἀναβολή
ἀναβάτας noun masc acc pl id.	ἀναβολήν noun fem acc sg id.
ἀναβάτῃ noun masc dat sg id.	ἀναβολῆς noun fem gen sg id.
ἀναβάτην noun masc acc sg id.	ἀναβράσαι vb 1st aor act inf . . . . ἀναβράσσω
ἀναβάτης noun masc nom sg id.	ἀναβράσσοντος vb pres act part
ἀναβεβηκόσι vb perf act part	masc and neut gen sg id.
masc and neut dat pl . . . . ἀναβαίνω	ἀναβῶ vb 2nd aor act subj 1st pers sg . . . . ἀναβαίνω
ἀναβεβηκότες vb perf act part masc nom pl id.	Αναβωθ pr noun
ἀναβεβλημένος vb perf m/p part	ἀναβῶμεν vb 2nd aor act subj 1st pers pl . . . . . . ἀναβαίνω
masc nom sg . . . . ἀναβάλλω	ἀναβῶσιν vb 2nd aor act subj 3rd pers pl id.
ἀναβῇ vb 2nd aor act subj 3rd pers sg . . . . ἀναβαίνω	Αναγ pr noun
ἀνάβηθι vb 2nd aor act impv 2nd pers sg id.	ἀνάγαγε vb 2nd aor act impv 2nd pers sg . . . . ἀνάγω
ἀναβῆναι vb 2nd aor act inf id.	ἀναγαγεῖν vb 2nd aor act inf id.
ἀναβήσει vb fut mid ind 2nd pers sg id.	ἀναγάγετε vb 2nd aor act impv 2nd pers pl id.
ἀναβήσεσθε vb fut mid ind 2nd pers pl id.	ἀναγάγῃς vb 2nd aor act subj 2nd pers sg id.
ἀναβήσεται vb fut mid ind 3rd pers sg id.	ἀναγαγόντες vb 2nd aor act part masc nom pl id.
ἀναβήσῃ vb fut mid ind 2nd pers sg,	ἀναγαγόντι vb 2nd aor act part masc and neut dat sg id.
2nd aor mid subj 2nd pers sg id.	ἀναγάγω vb 2nd aor act subj 1st pers sg id.
ἀναβήσομαι vb fut mid ind 1st pers sg id.	ἀναγαγών vb 2nd aor act part masc nom sg id.
ἀναβησόμεθα vb fut mid ind 1st pers pl id.	ἀναγγεῖλαι vb 1st aor act inf . . . . ἀναγγέλλω
ἀναβήσονται vb fut mid ind 3rd pers pl id.	ἀναγγείλαντες vb 1st aor act part masc nom pl id.
ἀνάβητε vb 2nd aor act subj 2nd pers pl,	ἀναγγείλατε vb 1st aor act impv 2nd pers pl id.
2nd aor act impv 2nd pers pl id.	ἀναγγειλάτω vb 1st aor act impv 3rd pers sg id.
ἀναβήτωσαν vb 2nd aor act impv 3rd pers pl id.	ἀναγγειλάτωσαν vb 1st aor act impv 3rd pers pl id.
ἀναβιβάζουσιν vb pres act ind 3rd pers pl . . . . ἀναβιβάζω	ἀναγγείλῃ vb 1st aor act subj 3rd pers sg id.
ἀναβιβάσαι vb 1st aor act inf id.	ἀναγγείλῃς vb 1st aor act subj 2nd pers sg id.
ἀναβιβάσας vb 1st aor act part masc nom sg id.	ἀναγγείλητε vb 1st aor act subj 2nd pers pl id.
ἀναβιβάσατε vb 1st aor act impv 2nd pers pl id.	ἀνάγγειλον vb 1st aor act impv 2nd pers sg id.
ἀναβιβασάτω vb 1st aor act impv 3rd pers sg id.	ἀναγγείλω vb 1st aor act subj 1st pers sg id.
ἀναβιβάσει vb fut act ind 3rd pers sg id.	ἀναγγείλωμεν vb 1st aor act subj 1st pers pl id.
ἀναβιβασθήσεται vb fut pass ind 3rd pers sg id.	ἀναγγείλωσιν vb 1st aor act subj 3rd pers pl id.
ἀναβίβασον vb 1st aor act impv 2nd pers sg id.	ἀναγγελεῖ vb fut act ind 3rd pers sg id.
ἀναβιβάσω vb fut act ind 1st pers sg id.	ἀναγγελεῖς vb fut act ind 2nd pers sg id.
ἀναβιβῶ vb fut act ind 1st pers sg id.	ἀναγγελεῖτε vb fut act ind 2nd pers pl id.
ἀναβίωσιν noun fem acc sg . . . . ἀναβίωσις	ἀναγγελῇ vb 2nd aor pass subj 3rd pers sg id.
ἀναβλαστήσει vb fut act ind 3rd pers sg . . . ἀναβλαστάνω	ἀναγγελήσεται vb fut pass ind 3rd pers sg id.
ἀναβλέψαι vb 1st aor act inf . . . . ἀναβλέπω	ἀνάγγελλε vb pres act impv 2nd pers sg id.
ἀναβλέψαντα vb 1st aor act part masc acc sg id.	ἀναγγέλλει vb pres act ind 3rd pers sg id.
ἀναβλέψαντες vb 1st aor act part masc nom pl id.	ἀναγγέλλειν vb pres act inf id.
ἀναβλέψας vb 1st aor act part masc nom sg id.	ἀναγγέλλετε vb pres act impv 2nd pers pl id.
ἀναβλέψασα vb 1st aor act part fem nom sg id.	ἀναγγέλλοντες vb pres act part masc nom pl id.
ἀναβλέψατε vb 1st aor act impv 2nd pers pl id.	ἀναγγέλλοντος vb pres act part masc and neut gen sg id.
ἀναβλέψει vb fut act ind 3rd pers sg id.	ἀναγγέλλουσιν vb pres act ind 3rd pers pl id.
ἀνάβλεψιν noun fem acc sg . . . . ἀνάβλεψις	ἀναγγέλλω vb pres act ind 1st pers sg id.
ἀνάβλεψον vb 1st aor act impv 2nd pers sg . . . . . ἀναβλέπω	ἀναγγέλλων vb pres act part masc nom sg id.
ἀναβλέψονται vb fut mid ind 3rd pers pl id.	ἀναγγελοῦμεν vb fut act ind 1st pers pl id.
ἀναβοῆσαι vb 1st aor act inf . . . . ἀναβοάω	ἀναγγελοῦσιν vb fut act ind 3rd pers pl id.
ἀναβοῆσαν vb 1st aor act part neut nom and acc sg id.	ἀναγγελῶ vb fut act ind 1st pers sg id.
ἀναβοήσας vb 1st aor act part masc nom sg id.	ἀναγέγραπται vb perf m/p ind 3rd pers sg . . . . . ἀναγράφω
ἀναβοήσετε vb fut act ind 2nd pers pl id.	ἀνάγει vb pres act ind 3rd pers sg . . . . ἀνάγω
ἀναβοήσῃς vb 1st aor act subj 2nd pers sg id.	ἀνάγειν vb pres act inf id.
ἀναβόησον vb 1st aor act impv 2nd pers sg id.	ἀνάγεις vb pres act ind 2nd pers sg id.

ἀναγινώσκειν vb pres act inf . . . . ἀναγινώσκω	ἀναγωγότερον comp adverb . . . . ἀναγώγως
ἀναγινώσκεις vb pres act ind 2nd pers sg id.	ἀνάγων vb pres act part masc nom sg . . . . ἀνάγω
ἀναγινώσκοντας vb pres act part masc acc pl id.	ἀναδεδειγμένον vb perf m/p part masc acc sg . ἀναδεικνύω
ἀναγινώσκοντος vb pres act part masc and neut gen sg id.	ἀναδέδειχα vb perf act ind 1st pers sg id.
ἀναγινώσκων vb pres act part masc nom sg id.	ἀναδεῖξαι vb 1st aor act inf id.
ἀναγκάζει vb pres act ind 3rd pers sg . . . . ἀναγκάζω	ἀναδείξας vb 1st aor act part masc nom sg id.
ἀναγκάζειν vb pres act inf id.	ἀναδείξει vb fut act ind 3rd pers sg id.
ἀναγκάζεσθαι vb pres m/p inf id.	ἀνάδειξιν noun fem acc sg . . . . ἀνάδειξις
ἀναγκάζοντα vb pres act part masc acc sg id.	ἀνάδειξον vb 1st aor act impv 2nd pers sg . . . . ἀναδεικνύω
ἀναγκάζοντες vb pres act part masc nom pl id.	ἀναδειχθέντι vb 1st aor pass part masc and neut dat sg id.
ἀναγκάζων vb pres act part masc nom sg id.	ἀναδειχθήσῃ vb fut pass ind 2nd pers sg id.
ἀναγκαίαν adj fem acc sg . . . . ἀναγκαῖος	ἀναδενδράδα noun fem acc sg . . . . ἀναδενδράς
ἀναγκαῖον adj masc acc sg, neut nom and acc sg id.	ἀναδενδράδες noun fem nom pl id.
ἀναγκαῖος adj masc nom sg id.	ἀναδεξάμενος vb 1st aor mid part
ἀναγκαιότατον superl adj masc acc sg,	masc nom sg . . . . ἀναδέχομαι
neut nom and acc sg id.	ἀναδούς vb 2nd aor act part masc nom sg . . . . . ἀναδίδωμι
ἀνάγκαις noun fem dat pl . . . . ἀνάγκη	ἀναδραμών vb 2nd aor act part masc nom sg . . . . ἀνατρέχω
ἀναγκαίων adj gen pl . . . . ἀναγκαῖος	ἀνάδυσις noun fem nom sg
ἀνάγκας noun fem acc pl . . . . ἀνάγκη	ἀναδώσει vb fut act ind 3rd pers sg . . . . ἀναδίδωμι
ἀναγκάσαι vb 1st aor act inf . . . . ἀναγκάζω	ἀναζεῖ vb pres act ind 3rd pers sg . . . . ἀναζέω
ἀναγκάσετε vb fut act ind 2nd pers pl id.	ἀναζεῖν vb pres act inf id.
ἀναγκασθείς vb 1st aor pass part masc nom sg id.	ἀναζέουσαι vb pres act part fem nom pl id.
ἀνάγκη noun fem nom sg	ἀναζευγνύειν vb pres act inf . . . . ἀναζευγνύω
ἀνάγκῃ noun fem dat sg . . . . ἀνάγκη	ἀναζεύξαντες vb 1st aor act part masc nom pl id.
ἀνάγκην noun fem acc sg id.	ἀναζεύξας vb 1st aor act part masc nom sg id.
ἀνάγκης noun fem gen sg id.	ἀναζευξάτωσαν vb 1st aor act impv
ἀναγκῶν noun fem gen pl id.	3rd pers pl id.
ἀναγνείαν noun fem acc sg . . . . ἀναγνεία	ἀναζητῆσαι vb 1st aor act opt 3rd pers sg . . . . . . ἀναζητέω
ἀναγνῶ vb 2nd aor act subj 3rd pers sg . . . . . . ἀναγινώσκω	ἀναζυγαῖς noun fem dat pl . . . . ἀναζυγή
ἀνάγνωθι vb 2nd aor act impv 2nd pers sg id.	ἀναζυγήν noun fem acc sg id.
ἀναγνῶναι vb 2nd aor act inf id.	ἀναζυγῆς noun fem gen sg id.
ἀναγνώσει noun fem dat sg . . . . ἀνάγνωσις	ἀναζωσαμένη vb 1st aor mid part
ἀναγνώσεσθε vb fut mid ind 2nd pers pl . . . . ἀναγινώσκω	fem nom sg . . . . ἀναζώννυμι
ἀναγνώσεται vb fut mid ind 3rd pers sg id.	Αναηλ pr noun
ἀναγνώσῃ vb fut mid ind 2nd pers sg id.	Αναθ pr noun
ἀναγνωσθέντων vb 1st aor pass part	ἀναθάλῃ vb 2nd aor act subj 3rd pers sg . . . . . . ἀναθάλλω
masc and neut gen pl id.	ἀναθάλλει vb pres act ind 3rd pers sg id.
ἀνάγνωσιν noun fem acc sg . . . . ἀνάγνωσις	ἀναθάλλουσα vb pres act part fem nom sg id.
ἀναγνῶσιν vb 2nd aor act subj 3rd pers pl . . . . ἀναγινώσκω	ἀναθάλλων vb pres act part masc nom sg id.
ἀναγνώσομαι vb fut mid ind 1st pers sg id.	ἀναθάλοι vb 2nd aor act opt 3rd pers sg id.
ἀναγνώστῃ noun masc dat sg . . . . ἀναγνώστης	Ἀναθεμα pr noun neut nom and acc sg
ἀναγνώστην noun masc acc sg id.	ἀνάθεμα noun neut nom and acc sg
ἀναγνώστης noun masc nom sg id.	ἀναθέματι noun neut dat sg . . . . ἀνάθεμα
ἀνάγον vb pres act part neut nom and acc sg . . . . . . ἀνάγω	ἀναθεματιεῖς vb fut act ind 2nd pers sg . . . . ἀναθεματίζω
ἀνάγοντες vb pres act part masc nom pl id.	ἀναθεματιεῖτε vb fut act ind 2nd pers pl id.
ἀναγόντων vb pres act part masc and neut gen pl id.	ἀναθεματίσαι vb 1st aor act inf id.
ἀναγορεύεσθαι vb pres m/p inf . . . . ἀναγορεύω	ἀναθεματισθήσεται vb fut pass ind 3rd pers sg id.
ἀνάγουσα vb pres act part fem nom sg . . . . ἀνάγω	ἀναθεματιῶ vb fut act ind 1st pers sg id.
ἀνάγουσιν vb pres act ind 3rd pers pl id.	ἀναθέματος noun neut gen sg . . . . ἀνάθεμα
ἀναγραφαῖς noun fem dat pl . . . . ἀναγραφή	ἀναθεμάτων noun neut gen pl id.
ἀναγράψαι vb 1st aor act inf . . . . ἀναγράφω	ἀναθέσθαι vb 2nd aor mid inf . . . . ἀνατίθημι
ἀνάγω vb pres act ind 1st pers sg	ἀναθῇ vb 2nd aor act subj 3rd pers sg id.

ἀνάθημα noun neut nom and acc sg

ἀναθήμασι noun neut dat pl . . . . ἀνάθημα

ἀναθήσεις vb fut act ind 2nd pers sg . . . . ἀνατίθημι

Αναθωθ pr noun

Αναθωθι pr noun

Αναθωθια pr noun

Αναθωθιτης pr noun masc nom sg

Αναια pr noun

ἀναιδεῖ adj dat sg . . . . ἀναιδής

ἀναίδεια noun fem nom sg

ἀναιδεῖς adj masc and fem nom and acc pl . . . . . . ἀναιδής

ἀναιδές adj neut nom and acc sg   id.

ἀναιδῆ adj masc and fem acc sg   id.

ἀναιδής adj masc and fem nom sg   id.

ἀναιδοῦς adj gen sg   id.

ἀναιδῶς adverb

ἀναιρεθέντα vb 1st aor pass part masc acc sg . . . . ἀναιρέω

ἀναιρέθη vb 1st aor pass ind 3rd pers sg   id.

ἀναιρεθῆναι vb 1st aor pass inf   id.

ἀναιρεθήσεται vb fut pass ind 3rd pers sg   id.

ἀναιρεθήσονται vb fut pass ind 3rd pers pl   id.

ἀναιρεθήτω vb 1st aor pass impv 3rd pers sg   id.

ἀναιρεῖ vb pres act ind 3rd pers sg   id.

ἀναιρεῖν vb pres act inf   id.

ἀναιρεῖτε vb pres act ind 2nd pers pl   id.

ἀναιρέσει noun fem dat sg . . . . ἀναίρεσις

ἀναίρεσιν noun fem acc sg   id.

Ἀναιρεσις pr noun fem nom sg

ἀναίρεσις noun fem nom sg

ἀναιροῦμαι vb pres m/p ind 1st pers sg . . . . ἀναιρέω

ἀναιρούμενος vb pres m/p part masc nom sg   id.

ἀναιροῦντες vb pres act part masc nom pl   id.

ἀναιρούντων vb pres act part masc and neut gen pl id.

ἀναιρῶν vb pres act part masc nom sg   id.

ἀναίτιον adj acc sg, neut nom sg . . . . ἀναίτιος

ἀναιτίως adverb

ἀνακαίεται vb pres m/p ind 3rd pers sg . . . . ἀνακαίω

ἀνακαινιεῖς vb fut act ind 2nd pers sg . . . . . . ἀνακαινίζω

ἀνακαινισθήσεται vb fut pass ind 3rd pers sg   id.

ἀνακαίνισον vb 1st aor act impv 2nd pers sg   id.

ἀνακαλεῖν vb pres act inf . . . . ἀνακαλέω

ἀνακαλεσάμενος vb 1st aor mid part masc nom sg   id.

ἀνακαλούμενα vb pres m/p part neut nom and acc pl id.

ἀνακαλύπτει vb pres act ind 3rd pers sg . . . . ἀνακαλύπτω

ἀνακαλύπτειν vb pres act inf   id.

ἀνακαλύπτων vb pres act part masc nom sg   id.

ἀνακαλυφθῆναι vb 1st aor pass inf   id.

ἀνακαλυφθήσεται vb fut pass ind 3rd pers sg   id.

ἀνακάλυψαι vb 1st aor mid impv 2nd pers sg   id.

ἀνακαλύψαι 1st aor act inf, 1st aor act opt 3rd pers sg id.

ἀνακαλύψει vb fut act ind 3rd pers sg   id.

ἀνακαλύψουσιν vb fut act ind 3rd pers pl   id.

ἀνακάμπτει vb pres act ind 3rd pers sg . . . . . . ἀνακάμπτω

ἀνακάμπτειν vb pres act inf   id.

ἀνακάμπτουσα vb pres act part fem nom sg   id.

ἀνακάμψαντες vb 1st aor act part masc nom pl   id.

ἀνακάμψατε vb 1st aor act impv 2nd pers pl   id.

ἀνακάμψει vb fut act ind 3rd pers sg   id.

ἀνακάμψουσιν vb fut act ind 3rd pers pl   id.

ἀνακαύσαντες vb 1st aor act part masc nom pl . . . ἀνακαίω

ἀνακαύσεις vb fut act ind 2nd pers sg   id.

ἀνακαύσω vb fut act ind 1st pers sg   id.

ἀνακείμενον vb pres m/p part masc acc sg . . . . ἀνάκειμαι

ἀνάκειται vb pres m/p ind 3rd pers sg   id.

ἀνακεκαλυμμένα vb perf m/p part

        neut nom and acc pl . . . . ἀνακαλύπτω

ἀνακεκαλυμμένον vb perf m/p part masc acc sg   id.

ἀνακεκαλυμμένους vb perf m/p part masc acc pl   id.

ἀνακέκληκεν vb perf act ind 3rd pers sg . . . . . . ἀνακαλέω

ἀνακέκλημαι vb perf m/p ind 1st pers sg   id.

ἀνακεκράξεται vb fut perf mid ind 3rd pers sg . ἀνακράζω

ἀνακληθέντας vb 1st aor pass part masc acc pl . . ἀνακαλέω

ἀνακλῖναι vb 1st aor act inf . . . . ἀνακλίνω

ἀνακλίσει noun fem dat sg . . . . ἀνάκλισις

ἀνάκλιτον noun neut nom and acc sg

ἀνακλώμενος vb pres m/p part masc nom sg . . . . ἀνακλάω

ἀνακοινωσαμένου vb 1st aor mid part

        masc and neut gen sg . . . . ἀνακοινόω

ἀνακομίσασθαι vb 1st aor mid inf . . . . ἀνακομίζω

ἀνακομισθέντων vb 1st aor pass part

        masc and neut gen pl   id.

ἀνακοπτόμενα vb pres m/p part

        neut nom and acc pl . . . . ἀνακόπτω

ἀνακόπτοντες vb pres act part masc nom pl   id.

ἀνάκραγε vb 2nd aor act impv 2nd pers sg . . . . . ἀνακράζω

ἀνακραγέτω vb 2nd aor act impv 3rd pers sg   id.

ἀνακραγόντων vb 2nd aor act part

        masc and neut gen pl   id.

ἀνακρίναντες vb 1st aor act part masc nom pl . . . ἀνακρίνω

ἀνακρινῶ vb fut act ind 1st pers sg   id.

ἀνακρίσεως noun fem gen sg . . . . ἀνάκρισις

ἀνακρουόμενοι vb pres m/p part masc nom pl . ἀνακρούω

ἀνακρουόμενον vb pres m/p part masc acc sg   id.

ἀνακρουομένῳ vb pres m/p part masc and neut dat sg id.

ἀνακρουομένων vb pres m/p part gen pl   id.

ἀνακύψαι vb 1st aor act inf . . . . ἀνακύπτω

ἀνακύψασα vb 1st aor act part fem nom sg   id.

ἀνάλαβε vb 2nd aor act impv 2nd pers sg . . . ἀναλαμβάνω

ἀναλαβεῖν vb 2nd aor act inf   id.

ἀναλάβετε vb 2nd aor act impv 2nd pers pl   id.

ἀναλαβέτω vb 2nd aor act impv 3rd pers sg   id.

ἀναλάβοι vb 2nd aor act opt 3rd pers sg   id.

ἀναλάβοιμι vb 2nd aor act opt 1st pers sg   id.

ἀναλαβόντες vb 2nd aor act part masc nom pl   id.

ἀναλαβοῦσα vb 2nd aor act part fem nom sg   ἀναλαμβάνω
ἀναλάβωμεν vb 2nd aor act subj 1st pers pl   id.
ἀναλαβών vb 2nd aor act part masc nom sg   id.
ἀναλαμβάνειν vb pres act inf   id.
ἀναλαμβάνεις vb pres act ind 2nd pers sg   id.
ἀναλαμβανόμενον vb pres m/p part masc acc sg,
      neut nom and acc sg   id.
ἀναλαμβάνων vb pres act part masc nom sg   id.
ἀναλάμψει vb fut act ind 3rd pers sg . . . . ἀναλάμπω
ἀναλάμψῃ vb 1st aor act subj 3rd pers sg   id.
ἀναλάμψουσιν vb fut act ind 3rd pers pl   id.
ἀνάλγητος adj masc nom sg
ἀναλελυκώς vb perf act part masc nom sg . . . . ἀναλύω
ἀναλεξάμενος vb 1st aor mid part masc nom sg . . ἀναλέγω
ἀνάλημμα noun neut nom and acc sg
ἀναλημπτέα verbal adj pl . . . . ἀναλημπτέον
ἀναλημπτῆρας noun masc acc pl . . . . ἀναλημπτήρ
ἀναλημφθείς vb 1st aor pass part
      masc nom sg . . . . ἀναλαμβάνω
ἀναλημφθῆναι vb 1st aor pass inf   id.
ἀναλημφθήσῃ vb fut pass ind 2nd pers sg   id.
ἀναλήμψεσθε vb fut mid ind 2nd pers pl   id.
ἀναλήμψεται vb fut mid ind 3rd pers sg   id.
ἀνάλημψιν noun fem acc sg . . . . ἀνάλημψις
ἀναλήμψομαι vb fut mid ind 1st pers sg . . . . ἀναλαμβάνω
ἀναληφθήσεται vb fut pass ind 3rd pers sg   id.
ἀναλίσκει vb pres act ind 3rd pers sg . . . . ἀναλίσκω
ἀναλίσκειν vb pres act inf   id.
ἀναλίσκεσθαι vb pres m/p inf   id.
ἀναλίσκον vb pres act part neut nom and acc sg   id.
ἀναλογισάμενοι vb 1st aor mid part
      masc nom pl . . . . ἀναλογίζομαι
ἀναλόγως adverb
ἀναλύει vb pres act ind 3rd pers sg . . . . ἀναλύω
ἀναλύειν vb pres act inf   id.
ἀναλυθήσονται vb fut pass ind 3rd pers pl   id.
ἀναλύοντες vb pres act part masc nom pl   id.
ἀναλύσαντες vb 1st aor act part masc nom pl   id.
ἀναλύσας vb 1st aor act part masc nom sg   id.
ἀναλύων vb pres act part masc nom sg   id.
ἀναλωθῇ vb 1st aor pass subj 3rd pers sg . . . . ἀναλίσκω
ἀναλωθήσεται vb fut pass ind 3rd pers sg   id.
ἀναλωθήσονται vb fut pass ind 3rd pers pl   id.
ἀναλώσας vb 1st aor act part masc nom sg   id.
ἀναλώσει vb fut act ind 3rd pers sg   id.
ἀναλώσῃ vb 1st aor act subj 3rd pers sg   id.
ἀνάλωσιν noun fem acc sg . . . . ἀνάλωσις
Αναμ pr noun
ἀναμάρτητον adj acc sg, neut nom sg . . . . . . ἀναμάρτητος
ἀναμαρτήτους adj masc and fem acc pl   id.
ἀναμαρτήτων adj gen pl   id.
Αναμεηλ pr noun

ἀναμείγνυται vb pres m/p ind 3rd pers sg . . . . ἀναμίγνυμι
ἀναμείνατε vb 1st aor act impv 2nd pers pl . . . . . . ἀναμένω
ἀνάμεινον vb 1st aor act impv 2nd pers sg   id.
ἀναμεῖξαι vb 1st aor act inf . . . . ἀναμίγνυμι
ἀναμείξεως noun fem gen sg . . . . ἀνάμιξις
ἀναμεμειγμένοι vb perf m/p part
      masc nom pl . . . . ἀναμίγνυμι
ἀναμεμειγμένον vb perf m/p part masc acc sg   id.
ἀναμεμειγμένος vb perf m/p part masc nom sg   id.
ἀναμεμεῖχθαι vb perf m/p inf   id.
ἀνάμενε vb pres act impv 2nd pers sg . . . . ἀναμένω
ἀναμένει vb pres act ind 3rd pers sg   id.
ἀναμενεῖτε vb fut act ind 2nd pers pl   id.
ἀναμένοντες vb pres act part masc nom pl   id.
ἀναμένω vb pres act ind 1st pers sg   id.
ἀναμένων vb pres act part masc nom sg   id.
ἀναμιμνήσκουσα vb pres act part
      fem nom sg . . . . ἀναμιμνήσκω
ἀναμιμνήσκουσαν vb pres act part fem acc sg   id.
ἀναμιμνήσκω vb pres act ind 1st pers sg   id.
ἀναμιμνήσκων vb pres act part masc nom sg   id.
ἀναμνῆσαι vb 1st aor act inf   id.
ἀναμνήσατε vb 1st aor act impv 2nd pers pl   id.
ἀναμνησθείη vb 1st aor pass opt 3rd pers sg   id.
ἀναμνησθήσεσθε vb fut pass ind 2nd pers pl   id.
ἀναμνησθήσεται vb fut pass ind 3rd pers sg   id.
ἀναμνήσθητε vb 1st aor pass subj 2nd pers pl   id.
ἀναμνησθῶσιν vb 1st aor pass subj 3rd pers pl   id.
ἀνάμνησιν noun fem acc sg . . . . ἀνάμνησις
ἀνάμνησις noun fem nom sg   id.
ἀναμοχλεύοντες vb pres act part
      masc nom pl . . . . ἀναμοχλεύω
ἀναμφισβητήτως adverb
Αναν pr noun
ἄνανδροι adj masc nom pl . . . . ἄνανδρος
ἄνανδρος adj masc nom sg   id.
Ανανεηλ pr noun
ἀνανεούμενοι vb pres m/p part masc nom pl . . . . . ἀνανεόω
ἀνανεῦσαι vb 1st aor act inf . . . . ἀνανεόω
ἀνανεύσῃ vb 1st aor act subj 3rd pers sg   id.
ἀνάνευσις noun fem nom sg
ἀνανεύων vb pres act part masc nom sg . . . . ἀνανεόω
ἀνανεωσάμενοι vb 1st aor mid part
      masc nom pl . . . . ἀνανεόω
ἀνανεώσασθαι vb 1st aor mid inf   id.
ἀνανεώσει vb fut act ind 3rd pers sg   id.
ἀνανεώσεως noun fem gen sg . . . . ἀνανέωσις
Ανανι pr noun
Ανανια pr noun
Ανανια pr noun masc voc and dat sg . . . . Ανανιας
Ανανιαν pr noun masc acc sg   id.
Ανανιας pr noun masc nom sg

Ανανιηλ   pr noun

Ανανιου   pr noun masc gen sg . . . . Ανανιας

ἀναντλήσεις   vb fut act ind 2nd pers sg . . . . ἀναντλέω

ἀνάξει   noun fem dat sg . . . . ἄναξις

ἀνάξει   vb fut act ind 3rd pers sg . . . . ἀνάγω

ἀναξηραίνει   vb pres act ind 3rd pers sg . . . . . ἀναξηραίνω

ἀναξηράνατε   vb 1st aor act impv 2nd pers pl   id.

ἀναξηρανεῖ   vb fut act ind 3rd pers sg   id.

ἀνάξια   adj neut nom and acc pl . . . . ἀνάξιος

ἀνάξιον   adj acc sg, neut nom sg   id.

ἀναξίου   adj gen sg   id.

ἀναξίῳ   adj dat sg   id.

ἀναξίως   adverb

ἀνάξομεν   vb fut act ind 1st pers pl . . . . ἀνάγω

ἀνάξω   vb fut act ind 1st pers sg   id.

ἀνάπαλιν   adverb

ἀνάπαυμα   noun neut nom and acc sg

ἀναπαυόμενα   vb pres m/p part

     neut nom and acc pl . . . . ἀναπαύω

ἀναπαυομένην   vb pres m/p part fem acc sg   id.

ἀναπαυόμενος   vb pres m/p part masc nom sg   id.

ἀναπαυομένων   vb pres m/p part gen pl   id.

ἀναπαύου   vb pres m/p impv 2nd pers sg   id.

ἀνάπαυσαι   vb 1st aor mid impv 2nd pers sg   id.

ἀναπαύσασθαι   vb 1st aor mid inf   id.

ἀναπαύσει   noun fem dat sg . . . . ἀνάπαυσις

ἀναπαύσει   vb fut act ind 3rd pers sg . . . . ἀναπαύω

ἀναπαύσεις   noun fem nom and acc pl . . . . ἀνάπαυσις

ἀναπαύσεται   vb fut mid ind 3rd pers sg . . . . . . ἀναπαύω

ἀναπαύσεως   noun fem gen sg . . . . ἀνάπαυσις

ἀναπαύσῃ   vb 1st aor act subj 3rd pers sg,

     fut mid ind 2nd pers sg . . . . ἀναπαύω

ἀναπαύσηται   vb 1st aor mid subj 3rd pers sg   id.

ἀνάπαυσιν   noun fem acc sg . . . . ἀνάπαυσις

ἀνάπαυσις   noun fem nom sg   id.

ἀναπαύσομαι   vb fut mid ind 1st pers sg . . . . . . ἀναπαύω

ἀναπαύσονται   vb fut mid ind 3rd pers pl   id.

ἀναπαύσω   vb 1st aor act subj 1st pers sg,

     fut act ind 1st pers sg   id.

ἀναπαύσωμαι   vb 1st aor mid subj 1st pers sg   id.

ἀναπαύσωνται   vb 1st aor mid subj 3rd pers pl   id.

ἀναπειθέτωσαν   vb pres act impv 3rd pers pl . . . . ἀναπείθω

ἀναπείρεσθαι   vb pres m/p inf . . . . ἀναπείρω

ἀνάπειρος   noun masc nom sg

ἀναπείρους   adj masc and fem acc pl . . . . ἀνάπηρος

ἀναπέπαυμαι   vb perf m/p ind 1st pers sg . . . . . ἀναπαύω

ἀναπέπαυται   vb perf m/p ind 3rd pers sg . . . . . ἀναπαύω

ἀναπεπλήρωνται   vb perf m/p ind 3rd pers pl .   ἀναπληρόω

ἀναπεποιημένα   vb perf m/p part

     neut nom and acc pl . . . . ἀναποιέω

ἀναπεποιημένη   vb perf m/p part fem nom sg   id.

ἀναπεποιημένην   vb perf m/p part fem acc sg   id.

ἀναπεποιημένης   vb perf m/p part fem gen sg . . . ἀναποιέω

ἀναπεποιημένους   vb perf m/p part masc acc pl   id.

ἀνέπεσε   vb 2nd aor act impv 2nd pers sg . . . . . . ἀναπίπτω

ἀναπεσεῖται   vb fut mid ind 3rd pers sg   id.

ἀναπεσών   vb 2nd aor act part masc nom sg   id.

ἀναπετάσας   vb 1st aor act part masc nom sg . . . ἀναπετάζω

ἀναπηδήσας   vb 1st aor act part masc nom sg . . . ἀναπηδάω

ἀναπηδύει   vb pres act ind 3rd pers sg . . . . ἀναπηδύω

ἀναπληροῦνται   vb pres m/p ind 3rd pers pl . . ἀναπληρόω

ἀναπληροῦσθαι   vb pres m/p inf   id.

ἀναπληρωθήσονται   vb fut pass ind 3rd pers pl   id.

ἀναπληρωθῶσιν   vb 1st aor pass subj 3rd pers pl   id.

ἀναπληρῶν   vb pres act part masc nom sg   id.

ἀναπληρώσῃ   vb 1st aor act subj 3rd pers sg   id.

ἀναπλήρωσιν   noun fem acc sg . . . . ἀναπλήρωσις

ἀναπληρώσω   vb 1st aor act subj 1st pers sg . . . ἀναπληρόω

ἀναπνεῦσαι   vb 1st aor act inf . . . . ἀναπνέω

ἀναποδισάντων   vb 1st aor act part

     masc and neut gen pl . . . . ἀναποδίζω

ἀναποδισμός   noun masc nom sg

ἀναπτεροῦσιν   vb pres act ind 3rd pers pl . . . . . ἀναπτερόω

ἀναπτερώσεως   noun fem gen sg . . . . ἀναπτέρωσις

ἀναπτομένη   vb pres m/p part fem nom sg . . . . . . ἀνάπτω

ἀνάπτον   vb pres act part neut nom and acc sg   id.

ἀνάπτοντες   vb pres act part masc nom pl   id.

ἀναπτύξουσιν   vb fut act ind 3rd pers pl . . . . . ἀναπτύσσω

ἀναπτυσσόμεναι   vb pres m/p part fem nom pl   id.

ἀναπτυσσόμενος   vb pres m/p part masc nom sg   id.

ἀνάπτω   vb pres act ind 1st pers sg

Αναρ   pr noun

Αναρεθ   pr noun

ἀναρίθμητα   adj neut nom and acc pl . . . . . . ἀναρίθμητος

ἀναρίθμητοι   adj masc and fem nom pl   id.

ἀναριθμήτοις   adj dat pl   id.

ἀναρίθμητον   adj acc sg, neut nom sg   id.

ἀναρίθμητος   adj masc and fem nom sg   id.

ἀναριθμήτους   adj masc and fem acc pl   id.

ἀναρρήξεις   vb fut act ind 2nd pers sg . . . . . . ἀναρρήγνυμι

ἀνασεσῳσμένοι   vb perf m/p part masc nom pl . . ἀνασῴζω

ἀνασεσῳσμένους   vb perf m/p part masc acc pl   id.

Ανασιβ   pr noun

ἀνασπάσει   vb fut act ind 3rd pers sg . . . . ἀνασπάω

ἀνασπάσῃ   vb 1st aor act subj 3rd pers sg   id.

Ανασσα   pr noun

ἀνάστα   vb 2nd aor act impv 2nd pers sg . . . . ἀνίστημι

ἀνασταθῇ   vb 1st aor pass subj 3rd pers sg   id.

ἀνασταθῇς   vb 1st aor pass subj 2nd pers sg   id.

ἀναστάντας   vb 2nd aor act part masc acc pl   id.

ἀναστάντες   vb 2nd aor act part masc nom pl   id.

ἀναστάντος   vb 2nd aor act part masc and neut gen sg   id.

ἀναστάς   vb 2nd aor act part masc nom sg   id.

ἀναστᾶσα   vb 2nd aor act part fem nom sg   id.

ἀναστάσεως noun fem gen sg . . . . ἀνάστασις
ἀνάστασιν noun fem acc sg   id.
ἀνάστασις noun fem nom sg   id.
ἀναστατώσει vb fut act ind 3rd pers sg . . . . . ἀναστατόω
ἀνάστεμα noun neut nom and acc sg . . . . ἀνάστημα
ἀναστενάζουσιν vb pres act ind 3rd pers pl . . ἀναστενάζω
ἀναστενάξας vb 1st aor act part masc nom sg   id.
ἀναστῇ vb 2nd aor act subj 3rd pers sg . . . . ἀνίστημι
ἀνάστηθι vb 2nd aor act impv 2nd pers sg   id.
ἀνάστημα noun neut nom and acc sg
ἀναστῆναι vb 2nd aor act inf . . . . ἀνίστημι
ἀναστήσαι vb 1st aor act opt 3rd pers sg   id.
ἀναστῆσαι vb 1st aor act inf   id.
ἀναστήσας vb 1st aor act part masc nom sg   id.
ἀναστήσει vb fut act ind 3rd pers sg   id.
ἀναστήσεις vb fut act ind 2nd pers sg   id.
ἀναστήσεσθαι vb fut mid inf   id.
ἀναστήσεται vb fut mid ind 3rd pers sg   id.
ἀναστήσετε vb fut act ind 2nd pers pl   id.
ἀναστήσῃ vb 1st aor act subj 3rd pers sg,
            fut mid ind 2nd pers sg   id.
ἀναστήσομαι vb fut mid ind 1st pers sg   id.
ἀναστησόμεθα vb fut mid ind 1st pers pl   id.
ἀνάστησον vb 1st aor act impv 2nd pers sg   id.
ἀναστήσονται vb fut mid ind 3rd pers pl   id.
ἀναστήσουσιν vb fut act ind 3rd pers pl   id.
ἀναστήσω vb 1st aor act subj 1st pers sg,
            fut act ind 1st pers sg   id.
ἀναστήσωμεν vb 1st aor act subj 1st pers pl   id.
ἀναστήσων vb fut act part masc nom sg   id.
ἀναστήσωσιν vb 1st aor act subj 3rd pers pl   id.
ἀνάστητε vb 2nd aor act impv 2nd pers pl   id.
ἀναστῆτε vb 2nd aor act subj 2nd pers pl   id.
ἀναστήτω vb 2nd aor act impv 3rd pers sg   id.
ἀναστήτωσαν vb 2nd aor act impv 3rd pers pl   id.
ἀναστραφήσεται vb fut pass ind 3rd pers sg . . . ἀναστρέφω
ἀναστράφητε vb 1st aor act impv 2nd pers pl   id.
ἀνάστρεφε vb pres act impv 2nd pers sg   id.
ἀναστρέφει vb pres act ind 3rd pers sg   id.
ἀναστρέφειν vb pres act inf   id.
ἀναστρέφεσθαι vb pres m/p inf   id.
ἀναστρέφεται vb pres m/p ind 3rd pers sg   id.
ἀναστρέφετε vb pres act ind 2nd pers pl   id.
ἀναστρεφέτω vb pres act impv 3rd pers sg   id.
ἀναστρεφέτωσαν vb pres act impv 3rd pers pl   id.
ἀναστρέφομαι vb pres m/p ind 1st pers sg   id.
ἀναστρεφόμενοι vb pres m/p part masc nom pl   id.
ἀναστρεφόμενον vb pres m/p part masc acc sg   id.
ἀναστρεφόμενος vb pres m/p part masc nom sg   id.
ἀναστρεφομένους vb pres m/p part masc acc pl   id.
ἀναστρέφοντος vb pres act part masc and neut gen sg id.
ἀναστρέφου vb pres m/p impv 2nd pers sg   id.

ἀναστρέφω vb pres act ind 1st pers sg . . . . ἀναστρέφω
ἀναστρέψαι vb 1st aor act inf   id.
ἀναστρέψαντες vb 1st aor act part
            masc nom pl   id.
ἀναστρέψας vb 1st aor act part masc nom sg   id.
ἀναστρέψατε vb 1st aor act impv 2nd pers pl   id.
ἀναστρέψει vb fut act ind 3rd pers sg   id.
ἀναστρέψεις vb fut act ind 2nd pers sg   id.
ἀνάστρεψον vb 1st aor act impv 2nd pers sg,
            fut act part neut nom and acc sg   id.
ἀναστρέψουσιν vb fut act ind 3rd pers pl   id.
ἀναστρέψω vb fut act ind 1st pers sg   id.
ἀναστρέψωμεν vb 1st aor act subj 1st pers pl   id.
ἀναστροφῇ noun fem dat sg . . . . ἀναστροφή
ἀναστροφῆς noun fem gen sg   id.
ἀναστῶ vb 2nd aor act subj 1st pers sg . . . . ἀνίστημι
ἀναστῶμεν vb 2nd aor act subj 1st pers pl   id.
ἀναστῶσιν vb 2nd aor act subj 3rd pers pl   id.
ἀνάσυραι vb 1st aor mid impv 2nd pers sg . . . . ἀνασύρω
ἀνασχίσας vb 1st aor act part masc nom sg . . . ἀνασχίζω
ἀνάσχισον vb 1st aor act impv 2nd pers sg   id.
ἀνασῴζεσθε vb pres m/p impv 2nd pers pl . . . . . ἀνασῴζω
ἀνασῳζέσθω vb pres m/p impv 3rd pers sg   id.
ἀνασῴζετε vb pres act ind 2nd pers pl   id.
ἀνασῳζόμενοι vb pres m/p part masc nom pl   id.
ἀνασῳζόμενον vb pres m/p part masc acc sg   id.
ἀνασῳζόμενος vb pres m/p part masc nom sg   id.
ἀνασῳζομένους vb pres m/p part masc acc pl   id.
ἀνασῳζομένων vb pres m/p part gen pl   id.
ἀνασῴζω vb pres act ind 1st pers sg   id.
ἀνασωθείς vb 1st aor pass part masc nom sg   id.
ἀνασωθέντων vb 1st aor pass part masc and neut gen pl id.
ἀνασωθήσονται vb fut pass ind 3rd pers pl   id.
ἀνατεθεματισμένον vb perf m/p part
            neut nom and acc sg . . . . ἀναθεματίζω
ἀνατεθέντα vb 1st aor pass part
            neut nom and acc pl . . . . ἀνατίθημι
ἀνατεθῇ vb 1st aor pass subj 3rd pers sg   id.
ἀνατεῖλαι vb 1st aor act opt 3rd pers sg . . . . ἀνατέλλω
ἀνατεῖλαι vb 1st aor act inf   id.
ἀνατειλάτω vb 1st aor act impv 3rd pers sg   id.
ἀνατείλῃ vb 1st aor act subj 3rd pers sg   id.
ἀνατείνας vb 1st aor act part masc nom sg . . . . . ἀνατείνω
ἀνατελεῖ vb fut act ind 3rd pers sg . . . . ἀνατέλλω
ἀνατέλλει vb pres act ind 3rd pers sg   id.
ἀνατέλλοντα vb pres act part masc acc sg,
            neut nom and acc pl   id.
ἀνατέλλοντος vb pres act part masc and neut gen sg   id.
ἀνατέλλουσα vb pres act part fem nom sg   id.
ἀνατέλλων vb pres act part masc nom sg   id.
ἀνατελοῦσιν vb fut act ind 3rd pers pl   id.
ἀνάτεμε vb pres act impv 2nd pers sg . . . . ἀνατέμνω

ἀνατέταλκεν   vb perf act ind 3rd pers sg . . . . . . ἀνατέλλω

ἀνατίκτουσα   vb pres act part fem nom sg . . . . . ἀνατίκτω

ἀνατιναγμός   noun masc nom sg

ἀνατλῶν   vb 1st aor act part neut nom and acc sg . . ἀνέτλην

ἀνατολαί   noun fem nom pl . . . . ἀνατολή

ἀνατολαῖς   noun fem dat pl   id.

ἀνατολάς   noun fem acc pl   id.

Ἀνατολη   pr noun fem nom sg

ἀνατολή   noun fem nom sg

ἀνατολῇ   noun fem dat sg . . . . ἀνατολή

Ἀνατολην   pr noun fem acc sg . . . . Ἀνατολη

ἀνατολήν   noun fem acc sg . . . . ἀνατολή

ἀνατολῆς   noun fem gen sg   id.

ἀνατολῶν   noun fem gen pl   id.

ἀνατραπῇ   vb 2nd aor pass subj 3rd pers sg . . . . ἀνατρέπω

ἀνατραφέντες   vb 2nd aor pass part

      masc nom pl . . . . ἀνατρέφω

ἀνατρέπει   vb pres act ind 3rd pers sg . . . . ἀνατρέπω

ἀνατρέποντες   vb pres act part masc nom pl   id.

ἀνατρέχων   vb pres act part masc nom sg . . . . . . ἀνατρέχω

ἀνατρέψαι   vb 1st aor act inf . . . . ἀνατρέπω

ἀνατρέψας   vb 1st aor act part masc nom sg   id.

ἀνατρέψει   vb fut act ind 3rd pers sg   id.

ἀνατροπῇ   noun fem dat sg . . . . ἀνατροπή

ἀνατροπῆς   noun fem gen sg   id.

ἀνατροφῆς   noun fem gen sg . . . . ἀνατροφή

ἀνατυπωσάμενοι   vb 1st aor mid part

      masc nom pl . . . . ἀνατυπόω

Αναφαθι   pr noun

ἀναφαίνεται   vb pres m/p ind 3rd pers sg . . . . . . ἀναφαίνω

ἀναφάλαντος   adj masc and fem nom sg

ἀναφαλαντώματι   noun neut dat sg . . . . . ἀναφαλάντωμα

ἀναφανείη   vb 2nd aor pass opt 3rd pers sg . . . . ἀναφαίνω

ἀναφανεῖται   vb fut mid ind 3rd pers sg   id.

ἀναφανῇς   vb 2nd aor pass subj 2nd pers sg   id.

ἀναφανοῦμαι   vb fut mid ind 1st pers sg   id.

ἀναφέρειν   vb pres act inf . . . . ἀναφέρω

ἀναφερέτω   vb pres act impv 3rd pers sg   id.

ἀναφερομένων   vb pres m/p part gen pl   id.

ἀναφέροντα   vb pres act part masc acc sg   id.

ἀναφέροντες   vb pres act part masc nom pl   id.

ἀναφέρουσι(ν)   vb pres act ind 3rd pers pl   id.

ἀναφέρων   vb pres act part masc nom sg   id.

ἀναφέρωσιν   vb pres act subj 3rd pers pl   id.

ἀναφθῇ   vb 1st aor pass subj 3rd pers sg . . . . ἀνάπτω

ἀναφθήσεται   vb fut pass ind 3rd pers sg   id.

ἀναφοράν   noun fem acc sg . . . . ἀναφορά

ἀναφορεῖς   noun masc nom and acc pl . . . . ἀναφορεύς

ἀναφορεῦσι   noun masc dat pl   id.

ἀναφορέων   noun masc gen pl   id.

ἀναφράσσεσθαι   vb pres m/p inf . . . . ἀναφράσσω

ἀναφύσει   vb fut act ind 3rd pers sg . . . . ἀναφύω

ἀναφωνεῖν   vb pres act inf . . . . ἀναφωνέω

ἀναφωνοῦντας   vb pres act part masc acc pl   id.

ἀναφωνοῦντες   vb pres act part masc nom pl   id.

ἀναφωνῶν   vb pres act part masc nom sg   id.

ἀναχανών   vb 2nd aor act part masc nom sg . . . . ἀναχάσκω

Αναχερεθ   pr noun

ἀναχθείς   vb 1st aor pass part masc nom sg . . . . ἀνάγω

ἀναχώρει   vb pres act impv 2nd pers sg . . . . ἀναχωρέω

ἀναχωρεῖν   vb pres act inf   id.

ἀναχωρῆσαι   vb 1st aor act inf   id.

ἀναχωρήσας   vb 1st aor act part masc nom sg   id.

ἀναχωρήσατε   vb 1st aor act impv 2nd pers pl   id.

ἀναχωροῦντες   vb pres act part masc nom pl   id.

ἀνάψαι   vb 1st aor act inf . . . . ἀνάπτω

ἀνάψει   vb fut act ind 3rd pers sg   id.

ἀνάψετε   vb fut act ind 2nd pers pl   id.

ἀναψύξῃ   vb 1st aor act subj 3rd pers sg . . . . ἀναψύχω

ἀνάψυξις   noun fem nom sg

ἀναψύξοντα   vb fut act part masc acc sg . . . . ἀναψύχω

ἀναψύξω   vb fut act ind 1st pers sg   id.

ἀναψυχήν   noun fem acc sg . . . . ἀναψυχή

ἀνάψω   vb fut act ind 1st pers sg . . . . ἀνάπτω

ἄνδρα   noun masc acc sg . . . . ἀνήρ

ἀνδραγαθῆσαι   vb 1st aor act inf . . . . ἀνδραγαθέω

ἀνδραγαθήσασι   vb 1st aor act part

      masc and neut dat pl   id.

ἀνδραγαθίαν   noun fem acc sg . . . . ἀνδραγαθία

ἀνδραγαθίας   noun fem gen sg and acc pl   id.

ἀνδραγαθιῶν   noun fem gen pl   id.

ἀνδράποδα   noun neut nom and acc pl . . . . . . ἀνδράποδον

ἄνδρας   noun masc acc pl . . . . ἀνήρ

ἀνδράσι   noun masc dat pl   id.

ἀνδρεία   adj fem nom sg . . . . ἀνδρεῖος

ἀνδρεία   noun fem nom sg

ἀνδρείᾳ   adj fem dat sg . . . . ἀνδρεῖος

ἀνδρείᾳ   noun fem dat sg . . . . ἀνδρεία

ἀνδρείαν   adj fem acc sg . . . . ἀνδρεῖος

ἀνδρείαν   noun fem acc sg . . . . ἀνδρεία

ἀνδρείας   adj fem acc pl . . . . ἀνδρεῖος

ἀνδρείας   noun fem gen sg . . . . ἀνδρεία

ἀνδρεῖοι   adj masc nom pl . . . . ἀνδρεῖος

ἀνδρεῖον   adj masc acc sg, neut nom and acc sg   id.

ἀνδρεῖος   adj masc nom sg   id.

ἀνδρειοτέρα   comp adj fem nom sg   id.

ἀνδρείου   adj masc and neut gen sg   id.

ἀνδρείους   adj masc acc pl   id.

ἀνδρείων   adj gen pl   id.

ἀνδρείως   adverb

ἀνδρειώσας   vb 1st aor act part masc nom sg . . . . ἀνδρειόω

ἄνδρες   noun masc nom pl . . . . ἀνήρ

ἀνδρί   noun masc dat sg   id.

ἀνδρίζεσθαι   vb pres dep inf . . . . ἀνδρίζομαι ἀνδρίζεσθε vb pres dep impv 2nd pers pl,

    pres dep ind 2nd pers pl . . . . ἀνδρίζομαι

ἀνδρίζου vb pres dep impv 2nd pers sg   id.

ἀνδριοῦμαι vb fut mid ind 1st pers sg   id.

ἀνδριούμεθα vb fut mid ind 1st pers pl   id.

ἄνδρισαι vb 1st aor mid impv 2nd pers sg   id.

ἀνδρογύναιον adj masc acc sg . . . . ἀνδρογύναιος

ἀνδρογύνων noun masc gen pl . . . . ἀνδρόγυνος

ἀνδρολογίαν noun fem acc sg . . . . ἀνδρολογία

Ἀνδρονικον pr noun masc acc sg . . . . Ἀνδρονικος

Ἀνδρονικου pr noun masc gen sg   id.

Ἀνδρονικῳ pr noun masc dat sg   id.

ἀνδρός noun masc gen sg . . . . ἀνήρ

ἀνδροφονήσαντα vb 1st aor act part

    masc acc sg . . . . ἀνδροφονέω

ἀνδροφόνος adj masc nom sg

ἀνδρωδῶς adverb

ἀνδρωθέντα vb 1st aor pass part masc acc sg . . . . . . ἀνδρόω

ἀνδρωθῶσιν vb 1st aor pass subj 3rd pers pl   id.

ἀνδρῶν noun masc gen pl . . . . ἀνήρ

ἀνέβαιναν vb impf act ind 3rd pers pl . . . . ἀναβαίνω

ἀνέβαινε(ν) vb impf act ind 3rd pers sg   id.

ἀνεβαίνετε vb impf act ind 2nd pers pl   id.

ἀνέβαινον vb impf act ind 3rd pers pl   id.

ἀνέβαλεν vb 2nd aor act ind 3rd pers sg . . . . . . ἀναβάλλω

ἀνεβάλετο vb 2nd aor mid ind 3rd pers sg   id.

ἀνέβαλον vb 2nd aor act ind 3rd pers pl   id.

ἀνεβάλου vb 2nd aor mid ind 2nd pers sg   id.

ἀνεβάστασεν vb 1st aor act ind 3rd pers sg . . ἀναβαστάζω

ἀνέβη vb 2nd aor act ind 3rd pers sg . . . . ἀναβαίνω

ἀνέβημεν vb 2nd aor act ind 1st pers pl   id.

ἀνέβην vb 2nd aor act ind 1st pers sg   id.

ἀνέβης vb 2nd aor act ind 2nd pers sg   id.

ἀνέβησαν vb 2nd aor act ind 3rd pers pl   id.

ἀνέβητε vb 2nd aor act ind 2nd pers pl   id.

ἀνεβίβασα vb 1st aor act ind 1st pers sg . . . . . . ἀναβιβάζω

ἀνεβίβασαν vb 1st aor act ind 3rd pers pl   id.

ἀνεβίβασας vb 1st aor act ind 2nd pers sg   id.

ἀνεβίβασεν vb 1st aor act ind 3rd pers sg   id.

ἀνεβιβάσθη vb 1st aor pass ind 3rd pers sg   id.

ἀνέβλεψα vb 1st aor act ind 1st pers sg . . . . ἀναβλέπω

ἀνέβλεψαν vb 1st aor act ind 3rd pers pl   id.

ἀνέβλεψεν vb 1st aor act ind 3rd pers sg   id.

ἀνεβόησα vb 1st aor act ind 1st pers sg . . . . ἀναβοάω

ἀνεβοήσαμεν vb 1st aor act ind 1st pers pl   id.

ἀνεβόησαν vb 1st aor act ind 3rd pers pl   id.

ἀνεβόησεν vb 1st aor act ind 3rd pers sg   id.

ἀνεβόων vb impf act ind 3rd pers pl   id.

ἀνέβρασεν vb 1st aor act ind 3rd pers sg . . . . . ἀναβράσσω

ἀνεγείραντος vb 1st aor act part

    masc and neut gen sg . . . . ἀνεγείρω

ἀνεγίγνωσκεν vb impf act ind 3rd pers sg . . . . ἀναγινώσκω

ἀνεγιγνώσκοντο vb impf m/p ind 3rd pers pl . ἀναγινώσκω

ἀνεγίνωσκε(ν) vb impf act ind 3rd pers sg   id.

ἀνεγίνωσκον vb impf act ind 1st pers sg, 3rd pers pl   id.

ἀνεγκλήτων adj gen pl . . . . ἀνέγκλητος

ἀνέγνω vb 2nd aor act ind 3rd pers sg . . . . . . ἀναγινώσκω

ἀνέγνων vb 2nd aor act ind 1st pers sg   id.

ἀνεγνωρίζετο vb impf m/p ind 3rd pers sg . . . ἀναγνωρίζω

ἀνέγνωσαν vb 2nd aor act ind 3rd pers pl . . . . ἀναγινώσκω

ἀνεγνώσθη vb 1st aor pass ind 3rd pers sg   id.

ἀνεγνώσθησαν vb 1st aor pass ind 3rd pers pl   id.

ἀνεγνωσμένον vb perf m/p part masc acc sg,

    neut nom and acc sg   id.

ἀνεγνωσμένῳ vb perf m/p part masc and neut dat sg   id.

ἀνεγράψαμεν vb 1st aor act ind 1st pers pl . . . . . ἀναγράφω

ἀνέδειξαν vb 1st aor act ind 3rd pers pl . . . . . . ἀναδεικνύω

ἀνέδειξας vb 1st aor act ind 2nd pers sg   id.

ἀνέδειξε(ν) vb 1st aor act ind 3rd pers sg   id.

ἀνεδείχθη vb 1st aor pass ind 3rd pers sg   id.

ἀνέδραμεν vb 2nd aor act ind 3rd pers sg . . . . . . ἀνατρέχω

ἀνεζεύγνυσαν vb 1st aor act ind 3rd pers pl . . ἀναζευγνύω

ἀνέζευξαν vb 1st aor act ind 3rd pers pl   id.

ἀνέζευξεν vb 1st aor act ind 3rd pers sg   id.

ἀνεζητήθη vb 1st aor pass ind 3rd pers sg . . . . . . ἀναζητέω

ἀνεζήτησας vb 1st aor act ind 2nd pers sg   id.

ἀνεζωπύρησεν vb 1st aor act ind 3rd pers sg . . ἀναζωπυρέω

ἀνεζωσμένοι vb perf m/p part masc nom pl . . . ἀναζώννυμι

ἀνέθαλεν vb 2nd aor act ind 3rd pers sg . . . . . . ἀναθάλλω

ἀνεθεμάτισαν vb 1st aor act ind 3rd pers pl . ἀναθεματίζω

ἀνεθεμάτισεν vb 1st aor act ind 3rd pers sg   id.

ἀνέθετο vb 2nd aor mid ind 3rd pers sg . . . . . . ἀνατίθημι

ἀνέθη vb 1st aor pass ind 3rd pers sg . . . . ἀνίημι

ἀνέθηκαν vb 1st aor act ind 3rd pers pl . . . . . . ἀνατίθημι

ἀνέθηκεν vb 1st aor act ind 3rd pers sg   id.

ἀνείκαστος adj masc and fem nom sg

ἀνείλατο vb 1st aor mid ind 3rd pers sg . . . . ἀναιρέω

ἀνεῖλεν vb 2nd aor act ind 3rd pers sg   id.

ἀνεῖλες vb 2nd aor act ind 2nd pers sg   id.

ἀνείλησεν vb 1st aor act ind 3rd pers sg . . . . ἀνειλέω

ἀνειλόμην vb 2nd aor mid ind 1st pers sg . . . . . . ἀναιρέω

ἀνεῖλον vb 2nd aor act ind 3rd pers pl   id.

ἀνειμένα vb perf m/p part neut nom and acc pl . . . . . ἀνίημι

ἀνειμέναι vb perf m/p part fem nom pl   id.

ἀνειμένης vb perf m/p part fem gen sg   id.

ἀνειμένον vb perf m/p part masc acc sg,

    neut nom and acc sg   id.

ἀνειμένος vb perf m/p part masc nom sg   id.

ἀνείς vb 2nd aor act part masc nom sg   id.

ἀνεῖται vb perf m/p ind 3rd pers sg   id.

ἀνεκαινίσθη vb 1st aor pass ind 3rd pers sg . . ἀνακαινίζω

ἀνεκάλεσεν vb 1st aor act ind 3rd pers sg . . . . . . ἀνακαλέω

ἀνεκαλύφθη vb 1st aor pass ind 3rd pers sg . . ἀνακαλύπτω

ἀνεκάλυψα vb 1st aor act ind 1st pers sg   id.

ἀνεκάλυψας vb 1st aor act ind 2nd pers sg .. ἀνακαλύπτω
ἀνεκάλυψεν vb 1st aor act ind 3rd pers sg id.
ἀνέκαμπτες vb impf act ind 2nd pers sg .... ἀνακάμπτω
ἀνεκάμψαμεν vb 1st aor act ind 1st pers pl id.
ἀνέκαμψεν vb 1st aor act ind 3rd pers sg id.
ἀνεκαύθη vb 1st aor pass ind 3rd pers sg .... ἀνακαίω
ἀνεκαύθησαν vb 1st aor pass ind 3rd pers pl id.
ἀνέκαυσαν vb 1st aor act ind 3rd pers pl id.
ἀνεκήρυξεν vb 1st aor act ind 3rd pers sg ... ἀνακηρύσσω
ἀνεκλιπής adj masc nom sg
ἀνέκοψε vb 1st aor act ind 3rd pers sg .... ἀνακόπτω
ἀνέκραγεν vb 2nd aor act ind 3rd pers sg .... ἀνακράζω
ἀνέκραγον vb 2nd aor act ind 3rd pers pl id.
ἀνέκραξαν vb 1st aor act ind 3rd pers pl id.
ἀνέκραξεν vb 1st aor act ind 3rd pers sg id.
ἀνέκρινε vb 1st aor act ind 3rd pers sg .... ἀνακρίνω
ἀνεκρούετο vb impf m/p ind 3rd pers sg ...... ἀνακρούω
ἀνεκρούοντο vb impf m/p ind 3rd pers pl id.
ἀνέλαβεν vb 2nd aor act ind 3rd pers sg ... ἀναλαμβάνω
ἀνελάβετε vb 2nd aor act ind 2nd pers pl id.
ἀνέλαβον vb 2nd aor act ind 1st pers sg, 3rd pers pl id.
ἀνέλαμψεν vb 1st aor act ind 3rd pers sg ...... ἀναλάμπω
ἄνελε vb 2nd aor act impv 2nd pers sg .... ἀναιρέω
ἀνελεήμονα adj masc and fem acc sg,
            neut nom and acc pl .... ἀνελεήμων
ἀνελεήμονας adj masc and fem acc pl id.
ἀνελεήμονες adj masc and fem nom pl id.
ἀνελεημονος adj gen sg id.
ἀνελεημόνων adj gen pl id.
ἀνελεημόνως adverb
ἀνελεήμοσι adj dat pl .... ἀνελεήμων
ἀνελεήμων adj masc and fem nom sg id.
ἀνελεῖ vb fut act ind 3rd pers sg .... ἀναιρέω
ἀνελεῖν vb 2nd aor act inf id.
ἀνελεῖς vb fut act ind 2nd pers sg id.
ἀνέλεξαν vb 1st aor act ind 3rd pers pl .... ἀναλέγω
ἀνέλεξεν vb 1st aor act ind 3rd pers sg id.
ἀνέλεσθε vb 2nd aor mid impv 2nd pers pl .... ἀναιρέω
ἀνελέτω vb 2nd aor act impv 3rd pers sg id.
ἀνέλῃ vb 2nd aor act subj 3rd pers sg id.
ἀνελήμφθη vb 1st aor pass ind 3rd pers sg ... ἀναλαμβάνω
ἀνελήμφθην vb 1st aor pass ind 1st pers sg id.
ἀνέλῃς vb 2nd aor pass subj 2nd pers sg .... ἀναιρέω
ἀνελογισάμην vb 1st aor mid ind
            1st pers sg .... ἀναλογίζομαι
ἀνελογίσατο vb 1st aor mid ind 3rd pers sg id.
ἀνέλοι vb 2nd aor act opt 3rd pers sg .... ἀναιρέω
ἀνελόμενος vb 2nd aor mid part masc nom sg id.
ἀνέλπιστον adj acc sg, neut nom sg .... ἀνέλπιστος
ἀνελπίστως adverb
ἀνελύθη vb 1st aor pass ind 3rd pers sg .... ἀναλύω
ἀνέλυσα vb 1st aor act ind 1st pers sg id.

ἀνέλυσαν vb 1st aor act ind 3rd pers pl .... ἀναλύω
ἀνέλυσεν vb 1st aor act ind 3rd pers sg id.
ἀνελῶ vb fut act ind 1st pers sg .... ἀναιρέω
ἀνέλωμεν vb 2nd aor pass subj 1st pers pl id.
ἀνελών vb 2nd aor act part masc nom sg id.
ἀνεμείναμεν vb 1st aor act ind 1st pers pl ...... ἀναμένω
ἀνεμνήσατε vb 1st aor act ind 2nd pers pl ... ἀναμιμνήσκω
ἀνεμνήσθη vb 1st aor pass ind 3rd pers sg id.
ἄνεμοι noun masc nom pl .... ἄνεμος
ἀνέμοις noun masc dat pl id.
ἄνεμον noun masc acc sg id.
ἄνεμος noun masc nom sg id.
ἀνέμου noun masc gen sg id.
ἀνέμους noun masc acc pl id.
ἀνεμόφθορα adj neut nom and acc pl ...... ἀνεμόφθορος
ἀνεμοφθορία noun fem nom sg
ἀνεμοφθορίᾳ noun fem dat sg .... ἀνεμοφθορία
ἀνεμόφθοροι adj masc and fem nom pl ..... ἀνεμόφθορος
ἀνεμόφθορον adj acc sg, neut nom sg id.
ἀνεμόφθορος adj masc and fem nom sg id.
ἀνεμποδίστοις adj dat pl .... ἀνεμπόδιστος
ἀνεμπόδιστος adj masc and fem nom sg id.
ἀνέμῳ noun masc dat sg .... ἄνεμος
ἀνέμων noun masc gen pl id.
ἀνενέασεν vb 1st aor act ind 3rd pers sg .... ἀνανεάζω
ἀνενέγκαι vb 1st aor act inf .... ἀναφέρω
ἀνενέγκας vb 1st aor act part masc nom sg id.
ἀνενεγκεῖν vb 2nd aor act inf id.
ἀνενεγκέτω vb 2nd aor act impv 3rd pers sg id.
ἀνενέγκῃς vb 1st aor act subj 2nd pers sg id.
ἀνενέγκητε vb 1st aor act subj 2nd pers pl id.
ἀνένεγκον vb 1st aor act impv 2nd pers sg id.
ἀνένευσαν vb 1st aor act ind 3rd pers pl .... ἀνανεύω
ἀνένευσεν vb 1st aor act ind 3rd pers sg id.
ἀνενεχθήσεται vb fut pass ind 3rd pers sg ...... ἀναφέρω
ἀνενήνοχα vb perf act ind 1st pers sg id.
ἀνενηνοχυῖα vb perf act part fem nom sg id.
ἀνέξει vb fut act ind 3rd pers sg .... ἀνέχω
ἀνεξέλεγκτος adj masc and fem nom sg
ἀνεξικακίαν noun fem acc sg .... ἀνεξικακία
ἀνεξιχνίαστα adj neut nom and acc pl .... ἀνεξιχνίαστος
ἀνεξιχνίαστον adj acc sg, neut nom sg id.
ἀνέξομαι vb fut mid ind 1st pers sg .... ἀνέχω
ἀνεπαύθημεν vb 1st aor pass ind 1st pers pl .... ἀναπαύω
ἀνεπαυσάμην vb 1st aor mid ind 1st pers sg id.
ἀνέπαυσαν vb 1st aor act ind 3rd pers pl id.
ἀνεπαύσαντο vb 1st aor mid ind 3rd pers pl id.
ἀνεπαύσατο vb 1st aor mid ind 3rd pers sg id.
ἀνέπαυσε(ν) vb 1st aor act ind 3rd pers sg id.
ἀνέπεισαν vb 1st aor act ind 3rd pers pl .... ἀναπείθω
ἀνέπεσα vb 1st aor act ind 1st pers sg .... ἀναπίπτω
ἀνέπεσαν vb 1st aor act ind 3rd pers pl id.

ἀνέπεσε(ν) vb 1st aor act ind 3rd pers sg . . . . ἀναπίπτω
ἀνεπήδησεν vb 1st aor act ind 3rd pers sg . . . . . . ἀναπηδάω
ἀνεπιεικεῖς adj masc and fem nom and acc pl . . . ἀνεπιεικής
ἀνεπιστρέπτως adverb
ἀνεπλάσατο vb 1st aor mid ind 3rd pers sg . . . . ἀναπλάσσω
ἀνεπληρώθη vb 1st aor pass ind 3rd pers sg . . . . . ἀναπληρόω
ἀνεπληρώθησαν vb 1st aor pass ind 3rd pers pl id.
ἀνεπλήρωσεν vb 1st aor act ind 3rd pers sg id.
ἀνεπόδισεν vb 1st aor act ind 3rd pers sg . . . . . . ἀναποδίζω
ἀνεπτερωμένη vb 1st aor mid part fem nom sg . . ἀναπτερόω
ἀνεπτέρωσαν vb 1st aor act ind 3rd pers pl id.
ἀνέπτυξεν vb 1st aor act ind 3rd pers sg . . . . . ἀναπτύσσω
ἀνερευνώμενοι vb pres m/p part masc nom pl . . . ἀνερευνάω
ἀνέρρηξαν vb 1st aor act ind 3rd pers pl . . . . ἀναρρήγνυμι
ἀνέρρηξεν vb 1st aor act ind 3rd pers sg id.
ἄνες vb 2nd aor act impv 2nd pers sg . . . . ἀνίημι
ἄνεσιν noun fem acc sg . . . . ἄνεσις
ἄνεσις noun fem nom sg id.
ἀνεσκαμμένη vb perf m/p part fem nom sg . . . . ἀνασκάπτω
ἀνέσκαψεν vb 1st aor act ind 3rd pers sg id.
ἀνέσπασεν vb 1st aor act ind 3rd pers sg . . . . ἀνασπάω
ἀνέστακεν vb perf act ind 3rd pers sg . . . . ἀνίστημι
ἀνεστάλη vb 2nd aor pass ind 3rd pers sg . . . . . ἀναστέλλω
ἀνεστάλησαν vb 2nd aor pass ind 3rd pers pl id.
ἀνεστέναξεν vb 1st aor act ind 3rd pers sg . . . . ἀναστενάζω
ἀνέστη vb 2nd aor act ind 3rd pers sg . . . . ἀνίστημι
ἀνέστηκεν vb perf act ind 3rd pers sg id.
ἀνέστημεν vb 2nd aor act ind 1st pers pl id.
ἀνέστην vb 2nd aor act ind 1st pers sg id.
ἀνέστης vb 2nd aor act ind 2nd pers sg . . . . ἀνίστημι
ἀνέστησα vb 1st aor act ind 1st pers sg id.
ἀνέστησαν vb 1st aor act ind 3rd pers pl id.
ἀνέστησεν vb 1st aor act ind 3rd pers sg id.
ἀνέστητε vb 2nd aor act ind 2nd pers pl id.
ἀνέστραπται vb perf m/p ind 3rd pers sg . . . . . ἀναστρέφω
ἀνεστρατοπέδευσεν vb 1st aor act ind
          3rd pers sg . . . . ἀναστρατοπεδεύω
ἀνεστρέφετο vb impf m/p ind 3rd pers sg . . . . . ἀναστρέφω
ἀνεστρέφοντο vb impf m/p ind 3rd pers pl id.
ἀνέστρεψα vb 1st aor act ind 1st pers sg id.
ἀνέστρεψαν vb 1st aor act ind 3rd pers pl id.
ἀνέστρεψεν vb 1st aor act ind 3rd pers sg id.
ἀνέσχεν vb 2nd aor act ind 3rd pers sg . . . . ἀνέχω
ἀνέσχιζον vb impf act ind
          1st pers sg and 3rd pers pl . . . . ἀνασχίζω
ἀνέσχον vb 2nd aor act ind
          1st pers sg and 3rd pers pl . . . . ἀνέχω
ἀνέσχοντο vb 2nd aor mid ind 3rd pers pl id.
ἀνέσχου vb 2nd aor mid ind 2nd pers sg id.
ἀνετάζοντες vb pres act part masc nom pl . . . . ἀνετάζω
ἀνέτειλαν vb 1st aor act ind 3rd pers pl . . . . ἀνατέλλω
ἀνέτειλεν vb 1st aor act ind 3rd pers sg id.
ἀνέτεινε vb 1st aor act ind 3rd pers sg . . . . ἀνατείνω
ἀνετράπη vb 2nd aor pass ind 3rd pers sg . . . . . . ἀνατρέπω
ἀνετράπην vb 2nd aor pass ind 1st pers sg id.
ἀνετράπησαν vb 2nd aor pass ind 3rd pers pl id.

ἀνετράφην vb 2nd aor pass ind 1st pers sg . . . . . . ἀνατρέφω
ἄνευ preposition
ἀνευράμενοι vb 1st aor mid part masc nom pl . . . ἀνευρίσκω
ἀνεφάνησαν vb 1st aor pass ind 3rd pers pl . . . . . . ἀναφαίνω
ἀνέφερεν vb impf act ind 3rd pers sg . . . . ἀναφέρω
ἀνεφέρετο vb impf m/p ind 3rd pers sg id.
ἀνέφερον vb impf act ind
          1st pers sg and 3rd pers pl id.
ἀνεφέροσαν vb impf act ind 3rd pers pl id.
ἀνέφικτος adj masc and fem nom sg
ἀνεφύη vb 2nd aor pass ind 3rd pers sg . . . . ἀναφύω
ἀνεφύησαν vb 2nd aor pass ind 3rd pers pl id.
ἀνεφύοντο vb impf m/p ind 3rd pers pl id.
ἀνέχεσθαι vb pres m/p inf . . . . ἀνέχω
ἀνέχεται vb pres m/p ind 3rd pers sg id.
ἀνέχομαι vb pres m/p ind 1st pers sg id.
ἀνεχώρησα vb 1st aor act ind 1st pers sg . . . . ἀναχωρέω
ἀνεχώρησας vb 1st aor act ind 2nd pers sg id.
ἀνεχώρησεν vb 1st aor act ind 3rd pers sg id.
ἀνεψιοῖς noun masc dat pl . . . . ἀνεψιός
ἀνεψιόν noun masc acc sg id.
ἀνεψιῷ noun masc dat sg id.
ἀνέψυξαν vb 1st aor act ind 3rd pers pl . . . . ἀναψύχω
ἀνέψυξεν vb 1st aor act ind 3rd pers sg id.
ἀνέψυχεν vb impf act ind 3rd pers sg id.
ἀνεψυχότα vb perf act part masc acc sg id.
ἀνεῳγμέναι vb perf m/p part fem nom pl . . . . ἀνοίγω
ἀνεῳγμένην vb perf m/p part fem acc sg id.
ἀνεῳγμένοι vb perf m/p part masc nom pl id.
ἀνεῳγμένον vb perf m/p part masc acc sg,
          neut nom and acc sg id.
ἀνεῳγμένος vb perf m/p part masc nom sg id.
ἀνεῳγμένους vb perf m/p part masc acc pl id.
ἀνεῳγότων vb perf act part masc and neut gen pl id.
ἀνέῳκτο vb plpf m/p ind 3rd pers sg id.
ἀνέῳξεν vb 1st aor act ind 3rd pers sg id.
ἀνεῳχθήσονται vb fut pass ind 3rd pers pl id.
ἀνῇ vb 2nd aor act subj 3rd pers sg . . . . ἀνίημι
ἀνήβων adj gen pl . . . . ἄνηβος
ἀνήγαγεν vb 2nd aor act ind 3rd pers sg . . . . ἀνάγω
ἀνήγαγες vb 2nd aor act ind 2nd pers sg id.
ἀνηγάγετε vb 2nd aor act ind 2nd pers pl id.
ἀνήγαγον vb 2nd aor act ind
          1st pers sg and 3rd pers pl id.
ἀνήγγειλα vb 1st aor act ind 1st pers sg . . . . ἀναγγέλλω
ἀνηγγείλαμεν vb 1st aor act ind 1st pers pl id.
ἀνήγγειλαν vb 1st aor act ind 3rd pers pl id.
ἀνήγγειλας vb 1st aor act ind 2nd pers sg id.
ἀνήγγειλεν vb 1st aor act ind 3rd pers sg id.
ἀνηγγέλη vb 2nd aor pass ind 3rd pers sg id.
ἀνήγγελκα vb perf act ind 1st pers sg id.
ἀνῆγον vb impf act ind
          1st pers sg and 3rd pers pl . . . . ἀνάγω
ἀνῆκα vb 1st aor act ind 1st pers sg . . . . ἀνίημι
ἀνῆκε(ν) vb 1st aor act ind 3rd pers sg id.
ἀνήκειν vb pres act inf . . . . ἀνήκω

ἀνηκέστοις adj dat pl . . . . ἀνήκεστος
ἀνήκεστον adj acc sg, neut nom sg   id.
ἀνήκεστος adj masc and fem nom sg   id.
ἀνήκοντα vb pres act part neut nom and acc pl . . . . . . ἀνήκω
ἀνήκοντας vb pres act part masc acc pl   id.
ἀνηκόντων vb pres act part masc and neut gen pl   id.
ἀνήκοοι adj masc and fem nom pl . . . . ἀνήκοος
ἀνήκοος adj masc and fem nom sg   id.
ἀνηκόων adj gen pl   id.
ἀνήλατος adj masc and fem nom sg
ἀνηλεεῖς adj masc and fem nom and acc pl . . . . . . ἀνηλεής
ἀνῆλθεν vb 2nd aor act ind 3rd pers sg . . . . ἀνέρχομαι
ἀνηλίσκετο vb impf m/p ind 3rd pers sg . . . . ἀναλίσκω
ἀνήλουν vb impf act ind
         1st pers sg and 3rd pers pl   id.
ἀνηλώθη vb 1st aor pass ind 3rd pers sg   id.
ἀνήλωσεν vb 1st aor act ind 3rd pers sg   id.
ἀνήλωται vb perf m/p ind 3rd pers sg   id.
Ανημελεχ pr noun
ἀνήνεγκα vb 1st aor act ind 1st pers sg . . . . ἀναφέρω
ἀνήνεγκαν vb 1st aor act ind 3rd pers pl   id.
ἀνήνεγκας vb 1st aor act ind 2nd pers sg   id.
ἀνήνεγκεν vb 1st aor act ind 3rd pers sg   id.
ἀνηνεγμένος vb perf m/p part masc nom sg   id.
ἀνηνέχθη vb aor pass ind 3rd pers sg   id.
ἀνήνυτον adj masc and fem acc sg . . . . ἀνήνυτος
ἀνήρ noun masc nom sg
ἀνηρέθη vb 1st aor pass ind 3rd pers sg . . . . ἀναιρέω
ἀνήρει vb impf act ind 3rd pers sg   id.
ἀνηρημένοι vb perf m/p part masc nom pl   id.
ἀνηρημένοις vb perf m/p part masc and neut dat pl   id.
ἀνηρημένους vb perf m/p part masc acc pl   id.
ἀνηρημένων vb perf m/p part gen pl   id.
ἀνηρῆσθαι vb perf m/p inf   id
ἀνήρουν vb impf act ind 1st pers sg and 3rd pers sg   id.
ἀνήρπαζον vb impf act ind
         1st pers sg and 3rd pers pl . . . . ἀναρπάζω
ἀνῇς vb 2nd aor act subj 2nd pers sg . . . . ἀνίημι
ἀνήσει vb fut act ind 3rd pers sg   id.
ἀνήσεις vb fut act ind 2nd pers sg   id.
ἀνήσομεν vb fut act ind 1st pers pl   id.
ἀνήσουσιν vb fut act ind 3rd pers pl   id.
ἀνήσω vb fut act ind 1st pers sg   id.
ἀνήταζον vb impf act ind
         1st pers sg and 3rd pers pl . . . . ἀνετάζω
ἀνήφθη vb 1st aor pass ind 3rd pers sg . . . . ἀνάπτω
ἀνήφθησαν vb 1st aor pass ind 3rd pers pl   id.
ἀνήχθησαν vb 1st aor pass ind 3rd pers pl . . . . ἀνάγω
ἀνῆψεν vb 1st aor act ind 3rd pers sg . . . . ἀνάπτω
ἀνθ' see ἀντί
ἀνθαιρεῖσθε vb pres m/p impv 2nd pers pl . . . . . . ἀνθαιρέω
ἀνθειστήκει vb plpf act ind 3rd pers sg . . . . . . ἀνθίστημι
ἀνθείτω vb pres act impv 3rd pers sg . . . . ἀνθέω
ἀνθέμιον noun neut nom and acc sg
ἀνθέξεται vb fut mid ind 3rd pers sg . . . . ἀντέχω
ἄνθεσι noun neut dat pl . . . . ἄνθος

ἀνθέστηκας vb perf act ind 2nd pers sg . . . . ἀνθίστημι
ἀνθεστήκασιν vb perf act ind 3rd pers pl   id.
ἀνθεστηκότα vb perf act part masc acc sg   id.
ἀνθεστηκότας vb perf act part masc acc pl   id.
ἀνθεστηκότων vb perf act part masc and neut gen pl   id.
ἀνθεστηκώς vb perf act part masc nom sg   id.
ἄνθη noun neut nom and acc pl . . . . ἄνθος
ἀνθήσαι vb 1st aor act opt 3rd pers sg . . . . ἀνθέω
ἄνθησαν vb 1st aor act part neut nom and acc sg   id.
ἀνθήσατε vb 1st aor act impv 2nd pers pl   id.
ἀνθήσει vb fut act ind 3rd pers sg   id.
ἀνθήσῃ vb 1st aor act subj 3rd pers sg   id.
ἄνθινον adj masc acc sg, neut nom and acc sg . . . . . ἄνθινος
ἀνθίστασθαι vb pres m/p inf . . . . ἀνθίστημι
ἀνθομολογήσει vb fut act ind
         3rd pers sg . . . . ἀνθομολογέομαι
ἀνθομολόγησιν noun fem acc sg . . . . ἀνθομολόγησις
ἀνθομολογησόμεθα vb fut mid ind
         1st pers pl . . . . ἀνθομολογέομαι
ἀνθομολογοῦμαι vb pres dep ind 1st pers sg   id.
ἀνθομολογούμενος vb pres dep part masc nom sg   id.
ἄνθος noun neut nom and acc sg
ἄνθους noun neut gen sg . . . . ἄνθος
ἄνθρακα noun masc acc sg . . . . ἄνθραξ
ἄνθρακας noun masc acc pl   id.
ἄνθρακες noun masc nom pl   id.
ἄνθρακι noun masc dat sg   id.
ἀνθρακιά noun fem nom sg
ἀνθρακιᾶς noun fem gen sg . . . . ἀνθρακιά
ἀνθράκινον adj masc acc sg,
         neut nom and acc sg . . . . ἀνθράκινος
ἄνθρακος noun masc gen sg . . . . ἄνθραξ
ἀνθράκων noun masc gen pl   id.
ἄνθραξ noun masc nom sg
ἄνθραξι noun masc dat pl   id.
ἀνθρωπαρέσκοις noun masc dat pl . . . . ἀνθρωπάρεσκος
ἀνθρωπάρεσκον noun masc acc sg   id.
ἀνθρωπαρέσκων noun masc gen pl   id.
ἄνθρωπε noun masc voc sg . . . . ἄνθρωπος
ἀνθρώπινα adj neut nom and acc pl . . . . ἀνθρώπινος
ἀνθρωπίνη adj fem nom sg   id.
ἀνθρωπίνης adj fem gen sg   id.
ἀνθρώπινοι adj masc nom pl   id.
ἀνθρώπινος adj masc nom sg   id.
ἀνθρωπίνου adj masc and neut gen sg   id.
ἀνθρωπίνων adj gen pl   id.
ἄνθρωποι noun masc nom pl . . . . ἄνθρωπος
ἀνθρώποις noun masc dat pl   id.
ἄνθρωπον noun masc acc sg   id.
ἄνθρωπος noun masc nom sg   id.
ἀνθρώπου noun masc gen sg   id.
ἀνθρώπους noun masc acc pl   id.
ἀνθρώπῳ noun masc dat sg   id.
ἀνθρώπων noun masc gen pl   id.
ἀνθυφαιρεθήσεται vb fut pass ind
         3rd pers sg . . . . ἀνθυφαιρέω

ἀνθωμολογεῖτο   vb impf dep ind
         3rd pers sg . . . . ἀνθομολογέομαι

Ανιαμ   pr noun

ἀνίατα   adj neut nom and acc pl . . . . ἀνίατος

ἀνίατον   adj acc sg, neut nom sg   id.

ἀνίατος   adj masc and fem nom sg   id.

ἀνιάτῳ   adj dat sg   id.

ἀνιέναι   vb pres act inf . . . . ἀνίημι

ἀνιερωθήσονται   vb fut pass ind 3rd pers pl . . . . . . ἀνιερόω

ἀνιερώσαντες   vb 1st aor act part masc nom pl   id.

ἀνίεται   vb pres m/p ind 3rd pers sg . . . . ἀνίημι

Ανιηλ   pr noun

ἀνίκητοι   adj masc and fem nom pl . . . . ἀνίκητος

ἀνίκητον   adj acc sg, neut nom sg   id.

ἀνίκητος   adj masc and fem nom sg   id.

ἀνικήτου   adj gen sg   id.

ἀνικήτους   adj masc and fem acc pl   id.

Ανιμ   pr noun

ἀνιόντος   vb pres act part masc and neut gen sg . . . . . . ἀνίημι

ἀνιπταμένου   vb pres dep part
         masc and neut gen sg . . . . ἀνίπταμαι

ἀνιστᾷ   vb pres act ind 3rd pers sg . . . . ἀνίστημι

ἀνιστάμενος   vb pres m/p part masc nom sg   id.

ἀνιστᾶν   vb pres act part neut nom and acc sg   id.

ἀνίστανται   vb pres m/p ind 3rd pers pl   id.

ἀνίστασθαι   vb pres m/p inf   id.

ἀνίσταται   vb pres m/p ind 3rd pers sg   id.

ἀνίστημι   vb pres act ind 1st pers sg   id.

ἀνίστησιν   vb pres act ind 3rd pers sg   id.

ἀνιστῶν   vb pres act part masc nom sg   id.

ἀνίσχυες   adj masc nom pl . . . . ἄνισχυς

Ανκαδης   pr noun

Αννα   pr noun

Ανναν   pr noun fem acc sg . . . . Αννας

Αννας   pr noun fem nom sg   id.

Αννας   pr noun fem gen sg . . . . Αννα

Αννιας   pr noun

Αννιουθ   pr noun

Αννουα   pr noun

Αννουνον   pr noun acc sg . . . . Αννουνος

Αννων   pr noun

ἀνόητοι   adj masc and fem nom pl . . . . ἀνόητος

ἀνοήτοις   adj dat pl   id.

ἀνόητον   adj acc sg, neut nom sg   id.

ἀνοητότερον   comp adj masc acc sg,
         neut nom and acc sg   id.

ἀνοήτου   adj gen sg   id.

ἀνοήτῳ   adj dat sg   id.

ἄνοια   noun fem nom sg

ἀνοίᾳ   noun fem dat sg . . . . ἄνοια

ἄνοιαν   noun fem acc sg   id.

ἀνοίας   noun fem gen sg   id.

ἄνοιγε   vb pres act impv 2nd pers sg . . . . ἀνοίγω

ἀνοίγει   vb pres act ind 3rd pers sg   id.

ἀνοίγειν   vb pres act inf   id.

ἀνοίγεις   vb pres act ind 2nd pers sg   id.

ἀνοιγῆναι   vb 2nd aor pass inf . . . . ἀνοίγω

ἀνοιγήσονται   vb fut pass ind 3rd pers pl   id.

ἀνοιγόμεναι   vb pres m/p part fem nom pl   id.

ἀνοίγονται   vb pres m/p ind 3rd pers pl   id.

ἀνοίγω   vb pres act ind 1st pers sg   id.

ἀνοίγων   vb pres act part masc nom sg   id.

ἀνοικοδομεῖν   vb pres act inf . . . . ἀνοικοδομέω

ἀνοικοδομεῖσθαι   vb pres m/p inf   id.

ἀνοικοδομεῖτε   vb pres act impv 2nd pers pl   id.

ἀνοικοδομηθῇ   vb 1st aor pass subj 3rd pers sg   id.

ἀνοικοδομηθήσεται   vb fut pass ind 3rd pers sg   id.

ἀνοικοδομήσει   vb fut act ind 3rd pers sg   id.

ἀνοικοδομήσεις   vb fut act ind 2nd pers sg   id.

ἀνοικοδομήσω   vb fut act ind 1st pers sg   id.

ἀνοικοδομήσωμεν   vb 1st aor act subj 1st pers pl   id.

ἀνοικοδομοῦνται   vb pres m/p ind 3rd pers pl   id.

ἀνοίκτου   adj masc and fem gen sg . . . . ἄνοικτος

ἀνοῖξαι   vb 1st aor act opt 3rd pers sg . . . . ἀνοίγω

ἀνοῖξαι   vb 1st aor act inf   id.

ἀνοίξαντα   vb 1st aor act part masc acc sg   id.

ἀνοίξαντες   vb 1st aor act part masc nom pl   id.

ἀνοίξαντος   vb 1st aor act part masc and neut gen sg   id.

ἀνοίξας   vb 1st aor act part masc nom sg   id.

ἀνοίξασα   vb 1st aor act part fem nom sg   id.

ἀνοίξατε   vb 1st aor act impv 2nd pers pl   id.

ἀνοίξει   vb fut act ind 3rd pers sg   id.

ἀνοίξεις   vb fut act ind 2nd pers sg   id.

ἀνοίξῃ   vb 1st aor act subj 3rd pers sg   id.

ἀνοίξῃς   vb 1st aor act subj 2nd pers sg   id.

ἀνοίξομεν   vb fut act ind 1st pers pl   id.

ἄνοιξον   vb 1st aor act impv 2nd pers sg   id.

ἀνοίξω   vb 1st aor act subj 1st pers sg,
         fut act ind 1st pers sg   id.

ἀνοίξωσιν   vb 1st aor act subj 3rd pers pl   id.

ἀνοίσατε   vb 1st aor act impv 2nd pers pl . . . . ἀναφέρω

ἀνοίσει   vb fut act ind 3rd pers sg   id.

ἀνοίσεις   vb fut act ind 2nd pers sg   id.

ἀνοίσετε   vb fut act ind 2nd pers pl   id.

ἀνοίσουσιν   vb fut act ind 3rd pers pl   id.

ἀνοίσω   vb fut act ind 1st pers sg   id.

ἀνοιχθέν   vb 1st aor pass part neut nom and acc sg . . . ἀνοίγω

ἀνοιχθήσεται   vb fut pass ind 3rd pers sg   id.

ἀνοιχθήσονται   vb fut pass ind 3rd pers pl   id.

ἄνομα   adj neut nom and acc pl . . . . ἄνομος

ἀνομβρήσει   vb fut act ind 3rd pers sg . . . . ἀνομβρέω

ἄνομε   adj masc and fem voc sg . . . . ἄνομος

ἀνομεῖ   vb pres act ind 3rd pers sg . . . . ἀνομέω

ἀνομηθῆναι   vb 1st aor pass inf   id.

ἀνόμημα   noun neut nom and acc sg

ἀνομήματα   noun neut nom and acc pl . . . . ἀνόμημα

ἀνομημάτων   noun neut gen pl   id.

ἀνομήσετε   vb fut act ind 2nd pers pl . . . . ἀνομέω

ἀνομήσητε   vb 1st aor act subj 2nd pers pl   id.

ἀνομήσωσιν   vb 1st aor act subj 3rd pers pl   id.

ἀνομία   noun fem nom sg

ἀνομίᾳ   noun fem dat sg . . . . ἀνομία ἀνομίαι noun fem nom pl . . . . ἀνομία

ἀνομίαις noun fem dat pl   id.

ἀνομίαν noun fem acc sg   id.

ἀνομίας noun fem gen sg and acc pl   id.

ἀνομιῶν noun fem gen pl   id.

ἄνομοι adj masc and fem nom pl . . . . ἄνομος

ἀνόμοιος adj masc and fem nom sg

ἀνόμοις adj dat pl . . . . ἄνομος

ἄνομον adj acc sg, neut nom sg   id.

ἄνομος adj masc and fem nom sg   id.

ἀνόμου adj gen sg   id.

ἀνομοῦντες vb pres act part masc nom pl . . . . ἀνομέω

ἀνόμους adj masc and fem acc pl . . . . ἄνομος

ἀνόμῳ adj dat sg   id.

ἀνόμων adj gen pl   id.

ἀνομῶν vb pres act part masc nom sg . . . . ἀνομέω

ἀνόμως adverb

ἀνόνητοι adj masc and fem nom pl . . . . ἀνόνητος

ἀνορθοῖ vb pres act ind 3rd pers sg . . . . ἀνορθόω

ἀνορθοῦται vb pres m/p ind 3rd pers sg   id.

ἀνορθῶσαι vb 1st aor act inf   id.

ἀνορθώσας vb 1st aor act part masc nom sg   id.

ἀνορθώσει vb fut act ind 3rd pers sg   id.

ἀνορθώσω vb fut act ind 1st pers sg   id.

ἀνορύσσοντες vb pres act part masc nom pl . . . . . ἀνορύσσω

ἀνορύσσων vb pres act part masc nom sg   id.

ἀνόσια adj neut nom and acc pl . . . . ἀνόσιος

ἀνοσίαν adj fem acc sg   id.

ἀνόσιε adj masc voc sg   id.

ἀνοσίου adj masc and neut gen sg   id.

ἀνοσίους adj masc and fem acc pl   id.

ἀνοσίως adverb

ἀνοσιώτατον superl adj masc acc sg,

          neut nom and acc sg . . . . ἀνόσιος

Ανουμ pr noun

Ανουν pr noun

ἄνους adj masc and fem nom sg

ἀνοχήν noun fem acc sg . . . . ἀνοχή

ἀντ’ see ἀντί

ἀνταγωνιστής noun masc nom sg

ἀντακούσεται vb fut mid ind 3rd pers sg . . . . . . ἀντακούω

ἀντάλλαγμα noun neut nom and acc sg

ἀνταλλάξει vb fut act ind 3rd pers sg . . . . ἀνταλλάσσω

ἀνταλλάξεται vb fut mid ind 3rd pers sg   id.

ἀντάμειψιν noun fem acc sg . . . . ἀντάμειψις

ἀνταναιρεθῇ vb 1st aor pass subj 3rd pers sg . . ἀνταναιρέω

ἀνταναιρεθήσονται vb fut pass ind 3rd pers pl   id.

ἀνταναιρεῖται vb pres m/p ind 3rd pers sg   id.

ἀνταναιροῦντες vb pres act part masc nom pl   id.

ἀνταναιρῶν vb pres act part masc nom sg   id.

ἀντανακλωμένη vb pres m/p part

          fem nom sg . . . . ἀντανακλάω

ἀντανελεῖς vb fut act ind 2nd pers sg . . . . ἀνταναιρέω

ἀντανέλῃς vb 2nd aor act subj 2nd pers sg   id.

ἀντανέστησαν vb 1st aor act ind 3rd pers pl . . ἀντανίστημι

ἀντανῃρέθην vb 1st aor pass ind 1st pers sg . . . ἀνταναιρέω

ἀνταπεδίδοσαν vb impf act ind 3rd pers pl . . ἀνταποδίδωμι

ἀνταπέδωκα vb 1st aor act ind 1st pers sg   id.

ἀνταπέδωκας vb 1st aor act ind 2nd pers sg   id.

ἀνταπεδώκατε vb 1st aor act ind 2nd pers pl   id.

ἀνταπέδωκεν vb 1st aor act ind 3rd pers sg   id.

ἀνταπεκρίθη vb 1st aor pass ind 3rd pers sg . . ἀνταποκρίνω

ἀνταπεκρίναντο vb 1st aor mid ind 3rd pers pl   id.

ἀνταπέστειλεν vb 1st aor act ind

          3rd pers sg . . . . ἀνταποστέλλω

ἀνταποδιδόντα vb pres act part masc acc sg . ἀνταποδίδωμι

ἀνταποδιδόντες vb pres act part masc nom pl   id.

ἀνταποδιδόντος vb pres act part masc and neut gen sg   id.

ἀνταποδίδοται vb pres m/p ind 3rd pers sg   id.

ἀνταποδίδοτε vb pres act ind 2nd pers pl   id.

ἀνταποδιδούς vb pres act part masc nom sg   id.

ἀνταποδιδοῦσι vb pres act part masc and neut dat pl   id.

ἀνταποδίδωσιν vb pres act ind 3rd pers sg   id.

ἀνταποδοθήσεται vb fut pass ind 3rd pers sg   id.

ἀνταπόδομα noun neut nom and acc sg

ἀνταπόδος vb 2nd aor act impv 2nd pers sg . . ἀνταποδίδωμι

ἀνταποδόσεις noun fem nom and acc pl . . . . . ἀνταπόδοσις

ἀνταποδόσεως noun fem gen sg   id.

ἀνταπόδοσιν noun fem acc sg   id.

ἀνταπόδοσις noun fem nom sg   id.

ἀνταπόδοτε vb 2nd aor act impv 2nd pers pl . ἀνταποδίδωμι

ἀνταποδοῦναι vb 2nd aor act inf   id.

ἀνταποδῷ vb 2nd aor act subj 1st and 3rd pers sg   id.

ἀνταποδῷς vb 2nd aor act subj 2nd pers sg   id.

ἀνταποδώσει vb fut act ind 3rd pers sg   id.

ἀνταποδώσεις vb fut act ind 2nd pers sg   id.

ἀνταποδώσομεν vb fut act ind 1st pers pl   id.

ἀνταποδώσω vb fut act ind 1st pers sg   id.

ἀνταποδώσων vb fut act part masc nom sg   id.

ἀνταποθανεῖται vb fut mid ind 3rd pers sg . ἀνταποθνήσκω

ἀνταποκρινόμενος vb pres m/p part

          masc nom sg . . . . ἀνταποκρίνω

ἀνταπόκρισιν noun fem acc sg . . . . ἀνταπόκρισις

ἀνταποτείσει vb fut act ind 3rd pers sg . . . . . . ἀνταποτίνω

ἀντάρῃ vb 1st aor act subj 3rd pers sg . . . . ἀνταίρω

ἀντέγραψαν vb 1st aor act ind 3rd pers pl . . . . . ἀντιγράφω

ἀντέγραψεν vb 1st aor act ind 3rd pers sg   id.

ἀντεδίδου vb impf act ind 3rd pers sg . . . . ἀντιδίδωμι

ἀντεδίδους vb impf act ind 2nd pers sg   id.

ἀντεδίκησεν vb 1st aor act ind 3rd pers sg . . . . . ἀντιδικέω

ἀντεῖπαν vb 1st aor act ind 3rd pers pl . . . . ἀντεῖπον

ἀντειπεῖν vb 2nd aor act inf   id.

ἀντεῖπεν vb 2nd aor act ind 3rd pers sg   id.

ἀντείπῃ vb 2nd aor act subj 3rd pers sg   id.

ἀντειπών vb 2nd aor act part masc nom sg   id.

ἀντείχοντο vb impf m/p ind 3rd pers pl . . . . ἀντέχω

ἀντεκάθισας vb 1st aor act ind 2nd pers sg . . . . ἀντικαθίζω

ἀντελάβετο vb 2nd aor mid ind

          3rd pers sg . . . . ἀντιλαμβάνομαι

ἀντελαβόμην vb 2nd aor mid ind 1st pers sg   id.

ἀντελάβοντο vb 2nd aor mid ind 3rd pers pl   id.

ἀντελάβου vb 2nd aor mid ind 2nd pers sg   id.

ἀντελαμβάνετο vb impf dep ind

    3rd pers sg . . . . ἀντιλαμβάνομαι

ἀντελαμβάνοντο vb impf dep ind 3rd pers pl   id.

ἀντερείδεται vb pres m/p ind 3rd pers sg . . . . . . ἀντερείδω

ἀντερεῖν vb fut act inf . . . . ἀντεῖπον

ἀντεροῦμεν vb fut act ind 1st pers pl   id.

ἀντεροῦσα vb fut act part fem nom sg   id.

ἀντέστη vb 2nd aor act ind 3rd pers sg . . . . ἀνθίστημι

ἀντέστης vb 2nd aor act ind 2nd pers sg   id.

ἀντέστησαν vb 1st aor act ind 3rd pers pl   id.

ἀντέσχε vb 2nd aor act ind 3rd pers sg . . . . ἀντέχω

ἀντεφιλοσόφησαν vb 1st aor act ind

    3rd pers pl . . . . ἀντιφιλοσοφέω

ἀντέχεσθαι vb pres m/p inf . . . . ἀντέχω

ἀντεχόμεθα vb pres m/p ind 1st pers pl   id.

ἀντεχόμενοι vb pres m/p part masc nom pl   id.

ἀντεχομένοις vb pres m/p part masc and neut dat pl   id.

ἀντεχόμενος vb pres m/p part masc nom sg   id.

ἀντεχομένους vb pres m/p part masc acc pl   id.

ἀντέχωνται vb pres m/p subj 3rd pers pl   id.

ἀντηγωνίζετο vb impf dep ind 3rd pers sg . . ἀνταγωνίζομαι

ἀντήχει vb impf act ind 3rd pers sg . . . . ἀντηχέω

ἀντί preposition

ἀντιβάλλων vb pres act part masc nom sg . . . . . ἀντιβάλλω

ἀντίγραφα noun neut nom and acc pl . . . . ἀντίγραφον

ἀντιγράφομεν vb pres act ind 1st pers pl . . . . . . ἀντιγράφω

ἀντίγραφον noun neut nom and acc sg

ἀντίδικοι noun masc nom pl . . . . ἀντίδικος

ἀντιδίκοις noun masc dat pl   id.

ἀντίδικον noun masc acc sg   id.

ἀντίδικος noun masc nom sg   id.

ἀντιδίκους noun masc acc pl   id.

ἀντιδικῶν vb pres act part masc nom sg . . . . ἀντιδικέω

ἀντιδοξῶν vb fut act part masc nom sg . . . . ἀντιδοκέω

ἀντίζηλον noun fem acc sg . . . . ἀντίζηλος

ἀντίζηλος noun fem nom sg   id.

ἀντιζήλου noun fem gen sg   id.

ἀντιθείς vb 2nd aor act part masc nom sg . . . . . . ἀντιτίθημι

ἀντίθετα adj neut nom and acc pl . . . . ἀντίθετος

ἀντίθετον adj acc sg, neut nom sg   id.

ἀντιθήσουσιν vb fut act ind 3rd pers pl . . . . ἀντιτίθημι

ἀντικαταλλασσόμενοι vb pres m/p part

    masc nom pl . . . . ἀντικαταλλάσσω

ἀντικαταλλασσόμενον vb pres m/p part

    neut nom and acc sg   id.

ἀντικαταστήσεται vb fut mid ind

    3rd pers sg . . . . ἀντικαθίστημι

ἀντικατέστησεν vb 1st aor act ind 3rd pers sg   id.

ἀντικείμενα vb pres m/p part

    neut nom and acc pl . . . . ἀντίκειμαι

ἀντικείμενοι vb pres m/p part masc nom pl   id.

ἀντικειμένοις vb pres m/p part masc and neut dat pl   id.

ἀντικείμενον vb pres m/p part masc acc sg   id.

ἀντικείμενος vb pres m/p part masc nom sg   id.

ἀντίκεισαι vb pres m/p ind 2nd pers sg   id.

ἀντικεῖσθαι vb pres m/p inf   id.

ἀντικείσομαι vb fut mid ind 1st pers sg . . . . . . ἀντίκειμαι

ἀντικρινόμενος vb pres dep part

    masc nom sg . . . . ἀντικρίνομαι

ἀντικρινοῦμαι vb fut mid ind 1st pers sg   id.

ἄντικρυς adverb

ἀντιλαβέσθαι vb 2nd aor mid inf . . . . . . ἀντιλαμβάνομαι

ἀντιλάβῃ vb 2nd aor act subj 3rd pers sg   id.

ἀντιλάβοιτο vb 2nd aor mid opt 3rd pers sg   id.

ἀντιλαβοῦ vb 2nd aor mid impv 2nd pers sg   id.

ἀντιλαμβάνεται vb pres dep ind 3rd pers sg   id.

ἀντιλαμβάνηται vb pres dep subj 3rd pers sg   id.

ἀντιλαμβανόμενον vb pres dep part masc acc sg   id.

ἀντιλαμβανόμενος vb pres dep part masc nom sg   id.

ἀντιλαμβανομένους vb pres dep part masc acc pl   id.

ἀντιλάμψαντος vb 1st aor act part

    masc and neut gen sg . . . . ἀντιλάμπω

ἀντίλεγε vb pres act impv 2nd pers sg . . . . ἀντιλέγω

ἀντιλέγοιεν vb pres act opt 3rd pers pl   id.

ἀντιλεγόμενος vb pres m/p part masc nom sg   id.

ἀντιλέγοντα vb pres act part masc acc sg   id.

ἀντιλέγοντας vb pres act part masc acc pl   id.

ἀντιλέγοντος vb pres act part masc and neut gen sg   id.

ἀντιλέγω vb pres act ind 1st pers sg   id.

ἀντιλέγων vb pres act part masc nom sg   id.

ἀντιλήμπτορες noun masc nom pl . . . . ἀντιλήπτωρ

ἀντιλήμπτωρ noun masc nom sg   id.

ἀντιλήμψει noun fem dat sg . . . . ἀντίληψις

ἀντιλήμψεις noun fem nom and acc pl   id.

ἀντιλήμψεται vb fut mid ind 3rd pers sg . ἀντιλαμβάνομαι

ἀντιλήμψεως noun fem gen sg . . . . ἀντίληψις

ἀντιλήμψῃ vb fut mid ind 2nd pers sg . . . . ἀντιλαμβάνομαι

ἀντιλήμψιν noun fem acc sg . . . . ἀντίληψις

ἀντιλήμψις noun fem nom sg   id.

ἀντιλήμψομαι vb fut mid ind 1st pers sg . ἀντιλαμβάνομαι

ἀντιλημψόμενος vb fut mid part masc nom sg   id.

ἀντιλήμψονται vb fut mid ind 3rd pers pl   id.

ἀντιλήπτωρ noun masc nom sg

ἀντιλήψεως noun fem gen sg . . . . ἀντίληψις

ἀντίληψιν noun fem acc sg   id.

Ἀντιλίβανον pr noun masc acc sg . . . . Ἀντιλιβανος

Ἀντιλιβανου pr noun masc gen sg   id.

Ἀντιλιβανῳ pr noun masc dat sg   id.

ἀντιλογία noun fem nom sg

ἀντιλογίαν noun fem acc sg . . . . ἀντιλογία

ἀντιλογίας noun fem gen sg and acc pl   id.

ἀντιλογιῶν noun fem gen pl   id.

ἀντιμαρτυρούσης vb pres act part

    fem gen sg . . . . ἀντιμαρτυρέω

ἀντίον adverb

ἀντίον noun neut nom and acc sg

Ἀντιοχε pr noun masc voc sg . . . . Ἀντιοχος

Ἀντιοχεια pr noun fem dat sg . . . . Ἀντιοχεια

Ἀντιοχειαν pr noun fem acc sg   id.

Ἀντιοχειας pr noun fem gen sg   id.

Ἀντιοχεῖς pr noun masc nom and acc pl . . . . . . Ἀντιοχευς

Ἀντιοχιδι pr noun fem dat sg . . . . Ἀντιοχις

Ἀντίοχον pr noun masc acc sg . . . . Ἀντίοχος
Ἀντίοχος pr noun masc nom sg   id.
Ἀντιόχου pr noun masc gen sg   id.
Ἀντιόχῳ pr noun masc dat sg   id.
ἀντιπάλους adj masc and fem acc pl . . . . ἀντίπαλος
ἀντιπάλων adj gen pl   id.
ἀντιπαραβεβλημένη vb perf m/p part
    fem nom sg . . . . ἀντιπαραβάλλω
ἀντιπαραγωγῇ noun fem dat sg . . . . ἀντιπαραγωγή
ἀντιπαρατάσσουσα vb pres act part
    fem nom sg . . . . ἀντιπαρατάσσω
ἀντιπαρῆγεν vb impf act ind 3rd pers sg . . . . . . ἀντιπαράγω
ἀντιπαρῆλθεν vb 2nd aor act ind
    3rd pers sg . . . . ἀντιπαρέρχομαι
Ἀντίπατρον pr noun masc acc sg . . . . Ἀντίπατρος
Ἀντίπατρος pr noun masc nom sg   id.
ἀντιπίπτειν vb pres act inf . . . . ἀντιπίπτω
ἀντιπίπτοντας vb pres act part masc acc pl   id.
ἀντιπίπτουσαι vb pres act part fem nom pl   id.
ἀντιποιηθήσεται vb fut pass ind 3rd pers sg . . . . . ἀντιποιέω
ἀντιποιήσασθαι vb 1st aor mid inf   id.
ἀντιποιήσεται vb fut mid ind 3rd pers sg   id.
ἀντιπολεμοῦντες vb pres act part
    masc nom pl . . . . ἀντιπολεμέω
ἀντιπολιτευόμενος vb pres m/p part
    masc nom sg . . . . ἀντιπολιτεύω
ἀντιπράττειν vb pres act inf . . . . ἀντιπράττω
ἀντιπρόσωπα adj neut nom and acc pl . . . . . ἀντιπρόσωπος
ἀντιπρόσωποι adj masc and fem nom pl   id.
ἀντιπρόσωπον adj acc sg, neut nom sg   id.
ἀντιπτώματι noun neut dat sg . . . . ἀντίπτωμα
ἀντιπτώματος noun neut gen sg   id.
ἀντίρρησις noun fem nom sg
ἀντιρρητορεύσαντα vb 1st aor act part
    masc acc sg . . . . ἀντιρρητορεύω
ἀντιστάντας vb 2nd aor act part masc acc pl . . . . ἀνθίστημι
ἀντιστάς vb 2nd aor act part masc nom sg   id.
ἀντιστῆναι vb 2nd aor act inf   id.
ἀντιστήριγμα noun neut nom and acc sg
ἀντιστηρίγματα noun neut nom and acc pl . . ἀντιστήριγμα
ἀντιστηρίζει vb pres act ind 3rd pers sg . . . . . . ἀντιστηρίζω
ἀντιστηριζόμενοι vb pres m/p part masc nom pl   id.
ἀντιστηρίσασθε vb 1st aor mid impv 2nd pers pl   id.
ἀντιστήσεται vb fut mid ind 3rd pers sg . . . . ἀνθίστημι
ἀντιστήσῃ vb 1st aor act subj 3rd pers sg   id.
ἀντιστήσονται vb fut mid ind 3rd pers pl   id.
ἀντιστήτω vb 2nd aor act impv 3rd pers sg   id.
ἀντιστῶσιν vb 2nd aor act subj 3rd pers pl   id.
ἀντιτάξεται vb fut mid ind 3rd pers sg . . . . . ἀντιτάσσομαι
ἀντιτάξομαι vb fut mid ind 1st pers sg   id.
ἀντιτάσσεται vb pres dep ind 3rd pers sg   id.
ἀντιτασσόμενον vb pres dep part masc acc sg   id.
ἀντιτασσόμενος vb pres dep part masc nom sg   id.
ἀντιφωνήσαντες vb 1st aor act part masc nom pl ἀντιφωνέω
ἀντίψυχον adj acc sg, neut nom sg . . . . ἀντίψυχος
ἀντλῆσαι vb 1st aor act inf . . . . ἀντλέω

ἀντλήσετε vb 1st aor act impv 2nd pers pl . . . . ἀντλέω
ἀντοφθαλμῆσαι vb 1st aor act inf . . . . ἀντοφθαλμέω
ἄντρον noun neut nom and acc sg
ἀντρώδη adj masc and fem acc sg . . . . ἀντρώδης
ἀνύδροις adj dat pl . . . . ἄνυδρος
ἄνυδρον adj acc sg, neut nom sg   id.
ἄνυδρος adj masc and fem nom sg   id.
ἀνύδρου adj gen sg   id.
ἀνύδρῳ adj dat sg   id.
ἀνύοντες vb pres act part masc nom pl . . . . ἀνύω
ἀνυπέρβλητος adj masc and fem nom sg
ἀνυπερθέτως adverb
ἀνυπόδετος adj masc and fem nom sg
ἀνυποδέτους adj masc and fem acc pl . . . . ἀνυπόδετος
ἀνυπόκριτον adj acc sg, neut nom sg . . . . ἀνυπόκριτος
ἀνυπομονήτῳ adj dat sg . . . . ἀνυπομόνητος
ἀνυπονόητος adj masc and fem nom sg
ἀνυπόστατον adj acc sg, neut nom sg . . . . . . ἀνυπόστατος
ἀνυπόστατος adj masc and fem nom sg   id.
ἀνυψοῖ vb pres act ind 3rd pers sg . . . . ἀνυψόω
ἀνυψούμενος vb pres m/p part masc nom sg   id.
ἀνυψώθη vb 1st aor pass ind 3rd pers sg   id.
ἀνυψώθην vb 1st aor pass ind 1st pers sg   id.
ἀνυψωθῆναι vb 1st aor pass inf   id.
ἀνυψῶν vb pres act part masc nom sg   id.
ἀνύψωσα vb 1st aor act ind 1st pers sg   id.
ἀνυψῶσαι vb 1st aor act inf   id.
ἀνύψωσαν vb 1st aor act ind 3rd pers pl   id.
ἀνυψώσει vb fut act ind 3rd pers sg   id.
ἀνύψωσεν vb 1st aor act ind 3rd pers sg   id.
ἀνυψώσουσιν vb fut act ind 3rd pers pl   id.
Ἀνω pr noun
ἄνω adverb
Ἀνωβ pr noun
ἄνωθεν adverb
ἀνῳκοδόμησαν vb 1st aor act ind 3rd pers pl . ἀνοικοδομέω
ἀνῳκοδόμησεν vb 1st aor act ind 3rd pers sg   id.
ἀνώμβρησαν vb 1st aor act ind 3rd pers pl . . . . . . ἀνομβρέω
ἀνώμβρησεν vb 1st aor act ind 3rd pers sg   id.
ἀνῶμεν vb 2nd aor act subj 1st pers pl . . . . ἀνίημι
Ανων pr noun
ἀνωνύμων adj gen pl . . . . ἀνώνυμος
ἀνωρθώθημεν vb 1st aor pass ind 1st pers pl . . . . . . ἀνορθόω
ἀνωρθώθησαν vb 1st aor pass ind 3rd pers pl   id.
ἀνωρθωμένος vb perf m/p part masc nom sg   id.
ἀνώρθωσεν vb 1st aor act ind 3rd pers sg   id.
Ανως pr noun
ἀνώτατα superl adj neut nom and acc pl . . . . ἀνώτερος
ἀνωτέραν comp adj fem acc sg   id.
ἀνωτέρας comp adj fem gen sg   id.
ἀνώτερον preposition
ἀνώτερος comp adj masc nom sg
ἀνωτέρω adverb . . . . ἄνω
ἀνωφελῆ adj masc and fem acc sg,
    neut nom and acc pl . . . . ἀνωφελής

ἀνωφελής adj masc and fem nom sg	ἀοικήτῳ adj dat sg . . . . ἀοίκητος
ἀνωφελοῦς adj gen sg . . . . ἀνωφελής	ἄοκνος adj masc and fem nom sg
Ανωχ pr noun	ἀορασίᾳ noun fem dat sg . . . . ἀορασία
ἄξει vb fut act ind 3rd pers sg . . . . ἄγω	ἀόρατος adj masc and fem nom sg
ἄξειν vb fut act inf id.	ἀοράτους adj masc and fem acc pl . . . . ἀόρατος
ἄξεις vb fut act ind 2nd pers sg id.	ἀοράτῳ adj dat sg id.
ἄξια adj neut nom and acc pl . . . . ἄξιος	Αουε pr noun
ἀξίᾳ adj fem nom sg id.	ἀπ᾽ see ἀπό
ἀξίαν adj fem acc sg id.	ἀπάγαγε vb 2nd aor act impv 2nd pers sg . . . . ἀπάγω
ἀξίαν noun fem acc sg . . . . ἀξία	ἀπαγαγεῖν vb 2nd aor act inf id.
ἄξιε adj masc voc sg . . . . ἄξιος	ἀπαγάγετε vb 2nd aor act impv 2nd pers pl id.
ἀξίναις noun fem dat pl . . . . ἀξίνη	ἀπαγάγῃ vb 2nd aor act subj 3rd pers sg id.
ἀξίνας noun fem acc pl id.	ἀπαγάγοι vb 2nd aor act opt 3rd pers sg id.
ἀξίνη noun fem nom sg id.	ἀπαγαγόντες vb 2nd aor act part masc nom pl id.
ἀξίνῃ noun fem dat sg id.	ἀπαγάγωμεν vb 2nd aor act subj 1st pers pl id.
ἀξίνην noun fem acc sg id.	ἀπαγγεῖλαι vb 1st aor act inf . . . . ἀπαγγέλλω
ἄξιοι adj masc nom pl . . . . ἄξιος	ἀπαγγείλας vb 1st aor act part masc nom sg id.
ἀξιοῖ vb pres act ind 3rd pers sg . . . . ἀξιόω	ἀπαγγείλασι vb 1st aor act part masc and neut dat pl id.
ἀξίοις adj masc and neut dat pl . . . . ἄξιος	ἀπαγγείλατε vb 1st aor act impv 2nd pers pl id.
ἀξιοῖς vb pres act ind 2nd pers sg . . . . ἀξιόω	ἀπαγγειλάτω vb 1st aor act impv 3rd pers sg id.
ἄξιον adj masc acc sg, neut nom and acc sg . . . . ἄξιος	ἀπαγγείλῃ vb 1st aor act subj 3rd pers sg id.
ἀξιόπιστον adj acc sg, neut nom sg . . . . ἀξιόπιστος	ἀπαγγείλητε vb 1st aor act subj 2nd pers pl id.
ἀξιόπιστος adj masc and fem nom sg id.	ἀπαγγείλατε vb 1st aor act impv 2nd pers pl id.
ἀξιοπιστότερα comp adj neut nom and acc pl id.	ἀπαγγείλω vb 1st aor act subj 1st pers sg id.
ἄξιος adj masc nom sg	ἀπαγγείλωμεν vb 1st aor act subj 1st pers pl id.
ἀξίου adj masc and neut gen sg . . . . ἄξιος	ἀπαγγείλωσιν vb 1st aor act subj 3rd pers pl id.
ἀξίου vb pres m/p impv 2nd pers sg . . . . ἀξιόω	ἀπαγγελεῖ vb fut act ind 3rd pers sg id.
ἀξιοῦμεν vb pres act ind 1st pers pl id.	ἀπαγγελεῖς vb fut act ind 2nd pers sg id.
ἀξιοῦντα vb pres act part masc acc sg id.	ἀπαγγελήσονται vb fut pass ind 3rd pers pl id.
ἀξιοῦντας vb pres act part masc acc pl id.	ἀπαγγελίᾳ noun fem dat sg . . . . ἀπαγγελία
ἀξιοῦντες vb pres act part masc nom pl id.	ἀπαγγέλλει vb pres act ind 3rd pers sg . . . . ἀπαγγέλλω
ἀξίους adj masc acc pl . . . . ἄξιος	ἀπαγγέλλειν vb pres act inf id.
ἀξιοῦσιν vb pres act ind 3rd pers pl . . . . ἀξιόω	ἀπαγγέλλον vb pres act part
ἀξιῶ vb pres act ind 1st pers sg id.	neut nom and acc sg id.
ἀξίῳ adj masc and neut dat sg . . . . ἄξιος	ἀπαγγέλλοντας vb pres act part masc acc pl id.
ἀξίωμα noun neut nom and acc sg	ἀπαγγέλλοντες vb pres act part masc nom pl id.
ἀξιώματα noun neut nom and acc pl . . . . ἀξίωμα	ἀπαγγέλλοντι vb pres act part masc and neut dat sg id.
ἀξιώματι noun neut dat sg id.	ἀπαγγέλλοντος vb pres act part masc and neut gen sg id.
ἀξιώματος noun neut gen sg id.	ἀπαγγέλλουσιν vb pres act ind 3rd pers pl id.
ἀξιῶν vb pres act part masc nom sg . . . . ἀξιόω	ἀπαγγέλλω vb pres act ind 1st pers sg id.
ἀξίως adverb	ἀπαγγέλλων vb pres act part masc nom sg id.
ἀξιῶσαι vb 1st aor act inf . . . . ἀξιόω	ἀπαγγελοῦσιν vb fut act ind 3rd pers pl id.
ἀξιώσαντες vb 1st aor act part masc nom pl id.	ἀπαγγελῶ vb fut act ind 1st pers sg id.
ἀξιώσει vb fut act ind 3rd pers sg id.	ἄπαγε vb pres act impv 2nd pers sg . . . . ἀπάγω
ἀξιώσῃ vb 1st aor act subj 3rd pers sg id.	ἀπάγει vb pres act ind 3rd pers sg id.
ἄξομεν vb fut act ind 1st pers pl . . . . ἄγω	ἀπαγέσθωσαν vb pres m/p impv 3rd pers pl id.
ἄξονας noun masc acc pl . . . . ἄξων	ἀπάγετε vb pres act impv 2nd pers pl id.
ἄξουσιν vb fut act ind 3rd pers pl . . . . ἄγω	ἀπάγξασθαι vb 1st aor mid inf . . . . ἀπάγχομαι
ἄξω vb fut act ind 1st pers sg id.	ἀπαγομένης vb pres m/p part fem gen sg . . . . ἀπάγω
ἄξων noun masc nom sg	ἀπαγωγῇ noun fem dat sg . . . . ἀπαγωγή
Αοζα pr noun	ἀπαδικήσεις vb fut act ind 2nd pers sg . . . . ἀπαδικέω
ἀοίδιμον adj acc sg, neut nom sg . . . . ἀοίδιμος	ἀπαιδευσία noun fem nom sg
ἀοίκητον adj acc sg, neut nom sg . . . . ἀοίκητος	ἀπαιδευσίαν noun fem acc sg . . . . ἀπαιδευσία
ἀοίκητος adj masc and fem nom sg id.	ἀπαιδευσίας noun fem gen sg id.
ἀοικήτου adj gen sg id.	ἀπαίδευτοι adj masc and fem nom pl . . . . ἀπαίδευτος
ἀοικήτους adj masc and fem acc pl id.	ἀπαιδεύτοις adj dat pl id.

ἀπαίδευτον adj acc sg, neut nom sg .... ἀπαίδευτος
ἀπαίδευτος adj masc and fem nom sg   id.
ἀπαιδεύτου adj gen sg   id.
ἀπαιδεύτῳ adj dat sg   id.
ἀπαιδεύτων adj gen pl   id.
ἀπαίρει vb pres act ind 3rd pers sg .... ἀπαίρω
ἀπαίρειν vb pres act inf   id.
ἀπαιτεῖτε vb pres act ind 2nd pers pl .... ἀπαιτέω
ἀπαιτηθείς vb 1st aor pass part masc nom sg   id.
ἀπαιτηθήσῃ vb fut pass ind 2nd pers sg   id.
ἀπαιτήσει noun fem dat sg .... ἀπαίτησις
ἀπαιτήσει vb fut act ind 3rd pers sg .... ἀπαιτέω
ἀπαιτήσεις vb fut act ind 2nd pers sg   id.
ἀπαίτησιν noun fem acc sg .... ἀπαίτησις
ἀπαιτοῦντες vb pres act part masc nom pl .... ἀπαιτέω
ἀπαιτούντων vb pres act part masc and neut gen pl id.
ἀπαιτῶν vb pres act part masc nom sg   id.
ἀπαλείφεται vb pres m/p ind 3rd pers sg .... ἀπαλείφω
ἀπαλειφόμενος vb pres m/p part masc nom sg   id.
ἀπαλεῖψαι vb 1st aor act inf   id.
ἀπάλειψον vb 1st aor act impv 2nd pers sg   id.
ἀπαλείψω vb fut act ind 1st pers sg   id.
ἀπαλή adj fem nom sg .... ἀπαλός
ἀπαλήν adj fem acc sg   id.
ἀπαλλαγείς vb 2nd aor pass part masc nom sg .. ἀπαλλάσσω
ἀπαλλαγέντες vb 2nd aor pass part masc nom pl   id.
ἀπαλλαγῆς vb 2nd aor pass subj 2nd pers sg   id.
ἀπαλλαγῶσι vb 2nd aor pass subj 3rd pers pl id.
ἀπαλλάξαι vb 1st aor act inf   id.
ἀπαλλαξάτω vb 1st aor act impv 3rd pers sg   id.
ἀπαλλάξει vb fut act ind 3rd pers sg   id.
ἀπαλλάξεις vb fut act ind 2nd pers sg   id.
ἀπαλλάξῃ vb 1st aor act subj 3rd pers sg   id.
ἀπαλλάξω vb fut act ind 1st pers sg   id.
ἀπαλλοτριωθῇ vb 1st aor pass subj
    3rd pers sg .... ἀπαλλοτριόω
ἀπαλλοτριώθητε vb 1st aor pass impv 2nd pers pl id.
ἀπαλλοτριώσει vb fut act ind 3rd pers sg   id.
ἀπαλλοτριώσετε vb fut act ind 2nd pers sg   id.
ἀπαλλοτρίωσις noun fem nom sg
ἀπαλλοτριώσουσιν vb fut act ind
    3rd pers pl .... ἀπαλλοτριόω
ἀπαλόν adj masc acc sg, neut nom and acc sg ...... ἀπαλός
ἀπαλός adj masc nom sg   id.
ἀπαλότητα noun fem acc sg .... ἀπαλότης
ἀπαλότητος noun fem gen sg   id.
ἀπαλούς adj masc acc pl .... ἀπαλός
ἀπαλυνεῖ vb pres act ind 3rd pers sg .... ἀπαλύνω
ἀπαλώτερα comp adj neut nom and acc pl .... ἀπαλός
Ἀπαμην pr noun fem acc sg .... Ἀπαμη
ἀπαμύνωσιν vb pres act ind 3rd pers pl .... ἀπαμύνω
ἄπαν adj neut nom and acc sg .... ἅπας
ἀπαναίνῃ vb pres act subj 3rd pers sg .... ἀπαναίνομαι
ἀπαναίνου vb pres dep impv 2nd pers sg   id.
ἀπαναστήσεται vb fut mid ind 3rd pers sg .... ἀπανίστημι
ἅπαντα adj masc acc sg, neut nom and acc pl .... ἅπας

ἅπαντα vb pres act impv 2nd pers sg .... ἀπαντάω
ἅπαντας adj masc acc pl .... ἅπας
ἅπαντες adj masc nom pl   id.
ἀπάντημα noun neut nom and acc sg
ἀπαντήν noun fem acc sg .... ἀπαντή
ἀπαντῆσαι vb 1st aor mid impv 2nd pers sg ..... ἀπαντάω
ἀπαντῆσαι vb 1st aor act inf   id.
ἀπαντήσαντες vb 1st aor act part masc nom pl   id.
ἀπαντήσας vb 1st aor act part masc nom sg   id.
ἀπαντησάτωσαν vb 1st aor act impv 3rd pers pl   id.
ἀπαντήσει noun fem dat sg .... ἀπάντησις
ἀπαντήσει vb fut act ind 3rd pers sg .... ἀπαντάω
ἀπαντήσεις vb fut act ind 2nd pers sg   id.
ἀπαντήσεται vb fut mid ind 3rd pers sg   id.
ἀπαντήσεως noun fem gen sg .... ἀπάντησις
ἀπαντήσῃ vb 1st aor act subj 3rd pers sg .... ἀπαντάω
ἀπαντήσητε vb 1st aor act subj 2nd pers pl   id.
ἀπάντησιν noun fem acc sg .... ἀπάντησις
ἀπαντήσομαι vb fut mid ind 1st pers sg .... ἀπαντάω
ἀπαντήσομεν vb fut act ind 1st pers pl   id.
ἀπάντησον vb 1st aor act impv 2nd pers sg   id.
ἀπαντήσονται vb fut mid ind 3rd pers pl   id.
ἀπαντήσωσιν vb 1st aor act subj 3rd pers pl id.
ἀπάντων adj gen pl .... ἅπας
ἀπαντῶντες vb pres act part masc nom pl .... ἀπαντάω
ἀπαντῶντι vb pres act part masc and neut dat sg id.
ἀπαντῶσα vb pres act part fem nom sg   id.
ἀπάνωθεν adverb
ἅπαξ adverb
ἀπάξει vb fut act ind 3rd pers sg .... ἀπάγω
ἀπάξομεν vb fut act ind 1st pers pl   id.
ἀπάξουσι vb fut act ind 3rd pers pl   id.
ἀπάξω vb fut act ind 1st pers sg   id.
ἀπαραιτήτοις adj dat pl .... ἀπαραίτητος
ἀπαραίτητον adj acc sg, neut nom sg   id.
ἀπαραλλάκτως adverb
ἀπάραντες vb 1st aor act part masc nom pl .... ἀπαίρω
ἀπαραπόδιστον adj acc sg .... ἀπαραπόδιστος
ἀπάρας vb 1st aor act part masc nom sg .... ἀπαίρω
ἀπαρασήμαντον adj acc sg, neut nom sg . ἀπαρασήμαντος
ἀπάρατε vb 1st aor act impv 2nd pers pl .... ἀπαίρω
ἀπαρεῖτε vb fut act ind 2nd pers pl   id.
ἀπαρνήσονται vb fut mid ind 3rd pers pl ..... ἀπαρνέομαι
ἄπαρον vb 1st aor act impv 2nd pers sg .... ἀπαίρω
ἀπαροῦσιν vb fut act ind 3rd pers pl   id.
ἀπάρσεις noun fem nom and acc pl .... ἄπαρσις
ἀπαρτία noun fem dat sg .... ἀπαρτία
ἀπαρτίαι noun fem nom pl   id.
ἀπαρτίαις noun fem dat pl   id.
ἀπαρτίαν noun fem acc sg   id.
ἀπαρχαί noun fem nom pl .... ἀπαρχή
ἀπαρχαῖς noun fem dat pl   id.
ἀπαρχάς noun fem acc pl   id.
ἀπαρχή noun fem nom sg   id.
ἀπαρχήν noun fem acc sg   id.
ἀπαρχῆς noun fem gen sg   id.

ἀπάρχου   vb pres m/p impv 2nd pers sg . . . . ἀπάρχω
ἀπαρχῶν   noun fem gen pl . . . . ἀπαρχή
ἀπάρωσιν   vb 1st aor act subj 3rd pers pl . . . . ἀπαίρω
ἅπας   adj masc nom sg
ἅπασαν   adj fem acc sg . . . . ἅπας
ἁπάσας   adj fem acc pl   id.
ἁπάσης   adj fem gen sg   id.
ἅπασι   adj masc and neut dat pl   id.
ἀπασπασάμενος   vb 1st aor mid part
        masc nom sg . . . . ἀπασπάζομαι
ἀπάτα   vb pres act impv 2nd pers sg . . . . ἀπατάω
ἀπατᾷ   vb pres act ind 3rd pers sg   id.
ἀπατάτω   vb pres act impv 3rd pers sg   id.
ἀπατηθεῖσαν   vb 1st aor pass part fem acc sg   id.
ἀπατηθῇς   vb 1st aor pass subj 2nd pers sg   id.
ἀπατηθήσεται   vb fut pass ind 3rd pers sg   id.
ἀπάτην   noun fem acc sg . . . . ἀπάτη
ἀπάτης   noun fem gen sg   id.
ἀπατῆσαι   vb 1st aor act inf . . . . ἀπατάω
ἀπατησάτω   vb 1st aor act impv 3rd pers sg   id.
ἀπατήσει   vb fut act ind 3rd pers sg   id.
ἀπατήσεις   vb fut act ind 2nd pers sg   id.
ἀπατήσῃ   vb 1st aor act subj 3rd pers sg   id.
ἀπάτησιν   noun fem acc sg . . . . ἀπάτησις
ἀπάτησον   vb 1st aor act impv 2nd pers sg . . . . ἀπατάω
ἀπατήσω   vb fut act ind 1st pers sg   id.
ἀπατῶν   vb pres act part masc nom sg   id.
ἀπαύγασμα   noun neut nom and acc sg
ἀπαυτομολήσει   vb fut act ind 3rd pers sg . . . . ἀπαυτομολέω
ἀπαυτομολῶ   vb pres act ind 1st pers sg   id.
ἀπαχθῆναι   vb 1st aor pass inf . . . . ἀπάγω
ἀπαχθῇς   vb 1st aor pass subj 2nd pers sg   id.
ἀπαχθήσονται   vb fut pass ind 3rd pers pl   id.
ἀπάχθητε   vb 1st aor pass impv 2nd pers pl   id.
ἀπέβαλεν   vb 2nd aor act ind 3rd pers sg . . . . ἀποβάλλω
ἀπέβαλον   vb 2nd aor act ind 3rd pers pl   id.
ἀπέβη   vb 2nd aor act ind 3rd pers sg . . . . ἀποβαίνω
ἀπέβην   vb 2nd aor act ind 1st pers sg   id.
ἀπέβησαν   vb 2nd aor act ind 3rd pers pl   id.
ἀπέβλεψεν   vb 1st aor act ind 3rd pers sg . . . . ἀποβλέπω
ἀπεγαλάκτισεν   vb 1st aor act ind
        3rd pers sg . . . . ἀπογαλακτίζω
ἀπεγαλακτίσθη   vb 1st aor pass ind 3rd pers sg   id.
ἀπέγνω   vb 2nd aor act ind 3rd pers sg . . . . ἀπογινώσκω
ἀπεγνωσμένων   vb perf m/p part gen pl   id.
ἀπεγράψατο   vb 1st aor mid ind 3rd pers sg . . . . . ἀπογράφω
ἀπέδειξα   vb 1st aor act ind 1st pers sg . . . . ἀποδεικνύω
ἀπέδειξεν   vb 1st aor act ind 3rd pers sg   id.
ἀπεδείχθησαν   vb 1st aor pass ind 3rd pers pl   id.
ἀπεδεκάτιζον   vb impf act ind
        1st pers sg and 3rd pers pl . . . . ἀποδεκατίζω
ἀπεδέξατο   vb 1st aor mid ind 3rd pers sg . . . . . ἀποδέχομαι
ἀπεδίδοσαν   vb impf act ind 3rd pers pl . . . . ἀποδίδωμι
ἀπεδίδουν   vb impf act ind 1st pers sg   id.
ἀπεδίδρασκεν   vb impf act ind 3rd pers sg . . . . ἀποδιδράσκω
ἀπεδίωξας   vb 1st aor act ind 2nd pers sg . . . . ἀποδιώκω

ἀπεδόθη   vb 1st aor pass ind 3rd pers sg . . . . ἀποδίδωμι
ἀπεδόθησαν   vb 1st aor pass ind 3rd pers pl   id.
ἀπεδοκίμασαν   vb 1st aor act ind 3rd pers pl . . ἀποδοκιμάζω
ἀπεδοκίμασας   vb 1st aor act ind 2nd pers sg   id.
ἀπεδοκίμασεν   vb 1st aor act ind 3rd pers sg   id.
ἀπέδομεν   vb 2nd aor act ind 1st pers pl . . . . ἀποδίδωμι
ἀπέδοντο   vb 2nd aor act mid ind 3rd pers pl   id.
ἀπέδοσθε   vb 2nd aor act mid ind 2nd pers pl   id.
ἀπέδοτο   vb 2nd aor act mid ind 3rd pers sg   id.
ἀπέδου   vb impf m/p ind 2nd pers sg . . . . ἀποδέω
ἀπέδρα   vb 2nd aor act ind 3rd pers sg . . . . ἀποδιδράσκω
ἀπέδραμεν   vb 2nd aor act ind 3rd pers sg . . . . ἀποτρέχω
ἀπέδρας   vb 2nd aor act ind 2nd pers sg . . . . . . ἀποδιδράσκω
ἀπέδρασα   vb 2nd aor act ind 1st pers sg   id.
ἀπέδρασαν   vb 2nd aor act ind 3rd pers pl   id.
ἀπέδρων   vb 2nd aor act ind 1st pers sg   id.
ἀπέδωκα   vb 1st aor act ind 1st pers sg . . . . ἀποδίδωμι
ἀπέδωκαν   vb 1st aor act ind 3rd pers pl   id.
ἀπέδωκας   vb 1st aor act ind 2nd pers sg   id.
ἀπέδωκεν   vb 1st aor act ind 3rd pers sg   id.
ἀπέθαναν   vb 2nd aor act ind 3rd pers pl . . . . ἀποθνήσκω
ἀπέθανε(ν)   vb 2nd aor act ind 3rd pers sg   id.
ἀπεθάνῃ   vb 2nd aor act subj 3rd pers sg   id.
ἀπεθάνομεν   vb 2nd aor act ind 1st pers pl   id.
ἀπέθανον   vb 2nd aor act ind
        1st pers sg and 3rd pers pl   id.
ἀπεθάνοσαν   vb 2nd aor act ind 3rd pers pl   id.
ἀπεθαύμασαν   vb 1st aor act ind 3rd pers pl . . ἀποθαυμάζω
ἀπέθεντο   vb 2nd aor mid ind 3rd pers pl . . . . ἀποτίθημι
ἀπεθέρισα   vb 1st aor act ind 1st pers sg . . . . ἀποθερίζω
ἀπέθετο   vb 2nd aor mid ind 3rd pers sg . . . . ἀποτίθημι
ἀπέθηκαν   vb 1st aor act ind 3rd pers pl   id.
ἀπέθηκεν   vb 1st aor act ind 3rd pers sg   id.
ἀπέθλιψεν   vb 1st aor act ind 3rd pers sg . . . . ἀποθλίβω
ἀπέθνησκεν   vb impf act ind 3rd pers sg . . . . ἀποθνήσκω
ἀπέθνησκον   vb impf act ind
        1st pers sg and 3rd pers pl   id.
ἀπεθνήσκοσαν   vb impf act ind 3rd pers pl   id.
ἀπείθει   vb pres act impv 2nd pers sg . . . . ἀπειθέω
ἀπειθεῖ   vb pres act ind 3rd pers sg   id.
ἀπειθεῖ   adj dat sg . . . . ἀπειθής
ἀπειθείᾳ   noun fem dat sg . . . . ἀπείθεια
ἀπείθειαν   noun fem acc sg   id.
ἀπειθείας   noun fem gen sg   id.
ἀπειθεῖν   vb pres act inf . . . . ἀπειθέω
ἀπειθεῖς   adj masc and fem nom and acc pl . . . . ἀπειθής
ἀπειθεῖς   vb pres act ind 2nd pers sg . . . . ἀπειθέω
ἀπειθείτω   vb pres act impv 3rd pers sg   id.
ἀπειθῆ   adj masc and fem acc sg . . . . ἀπειθής
ἀπειθής   adj masc and fem nom sg   id.
ἀπειθήσαντες   vb 1st aor act part masc nom pl . . . . . ἀπειθέω
ἀπειθήσασι   vb 1st aor act part masc and neut dat pl   id.
ἀπειθήσῃ   vb 1st aor act subj 3rd pers sg   id.
ἀπειθήσῃς   vb 1st aor act subj 2nd pers sg   id.
ἀπειθήσητε   vb 1st aor act subj 2nd pers pl   id.
ἀπειθήσουσιν   vb fut act ind 3rd pers pl   id.

ἀπειθοῦντα vb pres act part masc acc sg .... ἀπειθέω
ἀπειθοῦντας vb pres act part masc acc pl   id.
ἀπειθοῦντες vb pres act part masc nom pl   id.
ἀπειθοῦντι vb pres act part masc and neut dat sg   id.
ἀπειθούντων vb pres act part masc and neut gen pl   id.
ἀπειθοῦσιν vb pres act ind 3rd pers pl   id.
ἀπειθῶ vb pres act ind 1st pers sg   id.
ἀπειθῶν vb pres act part masc nom sg   id.
ἀπείκασεν vb 1st aor act ind 3rd pers sg .... ἀπεικάζω
ἀπεικάσματα noun neut nom and acc pl ...... ἀπείκασμα
ἀπειλαῖς noun fem dat pl .... ἀπειλή
ἀπειλάς noun fem acc pl   id.
ἀπειλεῖ vb pres act ind 3rd pers sg .... ἀπειλέω
ἀπειλή noun fem nom sg
ἀπειλῇ noun fem dat sg .... ἀπειλή
ἀπειληθῆναι vb 1st aor pass inf   id.
ἀπειλημμένων vb perf m/p part gen pl ...... ἀπολαμβάνω
ἀπειλήν noun fem acc sg .... ἀπειλή
ἀπειλῆς noun fem gen sg   id.
ἀπειλῆσαι vb 1st aor act inf .... ἀπειλέω
ἀπειλήσαντος vb 1st aor act part masc and neut gen sg   id.
ἀπειλήσει vb fut act ind 3rd pers sg   id.
ἀπειληφότες vb perf act part masc nom pl .... ἀπολαμβάνω
ἀπειλοῦντες vb pres act part masc nom pl .... ἀπειλέω
ἀπειλῶν vb pres act part masc nom sg   id.
ἀπείπασθε vb 1st aor mid ind 2nd pers pl .... ἀπεῖπον
ἀπείπατο vb 1st aor mid ind 3rd pers sg   id.
ἀπεῖπεν vb 2nd aor act ind 3rd pers sg   id.
ἀπεῖπον vb 2nd aor act ind 3rd pers pl   id.
ἀπείπω vb 2nd aor act subj 1st pers sg   id.
ἀπειραγάθων noun masc gen pl .... ἀπειράγαθος
ἀπείργει vb pres act ind 3rd pers sg .... ἀπείργω
ἀπειρημένας vb perf m/p part fem acc pl .... ἀπεῖπον
ἄπειρος adj masc nom sg
ἀπειρότατον superl adj masc acc sg,
    neut nom and acc sg .... ἄπειρος
ἀπείρου adj gen sg   id.
ἀπείρῳ adj dat sg   id.
ἀπεκαθίστων vb impf act ind 3rd pers pl .... ἀποκαθίστημι
ἀπεκάκησεν vb 1st aor act ind 3rd pers sg .... ἀποκακέω
ἀπεκαλύφθη vb 1st aor pass ind 3rd pers sg .... ἀποκαλύπτω
ἀπεκαλύφθην vb 1st aor pass ind 1st pers sg   id.
ἀπεκαλύφθησαν vb 1st aor pass ind 3rd pers pl   id.
ἀπεκάλυψα vb 1st aor act ind 1st pers sg   id.
ἀπεκάλυψαν vb 1st aor act ind 3rd pers pl   id.
ἀπεκάλυψας vb 1st aor act ind 2nd pers sg   id.
ἀπεκάλυψεν vb 1st aor act ind 3rd pers sg   id.
ἀπεκατέστη vb 2nd aor act ind 3rd pers sg .. ἀποκαθίστημι
ἀπεκατέστησεν vb 1st aor act ind 3rd pers sg   id.
ἀπεκδέδοσαι vb perf m/p ind 2nd pers sg ...... ἀπεκδίδωμι
ἀπεκέντησεν vb 1st aor act ind 3rd pers sg ..... ἀποκεντέω
ἀπεκεφάλισα vb 1st aor act ind 1st pers sg ... ἀποκεφαλίζω
ἀπέκλεισαν vb 1st aor act ind 3rd pers pl ...... ἀποκλείω
ἀπέκλεισε(ν) vb 1st aor act ind 3rd pers sg   id.
ἀπέκλινεν vb impf act ind 3rd pers sg .... ἀποκλίνω
ἀπέκνισεν vb 1st aor act ind 3rd pers sg .... ἀποκνίζω

ἀπεκόπησαν vb 1st aor act ind 3rd pers pl ...... ἀποκόπτω
ἀπεκόσμησεν vb 1st aor act ind 3rd pers sg ..... ἀποκοσμέω
ἀπέκοψαν vb 1st aor act ind 3rd pers pl .... ἀποκόπτω
ἀπέκοψεν vb 1st aor act ind 3rd pers sg   id.
ἀπεκρίθη vb 1st aor pass ind 3rd pers sg .... ἀποκρίνω
ἀπεκρίθην vb 1st aor pass ind 1st pers sg   id.
ἀπεκρίθης vb 1st aor pass ind 2nd pers sg   id.
ἀπεκρίθησαν vb 1st aor pass ind 3rd pers pl   id.
ἀπεκρίθητε vb 1st aor pass ind 2nd pers pl   id.
ἀπεκρίνατε vb 1st aor act ind 2nd pers pl   id.
ἀπεκρίνατο vb 1st aor mid ind 3rd pers sg   id.
ἀπεκρίνοντο vb impf m/p ind 3rd pers pl   id.
ἀπεκρύβη vb 2nd aor pass ind 3rd pers sg ..... ἀποκρύπτω
ἀπέκρυψεν vb 1st aor act ind 3rd pers sg   id.
ἀπέκταγκα vb perf act ind 1st pers sg .... ἀποκτείνω
ἀπεκτάγκασιν vb perf act ind 3rd pers pl   id.
ἀπεκτάγκατε vb perf act ind 2nd pers pl   id.
ἀπεκταμμένων vb perf m/p part gen pl   id.
ἀπεκτάνθη vb 1st aor pass ind 3rd pers sg   id.
ἀπεκτάσεις noun fem nom and acc pl ...... ἀπέκτασις
ἀπέκτεινα vb 1st aor act ind 1st pers sg ...... ἀποκτείνω
ἀπέκτειναν vb 1st aor act ind 3rd pers pl   id.
ἀπέκτεινας vb 1st aor act ind 2nd pers sg   id.
ἀπεκτείνατε vb 1st aor act ind 2nd pers pl   id.
ἀπέκτεινε(ν) vb 1st aor act ind 3rd pers sg   id.
ἀπέκτεννεν vb impf act ind 3rd pers sg   id.
ἀπέκτεννον vb impf act ind 1st pers sg and 3rd pers pl   id.
ἀπεκτέννοντο vb impf m/p ind 3rd pers pl   id.
ἀπεκτονῆσθαι vb 1st aor mid inf   id.
ἀπεκύλιον vb impf act ind
    1st pers sg and 3rd pers pl .... ἀποκυλίω
ἀπεκύλισε(ν) vb 1st aor act ind 3rd pers sg   id.
ἀπεκώλυσα vb 1st aor act ind 1st pers sg .... ἀποκωλύω
ἀπεκωλύσαμεν vb 1st aor act ind 1st pers pl   id.
ἀπεκώλυσαν vb 1st aor act ind 3rd pers pl   id.
ἀπεκώλυσεν vb 1st aor act ind 3rd pers sg   id.
ἀπέλαβον vb 2nd aor act ind 3rd pers pl ..... ἀπολαμβάνω
ἀπελάκτισεν vb 1st aor act ind 3rd pers sg .... ἀπολακτίζω
ἀπελάσατε vb 1st aor act impv 2nd pers pl ..... ἀπελαύνω
ἀπελάσω vb fut act ind 1st pers sg   id.
ἀπελαύνειν vb pres act inf   id.
ἀπελαύσατε vb 1st aor act ind 2nd pers pl .... ἀπολαύω
ἀπελέγετο vb impf m/p ind 3rd pers sg .... ἀπολέγω
ἀπελέγχων vb pres act part masc nom sg .... ἀπελέγχω
ἀπελείφθη vb 1st aor pass ind 3rd pers sg ...... ἀπολείπω
ἀπελέκητα adj neut nom and acc pl .... ἀπελέκητος
ἀπελεκήτους adj masc and fem acc pl   id.
ἀπελεκήτων adj gen pl   id.
ἀπελέπισεν vb 1st aor act ind 3rd pers sg ...... ἀπολεπίζω
ἀπελεύσει vb fut mid ind 2nd pers sg .... ἀπέρχομαι
ἀπελεύσεσθε vb fut mid ind 2nd pers pl   id.
ἀπελεύσεται vb fut mid ind 3rd pers sg   id.
ἀπελεύσῃ vb fut mid ind 2nd pers sg   id.
ἀπελεύσομαι vb fut mid ind 1st pers sg   id.
ἀπελευσόμεθα vb fut mid ind 1st pers pl   id.
ἀπελεύσονται vb fut mid ind 3rd pers pl   id.

ἀπεληλύθει vb plpf act ind 3rd pers sg . . . . ἀπέρχομαι
ἀπελήλυθεν vb perf act ind 3rd pers sg id.
ἀπέλθατε vb 1st aor act impv 2nd pers pl id.
ἀπελθάτω vb 1st aor act impv 3rd pers sg id.
ἄπελθε vb 2nd aor act impv 2nd pers sg id.
ἀπελθεῖν vb 2nd aor act inf id.
ἀπέλθετε vb 2nd aor act impv 2nd pers pl id.
ἀπελθέτω vb 2nd aor act impv 3rd pers sg id.
ἀπελθέτωσαν vb 2nd aor act impv 3rd pers pl id.
ἀπέλθῃ vb 2nd aor act subj 3rd pers sg id.
ἀπέλθῃς vb 2nd aor act subj 2nd pers sg id.
ἀπελθόντες vb 2nd aor act part masc nom pl id.
ἀπελθοῦσα vb 2nd aor act part fem nom sg id.
ἀπελθοῦσαν vb 2nd aor act part fem acc sg id.
ἀπέλθω vb 2nd aor act subj 1st pers sg id.
ἀπέλθωμεν vb 2nd aor act subj 1st pers pl id.
ἀπελθών vb 2nd aor act part masc nom sg id.
ἀπέλθωσιν vb 2nd aor act subj 3rd pers pl id.
ἀπέλιπεν vb 2nd aor act ind 3rd pers sg . . . . ἀπολείπω
ἀπέλιπον vb 2nd aor act ind 3rd pers pl id.
ἀπελογήσατο vb 1st aor mid ind 3rd pers sg . . ἀπολογέομαι
ἀπελπίσας vb 1st aor act part masc nom sg . . . . . . ἀπελπίζω
ἀπελύετο vb impf m/p ind 3rd pers sg . . . . ἀπολύω
ἀπελύθη vb 1st aor pass ind 3rd pers sg id.
ἀπελύθησαν vb 1st aor pass ind 3rd pers pl id.
ἀπέλυσαν vb 1st aor act ind 3rd pers pl id.
ἀπέλυσας vb 1st aor act ind 2nd pers sg id.
ἀπέλυσεν vb 1st aor act ind 3rd pers sg id.
ἀπεμάξατο vb 1st aor mid ind 3rd pers sg . . . . ἀπομάσσομαι
ἀπεμάχοντο vb impf dep ind 3rd pers pl . . . . . . ἀπομάχομαι
ἀπέναντι adverb
ἀπεναντίον adverb
ἀπενέγκαι vb 1st aor act inf . . . . ἀποφέρω
ἀπενέγκαιτο vb 1st aor mid opt 3rd pers sg id.
ἀπενεγκάμενος vb 1st aor mid part masc nom sg id.
ἀπενέγκαντι vb 1st aor act part masc and neut dat sg id.
ἀπενέγκας vb 1st aor act part masc nom sg id.
ἀπενέγκασθαι vb 1st aor mid inf id.
ἀπένεγκε vb 1st aor act impv 2nd pers sg id.
ἀπενεγκεῖν vb 2nd aor act inf id.
ἀπένειμεν vb 2nd aor act ind 3rd pers sg . . . . ἀπονέμω
ἀπενεχθήσονται vb fut pass ind 3rd pers pl . . . . . . ἀποφέρω
ἀπενηνεγμένος vb perf m/p part masc nom sg id.
ἀπένθητος adj masc nom sg
ἀπένιψαν vb 1st aor act ind 3rd pers pl . . . . ἀπονίπτω
ἀπένιψεν vb 1st aor act ind 3rd pers sg id.
ἀπενοήθησαν vb 1st aor pass ind 3rd pers pl . . . ἀπονοέομαι
ἀπεξαίνετο vb impf m/p ind 3rd pers sg . . . . ἀποξαίνω
ἀπεξήρανεν vb 1st aor act ind 3rd pers sg . . . . . ἀποξηραίνω
ἀπεξηράνθη vb 1st aor pass ind 3rd pers sg id.
ἀπεξυσμένους vb perf m/p part masc acc pl . . . . ἀποξύω
ἀπεπήδησαν vb 1st aor act ind 3rd pers pl . . . . . . ἀποπηδάω
ἀπεπήδησεν vb 1st aor act ind 3rd pers sg id.
ἀπεπίασεν vb 1st aor act ind 3rd pers sg . . . . ἀποπιάζω
ἀπέπιπτεν vb impf act ind 3rd pers sg . . . . ἀποπίπτω
ἀπεπλάνησαν vb 1st aor act ind 3rd pers pl . . . . ἀποπλανάω

ἀπεπλάνησεν vb 1st aor act ind 3rd pers sg . . . . ἀποπλανάω
ἀπέπλυνα vb 1st aor act ind 1st pers sg . . . . ἀποπλύνω
ἀπέπνιξεν vb 1st aor act ind 3rd pers sg . . . . ἀποπνίγω
ἀπεποιήσαντο vb 1st aor mid ind 3rd pers pl . . . . ἀποποιέω
ἀπεποιήσω vb 1st aor mid ind 2nd pers sg id.
ἀπεπρατιζόμην vb impf dep ind
      1st pers sg . . . . ἀποπρατίζομαι
ἅπερ rel pron neut nom and acc pl . . . . ὅσπερ
ἀπέραντον adj acc sg, neut nom sg . . . . ἀπέραντος
ἀπέραντος adj masc and fem nom sg id.
ἀπερείδομαι vb pres dep ind 1st pers sg
ἀπερείσηται vb 1st aor mid subj 3rd pers sg . . . ἀπερείδομαι
ἀπερικάθαρτος adj masc and fem nom sg
ἀπερίσπαστοι adj masc and fem nom pl . . . . ἀπερίσπαστος
ἀπερισπάστῳ adj dat sg id.
ἀπερίτμητα adj neut nom and acc pl . . . . ἀπερίτμητος
ἀπερίτμητοι adj masc and fem nom pl id.
ἀπερίτμητος adj masc and fem nom sg id.
ἀπεριτμήτου adj gen sg id.
ἀπεριτμήτους adj masc and fem acc pl id.
ἀπεριτμήτων adj gen pl id.
ἀπέρρηξεν vb 1st aor act ind 3rd pers sg . . . . . . ἀπορρήσσω
ἀπέρριμμαι vb perf m/p ind 1st pers sg . . . . ἀπορρίπτω
ἀπερριμμένην vb perf m/p part fem acc sg id.
ἀπερρίφη vb 2nd aor pass ind 3rd pers sg id.
ἀπερρίφης vb 2nd aor pass ind 2nd pers sg id.
ἀπερρίφησαν vb 2nd aor pass ind 3rd pers pl id.
ἀπέρριψα vb 1st aor act ind 1st pers sg id.
ἀπερρίψαμεν vb 1st aor act ind 1st pers pl id.
ἀπέρριψαν vb 1st aor act ind 3rd pers pl id.
ἀπέρριψας vb 1st aor act ind 2nd pers sg id.
ἀπέρριψεν vb 1st aor act ind 3rd pers sg id.
ἀπερρύη vb 2nd aor pass ind 3rd pers sg . . . . ἀπορρέω
ἀπέσαξεν vb 1st aor act ind 3rd pers sg . . . . ἀποσάττω
ἀπεσιώπησαν vb 1st aor act ind 3rd pers pl . . . . . ἀποσιωπάω
ἀπεσκάρισεν vb 1st aor act ind 3rd pers sg . . . . ἀποσκαρίζω
ἀπεσκλήρυνεν vb impf act ind 3rd pers sg . . ἀποσκληρύνω
ἀπεσκόπει vb impf act ind 3rd pers sg . . . . ἀποσκοπέω
ἀπεσκόπευον vb impf act ind
      1st pers sg and 3rd pers pl . . . . ἀποσκοπεύω
ἀπεσκοπεύσαμεν vb 1st aor act ind 1st pers pl id.
ἀπεσκοράκισεν vb 1st aor act ind
      3rd pers sg . . . . ἀποσκορακίζω
ἀπεσκύθιζον vb impf act ind
      1st pers sg and 3rd pers pl . . . . ἀποσκυθίζω
ἀπεσπασμένοι vb perf m/p part masc nom pl . . . ἀποσπάω
ἀπεσπασμένον vb perf m/p part neut nom and acc sg id.
ἀπέσται vb fut mid ind 3rd pers sg . . . . ἄπειμι
ἀπεστάλη vb 2nd aor pass ind 3rd pers sg . . . . ἀποστέλλω
ἀπεστάλην vb 2nd aor pass ind 1st pers sg id.
ἀπεστάλησαν vb 2nd aor pass ind 3rd pers pl id.
ἀπέσταλκα vb perf act ind 1st pers sg id.
ἀπεστάλκαμεν vb perf act ind 1st pers pl id.
ἀπεστάλκας vb perf act ind 2nd pers sg id.
ἀπεστάλκασιν vb perf act ind 3rd pers pl id.
ἀπεστάλκατε vb perf act ind 2nd pers pl id.

ἀπεστάλκει vb plpf act ind 3rd pers sg . . . . ἀποστέλλω
ἀπέσταλκεν vb perf act ind 3rd pers sg   id.
ἀπέσταλμαι vb perf m/p ind 1st pers sg   id.
ἀπεσταλμένα vb perf m/p part neut nom and acc pl   id.
ἀπεσταλμένοι vb perf m/p part masc nom pl   id.
ἀπεσταλμένον vb perf m/p part masc acc sg   id.
ἀπεστάτουν vb impf act ind
          1st pers sg and 3rd pers pl . . . . ἀποστατέω
ἀπέστειλα vb 1st aor act ind 1st pers sg . . . . ἀποστέλλω
ἀπεστείλαμεν vb 1st aor act ind 1st pers pl   id.
ἀπέστειλαν vb 1st aor act ind 3rd pers pl   id.
ἀπέστειλας vb 1st aor act ind 2nd pers sg   id.
ἀπεστείλατε vb 1st aor act ind 2nd pers pl   id.
ἀπέστειλε(ν) vb 1st aor act ind 3rd pers sg   id.
ἀπέστελλε(ν) vb impf act ind 3rd pers sg   id.
ἀπέστελλον vb impf act ind
          1st pers sg and 3rd pers pl   id.
ἀπεστενωμένη vb perf m/p part fem nom sg . . . . ἀποστενόω
ἀπεστέρησεν vb 1st aor act ind 3rd pers sg . . . . . ἀποστερέω
ἀπέστη vb 2nd aor act ind 3rd pers sg . . . . ἀφίστημι
ἀπέστημεν vb 2nd aor act ind 1st pers pl   id.
ἀπέστην vb 2nd aor act ind 1st pers sg   id.
ἀπέστης vb 2nd aor act ind 2nd pers sg   id.
ἀπέστησα vb 1st aor act ind 1st pers sg   id.
ἀπεστήσαμεν vb 1st aor act ind 1st pers pl   id.
ἀπέστησαν vb 1st aor act ind 3rd pers pl   id.
ἀπέστησε(ν) vb 1st aor act ind 3rd pers sg   id.
ἀπέστητε vb 1st aor act ind 2nd pers pl   id.
ἄπεστιν vb pres act ind 3rd pers sg . . . . ἄπειμι
ἀπεστραμμένην vb perf m/p part fem acc sg . . . . ἀποστρέφω
ἀπέστραπται vb perf m/p ind 3rd pers sg   id.
ἀπεστράφη vb 2nd aor pass ind 3rd pers sg   id.
ἀπεστράφης vb 2nd aor pass ind 2nd pers sg   id.
ἀπεστράφησαν vb 2nd aor pass ind 3rd pers pl   id.
ἀπεστράφητε vb 2nd aor pass ind 2nd pers pl   id.
ἀπέστρεφον vb impf act ind
          1st pers sg and 3rd pers pl   id.
ἀπέστρεψα vb 1st aor act ind 1st pers sg   id.
ἀπεστρέψαμεν vb 1st aor act ind 1st pers pl   id.
ἀπεστρεψάμην vb 1st aor mid ind 1st pers sg   id.
ἀπέστρεψαν vb 1st aor act ind 3rd pers pl   id.
ἀπεστρέψαντο vb 1st aor mid ind 3rd pers pl   id.
ἀπέστρεψας vb 1st aor act ind 2nd pers sg   id.
ἀπεστρέψατε vb 1st aor act ind 2nd pers pl   id.
ἀπεστρέψατο vb 1st aor mid ind 3rd pers sg   id.
ἀπέστρεψε(ν) vb 1st aor act ind 3rd pers sg   id.
ἀπεστρόφασιν vb perf act ind 3rd pers pl   id.
ἀπέσυρον vb impf act ind
          1st pers sg and 3rd pers pl . . . . ἀποσύρω
ἀπεσφενδονήθησαν vb 1st aor pass ind
          3rd pers pl . . . . ἀποσφενδονάω
ἀπέσχηκεν vb perf act ind 3rd pers sg . . . . ἀπέχω
ἀπεσχήμεθα vb perf m/p ind 1st pers pl   id.
ἀπεσχίσθη vb 1st aor pass ind 3rd pers sg . . . . ἀποσχίζω
ἀπέσχον vb 2nd aor act ind 3rd pers pl . . . . ἀπέχω
ἀπέταξεν vb 1st aor act ind 3rd pers sg . . . . ἀποτάσσω

ἀπέτασσε vb impf act ind 3rd pers sg . . . . ἀποτάσσω
ἀπέτεμεν vb 2nd aor act ind 3rd pers sg . . . . ἀποτέμνω
ἀπέτεμνεν vb impf act ind 3rd pers sg   id.
ἀπετηγάνισεν vb 1st aor act ind 3rd pers sg . . ἀποτηγανίζω
ἀπετίναξεν vb 1st aor act ind 3rd pers sg . . . . ἀποτινάσσω
ἀπετίννυον vb impf act ind
          1st pers sg and 3rd pers pl . . . . ἀποτιννύω
ἀπέτρεπεν vb impf act ind 3rd pers sg . . . . ἀποτρέπω
ἀπέτρεχεν vb impf act ind 3rd pers sg . . . . ἀποτρέχω
ἀπέτρεχον vb impf act ind
          1st pers sg and 3rd pers pl   id.
ἀπέτριψεν vb 1st aor act ind 3rd pers sg . . . . ἀποτρίβω
ἀπετρύγησαν vb 1st aor act ind 3rd pers pl . . . . . ἀποτρυγάω
ἀπετυμπανίσθη vb 1st aor pass ind
          3rd pers sg . . . . ἀποτυμπανίζω
ἀπετύφλωσεν vb 1st aor act ind 3rd pers sg . . . . ἀποτυφλόω
ἀπέτυχον vb 2nd aor act ind 3rd pers pl . . . . . . ἀποτυγχάνω
ἀπευθανατίζειν vb pres act inf . . . . ἀπευθανατίζω
ἀπεφήνατο vb 1st aor mid ind 3rd pers sg . . . . ἀποφαίνω
ἀπέφηνεν vb 1st aor act ind 3rd pers sg   id.
ἀπεφράγη vb 2nd aor pass ind 3rd pers sg . . . . . ἀποφράσσω
ἀπέφραξεν vb 1st aor act ind 3rd pers sg   id.
ἄπεχε vb pres act impv 2nd pers sg . . . . ἀπέχω
ἀπέχει vb pres act ind 3rd pers sg   id.
ἀπέχεσθαι vb pres m/p inf   id.
ἀπέχεσθε vb pres m/p ind 2nd pers pl   id.
ἀπέχεται vb pres m/p ind 3rd pers sg   id.
ἀπέχετε vb pres act ind 2nd pers pl   id.
ἀπέχῃ vb pres act subj 3rd pers sg   id.
ἀπεχθείας noun fem gen sg . . . . ἀπέχθεια
ἀπεχθεῖς adj masc and fem nom and acc pl . . . . ἀπεχθής
ἀπεχθῆ adj masc and fem acc sg   id.
ἀπεχθόμενος vb 2nd aor mid part
          masc nom sg . . . . ἀπεχθάνομαι
ἀπεχθῶς adverb
ἀπεχόμεθα vb pres m/p ind 1st pers pl . . . . ἀπέχω
ἀπέχομεν vb pres act ind 1st pers pl   id.
ἀπεχόμενος vb pres m/p part masc nom sg   id.
ἀπέχον vb pres act part neut nom and acc sg   id.
ἀπέχοντες vb pres act part masc nom pl   id.
ἀπέχοντι vb pres act part masc and neut dat sg   id.
ἀπέχου vb pres m/p impv 2nd pers sg   id.
ἀπεχούσαις vb pres act part fem dat pl   id.
ἀπέχουσαν vb pres act part fem acc sg   id.
ἀπέχουσιν vb pres act ind 3rd pers pl   id.
ἀπέχυννε vb impf act ind 3rd pers sg . . . . ἀποχέω
ἀπέχω vb pres act ind 1st pers sg
ἀπέχων vb pres act part masc nom sg . . . . ἀπέχω
ἀπεώσαντο vb 1st aor mid ind 3rd pers pl . . . . ἀπωθέω
ἀπήγαγεν vb 2nd aor act ind 3rd pers sg   id.
ἀπήγαγες vb 2nd aor act ind 2nd pers sg   id.
ἀπήγαγον vb 2nd aor act ind 3rd pers pl   id.
ἀπήγγειλα vb 1st aor act ind 1st pers sg . . . . ἀπαγγέλλω
ἀπηγγείλαμεν vb 1st aor act ind 1st pers pl   id.
ἀπήγγειλαν vb 1st aor act ind 3rd pers pl   id.
ἀπήγγειλας vb 1st aor act ind 2nd pers sg   id.

ἀπήγγειλεν vb 1st aor act ind 3rd pers sg . . . . . . ἀπαγγέλλω
ἀπηγγέλη vb 2nd aor pass ind 3rd pers sg   id.
ἀπήγγελκα vb perf act ind 1st pers sg   id.
ἀπηγγελκότες vb perf act part masc nom pl   id.
ἀπήγγελλον vb impf act ind
    1st pers sg and 3rd pers pl   id.
ἀπηγμένους vb perf m/p part masc acc pl . . . . ἀπάγω
ἀπηγμένῳ vb perf m/p part masc and neut dat sg   id.
ἀπήγξατο vb 1st aor mid ind 3rd pers sg . . . . . . ἀπάγχομαι
ἀπηγορευμένων vb perf m/p part gen pl . . . . ἀπαγορεύω
ἀπῄει vb impf act ind 3rd pers sg . . . . ἄπειμι
ἀπῆκτο vb plpf m/p ind 3rd pers sg . . . . ἀπάγω
ἀπήλεγχεν vb impf act ind 3rd pers sg . . . . ἀπελέγχω
ἀπήλειψα vb 1st aor act ind 1st pers sg . . . . ἀπαλείφω
ἀπηλευθερώθη vb 1st aor pass ind 3rd pers sg . ἀπελευθερόω
ἀπῆλθαν vb 1st aor act ind 3rd pers pl . . . . . . ἀπέρχομαι
ἀπήλθατε vb 1st aor act ind 2nd pers pl   id.
ἀπῆλθεν vb 2nd aor act ind 3rd pers sg   id.
ἀπῆλθες vb 2nd aor act ind 2nd pers sg   id.
ἀπῆλθον vb 2nd aor act ind 3rd pers pl   id.
ἀπήλθοσαν vb 2nd aor act ind 3rd pers pl   id.
ἀπηλιώτην noun masc acc sg . . . . ἀπηλιώτης
ἀπηλιώτου noun masc gen sg   id.
ἀπηλλάγην vb 1st aor pass ind 1st pers sg . . . . . ἀπαλλάσσω
ἀπήλλαξεν vb 1st aor act ind 3rd pers sg   id.
ἀπήλλαχεν vb perf act ind 3rd pers sg   id.
ἀπηλλοτριώθησαν vb 1st aor pass ind
    3rd pers pl . . . . ἀπαλλοτριόω
ἀπηλλοτριωμένας vb perf m/p part fem acc pl   id.
ἀπηλλοτριωμένος vb perf m/p part masc nom sg   id.
ἀπηλλοτρίωσαν vb 1st aor act ind 3rd pers pl   id.
ἀπηλπισμένοι vb 1st aor mid part masc nom pl . . . ἀπελπίζω
ἀπηλπισμένων vb perf m/p part gen pl   id.
ἀπήμαντον adj acc sg, neut nom sg . . . . ἀπήμαντος
ἀπημάντους adj masc and fem acc pl   id.
ἀπημαυρώθησαν vb 1st aor pass ind
    3rd pers pl . . . . ἀπαμαυρόω
ἀπηναισχύντησας vb 1st aor act ind
    2nd pers sg . . . . ἀπαναισχυντέω
ἀπήνεγκαν vb 1st aor act ind 3rd pers pl . . . . ἀποφέρω
ἀπήνεγκεν vb 1st aor act ind 3rd pers sg   id.
ἀπηνεστάτων superl adj gen pl . . . . ἀπηνής
ἀπηνέχθη vb 1st aor pass ind 3rd pers sg . . . . ἀποφέρω
ἀπηνεώθη vb 1st aor pass ind 3rd pers sg . . . . . . ἀπενεόομαι
ἀπηνήνατο vb 1st aor mid ind 3rd pers sg . . . . ἀπαναίνομαι
ἀπηνής adj masc nom sg
ἀπήντα vb impf act ind 3rd pers sg . . . . ἀπαντάω
ἀπήντηκα vb perf act ind 1st pers sg   id.
ἀπήντησαν vb 1st aor act ind 3rd pers pl   id.
ἀπήντησεν vb 1st aor act ind 3rd pers sg   id.
ἀπήραμεν vb 1st aor act ind 1st pers pl . . . . ἀπαίρω
ἀπῆραν vb 1st aor act ind 3rd pers pl   id.
ἀπηρείδοντο vb impf dep ind 3rd pers pl . . . . . ἀπερείδομαι
ἀπηρείσαντο vb 1st aor mid ind 3rd pers pl   id.
ἀπηρείσατο vb 1st aor mid ind 3rd pers sg   id.
ἀπῆρεν vb 1st aor act ind 3rd pers sg . . . . ἀπαίρω

ἀπήρεσεν vb 1st aor act ind 3rd pers sg . . . . ἀπαρέσκω
ἀπήρκασιν vb perf act ind 3rd pers pl . . . . ἀπαίρω
ἀπήρξαντο vb 1st aor mid ind 3rd pers pl . . . . . ἀπάρχομαι
ἀπήρξατο vb 1st aor mid ind 3rd pers sg   id.
ἀπῆρον vb impf act ind 1st pers sg and 3rd pers pl . . . ἀπαίρω
ἀπῄτει vb impf act ind 3rd pers sg . . . . ἀπαιτέω
ἀπήχθη vb 1st aor pass ind 3rd pers sg . . . . ἀπάγω
ἀπήχθησαν vb 1st aor pass ind 3rd pers pl   id.
ἀπίδῃ vb 2nd aor act subj 3rd pers sg . . . . ἀφοράω
ἀπιδών vb 2nd aor act part masc nom sg   id.
ἀπιέναι vb pres act inf . . . . ἄπειμι
ἀπιόντος vb pres act part masc and neut gen sg   id.
Ἆπις pr noun
ἀπιστία noun fem nom sg
ἄπιστον adj acc sg, neut nom sg . . . . ἄπιστος
ἀπίστου adj gen sg   id.
ἀπιστούμενος vb pres m/p part masc nom sg . . . . . . ἀπιστέω
ἀπιστοῦντες vb pres act part masc nom pl   id.
ἀπιστούσης vb pres act part fem gen sg   id.
ἀπιστοῦσι vb pres act part masc and neut dat pl   id.
ἀπίων noun fem gen pl . . . . ἄπιος
ἄπλαστος adj masc nom sg
ἀπλάτῳ adj dat sg . . . . ἄπλατος
ἀπλῆ adj fem nom sg . . . . ἀπλοῦς
ἀπληστεύου vb pres dep impv 2nd pers sg . . ἀπληστεύομαι
ἀπληστία noun fem nom sg
ἀπληστίαν noun fem acc sg . . . . ἀπληστία
ἄπληστοι adj masc and fem nom pl . . . . ἄπληστος
ἄπληστος adj masc and fem nom sg   id.
ἀπληστότερος comp adj masc nom sg   id.
ἀπλήστου adj gen sg   id.
ἀπλήστῳ adj dat sg   id.
ἀπλοσύνης noun fem gen sg . . . . ἀπλοσύνη
ἀπλότητι noun fem dat sg . . . . ἀπλότης
ἀπλότητος noun fem gen sg   id.
ἀπλῶς adverb
ἀπλώσῃς vb 1st aor act subj 2nd pers sg . . . . ἀπλόω
ἄπνουν adj acc sg, neut nom sg . . . . ἄπνοος
ἀπό preposition
ἀποβαίνῃ vb pres act subj 3rd pers sg . . . . ἀποβαίνω
ἀποβαλεῖ vb fut act ind 3rd pers sg . . . . ἀποβάλλω
ἀποβάλλεται vb pres m/p ind 3rd pers sg   id.
ἀποβάψαντας vb 1st aor act part masc acc pl . . . . ἀποβάπτω
ἀποβεβληκυῖα vb perf act part fem nom sg . . . . . ἀποβάλλω
ἀποβῇς vb 2nd aor act subj 2nd pers sg . . . . ἀποβαίνω
ἀποβήσεται vb fut mid ind 3rd pers sg   id.
ἀποβήσομαι vb fut mid ind 1st pers sg   id.
ἀποβησόμενον vb fut mid part neut nom and acc sg   id.
ἀποβιάζου vb pres mid impv 2nd pers sg . . . . ἀποβιάζομαι
ἀποβλέπει vb pres act ind 3rd pers sg . . . . ἀποβλέπω
ἀποβλέπετε vb pres act ind 2nd pers pl   id.
ἀποβλέποντες vb pres act part masc nom pl   id.
ἀποβλεπόντων vb pres act part masc and neut gen pl   id.
ἀποβλέπουσιν vb pres act ind 3rd pers pl   id.
ἀπόβλημα noun neut nom and acc sg
ἀποβλήματα noun neut nom and acc pl . . . . ἀπόβλημα

ἀπογαλακτίσῃ vb 1st aor act subj

    3rd pers sg . . . . ἀπογαλακτίζω

ἀπογαλακτίσῃς vb 1st aor act subj 2nd pers sg   id.

ἀπογαλακτίσω vb 1st aor act subj 1st pers sg   id.

ἀπογεγαλακτισμένοι vb perf m/p part masc nom pl   id.

ἀπογεγαλακτισμένον vb perf m/p part

    neut nom and acc sg   id.

ἀπογεύεσθαι vb pres dep inf . . . . ἀπογεύομαι

ἀπογευομένους vb pres dep part masc acc pl   id.

ἀπογευσάμενος vb 1st aor mid part masc nom sg   id.

ἀπογινώσκων vb pres act part masc nom sg . . . . ἀπογινώσκω

ἀπόγονοι adj masc and fem nom pl . . . . ἀπόγονος

ἀπόγονος adj masc and fem nom sg   id.

ἀπογόνων adj gen pl   id.

ἀπογραφαῖς noun fem dat pl . . . . ἀπογραφή

ἀπογραφή noun fem nom sg   id.

ἀπογραφῇ noun fem dat sg   id.

ἀπογραφήν noun fem acc sg   id.

ἀπογραφῆναι vb 2nd aor pass inf . . . . ἀπογράφω

ἀπογραφῆς noun fem gen sg . . . . ἀπογραφή

ἀπογραφομένους vb pres m/p part masc acc pl . . ἀπογράφω

ἀπογράφονται vb pres m/p ind 3rd pers pl   id.

ἀπογραφῶν noun fem gen pl . . . . ἀπογραφή

ἀπόγραψαι vb 1st aor mid impv 2nd pers sg . . . . ἀπογράφω

ἀπογραψάμενοι vb 1st aor mid part masc nom pl   id.

ἀποδεδειγμένα vb perf m/p part

    neut nom and acc pl . . . . ἀποδεικνύω

ἀποδεδειγμέναι vb perf m/p part fem nom pl   id.

ἀποδεδειγμένοις vb perf m/p part masc and neut dat pl   id.

ἀποδεδειγμένον vb perf m/p part masc acc sg,

    neut nom and acc sg   id.

ἀποδεδειγμένος vb perf m/p part masc nom sg . ἀποδεικνύω

ἀποδεδειγμένων vb perf m/p part gen pl   id.

ἀποδεδεμένους vb perf m/p part masc acc pl . . . . . . ἀποδέω

ἀποδεδοκιμασμένον vb perf m/p part masc acc sg,

    neut nom and acc sg . . . . ἀποδοκιμάζω

ἀποδεδομένοι vb perf m/p part masc nom pl . . . . ἀποδίδωμι

ἀποδεῖξαι vb 1st aor act inf . . . . ἀποδεικνύω

ἀποδείξαιμι vb 1st aor act opt 1st pers sg   id.

ἀποδείξεως noun fem gen sg . . . . ἀπόδειξις

ἀποδείξῃ vb 1st aor act subj 3rd pers sg . . . . . . ἀποδεικνύω

ἀπόδειξιν noun fem acc sg . . . . ἀπόδειξις

ἀποδειροτομουμένας vb pres m/p part

    fem acc pl . . . . ἀποδειροτομέω

ἀποδεκατῶσαι vb 1st aor act inf . . . . ἀποδεκατόω

ἀποδεκατώσει vb fut act ind 3rd pers sg   id.

ἀποδεκατώσεις vb fut act ind 2nd pers sg   id.

ἀποδεκατώσω vb fut act ind 1st pers sg   id.

ἀποδεξάμενοι vb 1st aor mid part masc nom pl . ἀποδέχομαι

ἀποδεξάμενος vb 1st aor mid part masc nom sg   id.

ἀποδεξαμένου vb 1st aor mid part

    masc and neut gen sg   id.

ἀποδεσμεύει vb pres act ind 3rd pers sg . . . . . . ἀποδεσμεύω

ἀπόδεσμος noun masc nom sg

ἀποδέχεσθαι vb pres dep inf . . . . ἀποδέχομαι

ἀποδεχθείς vb 2nd aor pass part masc nom sg   id.

ἀποδήσει vb fut act ind 3rd pers sg . . . . ἀποδέω

ἀποδιαστελεῖς vb fut act ind 2nd pers sg . . . ἀποδιαστέλλω

ἀποδιδόασιν vb pres act ind 3rd pers pl . . . . . . ἀποδίδωμι

ἀποδιδοῖ vb pres act opt 3rd pers sg   id.

ἀποδιδόμενον vb pres m/p part neut nom and acc sg   id.

ἀποδιδόναι vb pres act inf   id.

ἀποδιδόντες vb pres act part masc nom pl   id.

ἀποδίδοται vb pres m/p ind 3rd pers sg   id.

ἀποδιδούς vb pres act part masc nom sg   id.

ἀποδιδράσκει vb pres act ind 3rd pers sg . . . . ἀποδιδράσκω

ἀποδιδράσκειν vb pres act inf   id.

ἀποδιδράσκω vb pres act ind 1st pers sg

ἀποδίδωμι vb pres act ind 1st pers sg

ἀποδίδως vb pres act ind 2nd pers sg . . . . ἀποδίδωμι

ἀποδίδωσιν vb pres act ind 3rd pers sg   id.

ἀποδιεσταλμένοις vb perf m/p part

    masc and neut dat pl . . . . ἀποδιαστέλλω

ἀποδοθείη vb 1st aor pass opt 3rd pers sg . . . . . . ἀποδίδωμι

ἀποδοθήσεται vb fut pass ind 3rd pers sg   id.

ἀποδοκιμάζων vb pres act part masc nom sg . . ἀποδοκιμάζω

ἀποδοκιμάσῃς vb 1st aor act subj 2nd pers sg   id.

ἀποδοκιμασθήσεται vb fut pass ind 3rd pers sg   id.

ἀποδοκιμῶ vb fut act ind 1st pers sg   id.

ἀπόδομα noun neut nom and acc sg

ἀποδόμενοι vb 2nd aor mid part masc nom pl . . . ἀποδίδωμι

ἀποδόντος vb 2nd aor act part masc and neut gen sg   id.

ἀπόδος vb 2nd aor act impv 2nd pers sg   id.

ἀποδόσει noun fem dat sg . . . . ἀπόδοσις

ἀποδόσεως noun fem gen sg   id.

ἀποδόσθαι vb 2nd aor mid inf . . . . ἀποδίδωμι

ἀπόδοτε vb 2nd aor act impv 2nd pers pl   id.

ἀπόδου vb 2nd aor mid impv 2nd pers sg . . . . . . ἀποδίδωμι

ἀποδοῦναι vb 2nd aor act inf   id.

ἀποδούς vb 2nd aor act part masc nom sg   id.

ἀποδοχεῖα noun neut nom and acc pl . . . . ἀποδοχεῖον

ἀποδοχεῖον noun neut nom and acc sg   id.

ἀποδρᾷ vb 2nd aor act subj 3rd pers sg . . . . . ἀποδιδράσκω

ἀπόδραθι vb 1st aor act impv 2nd pers sg   id.

ἀποδραμεῖται vb fut mid ind 3rd pers sg . . . . . . ἀποτρέχω

ἀποδύρεσθαι vb pres dep inf . . . . ἀποδύρομαι

ἀποδῶ vb 2nd aor act subj 1st and 3rd pers sg,

    2nd aor mid subj 2nd pers sg . . . . ἀποδίδωμι

ἀποδώμεθα vb aor mid subj 1st pers pl   id.

ἀποδώσει vb fut act ind 3rd pers sg   id.

ἀποδώσειν vb fut act inf   id.

ἀποδώσεις vb fut act ind 2nd pers sg   id.

ἀποδώσεται vb fut mid ind 3rd pers sg   id.

ἀποδώσετε vb fut act ind 2nd pers pl   id.

ἀποδώσῃ vb fut mid ind 2nd pers sg   id.

ἀποδώσομαι vb fut mid ind 1st pers sg   id.

ἀποδώσομεν vb fut act ind 1st pers pl   id.

ἀποδώσονται vb fut mid ind 3rd pers pl   id.

ἀποδώσουσιν vb fut act ind 3rd pers pl   id.

ἀποδώσω vb fut act ind 1st pers sg   id.

ἀποδῶται vb 2nd aor mid subj 3rd pers sg   id.

ἀποθανεῖν vb 2nd aor act inf . . . . ἀποθνήσκω

ἀποθανεῖσθε vb fut mid ind 2nd pers pl ...... ἀποθνήσκω
ἀποθανεῖται vb fut mid ind 3rd pers sg id.
ἀποθανέτω vb 2nd aor act impv 3rd pers sg id.
ἀποθάνῃ vb 2nd aor act subj 3rd pers sg id.
ἀποθάνῃ vb fut mid ind 2nd pers sg id.
ἀποθάνῃς vb 2nd aor act subj 2nd pers sg id.
ἀποθάνητε vb 2nd aor act subj 2nd pers pl id.
ἀποθάνοι vb 2nd aor act opt 3rd pers sg id.
ἀποθάνοιμεν vb 2nd aor act opt 1st pers pl id.
ἀποθανόντας vb 2nd aor act part masc acc pl id.
ἀποθανόντες vb 2nd aor act part masc nom pl id.
ἀποθανόντων vb 2nd aor act part masc and neut gen pl id.
ἀποθανοῦμαι vb fut mid ind 1st pers sg id.
ἀποθανούμεθα vb fut mid ind 1st pers pl id.
ἀποθανοῦνται vb fut mid ind 3rd pers pl id.
ἀποθανοῦσι vb 2nd aor act part masc and neut dat pl id.
ἀποθάνω vb 2nd aor act subj 1st pers sg id.
ἀποθάνωμεν vb 2nd aor act subj 1st pers pl id.
ἀποθανών vb 2nd aor act part masc nom sg id.
ἀποθάνωσιν vb 2nd aor act subj 3rd pers pl id.
ἀποθαυμάζων vb pres act part masc nom sg .. ἀποθαυμάζω
ἀποθαυμάσας vb 1st aor act part masc nom sg id.
ἀποθεῖναι vb 2nd aor act inf .... ἀποτίθημι
ἀποθέμενος vb 2nd aor mid part masc nom sg id.
ἀπόθες vb 2nd aor act impv 2nd pers sg id.
ἀπόθεσθε vb 2nd aor mid impv 2nd pers pl id.
ἀποθῆκαι noun fem nom pl .... ἀποθήκη
ἀποθήκας noun fem acc pl id.
ἀποθήκην noun fem acc sg id.
ἀποθηκῶν noun fem gen pl id.
ἀποθησαυρίζων vb pres act part
    masc nom sg .... ἀποθησαυρίζω
ἀποθήσει vb fut act ind 3rd pers sg .... ἀποτίθημι
ἀποθήσεις vb fut act ind 2nd pers sg id.
ἀποθήσομεν vb fut act ind 1st pers pl id.
ἀποθνήσκει vb pres act ind 3rd pers sg .... ἀποθνήσκω
ἀποθνήσκειν vb pres act inf id.
ἀποθνήσκεις vb pres act ind 2nd pers sg id.
ἀποθνήσκετε vb pres act ind 2nd pers pl id.
ἀποθνησκέτω vb pres act impv 3rd pers sg id.
ἀποθνήσκομεν vb pres act ind 1st pers pl id.
ἀποθνήσκον vb pres act part neut nom and acc sg id.
ἀποθνήσκοντας vb pres act part masc acc pl id.
ἀποθνήσκοντες vb pres act part masc nom pl id.
ἀποθνήσκοντος vb pres act part masc and neut gen sg id.
ἀποθνησκόντων vb pres act part masc and neut gen pl id.
ἀποθνήσκουσιν vb pres act ind 3rd pers pl id.
ἀποθνήσκω vb pres act ind 1st pers sg id.
ἀποθνήσκων vb pres act part masc nom sg id.
ἀποικεσίᾳ noun fem dat sg .... ἀποικεσία
ἀποικεσίαν noun fem acc sg id.
ἀποικεσίας noun fem gen sg id.
ἀποικεσιῶν noun fem gen pl id.
ἀποικία noun fem dat sg .... ἀποικία
ἀποικίαν noun fem acc sg id.
ἀποικίας noun fem gen sg and acc pl id.

ἀποικιεῖ vb fut act ind 3rd pers sg .... ἀποικίζω
ἀποικίσαι vb 1st aor act inf id.
ἀποικισάντων vb 1st aor act part masc and neut gen pl id.
ἀποικισθέντας vb 1st aor pass part masc acc pl id.
ἀποικισθέντος vb 1st aor pass part masc and neut gen sg id.
ἀποικισθέντων vb 1st aor pass part masc and neut gen pl id.
ἀποικισθῆναι vb 1st aor pass inf id.
ἀποικισμόν noun masc acc sg .... ἀποικισμός
ἀποικισμοῦ noun masc gen sg id.
ἀποίσει vb fut act ind 3rd pers sg .... ἀποφέρω
ἀποίσῃ vb fut mid ind 2nd pers sg id.
ἀποίσονται vb fut mid ind 3rd pers pl id.
ἀποίσουσιν vb fut act ind 3rd pers pl id.
ἀποίσω vb fut act ind 1st pers sg id.
ἀποκαθαίρει vb pres act ind 3rd pers sg ..... ἀποκαθαίρω
ἀποκαθαίρονται vb pres m/p ind 3rd pers pl id.
ἀποκαθαρθέν vb 1st aor pass part neut nom and acc sg id.
ἀποκαθαριεῖ vb fut act ind 3rd pers sg ...... ἀποκαθαρίζω
ἀποκαθαρίσαι vb 1st aor act opt 3rd pers sg id.
ἀποκαθάρωμαι vb 1st aor act mid subj 1st pers sg . ἀποκαθαίρω
ἀποκαθημένη vb pres dep part fem nom sg .... ἀποκάθημαι
ἀποκαθημένην vb pres dep part fem acc sg id.
ἀποκαθημένης vb pres dep part fem gen sg id.
ἀποκαθίστησιν vb pres act ind 3rd pers sg .. ἀποκαθίστημι
ἀποκαθιστῶν vb pres act part masc nom sg ... ἀποκαθιστάω
ἀποκαιομένας vb pres m/p part fem acc pl .... ἀποκαίω
ἀποκάλυμμα noun neut nom and acc sg
ἀποκάλυπτε vb pres act impv 2nd pers sg ..... ἀποκαλύπτω
ἀποκαλύπτει vb pres act ind 3rd pers sg id.
ἀποκαλύπτεται vb pres m/p ind 3rd pers sg id.
ἀποκαλύπτων vb pres act part masc nom sg id.
ἀποκαλυφθείς vb 1st aor pass part masc nom sg id.
ἀποκαλυφθῆναι vb 1st aor pass inf id.
ἀποκαλυφθήσεται vb fut pass ind 3rd pers sg id.
ἀποκαλυφθήσομαι vb fut pass ind 1st pers sg id.
ἀποκάλυψαι vb 1st aor mid impv 2nd pers sg id.
ἀποκαλύψαι vb 1st aor act inf id.
ἀποκαλύψας vb 1st aor act part masc nom sg id.
ἀποκαλύψει vb fut act ind 3rd pers sg id.
ἀποκαλύψεις vb fut act ind 2nd pers sg id.
ἀποκαλύψεως noun fem gen sg .... ἀποκάλυψις
ἀποκαλύψῃ vb 1st aor act subj 3rd pers sg .... ἀποκαλύπτω
ἀποκαλύψῃς vb 1st aor act subj 2nd pers sg id.
ἀποκάλυψιν noun fem acc sg .... ἀποκάλυψις
ἀποκάλυψις noun fem nom sg id.
ἀποκάλυψον vb 1st aor act impv 2nd pers sg ... ἀποκαλύπτω
ἀποκαλύψω vb fut act ind 1st pers sg id.
ἀποκατασταθείς vb 1st aor pass part
    masc nom sg .... ἀποκαθίστημι
ἀποκατασταθέντων vb 1st aor pass part
    masc and neut gen pl id.
ἀποκατασταθῆναι vb 1st aor pass inf id.
ἀποκατασταθήσεσθε vb fut pass ind 2nd pers pl id.
ἀποκατασταθήσεται vb fut pass ind 3rd pers sg id.
ἀποκατασταθήσονται vb fut pass ind 3rd pers pl id.
ἀποκαταστῇ vb 2nd aor act subj 3rd pers sg id.

ἀποκατάστηθι vb 2nd aor act impv

    2nd pers sg . . . . ἀποκαθίστημι

ἀποκαταστήσαι vb 1st aor act opt 3rd pers sg   id.

ἀποκαταστήσαι vb 1st aor act inf   id.

ἀποκαταστήσατε vb 1st aor act impv 2nd pers pl   id.

ἀποκαταστήσει vb fut act ind 3rd pers sg   id.

ἀποκαταστήσον vb 1st aor act impv 2nd pers sg   id.

ἀποκαταστήσουσιν vb fut act ind 3rd pers pl   id.

ἀποκαταστήσω vb 1st aor act subj 1st pers sg,

    fut act ind 1st pers sg   id.

ἀποκαταστήτω vb 2nd aor act impv 3rd pers sg   id.

ἀποκατεστάθη vb 1st aor pass ind 3rd pers sg   id.

ἀποκείμενα vb pres m/p part

    neut nom and acc pl . . . . ἀπόκειμαι

ἀποκείμενον vb pres m/p part masc acc sg   id.

ἀπόκειται vb pres m/p ind 3rd pers sg   id.

ἀποκεκαλυμμένοι vb perf m/p part

    masc nom pl . . . . ἀποκαλύπτω

ἀποκεκλεισμέναι vb perf m/p part fem nom pl . . . ἀποκλείω

ἀποκέκλεισται vb perf m/p ind 3rd pers sg   id.

ἀποκεκομμένοι vb perf m/p part masc nom pl . . . . ἀποκόπτω

ἀποκεκομμένος vb perf m/p part masc nom sg   id.

ἀποκέκριται vb perf m/p ind 3rd pers sg . . . . ἀποκρίνω

ἀποκεκρυμμένον vb perf m/p part masc acc sg . . ἀποκρύπτω

ἀποκενοῖ vb pres act ind 3rd pers sg . . . . ἀποκενόω

ἀποκέντησιν noun fem acc sg . . . . ἀποκέντησις

ἀποκέντησον vb 1st aor act impv 2nd pers sg . . . ἀποκεντέω

ἀποκεντήσωσιν vb 1st aor act subj 3rd pers pl   id.

ἀποκεντοῦντος vb pres act part masc and neut gen sg   id.

ἀποκεντούντων vb pres act part masc and neut gen pl   id.

ἀποκενώσει vb fut act ind 3rd pers sg . . . . ἀποκενόω

ἀποκενώσῃ vb 1st aor act subj 3rd pers sg   id.

ἀποκεχωρηκώς vb perf act part masc nom sg . . . . ἀποχωρέω

ἀποκεχωρισμένῳ vb perf m/p part

    masc and neut dat sg . . . . ἀποχωρίζω

ἀποκιδαρώσει vb fut act ind 3rd pers sg . . . . . . ἀποκιδαρόω

ἀποκιδαρώσετε vb fut act ind 2nd pers pl   id.

ἀποκλαιομένη vb pres m/p part fem nom sg . . . . . ἀποκλαίω

ἀποκλαιόμενος vb pres m/p part masc nom sg   id.

ἀποκλαύσομαι vb fut mid ind 1st pers sg   id.

ἀποκλείσατε vb 1st aor act impv 2nd pers pl . . . . . ἀποκλείω

ἀποκλείσει vb fut act ind 3rd pers sg   id.

ἀποκλείσεις vb fut act ind 2nd pers sg   id.

ἀποκλεισθῆναι vb 1st aor pass inf   id.

ἀποκλεισθήσεται vb fut pass ind 3rd pers sg   id.

ἀπόκλεισμα noun neut nom and acc sg   id.

ἀπόκλεισον vb 1st aor act impv 2nd pers sg . . . . . ἀποκλείω

ἀποκλείσουσιν vb fut act ind 3rd pers pl   id.

ἀποκλύζειν vb pres act inf . . . . ἀποκλύζω

ἀπόκνιζε vb pres act impv 2nd pers sg . . . . ἀποκνίζω

ἀποκνίζων vb pres act part masc nom sg   id.

ἀποκνίσει vb fut act ind 3rd pers sg   id.

ἀποκνιῶ vb fut act ind 1st pers sg   id.

ἀποκομίζοντος vb pres act part

    masc and neut gen sg . . . . ἀποκομίζω

ἀποκομιοῦντας vb fut act part masc acc pl   id.

ἀποκόψει vb fut act ind 3rd pers sg . . . . ἀποκόπτω

ἀποκόψεις vb fut act ind 2nd pers sg . . . . ἀποκόπτω

ἀπόκρημνον adj acc sg, neut nom sg . . . . ἀπόκρημνος

ἀποκριθείς vb 1st aor pass part masc nom sg . . . . . ἀποκρίνω

ἀποκριθεῖσα vb 1st aor pass part fem nom sg   id.

ἀποκριθεῖσι vb 1st aor pass part masc and neut dat pl   id.

ἀποκριθέντα vb 1st aor pass part masc acc sg   id.

ἀποκριθέντες vb 1st aor pass part masc nom pl   id.

ἀποκριθῇ vb 1st aor pass subj 3rd pers sg   id.

ἀποκριθῆναι vb 1st aor pass inf   id.

ἀποκριθήσει vb fut pass ind 2nd pers sg   id.

ἀποκριθήσεσθε vb fut pass ind 2nd pers pl   id.

ἀποκριθήσεται vb fut pass ind 3rd pers sg   id.

ἀποκριθήσῃ vb fut pass ind 2nd pers sg   id.

ἀποκριθήσομαι vb fut pass ind 1st pers sg   id.

ἀποκριθήσονται vb fut pass ind 3rd pers pl   id.

ἀποκρίθητε vb 1st aor pass subj 2nd pers pl   id.

ἀποκρίθητι vb 1st aor pass impv 2nd pers sg   id.

ἀποκριθῶ vb 1st aor pass subj 1st pers sg   id.

ἀποκριθῶσιν vb 1st aor pass subj 3rd pers pl   id.

ἀποκρίνεσθαι vb pres m/p inf   id.

ἀποκρίνεσθε vb pres m/p ind 2nd pers pl   id.

ἀποκρίνεται vb pres m/p ind 3rd pers sg   id.

ἀποκρίνῃ vb pres m/p ind 2nd pers sg   id.

ἀποκρινόμενα vb pres m/p part neut nom and acc pl   id.

ἀποκρινόμενος vb pres m/p part masc nom sg   id.

ἀποκρίνου vb pres m/p impv 2nd pers sg   id.

ἀπόκρισιν noun fem acc sg . . . . ἀπόκρισις

ἀπόκρισις noun fem nom sg   id.

ἀποκρυβῇ vb 2nd aor pass subj 3rd pers sg . . . . . ἀποκρύπτω

ἀποκρύβηθι vb 2nd aor pass impv 2nd pers sg   id.

ἀποκρυβήν noun fem acc sg . . . . ἀποκρυβή

ἀποκρυβήσεται vb fut pass ind 3rd pers sg . . . . . ἀποκρύπτω

ἀποκρύπτεται vb pres m/p ind 3rd pers sg   id.

ἀποκρύπτομαι vb pres m/p ind 1st pers sg   id.

ἀποκρύπτων vb pres act part masc nom sg   id.

ἀπόκρυφα adj neut nom and acc pl . . . . ἀπόκρυφος

ἀπόκρυφα adverb   id.

ἀποκρυφή noun fem nom sg

ἀποκρυφήν noun fem acc sg . . . . ἀποκρυφή

ἀποκρύφοις adj dat pl . . . . ἀπόκρυφος

ἀπόκρυφος adj masc and fem nom sg   id.

ἀποκρύφους adj masc and fem acc pl   id.

ἀποκρύφῳ adj dat sg   id.

ἀποκρύφων adj gen pl   id.

ἀποκρυψάντων vb 1st aor act part

    masc and neut gen pl . . . . ἀποκρύπτω

ἀποκρύψῃς vb 1st aor act subj 2nd pers sg   id.

ἀποκρύψω vb fut act ind 1st pers sg   id.

ἀποκτεῖναι vb 1st aor act inf . . . . ἀποκτείνω

ἀποκτείναντα vb 1st aor act part masc acc sg   id.

ἀποκτείναντι vb 1st aor act part

    masc and neut dat sg   id.

ἀποκτείνας vb 1st aor act part masc nom sg   id.

ἀποκτείνατε vb 1st aor act impv 2nd pers pl   id.

ἀποκτείνειν vb pres act inf   id.

ἀποκτείνης vb 1st aor act subj 2nd pers sg . . . . ἀποκτείνω	ἀπολελυτρωμένη vb perf m/p part fem nom sg . ἀπολυτρόω	
ἀπόκτεινον vb 1st aor act impv 2nd pers sg id.	ἀπολεπίσει vb fut act ind 3rd pers sg . . . . ἀπολεπίζω	
ἀποκτείνουσιν vb pres act ind 3rd pers pl id.	ἀπολέσαι vb 1st aor act inf . . . . ἀπολλύω	
ἀποκτείνω vb 1st aor act subj 1st pers sg id.	ἀπολέσασι vb 1st aor act part masc and neut dat pl id.	
ἀποκτείνωμεν vb 1st aor act subj 1st pers pl id.	ἀπολέσει vb fut act ind 3rd pers sg id.	
ἀποκτείνωσιν vb 1st aor act subj 3rd pers pl id.	ἀπολέσεις vb fut act ind 2nd pers sg id.	
ἀποκτενεῖ vb fut act ind 3rd pers sg id.	ἀπολέση vb 1st aor act subj 3rd pers sg id.	
ἀποκτενεῖς vb fut act ind 2nd pers sg id.	ἀπολέσης vb 1st aor act subj 2nd pers sg id.	
ἀποκτενεῖτε vb fut act ind 2nd pers pl id.	ἀπολέσητε vb 1st aor act subj 2nd pers pl id.	
ἀποκτέννει vb pres act ind 3rd pers sg id.	ἀπολέσθαι vb 2nd aor mid inf id.	
ἀποκτέννειν vb pres act inf id.	ἀπολέσθωσαν vb 1st aor mid impv 3rd pers pl id.	
ἀποκτέννοντες vb pres act part masc nom pl id.	ἀπόλεσον vb 1st aor act impv 2nd pers sg id.	
ἀποκτέννουσα vb pres act part fem nom sg id.	ἀπολέσω vb 1st aor act subj 1st pers sg id.	
ἀποκτέννουσιν vb pres act ind 3rd pers pl id.	ἀπολέσωσιν vb 1st aor act subj 3rd pers pl id.	
ἀποκτέννων vb pres act part masc nom sg id.	ἀπολῇ vb fut mid ind 2nd pers sg id.	
ἀποκτενοῦμεν vb fut act ind 1st pers pl id.	ἀπολήγει vb pres act ind 3rd pers sg . . . . ἀπολήγω	
ἀποκτενοῦσι(ν) vb fut act ind 3rd pers pl id.	ἀπόλησθε vb 2nd aor mid subj 2nd pers pl . . . . . . ἀπολλύω	
ἀποκτενῶ vb fut act ind 1st pers sg id.	ἀπόληται vb 2nd aor mid subj 3rd pers sg id.	
ἀποκυήσασα vb 1st aor act part fem nom sg . . . . . ἀποκυέω	ἀπολιθωθήτωσαν vb 1st aor pass impv	
ἀποκυλίσωσιν vb 1st aor act subj 3rd pers pl . . . ἀποκυλίω	3rd pers pl . . . . ἀπολιθόω	
ἀποκωλῦσαι vb 1st aor act inf . . . . ἀποκωλύω	ἀπολιπέτω vb 2nd aor act impv 3rd pers sg . . . . ἀπολείπω	
ἀποκωλύσασα vb 1st aor act part fem nom sg id.	ἀπολιπών vb 2nd aor act part masc nom sg id.	
ἀποκωλύσης vb 1st aor act subj 2nd pers sg id.	ἀπόλλεις vb pres act ind 2nd pers sg . . . . ἀπόλλω	
ἀποκωφωθῇς vb 1st aor pass subj 2nd pers sg . . . ἀποκωφόω	Ἀπολλοφάνην pr noun masc acc sg . . . . . . Ἀπολλοφάνης	
ἀποκωφωθήση vb fut pass ind 2nd pers sg id.	ἀπολλύει vb pres act ind 3rd pers sg . . . . ἀπολλύω	
ἀποκωφωθήσονται vb fut pass ind 3rd pers pl id.	ἀπολλύειν vb pres act inf id.	
ἀπολαβόντες vb 2nd aor act part masc nom pl ἀπολαμβάνω	ἀπόλλυμαι vb pres m/p ind 1st pers sg id.	
ἀπολαβών vb 2nd aor act part masc nom sg id.	ἀπόλλυμεν vb pres act ind 1st pers pl id.	
ἀπολαμβάνων vb pres act part masc nom sg id.	ἀπολλύμενοι vb pres m/p part masc nom pl id.	
ἀπολαύειν vb pres act inf . . . . ἀπολαύω	ἀπολλύμενον vb pres m/p part masc acc sg id.	
ἀπόλαυσιν noun fem acc sg . . . . ἀπόλαυσις	ἀπολλύμενος vb pres m/p part masc nom sg id.	
ἀπολαύσωμεν vb 1st aor act subj 1st pers pl . . . . ἀπολαύω	ἀπολλυμένου vb pres m/p part masc and neut gen sg id.	
ἀπολεῖ vb fut act ind 3rd pers sg . . . . ἀπολλύω	ἀπολλυμένους vb pres m/p part masc acc pl id.	
ἀπόλειπε vb pres act impv 2nd pers sg . . . . ἀπολείπω	ἀπολλυμένῳ vb pres m/p part masc and neut dat sg id.	
ἀπολειπέσθω vb pres m/p impv 3rd pers sg id.	ἀπολλυμένων vb pres m/p part gen pl id.	
ἀπολείπετε vb pres act impv 2nd pers pl id.	ἀπολλύοντες vb pres act part masc nom pl id.	
ἀπολείπη vb pres act subj 3rd pers sg id.	ἀπόλλυσι vb pres act ind 3rd pers sg id.	
ἀπολειπόμενοι vb pres m/p part masc nom pl id.	ἀπόλλυται vb pres m/p ind 3rd pers sg id.	
ἀπολειπόμενος vb pres m/p part masc nom sg id.	ἀπόλλυτε vb pres act ind 2nd pers pl id.	
ἀπολείπουσα vb pres act part fem nom sg id.	ἀπολλύων vb pres act part masc nom sg id.	
ἀπολεῖς vb fut act ind 2nd pers sg . . . . ἀπολλύω	Ἀπολλώνιον pr noun masc acc sg . . . . Ἀπολλώνιος	
ἀπολεῖσθε vb fut mid ind 2nd pers pl id.	Ἀπολλώνιος pr noun masc nom sg id.	
ἀπολεῖται vb fut mid ind 3rd pers sg id.	Ἀπολλωνίου pr noun masc gen sg id.	
ἀπολεῖτε vb fut act ind 2nd pers pl id.	ἀπολογήματα noun neut nom and acc pl . . . . . . ἀπολόγημα	
ἀπολειφθῇ vb 1st aor pass subj 3rd pers sg . . . . . . ἀπολείπω	ἀπολογήσομαι vb fut mid ind 1st pers sg . . . ἀπολογέομαι	
ἀπολείψασα vb 1st aor act part fem nom sg id.	ἀπολογίαν noun fem acc sg . . . . ἀπολογία	
ἀπολείψει vb fut act ind 3rd pers sg id.	ἀπολογουμένων vb pres dep part gen pl . . . . ἀπολογέομαι	
ἀπολείψετε vb fut act ind 2nd pers pl id.	ἀπόλοιντο vb 2nd aor mid opt 3rd pers pl . . . . ἀπολλύω	
ἀπολείψω vb fut act ind 1st pers sg id.	ἀπόλοιο vb 2nd aor mid opt 2nd pers sg id.	
ἀπολελειμμένον vb perf m/p part masc acc sg id.	ἀπόλοιπα adj neut nom and acc pl . . . . ἀπόλοιπος	
ἀπολελύκαμεν vb perf act ind 1st pers pl . . . . ἀπολύω	ἀπόλοιπον adj acc sg, neut nom sg id.	
ἀπολελύσθωσαν vb perf m/p impv 3rd pers pl id.	ἀπολοίπου adj gen sg id.	

ἀπόλοιτο	vb 2nd aor mid opt 3rd pers sg	ἀπόλλύω
ἀπολόμενοι	vb 2nd aor mid part masc nom pl	id.
ἀπολομένους	vb 2nd aor mid part masc acc pl	id.
ἀπολοῦνται	vb fut mid ind 3rd pers pl	id.
ἀπολοῦσι	vb fut act ind 3rd pers pl	id.
ἀπολούσωμαι	vb 1st aor mid subj 1st pers sg	ἀπολούω
ἀπολύειν	vb pres act inf	ἀπολύω
ἀπολύεις	vb pres act ind 2nd pers sg	id.
ἀπολύεσθαι	vb pres m/p inf	id.
ἀπολυθῇ	vb 1st aor pass subj 3rd pers sg	id.
ἀπολυθῆναι	vb 1st aor pass inf	id.
ἀπολυθῶ	vb 1st aor pass subj 1st pers sg	id.
ἀπολύομαι	vb pres m/p ind 1st pers sg	id.
ἀπολῦσαι	vb 1st aor act inf	id.
ἀπολύσαντες	vb 1st aor act part masc nom pl	id.
ἀπολύσατε	vb 1st aor act impv 2nd pers pl	id.
ἀπολύσεως	noun fem gen sg	ἀπόλυσις
ἀπόλυσιν	noun fem acc sg	
ἀπόλυσον	vb 1st aor act impv 2nd pers sg	ἀπολύω
ἀπολυτρώσει	vb fut act ind 3rd pers sg	ἀπολυτρόω
ἀπολυτρώσεως	noun fem gen sg	ἀπολύτρωσις
ἀπολύω	vb pres act ind 1st pers sg	
ἀπολύων	vb pres act part masc nom sg	ἀπολύω
ἀπολῶ	vb fut act ind 1st pers sg	ἀπόλλύω
ἀπολώλαμεν	vb perf act ind 1st pers pl	id.
ἀπολώλεκας	vb perf act ind 2nd pers sg	id.
ἀπολωλεκός	vb perf act part neut nom and acc sg	id.
ἀπολωλεκόσι	vb perf act part masc and neut dat pl	id.
ἀπολωλεκότες	vb perf act part masc nom pl	id.
ἀπολωλεκότι	vb perf act part masc and neut dat sg	id.
ἀπολωλεκώς	vb perf act part masc nom sg	id.
ἀπόλωλεν	vb perf act ind 3rd pers sg	id.
ἀπολωλός	vb perf act part neut nom and acc sg	id.
ἀπολωλότα	vb perf act part neut nom and acc pl	id.
ἀπολωλότας	vb perf act part masc acc pl	id.
ἀπολωλότων	vb perf act part masc and neut gen pl	id.
ἀπολωλυιῶν	vb perf act part fem gen pl	id.
ἀπολώμεθα	vb 2nd aor mid subj 1st pers pl	id.
ἀπόλωνται	vb 2nd aor mid subj 3rd pers pl	id.
ἀπομανῶσιν	vb 2nd aor pass subj 3rd pers pl .	ἀπομαίνομαι
ἀπομαρτυρησάντων	vb 1st aor act part	
masc and neut gen pl	ἀπομαρτυρέω
ἀπομέμψεται	vb fut mid ind 3rd pers sg	ἀπομέμφομαι
ἀπομεριεῖ	vb fut act ind 3rd pers sg	ἀπομερίζω
ἀπομέρισον	vb 1st aor act impv 2nd pers sg	id.
ἀπόμοιραν	noun fem acc sg	ἀπόμοιρα
ἀπονείμαντες	vb 1st aor act part masc nom pl	ἀπονέμω
ἀπονείμας	vb 1st aor act part masc nom sg	id.
ἀπονενοῆσθαι	vb perf dep inf	ἀπονοέομαι
ἀπονιψαμένη	vb 1st aor mid part fem nom sg . . .	ἀπονίπτω
ἄπονοι	adj masc nom pl	ἄπονος
ἀπονοίᾳ	noun fem dat sg	ἀπόνοια

ἀπόνοιαν	noun fem acc sg	ἀπόνοια
ἀπονοίας	noun fem gen sg	id.
ἀπόντα	vb pres act part masc acc sg	ἄπειμι
ἀπόντες	vb pres act part masc nom pl	id.
ἀποξενωθῇ	vb 1st aor pass subj 3rd pers sg	ἀποξενόω
ἀποξενώσας	vb 1st aor act part masc nom sg	id.
ἀποξηράναντος	vb 1st aor act part	
masc and neut gen sg	ἀποξηραίνω
ἀποξηρανθήσονται	vb fut pass ind 3rd pers pl	id.
ἀποξυσθῆναι	vb 1st aor pass inf	ἀποξύω
ἀποξύσουσιν	vb fut act ind 3rd pers pl	id.
ἀποπαρθενῶσαι	vb 1st aor act inf	ἀποπαρθενόω
ἀποπειρᾶται	vb pres dep ind 3rd pers sg . . .	ἀποπειράομαι
ἀποπεμπτοῦν	vb pres act part	
neut nom and acc sg	ἀποπεμπτόω
ἀποπεμπτωσάτωσαν	vb 1st aor act impv 3rd pers pl	id.
ἀποπεσάτωσαν	vb 1st aor act impv 3rd pers pl . .	ἀποπίπτω
ἀποπεσεῖται	vb fut mid ind 3rd pers sg	id.
ἀποπέσοι	vb fut act opt 3rd pers sg	id.
ἀποπέσοιμι	vb 2nd aor act opt 1st pers sg	id.
ἀποπέσοιν	see ἀποπέσοιμι	
ἀποπεσοῦνται	vb fut mid ind 3rd pers pl	id.
ἀποπεσών	vb 2nd aor act part masc nom sg	id.
ἀποπηδήσεται	vb fut mid ind 3rd pers sg	ἀποπηδάω
ἀποπήδησον	vb 1st aor act impv 2nd pers sg	id.
ἀποπίπτοντα	vb pres act part neut nom and acc pl	ἀποπίπτω
ἀποπλανηθῇ	vb 1st aor pass subj 3rd pers sg . .	ἀποπλανάω
ἀποπλανηθῇς	vb 1st aor pass subj 2nd pers sg	id.
ἀποπλανηθῶσιν	vb 1st aor pass subj 3rd pers pl	id.
ἀποπλανήσει	noun fem dat sg	ἀπόπλάνησις
ἀποπλανήσει	vb fut act ind 3rd pers sg	ἀποπλανάω
ἀπόπλυνε	vb pres act impv 2nd pers sg	ἀποπλύνω
ἀποπλύνῃ	vb pres m/p subj 2nd pers sg	id.
ἀποπνέων	vb pres act part masc nom sg	ἀποπνέω
ἀποπνίγουσα	vb pres act part fem nom sg	ἀποπνίγω
ἀποποιήσηται	vb 1st aor mid subj 3rd pers sg . . .	ἀποποιέω
ἀποποιοῦ	vb pres m/p impv 2nd pers sg	id.
ἀποπομπαίου	adj masc and neut gen sg	ἀποπομπαῖος
ἀποπομπαίῳ	adj masc and neut dat sg	id.
ἀποπομπήν	noun fem acc sg	ἀποπομπή
ἀποπτύσαι	vb 1st aor act inf	ἀποπτύω
ἀπόπτωμα	noun neut nom and acc sg	
ἀπορηθείς	vb 1st aor pass part masc nom sg	ἀπορέω
ἀπορηθήσεται	vb fut pass ind 3rd pers sg	id.
ἀπορήσει	vb fut act ind 3rd pers sg	id.
ἀπορία	noun fem nom sg	
ἀπορίᾳ	noun fem dat sg	ἀπορία
ἀπορίαις	noun fem dat pl	id.
ἀπορίαν	noun fem acc sg	id.
ἀπορουμένη	vb pres m/p part fem nom sg	ἀπορέω
ἀπορουμένης	vb pres m/p part fem gen sg	id.
ἀπορούμενοι	vb pres m/p part masc nom pl	id.

ἀπορουμένων vb pres m/p part gen pl . . . . ἀπορέω
ἀποροῦντες vb pres act part masc nom pl   id.
ἀπορραγήσεται vb fut pass ind 3rd pers sg . . . ἀπορρήσσω
ἀπορρεούσας vb pres act part fem acc pl . . . . . . ἀπορρέω
ἀπορρήξει vb fut act ind 3rd pers sg . . . . ἀπορρήσσω
ἀπορρήξουσιν vb fut act ind 3rd pers pl   id.
ἀπόρρητα adj neut nom and acc pl . . . . ἀπόρρητος
ἀπόρριπτε vb pres act impv 2nd pers sg . . . . . . ἀπορρίπτω
ἀπορριφήσεσθε vb fut pass ind 2nd pers pl   id.
ἀπορριφήσονται vb fut pass ind 3rd pers pl   id.
ἀπορριφῆτε vb 2nd aor pass subj 2nd pers pl   id.
ἀπορριφῶμεν vb 2nd aor pass subj 1st pers sg   id.
ἀπορρῖψαι vb 1st aor act inf   id.
ἀπορρίψατε vb 1st aor act impv 2nd pers pl   id.
ἀπορριψάτω vb 1st aor act impv 3rd pers sg   id.
ἀπορρίψῃς vb 1st aor act subj 2nd pers sg   id.
ἀπορρίψω vb 1st aor act subj 1st pers sg,
              fut act ind 1st pers sg   id.
ἀπορρίψωμεν vb 1st aor act subj 1st pers pl   id.
ἀπόρροια noun fem nom sg
ἀπορρυήσεται vb fut mid ind 3rd pers sg . . . . . . ἀπορρέω
ἀπορρῶγας noun fem acc pl . . . . ἀπορρώξ
ἀπορρῶγος noun fem gen sg   id.
ἀπορῶν vb pres act part masc nom sg . . . . ἀπορέω
ἀποσβέννυται vb pres m/p ind 3rd pers sg . . ἀποσβέννυμι
ἀποσβέσει vb fut act ind 3rd pers sg   id.
ἀποσβεσθήσεται vb fut pass ind 3rd pers sg   id.
ἀποσειόμενος vb pres m/p part masc nom sg . . . . . ἀποσείω
ἀποσκεδάσεις vb fut act ind 2nd pers sg . . ἀποσκεδάννυμι
ἀποσκευαῖς noun fem dat pl . . . . ἀποσκευή
ἀποσκευάσαι vb 1st aor act inf . . . . ἀποσκευάζω
ἀποσκευή noun fem nom sg
ἀποσκευῇ noun fem dat sg . . . . ἀποσκευή
ἀποσκευήν noun fem acc sg   id.
ἀποσκευῆς noun fem gen sg   id.
ἀποσκηνώσας vb 1st aor act part masc nom sg   ἀποσκηνόω
ἀποσκηνώσῃς vb 1st aor act subj 2nd pers sg   id.
ἀποσκοπεύει vb pres act ind 3rd pers sg . . . . . ἀποσκοπεύω
ἀποσκοπευόντων vb pres act part masc and neut gen pl id.
ἀποσκοπεύσω vb fut act ind 1st pers sg   id.
ἀποσκορακιεῖ vb fut act ind 3rd pers sg . . . ἀποσκορακίζω
ἀποσκορακίσῃς vb 1st aor act subj 2nd pers sg   id.
ἀποσκορακισμόν noun masc acc sg . . . . ἀποσκορακισμός
ἀποσοβεῖ vb pres act ind 3rd pers sg . . . . ἀποσοβέω
ἀποσοβῶν vb pres act part masc nom sg   id.
ἀποσπάσαντες vb 1st aor act part masc nom pl . . ἀποσπάω
ἀποσπασθῶσιν vb 1st aor pass subj 3rd pers pl   id.
ἀπόσπασμα noun neut nom and acc sg
ἀποσπάσοι vb 2nd aor act opt 3rd pers sg . . . . . . ἀποσπάω
ἀποσπάσομεν vb fut act ind 1st pers pl   id.
ἀποσπῶ vb pres act ind 1st pers sg   id.
ἀποσπωμένων vb pres m/p part gen pl   id.

ἀπόστα vb 2nd aor act impv 2nd pers sg . . . . . . ἀφίστημι
ἀποστάζει vb pres act ind 3rd pers sg . . . . ἀποστάζω
ἀποστάζουσιν vb pres act ind 3rd pers pl   id.
ἀποσταθῇ vb 1st aor pass subj 3rd pers sg . . . . . ἀφίστημι
ἀποσταθήσεται vb fut pass ind 3rd pers sg   id.
ἀποσταίη vb 2nd aor act opt 3rd pers sg   id.
ἀποσταλάξει vb fut act ind 3rd pers sg . . . . . ἀποσταλάζω
ἀποσταλείς vb 2nd aor pass part masc nom sg . . ἀποστέλλω
ἀποσταλεῖσι vb 2nd aor pass part masc and neut dat pl id.
ἀποσταλέντες vb 2nd aor pass part masc nom pl   id.
ἀποσταλέντος vb 2nd aor pass part masc and neut gen sg id.
ἀποσταλῇ vb 2nd aor pass subj 3rd pers sg   id.
ἀποσταλήσονται vb fut pass ind 3rd pers pl   id.
ἀποστάντες vb 2nd aor act part masc nom pl . . . . ἀφίστημι
ἀποστάς vb 2nd aor act part masc nom sg   id.
ἀποστάσει noun fem dat sg . . . . ἀπόστασις
ἀποστάσεις noun fem nom and acc pl   id.
ἀποστασία noun fem nom sg
ἀποστασίᾳ noun fem dat sg . . . . ἀποστασία
ἀποστασίαν noun fem acc sg   id.
ἀποστασίου noun neut gen sg . . . . ἀποστάσιον
ἀποστάται noun masc nom pl . . . . ἀποστάτης
ἀποστάτας noun masc acc pl   id.
ἀποστατεῖν vb pres act inf . . . . ἀποστατέω
ἀποστατεῖτε vb pres act ind 2nd pers pl   id.
ἀποστάτην noun masc acc sg . . . . ἀποστάτης
ἀποστάτης noun masc nom sg   id.
ἀποστατῆσαι vb 1st aor act inf . . . . ἀποστατέω
ἀποστατήσῃ vb 1st aor act subj 3rd pers sg   id.
ἀποστάτιν noun fem acc sg . . . . ἀποστάτις
ἀποστάτις noun fem nom sg   id.
ἀποστατοῦντας vb pres act part masc acc pl . . . ἀποστατέω
ἀποστατῶν noun masc gen pl . . . . ἀποστάτης
ἀποστεῖλαι vb 1st aor act opt 3rd pers sg . . . . . ἀποστέλλω
ἀποστεῖλαι vb 1st aor act inf   id.
ἀποστείλαντα vb 1st aor act part masc acc sg   id.
ἀποστείλαντας vb 1st aor act part masc acc pl   id.
ἀποστείλαντες vb 1st aor act part masc nom pl   id.
ἀποστείλαντι vb 1st aor act part masc and neut dat sg id.
ἀποστείλας vb 1st aor act part masc nom sg   id.
ἀποστείλασα vb 1st aor act part fem nom sg   id.
ἀποστείλατε vb 1st aor act impv 2nd pers pl   id.
ἀποστειλάτω vb 1st aor act impv 3rd pers sg   id.
ἀποστείλῃ vb 1st aor act subj 3rd pers sg   id.
ἀποστείλῃς vb 1st aor act subj 2nd pers sg   id.
ἀπόστειλον vb 1st aor act impv 2nd pers sg   id.
ἀποστείλω vb 1st aor act subj 1st pers sg,
              fut act ind 1st pers sg   id.
ἀποστείλωμεν vb 1st aor act subj 1st pers pl   id.
ἀποστελεῖ vb fut act ind 3rd pers sg   id.
ἀποστελεῖς vb fut act ind 2nd pers sg   id.

ἀποστελεῖτε	vb fut act ind 2nd pers pl	ἀποστέλλω
ἀπόστελλε	vb pres act impv 2nd pers sg	id.
ἀποστέλλει	vb pres act ind 3rd pers sg	id.
ἀποστέλλειν	vb pres act inf	id.
ἀποστέλλεις	vb pres act ind 2nd pers sg	id.
ἀποστέλλετε	vb pres act impv 2nd pers pl	id.
ἀποστέλλομεν	vb pres act ind 1st pers pl	id.
ἀποστελλόμενα	vb pres m/p part neut nom and acc pl	id.
ἀποστελλόμενος	vb pres m/p part masc nom sg	id.
ἀποστέλλοντα	vb pres act part masc acc sg	id.
ἀποστέλλοντες	vb pres act part masc nom pl	id.
ἀποστέλλουσιν	vb pres act ind 3rd pers pl	id.
ἀποστέλλω	vb pres act ind 1st pers sg	id.
ἀποστέλλων	vb pres act part masc nom sg	id.
ἀποστελοῦμεν	vb fut act ind 1st pers pl	id.
ἀποστελοῦσι(ν)	vb fut act ind 3rd pers pl	id.
ἀποστελῶ	vb fut act ind 1st pers sg	id.
ἀποστερηθῆναι	vb 1st aor pass inf	ἀποστερέω
ἀποστερήσει	vb fut act ind 3rd pers sg	id.
ἀποστερήσῃς	vb 1st aor act subj 2nd pers sg	id.
ἀποστέρξεις	vb fut act ind 2nd pers sg	ἀποστέργω
ἀποστεροῦμεν	vb pres act ind 1st pers pl	ἀποστερέω
ἀποστεροῦντας	vb pres act part masc acc pl	id.
ἀποστερῶν	vb pres act part masc nom sg	id.
ἀποστῇ	vb 2nd aor act subj 3rd pers sg	ἀφίστημι
ἀπόστηθι	vb 2nd aor act impv 2nd pers sg	id.
ἀποστῆναι	vb 2nd aor act inf	id.
ἀποστῇς	vb 2nd aor act subj 2nd pers sg	id.
ἀποστῆσαι	vb 1st aor act inf	id.
ἀποστήσας	vb 1st aor act part masc nom sg	id.
ἀποστήσατε	vb 1st aor act impv 2nd pers pl	id.
ἀποστήσει	vb fut act ind 3rd pers sg	id.
ἀποστήσεται	vb fut mid ind 3rd pers sg	id.
ἀποστήσῃ	vb 1st aor act subj 3rd pers sg, fut mid ind 2nd pers sg	id.
ἀποστήσῃς	vb 1st aor act subj 2nd pers sg	id.
ἀποστησόμεθα	vb fut mid ind 1st pers pl	id.
ἀπόστησον	vb 1st aor act impv 2nd pers sg	id.
ἀποστήσουσι(ν)	vb fut act ind 3rd pers pl	id.
ἀποστήσω	vb 1st aor act subj 1st pers sg, fut act ind 1st pers sg	id.
ἀπόστητε	vb 2nd aor act impv 2nd pers pl	id.
ἀποστῆτε	vb 2nd aor act subj 2nd pers pl	id.
ἀποστήτω	vb 2nd aor act impv 3rd pers sg	id.
ἀποστήτωσαν	vb 2nd aor act impv 3rd pers pl	id.
ἀποστολαί	noun fem nom pl	ἀποστολή
ἀποστολαῖς	noun fem dat pl	id.
ἀποστολάς	noun fem acc pl	id.
ἀποστολή	noun fem nom sg	id.
ἀποστολῇ	noun fem dat sg	id.
ἀποστολήν	noun fem acc sg	id.

ἀποστραφειησαν	vb 2nd aor pass opt 3rd pers pl	ἀποστρέφω
ἀποστραφείς	vb 2nd aor pass part masc nom sg	id.
ἀποστραφεῖσα	vb 2nd aor pass part fem nom sg	id.
ἀποστραφέν	vb 2nd aor pass part neut nom and acc sg	id.
ἀποστραφέντες	vb 2nd aor pass part masc nom pl	id.
ἀποστραφῇ	vb 2nd aor pass subj 3rd pers sg	id.
ἀποστραφῆναι	vb 2nd aor pass inf	id.
ἀποστραφήσεσθε	vb fut pass ind 2nd pers pl	id.
ἀποστραφήσεται	vb fut pass ind 3rd pers sg	id.
ἀποστραφήσῃ	vb fut pass ind 2nd pers sg	id.
ἀποστραφήσομαι	vb fut pass ind 1st pers sg	id.
ἀποστραφήσονται	vb fut pass ind 3rd pers pl	id.
ἀποστράφητε	vb 2nd aor pass impv 2nd pers pl	id.
ἀποστραφῆτε	vb 2nd aor pass subj 2nd pers pl	id.
ἀποστράφητι	vb 2nd aor pass impv 2nd pers sg	id.
ἀποστραφήτω	vb 2nd aor pass impv 3rd pers sg	id.
ἀποστραφήτωσαν	vb 2nd aor pass impv 3rd pers pl	id.
ἀποστραφῶμεν	vb 2nd aor pass subj 1st pers pl	id.
ἀποστρεβλοῦσθαι	vb pres dep inf	ἀποστρεβλόομαι
ἀπόστρεφε	vb pres act impv 2nd pers sg	ἀποστρέφω
ἀποστρέφει	vb pres act ind 3rd pers sg	id.
ἀποστρέφειν	vb pres act inf	id.
ἀποστρέφεις	vb pres act ind 2nd pers sg	id.
ἀποστρέφεσθαι	vb pres m/p inf	id.
ἀποστρέφεται	vb pres m/p ind 3rd pers sg	id.
ἀποστρέφετε	vb pres act impv 2nd pers pl	id.
ἀποστρεφέτωσαν	vb pres act impv 3rd pers pl	id.
ἀποστρεφόμεθα	vb pres m/p ind 1st pers pl	id.
ἀποστρέφοντα	vb pres act part masc acc sg	id.
ἀποστρέφοντος	vb pres act part masc and neut gen sg	id.
ἀποστρέφου	vb pres m/p impv 2nd pers sg	id.
ἀποστρέφουσιν	vb pres act ind 3rd pers pl	id.
ἀποστρέφων	vb pres act part masc nom sg	id.
ἀποστρέφωνται	vb pres m/p subj 3rd pers pl	id.
ἀποστρέψαι	vb 1st aor act inf	id.
ἀποστρέψαντα	vb 1st aor act part masc acc sg	id.
ἀποστρέψαντας	vb 1st aor act part masc acc pl	id.
ἀποστρέψαντες	vb 1st aor act part masc nom pl	id.
ἀποστρέψαντος	vb 1st aor act part masc and neut gen sg	id.
ἀποστρέψας	vb 1st aor act part masc nom sg	id.
ἀποστρέψατε	vb 1st aor act impv 2nd pers pl	id.
ἀποστρέψει	vb fut act ind 3rd pers sg	id.
ἀποστρέψεις	vb fut act ind 2nd pers sg	id.
ἀποστρέψῃ	vb 1st aor act subj 3rd pers sg, fut mid ind 2nd pers sg	id.
ἀποστρέψῃς	vb 1st aor act subj 2nd pers sg	id.
ἀποστρέψητε	vb 1st aor act subj 2nd pers pl	id.
ἀποστρέψοιτο	vb fut mid opt 3rd pers sg	id.
ἀποστρέψομεν	vb fut act ind 1st pers pl	id.
ἀπόστρεψον	vb 1st aor act impv 2nd pers sg	id.
ἀποστρέψουσιν	vb fut act ind 3rd pers pl	id.

ἀποστρέψω vb fut act ind 1st pers sg . . . . ἀποστρέφω
ἀποστρέψωμεν vb 1st aor act subj 1st pers pl id.
ἀποστρέψωσιν vb 1st aor act subj 3rd pers pl id.
ἀποστροφαῖς noun fem dat pl . . . . ἀποστροφή
ἀποστροφάς noun fem acc pl id.
ἀποστροφή noun fem nom sg id.
ἀποστροφῇ noun fem dat sg id.
ἀποστροφήν noun fem acc sg id.
ἀποστροφῆς noun fem gen sg id.
ἀποστροφῶν noun fem gen pl id.
ἀποστύψει vb fut act ind 3rd pers sg . . . . ἀποστύφω
ἀποστῶμεν vb 2nd aor act subj 1st pers pl . . . . . . ἀφίστημι
ἀποσυνάξαι vb 1st aor act inf . . . . ἀποσυνάγω
ἀποσυνάξει vb fut act ind 3rd pers sg id.
ἀποσυνάξεις vb fut act ind 2nd pers sg id.
ἀποσυριεῖς vb fut act ind 2nd pers sg . . . . ἀποσυρίζω
ἀποσφάξαντας vb 1st aor act part masc acc pl . . ἀποσφάζω
ἀποσφράγισμα noun neut nom and acc sg
ἀπόσχῃ vb 2nd aor act subj 3rd pers sg . . . . ἀπέχω
ἀποσχίσθητε vb 1st aor pass impv 2nd pers pl . . . ἀποσχίζω
ἀπόσχου vb 2nd aor mid impv 2nd pers sg . . . . ἀπέχω
ἀποτάξασθαι vb 1st aor mid inf . . . . ἀποτάσσω
ἀποτείσαι vb vb 1st aor act opt 3rd pers sg . . . ἀποτίνω
ἀποτεισάτω vb 1st aor act impv 3rd pers sg id.
ἀποτείσει vb fut act ind 3rd pers sg id.
ἀποτείσεις vb fut act ind 2nd pers sg id.
ἀποτείσῃ vb 1st aor act subj 3rd pers sg id.
ἀποτείσῃς vb 1st aor act subj 2nd pers sg id.
ἀποτείσουσιν vb fut act ind 3rd pers pl id.
ἀποτείσω vb fut act ind 1st pers sg id.
ἀποτείσων vb fut act part masc nom sg id.
ἀποτελεῖ vb pres act ind 3rd pers sg . . . . ἀποτελέω
ἀπότεμε vb 2nd aor act impv 2nd pers sg . . . . . . ἀποτέμνω
ἀποτεμνομένας vb pres m/p part fem acc pl id.
ἀποτεμόντας vb 2nd aor act part masc acc pl id.
ἀποτενεῖτε vb fut act ind 2nd pers pl . . . . ἀποτείνω
ἀποτεταγμένοις vb perf m/p part
        masc and neut dat pl . . . . ἀποτάσσω
ἀποτεταγμένου vb perf m/p part masc and neut gen sg id.
ἀποτετίνακται vb perf m/p ind 3rd pers sg . . . ἀποτινάσσω
ἀποτεχθέντες vb 1st aor pass part masc nom pl . . ἀποτίκτω
ἀποτίκτει vb pres act ind 3rd pers sg id.
ἀποτινάγματος noun neut gen sg . . . . ἀποτίναγμα
ἀποτινάξομαι vb fut mid ind 1st pers sg . . . . . . ἀποτινάσσω
ἀποτιννύων vb pres act part masc nom sg . . . . . ἀποτιννύω
ἀποτομάς noun fem acc pl . . . . ἀποτομή
ἀπότομον adj acc sg, neut nom sg . . . . ἀπότομος
ἀπότομος adj masc and fem nom sg id.
ἀποτόμῳ adj dat sg id.
ἀποτόμως adverb
ἀποτραπέντες vb 2nd aor pass part masc nom pl . ἀποτρέπω
ἀποτρέπει vb pres act ind 3rd pers sg id.

ἀπότρεχε vb pres act impv 2nd pers sg . . . . ἀποτρέχω
ἀποτρέχει vb pres act ind 3rd pers sg id.
ἀποτρέχειν vb pres act inf id.
ἀποτρέχεις vb pres act ind 2nd pers sg id.
ἀποτρέχετε vb pres act impv 2nd pers pl id.
ἀποτρεχέτω vb pres act impv 3rd pers sg id.
ἀποτρέχητε vb pres act subj 2nd pers pl id.
ἀποτρέχομεν vb pres act ind 1st pers pl id.
ἀποτρέχοντες vb pres act part masc nom pl id.
ἀποτρέχουσιν vb pres act ind 3rd pers pl id.
ἀποτρέχω vb pres act ind 1st pers sg id.
ἀπότριψαι vb 1st aor mid impv 2nd pers sg . . . . . ἀποτρίβω
ἀποτρίψεται vb fut pass ind 3rd pers sg id.
ἀποτροπιάζεσθαι vb pres m/p inf . . . . ἀποτροπιάζω
ἀποτυμπανισθήσεται vb fut pass ind
        3rd pers sg . . . . ἀποτυμπανίζω
ἀποτυφλοῖ vb pres act ind 3rd pers sg . . . . ἀποτυφλόω
ἀποτυφλωθῆναι vb 1st aor pass inf id.
ἀποτυφλώσει noun fem dat sg . . . . ἀποτύφλωσις
ἀπούσης vb pres act part fem gen sg . . . . ἄπειμι
ἀποφέρει vb pres act ind 3rd pers sg . . . . ἀποφέρω
ἀποφέρουσιν vb pres act ind 3rd pers pl id.
ἀποφεύξεται vb fut mid ind 3rd pers sg . . . . ἀποφεύγω
ἀποφῆναι vb 1st aor act inf . . . . ἀποφαίνω
ἀποφηναμένων vb 1st aor mid part gen pl id.
ἀποφθέγγεσθαι vb pres dep inf . . . . ἀποφθέγγομαι
ἀποφθεγγόμενοι vb pres dep part masc nom pl id.
ἀποφθεγγομένους vb pres dep part masc acc pl id.
ἀπόφθεγμα noun neut nom and acc sg
ἀποφθέγματα noun neut nom and acc pl . . . . . . ἀπόφθεγμα
ἀποφθέγξονται vb fut mid ind 3rd pers pl . . ἀποφθέγγομαι
ἀποφυσώμενος vb pres m/p part masc nom sg . . ἀποφυσάω
ἀποχεεῖς vb fut act ind 2nd pers sg . . . . ἀποχέω
ἀποχωρήσει noun fem dat sg . . . . ἀποχώρησις
ἀποχωροῦντας vb pres act part masc acc pl . . . . . ἀποχωρέω
ἀποχωροῦσιν vb pres act ind 3rd pers pl id.
ἀποψύχων vb pres act part masc nom sg . . . . ἀποψύχω
ἄπρακτον adj acc sg, neut nom sg . . . . ἄπρακτος
ἄπρακτος adj masc and fem nom sg id.
ἀπρεπές adj neut nom and acc sg . . . . ἀπρεπής
ἀπρονοήτως adverb
ἀπροπτώτῳ adj dat sg . . . . ἀπρόπτωτος
ἀπροσδεεῖ adj dat sg . . . . ἀπροσδεής
ἀπροσδεεῖς adj masc and fem nom and acc pl id.
ἀπροσδεής adj masc and fem nom sg id.
ἀπροσδόκητον adj acc sg, neut nom sg . . . . ἀπροσδόκητος
ἀπροσδόκητος adj masc and fem nom sg id.
ἀπροσδοκήτως adverb
ἀπροσκόπους adj masc and fem acc pl . . . . . . ἀπρόσκοπος
ἀπροσκόπῳ adj dat sg id.
ἀπταίστους adj masc and fem acc pl . . . . ἄπταιστος
Απταλιμ pr noun

ἄπτεσθαι vb pres dep inf	. . . .	ἅπτομαι
ἄπτεσθε vb pres dep impv 2nd pers pl,		
pres dep ind 2nd pers pl		id.
ἀπτέσθω vb pres dep impv 3rd pers sg		id.
ἀπτόητος adj masc and fem nom sg		
ἀπτομένη vb pres dep part fem nom sg	. . . .	ἅπτομαι
ἀπτόμενος vb pres dep part masc nom sg		id.
ἀπτομένων vb pres dep part gen pl		id.
ἅπτονται vb pres dep ind 3rd pers pl		id.
ἅπτωνται vb pres dep subj 3rd pers pl		id.
ἄπυρον adj acc sg, neut nom sg	. . . .	ἄπυρος
Απφιν pr noun		
Απφους pr noun		
ἀπωθεῖς vb pres act ind 2nd pers sg	. . . .	ἀπωθέω
ἀπωθεῖται vb pres m/p ind 3rd pers sg		id.
ἀπωθοῦ vb pres m/p impv 2nd pers sg		id.
ἀπωθουμένοις vb pres m/p part		
masc and neut dat pl		id.
ἀπωθούμενος vb pres m/p part masc nom sg		id.
ἀπῴκισα vb 1st aor act ind 1st pers sg	. . . .	ἀποικίζω
ἀπῴκισαν vb 1st aor act ind 3rd pers pl		id.
ἀπῴκισας vb 1st aor act ind 2nd pers sg		id.
ἀπῴκισεν vb 1st aor act ind 3rd pers sg		id.
ἀπῳκίσθη vb 1st aor pass ind 3rd pers sg		id.
ἀπῴκισται vb perf m/p ind 3rd pers sg		id.
ἀπώλεια noun fem nom sg		
ἀπωλείᾳ noun fem dat sg	. . . .	ἀπώλεια
ἀπώλειαν noun fem acc sg		id.
ἀπωλείας noun fem gen sg		id.
ἀπώλεσα vb 1st aor act ind 1st pers sg	. . . .	ἀπολλύω
ἀπώλεσαν vb 1st aor act ind 3rd pers pl		id.
ἀπώλεσας vb 1st aor act ind 2nd pers sg		id.
ἀπώλεσεν vb 1st aor act ind 3rd pers sg		id.
ἀπώλετο vb 2nd aor mid ind 3rd pers sg		id.
ἀπωλόμην vb 2nd aor mid ind 1st pers sg		id.
ἀπώλοντο vb 2nd aor mid ind 3rd pers pl		id.
ἀπώλου vb 2nd aor mid ind 2nd pers sg		id.
ἀπώργισται vb perf mid ind 3rd pers sg	. . . .	ἀποργίζομαι
ἀπώρυγας noun fem acc pl	. . . .	ἀπῶρυξ
ἄπωσαι vb 1st aor mid impv 2nd pers sg	. . . .	ἀπωθέω
ἀπωσαμένη vb 1st aor mid part fem nom sg		id.
ἀπωσάμενοι vb 1st aor mid part masc nom pl		id.
ἀπωσάμενος vb 1st aor mid part masc nom sg		id.
ἀπωσαμένων vb 1st aor mid part gen pl		id.
ἀπωσάμην vb 1st aor mid ind 1st pers sg		id.
ἀπώσαντο vb 1st aor mid ind 3rd pers pl		id.
ἀπώσασθαι vb 1st aor mid inf		id.
ἀπωσάσθωσαν vb 1st aor mid impv 3rd pers pl		id.
ἀπώσατο vb 1st aor mid ind 3rd pers sg		id.
ἀπώσειεν vb 1st aor pass opt 3rd pers sg		id.
ἀπώσεται vb fut mid ind 3rd pers sg		id.

ἀπώσῃ vb 1st aor act subj 3rd pers sg,		
1st aor mid subj 2nd pers sg,		
fut mid ind 2nd pers sg	. . . .	ἀπωθέω
ἀπώσθη 1st aor pass ind 3rd pers sg		id.
ἀπωσθῆναι vb 1st aor pass inf		id.
ἀπωσθῇς vb 1st aor pass subj 2nd pers sg		id.
ἀπώσθησαν vb 1st aor pass ind 3rd pers pl		id.
ἀπωσθήσεται vb fut pass ind 3rd pers sg		id.
ἀπῶσμαι vb perf m/p ind 1st pers sg		id.
ἀπωσμένην vb perf m/p part fem acc sg		id.
ἀπωσμῶν noun masc gen pl	. . . .	ἀπωσμός
ἀπώσομαι vb fut mid ind 1st pers sg	. . . .	ἀπωθέω
ἀπῶσται vb perf m/p ind 3rd pers sg		id.
ἀπώσω vb 1st aor act subj 1st pers sg,		
1st aor mid ind 2nd pers sg		id.
ἀπωτέρω comp adverb		
ἀπῴχετο vb impf dep ind 3rd pers sg	. . . .	ἀποίχομαι
ἀπῴχοντο vb impf dep ind 3rd pers pl		id.
Αρα pr noun		
ἄρα particle		
ἆρα particle		
ἀρά noun fem nom sg		
ἀρᾷ noun fem dat sg	. . . .	ἀρά
Αραα pr noun		
Αρααβ pr noun		
Αραας pr noun		
Αραβα pr noun		
Ἄραβα pr noun masc acc sg	. . . .	Ἄραψ
Ἄραβας pr noun masc acc pl		id.
Ἄραβες pr noun masc nom pl		id.
Αραβι pr noun		
Ἀραβια pr noun fem nom sg		
Ἀραβίᾳ pr noun fem dat sg	. . . .	Ἀραβια
Ἀραβιαν pr noun fem acc sg		id.
Ἀραβιας pr noun fem gen sg		id.
Ἀραβισσαν pr noun fem acc sg	. . . .	Ἀραβισσα
Αραβωθ pr noun		
Αραβωθιτου pr noun masc gen sg	. . . .	Αραβωθιτης
Ἄραβων pr noun masc gen pl	. . . .	Ἄραψ
Αραδ pr noun		
Αραδιοι pr noun masc nom pl	. . . .	Αραδιος
Ἀραδιον pr noun masc acc sg		id.
Αραδιων pr noun masc gen pl		id.
Ἄραδον pr noun acc sg	. . . .	Ἄραδος
Αραηλ pr noun		
Αραθ pr noun		
ἄραι vb 1st aor act opt 3rd pers sg	. . . .	αἴρω
ἆραι vb 1st aor act inf		id.
ἀραί noun fem nom pl	. . . .	ἀρά
ἀραῖς noun fem dat pl		id.
Αραμ pr noun		
Αραμα pr noun		

Αραμιν pr noun

Αραν pr noun

ἀράν noun fem acc sg . . . . ἀρά

ἄραντες vb 1st aor act part masc nom pl . . . . αἴρω

Αραουριτης pr noun masc nom sg

Αραρατ pr noun

Αραρι pr noun

ἀραρότως adverb

ἄρας vb 1st aor act part masc nom sg . . . . αἴρω

ἀράς noun fem acc pl . . . . ἀρά

ἀρᾶς noun fem gen sg id.

ἀράσαι vb 1st aor mid impv 2nd pers sg . . . . ἀράομαι

ἀράσασθαι vb 1st aor mid inf id.

ἀράσηται vb 1st aor mid subj 3rd pers sg id.

ἀρᾶσθαι vb pres dep inf id.

ἀράσωμαι vb 1st aor mid subj 1st pers sg id.

ἀρᾶται vb pres dep ind 3rd pers sg id.

ἄρατε vb 1st aor act impv 2nd pers pl . . . . αἴρω

ἀράτω vb 1st aor act impv 3rd pers sg id.

Αραφωθ pr noun

Αραχι pr noun

ἀράχνη noun fem nom sg

ἀράχνην noun fem acc sg . . . . ἀράχνη

ἀράχνης noun fem gen sg id.

Ἀραψ pr noun masc nom sg

Αρβαττοις pr noun

Αρβεσεερ pr noun

Αρβηλα pr noun

Αρβηλοις pr noun masc dat pl . . . . Αρβηλος

Αρβο pr noun

Αρβοκ pr noun

ἀργά adj neut nom and acc pl . . . . ἀργός

ἀργῇ vb pres act subj 3rd pers sg . . . . ἀργέω

ἀργία noun fem nom sg

ἀργίᾳ noun fem dat sg . . . . ἀργία

ἀργίαν noun fem acc sg id.

ἀργίας noun fem gen sg id.

Αργοβ pr noun

ἀργοί adj masc nom pl . . . . ἀργός

ἀργοῖς adj masc and neut dat pl id.

ἀργοῦν vb pres act part neut nom and acc sg . . . . ἀργέω

ἀργοῦντας vb pres act part masc acc pl id.

ἀργυρᾶ adj neut nom and acc pl . . . . ἀργυροῦς

ἀργυραῖ adj fem nom pl id.

ἀργυρᾶν adj fem acc sg id.

ἀργυρᾶς adj fem gen sg and acc pl id.

ἀργυρικῇ adj fem dat sg . . . . ἀργυρικός

ἀργύριον noun neut nom and acc sg

ἀργυρίου noun neut gen sg . . . . ἀργύριον

ἀργυρίῳ noun neut dat sg id.

ἀργυροῖ adj masc nom pl . . . . ἀργυροῦς

ἀργυροῖς adj masc and neut dat pl id.

ἀργυροκοπεῖ vb pres act ind 3rd pers sg . . . . ἀργυροκοπέω

ἀργυροκόπος noun masc nom sg

ἀργυροκόπῳ noun masc dat sg . . . . ἀργυροκόπος

ἀργυρολόγητον noun masc acc sg . . . . . . ἀργυρολόγητος

ἄργυρον noun masc acc sg . . . . ἄργυρος

ἄργυρος noun masc nom sg id.

ἀργύρου noun masc gen sg id.

ἀργυροῦν adj masc acc sg, neut nom and acc sg . . ἀργυροῦς

ἀργυροῦς adj masc nom sg and acc pl id.

ἀργυροχόοις noun masc dat pl . . . . ἀργυροχόος

ἀργύρῳ noun masc dat sg . . . . ἄργυρος

ἀργυρώματα noun neut nom and acc pl . . . . ἀργύρωμα

ἀργυρωμάτων noun neut gen pl id.

ἀργυρῶν adj gen pl . . . . ἀργυροῦς

ἀργυρώνητοι adj masc nom pl . . . . ἀργυρώνητος

ἀργυρώνητον adj masc acc sg, neut nom and acc sg id.

ἀργυρώνητος adj masc nom sg id.

ἀργυρωνήτους adj masc acc pl id.

ἀργῷ adj masc and neut dat sg . . . . ἀργός

ἄρδην adverb

Αρεββα pr noun

Αρεε pr noun

ἀρεῖ vb fut act ind 3rd pers sg . . . . αἴρω

Ἄρειος pr noun masc nom sg

Ἀρειου pr noun masc gen sg . . . . Ἄρειος

ἀρεῖς vb fut act ind 2nd pers sg . . . . αἴρω

Αρεμ pr noun

Αρες pr noun

ἀρέσαι vb 1st aor act inf,

1st aor act opt 3rd pers sg . . . . ἀρέσκω

ἀρεσάτω vb 1st aor act impv 3rd pers sg id.

ἀρέσει vb fut act ind 3rd pers sg id.

ἀρέσῃ vb 1st aor act subj 3rd pers sg,

fut mid ind 2nd pers sg id.

ἀρέσκει vb pres act ind 3rd pers sg id.

ἀρέσκειαι noun fem nom pl . . . . ἀρέσκεια

ἀρέσκῃ vb pres act subj 3rd pers sg . . . . ἀρέσκω

ἀρέσκων vb pres act part masc nom sg id.

ἀρεστά adj neut nom and acc pl . . . . ἀρεστός

ἀρεστή adj fem nom sg id.

ἀρεστόν adj masc acc sg, neut nom and acc sg id.

ἀρεστῶν adj gen pl id.

ἀρεταί noun fem nom pl . . . . ἀρετή

ἀρεταλογίας noun fem gen sg and acc pl . . . . ἀρεταλογία

Ἀρεταν pr noun masc acc sg . . . . Ἀρετας

ἀρετάς noun fem acc pl . . . . ἀρετή

ἀρετή noun fem nom sg id.

ἀρετῇ noun fem dat sg id.

ἀρετήν noun fem acc sg id.

ἀρετῆς noun fem gen sg id.

ἀρετῶν noun fem gen pl id.

ἄρη vb 1st aor act subj 3rd pers sg . . . . αἴρω

ἀρήγειν vb pres act inf	. . . .	ἀρήγω
Αρημα pr noun		
Αρημωθ pr noun		
Αρης pr noun		
ἄρῃς vb 1st aor act subj 2nd pers sg	. . . .	αἴρω
Αρησα pr noun		
ἄρητε vb 1st aor act subj 2nd pers pl	. . . .	αἴρω
Αρθασασθα pr noun		
ἀρθεῖσα vb 1st aor pass part fem nom sg	. . . .	αἴρω
ἀρθῇ vb 1st aor pass subj 3rd pers sg		id.
ἀρθήσεται vb fut pass ind 3rd pers sg		id.
ἀρθήσονται vb fut pass ind 3rd pers pl		id.
ἀρθήτω vb 1st aor pass impv 3rd pers sg		id.
ἄρθρα noun neut nom and acc pl	. . . .	ἄρθρον
ἀρθρέμβολα noun neut nom and acc pl	. . . . .	ἀρθρέμβολον
ἀρθρεμβόλοις noun neut dat pl		id.
Αρια pr noun		
Ἀριαραθη pr noun dat sg	. . . .	Ἀριαραθης
αριηλ translit		
Αριηλ pr noun		
Αριηλι pr noun		
ἀριθμεῖ vb pres act ind 3rd pers sg	. . . .	ἀριθμέω
ἀριθμεῖν vb pres act inf		id.
ἀριθμηθείη vb 1st aor pass opt 3rd pers sg		id.
ἀριθμηθῆναι vb 1st aor pass inf		id.
ἀριθμηθήσεται vb fut pass ind 3rd pers sg		id.
ἀριθμηθήσονται vb fut pass ind 3rd pers pl		id.
ἀριθμῆσαι vb 1st aor act inf		id.
ἀριθμήσατε vb 1st aor act impv 2nd pers pl		id.
ἀριθμήσετε vb fut act ind 2nd pers pl		id.
ἀρίθμησον vb 1st aor act impv 2nd pers sg		id.
ἀριθμητά adj neut nom and acc pl	. . . .	ἀριθμητός
ἀριθμηταί vb pres m/p subj 3rd pers sg	. . . .	ἀριθμέω
ἀριθμητοί adj masc nom pl	. . . .	ἀριθμητός
ἀριθμοί noun masc nom pl	. . . .	ἀριθμός
ἀριθμόν noun masc acc sg		id.
ἀριθμός noun masc nom sg		id.
ἀριθμοῦ noun masc gen sg		id.
ἀριθμοῦντος vb pres act part masc and neut gen sg		ἀριθμέω
ἀριθμῷ noun masc dat sg	. . . .	ἀριθμός
ἀριθμῶν noun masc gen pl		id.
ἀριθμῶν vb pres act part masc nom sg	. . . .	ἀριθμέω
Αριμ pr noun		
Αριμα pr noun		
ἀριστᾶν vb pres act inf	. . . .	ἀριστάω
ἀριστείας noun fem gen sg	. . . .	ἀριστεία
ἀριστερά adj fem nom sg, neut nom and acc pl	.	ἀριστερός
ἀριστερᾷ adj fem dat sg		id.
ἀριστεραῖς adj fem dat pl		id.
ἀριστεράν adj fem acc sg		id.
ἀριστερᾶς adj fem gen sg		id.
ἀριστερόν adj masc acc sg, neut nom and acc sg		

ἀριστερῶν adj gen pl	. . . .	ἀριστερός
ἀριστεῦσαι vb 1st aor act inf	. . . .	ἀριστεύω
ἀριστῆσαι vb 1st aor act inf	. . . .	ἀριστάω
ἀρίστησον vb 1st aor act impv 2nd pers sg		id.
Ἀριστοβούλῳ pr noun masc dat sg	. . . .	Ἀριστοβουλος
ἄριστον noun neut nom and acc sg		
ἄριστος superl adj masc nom sg	. . . .	ἀγαθός
ἀρίστου noun neut gen sg	. . . .	ἄριστον
ἀρίστων superl adj gen pl	. . . .	ἀγαθός
Αρισωθ pr noun		
Αριφ pr noun		
Αριφου pr noun gen sg	. . . .	Αριφος
αριωθ translit		
Αριωργιμ pr noun		
Αριωχ pr noun		
Αριωχη pr noun masc dat sg	. . . .	Αριωχης
Αριωχης pr noun masc nom sg		id.
ἀρκεῖ vb pres act ind 3rd pers sg	. . . .	ἀρκέω
Αρκεσαιος pr noun		
ἀρκέσει vb fut act ind 3rd pers sg	. . . .	ἀρκέω
ἀρκεσθείς vb 1st aor pass part masc nom sg		id.
ἀρκέσουσιν vb fut act ind 3rd pers pl		id.
ἀρκεύθινα adj neut nom and acc pl	. . . .	ἀρκεύθινος
ἀρκευθίνων adj gen pl		id.
ἄρκευθος noun fem nom sg		
ἄρκοι noun masc or fem nom pl	. . . .	ἄρκος
ἄρκοις noun masc or fem dat pl		id.
ἄρκον noun masc or fem acc sg		id.
ἄρκος noun masc or fem nom sg		id.
ἄρκου noun masc or fem gen sg		id.
ἀρκοῦν vb pres act part neut nom and acc sg	. . . . . .	ἀρκέω
Ἀρκτοῦρον pr noun masc acc sg	. . . .	Ἀρκτοῦρος
ἄρκῳ noun masc dat sg	. . . .	ἄρκος
ἄρκων noun masc gen pl		id.
ἅρμα noun neut nom and acc sg		
Αρμαθαιμ pr noun		
Αρμαι pr noun		
Αρμαιθ pr noun		
ἅρμεσι noun neut dat pl	. . . .	ἅρμα
ἅρματα noun neut nom and acc pl		id.
ἁρματηλάτην noun masc acc sg	. . . .	ἁρματηλάτης
ἅρματι noun neut dat sg	. . . .	ἅρμα
ἅρματος noun neut gen sg		id.
ἁρμάτων noun neut gen pl		id.
Αρμε pr noun		
Ἀρμενιαν pr noun fem acc sg	. . . .	Ἀρμενια
ἁρμόζεται vb pres m/p ind 3rd pers sg	. . . .	ἁρμόζω
ἁρμόζουσα vb pres act part fem nom sg		id.
ἁρμόζουσαν vb pres act part fem acc sg		id.
ἁρμονίαν noun fem acc sg	. . . .	ἁρμονία
ἁρμονίας noun fem gen sg		id.
ἁρμόνιον adj acc sg, neut nom sg	. . . .	ἁρμόνιος

ἄρμοσαι vb 1st aor mid impv 2nd pers sg .... ἁρμόζω

ἁρμόσει vb fut act ind 3rd pers sg   id.

ἁρμῶν noun masc gen pl .... ἁρμός

Αρνα pr noun

ἄρνα noun masc acc sg .... ἀρήν

ἄρνας noun masc acc pl   id.

ἄρνασι noun masc dat pl   id.

ἀρνάσι see ἄρνασι

Αρναφαρ pr noun

ἄρνες noun masc nom pl .... ἀρήν

ἀρνησάμενοι vb 1st aor mid part masc nom pl .. ἀρνέομαι

ἀρνήσομαι vb fut act ind 1st pers sg   id.

ἀρνία noun neut nom and acc pl .... ἀρνίον

ἀρνίον noun neut nom and acc sg   id.

ἀρνός noun masc gen sg .... ἀρήν

ἀρνούμενοι vb pres dep part masc nom pl ...... ἀρνέομαι

Αρνων pr noun

ἀρνῶν noun masc gen pl .... ἀρήν

ἄρξαι vb 1st aor act inf, 1st aor act opt 3rd pers sg .... ἄρχω

ἀρξάμενον vb 1st aor mid part masc acc sg,

           neut nom and acc sg   id.

ἀρξάμενος vb 1st aor mid part masc nom sg   id.

ἀρξαμένου vb 1st aor mid part masc and neut gen sg   id.

ἀρξαμένῳ vb 1st aor mid part masc and neut dat sg   id.

ἄρξαντες vb 1st aor act part masc nom pl   id.

ἄρξασθαι vb 1st aor mid inf   id.

ἄρξασθε vb 1st aor mid impv 2nd pers pl   id.

ἄρξει vb fut act ind 3rd pers sg   id.

ἄρξεις vb fut act ind 2nd pers sg   id.

ἄρξεται vb fut mid ind 3rd pers sg   id.

ἄρξῃ vb fut mid ind 2nd pers sg   id.

ἄρξηται vb 1st aor mid subj 3rd pers sg   id.

ἄρξομαι vb fut mid ind 1st pers sg   id.

ἄρξον vb 1st aor act impv 2nd pers sg   id.

ἄρξουσιν vb fut act ind 3rd pers pl   id.

ἄρξω vb fut act ind 1st pers sg   id.

ἄρξωμαι vb 1st aor mid subj 1st pers sg   id.

ἀρξώμεθα vb 1st aor mid subj 1st pers pl   id.

Αροαδι pr noun

Αροηδις pr noun

Αροηλις pr noun

Αροηρ pr noun

Αρομ pr noun

ἆρον vb 1st aor act impv 2nd pers sg .... αἴρω

ἀροτῆρες noun masc nom pl .... ἀροτήρ

ἄροτρα noun neut nom and acc pl .... ἄροτρον

ἀροτρία vb pres act impv 2nd pers sg .... ἀροτριάω

ἀροτριαθήσεται vb fut pass ind 3rd pers sg   id.

ἀροτριᾶν vb pres act inf   id.

ἀροτριάσει vb fut act ind 3rd pers sg   id.

ἀροτριάσεις vb fut act ind 2nd pers sg   id.

ἀροτρίασις noun fem nom sg

ἀροτριώμενον vb pres m/p part masc acc sg .... ἀροτριάω

ἀροτριῶν vb pres act part masc nom sg   id.

ἀροτριῶντας vb pres act part masc acc pl   id.

ἄροτρον noun neut nom and acc sg

ἀροτρόποδι noun masc dat sg .... ἀροτρόπους

ἀρότρου noun neut gen sg .... ἄροτρον

Αρουδαῖος pr noun masc gen sg

Αρουηλ pr noun

Αρουκαῖον pr noun masc acc sg .... Αρουκαῖος

Αρουρ pr noun

ἄρουραν noun fem acc sg .... ἄρουρα

Αρους pr noun

ἀροῦσιν vb fut act ind 3rd pers pl .... αἴρω

Αρουφαιον pr noun masc acc sg .... Αρουφαιος

Αρουχαῖος pr noun masc nom sg

ἁρπαγαί noun fem nom pl .... ἁρπαγή

ἁρπαγή noun fem nom sg   id.

ἁρπαγήν noun fem acc sg   id.

ἁρπαγῆς noun fem gen sg   id.

ἅρπαγμα noun neut nom and acc sg

ἁρπάγματα noun neut nom and acc pl .... ἅρπαγμα

ἁρπάγματι noun neut dat sg   id.

ἁρπάζειν vb pres act inf .... ἁρπάζω

ἁρπάζοντες vb pres act part masc nom pl   id.

ἁρπάζων vb pres act part masc nom sg   id.

ἅρπαξ adj masc nom sg

ἁρπάσαι vb 1st aor act inf .... ἁρπάζω

ἁρπάσαντες vb 1st aor act part masc nom pl   id.

ἁρπάσατε vb 1st aor act impv 2nd pers pl   id.

ἁρπάσεις vb fut act ind 2nd pers sg   id.

ἁρπάσετε vb fut act ind 2nd pers pl   id.

ἁρπάσῃ vb 1st aor act subj 3rd pers sg   id.

ἁρπᾶται vb fut mid ind 3rd pers sg   id.

ἁρπῶμαι vb fut mid ind 1st pers sg   id.

ἀρραβῶνα noun masc acc sg .... ἀρραβών

Αρραν pr noun

ἄρρενα adj masc acc sg .... ἄρσην

ἀρρενωδῶς adverb

ἀρρένων noun masc gen pl .... ἄρσην

ἀρρήκτοις adj dat pl .... ἄρρηκτος

ἄρριζος adj masc and fem nom sg

ἀρρωστεῖν vb pres act inf .... ἀρρωστέω

ἀρρώστημα noun neut nom and acc sg

ἀρρωστήματι noun neut dat sg .... ἀρρώστημα

ἀρρωστῆσαι vb 1st aor act inf .... ἀρρωστέω

ἀρρωστία noun fem nom sg

ἀρρωστίᾳ noun fem dat sg .... ἀρρωστία

ἀρρωστίαν noun fem acc sg   id.

ἀρρωστίας noun fem gen sg   id.

ἄρρωστον adj acc sg, neut nom sg .... ἄρρωστος

Αρσαιον pr noun masc acc sg .... Αρσαιος

Ἀρσάκῃ pr noun masc dat sg .... Ἀρσάκης

Ἀρσακην pr noun masc acc sg . . . . Ἀρσακης
Ἀρσακης pr noun masc nom sg   id.
ἄρσεις noun fem nom and acc pl . . . . ἄρσις
ἄρσεν adj neut nom and acc sg . . . . ἄρσην
ἄρσενα adj neut nom and acc pl   id.
ἄρσενες adj masc and fem nom pl   id.
ἄρσενι adj dat sg   id.
ἀρσενικά adj neut nom and acc pl . . . . ἀρσενικός
ἀρσενικάς adj fem acc pl   id.
ἀρσενικόν adj masc acc sg, neut nom and acc sg   id.
ἀρσενικοῦ adj masc and neut gen sg   id.
ἀρσενικῷ adj masc and neut dat sg   id.
ἀρσενικῶν adj gen pl   id.
ἄρσενος adj gen sg . . . . ἄρσην
ἄρσεσιν noun fem dat pl . . . . ἄρσις
ἄρσεων noun fem gen pl   id.
ἄρσην adj masc and fem nom sg
ἄρσιν noun fem acc sg . . . . ἄρσις
Ἀρσινοη pr noun fem nom sg
Ἀρσινοην pr noun fem acc sg . . . . Ἀρσινοη
ἄρσις noun fem nom sg
Αρσωλα pr noun
Αρσων pr noun
ἀρτά noun neut nom and acc pl . . . . ἄρτος
ἀρτάβαι noun fem nom pl . . . . ἀρτάβη
ἀρτάβας noun fem acc pl   id.
Ἀρταξερξῃ pr noun masc dat sg . . . . Ἀρταξερξης
Ἀρταξερξην pr noun masc acc sg   id.
Ἀρταξερξης pr noun masc nom sg   id.
Ἀρταξερξου pr noun masc gen sg   id.
ἀρτῆρσι noun masc dat pl . . . . ἀρτήρ
ἄρτι adverb
ἀρτίως adverb
ἄρτοι noun masc nom pl . . . . ἄρτος
ἄρτοις noun masc dat pl   id.
ἀρτοκοπικόν adj masc acc sg,
          neut nom and acc sg . . . . ἀρτοκοπικός
ἄρτον noun masc acc sg . . . . ἄρτος
ἄρτος noun masc nom sg   id.
ἄρτου noun masc gen sg   id.
ἄρτους noun masc acc pl   id.
ἄρτῳ noun masc dat sg   id.
ἄρτων noun masc gen pl   id.
Αρφαδ pr noun
Αρφαθ pr noun
Αρφαξαδ pr noun
Αρχαβιν pr noun
Αρχαδ pr noun
ἀρχαί noun fem nom pl . . . . ἀρχή
ἀρχαία adj fem nom sg . . . . ἀρχαῖος
ἀρχαῖα adj neut nom and acc pl   id.
ἀρχαίαις adj fem dat pl   id.

ἀρχαίαν adj fem acc sg . . . . ἀρχαῖος
ἀρχαίας adj fem gen sg and acc pl   id.
ἀρχαῖον adj masc acc sg, neut nom and acc sg   id.
ἀρχαῖς noun fem dat pl . . . . ἀρχή
ἀρχαίων adj gen pl . . . . ἀρχαῖος
ἀρχάς noun fem acc pl . . . . ἀρχή
ἄρχε vb pres act impv 2nd pers sg . . . . ἄρχω
ἄρχει vb pres act ind 3rd pers sg   id.
ἄρχειν vb pres act inf   id.
ἄρχεις vb pres act ind 2nd pers sg   id.
ἄρχεται vb pres m/p ind 3rd pers sg   id.
ἄρχετε vb pres act ind 2nd pers pl   id.
ἀρχέτωσαν vb pres act impv 3rd pers pl   id.
ἀρχή noun fem nom sg
ἀρχῇ noun fem dat sg . . . . ἀρχή
ἀρχηγέτη noun masc dat sg . . . . ἀρχηγέτης
ἀρχηγοί noun masc nom pl . . . . ἀρχηγός
ἀρχηγοῖς noun masc dat pl   id.
ἀρχηγόν noun masc acc sg   id.
ἀρχηγός noun masc nom sg   id.
ἀρχηγούς noun masc acc pl   id.
ἀρχηγῶν noun masc gen pl   id.
ἀρχῆθεν adverb
ἀρχήν noun fem acc sg . . . . ἀρχή
ἀρχῆς noun fem gen sg   id.
Αρχι pr noun
ἀρχιδεσμοφύλακος noun masc gen sg . . ἀρχιδεσμοφύλαξ
ἀρχιδεσμοφύλαξ noun masc nom sg   id.
ἀρχιδεσμώτης noun masc nom sg
ἀρχιερᾶσθαι vb pres dep inf . . . . ἀρχιεράομαι
ἀρχιερατεύειν vb pres act inf . . . . ἀρχιερατεύω
ἀρχιερέα noun masc acc sg . . . . ἀρχιερεύς
ἀρχιερεῖ noun masc dat sg   id.
ἀρχιερεύς noun masc nom sg   id.
ἀρχιερέως noun masc gen sg   id.
ἀρχιερωσύνην noun fem acc sg . . . . ἀρχιερωσύνη
ἀρχιερωσύνης noun fem gen sg   id.
ἀρχιευνοῦχον noun masc acc sg . . . . ἀρχιευνοῦχος
ἀρχιευνοῦχος noun masc nom sg   id.
ἀρχιευνούχου noun masc gen sg   id.
ἀρχιευνούχῳ noun masc dat sg   id.
ἀρχιμάγειρον noun masc acc sg . . . . ἀρχιμάγειρος
ἀρχιμάγειρος noun masc nom sg   id.
ἀρχιμαγείρου noun masc gen sg   id.
ἀρχιμαγείρῳ noun masc dat sg   id.
ἀρχιοινοχοΐαν noun fem acc sg . . . . ἀρχιοινοχοΐα
ἀρχιοινοχόον noun masc acc sg . . . . ἀρχιοινοχόος
ἀρχιοινοχόος noun masc nom sg   id.
ἀρχιοινοχόου noun masc gen sg   id.
ἀρχιοινοχόῳ noun masc dat sg   id.
ἀρχιπατριῶται noun masc nom pl . . . . . . ἀρχιπατριώτης
ἀρχισιτοποιόν noun masc acc sg . . . . ἀρχισιτοποιός

ἀρχισιτοποιός noun masc nom sg
ἀρχισιτοποιοῦ noun masc gen sg . . . . ἀρχισιτοποιός
ἀρχισιτοποιῷ noun masc dat sg   id.
ἀρχιστράτηγον noun masc acc sg . . . . . ἀρχιστράτηγος
ἀρχιστράτηγος noun masc nom sg   id.
ἀρχιστρατήγου noun masc gen sg   id.
ἀρχιστρατήγῳ noun masc dat sg   id.
ἀρχισωματοφύλακα noun masc

     acc sg . . . . ἀρχισωματοφύλαξ
ἀρχισωματοφύλακες noun masc nom pl   id.
ἀρχιτέκτονα noun masc acc sg . . . . ἀρχιτέκτων
ἀρχιτεκτονεῖν vb pres act inf . . . . ἀρχιτεκτονέω
ἀρχιτεκτονῆσαι vb 1st aor act inf   id.
ἀρχιτέκτονι noun masc dat sg . . . . ἀρχιτέκτων
ἀρχιτεκτονίας noun fem gen sg . . . . ἀρχιτεκτονία
ἀρχιτέκτων noun masc nom sg
ἀρχίφυλοι noun masc nom pl . . . . ἀρχίφυλος
ἀρχιφύλους noun masc acc pl   id.
ἄρχομαι vb pres m/p ind 1st pers sg . . . . ἄρχω
ἀρχομένης vb pres m/p part fem gen sg   id.
ἄρχοντα noun masc acc sg . . . . ἄρχων
ἄρχοντας noun masc acc pl   id.
ἄρχοντες noun masc nom pl   id.
ἄρχοντι noun masc dat sg   id.
ἄρχοντος noun masc gen sg   id.
ἀρχόντων noun masc gen pl   id.
ἄρχου vb pres m/p impv 2nd pers sg . . . . ἄρχω
ἄρχουσα vb pres act part fem nom sg   id.
ἄρχουσαι vb pres act part fem nom pl   id.
ἀρχούσας vb pres act part fem acc pl   id.
ἄρχουσι(ν) noun masc dat pl . . . . ἄρχων
ἀρχουσῶν vb pres act part fem gen pl . . . . ἄρχω
Αρχυαῖοι pr noun
Αρχωβ pr noun
ἄρχων noun masc nom sg
ἀρῶ vb fut act ind 1st pers sg . . . . αἴρω
Αρωδαῖος pr noun masc nom sg
Αρωδιτης pr noun masc nom sg
Αρωεδ pr noun
Αρωθ pr noun
ἀρώμασι noun neut dat pl . . . . ἄρωμα
ἀρώματα noun neut nom and acc pl   id.
ἀρώματος noun neut gen sg   id.
ἀρωμάτων noun neut gen pl   id.
ἄρωμεν vb 1st aor act subj 1st pers pl . . . . αἴρω
Αρωνι pr noun
Αρωνιιμ pr noun
ἅς rel pron fem acc pl . . . . ὅς
Ασα pr noun
Ασαβαλ pr noun
Ασαβδανα pr noun
Ασαβια pr noun

Ασαβιαν pr noun masc acc sg . . . . Ασαβιας
Ασαβιας pr noun masc nom sg
Ασαδια pr noun
Ασαδιου pr noun . . . . Ασαδιας
Ασαηλ pr noun
Ασαηλος pr noun
Ασαια pr noun
Ασαια pr noun masc dat sg . . . . Ασαιας
Ασαιας pr noun masc nom sg   id.
ἀσάλευτον adj acc sg, neut nom sg . . . . ἀσάλευτος
Ασαν pr noun
Ασανα pr noun
Ασαρ pr noun
Ασαρα pr noun
Ασαραδδων pr noun
Ασαραι pr noun
ασαραμελ translit
ασαρημωθ translit
Ασαρμωθ pr noun
Ασαρσουλα pr noun
Ασας pr noun
Ασασανθαμαρ pr noun
ἄσατε vb 1st aor act impv 2nd pers pl . . . . ἄδω
ἀσάτωσαν vb 1st aor act impv 3rd pers pl   id.
Ασαφ pr noun
Ασβαν pr noun
Ασβανια pr noun
Ασβασαρεθ pr noun
Ασβηλ pr noun
Ασβίτου pr noun masc gen sg . . . . Ασβιτης
ἀσβόλην noun fem acc sg . . . . ἀσβόλη
Ασγαδ pr noun
Ασγαθ pr noun
Ασδωδ pr noun
ἀσεβεῖ adj dat sg . . . . ἀσεβής
ἀσέβεια noun fem nom sg
ἀσεβείᾳ noun fem dat sg . . . . ἀσέβεια
ἀσέβειαι noun fem nom pl   id.
ἀσεβείαις noun fem dat pl   id.
ἀσέβειαν noun fem acc sg   id.
ἀσεβείας noun fem gen sg and acc pl   id.
ἀσεβεῖν vb pres act inf . . . . ἀσεβέω
ἀσεβεῖς adj masc and fem nom and acc pl . . . . ἀσεβής
ἀσεβεῖτε vb pres act impv 2nd pers pl . . . . ἀσεβέω
ἀσεβειῶν noun fem gen pl . . . . ἀσέβεια
ἀσεβές adj neut nom and acc sg . . . . ἀσεβής
ἀσεβέσι adj dat pl   id.
ἀσεβέστατε superl adj masc voc sg   id.
ἀσεβῆ adj masc and fem acc sg, adj neut nom and acc pl id.
Ασεβηβιαν pr noun masc acc sg . . . . 'Ασεβηβιας
ἀσέβημα noun neut nom and acc sg
ἀσεβήματα noun neut nom and acc pl . . . . ἀσέβημα

ἀσεβής adj masc and fem nom sg
ἀσεβῆσαι vb 1st aor act inf . . . . ἀσεβέω
ἀσεβήσαντα vb 1st aor act part masc acc sg id.
ἀσεβήσαντας vb 1st aor act part masc acc pl id.
ἀσεβήσας vb 1st aor act part masc nom sg id.
ἀσεβήσει vb fut act ind 3rd pers sg id.
ἀσεβήσῃ vb 1st aor act subj 3rd pers sg id.
ἀσεβήσῃς vb 1st aor act subj 2nd pers sg id.
Ασεβι pr noun
Ασεβια pr noun
Ασεβιαν pr noun masc acc sg . . . . Ασεβια
ἀσεβοῦς adj gen sg . . . . ἀσεβής
ἀσεβοῦσιν vb pres act ind 3rd pers pl . . . . ἀσεβέω
Ασεβων pr noun
ἀσεβῶν adj gen pl . . . . ἀσεβής
ἀσεβῶν vb pres act part masc nom sg . . . . ἀσεβέω
Ασεδωθ pr noun
ἀσέλγεια noun fem nom sg
ἀσελγείαις noun fem dat pl . . . . ἀσέλγεια
ασελισι translit
Ασεμ pr noun
Ασεμωνα pr noun
Ασενα pr noun
Ασεννα pr noun
Ασενναιον pr noun masc acc sg . . . . Ασενναιος
Ασενναφαρ pr noun
Ασεννεθ pr noun
Ασεργαδδα pr noun
Ασεριηλ pr noun
Ασερναιν pr noun
Ασερσουαλ pr noun
Ασερσουσιμ pr noun
Ασερων pr noun
Ασεφηραθ pr noun
Ασηδωθ pr noun
Ασηλ pr noun
ἄσημα adj neut nom and acc pl . . . . ἄσημος
ἄσημον adj acc sg, neut nom sg id.
ἄσηπτα adj neut nom and acc pl . . . . ἄσηπτος
ἄσηπτον adj acc sg, neut nom sg id.
ἀσήπτους adj masc and fem acc pl id.
ἀσήπτων adj gen pl id.
Ασηρ pr noun
ασηρωθ translit
Ασηρωθ pr noun
ἀσθένεια noun fem nom sg
ἀσθενείᾳ noun fem dat sg . . . . ἀσθένεια
ἀσθένειαι noun fem nom pl id.
ἀσθένειαν noun fem acc sg id.
ἀσθενεῖς adj masc and fem nom and acc pl . . . . . . ἀσθενής
ἀσθενείτω vb pres act impv 3rd pers sg . . . . ἀσθενέω
ἀσθενές adj neut nom and acc sg . . . . ἀσθενής

ἀσθενῆ adj masc and fem acc sg,
    neut nom and acc pl . . . . ἀσθενής
ἀσθενής adj masc and fem nom sg id.
ἀσθενῆσαι vb 1st aor act inf . . . . ἀσθενέω
ἀσθενήσας vb 1st aor act part masc nom sg id.
ἀσθενήσει vb fut act ind 3rd pers sg id.
ἀσθενήσεις vb fut act ind 2nd pers sg id.
ἀσθενήσῃ vb 1st aor act subj 3rd pers sg id.
ἀσθενήσουσιν vb fut act ind 3rd pers pl id.
ἀσθενήσω vb 1st aor act subj 1st pers sg,
    fut act ind 1st pers sg id.
ἀσθενοῦμεν vb pres act ind 1st pers pl id.
ἀσθενοῦν vb pres act part neut nom and acc sg id.
ἀσθενοῦντας vb pres act part masc acc pl id.
ἀσθενοῦντες vb pres act part masc nom pl id.
ἀσθενοῦντος vb pres act part masc and neut gen sg id.
ἀσθενούντων vb pres act part masc and neut gen pl id.
ἀσθενούς adj gen sg . . . . ἀσθενής
ἀσθενοῦσαν vb pres act part fem acc sg . . . . ἀσθενέω
ἀσθενόψυχοι adj masc and fem nom pl . . . . . ἀσθενόψυχος
ἀσθενῶν adj gen pl . . . . ἀσθενής
ἀσθενῶν vb pres act part masc nom sg . . . . ἀσθενέω
Ασθηραν pr noun
ἄσθμα noun neut nom and acc sg
ἀσθμαίνει vb pres act ind 3rd pers sg . . . . ἀσθμαίνω
'Ασιαν pr noun fem acc sg . . . . 'Ασια
'Ασιας pr noun fem gen sg id.
Ασιβιας pr noun masc nom sg
ασιδα translit
Ασιδαιοι pr noun masc nom pl . . . . Ασιδαιος
Ασιδαίων pr noun masc gen pl id.
ἀσίδηρον adj acc sg, neut nom sg . . . . ἀσίδηρος
Ασιδων pr noun
Ασιεδωθ pr noun
Ασιηλ pr noun
Ασιηλι pr noun
Ασιθ pr noun
Ασιμαθ pr noun
Ασιμουθ pr noun
Ασιμωθ pr noun
ἀσινεῖς adj masc and fem nom and acc pl . . . . ἀσινής
ἀσινῆ adj masc and fem acc sg id.
Ασιρ pr noun
ἀσιτήσομεν vb fut act ind 1st pers pl . . . . ἀσιτέω
ἀσιτί adverb
ἀσιτοῦντες vb pres act part masc nom pl . . . . ἀσιτέω
Ασιφα pr noun
'Ασκαλων pr noun fem nom sg
'Ασκαλῶνα pr noun fem acc sg . . . . 'Ασκαλων
'Ασκαλῶνι pr noun fem dat sg id.
'Ασκαλωνῖται pr noun masc nom pl . . . . . . 'Ασκαλωνίτης
'Ασκαλωνιτη pr noun masc dat sg id.

'Ασκαλῶνος pr noun fem gen sg . . . . 'Ασκαλών
ἀσκεῖν vb pres act inf . . . . ἀσκέω
ἀσκήσεως noun fem gen sg . . . . ἄσκησις
ἀσκητάς noun masc acc pl . . . . ἀσκητής
ἀσκοί noun masc nom pl . . . . ἀσκός
ἀσκόν noun masc acc sg   id.
ἀσκοπυτίνην noun fem acc sg . . . . ἀσκοπυτίνη
ἀσκός noun masc nom sg
ἀσκοῦ noun masc gen sg . . . . ἀσκός
ἀσκούς noun masc acc pl   id.
ἀσκῷ noun masc dat sg   id.
Ασμα pr noun
ᾆσμα noun neut nom and acc sg
ᾄσματος noun neut gen sg . . . . ᾆσμα
ᾀσμάτων noun neut gen pl   id.
ἄσμενοι adj masc nom pl . . . . ἄσμενος
ἀσμένως adverb
Ασμοδαιον pr noun masc acc sg . . . . Ασμοδαιος
Ασμοδαῖος pr noun masc nom sg
Ασμοδαυν pr noun masc acc sg . . . . Ασμοδαυς
Ασμοδαυς pr noun masc nom sg
Ασμωθ pr noun
Ασνα pr noun
Ασοβαεσδ pr noun
Ασομ pr noun
ᾄσομαι vb fut mid ind 1st pers sg . . . . ᾄδω
ᾄσομεν vb fut act ind 1st pers pl   id.
ᾆσον vb 1st aor act impv 2nd pers sg   id.
ᾄσονται vb fut mid ind 3rd pers pl   id.
Ασορ pr noun
Ασορδαν pr noun
Ασοριωναιν pr noun
Ασουβ pr noun
Ασουβε pr noun
Ασουηρου pr noun masc gen sg . . . . Ασουηρος
Ασουρ pr noun
Ασουφε pr noun
ἀσπαζομένων vb pres dep part gen pl . . . . ἀσπάζομαι
ἀσπάλαθος noun masc nom sg
ἀσπάλαξ noun masc nom sg
ἀσπάσασθαι vb 1st aor mid inf . . . . ἀσπάζομαι
ἀσπασομένους vb fut mid part masc acc pl   id.
ἀσπίδα noun fem acc sg . . . . ἀσπίς
ἀσπίδας noun fem acc pl   id.
ἀσπίδες noun fem nom pl   id.
ἀσπίδι noun fem dat sg   id.
ἀσπιδίσκαις noun fem dat pl . . . . ἀσπιδίσκη
ἀσπιδίσκας noun fem acc pl   id.
ἀσπίδος noun fem gen sg . . . . ἀσπίς
ἀσπίδων noun fem gen pl   id.
ἀσπίς noun fem nom sg   id.
Ασρων pr noun

Ασρωνι pr noun
Ασσα pr noun
Ασσαθων pr noun
Ασσαλιμωθ pr noun
Ασσαρες pr noun
Ασσαρι pr noun
Ασσαφιωθ pr noun
Ασσηρ pr noun
Ασσουρ pr noun
Ασσουριμ pr noun
'Ασσυριας pr noun fem gen sg . . . . 'Ασσυρια
'Ασσυριοι pr noun masc nom pl . . . . 'Ασσυριος
'Ασσυριοις pr noun masc dat pl   id.
'Ασσυριον pr noun masc acc sg   id.
'Ασσυριος pr noun masc nom sg   id.
'Ασσυριου pr noun masc gen sg   id.
'Ασσυριους pr noun masc acc pl   id.
'Ασσυριων pr noun masc gen pl   id.
ἀσταθῆ adj masc and fem acc sg . . . . ἀσταθής
'Ασταρταις pr noun fem dat pl . . . . 'Ασταρτη
'Ασταρτεῖον pr noun neut nom and acc sg
'Ασταρτη pr noun fem dat sg . . . . 'Ασταρτη
'Ασταρτην pr noun fem acc sg   id.
Ασταρωθ pr noun
Ασταρωθι pr noun
Αστατωθι pr noun
Ασταωλ pr noun
ἄστεγον adj acc sg, neut nom sg . . . . ἄστεγος
ἄστεγος adj masc and fem nom sg   id.
ἀστέγους adj masc and fem acc pl   id.
ἀστεία adj fem nom sg . . . . ἀστεῖος
ἀστείαν adj fem acc sg   id.
ἀστεῖον adj masc acc sg, neut nom and acc sg   id.
ἀστεῖος adj masc nom sg   id.
ἀστείως adverb
ἄστεκτος adj masc and fem nom sg
ἀστέρας noun masc acc pl . . . . ἀστήρ
ἀστέρες noun masc nom pl   id.
ἀστέρων noun masc gen pl   id.
ἀστήρ noun masc nom sg   id.
Αστιν pr noun
ἀστόχει vb pres act impv 2nd pers sg . . . . ἀστοχέω
ἄστρα noun neut nom and acc pl . . . . ἄστρον
ἀστράγαλος noun masc nom sg
ἀστραγάλους noun masc acc pl . . . . ἀστράγαλος
ἀστραπαί noun fem nom pl . . . . ἀστραπή
ἀστραπάς noun fem acc pl   id.
ἀστραπή noun fem nom sg   id.
ἀστραπήν noun fem acc sg   id.
ἀστραπῆς noun fem gen sg   id.
ἀστράπτοντας vb pres act part masc acc pl . . . . . ἀστράπτω
ἀστραπῶν noun fem gen pl . . . . ἀστραπή

ἄστραψον vb 1st aor act impv 2nd pers sg . . . . . ἀστράπτω
ἄστροις noun neut dat pl . . . . ἄστρον
ἀστρολόγοι noun masc nom pl . . . . ἀστρολόγος
ἄστρον noun neut nom and acc sg
ἄστρων noun neut gen pl . . . . ἄστρον
Ἀστυαγης pr noun masc nom sg
ἀστυγείτονας adj masc and fem acc pl . . . . . ἀστυγείτων
Ασυβηρ pr noun
Ασυβηρι pr noun
Ασυηρος pr noun
ἀσυλία noun fem dat sg . . . . ἀσυλία
ἄσυλον adj acc sg, neut nom sg . . . . ἄσυλος
ἀσύλου adj gen sg . . . . id.
ἀσύμφορον adj acc sg, neut nom sg . . . . ἀσύμφορος
ἀσύμφωνον adj acc sg, neut nom sg . . . . ἀσύμφωνος
ἀσύμφωνος adj masc and fem nom sg . . . . id.
ἀσύνετοι adj masc and fem nom pl . . . . ἀσύνετος
ἀσύνετον adj acc sg, neut nom sg . . . . id.
ἀσύνετος adj masc and fem nom sg . . . . id.
ἀσυνέτου adj gen sg . . . . id.
ἀσυνέτῳ adj dat sg . . . . id.
ἀσυνέτων adj gen pl . . . . id.
ἀσυνετώτερος comp adj masc nom sg . . . . id.
ἀσυνθεσία noun fem dat sg . . . . ἀσυνθεσία
ἀσυνθεσίαν noun fem acc sg . . . . id.
ἀσυνθετῆσαι vb 1st aor act inf . . . . ἀσυνθετέω
ἀσυνθετήσητε vb 1st aor act subj 2nd pers pl . . . . . id.
ἀσύνθετος adj masc and fem nom sg
ἀσυνθέτου adj gen sg . . . . ἀσύνθετος
ἀσυνθετοῦντας vb pres act part masc acc pl . . . ἀσυνθετέω
ἀσυρῆ adj masc and fem acc sg . . . . ἀσυρής
ἀσφάλεια noun fem nom sg
ἀσφαλείᾳ noun fem dat sg . . . . ἀσφάλεια
ἀσφάλειαν noun fem acc sg . . . . id.
ἀσφαλείας noun fem gen sg . . . . id.
ἀσφαλεῖς adj masc and fem nom and acc pl . . . . . . ἀσφαλής
ἀσφαλές adj neut nom and acc sg . . . . id.
ἀσφαλῆ adj masc and fem acc sg, neut nom and acc pl . . id.
ἀσφαλής adj masc and fem nom sg . . . . id.
ἀσφαλισάμενος vb 1st aor mid part
     masc nom sg . . . . ἀσφαλίζω
ἀσφαλτοπίσσῃ noun fem dat sg . . . . ἀσφαλτόπισσα
ἄσφαλτος noun fem nom sg
ἀσφάλτου noun fem gen sg . . . . ἄσφαλτος
ἀσφάλτῳ noun fem dat sg . . . . id.
ἀσφαλτώσεις vb fut act ind 2nd pers sg . . . . ἀσφαλτόω
ἀσφαλῶς adverb
Ασφανες pr noun
Ασφαρ pr noun
Ασφαρασου pr noun gen sg . . . . Ασφαρασος
Ασχα pr noun
Ασχαζι pr noun

Ασχαν pr noun fem acc sg . . . . Ασχα
Ασχαναζ pr noun
Ασχαναζαιοις pr noun masc dat pl . . . . Ασχαναζαιος
ἄσχημον adj nom sg, neut acc sg . . . . ἀσχήμων
ἀσχήμονα adj masc and fem acc sg . . . . id.
ἀσχημονήσει vb fut act ind 3rd pers sg . . . . . . ἀσχημονέω
ἀσχήμονι adj dat sg . . . . ἀσχήμων
ἀσχημονοῦσα vb pres act part fem nom sg . . . . ἀσχημονέω
ἀσχημονοῦσαν vb pres act part fem acc sg . . . . . . id.
ἀσχημοσύνη noun fem nom sg
ἀσχημοσύνη noun fem dat sg . . . . ἀσχημοσύνη
ἀσχημοσύνην noun fem acc sg . . . . id.
ἀσχημοσύνης noun fem gen sg . . . . id.
ἀσχοληθήσεται vb fut pass ind 3rd pers sg . . . . . . ἀσχολέω
ἀσχολία noun fem nom sg
ἀσχολίαν noun fem acc sg . . . . ἀσχολία
Ασχωδ pr noun
ᾄσω vb fut act ind 1st pers sg . . . . ᾄδω
Ασωβ pr noun
Ασωθι pr noun
Ασωθιτου pr noun masc gen sg . . . . Ασωθιτης
ᾄσωμεν vb 1st aor act subj 1st pers pl . . . . ᾄδω
Ασωνειος pr noun masc nom sg
Ασωρ pr noun
Ασωρων pr noun
ἀσωτίαν noun fem acc sg . . . . ἀσωτία
ἀσωτίας noun fem gen sg and acc pl . . . . id.
ἄσωτος adj masc and fem nom sg
Αταδ pr noun
ἄτακτον adj acc sg, neut nom sg . . . . ἄτακτος
ἀταξία noun fem nom sg
Αταρ pr noun
ἀτάρ conjunction
Αταρα pr noun
ἀταραξίας noun fem gen sg . . . . ἀταραξία
ἀτάραχα adj neut nom and acc pl . . . . ἀτάραχος
ἀτάραχον adj acc sg, neut nom sg . . . . id.
ἀταράχους adj masc and fem acc pl . . . . id.
Αταρωθ pr noun
ἀτάφων adj gen pl . . . . ἄταφος
ἄτε adverb
ἀτειχίστοις adj dat pl . . . . ἀτείχιστος
ἀτείχιστος adj masc and fem nom sg . . . . id.
ἀτεκνία noun fem nom sg
ἀτεκνίαν noun fem acc sg . . . . ἀτεκνία
ἀτεκνίας noun fem gen sg . . . . id.
ἄτεκνοι adj masc and fem nom pl . . . . ἄτεκνος
ἄτεκνον adj acc sg, neut nom sg . . . . id.
ἄτεκνος adj masc and fem nom sg . . . . id.
ἀτεκνουμένη vb pres m/p part fem nom sg . . . . . . ἀτεκνόω
ἀτεκνοῦσα vb pres act part fem nom sg . . . . id.
ἀτεκνοῦσαν vb pres act part fem acc sg . . . . id.

ἀτεκνωθῆναι	vb 1st aor pass inf	ἀτεκνόω
ἀτεκνωθήσεται	vb fut pass ind 3rd pers sg	id.
ἀτεκνωθήσονται	vb fut pass ind 3rd pers pl	id.
ἀτεκνωθῶ	vb 1st aor pass subj 1st pers sg	id.
ἀτεκνώσει	vb fut act ind 3rd pers sg	id.
ἀτεκνώσεις	vb fut act ind 2nd pers sg	id.
ἀτελείας	noun fem gen sg	ἀτελεία
ἀτελέσι	adj dat pl	ἀτελής
ἀτέλεστα	adj neut nom and acc pl	ἀτέλεστος
ἀτελέστατον	superl adj masc acc sg	ἀτελής
ἀτέλεστοι	adj masc and fem nom pl	ἀτέλεστος
ἀτενίζοντας	vb pres act part masc acc pl	ἀτενίζω
ἀτενίσαι	vb 1st aor act inf	id.
ἄτερ	preposition	
Ατεργατειον	pr noun neut nom and acc sg	
Ατηρ	pr noun	
Ατητα	pr noun	
Ατθαριας	pr noun masc nom sg	
Ατιλ	pr noun	
ἄτιμα	adj neut nom and acc pl	ἄτιμος
ἀτιμάζει	vb pres act ind 3rd pers sg	ἀτιμάζω
ἀτιμάζοντα	vb pres act part masc acc sg	id.
ἀτιμαζόντων	vb pres act part masc and neut gen pl	id.
ἀτιμάζων	vb pres act part masc nom sg	id.
ἀτιμάζωνται	vb pres m/p subj 3rd pers pl	id.
ἀτιμάσαι	vb 1st aor act inf	id.
ἀτιμάσαντες	vb 1st aor act part masc nom pl	id.
ἀτιμασάντων	vb 1st aor act part masc and neut gen pl	id.
ἀτιμάσασι	vb 1st aor act part masc and neut dat pl	id.
ἀτιμάσῃς	vb 1st aor act subj 2nd pers sg	id.
ἀτιμασθῆναι	vb 1st aor pass inf	id.
ἀτιμασθήσεται	vb fut pass ind 3rd pers sg	id.
ἀτιμασθήσῃ	vb fut pass ind 2nd pers sg	id.
ἀτίμητον	adj acc sg, neut nom sg	ἀτίμητος
ἀτιμία	noun fem nom sg	
ἀτιμία	noun fem dat sg	ἀτιμία
ἀτιμίαν	noun fem acc sg	id.
ἀτιμίας	noun fem gen sg	id.
ἄτιμοι	adj masc and fem nom pl	ἄτιμος
ἄτιμον	adj acc sg, neut nom sg	id.
ἄτιμος	adj masc and fem nom sg	id.
ἀτιμότερος	comp adj masc nom sg	id.
ἀτιμωθήσεται	vb fut pass ind 3rd pers sg	ἀτιμόω
ἀτιμωθήσῃ	vb fut pass ind 2nd pers sg	id.
ἀτίμων	adj gen pl	ἄτιμος
ἀτιμώρητος	adj masc nom sg	
Ατιτα	pr noun	
Ατιφα	pr noun	
ἀτμίδα	noun fem acc sg	ἀτμίς
ἀτμίδας	noun fem acc pl	id.
ἀτμίδος	noun fem gen sg	id.
ἀτμίς	noun fem nom sg	

ἄτοπα	adj neut nom and acc pl	ἄτοπος
ἀτοπίαν	noun fem acc sg	ἀτοπία
ἄτοπον	adj acc sg, neut nom sg	ἄτοπος
Ατους	pr noun	
Ατουφα	pr noun	
ἄτρακτον	noun masc acc sg	ἄτρακτος
ἀτραπόν	noun fem acc sg	ἀτραπός
ἀτραπούς	noun fem acc pl	id.
ἀτραπῷ	noun fem dat sg	id.
ἄτρυγον	adj acc sg, neut nom sg	ἄτρυγος
ἄτρωτον	adj acc sg, neut nom sg	ἄτρωτος
ἀτρώτους	adj masc and fem acc pl	id.
ἀτρώτῳ	adj dat sg	
ἀττάκην	noun masc acc sg	ἀττάκης
Ἀττάλῳ	pr noun masc dat sg	Ἄτταλος
Ατταν	pr noun	
Ατταρατης	pr noun	
ἀττέλεβος	noun masc nom sg	
Αττους	pr noun	
ἀτυχίας	noun fem gen sg and acc pl	ἀτυχία
ἀτυχῶν	vb pres act part masc nom sg	ἀτυχέω
Αυα	pr noun	
Αυαραν	pr noun	
αὐγάζον	vb pres act part neut nom and acc sg	αὐγάζω
αὐγάζοντα	vb pres act part neut nom and acc pl	id.
αὐγάζοντι	vb pres act part masc and neut dat sg	id.
αὐγάζοντος	vb pres act part masc and neut gen sg	id.
αὐγάς	noun fem acc pl	αὐγή
αὐγάσματα	noun neut nom and acc pl	αὔγασμα
αὐγάσματι	noun neut dat sg	id.
αὐγήν	noun fem acc sg	αὐγή
Αυγιαν	pr noun fem acc sg	Αυγια
αὐθάδεια	noun fem nom sg	
αὐθάδης	adj masc and fem nom sg	
αὐθαιρέτως	adverb	
αὐθέντας	noun masc acc pl	αὐθέντης
αὐθεντίαν	noun fem acc sg	αὐθεντία
αὐθημερινοῦ	adj masc and neut gen sg	αὐθημερινός
αὐθημερόν	adverb	
αὐθωρί	adverb	
Αυιμ	pr noun	
αὐλαί	noun fem nom pl	αὐλή
αὐλαία	noun fem nom sg	
αὐλαία	noun fem dat sg	αὐλαία
αὐλαῖαι	noun fem nom pl	id.
αὐλαίαις	noun fem dat pl	id.
αὐλαίαν	noun fem acc sg	id.
αὐλαίας	noun fem gen sg and acc pl	id.
αὐλαῖς	noun fem dat pl	αὐλή
αὐλαιῶν	noun fem gen pl	αὐλαία
αὔλακας	noun masc acc pl	αὔλαξ
αὔλακες	noun masc nom pl	id.

αὔλαξι noun masc dat pl . . . . αὔλαξ

αὐλάρχαι noun masc nom pl . . . . αὐλάρχης

αὐλαρχίας noun fem gen sg . . . . αὐλαρχία

αὐλάς noun fem acc pl . . . . αὐλή

αὐλή noun fem nom sg   id.

αὐλῇ noun fem dat sg   id.

αὐλήν noun fem acc sg   id.

αὐλῆς noun fem gen sg   id.

αὐλίζεσθε vb pres m/p ind 2nd pers pl . . . . αὐλίζω

αὐλίζεται vb pres m/p ind 3rd pers sg   id.

αὐλίζων vb pres act part masc nom sg   id.

αὐλισθείη vb 1st aor pass opt 3rd pers sg   id.

αὐλισθείς vb 1st aor pass part masc nom sg   id.

αὐλισθῆναι vb 1st aor pass inf   id.

αὐλισθῇς vb 1st aor pass subj 2nd pers sg   id.

αὐλισθήσεται vb fut pass ind 3rd pers sg   id.

αὐλισθήσῃ vb fut pass ind 2nd pers sg   id.

αὐλισθήσομαι vb fut pass ind 1st pers sg   id.

αὐλισθησόμεθα vb fut pass ind 1st pers pl   id.

αὐλίσθητε vb 1st aor pass impv 2nd pers pl   id.

αὐλισθῆτε vb 1st aor pass subj 2nd pers pl   id.

αὐλίσθητι vb 1st aor pass impv 2nd pers sg   id.

αὐλισθήτω vb 1st aor pass impv 3rd pers sg   id.

αὐλισθῶμεν vb 1st aor pass subj 1st pers pl   id.

αὐλοί noun masc nom pl . . . . αὐλός

αὐλοῖς noun masc dat pl   id.

αὐλός noun masc nom sg   id.

αὐλοῦ noun masc gen sg   id.

Αυλων pr noun

αὐλών noun masc nom sg

αὐλῶν noun masc gen pl . . . . αὐλός

αὐλῶνα noun masc acc sg . . . . αὐλών

αὐλῶνας noun masc acc pl   id.

αὐλῶνι noun masc dat sg   id.

αὐλῶσι noun masc dat pl   id.

Αυν pr noun

Αυναν pr noun

αὐξάνεσθε vb pres m/p impv 2nd pers pl . . . . αὐξάνω

αὐξανόμενος vb pres m/p part masc nom sg   id.

αὐξάνου vb pres m/p impv 2nd pers sg   id.

αὐξανῶ vb fut act ind 1st pers sg   id.

αὐξηθέντες vb 1st aor pass part masc nom pl   id.

αὐξηθῇ vb 1st aor pass subj 3rd pers sg   id.

αὐξηθῇς vb 1st aor pass subj 2nd pers sg   id.

αὐξηθήσεται vb fut pass ind 3rd pers sg   id.

αὐξηθήσονται vb fut pass ind 3rd pers pl   id.

αὐξηθῆτε vb 1st aor pass subj 2nd pers pl   id.

αὐξήσαι vb 1st aor act opt 3rd pers sg   id.

αὔξησιν noun fem acc sg . . . . αὔξησις

αὐξήσον vb 1st aor act impv 2nd pers sg . . . . αὐξάνω

αὐξήσω vb 1st aor act subj 1st pers sg   id.

αὔξονται vb pres m/p ind 3rd pers pl   id.

αὔξουσαν vb pres act part fem acc sg . . . . αὐξάνω

αὔραν noun fem acc sg . . . . αὔρα

Αυρανιτιδος pr noun fem gen sg . . . . Αυρανιτις

Αυρανου pr noun masc gen sg . . . . Αυρανος

αὔρας noun fem gen sg . . . . αὔρα

αὔριον adverb

Αυση pr noun

Αυσιτιδι pr noun fem dat sg . . . . Αυσιτις

Αυσιτιδος pr noun fem gen sg   id.

αὐστηρίαν noun fem acc sg . . . . αὐστηρία

αὐστηρότερον comp adj masc acc sg,

      neut nom and acc sg . . . . αὐστηρός

αὐτά pers pron neut nom and acc pl . . . . αὐτός

αὗται dem pron fem nom pl . . . . οὗτος

αὐταί pers pron fem nom pl . . . . αὐτός

Αυταιας pr noun masc nom sg

αὐταῖς pers pron fem dat pl . . . . αὐτός

αὐταρκείας noun fem gen sg . . . . αὐτάρκεια

αὐτάρκη adj neut nom and acc pl . . . . αὐτάρκης

αὐτάρκης adj masc nom sg   id.

αὐτάρκησεν vb 1st aor act ind 3rd pers sg . . . . αὐταρκέω

αὐτάρκους adj gen sg . . . . αὐτάρκης

αὐτάς dem pron fem acc pl . . . . οὗτος

αὐτάς pers pron fem acc pl . . . . αὐτός

αὕτη dem pron fem nom sg . . . . οὗτος

αὐτή pers pron fem nom sg . . . . αὐτός

αὐτῇ dem pron fem dat sg . . . . οὗτος

αὐτῇ pers pron fem dat sg . . . . αὐτός

αὐτήν dem pron fem acc sg . . . . οὗτος

αὐτήν pers pron fem acc sg . . . . αὐτός

αὐτῆς dem pron fem gen sg . . . . οὗτος

αὐτῆς pers pron fem gen sg . . . . αὐτός

αὐτίκα adverb

αὐτό pers pron neut nom and acc sg . . . . αὐτός

αὐτοδέσποτος adj masc nom sg

αὐτόθεν adverb

αὐτόθι adverb

αὐτοί pers pron masc nom pl . . . . αὐτός

αὐτοῖς dem pron masc and neut dat pl . . . . οὗτος

αὐτοῖς pers pron masc and neut dat pl . . . . αὐτός

αὐτοκράτορες noun masc nom pl . . . . αὐτοκράτωρ

αὐτοκράτωρ noun masc nom sg   id.

αὐτόματα adj neut nom and acc pl . . . . αὐτόματος

αὐτομάτη adj fem nom sg   id.

αὐτόματος adj masc nom sg   id.

αὐτομόλησαν vb 1st aor act ind 3rd pers pl . . . . αὐτομολέω

αὐτομολησάντων vb 1st aor act part

      masc and neut gen pl   id.

αὐτομολήσασι vb 1st aor act part masc and neut dat pl   id.

αὐτομόλησεν vb 1st aor act ind 3rd pers sg   id.

αὐτομολούντων vb pres act part

      masc and neut gen pl   id.

αὐτόν dem pron masc acc sg . . . . οὗτος

αὐτόν pers pron masc acc sg . . . . αὐτός

αὐτός *see* αὐτός

αὐτός pers pron masc nom sg

αὐτοσχεδίως adverb

αὐτοῦ dem pron masc and neut gen sg . . . . ἑαυτοῦ

αὐτοῦ pers pron masc and neut gen sg . . . . αὐτός

αὐτοῦ adverb

αὐτούς dem pron masc acc pl . . . . οὗτος

αὐτούς pers pron masc acc pl . . . . αὐτός

αὐτόχθονες noun masc nom pl . . . . αὐτόχθων

αὐτόχθονι noun masc dat sg   id.

αὐτοχθόνων noun masc gen pl   id.

αὐτόχθοσι noun masc dat pl   id.

αὐτόχθων noun masc nom sg

αὐτῷ dem pron masc and neut dat sg . . . . οὗτος

αὐτῷ pers pron masc and neut dat sg . . . . αὐτός

αὐτῶν dem pron gen pl . . . . οὗτος

αὐτῶν pers pron gen pl . . . . αὐτός

αὐχένα noun masc acc sg . . . . αὐχήν

αὐχένας noun masc acc pl   id.

αὐχμοῦ noun masc gen sg . . . . αὐχμός

αὐχμώδει adj dat sg . . . . αὐχμώδης

αὐχμώδης adj masc and fem nom sg   id.

αὐχμώδους adj gen sg   id.

Αυωθ pr noun

ἀφ᾽ *see* ἀπό

ἀφαγνιεῖ vb fut act ind 3rd pers sg . . . . ἀφαγνίζω

ἀφαγνιεῖς vb fut act ind 2nd pers sg   id.

ἀφαγνιεῖτε vb fut act ind 2nd pers pl   id.

ἀφαγνίσαι vb 1st aor act inf   id.

ἀφαγνίσασθαι vb 1st aor mid inf   id.

ἀφαγνισθῇ vb 1st aor pass subj 3rd pers sg   id.

ἀφαγνισθήσεται vb fut pass ind 3rd pers sg   id.

ἀφαιρεθείη vb 1st aor pass opt 3rd pers sg . . . . ἀφαιρέω

ἀφαιρεθέντος vb 1st aor pass part masc and neut gen sg id.

ἀφαιρεθήσεται vb fut pass ind 3rd pers sg   id.

ἀφαιρεθήσῃ vb fut pass ind 2nd pers sg   id.

ἀφαιρεῖται vb pres m/p ind 3rd pers sg   id.

Αφαιρεμα pr noun

ἀφαίρεμα noun neut nom and acc sg

ἀφαιρέματα noun neut nom and acc pl . . . . ἀφαίρεμα

ἀφαιρέματος noun neut gen sg   id.

ἀφαιρεμάτων noun neut gen pl   id.

ἀφαιρέσεως noun fem gen sg . . . . ἀφαίρεσις

ἀφαίρεσιν noun fem acc sg   id.

ἀφαιρῆτε vb pres act subj 2nd pers pl . . . . ἀφαιρέω

ἀφαιρούμενος vb pres m/p part masc nom sg   id.

ἀφαιρουμένῳ vb pres m/p part masc and neut dat sg   id.

ἀφαιροῦνται vb pres m/p ind 3rd pers pl   id.

ἀφαιροῦσαν vb pres act part fem acc sg   id.

ἀφαιροῦσιν vb pres act ind 3rd pers pl   id.

ἀφαιρῶν vb pres act part masc nom sg . . . . ἀφαιρέω

ἀφαῖς noun fem dat pl . . . . ἀφή

Αφακα pr noun

Αφαληλ pr noun

ἀφαλλομένῳ vb pres dep part
    masc and neut dat sg . . . . ἀφάλλομαι

ἀφανεῖς adj masc and fem nom and acc pl . . . . ἀφανής

ἀφανής adj masc and fem nom sg   id.

ἀφανιεῖ vb fut act ind 3rd pers sg . . . . ἀφανίζω

ἀφανιεῖς vb fut act ind 2nd pers sg   id.

ἀφανιεῖτε vb fut act ind 2nd pers pl   id.

ἀφανίζεται vb pres m/p ind 3rd pers sg   id.

ἀφανίζοντας vb pres act part masc acc pl   id.

ἀφανίσαι vb 1st aor act inf,
    1st aor act opt 3rd pers sg   id.

ἀφανίσατε vb 1st aor act impv 2nd pers pl   id.

ἀφανίσει vb fut act ind 3rd pers sg   id.

ἀφανίσῃ vb 1st aor act subj 3rd pers sg   id.

ἀφανίσῃς vb 1st aor act subj 2nd pers sg   id.

ἀφανισθῇ vb 1st aor pass subj 3rd pers sg   id.

ἀφανισθῇς vb 1st aor pass subj 2nd pers sg   id.

ἀφανισθήσεται vb fut pass ind 3rd pers sg   id.

ἀφανισθήσονται vb fut pass ind 3rd pers pl   id.

ἀφανίσθητε vb 1st aor pass impv 2nd pers pl   id.

ἀφανισθῶσιν vb 1st aor pass subj 3rd pers pl   id.

ἀφανισμοῖς noun masc dat pl . . . . ἀφανισμός

ἀφανισμόν noun masc acc sg   id.

ἀφανισμός noun masc nom sg   id.

ἀφανισμοῦ noun masc gen sg   id.

ἀφανισμῷ noun masc dat sg   id.

ἀφάνισον vb 1st aor act impv 2nd pers sg . . . . ἀφανίζω

ἀφανίσω vb 1st aor act subj 1st pers sg   id.

ἀφανίσωμεν vb 1st aor act subj 1st pers pl   id.

ἀφανιῶ vb fut act ind 1st pers sg   id.

Αφαρ pr noun

Αφαρσαθαχαιοι pr noun

Αφαρσαιοι pr noun

Αφαρσαχαιοι pr noun

ἀφασίαν noun fem acc sg . . . . ἀφασία

ἄφαψαι vb 1st aor mid impv 2nd pers sg . . . . ἀφάπτω

ἀφάψεις vb fut act ind 2nd pers sg   id.

ἀφάψετε vb fut act ind 2nd pers pl   id.

ἀφεγγεῖ adj dat sg . . . . ἀφεγγής

ἄφεδρον noun fem acc sg . . . . ἄφεδρος

ἀφέδρου noun fem gen sg   id.

ἀφέδρῳ noun fem dat sg   id.

ἀφεθείς vb 1st aor pass part masc nom sg . . . . ἀφίημι

ἀφεθεῖσα vb 1st aor pass part fem nom sg   id.

ἀφεθέντες vb 1st aor pass part masc nom pl   id.

ἀφέθη vb 1st aor pass ind 3rd pers sg   id.

ἀφεθῆναι vb 1st aor pass inf   id.

ἀφέθησαν vb 1st aor pass ind 3rd pers pl   id.

ἀφεθήσεται vb fut pass ind 3rd pers sg .... ἀφίημι

ἀφειδῶς adverb

ἀφείλαντο vb 2nd aor mid ind 3rd pers pl ...... ἀφαιρέω

ἀφεῖλας vb 2nd aor act ind 2nd pers sg id.

ἀφείλατο vb 2nd aor mid ind 3rd pers sg id.

ἀφεῖλε(ν) vb 2nd aor act ind 3rd pers sg id.

ἀφεῖλον vb 2nd aor act ind

          1st pers sg and 3rd pers pl id.

ἀφείλου vb 2nd aor mid ind 2nd pers sg id.

ἀφείλω vb 1st aor mid ind 2nd pers sg id.

ἀφειμένη vb perf m/p part fem nom sg .... ἀφίημι

ἀφεῖναι vb 2nd aor act inf id.

ἀφείς vb 2nd aor act part masc nom sg id.

ἀφεῖς vb pres act ind 2nd pers sg id.

ἀφεῖσα vb 2nd aor act part fem nom sg id.

Αφεκ pr noun

Αφεκα pr noun

ἄφελε vb 2nd aor act impv 2nd pers sg .... ἀφαιρέω

ἀφελεῖ vb fut act ind 3rd pers sg id.

ἀφελεῖν vb 2nd aor act inf, fut act inf id.

ἀφελεῖς vb fut act ind 2nd pers sg id.

ἀφελεῖτε vb fut act ind 2nd pers pl id.

ἀφελέσθαι vb 2nd aor mid inf id.

ἀφέλεσθε vb 2nd aor mid impv 2nd pers pl id.

ἀφέλετε vb 2nd aor act impv 2nd pers pl id.

ἀφελέτω vb 2nd aor act impv 3rd pers sg id.

ἀφέλη vb 2nd aor act subj 3rd pers sg id.

ἀφέλης vb 2nd aor act subj 2nd pers sg id.

ἀφέληται vb 2nd aor mid subj 3rd pers sg id.

ἀφέλητε vb 2nd aor act subj 2nd pers pl id.

ἀφελομένη vb 2nd aor mid part fem nom sg id.

ἀφελόμενοι vb 2nd aor mid part masc nom pl id.

ἀφελόμενος vb 2nd aor mid part masc nom sg id.

ἀφελόντες vb 2nd aor act part masc nom pl id.

ἀφελοῦ vb 2nd aor mid impv 2nd pers sg id.

ἀφελοῦμαι vb fut mid ind 1st pers sg id.

ἀφελοῦνται vb fut mid ind 3rd pers pl id.

ἀφελοῦσιν vb fut act ind 3rd pers pl id.

ἀφελπίσης vb 1st aor act subj 2nd pers sg ...... ἀφελπίζω

ἀφελῶ vb fut act ind 1st pers sg .... ἀφαιρέω

ἀφέλωμαι vb 2nd aor mid subj 1st pers sg id.

ἀφέλωνται vb 2nd aor mid subj 3rd pers pl id.

ἀφέλωσιν vb 2nd aor act subj 3rd pers pl id.

ἀφέματα noun neut nom and acc pl .... ἄφεμα

ἀφέντες vb 2nd aor act part masc nom pl .... ἀφίημι

ἀφέξεσθε vb fut mid ind 2nd pers pl .... ἀπέχω

ἀφέξεται vb fut mid ind 3rd pers sg id.

ἀφεξόμεθα vb fut mid ind 1st pers pl id.

Αφερ pr noun

Αφεραϊμ pr noun

Αφερρα pr noun

ἄφες vb 2nd aor act impv 2nd pers sg .... ἀφίημι

ἀφέσει noun fem dat sg .... ἄφεσις

ἀφέσεις noun fem nom and acc pl id.

ἀφέσεως noun fem gen sg id.

ἄφεσιν noun fem acc sg id.

ἄφεσις noun fem nom sg id.

Αφεσση pr noun

ἀφέστακα vb perf act ind 1st pers sg .... ἀφίστημι

ἀφέστηκας vb perf act ind 2nd pers sg id.

ἀφέστηκεν vb perf act ind 3rd pers sg id.

ἀφεστηκός vb perf act part neut nom and acc sg id.

ἀφεστηκότα vb perf act part masc acc sg ...... ἀφίστημι

ἀφεστηκότας vb perf act part masc acc pl id.

ἀφεστηκότες vb perf act part masc nom pl id.

ἄφετε vb 2nd aor act impv 2nd pers pl .... ἀφίημι

ἀφέτω vb 2nd aor act impv 3rd pers sg id.

ἀφεύκτως adverb

ἀφή noun fem nom sg

ἀφῇ noun fem dat sg .... ἀφή

ἀφῇ vb 2nd aor act subj 3rd pers sg .... ἀφίημι

ἀφηγεῖσθαι vb pres dep inf .... ἀφηγέομαι

ἀφηγεῖται vb pres dep ind 3rd pers sg id.

ἀφηγῇ vb pres dep ind 2nd pers sg id.

ἀφηγήμασι noun neut dat pl .... ἀφήγημα

ἀφηγήσεται vb fut mid ind 3rd pers sg .... ἀφηγέομαι

ἀφηγήση vb fut mid ind 2nd pers sg id.

ἀφηγούμενε vb pres dep part masc voc sg id.

ἀφηγούμενοι vb pres dep part masc nom pl id.

ἀφηγουμένοις vb pres dep part masc and neut dat pl id.

ἀφηγουμενον vb pres dep part masc acc sg id.

ἀφηγούμενος vb pres dep part masc nom sg id.

ἀφηγουμένου vb pres dep part masc and neut gen sg id.

ἀφηγουμένους vb pres dep part masc acc pl id.

ἀφηγουμένῳ vb pres dep part masc and neut dat sg id.

ἀφηγουμένων vb pres dep part gen pl id.

ἀφῆκα vb 1st aor act ind 1st pers sg .... ἀφίημι

ἀφήκαμεν vb 1st aor act ind 1st pers pl id.

ἀφῆκαν vb 1st aor act ind 3rd pers pl id.

ἀφῆκας vb 1st aor act ind 2nd pers sg id.

ἀφῆκεν vb 1st aor act ind 3rd pers sg id.

ἀφήλαντο vb 1st aor mid ind 3rd pers pl ...... ἀφάλλομαι

ἀφήλατο vb 1st aor mid ind 3rd pers sg id.

ἀφήλπισεν vb 1st aor act ind 3rd pers sg .... ἀπελπίζω

ἀφήν noun fem acc sg .... ἀφή

ἀφῆπται vb perf m/p ind 3rd pers sg .... ἀφάπτω

ἀφηρέθη vb 1st aor pass ind 3rd pers sg .... ἀφαιρέω

ἀφήρηκα vb perf act ind 1st pers sg id.

ἀφηρημένα vb perf m/p part neut nom and acc pl id.

ἀφηρημένοι vb perf m/p part masc nom pl id.

ἀφηρημένος vb perf m/p part masc nom sg id.

ἀφήρηνται vb perf m/p ind 3rd pers sg id.

ἀφήρητο vb plpf m/p ind 3rd pers sg id.

ἀφῆς noun fem gen sg .... ἀφή

ἀφῆς vb 2nd aor act subj 2nd pers sg .... ἀφίημι	ἀφόδευμα noun neut nom and acc sg
ἀφήσει vb fut act ind 3rd pers sg id.	ἄφοδον noun fem acc sg .... ἄφοδος
ἀφήσεις vb fut act ind 2nd pers sg id.	ἀφόμοιον noun neut nom and acc sg
ἀφήσομεν vb fut act ind 1st pers pl id.	ἀφομοιωθέντες vb 1st aor pass part masc nom pl . ἀφομοιόω
ἀφήσουσιν vb fut act ind 3rd pers pl id.	ἀφομοιωθῆτε vb 1st aor pass subj 2nd pers pl id.
ἀφήσω vb fut act ind 1st pers sg id.	ἀφόρητον adj acc sg, neut nom sg .... ἀφόρητος
ἀφῆτε vb 1st aor act subj 2nd pers pl id.	ἀφορίᾳ noun fem dat sg .... ἀφορία
ἀφθαρσία noun fem nom sg	ἀφοριεῖ vb fut act ind 3rd pers sg .... ἀφορίζω
ἀφθαρσίᾳ noun fem dat sg .... ἀφθαρσία	ἀφοριεῖς vb fut act ind 2nd pers sg id.
ἀφθαρσίαν noun fem acc sg id.	ἀφοριεῖτε vb fut act ind 2nd pers pl id.
ἀφθαρσίας noun fem gen sg id.	ἀφορίζεται vb pres m/p ind 3rd pers sg id.
ἄφθαρτον adj acc sg, neut nom sg .... ἄφθαρτος	ἀφορίζοντες vb pres act part masc nom pl id.
ἀφθόνους adj masc and fem acc pl .... ἄφθονος	ἀφορίζω vb pres act ind 1st pers sg id.
ἀφθόνῳ adj dat sg id.	ἀφοριοῦσι vb fut act ind 3rd pers pl id.
ἀφθόνως adverb	ἀφόρισαι vb 1st aor mid impv 2nd pers sg id.
ἄφθορα adj neut nom and acc pl .... ἄφθορος	ἀφόρισαι vb 1st aor act inf id.
ἀφιδών vb 2nd aor act part masc nom sg .... ἀφοράω	ἀφορίσας vb 1st aor act part masc nom sg id.
ἀφίεμεν vb pres act ind 1st pers pl .... ἀφίημι	ἀφορισθεῖσαι vb 1st aor pass part fem nom pl id.
ἀφιέναι vb pres act inf id.	ἀφορίσθητε vb 1st aor pass impv 2nd pers pl id.
ἀφιερώσωμεν vb 1st aor act subj 1st pers pl ...... ἀφιερόω	ἀφορισθήτω vb 1st aor pass impv 3rd pers sg id.
ἀφιέσθω vb pres m/p impv 3rd pers sg .... ἀφίημι	ἀφόρισμα noun neut nom and acc sg
ἀφίεται vb pres m/p ind 3rd pers sg id.	ἀφορίσματα noun neut nom and acc pl .... ἀφόρισμα
ἀφιέτωσαν vb 2nd aor act impv 3rd pers pl id.	ἀφορίσματος noun neut gen sg id.
ἀφίημι vb pres act ind 1st pers sg id.	ἀφορισμοῖς noun masc dat pl .... ἀφορισμός
ἀφίησι vb pres act ind 3rd pers sg id.	ἀφορισμοῦ noun masc gen sg id.
ἀφίκετο vb 2nd aor mid ind 3rd pers sg ...... ἀφικνέομαι	ἀφορισμῶν noun masc gen pl id.
ἀφίκησθε vb 2nd aor mid subj 2nd pers pl id.	ἀφορίσωσιν vb 1st aor act subj 3rd pers pl .... ἀφορίζω
ἀφίκηται vb 2nd aor mid subj 3rd pers sg id.	ἀφορμή noun fem nom sg
ἀφικνεῖτο vb impf dep ind 3rd pers sg id.	ἀφορμήν noun fem acc sg .... ἀφορμή
ἀφίκοιτο vb 2nd aor mid opt 3rd pers sg id.	ἀφορμῆς noun fem gen sg id.
ἀφικομένων vb 2nd aor mid part gen pl id.	ἀφορολόγητον adj acc sg, neut nom sg .... ἀφορολόγητος
ἀφίκοντο vb 2nd aor mid ind 3rd pers pl id.	ἀφορῶντες vb pres act part masc nom pl .... ἀφοράω
ἀφίκου vb 2nd aor mid ind 2nd pers sg id.	Αφρα pr noun
ἀφικώμεθα vb 2nd aor mid subj 1st pers pl id.	ἄφρονα adj masc and fem acc sg .... ἄφρων
ἀφίξεται vb fut mid ind 3rd pers sg id.	ἄφρονας adj masc and fem acc pl id.
ἄφιξιν noun fem acc sg .... ἄφιξις	ἄφρονες adj masc and fem nom pl id.
ἀφίουσιν vb pres act ind 3rd pers pl .... ἀφίημι	ἀφρονέστατοι superl adj masc nom pl id.
ἀφιστᾷ vb pres act ind 3rd pers sg .... ἀφίστημι	ἀφρονέστατος superl adj masc nom sg id.
ἀφίσταντο vb impf m/p ind 3rd pers pl id.	ἄφρονι adj dat sg id.
ἀφίστασθαι vb pres m/p inf id.	ἄφρονος adj gen sg id.
ἀφίσταται vb pres m/p ind 3rd pers sg id.	ἀφρόνων adj gen pl id.
ἀφίστατο vb impf m/p ind 3rd pers sg id.	ἀφρόνως adverb
ἀφίστησιν vb pres act ind 3rd pers sg id.	ἄφροσι adj dat pl .... ἄφρων
ἀφίστω vb pres act subj 1st pers sg id.	ἀφροσύνη noun fem nom sg
ἀφίω vb pres act subj 1st pers sg .... ἀφίημι	ἀφροσύναις noun fem dat pl .... ἀφροσύνη
ἀφίων vb pres act part masc nom sg id.	ἀφροσύνη noun fem nom sg id.
ἀφιῶσι vb pres act subj 3rd pers pl id.	ἀφροσύνῃ noun fem dat sg id.
ἄφνω adverb	ἀφροσύνην noun fem acc sg id.
ἀφοβίας noun fem gen sg .... ἀφοβία	ἀφροσύνης noun fem gen sg id.
ἄφοβος adj masc and fem nom sg	ἄφρων adj masc and fem nom sg
ἀφόβους adj masc and fem acc pl .... ἄφοβος	ἄφρων noun masc nom sg
ἀφόβως adverb	ἀφυλάκτως adverb

ἀφυστέρησας vb 1st aor act part masc nom sg .. ἀφυστερέω

ἀφυστερήσῃς vb 1st aor act subj 2nd pers sg   id.

Αφφαιμ pr noun

αφφουσωθ translit

αφφω interjection

ἀφώδευσαν vb 1st aor act ind 3rd pers pl .... ἀφοδεύω

ἀφωμοιωμένα vb perf m/p part

       neut nom and acc pl .... ἀφομοιόω

ἀφωμοίωνται vb perf m/p ind 3rd pers pl   id.

ἄφωνος adj masc and fem nom sg

ἀφώνους adj masc and fem acc pl .... ἄφωνος

ἀφώριζεν vb impf act ind 3rd pers sg .... ἀφορίζω

ἀφώρισα vb 1st aor act ind 1st pers sg   id.

ἀφώρισεν vb 1st aor act ind 3rd pers sg   id.

ἀφωρίσθη vb 1st aor pass ind 3rd pers sg   id.

ἀφωρίσθησαν vb 1st aor pass ind 3rd pers pl   id.

ἀφωρισμένα vb perf m/p part neut nom and acc pl   id.

ἀφωρισμένας vb perf m/p part fem acc pl   id.

ἀφωρισμένη vb perf m/p part fem nom sg   id.

ἀφωρισμένην vb perf m/p part fem acc sg   id.

ἀφωρισμένοι vb perf m/p part masc nom pl   id.

ἀφωρισμένον vb perf m/p part neut nom and acc sg   id.

ἀφωρισμένους vb perf m/p part masc acc pl   id.

ἀφώρισται vb perf m/p ind 3rd pers sg   id.

Αχααβ pr noun

Αχαβαρ pr noun

Αχαζ pr noun

Αχαζιβ pr noun

Αχαλια pr noun

Αχαμανι pr noun

ἀχανεῖ adj dat sg .... ἀχανής

Αχαρ pr noun

ἄχαρις adj masc and fem nom sg

ἀχάριστα adj neut nom and acc pl .... ἀχάριστος

ἀχάριστος adj masc and fem nom sg   id.

ἀχαρίστου adj gen sg   id.

ἀχαρίστων adj gen pl   id.

ἀχαρίστως adverb

Αχασελωθ pr noun

ἀχάτην noun masc acc sg .... ἀχάτης

ἀχάτης noun masc nom sg   id.

ἄχει translit

Αχελ pr noun

Αχελγαι pr noun

Αχεχαρ pr noun

Αχζιβ pr noun

Αχζιφ pr noun

ἀχθείη vb 1st aor pass opt 3rd pers sg .... ἄγω

ἀχθείσης vb 1st aor pass part fem gen sg   id.

ἀχθέντων vb 1st aor pass part masc and neut gen pl   id.

ἀχθῆναι vb 1st aor pass inf   id.

ἀχθήσεσθε vb fut pass ind 2nd pers pl   id.

ἀχθήσεται vb fut pass ind 3rd pers sg .... ἄγω

ἀχθησομένους vb fut pass part masc acc pl   id.

ἀχθήσονται vb fut pass ind 3rd pers pl   id.

ἄχι translit

Αχια pr noun

Αχιαβ pr noun

Αχιαν pr noun

Αχιας pr noun

Αχιαχαρον pr noun masc acc sg .... Αχιαχαρος

Αχιαχαρος pr noun masc nom sg   id.

Αχιαχαρω pr noun masc dat sg   id.

Αχιβα pr noun

Αχιεζερ pr noun

Αχιεζερι pr noun

Αχιηλ pr noun

Αχιθαλαμ pr noun

Αχικαμ pr noun

Αχικαρ pr noun

Αχικαρον pr noun masc acc sg .... Αχικαρος

Αχικαρω pr noun masc dat sg   id.

Αχιλιδ pr noun

Αχιλουδ pr noun

Αχιλουθ pr noun

Αχιμ pr noun

Αχιμα pr noun

Αχιμαας pr noun

Αχιμαν pr noun

Αχιμελεχ pr noun

Αχιμι pr noun

Αχιμωθ pr noun

Αχινααμ pr noun

Αχινααν pr noun

Αχιναδαβ pr noun

Αχινοομ pr noun

Αχιου pr noun

Αχιουραογα pr noun

Αχιρε pr noun

Αχισααρ pr noun

Αχισαμαι pr noun

Αχισαμακ pr noun

Αχισαμαχ pr noun

Αχιτοφελ pr noun

Αχιτω3 pr noun

Αχιφα pr noun

Αχιχαρον pr noun masc acc sg .... Αχιχαρος

Αχιχαρος pr noun masc nom sg

Αχιχωδ pr noun

Αχιωρ pr noun

Αχλαι pr noun

Αχλια pr noun

Αχοβωρ pr noun

αχουχ translit

Αχραθαῖον pr noun masc acc sg . . . . Αχραθαῖος

Αχραθαῖος pr noun masc nom sg

Αχραν pr noun

ἀχρεῖον adj acc sg, neut nom sg . . . . ἀχρεῖος

ἀχρεῖος adj masc and fem nom sg   id.

ἀχρειότης noun fem nom sg

ἀχρειότητι noun fem dat sg . . . . ἀχρειότης

ἀχρειῶσαι vb 1st aor act inf . . . . ἀχρειόω

ἀχρειώσετε vb fut act ind 2nd pers pl   id.

ἀχρεῶσαι vb 1st aor act inf   id.

ἄχρηστα adj neut nom and acc pl . . . . ἄχρηστος

ἄχρηστον adj acc sg, neut nom sg   id.

ἄχρηστος adj masc and fem nom sg   id.

ἀχρήστων adj gen pl   id.

ἄχρι preposition

ἄχρις see ἄχρι

Αχσαν pr noun

Αχσαφ pr noun

ἄχυρα noun neut nom and acc pl . . . . ἄχυρον

ἀχύροις noun neut dat pl   id.

ἄχυρον noun neut nom and acc sg   id.

ἀχύρου noun neut gen sg   id.

Αχωι pr noun

Αχωρ pr noun

Αχωχι pr noun

ἅψαι vb 1st aor mid impv 2nd pers sg . . . . ἅπτομαι

Αψαλωμου pr noun masc gen sg . . . . Αψαλωμος

ἀψαμένη vb 1st aor mid part fem nom sg . . . . ἅπτομαι

ἀψάμενος vb 1st aor mid part masc nom sg   id.

ἅψαντες vb 1st aor act part masc nom pl . . . . ἅπτω

ἅψασθαι vb 1st aor mid inf . . . . ἅπτομαι

ἅψασθε vb 1st aor mid impv 2nd pers pl   id.

ἅψεσθε vb fut mid ind 2nd pers pl   id.

ἅψεται vb fut mid ind 3rd pers sg   id.

ἀψευδῆ adj masc and fem acc sg . . . . ἀψευδής

ἅψῃ vb fut mid ind 2nd pers sg . . . . ἅπτομαι

ἅψησθε vb 1st aor mid subj 2nd pers pl   id.

ἅψηται vb 1st aor mid subj 3rd pers sg   id.

ἅψονται vb fut mid ind 3rd pers pl   id.

ἀψύχοις adj dat pl . . . . ἄψυχος

ἀψύχῳ adj dat sg   id.

Αωδ pr noun

Αωδα pr noun fem nom sg

Αωδας pr noun fem gen sg . . . . Αωδα

Αωθ pr noun

Αωιτης pr noun masc nom sg

ἀωρία noun fem dat sg . . . . ἀωρία

ἀωρίας noun fem gen sg   id.

ἄωροι adj masc and fem nom pl . . . . ἄωρος

ἄωρον adj acc sg, neut nom sg   id.

ἄωρος adj masc and fem nom sg   id.

ἀώρῳ adj dat sg   id.

B β

β΄ indecl number

Βααδα pr noun

Βααζ pr noun

Βααλ pr noun

Βααλα pr noun

Βααλαθ pr noun

Βααλβεριθ pr noun

Βααλγαδ pr noun

Βααλεθβηρραμωθ pr noun

Βααλερμων pr noun

Βααλθαμαρ pr noun

Βααλια pr noun

Βααλιμ pr noun

Βααλιμαθ pr noun

Βααλσαμος pr noun

βααλταμ translit

Βααλφαρασιν pr noun

Βααλων pr noun

Βαανα pr noun

Βααανι pr noun

Βαασα pr noun

Βαβι pr noun

Βαβυλων pr noun fem nom sg

Βαβυλῶνα pr noun fem acc sg . . . . Βαβυλών

Βαβυλῶνι pr noun fem dat sg   id.

Βαβυλωνια pr noun fem dat sg . . . . Βαβυλωνια

Βαβυλωνιαν pr noun fem acc sg   id.

Βαβυλωνιας pr noun fem gen sg   id.

Βαβυλωνιοι pr noun masc nom pl . . . . Βαβυλωνιος

Βαβυλωνιοις pr noun masc dat pl   id.

Βαβυλωνιων pr noun masc gen pl   id.

Βαβυλῶνος pr noun fem gen sg . . . . Βαβυλών

Βαγαδιηλ pr noun

Βαγο pr noun

Βαγοι pr noun

Βαγουι pr noun

Βαγωα pr noun masc dat sg . . . . Βαγωας

Βαγωας pr noun masc nom sg

Βαγωου pr noun masc gen sg . . . . Βαγωας

Βαδαια pr noun

Βαδαν pr noun

Βαδδαργις pr noun

βαδδιν translit

Βαδεκαρ pr noun

βαδιεῖται vb fut mid ind 3rd pers sg . . . . Βαδίζω

βάδιζε vb pres act impv 2nd pers sg   id.

βαδίζει vb pres act ind 3rd pers sg   id.

βαδίζειν vb pres act inf   id.

βαδίζετε vb pres act impv 2nd pers pl,
        pres act ind 2nd pers pl   id.

βαδίζον vb pres act part neut nom and acc sg   id.

βαδίζοντες vb pres act part masc nom pl   id.

βαδίζουσιν vb pres act ind 3rd pers pl   id.

βαδίζων vb pres act part masc nom sg   id.

Βαδιηλ pr noun

βαδιοῦνται vb fut mid ind 3rd pers pl . . . . Βαδίζω

βαδίσαι vb 1st aor act inf   id.

βαδίσαντες vb 1st aor act part masc nom pl   id.

βαδίσας vb 1st aor act part masc nom sg   id.

βαδίσασα vb 1st aor act part fem nom sg   id.

βαδίσατε vb 1st aor act impv 2nd pers pl   id.

βαδίση vb 1st aor act subj 3rd pers sg   id.

βαδίσης vb 1st aor act subj 2nd pers sg   id.

βάδισον vb 1st aor act impv 2nd pers sg   id.

βαδίσωμεν vb 1st aor act subj 1st pers pl   id.

βάδων noun masc gen pl . . . . βάδος

Βαζαν pr noun

Βαζες pr noun

Βαζκαθ pr noun

Βαθαρωθ pr noun

βαθέα adj neut nom and acc pl . . . . βαθύς

βάθει noun neut dat sg . . . . βάθος

βαθεῖ adj masc and neut dat sg . . . . βαθύς

βαθεῖα adj fem nom sg   id.

βαθεῖαν adj fem acc sg   id.

βαθέος adj masc and neut gen sg   id.

βαθέων adj gen pl   id.

βαθέως adverb

βάθη noun neut nom and acc pl . . . . βάθος

Βαθησαρ pr noun

βαθμόν noun masc acc sg . . . . βαθμός

βαθμούς noun masc acc pl   id.

βάθος noun neut nom and acc sg

Βαθουηλ pr noun

Βαθουλ pr noun

βάθους noun neut gen sg . . . . βάθος

Βαθρεφαν pr noun

βαθύ adj neut nom and acc sg . . . . βαθύς

βαθύνατε vb 1st aor act impv 2nd pers pl . . . . βαθύνω

βαθύς adj masc nom sg

βαθύτερα comp adj neut nom and acc pl . . . . βαθύς

βαθύφονον adj acc sg, neut nom sg . . . . βαθύφονος

βαθύχειλον adj masc acc sg,
        neut nom and acc sg . . . . βαθύχειλος

Βαιαν pr noun

Βαιηρ pr noun

Βαιεαβαρα pr noun

Βαιθαγγαν pr noun

Βαιθαγλα pr noun

Βαιθακαδ pr noun

Βαιθαμμαρχαβωθ pr noun

Βαιθαναβρα pr noun

Βαιθαναθ pr noun

Βαιθαναμ pr noun

Βαιθαναν pr noun

Βαιθανι pr noun

Βαιθανωθ pr noun

Βαιθαρ pr noun

Βαιθαραβα pr noun

Βαιθαραμ pr noun

Βαιθαραν pr noun

Βαιθσσεττα pr noun

Βαιθσσιμωθ pr noun

Βαιθαχαρμα pr noun

Βαιθοχου pr noun

Βαιθβασι pr noun

Βαιθβηρα pr noun

Βοιθγεδωρ pr noun

Βαιθεγενεθ pr noun

Βαιθεγλιω pr noun

Βαιθενεθ pr noun

Βαιθεορ pr noun

Βαιθζαχαρια pr noun

Βαιθηλ pr noun

Βαιθηλβεριθ pr noun

Βαιθηλιτης pr noun masc nom sg

Βαιθηρ pr noun

Βαιθηρα pr noun

Βαιθθαμε pr noun

Βαιθθαπφουε pr noun

Βαιθλαβαθ pr noun

Βαιθλαεμ pr noun

Βαιθλεεμ pr noun

Βαιθλεεμιτης pr noun masc nom sg

Βαιθλωμων pr noun

Βαιθμαν pr noun

Βαιθμαρχαβωθ pr noun

Βαιθμαχα pr noun

Βαιθμαχερεβ pr noun

Βαιθοκ pr noun

Βαιθροοβ pr noun

Βαιθσααν pr noun

Βαιθσαμυς pr noun

Βαιθσαμυσιτου pr noun gen sg . . . . Βαιθσαμυσιτος

Βαιθσαν pr noun

Βαιθσαρισα pr noun

Βαιθσμας pr noun

Βαιθσουρ pr noun

Βαιθσουρα pr noun

Βαιθσουραν pr noun fem acc sg . . . . Βαιθσουρα

Βαιθσουροις pr noun fem dat pl   id.

Βαιθσουρων pr noun fem gen pl   id.

Βαιθφαλεθ pr noun

Βαιθφασης pr noun

Βαιθφογωρ pr noun

Βαιθχορ pr noun

Βαιθων pr noun

Βαιθωρων pr noun

βαίνειν vb pres act inf . . . . βαίνω

βαίνην noun fem acc sg . . . . βαίνη

Βαισαφουδ pr noun

Βαιτασμων pr noun

Βαιτηρους pr noun

Βαιτολιω pr noun

Βαιτομασθαιμ pr noun

Βαιτομεσθαιμ pr noun

Βαιτυλουα pr noun

Βαιφαλαδ pr noun

Βαιων pr noun

βαΐων noun neut gen pl . . . . βάϊον

Βακβακαρ pr noun

Βακβουκ pr noun

Βακηνορος pr noun masc gen sg . . . . Βακηνωρ

βακτηρία noun fem nom sg

βακτηρίαι noun fem nom pl . . . . βακτηρία

βακτηρίαν noun fem acc sg   id.

βακτηρίας noun fem gen sg   id.

Βακχα pr noun

Βακχιδην pr noun masc acc sg . . . . Βακχιδης

Βακχιδης pr noun masc nom sg   id.

Βακχιδου pr noun masc gen sg   id.

Βακχιρ pr noun

βακχουρίοις noun neut dat pl . . . . βακχούρια

Βακχουρος pr noun

Βακωκ pr noun

Βαλα pr noun

Βαλαα pr noun

Βαλααμ pr noun

Βαλααν pr noun

Βαλαδ pr noun

Βαλαδαν pr noun

Βαλαεννων pr noun

Βαλαερμων pr noun

Βαλακ pr noun

Βαλαμων pr noun

Βαλανας pr noun

βάλανοι noun fem nom pl . . . . βάλανος

βάλανον noun fem acc sg   id.

Βαλανος pr noun fem nom sg

βάλανος noun fem nom sg

βαλάνου noun fem gen sg . . . . βάλανος

βαλάνῳ noun fem dat sg   id.

Βαλασαν pr noun

Βαλγα pr noun

Βαλδαδ pr noun

βάλε vb 2nd aor act impv 2nd pers sg . . . . βάλλω

Βαλε pr noun

Βαλεγδαε pr noun

βαλεῖ vb fut act ind 3rd pers sg . . . . βάλλω

Βαλεϊ pr noun

βαλεῖν vb 2nd aor act inf, fut act inf . . . . βάλλω

βαλεῖτε vb fut act ind 2nd pers pl   id.

Βαλεκ pr noun

βάλετε vb 2nd aor act impv 2nd pers pl . . . . βάλλω

βάλῃ vb 2nd aor act subj 3rd pers sg   id.

Βαλλα pr noun

Βαλλαν pr noun fem acc sg . . . . Βαλλα

βαλλάντια noun neut nom and acc pl . . . . . . βαλλάντιον

βαλλάντιον noun neut nom and acc sg   id.

βαλλαντίου noun neut gen sg   id.

βαλλαντίῳ noun neut dat sg   id.

Βαλλας pr noun fem gen sg . . . . Βαλλα

βάλλει vb pres act ind 3rd pers sg . . . . βάλλω

βάλλειν vb pres act inf   id.

βάλλεσθαι vb pres m/p inf   id.

βάλλοντας vb pres act part masc acc pl   id.

βάλλοντες vb pres act part masc nom pl   id.

βάλλοντος vb pres act part masc and neut gen sg   id.

βάλλουσιν vb pres act ind 3rd pers pl   id.

βάλλων vb pres act part masc nom sg   id.

Βαλμαιναν pr noun

Βαλνουος pr noun

βαλοῦσιν vb fut act ind 3rd pers pl . . . . βάλλω

Βαλσαν pr noun

Βαλτασαρ pr noun

βαλῶ vb fut act ind 1st pers sg . . . . βάλλω

Βαλωθ pr noun

βάλωμεν vb 2nd aor act subj 1st pers pl . . . . βάλλω

βαλών vb 2nd aor act part masc nom sg   id.

βαμα translit

Βαμα pr noun

Βαμαηλ pr noun

Βαμεθ pr noun

βάμματα noun neut nom and acc pl . . . . βάμμα

βαμμάτων noun neut gen pl   id.

Βαμωθ pr noun

Βαμωθβααλ pr noun

Βαναι pr noun

Βαναια pr noun

Βαναια pr noun masc dat sg . . . . Βαναιας

Βαναιαν pr noun masc acc sg   id.

Βαναιας pr noun masc nom sg

Βαναιβακατ pr noun

Βαναιου pr noun masc gen sg . . . . Βαναιας

Βανηβαρακ pr noun

Βανηελαμ pr noun

Βανι pr noun

Βανναιας pr noun masc nom sg

Βαννου pr noun masc gen sg . . . . Βαννας

Βαννους pr noun

Βανουι pr noun

Βανουναι pr noun

Βαουριμ pr noun

βαπται adj fem nom pl . . . . βαπτός

βαπτίζει vb pres act ind 3rd pers sg . . . . βαπτίζω

βαπτιζόμενος vb pres m/p part masc nom sg   id.

βαρ translit

Βαραγα pr noun

Βαραδ pr noun

βάραθρον noun neut nom and acc sg

Βαραια pr noun

Βαρακ pr noun

βαρακηνιμ translit

Βαρακιμ pr noun

Βαραχια pr noun

Βαραχιας pr noun masc nom sg

Βαραχιηλ pr noun

Βαραχιου pr noun masc gen sg . . . . Βαραχιας

βάρβαρα adj neut nom and acc pl . . . . βάρβαρος

βαρβάροις adj dat pl   id.

βαρβάρου adj gen sg   id.

βαρβάρους adj masc and fem acc pl   id.

βαρβάρων adj gen pl   id.

βαρβάρως adverb

βαρβαρώτερον comp adj masc acc sg,
          neut nom and acc sg . . . . βάρβαρος

βαρέα adj neut nom and acc pl . . . . βαρύς

Βαρεα pr noun

βάρει noun fem dat sg . . . . βάρις

βαρεῖ adj masc and neut dat sg . . . . βαρύς

βαρεῖα adj fem nom sg   id.

βαρείᾳ adj fem dat sg   id.

βαρεῖαι adj fem nom pl   id.

βαρεῖαν adj fem acc sg   id.

βαρείας adj fem gen sg   id.

βάρεις noun fem acc pl . . . . βάρις

Βαρεκ pr noun

βαρέος adj masc and neut gen sg . . . . βαρύς

βάρεσιν noun fem dat pl . . . . βάρις

βάρεων noun fem gen pl   id.

βαρέως adverb

Βαρι pr noun

Βαρια pr noun

Βαριαϊ pr noun

Βαριγα pr noun

βαρκοννιμ translit

Βαρκους pr noun

Βαρνη pr noun

βάρος noun neut nom and acc sg

Βαρουμσεωριμ pr noun

Βαρουχ pr noun

Βαρσα pr noun

Βερσαμιτης pr noun masc nom sg

Βαρτακου pr noun masc gen sg . . . . Βαρτακος

βαρύ adj neut nom and acc sg . . . . βαρύς

βαρύγλωσσον adj acc sg, neut nom sg . . . . . βαρύγλωσσος

βαρυηχῆ adj masc and fem acc sg . . . . βαρυηχής

βαρύθυμον adj acc sg, neut nom sg . . . . βαρύθυμος

βαρυκάρδιοι adj masc and fem nom pl . . . . . βαρυκάρδιος

βαρύν adj masc acc sg . . . . βαρύς

βαρύνει vb pres act ind 3rd pers sg . . . . βαρύνω

βαρύνεσθαι vb pres m/p inf   id.

βαρυνέσθω vb pres m/p impv 3rd pers sg   id.

βαρύνεται vb pres m/p ind 3rd pers sg   id.

βαρύνετε vb pres act ind 2nd pers pl   id.

βαρύνῃς vb pres act subj 2nd pers sg   id.

βαρύνηται vb pres m/p subj 3rd pers sg   id.

βαρυνθεῖσα vb 1st aor pass part fem nom sg   id.

βαρυνθήσεται vb fut pass ind 3rd pers sg   id.

βαρυνθήσῃ vb fut pass ind 2nd pers sg   id.

βάρυνον vb 1st aor act impv 2nd pers sg   id.

βαρύνων vb pres act part masc nom sg   id.

βαρύς adj masc nom sg

βαρυτάτου superl adj masc and neut gen sg . . . . βαρύς

βαρυτέρα comp adj neut nom and acc pl   id.

βαρύτεροι comp adj masc nom pl   id.

βαρύτερον comp adj masc acc sg,
          neut nom and acc sg   id.

βαρύτερος comp adj masc nom sg   id.

βαρυτέρως adverb

βαρχαβωθ translit

Βαρχια pr noun

Βαρχους pr noun

Βαρωδις pr noun

Βασα pr noun

Βασαλωθ pr noun

Βασαμυς pr noun

Βασαν pr noun

Βασανι pr noun

βασανιεῖ vb fut act ind 3rd pers sg . . . . βασανίζω

βασάνιζε vb pres act impv 2nd pers sg . . . . βασανίζω	βασίλειον noun neut nom and acc sg	
βασανίζειν vb pres act inf	id.	βασιλεῖς noun masc nom pl . . . . βασιλεύς
βασανίζεσθαι vb pres m/p inf	id.	βασιλείων adj gen pl . . . . βασίλειος
βασανίζῃ vb pres m/p ind 2nd pers sg	id.	βασιλείων noun neut gen pl . . . . βασίλειον
βασανιζόμενον vb pres m/p part masc acc sg	id.	βασιλειῶν noun fem gen pl . . . . βασιλεία
βασανιζόμενος vb pres m/p part masc nom sg	id.	βασιλεῦ noun masc voc sg . . . . βασιλεύς
βασανιζομένους vb pres m/p part masc acc pl	id.	βασίλευε vb pres act impv 2nd pers sg . . . . βασιλεύω
βασανιζομένων vb pres m/p part gen pl	id.	βασιλεύει vb pres act ind 3rd pers sg	id.
βασανίζοντας vb pres act part masc acc pl	id.	βασιλεύειν vb pres act inf	id.
βασανιζόντων vb pres act part masc and neut gen pl	id.	βασιλευομένη vb pres m/p part fem dat sg	id.
βασανίζων vb pres act part masc nom sg	id.	βασιλεύοντα vb pres act part masc acc sg	id.
βασανίσαι vb 1st aor act inf	id.	βασιλεύοντας vb pres act part masc acc pl	id.
βασανίσαντα vb 1st aor act part neut nom and acc pl	id.	βασιλεύοντος vb pres act part	
βασανίσει vb fut act ind 3rd pers sg	id.	masc and neut gen sg	id.
βασανισθείς vb 1st aor pass part masc nom sg	id.	βασιλεύουσα vb pres act part fem nom sg	id.
βασανισμόν noun masc acc sg . . . . βασανισμός	βασιλεύουσιν vb pres act ind 3rd pers pl	id.
βασανισμούς noun masc acc pl	id.	βασιλεύς noun masc nom sg	
βασάνισον vb 1st aor act impv 2nd pers sg . . . . . βασανίζω	Βασιλευς pr noun masc nom sg	
βασανιστήρια noun neut nom and acc pl . βασανιστήριον	βασιλεῦσαι vb 1st aor act inf . . . . βασιλεύω
βασανιστηρίων noun neut gen pl	id.	βασιλεύσαντας vb 1st aor act part masc acc pl	id.
Βασανιτιδι pr noun fem dat sg . . . . Βασανιτις	βασιλεύσαντες vb 1st aor act part masc nom pl	id.
Βασανιτιδος pr noun fem gen sg	id.	βασιλεύσας vb 1st aor act part masc nom sg	id.
Βασανῖτιν pr noun fem acc sg	id.	βασιλευσάτω vb 1st aor act impv 3rd pers sg	id.
Βασανῖτις pr noun masc nom sg	id.	βασιλεύσει vb fut act ind 3rd pers sg	id.
βάσανοι noun fem nom pl . . . . βάσανος	βασιλεύσεις vb fut act ind 2nd pers sg	id.
βασάνοις noun fem dat pl	id.	βασιλεύσῃ vb 1st aor act subj 3rd pers sg	id.
βάσανον noun fem acc sg	id.	βασιλεύσητε vb 1st aor act subj 2nd pers pl	id.
βάσανος noun fem nom sg	id.	βασιλεῦσι noun masc dat pl . . . . βασιλεύς
βασάνου noun fem gen sg	id.	βασιλεύσομεν vb fut act ind 1st pers pl . . . . βασιλεύω
βασάνους noun fem acc pl	id.	βασίλευσον vb 1st aor act impv 2nd pers sg	id.
βασάνῳ noun fem dat sg	id.	βασιλεύσω vb fut act ind 1st pers sg	id.
βασάνων noun fem gen pl	id.	βασιλεύω vb pres act ind 1st pers sg	id.
βάσει noun fem dat sg . . . . βάσις	βασιλεύων vb pres act part masc nom sg	id.
βάσεις noun fem nom and acc pl	id.	βασιλέων noun masc gen pl . . . . βασιλεύς
Βασελλαν pr noun		βασιλέως noun masc gen sg	id.
Βασεμμαθ pr noun		βασιλικά adj neut nom and acc pl . . . . βασιλικός
βάσεως noun fem gen sg . . . . βάσις	βασιλικάς adj fem acc pl	id.
Βασηδωθ pr noun		βασιλικῇ adj fem dat sg	id.
Βασηζα pr noun		βασιλικήν adj fem acc sg	id.
Βασθαι pr noun		βασιλικῆς adj fem gen sg	id.
Βασι pr noun		βασιλικοί adj masc nom pl	id.
βασιλέα noun masc acc sg . . . . βασιλεύς	βασιλικοῖς adj masc and neut dat pl	id.
βασιλέας noun masc acc pl	id.	βασιλικόν adj masc acc sg, neut nom and acc sg	id.
βασιλεῖ noun masc dat sg	id.	βασιλικοῦ adj masc and neut gen sg	id.
βασίλεια noun neut nom and acc pl . . . . βασίλειον	βασιλικώτεροι comp adj masc nom pl	id.
βασίλεια noun fem nom sg		βασιλίσκον noun masc acc sg . . . . βασιλίσκος
βασιλείᾳ noun fem dat sg . . . . βασιλεία	βασιλίσκος noun masc nom sg	id.
βασιλεῖαι noun fem nom pl	id.	βασίλισσα noun fem nom sg	
βασιλείαις noun fem dat pl	id.	βασίλισσαι noun fem nom pl . . . . βασίλισσα
βασιλείαν noun fem acc sg	id.	βασίλισσαν noun fem acc sg	id.
βασιλείας noun fem gen sg and acc pl	id.		
βασιλείοις noun neut dat pl . . . . βασίλειον		

βασιλίσσῃ noun fem dat sg . . . . βασίλισσα
βασιλίσσῃ noun fem dat sg   id.
βασιλίσσης noun fem gen sg   id.
βάσιν noun fem acc sg . . . . βάσις
βάσις noun fem nom sg   id.
βασκαίνοντος vb pres act part
       masc and neut gen sg . . . . βασκαίνω
βασκαίνων vb pres act part masc nom sg   id.
Βασκαμα pr noun
βασκανεῖ vb fut act ind 3rd pers sg . . . . βασκαίνω
βασκανία noun fem nom sg
βασκανίας noun fem gen sg . . . . βασκανία
βάσκανος adj masc nom sg
βασκάνου adj masc gen sg . . . . βάσκανος
βασκάνῳ adj masc and neut dat sg   id.
Βασου pr noun
Βασουρωθ pr noun
Βασσαι pr noun
βάσταγμα noun neut nom and acc sg
βαστάγματα noun neut nom and acc pl . . . . βάσταγμα
βαστάζοντες vb pres act part masc nom pl . . . . . βαστάζω
βαστάξατε vb 1st aor act impv 2nd pers pl   id.
βάσταξον vb 1st aor act impv 2nd pers sg   id.
βαστάσας vb 1st aor act part masc nom sg   id.
βαστάσω vb fut act ind 1st pers sg   id.
Βασωδια pr noun
Βατανη pr noun
Βατνε pr noun
βάτος noun masc or fem nom sg
βάτου noun masc gen sg . . . . βάτος
βάτραχοι noun masc nom pl . . . . βάτραχος
βατράχοις noun masc dat pl   id.
βάτραχον noun masc acc sg   id.
βάτραχος noun masc nom sg   id.
βατράχους noun masc acc pl   id.
βατράχων noun masc gen pl   id.
βάτῳ noun masc dat sg . . . . βάτος
Βαυξ pr noun
βαφή noun fem nom sg
βαφῇ noun fem dat sg . . . . βαφή
βαφῇ vb 2nd aor pass subj 3rd pers sg . . . . βάπτω
βαφήσεται vb fut pass ind 3rd pers sg   id.
Βαχιρ pr noun
βάψαντες vb 1st aor act part masc nom pl . . . . βάπτω
βάψει vb fut act ind 3rd pers sg   id.
βάψεις vb fut act ind 2nd pers sg   id.
βδέλλη noun fem dat sg . . . . βδέλλα
βδέλυγμα noun neut nom and acc sg
βδελύγμασι noun neut dat pl . . . . βδέλυγμα
βδελύγματα noun neut nom and acc pl   id.
βδελύγματι noun neut dat sg   id.
βδελύγματος noun neut gen sg   id.

βδελυγμάτων noun neut gen pl . . . . βδέλυγμα
βδελυγμόν noun masc acc sg . . . . βδελυγμός
βδελυγμός noun masc nom sg   id.
βδελυκτός adj masc nom sg
βδελυκτούς adj masc acc pl . . . . βδελυκτός
βδελύξαι vb 1st aor act inf . . . . βδελύσσω
βδελύξεσθε vb fut mid ind 2nd pers pl   id.
βδελύξεται vb fut mid ind 3rd pers sg   id.
βδελύξετε vb fut act ind 2nd pers pl   id.
βδελύξῃ vb 1st aor act subj 3rd pers sg,
      1st aor mid subj 2nd pers sg,
      fut mid ind 2nd pers sg   id.
βδελύξητε vb 1st aor act subj 2nd pers pl   id.
βδελυρά adj neut nom and acc pl . . . . βδελυρός
βδελύσσεται vb pres m/p ind 3rd pers sg . . . . . . βδελύσσω
βδελύσσῃ vb pres m/p ind 2nd pers sg,
      pres m/p subj 2nd pers sg   id.
βδελύσσομαι vb pres m/p ind 1st pers sg   id.
βδελυσσόμενοι vb pres m/p part masc nom pl   id.
βδελυσσομένοις vb pres m/p part masc and neut dat pl id.
βδελυσσόμενον vb pres m/p part masc acc sg   id.
βδελυσσόμενος vb pres m/p part masc nom sg   id.
βδελύσσονται vb pres m/p ind 3rd pers pl   id.
βδελύττῃ vb pres m/p subj 2nd pers sg . . . . βδελύττω
βδελυχθήσεται vb fut pass ind 3rd pers sg . . . . . βδελύσσω
βεβαία adj fem dat sg . . . . βέβαιος
βεβαίαν adj fem acc sg   id.
βέβαιον adj masc acc sg, neut nom and acc sg   id.
βεβαίως adverb
βεβαίωσιν noun fem acc sg . . . . βεβαίωσις
βεβαίωσις noun fem nom sg   id.
βεβαίωσον vb 1st aor act impv 2nd pers sg . . . . . . βεβαιόω
βεβαρβαρωμένος vb perf m/p part masc nom sg   βαρβαρόω
βεβάρηται vb perf m/p ind 3rd pers sg . . . . βαρέω
βεβάρυνται vb perf m/p ind 3rd pers pl . . . . βαρύνω
βεβασίλευκεν vb perf act ind 3rd pers sg . . . . . . βασιλεύω
βεβήκει vb plpf act ind 3rd pers sg . . . . βαίνω
βεβηκότα vb perf act part masc acc sg   id.
βεβηκότες vb perf act part masc nom pl   id.
βέβηλα adj neut nom and acc pl . . . . βέβηλος
βέβηλε adj masc voc sg   id.
βέβηλοι adj masc and fem nom pl   id.
βεβηλοῖ vb pres act ind 3rd pers sg . . . . βεβηλόω
βεβηλοις adj masc and fem dat pl . . . . βέβηλος
βέβηλος adj masc and fem nom sg   id.
βεβηλου adj gen sg   id.
βεβηλοῦν vb pres act inf . . . . βεβηλόω
βεβηλοῦνται vb pres m/p ind 3rd pers pl   id.
βεβήλους adj masc and fem acc pl . . . . βέβηλος
βεβηλοῦσιν vb pres act ind 3rd pers pl . . . . βεβηλόω
βεβηλοῦται vb pres m/p ind 3rd pers sg   id.
βεβηλοῦτε vb pres act ind 2nd pers pl   id.

βεβηλῶ   vb pres act ind 1st pers sg . . . . βεβηλόω

βεβήλῳ   adj dat sg . . . . βέβηλος

βεβηλωθέν   vb 1st aor pass part neut nom and acc sg   βεβηλόω

βεβηλωθέντα   vb 1st aor pass part masc acc sg   id.

βεβηλωθῇ   vb 1st aor pass subj 3rd pers sg   id.

βεβηλωθήσεται   vb fut pass ind 3rd pers sg   id.

βεβηλωμένην   vb pres m/p part fem acc sg   id.

βεβηλωμένον   vb pres m/p part masc acc sg,

           neut nom and acc sg   id.

βεβηλωμένου   vb pres m/p part masc and neut gen sg   id.

βεβήλων   adj gen pl . . . . βέβηλος

βεβηλῶν   vb pres act part masc nom sg . . . . βεβηλόω

βεβηλῶνται   vb pres m/p subj 3rd pers pl   id.

βεβηλῶσαι   vb 1st aor act inf   id.

βεβηλώσει   noun fem dat sg . . . . βεβήλωσις

βεβηλώσει   vb fut act ind 3rd pers sg . . . . βεβηλόω

βεβηλώσεις   vb fut act ind 2nd pers sg   id.

βεβηλώσετε   vb fut act ind 2nd pers pl   id.

βεβηλώσεως   noun fem gen sg . . . . βεβήλωσις

βεβηλώσῃ   vb 1st aor act subj 3rd pers sg . . . . βεβηλόω

βεβήλωσιν   noun fem acc sg . . . . βεβήλωσις

βεβηλώσουσιν   vb fut act ind 3rd pers pl . . . . βεβηλόω

βεβηλώσω   vb 1st aor act subj 1st pers sg   id.

βεβηλώσωσιν   vb 1st aor act subj 3rd pers pl   id.

βεβλάστηκεν   vb perf act ind 3rd pers sg . . . . . . βλαστάνω

βεβλημένοι   vb perf m/p part masc nom pl . . . . βάλλω

βεβοήθηται   vb perf m/p ind 3rd pers sg . . . . βοηθέω

βεβούλευμαι   vb perf m/p ind 1st pers sg . . . . βουλεύω

βεβούλευνται   vb perf m/p ind 3rd pers pl   id.

βεβούλευται   vb perf m/p ind 3rd pers sg   id.

βεβουνισμένων   vb perf m/p part gen pl . . . . βουνίζω

βέβρωκα   vb perf act ind 1st pers sg . . . . βιβρώσκω

βέβρωκε   vb perf act ind 3rd pers sg   id.

βεβρώκει   vb plpf act ind 3rd pers sg   id.

βεβρωκέναι   vb perf act inf   id.

βεβρωμένα   vb perf m/p part neut nom and acc pl   id.

βεβρωμένοι   vb perf m/p part masc nom pl   id.

βεβρωμένος   vb perf m/p part masc nom sg   id.

βεβρῶσθαι   vb perf m/p inf   id.

Βεγεθων   pr noun

βεδεκ   translit

Βεελαμων   pr noun

Βεελιμ   pr noun

Βεελμαων   pr noun

Βεελμεων   pr noun

Βεελμων   pr noun

Βεελσαρου   pr noun masc gen sg . . . . Βεελσαρος

Βεελσεπφων   pr noun

Βεελτέεμος   pr noun

Βεελτεεμῳ   pr noun masc dat sg . . . . Βεελτεεμος

Βεελφεγωρ   pr noun

Βεερμι   pr noun

Βεζεκ   pr noun

Βεηρ   pr noun

Βεηρα   pr noun

Βεηρι   pr noun

Βεηρσαβεε   pr noun

Βεηρωθα   pr noun

βεθ   translit

Βεκτιλεθ   pr noun

Βελααν   pr noun

Βελασωρ   pr noun

Βελβαιμ   pr noun

Βελγα   pr noun

Βελγαι   pr noun

βέλει   noun neut dat sg . . . . βέλος

βέλεσι   noun neut dat pl   id.

βέλη   noun neut nom and acc pl   id.

Βελιαλ   pr noun

Βελισα   pr noun

Βελμαιν   pr noun

βέλος   noun neut nom and acc sg

βελοστάσεις   noun fem acc pl . . . . βελόστασις

βελοστάσεων   noun fem gen pl   id.

βέλους   noun neut gen sg . . . . βέλος

Βελσαττιμ   pr noun

βέλτιον   adj neut nom and acc sg . . . . βελτίων

βελτίους   adj masc and fem nom pl   id.

βέλτιστα   superl adj neut nom and acc pl . . . . . . βέλτιστος

βελτίστη   superl adj fem dat sg   id.

βελτίστου   superl adj masc and neut gen sg . . . . . βέλτιστος

βελτίω   adj masc acc sg . . . . βελτίων

βελτίων   adj masc and fem nom sg   id.

βελῶν   noun neut gen pl . . . . βέλος

Βεναμιουδ   pr noun

Βενι   pr noun

Βενιαμιν   pr noun

Βενναιας   pr noun masc nom sg

Βενωρ   pr noun

Βερεαν   pr noun fem acc sg . . . . Βερεα

Βερζαιθ   pr noun

Βερζελλαι   pr noun

Βερζελλι   pr noun

Βερθι   pr noun

Βερια   pr noun

Βεριγα   pr noun

Βέροιαν   pr noun fem acc sg . . . . Βέροια

βερσεχθαν   translit

Βερχια   pr noun

Βεσελεηλ   pr noun

Βεσεληλ   pr noun

Βεσεμιιν   pr noun

Βεσενανιμ   pr noun

Βεσι   pr noun

Βεσκασπασμυς pr noun

Βεσλεμος pr noun

Βεωρ pr noun

Βηβαι pr noun

Βηβι pr noun

βηθ translit (Heb. letter: ב)

Βηθαγγαβαριμ pr noun

Βηθαγλα pr noun

Βηθαζαρια pr noun

Βηθαλαμιν pr noun

Βηθαναθινιμ pr noun

Βηθαραβα pr noun

Βηθασμωθ pr noun

Βηθαχαρμ pr noun

Βηθδαγων pr noun

Βηθελισουβ pr noun

Βηθζαιθ pr noun

Βηθηλ pr noun

Βηθλεεμ pr noun

Βηθλεεμίτην pr noun masc acc sg . . . . Βηθλεεμίτης

Βηθμααλλων pr noun

Βηθμααλων pr noun

Βηθσεεδτα pr noun

Βηθσουρ pr noun

Βηλ pr noun

Βηλα pr noun

Βηλιου pr noun neut gen sg . . . . Βηλιον

Βῆλον pr noun masc acc sg . . . . Βῆλος

Βῆλος pr noun masc nom sg   id.

βῆμα noun neut nom and acc sg

βήμασι noun neut dat pl . . . . βῆμα

βήματα noun neut nom and acc pl   id.

βήματος noun neut gen sg   id.

Βην-Ιωναθου pr noun masc gen sg . . . . Βην-Ιωναθαν

Βηρβηθνεμα pr noun

Βηροτ pr noun

Βηρσαβεε pr noun

Βηρσαφης pr noun

βηρύλλιον noun neut nom and acc sg

βηρύλλῳ noun fem dat sg . . . . βήρυλλος

Βηρωθ pr noun

Βηρωθα pr noun

Βηρωθαῖοι pr noun masc nom pl . . . . Βηρωθαῖος

Βηρωθαῖος pr noun masc nom sg   id.

Βηρωθαιου pr noun masc gen sg   id.

Βησανα pr noun

Βησι pr noun

βία noun fem nom sg

βίᾳ noun fem dat sg . . . . βία

βιαζέσθωσαν vb pres dep impv 3rd pers pl . . . . . βιάζομαι

βιάζεται vb pres dep ind 3rd pers sg   id.

βιάζῃ vb pres dep ind 2nd pers sg   id.

βιαζομένων vb pres dep part gen pl . . . . βιάζομαι

βιάζου vb pres dep impv 2nd pers sg   id.

βιαζώμεθα vb pres dep subj 1st pers pl   id.

βιαίας adj fem gen sg . . . . βίαιος

βίαιον adj masc acc sg, neut nom and acc sg   id.

βίαιος adj masc nom sg   id.

βιαιοτέραν comp adj fem acc sg   id.

βιαιότερε comp adj masc voc sg   id.

βιαιοτέρων comp adj gen pl   id.

βιαίου adj masc and neut gen sg   id.

βιαίῳ adj masc and neut dat sg   id.

βιαίων adj gen pl   id.

βιαίως adverb

βίαν noun fem acc sg . . . . βία

βίας noun fem gen sg and acc pl   id.

βιασάμενος vb 1st aor mid part masc nom sg . . . βιάζομαι

βιάσασθαι vb 1st aor mid inf   id.

βιάσῃ vb 1st aor mid subj 3rd pers sg   id.

βιασώμεθα vb 1st aor mid subj 1st pers pl   id.

βιβασθῆναι vb 1st aor pass inf . . . . βιβάζω

βιβλία noun neut nom and acc pl . . . . βιβλίον

βιβλιαφόρων noun masc gen pl . . . . βιβλιαφόρος

βιβλιοθήκαις noun fem dat pl . . . . βιβλιοθήκη

βιβλιοθήκη noun fem dat sg

βιβλιοθήκην noun fem acc sg   id.

βιβλίοις noun neut dat pl . . . . βιβλίον

βιβλίον noun neut nom and acc sg   id.

βιβλίου noun neut gen sg   id.

βιβλιοφυλακίοις noun neut dat pl . . . . . . βιβλιοφυλάκιον

βιβλίῳ noun neut dat sg . . . . βιβλίον

βιβλίων noun neut gen pl   id.

βίβλοι noun fem nom pl . . . . βίβλος

βίβλοις noun fem dat pl   id.

βίβλον noun fem acc sg   id.

βίβλος noun fem nom sg   id.

βίβλου noun fem gen sg   id.

βίβλῳ noun fem dat sg   id.

βιβρώσκοντος vb pres act part
   masc and neut gen sg . . . . βιβρώσκω

βῖκον noun masc acc sg . . . . βῖκος

βίον noun masc acc sg . . . . βίος

βίος noun masc nom sg   id.

βιοτεύειν vb pres act inf . . . . βιοτεύω

βιότητος noun fem gen sg . . . . βιότης

βίου noun masc gen sg . . . . βίος

βιούντων vb pres act part masc and neut gen pl . . . . . . βιόω

βίους noun masc acc pl . . . . βίος

βιοῦσιν vb pres act ind 3rd pers pl . . . . βιόω

βιρα translit

βίῳ noun masc dat sg . . . . βίος

βιώσαντας vb 1st aor act part masc acc pl . . . . βιόω

βιώσεις vb fut act ind 2nd pers sg   id.

βιώσεως noun fem gen sg .... βίωσις

βιώσῃς vb 1st aor act subj 2nd pers sg .... βιόω

βιώσητε vb 1st aor act subj 2nd pers pl   id.

βιώσω vb fut act ind 1st pers sg   id.

βλαβερόν adj masc acc sg, neut nom and acc sg .. βλαβερός

βλάβη noun fem nom sg

βλάπτει vb pres act ind 3rd pers sg .... βλάπτω

βλάπτειν vb pres act inf   id.

βλάπτεσθαι vb pres m/p inf   id.

βλάπτομαι vb pres m/p ind 1st pers sg   id.

βλάπτουσιν vb pres act ind 3rd pers pl   id.

βλαστάνειν vb pres act inf .... βλαστάνω

βλάστημα noun neut nom and acc sg

βλαστήσατε vb 1st aor act impv 2nd pers pl .... βλαστάνω

βλαστησάτω vb 1st aor act impv 3rd pers sg   id.

βλαστήσει vb fut act ind 3rd pers sg   id.

βλαστήσῃ vb 1st aor act subj 3rd pers sg   id.

βλαστοί noun masc nom pl .... βλαστός

βλαστόν noun masc acc sg   id.

βλαστός noun masc nom sg   id.

βλαστοῦ noun masc gen sg   id.

βλαστούς noun masc acc pl   id.

βλαστῶντα vb pres act part masc acc sg .... βλαστάω

βλασφημεῖν vb pres act inf .... βλασφημέω

βλασφημεῖται vb pres m/p ind 3rd pers sg   id.

βλασφημήσῃ vb 1st aor act subj 3rd pers sg   id.

βλασφημίαν noun fem acc sg .... βλασφημία

βλασφημίας noun fem gen sg and acc pl   id.

βλασφημιῶν noun fem gen pl   id.

βλασφήμοις adj dat pl .... βλάσφημος

βλάσφημον adj acc sg, neut nom sg   id.

βλάσφημος adj masc and fem nom sg   id.

βλασφημοῦντες vb pres act part masc nom pl .. βλασφημέω

βλασφήμους adj masc acc pl .... βλάσφημος

βλέπε vb pres act impv 2nd pers sg .... βλέπω

βλέπει vb pres act ind 3rd pers sg   id.

βλέπειν vb pres act inf   id.

βλέπεις vb pres act ind 2nd pers sg   id.

βλέπετε vb pres act ind 2nd pers pl   id.

βλεπέτω vb pres act impv 3rd pers sg   id.

βλεπέτωσαν vb pres act impv 3rd pers pl   id.

βλεπόμενα vb pres m/p part neut nom and acc pl   id.

βλεπόμενος vb pres m/p part masc nom sg   id.

βλέπον vb pres act part neut nom and acc sg   id.

βλέποντα vb pres act part masc acc sg   id.

βλέποντες vb pres act part masc nom pl   id.

βλέποντος vb pres act part masc and neut gen sg id.

βλεπόντων vb pres act part masc and neut gen pl id.

βλέπουσα vb pres act part fem nom sg   id.

βλέπουσαι vb pres act part fem nom pl   id.

βλέπουσαν vb pres act part fem acc sg   id.

βλεπούσης vb pres act part fem gen sg   id.

βλέπουσιν vb pres act ind 3rd pers pl .... βλέπω

βλεπουσῶν vb pres act part fem gen pl   id.

βλέπω vb pres act ind 1st pers sg   id.

βλέπων vb pres act part masc nom sg   id.

βλέφαρα noun neut nom and acc pl .... βλέφαρον

βλεφάροις noun neut dat pl   id.

βλεφάρων noun neut gen pl   id.

βλέψετε vb fut act ind 2nd pers pl .... βλέπω

βλέψῃ vb fut mid ind 2nd pers sg   id.

βλέψητε vb 1st aor act subj 2nd pers pl   id.

βλέψον vb 1st aor act impv 2nd pers sg   id.

βλέψονται vb fut mid ind 3rd pers pl   id.

βληθέντος vb 1st aor pass part masc and neut gen sg . βάλλω

βοᾷ vb pres act ind 3rd pers sg .... βοάω

βοᾶν vb pres act inf

βόας noun masc or fem acc pl .... βοῦς

βοᾶς vb pres act ind 2nd pers sg .... βοάω

Βοασομ pr noun

βοᾶτε vb pres act impv 2nd pers pl,

        pres act ind 2nd pers pl .... βοάω

βόες noun masc or fem nom pl .... βοῦς

βοή noun fem nom sg

βοῇ noun fem dat sg .... βοή

βοηθέ noun masc voc sg .... βοηθός

βοηθεῖ vb pres act ind 3rd pers sg .... βοηθέω

βοήθεια noun fem nom sg

βοηθείᾳ noun fem dat sg .... βοήθεια

βοήθειαν noun fem acc sg   id.

βοηθείας noun fem gen sg   id.

βοηθεῖν vb pres act inf .... βοηθέω

βοηθεῖς vb pres act ind 2nd pers sg   id.

βοηθείτωσαν vb pres act impv 3rd pers pl   id.

βοηθηθῆναι vb 1st aor pass inf   id.

βοηθηθήσῃ vb fut pass ind 2nd pers sg   id.

βοηθηθήσονται vb fut pass ind 3rd pers pl   id.

βοηθήματα noun neut nom and acc pl .... βοήθημα

βοηθημάτων noun neut gen pl   id.

βοηθῆσαι vb 1st aor act opt 3rd pers sg .... βοηθέω

βοηθῆσαι vb 1st aor act inf   id.

βοηθήσασι vb 1st aor act part masc and neut dat pl id.

βοηθήσατε vb 1st aor act impv 2nd pers pl   id.

βοηθησάτωσαν vb 1st aor act impv 3rd pers pl   id.

βοηθήσει vb fut act ind 3rd pers sg   id.

βοηθήσῃ vb 1st aor act subj 3rd pers sg   id.

βοηθήσῃς vb 1st aor act subj 2nd pers sg   id.

βοήθησον vb 1st aor act impv 2nd pers sg   id.

βοηθήσων vb fut act part masc nom sg   id.

βοηθήσωσιν vb 1st aor act subj 3rd pers pl   id.

βοηθοί noun masc nom pl .... βοηθός

βοηθοῖς noun masc dat pl   id.

βοηθόν noun masc acc sg   id.

βοηθός noun masc nom sg

βοηθοῦ noun masc gen sg	βοηθός	βολίσι(ν) noun fem dat pl		βολίς
βοηθούμενος vb pres m/p part masc nom sg	βοηθέω	βομβήσει vb fut act ind 3rd pers sg		βομβέω
βοηθοῦντα vb pres act part masc acc sg	id.	βόμβησις noun fem nom sg		
βοηθοῦντες vb pres act part masc nom pl	id.	βομβήσουσιν vb fut act ind 3rd pers pl		βομβέω
βοηθοῦντος vb pres act part masc and neut gen sg	id.	Βοννι pr noun		
βοηθούντων vb pres act part masc and neut gen pl	id.	βοοζύγιον noun neut nom and acc sg		
βοηθούς noun masc acc pl	βοηθός	βοός noun masc gen sg		βοῦς
βοηθοῦσαν vb pres act part fem acc sg	βοηθέω	Βοος pr noun		
βοηθῷ noun masc dat sg	βοηθός	βοράν noun fem acc sg		βορά
βοηθῶν noun masc gen pl	id.	βόρβορος noun masc nom sg		
βοηθῶν vb pres act part masc nom sg	βοηθέω	βορβόρῳ noun masc dat sg		βόρβορος
βοῆς noun fem gen sg	βοή	βορέαν noun masc acc sg		βορέας
βοῆσαι vb 1st aor act inf	βοάω	βορέας noun masc nom sg		id.
βοήσαντες vb 1st aor act part masc nom pl	id.	βορέης noun masc nom sg		id.
βοήσας vb 1st aor act part masc nom sg	id.	βορέου noun masc gen sg		id.
βοήσατε vb 1st aor act impv 2nd pers pl	id.	Βορολιου pr noun masc gen sg		Βορολιας
βοήσει vb fut act ind 3rd pers sg	id.	βορρᾶ noun masc nom sg		βορέας
βοήσεσθε vb fut mid ind 2nd pers pl	id.	βορρᾷ noun masc dat sg		id.
βοήσεται vb fut mid ind 3rd pers sg	id.	βορρᾶν noun masc acc sg		id.
βοήσῃ vb 1st aor act subj 3rd pers sg,		βόσκε vb pres act impv 2nd pers sg		βόσκω
fut mid ind 2nd pers sg	id.	βόσκειν vb pres act inf		id.
βοήσομαι vb fut mid ind 1st pers sg	id.	βόσκεσθαι vb pres m/p inf		id.
βοησόμεθα vb fut mid ind 1st pers pl	id.	βόσκετε vb pres act ind 2nd pers pl		id.
βόησον vb 1st aor act impv 2nd pers sg	id.	βοσκηθῇ vb 1st aor pass subj 3rd pers sg		id.
βοήσονται vb fut mid ind 3rd pers pl	id.	βοσκηθήσεται vb fut pass ind 3rd pers sg		id.
βοήσουσιν vb fut act ind 3rd pers pl	id.	βοσκηθήσονται vb fut pass ind 3rd pers pl		id.
βοήσω vb fut act ind 1st pers sg	id.	βόσκημα noun neut nom and acc sg		
βοήσωμεν vb 1st aor act subj 1st pers pl	id.	βοσκήματα noun neut nom and acc pl		βόσκημα
βόθροις noun masc dat pl	βόθρος	βοσκημάτων noun neut gen pl		id.
βόθρον noun masc acc sg	id.	βοσκήσουσιν vb fut act ind 3rd pers pl		βόσκω
βόθρος noun masc nom sg	id.	βοσκήσω vb fut act ind 1st pers sg		id.
βόθρου noun masc gen sg	id.	βόσκουσιν vb pres act ind 3rd pers pl		id.
βόθυνον noun masc acc sg	βόθυνος	βόσκων vb pres act part masc nom sg		id.
βόθυνος noun masc nom sg	id.	Βοσορ pr noun		
βοθύνου noun masc gen sg	id.	Βοσοραν pr noun fem acc sg		Βοσορα
βοθύνους noun masc acc pl	id.	Βοσορρα pr noun		
βοΐ noun masc dat sg	βοῦς	Βοσορρας pr noun fem gen sg		Βοσορρα
βοΐδια noun neut nom and acc pl	βοΐδιον	βόστρυχοι noun masc nom pl		βόστρυχος
Βοκκα pr noun		βοστρύχους noun masc acc pl		id.
Βοκκι pr noun		βοτάνη noun fem nom sg		
βολαί noun fem nom pl	βολή	βοτάνῃ noun fem dat sg		βοτάνη
βολάς noun fem acc pl	id.	βοτάνην noun fem acc sg		id.
βόλβιτα noun neut nom and acc pl	βόλβιτον	Βοτανιν pr noun		
βολβίτοις noun neut dat pl	id.	βοτρύδια noun neut nom and acc pl		βοτρύδιον
βολβίτῳ noun neut dat sg	id.	βότρυες noun masc nom pl		βότρυς
βολβίτων noun neut gen pl	id.	βότρυϊ noun masc dat sg		id.
βολήν noun fem acc sg	βολή	βότρυν noun masc acc sg		id.
βολίδα noun fem acc sg	βολίς	βότρυος noun masc gen sg		id.
βολίδας noun fem acc pl	id.	βότρυς noun masc nom sg		id.
βολίδες noun fem nom pl	id.	βότρυσι noun masc dat pl		id.
βολίδι noun fem dat sg	id.	Βουα pr noun		
βολίς noun fem nom sg		βούβαλον noun masc acc sg		βούβαλος

Βουβαστου	pr noun gen sg	. . . .	Βουβαστος
Βουγαθαν	pr noun		
Βουγαῖον	pr noun masc acc sg	. . . .	Βουγαῖος
Βουγαῖος	pr noun masc nom sg		id.
Βουγαιου	pr noun masc gen sg		id.
Βουζι	pr noun		
Βουζιτης	pr noun masc nom sg		
Βουθαν	pr noun		
βούκεντρα	noun neut nom and acc pl	. . . . . .	βούκεντρον
Βουκιας	pr noun masc nom sg		
βουκόλια	noun neut nom and acc pl	. . . .	βουκόλιον
βουκόλιον	noun neut nom and acc sg		id.
βουκολίου	noun neut gen sg		id.
βουκολίων	noun neut gen pl		id.
Βουλα	pr noun		
βουλαί	noun fem nom pl	. . . .	βουλή
βουλαῖς	noun fem dat pl		id.
βουλάς	noun fem acc pl		id.
βούλει	vb pres dep ind 2nd pers sg	. . . .	βούλομαι
βούλεσθαι	vb pres dep inf		id.
βούλεσθε	vb pres dep ind 2nd pers pl		id.
βούλεται	vb pres dep ind 3rd pers sg		id.
βουλεύεσθε	vb pres m/p ind 2nd pers pl	. . . .	βουλεύω
βουλευόμενοι	vb pres m/p part masc nom pl		id.
βουλευομένων	vb pres m/p part gen pl		id.
βουλεύονται	vb pres m/p ind 3rd pers pl		id.
βουλεύοντες	vb pres act part masc nom pl		id.
βουλεύου	vb pres m/p impv 2nd pers sg		id.
βουλευσαμένους	vb 1st aor mid part masc acc pl		id.
βουλεύσασθαι	vb 1st aor mid inf		id.
βουλεύσασθε	vb 1st aor mid impv 2nd pers pl		id.
βουλεύσεται	vb fut mid ind 3rd pers sg		id.
βουλεύσησθε	vb 1st aor mid subj 2nd pers pl		id.
βουλεύσονται	vb fut mid ind 3rd pers pl		id.
βουλευσώμεθα	vb 1st aor mid subj 1st pers pl		id.
βουλεύσωνται	vb 1st aor mid subj 3rd pers pl		id.
βουλευτάς	noun masc acc pl	. . . .	βουλευτής
βουλευτήριον	noun neut nom and acc sg		
βουλευτηρίῳ	noun neut dat sg	. . . .	βουλευτήριον
βουλευτικῆς	adj fem gen sg	. . . .	βουλευτικός
βουλευτῶν	noun masc gen pl	. . . .	βουλευτής
βουλή	noun fem nom sg		
βουλῇ	vb pres dep ind 2nd pers sg,		
	pres dep subj 2nd pers sg	. . . .	βούλομαι
βουλῇ	noun fem dat sg	. . . .	βουλή
βουληθῇς	vb 1st aor pass subj 2nd pers sg	. . . . . .	βούλομαι
βουληθῶσιν	vb 1st aor pass subj 3rd pers pl		id.
βούλημα	noun neut nom and acc sg		
βουλήμασι	noun neut dat pl	. . . .	βούλημα
βουλήν	noun fem acc sg	. . . .	βουλή
βουλῆς	noun fem gen sg		id.
βουλήσεται	vb fut mid ind 3rd pers sg	. . . .	βούλομαι
βούλησθε	vb pres dep subj 2nd pers pl	. . . .	βούλομαι
βούληται	vb pres dep subj 3rd pers sg		id.
βούλοιτο	vb pres dep opt 3rd pers sg		id.
βούλομαι	vb pres dep ind 1st pers sg		id.
βουλόμεθα	vb pres dep ind 1st pers pl		id.
βουλομένῃ	vb pres dep part fem dat sg		id.
βουλόμενοι	vb pres dep part masc nom pl		id.
βουλομένοις	vb pres dep part masc and neut dat pl		id.
βουλόμενον	vb pres dep part masc acc sg		id.
βουλόμενος	vb pres dep part masc nom sg		id.
βουλομένους	vb pres dep part masc acc pl		id.
βούλονται	vb pres dep ind 3rd pers pl		id.
βούλωνται	vb pres dep subj 3rd pers pl		id.
βοῦν	noun masc or fem acc sg	. . . .	βοῦς
βουνοί	noun masc nom pl	. . . .	βουνός
βουνοῖς	noun masc dat pl		id.
βουνόν	noun masc acc sg		id.
βουνός	noun masc nom sg		id.
Βουνος	pr noun masc nom sg		
βουνοῦ	noun masc gen sg	. . . .	βουνός
βουνούς	noun masc acc pl		id.
βουνῷ	noun masc dat sg		id.
βουνῶν	noun masc gen pl		id.
βοῦς	noun masc or fem nom sg		
βουσί(ν)	noun masc or fem dat pl	. . . .	βοῦς
βούτομον	noun neut nom and acc sg		
βούτυρον	noun neut nom and acc sg		
βουτύρου	noun neut gen sg	. . . .	βούτυρον
βουτύρῳ	noun neut dat sg		id.
Βοχορι	pr noun		
βοῶν	noun masc or fem gen pl	. . . .	βοῦς
βοῶντες	vb pres act part masc nom pl	. . . .	βοάω
βοῶντος	vb pres act part masc and neut gen sg		id.
βοώντων	vb pres act part masc and neut gen pl		id.
βοῶσα	vb pres act part fem nom sg		id.
βραδέως	adverb		
βραδύγλωσσος	adj masc nom sg		
βραδυνεῖ	vb fut act ind 3rd pers sg	. . . .	βραδύνω
βραδύνῃ	vb 1st aor act subj 3rd pers sg		id.
βραδυνῶ	vb fut act ind 1st pers sg		id.
βραχέα	adj neut nom and acc pl	. . . .	βραχύς
βραχεῖ	adj masc and neut dat sg		id.
βραχεῖαν	adj fem acc sg		id.
βραχείας	adj fem gen sg		id.
βραχεῖς	adj masc acc pl		id.
βραχέως	adverb		
βραχήσεται	vb fut pass ind 3rd pers sg	. . . .	βρέχω
βραχίονα	noun masc acc sg	. . . .	βραχίων
βραχίονας	noun masc acc pl		id.
βραχίονες	noun masc nom pl		id.
βραχίονι	noun masc dat sg		id.
βραχίονος	noun masc gen sg		id.

βραχιόνων noun masc gen pl . . . . βραχίων	βρώσει noun fem dat sg . . . . βρῶσις
βραχίοσι noun masc dat pl id.	βρώσεως noun fem gen sg id.
βραχίων noun masc nom sg id.	βρώσιμον adj acc sg, neut nom sg . . . . βρώσιμος
βραχύ adj neut nom and acc sg . . . . βραχύς	βρῶσιν noun fem acc sg . . . . βρῶσις
βραχύ adv id.	βρῶσις noun fem nom sg id.
βραχύν adj masc acc sg id.	βρωτά adj neut nom and acc pl . . . . βρωτός
βραχυτελῆ adj masc and fem acc sg . . . . βραχυτελής	βρωτόν adj masc acc sg, neut nom and acc sg id.
βρέξαι vb 1st aor act inf . . . . βρέχω	βυβλίνας adj fem acc pl . . . . βύβλινος
βρέξει vb fut act ind 3rd pers sg id.	βυβλίῳ noun neut dat sg . . . . βυβλίον
βρέξω vb fut act ind 1st pers sg id.	Βυβλιων pr noun masc gen pl . . . . Βυβλιοι
βρέφη noun neut nom and acc pl . . . . βρέφος	βύβλοις noun fem dat pl . . . . βύβλος
βρέφους noun neut gen sg id.	βύβλος noun fem nom sg id.
βρεφῶν noun neut gen pl id.	βύβλῳ noun fem dat sg id.
βρεχομένη vb pres m/p part fem nom sg . . . . . . βρέχω	βυθεῖς noun masc dat pl . . . . βυθός
βρίθει vb pres act ind 3rd pers sg . . . . βρίθω	βυθόν noun masc acc sg id.
βρόμον noun masc acc sg . . . . βρόμος	βυθός noun masc nom sg id.
βρόμος noun masc nom sg id.	βυθοτρεφοῦς adj gen sg . . . . βυθοτρεφής
βρόμῳ noun masc dat sg id.	βυθοῦ noun masc gen sg . . . . βυθός
βρονταί noun fem nom pl . . . . βροντή	βυθῷ noun masc dat sg id.
βροντᾶς vb pres act ind 2nd pers sg . . . . βροντάω	βυούσης vb pres act part fem gen sg . . . . βύω
βροντή noun fem nom sg id.	βύρσαν noun fem acc sg . . . . βύρσα
βροντήν noun fem acc sg . . . . βροντή	βύρσης noun fem gen sg id.
βροντῆς noun fem gen sg id.	βύσσινα adj neut nom and acc pl . . . . βύσσινος
βροντήσει vb fut act ind 3rd pers sg . . . . βροντάω	βυσσίνας adj fem acc pl id.
βροτοί noun masc nom pl . . . . βροτός	βυσσίνη adj fem nom sg id.
βροτοῖς noun masc dat pl id.	βυσσίνη adj fem dat sg id.
βροτόν noun masc acc sg id.	βυσσίνην adj fem acc sg id.
βροτός noun masc nom sg id.	βυσσίνοις adj masc and neut dat pl id.
βροτῶν noun masc gen pl id.	βύσσινον adj masc acc sg, neut nom and acc sg id.
βροῦχον noun masc acc sg . . . . βροῦχος	βυσσίνους adj masc acc pl id.
βροῦχος noun masc nom sg id.	βυσσίνῳ adj masc and neut dat sg id.
βροῦχου noun masc gen sg id.	βύσσον noun fem acc sg . . . . βύσσος
βροχάς noun fem acc pl . . . . βροχή	βύσσος noun fem nom sg id.
βροχήν noun fem acc sg id.	βύσσου noun fem gen sg id.
βρόχοις noun masc dat pl . . . . βρόχος	βύσσῳ noun fem dat sg id.
βρόχους noun masc acc pl id.	Βωκαι pr noun
βρόχων noun masc gen pl id.	Βωλα pr noun
βρυγμῷ noun masc dat sg . . . . βρυγμός	βώλακας noun fem acc pl . . . . βῶλαξ
βρυγμῶν noun masc gen pl id.	βῶλον noun fem acc sg . . . . βῶλος
βρύξει vb fut act ind 3rd pers sg . . . . βρύχω	βώλους noun fem acc pl id.
βρωθείησαν vb 1st aor pass opt 3rd pers pl . . . . . βιβρώσκω	βώλῳ noun masc dat sg id.
βρωθῇ vb 1st aor pass subj 3rd pers sg id.	βωμοί noun masc nom pl . . . . βωμός
βρωθήσεται vb fut pass ind 3rd pers sg id.	βωμοῖς noun masc dat pl id.
βρωθήσονται vb fut pass ind 3rd pers pl id.	βωμόν noun masc acc sg id.
βρῶμα noun neut nom and acc sg id.	βωμός noun masc nom sg id.
βρώμασι noun neut dat pl . . . . βρῶμα	βωμοῦ noun masc gen sg id.
βρώματα noun neut nom and acc pl id.	βωμούς noun masc acc pl id.
βρώματος noun neut gen sg id.	βωμῶν noun masc gen pl id.
βρωμάτων noun neut gen pl id.	Βωραζη pr noun

Γ γ

γ´ indecl number		
Γααλ pr noun		
Γααλλα pr noun		
Γααμ pr noun		
Γααρ pr noun		
Γαας pr noun		
Γαβα pr noun		
Γαβαα pr noun		
Γαβααθ pr noun		
Γαβαε pr noun		
Γαβαεθ pr noun		
Γαβαηλ pr noun		
Γαβαηλῳ pr noun masc dat sg	. . . .	Γαβαηλος
Γαβαθα pr noun		
Γαβαθων pr noun		
Γαβαωθιαριμ pr noun		
Γαβαων pr noun		
Γαβαωνιτας pr noun masc acc pl	. . . .	Γαβαωνιτης
Γαβαωνιτης pr noun masc nom sg		id.
Γαβαωνιτῶν pr noun masc gen pl		id.
Γαββης pr noun		
Γαβε pr noun		
Γαβεε pr noun		
Γαβερ pr noun		
Γαβηρωθ-χαμααμ pr noun		
γαβης translit		
γαβιν translit		
γαβις translit		
Γαβλι pr noun		
Γαβρι pr noun		
Γαβρια pr noun		
Γαβριηλ pr noun		
Γαδ pr noun		
Γαδααμ pr noun		
Γαδαλια pr noun		
Γαδαραθι pr noun		
Γαδγαδ pr noun		
Γαδδι pr noun		
Γαδερ pr noun		
Γαδεωνι pr noun		
Γαδηλ pr noun		
Γαδηρα pr noun		
Γαδηρωθ pr noun		
Γαερ pr noun		
γάζα noun fem nom sg		
Γαζα pr noun fem nom sg		
Γαζαιοις pr noun masc dat pl	. . . .	Γαζαιος
γάζαις noun fem dat pl	. . . .	γάζα
Γαζαιῳ pr noun masc dat sg	. . . .	Γαζαιος
Γαζαν pr noun fem acc sg	. . . .	Γαζα
γάζαν noun fem acc sg	. . . .	γάζα
Γαζαν pr noun fem acc sg	. . . .	Γαζα
Γαζαρα pr noun fem nom sg		
Γαζαραν pr noun fem acc sg	. . . .	Γαζαρα
γαζαρηνοί noun masc nom pl	. . . .	γαζαρηνός
γαζαρηνούς noun masc acc pl		id.
γαζαρηνῶν noun masc gen pl		id.
Γαζαροις pr noun dat pl	. . . .	Γαζαρα
Γαζαρων pr noun gen pl		id.
Γαζεμ pr noun		
Γαζερ pr noun		
Γαζη pr noun fem dat sg	. . . .	Γαζα
Γαζηρα pr noun		
Γαζηρων pr noun		
γάζης noun fem gen sg	. . . .	γάζα
Γαζης pr noun fem gen sg	. . . .	Γαζα
Γαζμωθ pr noun		
Γαζουβα pr noun		
γαζοφύλακας noun masc acc pl	. . . .	γαζοφύλαξ
γαζοφύλακι noun masc dat sg		id.
γαζοφυλάκια noun neut nom and acc pl	. . .	γαζοφυλάκιον
γαζοφυλακίοις noun neut dat pl		id.
γαζοφυλάκιον noun neut nom and acc sg		id.
γαζοφυλακίου noun neut gen sg		id.
γαζοφυλακίῳ noun neut dat sg		id.
γαζοφυλακίων noun neut gen pl		id.
γαζοφύλαξι noun masc dat pl	. . . .	γαζοφύλαξ
Γαθεθ pr noun		
Γαθερ pr noun		
γαι translit		
Γαι pr noun		
Γαιαν pr noun		
Γαιβαα pr noun		
Γαιβαι pr noun		
Γαιβαλ pr noun		
Γαι-βαναι-εννομ pr noun		
Γαιβενενομ pr noun		
Γαιβηλ pr noun		
Γαιδαδ pr noun		
Γαιεννα pr noun		
Γαιθαν pr noun		
Γαιθβωρ pr noun		
Γαιιεφθαηλ pr noun		
Γαιμελε pr noun		
γαῖς noun fem dat pl	. . . .	γῆ
γαῖσον noun masc acc sg	. . . .	γαῖσος

γαίσῳ noun masc dat sg .... γαῖσος
Γαιφα pr noun
Γαιφαηλ pr noun
γαιῶν noun fem gen pl .... γαῖα
γάλα noun neut nom and acc sg
Γαλααδ pr noun
Γαλααδι pr noun
Γαλααδιτης pr noun masc nom sg
Γαλααδιτιδα pr noun fem acc sg .... Γαλααδιτις
Γαλααδιτιδι pr noun fem dat sg   id.
Γαλααδιτιδος pr noun fem gen sg   id.
Γαλααδῖτιν pr noun fem acc sg   id.
Γαλααδιτου pr noun masc gen sg .... Γαλααδιτης
Γαλααδιτῶν pr noun masc gen pl .... Γαλααδῖτις
γαλαθηνά adj neut nom and acc pl .... γαλαθηνός
γαλαθηνόν adj masc acc sg, neut nom and acc sg   id.
γαλαθηνοῦ adj masc and neut gen sg   id.
γάλακτι noun neut dat sg .... γάλα
γαλακτοποτοῦντες vb pres act part
          masc nom pl .... γαλακτοποτέω
γάλακτος noun neut gen sg .... γάλα
γαλακτοτροφίαι noun fem nom pl ...... γαλακτοτροφία
Γαλαλ pr noun
Γαλαμααν pr noun
Γαλαταις pr noun masc dat pl .... Γαλαται
Γαλατας pr noun masc acc pl   id.
Γαλγαλ pr noun
Γαλγαλα pr noun
Γαλγαλοις pr noun dat pl .... Γαλγαλα
Γαλγαλων pr noun gen pl   id.
γαλεάγρᾳ noun fem dat sg .... γαλεάγρα
Γαλεμ pr noun
Γαλεμαθ pr noun
Γαλεμεθ pr noun
γαλῆ noun fem nom sg
γαληνόν adj acc sg, neut nom sg .... γαληνός
Γαλιλαια pr noun fem nom sg
Γαλιλαιᾳ pr noun fem dat sg .... Γαλιλαια
Γαλιλαιαν pr noun fem acc sg   id.
Γαλιλαιας pr noun fem gen sg   id.
Γαλιλωθ pr noun
Γαλλιμ pr noun
Γαμαλα pr noun
Γαμαλι pr noun
Γαμαλιηλ pr noun
Γαμαριας pr noun masc nom sg
Γαμαριου pr noun masc gen sg .... Γαμαριας
γάμβρευσαι vb 1st aor mid impv 2nd pers sg .... γαμβρεύω
γαμβρεύσητε vb 1st aor act subj 2nd pers pl   id.
γαμβροί noun masc nom pl .... γαμβρός
γαμβρόν noun masc acc sg   id.
γαμβρός noun masc nom sg

γαμβροῦ noun masc gen sg .... γαμβρός
γαμβρούς noun masc acc pl   id.
γαμβρῷ noun masc dat sg   id.
γαμβρῶν noun masc gen pl   id.
Γαμερ pr noun
γαμετήν noun fem acc sg .... γαμετή
Γαμζω pr noun
Γαμηλος pr noun
γαμικόν adj masc acc sg, neut nom and acc sg .... γαμικός
γάμον noun masc acc sg .... γάμος
γάμος noun masc nom sg   id.
γάμου noun masc gen sg   id.
Γαμουλ pr noun
γάμους noun masc acc pl .... γάμος
Γαμωλ pr noun
γάμων noun masc gen pl .... γάμος
Γαναθων pr noun
Γαντβαθ pr noun
Γανοζα pr noun
γάρ particle
Γαραβεθθι pr noun
Γαραγαθα pr noun
Γαργασι pr noun
γαρεμ translit
Γαρηβ pr noun
Γαριζιν pr noun
Γαρσομος pr noun
γᾶς noun fem acc pl .... γῆ
Γας pr noun
γασβαρηνου noun masc gen sg .... γασβαρηνός
Γασιν pr noun
Γασιωνγαβερ pr noun
γαστέρα noun fem acc sg .... γαστήρ
γαστήρ noun fem nom sg   id.
γαστρί noun fem dat sg   id.
γαστριμαργίας noun fem gen sg .... γαστριμαργία
γαστρίμαργος adj masc and fem nom sg
γαστρός noun fem gen sg .... γαστήρ
Γαυλων pr noun
Γαυνι pr noun
γαυριᾷ vb pres act ind 3rd pers sg .... γαυριάω
γαυρίαμα noun neut nom and acc sg
γαυριωθήσεται vb fut pass ind 3rd pers sg ...... γαυριόω
γαυρωθέντα vb 1st aor pass part masc acc sg ...... γαυρόω
γε enclitic particle
Γεβαλ pr noun
Γεβεελαν pr noun
Γεβερε pr noun
Γεβωθῖτου pr noun masc gen sg .... Γεβωθιτης
γεγαυρωμένοι vb perf m/p part masc nom pl ...... γαυρόω
γεγαυρωμένος vb perf m/p part masc nom sg   id.
γεγένημαι vb perf mid ind 1st pers sg .... γίνομαι

γεγενημένας vb perf mid part fem acc pl . . . . γίνομαι

γεγενημένοις vb perf mid part masc and neut dat pl   id.

γεγενημένον vb perf mid part neut nom and acc sg   id.

γεγενημένος vb perf mid part masc nom sg   id.

γεγενημένων vb perf mid part gen pl   id.

γεγενῆσθαι vb perf mid inf   id.

γεγένηται vb perf mid ind 3rd pers sg   id.

γεγέννηκα vb perf act ind 1st pers sg . . . . γεννάω

γεγεννηκότων vb perf act part masc and neut gen pl   id.

γεγεννημένης vb perf m/p part fem gen sg   id.

γεγέννησαι vb perf m/p ind 2nd pers sg   id.

γεγήρακα vb perf act ind 1st pers sg . . . . γηράσκω

γεγήρακας vb perf act ind 2nd pers sg   id.

γεγήρακεν vb perf act ind 3rd pers sg   id.

γεγλυμμένα vb perf m/p part neut nom and acc pl . . . γλύφω

γεγλυμμένους vb perf m/p part masc acc pl   id.

γέγονα vb perf act ind 1st pers sg . . . . γίνομαι

γεγόναμεν vb perf act ind 1st pers pl   id.

γέγονας vb perf act ind 2nd pers sg   id.

γεγόνασι(ν) vb perf act ind 3rd pers pl   id.

γέγονε(ν) vb perf act ind 3rd pers sg   id.

γεγονέναι vb perf act inf   id.

γεγονός vb perf act part neut nom and acc sg   id.

γεγονόσι vb perf act part masc and neut dat pl   id.

γεγονότα vb perf act part masc acc sg, neut nom and acc pl id.

γεγονότας vb perf act part masc acc pl   id.

γεγονότες vb perf act part masc nom pl   id.

γεγονότος vb perf act part masc and neut gen sg   id.

γεγονότων vb perf act part masc and neut gen pl   id.

γεγονυῖαν vb perf act part fem acc sg   id.

γεγονυίας vb perf act part fem gen sg   id.

γεγονώς vb perf act part masc nom sg   id.

γεγραμμένα vb perf m/p part neut nom and acc pl . . . γράφω

γεγραμμέναι vb perf m/p part fem nom pl   id.

γεγραμμένας vb perf m/p part fem acc pl . . . . γράφω

γεγραμμένην vb perf m/p part fem acc sg   id.

γεγραμμένοι vb perf m/p part masc nom pl   id.

γεγραμμένοις vb perf m/p part masc and neut dat pl   id.

γεγραμμένον vb perf m/p part masc acc sg,

        neut nom and acc sg   id.

γεγραμμένος vb perf m/p part masc nom sg   id.

γεγραμμένους vb perf m/p part masc acc pl   id.

γεγραμμένων vb perf m/p part gen pl   id.

γέγραπται vb perf m/p ind 3rd pers sg   id.

γέγραφα vb perf act ind 1st pers sg   id.

γεγράφαμεν vb perf act ind 1st pers pl   id.

Γεδαν pr noun

γεδδουρ translit

Γεδδουρ pr noun

Γεδδων pr noun

Γεδδωρ pr noun

Γεδεων pr noun

Γεδηλ pr noun

Γεδουρ pr noun

Γεδσουρ pr noun

Γεδσων pr noun

Γεδσωνι pr noun

γεδωρ translit

Γεδωρ pr noun

Γεδωρίτης pr noun masc nom sg

Γεζουε pr noun

Γεθ pr noun

Γεθεδαν pr noun

Γεθερεμμων pr noun

Γεθθα pr noun

Γεθθαιμ pr noun

Γεθθαῖοι pr noun masc nom pl . . . . Γεθθαῖος

Γεθθαῖον pr noun masc acc sg   id.

Γεθθαῖος pr noun masc nom sg   id.

Γεθθαιου pr noun masc gen sg   id.

Γεθθαιῳ pr noun masc dat sg   id.

Γεθθεμ pr noun

Γεθρεμμων pr noun

Γεθχοβερ pr noun

γεῖσος noun neut nom and acc sg

γείσους noun neut gen sg . . . . γεῖσος

γεισῶν noun neut gen pl   id.

γειτνιῶν vb pres act part masc nom sg . . . . γειτνιάω

γειτνιῶντας vb pres act part masc acc pl   id.

γείτονα noun masc acc sg . . . . γείτων

γείτονες noun masc or fem nom pl   id.

γείτονος noun masc or fem gen sg   id.

γειτόνων noun masc or fem gen pl   id.

γείτοσι noun masc or fem dat pl   id.

γείτων noun masc or fem nom sg   id.

γειώραις noun masc dat pl . . . . γειώρας

γελᾷ vb pres act ind 3rd pers sg . . . . γελάω

Γελαμψουρ pr noun

γελάσαι vb 1st aor act inf . . . . γελάω

γελάσας vb 1st aor act part masc nom sg   id.

γελάσεις vb fut act ind 2nd pers sg   id.

γελάσομαι vb fut mid ind 1st pers sg   id.

γελάσονται vb fut mid ind 3rd pers pl   id.

γελάσω vb 1st aor act subj 1st pers sg   id.

Γελβουε pr noun

Γελγελ pr noun

Γελια pr noun

Γελλα pr noun

Γελμων pr noun

Γελμωναῖον pr noun acc sg . . . . Γελμωναῖος

γελοιάζειν vb pres act inf . . . . γελοιάζω

γελοιασμόν noun masc acc sg . . . . γελοιασμός

γελοιαστῶν noun masc gen pl . . . . γελοιαστής

γελοῖον adj masc acc sg, neut nom and acc sg . . . . . . γελοῖος

γελοῖος adj masc nom sg	
γελῶ vb pres act ind 1st pers sg . . . . γελάω	
Γελωνιτου pr noun masc gen sg . . . . Γελωνιτης	
Γελωραι pr noun	
γέλως noun masc nom sg	
γέλωτα noun masc acc sg . . . . γέλως	
γέλωτι noun masc dat sg id.	
γέλωτος noun masc gen sg id.	
Γεμεεθ pr noun	
γέμει vb pres act ind 3rd pers sg . . . . γέμω	
γέμειν vb pres act inf id.	
γεμίσας vb 1st aor act part masc nom sg . . . . γεμίζω	
γεμίσατε vb 1st aor act impv 2nd pers pl id.	
Γεμνα pr noun	
γέμον vb pres act part neut nom and acc sg . . . . γέμω	
γέμοντα vb pres act part neut nom and acc pl id.	
γέμουσα vb pres act part fem nom sg id.	
γενεά noun fem nom sg	
γενεᾷ noun fem dat sg . . . . γενεά	
γενεαί noun fem nom pl id.	
γενεαῖς noun fem dat pl id.	
γενεάν noun fem acc sg id.	
γενεάς noun fem acc pl id.	
γενεᾶς noun fem gen sg id.	
γενέθλιον adj fem acc sg . . . . γενέθλιος	
γένει noun neut dat sg . . . . γένος	
γένεια noun neut nom and acc pl . . . . γένειον	
γενείων noun neut gen pl id.	
γενέσει noun fem dat sg . . . . γένεσις	
γενέσεις noun fem nom and acc pl id.	
γενέσεσιν noun fem dat pl id.	
γενέσεως noun fem gen sg id.	
γενέσθαι vb 2nd aor mid inf . . . . γίνομαι	
γένεσθε vb 2nd aor mid impv 2nd pers pl id.	
γενέσθω vb 2nd aor mid impv 3rd pers sg id.	
γενέσθωσαν vb 2nd aor mid impv 3rd pers pl id.	
γένεσι noun neut dat pl . . . . γένος	
γενεσιάρχης noun masc nom sg	
γένεσιν noun fem acc sg . . . . γένεσις	
γενεσιουργός noun masc nom sg	
γένεσις noun fem nom sg	
γενετῆς noun fem gen sg . . . . γενετή	
γενέτιν noun fem acc sg . . . . γενέτις	
γενεῶν noun fem gen pl . . . . γενεά	
γένη noun neut nom and acc pl . . . . γένος	
γένη vb 2nd aor mid subj 2nd pers sg . . . . γίνομαι	
γενηθείς vb 1st aor pass part masc nom sg id.	
γενηθεῖσα vb 1st aor pass part fem nom sg id.	
γενηθείσῃ vb 1st aor pass part fem dat sg id.	
γενηθέντος vb 1st aor pass part masc and neut gen sg id.	
γενηθέντων vb 1st aor pass part masc and neut gen pl id.	
γενηθῇ vb 1st aor pass subj 3rd pers sg id.	

γενηθῆναι vb 1st aor pass inf . . . . γίνομαι	
γενηθῇς vb 1st aor pass subj 2nd pers sg id.	
γενήθητε vb 1st aor pass impv 2nd pers pl id.	
γενήθητι vb 1st aor pass impv 2nd pers sg id.	
γενηθήτω vb 1st aor pass impv 3rd pers sg id.	
γενηθήτωσαν vb 1st aor pass impv 3rd pers pl id.	
γενηθῶσιν vb 1st aor pass subj 3rd pers pl id.	
γένημα noun neut nom and acc sg	
γενήμασι noun neut dat pl . . . . γένημα	
γενήματα noun neut nom and acc pl id.	
γενήματι noun neut dat sg id.	
γενήματος noun neut gen sg id.	
γενημάτων noun neut gen pl id.	
γενήσεται vb fut mid ind 3rd pers sg . . . . γίνομαι	
γένησθε vb 2nd aor mid subj 2nd pers pl id.	
γενησόμενον vb fut mid part neut nom and acc sg id.	
γενησομένων vb fut mid part gen pl id.	
γένηται vb 2nd aor mid subj 3rd pers sg id.	
γενικῆς adj fem gen sg . . . . γενικός	
γεννᾷ vb pres act ind 3rd pers sg . . . . γεννάω	
γενναία adj fem nom sg . . . . γενναῖος	
γενναίᾳ adj fem dat sg id.	
γενναῖοι adj masc nom pl id.	
γενναῖον adj masc acc sg, neut nom and acc sg id.	
γενναῖος adj masc nom sg id.	
γενναιοτέρα comp adj fem nom sg id.	
γενναιοτέρων comp adj gen pl id.	
γενναιότητα noun fem acc sg . . . . γενναιότης	
γενναιότητος noun fem gen sg id.	
Γενναιου pr noun masc gen sg . . . . Γενναιος	
γενναίους adj masc acc pl . . . . γενναῖος	
γενναίῳ adj masc and neut dat sg id.	
γενναίως adverb	
γεννᾶται vb pres m/p ind 3rd pers sg . . . . γεννάω	
γεννηθεῖσι vb 1st aor pass part masc and neut dat pl id.	
γεννηθέντες vb 1st aor pass part masc nom pl id.	
γεννηθέντων vb 1st aor pass part masc and neut gen pl id.	
γεννηθήσεσθε vb fut pass ind 2nd pers pl id.	
γεννηθήσεται vb fut pass ind 3rd pers sg id.	
γεννηθῆτε vb 1st aor pass subj 2nd pers pl id.	
γεννήμασι noun neut dat pl . . . . γέννημα	
γεννήματα noun neut nom and acc pl id.	
γεννῆσαι vb 1st aor act inf . . . . γεννάω	
γεννήσαντα vb 1st aor act part masc acc sg id.	
γεννήσαντες vb 1st aor act part masc nom pl id.	
γεννήσαντος vb 1st aor act part masc and neut gen sg id.	
Γεννησαρ pr noun	
γεννήσασι vb 1st aor act part masc and neut dat pl . . γεννάω	
γεννήσει noun fem dat sg . . . . γέννησις	
γεννήσει vb fut act ind 3rd pers sg . . . . γεννάω	
γεννήσεις vb fut act ind 2nd pers sg id.	

γεννήσῃ vb 1st aor act subj 3rd pers sg,		
fut mid ind 2nd pers sg		γεννάω
γεννήσῃς vb 1st aor act subj 2nd pers sg		id.
γεννήσω vb fut act ind 1st pers sg		id.
γεννήσωσιν vb 1st aor act subj 3rd pers pl		id.
γεννητός adj masc nom sg		
Γεννουνι pr noun		
γεννώμενα vb pres m/p part neut nom and acc pl . . .		γεννάω
γεννωμένοις vb pres m/p part masc and neut dat pl		id.
γεννωμένων vb pres m/p part gen pl		id.
γεννῶνται vb pres m/p ind 3rd pers pl		id.
γεννῶσαν vb pres act part fem acc sg		id.
γενοίμεθα vb 2nd aor mid opt 1st pers pl		γίνομαι
γενοίμην vb 2nd aor mid opt 1st pers sg		id.
γένοιντο vb 2nd aor mid opt 3rd pers pl		id.
γένοιτο vb 2nd aor mid opt 3rd pers sg		id.
γενόμενα vb 2nd aor mid part neut nom and acc pl		id.
γενομένας vb 2nd aor mid part fem acc pl		id.
γενομένη vb 2nd aor mid part fem nom sg		id.
γενομένην vb 2nd aor mid part fem acc sg		id.
γενομένης vb 2nd aor mid part fem gen sg		id.
γενόμενοι vb 2nd aor mid part masc nom pl		id.
γενομένοις vb 2nd aor mid part masc and neut dat pl		id.
γενόμενον vb 2nd aor mid part masc acc sg,		
neut nom and acc sg		id.
γενόμενος vb 2nd aor mid part masc nom sg		id.
γενομένου vb 2nd aor mid part masc and neut gen sg		id.
γενομένους vb 2nd aor mid part masc acc pl		id.
γενομένῳ vb 2nd aor mid part masc and neut dat sg		id.
γενομένων vb 2nd aor mid part gen pl		id.
γένος noun neut nom and acc sg		
γενοῦ vb 2nd aor mid impv 2nd pers sg		γίνομαι
γένους noun neut gen sg		γένος
γένωμαι vb 2nd aor mid subj 1st pers sg		γίνομαι
γενώμεθα vb 2nd aor mid subj 1st pers pl		id.
γενῶν noun neut gen pl		γένος
γένωνται vb 2nd aor mid subj 3rd pers pl		γίνομαι
γεραιά adj fem nom sg		γεραιός
γεραιᾶς adj fem gen sg		id.
γεραιόν adj masc acc sg, neut nom and acc sg		id.
γεραιοῦ adj masc and neut gen sg		id.
γεραιρομένους vb pres m/p part masc acc pl		γεραίρω
γεραιῶν adj gen pl		γεραιός
Γεραρα pr noun		
Γεραροις pr noun dat pl		Γεραρα
Γεραρων pr noun gen pl		id.
γέρας noun neut nom and acc sg		
Γεργεσαῖοι pr noun masc nom pl		Γεργεσαῖος
Γεργεσαῖον pr noun masc acc sg		id.
Γεργεσαῖος pr noun masc nom sg		id.
Γεργεσαιου pr noun masc gen sg		id.
Γεργεσαιους pr noun masc acc pl		id.

Γεργεσαιων pr noun masc gen pl		Γεργεσαῖος
γέροντα noun masc acc sg		γέρων
γέροντες noun masc nom pl		id.
γέροντι noun masc dat sg		id.
γερόντων noun masc gen pl		id.
γερουσία noun fem nom sg		
γερουσίᾳ noun fem dat sg		γερουσία
γερουσίαν noun fem acc sg		id.
γερουσίας noun fem gen sg		id.
Γερρηνῶν pr noun masc gen pl		Γερρηνοι
γέρων noun masc nom sg		
Γεσεηλ pr noun		
Γεσεμ pr noun		
Γεσιρ pr noun		
Γεσιρι pr noun		
Γεσιωνγαβερ pr noun		
Γεσουρι pr noun		
γεύεται vb pres m/p ind 3rd pers sg		γεύω
γεῦμα noun neut nom and acc sg		
γευσάμενος vb 1st aor mid part masc nom sg		γεύω
γεύσασθαι vb 1st aor mid inf		id.
γεύσασθε vb 1st aor mid impv 2nd pers pl		id.
γευσάσθωσαν vb 1st aor mid impv 3rd pers pl		id.
γεύσει noun fem dat sg		γεῦσις
γεύσεται vb fut mid ind 3rd pers sg		γεύω
γεύσεως noun fem gen sg		γεῦσις
γεῦσιν noun fem acc sg		id.
γεύσομαι vb fut mid ind 1st pers sg		γεύω
γεῦσον vb 1st aor act impv 2nd pers sg		id.
γεύσωμαι vb 1st aor mid subj 1st pers sg		id.
γεφύραις noun fem dat pl		γέφυρα
γέφυραν noun fem acc sg		id.
γεῶδες adj neut nom and acc sg		γεώδης
γεώδους adj gen sg		id.
γεωμετρίας noun fem gen sg		γεωμετρία
γεωμετρικόν adj masc acc sg,		
neut nom and acc sg		γεωμετρικός
γεώργια noun neut nom and acc pl		γεώργιον
γεωργίαν noun fem acc sg		γεωργία
γεώργιον noun neut nom and acc sg		
γεωργίου noun neut gen sg		γεώργιον
γεωργοί noun masc nom pl		γεωργός
γεωργόν noun masc acc sg		id.
γεωργός noun masc nom sg		id.
γεωργοῦντες vb pres act part masc nom pl		γεωργέω
γεωργούντων vb pres act part masc and neut gen pl		id.
γεωργούς noun masc acc pl		γεωργός
γεωργοῦσιν vb pres act ind 3rd pers pl		γεωργέω
γεωργῷ noun masc dat sg		γεωργός
γῆ noun fem nom sg		
γῇ noun fem dat sg		γῆ
Γηβι pr noun		

γηγενεῖς adj masc and fem nom pl . . . . γηγενής
γηγενέσι adj dat pl   id.
γηγενοῦς adj gen sg   id.
γηγενῶν adj gen pl   id.
Γηζαμ pr noun
Γηλων pr noun
γῆμαι vb 1st aor act inf . . . . γαμέω
γήμαντες vb 1st aor act part masc nom pl   id.
γῆν noun fem acc sg . . . . γῆ
Γηρα pr noun
γήρᾳ noun neut dat sg . . . . γῆρας
γῆρας noun neut nom and acc sg   id.
γηράσαι vb 1st aor act inf . . . . γηράω
γηράσει vb fut act ind 3rd pers sg   id.
γηράσῃ vb 1st aor act subj 3rd pers sg   id.
γηράσκουσιν vb pres act ind 3rd pers pl . . . . γηράσκω
γήρει noun neut dat sg . . . . γῆρας
γήρους noun neut gen sg   id.
Γηρσαμ pr noun
Γηρσομ pr noun
Γηρσωμ pr noun
Γηρσων pr noun
Γηρσωνι pr noun
γήρως noun neut gen sg . . . . γῆρας
γῆς noun fem gen sg . . . . γῆ
Γησαμ pr noun
Γηων pr noun
Γιββιρ pr noun
γίγαντα noun masc acc sg . . . . γίγας
γίγαντας noun masc acc pl   id.
γίγαντες noun masc nom pl   id.
γίγαντος noun masc gen sg   id.
γιγάντων noun masc gen pl   id.
γιγάρτου noun neut gen sg . . . . γίγαρτον
γίγας noun masc nom sg
γίγνεσθαι vb pres mid inf . . . . γίνομαι
γιγνέσθω vb pres mid impv 3rd pers sg   id.
γίγνεται vb pres mid ind 3rd pers sg   id.
γίγνηται vb pres mid subj 3rd pers sg   id.
γιγνόμενα vb pres mid part neut nom and acc pl   id.
γιγνόμενον vb pres mid part masc acc sg   id.
γίγνωσκε vb pres act impv 2nd pers sg . . . . γινώσκω
γιγνώσκει vb pres act ind 3rd pers sg   id.
γιγνώσκοντας vb pres act part masc acc pl   id.
Γιεζι pr noun
γιμαλ translit (Heb letter: ג)
γίνεσθαι vb pres mid inf . . . . γίνομαι
γίνεσθε vb pres mid impv 2nd pers pl,
          pres mid ind 2nd pers pl   id.
γινέσθω vb pres mid impv 3rd pers sg   id.
γινέσθωσαν vb pres mid impv 3rd pers pl   id.
γίνεται vb pres mid ind 3rd pers sg   id.

γίνῃ vb pres mid ind 2nd pers sg,
          pres mid subj 2nd pers sg . . . . γίνομαι
γίνομαι vb pres mid ind 1st pers sg   id.
γινόμενα vb pres mid part neut nom and acc pl   id.
γινομέναις vb pres mid part fem dat pl   id.
γινομένας vb pres mid part fem acc pl   id.
γινομένη vb pres mid part fem nom sg   id.
γινομένῃ vb pres mid part fem dat sg   id.
γινομένην vb pres mid part fem acc sg   id.
γινόμενον vb pres mid part masc acc sg,
          neut nom and acc sg   id.
γινόμενος vb pres mid part masc nom sg   id.
γινομένῳ vb pres mid part masc and neut dat sg   id.
γινομένων vb pres mid part gen pl   id.
γίνονται vb pres mid ind 3rd pers pl   id.
γίνου vb pres mid impv 2nd pers sg   id.
γίνωσκε vb pres act impv 2nd pers sg . . . . γινώσκω
γινώσκει vb pres act ind 3rd pers sg   id.
γινώσκειν vb pres act inf   id.
γινώσκεις vb pres act ind 2nd pers sg   id.
γινώσκεται vb pres m/p ind 3rd pers sg   id.
γινώσκετε vb pres act ind 2nd pers pl   id.
γινώσκομεν vb pres act ind 1st pers pl   id.
γινώσκοντα vb pres act part neut nom and acc pl   id.
γινώσκοντες vb pres act part masc nom pl   id.
γινώσκουσαν vb pres act part fem acc sg   id.
γινώσκουσι(ν) vb pres act ind 3rd pers pl,
          pres act part masc and neut dat pl   id.
γινώσκω vb pres act ind 1st pers sg   id.
γινώσκων vb pres act part masc nom sg   id.
Γιων pr noun
γιώρας noun masc nom sg . . . . γειώρας
γλαῦκα noun fem acc sg . . . . γλαύξ
γλεύκους noun neut gen sg . . . . γλεῦκος
γλυκάζον vb pres act part neut nom and acc sg . . . . γλυκάζω
γλυκαίνειν vb pres act inf . . . . γλυκαίνω
γλυκανεῖ vb fut act ind 3rd pers sg   id.
γλυκανθῇ vb 1st aor pass subj 3rd pers sg   id.
γλυκανθήσεται vb fut pass ind 3rd pers sg   id.
γλύκασμα noun neut nom and acc sg
γλυκάσματα noun neut nom and acc pl . . . . γλύκασμα
γλυκασμάτων noun neut gen pl   id.
γλυκασμοί noun masc nom pl . . . . γλυκασμός
γλυκασμόν noun masc acc sg   id.
γλυκέα adj neut nom and acc pl . . . . γλυκύς
γλυκεῖα adj fem nom sg   id.
γλυκεῖς adj masc nom pl   id.
γλυκέος adj masc and neut gen sg   id.
γλυκεροῦ adj masc and neut gen sg . . . . γλυκερός
γλυκύ adj neut nom and acc sg . . . . γλυκύς
γλυκύς adj masc nom sg   id.
γλυκύτερα comp adj neut nom and acc pl   id.

γλυκύτερον comp adj neut nom and acc sg .... γλυκύς
γλυκύτητα noun fem acc sg .... γλυκύτης
γλύμμα noun neut nom and acc sg
γλύμματα noun neut nom and acc pl .... γλύμμα
γλύμματος noun neut gen sg   id.
γλυπτά adj neut nom and acc pl .... γλυπτός
γλυπτοῖς adj masc and neut dat pl   id.
γλυπτόν adj masc acc sg, neut nom and acc sg   id.
γλυπτούς adj masc acc pl   id.
γλυπτῷ adj masc and neut dat sg   id.
γλυπτῶν adj gen pl   id.
γλυφαί noun fem nom pl .... γλυφή
γλυφάς noun fem acc pl   id.
γλυφή noun fem nom sg   id.
γλυφήν noun fem acc sg   id.
γλυφῆς noun fem gen sg   id.
γλύφοντες vb pres act part masc nom pl .... γλύφω
γλυφῶν noun fem gen pl .... γλυφή
γλύψαι vb 1st aor act inf .... γλύφω
γλύψεις vb fut act ind 2nd pers sg   id.
γλῶσσα noun fem nom sg
γλῶσσαι noun fem nom pl .... γλῶσσα
γλώσσαις noun fem dat pl   id.
γλῶσσαν noun fem acc sg   id.
γλώσσας noun fem acc pl   id.
γλώσσῃ noun fem dat sg   id.
γλώσσης noun fem gen sg   id.
γλωσσόκομον noun neut nom and acc sg
γλωσσότμητον adj masc acc sg,
                neut nom and acc sg .... γλωσσότμητος
γλωσσοτομεῖν vb pres act inf .... γλωσσοτομέω
γλωσσοχαριτοῦντος vb pres act part
                masc and neut gen sg .... γλωσσοχαριτόω
γλωσσώδης adj masc and fem nom sg
γλωσσώδους adj gen sg .... γλωσσώδης
γλωσσῶν noun fem gen pl .... γλῶσσα
γλῶτταν noun fem acc sg .... γλῶττα
γλωττοτομῆσαι vb 1st aor act inf .... γλωττοτομέω
γλωττοτομήσεις vb fut act ind 2nd pers sg   id.
γνάθον noun fem acc sg .... γνάθος
γνάθῳ noun fem dat sg   id.
γναφέως noun masc gen sg .... γναφεύς
γνήσιον adj masc acc sg, neut nom and acc sg .... γνήσιος
γνησίως adverb
γνοίη vb 2nd aor act opt 3rd pers sg .... γινώσκω
γνόντες vb 2nd aor act part masc nom pl   id.
γνούς vb 2nd aor act part masc nom sg   id.
γνοφεράν adj fem acc sg .... γνοφερός
γνόφον noun masc acc sg .... γνόφος
γνόφος noun masc nom sg   id.
γνόφου noun masc gen sg   id.
γνόφῳ noun masc dat sg   id.

γνοφώδης adj masc and fem nom sg
γνῶ vb 2nd aor act subj 1st pers sg .... γινώσκω
γνῷ vb 2nd aor act subj 3rd pers sg   id.
γνῴην vb 2nd aor act opt 1st pers sg   id.
γνῶθι vb 2nd aor act impv 2nd pers sg   id.
γνῶμαι noun fem nom pl .... γνώμη
γνῶμεν vb 2nd aor act subj 1st pers pl .... γινώσκω
γνώμη noun fem nom sg
γνώμῃ noun fem dat sg .... γνώμη
γνώμην noun fem acc sg   id.
γνώμης noun fem gen sg   id.
γνῶναι vb 2nd aor act inf .... γινώσκω
γνωριεῖς vb fut act ind 2nd pers sg .... γνωρίζω
γνωριεῖτε vb fut act ind 2nd pers pl   id.
γνώριζε vb pres act impv 2nd pers sg   id.
γνωρίζεται vb pres m/p ind 3rd pers sg   id.
γνωρίζηται vb pres m/p subj 3rd pers sg   id.
γνωρίζομεν vb pres act ind 1st pers pl   id.
γνωρίζοντες vb pres act part masc nom pl   id.
γνωρίζω vb pres act ind 1st pers sg   id.
γνωρίζων vb pres act part masc nom sg   id.
γνώριμοι adj masc and fem nom pl .... γνώριμος
γνώριμον adj acc sg, neut nom sg   id.
γνώριμος adj masc and fem nom sg   id.
γνωρίμων adj gen pl   id.
γνωριοῦμεν vb fut act ind 1st pers pl .... γνωρίζω
γνωριοῦσιν vb fut act ind 3rd pers pl   id.
γνωρίσαι vb 1st aor act inf   id.
γνωρίσατε vb 1st aor act impv 2nd pers pl   id.
γνωρίσῃ vb 1st aor act subj 3rd pers sg   id.
γνωρίσητε vb 1st aor act subj 2nd pers pl   id.
γνωρισθῇς vb 1st aor pass subj 2nd pers sg   id.
γνώρισον vb 1st aor act impv 2nd pers sg   id.
γνωριστάς noun masc acc pl .... γνωριστής
γνωρίσω vb fut act ind 1st pers sg .... γνωρίζω
γνωρίσωσιν vb 1st aor act subj 3rd pers pl   id.
γνωριῶ vb fut act ind 1st pers sg   id.
γνῷς vb 2nd aor act subj 2nd pers sg .... γινώσκω
γνώσει noun fem dat sg .... γνῶσις
γνώσει vb fut mid ind 2nd pers sg .... γινώσκω
γνώσεσθε vb fut mid ind 2nd pers pl   id.
γνώσεται vb fut mid ind 3rd pers sg   id.
γνώσεων noun fem gen pl .... γνῶσις
γνώσεως noun fem gen sg   id.
γνώσῃ vb fut mid ind 2nd pers sg .... γινώσκω
γνωσθῇ vb 1st aor pass subj 3rd pers sg   id.
γνωσθῆναι vb 1st aor pass inf   id.
γνωσθήσεται vb fut pass ind 3rd pers sg   id.
γνωσθήσῃ vb fut pass ind 2nd pers sg   id.
γνωσθήσομαι vb fut pass ind 1st pers sg   id.
γνωσθήσονται vb fut pass ind 3rd pers pl   id.
γνώσθητι vb 1st aor pass impv 2nd pers sg   id.

γνωσθήτω	vb 1st aor pass impv 3rd pers sg	...... γινώσκω
γνωσθῶ	vb 1st aor pass subj 1st pers sg	id.
γνῶσιν	noun fem acc sg	.... γνῶσις
γνῶσιν	vb 2nd aor act subj 3rd pers pl	.... γινώσκω
γνῶσις	noun fem nom sg	
γνώσομαι	vb fut mid ind 1st pers sg	.... γινώσκω
γνωσόμεθα	vb fut mid ind 1st pers pl	id.
γνώσονται	vb fut mid ind 3rd pers pl	id.
γνωστά	adj neut nom and acc pl	.... γνωστός
γνωσταί	adj fem nom pl	id.
γνώστας	noun masc acc pl	.... γνώστης
γνωστέ	adj masc voc sg	.... γνωστός
γνωστέον	verbal adj sg	
γνωστή	adj fem nom sg	.... γνωστός
γνώστης	noun masc nom sg	
γνωστοί	adj masc nom pl	.... γνωστός
γνωστοῖς	adj masc and neut dat pl	id.
γνωστόν	adj masc acc sg, neut nom and acc sg	id.
γνωστός	adj masc nom sg	id.
γνωστούς	adj masc acc pl	id.
γνωστῶς	adverb	
γνῶτε	vb 2nd aor act impv 2nd pers pl,	
	2nd aor act subj 2nd pers pl	.... γινώσκω
γνώτω	vb 2nd aor act impv 3rd pers sg	id.
γνώτωσαν	vb 2nd aor act impv 3rd pers pl	id.
Γοβ	pr noun	
γογγύζοντες	vb pres act part masc nom pl	...... γογγύζω
γογγύζουσιν	vb pres act ind 3rd pers pl	id.
γογγύζων	vb pres act part masc nom sg	id.
γογγύσει	vb fut act ind 3rd pers sg	id.
γόγγυσιν	noun fem acc sg	.... γόγγυσις
γογγυσμόν	noun masc acc sg	.... γογγυσμός
γογγυσμός	noun masc nom sg	id.
γογγυσμοῦ	noun masc gen sg	id.
γογγυσμῶν	noun masc gen pl	id.
γογγύσουσιν	vb fut act ind 3rd pers pl	.... γογγύζω
Γοδολια	pr noun	
Γοδολια	pr noun masc dat sg	.... Γοδολιας
Γοδολιαν	pr noun masc acc sg	id.
Γοδολιας	pr noun masc nom sg	id.
Γοδολιου	pr noun masc gen sg	id.
Γοδολλαθι	pr noun	
γοεροῖς	adj masc and neut dat pl	.... γοερός
γοητείας	noun fem gen sg	.... γοητεία
Γοθνι	pr noun	
Γοθολια	pr noun fem nom sg	
Γοθολιαν	pr noun fem acc sg	.... Γοθολια
Γοθολιας	pr noun fem gen sg	id.
Γοθολιου	pr noun masc gen sg	.... Γοθολιας
Γοθομ	pr noun	
Γοθονιηλ	pr noun	
Γολαθμαιν	pr noun	

Γολγολ	pr noun	
Γολιαδ	pr noun	
Γολιαθ	pr noun	
Γομερ	pr noun	
γόμον	noun masc acc sg	.... γόμος
γομορ	translit	
Γομορ	pr noun	
Γομορρα	pr noun	
Γομορρας	pr noun fem gen sg	.... Γομορρα
γόμος	noun masc nom sg	
γομφιάσεις	vb fut act ind 2nd pers sg	.... γομφιάζω
γομφιασμόν	noun masc acc sg	.... γομφιασμός
γόνασι	noun neut dat pl	.... γόνυ
γόνατα	noun neut nom and acc pl	id.
γονάτων	noun neut gen pl	id.
γονεῖς	noun masc nom and acc pl	.... γονεύς
γονεῦσι	noun masc dat pl	id.
γονέων	noun masc gen pl	id.
γόνοι	noun masc nom pl	.... γόνος
γόνον	noun masc acc sg	id.
γονορρυῇ	adj masc and fem acc sg	.... γονορρυής
γονορρυής	adj masc and fem nom sg	id.
γονορρυοῦς	adj gen sg	id.
γόνυ	noun neut nom and acc sg	
γόου	noun masc gen sg	.... γόος
γόους	noun masc acc pl	id.
Γοργιαν	pr noun masc acc sg	.... Γοργιας
Γοργιας	pr noun masc nom sg	id.
Γοργιου	pr noun masc gen sg	id.
Γορτυναν	pr noun fem acc sg	.... Γορτυνα
Γοσομ	pr noun	
Γουγ	pr noun	
Γουδιηλ	pr noun	
γοῦν	particle	
Γουνι	pr noun	
Γοφερα	pr noun	
Γοωθαμ	pr noun	
γόων	noun masc gen pl	.... γόος
γράμμα	noun neut nom and acc sg	
γράμμασι	noun neut dat pl	.... γράμμα
γράμματα	noun neut nom and acc pl	id.
γραμματέα	noun masc acc sg	.... γραμματεύς
γραμματεῖ	noun masc dat sg	id.
γραμματείας	noun fem gen sg	.... γραμματεία
γραμματεῖς	noun masc nom and acc pl	...... γραμματεύς
γραμματεύειν	vb pres act inf	.... γραμματεύω
γραμματεύοντα	vb pres act part masc acc sg	id.
γραμματεύς	noun masc nom sg	
γραμματεῦσι	noun masc dat pl	.... γραμματεύς
γραμματέων	noun masc gen pl	id.
γραμματέως	noun masc gen sg	id.
γραμματικῇ	adj fem dat sg	.... γραμματικός

γραμματικοί adj masc nom pl . . . . γραμματικός
γραμματικούς adj masc acc pl   id.
γραμματοεισαγωγείς noun masc
        nom and acc pl . . . . γραμματοεισαγωγεύς
γραμμάτων noun neut gen pl . . . . γράμμα
γραπτῷ noun neut dat sg . . . . γραπτόν
γραπτῶν noun neut gen pl   id.
γράφει vb pres act ind 3rd pers sg . . . . γράφω
γράφειν vb pres act inf   id.
γραφείῳ noun neut dat sg . . . . γραφεῖον
γραφέν vb 2nd aor pass part neut nom and acc sg . . . . γράφω
γραφέντα vb 2nd aor pass part neut nom and acc pl   id.
γραφέντες vb 2nd aor pass part masc nom pl   id.
γραφέντος vb 2nd aor pass part masc and neut gen sg   id.
γραφέντων vb 2nd aor pass part masc and neut gen pl   id.
γράφεται vb pres m/p ind 3rd pers sg   id.
γραφή noun fem nom sg
γραφῇ noun fem dat sg . . . . γραφή
γραφήν noun fem acc sg   id.
γραφῆναι vb 2nd aor pass inf . . . . γράφω
γραφῆς noun fem gen sg . . . . γραφή
γραφήσονται vb fut pass ind 3rd pers pl . . . . γράφω
γραφήτω vb 2nd aor pass impv 3rd pers sg   id.
γραφήτωσαν vb 2nd aor pass impv 3rd pers pl   id.
γραφίδι noun fem dat sg . . . . γραφίς
γραφικούς adj masc acc pl . . . . γραφικός
γράφομεν vb pres act ind 1st pers pl . . . . γράφω
γράφοντας vb pres act part masc acc pl   id.
γράφοντες vb pres act part masc nom pl   id.
γράφοντι vb pres act part masc and neut dat sg   id.
γραφόντων vb pres act part masc and neut gen pl   id.
γράφουσαν vb pres act part fem acc sg   id.
γραφούσης vb pres act part fem gen sg   id.
γράφουσι(ν) vb pres act ind 3rd pers pl,
        pres act part masc and neut dat pl   id.
γράφων vb pres act part masc nom sg   id.
γράφωνται vb pres m/p subj 3rd pers pl   id.
γράψαι vb 1st aor act inf   id.
γράψαντες vb 1st aor act part masc nom pl   id.
γράψασα vb 1st aor act part fem nom sg   id.
γράψατε vb 1st aor act impv 2nd pers pl   id.
γράψει vb fut act ind 3rd pers sg   id.
γράψεις vb fut act ind 2nd pers sg   id.
γράψετε vb fut act ind 2nd pers pl   id.
γράψον vb 1st aor act impv 2nd pers sg   id.
γράψω vb fut act ind 1st pers sg   id.
γρηγορεῖν vb pres act inf . . . . γρηγορέω
γρηγόρησιν noun fem acc sg . . . . γρηγόρησις
γρηγόρησις noun fem nom sg   id.
γρηγόρησον vb 1st aor act impv 2nd pers sg . . . . γρηγορέω
γρηγορήσω vb fut act ind 1st pers sg   id.
γρηγορούντων vb pres act part masc and neut gen pl   id.

γρύξει vb fut act ind 3rd pers sg . . . . γρύζω
γρύπα noun masc acc sg . . . . γρύψ
γυμνά adj neut nom and acc pl . . . . γυμνός
γυμναί adj fem nom pl   id.
γυμνασίαν noun fem acc sg . . . . γυμνασία
γυμνάσιον noun neut nom and acc sg
γυμνή adj fem nom sg . . . . γυμνός
γυμνήν adj fem acc sg   id.
γυμνοί adj masc nom pl   id.
γυμνοῖς adj masc and neut dat pl   id.
γυμνόν adj masc acc sg, neut nom and acc sg   id.
γυμνός adj masc nom sg   id.
γυμνότερος comp adj masc nom sg   id.
γυμνότητι noun fem dat sg . . . . γυμνότης
γυμνούς adj masc acc pl . . . . γυμνός
γυμνῶν adj gen pl   id.
γύμνωσιν noun fem acc sg . . . . γύμνωσις
γύναι noun fem voc sg . . . . γυνή
γυναῖκα noun fem acc sg   id.
γυναῖκας noun fem acc pl   id.
γυναικεῖα adj neut nom and acc pl . . . . γυναικεῖος
γυναικείαν adj fem acc sg   id.
γυναικείοις adj masc and neut dat pl   id.
γυναικεῖον adj masc acc sg, neut nom and acc sg   id.
γυναικείῳ adj masc and neut dat sg   id.
γυναῖκες noun fem nom pl . . . . γυνή
γυναικί noun fem dat sg   id.
γυναικός noun fem gen sg   id.
γυναικῶν noun fem gen pl   id.
γυναικῶνα noun masc acc sg . . . . γυναικών
γυναικῶνι noun masc dat sg   id.
γυναικῶνος noun masc gen sg   id.
γυναιξί(ν) noun fem dat pl . . . . γυνή
γύναιον noun neut nom and acc sg
γυνή noun fem nom sg
γῦπα noun masc acc sg . . . . γύψ
γυπός noun masc gen sg   id.
γῦρον noun masc acc sg . . . . γῦρος
γύψ noun masc nom sg
γυψί noun masc dat pl . . . . γύψ
Γωγ pr noun
Γωζαν pr noun
Γωθι pr noun
Γωιμ pr noun
Γωλα pr noun
γωλαθ translit
Γωλαμ pr noun
Γωλαν pr noun
γωληλα translit
Γωλων pr noun
Γωναθ pr noun
Γωνι pr noun

γωνίᾳ noun fem dat sg .... γωνία
γωνίαι noun fem nom pl   id.
γωνιαῖον adj masc acc sg, neut nom and acc sg ... γωνιαῖος
γωνίαις noun fem dat pl .... γωνία

γωνίαν noun fem acc sg .... γωνία
γωνίας noun fem gen sg and acc pl   id.
γωνιῶν noun fem gen pl   id.
Γωυνι pr noun

Δ δ

δ΄ indecl number
δ΄ particle .... δέ
Δαβασθαι pr noun
Δαββων pr noun
δαβιρ translit
Δαβιρ pr noun
Δαβιρωθ pr noun
Δαβιρων pr noun
Δαβραθ pr noun
Δαβρι pr noun
Δαβωρ pr noun
Δαγων pr noun
Δαδαν pr noun
δαδουχίας noun fem gen sg .... δαδουχία
Δαεμια pr noun
Δαθαν pr noun
Δαθεμα pr noun
Δαιβαν pr noun
Δαιβων pr noun
Δαιδαν pr noun
δαίμονι noun masc dat sg .... δαίμων
δαιμόνια noun neut nom and acc pl .... δαιμόνιον
δαιμονίοις noun neut dat pl   id.
δαιμόνιον noun neut nom and acc sg   id.
δαιμονίου noun neut gen sg   id.
δαιμονίων noun neut gen pl   id.
Δαισαν pr noun
Δαισων pr noun
Δακεθ pr noun
δάκῃ vb 2nd aor act subj 3rd pers sg .... δάκνω
δάκνοντας vb pres act part masc acc pl   id.
δάκνοντες vb pres act part masc nom pl   id.
δάκνων vb pres act part masc nom sg   id.
δάκρυα noun neut nom and acc pl .... δάκρυον
δακρύει vb pres act ind 3rd pers sg .... δακρύω
δακρύειν vb pres act inf   id.
δακρυέτωσαν vb pres act impv 3rd pers pl   id.
δάκρυον noun neut nom and acc sg
δακρύσας vb 1st aor act part masc nom sg .... δακρύω
δακρύσει vb fut act ind 3rd pers sg   id.
δάκρυσι noun neut dat pl .... δάκρυ
δακρύω vb pres act ind 1st pers sg

δακρύων noun neut gen pl .... δάκρυον
δακτυλήθρας noun fem gen sg and acc pl .... δακτυλήθρα
δακτύλιοι noun masc nom pl .... δακτύλιος
δακτυλίοις noun masc dat pl   id.
δακτύλιον noun masc acc sg   id.
δακτύλιος noun masc nom sg   id.
δακτυλίου noun masc gen sg   id.
δακτυλίους noun masc acc pl   id.
δακτυλίῳ noun masc dat sg   id.
δακτιλίων noun masc gen pl   id.
δάκτυλοι noun masc nom pl .... δάκτυλος
δακτύλοις noun masc dat pl   id.
δάκτυλον noun masc acc sg   id.
δάκτυλος noun masc nom sg   id.
δακτύλους noun masc acc pl   id.
δακτύλῳ noun masc dat sg   id.
δακτύλων noun masc gen pl   id.
Δαλαον pr noun
Δαλαια pr noun
Δαλαιας pr noun
Δαλαλ pr noun
Δαλαν pr noun
Δαλια pr noun
Δαλιδα pr noun
Δαλιλα pr noun
δαλόν noun masc acc sg .... δαλός
δαλός noun masc nom sg   id.
Δαλουια pr noun
δαλῶν noun masc gen pl .... δαλός
δαμάζει vb pres act ind 3rd pers sg .... δαμάζω
δαμάζων vb pres act part masc nom sg   id.
δαμάλει noun fem dat sg .... δάμαλις
δαμάλεις noun fem nom and acc pl   id.
δαμάλεσιν noun fem dat pl   id.
δαμάλεων noun fem gen pl   id.
δαμάλεως noun fem gen sg   id.
δάμαλιν noun fem acc sg   id.
δάμαλις noun fem nom sg   id.
Δαμαν pr noun
δαμάσει vb fut act ind 3rd pers sg .... δαμάζω
Δαμασεκ pr noun
Δαμοσκηνῆς pr noun fem gen sg .... Δαμασκηνή

Δαμασκον pr noun fem acc sg . . . . Δαμασκός

Δαμασκος pr noun fem nom sg   id.

Δαμασκοῦ pr noun fem gen sg   id.

Δαμασκῷ pr noun fem dat sg   id.

Δαν pr noun

δανείζει vb pres act ind 3rd pers sg . . . . δανείζω

δανείζεται vb pres m/p ind 3rd pers sg   id.

δανειζόμενος vb pres m/p part masc nom sg   id.

δανείζων vb pres act part masc nom sg   id.

δάνειον noun neut nom and acc sg

δανείσῃς vb 1st aor act subj 2nd pers sg . . . . δανείζω

δανεισμοῦ noun masc gen sg . . . . δανεισμός

δάνεισον vb 1st aor act impv 2nd pers sg . . . . δανείζω

δανειστής noun masc nom sg

δανειστοῦ noun masc gen sg . . . . δανειστής

Δανι pr noun

Δανιδαν pr noun

δανιεῖ vb fut act ind 3rd pers sg . . . . δανείζω

δανιεῖς vb fut act ind 2nd pers sg   id.

δανίζει vb pres act ind 3rd pers sg   id.

δανιζόμενος vb pres m/p part masc nom sg   id.

δανιῇ vb fut mid ind 2nd pers sg   id.

Δανιηλ pr noun

δανιοῦσιν vb fut act ind 3rd pers pl . . . . δανείζω

δανιστής noun masc nom sg

δανιστοῦ noun masc gen sg . . . . δανιστής

Δανιτῶν pr noun

δάνος noun neut nom and acc sg

δαπάνας noun fem acc pl . . . . δαπάνη

δαπανᾶται vb pres m/p ind 3rd pers sg . . . . δαπανάω

δαπάνη noun fem nom sg

δαπάνημα noun neut nom and acc sg

δαπανήμασι noun neut dat pl . . . . δαπάνημα

δαπανήματα noun neut nom and acc pl   id.

δαπάνην noun fem acc sg . . . . δαπάνη

δαπανῆσαι vb 1st aor act inf . . . . δαπανάω

δαπανήσει vb fut act ind 3rd pers sg   id.

δαπανωμένης vb pres m/p part fem gen sg   id.

Δαρα pr noun

Δαρδα pr noun

Δαρεῖε pr noun masc voc sg . . . . Δαρεῖος

Δαρεῖον pr noun masc acc sg

Δαρεῖος pr noun masc nom sg

Δαρειου pr noun masc gen sg

Δαρειφ pr noun masc dat sg   id.

Δαρκων pr noun

Δαρωμ pr noun

δασέα adj neut nom and acc pl . . . . δασύς

δασεῖαι adj fem nom pl   id.

δασεῖς adj masc nom and acc pl   id.

Δασεμ pr noun

δασέος adj masc and neut gen sg . . . . δασύς

δάσεσι noun neut dat pl . . . . δάσος

δασέως adverb

δάσος noun neut nom and acc sg

δασύποδα noun masc acc sg . . . . δασύπους

δασύς adj masc nom sg

Δαυιδ pr noun

Δαφνης pr noun fem gen sg . . . . Δαφνη

δαψιλές adj neut nom and acc sg . . . . δαψιλής

δαψιλέσι adj dat pl   id.

δαψιλῆ adj masc and fem acc sg   id.

δαψιλῆ adj dat sg   id.

δέ conjunction and particle

Δεββα pr noun

Δεββωρα pr noun

Δεββωρας pr noun fem gen sg . . . . Δεββωρα

Δεβερι pr noun

Δεβηλαιμ pr noun

Δεβλαθα pr noun

Δεβλαθαιμ pr noun

δεβραθα translit

δεδανεισμένος vb perf m/p part masc nom sg . . . . δανείζω

δεδαπανημένα vb perf m/p part

         neut nom and acc pl . . . . δαπανάω

δεδέημαι vb perf m/p ind 1st pers sg . . . . δέω

δεδειγμένον vb perf m/p part masc acc sg,

         neut nom and acc sg . . . . δεικνύω

δέδειχα vb perf act ind 1st pers sg   id.

δεδεμένοι vb perf m/p part masc nom pl . . . . δέω

δεδεμένος vb perf m/p part masc nom sg   id.

δεδεμένους vb perf m/p part masc acc pl   id.

δέδεται vb perf m/p ind 3rd pers sg   id.

δεδηγμένος vb perf m/p part masc nom sg . . . . δάκνω

δεδηλωμένα vb perf m/p part neut nom and acc pl . . . δηλόω

δεδηλώσθω vb perf m/p impv 3rd pers sg   id.

δεδημιουργημένους vb perf m/p part

         masc acc pl . . . . δημιουργέω

δεδιδαγμένη vb perf m/p part fem nom sg . . . . διδάσκω

δεδιδαγμένοι vb perf m/p part masc nom pl   id.

δεδίδαχεν vb perf act ind 3rd pers sg   id.

δεδικαιωμένα vb perf m/p part neut nom and acc pl δικαιόω

δεδικαίωται vb perf m/p ind 3rd pers sg   id.

δεδικτυωμένοι vb perf m/p part masc nom pl . . . . δικτυόω

δεδίψηκεν vb perf act ind 3rd pers sg . . . . διψάω

δεδογμάτικα vb perf act ind 1st pers sg . . . . δογματίζω

δεδογματισμένον vb perf m/p part neut nom and acc sg id.

δεδογμένα vb perf m/p part neut nom and acc pl . . . . . δοκέω

δέδοικας vb perf act ind 2nd pers sg . . . . δείδω

δεδοίκασιν vb perf act ind 3rd pers pl   id.

δεδοικότες vb perf act part masc nom pl   id.

δεδοικώς vb perf act part masc nom sg   id.

δεδοκίμακας vb perf act ind 2nd pers sg . . . . δοκιμάζω

δεδοκιμασμένοις vb perf m/p part masc and neut dat pl id.

δεδοκιμασμένον vb perf m/p part masc acc sg,	δεήθητε vb 1st aor pass impv 2nd pers pl .... δέω
neut nom and acc sg .... δοκιμάζω	δεήθητι vb 1st aor pass impv 2nd pers sg id.
δεδοκιμασμένος vb perf m/p part masc nom sg id.	δεηθῶμεν vb 1st aor pass subj 1st pers pl id.
δεδοκιμασμένους vb perf m/p part masc acc pl id.	δεηθῶσιν vb 1st aor pass subj 3rd pers pl id.
δεδοκιμασμένων vb perf m/p part gen pl id.	δεήσει noun fem dat sg .... δέησις
δέδοκται vb perf m/p ind 3rd pers sg .... δοκέω	δεήσει vb fut act ind 3rd pers sg .... δέω
δεδομένα vb perf m/p part neut nom and acc pl ..... δίδωμι	δεήσεις noun fem acc pl .... δέησις
δεδομέναι vb perf m/p part fem nom pl id.	δεήσεων noun fem gen pl id.
δεδομένη vb perf m/p part fem nom sg id.	δεήσεως noun fem gen sg id.
δεδομένης vb perf m/p part fem gen sg id.	δέησιν noun fem acc sg id.
δεδομένοι vb perf m/p part masc nom pl id.	δέησις noun fem nom sg id.
δεδομένον vb perf m/p part neut nom and acc sg id.	δέηται vb pres m/p subj 3rd pers sg .... δέω
δεδομένους vb perf m/p part masc acc pl id.	ξεθήσῃ vb fut pass ind 2nd pers sg id.
δεδομένων vb perf m/p part gen pl id.	ξεθήσονται vb fut pass ind 3rd pers pl id.
δέδονται vb perf m/p ind 3rd pers pl id.	δεῖ vb pres act ind 3rd pers sg id.
δεδοξασμένα vb perf m/p part neut nom and acc pl . δοξάζω	δεικνύντας vb pres act part masc acc pl .... δεικνύω
δεδοξασμένη vb perf m/p part fem nom sg id.	δεικνύουσιν vb pres act ind 3rd pers pl id.
δεδοξασμένοι vb perf m/p part masc nom pl id.	δεικνύς vb pres act part masc nom sg .... δείκνυμι
δεδοξασμένοις vb perf m/p part masc and neut dat pl id.	δεικνύω vb pres act ind 1st pers sg,
δεδοξασμένον vb perf m/p part masc acc sg,	pres act subj 1st pers sg .... δεικνύω
neut nom and acc sg id.	δεικνύων vb pres act part masc nom sg id.
δεδοξασμένος vb perf m/p part masc nom sg id.	δειλαία adj fem nom sg .... δείλαιος
δεδοξασμένους vb perf m/p part masc acc pl id.	δείλαιαι adj fem nom pl id.
δεδοξασμένῳ vb perf m/p part masc and neut dat sg id.	δείλαιοι adj masc nom pl id.
δεδοξασμένων vb perf m/p part gen pl id.	δειλαῖς adj fem dat pl .... δειλός
δεδόξασται vb perf m/p ind 3rd pers sg id.	δειλανδρῆσαι vb 1st aor act inf .... δειλανδρέω
δεδόσθαι vb perf m/p inf .... δίδωμι	δειλανδρήσωμεν vb 1st aor act subj 1st pers pl id.
δέδοται vb perf m/p ind 3rd pers sg	δειλανδροῦντες vb pres act part masc nom pl id.
δεδούλευκα vb perf act ind 1st pers sg .... δουλεύω	δειλανθῇ vb 1st aor pass subj 3rd pers sg .... δειλαίνω
δεδυκότος vb perf act part masc and neut gen sg ..... δύω	δειλή adj fem nom sg .... δειλός
δέδωκα vb perf act ind 1st pers sg .... δίδωμι	δείλης noun fem gen sg .... δείλη
δεδώκαμεν vb perf act ind 1st pers pl id.	δειλία noun fem nom sg
δέδωκας vb perf act ind 2nd pers sg id.	δειλία vb pres act impv 2nd pers sg .... δειλιάω
δεδώκατε vb perf act ind 2nd pers pl id.	δειλίᾳ noun fem dat sg .... δειλία
δεδώκει vb plpf act ind 3rd pers sg id.	δειλίαν noun fem acc sg id.
δεδώκειν vb plpf act ind 1st pers sg id.	δειλιᾶν vb pres act inf .... δειλιάω
δέδωκεν vb perf act ind 3rd pers sg id.	δειλιάνῃ vb 1st aor act subj 3rd pers sg .... δειλιαίνω
δεδωκότας vb perf act part masc acc pl id.	δειλίας noun fem gen sg .... δειλία
δεδωκότες vb perf act part masc nom pl id.	δειλιάσει vb fut act ind 3rd pers sg .... δειλιάω
δεδωρημένῳ vb perf dep part masc and neut dat sg δωρέομαι	δειλιάσῃ vb 1st aor act subj 3rd pers sg id.
δεδώρηται vb perf dep ind 3rd pers sg id.	δειλιάσῃς vb 1st aor act subj 2nd pers sg id.
δεδωροκοπημένοις vb perf m/p part	δειλιάσητε vb 1st aor act subj 2nd pers pl id.
masc and neut dat pl .... δωροκοπέω	δειλιάσουσιν vb fut act ind 3rd pers pl id.
δέεσθαι vb pres m/p inf .... δέω	δειλιάσω vb fut act ind 1st pers sg id.
δέῃ vb pres act subj 3rd pers sg id.	δειλινήν adj fem acc sg .... δειλινός
δεηθείς vb 1st aor pass part masc nom sg id.	δειλινῆς adj fem gen sg id.
δεηθέντος vb 1st aor pass part masc and neut gen sg id.	δειλινόν adj masc acc sg, neut nom and acc sg id.
δεηθῆναι vb 1st aor pass inf id.	δειλοί adj masc nom pl .... δειλός
δεηθήσεται vb fut pass ind 3rd pers sg id.	δειλοῖς adj masc and neut dat pl id.
δεηθήσῃ vb fut pass ind 2nd pers sg id.	δειλόν adj masc acc sg, neut nom and acc sg id.
δεηθήσομαι vb fut pass ind 1st pers sg id.	δειλός adj masc nom sg id.
δεηθήσονται vb fut pass ind 3rd pers pl id.	δειλοῦ adj masc and neut gen sg id.

δειλούμενον vb pres dep part masc acc sg . . . . . . δειλόομαι
δειλούς adj masc acc pl . . . . δειλός
δειλόψυχοι adj masc and fem nom pl . . . . δειλόψυχος
δειλόψυχος adj masc and fem nom sg   id.
δειλωθῆτε vb 1st aor pass subj 2nd pers pl . . . . . δειλόομαι
δείματα noun neut nom and acc pl . . . . δεῖμα
δεῖν vb pres act inf . . . . δέω
δεινά adj neut nom and acc pl . . . . δεινός
δειναῖς adj fem dat pl   id.
δεινή adj fem nom sg   id.
δεινήν adj fem acc sg   id.
δεινοῖς adj masc and neut dat pl   id.
δεινόν adj masc acc sg, neut nom and acc sg   id.
δεινός adj masc nom sg   id.
δεινούς adj masc acc pl   id.
δεινῷ adj masc and neut dat sg   id.
δεινῶν adj gen pl   id.
δεινῶς adverb
δεῖξαι vb 1st aor act inf . . . . δεικνύω
δείξας vb 1st aor act part masc nom sg   id.
δείξασα vb 1st aor act part fem nom sg   id.
δείξει vb fut act ind 3rd pers sg   id.
δείξεις vb fut act ind 2nd pers sg   id.
δείξῃ vb 1st aor act subj 3rd pers sg   id.
δείξῃς vb 1st aor act subj 2nd pers sg   id.
δείξητε vb 1st aor act subj 2nd pers pl   id.
δεῖξον vb 1st aor act impv 2nd pers sg   id.
δείξουσιν vb fut act ind 3rd pers pl   id.
δείξω vb fut act ind 1st pers sg   id.
δείξωσιν vb 1st aor act subj 3rd pers pl   id.
δειπνεῖν vb pres act inf . . . . δειπνέω
δειπνῆσαι vb 1st aor act inf   id.
δειπνήσουσιν vb fut act ind 3rd pers pl   id.
δεῖπνον noun neut nom and acc sg
δείπνου noun neut gen sg . . . . δεῖπνον
δειπνοῦντες vb pres act part masc nom pl . . . . δειπνέω
δείπνῳ noun neut dat sg . . . . δεῖπνον
Δεῖρα pr noun
δεῖραι vb 1st aor act inf . . . . δέρω
δεῖσθαι vb pres m/p inf . . . . δέω
δεῖται vb pres m/p ind 3rd pers sg   id.
δειχθῆναι vb 1st aor pass inf . . . . δεικνύω
δειχθήτω vb 1st aor pass impv 3rd pers sg   id.
δέκα indecl number
δεκαδάρχους noun masc acc pl . . . . δεκάδαρχος
δεκαέξ indecl number
δεκαμηνιαίῳ adj masc and neut dat sg . . . . δεκαμηνιαῖος
δεκάμηνοι noun masc nom pl . . . . δεκάμηνος
δεκαπήχεσι adj masc and neut dat pl . . . . δεκάπηχυς
δεκαπλασιάσατε vb 1st aor act impv
      2nd pers pl . . . . δεκαπλασιάζω
δεκαπλασίονας adj masc and fem acc pl . . . . δεκαπλασίων

δεκαπλασίως adverb
δέκατα adj neut nom and acc pl . . . . δέκατος
δεκάται adj fem nom pl   id.
δεκάταις adj fem dat pl   id.
δεκάτας adj fem acc pl   id.
δεκάτη adj fem nom sg   id.
δεκάτῃ adj fem dat sg   id.
δεκάτην adj fem acc sg   id.
δεκάτης adj fem gen sg   id.
δέκατον adj masc acc sg, neut nom and acc sg   id.
δέκατος adj masc nom sg   id.
δεκάτου adj masc and neut gen sg   id.
δεκατοῦντες vb pres act part masc nom pl . . . . δεκατόω
δεκάτῳ adj masc and neut dat sg . . . . δέκατος
δεκάτων adj gen pl   id.
δεκατῶν noun fem gen pl . . . . δεκάτη
δεκαχόρδῳ adj dat sg . . . . δεκάχορδος
Δεκλα pr noun
Δεκμων pr noun
δεκτά adj neut nom and acc pl . . . . δεκτός
δεκταί adj fem nom pl   id.
δεκτή adj fem nom sg   id.
δεκτήν adj fem acc sg   id.
δεκτοί adj masc nom pl   id.
δεκτόν adj masc acc sg, neut nom and acc sg   id.
δεκτός adj masc nom sg   id.
δεκτοῦ adj masc and neut gen sg   id.
δεκτῷ adj masc and neut dat sg   id.
δεκτῶν adj gen pl   id.
δελθ translit (Heb letter: ד)
δέλτοις noun fem dat pl . . . . δέλτος
Δελφων pr noun
Δεμνα pr noun
δένδρα noun neut nom and acc pl . . . . δένδρον
δένδρει noun neut dat sg . . . . δένδρος
δένδρον noun neut nom and acc sg
δενδροτομῶν vb pres act part masc nom sg . . δενδροτομέω
δένδρου noun neut gen sg . . . . δένδρον
δένδρῳ noun neut dat sg   id.
δένδρων noun neut gen pl   id.
Δενεθι pr noun
Δενναβα pr noun
δέξαι vb 1st aor mid impv 2nd pers sg . . . . δέχομαι
δεξαμενάς noun fem acc pl . . . . δεξαμενή
δεξαμένη vb 1st aor mid part fem nom sg . . . . δέχομαι
δεξάμενος vb 1st aor mid part masc nom sg   id.
δέξασθαι vb 1st aor mid inf   id.
δέξασθε vb 1st aor mid impv 2nd pers pl   id.
δεξάσθω vb 1st aor mid impv 3rd pers sg   id.
δέξεται vb fut mid ind 3rd pers sg   id.
δέξῃ vb 1st aor mid subj 2nd pers sg,
      fut mid ind 2nd pers sg   id.

δέξηται vb 1st aor mid subj 3rd pers sg .... δέχομαι

δεξιά adj fem nom sg, neut nom and acc pl .... δεξιός

δεξιᾷ adj fem dat sg id.

δεξιαῖς adj fem dat pl id.

δεξιάν adj fem acc sg id.

δεξιάς adj fem acc pl id.

δεξιᾶς adj fem gen sg id.

δεξιασθείς vb 1st aor pass part masc nom sg ..... δεξιάζω

δεξιοῖς adj masc and neut dat pl .... δεξιός

δεξιόν adj masc acc sg, neut nom and acc sg id.

δεξιός adj masc nom sg id.

δεξιοῦ adj masc and neut gen sg id.

δεξιῷ adj masc and neut dat sg id.

δεξιῶν adj gen pl id.

δέξομαι vb fut mid ind 1st pers sg .... δέχομαι

δέομαι vb pres m/p ind 1st pers sg .... δέω

δεόμεθα vb pres m/p ind 1st pers pl id.

δεόμενοι vb pres m/p part masc nom pl id.

δεομένοις vb pres m/p part masc and neut dat pl id.

δεόμενον vb pres m/p part masc acc sg,

neut nom and acc sg id.

δεόμενος vb pres m/p part masc nom sg id.

δεομένου vb pres m/p part masc and neut gen sg id.

δεομένων vb pres m/p part gen pl id.

δέον vb pres act part neut nom and acc sg id.

δέοντα vb pres act part masc acc sg, neut nom and acc pl id.

δέος noun neut nom and acc sg

δέους noun neut gen sg .... δέος

δέρμα noun neut nom and acc sg

δέρματα noun neut nom and acc pl .... δέρμα

δέρματι noun neut dat sg id.

δερματίνην adj fem acc sg .... δερμάτινος

δερμάτινον adj masc acc sg, neut nom and acc sg id.

δερματίνου adj masc and neut gen sg id.

δερματίνους adj masc acc pl id.

δερματίνῳ adj masc and neut dat sg id.

δέρματος noun neut gen sg .... δέρμα

δέρρει noun fem dat sg .... δέρρις

δέρρεις noun fem nom and acc pl id.

δέρρεσι(ν) noun fem dat pl id.

δέρρεων noun fem gen pl id.

δέρρεως noun fem gen sg id.

δέρριν noun fem acc sg id.

Δεσεθ pr noun

δέσει noun fem dat sg .... δέσις

δεσμά noun masc nom and acc pl .... δεσμός

δεσμεύειν vb pres act inf .... δεσμεύω

δεσμεύεις vb pres act ind 2nd pers sg id.

δεσμεύοντας vb pres act part masc acc pl id.

δεσμεύοντες vb pres act part masc nom pl id.

δεσμεύων vb pres act part masc nom sg id.

δέσμην noun fem acc sg .... δέσμη

δέσμιαι adj fem nom pl .... δέσμιος

δέσμιοι adj masc nom pl id.

δέσμιον adj masc acc sg, neut nom and acc sg id.

δεσμίους adj masc acc pl id.

δεσμίων adj gen pl id.

δεσμοί noun masc nom pl .... δεσμός

δεσμοῖς noun masc dat pl id.

δεσμόν noun masc acc sg id.

δεσμός noun masc nom sg id.

δεσμοῦ noun masc gen sg id.

δεσμούς noun masc acc pl id.

δεσμοφύλακι noun masc dat sg .... δεσμοφύλαξ

δεσμῷ noun masc dat sg .... δεσμός

δεσμῶν noun masc gen pl id.

δεσμῶται noun masc nom pl .... δεσμώτης

δεσμώτας noun masc acc pl id.

δεσμωτήριον noun neut nom and acc sg

δεσμωτηρίου noun neut gen sg .... δεσμωτήριον

δεσμωτηρίῳ noun neut dat sg id.

δεσμώτου noun masc gen sg .... δεσμώτης

δεσπόζει vb pres act ind 3rd pers sg .... δεσπόζω

δεσπόζειν vb pres act inf id.

δεσπόζεις vb pres act ind 2nd pers sg id.

δεσπόζῃ vb pres act subj 3rd pers sg id.

δεσπόζοντα vb pres act part masc acc sg id.

δεσπόζοντι vb pres act part masc and neut dat sg id.

δεσπόζων vb pres act part masc nom sg id.

δεσπόσεις vb fut act ind 2nd pers sg id.

δέσποτα noun masc voc sg .... δεσπότης

δεσπόταις noun masc dat pl id.

δεσποτεία noun fem nom sg

δεσποτείας noun fem gen sg .... δεσποτεία

δεσποτεύοντος vb pres act part

masc and neut gen sg .... δεσποτεύω

δεσπότῃ noun masc dat sg .... δεσπότης

δεσπότην noun masc acc sg id.

δεσπότης noun masc nom sg id.

δεσπότου noun masc gen sg id.

δεσποτῶν noun masc gen pl id.

Δεσσα pr noun

Δεσσαου pr noun masc gen sg .... Δεσσαος

δεῦρο adverb and interjection

δεῦτε adverb and interjection

δευτέρα adj fem nom sg .... δεύτερος

δευτέρᾳ adj fem dat sg id.

δευτέραν adj fem acc sg id.

δευτέρας adj fem gen sg and acc pl id.

δευτερεῦον vb pres act part neut nom and acc sg δευτερεύω

δευτερεύοντα vb pres act part masc acc sg id.

δευτερεύων vb pres act part masc nom sg id.

δευτέριον adj masc acc sg, neut nom and acc sg .. δευτέριος

δεύτεροι adj masc nom pl .... δεύτερος

δεύτερον adj masc acc sg, neut nom and acc sg ... δεύτερος
δευτερονόμιον noun neut nom and acc sg
Δευτερονομιω pr noun neut dat sg ...... Δευτερονομιον
δεύτερος adj masc nom sg
δευτέρου adj masc and neut gen sg .... δεύτερος
δευτέρῳ adj masc and neut dat sg id.
δευτερῶσαι vb 1st aor act inf .... δευτερόω
δευτερώσατε vb 1st aor act impv 2nd pers pl id.
δευτερώσεως noun fem gen sg .... δευτέρωσις
δευτερώσῃ vb 1st aor act subj 3rd pers sg ..... δευτερόω
δευτερώσῃς vb 1st aor act subj 2nd pers sg id.
δευτερώσητε vb 1st aor act subj 2nd pers pl id.
δευτερώσω vb 1st aor act subj 1st pers sg id.
Δεφρωνα pr noun
δέχεσθαι vb pres dep inf .... δέχομαι
δέχεσθε vb pres dep ind 2nd pers pl id.
δεχθήσεται vb fut pass ind 3rd pers sg id.
δεχόμενος vb pres dep part masc nom sg id.
δή particle
Δηβων pr noun
δήγμασι noun neut dat pl .... δήγμα
δήγματα noun neut nom and acc pl id.
δηλαϊστή adj fem nom sg .... δηλαϊστός
Δηλαναθ pr noun
δήλοις adj masc and neut dat pl .... δῆλος
δήλον adj masc acc sg, neut nom and acc sg id.
Δῆλον pr noun acc sg .... Δῆλος
δήλους adj masc acc pl .... δῆλος
δηλωθῆναι vb 1st aor pass inf .... δηλόω
δήλων adj gen pl .... δῆλος
δηλῶσαι vb 1st aor act inf .... δηλόω
δηλώσατε vb 1st aor act impv 2nd pers pl id.
δηλώσει vb fut act ind 3rd pers sg id.
δηλώσεις vb fut act ind 2nd pers sg id.
δηλώσετε vb fut act ind 2nd pers pl id.
δηλώσῃ vb 1st aor act subj 3rd pers sg id.
δηλώσητε vb 1st aor act subj 2nd pers pl id.
δήλωσιν noun fem acc sg .... δήλωσις
δήλωσις noun fem nom sg id.
δηλώσομεν vb fut act ind 1st pers pl .... δηλόω
δηλώσουσιν vb fut act ind 3rd pers pl id.
δηλώσω vb fut act ind 1st pers sg id.
δηλώσων vb fut act part masc nom sg id.
δημαγωγίας noun fem acc pl .... δημαγωγία
δημευθήσεται vb fut pass ind 3rd pers sg .... δημεύω
δημηγορεῖν vb pres act inf .... δημηγορέω
δημηγορῶν vb pres act part masc nom sg id.
Δημητριον pr noun masc acc sg .... Δημητριος
Δημητριος pr noun masc nom sg id.
Δημητριου pr noun masc gen sg id.
Δημητριω pr noun masc dat sg id.
δήμιον adj acc sg, neut nom sg .... δήμιος

δήμιος adj masc and fem nom sg
δημιουργός noun masc nom sg
δημιουργοῦντας vb pres act part masc acc pl . δημιουργέω
δημιουργῶν noun masc gen pl .... δημιουργός
δῆμοι noun masc nom pl .... δῆμος
δήμοις noun masc dat pl id.
δῆμον noun masc acc sg id.
δῆμος noun masc nom sg id.
δημοσίᾳ adj fem dat sg .... δημόσιος
δημοτελής adj masc and fem nom sg
δημότης noun masc nom sg
δήμου noun masc gen sg .... δῆμος
δήμους noun masc acc pl id.
Δημοφων pr noun masc nom sg
δήμῳ noun masc dat sg .... δῆμος
δήμων noun masc gen pl id.
δήξεται vb fut mid ind 3rd pers sg .... δάκνω
δήξονται vb fut mid ind 3rd pers pl id.
δῆσαι vb 1st aor act inf .... δέω
δήσαντες vb 1st aor act part masc nom pl id.
δήσας vb 1st aor act part masc nom sg id.
δήσεις vb fut act ind 2nd pers sg id.
δήσομεν vb fut act ind 1st pers pl id.
δήσουσι(ν) vb fut act ind 3rd pers pl id.
δήσωμεν vb 1st aor act subj 1st pers pl id.
Δησων pr noun
δήσωσιν vb 1st aor act subj 3rd pers pl .... δέω
δηχθείς vb aor pass part masc nom sg .... δάκνω
δι' see διά
διά preposition
διαβάθρας noun fem gen sg .... διαβάθρα
διάβαινε vb pres act impv 2nd pers sg .... διαβαίνω
διαβαίνει vb pres act ind 3rd pers sg id.
διαβαίνειν vb pres act inf id.
διαβαίνεις vb pres act ind 2nd pers sg id.
διαβαίνετε vb pres act impv 2nd pers pl,
        pres act ind 2nd pers pl id.
διαβαίνῃς vb pres act subj 2nd pers sg id.
διαβαίνομεν vb pres act ind 1st pers pl id.
διαβαίνοντα vb pres act part masc acc sg id.
διαβαίνοντες vb pres act part masc nom pl id.
διαβαίνοντος vb pres act part masc and neut gen sg id.
διαβαίνω vb pres act ind 1st pers sg id.
διαβαίνων vb pres act part masc nom sg id.
διαβάλλων vb pres act part masc nom sg ... διαβάλλω
διαβαλόντας vb 2nd aor act part masc acc pl
διαβάντες vb 2nd aor act part masc nom pl ..... διαβαίνω
διαβάς vb 2nd aor act part masc nom sg
διαβάσει noun fem dat sg .... διάβασις
διαβάσεις noun fem nom and acc pl id.
διαβάσεων noun fem gen pl id.
διαβάσεως noun fem gen sg id.

διαβάσης vb 2nd aor act part fem gen sg . . . . διαβαίνω
διάβασιν noun fem acc sg . . . . διάβασις
διάβασις noun fem nom sg   id.
διαβῇ vb 2nd aor act subj 3rd pers sg . . . . διαβαίνω
διάβηθι vb 2nd aor act impv 2nd pers sg   id.
διαβήματα noun neut nom and acc pl . . . . διάβημα
διαβῆναι vb 2nd aor act inf . . . . διαβαίνω
διαβῇς vb 2nd aor act subj 2nd pers sg   id.
διαβήσεσθε vb fut mid ind 2nd pers pl   id.
διαβήσεται vb fut mid ind 3rd pers sg   id.
διαβήσῃ vb fut mid ind 2nd pers sg   id.
διαβήσομαι vb fut mid ind 1st pers sg   id.
διαβησόμεθα vb fut mid ind 1st pers pl   id.
διαβήσονται vb fut mid ind 3rd pers pl   id.
διάβητε vb 2nd aor act impv 2nd pers pl   id.
διαβῆτε vb 2nd aor act subj 2nd pers pl   id.
διαβήτω vb 2nd aor act impv 3rd pers sg   id.
διαβιασάμενοι vb 1st aor mid part
       masc nom pl . . . . διαβιάζομαι
διαβιβάσαι vb 1st aor act inf . . . . διαβιβάζω
διαβιβάσετε vb fut act ind 2nd pers pl   id.
διαβιβάσῃς vb 1st aor act subj 2nd pers sg   id.
διαβιώσῃ vb 1st aor act subj 3rd pers sg . . . . διαβιόω
διαβοήσετε vb fut act ind 2nd pers pl . . . . διαβοάω
διαβολαῖς noun fem dat pl . . . . διαβολή
διάβολε noun masc voc sg . . . . διάβολος
διαβολή noun fem nom sg
διαβολήν noun fem acc sg . . . . διαβολή
διαβολῆς noun fem gen sg   id.
διάβολον noun masc acc sg . . . . διάβολος
διάβολος noun masc nom sg   id.
διαβόλου noun masc gen sg   id.
διαβόλῳ noun masc dat sg   id.
διαβουλευόμενοι vb pres dep part
       masc nom pl . . . . διαβουλεύομαι
διαβούλια noun neut nom and acc pl . . . . διαβούλιον
διαβουλίοις noun neut dat pl   id.
διαβούλιον noun neut nom and acc sg   id.
διαβουλίου noun neut gen sg   id.
διαβουλίων noun fem gen pl . . . . διαβουλία
διαβῶ vb 2nd aor act subj 1st pers sg . . . . διαβαίνω
διαβῶμεν vb 2nd aor act subj 1st pers pl   id.
διαβῶσιν vb 2nd aor act subj 3rd pers pl   id.
διαγαγόντι vb 2nd aor act part masc and neut dat sg . . διάγω
διαγαγών vb 2nd aor act part masc nom sg   id.
διαγγείλῃ vb 1st aor act subj 3rd pers sg . . . . . . διαγγέλλω
διαγγελεῖτε vb fut act ind 2nd pers pl   id.
διαγγελῇ vb 2nd aor pass subj 3rd pers sg   id.
διαγγελήσονται vb fut pass ind 3rd pers pl   id.
διάγγελλε vb pres act impv 2nd pers sg   id.
διαγγέλλων vb pres act part masc nom sg   id.
διαγγέλματα noun neut nom and acc pl . . . . . . διάγγελμα

διαγεγλυμμένα vb perf m/p part
       neut nom and acc pl . . . . διαγλύφω
διαγεγλυμμένοι vb perf m/p part masc nom pl   id.
διαγεγλυμμένος vb perf m/p part masc nom sg   id.
διαγεγραμμένα vb perf m/p part
       neut nom and acc pl . . . . διαγράφω
διαγεγραμμέναι vb perf m/p part fem nom pl   id.
διάγει vb pres act ind 3rd pers sg . . . . διάγω
διάγειν vb pres act inf   id.
διαγίνωνται vb pres mid subj 3rd pers pl . . . . . . διαγίνομαι
διαγινώσκεται vb pres m/p ind 3rd pers sg . . . διαγινώσκω
διαγλύψεις vb fut act ind 2nd pers sg . . . . διαγλύφω
διάγνωθι vb 2nd aor act impv 2nd pers sg . . . . διαγινώσκω
διαγνώσεως noun fem gen sg . . . . διάγνωσις
διαγνωσθῇ vb 1st aor pass subj 3rd pers sg . . . διαγινώσκω
διαγογγύζετε vb pres act ind 2nd pers pl . . . . . διαγογγύζω
διαγογγύσει vb fut act ind 3rd pers sg   id.
διαγορεύει vb pres act ind 3rd pers sg . . . . . . διαγορεύω
διαγράφειν vb pres act inf . . . . διαγράφω
διαγραφήν noun fem acc sg . . . . διαγραφή
διαγραψάτωσαν vb 1st aor act impv 3rd pers pl . διαγράφω
διαγράψεις vb fut act ind 2nd pers sg   id.
διαγράψω vb fut act ind 1st pers sg   id.
διαγράψωμεν vb 1st aor act subj 1st pers pl   id.
διαγωγήν noun fem acc sg . . . . διαγωγή
διάγων vb pres act part masc nom sg . . . . διάγω
διαδεξάμενον vb 1st aor mid part masc acc sg . . διαδέχομαι
διαδέχεσθαι vb pres dep inf   id.
διαδέχεται vb pres dep ind 3rd pers sg   id.
διαδεχόμενον vb pres dep part masc acc sg   id.
διαδεχόμενος vb pres dep part masc nom sg   id.
διαδεχομένους vb pres dep part masc acc pl   id.
διάδηλοι noun masc nom pl . . . . διάδηλος
διαδήλους adj masc acc pl   id.
διάδημα noun neut nom and acc sg
διαδήματα noun neut nom and acc pl . . . . διάδημα
διαδήματος noun neut gen sg   id.
διαδιδούσης vb pres act part fem gen sg . . . . . . διαδίδωμι
διαδοθείσης vb 1st aor pass part fem gen sg   id.
διάδος vb 2nd aor act impv 2nd pers sg   id.
διάδοτε vb 2nd aor act impv 2nd pers pl   id.
διαδοῦναι vb 2nd aor act inf   id.
διάδοχοι noun masc nom pl . . . . διάδοχος
διάδοχον noun masc acc sg   id.
διάδοχος noun masc nom sg   id.
διαδόχου noun masc gen sg   id.
διαδόχους noun masc acc pl   id.
διαδραμοῦνται vb fut mid ind 3rd pers pl . . . . . διατρέχω
διαδράς vb 1st aor act part masc nom sg . . . . διαδιδράσκω
διαδώσει vb fut act ind 3rd pers sg . . . . διαδίδωμι
διαδώσουσιν vb fut act ind 3rd pers pl   id.
διαζόμενοι vb pres dep part masc nom pl . . . . . . διάζομαι

διαθερμάναντος vb 1st aor act part
 masc and neut gen sg . . . . διαθερμαίνω
διαθέσει noun fem dat sg . . . . διάθεσις
διαθέσθαι vb 2nd aor mid inf . . . . διατίθημι
διάθεσθε vb 2nd aor mid impv 2nd pers pl id.
διάθεσιν noun fem acc sg . . . . διάθεσις
διάθεσις noun fem nom sg id.
διαθῆκαι noun fem nom pl . . . . διαθήκη
διαθήκαις noun fem dat pl id.
διαθήκας noun fem acc pl id.
διαθήκη noun fem nom sg id.
διαθήκῃ noun fem dat sg id.
διαθήκην noun fem acc sg id.
διαθήκης noun fem gen sg id.
διαθήσεσθε vb fut mid ind 2nd pers pl . . . . διατίθημι
διαθήσεται vb fut mid ind 3rd pers sg id.
διαθήσῃ vb fut mid ind 2nd pers sg id.
διάθησθε vb 2nd aor mid subj 2nd pers pl id.
διαθήσομαι vb fut mid ind 1st pers sg id.
διαθησόμεθα vb fut mid ind 1st pers pl id.
διάθου vb 2nd aor mid impv 2nd pers sg id.
διαθρέψαι vb 1st aor act inf . . . . διατρέφω
διαθρέψει vb fut act ind 3rd pers sg id.
διαθρέψεις vb fut act ind 2nd pers sg id.
διαθρέψω vb fut act ind 1st pers sg id.
διάθρυπτε vb pres act impv 2nd pers sg . . . . . . διαθρύπτω
διαθρύψεις vb fut act ind 2nd pers sg id.
διαθῶ vb 2nd aor act subj 1st pers sg . . . . διατίθημι
διαθῶμαι vb 2nd aor mid subj 1st pers sg id.
διαθώμεθα vb 2nd aor mid subj 1st pers pl id.
διαιρεθήσεται vb fut pass ind 3rd pers sg . . . . διαιρέω
διαιρεθῶσιν vb 1st aor pass subj 3rd pers pl id.
διαιρεῖται vb pres m/p ind 3rd pers sg id.
διαιρέσεις noun masc and fem nom and acc pl . . . διαίρεσις
διαιρέσεσιν noun fem dat pl id.
διαιρέσεως noun fem gen sg id.
διαίρεσιν noun fem acc sg id.
διαίρεσις noun fem nom sg id.
διαιρούμενοι vb pres m/p part masc nom pl . . . . . διαιρέω
διαιρῶν vb pres act part masc nom sg id.
δίαιτα noun fem nom sg
δίαιταις noun fem dat pl . . . . δίαιτα
δίαιταν noun fem acc sg id.
διαίτῃ noun fem dat sg id.
διαιτηθῆναι vb 1st aor pass inf . . . . διαιτέω
διαίτης noun fem gen sg . . . . δίαιτα
διακαθιζάνῃς vb pres act subj 2nd pers sg . . διακαθιζάνω
διακαρτερήσωμεν vb 1st aor act subj
  1st pers pl . . . . διακαρτερέω
διακατασχεῖν vb 2nd aor act inf . . . . διακατέχω
διακειμένους vb pres m/p part masc acc pl . . . . . διάκειμαι
διακειμένῳ vb pres m/p part masc and neut dat sg id.

διακεκοσμημένος vb perf m/p part
 masc nom sg . . . . διακοσμέω
διακένῳ noun masc dat sg . . . . διάκενος
διακεχρισμένα vb perf m/p part
 neut nom and acc pl . . . . διαχρίω
διακεχυμένοι vb perf m/p part masc nom pl . . . . . διαχέω
διακέχυται vb perf m/p ind 3rd pers sg id.
διακεχωρισμένοι vb perf m/p part masc nom pl διαχωρίζω
διακεχωρισμένος vb perf m/p part masc nom sg id.
διακεχωρισμένων vb perf m/p part gen pl id.
διακινδυνεύοντας vb pres act part
 masc acc pl . . . . διακινδυνεύω
διακλέπτεται vb pres m/p ind 3rd pers sg . . . . . διακλέπτω
διακλῶν vb pres act part masc nom sg . . . . διακλάω
διακομίσαντες vb 1st aor act part masc nom pl . διακομίζω
διακομισθείς vb 1st aor pass part masc nom sg id.
διακομισθέντες vb 1st aor pass part masc nom pl id.
διακονίαν noun fem acc sg . . . . διακονία
διάκονοι noun masc nom pl . . . . διάκονος
διακόνοις noun masc dat pl id.
διακόνῳ noun masc dat sg id.
διακοπάς noun fem acc pl . . . . διακοπή
Διακοπη pr noun fem nom sg . . . . Διακοπη
διακοπή noun fem nom sg
διακοπήν noun fem acc sg . . . . διακοπή
διακοπῆς noun fem gen sg id.
διακόπτεται vb pres m/p ind 3rd pers sg . . . . . διακόπτω
διακόπτοντος vb pres act part masc and neut gen sg id.
διακοπῶν noun fem gen pl . . . . διακοπή
διακόσια adj neut nom and acc pl . . . . διακόσιοι
διακόσιαι adj fem nom pl id.
διακοσίας adj fem acc pl id.
διακόσιοι adj masc nom pl id.
διακοσίοις adj masc and neut dat pl id.
διακοσίους adj masc acc pl id.
διακοσίων adj gen pl id.
διακόσμησιν noun fem acc sg . . . . διακόσμησις
διακούετε vb pres act impv 2nd pers pl . . . . διακούω
διακούων vb pres act part masc nom sg id.
διακόψαι vb 1st aor act inf . . . . διακόπτω
διάκοψον vb 1st aor act impv 2nd pers sg id.
διακρατοῦσιν vb pres act ind 3rd pers pl . . . . . διακρατέω
διακριβοῦν vb pres act inf . . . . διακριβόω
διακριθήσομαι vb fut pass ind 1st pers sg . . . . . . διακρίνω
διακρῖναι vb 1st aor act inf id.
διάκρινε vb pres act impv 2nd pers sg id.
διακρίνει vb pres act ind 3rd pers sg id.
διακρινεῖ vb fut act ind 3rd pers sg id.
διακρίνειν vb pres act inf id.
διακρινεῖς vb fut act ind 2nd pers sg id.
διακρίνομεν vb pres act ind 1st pers pl id.
διακρινόμενον vb pres m/p part masc acc sg id.

διακρίνοντες	vb pres act part masc nom pl	διακρίνω
διακρινοῦσιν	vb fut act ind 3rd pers pl	id.
διακρίνω	vb pres act ind 1st pers sg	id.
διακρινῶ	vb fut act ind 1st pers sg	id.
διακρίνωσιν	vb 1st aor act subj 3rd pers pl	id.
διάκρισιν	noun fem acc sg	διάκρισις
διακυβερνᾷ	vb pres act ind 3rd pers sg . . .	διακυβερνάω
διακυβερνῶν	vb pres act part masc nom sg	id.
διακύπτειν	vb pres act inf	διακύπτω
διακύψῃ	vb 1st aor act subj 3rd pers sg	id.
διακωλύειν	vb pres act inf	διακωλύω
διακωλῦσαι	vb 1st aor act inf	id.
διαλέγεσθαι	vb pres dep inf	διαλέγομαι
διαλεγῆναι	vb 2nd aor pass inf	id.
διαλέγομαι	vb pres dep ind 1st pers sg	id.
διαλεγόμενοι	vb pres dep part masc nom pl	id.
διαλείψει	vb fut act ind 3rd pers sg	διαλείπω
διαλείψεις	vb fut act ind 2nd pers sg	id.
διάλεκτον	noun fem acc sg	διάλεκτος
διαλέκτῳ	noun fem dat sg	id.
διαλέλυται	vb perf m/p ind 3rd pers sg	διαλύω
διάλευκα	adj neut nom and acc pl	διάλευκος
διάλευκοι	adj masc and fem nom pl	id.
διάλευκον	adj acc sg, neut nom sg	id.
διαλεύκους	adj masc and fem acc pl	id.
διαλεχθῆναι	vb 1st aor pass inf	διαλέγομαι
διαλεχθήσεται	vb fut pass ind 3rd pers sg	id.
διαλήμψεσθε	vb fut mid ind 2nd pers pl	διαλαμβάνω
διάλημψιν	noun fem acc sg	διάλημψις
διαλιπεῖν	vb 2nd aor act inf	διαλείπω
διαλιπέτω	vb 2nd aor act impv 3rd pers sg	id.
διαλιπέτωσαν	vb 2nd aor act impv 3rd pers pl	id.
διαλίπητε	vb 2nd aor act subj 2nd pers pl	id.
διαλλαγή	noun fem nom sg	
διαλλαγῇ	vb 2nd aor pass subj 3rd pers sg	διαλλάσσω
διαλλαγήσεται	vb fut pass ind 3rd pers sg	id.
διαλλάξαι	vb 1st aor act inf	id.
διαλλάξας	vb 1st aor act part masc nom sg	id.
διαλλάσσεται	vb pres m/p ind 3rd pers sg	id.
διαλλάσσοντα	vb pres act part masc acc sg	id.
διαλλάσσουσιν	vb pres act ind 3rd pers pl	id.
διαλλάσσων	vb pres act part masc nom sg	id.
διαλλόμενος	vb pres dep part masc nom sg	διάλλομαι
διαλογή	noun fem nom sg	
διαλογεῖσθε	vb fut mid ind 2nd pers pl	διαλογίζομαι
διαλογιζόμενος	vb pres dep part masc nom sg	id.
διαλογίζονται	vb pres dep ind 3rd pers pl	id.
διαλογιοῦνται	vb fut mid ind 3rd pers pl	id.
διαλογισάσθω	vb 1st aor mid impv 3rd pers sg	id.
διαλογισμοί	noun masc nom pl	διαλογισμός
διαλογισμοῖς	noun masc dat pl	id.
διαλογισμόν	noun masc acc sg	id.

διαλογισμός	noun masc nom sg	
διαλογισμούς	noun masc acc pl	διαλογισμός
διαλογισμῷ	noun masc dat sg	id.
διαλοιδόρησις	noun fem nom sg	
διάλυε	vb pres act impv 2nd pers sg	διαλύω
διαλυθῇ	vb 1st aor pass subj 3rd pers sg	id.
διαλυθήσεται	vb fut pass ind 3rd pers sg	id.
διαλῦον	vb pres act part neut nom and acc sg	id.
διαλῦσαι	vb 1st aor act inf	id.
διαλύσει	noun fem dat sg	διάλυσις
διαλύσει	vb fut act ind 3rd pers sg	διαλύω
διαμαρτάνοντες	vb pres act part	
	masc nom pl	διαμαρτάνω
διαμάρτητε	vb 2nd aor act subj 2nd pers pl . .	διαμαρτυρέω
διαμαρτύραι	vb 1st aor mid impv	
	2nd pers sg	διαμαρτύρομαι
διαμαρτύρῃ	vb pres dep subj 2nd pers sg	id.
διαμαρτυρῇ	vb fut mid ind 2nd pers sg	id.
διαμαρτυρία	noun fem dat sg	διαμαρτυρία
διαμαρτυρίας	noun fem gen sg	id.
διαμαρτύρομαι	vb pres dep ind 1st pers sg	
διαμαρτυρόμενος	vb pres dep part	
	masc nom sg	διαμαρτύρομαι
διαμαρτύρωμαι	vb pres dep subj 1st pers sg	id.
διαμαρτύρωνται	vb pres dep subj 3rd pers pl	id.
διαμασῶ	vb pres dep impv 2nd pers sg	διαμασάομαι
διαμάχεσθαι	vb pres dep inf	διαμάχομαι
διαμαχήσεται	vb fut pass ind 3rd pers sg	id.
διαμάχου	vb pres dep impv 2nd pers sg	id.
διαμείνῃ	vb 1st aor act subj 3rd pers sg	διαμένω
διαμελισθήσεται	vb fut pass ind 3rd pers sg	διαμελίζω
διαμεμαρτύρημαι	vb perf m/p ind	
	1st pers sg	διαμαρτυρέω
διαμεμαρτυρημένοι	vb perf m/p part masc nom pl	id.
διαμεμαρτύρησαι	vb perf m/p ind 2nd pers sg	id.
διαμεμαρτύρηται	vb perf m/p ind 3rd pers sg	id.
διαμεμάχισται	vb perf dep ind 3rd pers sg .	διαμαχίζομαι
διάμενε	vb pres act impv 2nd pers sg	διαμένω
διαμένει	vb pres act ind 3rd pers sg	id.
διαμενεῖ	vb fut act ind 3rd pers sg	id.
διαμενεῖν	vb fut act inf	id.
διαμενεῖς	vb fut act ind 2nd pers sg	id.
διαμενοῦσιν	vb fut act ind 3rd pers pl	id.
διαμένον	vb pres act part masc nom sg	id.
διαμερίζοντα	vb pres act part masc acc sg	διαμερίζω
διαμερίσας	vb 1st aor act part masc nom sg	id.
διαμερίσετε	vb fut act ind 2nd pers pl	id.
διαμερισθήσεται	vb fut pass ind 3rd pers sg	id.
διαμερισμοί	noun masc nom pl	διαμερισμός
διαμερισμόν	noun masc acc sg	id.
διαμέρισον	vb 1st aor act impv 2nd pers sg	διαμερίζω
διαμεριῶ	vb fut act ind 1st pers sg	id.

διαμετρῆσαι vb 1st aor act inf . . . . διαμετρέω
διαμετρήσεις vb fut act ind 2nd pers sg   id.
διαμετρήσεως noun fem gen sg . . . . διαμέτρησις
διαμέτρησιν noun fem acc sg   id.
διαμέτρησις noun fem nom sg   id.
διαμετρήσω vb fut act ind 1st pers sg . . . . διαμετρέω
διαναπαύσει vb fut act ind 3rd pers sg . . . . . . διαναπαύω
διαναστᾶσα vb 2nd aor act part fem nom sg . . . διανίστημι
διανενησμένον vb perf m/p part

      neut nom and acc sg . . . . διανήθω
διανενησμένου vb perf m/p part masc and neut gen sg   id.
διανενησμένῳ vb perf m/p part masc and neut dat sg   id.
διανενόημαι vb perf dep ind 1st pers sg . . . . . διανοέομαι
διανεύοντες vb pres act part masc nom pl . . . . διανεύω
διανεύων vb pres act part masc nom sg   id.
διανιστάμενος vb pres m/p part masc nom sg . . διανίστημι
διανισταμένους vb pres m/p part masc acc pl   id.
διανοεῖσθαι vb pres dep inf . . . . διανοέομαι
διανοεῖται vb pres dep ind 3rd pers sg   id.
διανοηθείς vb 1st aor pass part masc nom sg   id.
διανοηθῆναι vb 1st aor pass inf   id.
διανοηθήσεται vb fut pass ind 3rd pers sg   id.
διανοηθήσῃ vb fut pass ind 2nd pers sg   id.
διανοηθήσονται vb fut pass ind 3rd pers pl   id.
διανοήθητι vb 1st aor pass impv 2nd pers sg   id.
διανοηθῶσι vb 1st aor pass subj 3rd pers pl   id.
διανόημα noun neut nom and acc sg
διανοήματα noun neut nom and acc pl . . . . διανόημα
διανοήματος noun neut gen sg   id.
διανοημάτων noun neut gen pl   id.
διανόησιν noun fem acc sg . . . . διανόησις
διάνοια noun fem nom sg
διανοίᾳ noun fem dat sg . . . . διάνοια
διάνοιαι noun fem nom pl   id.
διανοίαις noun fem dat pl   id.
διάνοιαν noun fem acc sg   id.
διανοίας noun fem gen sg and acc pl   id.
διανοίγειν vb pres act inf . . . . διανοίγω
διανοιγόμενος vb pres m/p part masc nom sg   id.
διανοῖγον vb pres act part neut nom and acc sg   id.
διανοίγοντος vb pres act part masc and neut gen sg   id.
διανοιγόντων vb pres act part masc and neut gen pl   id.
διανοῖξαι vb 1st aor act opt 3rd sg   id.
διανοῖξαι vb 1st aor act inf   id.
διανοίξεις vb fut act ind 2nd pers sg   id.
διανοῖξον vb 1st aor act impv 2nd pers sg   id.
διανοίξουσιν vb fut act ind 3rd pers pl   id.
διανοίξω vb fut act ind 1st pers sg   id.
διανοιχθήσεται vb fut pass ind 3rd pers sg   id.
διανοιχθήσονται vb fut pass ind 3rd pers pl   id.
διανοιῶν noun fem gen pl . . . . διάνοια
διανοοῦ vb pres dep impv 2nd pers sg . . . . διανοέομαι

διανοούμενοι vb pres dep part masc nom pl . . . διανοέομαι
διανοούμενος vb pres dep part masc nom sg   id.
διανοουμένου vb pres dep part masc and neut gen sg   id.
διανοουμένους vb pres dep part masc acc pl   id.
διανοουμένων vb pres dep part gen pl   id.
διανυκτερεύων vb pres act part masc nom sg διανυκτερεύω
διάξω vb fut act ind 1st pers sg . . . . διάγω
διαπαύσετε vb fut act ind 2nd pers pl . . . . διαπαύω
διαπαύσῃ vb 1st aor act subj 3rd pers sg   id.
διαπειλησάμενοι vb 1st aor mid part

      masc nom pl . . . . διαπειλέω
διαπειλήσῃ vb fut mid ind 2nd pers sg   id.
διαπειράζεις vb pres act ind 2nd pers sg . . . . . διαπειράζω
διαπείραντες vb 1st aor act part masc nom pl . . . . διαπείρω
διαπέμπεται vb pres m/p ind 3rd pers sg . . . . . . διαπέμπω
διαπεμφθῆναι vb 1st aor pass inf   id.
διαπεμψάμενος vb 1st aor mid part masc nom sg   id.
διαπεμψαμένων vb 1st aor mid part gen pl   id.
διαπεπετακότα vb perf act part

      neut nom and acc pl . . . . διαπετάζω
διαπεπετασμένα vb perf m/p part neut nom and acc pl id.
διαπεπετασμέναι vb perf m/p part fem nom pl   id.
διαπεπετασμένων vb perf m/p part gen pl   id.
διαπεπτωκότα vb perf act part masc acc sg,

      neut nom and acc pl . . . . διαπίπτω
διαπερᾶσαι vb 1st aor act inf . . . . διαπεράω
διαπεράσει vb fut act ind 3rd pers sg   id.
διαπεράσομεν vb fut act ind 1st pers pl   id.
διαπερῶντες vb pres act part masc nom pl   id.
διαπεσεῖν vb 2nd aor act inf . . . . διαπίπτω
διαπεσεῖται vb fut mid ind 3rd pers sg   id.
διαπέσῃ vb 2nd aor act subj 3rd pers sg   id.
διαπέσητε vb 1st aor act subj 2nd pers pl   id.
διαπετάσασα vb 1st aor act part fem nom sg . . . διαπετάζω
διαπετάσῃ vb 1st aor act subj 3rd pers sg   id.
διαπεφεύγασιν vb perf act ind 3rd pers pl . . . . . . διαφεύγω
διαπεφευγότα vb perf act part masc acc sg   id.
διαπεφευγώς vb perf act part masc nom sg   id.
διαπεφυλαγμένη vb perf m/p part

      fem nom sg . . . . διαφυλάσσω
διαπεφωνήκαμεν vb perf act ind 1st pers pl . . . . . διαφωνέω
διαπεφώνηκεν vb perf act ind 3rd pers sg   id.
διαπίπτειν vb pres act inf . . . . διαπίπτω
διαπίπτουσαν vb pres act part fem acc sg   id.
διαπίπτων vb pres act part masc nom sg   id.
διαπλατύνηται vb pres m/p subj 3rd pers sg . . διαπλατύνω
διαπληκτιζομένους vb pres dep part

      masc acc pl . . . . διαπληκτίζομαι
διαπνεύσῃ vb 1st aor act subj 3rd pers sg . . . . διαπνέω
διάπνευσον vb 1st aor act impv 2nd pers sg   id.
διαπονηθήσεται vb fut pass ind 3rd pers sg . . . . διαπονέω
διαπονοῦντες vb pres act part masc nom pl   id.

διαπορεύεσθαι vb pres dep inf	διαπορεύομαι
διαπορευέσθω vb pres dep impv 3rd pers sg	id.
διαπορεύεται vb pres dep ind 3rd pers sg	id.
διαπορεύηται vb pres dep subj 3rd pers sg	id.
διαπορευθείς vb 1st aor pass part masc nom sg	id.
διαπορευόμενα vb pres dep part	
neut nom and acc pl	id.
διαπορευομένης vb pres dep part fem gen sg	id.
διαπορευόμενοι vb pres dep part masc nom pl	id.
διαπορευόμενον vb pres dep part masc acc sg,	
neut nom and acc sg	id.
διαπορευόμενος vb pres dep part masc nom sg	id.
διαπορευομένου vb pres dep part masc and neut gen sg	id.
διαπορευομένους vb pres dep part masc acc pl	id.
διαπορευομένων vb pres dep part gen pl	id.
διαπορεύονται vb pres dep ind 3rd pers pl	id.
διαπορεύου vb pres dep impv 2nd pers sg	id.
διαπορεύσεται vb fut mid ind 3rd pers sg	id.
διαπραξάμενοι vb 1st aor mid part	
masc nom pl	διαπράσσω
διάπρασις noun fem nom sg	
διαπρεπεῖς adj masc and fem nom and acc pl . . .	διαπρεπής
διαπτώσεως noun fem gen sg	διάπτωσις
διάπτωσις noun fem nom sg	id.
διάπυρον adj acc sg, neut nom sg	διάπυρος
διάπυρος adj masc and fem nom sg	id.
διαπυρούμενος vb pres m/p part masc nom sg . .	διαπυρόω
διαρπαγή noun fem nom sg	
διαρπαγῇ noun fem dat sg	διαρπαγή
διαρπαγῇ vb 2nd aor pass subj 3rd pers sg	διαρπάζω
διαρπαγήν noun fem acc sg	διαρπαγή
διαρπαγήσεται vb fut pass ind 3rd pers sg	διαρπάζω
διαρπαγήσονται vb fut pass ind 3rd pers pl	id.
διαρπαζόμενος vb pres m/p part masc nom sg	id.
διαρπάζοντες vb pres act part masc nom pl	id.
διαρπαζόντων vb pres act part masc and neut gen pl	id.
διαρπάζουσιν vb pres act ind 3rd pers pl	id.
διαρπάσαι vb 1st aor act inf	id.
διαρπασάτωσαν vb 1st aor act impv 3rd pers pl	id.
διαρπασθῆναι vb 1st aor pass inf	id.
διαρπάσωμεν vb 1st aor act subj 1st pers pl	id.
διαρπῶνται vb fut mid ind 3rd pers pl	id.
διαρραγήσονται vb fut pass ind 3rd pers pl .	διαρρήγνυμι
διαρραγῶσιν vb 2nd aor pass subj 3rd pers pl	id.
διαρρῆξαι vb 1st aor act inf	id.
διαρρήξαντες vb 1st aor act part masc nom pl	id.
διαρρήξατε vb 1st aor act impv 2nd pers pl	id.
διαρρήξει vb fut act ind 3rd pers sg	id.
διαρρήξετε vb fut act ind 2nd pers pl	id.
διαρρήξω vb fut act ind 1st pers sg	id.
διαρρήξωμεν vb 1st aor act subj 1st pers pl	id.
διαρρησσων vb pres act part masc nom sg	id.

διαρριττοῦνται vb pres m/p ind 3rd pers pl . . .	διαρρίπτω
διαρρίψατε vb 1st aor act impv 2nd pers pl	id.
διαρρυῆναι vb 1st aor act inf	διαρρέω
διαρτηθῆναι vb 1st aor pass inf	διαρτάω
διασαλεύθητι vb 1st aor pass impv 2nd pers sg .	διασαλεύω
διασαφεῖ vb pres act ind 3rd pers sg	διασαφέω
διασαφῆσαι vb 1st aor act inf	id.
διασαφήσητε vb 1st aor act subj 2nd pers pl	id.
διασάφησις noun fem nom sg	
διασεισθέντες vb 1st aor pass part masc nom pl . . .	διασείω
διασέσωσμαι vb perf m/p ind 1st pers sg	διασῴζω
διασεσωσμένη vb perf m/p part fem nom sg	id.
διασεσωσμένοι vb perf m/p part masc nom pl	id.
διασεσωσμένον vb perf m/p part masc acc sg,	
neut nom and acc sg	id.
διασεσωσμένος vb perf m/p part masc nom sg	id.
διασέσωται vb perf m/p ind 3rd pers sg	id.
διασκεδάζει vb pres act ind 3rd pers sg	διασκεδάζω
διασκεδάννυται vb pres m/p ind 3rd pers sg	id.
διασκεδάσαι vb 1st aor act inf	id.
διασκεδάσει vb fut act ind 3rd pers sg	id.
διασκεδάσεις vb fut act ind 2nd pers sg	id.
διασκεδάσῃς vb 1st aor act subj 2nd pers sg	id.
διασκεδασθῇ vb 1st aor pass subj 3rd pers sg	id.
διασκεδασθήσεται vb fut pass ind 3rd pers sg	id.
διασκέδασον vb 1st aor act impv 2nd pers sg	id.
διασκεδάσουσιν vb fut act ind 3rd pers pl	id.
διασκεδάσω vb 1st aor act subj 1st pers sg,	
fut act ind 1st pers sg	id.
διασκευή noun fem dat sg	διασκευή
διασκευήν noun fem acc sg	id.
διασκορπιεῖ vb fut act ind 3rd pers sg	διασκορπίζω
διασκορπίζεις vb pres act ind 2nd pers sg	id.
διασκορπίζηται vb pres m/p subj 3rd pers sg	id.
διασκορπίζοντες vb pres act part masc nom pl	id.
διασκορπίσαι vb 1st aor act inf	id.
διασκορπίσαντα vb 1st aor act part neut nom and acc pl	id.
διασκορπίσατε vb 1st aor act impv 2nd pers pl	id.
διασκορπίσεις vb fut act ind 2nd pers sg	id.
διασκορπίσῃ vb 1st aor act subj 3rd pers sg	id.
διασκορπισθήσονται vb fut pass ind 3rd pers pl	id.
διασκορπισθῆτε vb 1st aor pass subj 2nd pers pl	id.
διασκορπισθήτωσαν vb 1st aor pass impv 3rd pers pl	id.
διασκορπισμόν noun masc acc sg	διασκορπισμός
διασκορπισμῷ noun masc dat sg	id.
διασκόρπισον vb 1st aor act impv	
2nd pers sg	διασκορπίζω
διασκορπιῶ vb fut act ind 1st pers sg	id.
δίασμα noun neut nom and acc sg	
διάσματι noun neut dat sg	δίασμα
διάσματος noun neut gen sg	id.
διάσπα vb pres act impv 2nd pers sg	διασπάω

διασπαρῇ vb 2nd aor pass subj 3rd pers sg . . . . . διασπείρω
διασπαρῆναι vb 2nd aor pass inf id.
διασπαρήσεσθε vb fut pass ind 2nd pers pl id.
διασπάρητε vb 1st aor act impv 2nd pers pl id.
διασπάσαι vb 1st aor act inf . . . . διασπάω
διασπάσει vb fut act ind 3rd pers sg id.
διασπασμόν noun masc acc sg . . . . διασπασμός
διασπᾶται vb pres m/p ind 3rd pers sg . . . . διασπάω
διασπεῖραι vb 1st aor act inf . . . . διασπείρω
διασπείρω vb pres act subj 1st pers sg id.
διασπερεῖ vb fut act ind 3rd pers sg id.
διασπερῶ vb fut act ind 1st pers sg id.
διασπορά noun fem nom sg
διασπορᾷ noun fem dat sg . . . . διασπορά
διασποράν noun fem acc sg id.
διασποράς noun fem acc pl id.
διασπορᾶς noun fem gen sg id.
διασταλήσεται vb fut pass ind 3rd pers sg . . . . διαστέλλω
διασταλήσονται vb fut pass ind 3rd pers pl id.
διαστάλητε vb 2nd aor pass subj 2nd pers pl id.
διαστάλσεις noun fem nom and acc pl . . . . . . διάσταλσις
διάστασιν noun fem acc sg . . . . διάστασις
διαστεῖλαι vb 1st aor act inf . . . . διαστέλλω
διαστείλας vb 1st aor act part masc nom sg id.
διαστείλασθαι vb 1st aor mid inf id.
διαστείλῃ vb 1st aor act subj 3rd pers sg,
     1st aor mid subj 2nd pers sg id.
διάστειλον vb 1st aor act impv 2nd pers sg id.
διαστελεῖ vb fut act ind 3rd pers sg id.
διαστελεῖς vb fut act ind 2nd pers sg id.
διαστελεῖσθε vb fut mid ind 2nd pers pl id.
διαστελεῖτε vb fut act ind 2nd pers pl id.
διαστέλλειν vb pres act inf id.
διαστέλλουσα vb pres act part fem nom sg id.
διαστελοῦσιν vb fut act ind 3rd pers pl id.
διαστελῶ vb fut act ind 1st pers sg id.
διάστημα noun neut nom and acc sg
διαστήματι noun neut dat sg . . . . διάστημα
διαστήματος noun neut gen sg id.
διαστημάτων noun neut gen pl id.
διαστήσεις vb fut act ind 2nd pers sg . . . . διΐστημι
διαστήσῃς vb 1st aor act subj 2nd pers sg id.
διαστολή noun fem nom sg
διαστολήν noun fem acc sg . . . . διαστολή
διαστολῆς noun fem gen sg id.
διαστράπτον vb pres act part
     neut nom and acc sg . . . . διαστράπτω
διαστραφήσεσθε vb fut pass ind 2nd pers pl . . . διαστρέφω
διαστραφῶσιν vb 2nd aor pass subj 3rd pers pl id.
διαστρέφειν vb pres act inf id.
διαστρέφετε vb pres act ind 2nd pers pl id.
διαστρέφοντες vb pres act part masc nom pl

διαστρέφω vb pres act ind 1st pers sg
διαστρέφων vb pres act part masc nom sg . . . . . διαστρέφω
διαστρέψει vb fut act ind 3rd pers sg id.
διαστρέψεις vb fut act ind 2nd pers sg id.
διαστρέψῃ vb 1st aor act subj 3rd pers sg id.
διαστροφῇ noun fem dat sg . . . . διαστροφή
διασυρίζον vb pres act part neut nom and acc sg διασυρίζω
διασφαγαί noun fem nom pl . . . . διασφαγή
διασῴζει vb pres act ind 3rd pers sg . . . . διασῴζω
διασῴζεσθαι vb pres m/p inf id.
διασῴζεται vb pres m/p ind 3rd pers sg id.
διασῳζόμενοι vb pres m/p part masc nom pl id.
διασῳζόμενον vb pres m/p part masc acc sg id.
διασῳζόμενος vb pres m/p part masc nom sg id.
διασῳζομένων vb pres m/p part gen pl id.
διασῴζονται vb pres m/p ind 3rd pers pl id.
διασῴζουσα vb pres act part fem nom sg id.
διασῴζων vb pres act part masc nom sg id.
διασωθείη vb 1st aor pass opt 3rd pers sg id.
διασωθείς vb 1st aor pass part masc nom sg id.
διασωθέντι vb 1st aor pass part masc and neut dat sg id.
διασωθῇ vb 1st aor pass subj 3rd pers sg id.
διασωθῆναι vb 1st aor pass inf id.
διασωθῆς vb 1st aor pass subj 2nd pers sg id.
διασωθήσεσθε vb fut pass ind 2nd pers pl id.
διασωθήσεται vb fut pass ind 3rd pers sg id.
διασωθήσομαι vb fut pass ind 1st pers sg id.
διασωθήσονται vb fut pass ind 3rd pers pl id.
διασωθῆτε vb 1st aor pass subj 2nd pers pl id.
διασώθητι vb 1st aor pass impv 2nd pers sg id.
διασωθῶσιν vb 1st aor pass subj 3rd pers pl id.
διασῶσαι vb 1st aor act opt 3rd pers sg id.
διασῶσαι vb 1st aor act inf id.
διασώσαντι vb 1st aor act part masc and neut dat sg id.
διασωσάτω vb 1st aor act impv 3rd pers sg id.
διασώσει vb fut act ind 3rd pers sg id.
διασώσῃ vb 1st aor act subj 3rd pers sg id.
διασώσω vb fut act ind 1st pers sg id.
διαταγή noun fem nom sg
διατάγματα noun neut nom and acc pl . . . . διάταγμα
διατάγματος noun neut gen sg id.
διαταξαμένου vb 1st aor mid part
     masc and neut gen sg . . . . διατάσσω
διατάξας vb 1st aor act part masc nom sg id.
διατάξει noun fem dat sg . . . . διάταξις
διατάξεις noun fem nom and acc pl id.
διατάξεις vb fut act ind 2nd pers sg . . . . διατάσσω
διατάξεως noun fem gen sg . . . . διάταξις
διάταξιν noun fem acc sg id.
διάταξον vb 1st aor act impv 2nd pers sg . . . . . . διατάσσω
διατείνας vb 1st aor act part masc nom sg . . . . . . διατείνω
διατείνει vb pres act ind 3rd pers sg id.

διατελεῖν vb pres act inf . . . . διατελέω	διαθεύξη vb fut mid ind 2nd pers sg . . . . διαφεύγω
διατενεῖς vb fut act ind 2nd pers sg . . . . διατείνω	διαφθορῇ vb 2nd aor pass subj 3rd pers sg . . . . . . διαφθείρω
διατεταγμένα vb perf m/p part	διαφθαρῆναι vb 2nd aor pass inf id.
neut nom and acc pl . . . . διατάσσω	διαφθαρήσεται vb fut pass ind 3rd pers sg id.
διατεταγμέναι vb perf m/p part fem nom pl id.	διαφθεῖραι vb 1st aor act inf id.
διατεταγμένας vb perf m/p part fem acc pl id.	διαφθείρατε vb 1st aor act impv 2nd pers pl id.
διατεταγμένη vb perf m/p part fem nom sg id.	διαφθείρειν vb pres act inf id.
διατεταγμένην vb perf m/p part fem acc sg id.	διαφθείρῃ vb pres act subj 3rd pers sg id.
διατεταγμένοι vb perf m/p part masc nom pl id.	διαφθείρῃς vb pres act subj 2nd pers sg id.
διατεταγμένους vb perf m/p part masc acc pl id.	διάφθειρον vb 2nd aor act impv 2nd pers sg id.
διατεταμένων vb perf m/p part gen pl . . . . διατείνω	διαφθεῖρον vb pres act part neut nom and acc sg id.
διατετηρημένον vb perf m/p part	διαφθείροντα vb pres act part masc acc sg id.
neut nom and acc sg . . . . διατηρέω	διαφθείροντες vb pres act part masc nom pl id.
διατετραμμένα vb perf m/p part	διαφθείροντι vb pres act part masc and neut dat sg id.
neut nom and acc pl . . . . διατρέπω	διαφθείροντος vb pres act part masc and neut gen sg id.
διατετραμμένη vb perf m/p part fem nom sg id.	διαφθειρόντων vb pres act part masc and neut gen pl id.
διατηρεῖ vb pres act ind 3rd pers sg . . . . διατηρέω	διαφθείρω vb pres act ind 1st pers sg id.
διατηρήσας vb 1st aor act part masc nom sg id.	διαφθείρωμεν vb pres act subj 1st pers pl id.
διατηρήσει vb fut act ind 3rd pers sg id.	διαφθείρων vb pres act part masc nom sg id.
διατηρήσεις vb fut act ind 2nd pers sg id.	διαφθερεῖ vb fut act ind 3rd pers sg id.
διατηρήσετε vb fut act ind 2nd pers pl id.	διαφθερῶ vb fut act ind 1st pers sg id.
διατήρησιν noun fem acc sg . . . . διατήρησις	διαφθορά noun fem nom sg
διατήρησον vb 1st aor act impv 2nd pers sg . . . . διατηρέω	διαφθορᾷ noun fem dat sg . . . . διαφθορά
διατηροῦσιν vb pres act ind 3rd pers pl id.	διαφθοραῖς noun fem dat pl id.
διατηρῶν vb pres act part masc nom sg id.	διαφθοράν noun fem acc sg id.
διατίθεμαι vb pres m/p ind 1st pers sg . . . . διατίθημι	διαφθορᾶς noun fem gen sg id.
διατιθέμεθα vb pres m/p ind 1st pers pl id.	διαφθορῶν noun fem gen pl id.
διατιθεμένους vb pres m/p part masc acc pl id.	διαφλέξει vb fut act ind 3rd pers sg . . . . διαφλέγω
διατίθεται vb pres m/p ind 3rd pers sg id.	διάφορα adj neut nom and acc pl . . . . διάφορος
διατόνια noun neut nom and acc pl . . . . διατόνιον	διαφορά noun fem nom sg
διατραφῇ vb 2nd aor pass subj 3rd pers sg . . . . . . διατρέφω	διαφοράν noun fem acc sg . . . . διαφορά
διατραφήσεται vb fut pass ind 3rd pers sg id.	διαφοράς noun fem acc pl id.
διατρέπων vb pres act part masc nom sg . . . . διατρέπω	διαφόρημα noun neut nom and acc sg
διατρέφειν vb pres act inf . . . . διατρέφω	διάφορον adj acc sg, neut nom sg . . . . διάφορος
διατρέχουσαι vb pres act part fem nom pl . . . . . διατρέχω	διαφόρου adj gen sg id.
διατριβαί noun fem nom pl . . . . διατριβή	διαφοροῦντες vb pres act part masc nom pl . . . . . διαφορέω
διατριβαῖς noun fem dat pl id.	διαφόρων adj gen pl . . . . διάφορος
διατρίβετε vb pres act ind 2nd pers pl . . . . διατρίβω	διαφόρος adverb
διατριβή noun fem nom sg	διαφυγεῖν vb 2nd aor act inf . . . . διαφεύγω
διατρίψει vb fut act ind 3rd pers sg . . . . διατρίβω	διαφύγῃ vb 2nd aor act subj 3rd pers sg id.
διατροφή noun fem nom sg	διαφύγῃς vb 2nd aor act subj 2nd pers sg id.
διαφανεῖς adj masc and fem nom and acc pl . . . . . διαφανής	διαφυγόντες vb 2nd aor act part masc nom pl id.
διαφανῆ adj masc and fem acc sg, neut nom and acc pl id.	διαφυλάξαι vb 1st aor act inf . . . . διαφυλάσσω
διαφαύσῃ vb 1st aor act subj 3rd pers sg . . . . . . διεφαύσκω	διαφυλάξας vb 1st aor act part masc nom sg id.
διαφέρει vb pres act ind 3rd pers sg . . . . διαφέρω	διαφυλάξει vb fut act ind 3rd pers sg id.
διαφέρειν vb pres act inf id.	διαφυλάξῃ vb 1st aor act subj 3rd pers sg id.
διαφερόμενον vb pres m/p part masc acc sg,	διαφυλάξῃς vb 1st aor act subj 2nd pers sg id.
neut nom and acc sg id.	διαφύλαξον vb 1st aor act impv 2nd pers sg id.
διαφέροντα vb pres act part masc acc sg,	διαφυλάσσειν vb pres act inf id.
neut nom and acc pl id.	διαφυλάσσοντας vb pres act part masc acc pl id.
διαφέροντας vb pres act part masc acc pl id.	διαφυλάσσων vb pres act part masc nom sg id.
διαφεύξεται vb fut mid ind 3rd pers sg . . . . διαφεύγω	διαφυλάττειν vb pres act inf . . . . διαφυλάττω

διαφυλαχθήσεται vb fut pass ind 3rd pers sg . διαφυλάσσω
διαφωνήσει vb fut act ind 3rd pers sg .... διαφωνέω
διαφώσαι vb 1st aor act inf .... διαφώσκω
διαφωτίσαι vb 1st aor act inf .... διαφωτίζω
διαχέηται vb pres m/p subj 3rd pers sg .... διαχέω
διαχεῖται vb pres m/p ind 3rd pers sg   id.
διαχεομένης vb pres m/p part fem gen sg   id.
διαχρύσους adj masc and fem acc pl .... διάχρυσος
διαχρύσῳ adj dat sg   id.
διαχυθῇ vb 1st aor pass subj 3rd pers sg .... διαχέω
διαχυθήσεται vb fut pass ind 3rd pers sg   id.
διαχυθήσομαι vb fut pass ind 1st pers sg   id.
διαχυθήσονται vb fut pass ind 3rd pers pl   id.
διαχύσει noun fem dat sg .... διάχυσις
διαχωρίζει vb pres act ind 3rd pers sg .... διαχωρίζω
διαχωρίζειν vb pres act inf   id.
διαχωρίζον vb pres act part neut nom and acc sg   id.
διαχωρίσατε vb 1st aor act impv 2nd pers pl   id.
διαχωρισθῆναι vb 1st aor pass inf   id.
διαχωρισθήσεται vb fut pass ind 3rd pers sg   id.
διαχωρίσθητι vb 1st aor pass impv 2nd pers sg   id.
διαχώρισον vb 1st aor act impv 2nd pers sg   id.
διάψαλμα noun neut nom and acc sg
διαψάλματος noun neut gen sg .... διάψαλμα
διαψεύσῃ vb fut mid ind 2nd pers sg .... διαψεύδομαι
διαψιθυρίσει vb fut act ind 3rd pers sg ...... διαψιθυρίζω
δίγλωσσον adj acc sg, neut nom sg .... δίγλωσσος
δίγλωσσος adj masc and fem nom sg   id.
διγλώσσου adj gen sg   id.
διγομίας noun fem gen sg .... διγομία
διδακτοί adj masc nom pl .... διδακτός
διδακτός adj masc nom sg   id.
διδακτούς adj masc acc pl   id.
διδάξαι vb 1st aor act inf .... διδάσκω
διδάξατε vb 1st aor act impv 2nd pers pl   id.
διδάξει vb fut act ind 3rd pers sg   id.
διδάξεις vb fut act ind 2nd pers sg   id.
διδάξετε vb fut act ind 2nd pers pl   id.
διδάξῃς vb 1st aor act subj 2nd pers sg   id.
δίδαξον vb 1st aor act impv 2nd pers sg   id.
διδάξουσιν vb fut act ind 3rd pers pl   id.
διδάξω vb 1st aor act subj 1st pers sg,
        fut act ind 1st pers sg   id.
διδάξωσιν vb 1st aor act subj 3rd pers pl   id.
διδασκαλίαν noun fem acc sg .... διδασκαλία
διδασκαλίας noun fem gen sg and acc pl   id.
διδασκάλῳ noun masc dat sg .... διδάσκαλος
δίδασκε vb pres act impv 2nd pers sg .... διδάσκω
διδάσκει vb pres act ind 3rd pers sg   id.
διδάσκειν vb pres act inf   id.
διδάσκοντα vb pres act part masc acc sg   id.
διδάσκοντας vb pres act part masc acc pl   id.

διδάσκοντες vb pres act part masc nom pl .... διδάσκω
διδάσκοντος vb pres act part masc and neut gen sg   id.
διδάσκουσα vb pres act part fem nom sg   id.
διδάσκουσι vb pres act part masc and neut dat pl   id.
διδάσκω vb pres act ind 1st pers sg   id.
διδάσκων vb pres act part masc nom sg   id.
διδαχήν noun fem acc sg .... διδαχή
διδαχθέντες vb 1st aor pass part masc nom pl .... διδάσκω
διδαχθήσεσθε vb fut pass ind 2nd pers pl   id.
διδαχθῶσιν vb 1st aor pass subj 3rd pers pl   id.
διδόασιν vb pres act ind 3rd pers pl .... δίδωμι
διδοῖ vb pres act ind 3rd pers sg   id.
διδοῖς vb pres act ind 2nd pers sg   id.
διδόμενα vb pres m/p part neut nom and acc pl   id.
διδομένη vb pres m/p part fem nom sg   id.
διδομένης vb pres m/p part fem gen sg   id.
διδόμενον vb pres m/p part masc acc sg,
        neut nom and acc sg   id.
διδόναι vb pres act inf   id.
διδόντα vb pres act part masc acc sg   id.
διδόντες vb pres act part masc nom pl   id.
διδόντι vb pres act part masc and neut dat sg   id.
διδόντος vb pres act part masc and neut gen sg   id.
διδόντων vb pres act part masc and neut gen pl   id.
δίδοσθαι vb pres m/p inf   id.
δίδοται vb pres m/p ind 3rd pers sg   id.
δίδοτε vb pres act ind 2nd pers pl   id.
δίδου vb pres act impv 2nd pers sg   id.
διδούς vb pres act part masc nom sg   id.
δίδραχμα noun neut nom and acc pl .... δίδραχμον
δίδραχμον noun neut nom and acc sg   id.
διδράχμου noun neut gen sg   id.
διδράχμων noun neut gen pl   id.
δίδυμα adj neut nom and acc pl .... δίδυμος
διδυμεύουσαι vb pres act part fem nom pl ..... διδυμεύω
δίδυμοι adj masc nom pl .... δίδυμος
διδύμου adj gen sg   id.
διδύμων adj gen pl   id.
δίδωμι vb pres act ind 1st pers sg
δίδως vb pres act ind 2nd pers sg .... δίδωμι
δίδωσιν vb pres act ind 3rd pers sg   id.
διδῶσιν vb pres act subj 3rd pers pl   id.
διέβαιναν vb impf act ind 3rd pers pl .... διαβαίνω
διέβαινεν vb impf act ind 3rd pers sg   id.
διέβαινον vb impf act ind 3rd pers pl   id.
διέβαλον vb 2nd aor act ind 3rd pers pl .... διαβάλλω
διέβη vb 2nd aor act ind 3rd pers sg .... διαβαίνω
διέβην vb 2nd aor act ind 1st pers sg   id.
διέβησαν vb 2nd aor act ind 3rd pers pl   id.
διέβητε vb 2nd aor act ind 2nd pers pl   id.
διεβίβασαν vb 1st aor act ind 3rd pers pl ...... διαβιβάζω
διεβίβασεν vb 1st aor act ind 3rd pers sg   id.

διεβοήθη vb 1st aor pass ind 3rd pers sg	. . . .	διαβοάω
διεγγυῶμεν vb pres act ind 1st pers pl	. . . .	διεγγυάω
διεγείρας vb 1st aor act part masc nom sg	. . . . . .	διεγείρω
διεγείρασα vb 1st aor act part fem nom sg		id.
διεγειρομένας vb pres m/p part fem acc pl		id.
διεγερθείς vb 1st aor pass part masc nom sg		id.
διεγνώκει vb plpf act ind 3rd pers sg	. . . . . .	διαγινώσκω
διεγνώκειν vb plpf act ind 1st pers sg		id.
διέγνωσαν vb 2nd aor act ind 3rd pers pl		id.
διεγνωσμένον vb perf m/p part masc acc sg		id.
διεγόγγυζεν vb impf act ind 3rd pers sg	. . . . . .	διαγογγύζω
διεγογγύζετε vb impf act ind 2nd pers pl		id.
διεγόγγυζον vb impf act ind 3rd pers pl		id.
διεγόγγυσαν vb 1st aor act ind 3rd pers pl		id.
διεδέχετο vb impf dep ind 3rd pers sg	. . . . . .	διαδεχομαι
διέδησαν vb 1st aor act ind 3rd pers pl	. . . .	διαδέω
διεδίδρασκον vb impf act ind 3rd pers pl	. . .	διαδιδράσκω
διεδόθη vb 1st aor pass ind 3rd pers sg	. . . .	διαδίδωμι
διέδυ vb 2nd aor act ind 3rd pers sg	. . . .	διαδύομαι
διέδωκα vb 1st aor act ind 1st pers sg	. . . .	διαδίδωμι
διέζη vb 2nd aor pass ind 3rd pers sg	. . . .	διαζάω
διεθέμην vb 2nd aor mid ind 1st pers sg	. . . . . .	διατίθημι
διέθεντο vb 2nd aor mid ind 3rd pers pl		id.
διεθέρμαινεν vb impf act ind 3rd pers sg	. . .	διαθερμαίνω
διεθερμάνθη vb 1st aor pass ind 3rd pers sg		id.
διέθετο vb 2nd aor mid ind 3rd pers sg	. . . .	διατίθημι
διέθηκεν vb 1st aor act ind 3rd pers sg		id.
διέθου vb 2nd aor mid ind 2nd pers sg		id.
διέθρεψας vb 1st aor act ind 2nd pers sg	. . . . . .	διατρέφω
διέθρεψεν vb 1st aor act ind 3rd pers sg		id.
διεθρύβη vb 2nd aor pass ind 3rd pers sg	. . . . . .	διαθρύπτω
διεθρύβησαν vb 2nd aor pass ind 3rd pers pl		id.
διείλαντο vb 2nd aor mid ind 3rd pers pl	. . . .	διαιρέω
διείλεν vb 2nd aor act ind 3rd pers sg		id.
διειλήφαμεν vb perf act ind 1st pers pl	. . . . .	διαλαμβάνω
διειληφότες vb perf act part masc nom pl		id.
διείλον vb 2nd aor act ind 3rd pers pl	. . . .	διαιρέω
διείς vb 2nd aor act part masc nom sg	. . . .	διΐημι
διεκάθισαν vb 1st aor act ind 3rd pers pl	. . . . . .	διακαθίζω
διέκαιον vb impf act ind		
1st pers sg and 3rd pers pl	. . . .	διακαίω
διέκαμψεν vb 1st aor act ind 3rd pers sg	. . . . .	διακάμπτω
διεκαρτέρει vb impf act ind 3rd pers sg	. . . .	διακαρτερέω
διεκβαλεῖ vb fut act ind 3rd pers sg	. . . .	διεκβάλλω
διεκβάλλει vb pres act ind 3rd pers sg		id.
διεκβολαί noun fem nom pl	. . . .	διεκβολή
διεκβολάς noun fem acc pl		id.
διεκβολῇ noun fem dat sg		id.
διεκβολήν noun fem acc sg		id.
διεκβολῆς noun fem gen sg		id.
διεκίνει vb impf act ind 3rd pers sg	. . . .	διακινεω
διεκλέπτετο vb impf m/p ind 3rd pers sg	. . . . . .	διακλέπτω

διεκολυμβησαν vb 1st aor act ind		
3rd pers pl	. . . .	διακολυμβάω
διεκόμισαν vb 1st aor act ind 3rd pers pl	. . . . .	διακομίζω
διεκόμισας vb 1st aor act ind 2nd pers sg		id.
διεκομίσθη vb 1st aor pass ind 3rd pers sg		id.
διεκόπη vb 2nd aor pass ind 3rd pers sg	. . . .	διακόπτω
διέκοπτον vb impf act ind 3rd pers pl		id.
διεκόπτοντο vb impf m/p ind 3rd pers pl		id.
διέκοψαν vb 1st aor act ind 3rd pers pl		id.
διέκοψας vb 1st aor act ind 2nd pers sg		id.
διέκοψεν vb 1st aor act ind 3rd pers sg		id.
διεκράτησαν vb 1st aor act ind 3rd pers pl	. . . .	διακρατέω
διεκρίθην vb 1st aor pass ind 1st pers sg	. . . . . .	διακρίνω
διέκρινας vb 1st aor act ind 2nd pers sg		id.
διέκρινεν vb 1st aor act ind 3rd pers sg		id.
διέκυπτεν vb impf act ind 3rd pers sg	. . . .	διακύπτω
διέκυψαν vb 1st aor act ind 3rd pers pl		id.
διέκυψεν vb 1st aor act ind 3rd pers sg		id.
διέλαβεν vb 2nd aor act ind 3rd pers sg	. . . . .	διαλαμβάνω
διέλαθον vb 2nd aor act ind 3rd pers pl	. . . . .	διαλανθάνω
διελάμβανον vb impf act ind		
1st pers sg and 3rd pers pl	. . . .	διαλαμβάνω
διελεγχθήσεται vb fut pass ind 3rd pers sg	. . . . .	διελέγχω
διελεγχθῶμεν vb 1st aor pass subj 1st pers pl		id.
διελεῖ vb fut act ind 3rd pers sg	. . . .	διαιρέω
διελεῖν vb 2nd aor act inf, fut act inf		id.
διέλειπον vb impf act ind		
1st pers sg and 3rd pers pl	. . . .	διαλείπω
διελεῖσθε vb fut mid ind 2nd pers pl	. . . .	διαιρέω
διελεῖται vb fut mid ind 3rd pers sg		id.
διελεῖτε vb fut act ind 2nd pers pl		id.
διελέξαντο vb 1st aor mid ind 3rd pers pl	. . . . .	διαλέγομαι
διελέσθαι vb 2nd aor mid inf	. . . .	διαιρέω
διέλετε vb 2nd aor act impv 2nd pers pl		id.
διελεύσεται vb fut mid ind 3rd pers sg	. . . .	διέρχομαι
διελεύσῃ vb fut mid ind 2nd pers sg		id.
διελεύσομαι vb fut mid ind 1st pers sg		id.
διελευσόμεθα vb fut mid ind 1st pers pl		id.
διελεύσονται vb fut mid ind 3rd pers pl		id.
διελήλυθα vb perf act ind 1st pers sg		id.
διεληλύθασιν vb perf act ind 3rd pers pl		id.
διελήλυθεν vb perf act ind 3rd pers sg		id.
διέλης vb 2nd aor act subj 2nd pers sg	. . . .	διαιρέω
διέλθατε vb 1st aor act impv 2nd pers pl	. . . . . .	διέρχομαι
διελθάτω vb 1st aor act impv 3rd pers sg		id.
διέλθε vb 2nd aor act impv 2nd pers sg		id.
διελθεῖν vb 2nd aor act inf		id.
διέλθετε vb 2nd aor act impv 2nd pers pl		id.
διελθέτω vb 2nd aor act impv 3rd pers sg		id.
διελθέτωσαν vb 2nd aor act impv 3rd pers pl		id.
διέλθη vb 2nd aor act subj 3rd pers sg		id.
διέλθῃς vb 2nd aor act subj 2nd pers sg		id.

διέλθοι vb 2nd aor act opt 3rd pers sg .... διέρχομαι
διελθόντες vb 2nd aor act part masc nom pl   id.
διελθόντων vb 2nd aor act part masc and neut gen pl   id.
διελθοῦσαι vb 2nd aor act part fem nom pl   id.
διέλθωμεν vb 2nd aor act subj 1st pers pl   id.
διελθών vb 2nd aor act part masc nom sg   id.
διέλθωσιν vb 2nd aor act subj 3rd pers pl   id.
διελίμπανεν vb impf act ind 3rd pers sg ..... διαλιμπάνω
διέλιπεν vb 2nd aor act ind 3rd pers sg .... διαλείπω
διελίπομεν vb 2nd aor act ind 1st pers pl   id.
διέλιπον vb 2nd aor act ind 3rd pers pl   id.
διελογίζετο vb impf dep ind 3rd pers sg .... διαλογίζομαι
διελογίζοντο vb impf dep ind 3rd pers pl   id.
διελογισάμην vb 1st aor mid ind 1st pers sg   id.
διελογίσαντο vb 1st aor mid ind 3rd pers pl   id.
διελογίσατο vb 1st aor mid ind 3rd pers sg   id.
διελοῦνται vb fut mid ind 3rd pers pl .... διαιρέω
διελοῦσιν vb fut act ind 3rd pers pl   id.
διέλυεν vb impf act ind 3rd pers sg .... διαλύω
διελύθησαν vb 1st aor pass ind 3rd pers pl   id.
διελύοντο vb impf m/p ind 3rd pers pl   id.
διελύσαμεν vb 1st aor act ind 1st pers pl   id.
διεμαρτυράμην vb 1st aor mid ind
         1st pers sg .... διαμαρτυρέω
διεμαρτύραντο vb 1st aor mid ind 3rd pers pl   id.
διεμαρτύρατο vb 1st aor mid ind 3rd pers sg   id.
διεμαρτύρω vb 1st aor mid ind 2nd pers sg   id.
διεμβαλοῦσιν vb fut act ind 3rd pers pl ...... διεμβάλλω
διέμεινεν vb 1st aor act ind 3rd pers sg .... διαμένω
διεμέριζεν vb impf act ind 3rd pers sg .... διαμερίζω
διεμερίσαντο vb 1st aor mid ind 3rd pers pl   id.
διεμέρισας vb 1st aor act ind 2nd pers sg   id.
διεμέρισεν vb 1st aor act ind 3rd pers sg   id.
διεμερίσθη vb 1st aor pass ind 3rd pers sg   id.
διεμερίσθησαν vb 1st aor pass ind 3rd pers pl   id.
διεμέτρησεν vb 1st aor act ind 3rd pers sg ..... διαμετρέω
διεμπιπλαμένων vb pres mid part gen pl .... διεμπίμπλημι
διενέβαλεν vb 2nd aor act ind 3rd pers sg ..... διεμβάλλω
διενέγκας vb 1st aor act part masc nom sg .... διαφέρω
διένειμεν vb 1st aor act ind 3rd pers sg .... διανέμω
διενεχθῆναι vb 1st aor pass inf .... διαφέρω
διενηνεγμένων vb perf m/p part gen pl   id.
διενοεῖτο vb impf dep ind 3rd pers sg .... διανοέομαι
διενοήθη vb 1st aor pass ind 3rd pers sg   id.
διενοήθην vb 1st aor pass ind 1st pers sg   id.
διενοήθης vb 1st aor pass ind 2nd pers sg   id.
διενοήθησαν vb 1st aor pass ind 3rd pers pl   id.
διενοούμην vb impf dep ind 1st pers sg   id.
διεξαγαγόντα vb perf act part masc acc sg ...... διεξάγω
διέξαγε vb pres act impv 2nd pers sg   id.
διεξάγειν vb pres act inf   id.
διεξάγεται vb pres m/p ind 3rd pers sg   id.

διεξάγων vb pres act part masc nom sg .... διεξάγω
διέξανε vb 1st aor act ind 3rd pers sg .... διαξαίνω
διεξέκυπτον vb impf act ind 3rd pers pl ..... διεκκύπτω
διεξελεύσῃ vb fut mid ind 2nd pers sg ...... διεξέρχομαι
διεξέλθοι vb 2nd aor act opt 3rd pers sg   id.
διεξῄεσαν vb impf act ind 3rd pers pl .... διέξειμι
διεξῆλθεν vb 2nd aor act ind 3rd pers sg .... διεξέρχομαι
διέξοδοι noun fem nom pl .... διέξοδος
διεξόδοις noun fem dat pl   id.
διέξοδον noun fem acc sg   id.
διέξοδος noun fem nom sg   id.
διεξόδους noun fem acc pl   id.
διεξώδευσε vb 1st aor act ind 3rd pers sg ...... διεξοδεύω
διεπαρετηροῦντο vb impf m/p ind
         3rd pers pl .... διαπαρατηρέω
διεπαρθενεύθησαν vb 1st aor pass ind
         3rd pers pl .... διαπαρθενεύω
διεπαρθένευσαν vb 1st aor act ind 3rd pers pl   id.
διέπεις vb pres act ind 2nd pers sg .... διέπω
διέπεμψαν vb 1st aor act ind 3rd pers pl ...... διαπέμπω
διεπέμψατο vb 1st aor mid ind 3rd pers sg   id.
διεπέρασαν vb 1st aor act ind 3rd pers pl ..... διαπεράω
διεπέρασεν vb 1st aor act ind 3rd pers sg   id.
διέπεσαν vb 1st aor act ind 3rd pers pl .... διαπίπτω
διέπεσεν vb 1st aor act ind 3rd pers sg   id.
διεπέτασα vb 1st aor act ind 1st pers sg .... διαπετάζω
διεπετάσαμεν vb 1st aor act ind 1st pers pl   id.
διεπέτασεν vb 1st aor act ind 3rd pers sg   id.
διέπῃ vb pres act subj 3rd pers sg .... διέπω
διεπορεύετο vb impf dep ind 3rd pers sg ... διαπορεύομαι
διεπορευόμην vb impf dep ind 1st pers sg   id.
διέπρισεν vb 1st aor act ind 3rd pers sg .... διαπρίω
διερεθίζον vb pres act part neut nom and acc sg .. διερεθίζω
διερευνήσει vb fut act ind 3rd pers sg .... διερευνάω
διερευνῶσιν vb pres act ind 3rd pers pl   id.
διερμηνεύεται vb pres m/p ind 3rd pers sg ... διερμηνεύω
διερράγη vb 2nd aor pass ind 3rd pers sg .... διαρρήγνυμι
διερράγησαν vb 2nd aor pass ind 3rd pers pl   id.
διέρραγκα vb perf act ind 1st pers sg .... διαρραίνω
διερρηγμένα vb perf m/p part
         neut nom and acc pl .... διαρρήγνυμι
διερρηγμένοι vb perf m/p part masc nom pl   id.
διερρήγνυντο vb impf m/p ind 3rd pers pl   id.
διερρηγότα vb perf act part neut nom and acc pl   id.
διέρρηξα vb 1st aor act ind 1st pers sg   id.
διέρρηξαν vb 1st aor act ind 3rd pers pl   id.
διέρρηξας vb 1st aor act ind 2nd pers sg   id.
διέρρηξεν vb 1st aor act ind 3rd pers sg   id.
διερρηχότες vb perf act part masc nom pl   id.
διερρηχώς vb perf act part masc nom sg   id.
διερρύθμισα vb 1st aor act ind 1st pers sg ... διαρρυθμίζω

διερρωγότα	vb perf act part	
	neut nom and acc pl	διαρρήγνυμι
διερρωγότας	vb perf act part masc acc pl	id.
διερχομένη	vb pres dep part fem nom sg	διέρχομαι
διεσαφεῖτο	vb impf m/p ind 3rd pers sg	διασαφέω
διεσάφησα	vb 1st aor act ind 1st pers sg	id.
διεσάφησαν	vb 1st aor act ind 3rd pers pl	id.
διεσάφησεν	vb 1st aor act ind 3rd pers sg	id.
διέσεως	noun fem gen sg	δίεσις
διεσκεδάσαμεν	vb 1st aor act ind 1st pers pl . .	διασκεδάζω
διεσκέδασαν	vb 1st aor act ind 3rd pers pl	id.
διεσκέδασεν	vb 1st aor act ind 3rd pers sg	id.
διεσκεδάσθαι	vb perf m/p inf	id.
διεσκέδασται	vb perf m/p ind 3rd pers sg	id.
διεσκευάσθησαν	vb 1st aor pass ind	
	3rd pers pl	διασκευάζω
διεσκευασμένοι	vb perf m/p part masc nom pl	id.
διεσκίρτησαν	vb 1st aor act ind 3rd pers pl . . .	διασκιρτάω
διεσκόρπισας	vb 1st aor act ind 2nd pers sg .	διασκορπίζω
διεσκορπίσατε	vb 1st aor act ind 2nd pers pl	id.
διεσκόρπισεν	vb 1st aor act ind 3rd pers sg	id.
διεσκορπίσθη	vb 1st aor pass ind 3rd pers sg	id.
διεσκορπίσθησαν	vb 1st aor pass ind 3rd pers pl	id.
διεσκορπίσθητε	vb 1st aor pass ind 2nd pers pl	id.
διεσκορπισμένον	vb perf m/p part neut nom and acc sg	id.
διεσπάρη	vb 2nd aor pass ind 3rd pers sg	διασπείρω
διεσπάρησαν	vb 2nd aor pass ind 3rd pers pl	id.
διεσπαρμένοι	vb perf m/p part masc nom pl	id.
διεσπαρμένον	vb perf m/p part masc acc sg,	
	neut nom and acc sg	id.
διεσπαρμένος	vb perf m/p part masc nom sg	id.
διεσπαρμένους	vb perf m/p part masc acc pl	id.
διέσπασας	vb 1st aor act ind 2nd pers sg	διασπάω
διέσπασεν	vb 1st aor act ind 3rd pers sg	id.
διεσπάσθησαν	vb 1st aor pass ind 3rd pers pl	id.
διέσπειρα	vb 1st aor act ind 1st pers sg	διασπείρω
διέσπειρας	vb 1st aor act ind 2nd pers sg	id.
διέσπειρεν	vb 1st aor act ind 3rd pers sg	id.
διεστάλη	vb 2nd aor pass ind 3rd pers sg	διαστέλλω
διεστάλησαν	vb 2nd aor pass ind 3rd pers pl	id.
διεσταλμένα	vb perf m/p part neut nom and acc pl	id.
διεσταλμένον	vb perf m/p part masc acc sg	id.
διέστειλα	vb 1st aor act ind 1st pers sg	id.
διέστειλαν	vb 1st aor act ind 3rd pers pl	id.
διέστειλας	vb 1st aor act ind 2nd pers sg	id.
διεστείλατο	vb 1st aor mid ind 3rd pers sg	id.
διέστειλεν	vb 1st aor act ind 3rd pers sg	id.
διεστείλω	vb 1st aor mid ind 2nd pers sg	id.
διέστελλεν	vb impf act ind 3rd pers sg	id.
διέστελλον	vb impf act ind 1st pers sg and 3rd pers pl	id.
διέστη	vb 2nd aor act ind 3rd pers sg	διΐστημι
διεστηκώς	vb perf act part masc nom sg	id.

διέστησαν	vb 2nd aor act ind 3rd pers pl	διΐστημι
διεστήσατο	vb 1st aor mid ind 3rd pers sg	id.
διέστησεν	vb 1st aor act ind 3rd pers sg	id.
διεστραμμένα	vb perf m/p part	
	neut nom and acc pl	διαστρέφω
διεστραμμέναι	vb perf m/p part fem nom pl	id.
διεστραμμένας	vb perf m/p part fem acc pl	id.
διεστραμμένη	vb perf m/p part fem nom sg	id.
διεστραμμένῃ	vb perf m/p part fem dat sg	id.
διεστραμμένον	vb perf m/p part masc acc sg,	
	neut nom and acc sg	id.
διεστραμμένως	adverb	
διεστράφησαν	vb 2nd aor pass ind 3rd pers pl . .	διαστρέφω
διεστρέφετε	vb impf act ind 2nd pers pl	id.
διέστρεφον	vb impf act ind 1st pers sg	id.
διέστρεψαν	vb 1st aor act ind 3rd pers pl	id.
διέστρεψεν	vb 1st aor act ind 3rd pers sg	id.
διέστρωσαν	vb 1st aor act ind 3rd pers pl . .	διαστρώννυμι
διεσφαλμένος	vb perf m/p part masc nom sg . . .	διασφάλλω
διέσχισεν	vb 1st aor act ind 3rd pers sg	διασχίζω
διεσχίσθησαν	vb 1st aor pass ind 3rd pers pl	id.
διεσῴζοντο	vb impf m/p ind 3rd pers pl	διασῴζω
διεσώθη	vb 1st aor pass ind 3rd pers sg	id.
διεσώθημεν	vb 1st aor pass ind 1st pers pl	id.
διεσώθην	vb 1st aor pass ind 1st pers sg	id.
διεσώθησαν	vb 1st aor pass ind 3rd pers pl	id.
διέσωσα	vb 1st aor act ind 1st pers sg	id.
διέσωσεν	vb 1st aor act ind 3rd pers sg	id.
διετάκη	vb 2nd aor pass ind 3rd pers sg	διατήκω
διέταξας	vb 1st aor act ind 2nd pers sg	διατάσσω
διετάξατε	vb 1st aor act ind 2nd pers pl	id.
διέταξεν	vb 1st aor act ind 3rd pers sg	id.
διετάξω	vb 1st aor mid ind 2nd pers sg	id.
διέτασσον	vb impf act ind 1st pers sg and 3rd pers pl	id.
διέτειναν	vb 1st aor act ind 3rd pers pl	διατείνω
διετελεῖτε	vb impf act ind 2nd pers pl	διατελέω
διετέλεσα	vb 1st aor act ind 1st pers sg	id.
διετέλεσαν	vb 1st aor act ind 3rd pers pl	id.
διετέλουν	vb impf act ind 3rd pers pl	id.
διετῆ	adj masc and fem acc sg	διετής
διετηρήθη	vb 1st aor pass ind 3rd pers sg	διατηρέω
διετηρήθης	vb 1st aor pass ind 2nd pers sg	id.
διετήρησεν	vb 1st aor act ind 3rd pers sg	id.
διετηρίδα	noun fem acc sg	διετηρίς
διέτιλεν	vb 2nd aor act ind 3rd pers sg	διατίλλω
διετράπη	vb 2nd aor pass ind 3rd pers sg	διατρέπω
διετράπην	vb 2nd aor pass ind 1st pers sg	id.
διετράφησαν	vb 2nd aor pass ind 3rd pers pl	διατρέφω
διέτρεφεν	vb impf act ind 3rd pers sg	id.
διέτρεχεν	vb impf act ind 3rd pers sg	διατρέχω
διέτρεχον	vb impf act ind 1st pers sg and 3rd pers pl	id.
διέτριβεν	vb impf act ind 3rd pers sg	διατρίβω

διέτριψε vb 1st aor act ind 3rd pers sg . . . . διατρίβω

διετυποῦτο vb impf m/p ind 3rd pers sg . . . . . . διατυπόω

διευλαβηθείς vb 1st aor pass part

    masc nom sg . . . . διευλαβέομαι

διευλαβοῦ vb impf dep ind 2nd pers sg id.

διευλαβοῦντο vb impf dep ind 3rd pers pl id.

διεφαίνετο vb impf m/p ind 3rd pers sg . . . . διαφαίνω

διέφαυσεν vb 1st aor act ind 3rd pers sg . . . . . διαφαύσκω

διεφέρετο vb impf m/p ind 3rd pers sg . . . . διαφέρω

διεφθάρη vb 2nd aor pass ind 3rd pers sg . . . . . . διαφθείρω

διεφθάρησαν vb 2nd aor pass ind 3rd pers pl id.

διεφθάρητε vb 2nd aor pass ind 2nd pers pl id.

διεφθαρμένα vb perf m/p part neut nom and acc pl id.

διεφθαρμέναις vb perf m/p part fem dat pl id.

διεφθαρμένας vb perf m/p part fem acc pl id.

διεφθαρμένοι vb perf m/p part masc nom pl id.

διεφθαρμένον vb perf m/p part masc acc sg,

    neut nom and acc sg id.

διέφθαρται vb perf m/p ind 3rd pers sg id.

διέφθαρτο vb plpf m/p ind 3rd pers sg id.

διέφθειραν vb 1st aor act ind 3rd pers pl id.

διέφθειρας vb 1st aor act ind 2nd pers sg id.

διεφθείρατε vb 1st aor act ind 2nd pers pl id.

διέφθειρε vb impf act ind 3rd pers sg id.

διέφθειρον vb impf act ind 3rd pers pl id.

διεφθείροντο vb impf m/p ind 3rd pers pl id.

διέφυγεν vb 2nd aor act ind 3rd pers sg . . . . διαφεύγω

διεφύλαξαν vb 1st aor act ind 3rd pers pl . . . . διαφυλάσσω

διεφύλαξεν vb 1st aor act ind 3rd pers sg id.

διεφύλαττεν vb impf act ind 3rd pers sg . . . . . διαφυλάττω

διεφύλαττον vb impf act ind 1st pers sg and 3rd pers pl id.

διεφυλάχθη vb 1st aor pass ind 3rd pers sg . . . διαφυλάσσω

διεφώνησεν vb 1st aor act ind 3rd pers sg . . . . . . διαφωνέω

διέχεας vb 1st aor act ind 2nd pers sg . . . . διαχέω

διεχεῖτο vb impf m/p ind 3rd pers sg id.

διεχύθη vb 1st aor pass ind 3rd pers sg id.

διεχώρισεν vb 1st aor act ind 3rd pers sg . . . . . . διαχωρίζω

διεχωρίσθησαν vb 1st aor pass ind 3rd pers pl id.

διεψεύσατο vb 1st aor mid ind 3rd pers sg . . διαψεύδομαι

διεψευσμένος vb perf dep part masc nom sg id.

διήγαγεν vb 2nd aor act ind 3rd pers sg . . . . διάγω

διήγαγες vb 2nd aor act ind 2nd pers sg id.

διήγαγον vb 2nd aor act ind 1st pers sg and 3rd pers pl id.

διηγγέλη vb 2nd aor pass ind 3rd pers sg . . . . . . διαγγέλλω

διηγεῖσθαι vb pres dep inf . . . . διηγέομαι

διηγεῖσθε vb pres dep impv 2nd pers pl id.

διηγεῖτο vb impf dep ind 3rd pers sg id.

διῆγεν vb impf act ind 3rd pers sg . . . . διάγω

διηγῇ vb pres dep ind 2nd pers sg . . . . διηγέομαι

διήγημα noun neut nom and acc sg

διηγήμασι noun neut dat pl . . . . διήγημα

διηγήματι noun neut dat sg id.

διηγήματος noun neut gen sg . . . . διήγημα

διηγήσαι vb 1st aor mid impv 2nd pers sg . . . . . διηγέομαι

διηγησάμεθα vb 1st aor mid ind 1st pers pl id.

διηγησάμην vb 1st aor mid ind 1st pers sg id.

διηγήσαντο vb 1st aor mid ind 3rd pers pl id.

διηγήσασθαι vb 1st aor mid inf id.

διηγήσασθε vb 1st aor mid impv 2nd pers pl id.

διηγησάσθω vb 1st aor mid impv 3rd pers sg id.

διηγήσατο vb 1st aor mid ind 3rd pers sg id.

διηγήσεται vb fut mid ind 3rd pers sg id.

διηγήσεως noun fem gen sg . . . . διήγησις

διηγήσησθε vb 1st aor mid subj 2nd pers pl . . . . . διηγέομαι

διήγησιν noun fem acc sg . . . . διήγησις

διήγησις noun fem nom sg id.

διηγήσομαι vb fut mid ind 1st pers sg . . . . διηγέομαι

διηγήσονται vb fut mid ind 3rd pers pl id.

διῆγον vb impf act ind 1st pers sg and 3rd pers pl . . . . διάγω

διηγορευμένοις vb perf m/p part

    masc and neut dat pl . . . . διαγορεύω

διηγοῦ vb pres dep impv 2nd pers sg . . . . διηγέομαι

διηγούμενοι vb pres dep part masc nom pl id.

διηγούμενος vb pres dep part masc nom sg id.

διηγοῦνται vb pres dep ind 3rd pers pl id.

διηγοῦντο vb impf dep ind 3rd pers pl id.

διηγῶνται vb pres dep subj 3rd pers pl id.

διηθεῖται vb pres m/p ind 3rd pers sg . . . . διηθέω

διήκει vb pres act ind 3rd pers sg . . . . διήκω

διηκριβασάμην vb 1st aor mid ind 1st pers sg . . διακριβόω

διήλασεν vb 1st aor act ind 3rd pers sg . . . . διελαύνω

διῆλθεν vb 2nd aor act ind 3rd pers sg . . . . διέρχομαι

διῆλθες vb 2nd aor act ind 2nd pers sg id.

διήλθομεν vb 2nd aor act ind 1st pers pl id.

διῆλθον vb 2nd aor act ind 1st pers sg and 3rd pers pl id.

διήλθοσαν vb 2nd aor act ind 3rd pers pl id.

διηλλαγμένοις vb perf m/p part

    masc and neut dat pl . . . . διαλλάσσω

διήλωσεν vb 1st aor act ind 3rd pers sg . . . . διηλόω

διήνεγκεν vb 1st aor act ind 3rd pers sg . . . . διαφέρω

διηνεκῶς adverb

διηνέχθη vb 1st aor pass ind 3rd pers sg . . . . διαφέρω

διηνθισμέναι vb perf m/p part fem nom pl . . . . . . διανθίζω

διήνοικται vb perf m/p ind 3rd pers sg . . . . διανοίγω

διήνοιξα vb 1st aor act ind 1st pers sg id.

διήνοιξαν vb 1st aor act ind 3rd pers pl id.

διήνοιξεν vb 1st aor act ind 3rd pers sg id.

διηνοίχθησαν vb 1st aor pass ind 3rd pers pl id.

διήνυσαν vb 1st aor act ind 3rd pers pl . . . . διανύω

διηπειλεῖτο vb impf m/p ind 3rd pers sg . . . . διαπειλέω

διηρέθη vb 1st aor pass ind 3rd pers sg . . . . διαιρέω

διηρέθησαν vb 1st aor pass ind 3rd pers pl id.

διηρημένη vb perf m/p part fem nom sg id.

διήρηται vb perf m/p ind 3rd pers sg id.

διηριθμήσαντο	vb 1st aor mid ind 3rd pers pl	. . . διαριθμέω
διηρκέσθη	vb 1st aor pass ind 3rd pers sg	. . . . . . διαρκέω
διηρπάγη	vb 2nd aor pass ind 3rd pers sg	. . . . . . διαρπάζω
διήρπαζον	vb impf act ind 3rd pers pl	id.
διηρπάζοντο	vb impf m/p ind 3rd pers pl	id.
διηρπάζοσαν	vb impf act ind 3rd pers pl	id.
διήρπασαν	vb 1st aor act ind 3rd pers pl	id.
διήρπασεν	vb 1st aor act ind 3rd pers sg	id.
διηρπασμένη	vb perf m/p part fem nom sg	id.
διηρπασμένοι	vb perf m/p part masc nom pl	id.
διηρπασμένον	vb perf m/p part masc acc sg,	
	neut nom and acc sg	id.
διηρπασμένος	vb perf m/p part masc nom sg	id.
διήρτισαι	vb perf m/p ind 2nd pers sg	. . . . διαρτίζω
διηρτίσμεθα	vb perf m/p ind 1st pers pl	id.
διήτησεν	vb 1st aor act ind 3rd pers sg	. . . . διαιτέω
διητῶντο	vb impf m/p ind 3rd pers pl	. . . . διαιτάω
διηχεῖτο	vb impf m/p ind 3rd pers sg	. . . . διηχέω
δίθυμος	adj masc and fem nom sg	
διϊκνείσθω	vb pres dep impv 3rd pers sg	. . . . . διϊκνέομαι
διιπτάντος	vb pres act part masc and neut gen sg	. διΐπταμαι
διίστησιν	vb pres act ind 3rd pers sg	. . . . διΐστημι
διιστῶσιν	vb pres act subj 3rd pers pl	id.
δικάζειν	vb pres act inf	. . . . δικάζω
δικάζεσθε	vb pres m/p ind 2nd pers pl	id.
δικαζέσθω	vb pres m/p impv 3rd pers sg	id.
δικάζηται	vb pres m/p subj 3rd pers sg	id.
δικαζόμενον	vb pres m/p part masc acc sg	id.
δικάζονται	vb pres m/p ind 3rd pers pl	id.
δικάζου	vb pres m/p impv 2nd pers sg	id.
δικάζωσιν	vb pres act subj 3rd pers pl	id.
δίκαια	adj neut nom and acc pl	. . . . δίκαιος
δικαία	adj fem nom sg	id.
δικαίᾳ	adj fem dat sg	id.
δικαίαν	adj fem acc sg	id.
δικαίας	adj fem gen sg	id.
δίκαιοι	adj masc nom pl	id.
δικαίοις	adj masc and neut dat pl	id.
δικαιοκρίτου	noun masc gen sg	. . . . δικαιοκρίτης
δικαιολογίαν	noun fem acc sg	. . . . δικαιολογία
δίκαιον	adj masc acc sg, neut nom and acc sg	. . . . . δίκαιος
δίκαιος	adj masc nom sg	id.
δικαιοσύναι	noun fem nom pl	. . . . δικαιοσύνη
δικαιοσύναις	noun fem dat pl	id.
δικαιοσύνας	noun fem acc pl	id.
δικαιοσύνη	noun fem nom sg	id.
δικαιοσύνῃ	noun fem dat sg	id.
δικαιοσύνην	noun fem acc sg	id.
δικαιοσύνης	noun fem gen sg	id.
δικαιοσυνῶν	noun fem gen pl	id.
δικαιοτάτοις	superl adj masc and neut dat pl	. . . . . . δίκαιος
δικαιότερον	comp adj masc acc sg, neut nom and acc sg	id.

δικαίου	adj masc and neut gen sg	. . . . δίκαιος
δικαιοῦ	vb pres m/p impv 2nd pers sg	. . . . δικαιόω
δικαιοῦντες	vb pres act part masc nom pl	id.
δικαίους	adj masc acc pl	. . . . δίκαιος
δικαιοῦται	vb pres m/p ind 3rd pers sg	. . . . δικαιόω
δικαίῳ	adj masc and neut dat sg	. . . . δίκαιος
δικαιωθῇ	vb 1st aor pass subj 3rd pers sg	. . . . δικαιόω
δικαιωθῆναι	vb 1st aor pass inf	id.
δικαιωθῇς	vb 1st aor pass subj 2nd pers sg	id.
δικαιωθήσεται	vb fut pass ind 3rd pers sg	id.
δικαιωθήσονται	vb fut pass ind 3rd pers pl	id.
δικαιωθήτωσαν	vb 1st aor pass impv 3rd pers pl	id.
δικαιωθῶμεν	vb 1st aor pass subj 1st pers pl	id.
δικαιωθῶσιν	vb 1st aor pass subj 3rd pers pl	id.
δικαίωμα	noun neut nom and acc sg	
δικαιώμασι	noun neut dat pl	. . . . δικαίωμα
δικαιώματα	noun neut nom and acc pl	id.
δικαιώματος	noun neut gen sg	id.
δικαιωμάτων	noun neut gen pl	id.
δικαίων	adj gen pl	. . . . δίκαιος
δικαίως	adverb	
δικαιῶσαι	vb 1st aor act inf	. . . . δικαιόω
δικαιώσαισαν	vb 1st aor act opt 3rd pers pl	id.
δικαιώσας	vb 1st aor act part masc nom sg	id.
δικαιώσατε	vb 1st aor act impv 2nd pers pl	id.
δικαιώσει	noun fem dat sg	. . . . δικαίωσις
δικαιώσει	vb fut act ind 3rd pers sg	. . . . δικαιόω
δικαιώσεις	vb fut act ind 2nd pers sg	id.
δικαίωσις	noun fem nom sg	
δικαιώσουσιν	vb fut act ind 3rd pers pl	. . . . δικαιόω
δικαιώσω	vb fut act ind 1st pers sg	id.
δικαιώσωσιν	vb 1st aor act subj 3rd pers pl	id.
δίκας	noun fem acc pl	. . . . δίκη
δικάσαι	vb 1st aor act opt 3rd pers sg	. . . . δικάζω
δικάσαντας	vb 1st aor act part masc acc pl	id.
δικασάσθω	vb 1st aor mid impv 3rd pers sg	id.
δικάσει	vb fut act ind 3rd pers sg	id.
δικάσηται	vb 1st aor mid subj 3rd pers sg	id.
δίκασον	vb 1st aor act impv 2nd pers sg	id.
δικασταί	noun masc nom pl	. . . . δικαστής
δικαστάς	noun masc acc pl	id.
δικαστήν	noun masc acc sg	id.
Δικαστηριον	pr noun neut nom and acc sg	. . Δικαστηριον
δικαστοῦ	noun masc gen sg	. . . . δικαστής
δικάσω	vb fut act ind 1st pers sg	. . . . δικάζω
δίκη	noun fem nom sg	
δίκῃ	noun fem dat sg	. . . . δίκη
δίκην	noun fem acc sg	id.
δίκης	noun fem gen sg	id.
δίκτυα	noun neut nom and acc pl	. . . . δίκτυον
δικτύοις	noun neut dat pl	id.
δίκτυον	noun neut nom and acc sg	id.

δικτύου noun neut gen sg . . . . δίκτυον
δικτύῳ noun neut dat sg   id.
δικτύων noun neut gen pl   id.
δικτυωταί adj fem nom pl . . . . δικτυωτός
δικτυωτῆς adj fem gen sg   id.
δικτυωτόν adj masc acc sg, neut nom and acc sg   id.
δικτυωτοῦ adj masc and neut gen sg   id.
δικτυωτῷ adj masc and neut dat sg   id.
διμερής adj fem nom sg
δίμετρον noun neut acc sg
δίμετρον adj acc sg, neut nom sg . . . . δίμετρος
Διμετρον pr noun neut nom and acc sg . . . . Διμετρον
Διμωνα pr noun
Δινα pr noun
δῖναι noun fem nom pl . . . . δίνη
Διναῖοι pr noun
Διναν pr noun fem acc sg . . . . Δινα
δίνας noun fem acc pl . . . . δίνη
Δινας pr noun fem gen sg . . . . Δινα
Διναχ pr noun
διό conjunction
διοδεύειν vb pres act inf . . . . διοδεύω
διοδεύεσθαι vb pres m/p inf   id.
διοδεύοντες vb pres act part masc nom pl   id.
διοδεύοντος vb pres act part masc and neut gen sg   id.
διοδεύουσιν vb pres act ind 3rd pers pl   id.
διόδευσον vb 1st aor act impv 2nd pers sg   id.
διοδεύων vb pres act part masc nom sg   id.
διόδοις noun fem dat pl . . . . δίοδος
δίοδον noun fem acc sg   id.
δίοδος noun fem nom sg   id.
διόδους noun fem acc pl   id.
διόδων noun fem gen pl   id.
διοικεῖ vb pres act ind 3rd pers sg . . . . διοικέω
διοικεῖς vb pres act ind 2nd pers sg   id.
διοίκησιν noun fem acc sg . . . . διοίκησις
διοικήσω vb fut act ind 1st pers sg . . . . διοικέω
διοικηταῖς noun masc dat pl . . . . διοικητής
διοικητάς noun masc acc pl   id.
διοικητής noun masc nom sg   id.
διοικοδομήσωμεν vb 1st aor act subj
      1st pers pl . . . . διοικοδομέω
διοικῶν vb pres act part masc nom sg . . . . διοικέω
διοίσει vb fut act ind 3rd pers sg . . . . διαφέρω
διολέσαι vb 1st aor act inf . . . . διόλλυμι
διόλου adverb
Διονυσιων pr noun neut gen pl . . . . Διονυσια
Διονυσου pr noun masc gen sg . . . . Διονυσος
Διονυσῳ pr noun masc dat sg   id.
διόπερ conjunction
διοργίζεσθαι vb pres m/p inf . . . . διοργίζω
διοργισθείς vb 1st aor pass part masc nom sg   id.

διορθοῦντες vb pres act part masc nom pl . . . . . . διορθόω
διορθωθῇ vb 1st aor pass subj 3rd pers sg   id.
διορθωθήσεται vb fut pass ind 3rd pers sg   id.
διορθώσατε vb 1st aor act impv 2nd pers pl   id.
διορθώσῃ vb 1st aor act subj 3rd pers sg   id.
διορθώσητε vb 1st aor act subj 2nd pers pl   id.
διορθωτής noun masc nom sg
διοριεῖ vb fut act ind 3rd pers sg . . . . διορίζω
διορίζει vb pres act ind 3rd pers sg   id.
διορίζον vb pres act part neut nom and acc sg   id.
διορίζοντα vb pres act part masc acc sg,
            neut nom and acc pl   id.
διορίζοντος vb pres act part masc and neut gen sg   id.
διορίζων vb pres act part masc nom sg   id.
διορύγμασι noun neut dat pl . . . . διόρυγμα
διορύγματι noun neut dat sg   id.
διορύξει vb fut act ind 3rd pers sg . . . . διορύσσω
διόρυξον vb 1st aor act impv 2nd pers sg   id.
διορῶντες vb pres act part masc nom pl . . . . διοράω
Διος pr noun masc gen sg . . . . Ζευς
Διοσπολει pr noun fem dat sg . . . . Διόσπολις
διότι conjunction
δίπηχυ adj neut nom and acc sg . . . . δίπηχυς
διπλᾶ adj neut nom and acc pl . . . . διπλοῦς
διπλᾶς adj fem acc pl   id.
διπλάσια adj neut nom and acc pl . . . . διπλάσιος
διπλασιαζόντων vb pres act part gen pl . . . . . διπλασιάζω
διπλασιασμόν noun masc acc sg . . . . διπλασιασμός
διπλασίασον vb 1st aor act impv 2nd pers sg . διπλασιάζω
διπλάσιος adj masc nom sg
διπλῆ adj fem nom sg . . . . διπλοῦς
διπλῆς adj fem gen sg   id.
διπλοΐδα noun fem acc sg . . . . διπλοΐς
διπλοΐδι noun fem dat sg   id.
διπλοΐδος noun fem gen sg   id.
διπλοῦν adj masc acc sg, neut nom and acc sg . . . . διπλοῦς
διπλοῦς adj masc nom sg   id.
διπλῷ adj masc and neut dat sg   id.
δίς adverb
δίσκου noun masc gen sg . . . . δίσκος
δισμύριοι adj masc nom pl
δισμυρίους adj masc acc pl . . . . δισμύριοι
δισμυρίων adj gen pl   id.
δισσά adj neut nom and acc pl . . . . δισσός
δισσάς adj fem acc pl   id.
δισσῇ adj fem dat sg   id.
δισσόν adj masc acc sg, neut nom and acc sg   id.
δισσῶς adverb
δίστομοι adj masc and fem nom pl . . . . δίστομος
δίστομον adj acc sg, neut nom sg   id.
δίστομος adj masc and fem nom sg   id.
διστόμου adj gen sg   id.

δισχίλια   adj neut nom and acc pl .... δισχίλιοι
δισχιλία   adj fem dat sg .... δισχίλιος
εισχίλιαι   adj fem nom pl .... δισχίλιοι
εισχιλίαν   adj fem acc sg .... δισχίλιος
δισχιλίας   adj fem acc pl .... δισχίλιοι
δισχίλιοι   adj masc nom pl   id.
δισχιλίοις   adj masc and neut dat pl   id.
δισχιλίους   adj masc acc pl   id.
δισχιλίων   adj gen pl   id.
διτάλαντον   noun neut nom and acc sg
διυλισμένον   vb perf m/p part masc acc sg .... διυλίζω
διυφασμένον   vb perf m/p part
          neut nom and acc sg .... διυφαίνω
διφθέρας   noun fem acc pl .... διφθέρα
δίφραξ   noun fem nom sg
διφρεύουσιν   vb pres act ind 3rd pers pl .... διφρεύω
δίφρον   noun masc acc sg .... δίφρος
δίφρος   noun masc nom sg   id.
δίφρου   noun masc gen sg   id.
δίφρους   noun masc acc pl   id.
δίζα   adverb
διχηλεῖ   vb pres act ind 3rd pers sg .... διχηλέω
διχηλοῦν   vb pres act part neut nom and acc sg   id.
διχηλούντων   vb pres act part masc and neut gen pl   id.
διχηλοῦσιν   vb pres act ind 3rd pers pl   id.
διχομηνία   noun fem nom sg
διχοστασίας   noun fem gen sg .... διχοστασία
διχοτόμημα   noun neut nom and acc sg
διχοτομήματα   noun neut nom and acc pl .... διχοτόμημα
διχοτομημάτων   noun neut gen pl   id.
διχοτομήσεις   vb fut act ind 2nd pers sg ...... διχοτομέω
δίψα   noun fem nom sg
διψᾷ   vb pres act ind 3rd pers sg .... διψάω
δίψαν   noun fem acc sg .... δίψα
δίψει   noun neut dat sg .... δίψος
δίψη   noun fem dat sg .... δίψα
δίψης   noun fem gen sg   id.
διψήσαντες   vb 1st aor act part masc nom pl .... διψάω
διψήσεις   vb fut act ind 2nd pers sg   id.
διψήσετε   vb fut act ind 2nd pers pl   id.
διψήσουσιν   vb fut act ind 3rd pers pl   id.
διψήσωσιν   vb 1st aor act subj 3rd pers pl   id.
δίψους   noun neut gen sg .... δίψος
διψώδεσι   adj fem dat pl .... διψώδης
διψῶν   vb pres act part masc nom sg .... διψάω
διψῶντας   vb pres act part masc acc pl   id.
διψῶντες   vb pres act part masc nom pl   id.
διψῶντι   vb pres act part masc and neut dat sg   id.
διψώντων   vb pres act part masc and neut gen pl   id.
διψῶσα   vb pres act part fem nom sg   id.
διψῶσαν   vb pres act part fem acc sg   id.
διψώσας   vb pres act part fem acc pl   id.

διψώσῃ   vb pres act part fem dat sg .... διψάω
διψῶσι   vb pres act ind 3rd pers pl   id.
διωγμόν   noun masc acc sg .... διωγμός
διωγμός   noun masc nom sg   id.
διωγμοῦ   noun masc gen sg   id.
διωδεύθη   vb 1st aor pass ind 3rd pers sg .... διοδεύω
ειωδεύσαμεν   vb 1st aor act ind 1st pers pl   id.
διώδευσαν   vb 1st aor act ind 3rd pers pl   id.
διώδευσεν   vb 1st aor act ind 3rd pers sg   id.
διωθεῖσθε   vb pres m/p ind 2nd pers pl .... διωθέω
διώκει   vb pres act ind 3rd pers sg .... διώκω
διώκειν   vb pres act inf   id.
διώκετε   vb pres act ind 2nd pers pl   id.
διώκῃ   vb pres act subj 3rd pers sg   id.
διώκῃς   vb pres act subj 2nd pers sg   id.
διωκόμενοι   vb pres m/p part masc nom pl   id.
διωκόμενον   vb pres m/p part masc acc sg   id.
διωκόμενος   vb pres m/p part masc nom sg   id.
διώκοντας   vb pres act part masc acc pl   id.
διώκοντες   vb pres act part masc nom pl   id.
διώκοντος   vb pres act part masc and neut gen sg   id.
διωκόντων   vb pres act part masc and neut gen pl   id.
διώκω   vb pres act ind 1st pers sg   id.
διώκων   vb pres act part masc nom sg   id.
διόλλυντο   vb impf m/p ind 3rd pers pl .... διόλλυμι
διῶξαι   vb 1st aor act inf .... διώκω
διώξας   vb 1st aor act part masc nom sg   id.
διώξεσθε   vb fut mid ind 2nd pers pl   id.
διώξεται   vb fut mid ind 3rd pers sg   id.
διάξῃ   vb fut mid ind 2nd pers sg   id.
διάξῃς   vb 1st aor act subj 2nd pers sg   id.
διώξομεν   vb fut act ind 1st pers pl   id.
δίωξον   vb 1st aor act impv 2nd pers sg   id.
διώξονται   vb fut mid ind 3rd pers pl   id.
διώξουσιν   vb fut act ind 3rd pers pl   id.
διώξω   vb fut act ind 1st pers sg   id.
διωρθώθησαν   vb 1st aor pass ind 3rd pers pl ..... διορθόω
διώρισα   vb 1st aor act ind 1st pers sg .... διορίζω
διώρισεν   vb 1st aor act ind 3rd pers sg   id.
διώροφα   adj neut nom and acc pl .... διώροφος
διώρυγας   noun fem acc pl .... διῶρυξ
διώρυγες   noun fem nom pl   id.
διώρυγος   noun fem gen sg   id.
διῶρυξ   noun fem nom sg   id.
διώρυξα   vb 1st aor act ind 1st pers sg .... διορύσσω
διώρυξεν   vb 1st aor act ind 3rd pers sg   id.
διωστῆρας   noun masc acc pl .... διωστήρ
διωστῆρσι   noun masc dat pl   id.
διωχθεῖσα   vb 1st aor pass part fem nom sg .... διώκω
διωχθέντες   vb 1st aor pass part masc nom pl   id.
δόγμα   noun neut nom and acc sg
δόγμασι   noun neut dat pl .... δόγμα

δόγματα   noun neut nom and acc pl . . . . δόγμα

δόγματι   noun neut dat sg   id.

δογματίζεται   vb pres m/p ind 3rd pers sg . . . . . δογματίζω

δογματισάτω   vb 1st aor act impv 3rd pers sg   id.

δογμάτων   noun neut gen pl . . . . δόγμα

δοθείη   vb 1st aor pass opt 3rd pers sg . . . . δίδωμι

δοθεῖσα   vb 1st aor pass part fem nom sg   id.

δοθεῖσαν   vb 1st aor pass part fem acc sg   id.

δοθείσας   vb 1st aor pass part fem acc pl   id.

δοθέν   vb 1st aor pass part neut nom and acc sg   id.

δοθέντος   vb 1st aor pass part masc and neut gen sg   id.

δοθῇ   vb 1st aor pass subj 3rd pers sg   id.

δοθῆναι   vb 1st aor pass inf   id.

δοθήσεται   vb fut pass ind 3rd pers sg   id.

δοθήσῃ   vb fut pass ind 2nd pers sg   id.

δοθήσονται   vb fut pass ind 3rd pers pl   id.

δοθήτω   vb 1st aor pass impv 3rd pers sg   id.

δόκει   vb pres act impv 2nd pers sg . . . . δοκέω

δοκεῖ   vb pres act ind 3rd pers sg   id.

δοκεῖν   vb pres act inf   id.

δοκεῖς   vb pres act ind 2nd pers sg   id.

δοκῇ   vb pres act subj 3rd pers sg   id.

δοκιμάζει   vb pres act ind 3rd pers sg . . . . δοκιμάζω

δοκιμάζεται   vb pres m/p ind 3rd pers sg   id.

δοκιμαζομένη   vb pres m/p part fem nom sg   id.

δοκιμάζουσα   vb pres act part fem nom sg   id.

δοκιμάζων   vb pres act part masc nom sg   id.

δοκιμάσαι   vb 1st aor act inf   id.

δοκιμάσας   vb 1st aor act part masc nom sg   id.

δοκιμασία   noun fem nom sg

δοκιμασίας   noun fem gen sg . . . . δοκιμασία

δοκίμασον   vb 1st aor act impv 2nd pers sg . . . . . δοκιμάζω

δοκιμαστήν   noun masc acc sg . . . . δοκιμαστής

δοκιμάσωμεν   vb 1st aor act subj 1st pers pl . . . . . δοκιμάζω

δοκίμιον   noun neut nom and acc sg

δόκιμον   adj acc sg, neut nom sg . . . . δόκιμος

δοκίμου   adj gen sg   id.

δοκιμῶ   vb fut act ind 1st pers sg . . . . δοκιμάζω

δοκίμῳ   adj dat sg . . . . δόκιμος

δοκοί   noun fem nom pl . . . . δοκός

δοκόν   noun fem acc sg   id.

δοκός   noun fem nom sg   id.

δοκοῦντα   vb pres act part masc acc sg,

       neut nom and acc pl . . . . δοκέω

δοκοῦντες   vb pres act part masc nom pl   id.

δοκούς   noun fem acc pl . . . . δοκός

δοκοῦσα   vb pres act part fem nom sg . . . . δοκέω

δοκοῦσαι   vb pres act part fem nom pl   id.

δοκοῦσι   vb pres act part masc and neut dat pl   id.

δοκῶ   vb pres act ind 1st pers sg   id.

δοκῶμεν   vb pres act subj 1st pers pl   id.

δοκῶν   noun fem gen pl . . . . δοκός

δοκῶν   vb pres act part masc nom sg . . . . δοκέω

δόκωσις   noun fem nom sg

δόλια   adj neut nom and acc pl . . . . δόλιος

δολία   adj fem nom sg   id.

δολίᾳ   adj fem dat sg   id.

δολίαι   adj fem nom pl   id.

δολίαν   adj fem acc sg   id.

δολίας   adj fem gen sg   id.

δόλιοι   adj masc nom pl   id.

δολίοις   adj masc and neut dat pl   id.

δόλιον   adj masc acc sg, neut nom and acc sg   id.

δόλιος   adj masc nom sg   id.

δολιότητα   noun fem acc sg . . . . δολιότης

δολιότητας   noun fem acc pl   id.

δολιότητι   noun fem dat sg   id.

δολιότητος   noun fem gen sg   id.

δολίου   adj masc and neut gen sg . . . . δόλιος

δολιοῦσθαι   vb pres m/p inf . . . . δολιόω

δολιοῦσιν   vb pres act ind 3rd pers pl   id.

δολίῳ   adj masc and neut dat sg . . . . δόλιος

δολίων   adj gen pl   id.

δολίως   adverb

δόλον   noun masc acc sg . . . . δόλος

δόλος   noun masc nom sg   id.

δόλου   noun masc gen sg   id.

δόλους   noun masc acc pl   id.

δόλῳ   noun masc dat sg   id.

δόμα   noun neut nom and acc sg

δόμασι   noun neut dat pl . . . . δόμα

δόματα   noun neut nom and acc pl   id.

δόματι   noun neut dat sg   id.

δόματος   noun neut gen sg   id.

δομάτων   noun neut gen pl   id.

δόμοι   noun masc nom pl . . . . δόμος

δόμος   noun masc nom sg   id.

δόμου   noun masc gen sg   id.

δόμων   noun masc gen pl   id.

δόντας   vb 2nd aor act part masc acc pl . . . . δίδωμι

δόντες   vb 2nd aor act part masc nom pl   id.

δόντι   vb 2nd aor act part masc and neut dat sg   id.

δόντος   vb 2nd aor act part masc and neut gen sg   id.

δόξα   noun fem nom sg

δοξάζει   vb pres act ind 3rd pers sg . . . . δοξάζω

δοξάζειν   vb pres act inf   id.

δοξάζεται   vb pres m/p ind 3rd pers sg   id.

δοξάζετε   vb pres act impv 2nd pers pl   id.

δοξαζόμενος   vb pres m/p part masc nom sg   id.

δοξάζοντας   vb pres act part masc acc pl   id.

δοξάζοντες   vb pres act part masc nom pl   id.

δοξάζου   vb pres m/p impv 2nd pers sg   id.

δοξάζω   vb pres act ind 1st pers sg   id.

δοξάζων   vb pres act part masc nom sg   id.

δόξαι noun fem nom pl	....	δόξα
δόξαις noun fem dat pl		id.
δόξαν noun fem acc sg		id.
δόξαντα vb 1st aor act part masc acc sg	....	δοκέω
δόξαντες vb 1st aor act part masc nom pl		id.
δόξας noun fem acc pl	....	δόξα
δοξάσαι vb 1st aor act inf	....	δοξάζω
δοξάσας vb 1st aor act part masc nom sg		id.
δοξάσατε vb 1st aor act impv 2nd pers pl		id.
δοξάσει vb fut act ind 3rd pers sg		id.
δοξάσεις vb fut act ind 2nd pers sg		id.
δοξασθείς vb 1st aor pass part masc nom sg		id.
δοξασθῇ vb 1st aor pass subj 3rd pers sg		id.
δοξασθῆναι vb 1st aor pass inf		id.
δοξασθήσεσθε vb fut pass ind 2nd pers pl		id.
δοξασθήσεται vb fut pass ind 3rd pers sg		id.
δοξασθήσομαι vb fut pass ind 1st pers sg		id.
δόξασμα noun neut nom and acc sg		
δοξάσομεν vb fut act ind 1st pers pl	....	δοξάζω
δόξασον vb 1st aor act impv 2nd pers sg		id.
δοξάσουσι(ν) vb fut act ind 3rd pers pl		id.
δόξαστον adj masc acc sg, neut nom and acc sg	..	δόξαστος
δοξάσω vb fut act ind 1st pers sg	....	δοξάζω
δοξάσωμεν vb 1st aor act subj 1st pers pl		id.
δόξει vb fut act ind 3rd pers sg	....	δοκέω
δόξῃ noun fem dat sg	....	δόξα
δόξῃ vb 1st aor act subj 3rd pers sg	....	δοκέω
δόξης noun fem gen sg	....	δόξα
δοξικήν adj fem acc sg	....	δοξικός
δοξολογοῦμεν vb pres act ind 1st pers pl	......	δοξολογέω
δοξῶν noun fem gen pl	....	δόξα
δορά noun fem nom sg		
δοράν noun fem acc sg	....	δορά
δόρασι noun neut dat pl	....	δόρυ
δόρατα noun neut nom and acc pl		id.
δόρατι noun neut dat sg		id.
δόρατος noun neut gen sg		id.
δορατοφόροι noun masc nom pl	....	δορατοφόρος
δοριάλωτον adj acc sg, neut nom sg	....	δοριάλωτος
δοριαλώτους adj masc and fem acc pl		id.
δορκάδα noun fem acc sg	....	δορκάς
δορκάδες noun fem nom pl		id.
δορκάδι noun fem dat sg		id.
δορκάδιον noun neut nom and acc sg		
δορκάδος noun fem gen sg	....	δορκάς
δορκάδων noun fem gen pl		id.
δορκάς noun fem nom sg		id.
Δορκων pr noun		
δόρκωνι noun masc dat sg	....	δόρκων
δόρυ noun neut nom and acc sg		
Δορυμενους pr noun masc gen sg	....	Δορυμενης
δορυφορίας noun fem gen sg	....	δορυφορία
δορυφόροι noun masc nom pl	....	δορυφόρος
δορυφόροις noun masc dat pl		id.
δορυφόρων noun masc gen pl		id.
δός vb 2nd aor act impv 2nd pers sg	....	δίδωμι
δόσει noun fem dat sg	....	δόσις
δόσεσιν noun fem dat pl		id.
δόσεως noun fem gen sg		id.
Δοσιθεον pr noun masc acc sg	....	Δοσιθεος
δόσιν noun fem acc sg	....	δόσις
δόσις noun fem nom sg		id.
δότε vb 2nd aor act impv 2nd pers pl	....	δίδωμι
δότην noun masc acc sg	....	δότης
δοτέν adj masc acc sg, neut nom and acc sg	....	δοτός
δότω vb 2nd aor act impv 3rd pers sg	....	δίδωμι
δότωσαν vb 2nd aor act impv 3rd pers pl		id.
Δουδι pr noun		
δοῦλα adj neut nom and acc pl	....	δοῦλος
δοῦλαι noun fem nom pl	....	δούλη
δούλας noun fem acc pl		id.
δουλεία noun fem nom sg		
δουλεία noun fem dat sg	....	δουλεία
δουλείαν noun fem acc sg		id.
δουλείας noun fem gen sg		id.
δούλευε vb pres act impv 2nd pers sg	....	δουλεύω
δουλεύειν vb pres act inf		id.
δουλεύοντα vb pres act part masc acc sg		id.
δουλεύοντας vb pres act part masc acc pl		id.
δουλεύοντες vb pres act part masc nom pl		id.
δουλεύοντος vb pres act part masc and neut gen sg		id.
δουλεύουσι(ν) vb pres act ind 3rd pers pl, pres act part masc and neut dat pl		id.
δουλεῦσαι vb 1st aor act inf		id.
δουλεύσαντες vb 1st aor act part masc nom pl		id.
δουλεύσατε vb 1st aor act impv 2nd pers pl		id.
δουλευσάτω vb 1st aor act impv 3rd pers sg		id.
δουλευσάτωσαν vb 1st aor act impv 3rd pers pl		id.
δουλεύσει vb fut act ind 3rd pers sg		id.
δουλεύσεις vb fut act ind 2nd pers sg		id.
δουλεύσετε vb fut act ind 2nd pers pl		id.
δουλεύσῃς vb 1st aor act subj 2nd pers sg		id.
δουλεύσητε vb 1st aor act subj 2nd pers pl		id.
δουλεύσομεν vb fut act ind 1st pers pl		id.
δούλευσον vb 1st aor act impv 2nd pers sg		id.
δουλεύσουσιν vb fut act ind 3rd pers pl		id.
δουλεύσω vb 1st aor act subj 1st pers sg, fut act ind 1st pers sg		id.
δουλεύσωμεν vb 1st aor act subj 1st pers pl		id.
δουλεύσωσιν vb 1st aor act subj 3rd pers pl		id.
δουλεύων vb pres act part masc nom sg		id.
δούλη noun fem nom sg		
δούλῃ noun fem dat sg	....	δούλη
δούλην noun fem acc sg		id.

δούλης noun fem gen sg . . . . δούλη
δοῦλοι noun masc nom pl . . . . δοῦλος
δούλοις noun masc dat pl   id.
δοῦλον noun masc acc sg   id.
δοῦλος noun masc nom sg   id.
δούλου noun masc gen sg   id.
δούλους noun masc acc pl   id.
δουλοῦται vb pres m/p ind 3rd pers sg . . . . δουλόω
δούλῳ noun masc dat sg . . . . δοῦλος
δουλωθέντες vb 1st aor pass part masc nom pl . . . . . δουλόω
δουλωθῆναι vb 1st aor pass inf   id.
δούλων noun masc gen pl . . . . δοῦλος
δουλώσουσιν vb fut act ind 3rd pers pl . . . . δουλόω
δοῦναι vb 2nd aor act inf . . . . δίδωμι
δούς vb 2nd aor act part masc nom sg   id.
δοῦσα vb 2nd aor act part fem nom sg   id.
δοχήν noun fem acc sg . . . . δοχή
δράγμα noun neut nom and acc sg
δράγμασι noun neut dat pl . . . . δράγμα
δράγματα noun neut nom and acc pl   id.
δραγμάτων noun neut gen pl   id.
δράκα noun fem acc sg . . . . δράξ
δράκας noun fem acc pl   id.
δράκεσι noun neut dat pl . . . . δράκος
δρακί noun fem dat sg . . . . δράξ
δράκοντα noun masc acc sg . . . . δράκων
δράκοντες noun masc nom pl   id.
δράκοντι noun masc dat sg   id.
δράκοντος noun masc gen sg   id.
δρακόντων noun masc gen pl   id.
δρακός noun fem gen sg . . . . δράξ
δράκων noun masc nom sg
δρακῶν noun fem gen pl . . . . δράξ
δρᾶμα noun neut nom and acc sg
δράμε vb 2nd aor act impv 2nd pers sg . . . . τρέχω
δραμεῖν vb 2nd aor act inf   id.
δραμεῖται vb fut mid ind 3rd pers sg   id.
δραμοῦμαι vb fut mid ind 1st pers sg   id.
δραμοῦμεν vb fut act ind 1st pers pl   id.
δραμοῦνται vb fut mid ind 3rd pers pl   id.
δραμοῦσα vb 2nd aor act part fem nom sg   id.
δράμω vb 2nd aor act subj 1st pers sg   id.
δραμών vb 2nd aor act part masc nom sg   id.
δράξ noun fem nom sg
δραξάμενος vb 1st aor mid part masc nom sg . . δράσσομαι
δράξασθε vb 1st aor mid impv 2nd pers pl   id.
δράξεται vb fut mid ind 3rd pers sg   id.
δραπέτου noun masc gen sg . . . . δραπέτης
δράσαντας vb 1st aor act part masc acc pl . . . . δράω
δράσαντι vb 1st aor act part masc and neut dat sg   id.
δρασσόμενοι vb pres dep part masc nom pl . . . . δράσσομαι
δρασσόμενος vb pres dep part masc nom sg   id.

δραχμάς noun fem acc pl . . . . δραχμή
δραχμή noun fem nom sg   id.
δραχμήν noun fem acc sg   id.
δρέπανα noun neut nom and acc pl . . . . δρέπανον
δρεπανηφόρα adj neut nom and acc pl . . . . δρεπανηφόρος
δρεπάνοις noun neut dat pl . . . . δρέπανον
δρέπανον noun neut nom and acc sg   id.
δρεπάνῳ noun neut dat sg   id.
Δριμυλου pr noun masc gen sg . . . . Δριμυλος
δρομεύς noun masc nom sg
δρομέως noun masc gen sg . . . . δρομεύς
δρόμον noun masc acc sg . . . . δρόμος
δρόμος noun masc nom sg   id.
δρόμου noun masc gen sg   id.
δρόμῳ noun masc dat sg   id.
δροσίσας vb 1st aor act part masc nom sg . . . . δροσίζω
δρόσοι noun fem nom pl . . . . δρόσος
δρόσον noun fem acc sg   id.
δρόσος noun fem nom sg   id.
δρόσου noun fem gen sg   id.
δρόσους noun fem acc pl   id.
δρόσῳ noun fem dat sg   id.
δρύες noun fem nom pl . . . . δρῦς
δρυί noun fem dat sg   id.
δρυμοί noun masc nom pl . . . . δρυμός
δρυμοῖς noun masc dat pl   id.
δρυμόν noun masc acc sg   id.
δρυμός noun masc nom sg   id.
δρυμοῦ noun masc gen sg   id.
δρυμούς noun masc acc pl   id.
δρυμῷ noun masc dat sg   id.
δρυμῶν noun masc gen pl   id.
δρῦν noun fem acc sg . . . . δρῦς
δρυός noun fem gen sg   id.
δρῦς noun fem nom sg   id.
δρῶντες vb pres act part masc nom pl . . . . δράω
δύειν vb pres act inf . . . . δύω
δυεῖν dual number . . . . δύο
δύη vb pres act subj 3rd pers sg . . . . δύω
δῦναι vb 2nd aor act inf   id.
δυναίμην vb pres dep opt 1st pers sg . . . . δύναμαι
δύναιντο vb pres dep opt 3rd pers pl   id.
δύναιτ᾽ see δύναιτο
δύναιτο vb pres dep opt 3rd pers sg   id.
δύναμαι vb pres dep ind 1st pers sg   id.
δυνάμεθα vb pres dep ind 1st pers pl   id.
δυνάμει noun fem dat sg . . . . δύναμις
δυνάμεις noun fem nom and acc pl   id.
δυνάμενα vb pres dep part neut nom and acc pl . . . δύναμαι
δυνάμενοι vb pres dep part masc nom pl   id.
δυναμένοις vb pres dep part masc and neut dat pl   id.

δυνάμενον vb pres dep part masc acc sg,		
neut nom and acc sg	δύναμαι	
δυνάμενος vb pres dep part masc nom sg	id.	
δυναμένου vb pres dep part masc and neut gen sg	id.	
δυναμένους vb pres dep part masc acc pl	id.	
δυναμένῳ vb pres dep part masc and neut dat sg	id.	
δυνάμεσιν noun fem dat pl	δύναμις	
δυνάμεων noun fem gen pl	id.	
δυνάμεως noun fem gen sg	id.	
δύναμιν noun fem acc sg	id.	
δύναμις noun fem nom sg	id.	
δυναμώσει vb fut act ind 3rd pers sg	δυναμόω	
δυνάμωσον vb 1st aor act impv 2nd pers sg	id.	
δύνανται vb pres dep ind 3rd pers pl	δύναμαι	
δύνασαι vb pres dep ind 2nd pers sg	id.	
δύνασθαι vb pres dep inf	id.	
δύνασθε vb pres dep ind 2nd pers pl	id.	
δυνασθῆτε vb 1st aor pass subj 2nd pers pl	id.	
δυνάστα noun masc voc sg	δυνάστης	
δυνάσται noun masc nom pl	id.	
δυνάσταις noun masc dat pl	id.	
δυνάστας noun masc acc pl	id.	
δυναστεία noun fem nom sg		
δυναστείᾳ noun fem dat sg	δυναστεία	
δυναστεῖαι noun fem nom pl	id.	
δυναστείαις noun fem dat pl	id.	
δυναστείαν noun fem acc sg	id.	
δυναστείας noun fem gen sg and acc pl	id.	
δυναστεύειν vb pres act inf	δυναστεύω	
δυναστεύματα noun neut nom and acc pl	δυνάστευμα	
δυναστεύοντα vb pres act part masc acc sg	δυναστεύω	
δυναστεύοντι vb pres act part masc and neut dat sg	id.	
δυναστευόντων vb pres act part masc and neut gen pl	id.	
δυναστευούσης vb pres act part fem gen sg	id.	
δυναστεύουσι vb pres act part masc and neut dat pl	id.	
δυναστεῦσαι vb 1st aor act inf	id.	
δυναστεύσει vb fut act ind 3rd pers sg	id.	
δυναστεύσῃ vb 1st aor act subj 3rd pers sg	id.	
δυναστεύων vb pres act part masc nom sg	id.	
δυνάστῃ noun masc dat sg	δυνάστης	
δυνάστην noun masc acc sg	id.	
δυνάστης noun masc nom sg	id.	
δυνάστου noun masc gen sg	id.	
δυναστῶν noun masc gen pl	id.	
δυνατά adj neut nom and acc pl	δυνατός	
δύναται vb pres dep ind 3rd pers sg	δύναμαι	
δυνατέ adj masc voc sg	δυνατός	
δυνατή adj fem nom sg	id.	
δυνατοί adj masc nom pl	id.	
δυνατοῖς adj masc and neut dat pl	id.	
δυνατόν adj masc acc sg, neut nom and acc sg	id.	
δυνατός adj masc nom sg	id.	

δυνατοῦ adj masc and neut gen sg	δυνατός	
δυνατούς adj masc acc pl	id.	
δυνατῶν adj gen pl	id.	
δυνατῶς adverb		
δυνατωτέρα comp adj fem nom sg	δυνατός	
δυνατώτεροι comp adj masc nom pl	id.	
δυνατώτερον comp adj masc acc sg, neut nom and acc sg	id.	
δυνατώτερος comp adj masc nom sg	id.	
δύνει vb pres act ind 3rd pers sg	δύω	
δύνῃ vb pres dep ind 2nd pers sg,		
pres dep subj 2nd pers sg	δύναμαι	
δυντθεὶς vb 1st aor pass part masc nom sg	id.	
δυντθῇ vb 1st aor pass subj 3rd pers sg	id.	
δυνηθῆναι vb 1st aor pass inf	id.	
δυνηθῇς vb 1st aor pass subj 2nd pers sg	id.	
δυνηθῶ vb 1st aor pass subj 1st pers sg	id.	
δυνηθῶσιν vb 1st aor pass subj 3rd pers pl	id.	
δυνήσει vb fut act ind 3rd pers sg	id.	
δυνήσεσθε vb fut mid ind 2nd pers pl	id.	
δυνήσεται vb fut mid ind 3rd pers sg	id.	
δυνήσῃ vb fut mid ind 2nd pers sg	id.	
δύνησθε vb pres dep subj 2nd pers pl	id.	
δυνήσομαι vb fut mid ind 1st pers sg	id.	
δυνησόμεθα vb fut mid ind 1st pers pl	id.	
δυνήσονται vb fut mid ind 3rd pers pl	id.	
δύνηται vb pres dep subj 3rd pers sg	id.	
δύνοντος vb pres act part masc and neut gen sg	δύω	
δύνωμαι vb pres dep subj 1st pers sg	δύναμαι	
δυνώμεθα vb pres dep subj 1st pers pl	id.	
δύνωνται vb pres dep subj 3rd pers pl	id.	
δύο indecl number		
δυσάθλιον adj masc and fem acc sg	δυσάθλιος	
δυσαιάκτου adj gen sg	δυσαίακτος	
δυσάλυκτον adj acc sg, neut nom sg	δυσάλυκτος	
δυσβάστακτον adj acc sg, neut nom sg	δυσβάστακτος	
δυσδιήγητοι adj masc and fem nom pl	δυσδιήγητος	
δύσεται vb fut mid ind 3rd pers sg	δύω	
δυσημερίαν noun fem acc sg	δυσημερία	
δυσί dual number dat	δύο	
δύσιν noun fem acc sg	δύσις	
δυσκαταπαύστῳ adj dat sg	δυσκατάπαυστος	
δυσκλεεστάτης superl adj fem gen sg	δυσκλεής	
δυσκλεῆ adj masc acc sg	id.	
δύσκολα adj neut nom and acc pl	δύσκολος	
δυσκολίας noun fem gen sg	δυσκολία	
δύσκωφον adj acc sg, neut nom sg	δύσκωφος	
δυσμαῖς noun fem dat pl	δυσμή	
δυσμάς noun fem acc pl and gen sg	id.	
δυσμένειαν noun fem acc sg	δυσμένεια	
δυσμενείς noun masc acc pl	id.	
δυσμενεῖς adj masc nom and acc pl	δυσμενής	
δυσμενέσι adj masc and neut dat pl	id.	

δυσμενῆ adj masc and fem acc sg . . . . δυσμενής

δυσμενής adj masc and fem nom sg   id.

δυσμενῶς adverb

δυσμῶν noun fem gen pl . . . . δυσμή

δυσνοεῖν vb pres act inf . . . . δυσνοέω

δυσνοοῦν vb pres act part neut nom and acc sg   id.

δύσονται vb fut mid ind 3rd pers pl . . . . δύω

δύσουσιν vb fut act ind 3rd pers pl   id.

δυσπετημάτων noun neut gen pl . . . . δυσπέτημα

δυσπολιόρκητον adj acc sg,

              neut nom sg . . . . δυσπολιόρκητος

δυσπρόσιτον adj acc sg, neut nom sg . . . . . . δυσπρόσιτος

δυσσεβείας noun fem gen sg . . . . δυσσέβεια

δυσσεβεῖς adj masc and fem nom and acc pl . . . . δυσσεβής

δυσσεβῆ adj masc and fem acc sg   id.

δυσσέβημα noun neut nom and acc sg

δυσσεβήματα noun neut nom and acc pl . . . . . δυσσέβημα

δυσσεβής adj masc and fem nom sg

δυσσεβοῦντας vb pres act part masc acc pl . . . . δυσσεβέω

δυσσεβοῦς adj gen sg . . . . δυσσεβής

Δυστρου pr noun neut gen sg . . . . Δυστρος

δυσφημίας noun fem gen sg and acc pl . . . . δυσφημία

δυσφημιῶν noun fem gen pl   id.

δυσφήμοις adj dat pl . . . . δύσφημος

δυσφήμου adj gen sg   id.

δυσφόρως adverb

δυσχερεῖ adj dat sg . . . . δυσχερής

δυσχέρειαν noun fem acc sg . . . . δυσχέρεια

δυσχερές adj neut nom and acc sg . . . . δυσχερής

δυσχερής adj masc and fem nom sg   id.

δυσχερῶν adj gen pl   id.

δύσχρηστος adj masc nom sg

δυσώδεις adj masc and fem nom and acc pl . . . . . . δυσώδης

δῶ vb 2nd aor act subj 1st and 3rd pers sg . . . . δίδωμι

Δωδαι pr noun

Δωδαμ pr noun

δώδεκα indecl number

δωδεκαετοῦς adj gen sg . . . . δωδεκαετής

δωδεκάμηνον noun neut nom and acc sg

δωδεκάτη adj fem dat sg . . . . δωδέκατος

δωδέκατον adj masc acc sg, neut nom and acc sg   id.

δωδέκατος adj masc nom sg   id.

δωδεκάτου adj masc and neut gen sg   id.

δωδεκάτῳ adj masc and neut dat sg   id.

Δωδια pr noun

Δωδω pr noun

δώῃ vb 2nd aor act opt 3rd pers sg,

              2nd aor act subj 3rd pers sg . . . . δίδωμι

Δωηκ pr noun

δώῃς vb 2nd aor act opt 2nd pers sg . . . . δίδωμι

Δωθαϊμ pr noun

Δωκ pr noun

δῶμα noun neut nom and acc sg

Δωμανα pr noun

δώματα noun neut nom and acc pl . . . . δῶμα

δώματι noun neut dat sg   id.

δώματος noun neut gen sg   id.

δωμάτων noun neut gen pl   id.

δῶμεν vb 2nd aor act subj 1st pers pl . . . . δίδωμι

Δωρ pr noun

δῶρα noun neut nom and acc pl . . . . δῶρον

Δωρα pr noun

δωρεᾷ noun fem dat sg . . . . δωρεά

δωρεάν noun fem acc sg   id.

δωρεάς noun fem gen sg and acc pl   id.

δωρεῖται vb pres dep ind 3rd pers sg . . . . δωρέομαι

δωρήματα noun neut nom and acc pl . . . . δώρημα

δώρησαι vb 1st aor mid impv 2nd pers sg . . . . δωρέομαι

δωροδεκτῶν noun masc gen pl . . . . δωροδέκτης

δώροις noun neut dat pl . . . . δῶρον

δωροκόπει vb pres act impv 2nd pers sg . . . . . . δωροκοπέω

δωρολήμπτης noun masc nom sg

δῶρον noun neut nom and acc sg

δώρου noun neut gen sg . . . . δῶρον

δωροῦμαι vb pres dep ind 1st pers sg . . . . δωρέομαι

δώρων noun neut gen pl . . . . δῶρον

δῷς vb 2nd aor act subj 2nd pers sg . . . . δίδωμι

δώσει vb fut act ind 3rd pers sg   id.

δώσειν vb fut act inf   id.

δώσεις vb fut act ind 2nd pers sg   id.

δώσετε vb fut act ind 2nd pers pl   id.

δῶσι(ν) vb 2nd aor act subj 3rd pers pl   id.

Δωσιθεος pr noun masc nom sg

δώσομεν vb fut act ind 1st pers pl . . . . δίδωμι

δώσουσι(ν) vb fut act ind 3rd pers pl   id.

δώσω vb fut act ind 1st pers sg   id.

Δωταιας pr noun fem gen sg . . . . Δωταια

δῶτε vb 2nd aor act subj 2nd pers pl . . . . δίδωμι

E ε

ε′ indecl number	ἐβαρύνθη vb 1st aor pass ind 3rd pers sg . . . . βαρύνω
ἔα interjection	ἐβαρύνθης vb 1st aor pass ind 2nd pers sg id.
ἐᾷ vb pres act ind 3rd pers sg . . . . ἐάω	ἐβαρύνθησαν vb 1st aor pass ind 3rd pers pl id.
ἐάλω vb 2nd aor act ind 3rd pers sg . . . . ἁλίσκω	ἐβαρυόπησαν vb 1st aor act ind 3rd pers pl . . . . . . βαρυωπέω
ἐάλωκεν vb perf act ind 3rd pers sg id.	ἐβασανίζετο vb impf m/p ind 3rd pers sg . . . . βασανίζω
ἐαλωκυίας vb perf act part fem gen sg id.	ἐβασάνιζον vb impf act ind 3rd pers pl id.
ἐάλως vb 2nd aor act ind 2nd pers sg id.	ἐβασανίζοντο vb impf m/p ind 3rd pers pl id.
ἐάλωσαν vb 2nd aor act ind 3rd pers pl id.	ἐβασάνισας vb 1st aor act ind 2nd pers sg id.
ἐάν particle	ἐβασάνισεν vb 1st aor act ind 3rd pers sg id.
ἐᾶν vb pres act inf . . . . ἐάω	ἐβασανίσθησαν vb 1st aor pass ind 3rd pers pl id.
ἐάνπερ particle	ἐβασίλευσα vb 1st aor act ind 1st pers sg . . . . βασιλεύω
ἔαρ noun neut nom and acc sg	ἐβασίλευσαν vb 1st aor act ind 3rd pers pl id.
ἔαρι noun neut dat sg . . . . ἔαρ	ἐβασίλευσας vb 1st aor act ind 2nd pers sg id.
ἔαρος noun neut gen sg id.	ἐβασιλεύσατε vb 1st aor act ind 2nd pers pl id.
ἐᾷς vb pres act ind 2nd pers sg . . . . ἐάω	ἐβασίλευσεν vb 1st aor act ind 3rd pers sg id.
ἐᾶσαι vb 1st aor act inf id.	ἐβάσταξεν vb 1st aor act ind 3rd pers sg . . . . βαστάζω
Εασακεμ pr noun	ἐβάφη vb 2nd aor pass ind 3rd pers sg . . . . βάπτω
ἐάσατε vb 1st aor act impv 2nd pers pl . . . . ἐάω	ἐβάφησαν vb 2nd aor pass ind 3rd pers pl id.
ἐάσεις vb fut act ind 2nd pers sg id.	ἔβαψας vb 1st aor act ind 2nd pers sg id.
ἐάσῃ vb 1st aor act subj 3rd pers sg id.	ἔβαψεν vb 1st aor act ind 3rd pers sg id.
ἐᾶσθαι vb pres m/p inf id.	ἐβδελυγμένα vb perf m/p part neut
ἔασον vb 1st aor act impv 2nd pers sg id.	nom and acc pl . . . . βδελύσσω
ἑαυτά refl pron neut nom and acc pl . . . . ἑαυτοῦ	ἐβδελυγμένοι vb perf m/p part masc nom pl id.
ἑαυταῖς refl pron fem dat pl id.	ἐβδελυγμένον vb perf m/p part masc acc sg id.
ἑαυτάς refl pron fem acc pl id.	ἐβδελυγμένος vb perf m/p part masc nom sg id.
ἑαυτῇ refl pron fem dat sg id.	ἐβδελυγμένων vb perf m/p part gen pl id.
ἑαυτήν refl pron fem acc sg id.	ἐβδέλυκται vb perf m/p ind 3rd pers sg id.
ἑαυτῆς refl pron fem gen sg id.	ἐβδελυξάμεθα vb 1st aor mid ind 1st pers pl id.
ἑαυτό refl pron neut nom and acc sg id.	ἐβδελυξάμην vb 1st aor mid ind 1st pers sg id.
ἑαυτοῖς refl pron masc and neut dat pl id.	ἐβδελύξαντο vb 1st aor mid ind 3rd pers pl id.
ἑαυτόν refl pron masc acc sg id.	ἐβδελύξατε vb 1st aor act ind 2nd pers pl id.
ἑαυτοῦ refl pron masc and neut gen sg id.	ἐβδελύξατο vb 1st aor mid ind 3rd pers sg id.
ἑαυτούς refl pron masc acc pl id.	ἐβδελύσσοντο vb impf m/p ind 3rd pers pl id.
ἑαυτῷ refl pron masc and neut dat sg id.	ἐβδελύχθη vb 1st aor pass ind 3rd pers sg id.
ἑαυτῶν refl pron gen pl id.	ἐβδελύχθησαν vb 1st aor pass ind 3rd pers pl id.
ἐβάδισεν vb 1st aor act ind 3rd pers sg . . . . βαδίζω	ἕβδομα adj neut nom and acc pl . . . . ἕβδομος
ἐβαθύνθησαν vb 1st aor pass ind 3rd pers pl . . . . . . βαθύνω	ἑβδομάδα noun fem acc sg . . . . ἑβδομάς
ἔβαλαν vb 1st aor act ind 3rd pers pl . . . . βάλλω	ἑβδομάδας noun fem acc pl id.
ἔβαλεν vb 2nd aor act ind 3rd pers sg id.	ἑβδομάδες noun fem nom pl id.
ἔβαλες vb 2nd aor act ind 2nd pers sg id.	ἑβδομάδος noun fem gen sg id.
ἔβαλλον vb impf act ind 3rd pers pl id.	ἑβδομάδων noun fem gen pl id.
ἐβάλομεν vb 2nd aor act ind 1st pers pl id.	ἑβδόμαις adj fem dat pl . . . . ἕβδομος
ἔβαλον vb 2nd aor act ind 3rd pers pl id.	ἑβδομάς noun fem nom sg
ἐβάλοσαν vb 2nd aor act ind 3rd pers pl id.	ἑβδόμη adj fem nom sg . . . . ἕβδομος
ἐβαπτίζετο vb impf m/p ind 3rd pers sg . . . . βαπτίζω	ἑβδόμῃ adj fem dat sg id.
ἐβαπτίσατο vb 1st aor mid ind 3rd pers sg id.	ἑβδομήκοντα indecl number
ἐβαρυθύμησεν vb 1st aor act ind 3rd pers sg . . . . βαρυθυμέω	ἑβδομηκοντάκις adverb
ἐβάρυναν vb 1st aor act ind 3rd pers pl . . . . βαρύνω	ἑβδομηκοστόν adj masc acc sg,
ἐβάρυνας vb 1st aor act ind 2nd pers sg id.	neut nom and acc sg . . . . ἑβδομηκοστός
ἐβαρύνατε vb 1st aor act ind 2nd pers pl id.	ἑβδομηκοστοῦ adj masc and neut gen sg id.
ἐβάρυνεν vb impf act ind 3rd pers sg,	ἑβδομηκοστῷ adj masc and neut dat sg id.
1st aor act ind 3rd pers sg id.	ἑβδόμην adj fem acc sg . . . . ἕβδομος

ἑβδόμης adj fem gen sg . . . . ἕβδομος

ἕβδομον adj masc acc sg, neut nom and acc sg   id.

ἕβδομος adj masc nom sg   id.

ἑβδόμου adj masc and neut gen sg   id.

ἑβδόμῳ adj masc and neut dat sg   id.

Εβεαρ pr noun

ἐβεβαίωσας vb 1st aor act ind 2nd pers sg . . . . βεβαιόω

ἐβεβηλούμην vb impf m/p ind 1st pers sg . . . . βεβηλόω

ἐβεβήλουν vb impf act ind 3rd pers pl   id.

ἐβεβηλοῦσαν vb impf act ind 3rd pers pl   id.

ἐβεβηλώθη vb 1st aor pass ind 3rd pers sg   id.

ἐβεβήλωσαν vb 1st aor act ind 3rd pers pl   id.

ἐβεβήλωσας vb 1st aor act ind 2nd pers sg   id.

ἐβεβηλώσατε vb 1st aor act ind 2nd pers pl   id.

ἐβεβήλωσεν vb 1st aor act ind 3rd pers sg   id.

Εβελμαωλα pr noun

Εβελχαρμιν pr noun

Εβερ pr noun

Εβια pr noun

ἐβιάσατο vb 1st aor mid ind 3rd pers sg . . . . βιάζομαι

ἐβιάσθης vb 1st aor pass ind 2nd pers sg   id.

ἐβλάβησαν vb 2nd aor pass ind 3rd pers pl . . . . βλάπτω

Εβλαζερ pr noun

ἐβλάστησα vb 1st aor act ind 1st pers sg . . . . βλαστάνω

ἐβλάστησεν vb 1st aor act ind 3rd pers sg   id.

ἐβλασφήμησαν vb 1st aor act ind 3rd pers pl . . . . βλασφημέω

ἐβλασφήμησας vb 1st aor act ind 2nd pers sg   id.

ἐβλασφήμησεν vb 1st aor act ind 3rd pers sg   id.

ἐβλασφήμουν vb impf act ind 3rd pers pl   id.

ἔβλεπεν vb impf act ind 3rd pers sg . . . . βλέπω

ἔβλεπον vb impf act ind 3rd pers pl   id.

ἐβλέποντο vb impf m/p ind 3rd pers pl   id.

ἔβλεψεν vb 1st aor act ind 3rd pers sg   id.

ἐβλήθη vb 1st aor pass ind 3rd pers sg . . . . βάλλω

ἐβλήθησαν vb 1st aor pass ind 3rd pers pl   id.

ἐβόα vb impf act ind 3rd pers sg . . . . βοάω

ἐβοήθει vb impf act ind 3rd pers sg . . . . βοηθέω

ἐβοηθήθην vb 1st aor pass ind 1st pers sg   id.

ἐβοήθησα vb 1st aor act ind 1st pers sg   id.

ἐβοήθησαν vb 1st aor act ind 3rd pers pl   id.

ἐβοήθησας vb 1st aor act ind 2nd pers sg   id.

ἐβοήθησεν vb 1st aor act ind 3rd pers sg   id.

ἐβοήθουν vb impf act ind 3rd pers pl   id.

ἐβόησα vb 1st aor act ind 1st pers sg . . . . βοάω

ἐβόησαν vb 1st aor act ind 3rd pers pl   id.

ἐβόησας vb 1st aor act ind 2nd pers sg   id.

ἐβόησατε vb 1st aor act ind 2nd pers pl   id.

ἐβόησεν vb 1st aor act ind 3rd pers sg   id.

ἐβόμβησεν vb 1st aor act ind 3rd pers sg . . . . βομβέω

ἔβοσκεν vb impf act ind 3rd pers sg . . . . βόσκω

ἐβόσκησαν vb 1st aor act ind 3rd pers pl   id.

ἐβόσκοντο vb impf m/p ind 3rd pers pl   id.

ἐβούλετο vb impf dep ind 3rd pers sg . . . . βούλομαι

ἐβουλεύετο vb impf m/p ind 3rd pers sg . . . . βουλεύω

ἐβουλεύοντο vb impf m/p ind 3rd pers pl   id.

ἐβουλεύσαντο vb 1st aor mid ind 3rd pers pl   id.

ἐβουλεύσασθε vb 1st aor mid ind 2nd pers pl . . . . . βουλεύω

ἐβουλεύσατο vb 1st aor mid ind 3rd pers sg   id.

ἐβούλευσεν vb 1st aor act ind 3rd pers sg   id.

ἐβουλεύσω vb 1st aor mid ind 2nd pers sg   id.

ἐβουλήθη vb 1st aor pass ind 3rd pers sg . . . . βούλομαι

ἐβουλήθημεν vb 1st aor pass ind 1st pers pl   id.

ἐβουλήθην vb 1st aor pass ind 1st pers sg   id.

ἐβουλήθης vb 1st aor pass ind 2nd pers sg   id.

ἐβουλήθησαν vb 1st aor pass ind 3rd pers pl   id.

ἐβουλόμην vb impf dep ind 1st pers sg   id.

ἐβούλοντο vb impf dep ind 3rd pers pl   id.

ἐβούλου vb impf dep ind 2nd pers sg   id.

ἐβούνισεν vb 1st aor act ind 3rd pers sg . . . . βουνίζω

ἐβόων vb impf act ind 3rd pers pl . . . . βοάω

ἐβράβευσεν vb 1st aor act ind 3rd pers sg . . . . βραβεύω

ἐβραγχίασεν vb 1st aor act ind 3rd pers sg . . . . . . βραγχιάω

ἐβραδύναμεν vb 1st aor act ind 1st pers pl . . . . βραδύνω

Εβραιαι adj fem nom pl . . . . Εβραιος

Εβραιαν adj fem acc sg   id.

Εβραιας adj fem gen sg and acc pl   id.

Εβραΐδι pr noun fem dat sg . . . . Εβραΐς

Εβραιοι adj masc nom pl . . . . Εβραιος

Εβραιοις adj masc dat pl   id.

Εβραιον adj masc acc sg   id.

Εβραιος adj masc nom sg   id.

Εβραιους adj masc acc pl   id.

Εβραϊστι pr noun

Εβραιων adj gen pl . . . . Εβραιος

ἔβρεξεν vb 1st aor act ind 3rd pers sg . . . . βρέχω

ἐβρόντησεν vb 1st aor act ind 3rd pers sg . . . . βροντάω

ἔβρυξαν vb 1st aor act ind 3rd pers pl . . . . βρύχω

ἔβρυξεν vb 1st aor act ind 3rd pers sg   id.

ἐβρώθη vb 1st aor pass ind 3rd pers sg . . . . βιβρώσκω

Εβρωνα pr noun

ἐβύθισαν vb 1st aor act ind 3rd pers pl . . . . βυθίζω

ἐγάμησεν vb 1st aor act ind 3rd pers sg . . . . γαμεω

ἐγαυρίασαν vb 1st aor act ind 3rd pers pl . . . . γαυριάω

Εγγαδδι pr noun

ἐγγαστριμύθοις adj dat pl . . . . ἐγγαστρίμυθος

ἐγγαστρίμυθον adj acc sg, neut nom sg   id.

ἐγγαστρίμυθος adj masc and fem nom sg   id.

ἐγγαστριμύθους adj masc and fem acc pl   id.

ἐγγαστριμύθῳ adj dat sg   id.

ἐγγαστριμύθων adj gen pl   id.

ἐγγεγλυμμένα vb perf m/p part

         neut nom and acc pl . . . . ἐγγλύφω

ἐγγεγραμμένα vb perf m/p part

         neut nom and acc pl . . . . ἐγγράφω

ἐγγεγραμμένος vb perf m/p part masc nom sg   id.

ἐγγιεῖ vb fut act ind 3rd pers sg . . . . ἐγγίζω

ἔγγιζε vb pres act impv 2nd pers sg   id.

ἐγγίζει vb pres act ind 3rd pers sg   id.

ἐγγίζειν vb pres act inf   id.

ἐγγίζῃ vb pres act subj 3rd pers sg   id.

ἐγγίζοντας vb pres act part masc acc pl   id.

ἐγγίζοντες vb pres act part masc nom pl   id.

ἐγγίζοντι vb pres act part masc and neut dat sg	. . . . . . ἐγγίζω	
ἐγγίζοντος vb pres act part masc and neut gen sg	id.	
ἐγγιζόντων vb pres act part masc and neut gen pl	id.	
ἐγγίζουσα vb pres act part fem nom sg	id.	
ἐγγιζούσαις vb pres act part fem dat pl	id.	
ἐγγιζούσῃ vb pres act part fem dat sg	id.	
ἐγγιζούσης vb pres act part fem gen sg	id.	
ἐγγίζουσι(ν) vb pres act ind 3rd pers pl,		
pres act part masc and neut dat pl	id.	
ἐγγίζων vb pres act part masc nom sg	id.	
ἐγγιοῦσι(ν) vb fut act ind 3rd pers pl	id.	
ἐγγίσαι vb 1st aor act inf	id.	
ἐγγίσας vb 1st aor act part masc nom sg	id.	
ἐγγίσασα vb 1st aor act part fem nom sg	id.	
ἐγγίσατε vb 1st aor act impv 2nd pers pl	id.	
ἐγγισάτω vb 1st aor act impv 3rd pers sg	id.	
ἐγγισάτωσαν vb 1st aor act impv 3rd pers pl	id.	
ἐγγίσῃ vb 1st aor act subj 3rd pers sg	id.	
ἐγγίσῃς vb 1st aor act subj 2nd pers sg	id.	
ἐγγίσητε vb 1st aor act subj 2nd pers pl	id.	
ἔγγισον vb 1st aor act impv 2nd pers sg	id.	
ἔγγιστα superl adverb	. . . . ἐγγύς	
ἐγγίσωμεν vb 1st aor act subj 1st pers pl	. . . . ἐγγίζω	
ἐγγίσωσιν vb 1st aor act subj 3rd pers pl	id.	
ἐγγίων comp adj masc nom sg	. . . . ἐγγύς	
ἐγγλυφῆναι vb 2nd aor pass inf	. . . . ἐγγλύφω	
ἔγγραπτον adj acc sg, neut nom sg	. . . . ἔγγραπτος	
ἐγγραφέσθωσαν vb pres m/p impv 3rd pers pl	. . . . . ἐγγράφω	
ἐγγραφή noun fem nom sg	. . . . ἐγγραφή	
ἐγγυᾶσθαι vb pres m/p inf	. . . . ἐγγυαω	
ἐγγύη noun fem nom sg		
ἐγγύῃ noun fem dat sg	. . . . ἐγγύη	
ἐγγύην noun fem acc sg	id.	
ἐγγυήσεται vb fut mid ind 3rd pers sg	. . . . ἐγγυάω	
ἐγγυήσῃ vb 1st aor mid subj 2nd pers sg,		
fut mid ind 2nd pers sg	id.	
ἐγγύθεν adverb		
ἔγγυον adj acc sg, neut nom sg	. . . . ἔγγυος	
ἐγγύου adj gen sg	id.	
ἐγγύς adverb		
ἐγγύτατοι superl adj masc nom pl	. . . . ἐγγύς	
ἐγγυώμενος vb pres m/p part masc nom sg	. . . . ἐγγυάω	
ἐγεγόνει vb plpf act ind 3rd pers sg	. . . . γίνομαι	
ἐγέγραπτο vb plpf m/p ind 3rd pers sg	. . . . γράφω	
ἐγεῖραι vb 1st aor act inf	. . . . ἐγείρω	
ἐγείραντες vb 1st aor act part masc nom pl	id.	
ἐγείραντος vb 1st aor act part masc and neut gen sg	id.	
ἐγείρας vb 1st aor act part masc nom sg	id.	
ἐγείρατε vb 1st aor act impv 2nd pers pl	id.	
ἐγείρει vb pres act ind 3rd pers sg	id.	
ἐγείρεσθαι vb pres m/p inf	id.	
ἐγείρητε vb pres act subj 2nd pers pl,		
1st aor act subj 2nd pers pl	id.	
ἐγειρόμενοι vb pres m/p part masc nom pl	id.	
ἐγειρομένῳ vb pres m/p part masc and neut dat sg	id.	
ἔγειρον vb 1st aor act impv 2nd pers sg	id.	

ἐγείρονται vb pres m/p ind 3rd pers pl	. . . . ἐγείρω	
ἐγείροντες vb pres act part masc nom pl	id.	
ἐγείρου vb pres m/p impv 2nd pers sg	id.	
ἐγείρω vb pres act ind 1st pers sg	id.	
ἐγείρων vb pres act part masc nom sg	id.	
ἐγέλασα vb 1st aor act ind 1st pers sg	. . . . γελάω	
ἐγέλασαν vb 1st aor act ind 3rd pers pl	id.	
ἐγέλασας vb 1st aor act ind 2nd pers sg	id.	
ἐγέλασε(ν) vb 1st aor act ind 3rd pers sg	id.	
ἔγεμον vb impf act ind 3rd pers pl	. . . . γέμω	
ἐγενεαλογήθη vb 1st aor pass ind 3rd pers sg	. . . γενεαλογέω	
ἐγένεσθε vb 2nd aor mid ind 2nd pers pl	. . . . γίνομαι	
ἐγένετο vb 2nd aor mid ind 3rd pers sg	id.	
ἐγενήθη vb 1st aor pass ind 3rd pers sg	id.	
ἐγενήθημεν vb 1st aor pass ind 1st pers pl	id.	
ἐγενήθην vb 1st aor pass ind 1st pers sg	id.	
ἐγενήθης vb 1st aor pass ind 2nd pers sg	id.	
ἐγενήθησαν vb 1st aor pass ind 3rd pers pl	id.	
ἐγενήθητε vb 1st aor pass ind 2nd pers pl	id.	
ἐγεννήθη vb 1st aor pass ind 3rd pers sg	. . . . γεννάω	
ἐγεννήθην vb 1st aor pass ind 1st pers sg	id.	
ἐγεννήθης vb 1st aor pass ind 2nd pers sg	id.	
ἐγεννήθησαν vb 1st aor pass ind 3rd pers pl	id.	
ἐγέννησα vb 1st aor act ind 1st pers sg	id.	
ἐγέννησαν vb 1st aor act ind 3rd pers pl	id.	
ἐγέννησας vb 1st aor act ind 2nd pers sg	id.	
ἐγέννησε(ν) vb 1st aor act ind 3rd pers sg	id.	
ἐγεννῶσον vb 1st aor act ind 3rd pers pl	id.	
ἐγενόμεθα vb 2nd aor mid ind 1st pers pl	. . . . γίνομαι	
ἐγενόμην vb 2nd aor mid ind 1st pers sg	id.	
ἐγένοντο vb 2nd aor mid ind 3rd pers pl	id.	
ἐγένου vb 2nd aor mid ind 2nd pers sg	id.	
ἐγερεῖ vb fut act ind 3rd pers sg	. . . . ἐγείρω	
ἐγερθῇ vb 1st aor pass subj 3rd pers sg	id.	
ἐγερθήσεται vb fut pass ind 3rd pers sg	id.	
ἐγερθήσῃ vb fut pass ind 2nd pers sg	id.	
ἐγερθήσονται vb fut pass ind 3rd pers pl	id.	
ἐγέρθητε vb 1st aor pass subj 2nd pers pl	id.	
ἐγερθῶσι vb 1st aor pass subj 3rd pers pl	id.	
ἐγεροῦσι vb fut act ind 3rd pers pl	id.	
ἐγέρσει noun fem dat sg	. . . . ἔγερσις	
ἔγερσιν noun fem acc sg	id.	
ἐγευσάμην vb 1st aor mid ind 1st pers sg	. . . . γεύω	
ἐγεύσατο vb 1st aor mid ind 3rd pers sg	id.	
ἐγήρασα vb 1st aor act ind 1st pers sg	. . . . γηράω	
ἐγήρασεν vb 1st aor act ind 3rd pers sg	id.	
ἐγηροβόσκησεν vb 1st aor act ind 3rd pers sg	. . . γηροβόσκω	
ἐγίνετο vb impf mid ind 3rd pers sg	. . . . γίνομαι	
ἐγινόμην vb impf mid ind 1st pers sg	id.	
ἐγίνοντο vb impf mid ind 3rd pers pl	id.	
ἐγίνου vb impf mid ind 2nd pers sg	id.	
ἐγίνωσκον vb impf act ind		
1st pers sg and 3rd pers pl	. . . . γινώσκω	
ἐγκάθετοι adj masc and fem nom pl	. . . . ἐγκάθετος	
ἐγκάθετος adj masc and fem nom sg	id.	
ἐγκαθήμενοι vb pres mid part masc nom pl	. . . . . ἐγκάθημαι	

ἐγκαθημένοις vb pres mid part	ἐγκαταλιπεῖν vb 2nd aor act inf . . . . ἐγκαταλείπω
masc and neut dat pl . . . . ἐγκάθημαι	ἐγκαταλίπῃ vb 2nd aor act subj 3rd pers sg id.
ἐγκαθήμενον vb pres mid part masc acc sg id.	ἐγκαταλίπῃς vb 2nd aor act subj 2nd pers sg id.
ἐγκαθήμενος vb pres mid part masc nom sg id.	ἐγκαταλίπητε vb 2nd aor act subj 2nd pers pl id.
ἐγκαθημένους vb pres mid part masc acc pl id.	ἐγκαταλίποι vb 2nd aor act opt 3rd pers sg id.
ἐγκάθηνται vb pres mid ind 3rd pers pl id.	ἐγκαταλίποιτο vb 2nd aor mid opt 3rd pers sg id.
ἐγκαθήσονται vb fut mid ind 3rd pers pl id.	ἐγκαταλιπόντες vb 2nd aor act part masc nom pl id.
ἐγκάθηται vb pres mid ind 3rd pers sg id.	ἐγκαταλίπω vb 2nd aor act subj 1st pers sg id.
ἐγκαθίσατε vb 1st aor act impv 2nd pers pl . . . . . . ἐγκαθίζω	ἐγκαταλίπωμεν vb 2nd aor act subj 1st pers pl id.
ἐγκαθίσῃ vb 1st aor act subj 3rd pers sg id.	ἐγκαταλιπών vb 2nd aor act part masc nom sg id.
ἐγκαίειν vb pres act inf . . . . ἐγκαίω	ἐγκαταλίπωσιν vb 2nd aor act subj 3rd pers pl id.
ἐγκαίνια noun neut nom and acc pl	ἐγκαταπαίζεσθαι vb pres m/p inf . . . . ἐγκαταπαίζω
ἐγκαινιεῖ vb fut act ind 3rd pers sg . . . . ἐγκαινίζω	ἐγκατελείφθη vb 1st aor pass ind 3rd pers sg . . ἐγκαταλείπω
ἐγκαινίζεσθε vb pres m/p impv 2nd pers pl id.	ἐγκατελείφθημεν vb 1st aor pass ind 1st pers pl id.
ἐγκαινίοις noun neut dat pl . . . . ἐγκαίνια	ἐγκατελείφθησαν vb 1st aor pass ind 3rd pers pl id.
ἐγκαινίσαι vb 1st aor act inf . . . . ἐγκαινίζω	ἐγκατέλιπαν vb 1st aor act ind 3rd pers pl id.
ἐγκαινισμόν noun masc acc sg . . . . ἐγκαινισμός	ἐγκατελίπατε vb 1st aor act ind 2nd pers pl id.
ἐγκαινισμός noun masc nom sg id.	ἐγκατέλιπε(ν) vb 2nd aor act ind 3rd pers sg id.
ἐγκαινισμοῦ noun masc gen sg id.	ἐγκατέλιπες vb 2nd aor act ind 2nd pers sg id.
ἐγκαίνισον vb 1st aor act impv 2nd pers sg . . . . . . ἐγκαινίζω	ἐγκατελίπετε vb 2nd aor act ind 2nd pers pl id.
ἐγκαινίσωμεν vb 1st aor act subj 1st pers pl id.	ἐγκατελίπομεν vb 2nd aor act ind 1st pers pl id.
ἐγκαίνωσις noun fem nom sg	ἐγκατέλιπον vb 2nd aor act ind 1st pers sg and 3rd pers pl id.
ἐγκαλέσει vb fut act ind 3rd pers sg . . . . ἐγκαλέω	ἐγκάτοις noun neut dat pl . . . . ἔγκατον
ἐγκαλουμένης vb pres m/p part fem gen sg id.	ἐγκαυχᾷ vb pres dep ind 2nd pers sg . . . . ἐγκαυχάομαι
ἐγκαλῶν vb pres act part masc nom sg id.	ἐγκαυχᾶσθαι vb 1st aor mid inf id.
ἔγκαρπον adj acc sg, neut nom sg . . . . ἔγκαρπος	ἐγκαυχώμενοι vb pres dep part masc nom pl id.
ἔγκατα noun neut nom and acc pl	ἔγκειται vb pres m/p ind 3rd pers sg . . . . ἔγκειμαι
ἐγκατάλειμμα noun neut nom and acc sg	ἐγκεκήδευνται vb perf dep ind 3rd pers pl . . . . ἐγκηδεύομαι
ἐγκαταλείμματα noun neut nom and acc pl . ἐγκατάλειμμα	ἐγκεκολαμμένα vb perf m/p part
ἐγκαταλείπει vb pres act ind 3rd pers sg . . . . . ἐγκαταλείπω	neut nom and acc pl . . . . ἐγκολάπτω
ἐγκαταλείποντας vb pres act part masc acc pl id.	ἐγκεκρυμμένα vb perf m/p part
ἐγκαταλείποντες vb pres act part masc nom pl id.	neut nom and acc pl . . . . ἐγκρύπτω
ἐγκαταλείπων vb pres act part masc nom sg id.	ἐγκεκρυμμένη vb perf m/p part fem nom sg id.
ἐγκαταλειφθήσεται vb fut pass ind 3rd pers sg id.	ἐγκέκρυπται vb perf m/p ind 3rd pers sg id.
ἐγκαταλειφθῶ vb 1st aor pass subj 1st pers sg id.	ἐγκέχηναν vb perf act ind 3rd pers pl . . . . ἐγχάσκω
ἐγκαταλείψει vb fut act ind 3rd pers sg id.	ἐγκισσῆσαι vb 1st aor act inf . . . . ἐγκισσάω
ἐγκαταλείψεις vb fut act ind 2nd pers sg id.	ἐγκισσήσωσιν vb 1st aor act subj 3rd pers pl id.
ἐγκαταλείψομεν vb fut act ind 1st pers pl id.	ἐγκλείσθητι vb 1st aor pass impv 2nd pers sg . . . . . . ἐγκλείω
ἐγκαταλείψουσιν vb fut act ind 3rd pers pl id.	ἐγκληθείς vb 1st aor pass part masc nom sg . . . . . . ἐγκαλέω
ἐγκαταλείψω vb fut act ind 1st pers sg id.	ἔγκληρον adj acc sg, neut nom sg . . . . ἔγκληρος
ἐγκαταλελειμμέναι vb perf m/p part	ἐγκλοίωσαι vb 1st aor mid impv 2nd pers sg . . . . . . ἐγκλοιόω
fem nom pl id.	ἐγκοίλια adj neut nom and acc pl . . . . ἐγκοίλιος
ἐγκαταλελειμμέναις vb perf m/p part fem dat pl id.	ἐγκοιλοτέρα comp adj fem nom sg . . . . ἔγκοιλος
ἐγκαταλελειμμένη vb perf m/p part fem nom sg id.	ἐγκολαπτά adj neut nom and acc pl . . . . ἐγκολαπτός
ἐγκαταλελειμμένην vb perf m/p part fem acc sg id.	ἐγκολληθήσεται vb fut pass ind 3rd pers sg . . . . . ἐγκολλάω
ἐγκαταλελειμμένοι vb perf m/p part masc nom pl id.	ἔγκοποι adj masc and fem nom pl . . . . ἔγκοπος
ἐγκαταλελειμμένον vb perf m/p part masc acc sg id.	ἔγκοπον adj acc sg, neut nom sg id.
ἐγκαταλελειμμένους vb perf m/p part masc acc pl id.	ἐγκοσμούμενον vb pres m/p part masc acc sg . . . . ἐγκοσμέω
ἐγκαταλέλειπται vb perf m/p ind 3rd pers sg id.	ἐγκότημα noun neut nom and acc sg
ἐγκαταλέλοιπα vb perf act ind 1st pers sg id.	ἐγκράτεια noun fem nom sg
ἐγκαταλελοίπατε vb perf act ind 2nd pers pl id.	ἐγκρατεῖς adj masc and fem nom and acc pl . . . . . . ἐγκρατής
ἐγκαταλέλοιπεν vb perf act ind 3rd pers sg id.	ἐγκρατεῖς vb pres act ind 2nd pers sg . . . . ἐγκρατέω
ἐγκαταλελοιπώς vb perf act part masc nom sg id.	ἐγκρατής adj masc and fem nom sg
ἐγκαταλιμπανόντων vb pres act part	ἐγκρατοῦς adj gen sg . . . . ἐγκρατής
masc and neut gen pl . . . . ἐγκαταλιμπάνω	ἐγκρίς noun fem nom sg
ἐγκατάλιπε vb 2nd aor act impv 2nd pers sg . . ἐγκαταλείπω	ἐγκρούσῃς vb 1st aor act subj 2nd pers sg . . . . ἐγκρούω

ἐγκρυβῶσιν vb 2nd aor pass subj 3rd pers pl . . . . . ἐγκρύπτω
ἐγκρύπτων vb pres act part masc nom sg   id.
ἐγκρυφίαν noun masc acc sg . . . . ἐγκρυφίας
ἐγκρυφίας noun masc nom sg   id.
ἐγκρύψεις vb fut act ind 2nd pers sg . . . . ἐγκρύπτω
ἐγκτήσασθε vb 1st aor mid impv 2nd pers pl . . . . ἐγκτάομαι
ἐγκτησιν noun fem acc sg . . . . ἐγκτησις
ἔγκτητα adj neut nom and acc pl . . . . ἔγκτητος
ἔγκτητον adj acc sg, neut nom sg   id.
ἐγκτήτου adj gen sg   id.
ἐγκύκλιον adj masc and fem acc sg . . . . ἐγκύκλιος
ἐγκυλισθήσονται vb fut pass ind 3rd pers pl . . . . ἐγκυλίω
ἐγκυλισθῶμεν vb 1st aor pass subj 1st pers pl   id.
ἔγκυος adj masc and fem nom sg
ἐγκύψας vb 1st aor act part masc nom sg . . . . ἐγκύπτω
ἐγκωμιάζεται vb pres m/p ind 3rd pers sg . . . . . ἐγκωμιάζω
ἐγκωμιαζέτω vb pres act impv 3rd pers sg   id.
ἐγκωμιαζομένων vb pres m/p part gen pl   id.
ἐγκωμιαζόντων vb pres act part masc and neut gen pl id.
ἐγκωμιάζουσιν vb pres act ind 3rd pers pl   id.
ἐγκωμίῳ noun neut dat sg . . . . ἐγκώμιον
ἐγκωμίων noun neut gen pl   id.
Εγλα pr noun
Εγλαμ pr noun
Εγλι pr noun
ἐγλύκανας vb 1st aor act ind 2nd pers sg . . . . γλυκαίνω
ἐγλυκάνθη vb 1st aor pass ind 3rd pers sg   id.
ἐγλυκάνθησαν vb 1st aor pass ind 3rd pers pl   id.
ἐγλύφην 2nd aor pass ind 1st pers sg . . . . γλύφω
ἔγλυψαν vb 1st aor act ind 3rd pers pl   id.
ἔγλυψεν vb 1st aor act ind 3rd pers sg   id.
Εγλωμ pr noun
ἐγνόφωσεν vb 1st aor act ind 3rd pers sg . . . . γνοφόω
ἔγνω vb 2nd aor act ind 3rd pers sg . . . . γινώσκω
ἔγνωκα vb perf act ind 1st pers sg   id.
ἐγνώκαμεν vb perf act ind 1st pers pl   id.
ἔγνωκεν vb perf act ind 3rd pers sg   id.
ἐγνωκότας vb perf act part masc acc pl   id.
ἐγνωκότες vb perf act part masc nom pl   id.
ἔγνωμεν vb 2nd aor act ind 1st pers pl   id.
ἔγνων vb 2nd aor act ind 1st pers sg   id.
ἐγνώρισα vb 1st aor act ind 1st pers sg . . . . γνωρίζω
ἐγνωρίσαμεν vb 1st aor act ind 1st pers pl   id.
ἐγνώρισαν vb 1st aor act ind 3rd pers pl   id.
ἐγνώρισας vb 1st aor act ind 2nd pers sg   id.
ἐγνώρισεν vb 1st aor act ind 3rd pers sg   id.
ἐγνωρίσθην vb 1st aor pass ind 1st pers sg   id.
ἐγνώρισται vb perf m/p ind 3rd pers sg   id.
ἔγνως vb 2nd aor act ind 2nd pers sg . . . . γινώσκω
ἔγνωσαν vb 2nd aor act ind 3rd pers pl   id.
ἐγνώσθη vb 1st aor pass ind 3rd pers sg   id.
ἐγνώσθην vb 1st aor pass ind 1st pers sg   id.
ἐγνώσθης vb 1st aor pass ind 2nd pers sg   id.
ἔγνωσται vb perf m/p ind 3rd pers sg   id.
ἔγνωτε vb 2nd aor act ind 2nd pers pl   id.
ἐγόγγυζεν vb impf act ind 3rd pers sg . . . . γογγύζω

ἐγόγγυσαν vb 1st aor act ind 3rd pers pl . . . . γογγύζω
ἐγόγγυσας vb 1st aor act ind 2nd pers sg   id.
ἐγόγγυσεν vb 1st aor act ind 3rd pers sg   id.
ἐγομφίασαν vb 1st aor act ind 3rd pers pl . . . . . . γομφιάζω
ἔγραφεν vb impf act ind 3rd pers sg . . . . γράφω
ἐγράφη vb 2nd aor pass ind 3rd pers sg   id.
ἔγραφον vb impf act ind 3rd pers pl   id.
ἔγραψα vb 1st aor act ind 1st pers sg   id.
ἐγράψαμεν vb 1st aor act ind 1st pers pl   id.
ἔγραψαν vb 1st aor act ind 3rd pers pl   id.
ἔγραψας vb 1st aor act ind 2nd pers sg   id.
ἔγραψε ν) vb 1st aor act ind 3rd pers sg   id.
Εγρεβηλ pr noun
ἐγρήγορα vb perf act ind 1st pers sg . . . . ἐγείρω
ἐγρηγορήθη vb 1st aor pass ind 3rd pers sg . . . . . γρηγορέω
ἐγρηγόρησεν vb 1st aor act ind 3rd pers sg   id.
ἐγρήγοροι vb perf act opt 3rd pers sg . . . . ἐγείρω
ἐγρηγόρουν vb impf act ind 1st pers sg . . . . γρηγορέω
ἔγρυξεν vb 1st aor act ind 3rd pers sg . . . . γρύζω
ἐγύμναζον vb impf act ind 3rd pers pl . . . . γυμνάζω
ἐγυμνώθη vb 1st aor pass ind 3rd pers sg . . . . γυμνόω
ἐγύμνωσαν vb 1st aor act ind 3rd pers pl   id.
ἐγύμνωσεν vb 1st aor act ind 3rd pers sg   id.
ἐγύρωσεν vb 1st aor act ind 3rd pers sg . . . . γυρόω
ἔγχει vb pres act impv 2nd pers sg . . . . ἐγχέω
ἐγχείρημα noun neut nom and acc sg
ἐγχειρήματος noun neut gen sg . . . . ἐγχείρημα
ἐγχειρίδιον noun neut nom and acc sg
ἐγχρῖσαι vb 1st aor act inf . . . . ἐγχρίω
ἐγχρίσῃ vb 1st aor mid subj 2nd pers sg   id.
ἔγχρισον vb 1st aor act impv 2nd pers sg   id.
ἐγχρονίζει vb pres act ind 3rd pers sg . . . . ἐγχρονίζω
ἐγχρονιζόντων vb pres act part masc and neut gen pl id.
ἐγχρονίσῃς vb 1st aor act subj 2nd pers sg   id.
ἐγχώριαι adj masc and fem nom pl . . . . ἐγχώριος
ἐγχώριος adj masc and fem nom sg   id.
ἐγχωρίου adj gen sg   id.
ἐγχωρίῳ adj dat sg   id.
ἐγχωρίων adj gen pl   id.
ἐγώ pers pron nom sg
ἔγωγε = εγω + γε
ἔδακνεν vb impf act ind 3rd pers sg . . . . δάκνω
ἔδακνον vb impf act ind 3rd pers pl   id.
ἐδάκρυσας vb 1st aor act ind 2nd pers sg . . . . δακρύω
ἐδάκρυσεν vb 1st aor act ind 3rd pers sg   id.
Εδαν pr noun
ἐδανεισάμεθα vb 1st aor mid ind 1st pers pl . . . . . δανείζω
Εδανια pr noun
ἐδαπανήθη vb 1st aor pass ind 3rd pers sg . . . . . . δαπανάω
ἐδαπάνησεν vb 1st aor act ind 3rd pers sg   id.
ἐδαπάνων vb impf act ind 1st pers sg and 3rd pers pl id.
ἐδαπανῶντο vb impf m/p ind 3rd pers pl   id.
ἐδάφει noun neut dat sg . . . . ἔδαφος
ἐδαφιεῖ vb fut act ind 3rd pers sg . . . . ἐδαφίζω
ἐδαφιοῦσιν vb fut act ind 3rd pers pl   id.
ἐδαφισθήσῃ vb fut pass ind 2nd pers sg   id.

ἐδαφισθήσονται vb fut pass ind 3rd pers pl . . . . . ἐδαφίζω	ἐδήσατο vb 1st aor mid ind 3rd pers sg . . . . δέω
ἔδαφος noun neut nom and acc sg	ἔδησεν vb 1st aor act ind 3rd pers sg id.
ἐδάφους noun neut gen sg . . . . ἔδαφος	ἐδιάσατο vb 1st aor mid ind 3rd pers sg . . . . διάζομαι
ἐδαψιλεύσατο vb 1st aor mid ind 3rd pers sg . δαψιλεύομαι	ἐδίδαξα vb 1st aor act ind 1st pers sg . . . . διδάσκω
Εδδεκελ pr noun	ἐδίδαξαν vb 1st aor act ind 3rd pers pl id.
Εδδι pr noun	ἐδίδαξας vb 1st aor act ind 2nd pers sg id.
Εδδινους pr noun	ἐδίδαξεν vb 1st aor act ind 3rd pers sg id.
ἐδεδοίκειν vb plpf act ind 1st pers sg . . . . δείδω	ἐδίδασκεν vb impf act ind 3rd pers sg id.
ἐδέετο vb impf dep ind 3rd pers sg . . . . δέομαι	ἐδίδασκον vb impf act ind 3rd pers pl id.
ἐδεήθη vb 1st aor pass ind 3rd pers sg id.	ἐδιδάχθην vb 1st aor pass ind 1st pers sg id.
ἐδεήθημεν vb 1st aor pass ind 1st pers pl id.	ἐδιδάχθησαν vb 1st aor pass ind 3rd pers pl id.
ἐδεήθην vb 1st aor pass ind 1st pers sg id.	ἐδίδετο vb impf m/p ind 3rd pers sg . . . . δίδωμι
ἐδεήθης vb 1st aor pass ind 2nd pers sg id.	ἐδίδοσαν vb impf act ind 3rd pers pl id.
ἐδεήθησαν vb 1st aor pass ind 3rd pers pl id.	ἐδίδοτο vb impf m/p ind 3rd pers sg id.
ἐδέθη vb 1st aor pass ind 3rd pers sg . . . . δέω	ἐδίδου vb impf m/p ind 3rd pers sg id.
ἐδέθησαν vb 1st aor pass ind 3rd pers pl id.	ἐδίδουν vb impf m/p ind 1st pers sg and 3rd pers pl id.
ἔδει vb impf act ind 3rd pers sg id.	ἐδίδους vb impf m/p ind 2nd pers sg id.
Εδεϊα pr noun	Εδιηλ pr noun
ἐδειλίασαν vb 1st aor act ind 3rd pers pl . . . . δειλιάω	ἐδίκαζεν vb impf act ind 3rd pers sg . . . . δικάζω
ἐδειλίασεν vb 1st aor act ind 3rd pers sg id.	ἐδικαιώθη vb 1st aor pass ind 3rd pers sg . . . . δικαιόω
ἐδειλώθησαν vb 1st aor pass ind 3rd pers pl . . . . . δειλόομαι	ἐδικαίωσα vb 1st aor act ind 1st pers sg id.
ἐδείναζον vb impf act ind 3rd pers pl . . . . δεινάζω	ἐδικαιώσαμεν vb 1st aor act ind 1st pers pl id.
ἔδειξα vb 1st aor act ind 1st pers sg . . . . δεικνύω	ἐδικαίωσαν vb 1st aor act ind 3rd pers pl id.
ἔδειξαν vb 1st aor act ind 3rd pers pl id.	ἐδικαίωσας vb 1st aor act ind 2nd pers sg id.
ἔδειξας vb 1st aor act ind 2nd pers sg id.	ἐδικαίωσεν vb 1st aor act ind 3rd pers sg id.
ἔδειξεν vb 1st aor act ind 3rd pers sg id.	ἐδίκασας vb 1st aor act ind 2nd pers sg . . . . δικάζω
ἐδεῖτο vb impf dep ind 3rd pers sg . . . . δέομαι	ἐδίψησα vb 1st aor act ind 1st pers sg . . . . διψάω
ἐδείχθη vb 1st aor pass ind 3rd pers sg . . . . δεικνύω	ἐδίψησαν vb 1st aor act ind 3rd pers pl id.
Εδεμ pr noun	ἐδίψησεν vb 1st aor act ind 3rd pers sg id.
Εδεν pr noun	ἐδίωκε(ν) vb impf act ind 3rd pers sg . . . . διώκω
Εδενε pr noun	ἐδίωκον vb impf act ind 3rd pers pl id.
Εδενι pr noun	ἐδίωξαν vb 1st aor act ind 3rd pers pl id.
ἐδεξάμεθα vb 1st aor mid ind 1st pers pl . . . . δέχομαι	ἐδίωξε(ν) vb 1st aor act ind 3rd pers sg id.
ἐδεξάμην vb 1st aor mid ind 1st pers sg id.	ἐδιώχθημεν vb 1st aor pass ind 1st pers pl id.
ἐδέξαντο vb 1st aor mid ind 3rd pers pl id.	ἐδιώχθησαν vb 1st aor pass ind 3rd pers pl id.
ἐδέξασθε vb 1st aor mid ind 2nd pers pl id.	Εδνα pr noun nom sg
ἐδέξατο vb 1st aor mid ind 3rd pers sg id.	Εδναν pr noun acc sg . . . . Εδνα
ἐδέοντο vb impf dep ind 3rd pers pl . . . . δέομαι	Εδνας pr noun
Εδερ pr noun	ἐδογμάτισαν vb 1st aor act ind 3rd pers pl . . . . . δογματίζω
ἔδεσθε vb fut mid ind 2nd pers pl . . . . ἐσθίω	ἐδογματίσθη vb 1st aor pass ind 3rd pers sg id.
ἐδέσμασι noun neut dat pl . . . . ἔδεσμα	ἐδόθη vb 1st aor pass ind 3rd pers sg . . . . δίδωμι
ἐδέσματα noun neut nom and acc pl id.	ἐδόθησαν vb 1st aor pass ind 3rd pers pl id.
ἐδεσμάτων noun neut gen pl id.	ἐδοκίμασα vb 1st aor act ind 1st pers sg . . . . δοκιμάζω
ἐδέσμευον vb impf act ind 3rd pers pl . . . . δεσμεύω	ἐδοκίμασαν vb 1st aor act ind 3rd pers pl id.
ἔδεται vb fut mid ind 3rd pers sg . . . . ἐσθίω	ἐδοκίμασας vb 1st aor act ind 2nd pers sg id.
ἐδευτερολόγησεν vb 1st aor act ind	ἐδοκίμασεν vb 1st aor act ind 3rd pers sg id.
3rd pers sg . . . . δευτερολογέω	ἐδοκιμάσθη vb 1st aor pass ind 3rd pers sg id.
ἐδευτέρωσαν vb 1st aor act ind 3rd pers pl . . . . . . δευτερόω	ἐδοκιμάσθην vb 1st aor pass ind 1st pers sg id.
ἐδευτέρωσεν vb 1st aor act ind 3rd pers sg id.	ἐδόκουν vb impf act ind 3rd pers pl . . . . δοκέω
ἐδέχοντο vb impf dep ind 3rd pers pl . . . . δέχομαι	ἐδολιοῦσαν vb impf act ind 3rd pers pl . . . . δολιόω
ἐδηλοῦτο vb impf m/p ind 3rd pers sg . . . . δηλόω	ἐδόλωσεν vb 1st aor act ind 3rd pers sg . . . . δολόω
ἐδηλώθη vb 1st aor pass ind 3rd pers sg id.	ἔδονται vb fut mid ind 3rd pers pl . . . . ἐσθίω
ἐδήλωσα vb 1st aor act ind 1st pers sg id.	ἐδόξαζεν vb impf act ind 3rd pers sg . . . . δοξάζω
ἐδήλωσας vb 1st aor act ind 2nd pers sg id.	ἐδόξαζον vb impf act ind 3rd pers pl id.
ἐδήλωσε(ν) vb 1st aor act ind 3rd pers sg id.	ἔδοξαν vb 1st aor act ind 3rd pers pl . . . . δοκέω
ἔδησαν vb 1st aor act ind 3rd pers pl . . . . δέω	ἐδόξασα vb 1st aor act ind 1st pers sg . . . . δοξάζω

ἐδοξάσαμεν vb 1st aor act ind 1st pers pl . . . . δοξάζω	Εζεκιαν pr noun masc acc sg . . . . Εζεκιας
ἐδόξασαν vb 1st aor act ind 3rd pers pl id.	Εζεκιες pr noun masc nom sg id.
ἐδόξασας vb 1st aor act ind 2nd pers sg id.	Εζεκιου pr noun masc gen sg id.
ἐδόξασεν vb 1st aor act ind 3rd pers sg id.	Εζεκρι pr noun
ἐδοξάσθη vb 1st aor pass ind 3rd pers sg id.	Εζερ pr noun
ἐδοξάσθην vb 1st aor pass ind 1st pers sg id.	Εζερεελ pr noun
ἐδοξάσθης vb 1st aor pass ind 2nd pers sg id.	Εζερηλ pr noun
ἐδοξάσθησαν vb 1st aor pass ind 3rd pers pl id.	Εζεριου pr noun masc gen sg . . . . Εζεριας
ἔδοξε(ν) vb 1st aor act ind 3rd pers sg . . . . δοκέω	ἔζεσεν vb 1st aor act ind 3rd pers sg . . . . ζέω
ἐδούλευον vb impf act ind 3rd pers pl . . . . δουλεύω	ἐζευγίσθησαν vb 1st aor pass ind 3rd pers pl . . . . . . ζευγίζω
ἐδούλευσα vb 1st aor act ind 1st pers sg id.	ἐζευγμενην vb perf m/p part fem acc sg . . . . ζευγνύω
ἐδουλεύσαμεν vb 1st aor act ind 1st pers pl id.	ἔζευξαν vb 1st aor act ind 3rd pers pl id.
ἐδούλευσαν vb 1st aor act ind 3rd pers pl id.	ἔζευξεν vb 1st aor act ind 3rd pers sg id.
ἐδούλευσας vb 1st aor act ind 2nd pers sg id.	ἔζη vb impf act ind 3rd pers sg . . . . ζάω
ἐδουλεύσατε vb 1st aor act ind 2nd pers pl id.	ἐζήλουν vb impf act ind 3rd pers pl . . . . ζηλόω
ἐδούλευσεν vb 1st aor act ind 3rd pers sg id.	ἐζήλωκα vb perf act ind 1st pers sg id.
ἐδουλοῦντο vb impf m/p ind 3rd pers pl . . . . δουλόω	ἐζήλωσα vb 1st aor act ind 1st pers sg id.
ἐδούλωσαν vb 1st aor act ind 3rd pers pl id.	ἐζήλωσαν vb 1st aor act ind 3rd pers pl id.
Εδραι pr noun	ἐζήλοσεν vb 1st aor act ind 3rd pers sg id.
ἔδραι noun fem nom pl . . . . ἔδρα	ἐζημιώθησαν vb 1st aor pass ind 3rd pers pl . . . . . . ζημιόω
Εδραϊ pr noun	ἐζημίωσεν vb 1st aor act ind 3rd pers sg id.
Εδραϊν pr noun	ἔζησα vb 1st aor act ind 1st pers sg . . . . ζάω
ἔδραις noun fem dat pl . . . . ἔδρα	ἔζησαν vb 1st aor act ind 3rd pers pl id.
Εδραμ pr noun	ἔζησας vb 1st aor act ind 2nd pers sg id.
ἔδραμε(ν) vb 2nd aor act ind 3rd pers sg . . . . τρέχω	ἔζησεν vb 1st aor act ind 3rd pers sg id.
ἐδράμομεν vb 2nd aor act ind 1st pers pl id.	ἐζήτει vb impf act ind 3rd pers sg . . . . ζητέω
ἔδραμον vb 2nd aor act ind 1st pers sg and 3rd pers pl id.	ἐζητεῖτε vb impf act ind 2nd pers pl id.
ἐδράξατο vb 1st aor mid ind 3rd pers sg . . . . δράσσομαι	ἐζητήθη vb 1st aor pass ind 3rd pers sg id.
ἔδρας noun fem gen sg and acc pl . . . . ἔδρα	ἐζήτησα vb 1st aor act ind 1st pers sg id.
ἐδράσει vb fut act ind 3rd pers sg . . . . ἑδράζω	ἐζητήσαμεν vb 1st aor act ind 1st pers pl id.
ἐδρασθῆναι vb 1st aor pass inf id.	ἐζήτησαν vb 1st aor act ind 3rd pers pl id.
ἔδυ vb 2nd aor act ind 3rd pers sg . . . . δύω	ἐζήτησας vb 1st aor act ind 2nd pers sg id.
ἐδυναμώθη vb 1st aor pass ind 3rd pers sg . . . . δυναμόω	ἐζητήσατε vb 1st aor act ind 2nd pers pl id.
ἐδύναντο vb impf dep ind 3rd pers pl . . . . δύναμαι	ἐζήτησε(ν) vb 1st aor act ind 3rd pers sg id.
ἐδυνάσθη vb 1st aor pass ind 3rd pers sg id.	ἐζήτουν vb impf act ind 1st pers sg and 3rd pers pl id.
ἐδυνάσθης vb 1st aor pass ind 2nd pers sg id.	Εζουρ pr noun
ἐδυνάσθησαν vb 1st aor pass ind 3rd pers pl id.	Εζραϊτην pr noun masc acc sg . . . . Εζραϊτης
ἐδυνάστευσε vb 1st aor act ind 3rd pers sg . . . . . δυναστεύω	Εζρι pr noun
ἐδύνατο vb impf dep ind 3rd pers sg . . . . δύναμαι	Εζρικαμ pr noun
ἔδυνεν vb 2nd aor act ind 3rd pers sg . . . . δύω	Εζριλ pr noun
ἐδυνήθησαν vb 1st aor pass ind 3rd pers pl . . . . . . δύναμαι	ἐζυγωμένα vb perf m/p part neut nom and acc pl . . . . . ζυγόω
ἔδυσαν vb 1st aor act ind 3rd pers pl . . . . δύω	ἐζυμώθη vb 1st aor pass ind 3rd pers sg . . . . ζυμόω
ἐδυστόκησεν vb 1st aor act ind 3rd pers sg . . . . . . δυστοκέω	ἐζυμωμένη vb perf m/p part fem nom sg id.
ἐδυσφήμησαν vb 1st aor act ind 3rd pers pl . . . . . . δυσφημέω	ἐζυμωμένοι vb perf m/p part masc nom pl id.
ἐδυσφόρουν vb impf act ind 3rd pers pl . . . . . . δυσφορέω	ἐζωγραφημένους vb perf m/p part masc acc pl . . . ζωγραφέω
ἔδωκα vb 1st aor act ind 1st pers sg . . . . δίδωμι	ἐζωγράφησα vb 1st aor act ind 1st pers sg id.
ἔδωκαν vb 1st aor act ind 3rd pers pl id.	ἐζώγρησαν vb 1st aor act ind 3rd pers pl . . . . ζωγρέω
ἔδωκας vb 1st aor act ind 2nd pers sg id.	ἐζωγρήσατε vb 1st aor act ind 2nd pers pl id.
ἐδώκατε vb 1st aor act ind 2nd pers pl id.	ἐζώγρησεν vb 1st aor act ind 3rd pers sg id.
ἔδωκε(ν) vb 1st aor act ind 3rd pers sg id.	ἐζωογόνει vb impf act ind 3rd pers sg . . . . ζωογονέω
Εδωμ pr noun	ἐζωογονεῖτε vb impf act ind 2nd pers pl id.
ἐδωρήσατο vb 1st aor mid ind 3rd pers sg . . . . δωρέομαι	ἐζωογονήκειτε vb plpf act ind 3rd pers pl id.
Εζεκηλ pr noun	ἐζωογονήσατε vb 1st aor act ind 2nd pers pl id.
Εζεκια pr noun	ἐζωογόνησεν vb 1st aor act ind 3rd pers sg id.
Εζεκια pr noun masc dat sg . . . . Εζεκιας	ἐζωογόνουν vb impf act ind 3rd pers pl id.
Εζεκιαν pr noun	ἐζωοποίησεν vb 1st aor act ind 3rd pers pl . . . . . . ζωοποιέω

ἐζωοποίησας vb 1st aor act ind 2nd pers sg . . . . . ζωοποιέω

ἐζωπύρησεν vb 1st aor act ind 3rd pers sg . . . . ζωπυρέω

Ἐζωρα pr noun

ἔζωσα vb 1st aor act ind 1st pers sg . . . . ζωννύω

ἐζώσατο vb 1st aor mid ind 3rd pers sg   id.

ἔζωσεν vb 1st aor act ind 3rd pers sg   id.

ἐζωσμένοι vb perf m/p part masc nom pl   id.

ἐζωσμένος vb perf m/p part masc nom sg   id.

ἐζωσμένους vb perf m/p part masc acc pl   id.

ἐθαμβήθη vb 1st aor pass ind 3rd pers sg . . . . θαμβέω

ἐθαμβήθην vb 1st aor pass ind 1st pers sg   id.

ἐθάμβησαν vb 1st aor act ind 3rd pers pl   id.

ἐθάμβησεν vb 1st aor act ind 3rd pers sg   id.

ἐθανάτου vb impf act ind 3rd pers sg . . . . θανατόω

ἐθανατοῦντο vb impf m/p ind 3rd pers pl   id.

ἐθανατώθη vb 1st aor pass ind 3rd pers sg   id.

ἐθανατώθησαν vb 1st aor pass ind 3rd pers pl   id.

ἐθανάτωσα vb 1st aor act ind 1st pers sg   id.

ἐθανάτωσαν vb 1st aor act ind 3rd pers pl   id.

ἐθανάτωσας vb 1st aor act ind 2nd pers sg   id.

ἐθανάτωσεν vb 1st aor act ind 3rd pers sg   id.

ἔθαπτες vb impf act ind 2nd pers sg . . . . θάπτω

ἔθαπτον vb impf act ind 1st pers sg and 3rd pers pl   id.

ἐθαυμάζετο vb impf m/p ind 3rd pers sg . . . . θαυμάζω

ἐθαύμαζον vb impf act ind 1st pers sg and 3rd pers pl   id.

ἐθαύμασα vb 1st aor act ind 1st pers sg   id.

ἐθαύμασαν vb 1st aor act ind 3rd pers pl   id.

ἐθαύμασας vb 1st aor act ind 2nd pers sg   id.

ἐθαύμασε(ν) vb 1st aor act ind 3rd pers sg   id.

ἐθαυμάσθησαν vb 1st aor pass ind 3rd pers pl   id.

ἐθαυμαστώθη vb 1st aor pass ind 3rd pers sg . . . . θαυμαστόω

ἐθαυμαστώθην vb 1st aor pass ind 1st pers sg   id.

ἐθαυμάστωσεν vb 1st aor act ind 3rd pers sg   id.

ἔθαψα vb 1st aor act ind 1st pers sg . . . . θάπτω

ἔθαψαν vb 1st aor act ind 3rd pers pl   id.

ἐθάψατε vb 1st aor act ind 2nd pers pl   id.

ἔθαψεν vb 1st aor act ind 3rd pers sg   id.

ἐθεασάμην vb 1st aor mid ind 1st pers sg . . . . θεάομαι

ἐθεάσατο vb 1st aor mid ind 3rd pers sg   id.

ἐθελοκωφῶν vb pres act part masc nom sg . . . . . ἐθελοκωφέω

ἐθεμελιώθη vb 1st aor pass ind 3rd pers sg . . . . θεμελιόω

ἐθεμελίωσα vb 1st aor act ind 1st pers sg   id.

ἐθεμελίωσαν vb 1st aor act ind 3rd pers pl   id.

ἐθεμελίωσας vb 1st aor act ind 2nd pers sg   id.

ἐθεμελίωσεν vb 1st aor act ind 3rd pers sg   id.

ἐθέμην vb 2nd aor mid ind 1st pers sg . . . . τίθημι

ἔθεντο vb 2nd aor mid ind 3rd pers pl   id.

Εθερ pr noun

ἐθεράπευεν vb impf act ind 3rd pers sg . . . . θεραπεύω

ἐθεραπεύετο vb impf m/p ind 3rd pers sg   id.

ἐθεράπευον vb impf act ind 3rd pers pl   id.

ἐθεράπευσεν vb 1st aor act ind 3rd pers sg   id.

ἐθέριζον vb impf act ind 3rd pers pl . . . . θερίζω

ἐθέρισαν vb 1st aor act ind 3rd pers pl   id.

ἐθερμαίνετο vb impf m/p ind 3rd pers sg . . . . θερμαίνω

ἐθερμάνθη vb 1st aor pass ind 3rd pers sg   id.

ἐθερμάνθην vb 1st aor pass ind 1st pers sg . . . . . θερμαίνω

ἐθερμάνθησαν vb 1st aor pass ind 3rd pers pl   id.

ἐθερμάνθητε vb 1st aor pass ind 2nd pers pl   id.

ἔθεσαν vb 2nd aor act ind 3rd pers pl . . . . τίθημι

ἔθεσθε vb 2nd aor mid ind 2nd pers pl   id.

ἔθετο vb 2nd aor mid ind 3rd pers sg   id.

ἐθεώρει vb impf act ind 3rd pers sg . . . . θεωρέω

ἐθεώρεις vb impf act ind 2nd pers sg   id.

ἐθεωρεῖτε vb impf act ind 2nd pers pl   id.

ἐθεωρεῖτο vb impf m/p ind 3rd pers sg   id.

ἐθεωρήθη vb 1st aor pass ind 3rd pers sg   id.

ἐθεωρήθησαν vb 1st aor pass ind 3rd pers pl   id.

ἐθεωροῦμεν vb impf act ind 1st pers pl   id.

ἐθεώρουν vb impf act ind 1st pers sg and 3rd pers pl   id.

ἔθη noun neut nom and acc pl . . . . ἔθος

ἔθηκα vb 1st aor act ind 1st pers sg . . . . τίθημι

ἐθήκαμεν vb 1st aor act ind 1st pers pl   id.

ἔθηκαν vb 1st aor act ind 3rd pers pl   id.

ἔθηκας vb 1st aor act ind 2nd pers sg   id.

ἔθηκεν vb 1st aor act ind 3rd pers sg   id.

ἐθήλαζεν vb impf act ind 3rd pers sg . . . . θηλάζω

ἐθήλασα vb 1st aor act ind 1st pers sg   id.

ἐθήλασαν vb 1st aor act ind 3rd pers pl   id.

ἐθήλασεν vb 1st aor act ind 3rd pers sg   id.

ἐθηρεύθη vb 1st aor pass ind 3rd pers sg . . . . θηρεύω

ἐθηρεύσαμεν vb 1st aor act ind 1st pers pl   id.

ἐθήρευσαν vb 1st aor act ind 3rd pers pl   id.

ἐθησαύρισαν vb 1st aor act ind 3rd pers pl . . . . . θησαυρίζω

ἐθησαύρισεν vb 1st aor act ind 3rd pers sg   id.

Εθθι pr noun

Εθι pr noun

ἐθίσῃς vb 1st aor act subj 2nd pers sg . . . . ἐθίζω

ἐθισμόν noun masc acc sg . . . . ἐθισμός

ἐθισμούς noun masc acc pl   id.

ἐθισμῷ noun masc dat sg   id.

ἔθλασαν vb 1st aor act ind 3rd pers pl . . . . θλάω

ἔθλασας vb 1st aor act ind 2nd pers sg   id.

ἔθλασεν vb 1st aor act ind 3rd pers sg   id.

ἐθλάσθης vb 1st aor pass ind 2nd pers sg   id.

ἔθλιβε vb impf act ind 3rd pers sg . . . . θλίβω

ἐθλίβετο vb impf m/p ind 3rd pers sg   id.

ἐθλίβη vb 2nd aor pass ind 3rd pers sg   id.

ἐθλίβησαν vb 2nd aor pass ind 3rd pers pl   id.

ἐθλίβητε vb 2nd aor pass ind 2nd pers pl   id.

ἔθλιβον vb impf act ind 3rd pers pl   id.

ἔθλιψαν vb 1st aor act ind 3rd pers pl   id.

ἔθλιψεν vb 1st aor act ind 3rd pers sg   id.

ἔθλων vb impf act ind 3rd pers pl . . . . θλάω

Εθναν pr noun

ἐθνάρχῃ noun masc dat sg . . . . ἐθνάρχης

ἐθνάρχης noun masc nom sg   id.

ἔθνει noun neut dat sg . . . . ἔθνος

ἔθνεσι noun neut dat pl   id.

ἔθνη noun neut nom and acc pl   id.

ἐθνηδόν adverb

ἔθνησκον vb impf act ind 3rd pers pl . . . . θνήσκω

ἐθνοπάτορα noun masc acc sg . . . . ἐθνοπάτωρ
ἐθνοπλήθους adj gen sg . . . . ἐθνοπλήθης
ἔθνος noun neut nom and acc sg
ἔθνους noun neut gen sg . . . . ἔθνος
ἐθνῶν noun neut gen pl   id.
ἐθορυβήθην vb 1st aor pass ind 3rd pers sg . . . . . . θορυβέω
ἐθορυβοῦντο vb impf m/p ind 3rd pers pl   id.
ἔθος noun neut nom and acc sg
ἔθου vb 2nd aor mid ind 2nd pers sg . . . . τίθημι
ἔθραυσας vb 1st aor act ind 2nd pers sg . . . . θραύω
ἔθραυσε(ν) vb 1st aor act ind 3rd pers sg   id.
ἐθραύσθη vb 1st aor pass ind 3rd pers sg   id.
ἔθρεψα vb 1st aor act ind 1st pers sg . . . . τρέφω
ἐθρήνει vb impf act ind 3rd pers sg . . . . θρηνέω
ἐθρήνησεν vb 1st aor act ind 3rd pers sg   id.
ἐθρηνοῦσαν vb impf act ind 3rd pers pl   id.
ἐθρησκεύετο vb impf m/p ind 3rd pers sg . . . . . . θρησκεύω
ἐθρήσκευον vb impf act ind 3rd pers pl   id.
ἐθροήθη vb 1st aor pass ind 3rd pers sg . . . . θροέω
ἐθρονίσθη vb 1st aor pass ind 3rd pers sg . . . . θρονίζω
ἐθρύλουν vb impf act ind 3rd pers pl . . . . θρυλέω
ἔθυεν vb impf act ind 3rd pers sg . . . . θύω
ἐθυμία vb impf act ind 3rd pers sg . . . . θυμιάω
ἐθυμίασαν vb 1st aor act ind 3rd pers pl . . . . θυμιάζω
ἐθυμιάσατε vb 1st aor act ind 2nd pers pl   id.
ἐθυμίασεν vb 1st aor act ind 3rd pers sg   id.
ἐθυμιᾶτε vb impf act ind 2nd pers pl . . . . θυμιάω
ἐθυμίων vb impf act ind 3rd pers pl   id.
ἐθυμιῶσαν vb 1st aor act ind 3rd pers pl   id.
ἐθυμώθη vb 1st aor pass ind 3rd pers sg . . . . θυμόω
ἐθυμώθην vb 1st aor pass ind 1st pers sg   id.
ἐθυμώθης vb 1st aor pass ind 2nd pers sg   id.
ἐθυμώθησαν vb 1st aor pass ind 3rd pers pl   id.
ἐθύμωσεν vb 1st aor act ind 3rd pers sg   id.
ἔθυον vb impf act ind 3rd pers pl . . . . θύω
ἐθύρωσαν vb 1st aor act ind 3rd pers pl . . . . θυρόω
ἔθυσα vb 1st aor act ind 1st pers sg . . . . θύω
ἔθυσαν vb 1st aor act ind 3rd pers pl   id.
ἔθυσας vb 1st aor act ind 2nd pers sg   id.
ἔθυσεν vb 1st aor act ind 3rd pers sg   id.
ἐθυσίαζεν vb impf act ind 3rd pers sg . . . . θυσιάζω
ἐθυσίαζον vb impf act ind 3rd pers pl   id.
ἐθυσίασαν vb 1st aor act ind 3rd pers pl   id.
ἐθυσίασεν vb 1st aor act ind 3rd pers sg   id.
ἐθῶν noun neut gen pl . . . . ἔθος
εἰ conjunctive particle
εἶ vb pres act ind 2nd pers sg . . . . εἰμί
εἰάθησαν vb 1st aor pass ind 3rd pers pl . . . . ἐάω
εἴασα vb 1st aor act ind 1st pers sg   id.
εἴασαν vb 1st aor act ind 3rd pers pl   id.
εἴασεν vb 1st aor act ind 3rd pers sg   id.
εἴδαμεν vb 1st aor act ind 1st pers pl . . . . ὁράω
εἶδαν vb 1st aor act ind 3rd pers pl   id.
εἶδε(ν) vb 2nd aor act ind 3rd pers sg   id.
εἴδει noun neut dat sg . . . . εἶδος
εἰδέναι vb perf act inf . . . . οἶδα

εἶδες vb 2nd aor act ind 2nd pers sg . . . . ὁράω
εἴδεσι noun neut dat pl . . . . εἶδος
εἴδετε vb 2nd aor act ind 2nd pers pl . . . . ὁράω
εἰδέχθειαν noun fem acc sg . . . . εἰδέχθεια
εἴδη noun neut nom and acc pl . . . . εἶδος
εἰδῇς vb perf act subj 2nd pers sg . . . . οἶδα
εἰδῆσαι vb 1st aor act inf   id.
εἴδησαν vb 1st aor act ind 3rd pers pl . . . . ὁράω
εἴδησιν noun fem acc sg . . . . εἴδησις
εἰδήσουσιν vb fut perf act ind 3rd pers pl . . . . οἶδα
εἰδῆτε vb perf act subj 2nd pers pl   id.
εἴδομεν vb 2nd aor act ind 1st pers pl . . . . ὁράω
εἶδον vb 2nd aor act ind 1st pers sg and 3rd pers pl   id.
εἶδος noun neut nom and acc sg
Εἶδος pr noun neut nom and acc sg . . . . Εἶδος
εἴδοσαν vb 2nd aor act ind 3rd pers pl . . . . ὁράω
εἰδόσι vb perf act part masc and neut dat pl . . . . οἶδα
εἰδότα vb perf act part masc acc sg   id.
εἰδότας vb perf act part masc acc pl   id.
εἰδότες vb perf act part masc nom pl   id.
εἰδότι vb perf act part masc and neut dat sg   id.
εἰδότος vb perf act part masc and neut gen sg   id.
εἰδότων vb perf act part masc and neut gen pl   id.
εἰδυῖα vb perf act part fem nom sg   id.
εἰδυῖαν vb perf act part fem acc sg   id.
εἴδαλα noun neut nom and acc pl . . . . εἴδωλον
εἰδάλια noun neut nom and acc pl . . . . εἰδώλιον
εἰδάλιον noun neut nom and acc sg   id.
εἰδαλίῳ noun neut dat sg   id.
εἰδαλοθύτων adj gen pl . . . . εἰδωλόθυτος
εἰδάλοις noun neut dat pl . . . . εἴδωλον
εἴδαλον noun neut nom and acc sg   id.
εἰδάλῳ noun neut dat sg   id.
εἰδάλων noun neut gen pl   id.
εἰδάς vb perf act part masc nom sg . . . . οἶδα
εἰδᾶσιν vb perf act subj 3rd pers pl   id.
εἴη vb pres act opt 3rd pers sg . . . . εἰμί
εἴησαν vb pres act opt 3rd pers pl   id.
εἶθ' see εἶθε
εἶθ' see εἶτα
εἶθε interjection
εἰθισμενην vb perf m/p part fem acc sg . . . . ἐθίζω
εἰκάδι noun fem dat sg . . . . εἰκάς
εἰκάδος noun fem gen sg   id.
εἰκάζε vb pres act ind 3rd pers sg . . . . εἰκάζω
εἰκάζομεν vb pres act ind 1st pers pl   id.
εἰκάσαι vb 1st aor act inf   id.
εἰκασθῇ vb 1st aor pass subj 3rd pers sg   id.
εἰκῇ adverb
εἰκένα noun fem acc sg . . . . εἰκών
εἰκένας noun fem acc pl   id.
εἰκένι noun fem dat sg   id.
εἰκένος noun fem gen sg   id.
εἰκοσαετοῦς adj gen sg . . . . εἰκοσαετής
εἴκοσι indecl number
εἰκοστῇ adj fem dat sg . . . . εἰκοστός

εἰκοστός adj masc nom sg	
εἰκοστοῦ adj masc and neut gen sg	εἰκοστός
εἰκοστῷ adj masc and neut dat sg	id.
εἰκότως adverb	
εἰκών noun fem nom sg	
εἵλατο vb 1st aor mid ind 3rd pers sg	αἱρέω
εἰλημένος vb perf m/p part masc nom sg	εἰλέω
εἰλημμένων vb perf m/p part gen pl	λαμβάνω
εἵλησεν vb 1st aor act ind 3rd pers sg	εἰλέω
εἴληφα vb perf act ind 1st pers sg	λαμβάνω
εἰλήφαμεν vb perf act ind 1st pers pl	id.
εἴληφας vb perf act ind 2nd pers sg	id.
εἰλήφασι(ν) vb perf act ind 3rd pers pl	id.
εἴληφε(ν) vb perf act ind 3rd pers sg	id.
εἰληφέναι vb perf act inf	id.
εἰληφότας vb perf act part masc acc pl	id.
εἰληφότες vb perf act part masc nom pl	id.
εἰληφώς vb perf act part masc nom sg	id.
εἰλικρινής adj masc and fem nom sg	
εἷλκεν vb impf act ind 3rd pers sg	ἕλκω
εἷλκον vb impf act ind 3rd pers pl	id.
εἵλκοντο vb impf m/p ind 3rd pers pl	id.
εἵλκυσα vb 1st aor act ind 1st pers sg	ἑλκύω
εἵλκυσαν vb 1st aor act ind 3rd pers pl	id.
εἵλκυσας vb 1st aor act ind 2nd pers sg	id.
εἵλκυσεν vb 1st aor act ind 3rd pers sg	id.
εἱλκύσθη vb 1st aor pass ind 3rd pers sg	id.
εἵλοντο vb 2nd aor mid ind 3rd pers pl	αἱρέω
εἵλου vb 2nd aor mid ind 2nd pers sg	
εἰμι see εἰμί	
εἰμί vb pres act ind 1st pers sg	id.
εἶναι vb pres act inf	id.
εἵνεκεν preposition	ἕνεκα
εἶξαι vb 1st aor act inf	εἴκω
εἶξεν vb 1st aor act ind 3rd pers sg	id.
εἶπα vb 1st aor act ind 1st pers sg	εἶπον
εἶπαι vb 1st aor act inf	id.
εἴπαισαν vb 1st aor act opt 3rd pers pl	id.
εἴπαμεν vb 1st aor act ind 1st pers pl	id.
εἶπαν vb 1st aor act ind 3rd pers pl	id.
εἴπαντες vb 1st aor act part masc nom pl	id.
εἴπας vb 1st aor act part masc nom sg	id.
εἴπας vb 1st aor act ind 2nd pers pl	id.
εἴπατε vb 1st aor act impv 2nd pers pl, 1st aor act ind 2nd pers pl	id.
εἰπάτω vb 1st aor act impv 3rd pers sg	id.
εἰπάτωσαν vb 1st aor act impv 3rd pers pl	id.
εἶπεν see εἶπεν	
εἶπε vb 2nd aor act ind 3rd pers sg	id.
εἰπέ vb 2nd aor act impv 2nd pers sg	id.
εἰπεῖν vb 2nd aor act inf	id.
εἶπεν vb 2nd aor act ind 3rd pers sg	id.
εἴπερ conjunction	
εἴπῃ vb 2nd aor act subj 3rd pers sg	εἶπον
εἴπῃς vb 2nd aor act subj 2nd pers sg	id.
εἴπητε vb 2nd aor act subj 2nd pers pl	id.

εἴποι vb 2nd aor act opt 3rd pers sg	εἶπον
εἴποιεν vb 2nd aor act opt 3rd pers pl	id.
εἴποιμι vb 2nd aor act opt 1st pers sg	id.
εἶπον vb 2nd aor act ind 1st pers sg and 3rd pers pl	id.
εἰπόν vb 2nd aor act impv 2nd pers sg	id.
εἰπόντα vb 2nd aor act part masc acc sg	id.
εἰπόντας vb 2nd aor act part masc acc pl	id.
εἰπόντες vb 2nd aor act part masc nom pl	id.
εἰπόντος vb 2nd aor act part masc and neut gen sg	id.
εἰπόντων vb 2nd aor act part masc and neut gen pl	id.
εἴποσαν vb 2nd aor act ind 3rd pers pl	id.
εἰπούσῃ vb 2nd aor act part fem dat sg	id.
εἴπω vb 2nd aor act subj 1st pers sg	id.
εἴπωμεν vb 2nd aor act subj 1st pers pl	id.
εἰπών vb 2nd aor act part masc nom sg	id.
εἴπωσιν vb 2nd aor act subj 3rd pers pl	id.
εἰργάσαντο vb 1st aor mid ind 3rd pers pl	ἐργάζομαι
εἰργάσατο vb 1st aor mid ind 3rd pers sg	id.
εἰργασμένον vb perf dep part neut nom and acc sg	id.
εἰργασμένος vb perf dep part masc nom sg	id.
εἰργασμένου vb perf dep part masc and neut gen sg	id.
εἴργασται vb perf dep ind 3rd pers sg	id.
εἰργάσω vb 1st aor mid ind 2nd pers sg	id.
εἶργον vb impf act ind 3rd pers pl	εἴργω
εἴρηκα vb perf act ind 1st pers sg	εἶπον
εἴρηκας vb perf act ind 2nd pers sg	id.
εἰρήκατε vb perf act ind 2nd pers pl	id.
εἴρηκεν vb perf act ind 3rd pers sg	id.
εἰρηκόσι vb perf act part masc and neut dat pl	id.
εἰρημένα vb perf m/p part neut nom and acc pl	id.
εἰρημένων vb perf m/p part gen pl	id.
εἰρηνεύειν vb pres act inf	εἰρηνεύω
εἰρηνεύοντα vb pres act part masc acc sg	id.
εἰρηνεύοντας vb pres act part masc acc pl	id.
εἰρηνεύοντες vb pres act part masc nom pl	id.
εἰρηνεύοντι vb pres act part masc and neut dat sg	id.
εἰρηνευόντων vb pres act part masc and neut gen pl	id.
εἰρήνευσα vb 1st aor act ind 1st pers sg	id.
εἰρηνεῦσαι vb 1st aor act inf	id.
εἰρηνεύσει vb fut act ind 3rd pers sg	id.
εἰρήνευσεν vb 1st aor act ind 3rd pers sg	id.
εἰρηνεύσουσιν vb fut act ind 3rd pers pl	id.
εἰρηνεύων vb pres act part masc nom sg	id.
Εἰρήνη pr noun fem nom sg	
εἰρήνη noun fem nom sg	
εἰρήνῃ noun fem dat sg	εἰρήνη
εἰρήνην noun fem acc sg	
εἰρήνης noun fem gen sg	id.
εἰρηνικά adj neut nom and acc pl	εἰρηνικός
εἰρηνικάς adj fem acc pl	id.
εἰρηνική adj fem nom sg	id.
εἰρηνικῇ adj fem dat sg	id.
εἰρηνικῆς adj fem gen sg	id.
εἰρηνικοί adj masc nom pl	id.
εἰρηνικοῖς adj masc and neut dat pl	id.
εἰρηνικόν adj masc acc sg, neut nom and acc sg	id.

εἰρηνικός   adj masc nom sg

εἰρηνικούς   adj masc acc pl . . . . εἰρηνικός

εἰρηνικῷ   adj masc and neut dat sg   id.

εἰρηνικῶν   adj gen pl   id.

εἰρηνικῶς   adverb

εἰρηνοποιεῖ   vb pres act ind 3rd pers sg . . . . . . εἰρηνοποιέω

εἴρηνται   vb perf m/p ind 3rd pers pl . . . . εἶπον

εἰρήσθω   vb perf m/p impv 3rd pers sg   id.

εἱρκτήν   noun fem acc sg . . . . εἱρκτή

εἷρξαν   vb 1st aor act ind 3rd pers pl . . . . εἵργω

εἵρχθησαν   vb 1st aor pass ind 3rd pers pl   id.

Εἴρωθ   pr noun

εἰρωνείας   noun fem gen sg . . . . εἰρωνεία

εἰς   preposition

εἷς   adj masc nom sg

εἰσάγαγε   vb 2nd aor act impv 2nd pers sg . . . . εἰσάγω

εἰσαγαγεῖν   vb 2nd aor act inf   id.

εἰσαγάγετε   vb 2nd aor act impv 2nd pers pl   id.

εἰσαγάγῃ   vb 2nd aor act subj 3rd pers sg   id.

εἰσαγάγῃς   vb 2nd aor act subj 2nd pers sg   id.

εἰσαγάγητε   vb 2nd aor act subj 2nd pers pl   id.

εἰσαγαγών   vb 2nd aor act part masc nom sg   id.

εἴσαγε   vb pres act impv 2nd pers sg   id.

εἰσάγει   vb pres act ind 3rd pers sg   id.

εἰσαγειόχατε   vb perf act ind 2nd pers pl   id.

εἰσάγεις   vb pres act ind 2nd pers sg   id.

εἰσαγόμεθα   vb pres m/p ind 1st pers pl   id.

εἰσαγομένοις   vb pres m/p part masc and neut dat pl   id.

εἰσάγουσιν   vb pres act ind 3rd pers pl   id.

εἰσάγω   vb pres act ind 1st pers sg   id.

εἰσάγων   vb pres act part masc nom sg   id.

εἰσακήκοα   vb perf act ind 1st pers sg . . . . εἰσακούω

εἰσακήκοεν   vb perf act ind 3rd pers sg   id.

εἰσάκουε   vb pres act impv 2nd pers sg   id.

εἰσακούει   vb pres act ind 3rd pers sg   id.

εἰσακούειν   vb pres act inf   id.

εἰσακούεις   vb pres act ind 2nd pers sg   id.

εἰσακούετε   vb pres act ind 2nd pers pl   id.

εἰσακούῃ   vb pres act subj 3rd pers sg   id.

εἰσακούοντες   vb pres act part masc nom pl   id.

εἰσακούοντι   vb pres act part masc and neut dat sg   id.

εἰσακούσαι   vb 1st aor act opt 3rd pers sg   id.

εἰσακοῦσαι   vb 1st aor act inf   id.

εἰσακούσας   vb 1st aor act part masc nom sg   id.

εἰσακούσατε   vb 1st aor act impv 2nd pers pl   id.

εἰσακουσάτω   vb 1st aor act impv 3rd pers sg   id.

εἰσακούσει   vb fut act ind 3rd pers sg   id.

εἰσακούσεται   vb fut mid ind 3rd pers sg   id.

εἰσακούσῃ   vb 1st aor act subj 3rd pers sg,

         1st aor mid subj 2nd pers sg,

         fut mid ind 2nd pers sg   id.

εἰσακούσῃς   vb 1st aor act subj 2nd pers sg   id.

εἰσακούσητε   vb 1st aor act subj 2nd pers pl   id.

εἰσακουσθήσεται   vb fut pass ind 3rd pers sg   id.

εἰσακούσομαι   vb fut mid ind 1st pers sg   id.

εἰσάκουσον   vb 1st aor act impv 2nd pers sg   id.

εἰσακούσονται   vb fut mid ind 3rd pers pl . . . . εἰσακούω

εἰσακούσω   vb fut act ind 1st pers sg   id.

εἰσακούσωσιν   vb 1st aor act subj 3rd pers pl   id.

εἰσακούων   vb pres act part masc nom sg   id.

εἰσάξει   vb fut act ind 3rd pers sg . . . . εἰσάγω

εἰσάξεις   vb fut act ind 2nd pers sg   id.

εἰσάξετε   vb fut act ind 2nd pers pl   id.

εἰσάξουσιν   vb fut act ind 3rd pers pl   id.

εἰσάξω   vb fut act ind 1st pers sg   id.

εἰσαχθέντας   vb 1st aor pass part masc acc pl   id.

εἰσβαλεῖν   vb 2nd aor act inf, fut act inf . . . . εἰσβάλλω

εἰσβαλλόντων   vb pres act part masc and neut gen pl   id.

εἰσβλέψαντες   vb 1st aor act part masc nom pl . . . . εἰσβλέπω

εἰσβλέψας   vb 1st aor act part masc nom sg   id.

εἰσβλεψον   vb 1st aor act impv 2nd pers sg   id.

εἰσδεξάμενοι   vb 1st aor mid part masc nom pl .   εἰσδέχομαι

εἰσδέξασθαι   vb 1st aor mid inf   id.

εἰσδέξεται   vb fut mid ind 3rd pers sg   id.

εἰσδέξομαι   vb fut mid ind 1st pers sg   id.

εἰσδέξονται   vb fut mid ind 3rd pers pl   id.

εἰσδέξωμαι   vb 1st aor mid subj 1st pers sg   id.

εἰσδέχεσθαι   vb pres dep inf   id.

εἰσδέχεται   vb pres dep ind 3rd pers sg   id.

εἰσδέχομαι   vb pres dep ind 1st pers sg   id.

εἰσδραμών   vb 2nd aor act part masc nom sg . . . . εἰστρέχω

εἰσεδέχθη   vb 1st aor pass ind 3rd pers sg . . . . εἰσδέχομαι

εἰσέδυ   vb 2nd aor act ind 3rd pers sg . . . . εἰσδύω

εἰσέδυσαν   vb 1st aor act ind 3rd pers pl   id.

εἰσεῖδεν   vb 2nd aor act ind 3rd pers sg . . . . εἰσοράω

εἰσελεύσει   vb fut act ind 2nd pers sg . . . . εἰσέρχομαι

εἰσελεύσεσθαι   vb fut mid inf   id.

εἰσελεύσεσθε   vb fut mid ind 2nd pers pl   id.

εἰσελεύσεται   vb fut mid ind 3rd pers sg   id.

εἰσελεύσῃ   vb fut mid ind 2nd pers sg   id.

εἰσελεύσομαι   vb fut mid ind 1st pers sg   id.

εἰσελευσόμεθα   vb fut mid ind 1st pers pl   id.

εἰσελεύσονται   vb fut mid ind 3rd pers pl   id.

εἰσελήλυθα   vb perf act ind 1st pers sg   id.

εἰσελήλυθας   vb perf act ind 2nd pers sg   id.

εἰσεληλύθασιν   vb perf act ind 3rd pers pl   id.

εἰσεληλύθει   vb plpf act ind 3rd pers sg   id.

εἰσεληλύθεν   vb perf act ind 3rd pers sg   id.

εἰσεληλυθέναι   vb perf act inf   id.

εἰσεληλυθός   vb perf act part neut nom and acc sg   id.

εἰσελεάτε   vb 1st aor mid ind 2nd pers pl   id.

εἰσελεάτω   vb 1st aor act impv 3rd pers sg   id.

εἰσελεάτωσαν   vb 1st aor act impv 3rd pers pl   id.

εἴσελθε   vb 2nd aor act impv 2nd pers sg   id.

εἰσελθεῖν   vb 2nd aor act inf   id.

εἰσέλθετε   vb 2nd aor act impv 2nd pers pl   id.

εἰσελθέτο   vb 2nd aor act impv 3rd pers sg   id.

εἰσελθέτοσαν   vb 2nd aor act impv 3rd pers pl   id.

εἰσέλθῃ   vb 2nd aor act subj 3rd pers sg   id.

εἰσέλθῃς   vb 2nd aor act subj 2nd pers sg   id.

εἰσέλθητε   vb 2nd aor act subj 2nd pers pl   id.

εἰσέλθοι   vb 2nd aor act opt 3rd pers sg   id.

εἰσέλθοις   vb 2nd aor act opt 2nd pers sg . . . . . . εἰσέρχομαι

εἰσέλθοισαν   vb 2nd aor act opt 3rd pers pl   id.

εἰσελθόντα   vb 2nd aor act part masc acc sg,
       neut nom and acc pl   id.

εἰσελθόντας   vb 2nd aor act part masc acc pl   id.

εἰσελθόντες   vb 2nd aor act part masc nom pl   id.

εἰσελθόντος   vb 2nd aor act part masc and neut gen sg   id.

εἰσελθόντων   vb 2nd aor act part masc and neut gen pl   id.

εἰσελθοῦσα   vb 2nd aor act part fem nom sg   id.

εἰσελθοῦσαι   vb 2nd aor act part fem nom pl   id.

εἰσελθούσῃ   vb 2nd aor act part fem dat sg   id.

εἰσελθούσης   vb 2nd aor act part fem gen sg   id.

εἰσέλθω   vb 2nd aor act subj 1st pers sg   id.

εἰσέλθωμεν   vb 2nd aor act subj 1st pers pl   id.

εἰσελθών   vb 2nd aor act part masc nom sg   id.

εἰσέλθωσιν   vb 2nd aor act subj 3rd pers pl   id.

εἰσενέγκαι   vb 1st aor act inf . . . . εἰσφέρω

εἰσενέγκαντες   vb 1st aor act part masc nom pl   id.

εἰσενέγκας   vb 1st aor act part masc nom sg   id.

εἰσένεγκε   vb 2nd aor act impv 2nd pers sg   id.

εἰσενεγκεῖν   vb 2nd aor act inf   id.

εἰσένεγκον   vb 1st aor act impv 2nd pers sg   id.

εἰσενέγκωσιν   vb 1st aor act subj 3rd pers pl   id.

εἰσενεχθέν   vb 1st aor pass part neut nom and acc sg   id.

εἰσενεχθέντος   vb 1st aor pass part masc and neut gen sg   id.

εἰσενεχθῇ   vb 1st aor pass subj 3rd pers sg   id.

εἰσενεχθῆναι   vb 1st aor pass inf   id.

εἰσενεχθήσεται   vb fut pass ind 3rd pers sg   id.

εἰσενηνεγμένος   vb perf m/p part masc nom sg   id.

εἰσέπεμψεν   vb 1st aor act ind 3rd pers sg . . . . εἰσπέμπω

εἰσεπήδησαν   vb 1st aor act ind 3rd pers pl . . . . . . εἰσπηδάω

εἰσεπορεύεσθε   vb impf dep ind 2nd pers pl . . . εἰσπορεύομαι

εἰσεπορεύετο   vb impf dep ind 3rd pers sg   id.

εἰσεπορεύθη   vb 1st aor pass ind 3rd pers sg   id.

εἰσεπορευόμην   vb impf dep ind 1st pers sg   id.

εἰσεπορεύοντο   vb impf dep ind 3rd pers pl   id.

εἰσέρχεσθε   vb pres dep ind 2nd pers pl . . . . εἰσέρχομαι

εἰσερχόμενον   vb pres dep part masc acc sg   id.

εἰσεσπάσαντο   vb 1st aor mid ind 3rd pers pl . . . . . . εἰσπάω

εἰσεφέρετε   vb impf act ind 2nd pers pl . . . . εἰσφέρω

εἰσέφερον   vb impf act ind 1st pers sg and 3rd pers pl   id.

εἰσήγαγεν   vb 2nd aor act ind 3rd pers sg . . . . εἰσάγω

εἰσήγαγες   vb 2nd aor act ind 2nd pers sg   id.

εἰσηγάγετε   vb 2nd aor act ind 2nd pers pl   id.

εἰσήγαγον   vb 2nd aor act ind 1st pers sg and 3rd pers pl   id.

εἰσηγάγοσαν   vb 2nd aor act ind 3rd pers pl   id.

εἰσῄει   vb impf act ind 3rd pers sg . . . . εἴσειμι

εἰσήκουσα   vb 1st aor act ind 1st pers sg . . . . εἰσακούω

εἰσηκούσαμεν   vb 1st aor act ind 1st pers pl   id.

εἰσήκουσαν   vb 1st aor act ind 3rd pers pl   id.

εἰσήκουσας   vb 1st aor act ind 2nd pers sg   id.

εἰσηκούσατε   vb 1st aor act ind 2nd pers pl   id.

εἰσήκουσε(ν)   vb 1st aor act ind 3rd pers sg   id.

εἰσηκούσθη   vb 1st aor pass ind 3rd pers sg   id.

εἰσηκούσθημεν   vb 1st aor pass ind 1st pers pl   id.

εἰσήλθαμεν   vb 1st aor act ind 1st pers pl . . . . εἰσέρχομαι

εἰσῆλθαν   vb 1st aor act ind 3rd pers pl . . . . εἰσέρχομαι

εἰσήλθατε   vb 1st aor act ind 2nd pers pl   id.

εἰσῆλθε(ν)   vb 2nd aor act ind 3rd pers sg   id.

εἰσῆλθες   vb 2nd aor act ind 2nd pers sg   id.

εἰσήλθετε   vb 2nd aor act ind 2nd pers pl   id.

εἰσήλθομεν   vb 2nd aor act ind 1st pers pl   id.

εἰσῆλθον   vb 2nd aor act ind 1st pers sg and 3rd pers pl   id.

εἰσήλθοσαν   vb 2nd aor act ind 3rd pers pl   id.

εἰσήνεγκαν   vb 1st aor act ind 3rd pers pl . . . . εἰσφέρω

εἰσηνέγκατε   vb 1st aor act ind 2nd pers pl   id.

εἰσήνεγκεν   vb 1st aor act ind 3rd pers sg   id.

εἰσηνέχθη   vb 1st aor pass ind 3rd pers sg   id.

εἰσήρχετο   vb impf dep ind 3rd pers sg . . . . εἰσέρχομαι

εἰσήχθη   vb 1st aor pass ind 3rd pers sg . . . . εἰσάγω

εἰσήχθησαν   vb 1st aor pass ind 3rd pers pl   id.

εἰσι   *see* εἰσί(ν)

εἰσί(ν)   vb pres act ind 3rd pers pl . . . . εἰμί

εἰσιέναι   vb pres act inf . . . . εἴσειμι

εἰσιόντι   vb pres act part masc and neut dat sg   id.

εἰσκυκλεῖσθαι   vb pres m/p inf . . . . εἰσκυκλέω

εἰσκύπτουσαν   vb pres act part fem acc sg . . . . εἰσκύπτω

εἰσόδια   noun neut nom and acc pl . . . . εἰσόδιον

εἰσοδιαζόμενον   vb pres m/p part
       neut nom and acc sg . . . . εἰσοδιάζω

εἰσοδιασθέν   vb 1st aor pass part neut nom and acc sg   id.

εἰσόδοις   noun fem dat pl . . . . εἴσοδος

εἴσοδον   noun fem acc sg   id.

εἴσοδος   noun fem nom sg   id.

εἰσόδου   noun fem gen sg   id.

εἰσόδῳ   noun fem dat sg   id.

εἰσόδων   noun fem gen pl   id.

εἰσοίσει   vb fut act ind 3rd pers sg . . . . εἰσφέρω

εἰσοίσεις   vb fut act ind 2nd pers sg   id.

εἰσοίσομεν   vb fut act ind 1st pers pl   id.

εἰσοίσουσιν   vb fut act ind 3rd pers pl   id.

εἰσοίσω   vb fut act ind 1st pers sg   id.

εἰσπεπορευμένους   vb perf dep part
       masc acc pl . . . . εἰσπορεύομαι

εἰσπεπορευμένων   vb perf dep part gen pl   id.

εἰσπεπόρευνται   vb perf dep ind 3rd pers pl   id.

εἰσπηδήσῃ   vb 1st aor act subj 3rd pers sg . . . . εἰσπηδάω

εἰσπλέουσι   vb pres act ind 3rd pers pl . . . . εἰσπλέω

εἰσπλεύσαντα   vb 1st aor act part masc acc sg   id.

εἰσπορεύεσθαι   vb pres dep inf . . . . εἰσπορεύομαι

εἰσπορεύεσθε   vb pres dep impv 2nd pers pl,
       pres dep ind 2nd pers pl   id.

εἰσπορευέσθω   vb pres dep impv 3rd pers sg   id.

εἰσπορευέσθωσαν   vb pres dep impv 3rd pers pl   id.

εἰσπορεύεται   vb pres dep ind 3rd pers sg   id.

εἰσπορεύῃ   vb pres dep ind 2nd pers sg   id.

εἰσπορεύησθε   vb pres dep subj 2nd pers pl   id.

εἰσπορεύηται   vb pres dep subj 3rd pers sg   id.

εἰσπορευθέντες   vb 1st aor pass part masc nom pl   id.

εἰσπορεύομαι   vb pres dep ind 1st pers sg   id.

εἰσπορευόμεθα   vb pres dep ind 1st pers pl   id.

εἰσπορευόμενα   vb pres dep part neut nom and acc pl   id.

εἰσπορευομένη vb pres dep part fem nom sg .. εἰσπορεύομαι
εἰσπορευομένην vb pres dep part fem acc sg   id.
εἰσπορευόμενοι vb pres dep part masc nom pl   id.
εἰσπορευομένοις vb pres dep part masc and neut dat pl   id.
εἰσπορευόμενον vb pres dep part masc acc sg,
　　　　neut nom and acc sg   id.
εἰσπορευόμενος vb pres dep part masc nom sg   id.
εἰσπορευομένου vb pres dep part masc and neut gen sg   id.
εἰσπορευομένους vb pres dep part masc acc pl   id.
εἰσπορευομένῳ vb pres dep part masc and neut dat sg   id.
εἰσπορευομένων vb pres dep part gen pl   id.
εἰσπορεύονται vb pres dep ind 3rd pers pl   id.
εἰσπορεύσεται vb fut mid ind 3rd pers sg   id.
εἰσπορευσόμεθα vb fut mid ind 1st pers pl   id.
εἰσπορεύωμαι vb pres dep subj 1st pers sg   id.
εἰσπορεύωνται vb pres dep subj 3rd pers pl   id.
εἰστήκει vb plpf act ind 3rd pers sg .... ἵστημι
εἰστήκειμεν vb plpf act ind 1st pers pl   id.
εἰστήκειν vb plpf act ind 1st pers sg   id.
εἰστήκεις vb plpf act ind 2nd pers sg   id.
εἰστήκεισαν vb plpf act ind 3rd pers pl   id.
εἰσφέρειν vb pres act inf .... εἰσφέρω
εἰσφερομένου vb pres m/p part masc and neut gen sg   id.
εἰσφερόντων vb pres act part masc and neut gen pl   id.
εἰσφέρουσιν vb pres act ind 3rd pers pl   id.
εἰσφορά noun fem nom sg
εἰσφοράν noun fem acc sg .... εἰσφορά
εἰσφορᾶς noun fem gen sg   id.
εἴτ᾽ see εἶτα
εἶτα adverb
εἴτε conjunction
εἴτοι conjunction
εἶχε(ν) vb impf act ind 3rd pers sg .... ἔχω
εἴχετο vb impf m/p ind 3rd pers sg   id.
εἶχον vb impf act ind 3rd pers pl   id.
εἴωθα vb perf act ind 1st pers sg .... ἔθω
εἴωθεν vb perf act ind 3rd pers sg   id.
εἰωθός vb perf act part neut nom and acc sg   id.
εἴων vb impf act ind 3rd pers pl .... ἐάω
ἐκ preposition
ἐκάησαν vb 1st aor act ind 3rd pers pl .... καίω
ἐκάθαιρεν vb impf act ind 3rd pers sg .... καθαίρω
ἐκαθάριζεν vb impf act ind 3rd pers sg .... καθαρίζω
ἐκαθάρισα vb 1st aor act ind 1st pers sg   id.
ἐκαθάρισαν vb 1st aor act ind 3rd pers pl   id.
ἐκαθάρισεν vb 1st aor act ind 3rd pers sg   id.
ἐκαθαρίσθη vb 1st aor pass ind 3rd pers sg   id.
ἐκαθαρίσθημεν vb 1st aor pass ind 1st pers pl   id.
ἐκαθαρίσθης vb 1st aor pass ind 2nd pers sg   id.
ἐκαθαριώθησαν vb 1st aor pass ind 3rd pers pl   id.
ἐκάθευδεν vb impf act ind 3rd pers sg .... καθεύδω
ἐκάθευδον vb impf act ind 1st pers sg   id.
ἐκαθήμην vb impf mid ind 1st pers sg .... κάθημαι
ἐκάθηντο vb impf mid ind 3rd pers pl   id.
ἐκάθητο vb impf mid ind 3rd pers sg   id.
ἐκάθισα vb 1st aor act ind 1st pers sg .... καθίζω

ἐκαθίσαμεν vb 1st aor act ind 1st pers pl .... καθίζω
ἐκάθισαν vb 1st aor act ind 3rd pers pl   id.
ἐκάθισας vb 1st aor act ind 2nd pers sg   id.
ἐκαθίσατε vb 1st aor act ind 2nd pers pl   id.
ἐκάθισε(ν) vb 1st aor act ind 3rd pers sg   id.
ἐκάθου vb impf mid ind 2nd pers sg .... κάθημαι
ἐκαίετο vb impf m/p ind 3rd pers sg .... καίω
ἐκαίνιζεν vb impf act ind 3rd pers sg .... καινίζω
ἐκακηγόρει vb impf act ind 3rd pers sg .... κακηγορέω
ἐκακολόγει vb impf act ind 3rd pers sg .... κακολογέω
ἐκακολόγουν vb impf act ind 3rd pers pl   id.
ἐκακοπάθησας vb 1st aor act ind 2nd pers sg ... κακοπαθέω
ἐκακοποίησα vb 1st aor act ind 1st pers sg ..... κακοποιέω
ἐκακοποιήσατε vb 1st aor act ind 2nd pers pl   id.
ἐκακοποίησεν vb 1st aor act ind 3rd pers sg   id.
ἐκακουχήθη vb 1st aor pass ind 3rd pers sg ..... κακουχέω
ἐκακουχήθης vb 1st aor pass ind 2nd pers sg   id.
ἐκακώθη vb 1st aor pass ind 3rd pers sg .... κακόω
ἐκακώθην vb 1st aor pass ind 1st pers sg   id.
ἐκακώθησαν vb 1st aor pass ind 3rd pers pl   id.
ἐκάκωσα vb 1st aor act ind 1st pers sg   id.
ἐκάκωσαν vb 1st aor act ind 3rd pers pl   id.
ἐκάκωσας vb 1st aor act ind 2nd pers sg   id.
ἐκάκωσεν vb 1st aor act ind 3rd pers sg   id.
ἐκαλαμήσαντο vb 1st aor mid ind 3rd pers pl .. καλαμάομαι
ἐκάλει vb impf act ind 3rd pers sg .... καλέω
ἐκάλεσα vb 1st aor act ind 1st pers sg   id.
ἐκάλεσαν vb 1st aor act ind 3rd pers pl   id.
ἐκάλεσας vb 1st aor act ind 2nd pers sg   id.
ἐκαλέσατε vb 1st aor act ind 2nd pers pl   id.
ἐκάλεσε(ν) vb 1st aor act ind 3rd pers sg   id.
ἐκαλλιώθησαν vb 1st aor pass ind 3rd pers pl ..... καλλιόω
ἐκαλλωπίσατο vb 1st aor mid ind 3rd pers sg ... καλλωπίζω
ἐκάλουν vb impf act ind 1st pers sg and 3rd pers pl ... καλέω
ἐκάλυπτεν vb impf act ind 3rd pers sg .... καλύπτω
ἐκαλύπτετε vb impf act ind 2nd pers pl   id.
ἐκάλυψα vb 1st aor act ind 1st pers sg   id.
ἐκάλυψαν vb 1st aor act ind 3rd pers pl   id.
ἐκάλυψας vb 1st aor act ind 2nd pers sg   id.
ἐκάλυψεν vb 1st aor act ind 3rd pers sg   id.
ἐκάμμυσαν vb 1st aor act ind 3rd pers pl .... καμμύω
ἐκάμφθησαν vb 1st aor pass ind 3rd pers pl .... κάμπτω
ἔκαμναν vb 1st aor act ind 3rd pers pl   id.
ἔκαμψεν vb 1st aor act ind 3rd pers sg   id.
ἐκαπνίζετο vb impf m/p ind 3rd pers sg .... καπνίζω
ἐκάπνισεν vb 1st aor act ind 3rd pers sg   id.
ἐκαρδίωσας vb 1st aor act ind 2nd pers sg .... καρδιόω
ἐκαρπίσαντο vb 1st aor mid ind 3rd pers pl .... καρπίζομαι
ἐκάρπωσα vb 1st aor act ind 1st pers sg .... καρπόω
ἐκαρτέρησα vb 1st aor act ind 1st pers sg ...... καρτερέω
ἕκαστα adj neut nom and acc pl .... ἕκαστος
ἑκάστη adj fem nom sg   id.
ἑκάστῃ adj fem dat sg   id.
ἑκάστην adj fem acc sg   id.
ἑκάστης adj fem gen sg   id.
ἕκαστον adj masc acc sg, neut nom and acc sg   id.

ἕκαστος adj masc nom sg

ἑκάστου adj masc and neut gen sg . . . . ἕκαστος

ἑκάστῳ adj masc and neut dat sg id.

ἑκάστων adj gen pl id.

ἑκατέραις adj fem dat pl . . . . ἑκάτερος

ἑκατέρας adj fem gen sg id.

ἑκάτεροι adj masc nom pl id.

ἑκάτερον adj masc acc sg, neut nom and acc sg id.

ἑκάτερος adj masc nom sg id.

ἑκατέρου adj masc and neut gen sg id.

ἑκατέρῳ adj masc and neut dat sg id.

ἑκατέρωθεν adverb

ἑκατέρων adj gen pl . . . . ἑκάτερος

ἑκατόν indecl number

ἑκατοντάδας noun fem acc pl . . . . ἑκατοντάς

ἑκατοντάδων noun fem gen pl id.

ἑκατονταετεῖ adj dat sg . . . . ἑκατονταετής

ἑκατονταπλασίονα adj masc and fem

      acc sg . . . . ἑκατονταπλασίων

ἑκατονταπλασίως adverb

ἑκατοντάρχαις noun masc dat pl . . . . ἑκατοντάρχης

ἑκατόνταρχοι noun masc nom pl . . . . . . ἑκατόνταρχος

ἑκατοντάρχοις noun masc dat pl id.

ἑκατοντάρχους noun masc acc pl id.

ἑκατοντάρχων noun masc gen pl id.

ἑκατοστεύουσαν vb pres act part fem acc sg . . ἑκατοστεύω

ἑκατοστοῦ adj masc and neut gen sg . . . . ἑκατοστός

ἑκατοστῷ adj masc and neut dat sg id.

ἐκαυχῶντο vb impf dep ind 3rd pers pl . . . . καυχάομαι

ἐκβαίνει vb pres act ind 3rd pers sg . . . . ἐκβαίνω

ἐκβαίνων vb pres act part masc nom sg id.

ἔκβαλε vb 2nd aor act impv 2nd pers sg . . . . ἐκβάλλω

ἐκβαλεῖ vb fut act ind 3rd pers sg id.

ἐκβαλεῖν vb 2nd aor act inf id.

ἐκβάλετε vb 2nd aor act impv 2nd pers pl id.

ἐκβάλῃ vb 2nd aor act subj 3rd pers sg id.

ἐκβάλῃς vb 2nd aor act subj 2nd pers sg id.

ἐκβάλλει vb pres act ind 3rd pers sg id.

ἐκβάλλεις vb pres act ind 2nd pers sg id.

ἐκβάλλοντας vb pres act part masc acc pl id.

ἐκβάλλοντες vb pres act part masc nom pl id.

ἐκβάλλουσιν vb pres act ind 3rd pers pl id.

ἐκβάλλω vb pres act ind 1st pers sg id.

ἐκβαλόντας vb 2nd aor act part masc acc pl id.

ἐκβαλοῦσιν vb fut act ind 3rd pers pl id.

ἐκβάλω vb 2nd aor act subj 1st pers sg id.

ἐκβαλῶ vb fut act ind 1st pers sg id.

ἐκβαλών vb 2nd aor act part masc nom sg id.

ἐκβάσει noun fem dat sg . . . . ἔκβασις

ἐκβάσεις noun fem nom and acc pl id.

ἐκβάσεων noun fem gen pl id.

Ἐκβάτανα pr noun

Ἐκβατάνοις pr noun dat pl . . . . Ἐκβάτανα

Ἐκβατάνων pr noun gen pl id.

ἐκβεβλημένη vb perf m/p part fem nom sg . . . . ἐκβάλλω

ἐκβεβλημένην vb perf m/p part fem acc sg id.

ἐκβεβλημένης vb perf m/p part fem gen sg . . . . ἐκβάλλω

ἐκβῆναι vb 2nd aor act inf . . . . ἐκβαίνω

ἔκβητε vb 2nd aor act impv 2nd pers pl id.

ἐκβιάζεται vb pres m/p ind 3rd pers sg . . . . ἐκβιάζω

ἐκβιάσαι vb 1st aor act inf id.

ἐκβλαστῆσαι vb 1st aor act inf . . . . ἐκβλαστάνω

ἐκβλαστήσει vb fut act ind 3rd pers sg id.

ἐκβλαστήσῃ vb 1st aor act subj 3rd pers sg id.

ἐκβληθήτωσαν vb 1st aor pass impv 3rd pers pl . . . . ἐκβάλλω

ἐκβλύζωσιν vb pres act subj 3rd pers pl . . . . ἐκβλύζω

ἐκβολή noun fem dat sg . . . . ἐκβολή

ἐκβολήν noun fem acc sg id.

ἔκβολος adj masc and fem nom sg

ἐκβρασμός noun masc nom sg

ἐκγελάσεται vb fut mid ind 3rd pers sg . . . . ἐκγελάω

ἐκγελάσῃ vb fut mid ind 2nd pers sg id.

ἔκγονα adj neut nom and acc pl . . . . ἔκγονος

ἐκγόνοις adj dat pl id.

ἔκγονον adj acc sg, neut nom sg id.

ἐκγόνους adj masc and fem acc pl id.

ἐκγόνων adj gen pl id.

ἐκδανείσῃς vb 1st aor act subj 2nd pers sg . . . . ἐκδανείζω

ἐκδέδεκται vb perf dep ind 3rd pers sg . . . . ἐκδέχομαι

ἐκδεδίκηται vb perf m/p ind 3rd pers sg . . . . ἐκδικέω

ἐκδεδομένη vb perf m/p part fem nom sg . . . . δίδωμι

ἐκδεδομένῃ vb perf m/p part fem dat sg id.

ἐκδεδομένῳ vb perf m/p part masc and neut dat sg id.

ἐκδέδοσαι vb perf m/p ind 2nd pers sg id.

ἐκδειματούμενοι vb pres m/p part

      masc nom pl . . . . ἐκδειματόω

ἐκδείραντες vb 1st aor act part masc nom pl . . . . ἐκδέρω

ἐκδεκτέον verbal adj sg

ἔκδεξαι vb 1st aor mid impv 2nd pers sg . . . . ἐκδέχομαι

ἐκδέξεται vb fut mid ind 3rd pers sg id.

ἐκδέξῃ vb fut mid ind 2nd pers sg id.

ἐκδέξομαι vb fut mid ind 1st pers sg id.

ἐκδέχεται vb pres dep ind 3rd pers sg id.

ἐκδέχομαι vb pres dep ind 1st pers sg id.

ἐκδεχόμενοι vb pres dep part masc nom pl id.

ἐκδεχόμενος vb pres dep part masc nom sg id.

ἐκδεχομένου vb pres dep part masc and neut gen sg id.

ἐκδεχομένους vb pres dep part masc acc pl id.

ἔκδηλον adj acc sg, neut nom sg . . . . ἔκδηλος

ἐκδημίαν noun fem acc sg . . . . ἐκδημία

ἐκδήσεις vb fut act ind 2nd pers sg . . . . ἐκδέω

ἐκδιαιτηθῆναι vb 1st aor pass inf . . . . ἐκδιαιτέω

ἐκδιδάσκει vb pres act ind 3rd pers sg . . . . ἐκδιδάσκω

ἐκδιδύσκειν vb pres act inf . . . . ἐκδιδύσκω

ἐκδιδυσκόμενος vb pres m/p part masc nom sg id.

ἐκδιδύσκων vb pres act part masc nom sg id.

ἐκδιηγῆσαι vb 1st aor mid impv 2nd pers sg . . . ἐκδιηγέομαι

ἐκδιηγήσασθαι vb 1st aor mid inf id.

ἐκδιηγήσάσθωσαν vb 1st aor mid impv 3rd pers pl id.

ἐκδιηγήσεται vb fut mid ind 3rd pers sg id.

ἐκδιηγήσομαι vb fut mid ind 1st pers sg id.

ἐκδιηγῆται vb pres dep subj 3rd pers sg id.

ἐκδιηγῶνται vb pres dep subj 3rd pers pl . . . . . ἐκδιηγέομαι
ἐκδικᾷ vb pres act subj 3rd pers sg . . . . ἐκδικάω
ἐκδικᾶται vb fut mid ind 3rd pers sg . . . . ἐκδικάζω
ἔκδικε adj masc and fem voc sg . . . . ἔκδικος
ἐκδίκει vb pres act impv 3rd pers sg . . . . ἐκδικέω
ἐκδικεῖ vb pres act ind 3rd pers sg   id.
ἐκδικεῖται vb pres m/p ind 3rd pers sg   id.
ἐκδικεῖτε vb pres act ind 2nd pers pl   id.
ἐκδικηθῆναι vb 1st aor pass inf   id.
ἐκδικηθήσεται vb fut pass ind 3rd pers sg   id.
ἐκδικηθήτω vb 1st aor pass impv 3rd pers sg   id.
ἐκδικῆσαι vb 1st aor act opt 3rd pers sg   id.
ἐκδικῆσαι vb 1st aor act inf   id.
ἐκδικήσατε vb 1st aor act impv 2nd pers pl   id.
ἐκδικήσει noun fem dat sg . . . . ἐκδίκησις
ἐκδικήσει vb fut act ind 3rd pers sg . . . . ἐκδικέω
ἐκδικήσειν vb fut act inf   id.
ἐκδικήσεις noun fem nom and acc pl . . . . ἐκδίκησις
ἐκδικήσεις vb fut act ind 2nd pers sg . . . . ἐκδικέω
ἐκδικήσεων noun fem gen pl . . . . ἐκδίκησις
ἐκδικήσεως noun fem gen sg   id.
ἐκδικήσῃ vb 1st aor act subj 3rd pers sg . . . . ἐκδικέω
ἐκδικήσῃς vb 1st aor act subj 2nd pers sg   id.
ἐκδίκησιν noun fem acc sg . . . . ἐκδίκησις
ἐκδίκησις noun fem nom sg
ἐκδίκησον vb 1st aor act impv 2nd pers sg . . . . ἐκδικέω
ἐκδικήσουσιν vb fut act ind 3rd pers pl   id.
ἐκδικήσω vb fut act ind 1st pers sg   id.
ἐκδικητήν noun masc acc sg . . . . ἐκδικητής
ἔκδικον adj acc sg, neut nom sg . . . . ἔκδικος
ἔκδικος adj masc and fem nom sg
ἐκδικούμενα vb pres m/p part neut nom and acc pl . . . ἐκδικέω
ἐκδικοῦσα vb pres act part fem nom sg   id.
ἐκδικοῦσαν vb pres act part fem acc sg   id.
ἐκδικῶ vb pres act ind 1st pers sg   id.
ἐκδικῶν vb pres act part masc nom sg   id.
ἐκδιωκόμενος vb pres m/p part masc nom sg . . . . . . ἐκδιώκω
ἐκδιώκοντες vb pres act part masc nom pl   id.
ἐκδιώκοντος vb pres act part masc and neut gen sg   id.
ἐκδιῶξαι vb 1st aor act inf   id.
ἐκδιώξουσιν vb fut act ind 3rd pers pl   id.
ἐκδιώξω vb fut act ind 1st pers sg   id.
ἐκδιωχθήσονται vb fut pass ind 3rd pers pl   id.
ἐκδοθῶσι vb 1st aor pass subj 3rd pers pl . . . . ἐκδίδωμι
ἐκδόσθαι vb 2nd aor mid inf   id.
ἔκδοσθε vb 2nd aor mid impv 2nd pers pl   id.
ἔκδοτον adj acc sg, neut nom sg . . . . ἔκδοτος
ἔκδου vb pres m/p impv 2nd pers sg . . . . ἐκδέω
ἐκδοῦναι vb 2nd aor act inf . . . . ἐκδίδωμι
ἐκδύνει vb pres act ind 3rd pers sg . . . . ἐκδύνω
ἔκδυσαι vb 1st aor mid impv 2nd pers sg   id.
ἐκδύσαντες vb 1st aor act part masc nom pl   id.
ἐκδύσασθε vb 1st aor mid impv 2nd pers pl   id.
ἐκδύσεται vb fut mid ind 3rd pers sg   id.
ἐκδύσῃ vb fut mid ind 2nd pers sg   id.
ἔκδυσον vb 1st aor act impv 2nd pers sg   id.

ἐκδύσονται vb fut mid ind 3rd pers pl . . . . ἐκδύνω
ἐκδύσουσιν vb fut act ind 3rd pers pl   id.
ἐκδύσω vb fut act ind 1st pers sg   id.
ἐκδώσειν vb fut act inf . . . . ἐκδίδωμι
ἐκδώσουσι(ν) vb fut act ind 3rd pers pl   id.
ἐκεῖ adverb
ἐκεῖθεν adverb
ἐκεῖνα dem pron neut nom and acc pl . . . . ἐκεῖνος
ἐκεῖναι dem pron fem nom pl   id.
ἐκείναις dem pron fem dat pl   id.
ἐκείνας dem pron fem acc pl   id.
ἐκείνη dem pron fem nom sg   id.
ἐκείνῃ dem pron fem dat sg   id.
ἐκείνην dem pron fem acc sg   id.
ἐκείνης dem pron fem gen sg   id.
ἐκεῖνο dem pron neut nom and acc sg   id.
ἐκεῖνοι dem pron masc nom pl   id.
ἐκείνοις dem pron masc and neut dat pl   id.
ἐκεῖνον dem pron masc acc sg   id.
ἐκεῖνος dem pron masc nom sg   id.
ἐκείνου dem pron masc and neut gen sg   id.
ἐκείνους dem pron masc acc pl   id.
ἔκειντο vb impf m/p ind 3rd pers pl . . . . κεῖμαι
ἐκείνῳ dem pron masc and neut dat sg . . . . ἐκεῖνος
ἐκείνων dem pron gen pl   id.
ἐκείρατο vb 1st aor mid ind 3rd pers sg . . . . κείρω
ἐκείρετο vb impf m/p ind 3rd pers sg   id.
ἐκεῖσε adverb
ἐκέκραγεν vb 2nd aor act ind 3rd pers sg . . . . κράζω
ἐκέκραγον vb 2nd aor act ind 3rd pers pl   id.
ἐκέκραξα vb 1st aor act ind 1st pers sg   id.
ἐκέκραξαν vb 1st aor act ind 3rd pers pl   id.
ἐκεκράξατε vb 1st aor act ind 2nd pers pl   id.
ἐκέκραξεν vb 1st aor act ind 3rd pers sg   id.
ἐκελεκτός adj masc nom sg
ἐκέλευον vb impf act ind 3rd pers pl . . . . κελεύω
ἐκέλευσαν vb 1st aor act ind 3rd pers pl   id.
ἐκέλευσε(ν) vb 1st aor act ind 3rd pers sg   id.
ἐκενώθη vb 1st aor pass ind 3rd pers sg . . . . κενόω
ἐκενώθησαν vb 1st aor pass ind 3rd pers pl   id.
ἐκέρασα vb 1st aor act ind 1st pers sg . . . . κεράννυμι
ἐκέρασεν vb 1st aor act ind 3rd pers sg   id.
ἐκεράτιζες vb impf act ind 2nd pers sg . . . . κερατίζω
ἐκερατίζετε vb impf act ind 2nd pers pl   id.
ἐκζεόντων vb pres act part masc and neut gen pl . . . . . . ἐκζέω
ἐκζέσῃς vb 1st aor act subj 2nd pers sg   id.
ἐκζητεῖ vb pres act ind 3rd pers sg . . . . ἐκζητέω
ἐκζητεῖται vb pres m/p ind 3rd pers sg   id.
ἐκζητεῖτε vb pres act ind 2nd pers pl   id.
ἐκζητῆσαι vb 1st aor act opt 3rd pers sg   id.
ἐκζητῆσαι vb 1st aor act inf   id.
ἐκζητήσαντες vb 1st aor act part masc nom pl   id.
ἐκζητήσατε vb 1st aor act impv 2nd pers pl   id.
ἐκζητήσει vb fut act ind 3rd pers sg   id.
ἐκζητήσεις vb fut act ind 2nd pers sg   id.
ἐκζητήσετε vb fut act ind 2nd pers pl   id.

ἐκζητήσῃ vb 1st aor act subj 3rd pers sg .... ἐκζητέω	ἐκινήθησαν vb 1st aor pass ind 3rd pers pl .... κινέω
ἐκζητήσῃς vb 1st aor act subj 2nd pers sg id.	ἐκίνησαν vb 1st aor act ind 3rd pers pl id.
ἐκζητήσητε vb 1st aor act subj 2nd pers pl id.	ἐκίνησεν vb 1st aor act ind 3rd pers sg id.
ἐκζητήσομεν vb fut act ind 1st pers pl id.	ἐκίρνων vb impf act ind 1st pers sg .... κιρνάω
ἐκζητήσουσιν vb fut act ind 3rd pers pl id.	ἐκίσσησεν vb 1st aor act ind 3rd pers sg .... κισσάω
ἐκζητήσω vb 1st aor act subj 1st pers sg,	ἐκκαῇ vb 2nd aor pass subj 3rd pers sg .... ἐκκαίω
fut act ind 1st pers sg id.	ἐκκαῆναι vb 2nd aor pass inf id.
ἐκζητήσωσιν vb 1st aor act subj 3rd pers pl id.	ἐκκαήσεται vb fut pass ind 3rd pers sg id.
ἐκζητηταί noun masc nom pl .... ἐκζητητής	ἐκκαθαριεῖ vb fut act ind 3rd pers sg .... ἐκκαθαρίζω
ἐκζητοῦμεν vb pres act ind 1st pers pl .... ἐκζητέω	ἐκκαθαριεῖς vb fut act ind 2nd pers sg id.
ἐκζητοῦντα vb pres act part masc acc sg id.	ἐκκαθαριοῦμεν vb fut act ind 1st pers pl id.
ἐκζητοῦντας vb pres act part masc acc pl id.	ἐκκάθαρον vb 2nd aor act impv 2nd pers sg id.
ἐκζητοῦντες vb pres act part masc nom pl id.	ἐκκαθαρῶ vb fut act ind 1st pers sg .... ἐκκαθαίρω
ἐκζητοῦσι(ν) vb pres act ind 3rd pers pl,	ἐκκαίδεκα indecl number
pres act part masc and neut dat pl id.	ἐκκαιδεκάτη adj fem dat sg .... ἐκκαιδέκατος
ἐκζητῶν vb pres act part masc nom sg id.	ἐκκαιδέκατος adj masc nom sg id.
ἐκήρυξαν vb 1st aor act ind 3rd pers pl .... κηρύσσω	ἐκκαιε vb pres act impv 2nd pers sg .... ἐκκαίω
ἐκήρυξε(ν) vb 1st aor act ind 3rd pers sg id.	ἐκκαίει vb pres act ind 3rd pers sg id.
ἐκήρυσσεν vb impf act ind 3rd pers sg id.	ἐκκαίων vb pres act part masc nom sg id.
ἐκηρύχθη vb 1st aor pass ind 3rd pers sg id.	ἐκκαλέσῃ vb 1st aor act subj 3rd pers sg,
ἐκθαμβήσει vb fut act ind 3rd pers sg .... ἐκθαμβέω	fut mid ind 2nd pers sg .... ἐκκαλέω
ἔκθαμβον adj acc sg, neut nom sg .... ἔκθαμβος	ἐκκαλύπτει vb pres act ind 3rd pers sg .... ἐκκαλύπτω
Εκθανααδ pr noun	Εκκας pr noun
ἐκθαυμάσει vb fut act ind 3rd pers sg .... ἐκθαυμάζω	ἐκκαυθῇ vb 1st aor pass subj 3rd pers sg .... ἐκκαίω
ἔκθεμα noun neut nom and acc sg	ἐκκαυθήσεται vb fut pass ind 3rd pers sg id.
ἐκθέντες vb 2nd aor act part masc nom pl ...... ἐκτίθημι	ἐκκαυθήσονται vb fut pass ind 3rd pers pl id.
ἐκθεριζόντων vb pres act part masc and neut gen pl . ἐκθερίζω	ἐκκαῦσαι vb 1st aor act inf id.
ἐκθερίσαι vb 1st aor act inf id.	ἐκκαύσας vb 1st aor act part masc nom sg id.
ἐκθερίσεις vb fut act ind 2nd pers sg id.	ἐκκαύσει vb fut act ind 3rd pers sg id.
ἔκθες vb 2nd aor act impv 2nd pers sg .... ἐκτίθημι	ἐκκαύσῃ vb 1st aor act subj 3rd pers sg,
ἐκθέσει noun fem dat sg .... ἔκθεσις	fut mid ind 2nd pers sg id.
ἔκθεσιν noun fem acc sg id.	ἐκκαύσω vb 1st aor act subj 1st pers sg,
ἔκθεσμον adj acc sg, neut nom sg .... ἔκθεσμος	fut act ind 1st pers sg id.
ἐκθηλάσαντες vb 1st aor act part masc nom pl ... ἐκθηλάζω	ἐκκεκαυμένη vb perf m/p part fem nom sg id.
ἐκθήσει vb fut act ind 3rd pers sg .... ἐκτίθημι	ἐκκέκαυται vb perf m/p ind 3rd pers sg id.
ἐκθλίβειν vb pres act inf .... ἐκθλίβω	ἐκκεκεντημένοι vb perf m/p part masc nom pl .... ἐκκεντέω
ἐκθλιβῇ vb pres pass subj 3rd pers sg id.	ἐκκεκεντημένον vb perf m/p part masc acc sg id.
ἐκθλίβοντες vb pres act part masc nom pl id.	ἐκκεκεντημένων vb perf m/p part gen pl id.
ἐκθλιβόντων vb pres act part masc and neut gen pl id.	ἐκκεκολαμμένους vb perf m/p part masc acc pl . ἐκκολάπτω
ἐκθλίβουσιν vb pres act ind 3rd pers pl id.	ἐκκεκομμένα vb perf m/p part neut nom and acc pl . ἐκκόπτω
ἐκθλίβων vb pres act part masc nom sg id.	ἐκκεκομμένον vb perf m/p part masc acc sg,
ἐκθλίψει vb fut act ind 3rd pers sg id.	neut nom and acc sg id.
ἐκθλίψουσιν vb fut act ind 3rd pers pl id.	ἐκκέκυφεν vb perf act ind 3rd pers sg .... ἐκκύπτω
ἐκθλίψω vb fut act ind 1st pers sg id.	ἐκκενοῦτε vb pres act impv 2nd pers pl .... ἐκκενόω
ἐκθρέψαι vb 1st aor act inf .... ἐκτρέφω	ἐκκέντησον vb 1st aor act impv 2nd pers sg ...... ἐκκεντέω
ἐκθρέψαντι vb 1st aor act part masc and neut dat sg	ἐκκενωθέν vb 1st aor pass part neut nom and acc sg . ἐκκενόω
ἐκθρέψασαν vb 1st aor act part fem acc sg id.	ἐκκενωθήσονται vb fut pass ind 3rd pers pl id.
ἐκθρέψουσιν vb fut act ind 3rd pers pl id.	ἐκκενώσουσιν vb fut act ind 3rd pers pl id.
ἐκθρέψω vb fut act ind 1st pers sg id.	ἐκκενώσω vb fut act ind 1st pers sg id.
ἐκθρέψωσιν vb 1st aor act subj 3rd pers pl id.	ἐκκενώσωμεν vb 1st aor act subj 1st pers pl id.
ἔκθυμος adj masc and fem nom sg	ἐκκέχυκα vb perf act ind 1st pers sg .... ἐκχέω
ἐκθῶμεν vb 2nd aor act subj 1st pers pl .... ἐκτίθημι	ἐκκεχυμένα vb perf m/p part neut nom and acc pl id.
ἐκινδύνευεν vb impf act ind 3rd pers sg .... κινδυνεύω	ἐκκεχυμένου vb perf m/p part masc and neut gen sg id.
ἐκινδύνευσα vb 1st aor act ind 1st pers sg id.	ἐκκήρυκτον adj acc sg, neut nom sg .... ἐκκήρυκτος
ἐκινεῖτο vb impf m/p ind 3rd pers sg .... κινέω	Εκκης pr noun
ἐκινήθη vb 1st aor pass ind 3rd pers sg id.	ἐκκλάσει vb fut act ind 3rd pers sg .... ἐκκλάω

ἐκκλησία   noun fem nom sg

ἐκκλησίᾳ   noun fem dat sg . . . . ἐκκλησία

ἐκκλησίαις   noun fem dat pl   id.

ἐκκλησίαν   noun fem acc sg   id.

ἐκκλησίας   noun fem gen sg and acc pl   id.

ἐκκλησιάσας   vb 1st aor act part masc nom sg . . ἐκκλησιάζω

ἐκκλησιάσατε   vb 1st aor act impv 2nd pers pl   id.

ἐκκλησίασον   vb 1st aor act impv 2nd pers sg   id.

Ἐκκλησιαστης   pr noun masc nom sg

Ἐκκλησιαστοῦ   pr noun masc gen sg . . . . . . Ἐκκλησιαστης

ἔκκλητον   adj acc sg, neut nom sg . . . . ἔκκλητος

ἐκκλῖναι   vb 1st aor act inf . . . . ἐκκλίνω

ἐκκλίνας   vb 1st aor act part masc nom sg   id.

ἐκκλινατε   vb 1st aor act impv 2nd pers pl   id.

ἐκκλινάτω   vb 1st aor act impv 3rd pers sg   id.

ἔκκλινε   vb pres act impv 2nd pers sg   id.

ἐκκλίνει   vb pres act ind 3rd pers sg   id.

ἐκκλινεῖ   vb fut act ind 3rd pers sg   id.

ἐκκλίνειν   vb pres act inf   id.

ἐκκλινεῖς   vb fut act ind 2nd pers sg   id.

ἐκκλινεῖτε   vb fut act ind 2nd pers pl   id.

ἐκκλίνῃ   vb pres act subj 3rd pers sg   id.

ἐκκλίνῃς   vb pres act subj 2nd pers sg   id.

ἐκκλίνητε   vb pres act subj 2nd pers pl   id.

ἐκκλινομένων   vb pres m/p part gen pl   id.

ἔκκλινον   vb 1st aor act impv 2nd pers sg   id.

ἐκκλίνοντας   vb pres act part masc acc pl   id.

ἐκκλίνοντες   vb pres act part masc nom pl   id.

ἐκκλίνοντος   vb pres act part masc and neut gen sg   id.

ἐκκλινοῦμεν   vb fut act ind 1st pers pl   id.

ἐκκλινούσας   vb pres act part fem acc pl   id.

ἐκκλίνουσιν   vb pres act ind 3rd pers pl   id.

ἐκκλινοῦσιν   vb fut act ind 3rd pers pl   id.

ἐκκλίνω   vb pres act ind 1st pers sg   id.

ἐκκλινῶ   vb fut act ind 1st pers sg   id.

ἐκκλίνωμεν   vb pres act subj 1st pers pl   id.

ἐκκλίνων   vb pres act part masc nom sg   id.

ἐκκλίνωσιν   vb pres act subj 3rd pers pl   id.

ἐκκλύσει   vb fut act ind 3rd pers sg . . . . ἐκκλύζω

ἐκκόλαμμα   noun neut nom and acc sg

ἐκκομιδήν   noun fem acc sg . . . . ἐκκομιδή

ἐκκοπῇ   vb 2nd aor pass subj 3rd pers sg . . . . ἐκκόπτω

ἐκκοπήσονται   vb fut pass ind 3rd pers pl   id.

ἐκκοπῆτε   vb 2nd aor pass subj 2nd pers pl   id.

ἐκκοπτομένου   vb pres m/p part masc and neut gen sg   id.

ἐκκόπτουσιν   vb pres act ind 3rd pers pl   id.

ἐκκόπτων   vb pres act part masc nom sg   id.

ἐκκόψαι   vb 1st aor act inf   id.

ἐκκόψαισαν   vb 1st aor act opt 3rd pers pl   id.

ἐκκόψας   vb 1st aor act part masc nom sg   id.

ἐκκόψατε   vb 1st aor act impv 2nd pers pl   id.

ἐκκόψειας   vb 1st aor act opt 2nd pers sg   id.

ἐκκόψεις   vb fut act ind 2nd pers sg   id.

ἐκκόψετε   vb fut act ind 2nd pers pl   id.

ἐκκόψῃ   vb 1st aor act subj 3rd pers sg   id.

ἐκκόψον   vb 1st aor act impv 2nd pers sg   id.

ἐκκόψουσιν   vb fut act ind 3rd pers pl . . . . ἐκκόπτω

ἐκκόψω   vb fut act ind 1st pers sg   id.

ἐκκόψωμεν   vb 1st aor act subj 1st pers pl   id.

ἐκκρέμαται   vb pres dep ind 3rd pers sg . . . . ἐκκρέμαμαι

ἐκκρουσθῇ   vb 1st aor pass subj 3rd pers sg . . . . ἐκκρούω

ἐκκύπτον   vb pres act part neut nom and acc sg . . . . . ἐκκύπτω

ἐκκύπτουσα   vb pres act part fem nom sg   id.

ἐκκύπτων   vb pres act part masc nom sg   id.

ἔκλαβε   vb 2nd aor act impv 2nd pers sg . . . . ἐκλαμβάνω

ἐκλάβοι   vb 2nd aor act opt 3rd pers sg   id.

ἔκλαιεν   vb impf act ind 3rd pers sg . . . . κλαίω

ἔκλαιες   vb impf act ind 2nd pers sg   id.

ἐκλαιετε   vb impf act ind 2nd pers pl   id.

ἔκλαιον   vb impf act ind 3rd pers pl   id.

ἐκλαίοσαν   vb impf act ind 3rd pers pl   id.

ἔκλαμπροι   adj masc and fem nom pl . . . . ἔκλαμπρος

ἐκλάμπων   vb pres act part masc nom sg . . . . ἐκλάμπω

ἐκλάμψει   vb fut act ind 3rd pers sg   id.

ἐκλάμψεις   noun fem nom and acc pl . . . . ἔκλαμψις

ἐκλάμψουσιν   vb fut act ind 3rd pers pl . . . . ἐκλάμπω

ἐκλάπην   vb 2nd aor pass ind 1st pers sg . . . . κλέπτω

ἔκλασεν   vb 1st aor act ind 3rd pers sg . . . . κλάω

ἔκλαυσα   vb 1st aor act ind 1st pers sg . . . . κλαίω

ἐκλαυσαμεν   vb 1st aor act ind 1st pers pl   id.

ἔκλαυσαν   vb 1st aor act ind 3rd pers pl   id.

ἔκλαυσας   vb 1st aor act ind 2nd pers sg   id.

ἐκλαύσατε   vb 1st aor act ind 2nd pers pl   id.

ἔκλαυσε(ν)   vb 1st aor act ind 3rd pers sg   id.

ἐκλεγείσης   vb 2nd aor pass part fem gen sg . . . . ἐκλέγω

ἐκλεγέντες   vb 2nd aor pass part masc nom pl   id.

ἐκλέγεσθαι   vb pres m/p inf, 2nd aor mid inf   id.

ἐκλέγεται   vb pres m/p ind 3rd pers sg   id.

ἐκλεγῆναι   vb 2nd aor pass inf   id.

ἐκλεγῶσιν   vb 2nd aor pass subj 3rd pers pl   id.

ἐκλείετο   vb impf m/p ind 3rd pers sg . . . . κλείω

ἐκλείξαι   vb 1st aor act opt 3rd pers sg . . . . ἐκλείχω

ἐκλείξει   vb fut act ind 3rd pers sg   id.

ἐκλείξουσιν   vb fut act ind 3rd pers pl   id.

ἐκλείπει   vb pres act ind 3rd pers sg . . . . ἐκλείπω

ἐκλείπειν   vb pres act inf   id.

ἐκλειπέτω   vb pres act impv 3rd pers sg   id.

ἐκλείπῃ   vb pres act subj 3rd pers sg   id.

ἐκλείπομεν   vb pres act ind 1st pers pl   id.

ἐκλεῖπον   vb pres act part neut nom and acc sg   id.

ἐκλείποντα   vb pres act part masc acc sg   id.

ἐκλείποντας   vb pres act part masc acc pl   id.

ἐκλείποντες   vb pres act part masc nom pl   id.

ἐκλειπούσας   vb pres act part fem acc pl   id.

ἐκλείπουσι(ν)   vb pres act ind 3rd pers pl,

       pres act part masc and neut dat pl   id.

ἐκλείπω   vb pres act ind 1st pers sg   id.

ἐκλείπων   vb pres act part masc nom sg   id.

ἔκλεισαν   vb 1st aor act ind 3rd pers pl . . . . κλείω

ἔκλεισεν   vb 1st aor act ind 3rd pers sg   id.

ἐκλείσθη   vb 1st aor pass ind 3rd pers sg   id.

ἐκλείχεσθαι   vb pres m/p inf . . . . ἐκλείχω

ἐκλείψει noun fem dat sg . . . . ἔκλειψις	ἐκλέψατε vb 1st aor act ind 2nd pers pl . . . . κλέπτω
ἐκλείψει vb fut act ind 3rd pers sg . . . . ἐκλείπω	ἔκλεψεν vb 1st aor act ind 3rd pers sg id.
ἐκλείψειν vb fut act inf id.	ἐκληδονίζετο vb impf m/p ind 3rd pers sg . . . . . . κληδονίζω
ἐκλείψετε vb fut act ind 2nd pers pl id.	ἐκλήθη vb 1st aor pass ind 3rd pers sg . . . . καλέω
ἐκλείψεως noun fem gen sg . . . . ἔκλειψις	ἐκλήθης vb 1st aor pass ind 2nd pers sg id.
ἔκλειψιν noun fem acc sg id.	ἐκλήθησαν vb 1st aor pass ind 3rd pers pl id.
ἔκλειψις noun fem nom sg id.	ἐκληροδότησεν vb 1st aor act ind 3rd pers sg . . κληροδοτέω
ἐκλείψομεν vb fut act ind 1st pers pl . . . . ἐκλείπω	ἐκληρονόμησα vb 1st aor act ind 1st pers sg . . . κληρονομέω
ἐκλείψουσιν vb fut act ind 3rd pers pl id.	ἐκληρονομήσαμεν vb 1st aor act ind 1st pers pl id.
ἐκλείψω vb fut act ind 1st pers sg id.	ἐκληρονόμησαν vb 1st aor act ind 3rd pers pl id.
ἐκλεκτά adj neut nom and acc pl . . . . ἐκλεκτός	ἐκληρονόμησας vb 1st aor act ind 2nd pers sg id.
ἐκλεκταί adj fem nom pl id.	ἐκληρονόμησεν vb 1st aor act ind 3rd pers sg id.
ἐκλεκτάς adj fem acc pl id.	ἐκλίθη vb 1st aor pass ind 3rd pers sg . . . . κλίνω
ἐκλεκτή adj fem nom sg id.	ἐκλίθησαν vb 1st aor pass ind 3rd pers pl id.
ἐκλεκτήν adj fem acc sg id.	ἐκλικμήσει vb fut act ind 3rd pers sg . . . . ἐκλικμάω
ἐκλεκτῆς adj fem gen sg id.	ἐκλιμίαν noun fem acc sg . . . . ἐκλιμία
ἐκλεκτοί adj masc nom pl id.	ἐκλιμπάνον vb pres act part neut nom and acc sg . ἐκλιμπάνω
ἐκλεκτοῖς adj masc and neut dat pl id.	ἔκλινα vb 1st aor act ind 1st pers sg . . . . κλίνω
ἐκλεκτόν adj masc acc sg, neut nom and acc sg id.	ἔκλιναν vb 1st aor act ind 3rd pers pl id.
ἐκλεκτός adj masc nom sg id.	ἐκλίνατε vb 1st aor act ind 2nd pers pl id.
ἐκλεκτοῦ adj masc and neut gen sg id.	ἔκλινεν vb impf act ind 3rd pers sg,
ἐκλεκτούς adj masc acc pl id.	1st aor act ind 3rd pers sg id.
ἐκλεκτῶν adj gen pl id.	ἐκλιπεῖν vb 2nd aor act inf . . . . ἐκλείπω
ἐκλελεγμένη vb perf m/p part fem nom sg . . . . ἐκλέγω	ἐκλιπέτω vb 2nd aor act impv 3rd pers sg id.
ἐκλελειμμένη vb perf m/p part fem nom sg . . . . ἐκλείπω	ἐκλιπέτωσαν vb 2nd aor act impv 3rd pers pl id.
ἐκλελειμμένος vb perf m/p part masc nom sg id.	ἐκλίπῃ vb 2nd aor act subj 3rd pers sg id.
ἐκλέλεκται vb perf m/p ind 3rd pers sg . . . . ἐκλέγω	ἐκλίποι vb 2nd aor act opt 3rd pers sg id.
ἐκλελοίπασιν vb perf act ind 3rd pers pl . . . . ἐκλείπω	ἐκλίποισαν vb 1st aor act opt 3rd pers pl id.
ἐκλέλοιπεν vb perf act ind 3rd pers sg id.	ἐκλιπόντες vb 2nd aor act part masc nom pl id.
ἐκλελοιπέναι vb perf act inf id.	ἐκλίπω vb 2nd aor act subj 1st pers sg id.
ἐκλελοιπότας vb perf act part masc acc pl id.	ἐκλιπών vb 2nd aor act part masc nom sg id.
ἐκλελοχισμένος vb perf m/p part masc nom sg . . . ἐκλοχίζω	ἐκλίπωσιν vb 2nd aor act subj 3rd pers pl id.
ἐκλελυκότα vb perf act part masc acc sg . . . . ἐκλύω	ἐκλογῇ noun fem dat sg . . . . ἐκλογή
ἐκλελύμεθα vb perf m/p ind 1st pers pl id.	ἐκλογῆς noun fem gen sg id.
ἐκλελυμένοι vb perf m/p part masc nom pl id.	ἐκλογιστής noun masc nom sg
ἐκλελυμένοις vb perf m/p part masc and neut dat pl id.	ἐκλογιστίαν noun fem acc sg . . . . ἐκλογιστία
ἐκλελυμένος vb perf m/p part masc nom sg id.	ἐκλοποφόρησας vb 1st aor act ind 2nd pers sg . κλοποφορέω
ἐκλελυμένῳ vb perf m/p part masc and neut dat sg id.	ἐκλύει vb pres act ind 3rd pers sg . . . . ἐκλύω
ἔκλεξαι vb 1st aor mid impv 2nd pers sg . . . . ἐκλέγω	ἐκλύειν vb pres act inf id.
ἐκλεξάμενος vb 1st aor mid part masc nom sg id.	ἐκλύεσθαι vb pres m/p inf id.
ἐκλέξασθαι vb 1st aor mid inf id.	ἐκλύέσθω vb pres m/p impv 3rd pers sg id.
ἐκλέξασθε vb 1st aor mid impv 2nd pers pl id.	ἐκλυέσθωσαν vb pres m/p impv 3rd pers pl id.
ἐκλεξάσθωσαν vb 1st aor mid impv 3rd pers pl id.	ἐκλυθέντας vb 1st aor pass part masc acc pl id.
ἐκλέξεται vb fut mid ind 3rd pers sg id.	ἐκλυθήσεσθε vb fut pass ind 2nd pers pl id.
ἐκλέξῃ vb 1st aor act subj 3rd pers sg,	ἐκλυθήσεται vb fut pass ind 3rd pers sg id.
fut mid ind 2nd pers sg id.	ἐκλυθήσονται vb fut pass ind 3rd pers pl id.
ἐκλέξηται vb 1st aor mid subj 3rd pers sg id.	ἐκλύθητε vb 1st aor pass impv 2nd pers pl id.
ἐκλέξομαι vb fut mid ind 1st pers sg id.	ἐκλυθῶσιν vb 1st aor pass subj 3rd pers pl id.
ἐκλέξω vb fut act ind 1st pers sg id.	ἐκλυόμενος vb pres m/p part masc nom sg id.
ἐκλέξωμαι vb 1st aor mid subj 1st pers sg id.	ἐκλυομένων vb pres m/p part gen pl id.
ἐκλέξωνται vb 1st aor mid subj 3rd pers pl id.	ἐκλύου vb pres m/p impv 2nd pers sg id.
ἔκλεπτον vb impf act ind 1st pers sg and 3rd pers pl . . κλέπτω	ἐκλύουσιν vb pres act ind 3rd pers sg id.
ἐκλευκανθῶσιν vb 1st aor pass subj 3rd pers pl . ἐκλευκαίνω	ἐκλύσατε vb 1st aor act impv 2nd pers pl id.
ἔκλευκον adj acc sg, neut nom sg . . . . ἔκλευκος	ἐκλύσει noun fem dat sg . . . . ἔκλυσις
ἔκλεψαν vb 1st aor act ind 3rd pers pl . . . . κλέπτω	ἐκλύσεις vb fut act ind 2nd pers sg . . . . ἐκλύω
ἔκλεψας vb 1st aor act ind 2nd pers sg id.	ἐκλύσεως noun fem gen sg . . . . ἔκλυσις

ἐκλύσῃς   vb 1st aor act subj 2nd pers sg . . . . ἐκλύω

ἔκλυσιν   noun fem acc sg . . . . ἔκλυσις

ἐκλύτρωσιν   noun fem acc sg . . . . ἐκλύτρωσις

ἐκλύων   vb pres act part masc nom sg . . . . ἐκλύω

ἐκμάξῃ   vb 1st aor act subj 3rd pers sg . . . . ἐκμάσσω

ἐκμάσσονται   vb pres m/p ind 3rd pers pl   id.

ἐκμελιζόμενος   vb pres m/p part masc nom sg . . . . ἐκμελίζω

ἐκμεμαχώς   vb perf act part masc nom sg . . . . ἐκμάσσω

ἐκμεμελετηκότα   vb perf act part masc acc sg . . ἐκμελετάω

ἐκμετρηθήσεται   vb fut pass ind 3rd pers sg . . . . ἐκμετρέω

ἐκμετρήσουσιν   vb fut act ind 3rd pers pl   id.

ἐκμιανθῆναι   vb 1st aor pass inf . . . . ἐκμιαίνω

ἐκμυελιεῖ   vb fut act ind 3rd pers sg . . . . ἐκμυελίζω

ἐκμυκτηριεῖ   vb fut act ind 3rd pers sg . . . . . . ἐκμυκτηρίζω

ἐκνεύοντες   vb pres act part masc nom pl . . . . ἐκνεύω

ἐκνεύσει   vb fut act ind 3rd pers sg   id.

ἔκνευσον   vb 1st aor act impv 2nd pers sg   id.

ἐκνήψατε   vb 1st aor act impv 2nd pers pl . . . . εκνήφω

ἐκνήψει   vb fut act ind 3rd pers sg   id.

ἔκνηψιν   noun fem acc sg . . . . ἔκνηψις

ἔκνηψον   vb 1st aor act impv 2nd pers sg . . . . ἐκνήφω

ἐκνήψουσιν   vb fut act ind 3rd pers pl   id.

ἐκοιλοστάθμησεν   vb 1st aor act ind

     3rd pers sg . . . . κοιλοσταθμέω

ἐκοιμήθη   vb 1st aor pass ind 3rd pers sg . . . . κοιμάω

ἐκοιμήθημεν   vb 1st aor pass ind 1st pers pl   id.

ἐκοιμήθην   vb 1st aor pass ind 1st pers sg   id.

ἐκοιμήθης   vb 1st aor pass ind 2nd pers sg   id.

ἐκοιμήθησαν   vb 1st aor pass ind 3rd pers pl   id.

ἐκοίμισαν   vb 1st aor act ind 3rd pers pl . . . . κοιμίζω

ἐκοίμισεν   vb 1st aor act ind 3rd pers sg   id.

ἐκοιμῶντο   vb impf m/p ind 3rd pers pl . . . . κοιμάω

ἐκοινολογοῦντο   vb impf dep ind

     3rd pers pl . . . . κοινολογέομαι

ἐκοινώνησεν   vb 1st aor act ind 3rd pers sg . . . . κοινωνέω

ἐκοίνωσας   vb 1st aor act ind 2nd pers sg . . . . κοινόω

ἐκολάζοντο   vb impf m/p ind 3rd pers pl . . . . κολάζω

ἐκόλασας   vb 1st aor act ind 2nd pers sg   id.

ἐκολάσθησαν   vb 1st aor pass ind 3rd pers pl   id.

ἐκόλαψεν   vb 1st aor act ind 3rd pers sg . . . . κολάπτω

ἐκολλήθη   vb 1st aor pass ind 3rd pers sg . . . . κολλάω

ἐκολλήθην   vb 1st aor pass ind 1st pers sg   id.

ἐκολλήθησαν   vb 1st aor pass ind 3rd pers pl   id.

ἐκόλλησα   vb 1st aor act ind 1st pers sg   id.

ἐκόλλησεν   vb 1st aor act ind 3rd pers sg   id.

ἐκολλύρισεν   vb 1st aor act ind 3rd pers sg . . . . κολλυρίζω

ἐκολλῶντο   vb impf m/p ind 3rd pers pl . . . . κολλάω

ἐκόμισαν   vb 1st aor act ind 3rd pers pl . . . . κομίζω

ἐκομίσαντο   vb 1st aor mid ind 3rd pers pl   id.

ἐκομίσατο   vb 1st aor mid ind 3rd pers sg   id.

ἐκόμισεν   vb 1st aor act ind 3rd pers sg   id.

ἐκονδύλιζον   vb impf act ind 3rd pers pl . . . . . . κονδυλίζω

ἐκόπασεν   vb 1st aor act ind 3rd pers sg . . . . κοπάζω

ἐκοπίας   vb impf act ind 2nd pers sg . . . . κοπιάω

ἐκοπίασα   vb 1st aor act ind 1st pers sg   id.

ἐκοπιάσαμεν   vb 1st aor act ind 1st pers pl   id.

ἐκοπίασαν   vb 1st aor act ind 3rd pers pl   id.

ἐκοπίασας   vb 1st aor act ind 2nd pers sg   id.

ἐκοπιάσατε   vb 1st aor act ind 2nd pers pl   id.

ἐκοπίασεν   vb 1st aor act ind 3rd pers sg   id.

ἐκοπίων   vb impf act ind 3rd pers pl   id.

ἔκοπτον   vb impf act ind 3rd pers pl . . . . κόπτω

ἐκόπωσας   vb 1st aor act ind 2nd pers sg . . . . κοπόω

ἐκοσμήθη   vb 1st aor pass ind 3rd pers sg . . . . κοσμέω

ἐκοσμήθης   vb 1st aor pass ind 2nd pers sg   id.

ἐκόσμησα   vb 1st aor act ind 1st pers sg   id.

ἐκόσμησεν   vb 1st aor act ind 3rd pers sg   id.

ἐκόσμου   impf m/p ind 2nd pers sg   id.

ἐκούσια   adj neut nom and acc pl . . . . ἑκούσιος

ἑκουσιαζόμενοι   vb pres dep part

     masc nom pl . . . . ἑκουσιάζομαι

ἑκουσιαζόμενος   vb pres dep part masc nom sg   id.

ἑκουσιαζομένους   vb pres dep part masc acc pl   id.

ἑκουσιαζομένῳ   vb pres dep part masc and neut dat sg   id.

ἑκουσιαζομένων   vb pres dep part gen pl   id.

ἑκουσιασθῆναι   vb 1st aor pass inf   id.

ἑκουσιασμοῦ   noun masc gen sg . . . . ἑκουσιασμός

ἑκουσίοις   adj masc and neut dat pl . . . . ἑκούσιος

ἑκούσιον   adj masc acc sg, neut nom and acc sg   id.

ἑκουσίου   adj masc and neut gen sg   id.

ἑκουσίῳ   adj masc and neut dat sg   id.

ἑκουσίων   adj gen pl   id.

ἑκουσίως   adverb

ἐκούφισας   vb 1st aor act ind 2nd pers sg . . . . κουφίζω

ἔκοψα   ▪ vb 1st aor act ind 1st pers sg . . . . κόπτω

ἐκόψαμεν   vb 1st aor act ind 1st pers pl   id.

ἔκοψαν   vb 1st aor act ind 3rd pers pl   id.

ἐκόψαντο   vb 1st aor mid ind 3rd pers pl   id.

ἐκόψατο   vb 1st aor mid ind 3rd pers sg   id.

ἔκοψεν   vb 1st aor act ind 3rd pers sg   id.

ἐκπαιδεῦσαι   vb 1st aor act inf . . . . ἐκπαιδεύω

ἐκπαίζοντες   vb pres act part masc nom pl . . . . . . ἐκπαίζω

ἐκπειράσεις   vb fut act ind 2nd pers sg . . . . ἐκπειράζω

ἐκπειράσῃ   vb 1st aor act subj 3rd pers sg   id.

ἐκπέμπων   vb pres act part masc nom sg . . . . ἐκπέμπω

ἐκπέμψαι   vb 1st aor act inf   id.

ἐκπέμψατε   vb 1st aor act impv 2nd pers pl   id.

ἐκπέμψει   vb fut act ind 3rd pers sg   id.

ἐκτεπηδηκέναι   vb perf act inf . . . . ἐκπηδάω

ἐκτεπιεσμένην   vb perf m/p part fem acc sg . . . . ἐκπιέζω

ἐκπεπορευμένοι   vb perf dep part

     masc nom pl . . . . ἐκπορεύομαι

ἐκπεπορευμένων   vb perf dep part gen pl   id.

ἐκπεπόρευσθε   vb perf dep ind 2nd pers pl   id.

ἐκπεπόρθηκαν vb perf act ind 3rd pers pl . . . . . ἐκπορθέω

ἐκπεπόρνευκεν vb perf act ind 3rd pers sg . . . . ἐκπορνεύω

ἐκπεπτωκότα vb perf act part masc acc sg . . . . . . ἐκπίπτω

ἐκπεριπορεύεται vb pres dep ind

      3rd pers sg . . . . ἐκπεριπορεύομαι

ἐκπέσῃ vb 2nd aor act subj 3rd pers sg . . . . ἐκπίπτω

ἐκπέσοι vb 2nd aor act opt 3rd pers sg   id.

ἐκπεσόν vb 2nd aor act part neut nom and acc sg   id.

ἐκπετάζω vb pres act ind 1st pers sg

ἐκπετάζων vb pres act part masc nom sg . . . . . . ἐκπετάζω

ἐκπετάσαντες vb 1st aor act part masc nom pl   id.

ἐκπετασθέν vb 1st aor pass part neut nom and acc sg id.

ἐκπέτασον vb 1st aor act impv 2nd pers sg   id.

ἐκπετάσω vb fut act ind 1st pers sg . . . . ἐκπετάζω

ἐκπέφευγας vb perf act ind 2nd pers sg . . . . ἐκφεύγω

ἐκπέφευγεν vb perf act ind 3rd pers sg   id.

ἐκπεφευγότες vb perf act part masc nom pl   id.

ἐκπεφευγώς vb perf act part masc nom sg   id.

ἐκπηδήσας vb 1st aor act part masc nom sg . . . . . . ἐκπηδάω

ἐκπηδήσασα vb 1st aor act part fem nom sg   id.

ἐκπηδήσεται vb fut mid ind 3rd pers sg   id.

ἐκπηδήσῃ vb 1st aor act subj 3rd pers sg   id.

ἐκπηδῶν vb pres act part masc nom sg   id.

ἐκπιέζῃς vb pres act subj 2nd pers sg . . . . ἐκπιέζω

ἐκπιεζοῦντες vb pres act part masc nom pl   id.

ἐκπιέζων vb pres act part masc nom sg   id.

ἐκπίνει vb pres act ind 3rd pers sg . . . . ἐκπίνω

ἐκπίονται vb fut mid ind 3rd pers pl   id.

ἐκπλαγείς vb 2nd aor pass part masc nom sg . . . . ἐκπλήσσω

ἐκπλαγέντες vb 2nd aor pass part masc nom pl   id.

ἐκπλαγῇς vb 2nd aor pass subj 2nd pers sg   id.

ἐκπληροῦν vb pres act inf . . . . ἐκπληρόω

ἐκπληρῶσαι vb 1st aor act inf   id.

ἐκπληρώσειν vb fut act inf   id.

ἐκπλήρωσιν noun fem acc sg . . . . ἐκπλήρωσις

ἐκπλήσσεσθαι vb pres m/p inf . . . . ἐκπλήσσω

ἐκπλυνεῖ vb fut act ind 3rd pers sg . . . . ἐκπλύνω

ἐκποιεῖ vb pres act ind 3rd pers sg . . . . ἐκποιέω

ἐκποιῇ vb pres act subj 3rd pers sg   id.

ἐκποιήσει vb fut act ind 3rd pers sg   id.

ἐκπολεμῆσαι vb 1st aor act inf . . . . ἐκπολεμέω

ἐκπολεμήσαντες vb 1st aor act part masc nom pl   id.

ἐκπολεμήσας vb 1st aor act part masc nom sg   id.

ἐκπολεμήσομεν vb fut act ind 1st pers pl   id.

ἐκπολεμήσωμεν vb 1st aor act subj 1st pers pl   id.

ἐκπολιορκησάτωσαν vb 1st aor act impv

      3rd pers pl . . . . ἐκπολιορκέω

ἐκπορεύεσθαι vb pres dep inf . . . . ἐκπορεύομαι

ἐκπορεύεσθε vb pres dep impv 2nd pers pl,

    pres dep ind 2nd pers pl   id.

ἐκπορεύεσθω vb pres dep impv 3rd pers sg   id.

ἐκπορεύεται vb pres dep ind 3rd pers sg   id.

ἐκπορεύῃ vb pres dep ind 2nd pers sg,

    pres dep subj 2nd pers sg . . . . ἐκπορεύομαι

ἐκπορεύομαι vb pres dep ind 1st pers sg   id.

ἐκπορευόμενα vb pres dep part neut nom and acc pl   id.

ἐκπορευόμεναι vb pres dep part fem nom pl   id.

ἐκπορευομένη vb pres dep part fem nom sg   id.

ἐκπορευομένης vb pres dep part fem gen sg   id.

ἐκπορευόμενοι vb pres dep part masc nom pl   id.

ἐκπορευομένοις vb pres dep part masc and neut dat pl   id.

ἐκπορευόμενον vb pres dep part masc acc sg,

    neut nom and acc sg   id.

ἐκπορευομένου vb pres dep part masc and neut gen sg   id.

ἐκπορευομένους vb pres dep part masc acc pl   id.

ἐκπορευομένῳ vb pres dep part masc and neut dat sg   id.

ἐκπορευομένων vb pres dep part gen pl   id.

ἐκπορεύονται vb pres dep ind 3rd pers pl   id.

ἐκπορεύσῃ vb 1st aor mid subj 2nd pers sg   id.

ἐκπορθεῖσθαι vb pres m/p inf . . . . ἐκπορθέω

ἐκπορθήσας vb 1st aor act part masc nom sg   id.

ἐκπορνεύειν vb pres act inf . . . . ἐκπορνεύω

ἐκπορνεύετε vb pres act ind 2nd pers pl   id.

ἐκπορνεύουσα vb pres act part fem nom sg   id.

ἐκπορνευούσῃ vb pres act part fem dat sg   id.

ἐκπορνεύουσιν vb pres act ind 3rd pers pl   id.

ἐκπορνεῦσαι vb 1st aor act inf   id.

ἐκπορνεύσασι vb 1st aor act part masc and neut dat pl   id.

ἐκπορνεύσει vb fut act ind 3rd pers sg   id.

ἐκπορνεύσουσιν vb fut act ind 3rd pers pl   id.

ἐκπορνεύσωσιν vb 1st aor act subj 3rd pers pl   id.

ἐκπρεπεῖς adj masc and fem nom and acc pl . . . . . ἐκπρεπής

ἐκπρεπέσι adj dat pl   id.

ἐκπρεπῆ adj masc and fem acc sg   id.

ἐκπρίου vb pres m/p impv 2nd pers sg . . . . ἐκπρίω

ἐκπρίσας vb 1st aor act part masc nom sg   id.

ἐκπυροῦν vb pres act inf . . . . ἐκπυρόω

ἐκπυρωθέντων vb 1st aor pass part masc and neut gen pl id.

ἐκραγείη vb 2nd aor pass opt 3rd pers sg . . . . . . ἐκρήγνυμι

ἔκραζον vb impf act ind 3rd pers pl . . . . κράζω

ἔκραξας vb 1st aor act ind 2nd pers sg   id.

ἔκραξεν vb 1st aor act ind 3rd pers sg   id.

ἐκραταιοῦτε vb impf act ind 2nd pers pl . . . . . . κραταιόω

ἐκραταιοῦτο vb impf m/p ind 3rd pers sg   id.

ἐκραταιώθη vb 1st aor pass ind 3rd pers sg   id.

ἐκραταιώθην vb 1st aor pass ind 1st pers sg   id.

ἐκραταιώθησαν vb 1st aor pass ind 3rd pers pl   id.

ἐκραταίωσα vb 1st aor act ind 1st pers sg   id.

ἐκραταίωσαν vb 1st aor act ind 3rd pers pl   id.

ἐκραταίωσας vb 1st aor act ind 2nd pers sg   id.

ἐκραταίωσεν vb 1st aor act ind 3rd pers sg   id.

ἐκράτει vb impf act ind 3rd pers sg . . . . κρατέω

ἐκρατήθη vb 1st aor pass ind 3rd pers sg   id.

ἐκρατήθησαν vb 1st aor pass ind 3rd pers pl   id.

ἐκράτησα vb 1st aor act ind 1st pers sg . . . . κρατέω
ἐκρατήσαμεν vb 1st aor act ind 1st pers pl   id.
ἐκράτησαν vb 1st aor act ind 3rd pers pl   id.
ἐκράτησας vb 1st aor act ind 2nd pers sg   id.
ἐκράτησε(ν) vb 1st aor act ind 3rd pers sg   id.
ἐκραύγασεν vb 1st aor act ind 3rd pers sg . . . . . . κραυγάζω
ἐκρεανόμησεν vb 1st aor act ind 3rd pers sg . . . κρεανομέω
ἐκρέμασα vb 1st aor act ind 1st pers sg . . . . κρεμάζω
ἐκρεμάσαμεν vb 1st aor act ind 1st pers pl   id.
ἐκρέμασαν vb 1st aor act ind 3rd pers pl   id.
ἐκρέμασεν vb 1st aor act ind 3rd pers sg   id.
ἐκρεμάσθη vb 1st aor pass ind 3rd pers sg   id.
ἐκρεμάσθησαν vb 1st aor pass ind 3rd pers pl   id.
ἐκρεριμμένην vb perf m/p part fem acc sg . . . . ἐκρίπτω
ἔκρηγμα noun neut nom and acc sg
ἐκρήμνισαν vb 1st aor act ind 3rd pers pl . . . . . . κρτμνίζω
ἐκριζοῖ vb pres act ind 3rd pers sg . . . . ἐκριζόω
ἐκριζοῦν vb pres act inf   id.
ἐκριζωθήσεται vb fut pass ind 3rd pers sg   id.
ἐκριζῶσαι vb 1st aor act inf   id.
ἐκριζωτής noun masc nom sg
ἐκρίθη vb 1st aor pass ind 3rd pers sg . . . . κρίνω
ἐκρίθησαν vb 1st aor pass ind 3rd pers pl   id.
ἔκρινα vb 1st aor act ind 3rd pers sg   id.
ἐκρίναμεν vb 1st aor act ind 1st pers pl   id.
ἔκριναν vb 1st aor act ind 3rd pers pl   id.
ἔκρινας vb 1st aor act ind 2nd pers sg   id.
ἐκρίνατε vb 1st aor act ind 2nd pers pl   id.
ἔκρινεν vb 1st aor act ind 3rd pers sg,
    impf act ind 3rd pers sg   id.
ἔκρινον vb impf act ind 3rd pers pl   id.
ἐκρίνοντο vb impf m/p ind 3rd pers pl   id.
ἐκρίνοσαν vb impf act ind 3rd pers pl   id.
ἐκριπτεῖ vb pres act ind 3rd pers sg . . . . ἐκριπτέω
ἐκριφήσεται vb fut pass ind 3rd pers sg . . . . ἐκρίπτω
ἐκρίψας vb 1st aor act part masc nom sg   id.
ἐκρίψειν vb fut act inf   id.
ἐκρότησαν vb 1st aor act ind 3rd pers pl . . . . κροτέω
ἐκρότησας vb 1st aor act ind 2nd pers sg   id.
ἔκρουσαν vb 1st aor act ind 3rd pers pl . . . . κρούω
ἔκρουσε vb 1st aor act ind 3rd pers sg   id.
ἐκρύβη vb 2nd aor pass ind 3rd pers sg . . . . κρύπτω
ἐκρύβην vb 2nd aor pass ind 1st pers sg   id.
ἐκρύβης vb 2nd aor pass ind 2nd pers sg   id.
ἐκρύβησαν vb 2nd aor pass ind 3rd pers pl   id.
ἐκρυήσεται vb fut mid ind 3rd pers sg . . . . ἐκρέω
ἔκρυσις noun fem nom sg
ἔκρυψα vb 1st aor act ind 1st pers sg . . . . κρύπτω
ἔκρυψαν vb 1st aor act ind 3rd pers pl   id.
ἔκρυψας vb 1st aor act ind 2nd pers sg   id.
ἔκρυψεν vb 1st aor act ind 3rd pers sg   id.

ἐκσεσορκισμένα vb perf mid part
    neut nom and acc pl . . . . ἐκσαρκίζω
ἐκσεσοβημένοι vb perf m/p part masc nom pl . . . . ἐκσοβέω
ἐκσιφωνισθείη vb 1st aor pass opt 3rd pers sg . . ἐκσιφωνίζω
ἐκσπάσαι vb 1st aor act inf . . . . ἐκσπάω
ἐκσπάσας vb 1st aor act part masc nom sg   id.
ἐκσπάσατε vb 1st aor act impv 2nd pers pl   id.
ἐκσπάσει vb fut act ind 3rd pers sg   id.
ἐκσπάσῃ vb 1st aor act subj 3rd pers sg   id.
ἐκσπασθῆναι vb 1st aor pass inf   id.
ἐκσπασθήσονται vb fut pass ind 3rd pers pl   id.
ἐκσπασθῶσιν vb 1st aor pass subj 3rd pers pl   id.
ἐκσπάσω vb fut act ind 1st pers sg   id.
ἐκσπεσωμεν vb 1st aor act subj 1st pers pl   id.
ἐκσπερματιεῖ vb fut act ind 3rd pers sg . . . . ἐκσπερματίζω
ἐκσπονδυλιζόμενος vb pres dep part
    masc nom sg . . . . ἐκσπονδυλίζομαι
ἐκστάσει noun fem dat sg . . . . ἔκστασις
ἐκστάσεως noun fem gen sg   id.
ἔκστασιν noun fem acc sg   id.
ἔκστασις noun fem nom sg   id.
ἐκστῇς vb 2nd aor act subj 2nd pers sg . . . . ἐξίστημι
ἐκστήσει vb fut act ind 3rd pers sg   id.
ἐκστήσεται vb fut mid ind 3rd pers sg   id.
ἐκστήσῃ vb fut mid ind 2nd pers sg   id.
ἐκστήσονται vb fut mid ind 3rd pers pl   id.
ἐκστήσω vb fut act ind 1st pers sg   id.
ἔκστητε vb 2nd aor act impv 2nd pers pl   id.
ἐκστρατεύει vb pres act ind 3rd pers sg . . . . . ἐκστρατεύω
ἐκστρέφετε vb pres act ind 2nd pers pl . . . . ἐκστρέφω
ἐκστρέψει vb fut act ind 3rd pers sg   id.
ἐκσυριεῖ vb fut act ind 3rd pers sg . . . . ἐκσυρίζω
ἐκταγείσης vb 2nd aor pass part fem gen sg . . . . . . ἐκτάσσω
ἐκταθήσεται vb fut pass ind 3rd pers sg . . . . . . ἐκτείνω
ἐκτάξαντα vb 1st aor act part masc acc sg . . . . . . ἐκτάσσω
ἐκταρασσόμενοι vb pres m/p part
    masc nom pl . . . . ἐκταράσσω
ἐκταράσσοντες vb pres act part masc nom pl   id.
ἐκτάσει noun fem dat sg . . . . ἔκτασις
ἐκτάσεως noun fem gen sg   id.
ἐκτάσσοντα vb pres act part masc acc sg . . . . ἐκτάσσω
ἐκτεθέν vb 1st aor pass part neut nom and acc sg . . ἐκτίθημι
ἐκτεθέντος vb 1st aor pass part masc and neut gen sg   id.
ἐκτεθλιμμένον vb perf m/p part
    neut nom and acc sg . . . . ἐκθλίβω
ἐκτεῖναι vb 1st aor act inf . . . . ἐκτείνω
ἐκτείναντες vb 1st aor act part masc nom pl   id.
ἐκτείνας vb 1st aor act part masc nom sg   id.
ἐκτείνασα vb 1st aor act part fem nom sg   id.
ἐκτείνει vb pres act ind 3rd pers sg   id.
ἐκτείνειν vb pres act inf   id.
ἐκτείνεται vb pres m/p ind 3rd pers sg   id.

ἐκτείνῃ   vb pres act subj 3rd pers sg,

     1st aor act subj 3rd pers sg .... ἐκτείνω

ἐκτείνῃς   vb pres act subj 2nd pers sg,

     1st aor act subj 2nd pers sg   id.

ἐκτείνητε   vb pres act subj 2nd pers pl,

     1st aor act subj 2nd pers pl   id.

ἔκτεινον   vb 1st aor act impv 2nd pers sg   id.

ἐκτείνοντες   vb pres act part masc nom pl   id.

ἐκτείνου   vb pres m/p impv 2nd pers sg   id.

ἐκτείνω   vb pres act subj 1st pers sg,

     1st aor act subj 1st pers sg   id.

ἐκτείνων   vb pres act part masc nom sg   id.

ἐκτείνωσιν   vb pres act subj 3rd pers pl,

     1st aor act subj 3rd pers pl   id.

ἐκτείσει   vb fut act ind 3rd pers sg .... ἐκτίνω

ἐκτέκῃ   vb 2nd aor act subj 3rd pers sg .... ἐκτίκτω

ἐκτελέσαι   vb 1st aor act inf,

     1st aor act opt 3rd pers sg .... ἐκτελέω

ἐκτεμεῖν   vb 2nd aor act inf .... ἐκτέμνω

ἐκτέμνεις   vb pres act ind 2nd pers sg   id.

ἐκτεμών   vb 2nd aor act part masc nom sg   id.

ἐκτενεῖ   vb fut act ind 3rd pers sg .... ἐκτείνω

ἐκτενεία   noun fem dat sg .... ἐκτένεια

ἐκτενεῖς   vb fut act ind 2nd pers sg .... ἐκτείνω

ἐκτενές   adj neut nom and acc sg .... ἐκτενής

ἐκτενῆ   adj masc and fem acc sg   id.

ἐκτενίαν   noun fem acc sg .... ἐκτενία

ἐκτενίας   noun fem gen sg   id.

ἐκτενῶ   vb fut act ind 1st pers sg .... ἐκτείνω

ἐκτενῶς   adverb

ἐκτεταγμένοι   vb perf m/p part masc nom pl ..... ἐκτάσσω

ἐκτέτακα   vb perf act ind 1st pers sg .... ἐκτείνω

ἐκτεταμέναι   vb perf m/p part fem nom pl   id.

ἐκτεταμένη   vb perf m/p part fem nom sg   id.

ἐκτεταμένῃ   vb perf m/p part fem dat sg   id.

ἐκτεταμένον   vb perf m/p part neut nom and acc sg   id.

ἐκτετελεκότες   vb perf act part masc nom pl ..... ἐκτελέω

ἐκτετιναγμένοι   vb perf m/p part masc nom pl .. ἐκτινάσσω

ἐκτετιναγμένος   vb perf m/p part masc nom sg   id.

ἐκτετιναγμένων   vb perf m/p part gen pl   id.

ἐκτετυπωμένα   vb perf m/p part

     neut nom and acc pl .... ἐκτυπόω

ἐκτετυπωμένοι   vb perf m/p part masc nom pl   id.

ἐκτετύφλωνται   vb perf m/p ind 3rd pers pl ..... ἐκτυφλόω

ἔκτη   adj fem nom sg .... ἔκτος

ἔκτῃ   adj fem dat sg   id.

ἐκτήκει   vb pres act ind 3rd pers sg .... ἐκτήκω

ἐκτήκουσαν   vb pres act part fem acc sg   id.

ἔκτην   adj fem acc sg .... ἔκτος

ἐκτησάμην   vb 1st aor mid ind 1st pers sg .... κτάομαι

ἐκτήσαντο   vb 1st aor mid ind 3rd pers pl   id.

ἐκτήσατο   vb 1st aor mid ind 3rd pers sg   id.

ἐκτήσω   vb 1st aor mid ind 2nd pers sg .... κτάομαι

ἐκτίθεμαι   vb pres m/p ind 1st pers sg .... ἐκτίθημι

ἐκτιθέσθωσαν   vb pres m/p impv 3rd pers pl   id.

ἐκτῖλαι   vb 1st aor act opt 3rd pers sg .... ἐκτίλλω

ἐκτῖλαι   vb 1st aor act inf   id.

ἐκτίλατε   vb 1st aor act impv 2nd pers pl   id.

ἐκτιλήσεται   vb fut mid ind 3rd pers sg   id.

ἐκτιλήσονται   vb fut mid ind 3rd pers pl   id.

ἐκτίλλω   vb pres act ind 1st pers sg   id.

ἐκτίλω   vb 1st aor act subj 1st pers sg   id.

ἐκτιναγμός   noun masc nom sg

ἐκτινάξαι   vb 1st aor mid impv 2nd pers sg .... ἐκτινάσσω

ἐκτινάξαι   vb 1st aor act opt 3rd pers sg   id.

ἐκτινάξαντι   vb 1st aor act part masc and neut dat sg   id.

ἐκτινάξαντος   vb 1st aor act part masc and neut gen sg   id.

ἐκτινάξατε   vb 1st aor act impv 2nd pers pl   id.

ἐκτινάξει   vb fut act ind 3rd pers sg   id.

ἐκτινάξω   vb fut act ind 1st pers sg   id.

ἐκτινάσσεται   vb pres m/p ind 3rd pers sg   id.

ἐκτινάσσοντες   vb pres act part masc nom pl   id.

ἐκτιναχθήσομαι   vb fut pass ind 1st pers sg   id.

ἔκτισα   vb 1st aor act ind 1st pers sg .... κτίζω

ἔκτισαν   vb 1st aor act ind 3rd pers pl   id.

ἔκτισας   vb 1st aor act ind 2nd pers sg   id.

ἔκτισεν   vb 1st aor act ind 3rd pers sg   id.

ἐκτίσθη   vb 1st aor pass ind 3rd pers sg   id.

ἐκτίσθης   vb 1st aor pass ind 2nd pers sg   id.

ἐκτίσθησαν   vb 1st aor pass ind 3rd pers pl   id.

ἐκτισμένῃ   vb perf m/p part fem dat sg   id.

ἐκτισμένην   vb perf m/p part fem acc sg   id.

ἔκτισται   vb perf m/p ind 3rd pers sg   id.

ἐκτοκιεῖς   vb fut act ind 2nd pers sg .... ἐκτοκίζω

ἐκτομίαν   noun masc acc sg .... ἐκτομίας

ἔκτον   adj masc acc sg, neut nom and acc sg .... ἔκτος

ἕκτος   adj masc nom sg   id.

ἐκτός   preposition

ἔκτου   adj masc and neut gen sg .... ἔκτος

ἐκτραφέντα   vb 2nd aor pass part

     neut nom and acc pl .... ἐκτρέφω

ἐκτραφέντων   vb 2nd aor pass part

     masc and neut gen pl   id.

ἐκτρέπων   vb pres act part masc nom sg .... ἐκτρέπω

ἐκτρέφει   vb pres act ind 3rd pers sg .... ἐκτρέφω

ἐκτρίβει   vb pres act ind 3rd pers sg .... ἐκτρίβω

ἐκτριβέτω   vb pres act impv 3rd pers sg   id.

ἐκτριβῇ   noun fem dat sg .... ἐκτριβή

ἐκτριβῇ   vb 2nd aor pass subj 3rd pers sg .... ἐκτρίβω

ἐκτριβῆναι   vb 2nd aor pass inf   id.

ἐκτριβῆς   vb 2nd aor pass subj 2nd pers sg   id.

ἐκτριβήσεσθε   vb fut pass ind 2nd pers pl   id.

ἐκτριβήσεται   vb fut pass ind 3rd pers sg   id.

ἐκτριβήσῃ   vb fut pass ind 2nd pers sg   id.

ἐκτριβήσομαι vb fut pass ind 1st pers sg	ἐκτρίβω	
ἐκτρίβητε vb 2nd aor pass impv 2nd pers pl	id.	
ἐκτρίβοντες vb pres act part masc nom pl	id.	
ἐκτριβῶμεν vb 2nd aor pass subj 1st pers pl	id.	
ἐκτριβῶσιν vb 2nd aor pass subj 3rd pers pl	id.	
ἐκτρῖψαι vb 1st aor act inf	id.	
ἐκτρίψει vb fut act ind 3rd pers sg	id.	
ἐκτρίψεις vb fut act ind 2nd pers sg	id.	
ἐκτρίψῃ vb 1st aor act subj 3rd pers sg	id.	
ἐκτρίψητε vb 1st aor act subj 2nd pers pl	id.	
ἔκτριψον vb 1st aor act impv 2nd pers sg	id.	
ἐκτρίψουσιν vb fut act ind 3rd pers pl	id.	
ἐκτρίψω vb fut act ind 1st pers sg	id.	
ἐκτρίψωμεν vb 1st aor act subj 1st pers pl	id.	
ἐκτρυγήσεις vb fut act ind 2nd pers sg	ἐκτρυγάω	
ἐκτρώγων vb pres act part masc nom sg	ἐκτρώγω	
ἔκτρωμα noun neut nom and acc sg		
ἐκτύπωμα noun neut nom and acc sg		
ἐκτυπώσεις vb fut act ind 2nd pers sg	ἐκτυπόω	
ἐκτύπωσιν noun fem acc sg	ἐκτύπωσις	
ἐκτυφλοῖ vb pres act ind 3rd pers sg	ἐκτυφλόω	
ἐκτυφλούμενος vb pres m/p part masc nom sg	id.	
ἐκτυφλωθήσεται vb fut pass ind 3rd pers sg	id.	
ἐκτυφλώσῃ vb 1st aor act subj 3rd pers sg	id.	
ἕκτῳ adj masc and neut dat sg	ἕκτος	
ἐκύκλευσαν vb 1st aor act ind 3rd pers pl	κυκλεύω	
ἐκύκλου noun masc gen sg	κύκλος	
ἐκύκλουν vb impf act ind 3rd pers pl	κυκλόω	
ἐκυκλώθη vb 1st aor pass ind 3rd pers sg	id.	
ἐκύκλωσα vb 1st aor act ind 1st pers sg	id.	
ἐκυκλώσαμεν vb 1st aor act ind 1st pers pl	id.	
ἐκύκλωσαν vb 1st aor act ind 3rd pers pl	id.	
ἐκύκλωσεν vb 1st aor act ind 3rd pers sg	id.	
ἐκύλισαν vb 1st aor act ind 3rd pers pl	κυλίω	
ἐκύομεν vb impf act ind 1st pers pl	κύω	
ἐκυρίευον vb impf act ind 3rd pers pl	κυριεύω	
ἐκυρίευσαν vb 1st aor act ind 3rd pers pl	id.	
ἐκυριεύσατε vb 1st aor act ind 2nd pers pl	id.	
ἐκυρίευσε(ν) vb 1st aor act ind 3rd pers sg	id.	
ἐκυρώθη vb 1st aor pass ind 3rd pers sg	κυρόω	
ἐκύρωσας vb 1st aor act ind 2nd pers sg	id.	
ἐκύρωσεν vb 1st aor act ind 3rd pers sg	id.	
ἔκυψαν vb 1st aor act ind 3rd pers pl	κύπτω	
ἔκυψεν vb 1st aor act ind 3rd pers sg	id.	
ἔκφαινε vb pres act impv 2nd pers sg	ἐκφαίνω	
ἐκφαίνει vb pres act ind 3rd pers sg	id.	
ἐκφαινομένης vb pres m/p part fem gen sg	id.	
ἐκφαίνων vb pres act part masc nom sg	id.	
ἐκφᾶναι vb 1st aor act inf	id.	
ἐκφανεῖ vb fut act ind 3rd pers sg	id.	
ἐκφανῶ vb fut act ind 1st pers sg	id.	
ἐκφάνωσιν vb 2nd aor act subj 3rd pers pl	id.	

ἐκφαυλίσαντα vb 1st aor act part masc acc sg . .	ἐκφαυλίζω	
ἐκφέρει vb pres act ind 3rd pers sg	ἐκφέρω	
ἐκφέρειν vb pres act inf	id.	
ἐκφέρετε vb pres act impv 2nd pers pl	id.	
ἐκφέροντα vb pres act part neut nom and acc pl	id.	
ἐκφέροντες vb pres act part masc nom pl	id.	
ἐκφέρων vb pres act part masc nom sg	id.	
ἐκφεύγει vb pres act ind 3rd pers sg	ἐκφεύγω	
ἐκφευγέτωσαν vb pres act impv 3rd pers pl	id.	
ἐκφεύξεσθαι vb fut mid inf	id.	
ἐκφεύξεται vb fut mid ind 3rd pers sg	id.	
ἐκφεύξῃ vb fut mid ind 2nd pers sg	id.	
ἐκφεύξομαι vb fut mid ind 1st pers sg	id.	
ἐκφεύξονται vb fut mid ind 3rd pers pl	id.	
ἐκφλεγομένη vb pres m/p part fem nom sg	ἐκφλέγω	
ἐκφοβεῖς vb pres act ind 2nd pers sg	ἐκφοβέω	
ἐκφοβήσασα vb 1st aor act part fem nom sg	id.	
ἔκφοβος adj masc nom sg		
ἐκφοβοῦντα vb pres act part neut nom and acc pl . .	ἐκφοβέω	
ἐκφοβῶν vb pres act part masc nom sg	id.	
ἐκφοράν noun fem acc sg	ἐκφορά	
ἐκφόρια noun neut nom and acc pl	ἐκφόριον	
ἐκφυγεῖν vb 2nd aor act inf	ἐκφεύγω	
ἐκφύγῃ vb 2nd aor act subj 3rd pers sg	id.	
ἐκφυγῆς noun fem gen sg	ἐκφυγή	
ἐκφύγῃς vb 2nd aor act subj 2nd pers sg	ἐκφεύγω	
ἐκφυγόντα vb 2nd aor act part neut nom and acc pl	id.	
ἐκφύσα vb pres act impv 2nd pers sg	ἐκφυσάω	
ἐκφυσῆσαι vb 1st aor act inf	id.	
ἐκφυσήσω vb fut act ind 1st pers sg	id.	
ἐκφυσῶν vb pres act part masc nom sg	id.	
ἐκφωνήσας vb 1st aor act part masc nom sg	ἐκφωνέω	
ἐκχέαι vb 1st aor act inf	ἐκχέω	
ἔκχεε vb pres act impv 2nd pers sg	id.	
ἐκχέει vb pres act ind 3rd pers sg	id.	
ἐκχεεῖ vb fut act ind 3rd pers sg	id.	
ἐκχέειν vb pres act inf	id.	
ἐκχεεῖς vb fut act ind 2nd pers sg	id.	
ἐκχεεῖτε vb fut act ind 2nd pers pl	id.	
ἐκχέετε vb pres act ind 2nd pers pl	id.	
ἐκχέῃ vb pres act subj 3rd pers sg	id.	
ἐκχέῃς vb pres act subj 2nd pers sg	id.	
ἐκχέητε vb pres act subj 2nd pers pl	id.	
ἐκχεῖσθαι vb pres m/p inf	id.	
ἔκχεον vb 1st aor act impv 2nd pers sg	id.	
ἐκχέοντα vb pres act part masc acc sg	id.	
ἐκχέοντος vb pres act part masc and neut gen sg	id.	
ἐκχεόντων vb pres act part masc and neut gen pl	id.	
ἐκχέουσα vb pres act part fem nom sg	id.	
ἐκχέουσαι vb pres act part fem nom pl	id.	
ἐκχεούσης vb pres act part fem gen sg	id.	
ἐκχέουσιν vb pres act ind 3rd pers pl	id.	

ἐκχεοῦσιν	vb fut act ind 3rd pers pl	ἐκχέω
ἐκχέω	vb pres act ind 1st pers sg	id.
ἐκχεῶ	vb fut act ind 1st pers sg	id.
ἐκχέων	vb pres act part masc nom sg	id.
ἐκχέωσιν	vb pres act subj 3rd pers pl	id.
ἐκχυθέντες	vb 1st aor pass part masc nom pl	id.
ἐκχυθέντος	vb 1st aor pass part masc and neut gen sg	id.
ἐκχυθῇς	vb 1st aor pass subj 2nd pers sg	id.
ἐκχυθήσεται	vb fut pass ind 3rd pers sg	id.
ἐκχυθήσονται	vb fut pass ind 3rd pers pl	id.
ἐκχύσεως	noun fem gen sg	ἔκχυσις
ἔκχυσις	noun fem nom sg	
ἐκχωρείτω	vb pres act impv 3rd pers sg	ἐκχωρέω
ἐκχωρήσατε	vb 1st aor act impv 2nd pers pl	id.
ἐκχώρησον	vb 1st aor act impv 2nd pers sg	id.
ἐκψύξει	vb fut act ind 3rd pers sg	ἐκψύχω
ἐκωθωνίζοντο	vb impf dep ind 3rd pers pl	κωθωνίζομαι
ἐκωλύθη	vb 1st aor pass ind 3rd pers sg	κωλύω
ἐκωλύθησαν	vb 1st aor pass ind 3rd pers pl	id.
ἐκώλυον	vb impf act ind 3rd pers pl	id.
ἐκωλύοντο	vb impf m/p ind 3rd pers pl	id.
ἐκώλυσα	vb 1st aor act ind 1st pers sg	id.
ἐκώλυσας	vb 1st aor act ind 2nd pers sg	id.
ἐκώλυσεν	vb 1st aor act ind 3rd pers sg	id.
ἑκών	adj masc nom sg	
ἐκώφευσαν	vb 1st aor act ind 3rd pers pl	κωφεύω
ἐκωφώθην	vb 1st aor pass ind 1st pers sg	κωφόω
Ελα	pr noun	
ἔλαβαν	vb 2nd aor act ind 3rd pers pl	λαμβάνω
ἔλαβε(ν)	vb 2nd aor act ind 3rd pers sg	id.
ἔλαβες	vb 2nd aor act ind 2nd pers sg	id.
ἐλάβετε	vb 2nd aor act ind 2nd pers pl	id.
ἐλάβετο	vb 2nd aor mid ind 3rd pers sg	id.
ἐλάβομεν	vb 2nd aor act ind 1st pers pl	id.
ἔλαβον	vb 2nd aor act ind 1st pers sg and 3rd pers pl	id.
ἐλάβοντο	vb 2nd aor mid ind 3rd pers pl	id.
ἐλάβοσαν	vb 2nd aor act ind 3rd pers pl	id.
ἔλαθεν	vb 2nd aor act ind 3rd pers sg	λανθάνω
ἔλαθες	vb 2nd aor act ind 2nd pers sg	id.
ἔλαθον	vb 2nd aor act ind 3rd pers pl	id.
ἐλαία	noun fem nom sg	
ἐλαίᾳ	noun fem dat sg	ἐλαία
ἐλαῖαι	noun fem nom pl	
ἐλαιαλογήσῃς	vb 1st aor act subj 3rd pers sg	ἐλαιολογέω
ἐλαίαν	noun fem acc sg	ἐλαία
ἐλαίας	noun fem gen sg and acc pl	ἐλαία
ἐλάϊνον	adj masc acc sg, neut nom and acc sg	ἐλάϊνος
ἔλαιον	noun neut nom and acc sg	
ἐλαίου	noun neut gen sg	ἔλαιον
ἐλαίῳ	noun neut dat sg	id.
ἐλαίων	noun neut gen pl	id.
ἐλαιῶν	noun fem gen pl	ἐλαία

ἐλαιῶνα	noun masc acc sg	ἐλαιών
ἐλαιῶνας	noun masc acc pl	id.
ἐλαιώνων	noun masc gen pl	id.
ἐλάλει	vb impf act ind 3rd pers sg	λαλέω
ἐλαλήθη	vb 1st aor pass ind 3rd pers sg	id.
ἐλάλησα	vb 1st aor act ind 1st pers sg	id.
ἐλαλήσαμεν	vb 1st aor act ind 1st pers pl	id.
ἐλάλησαν	vb 1st aor act ind 3rd pers pl	id.
ἐλάλησας	vb 1st aor act ind 2nd pers sg	id.
ἐλαλήσατε	vb 1st aor act ind 2nd pers pl	id.
ἐλάλησε(ν)	vb 1st aor act ind 3rd pers sg	id.
ἐλάλουν	vb impf act ind 1st pers sg and 3rd pers pl	id.
ἐλάμβανεν	vb impf act ind 3rd pers sg	λαμβάνω
ἐλαμβάνετε	vb impf act ind 2nd pers pl	id.
ἐλάμβανον	vb impf act ind 3rd pers pl	id.
ἐλαμβάνοσαν	vb impf act ind 3rd pers pl	id.
Ελαμι	pr noun	
ἔλαμψαν	vb 1st aor act ind 3rd pers pl	λάμπω
ἐλάξευσα	vb 1st aor act ind 1st pers sg	λαξεύω
ἐλάξευσεν	vb 1st aor act ind 3rd pers sg	id.
Ελασα	pr noun	
ἐλάσεις	vb fut act ind 2nd pers sg	ἐλαύνω
ἔλασμα	noun masc nom sg	
ἐλάσσονι	comp adj masc and neut dat sg	ἐλάσσων
ἐλασσονοῦσι	vb pres act ind 3rd pers pl	ἐλασσονόω
ἐλασσούμενον	vb pres m/p part masc acc sg	ἐλασσόω
ἐλασσούμενος	vb pres m/p part masc nom sg	id.
ἐλασσουμένῳ	vb pres m/p part masc and neut dat sg	id.
ἐλάσσω	comp adj masc and fem acc sg	ἐλάσσων
ἐλάσσων	comp adj masc and fem nom sg	id.
ἐλατά	adj neut nom and acc pl	ἐλατός
ἐλάται	noun fem nom pl	ἐλάτη
ἐλαταῖς	noun fem dat pl	id.
ἐλατάς	noun fem acc pl	id.
ἐλάτης	noun fem gen sg	id.
ἐλατίνους	adj masc acc pl	ἐλάτινος
ἐλατομήθη	vb 1st aor pass ind 3rd pers sg	λατομέω
ἐλατόμησας	vb 1st aor act ind 2nd pers sg	id.
ἐλατομήσατε	vb 1st aor act ind 2nd pers pl	id.
ἐλατόμησεν	vb 1st aor act ind 3rd pers sg	id.
ἐλατούς	adj masc acc pl	ἐλατός
ἐλάτρευον	vb impf act ind 3rd pers pl	λατρεύω
ἐλατρεύσαμεν	vb 1st aor act ind 1st pers pl	id.
ἐλάτρευσαν	vb 1st aor act ind 3rd pers pl	id.
ἐλάτρευσας	vb 1st aor act ind 2nd pers sg	id.
ἐλατρεύσατε	vb 1st aor act ind 2nd pers pl	id.
ἐλάτρευσεν	vb 1st aor act ind 3rd pers sg	id.
ἔλαττον	comp adj neut nom and acc sg	ἐλάττων
ἔλαττον	adverb	
ἐλαττονῇ	vb pres mid ind 2nd pers sg	ἐλαττονέω
ἐλαττονήσει	vb fut act ind 3rd pers sg	id.
ἐλαττονοῦνται	vb pres m/p ind 3rd pers pl	ἐλαττονόω

ἐλαττονοῦται vb pres m/p ind 3rd pers sg . . . . . ἐλαττονόω
ἐλαττονωθέντες vb 1st aor pass part masc nom pl   id.
ἐλαττονώθη vb 1st aor pass ind 3rd pers sg   id.
ἐλαττονωθῇ vb 1st aor pass subj 3rd pers sg   id.
ἐλαττονωθῶσιν vb 1st aor pass subj 3rd pers pl   id.
ἐλαττόνων comp adj gen pl . . . . ἐλάττων
ἐλαττονώσῃ vb 1st aor act subj 3rd pers sg . . . . ἐλαττονόω
ἐλάττοσι comp adj dat pl . . . . ἐλάττων
ἐλαττοῦμαι vb pres m/p ind 1st pers sg . . . . ἐλαττόω
ἐλαττούμενον vb pres m/p part masc acc sg   id.
ἐλαττούμενος vb pres m/p part masc nom sg   id.
ἐλάττους comp adj masc and fem nom and acc pl . . ἐλάττων
ἐλαττοῦσιν vb pres act ind 3rd pers pl . . . . ἐλαττόω
ἐλάττω comp adj masc and fem acc sg . . . . ἐλάττων
ἐλαττωθῇ vb 1st aor pass subj 3rd pers sg . . . . ἐλαττόω
ἐλαττωθήσεται vb fut pass ind 3rd pers sg   id.
ἐλαττωθήσονται vb fut pass ind 3rd pers pl   id.
ἐλαττωθῶσιν vb 1st aor pass subj 3rd pers pl   id.
ἐλάττωμα noun neut nom and acc sg
ἐλαττώματος noun neut gen sg . . . . ἐλάττωμα
ἐλάττων comp adj masc and fem nom sg
ἐλαττῶν vb pres act part masc nom sg . . . . ἐλαττόω
ἐλαττῶσαι vb 1st aor act inf   id.
ἐλαττώσει noun fem dat sg . . . . ἐλάττωσις
ἐλαττώσει vb fut act ind 3rd pers sg . . . . ἐλαττόω
ἐλαττώσεις vb fut act ind 2nd pers sg   id.
ἐλαττώσετε vb fut act ind 2nd pers pl   id.
ἐλαττώσεως noun fem gen sg . . . . ἐλάττωσις
ἐλαττώσῃς vb 1st aor act subj 2nd pers sg . . . . . . ἐλαττόω
ἐλάττωσιν noun fem acc sg . . . . ἐλάττωσις
ἐλάττωσις noun fem nom sg   id.
ἐλαύνειν vb pres act inf . . . . ἐλαύνω
ἐλαῦνον vb pres act part neut nom and acc sg   id.
ἐλαύνοντα vb pres act part masc acc sg   id.
ἐλαύνονται vb pres m/p ind 3rd pers pl   id.
ἐλαύνων vb pres act part masc nom sg   id.
ἔλαφοι noun masc nom pl . . . . ἔλαφος
ἐλάφοις adj fem dat pl   id.
ἔλαφον noun masc acc sg   id.
ἔλαφος noun masc or fem nom sg   id.
ἐλάφου noun masc gen sg   id.
ἐλάφους noun masc acc pl   id.
ἐλαφραί adj fem nom pl . . . . ἐλαφρός
ἐλαφρόν adj masc acc sg, neut nom and acc sg   id.
ἐλαφρός adj masc nom sg   id.
ἐλαφρότερος comp adj masc nom sg   id.
ἐλαφύρευσεν vb 1st aor act ind 3rd pers sg . . . . . λαφυρεύω
ἐλάφων noun masc gen pl . . . . ἔλαφος
ἐλάχιστα superl adj neut nom and acc pl . . . . ἐλάττων
ἐλαχίστης superl adj fem gen sg   id.
ἐλάχιστοι superl adj masc nom pl   id.

ἐλάχιστον superl adj masc acc sg,
        neut nom and acc sg . . . . ἐλάττων
ἐλάχιστος superl adj masc nom sg   id.
ἐλαχίστου superl adj masc and neut gen sg   id.
ἐλαχίστῳ superl adj masc and neut dat sg   id.
ἐλαχίστων superl adj gen pl   id.
ἔλαχον vb 2nd aor act ind 1st pers sg . . . . λαγχάνω
Ελβων pr noun
Ελβωυδαδ pr noun
Ελδοα pr noun
Ελδαδ pr noun
ἐλέα vb pres act impv 2nd pers sg . . . . ἐλεάω
ἐλεᾷ vb pres act ind 3rd pers sg   id.
Ελεαδ pr noun
Ελεαδα pr noun
Ελεαζαρ pr noun
Ελεαζαρον pr noun masc acc sg . . . . Ελεαζαρος
Ελεαζαρος pr noun masc nom sg   id.
Ελεαζαρου pr noun masc gen sg   id.
Ελεαλη pr noun
ἐλέανα vb 1st aor act ind 1st pers sg . . . . λεαίνω
Ελεαναν pr noun
ἐλέαναν vb 1st aor act ind 3rd pers pl . . . . λεαίνω
Ελεασα pr noun
ἔλεγεν vb impf act ind 3rd pers sg . . . . λέγω
ἔλεγες vb impf act ind 2nd pers sg   id.
ἐλέγετε vb impf act ind 2nd pers pl   id.
ἐλέγετο vb impf m/p ind 3rd pers sg   id.
ἐλεγμοῖς noun masc dat pl . . . . ἐλεγμός
ἐλεγμόν noun masc acc sg   id.
ἐλεγμός noun masc nom sg   id.
ἐλεγμοῦ noun masc gen sg   id.
ἐλεγμούς noun masc acc pl   id.
ἐλεγμῷ noun masc dat sg   id.
ἐλέγξαι vb 1st aor act inf,
        1st aor act opt 3rd pers sg . . . . ἐλέγχω
ἐλέγξαιτο vb 1st aor mid opt 3rd pers sg   id.
ἐλεγξάτωσαν vb 1st aor act impv 3rd pers pl   id.
ἐλέγξει vb fut act ind 3rd pers sg   id.
ἐλέγξεις vb fut act ind 2nd pers sg   id.
ἐλέγξῃ vb 1st aor act subj 3rd pers sg   id.
ἐλέγξῃς vb 1st aor act subj 2nd pers sg   id.
ἔλεγξις noun fem nom sg
ἔλεγξον vb 1st aor act impv 2nd pers sg . . . . ἐλέγχω
ἐλέγξω vb fut act ind 1st pers sg   id.
ἐλέγομεν vb impf act ind 1st pers pl . . . . λέγω
ἔλεγον vb impf act ind 1st pers sg and 3rd pers pl   id.
ἔλεγχε vb pres act impv 2nd pers sg . . . . ἐλέγχω
ἐλέγχει vb pres act ind 3rd pers sg   id.
ἐλέγχειν vb pres act inf   id.
ἐλέγχεις vb pres act ind 2nd pers sg   id.
ἐλέγχεσθαι vb pres m/p inf   id.

ἐλέγχεται	vb pres m/p ind 3rd pers sg	ἐλέγχω
ἐλέγχῃ	vb pres act subj 3rd pers sg	id.
ἐλέγχῃς	vb pres act subj 2nd pers sg	id.
ἐλεγχθῇ	vb 1st aor pass subj 3rd pers sg	id.
ἐλεγχθήσεται	vb fut pass ind 3rd pers sg	id.
ἔλεγχοι	noun masc nom pl	ἔλεγχος
ἐλέγχοις	noun masc dat pl	id.
ἐλεγχόμενος	vb pres m/p part masc nom sg	ἐλέγχω
ἔλεγχον	noun masc acc sg	ἔλεγχος
ἐλέγχοντα	vb pres act part masc acc sg	ἐλέγχω
ἐλέγχοντας	vb pres act part masc acc pl	id.
ἐλέγχοντες	vb pres act part masc nom pl	id.
ἔλεγχος	noun masc nom sg	
ἐλέγχου	noun masc gen sg	ἔλεγχος
ἐλέγχους	noun masc acc pl	id.
ἐλέγχουσα	vb pres act part fem nom sg	ἐλέγχω
ἐλέγχων	noun masc gen pl	ἔλεγχος
ἐλέγχων	vb pres act part masc nom sg	ἐλέγχω
ἐλέει	noun neut dat sg	ἔλεος
ἐλεεῖν	vb pres act inf	ἐλεέω
ἐλεεινός	adj masc nom sg	
ἐλεεῖς	vb pres act ind 2nd pers sg	ἐλεέω
ἐλέη	noun neut nom and acc pl	ἔλεος
ἐλεηθῆναι	vb 1st aor pass inf	ἐλεέω
ἐλεηθήσεται	vb fut pass ind 3rd pers sg	id.
ἐλεηθησόμεθα	vb fut pass ind 1st pers pl	id.
ἐλεηθήσονται	vb fut pass ind 3rd pers pl	id.
Ελεηλ	pr noun	
ἐλεήμονα	adj masc and fem acc sg	ἐλεήμων
ἐλεήμονος	adj gen sg	id.
ἐλεημοποιοῦ	adj gen sg	ἐλεημοποιός
ἐλεημοσύναι	noun fem nom pl	ἐλεημοσύνη
ἐλεημοσύναις	noun fem dat pl	id.
ἐλεημοσύνας	noun fem acc pl	id.
ἐλεημοσύνη	noun fem nom sg	id.
ἐλεημοσύνῃ	noun fem dat sg	id.
ἐλεημοσύνην	noun fem acc sg	id.
ἐλεημοσύνης	noun fem gen sg	id.
ἐλεήμων	adj masc and fem nom sg	
ἐλεήσαι	vb 1st aor act opt 3rd pers sg	ἐλεέω
ἐλεῆσαι	vb 1st aor act inf	id.
ἐλεήσαντος	vb 1st aor act part masc and neut gen sg	id.
ἐλεήσας	vb 1st aor act part masc nom sg	id.
ἐλεήσατε	vb 1st aor act impv 2nd pers pl	id.
ἐλεήσει	vb fut act ind 3rd pers sg	id.
ἐλεήσεις	vb fut act ind 2nd pers sg	id.
ἐλεήσῃ	vb 1st aor act subj 3rd pers sg	id.
ἐλεήσῃς	vb 1st aor act subj 2nd pers sg	id.
ἐλεήσητε	vb 1st aor act subj 2nd pers pl	id.
ἐλέησον	vb 1st aor act impv 2nd pers sg	id.
ἐλεήσοντα	vb fut act part masc acc sg	id.

ἐλεήσω	vb 1st aor act subj 1st pers sg,	
	fut act ind 1st pers sg	ἐλεέω
ἐλεήσωμεν	vb 1st aor act subj 1st pers pl	id.
ἐλεήσωσιν	vb 1st aor act subj 3rd pers pl	id.
ἔλει	noun neut dat sg	ἔλος
ἔλειξαν	vb 1st aor act ind 3rd pers pl	λείχω
ἐλειτούργει	vb impf act ind 3rd pers sg	λειτουργέω
ἐλειτούργησα	vb 1st aor act ind 1st pers sg	id.
ἐλειτούργησαν	vb 1st aor act ind 3rd pers pl	id.
ἐλειτούργουν	vb impf act ind 3rd pers pl	id.
Ελεκεθ	pr noun	
ἔλεξεν	vb 1st aor act ind 3rd pers sg	λέγω
ἔλεον	noun masc acc sg	ἔλεος
ἐλεοπόλει	noun fem dat sg	ἐλεόπολις
ἐλεόπολιν	noun fem acc sg	id.
ἔλεος	noun masc nom sg or neut nom and acc sg	
ἐλέου	noun masc gen sg	ἔλεος
ἐλέους	noun neut gen sg	id.
ἐλέπισεν	vb 1st aor act ind 3rd pers sg	λεπίζω
ἐλεπίσθη	vb 1st aor pass ind 3rd pers sg	id.
ἐλέπτυνα	vb 1st aor act ind 1st pers sg	λεπτύνω
ἐλέπτυναν	vb 1st aor act ind 3rd pers pl	id.
ἐλέπτυνεν	vb 1st aor act ind 3rd pers sg	id.
ἐλεπτύνθησαν	vb 1st aor pass ind 3rd pers pl	id.
ἔλεσθε	vb 2nd aor mid impv 2nd pers pl	αἱρέω
ἐλεύθερα	adj neut nom and acc pl	ἐλεύθερος
ἐλευθέραν	adj fem acc sg	id.
ἐλευθέρας	adj fem gen sg	id.
ἐλευθερία	noun fem nom sg	
ἐλευθερίᾳ	noun fem dat sg	ἐλευθερία
ἐλευθερίαν	noun fem acc sg	id.
ἐλευθερίας	noun fem gen sg	id.
ἐλεύθεροι	adj masc nom pl	ἐλεύθερος
ἐλευθεροῖ	vb pres act ind 3rd pers sg	ἐλευθερόω
ἐλευθέροις	adj masc and neut dat pl	ἐλεύθερος
Ἐλευθερον	pr noun masc acc sg	Ἐλεύθερος
ἐλεύθερον	adj masc acc sg, neut nom and acc sg	ἐλεύθερος
ἐλεύθερος	adj masc nom sg	id.
Ἐλευθερου	pr noun masc gen sg	Ἐλεύθερος
ἐλευθέρου	adj masc and neut gen sg	ἐλεύθερος
ἐλευθέρους	adj masc acc pl	id.
ἐλευθέρων	adj gen pl	id.
ἐλευθερῶσαι	vb 1st aor act inf	ἐλευθερόω
ἐλευθέρωσον	vb 1st aor act impv 2nd pers sg	id.
ἐλευθερώτεροι	comp adj masc nom pl	ἐλεύθερος
ἐλεύκανεν	vb 1st aor act ind 3rd pers sg	λευκαίνω
ἐλεύσεται	vb fut mid ind 3rd pers sg	ἔρχομαι
ἐλεύσῃ	vb fut mid ind 2nd pers sg	id.
ἐλεύσομαι	vb fut mid ind 1st pers sg	id.
ἐλευσόμεθα	vb fut mid ind 1st pers pl	id.
ἐλεύσονται	vb fut mid ind 3rd pers pl	id.
ἐλευστέον	verbal adj sg	

ἐλέφαντα noun masc acc sg	. . . .	ἐλέφας
ἐλεφαντάρχην noun masc acc sg	. . . .	ἐλεφαντάρχης
ἐλεφαντάρχης noun masc nom sg		id.
ἐλέφαντας noun masc acc pl	. . . .	ἐλέφας
ἐλέφαντες noun masc nom pl		id.
ἐλέφαντι noun masc dat sg		id.
ἐλεφάντινοι adj masc nom pl	. . . .	ἐλεφάντινος
ἐλεφάντινον adj masc acc sg, neut nom and acc sg		id.
ἐλεφάντινος adj masc nom sg		id.
ἐλεφαντίνους adj masc acc pl		id.
ἐλεφαντίνων adj gen pl		id.
ἐλέφαντος noun masc gen sg	. . . .	ἐλέφας
ἐλεφάντων noun masc gen pl		id.
ἐλέφασι noun masc dat pl		id.
ἐλεῶ vb pres act subj 1st pers sg	. . . .	ἐλεέω
ἐλεῶν noun masc gen pl	. . . .	ἔλεος
ἐλεῶν vb pres act part masc nom sg	. . . .	ἐλεέω
ἐλεῶντες vb pres act part masc nom pl	. . . .	ἐλεάω
ἐλεῶντι vb pres act part masc and neut dat sg		id.
ἐλεῶσιν vb pres act subj 3rd pers pl		id.
Ελζαβαδ pr noun		
ἔλη noun neut nom and acc pl	. . . .	ἕλος
ἔληγεν vb impf act ind 3rd pers sg	. . . .	λήγω
ἐλήλυθα vb perf act ind 1st pers sg	. . . .	ἔρχομαι
ἐληλύθασιν vb perf act ind 3rd pers pl		id.
ἐληλύθει vb plpf act ind 3rd pers sg		id.
ἐληλυθότος vb perf act part masc and neut gen sg		id.
ἐληλυθώς vb perf act part masc nom sg		id.
ἐλήμφθη vb 1st aor pass ind 3rd pers sg	. . . .	λαμβάνω
ἐλήμφθης vb 1st aor pass ind 2nd pers sg		id.
ἐλήμφθησαν vb 1st aor pass ind 3rd pers pl		id.
ἔληξεν vb 1st aor act ind 3rd pers sg	. . . .	λήγω
ἔλθατε vb 1st aor act impv 2nd pers pl	. . . .	ἔρχομαι
ἐλθάτω vb 1st aor act impv 3rd pers sg		id.
ἐλθάτωσαν vb 1st aor act impv 3rd pers pl		id.
ἐλθέ vb 2nd aor act impv 2nd pers sg		id.
ἐλθεῖν vb 2nd aor act inf		id.
Ελθεκεν pr noun		
Ελθεκω pr noun		
ἔλθετε vb 2nd aor act impv 2nd pers pl	. . . .	ἔρχομαι
ἐλθέτω vb 2nd aor act impv 3rd pers sg		id.
ἐλθέτωσαν vb 2nd aor act impv 3rd pers pl		id.
ἔλθη vb 2nd aor act subj 3rd pers sg		id.
ἔλθης vb 2nd aor act subj 2nd pers sg		id.
ἔλθητε vb 2nd aor act subj 2nd pers pl		id.
ἔλθοι vb 2nd aor act opt 3rd pers sg		id.
ἔλθοιμι vb 2nd aor act opt 1st pers sg		id.
ἔλθοις vb 2nd aor act opt 2nd pers sg		id.
ἔλθοισαν vb 2nd aor act opt 3rd pers pl		id.
ἐλθόν vb 2nd aor act part neut nom and acc sg		id.
ἐλθόντα vb 2nd aor act part masc acc sg		id.
ἐλθόντας vb 2nd aor act part masc acc pl		id.

ἐλθόντες vb 2nd aor act part masc nom pl	. . . .	ἔρχομαι
ἐλθόντι vb 2nd aor act part masc and neut dat sg		id.
ἐλθόντος vb 2nd aor act part masc and neut gen sg		id.
ἐλθόντων vb 2nd aor act part masc and neut gen pl		id.
Ελθουλα pr noun		
Ελθουλαδ pr noun		
ἐλθοῦσα vb 2nd aor act part fem nom sg	. . . .	ἔρχομαι
ἐλθοῦσαν vb 2nd aor act part fem acc sg		id.
ἐλθούςῃ vb 2nd aor act part fem dat sg		id.
ἔλθω vb 2nd aor act subj 1st pers sg		id.
Ελθωδαδ pr noun		
ἔλθωμεν vb 2nd aor act subj 1st pers pl	. . . .	ἔρχομαι
ἔλθων vb 2nd aor act part masc nom sg		id.
ἔλθωσι(ν) vb 2nd aor act subj 3rd pers pl		id.
Ελια pr noun		
Ελιαβ pr noun		
Ελιαβα pr noun		
Ελιοδα pr noun		
Ελιοδαε pr noun		
Ελιοδας pr noun		
Ελιαζαι pr noun		
Ελιαζερ pr noun		
Ελιαθα pr noun		
Ελιακιμ pr noun		
Ελιαλις pr noun		
Ελιανα pr noun		
Ελιαρεφ pr noun		
Ελιασιβ pr noun		
Ελιασιβος pr noun masc nom sg		
Ελιασιβου pr noun masc gen sg	. . . .	Ἐλιασιβος
Ελιασιμος pr noun		
Ελιασις pr noun		
Ελιασου pr noun		
Ελιαωνιας pr noun masc nom sg		
Ελιβαμας pr noun		
Ελιβεμα pr noun		
Ελιβεμας pr noun fem gen sg	. . . .	Ελιβεμα
ἐλιγήσεται vb fut pass ind 3rd pers sg	. . . .	ἐλίσσω
Ελιδαε pr noun		
Ελιε pr noun		
Ελιεζερ pr noun		
Ελιηλ pr noun		
Ελιηλι pr noun		
Ελιθεναν pr noun		
ἐλιθοβόλησαν vb 1st aor act ind 3rd pers pl	. . .	λιθοβολέω
Ελικα pr noun		
ἕλικι noun fem dat sg	. . . .	ἕλιξ
ἐλίκμησα vb 1st aor act ind 1st pers sg	. . . .	λικμάω
ἑλικτά adj neut nom and acc pl	. . . .	ἑλικτός
ἑλικτῃ adj fem nom sg		id.
ἐλιμαγχόνησεν vb 1st aor act ind 3rd pers sg	.	λιμαγχονέω
Ελιμελεκ pr noun		

Ελιμουθ pr noun
Ελιου pr noun
Ελιουν pr noun masc acc sg .... Ελιους
Ελιους pr noun masc nom sg
ἐλίπανας vb 1st aor act ind 2nd pers sg .... λιπαίνω
ἐλίπανεν vb 1st aor act ind 3rd pers sg   id.
ἐλιπάνθη vb 1st aor pass ind 3rd pers sg   id.
ἐλιπάνθησαν vb 1st aor pass ind 3rd pers pl   id.
ἔλιπεν vb 2nd aor act ind 3rd pers sg .... λείπω
ἔλιπον vb 2nd aor act ind 3rd pers pl   id.
Ελισα pr noun
Ελισαβεθ pr noun
Ελισαε pr noun
Ελισαι pr noun
Ελισαιε pr noun
Ελισαμα pr noun
Ελισαμαε pr noun
Ελισαφ pr noun
Ελισαφαν pr noun
Ελισουβ pr noun
Ελισουρ pr noun
Ελισους pr noun
ἐλιτάνευον vb impf act ind 3rd pers pl .... λιτανεύω
Ελιφαλαθ pr noun
Ελιφαλατ pr noun
Ελιφαλατος pr noun
Ελιφαλεθ pr noun
Ελιφαλετ pr noun
Ελιφαλια pr noun
Ελιφαλιας pr noun masc nom sg
Ελιφας pr noun
ἐλιχθείη vb 1st aor pass opt 3rd pers sg .... ἐλίσσω
Ελιωηναι pr noun
Ελιωναις pr noun
Ελιωνας pr noun
Ελκαι pr noun
Ελκανα pr noun
ἕλκει noun neut dat sg .... ἕλκος
ἕλκει vb pres act ind 3rd pers sg .... ἕλκω
Ελκεσαιου pr noun masc gen sg .... Ελκεσαιος
ἕλκη noun neut nom and acc pl .... ἕλκος
Ελκια pr noun
ἕλκοντα vb pres act part neut nom and acc pl .... ἕλκω
ἕλκοντες vb pres act part masc nom pl   id.
ἕλκοντος vb pres act part masc and neut gen sg   id.
ἑλκόντων vb pres act part masc and neut gen pl   id.
ἕλκος noun neut nom and acc sg
ἕλκους noun neut gen sg .... ἕλκος
ἕλκουσα vb pres act part fem nom sg .... ἕλκω
ἑλκύσαι vb 1st aor act inf,
         1st aor act opt 3rd pers sg .... ἑλκύω
ἑλκύσει vb fut act ind 3rd pers sg   id.

ἕλκυσον vb 1st aor act impv 2nd pers sg .... ἑλκύω
Ελκωθαιμ pr noun
ἕλκων vb pres act part masc nom sg .... ἕλκω
Ἑλλαδα pr noun fem acc sg .... Ἑλλας
Ἑλλαδος pr noun fem gen sg   id.
Ελλαναθαν pr noun
Ελλαναν pr noun
Ἑλλας pr noun fem nom sg
Ελλασαρ pr noun
ἐλλεῖπον vb pres act part neut nom and acc sg ..... ἐλλείπω
Ελληλ pr noun
Ἑλληνας pr noun masc acc pl .... Ἑλλην
Ἑλληνες pr noun masc nom pl   id.
Ἑλληνιδας pr noun fem acc pl .... Ἑλληνις
Ἑλληνικα adj neut nom and acc pl .... Ἑλληνικος
Ἑλληνικά noun neut nom and acc pl .... Ἑλληνικόν
Ἑλληνικας adj fem acc pl .... Ἑλληνικος
Ἑλληνικην adj fem acc sg   id.
Ἑλληνικῆς adj fem gen sg   id.
Ἑλληνικον adj masc acc sg   id.
Ἑλληνικοῦ adj masc gen sg   id.
Ἑλληνισμοῦ pr noun masc gen sg .... Ἑλληνισμός
Ἑλληνων pr noun masc gen pl .... Ἑλλην
Ελλης pr noun
Ἑλλησι pr noun masc dat pl .... Ἑλλην
ἐλλιπής adj masc nom sg
ελλουλιμ translit
Ελμωδαδ pr noun
ελμωνι translit
Ελνααμ pr noun
Ελναθαν pr noun
Ελναταν pr noun
ἐλογίζετο vb impf dep ind 3rd pers sg .... λογίζομαι
ἐλογίζοντο vb impf dep ind 3rd pers pl   id.
ἐλογισάμεθα vb 1st aor mid ind 1st pers pl   id.
ἐλογισάμην vb 1st aor mid ind 1st pers sg   id.
ἐλογίσαντο vb 1st aor mid ind 3rd pers pl   id.
ἐλογίσατο vb 1st aor mid ind 3rd pers sg   id.
ἐλογίσθη vb 1st aor pass ind 3rd pers sg   id.
ἐλογίσθημεν vb 1st aor pass ind 1st pers pl   id.
ἐλογίσθησαν vb 1st aor pass ind 3rd pers pl   id.
ἐλογίσω vb 1st aor mid ind 2nd pers sg   id.
ἐλοιδορεῖτο vb impf m/p ind 3rd pers sg .... λοιδορέω
ἐλοιδορήθησαν vb 1st aor pass ind 3rd pers pl   id.
ἐλοιδόρησαν vb 1st aor act ind 3rd pers pl   id.
ἐλοιδόρουν vb impf act ind 3rd pers pl   id.
ἕλος noun neut nom and acc sg
Ελουλ pr noun
ἐλούου vb impf m/p ind 2nd pers sg .... λούω
ἔλουσα vb 1st aor act ind 1st pers sg   id.
ἐλουσάμην vb 1st aor mid ind 1st pers sg   id.
ἐλούσαντο vb 1st aor mid ind 3rd pers pl   id.

ἐλούσατο vb 1st aor mid ind 3rd pers sg . . . . λούω

ἔλουσεν vb 1st aor act ind 3rd pers sg   id.

ἐλούσθης vb 1st aor pass ind 2nd pers sg   id.

ἐλπίδα noun fem acc sg . . . . ἐλπίς

ἐλπίδας noun fem acc pl   id.

ἐλπίδες noun fem nom pl   id.

ἐλπίδι noun fem dat sg   id.

ἐλπίδος noun fem gen sg   id.

ἐλπίδων noun fem gen pl   id.

ἐλπιεῖ vb fut act ind 3rd pers sg . . . . ἐλπίζω

ἐλπιεῖς vb fut act ind 2nd pers sg   id.

ἐλπίζει vb pres act ind 3rd pers sg   id.

ἐλπίζειν vb pres act inf   id.

ἐλπίζεις vb pres act ind 2nd pers sg   id.

ἐλπίζετε vb pres act ind 2nd pers pl   id.

ἐλπιζέτω vb pres act impv 3rd pers sg   id.

ἐλπίζομεν vb pres act ind 1st pers pl   id.

ἐλπίζον vb pres act part neut nom and acc sg   id.

ἐλπίζοντα vb pres act part masc acc sg   id.

ἐλπίζοντας vb pres act part masc acc pl   id.

ἐλπίζοντες vb pres act part masc nom pl   id.

ἐλπιζόντων vb pres act part masc and neut gen pl   id.

ἐλπιζούσης vb pres act part fem gen sg   id.

ἐλπίζουσι(ν) vb pres act ind 3rd pers pl,

pres act part masc and neut dat pl   id.

ἐλπίζω vb pres act ind 1st pers sg   id.

ἐλπίζων vb pres act part masc nom sg   id.

ἐλπιοῦμεν vb fut act ind 1st pers pl   id.

ἐλπιοῦσιν vb fut act ind 3rd pers pl   id.

ἐλπίς noun fem nom sg

ἐλπίσαντας vb 1st aor act part masc acc pl . . . . ἐλπίζω

ἐλπίσατε vb 1st aor act impv 2nd pers pl   id.

ἐλπισάτω vb 1st aor act impv 3rd pers sg   id.

ἐλπισάτωσαν vb 1st aor act impv 3rd pers pl   id.

ἐλπίσιν noun fem dat pl . . . . ἐλπίς

ἔλπισον vb 1st aor act impv 2nd pers sg . . . . ἐλπίζω

ἐλπιῶ vb fut act ind 1st pers sg   id.

Ελραγα pr noun

Ἐλυμαΐδα pr noun fem acc sg . . . . Ἐλυμαΐς

Ἐλυμαΐδι pr noun fem dat sg   id.

Ἐλυμαΐς pr noun fem nom sg   id.

Ἐλυμαιων pr noun masc gen pl . . . . Ἐλύμαιος

ἐλυμήναντο vb 1st aor mid ind 3rd pers pl . . . . . . λυμαίνω

ἐλυμήνατο vb 1st aor mid ind 3rd pers sg   id.

ἐλυμήνω vb 1st aor mid ind 2nd pers sg   id.

ἐλύπεις vb impf act ind 2nd pers sg . . . . λυπέω

ἐλυπεῖτο vb impf m/p ind 3rd pers sg   id.

ἐλυπήθη vb 1st aor pass ind 3rd pers sg   id.

ἐλυπήθην vb 1st aor pass ind 1st pers sg   id.

ἐλυπήθησαν vb 1st aor pass ind 3rd pers pl   id.

ἐλύπησα vb 1st aor act ind 1st pers sg   id.

ἐλύπησαν vb 1st aor act ind 3rd pers pl   id.

ἐλυπήσατε vb 1st aor act ind 2nd pers pl . . . . λυπέω

ἐλύπησε(ν) vb 1st aor act ind 3rd pers sg   id.

ἐλυποῦντο vb impf m/p ind 3rd pers pl   id.

ἔλυσα vb 1st aor act ind 1st pers sg . . . . λύω

ἔλυσαν vb 1st aor act ind 3rd pers pl   id.

ἔλυσας vb 1st aor act ind 2nd pers sg   id.

ἔλυσεν vb 1st aor act ind 3rd pers sg   id.

ἐλυτρωσάμην vb 1st aor mid ind 1st pers sg . . . . . . λυτρόω

ἐλυτρώσαντο vb 1st aor mid ind 3rd pers pl   id.

ἐλυτρώσατο vb 1st aor mid ind 3rd pers sg   id.

ἐλυτρώσω vb 1st aor mid ind 2nd pers sg   id.

Ελφααλ pr noun

Ελφαλ pr noun

Ελφαλατ pr noun

ελωαι translit

Ελωι pr noun

Ελωμ pr noun

ἑλώμεθα vb 2nd aor mid subj 1st pers pl . . . . αἱρέω

ἐμά adj neut nom and acc pl . . . . ἐμός

ἐμαγείρευσας vb 1st aor act ind 2nd pers sg . . . μαγειρεύω

ἐμαδόρωσα vb 1st aor act ind 1st pers sg . . . . μαδαρόω

Εμαθ pr noun

ἔμαθεν vb 2nd aor act ind 3rd pers sg . . . . μανθάνω

Εμαθις pr noun

ἔμαθον vb 2nd aor act ind

1st pers sg and 3rd pers pl . . . . μανθάνω

ἐμαί adj fem nom pl . . . . ἐμός

ἐμαίμασσεν vb impf act ind 3rd pers sg . . . . . . μαιμάσσω

ἐμαῖς adj fem dat pl . . . . ἐμός

Εμακ pr noun

ἐμακάριζεν vb impf act ind 3rd pers sg . . . . μακαρίζω

ἐμακάριζον vb impf act ind 3rd pers pl   id.

ἐμακάρισα vb 1st aor act ind 1st pers sg   id.

ἐμακάρισαν vb 1st aor act ind 3rd pers pl   id.

ἐμακάρισεν vb 1st aor act ind 3rd pers sg   id.

ἐμακροημέρευσαν vb 1st aor act ind

3rd pers pl . . . . μακροημερεύω

ἐμακροθύμησεν vb 1st aor act ind

3rd pers sg . . . . μακροθυμέω

ἐμακροτόνησαν vb 1st aor act ind

3rd pers pl . . . . μακροτονέω

ἐμάκρυνα vb 1st aor act ind 1st pers sg . . . . μακρύνω

ἐμάκρυναν vb 1st aor act ind 3rd pers pl   id.

ἐμάκρυνας vb 1st aor act ind 2nd pers sg   id.

ἐμάκρυνεν vb 1st aor act ind 3rd pers sg,

impf act ind 3rd pers sg   id.

ἐμακρύνθη vb 1st aor pass ind 3rd pers sg   id.

ἐμακρύνθησαν vb 1st aor pass ind 3rd pers pl   id.

ἐμαλακίσθη vb 1st aor pass ind 3rd pers sg . . μαλακίζομαι

ἐμαλακίσθην vb 1st aor pass ind 1st pers sg   id.

ἐμαλάκυνεν vb impf act ind 3rd pers sg . . . . . . μαλακύνω

ἐμάνθανες vb impf act ind 2nd pers sg . . . . μανθάνω

ἐμαντεύοντο vb impf dep ind 3rd pers pl	....	μαντεύομαι
ἐμάραναν vb 1st aor act ind 3rd pers pl	....	μαραίνω
ἐμαράνθη vb 1st aor pass ind 3rd pers sg		id.
ἐμαρτύρησεν vb 1st aor act ind 3rd pers sg	.....	μαρτυρέω
ἐμάς adj fem acc pl	....	ἐμός
ἐμαστίγου vb impf act ind 3rd pers sg	....	μαστιγόω
ἐμαστίγουν vb impf act ind 3rd pers pl		id.
ἐμαστιγώθησαν vb 1st aor pass ind 3rd pers pl		id.
ἐμαστίγωσας vb 1st aor act ind 2nd pers sg		id.
ἐμαστίγωσεν vb 1st aor act ind 3rd pers sg		id.
ἐμάστιξεν vb 1st aor act ind 3rd pers sg	....	μαστίζω
ἐμασῶντο vb impf m/p ind 3rd pers pl	....	μασάω
ἐματαιώθην vb 1st aor pass ind 1st pers sg	.....	ματαιόω
ἐματαιώθησαν vb 1st aor pass ind 3rd pers pl		id.
ἐμαυτῇ dem pron fem dat sg	....	ἐμαυτοῦ
ἐμαυτήν dem pron fem acc sg		id.
ἐμαυτόν dem pron masc acc sg		id.
ἐμαυτοῦ dem pron masc and neut gen sg		id.
ἐμαυτῷ dem pron masc and neut dat sg		id.
ἐμαχεσάμην vb 1st aor mid ind 1st pers sg	......	μάχομαι
ἐμαχέσαντο vb 1st aor mid ind 3rd pers pl		id.
ἐμαχέσατο vb 1st aor mid ind 3rd pers sg		id.
ἐμβάλατε vb 1st aor act impv 2nd pers pl	....	ἐμβάλλω
ἔμβαλε vb 2nd aor act impv 2nd pers sg		id.
ἐμβαλεῖ vb fut act ind 3rd pers sg		id.
ἐμβαλεῖν vb 2nd aor act inf, fut act inf		id.
ἐμβαλεῖς vb fut act ind 2nd pers sg		id.
ἐμβαλεῖτε vb fut act ind 2nd pers pl		id.
ἐμβάλετε vb 2nd aor act impv 2nd pers pl		id.
ἐμβάλῃ vb 2nd aor act subj 3rd pers sg		id.
ἐμβάλῃς vb 2nd aor act subj 2nd pers sg		id.
ἐμβάληται vb 2nd aor mid subj 3rd pers sg		id.
ἐμβάλλοντες vb pres act part masc nom pl		id.
ἐμβαλόντες vb 2nd aor act part masc nom pl		id.
ἐμβαλοῦσιν vb fut act ind 3rd pers pl		id.
ἐμβαλῶ vb fut act ind 1st pers sg		id.
ἐμβάλωμεν vb 2nd aor act subj 1st pers pl		id.
ἐμβαλών vb 2nd aor act part masc nom sg		id.
ἐμβάλωσιν vb 2nd aor act subj 3rd pers pl		id.
ἐμβάς vb 2nd aor act part masc nom sg	....	ἐμβαίνω
ἐμβατεύειν vb pres act inf	....	ἐμβατεύω
ἐμβατεῦσαι vb 1st aor act inf		id.
ἐμβέβληται vb perf m/p ind 3rd pers sg	....	ἐμβάλλω
ἔμβηθι vb 2nd aor act impv 2nd pers sg	....	ἐμβαίνω
ἐμβῆναι vb 2nd aor act inf		id.
ἐμβιβάζω vb pres act ind 1st pers sg		
ἐμβιώσεως noun fem gen sg	....	ἐμβίωσις
ἐμβίωσιν noun fem acc sg		id.
ἔμβλεπε vb pres act impv 2nd pers sg	....	ἐμβλέπω
ἐμβλέπειν vb pres act inf		id.
ἐμβλέποντες vb pres act part masc nom pl		id.

ἐμβλέπουσιν vb pres act ind 3rd pers pl	....	ἐμβλέπω
ἐμβλέπων vb pres act part masc nom sg		id.
ἐμβλέψας vb 1st aor act part masc nom sg		id.
ἐμβλέψατε vb 1st aor act impv 2nd pers pl		id.
ἐμβλέψεται vb fut mid ind 3rd pers sg		id.
ἔμβλεψον vb 1st aor act impv 2nd pers sg		id.
ἐμβλέψονται vb fut mid ind 3rd pers pl		id.
ἐμβληθῆναι vb 1st aor pass inf	....	ἐμβάλλω
ἐμβληθήσεσθε vb fut pass ind 2nd pers pl		id.
ἐμβληθήσεται vb fut pass ind 3rd pers sg		id.
ἐμβολῆς noun fem gen sg	....	ἐμβολή
ἐμβριμήματι noun neut dat sg	....	ἐμβρίμημα
ἐμβριμήσονται vb fut mid ind 3rd pers pl	...	ἐμβριμάομαι
ἐμέ pers pron acc sg	....	ἐγώ
ἐμεγαλαύχησεν vb 1st aor act ind		
3rd pers sg	....	μεγαλαυχέω
ἐμεγαλαύχουν vb impf act ind 3rd pers pl		id.
ἐμεγαλορημόνησας see ἐμεγαλορρημόνησας		
ἐμεγαλορρημόνησαν vb 1st aor act ind		
3rd pers pl	....	μεγαλορρημονέω
ἐμεγαλορρημόνησας vb 1st aor act ind		
2nd pers sg		id.
ἐμεγαλορρημόνησεν vb 1st aor act ind 3rd pers sg		id.
ἐμεγάλυνα vb 1st aor act ind 1st pers sg	....	μεγαλύνω
ἐμεγάλυνας vb 1st aor act ind 2nd pers sg		id.
ἐμεγάλυνεν vb 1st aor act ind 3rd pers sg		id.
ἐμεγαλύνετο vb impf m/p ind 3rd pers sg		id.
ἐμεγαλύνθη vb 1st aor pass ind 3rd pers sg		id.
ἐμεγαλύνθην vb 1st aor pass ind 1st pers sg		id.
ἐμεγαλύνθης vb 1st aor pass ind 2nd pers sg		id.
ἐμεγαλύνθησαν vb 1st aor pass ind 3rd pers pl		id.
ἐμεγαλύνοντο vb impf m/p ind 3rd pers pl		id.
ἐμέθυσα vb 1st aor act ind 1st pers sg	....	μεθύω
ἐμέθυσας vb 1st aor act ind 2nd pers sg		id.
ἐμέθυσεν vb 1st aor act ind 3rd pers sg		id.
ἐμεθύσθη vb 1st aor pass ind 3rd pers sg		id.
ἐμεθύσθησαν vb 1st aor pass ind 3rd pers pl		id.
ἔμεινα vb 1st aor act ind 1st pers sg	....	μένω
ἔμεινεν vb 1st aor act ind 3rd pers sg		id.
Εμεκ pr noun		
Εμεκαχωρ pr noun		
Εμεκραφαϊν pr noun		
ἐμελέτησα vb 1st aor act ind 1st pers sg	....	μελετάω
ἐμελετήσαμεν vb 1st aor act ind 1st pers pl		id.
ἐμελέτησαν vb 1st aor act ind 3rd pers pl		id.
ἐμελέτων vb impf act ind 1st pers sg and 3rd pers pl		id.
ἐμέλισα vb 1st aor act ind 1st pers sg	....	μελίζω
ἐμέλισαν vb 1st aor act ind 3rd pers pl		id.
ἐμέλισεν vb 1st aor act ind 3rd pers sg		id.
ἔμελλεν vb impf act ind 3rd pers sg	....	μέλλω
ἔμελλον vb impf act ind 3rd pers pl		id.
ἐμελῴδει vb impf act ind 3rd pers sg	....	μελῳδέω

Εμεμαων pr noun		
ἐμεμνήμην vb plpf m/p ind 1st pers sg	....	μιμνήσκω
ἐμέμνηντο vb plpf m/p ind 3rd pers pl		id.
ἔμενεν vb impf act ind 3rd pers sg	....	μένω
ἔμενον vb impf act ind 3rd pers pl		id.
ἐμέρισα vb 1st aor act ind 1st pers sg	....	μερίζω
ἐμέρισαν vb 1st aor act ind 3rd pers pl		id.
ἐμερίσαντο vb 1st aor mid ind 3rd pers pl		id.
ἐμερίσατο vb 1st aor mid ind 3rd pers sg		id.
ἐμέρισεν vb 1st aor act ind 3rd pers sg		id.
ἐμερίσθη vb 1st aor pass ind 3rd pers sg		id.
ἐμερίσθησαν vb 1st aor pass ind 3rd pers pl		id.
Εμερων pr noun		
ἔμεσον vb 1st aor act impv 2nd pers sg	....	ἐμέω
ἐμετεωρίζετο vb impf m/p ind 3rd pers sg	.....	μετεωρίζω
ἐμετεωρίζοντο vb impf m/p ind 3rd pers pl		id.
ἐμετεωρίσθησαν vb 1st aor pass ind 3rd pers pl		id.
ἔμετον noun masc acc sg	....	ἔμετος
ἐμέτρησεν vb 1st aor act ind 3rd pers sg	....	μετρέω
ἐμή adj fem nom sg	....	ἐμός
ἐμῇ adj fem dat sg		id.
ἐμήκυνεν vb impf act ind 3rd pers sg	....	μηκύνω
ἐμήν adj fem acc sg	....	ἐμός
ἐμηνύθη vb 1st aor pass ind 3rd pers sg	....	μηνύω
Εμηρ pr noun		
ἐμῆς adj fem gen sg	....	ἐμός
ἐμηχανῶντο vb impf dep ind 3rd pers pl	.....	μηχανάομαι
ἐμίαινεν vb impf act ind 3rd pers sg	....	μιαίνω
ἐμιαίνεσθε vb impf m/p ind 2nd pers pl		id.
ἐμιαίνετο vb impf m/p ind 3rd pers sg		id.
ἐμίαινον vb impf act ind 3rd pers pl		id.
ἐμιαίνου vb impf m/p ind 2nd pers sg		id.
ἐμιαίωσαν vb 1st aor act ind 3rd pers pl	....	μιαιόω
ἐμίαναν vb 1st aor act ind 3rd pers pl	....	μιαίνω
ἐμίανας vb 1st aor act ind 2nd pers sg		id.
ἐμιάνατε vb 1st aor act ind 2nd pers pl		id.
ἐμίανεν vb 1st aor act ind 3rd pers sg		id.
ἐμιάνθη vb 1st aor pass ind 3rd pers sg		id.
ἐμιάνθην vb 1st aor pass ind 1st pers sg		id.
ἐμιάνθησαν vb 1st aor pass ind 3rd pers pl		id.
ἐμιαροφάγησαν vb 1st aor act ind 3rd pers pl	.	μιαροφαγέω
ἐμίγησαν vb 2nd aor pass ind 3rd pers pl	....	μίγνυμι
ἔμιξεν vb 1st aor act ind 3rd pers sg		id.
Εμιουδ pr noun		
ἐμίσει vb impf act ind 3rd pers sg	....	μισέω
ἐμίσεις vb impf act ind 2nd pers sg		id.
ἐμισεῖτε vb impf act ind 2nd pers pl		id.
ἐμίσησα vb 1st aor act ind 1st pers sg		id.
ἐμίσησαν vb 1st aor act ind 3rd pers pl		id.
ἐμίσησας vb 1st aor act ind 2nd pers sg		id.
ἐμισήσατε vb 1st aor act ind 2nd pers pl		id.
ἐμίσησεν vb 1st aor act ind 3rd pers sg		id.
ἐμισθοῦντο vb impf m/p ind 3rd pers sg	......	μισθόομαι
ἐμισθωσάμην vb 1st aor mid ind 1st pers sg		id.
ἐμισθώσαντο vb 1st aor mid ind 3rd pers pl		id.
ἐμισθώσατο vb 1st aor mid ind 3rd pers sg		id.
ἐμίσουν vb impf act ind 1st pers sg and 3rd pers pl	...	μισέω
Εμμαθ pr noun		
ἐμμανεῖς adj masc and fem nom and acc pl	......	ἐμμανής
Εμμανουηλ pr noun		
ἐμμείνασαι vb 1st aor act part fem nom pl	....	ἐμμένω
ἐμμείνατε vb 1st aor act impv 2nd pers pl		id.
ἐμμείνῃ vb 1st aor act subj 3rd pers sg		id.
ἐμμελέτημα noun neut nom and acc sg		
ἔμμενε vb pres act impv 2nd pers sg	....	ἐμμένω
ἐμμενεῖ vb fut act ind 3rd pers sg		id.
ἐμμενέτω vb pres act impv 3rd pers sg		id.
ἐμμένοντες vb pres act part masc nom pl		id.
ἐμμένων vb pres act part masc nom sg		id.
Εμμηρ pr noun		
Εμμηρου pr noun		
ἐμμολυνθήσεται vb fut pass ind 3rd pers sg	....	ἐμμολύνω
ἔμμονον adj acc sg, neut nom sg	....	ἔμμονος
ἔμμονος adj masc and fem nom sg		id.
Εμμωθ pr noun		
Εμμωρ pr noun		
ἐμνημόνευον vb impf act ind 3rd pers pl	......	μνημονεύω
ἐμνήσθη vb 1st aor pass ind 3rd pers sg	......	μιμνήσκω
ἐμνήσθημεν vb 1st aor pass ind 1st pers pl		id.
ἐμνήσθην vb 1st aor pass ind 1st pers sg		id.
ἐμνήσθης vb 1st aor pass ind 2nd pers sg		id.
ἐμνήσθησαν vb 1st aor act ind 3rd pers pl		id.
ἐμνησικάκησαν vb 1st aor act ind 3rd pers pl	.	μνησικακέω
ἐμοί pers pron dat sg	....	ἐγώ
ἐμοῖς adj masc and neut dat pl	....	ἐμός
ἐμοιχᾶτε vb impf dep ind 3rd pers sg	....	μοιχάομαι
ἐμοιχεύθη vb 1st aor pass ind 3rd pers sg	....	μοιχεύω
ἐμοίχευσεν vb 1st aor act ind 3rd pers sg		id.
ἐμοιχῶντο vb impf dep ind 3rd pers pl	....	μοιχάομαι
ἐμόλυνα vb 1st aor act ind 1st pers sg	....	μολύνω
ἐμόλυναν vb 1st aor act ind 3rd pers pl		id.
ἐμολύνετο vb impf m/p ind 3rd pers sg		id.
ἐμολύνθησαν vb 1st aor pass ind 3rd pers pl		id.
ἐμόν adj masc acc sg, neut nom and acc sg	....	ἐμός
ἐμονομάχησεν vb 1st aor act ind 3rd pers sg	...	μονομαχέω
ἐμός adj masc nom sg		
Εμσφεως pr noun		
ἐμοῦ pers pron gen sg	....	ἐγώ
ἐμοῦ poss adj masc and neut gen sg	....	ἐμός
ἐμούς poss adj masc acc pl		id.
ἐμόχθησα vb 1st aor act ind 1st pers sg	....	μοχθέω
ἐμόχθησας vb 1st aor act ind 2nd pers sg		id.
ἐμόχθησεν vb 1st aor act ind 3rd pers sg		id.
ἐμπαγῆναι vb 2nd aor pass inf	....	ἐμπήγνυμι

ἐμπαγῶ vb 2nd aor pass subj 1st pers sg . . . . . . ἐμπήγνυμι

ἐμπαίγματα noun neut nom and acc pl . . . . ἔμπαιγμα

ἐμπαιγμόν noun masc acc sg . . . . ἐμπαιγμός

ἐμπαιγμός noun masc nom sg   id.

ἐμπαιγμούς noun masc acc pl   id.

ἐμπαιγμῶν noun masc gen pl   id.

ἐμπαίζει vb pres act ind 3rd pers sg . . . . ἐμπαίζω

ἐμπαίζειν vb pres act inf   id.

ἐμπαιζόμενον vb pres m/p part masc acc sg,

       neut nom and acc sg   id.

ἐμπαίζοντας vb pres act part masc acc pl   id.

ἐμπαίζοντες vb pres act part masc nom pl   id.

ἐμπαίζων vb pres act part masc nom sg   id.

ἐμπαῖκται noun masc nom pl . . . . ἐμπαίκτης

ἐμπαῖξαι vb 1st aor act inf . . . . ἐμπαίζω

ἐμπαίξεται vb fut mid ind 3rd pers sg   id.

ἐμπαίξονται vb fut mid ind 3rd pers pl   id.

ἐμπαίξουσιν vb fut act ind 3rd pers pl   id.

ἐμπαίξωσιν vb 1st aor act subj 3rd pers pl   id.

ἐμπαραγίνεται vb pres dep ind

       3rd pers sg . . . . ἐμπαραγίνομαι

ἐμπειρεῖ vb pres act ind 3rd pers sg . . . . ἐμπειρέω

ἐμπειρίᾳ noun fem dat sg . . . . ἐμπειρία

ἔμπειρος adj masc and fem nom sg

ἐμπειρῶ vb pres act ind 1st pers sg . . . . ἐμπειρέω

ἐμπείρων adj gen pl . . . . ἔμπειρος

ἐμπεπαιγμένα vb perf m/p part

       neut nom and acc pl . . . . ἐμπαίζω

ἐμπεπαιγμένης vb perf m/p part fem gen sg   id.

ἐμπέπαιχα vb perf act ind 1st pers sg   id.

ἐμπέπαιχας vb perf act ind 2nd pers sg   id.

ἐμπεπηγός vb perf act part neut nom and acc sg . ἐμπήγνυμι

ἐμπέπλησται vb perf m/p ind 3rd pers sg . . . . . . ἐμπίμπλημι

ἐμπεποδοστάτηκας vb perf act ind

       2nd pers sg . . . . ἐμποδοστατέω

ἐμπεπορπημένοι vb perf m/p part masc nom pl . . ἐμπορπάω

ἐμπεπτωκότας vb perf act part masc acc pl . . . . . . ἐμπίπτω

ἐμπεπυρισμέναι vb perf m/p part fem nom pl . . . ἐμπυρίζω

ἐμπεπυρισμένη vb perf m/p part fem nom sg   id.

ἐμπεπυρισμένον vb perf m/p part masc acc sg,

       neut nom and acc sg   id.

ἐμπεπυρισμένους vb perf m/p part masc acc pl   id.

ἐμπεπύρισται vb perf m/p ind 3rd pers sg   id.

ἐμπεριπατεῖ vb pres act ind 3rd pers sg . . . . . . ἐμπεριπατέω

ἐμπεριπατήσας vb 1st aor act part masc nom sg   id.

ἐμπεριπατήσω vb fut act ind 1st pers sg   id.

ἐμπεριπατούντων vb pres act part masc and neut gen pl id.

ἐμπεριπατῶν vb pres act part masc nom sg   id.

ἐμπεσεῖν vb 2nd aor act inf . . . . ἐμπίπτω

ἐμπεσεῖται vb fut mid ind 3rd pers sg   id.

ἐμπέσῃ vb 2nd aor act subj 3rd pers sg   id.

ἐμπεσῇ vb fut mid ind 2nd pers sg   id.

ἐμπέσῃς vb 2nd aor act subj 2nd pers sg   ἐμπίπτω

ἐμπέσοι vb 2nd aor act opt 3rd pers sg   id.

ἐμπεσόντα vb 2nd aor act part masc acc sg   id.

ἐμπεσόντες vb 2nd aor act part masc nom pl   id.

ἐμπεσοῦμαι vb fut mid ind 1st pers sg   id.

ἐμπεσούμεθα vb fut mid ind 1st pers pl   id.

ἐμπεσοῦνται vb fut mid ind 3rd pers pl   id.

ἐμπέσω vb 1st aor act subj 1st pers sg   id.

ἐμπέσωμεν vb 1st aor act subj 1st pers pl   id.

ἐμπεσών vb 2nd aor act part masc nom sg   id.

ἐμπεφραγμένοι vb perf m/p part masc nom pl . . . ἐμφράσσω

ἐμπιμπλαμένη vb pres m/p part fem nom sg . . . ἐμπίμπλημι

ἐμπίμπλανται vb pres m/p ind 3rd pers pl   id.

ἐμπίμπλαται vb pres m/p ind 3rd pers sg   id.

ἐμπιπλᾷ vb pres act ind 3rd pers sg . . . . ἐμπιπλάω

ἐμπιπλαμένη vb pres m/p part fem nom sg   id.

ἐμπιπλάμενος vb pres m/p part masc nom sg   id.

ἐμπιπλᾷς vb pres act ind 2nd pers sg   id.

ἐμπίπλασθε vb pres m/p ind 2nd pers pl   id.

ἐμπίπλαται vb pres m/p ind 3rd pers sg   id.

ἐμπιπλῶν vb pres act part masc nom sg   id.

ἐμπιπλῶντα vb pres act part masc acc sg   id.

ἔμπιπτε vb pres act impv 2nd pers sg . . . . ἐμπίπτω

ἐμπίπτει vb pres act ind 3rd pers sg   id.

ἐμπίπτοντα vb pres act part masc acc sg   id.

ἐμπίπτοντας vb pres act part masc acc pl   id.

ἐμπίπτοντος vb pres act part masc and neut gen sg   id.

ἐμπιστευθέντα vb 1st aor pass part masc acc sg,

       neut nom and acc pl . . . . ἐμπιστεύω

ἐμπιστευθήσεσθε vb fut pass ind 2nd pers pl   id.

ἐμπιστευθήσεται vb fut pass ind 3rd pers sg   id.

ἐμπιστευθήτωσαν vb 1st aor pass impv 3rd pers pl   id.

ἐμπιστεύσαι vb 1st aor act opt 3rd pers sg   id.

ἐμπιστεύσαντας vb 1st aor act part masc acc pl   id.

ἐμπιστεύσας vb 1st aor act part masc nom sg   id.

ἐμπιστεύσατε vb 1st aor act impv 2nd pers pl   id.

ἐμπιστεύσει vb fut act ind 3rd pers sg   id.

ἐμπιστεύσειν vb fut act inf   id.

ἐμπιστεύσῃ vb 1st aor act subj 3rd pers sg   id.

ἐμπιστεύσῃς vb 1st aor act subj 2nd pers sg   id.

ἐμπιστεύων vb pres act part masc nom sg   id.

ἐμπλακέντες vb 2nd aor pass part masc nom pl . . . ἐμπλέκω

ἐμπλακήσεται vb fut pass ind 3rd pers sg   id.

ἔμπλασον vb 1st aor act impv 2nd pers sg . . . . . . ἐμπλάσσω

ἐμπλατύνει vb pres act ind 3rd pers sg . . . . ἐμπλατύνω

ἐμπλατύνῃ vb pres act subj 3rd pers sg   id.

ἐμπλάτυνον vb pres act part neut nom and acc sg   id.

ἐμπλατύνω vb pres act ind 1st pers sg   id.

ἐμπλατύνων vb pres act part masc nom sg   id.

ἐμπλατύνωσιν vb pres act subj 3rd pers pl   id.

ἐμπληθυνθείς vb 1st aor pass part masc nom sg . ἐμπληθύνω

ἐμπλῆσαι vb 1st aor act inf . . . . ἐμπίμπλημι

ἐμπλήσαιμι	vb 1st aor act opt 1st pers sg	ἐμπίμπλημι
ἐμπλησάντων	vb 1st aor act part masc and neut gen pl	id.
ἐμπλήσει	vb fut act ind 3rd pers sg	id.
ἐμπλήσεις	vb fut act ind 2nd pers sg	id.
ἐμπλήσῃ	vb 1st aor act subj 3rd pers sg	id.
ἐμπλήσῃς	vb 1st aor act subj 2nd pers sg	id.
ἐμπλησθείη	vb 1st aor pass opt 3rd pers sg	id.
ἐμπλησθείς	vb 1st aor pass part masc nom sg	id.
ἐμπλησθέντες	vb 1st aor pass part masc nom pl	id.
ἐμπλησθέντι	vb 1st aor pass part masc and neut dat sg	id.
ἐμπλησθῇ	vb 1st aor pass subj 3rd pers sg	id.
ἐμπλησθῆναι	vb 1st aor pass inf	id.
ἐμπλησθῇς	vb 1st aor pass subj 2nd pers sg	id.
ἐμπλησθήσεσθε	vb fut pass ind 2nd pers pl	id.
ἐμπλησθήσεται	vb fut pass ind 3rd pers sg	id.
ἐμπλησθήσῃ	vb fut pass ind 2nd pers sg	id.
ἐμπλησθήσονται	vb fut pass ind 3rd pers pl	id.
ἐμπλήσθητε	vb 1st aor pass impv 2nd pers pl	id.
ἐμπλησθῆτε	vb 1st aor pass subj 2nd pers pl	id.
ἐμπλήσθητι	vb 1st aor pass impv 2nd pers sg	id.
ἐμπλησθήτω	vb 1st aor pass impv 3rd pers sg	id.
ἐμπλησθῶσι(ν)	vb 1st aor pass subj 3rd pers pl	id.
ἔμπλησον	vb 1st aor act impv 2nd pers sg	id.
ἐμπλήσω	vb 1st aor act subj 1st pers sg,	
	fut act ind 1st pers sg	id.
ἐμπλήσωσι	vb 1st aor act subj 3rd pers pl	id.
ἐμπλόκια	noun neut nom and acc pl	ἐμπλόκιον
ἐμπλόκιον	noun neut nom and acc sg	id.
ἐμπλοκίου	noun neut gen sg	id.
ἐμπνέον	vb pres act part neut nom and acc sg	ἐμπνέω
ἐμπνεύσαντα	vb 1st aor act part masc acc sg	id.
ἐμπνεύσεως	noun fem gen sg	ἔμπνευσις
ἔμπνουν	adj acc sg, neut nom sg	ἔμπνους
ἔμπνους	adj masc and fem nom sg	
ἐμποδίσῃς	vb 1st aor act subj 2nd pers sg	ἐμποδίζω
ἐμποδισθῇς	vb 1st aor pass subj 2nd pers sg	id.
ἐμπόδισον	vb 1st aor act impv 2nd pers sg	id.
ἐμποδιστικῶν	adj gen pl	ἐμποδιστικός
ἐμποδοστάτης	noun masc nom sg	
ἐμποιῇ	vb pres m/p ind 2nd pers sg	ἐμποιέω
ἐμποιούμενοι	vb pres m/p part masc nom pl	id.
ἐμπολήσομεν	vb fut act ind 1st pers pl	ἐμπολάω
ἐμπόνου	adj fem gen sg	ἔμπονος
ἐμπορεύεσθαι	vb pres dep inf	ἐμπορεύομαι
ἐμπορεύεσθε	vb pres dep impv 2nd pers pl,	
	vb pres dep ind 2nd pers pl	id.
ἐμπορευέσθωσαν	vb pres dep impv 3rd pers pl	id.
ἐμπορευομένη	vb pres dep part fem nom sg	id.
ἐμπορευομένων	vb pres dep part gen pl	id.
ἐμπορεύονται	vb pres dep ind 3rd pers pl	id.
ἐμπορευσόμεθα	vb fut mid ind 1st pers pl	id.
ἐμπόρια	noun neut nom and acc pl	ἐμπόριον

εμπορία	noun fem nom sg	
ἐμπορίᾳ	noun fem dat sg	ἐμπορία
ἐμπορίαν	noun fem acc sg	id.
ἐμπορίας	noun fem gen sg and acc pl	id.
ἐμπόριον	noun neut nom and acc sg	
ἐμπορίῳ	noun neut dat sg	ἐμπόριον
ἔμπεροι	noun masc nom pl	ἔμπορος
ἐμπέροις	noun masc dat pl	id.
ἔμπερος	noun masc nom sg	id.
ἐμπόρου	noun masc gen sg	id.
ἐμπόρους	noun masc acc pl	id.
ἐμπορποῦσθαι	vb pres m/p inf	ἐμπορπόω
ἐμπόρων	noun masc gen pl	ἔμπορος
ἐμπρῆσαι	vb 1st aor act inf	ἐμπίμπρημι
ἐμπρήσαντας	vb 1st aor act part masc acc pl	id.
ἐμπρήσατε	vb 1st aor act impv 2nd pers pl	id.
ἐμπρήσειν	vb fut act inf	id.
ἐμπρήσεις	vb fut act ind 2nd pers sg	id.
ἐμπρήσομεν	vb fut act ind 1st pers pl	id.
ἐμπρήσουσιν	vb fut act ind 3rd pers pl	id.
ἔμπροσθε	see ἔμπροσθεν	
ἔμπροσθεν	adverb and preposition	
ἐμπρόσθια	noun neut nom and acc pl	ἐμπρόσθιον
ἐμπροσθίους	adj masc and fem acc pl	ἐμπρόσθιος
ἐμπροσθίων	adj gen pl	id.
ἐμπτύσεται	vb fut mid ind 3rd pers sg	ἐμπτύω
ἐμπτυσμάτων	noun neut gen pl	ἔμπτυσμα
ἐμπυριεῖ	vb fut act ind 3rd pers sg	ἐμπυρίζω
ἐμπυρίζεται	vb pres m/p ind 3rd pers sg	id.
ἐμπυρίζοντες	vb pres act part masc nom pl	id.
ἐμπυρίζουσιν	vb pres act ind 3rd pers pl	id.
ἐμπυρισθεῖσι	vb 1st aor pass part masc and neut dat pl	id.
ἐμπυρισθῇς	vb 1st aor pass subj 2nd pers sg	id.
ἐμπυρισθήσονται	vb fut pass ind 3rd pers pl	id.
ἐμπυρισμόν	noun masc acc sg	εμπυρισμός
ἐμπυρισμός	noun masc nom sg	id.
ἐμπυρισμῷ	noun masc dat sg	id.
Ἐμπυρισμῷ	pr noun masc dat sg	Ἐμπυρισμός
ἐμπυριστήν	adj masc acc sg	εμπυριστής
ἐμπυρίσομεν	vb 1st aor act subj 1st pers pl	ἐμπυρίζω
ἐμπυριῶ	vb fut act ind 1st pers sg	id.
ἔμπυροι	adj masc and fem nom pl	ἔμπυρος
ἐμπύρων	adj gen pl	id.
ἐμυκτήριζον	vb impf act ind 3rd pers pl	μυκτηρίζω
ἐμυκτήρισαν	vb 1st aor act ind 3rd pers pl	id.
ἐμυκτήρισεν	vb 1st aor act ind 3rd pers sg	id.
ἐμφανές	adj neut nom and acc sg	ἐμφανής
ἐμφανῆ	adj masc and fem acc sg, neut nom and acc pl	id.
ἐμφάνηθι	vb 2nd aor pass impv 2nd pers sg	ἐμφαίνω
ἐμφανής	adj masc and fem nom sg	
ἐμφανίζεται	vb pres m/p ind 3rd pers sg	ἐμφανίζω
ἐμφανισμοῦ	noun masc gen sg	ἐμφανισμός

ἐμφάνισον   vb 1st aor act impv 2nd pers sg   ..... ἐμφανίζω

ἐμφανῶς   adverb

ἐμφάσει   noun fem dat sg .... ἔμφασις

ἐμφέρεσθαι   vb pres m/p inf .... ἐμφέρω

ἔμφοβος   adj masc and fem nom sg

ἐμφραγμός   noun masc nom sg

ἐμφράξαι   vb 1st aor act inf .... ἐμφράσσω

ἐμφράξει   vb fut act ind 3rd pers sg   id.

ἐμφράξετε   vb fut act ind 2nd pers pl   id.

ἔμφραξον   vb 1st aor act impv 2nd pers sg   id.

ἐμφράξουσι   vb fut act ind 3rd pers pl   id.

ἐμφραχθείη   vb 1st aor pass opt 3rd pers sg   id.

ἐμφραχθήσεται   vb fut pass ind 3rd pers sg   id.

ἐμφυσῆσαι   vb 1st aor act inf .... ἐμφυσάω

ἐμφυσήσαντα   vb 1st aor act part masc acc sg   id.

ἐμφύσησον   vb 1st aor act impv 2nd pers sg   id.

ἐμφυσήσω   vb fut act ind 1st pers sg   id.

ἐμφυσιοῦντες   vb pres act part masc nom pl ..... ἐμφυσιόω

ἐμφυσῶν   vb pres act part masc nom sg .... ἐμφυσάω

ἔμφυτος   adj masc and fem nom sg

ἐμῷ   adj masc and neut dat sg .... ἐμός

ἐμῶν   adj gen pl   id.

ἐμωράνθη   vb 1st aor pass ind 3rd pers sg .... μωραίνω

ἐμωράνθην   vb 1st aor pass ind 1st pers sg   id.

ἐν   preposition

ἕν   adj neut nom and acc sg .... εἷς

ἔν   (before enclitic)   see ἐν

ἕνα   adj masc acc sg .... εἷς

Ενααλα   pr noun

ἐναγκαλίζῃ   vb pres dep subj 2nd pers sg .. ἐναγκαλίζομαι

ἐναγκαλίζομαι   vb pres dep ind 1st pers sg

ἐναγκαλισμάτων   noun neut gen pl .... ἐναγκάλισμα

ἐναγωνίσασθε   vb 1st aor mid impv

     2nd pers pl .... ἐναγωνίζομαι

Εναθ   pr noun

Ενακ   pr noun

Ενακιμ   pr noun

ἐνακισχιλίους   adj masc acc pl .... ἐνακισχίλιοι

ἐνακισχιλίων   adj gen pl   id.

ἐνακούουσιν   vb pres act ind 3rd pers pl .... ἐνακούω

ἐνακουσθήσεται   vb fut pass ind 3rd pers sg   id.

ἐναλλαγή   noun fem nom sg

ἐναλλάξ   adverb

ἐνάλλεσθε   vb pres dep ind 2nd pers pl .... ἐνάλλομαι

ἐναλλόμενος   vb pres dep part masc nom sg   id.

ἐναλοῦμαι   vb fut mid ind 1st pers sg   id.

ἔναντι   adverb and preposition

ἐναντία   adj neut nom and acc pl .... ἐναντίος

ἐναντίας   adj fem gen sg   id.

ἐναντίοι   adj masc nom pl   id.

ἐναντίον   adverb and preposition

ἐναντιοῦ   vb pres dep impv 2nd pers sg ...... ἐναντιόομαι

ἐναντιουμένους   vb pres dep part

     masc acc pl .... ἐναντιόομαι

ἐναντιοῦται   vb pres dep ind 3rd pers sg   id.

ἐναντιωθῆναι   vb 1st aor pass inf   id.

ἐναντιωθησόμενα   vb fut pass part neut nom and acc pl   id.

ἐναντίων   adj gen pl .... ἐναντίος

ἐναπέθανεν   vb 2nd aor act ind 3rd pers sg ... ἐναποθνήσκω

ἐναπερείσασθαι   vb 1st aor mid inf .... ἐναπερείδω

ἐναποσφραγίζομεν   vb pres act ind

     1st pers pl .... ἐναποσφραγίζω

ἐνάρετον   adj acc sg, neut nom sg .... ἐνάρετος

ἐναρίθμιος   adj masc and fem nom sg

ἐνάρκησεν   vb 1st aor act ind 3rd pers sg .... ναρκάω

ἐναρμοσάμενοι   vb 1st aor mid part

     masc nom pl .... ἐναρμόζω

ἐναρμόσασθε   vb 1st aor mid impv 2nd pers pl   id.

ἔναρξαι   vb 1st aor mid impv 2nd pers sg ...... ἐνάρχομαι

ἐνάρχεται   vb pres dep ind 3rd pers sg   id.

ἐναρχόμενος   vb pres dep part masc nom sg   id.

ἐναρχομένου   vb pres dep part masc and neut gen sg   id.

ἐναρχομένους   vb pres dep part masc acc pl   id.

ἐνάρχου   vb pres dep impv 2nd pers sg   id.

ἐνατενίσας   vb 1st aor act part masc nom sg ..... ἐνατενίζω

ἐνάτη   adj fem dat sg .... ἔνατος

ἐνάτης   adj fem gen sg   id.

ἔνατος   adj masc nom sg   id.

Ενατου   pr noun

ἐνάτου   adj masc and neut gen sg .... ἔνατος

ἐνάτῳ   adj masc and neut dat sg   id.

ἐναφήσω   vb fut act ind 1st pers sg .... ἐναφίημι

Εναχ   pr noun

Ενγαδδι   pr noun

ἐνδεδεμένα   vb perf m/p part neut nom and acc pl .... ἐνδέω

ἐνδεδεμένη   vb perf m/p part fem nom sg   id.

ἐνδεδεμένοι   vb perf m/p part masc nom pl   id.

ἐνδέδεσαι   vb perf m/p ind 2nd pers sg   id.

ἐνδεδυκότα   vb perf act part masc acc sg .... ἐνδύω

ἐνδεδυκότας   vb perf act part masc acc pl   id.

ἐνδεδυκότι   vb perf act part masc and neut dat sg   id.

ἐνδεδυκότος   vb perf act part masc and neut gen sg   id.

ἐνδεδυκώς   vb perf act part masc nom sg   id.

ἐνδεδυμένοι   vb perf m/p part masc nom pl   id.

ἐνδεδυμένος   vb perf m/p part masc nom sg   id.

ἐνδεδυμένου   vb perf m/p part masc and neut gen sg   id.

ἐνδεδυμένους   vb perf m/p part masc acc pl   id.

ἐνδεδυμένῳ   vb perf m/p part masc and neut dat sg   id.

ἐνδεδυμένων   vb perf m/p part gen pl   id.

ἐνδεεῖ   adj dat sg .... ἐνδεής

ἐνδεεῖς   adj masc and fem nom and acc pl   id.

ἐνδεεῖται   vb fut mid ind 3rd pers sg .... ἐνδέω

ἐνδεέσι   adj dat pl .... ἐνδεής

ἐνδεῆ   adj masc and fem acc sg, neut nom and acc pl   id.

ἐνδεηθήσεται vb fut pass ind 3rd pers sg . . . . ἐνδέω	ἐνδοξασθήσομαι vb fut pass ind
ἐνδεηθήσῃ vb fut pass ind 2nd pers sg id.	1st pers sg . . . . ἐνδοξάζομαι
ἐνδεής adj masc and fem nom sg	ἐνδοξασθήσονται vb fut pass ind 3rd pers pl id.
ἔνδεια noun fem nom sg	ἐνδοξάσθητι vb 1st aor pass impv 2nd pers sg id.
ἐνδείᾳ noun fem dat sg . . . . ἔνδεια	ἔνδοξοι adj masc and fem nom pl . . . . ἔνδοξος
ἔνδειαν noun fem acc sg id.	ἐνδόξοις adj dat pl id.
ἐνδείας noun fem gen sg id.	ἔνδοξον adj acc sg, neut nom sg id.
ἐνδεικνύμενοι vb pres m/p part masc nom pl . . . . ἐνδεικνύω	ἔνδοξος adj masc and fem nom sg id.
ἐνδεικνύμενος vb pres m/p part masc nom sg id.	ἐνδοξότατος superl adj masc nom sg id.
ἐνδείκνυσαι vb pres m/p ind 2nd pers sg id.	ἐνδοξότερον comp adj masc acc sg, neut nom and acc sg id.
ἐνδείκτης noun masc nom sg	ἐνδόξου adj gen sg id.
ἐνδειξόμενος vb fut mid part masc nom sg . . . . ἐνδεικνύω	ἐνδόξους adj masc and fem acc pl id.
ἐνδείξωμαι vb 1st aor mid subj 1st pers sg id.	ἐνδόξῳ adj dat sg id.
ἐνδειχθῇ vb 1st aor pass subj 3rd pers sg id.	ἐνδόξων adj gen pl id.
ἔνδεκα indecl number	ἐνδόξως adverb
ἐνδεκάτη adj fem dat sg . . . . ἐνδέκατος	ἐνδόσθια noun neut nom and acc pl
ἐνδέκατος adj masc nom sg id.	ἐνδοσθίοις noun neut dat pl . . . . ἐνδόσθια
ἐνδεκάτου adj masc and neut gen sg id.	ἐνδοσθίων noun neut gen pl id.
ἐνδεκάτῳ adj masc and neut dat sg id.	ἔνδυμα noun neut nom and acc sg
ἐνδελεχεῖς adj masc and fem nom and acc pl . . . . ἐνδελεχής	ἐνδύμασι noun neut dat pl . . . . ἔνδυμα
ἐνδελεχήσει vb fut act ind 3rd pers sg . . . . ἐνδελεχέω	ἐνδύματα noun neut nom and acc pl id.
ἐνδελεχιεῖ vb fut act ind 3rd pers sg . . . . ἐνδελεχίζω	ἐνδύματος noun neut gen sg id.
ἐνδελέχιζε vb pres act impv 2nd pers sg id.	ἐνδυμάτων noun neut gen pl id.
ἐνδελεχίζοντι vb pres act part masc and neut dat sg id.	ἐνδύουσιν vb pres act ind 3rd pers pl . . . . ἐνδύω
ἐνδελεχίζων vb pres act part masc nom sg id.	ἔνδυσαι vb 1st aor mid impv 2nd pers sg id.
ἐνδελεχισθήσεται vb fut pass ind 3rd pers sg id.	ἐνδύσαιντο vb 1st aor mid opt 3rd pers pl id.
ἐνδελεχισμόν noun masc acc sg . . . . ἐνδελεχισμός	ἐνδύσασθαι vb 1st aor mid inf id.
ἐνδελεχισμός noun masc nom sg id.	ἐνδύσασθε vb 1st aor mid impv 2nd pers pl id.
ἐνδελεχισμοῦ noun masc gen sg id.	ἐνδυσάσθωσαν vb 1st aor mid impv 3rd pers pl id.
ἐνδελεχοῦς adj gen sg . . . . ἐνδελεχής	ἐνδύσατε vb 1st aor act impv 2nd pers pl id.
ἐνδελεχῶς adverb	ἐνδύσεις vb fut act ind 2nd pers sg id.
ἐνδεοῦς adj gen sg . . . . ἐνδεής	ἐνδύσεται vb fut mid ind 3rd pers sg id.
ἔνδεσμον noun masc acc sg . . . . ἔνδεσμος	ἐνδύσεως noun fem gen sg . . . . ἔνδυσις
ἐνδέσμους noun masc acc pl id.	ἐνδύσῃ vb fut mid ind 2nd pers sg . . . . ἐνδύω
ἐνδέχεται vb pres dep ind 3rd pers sg . . . . ἐνδέχομαι	ἐνδύσηται vb 1st aor mid subj 3rd pers sg id.
ἐνδεχόμενα vb pres dep part neut nom and acc pl id.	ἔνδυσιν noun fem acc sg . . . . ἔνδυσις
ἐνδεχομένως adverb	ἔνδυσον vb 1st aor act impv 2nd pers sg . . . . ἐνδύω
ἐνδιαβάλλειν vb pres act inf . . . . ἐνδιαβάλλω	ἐνδύσονται vb fut mid ind 3rd pers pl id.
ἐνδιαβάλλοντες vb pres act part masc nom pl	ἐνδύσουσιν vb fut act ind 3rd pers pl id.
ἐνδιαβαλλόντων vb pres act part masc and neut gen pl id.	ἐνδύσω vb fut act ind 1st pers sg id.
ἐνδιατρίψει vb fut act ind 3rd pers sg . . . . ἐνδιατρίβω	ἐνδύσωμαι vb 1st aor mid subj 1st pers sg id.
ἐνδιδύσκεσθαι vb pres m/p inf . . . . ἐνδιδύσκω	ἐνδώσει vb fut act ind 3rd pers sg . . . . ἐνδίδωμι
ἐνδιδύσκοντα vb pres act part masc acc sg	ἐνδῶσιν vb 2nd aor act subj 3rd pers pl id.
ἐνδιδύσκονται vb pres m/p ind 3rd pers pl id.	ἐνέβαλεν vb 2nd aor act ind 3rd pers sg . . . . ἐμβάλλω
ἐνδιέβαλλον vb impf act ind 3rd pers pl . . . . . ἐνδιαβάλλω	ἐνεβάλετο vb 2nd aor mid ind 3rd pers sg id.
ἐνδογενοῦς adj gen sg . . . . ἐνδογενής	ἐνεβάλλετε vb impf act ind 2nd pers pl id.
ἔνδοθεν adverb	ἐνέβαλλον vb impf act ind 3rd pers pl id.
ἔνδον adverb	ἐνέβαλον vb 2nd aor act ind 1st pers sg and 3rd pers pl id.
ἔνδοξα adj neut nom and acc pl . . . . ἔνδοξος	ἐνεβάλοσαν vb 2nd aor act ind 3rd pers pl id.
ἐνδοξάζεσθαι vb pres dep inf . . . . ἐνδοξάζομαι	ἐνέβη vb 2nd aor act ind 3rd pers sg . . . . ἐμβαίνω
ἐνδοξαζόμενος vb pres dep part masc nom sg id.	ἐνέβλεπον vb impf act ind
ἐνδοξαζομένου vb pres dep part masc and neut gen sg id.	1st pers sg and 3rd pers pl . . . . ἐμβλέπω

ἐνεβλέποντο vb impf m/p ind 3rd pers pl . . . . ἐμβλέπω
ἐνεβλέψατε vb 1st aor act ind 2nd pers pl   id.
ἐνέβλεψεν vb 1st aor act ind 3rd pers sg   id.
ἐνεβλήθησαν vb 1st aor pass ind 3rd pers pl . . . . . ἐμβάλλω
ἐνέγκαι vb 1st aor act inf . . . . φέρω
ἐνέγκαισαν vb 1st aor act opt 3rd pers pl   id.
ἐνέγκαντα vb 1st aor act part masc acc sg   id.
ἐνέγκαντες vb 1st aor act part masc nom pl   id.
ἐνέγκαντος vb 1st aor act part masc and neut gen sg   id.
ἐνέγκας vb 1st aor act part masc nom sg   id.
ἐνέγκατε vb 1st aor act impv 2nd pers pl   id.
ἐνεγκάτωσαν vb 1st aor act impv 3rd pers pl   id.
ἔνεγκε vb 2nd aor act impv 2nd pers sg   id.
ἐνεγκεῖν vb 2nd aor act inf   id.
ἐνέγκετε vb 2nd aor act impv 2nd pers pl   id.
ἐνέγκῃ vb 1st aor act subj 3rd pers sg   id.
ἐνέγκητε vb 1st aor act subj 2nd pers pl   id.
ἔνεγκον vb 1st aor act impv 2nd pers sg   id.
ἐνέγκωσιν vb 1st aor act subj 3rd pers pl   id.
ἐνεγυήσω vb 1st aor mid ind 2nd pers sg . . . . ἐγγυάω
ἐνεδεδύκει vb plpf act ind 3rd pers sg . . . . ἐνδύω
ἐνεδεδύκειν vb plpf act ind 1st pers sg   id.
ἐνεδειξάμεθα vb 1st aor mid ind 1st pers pl . . . . . ἐνδεικνύω
ἐνεδείξαντο vb 1st aor mid ind 3rd pers pl   id.
ἐνεδείχθη vb 1st aor pass ind 3rd pers sg   id.
ἐνεδίδου vb impf act ind 3rd pers sg . . . . ἐνδίδωμι
ἐνεδιδύσκοντο vb impf m/p ind 3rd pers pl . . . . ἐνδιδύσκω
ἔνεδρα noun neut nom and acc pl . . . . ἔνεδρον
ἐνέδρᾳ noun fem dat sg . . . . ἐνέδρα
ἐνέδραν noun fem acc sg   id.
ἐνέδρας noun fem gen sg   id.
ἐνέδρευε vb pres act impv 2nd pers sg . . . . ἐνεδρεύω
ἐνεδρεύει vb pres act ind 3rd pers sg   id.
ἐνεδρεύειν vb pres act inf   id.
ἐνεδρεύοντας vb pres act part masc acc pl   id.
ἐνεδρεύοντες vb pres act part masc nom pl   id.
ἐνεδρεύοντος vb pres act part masc and neut gen sg   id.
ἐνεδρευόντων vb pres act part masc and neut gen pl   id.
ἐνεδρεύουσα vb pres act part fem nom sg   id.
ἐνεδρεύσατε vb 1st aor act impv 2nd pers pl   id.
ἐνεδρεύσει vb fut act ind 3rd pers sg   id.
ἐνεδρεύσῃ vb fut mid ind 2nd pers sg,
        1st aor act subj 3rd pers sg   id.
ἐνεδρεύσον vb 1st aor act impv 2nd pers sg   id.
ἐνεδρεύσωμεν vb 1st aor act subj 1st pers pl   id.
ἐνεδρεύων vb pres act part masc nom sg   id.
ἔνεδρον noun neut nom and acc sg
ἐνέδρου noun neut gen sg . . . . ἔνεδρον
ἐνέδρων noun neut gen pl   id.
ἐνεδυνάμωσεν vb 1st aor act ind 3rd pers sg . . . ἐνδυναμόω
ἐνεδυόμην vb impf m/p ind 1st pers sg . . . . ἐνδύω
ἐνέδυσα vb 1st aor act ind 1st pers sg   id.

ἐνεδυσάμην vb 1st aor mid ind 1st pers sg . . . . ἐνδύω
ἐνέδυσαν vb 1st aor act ind 3rd pers pl   id.
ἐνεδύσαντο vb 1st aor mid ind 3rd pers pl   id.
ἐνέδυσας vb 1st aor act ind 2nd pers sg   id.
ἐνεδύσατο vb 1st aor mid ind 3rd pers sg   id.
ἐνέδυσε(ν) vb 1st aor act ind 3rd pers sg   id.
ἐνεδύσω vb 1st aor mid ind 2nd pers sg   id.
ἐνεθρόνισεν vb 1st aor act ind 3rd pers sg . . . . . ἐνθρονίζω
ἐνέθρυψεν vb 1st aor act ind 3rd pers sg . . . . ἐνθρύπτω
ἐνεθυμεῖτο vb impf dep ind 3rd pers sg . . . . ἐνθυμέομαι
ἐνεθυμήθη vb 1st aor pass ind 3rd pers sg   id.
ἐνεθυμήθησαν vb 1st aor pass ind 3rd pers pl   id.
ἐνειλημένη vb perf m/p part fem nom sg . . . . ἐνειλέω
ἐνεῖρας vb 1st aor act ind 2nd pers sg . . . . ἐνείρω
ἐνεῖχον vb impf act ind 3rd pers pl . . . . ἐνέχω
ἕνεκα preposition
ἐνεκαθήμεθα vb impf dep ind 1st pers pl . . . . . . ἐγκάθημαι
ἐνεκάθηντο vb impf dep ind 3rd pers pl   id.
ἐνεκάθησθε vb impf dep ind 2nd pers pl   id.
ἐνεκάθητο vb impf dep ind 3rd pers sg   id.
ἐνεκάθισα vb 1st aor act ind 1st pers sg . . . . ἐγκαθίζω
ἐνεκάθισαν vb 1st aor act ind 3rd pers pl   id.
ἐνεκάθισας vb 1st aor act ind 2nd pers sg   id.
ἐνεκαίνισαν vb 1st aor act ind 3rd pers pl . . . . . ἐγκαινίζω
ἐνεκαίνισας vb 1st aor act ind 2nd pers sg   id.
ἐνεκαίνισεν vb 1st aor act ind 3rd pers sg   id.
ἐνεκαινίσθη vb 1st aor pass ind 3rd pers sg   id.
ἐνεκάλεσαν vb 1st aor act ind 3rd pers pl . . . . ἐγκαλέω
ἐνεκάλεσεν vb 1st aor act ind 3rd pers sg   id.
ἐνεκαρτέρουν vb impf act ind 3rd pers pl . . . . ἐγκαρτερέω
ἐνεκαυχήσαντο vb 1st aor mid ind
        3rd pers pl . . . . ἐγκαυχάομαι
ἐνέκειτο vb impf m/p ind 3rd pers sg . . . . ἔγκειμαι
ἕνεκεν preposition
ἐνεκεντρίζοντο vb impf m/p ind 3rd pers pl . . . ἐγκεντρίζω
ἐνεκίσσησεν vb 1st aor act ind 3rd pers sg . . . . . ἐγκισσάω
ἐνεκίσσων vb impf act ind 3rd pers pl   id.
ἐνεκότει vb impf act ind 3rd pers sg . . . . ἐγκοτέω
ἐνεκότουν vb impf act ind 3rd pers pl   id.
ἐνεκρατευσάμην vb 1st aor mid ind
        1st pers sg . . . . ἐγκρατεύομαι
ἐνεκρατεύσατο vb 1st aor mid ind 3rd pers sg   id.
ἐνέκρουσεν vb 1st aor act ind 3rd pers sg . . . . . . ἐγκρούω
ἐνέκρυψεν vb 1st aor act ind 3rd pers sg . . . . . . ἐγκρύπτω
ἐνεκυλίσθης vb 1st aor pass ind 2nd pers sg . . . . . ἐγκυλίω
Ενεμασσαρ pr noun
ἐνέμειναν vb 1st aor act ind 3rd pers pl . . . . ἐμμένω
ἐνεμείνατε vb 1st aor act ind 2nd pers pl   id.
ἐνέμεινε(ν) vb 1st aor act ind 3rd pers sg   id.
ἔνεμεν vb impf act ind 3rd pers sg . . . . νέμω
ἐνέμεσθε vb impf m/p ind 2nd pers pl   id.
Ενεμεσσαρος pr noun masc nom sg

Ενεμεσσαρου pr noun masc gen sg . . . . Ενεμεσσαρος
Ενεμετιιμ pr noun
ἐνέμετο vb impf m/p ind 3rd pers sg . . . . νέμω
ἐνεμήθησαν vb 1st aor pass ind 3rd pers pl   id.
ἐνέμοντο vb impf m/p ind 3rd pers pl   id.
ἐνενήκοντα indecl number
ἐνενηκονταετῆ adj masc and fem acc sg,
          neut nom and acc pl . . . . ἐνενηκονταετής
ἐνενοήθης vb 1st aor pass ind 2nd pers sg . . . . ἐννοέω
ἐνενόησαν vb 1st aor act ind 3rd pers pl   id.
ἐνεξουσιαζόμενος vb pres dep part
          masc nom sg . . . . ἐνεξουσιάζομαι
ἐνεξουσιάσθης vb 1st aor pass ind 2nd pers sg   id.
ἐνεοί adj masc nom pl . . . . ἐνεός
ἐνεόν adj masc acc sg, neut nom and acc sg   id.
ἐνεπάγην vb 2nd aor pass ind 1st pers sg . . . . . . ἐμπήγνυμι
ἐνεπάγησαν vb 2nd aor pass ind 3rd pers pl   id.
ἐνέπαιζεν vb impf act ind 3rd pers sg . . . . ἐμπαίζω
ἐνέπαιζετο vb impf m/p ind 3rd pers sg   id.
ἐνέπαιζον vb impf act ind 3rd pers pl   id.
ἐνέπαιξαν vb 1st aor act ind 3rd pers pl   id.
ἐνέπαιξεν vb 1st aor act ind 3rd pers sg   id.
ἐνεπεπύριστο vb plpf m/p ind 3rd pers sg . . . . . . ἐμπυρίζω
ἐνεπεριεπατήσαμεν vb 1st aor act ind
          1st pers pl . . . . ἐμπεριπατέω
ἐνέπεσαν vb 1st aor act ind 3rd pers pl . . . . εμπίπτω
ἐνέπεσεν vb 1st aor act ind 3rd pers sg   id.
ἐνέπεσον vb 2nd aor act ind 3rd pers pl   id.
ἐνεπήδησεν vb 1st aor act ind 3rd pers sg . . . . . . ἐμπηδάω
ἐνέπηξεν vb 1st aor act ind 3rd pers sg . . . . . . ἐμπήγνυμι
ἐνεπίμπλασαν vb impf act ind 3rd pers pl . . . . . ἐμπίμπλημι
ἐνεπίμπλων vb impf act ind 3rd pers pl   id.
ἐνεπίμπρα vb 1st aor act ind 3rd pers sg . . . . . ἐμπίμπρημι
ἐνεπίμπρων vb impf act ind 3rd pers pl   id.
ἐνέπιπλω vb 1st aor mid ind 2nd pers sg . . . . ἐμπίπλημι
ἐνεπιπλῶντο vb impf m/p ind 3rd pers pl . . . . . . ἐμπιπλάω
ἐνεπίστευσαν vb 1st aor act ind 3rd pers pl . . . . ἐμπιστεύω
ἐνεπιστεύσατε vb 1st aor act ind 2nd pers pl   id.
ἐνεπίστευσεν vb 1st aor act ind 3rd pers sg   id.
ἐνέπλησα vb 1st aor act ind 1st pers sg . . . . ἐμπίμπλημι
ἐνέπλησαν vb 1st aor act ind 3rd pers pl   id.
ἐνέπλησας vb 1st aor act ind 2nd pers sg   id.
ἐνεπλήσατε vb 1st aor act ind 2nd pers pl   id.
ἐνέπλησεν vb 1st aor act ind 3rd pers sg   id.
ἐνεπλήσθη vb 1st aor pass ind 3rd pers sg   id.
ἐνεπλήσθημεν vb 1st aor pass ind 1st pers pl   id.
ἐνεπλήσθην vb 1st aor pass ind 1st pers sg   id.
ἐνεπλήσθης vb 1st aor pass ind 2nd pers sg   id.
ἐνεπλήσθησαν vb 1st aor pass ind 3rd pers pl   id.
ἐνεπόδιζον vb impf act ind 3rd pers pl . . . . ἐμποδίζω
ἐνεποδίσθη vb 1st aor pass ind 3rd pers sg   id.
ἐνεποδίσθησαν vb 1st aor pass ind 3rd pers pl   id.

ἐνεπορεύετο vb impf dep ind 3rd pers sg . . . . ἐμπορεύομαι
ἐνεπορεύοντο vb impf dep ind 3rd pers pl   id.
ἐνέπρησαν vb 1st aor act ind 3rd pers pl . . . . . . ἐμπίμπρημι
ἐνέπρησεν vb 1st aor act ind 3rd pers sg   id.
ἐνεπρήσθη vb 1st aor pass ind 3rd pers sg   id.
ἐνεπρήσθησαν vb 1st aor pass ind 3rd pers pl   id.
ἐνέπτυσεν vb 1st aor act ind 3rd pers sg . . . . ἐμπτύω
ἐνεπυρίσαμεν vb 1st aor act ind 3rd pers sg . . . ἐμπυρίζω
ἐνεπύρισαν vb 1st aor act ind 3rd pers pl   id.
ἐνεπυρίσατε vb 1st aor act ind 2nd pers pl   id.
ἐνεπύρισε(ν) vb 1st aor act ind 3rd pers sg   id.
ἐνεπυρίσθη vb 1st aor pass ind 3rd pers sg   id.
ἐνεπυρίσθησαν vb 1st aor pass ind 3rd pers pl   id.
ἐνεργάσασθαι vb 1st aor mid inf . . . . ἐνεργάζομαι
ἐνεργεῖ vb pres act ind 3rd pers sg . . . . ἐνεργέω
ἐνέργεια noun fem nom sg
ἐνεργείᾳ noun fem dat sg . . . . ἐνέργεια
ἐνέργειαν noun fem acc sg   id.
ἐνεργείας noun fem gen sg
ἐνεργεῖν vb pres act inf . . . . ἐνεργέω
ἐνεργεῖται vb pres m/p ind 3rd pers sg   id.
ἐνεργούς adj masc and fem acc pl . . . . ἐνεργός
ἐνεργοῦσαν vb pres act part fem acc sg . . . . ἐνεργέω
ἐνεργῶν vb pres act part masc nom sg   id.
ἐνέσεισαν vb 1st aor act ind 3rd pers pl . . . . ἐνσείω
ἐνέσεισε(ν) vb 1st aor act ind 3rd pers sg   id.
ἐνέστη vb 2nd aor act ind 3rd pers sg . . . . ἐνίστημι
ἐνεστηκότος vb perf act part masc and neut gen sg   id.
ἐνεστιν vb pres act ind 3rd pers sg . . . . ἔνειμι
ἐνεστός vb perf act part neut nom and acc sg . . . . . ἐνίστημι
ἐνεστῶσαν vb perf act part fem acc sg   id.
ἐνεστώσης vb perf act part fem gen sg   id.
ἐνεστῶσιν vb perf act part masc and neut dat pl   id.
ἐνεστῶτα vb perf act part masc acc sg   id.
ἐνεστῶτος vb perf act part masc and neut gen sg   id.
ἐνέσχηται vb perf m/p ind 3rd pers sg . . . . ἐνέχω
ἐνετάγη vb 2nd aor pass ind 3rd pers sg . . . . ἐντάσσω
ἐνέταξεν vb 1st aor act ind 3rd pers sg   id.
ἐνεταφίασαν vb 1st aor act ind 3rd pers pl . . . . ἐνταφιάζω
ἐνετειλάμεθα vb 1st aor mid ind 1st pers pl . . . ἐντέλλομαι
ἐνετειλάμην vb 1st aor mid ind 1st pers sg   id.
ἐνετείλαντο vb 1st aor mid ind 3rd pers pl   id.
ἐνετείλατο vb 1st aor mid ind 3rd pers sg   id.
ἐνετείλω vb 1st aor mid ind 2nd pers sg   id.
ἐνέτεινα vb 1st aor act ind 1st pers sg . . . . ἐντείνω
ἐνέτειναν vb 1st aor act ind 3rd pers pl   id.
ἐνέτεινεν vb 1st aor act ind 3rd pers sg   id.
ἐνετέλλεσθε vb impf dep ind 2nd pers pl . . . . . . ἐντέλλομαι
ἐνετίναξαν vb 1st aor act ind 3rd pers pl . . . . . . ἐντινάσσω
ἐνετίνασσον vb impf act ind 3rd pers pl   id.
ἐνετράπη vb 2nd aor pass ind 3rd pers sg . . . . ἐντρέπω
ἐνετράπην vb 2nd aor pass ind 1st pers sg   id.

ἐνετράπης vb 2nd aor pass ind 2nd pers sg ..... ἐντρέπω

ἐνετράπησαν vb 2nd aor pass ind 3rd pers pl   id.

ἐνετρυφήσατε vb 1st aor act ind 2nd pers pl .... ἐντρυφάω

ἐνετύγχανον vb impf act ind 3rd pers pl ...... ἐντυγχάνω

ἐνέτυχον vb 2nd aor act ind 1st pers sg and 3rd pers pl   id.

ἐνευλογεῖσθαι vb pres m/p inf .... ἐνευλογέω

ἐνευλογεῖται vb pres m/p ind 3rd pers sg   id.

ἐνευλογηθῆναι vb 1st aor pass inf   id.

ἐνευλογηθήσονται vb fut pass ind 3rd pers pl   id.

ἐνευροκόπησαν vb 1st aor act ind 3rd pers pl . νευροκοπέω

ἐνευροκόπησεν vb 1st aor act ind 3rd pers sg   id.

ἐνευφραίνετο vb impf dep ind 3rd pers sg .. ἐνευφραίνομαι

ἐνέφαινεν vb impf act ind 3rd pers sg .... ἐμφαίνω

ἐνεφάνιζεν vb impf act ind 3rd pers sg .... ἐμφανίζω

ἐνεφανίζετο vb impf m/p ind 3rd pers sg   id.

ἐνεφάνισαν vb 1st aor act ind 3rd pers pl   id.

ἐνεφάνισεν vb 1st aor act ind 3rd pers sg   id.

ἐνεφράγη vb 2nd aor pass ind 3rd pers sg ...... ἐμφράσσω

ἐνέφραξαν vb 1st aor act ind 3rd pers pl   id.

ἐνέφραξεν vb 1st aor act ind 3rd pers sg   id.

ἐνεφύσησεν vb 1st aor act ind 3rd pers sg .... ἐμφυσάω

ἐνεφυσιώθησαν vb 1st aor pass ind 3rd pers pl .. ἐμφυσιόω

ἐνέχεεν vb impf act ind 3rd pers sg .... ἐγχέω

ἐνέχει vb pres act ind 3rd pers sg .... ἐνέχω

ἐνεχείρησαν vb 1st aor act ind 3rd pers pl ...... ἐγχειρέω

ἐνεχείρησεν vb 1st aor act ind 3rd pers sg   id.

ἐνέχεται vb pres m/p ind 3rd pers sg .... ἐνέχω

ἐνεχθέντος vb 1st aor pass part masc and neut gen sg .. φέρω

ἐνεχρίοσαν vb impf act ind 3rd pers pl .... ἐγχρίω

ἐνεχυράζει vb pres act ind 3rd pers sg .... ἐνεχυράζω

ἐνεχυράζετε vb pres act impv 2nd pers pl   id.

ἐνεχυράσαι vb 1st aor act inf   id.

ἐνεχυράσεις vb fut act ind 2nd pers sg   id.

ἐνεχύρασεν vb 1st aor act ind 3rd pers sg   id.

ἐνεχυράσῃς vb 1st aor act subj 2nd pers sg   id.

ἐνεχύρασμα noun neut nom and acc sg

ἐνεχυρασμόν noun masc acc sg .... ἐνεχυρασμός

ἐνεχυράσω vb fut act ind 1st pers sg .... ἐνεχυράζω

ἐνέχυρον noun neut nom and acc sg

ἐνεχύρῳ noun neut dat sg .... ἐνεχύρον

ἐνήδρευσαν vb 1st aor act ind 3rd pers pl ...... ἐνεδρεύω

ἐνήδρευσεν vb 1st aor act ind 3rd pers sg   id.

ἐνήθλει vb impf act ind 3rd pers sg .... ἐναθλέω

ἐνῆκας vb 1st aor act ind 2nd pers sg .... ἐνίημι

ἐνήλατο vb 1st aor mid ind 3rd pers sg .... ἐνάλλομαι

ἐνηλίκων noun masc gen pl .... ἐνῆλιξ

Ενηνιος pr noun

ἐνήνοχα vb perf act ind 1st pers sg .... φέρω

ἐνήνοχας vb perf act ind 2nd pers sg   id.

ἐνηνόχατε vb perf act ind 2nd pers pl   id.

ἐνήνοχεν vb perf act ind 3rd pers sg   id.

ἐνήργει vb impf act ind 3rd pers sg .... ἐνεργέω

ἐνήργησεν vb 1st aor act ind 3rd pers sg .... ἐνεργέω

ἐνῆρκτο vb plpf dep ind 3rd pers sg .... ἐνάρχομαι

ἐνήρξατο vb 1st aor mid ind 3rd pers sg   id.

ἔνησαν vb 1st aor act ind 3rd pers pl .... νήθω

ἔνησαν vb impf act ind 3rd pers pl .... ἔνειμι

ἐνήστευε vb impf act ind 3rd pers sg .... νηστεύω

ἐνήστευες vb impf act ind 2nd pers sg   id.

ἐνήστευον vb impf act ind 3rd pers pl   id.

ἐνήστευσα vb 1st aor act ind 1st pers sg   id.

ἐνηστεύσαμεν vb 1st aor act ind 1st pers pl   id.

ἐνήστευσαν vb 1st aor act ind 3rd pers pl   id.

ἐνήστευσε(ν) vb 1st aor act ind 3rd pers sg   id.

ἔνθα adverb

ἐνθάδε adverb

ἐνθέματι noun neut dat sg .... ἔνθεμα

ἐνθέμια noun neut nom and acc pl .... ἐνθέμιον

ἐνθέμιον noun neut nom and acc sg   id.

ἔνθεν adverb

ἐνθέντες vb 2nd aor act part masc nom pl .... ἐντίθημι

ἔνθεσθε vb 2nd aor mid impv 2nd pers pl   id.

ἐνθέσμου adj gen sg .... ἔνθεσμος

ἐνθουσιάζουσι vb pres act part

      masc and neut dat pl .... ἐνθουσιάζω

ἐνθυμηθείς vb 1st aor pass part masc nom sg .. ἐνθυμέομαι

ἐνθυμηθέντες vb 1st aor pass part masc nom pl   id.

ἐνθυμηθῆναι vb 1st aor pass inf   id.

ἐνθυμηθῇς vb 1st aor pass subj 2nd pers sg   id.

ἐνθυμηθήσεται vb fut pass ind 3rd pers sg   id.

ἐνθυμήθητι vb 1st aor pass impv 2nd pers sg   id.

ἐνθυμηθῶμεν vb 1st aor pass subj 1st pers pl   id.

ἐνθύμημα noun neut nom and acc sg

ἐνθυμήμασι noun neut dat pl .... ἐνθύμημα

ἐνθυμήματα noun neut nom and acc pl   id.

ἐνθυμήματος noun neut gen sg   id.

ἐνθυμημάτων noun neut gen pl   id.

ἐνθύμιον adj masc acc sg, neut nom and acc sg .. ἐνθύμιον

ἐνθυμίου adj masc and neut gen sg   id.

ἐνθυμούμενος vb pres dep part masc nom sg .. ἐνθυμέομαι

ἐνθυμοῦνται vb pres dep ind 3rd pers pl   id.

ἐνί adj masc and neut dat sg .... εἷς

ἔνι vb pres act ind 3rd pers sg .... ἔνειμι

ἐνιαύσιαι adj fem nom pl .... ἐνιαύσιος

ἐνιαυσίαν adj fem acc sg   id.

ἐνιαυσίας adj fem gen sg and acc pl   id.

ἐνιαύσιοι adj masc nom pl   id.

ἐνιαυσίοις adj masc and neut dat pl   id.

ἐνιαύσιον adj masc acc sg, neut nom and acc sg   id.

ἐνιαυσίους adj masc acc pl   id.

ἐνιαυτόν noun masc acc sg .... ἐνιαυτός

ἐνιαυτός noun masc nom sg   id.

ἐνιαυτοῦ noun masc gen sg   id.

ἐνιαυτούς noun masc acc pl   id.

ἐνιαυτῷ noun masc dat sg	. . . .	ἐνιαυτός
ἐνιαυτῶν noun masc gen pl		id.
ἐνιδών vb 2nd aor act part masc nom sg	. . . .	ἐνοράω
ἐνιέντες vb pres act part masc nom pl	. . . .	ἐνίημι
ἐνίκα vb impf act ind 3rd pers sg	. . . .	νικάω
ἐνικήθη vb 1st aor pass ind 3rd pers sg		id.
ἐνικήθημεν vb 1st aor pass ind 1st pers pl		id.
ἐνίκησαν vb 1st aor act ind 3rd pers pl		id.
ἐνίκησας vb 1st aor act ind 2nd pers sg		id.
ἐνίκησεν vb 1st aor act ind 3rd pers sg		id.
ἔνιοι adj masc nom pl		
ἐνίοις adj masc and neut dat pl	. . . .	ἔνιοι
ἐνίοτε adverb		
ἐνίπτοντο vb impf m/p ind 3rd pers pl	. . . .	νίπτω
ἐνισταμένου vb pres m/p part		
masc and neut gen sg	. . . .	ἐνίστημι
ἐνίσχυον vb impf act ind 3rd pers pl,		
pres act part neut nom and acc sg	. . . .	ἐνισχύω
ἐνισχύοντος vb pres act part masc and neut gen sg		id.
ἐνισχύουσα vb pres act part fem nom sg		id.
ἐνισχῦσαι vb 1st aor act inf		id.
ἐνίσχυσαν vb 1st aor act ind 3rd pers pl		id.
ἐνίσχυσας vb 1st aor act ind 2nd pers sg		id.
ἐνισχύσας vb 1st aor act part masc nom sg		id.
ἐνισχύσατε vb 1st aor act impv 2nd pers pl,		
1st aor act ind 2nd pers pl		id.
ἐνισχυσάτωσαν vb 1st aor act impv 3rd pers pl		id.
ἐνίσχυσε(ν) vb 1st aor act ind 3rd pers sg		id.
ἐνισχύσει vb fut act ind 3rd pers sg		id.
ἐνισχύσεις vb fut act ind 2nd pers sg		id.
ἐνισχύσῃς vb 1st aor act subj 2nd pers sg		id.
ἐνισχύσητε vb 1st aor act subj 2nd pers pl		id.
ἐνίσχυσον vb 1st aor act impv 2nd pers sg		id.
ἐνισχύσουσιν vb fut act ind 3rd pers pl		id.
ἐνισχύσω vb fut act ind 1st pers sg		id.
ἐνισχύσωμεν vb 1st aor act subj 1st pers pl		id.
ἐνισχύων vb pres act part masc nom sg		id.
ἐνιψάμην vb 1st aor mid ind 1st pers sg	. . . .	νίπτω
ἐνίψαντο vb 1st aor mid ind 3rd pers pl		id.
Ενναθωθ pr noun		
ἐννακόσια adj neut nom and acc pl	. . . .	ἐννακόσιοι
ἐννακόσιοι adj masc nom pl		id.
Ενναταν pr noun		
ἐννέα indecl number		
ἐννεακαίδεκα indecl number		
ἐννεακαιδέκατος adj masc nom sg		
ἐννεμομένους vb pres m/p part masc acc pl	. . . .	ἐννέμω
ἐννεύει vb pres act ind 3rd pers sg	. . . .	ἐννεύω
ἐννεύμασι noun neut dat pl	. . . .	ἔννευμα
ἐννεύων vb pres act part masc nom sg	. . . .	ἐννεύω
ἐννοηθῇ vb 1st aor pass subj 3rd pers sg	. . . .	ἐννοέω
ἐννοηθήσεται vb fut pass ind 3rd pers sg		id.
ἐννοήθητε vb 1st aor pass subj 2nd pers pl	. . . .	ἐννοέω
ἐννοήθητι vb 1st aor pass impv 2nd pers sg		id.
ἐννοηθῶσιν vb 1st aor pass subj 3rd pers pl		id.
ἐννοήματος noun neut gen sg	. . . .	ἐννόημα
ἐννόησον vb 1st aor act impv 2nd pers sg	. . . .	ἐννοέω
ἔννοια noun fem nom sg		
ἐννοίᾳ noun fem dat sg	. . . .	ἔννοια
ἔννοιαν noun fem acc sg		id.
ἐννοίας noun fem gen sg and acc pl		id.
ἐννοιῶν noun fem gen pl		id.
Εννομ pr noun		
ἐννόμου adj gen sg	. . . .	ἔννομος
ἐννόμως adverb		
ἐννοούμενοι vb pres m/p part masc nom pl	. . . .	ἐννοέω
ἐννοσσεύουσα vb pres act part fem nom sg	. . .	ἐννοσσεύω
ἐννοσσεύσουσιν vb fut act ind 3rd pers pl		id.
ἐννοσσοποιησάμενα vb 1st aor mid part		
neut nom and acc pl	. . . .	ἐννοσσοποιέω
ἔννυχον adj masc and fem acc sg	. . . .	ἔννυχος
Ενναν pr noun		
ἐνόησαν vb 1st aor act ind 3rd pers pl	. . . .	νοέω
ἐνόησας vb 1st aor act ind 2nd pers sg		id.
ἐνόησεν vb 1st aor act ind 3rd pers sg		id.
ἐνοικεῖν vb pres act inf	. . . .	ἐνοικέω
ἐνοικεῖτε vb pres act ind 2nd pers pl		id.
ἐνοικείωται vb pres dep subj 3rd pers sg	. . . .	ἐνοικειόομαι
ἐνοικήσει vb fut act ind 3rd pers sg	. . . .	ἐνοικέω
ἐνοικήσῃ vb 1st aor act subj 3rd pers sg,		
fut mid ind 2nd pers sg		id.
ἐνοικήσουσιν vb fut act ind 3rd pers pl		id.
ἐνοίκισον vb 1st aor act impv 2nd pers sg	. . . .	ἐνοικίζω
ἔνοικος adj masc and fem nom sg		
ἐνοικοῦντας vb pres act part masc acc pl	. . . .	ἐνοικέω
ἐνοικοῦντες vb pres act part masc nom pl		id.
ἐνοικούντων vb pres act part masc and neut gen pl		id.
ἐνοίκους adj masc and fem acc pl	. . . .	ἔνοικος
ἐνοικοῦσι(ν) vb pres act ind 3rd pers pl,		
pres act part masc and neut dat pl	. . . .	ἐνοικέω
ἐνοίκων noun masc gen pl	. . . .	ἔνοικος
ἐνοικῶν vb pres act part masc nom sg	. . . .	ἐνοικέω
ἐνομίζομεν vb impf act ind 1st pers pl	. . . .	νομίζω
ἐνόμισαν vb 1st aor act ind 3rd pers pl		id.
ἐνομοθέτησας vb 1st aor act ind 2nd pers sg	. . .	νομοθετέω
ἐνόντα vb pres act part neut nom and acc pl	. . . .	ἔνειμι
ἐνοοῦσαν vb impf act ind 3rd pers pl	. . . .	νοέω
ἐνοπλισάμενοι vb 1st aor mid part masc nom pl	.	ἐνοπλίζω
ἔνοπλοι adj masc and fem nom pl	. . . .	ἔνοπλος
ἐνόπλου adj gen sg		id.
ἐνόπλους adj masc and fem acc pl		id.
ἐνόπλων adj gen pl		id.
ἐνόρκιον noun masc acc sg	. . . .	ἐνόρκιος
ἔνορκοι adj masc and fem nom pl	. . . .	ἔνορκος

ἐνόρκως   adverb

ἑνός   adj masc and neut gen sg . . . . εἷς

ἐνόσουν   vb impf act ind 3rd pers pl . . . . νοσέω

ἐνόσσευον   vb impf act ind 3rd pers pl . . . . νοσσεύω

ἐνόσσευσαν   vb 1st aor act ind 3rd pers pl   id.

ἐνόσσευσεν   vb 1st aor act ind 3rd pers sg   id.

ἐνοσφίσαντο   vb 1st aor mid ind 3rd pers pl . . . νοσφίζομαι

ἐνουθέτει   vb impf act ind 3rd pers sg . . . . νουθετέω

ἐνουθέτησας   vb 1st aor act ind 2nd pers sg   id.

ἐνούσης   vb pres act part fem gen sg . . . . ἔνειμι

ἐνοῦσι   vb pres act part masc and neut dat pl   id.

ἐνοχλεῖσθαι   vb 1st aor mid inf . . . . ἐνοχλέω

ἐνοχλεῖται   vb pres m/p ind 3rd pers sg   id.

ἐνοχλῆσαι   vb 1st aor act inf   id.

ἐνοχλῆται   vb pres m/p subj 3rd pers sg   id.

ἐνοχλούμενα   vb pres m/p part neut nom and acc pl   id.

ἐνοχλοῦσα   vb pres act part fem nom sg   id.

ἔνοχοι   adj masc and fem nom pl . . . . ἔνοχος

ἔνοχον   adj acc sg, neut nom sg   id.

ἔνοχος   adj masc and fem nom sg   id.

ἐνόχου   adj gen sg   id.

ἐνόχους   adj masc and fem acc pl   id.

ἐνσείσας   vb 1st aor act part masc nom sg . . . . ἐνσείω

ἐνσείσεις   vb fut act ind 2nd pers sg   id.

ἐνσιτοῦνται   vb pres dep ind 3rd pers pl . . . . . . ἐνσιτέομαι

ἐνσκολιευόμενος   vb pres dep part

        masc nom sg . . . . ἐνσκολιεύομαι

ἐνστάντος   vb 2nd aor act part

        masc and neut gen sg . . . . ἐνίστημι

ἐνστάσης   vb 2nd aor act part fem gen sg   id.

ἐνστασῶν   vb 2nd aor act part fem gen pl   id.

ἐνστῇ   vb 2nd aor act subj 3rd pers sg   id.

ἐντακήσεσθε   vb fut mid ind 2nd pers pl . . . . ἐντήκω

ἐντάλμασι   noun neut dat pl . . . . ἔνταλμα

ἐντάλματα   noun neut nom and acc pl   id.

ἐνταλμάτων   noun neut gen pl   id.

ἔνταξον   vb 1st aor act impv 2nd pers sg . . . . ἐντάσσω

ἐντάσσω   vb pres act ind 1st pers sg   id.

ἐνταῦθα   adverb

ἐνταφιάσαι   vb 1st aor act inf . . . . ἐνταφιάζω

ἐνταφιασταί   noun masc nom pl . . . . ἐνταφιαστής

ἐνταφιασταῖς   noun masc dat pl   id.

ἐντεθεικότος   vb perf act part masc and neut gen sg   ἐντίθημι

ἐντεθρυμμένους   vb perf m/p part masc acc pl . . . ἐνθρύπτω

ἐντεθυμημένης   vb perf dep part fem gen sg . . ἐνθυμέομαι

ἔντειλαι   vb 1st aor mid impv 2nd pers sg . . . . . ἐντέλλομαι

ἐντειλάμενος   vb 1st aor mid part masc nom sg   id.

ἐντειλαμένου   vb 1st aor mid part masc and neut gen sg   id.

ἐντείλασθαι   vb 1st aor mid inf   id.

ἐντείλασθε   vb 1st aor mid impv 2nd pers pl   id.

ἐντείλῃ   vb 1st aor mid subj 2nd pers sg   id.

ἐντείληται   vb 1st aor mid subj 3rd pers sg   id.

ἐντείλωμαι   vb 1st aor mid subj 1st pers sg . . . . . ἐντέλλομαι

ἐντείνατε   vb 1st aor act impv 2nd pers pl . . . . ἐντείνω

ἔντεινον   vb 1st aor act impv 2nd pers sg   id.

ἐντείνοντες   vb pres act part masc nom pl   id.

ἐντείνοντι   vb pres act part masc and neut dat sg   id.

ἐντείνων   vb pres act part masc nom sg   id.

ἐντελεῖσθε   vb fut dep ind 2nd pers pl . . . . ἐντέλλομαι

ἐντελεῖται   vb fut mid ind 3rd pers sg   id.

ἐντελῇ   vb fut mid ind 2nd pers sg   id.

ἐντέλλεσθαι   vb pres dep inf   id.

ἐντέλλεται   vb pres dep ind 3rd pers sg   id.

ἐντέλλομαι   vb pres dep ind 1st pers sg   id.

ἐντελλόμεθα   vb pres dep ind 1st pers pl   id.

ἐντελλόμενος   vb pres dep part masc nom sg   id.

ἐντελλομένου   vb pres dep part masc and neut gen sg   id.

ἐντελοῦμαι   vb fut mid ind 1st pers sg   id.

ἐντενεῖ   vb fut act ind 3rd pers sg . . . . ἐντείνω

ἐντενεῖς   vb fut act ind 2nd pers sg   id.

ἔντερα   noun neut nom and acc pl . . . . ἔντερον

ἐντέρῳ   noun neut dat sg   id.

ἐντεταγμένη   vb perf m/p part fem nom sg . . . . ἐντάσσω

ἐντεταγμένον   vb perf m/p part masc acc sg,

        neut nom and acc sg   id.

ἐντέταλμαι   vb perf dep ind 1st pers sg . . . . ἐντέλλομαι

ἐντέταλσαι   vb perf dep ind 2nd pers sg   id.

ἐντέταλται   vb perf dep ind 3rd pers sg   id.

ἐντεταμένα   vb perf m/p part neut nom and acc pl . . . ἐντείνω

ἐντεταμένον   vb perf m/p part masc acc sg,

        neut nom and acc sg   id.

ἐντεταμένου   vb perf m/p part masc and neut gen sg   id.

ἐντέτηκε   vb perf act ind 3rd pers sg . . . . ἐντήκω

ἐντέτραμμαι   vb perf m/p ind 1st pers sg . . . . ἐντρέπω

ἐντεῦθεν   adverb

ἐντεύξεως   noun fem gen sg . . . . ἔντευξις

ἐντίθεται   vb pres m/p ind 3rd pers sg . . . . ἐντίθημι

ἔντιμε   adj masc and fem voc sg . . . . ἔντιμος

ἔντιμοι   adj masc and fem nom pl   id.

ἐντίμοις   adj dat pl   id.

ἔντιμον   adj acc sg, neut nom sg   id.

ἔντιμος   adj masc and fem nom sg   id.

ἐντιμοτέρα   comp adj fem nom sg   id.

ἐντιμοτέρους   comp adj masc acc pl   id.

ἐντίμου   adj gen sg   id.

ἐντίμους   adj masc and fem acc pl   id.

ἐντίμῳ   adj dat sg   id.

ἐντιμωθήτω   vb 1st aor pass impv 3rd pers sg . . . ἐντιμάομαι

ἐντίμων   adj gen pl . . . . ἔντιμος

ἐντίμως   adverb

ἐντιναγμῷ   noun masc dat sg . . . . ἐντιναγμός

ἐντινάξαντες   vb 1st aor act part masc nom pl . . ἐντινάσσω

ἐντολαί   noun fem nom pl . . . . ἐντολή

ἐντολαῖς   noun fem dat pl   id.

ἐντολάς noun fem acc pl	. . . .	ἐντολή
ἐντολή noun fem nom sg		id.
ἐντολῇ noun fem dat sg		id.
ἐντολήν noun fem acc sg		id.
ἐντολῆς noun fem gen sg		id.
ἐντολῶν noun fem gen pl		id.
ἐντομίδας noun fem acc pl	. . . .	ἐντομίς
ἐντός adverb and preposition		
ἐντραπείησαν vb 2nd aor pass opt 3rd pers pl	. . . .	ἐντρέπω
ἐντραπῇ vb 2nd aor pass subj 3rd pers sg		id.
ἐντράπηθι vb 2nd aor pass impv 2nd pers sg		id.
ἐντραπῆναι vb 2nd aor pass inf		id.
ἐντραπῇς vb 2nd aor pass subj 2nd pers sg		id.
ἐντραπήσεται vb fut pass ind 3rd pers sg		id.
ἐντραπήσῃ vb fut pass ind 2nd pers sg		id.
ἐντραπήσονται vb fut pass ind 3rd pers pl		id.
ἐντράπητε vb 2nd aor pass impv 2nd pers pl		id.
ἐντραπήτωσαν vb 2nd aor pass impv 3rd pers pl		id.
ἐντραπῶ vb 2nd aor pass subj 1st pers sg		id.
ἐντραπῶμεν vb 2nd aor pass subj 1st pers pl		id.
ἐντραπῶσιν vb 2nd aor pass subj 3rd pers pl		id.
ἐντρεχής adj masc and fem nom sg		
ἔντριτον adj acc sg, neut nom sg	. . . .	ἔντριτος
ἔντρομοι adj masc and fem nom pl	. . . .	ἔντρομος
ἔντρομος adj masc and fem nom sg		id.
ἐντροπή noun fem nom sg		
ἐντροπήν noun fem acc sg	. . . .	ἐντροπή
ἐντροπῆς noun fem gen sg		id.
ἐντρυφήματα noun neut nom and acc pl	. . . . . .	ἐντρύφημα
ἐντρυφήσατε vb 1st aor act ind 2nd pers pl	. . . . .	ἐντρυφάω
ἐντρυφήσει vb fut act ind 3rd pers sg		id.
ἐντρυφῶν vb pres act part neut nom and acc sg		id.
ἐντυγχάνειν vb pres act inf	. . . .	ἐντυγχάνω
ἐντυγχάνοντας vb pres act part masc acc pl		id.
ἐντυγχάνοντες vb pres act part masc nom pl		id.
ἐντυγχανόντων vb pres act part masc and neut gen pl		id.
ἐντυγχάνουσιν vb pres act part masc and neut dat pl		id.
ἐντυχεῖν vb 2nd aor act inf		id.
ἐντυχίαν noun fem acc sg	. . . .	ἐντυχία
ἐντύχωσιν vb 2nd aor act subj 3rd pers pl	. . . . .	ἐντυγχάνω
ἔνυδρα adj neut nom and acc pl	. . . .	ἔνυδρος
ἐνύδρων adj gen pl		id.
ἔνυξεν vb 1st aor act ind 3rd pers sg	. . . .	νύσσω
ἐνύπνια noun neut nom and acc pl	. . . .	ἐνύπνιον
ἐνυπνιάζεσθε vb pres dep ind 2nd pers pl	. .	ἐνυπνιάζομαι
ἐνυπνιάζεται vb pres dep ind 3rd pers sg		id.
ἐνυπνιαζόμενοι vb pres dep part masc nom pl		id.
ἐνυπνιαζόμενος vb pres dep part masc nom sg		id.
ἐνυπνιαζομένου vb pres dep part masc and neut gen sg		id.
ἐνυπνιαζομένων vb pres dep part gen pl		id.
ἐνυπνιασάμην vb 1st aor mid ind 1st pers sg		id.
ἐνυπνιασθείς vb 1st aor pass part masc nom sg		id.

ἐνιπνιάσθη vb 1st aor pass ind 3rd pers sg	.	ἐνυπνιάζομαι
ἐνιπνιάσθην vb 1st aor pass ind 1st pers sg		id.
ἐνιπνιάσθης vb 1st aor pass ind 2nd pers sg		id.
ἐνιπνιασθήσονται vb fut pass ind 3rd pers pl		id.
ἐνιπνιαστής noun masc nom sg		
ἐνυπνίοις noun neut dat pl	. . . .	ἐνύπνιον
ἐνύπνιον noun neut nom and acc sg		id.
ἐνυπνίου noun neut gen sg		id.
ἐνυπνίῳ noun neut dat sg		id.
ἐνυπνίων noun neut gen pl		id.
ἐνυποταγήσεται vb fut mid ind 3rd pers sg	.	ἐνυποτάσσω
ἐνύσταξαν vb 1st aor act ind 3rd pers pl	. . . .	νυστάζω
ἐνύσταξεν vb 1st aor act ind 3rd pers sg		id.
ἔνυστρον noun neut nom and acc sg		
ενφωθ translit		
Ενωβ pr noun		
ἐνώτια adj neut nom and acc pl	. . . .	ἐνώπιος
ἐνώπιον adj acc sg, neut nom sg		id.
ἐνώπιον adverb and preposition		
ενωπιος adj masc and fem nom sg		
ενωπίους adj masc and fem acc pl	. . . .	ἐνώπιος
ενωπίῳ adj dat sg		id.
ἐνωπλισμένοι vb perf m/p part masc nom pl	. . . .	ἐνοπλίζω
ἐνωπλισμένος vb perf m/p part masc nom sg		id.
Ενως pr noun		
ἐνώτια noun neut nom and acc pl	. . . .	ἐνώτιον
ἐνωτιεῖται vb fut mid ind 3rd pers sg	. . . .	ἐνωτίζομαι
ἐνωτίζεσθε vb pres dep impv 2nd pers pl		id.
ἐνωτίζου vb pres dep impv 2nd pers sg		id.
ἐνώτιον noun neut nom and acc sg		
ἐνωτίσαι vb 1st aor act mid impv 2nd pers sg	. . . . .	ἐνωτίζομαι
ἐνωτίσασθε vb 1st aor act mid impv 2nd pers pl		id.
ἐνωτίσατο vb 1st aor act mid ind 3rd pers sg		id.
ἐνωτίσῃ vb 1st aor act mid subj 2nd pers sg		id.
ἐνωτισθήσονται vb fut pass ind 3rd pers pl		id.
ἐνωτίων noun neut gen pl	. . . .	ἐνώτιον
Ενωχ pr noun		
ἐξ see ἐκ		
ἕξ indecl number		
ἐξάγαγε vb 2nd aor act impv 2nd pers sg	. . . .	ἐξάγω
ἐξαγαγεῖν vb 2nd aor act inf		id.
ἐξαγάγετε vb 2nd aor act impv 2nd pers pl		id.
ἐξαγαγέτω vb 2nd aor act impv 3rd pers sg		id.
ἐξαγαγέτωσαν vb 2nd aor act impv 3rd pers pl		id.
ἐξαγάγῃς vb 2nd aor act subj 2nd pers sg		id.
ἐξαγάγοι vb 2nd aor act opt 3rd pers sg		id.
ἐξαγαγόντα vb 2nd aor act part masc acc sg		id.
ἐξαγαγόντες vb 2nd aor act part masc nom pl		id.
ἐξαγαγόντι vb 2nd aor act part masc and neut dat sg		id.
ἐξαγαγόντος vb 2nd aor act part masc and neut gen sg		id.
ἐξαγαγών vb 2nd aor act part masc nom sg		id.
ἐξαγαγῶν see ἐξαγαγών		

ἐξαγγεῖλαι vb 1st aor act inf . . . . ἐξαγγέλλω
ἐξαγγειλάτωσαν vb 1st aor act impv 3rd pers pl   id.
ἐξαγγείλω vb 1st aor act subj 1st pers sg   id.
ἐξαγγελεῖ vb fut act ind 3rd pers sg   id.
ἐξαγγέλλει vb pres act ind 3rd pers sg   id.
ἐξαγγελοῦμεν vb fut act ind 1st pers pl   id.
ἐξάγομεν vb pres act ind 1st pers pl . . . . ἐξάγω
ἐξαγομένης vb pres m/p part fem gen sg   id.
ἐξαγοράζετε vb pres act ind 2nd pers pl . . . . . ἐξαγοράζω
ἐξαγορεύοντες vb pres act part masc nom pl . . . ἐξαγορεύω
ἐξαγορεύοντος vb pres act part masc and neut gen sg   id.
ἐξαγορεῦσαι vb 1st aor act inf   id.
ἐξαγορεύσει vb fut act ind 3rd pers sg   id.
ἐξαγορεύσῃ vb 1st aor act subj 3rd pers sg   id.
ἐξαγορεύσουσιν vb fut act ind 3rd pers pl   id.
ἐξαγορεύσω vb fut act ind 1st pers sg   id.
ἐξαγορεύω vb pres act ind 1st pers sg   id.
ἐξαγορίαις noun fem dat pl . . . . ἐξαγορία
ἐξάγουσιν vb pres act ind 3rd pers pl . . . . ἐξάγω
ἐξάγων vb pres act part masc nom sg   id.
ἐξάδελφοι noun masc nom pl . . . . ἐξάδελφος
ἐξάδελφος noun masc nom sg   id.
ἔξαιμος adj masc and fem nom sg
ἐξαιρεθήσεται vb fut pass ind 3rd pers sg . . . . ἐξαιρέω
ἐξαίρει vb pres act ind 3rd pers sg . . . . ἐξαίρω
ἐξαίρειν vb pres act inf   id.
ἐξαιρεῖσθαι vb pres m/p inf . . . . ἐξαιρέω
ἐξαιρεῖσθε vb pres m/p ind 2nd pers pl   id.
ἐξαίρεσθαι vb pres m/p inf . . . . ἐξαίρω
ἐξαίρετοι adj masc and fem nom pl . . . . ἐξαίρετος
ἐξαίρετον adj acc sg, neut nom sg   id.
ἐξαίρῃ vb pres act subj 3rd pers sg . . . . ἐξαίρω
ἐξαιρῇ vb pres m/p ind 2nd pers sg   id.
ἐξαίρομεν vb pres act ind 1st pers pl   id.
ἐξαιρόμενον vb pres m/p part masc acc sg,
       neut nom and acc sg   id.
ἐξαῖρον vb pres act part neut nom and acc sg   id.
ἐξαιρούμενος vb pres m/p part masc nom sg . . . . . ἐξαιρέω
ἐξαιρουμένων vb pres m/p part gen pl   id.
ἐξαίρουσαν vb pres act part fem acc sg . . . . ἐξαίρω
ἐξαίρων vb pres act part masc nom sg   id.
ἐξαίσια adj neut nom and acc pl . . . . ἐξαίσιος
ἐξαίσιον adj acc sg, neut nom sg   id.
ἐξαίσιος adj masc and fem nom sg   id.
ἐξαισίῳ adj dat sg   id.
ἐξαίφνης adverb
ἐξάκις adverb
ἑξακισχίλιαι adj fem nom pl . . . . ἑξακισχίλιοι
ἑξακισχίλιοι adj masc nom pl   id.
ἑξακισχιλίους adj masc acc pl   id.
ἐξακολούθει vb pres act impv 2nd pers sg . . . ἐξακολουθέω
ἐξακολουθῆσαι vb 1st aor act inf   id.

ἐξακολουθοῦμεν vb pres act ind 1st pers pl . ἐξακολουθέω
ἑξακόσια adj neut nom and acc pl . . . . ἑξακόσιοι
ἑξακόσιαι adj fem nom pl   id.
ἑξακοσίας adj fem acc pl   id.
ἑξακόσιοι adj masc nom pl   id.
ἑξακοσιοστῷ adj masc and neut dat sg . . . . ἑξακοσιοστός
ἑξακοσίους adj masc acc pl . . . . ἑξακόσιοι
ἑξακοσίων adj masc and neut gen pl   id.
ἐξακριβάζεται vb pres dep ind
       3rd pers sg . . . . ἐξακριβάζομαι
ἐξακριβάσασθαι vb 1st aor mid inf   id.
ἐξάλειπτρον noun neut nom and acc sg
ἐξαλείφεις vb pres act ind 2nd pers sg . . . . ἐξαλείφω
ἐξαλειφθείη vb 1st aor pass opt 3rd pers sg   id.
ἐξαλειφθῇ vb 1st aor pass subj 3rd pers sg   id.
ἐξαλειφθῆναι vb 1st aor pass inf   id.
ἐξαλειφθήσεται vb fut pass ind 3rd pers sg   id.
ἐξαλειφθήτω vb 1st aor pass impv 3rd pers sg   id.
ἐξαλειφθήτωσαν vb 1st aor pass impv 3rd pers pl   id.
ἐξαλείφων vb pres act part masc nom sg   id.
ἐξαλεῖψαι vb 1st aor act inf   id.
ἐξαλείψει vb fut act ind 3rd pers sg   id.
ἐξαλείψεις vb fut act ind 2nd pers sg   id.
ἐξαλείψῃ vb 1st aor act subj 3rd pers sg   id.
ἐξαλείψῃς vb 1st aor act subj 2nd pers sg   id.
ἐξάλειψιν noun fem acc sg . . . . ἐξάλειψις
ἐξάλειψις noun fem nom sg   id.
ἐξάλειψον vb 1st aor act impv 2nd pers sg . . . . . . ἐξαλείφω
ἐξαλείψουσιν vb fut act ind 3rd pers pl   id.
ἐξαλείψω vb fut act ind 1st pers sg   id.
ἔξαλλα adj neut nom and acc pl . . . . ἔξαλλος
ἐξαλλασσούσας vb pres act part fem acc pl . . . ἐξαλλάσσω
ἔξαλλοι adj masc and fem nom pl . . . . ἔξαλλος
ἐξάλλοις adj dat pl   id.
ἐξαλλοιῶσαι vb 1st aor act inf . . . . ἐξαλλοιόω
ἔξαλλον adj acc sg, neut nom sg . . . . ἔξαλλος
ἐξαλλοτριωθῆναι vb 1st aor pass inf . . . . . . ἐξαλλοτριόω
ἐξάλλων adj gen pl . . . . ἔξαλλος
ἐξαλυνται vb fut mid ind 3rd pers pl . . . . ἐξάλλομαι
ἐξαμαρτάνει vb pres act ind 3rd pers sg . . . . . ἐξαμαρτάνω
ἐξαμαρτάνοντες vb pres act part masc nom pl   id.
ἐξαμαρτῆσαι vb 1st aor act inf   id.
ἐξάμηνον noun masc acc sg . . . . ἐξάμηνος
ἐξαναλωθήσεται vb fut pass ind 3rd pers sg . . ἐξαναλίσκω
ἐξαναλωθήσονται vb fut pass ind 3rd pers pl   id.
ἐξαναλῶσαι vb 1st aor act inf   id.
ἐξαναλώσει vb fut act ind 3rd pers sg   id.
ἐξαναλώσεις vb fut act ind 2nd pers sg   id.
ἐξαναλώσῃ vb 1st aor act subj 3rd pers sg   id.
ἐξαναλώσω vb 1st aor act subj 1st pers sg,
       fut act ind 1st pers sg   id.
ἐξαναστάντες vb 2nd aor act part masc nom pl . ἐξανίστημι

ἐξαναστάντων	vb 2nd aor act part masc gen pl	. ἐξανίστημι	ἐξαπεστείλατε	vb 1st aor act ind 2nd pers pl	. ἐξαποστέλλω

ἐξαναστάντων vb 2nd aor act part masc gen pl . ἐξανίστημι
ἐξαναστάς vb 2nd aor act part masc nom sg   id.
ἐξανάστασιν noun fem acc sg . . . . ἐξανάστασις
ἐξαναστῇς vb 2nd aor act subj 2nd pers sg . . . . ἐξανίστημι
ἐξαναστήσεσθε vb fut mid ind 2nd pers pl   id.
ἐξαναστήσεται vb fut mid ind 3rd pers sg   id.
ἐξαναστήσῃ vb fut mid ind 2nd pers sg   id.
ἐξαναστήσονται vb fut mid ind 3rd pers pl   id.
ἐξαναστήσουσιν vb fut act ind 3rd pers pl   id.
ἐξαναστήσωμεν vb 1st aor act subj 1st pers pl   id.
ἐξαναστῶμεν vb 2nd aor act subj 1st pers pl   id.
ἐξανατέλλοντι vb pres act part
        masc and neut dat sg . . . . ἐξανατέλλω
ἐξανατέλλων vb pres act part masc nom sg   id.
ἐξανατελῶ vb fut act ind 1st pers sg   id.
ἐξανέστη vb 2nd aor act ind 3rd pers sg . . . . . . ἐξανίστημι
ἐξανέστηκεν vb perf act ind 3rd pers sg   id.
ἐξανέστησαν vb aor act ind 3rd pers pl   id.
ἐξανέστησας vb 1st aor act ind 2nd pers sg   id.
ἐξανέστησεν vb 1st aor act ind 3rd pers sg   id.
ἐξανέτειλεν vb 1st aor act ind 3rd pers sg . . . . ἐξανατέλλω
ἐξανηλώθη vb 1st aor pass ind 3rd pers sg . . . . ἐξαναλίσκω
ἐξανηλώμεθα vb perf m/p ind 1st pers pl   id.
ἐξανήλωσα vb 1st aor act ind 1st pers sg   id.
ἐξανήλωσαν vb 1st aor act ind 3rd pers pl   id.
ἐξανθεῖ vb pres act ind 3rd pers sg . . . . ἐξανθέω
ἐξανθήσει vb fut act ind 3rd pers sg   id.
ἐξανθήσῃ vb 1st aor act subj 3rd pers sg   id.
ἐξανθήσουσιν vb fut act ind 3rd pers pl   id.
ἐξανθοῦντα vb pres act part neut nom and acc pl   id.
ἐξανθοῦσα vb pres act part fem nom sg   id.
ἐξανθούσης vb pres act part fem gen sg   id.
ἐξανίσταιτο vb pres m/p opt 3rd pers sg . . . . . ἐξανίστημι
ἐξανίστασο vb pres m/p impv 2nd pers sg   id.
ἐξαντλῆσαι vb 1st aor act inf . . . . ἐξαντλέω
ἐξαντλήσει vb fut act ind 3rd pers sg   id.
ἐξάξει vb fut act ind 3rd pers sg . . . . ἐξάγω
ἐξάξεις vb fut act ind 2nd pers sg   id.
ἐξάξετε vb fut act ind 2nd pers pl   id.
ἐξάξομεν vb fut act ind 1st pers pl   id.
ἐξάξουσιν vb fut act ind 3rd pers pl   id.
ἐξάξω vb fut act ind 1st pers sg   id.
ἐξαπατῆσαι vb 1st aor act inf . . . . ἐξαπατάω
ἐξαπέσταλκα vb perf act ind 1st pers sg . . . . ἐξαποστέλλω
ἐξαπέσταλκας vb perf act ind 2nd pers sg   id.
ἐξαπέσταλκεν vb perf act ind 3rd pers sg   id.
ἐξαπέσταλμαι vb perf m/p ind 1st pers sg   id.
ἐξαπεσταλμέναι vb perf m/p part fem nom pl   id.
ἐξαπέστειλα vb 1st aor act ind 1st pers sg   id.
ἐξαπεστείλαμεν vb 1st aor act ind 1st pers pl   id.
ἐξαπέστειλαν vb 1st aor act ind 3rd pers pl   id.
ἐξαπέστειλας vb 1st aor act ind 2nd pers sg   id.

ἐξαπεστείλατε vb 1st aor act ind 2nd pers pl . ἐξαποστέλλω
ἐξαπέστειλεν vb 1st aor act ind 3rd pers sg   id.
ἐξαπεστέλλετε vb impf act ind 2nd pers pl   id.
ἐξαπεστέλλοντο vb impf m/p ind 3rd pers pl   id.
ἐξαπεστέλλοσαν vb impf act ind 3rd pers pl   id.
ἐξάπινα adverb
ἐξαπίνης adverb
ἐξαπολλυμένων vb pres m/p part gen pl . . . . . ἐξαπόλλυμι
ἐξαποσταλέν vb 2nd aor pass part
        neut nom and acc sg . . . . ἐξαποστέλλω
ἐξαποστείλαι vb 1st aor act opt 3rd pers sg   id.
ἐξαποστεῖλαι vb 1st aor act inf   id.
ἐξαποστείλας vb 1st aor act part masc nom sg   id.
ἐξαποστείλατε vb 1st aor act impv 2nd pers pl   id.
ἐξαποστειλάτωσαν vb 1st aor act impv 3rd pers pl   id.
ἐξαποστείλῃ vb 1st aor act subj 3rd pers sg   id.
ἐξαποστείλῃς vb 1st aor act subj 2nd pers sg   id.
ἐξαποστείλητε vb 1st aor act subj 2nd pers pl   id.
ἐξαπόστειλον vb 1st aor act impv 2nd pers sg   id.
ἐξαποστείλω vb 1st aor act subj 1st pers sg   id.
ἐξαποστελεῖ vb fut act ind 3rd pers sg   id.
ἐξαποστελεῖς vb fut act ind 2nd pers sg   id.
ἐξαποστελεῖτε vb fut act ind 2nd pers pl   id.
ἐξαποστέλλειν vb pres act inf   id.
ἐξαποστέλλῃ vb pres act subj 3rd pers sg   id.
ἐξαποστέλλῃς vb pres act subj 2nd pers sg   id.
ἐξαποστελλομένους vb pres m/p part masc acc pl   id.
ἐξαποστελλομένων vb pres m/p part gen pl   id.
ἐξαποστέλλοντας vb pres act part masc acc pl   id.
ἐξαποστέλλοντες vb pres act part masc nom pl   id.
ἐξαποστέλλουσιν vb pres act ind 3rd pers pl   id.
ἐξαποστέλλω vb pres act ind 1st pers sg   id.
ἐξαποστέλλων vb pres act part masc nom sg   id.
ἐξαποστελῶ vb fut act ind 1st pers sg   id.
ἐξαποστολήν noun fem acc sg . . . . ἐξαποστολή
ἐξάπτῃ vb pres act subj 3rd pers sg . . . . ἐξάπτω
ἐξάραι vb 1st aor act opt 3rd pers sg . . . . ἐξαίρω
ἐξᾶραι vb 1st aor act inf   id.
ἐξάραντες vb 1st aor act part masc nom pl   id.
ἐξάρας vb 1st aor act part masc nom sg   id.
ἐξάρατε vb 1st aor act impv 2nd pers pl   id.
ἐξαρεῖ vb fut act ind 3rd pers sg   id.
ἐξαρεῖς vb fut act ind 2nd pers sg   id.
ἐξαρεῖτε vb fut act ind 2nd pers pl   id.
ἐξάρῃ vb 1st aor act subj 3rd pers sg   id.
ἐξάρητε vb 1st aor act subj 2nd pers pl   id.
ἐξαρθῇ vb 1st aor pass subj 3rd pers sg   id.
ἐξαρθῆναι vb 1st aor pass inf   id.
ἐξαρθῇς vb 1st aor pass subj 2nd pers sg   id.
ἐξαρθήσεσθε vb fut pass ind 2nd pers pl   id.
ἐξαρθήσεται vb fut pass ind 3rd pers sg   id.
ἐξαρθήσῃ vb fut pass ind 2nd pers sg   id.

ἐξαρθήσονται vb fut pass ind 3rd pers pl . . . . ἐξαίρω

ἔξαρθρος adj masc and fem nom sg

ἐξαριθμηθήσεται vb fut pass ind 3rd pers sg . . ἐξαριθμέω

ἐξαριθμῆσαι vb 1st aor act inf id.

ἐξαριθμήσασθαι vb 1st aor mid inf id.

ἐξαριθμήσει vb fut act ind 3rd pers sg id.

ἐξαριθμήσεις vb fut act ind 2nd pers sg id.

ἐξαριθμήσεται vb fut mid ind 3rd pers sg id.

ἐξαριθμήσομαι vb fut mid ind 1st pers sg id.

ἐξαρκέσει vb fut act ind 3rd pers sg . . . . ἐξαρκέω

ἐξαρνήσομαι vb fut mid ind 1st pers sg . . . . . ἐξαρνέομαι

ἐξάρξατε vb 1st aor act impv 2nd pers pl . . . . ἐξάρχω

ἔξαρον vb 1st aor act impv 2nd pers sg . . . . ἐξαίρω

ἐξαροῦμεν vb fut act ind 1st pers pl id.

ἐξαροῦσιν vb fut act ind 3rd pers pl id.

ἐξαρπάσαι vb 1st aor act inf . . . . ἐξαρπάζω

ἐξάρσει noun fem dat sg . . . . ἔξαρσις

ἐξάρχειν vb pres act inf . . . . ἐξάρχω

ἐξάρχετε vb pres act impv 2nd pers pl,

pres act ind 2nd pers pl id.

ἐξαρχόντων vb pres act part masc and neut gen pl id.

ἐξαρῶ vb fut act ind 1st pers sg . . . . ἐξαίρω

ἐξάρωμεν vb 1st aor act subj 1st pers pl id.

ἐξάρωσιν vb 1st aor act subj 3rd pers pl id.

ἐξασκεῖ vb pres act ind 3rd pers sg . . . . ἐξασκέω

ἐξασκήσαντες vb 1st aor act part masc nom pl id.

ἐξαστράπτον vb pres act part

neut nom and acc sg . . . . ἐξαστράπτω

ἐξαστραπτόντων vb pres act part

masc and neut gen pl id.

ἐξαστράπτων vb pres act part masc nom sg id.

ἐξατιμωθήσῃ vb fut pass ind 2nd pers sg . . . . ἐξατιμόω

ἐξαφεῖναι vb 2nd aor act inf . . . . ἐξαφίημι

ἐξαφθεῖσα vb 1st aor pass part fem nom sg . . . . ἐξάπτω

ἐξαχθήσεται vb fut pass ind 3rd pers sg . . . . ἐξάγω

ἐξάψουσιν vb fut act ind 3rd pers pl . . . . ἐξάπτω

ἐξέβαλεν vb 2nd aor act ind 3rd pers sg . . . . ἐκβάλλω

ἐξέβαλες vb 2nd aor act ind 2nd pers sg id.

ἐξεβάλετε vb 2nd aor act ind 2nd pers pl id.

ἐξεβάλλοντο vb impf m/p ind 3rd pers pl id.

ἐξέβαλον vb 2nd aor act ind 1st pers sg and 3rd pers pl id.

ἐξέβη vb 2nd aor act ind 3rd pers sg . . . . ἐκβαίνω

ἐξέβησαν vb 2nd aor act ind 3rd pers pl id.

ἐξεβιάζοντο vb impf m/p ind 3rd pers pl . . . . ἐκβιάζω

ἐξεβιάσαντο vb 1st aor mid ind 3rd pers pl id.

ἐξεβιάσατο vb 1st aor mid ind 3rd pers sg id.

ἐξεβλήθη vb 1st aor pass ind 3rd pers sg . . . . ἐκβάλλω

ἐξεβόησεν vb 1st aor act ind 3rd pers sg . . . . ἐκβοάω

ἐξέβρασα vb 1st aor act ind 1st pers sg . . . . ἐκβράζω

ἐξέβρασεν vb 1st aor act ind 3rd pers sg id.

ἐξεβράσθη vb 1st aor pass ind 3rd pers sg id.

ἐξεγεῖραι vb 1st aor act inf . . . . ἐξεγείρω

ἐξεγείρατε vb 1st aor act impv 2nd pers pl . . . . . . ἐξεγείρω

ἐξεγείρει vb pres act ind 3rd pers sg id.

ἐξεγειρέσθωσαν vb pres m/p impv 3rd pers pl id.

ἐξεγείρηται vb pres mid subj 3rd pers sg id.

ἐξεγείρητε vb pres act subj 2nd pers pl id.

ἐξεγειρόμενος vb pres m/p part masc nom sg id.

ἐξεγειρομένου vb pres m/p part masc and neut gen sg id.

ἐξέγειρον vb 1st aor act impv 2nd pers sg id.

ἐξεγείροντα vb pres act part masc acc sg id.

ἐξεγειρόντων vb pres act part masc and neut gen pl id.

ἐξεγείρου vb pres m/p impv 2nd pers sg id.

ἐξεγείρω vb pres act ind 1st pers sg id.

ἐξεγείρων vb pres act part masc nom sg id.

ἐξεγέλα vb impf act ind 3rd pers sg . . . . ἐκγελάω

ἐξεγέλασαν vb 1st aor act ind 3rd pers pl id.

ἐξεγέννησα vb 1st aor act ind 1st pers sg . . . . ἐκγεννάω

ἐξεγερθείς vb 1st aor pass part masc nom sg . . . . . ἐξεγείρω

ἐξεγερθῇ vb 1st aor pass subj 3rd pers sg id.

ἐξεγερθήσεται vb fut pass ind 3rd pers sg id.

ἐξεγερθήσομαι vb fut pass ind 1st pers sg id.

ἐξεγερθήσονται vb fut pass ind 3rd pers pl id.

ἐξεγέρθητε vb 1st aor pass impv 2nd pers pl id.

ἐξεγέρθητι vb 1st aor pass impv 2nd pers sg id.

ἐξέγερσις noun fem nom sg

ἐξεγήγερται vb perf m/p ind 3rd pers sg . . . . ἐξεγείρω

ἐξεγράψαντο vb 1st aor mid ind 3rd pers pl . . . . . ἐκγράφω

ἐξέδειραν vb 1st aor act ind 3rd pers pl . . . . ἐκδέρω

ἐξέδετο vb 2nd aor m/p ind 3rd pers sg . . . . ἐκδίδωμι

ἐξέδησεν vb 1st aor act ind 3rd pers sg . . . . ἐκδέω

ἐξεδιήτησεν vb 1st aor act ind 3rd pers sg . . . . . . ἐκδιαιτάω

ἐξεδίκα vb impf act ind 3rd pers sg . . . . ἐκδικάω

ἐξεδικήθη vb 1st aor pass ind 3rd pers sg . . . . ἐκδικέω

ἐξεδίκησα vb 1st aor act ind 1st pers sg id.

ἐξεδίκησαν vb 1st aor act ind 3rd pers pl id.

ἐξεδίκησεν vb 1st aor act ind 3rd pers sg id.

ἐξεδίωκον vb impf act ind 1st pers sg . . . . ἐκδιώκω

ἐξεδίωξαν vb 1st aor act ind 3rd pers pl id.

ἐξεδιώχθη vb 1st aor pass ind 3rd pers sg id.

ἐξεδόθη vb 1st aor pass ind 3rd pers sg . . . . ἐκδίδωμι

ἐξέδοσαν vb 2nd aor act ind 3rd pers pl id.

ἐξέδοτο vb 2nd aor mid ind 3rd pers sg id.

ἐξέδρα noun fem nom sg

ἐξέδραι noun fem nom pl . . . . ἐξέδρα

ἐξέδραις noun fem dat pl id.

ἐξέδραμεν vb 2nd aor act ind 3rd pers sg . . . . ἐκτρέχω

ἐξέδραν noun fem acc sg . . . . ἐξέδρα

ἐξεδρῶν noun fem gen pl id.

ἐξεδυσάμην vb 1st aor mid ind 1st pers sg . . . . ἐκδύω

ἐξέδυσαν vb 1st aor act ind 3rd pers pl id.

ἐξεδύσατο vb 1st aor mid ind 3rd pers sg id.

ἐξέδυσεν vb 1st aor act ind 3rd pers sg id.

ἐξέζεσεν vb 1st aor act ind 3rd pers sg . . . . ἐκζέω

ἐξεζητημένα   vb perf m/p part neut nom and acc pl .   ἐκζητέω
ἐξεζήτησα   vb 1st aor act ind 1st pers sg   id.
ἐξεζητήσαμεν   vb 1st aor act ind 1st pers pl   id.
ἐξεζήτησαν   vb 1st aor act ind 3rd pers pl   id.
ἐξεζήτησεν   vb 1st aor act ind 3rd pers sg   id.
ἐξεζήτουν   vb impf act ind 3rd pers pl   id.
ἐξέθηκε   vb 1st aor act ind 3rd pers sg . . . . ἐκτίθημι
ἐξεθλίβετε   vb impf act ind 2nd pers pl . . . . ἐκθλίβω
ἐξέθλιψα   vb 1st aor act ind 1st pers sg   id.
ἐξέθλιψαν   vb 1st aor act ind 3rd pers pl   id.
ἐξέθλιψεν   vb 1st aor act ind 3rd pers sg   id.
ἐξέθρεψα   vb 1st aor act ind 1st pers sg . . . . ἐκτρέφω
ἐξέθρεψαν   vb 1st aor act ind 3rd pers pl   id.
ἐξέθρεψας   vb 1st aor act ind 2nd pers sg   id.
ἐξέθρεψεν   vb 1st aor act ind 3rd pers sg   id.
ἕξει   noun fem dat sg . . . . ἕξις
ἕξει   vb fut act ind 3rd pers sg . . . . ἔχω
ἐξεικονισμένον   vb perf m/p part masc acc sg,
      neut nom and acc sg . . . . ἐξεικονίζω
ἐξειλάμεθα   vb 1st aor mid ind 1st pers pl . . . . ἐξαιρέω
ἐξειλάμην   vb 1st aor mid ind 1st pers sg   id.
ἐξείλαντο   vb 1st aor mid ind 3rd pers pl   id.
ἐξείλατο   vb 1st aor mid ind 3rd pers sg   id.
ἐξείλεν   vb 2nd aor act ind 3rd pers sg   id.
ἐξείλετο   vb 2nd aor mid ind 3rd pers sg   id.
ἐξείλκυσαν   vb 1st aor act ind 3rd pers pl . . . . ἐξέλκω
ἐξειλκύσθησαν   vb 1st aor pass ind 3rd pers pl   id.
ἐξείλου   vb 2nd aor mid ind 2nd pers sg . . . . ἐξαιρέω
ἐξείλω   vb 2nd aor act ind 1st pers sg   id.
ἕξειν   vb fut act inf . . . . ἔχω
ἐξεῖναι   vb 2nd aor act inf . . . . ἐξίημι
ἐξειργάσατο   vb 1st aor mid ind 3rd pers sg . . ἐξεργάζομαι
ἐξειργάσω   vb 1st aor mid ind 2nd pers sg   id.
ἕξεις   vb fut act ind 2nd pers sg . . . . ἔχω
ἐξείχετο   vb impf m/p ind 3rd pers sg . . . . ἐξέχω
ἐξείχοντο   vb impf m/p ind 3rd pers pl   id.
ἐξεκάθαρα   vb 1st aor act ind 1st pers sg . . . . . . ἐκκαθαίρω
ἐξεκαλοῦντο   vb impf m/p ind 3rd pers pl . . . . ἐκκαλέω
ἐξεκαύθη   vb 1st aor pass ind 3rd pers sg . . . . ἐκκαίω
ἐξεκαύθησαν   vb 1st aor pass ind 3rd pers pl   id.
ἐξέκαυσα   vb 1st aor act ind 1st pers sg   id.
ἐξέκαυσαν   vb 1st aor act ind 3rd pers pl   id.
ἐξεκαύσατε   vb 1st aor act ind 2nd pers pl   id.
ἐξέκαυσεν   vb 1st aor act ind 3rd pers sg   id.
ἐξεκενοῦντο   vb impf m/p ind 3rd pers pl . . . . ἐκκενόω
ἐξεκέντησα   vb 1st aor act ind 1st pers sg . . . . ἐκκεντέω
ἐξεκέντησαν   vb 1st aor act ind 3rd pers pl   id.
ἐξεκέντησεν   vb 1st aor act ind 3rd pers sg   id.
ἐξεκενώθη   vb 1st aor pass ind 3rd pers sg . . . . ἐκκενόω
ἐξεκενώθησαν   vb 1st aor pass ind 3rd pers pl   id.
ἐξεκένωσαν   vb 1st aor act ind 3rd pers pl   id.
ἐξεκένωσας   vb 1st aor act ind 2nd pers sg   id.

ἐξεκένωσεν   vb 1st aor act ind 3rd pers sg . . . . ἐκκενόω
ἐξεκινήθη   vb 1st aor pass ind 3rd pers sg . . . . ἐκκινέω
ἐξεκκλησίασαν   vb 1st aor act ind
      3rd pers pl . . . . ἐξεκκλησιάζω
ἐξεκκλησίασε(ν)   vb 1st aor act ind 3rd pers sg   id.
ἐξεκκλησιάσθη   vb 1st aor pass ind 3rd pers sg   id.
ἐξεκκλησιάσθησαν   vb 1st aor pass ind 3rd pers pl   id.
ἐξέκλινα   vb 1st aor act ind 1st pers sg . . . . ἐκκλίνω
ἐξεκλίναμεν   vb 1st aor act ind 1st pers pl   id.
ἐξέκλιναν   vb 1st aor act ind 3rd pers pl   id.
ἐξέκλινας   vb 1st aor act ind 2nd pers sg   id.
ἐξεκλίνατε   vb 1st aor act ind 2nd pers pl   id.
ἐξέκλινεν   vb impf act ind 3rd pers sg,
      1st aor act ind 3rd pers sg   id.
ἐξέκλινον   vb impf act ind 3rd pers pl   id.
ἐξεκόπη   vb 2nd aor pass ind 3rd pers sg . . . . ἐκκόπτω
ἐξέκοψαν   vb 1st aor act ind 3rd pers pl   id.
ἐξέκοψας   vb 1st aor act ind 2nd pers sg   id.
ἐξέκοψεν   vb 1st aor act ind 3rd pers sg   id.
ἐξέκυψαν   vb 1st aor act ind 3rd pers pl . . . . ἐκκύπτω
ἐξέκυψεν   vb 1st aor act ind 3rd pers sg   id.
ἐξελάλησεν   vb 1st aor act ind 3rd pers sg . . . . ἐκλαλέω
ἐξέλαμπεν   vb impf act ind 3rd pers sg . . . . ἐκλάμπω
ἐξελατόμησαν   vb 1st aor act ind 3rd pers pl . . . ἐκλατομέω
ἐξελατόμησας   vb 1st aor act ind 2nd pers sg   id.
ἐξελαύνων   vb pres act part masc nom sg . . . . ἐξελαύνω
ἔξελε   vb 2nd aor act impv 2nd pers sg . . . . ἐξαιρέω
ἐξελέγησαν   vb 1st aor act ind 3rd pers pl . . . . ἐκλέγω
ἐξελέγξει   vb fut act ind 3rd pers sg . . . . ἐξελέγχω
ἐξελέγχεις   vb pres act ind 2nd pers sg   id.
ἐξελέγχων   vb pres act part masc nom sg   id.
ἐξελεῖν   vb 2nd aor act inf . . . . ἐξαιρέω
ἐξέλειξαν   vb 1st aor act ind 3rd pers pl . . . . ἐκλείχω
ἐξελεῖσθε   vb fut mid ind 2nd pers pl . . . . ἐξαιρέω
ἐξελεῖται   vb fut mid ind 3rd pers sg   id.
ἐξελεξάμην   vb 1st aor mid ind 1st pers sg . . . . ἐκλέγω
ἐξελέξαντο   vb 1st aor mid ind 3rd pers pl   id.
ἐξελέξασθε   vb 1st aor mid ind 2nd pers pl   id.
ἐξελέξατο   vb 1st aor mid ind 3rd pers sg   id.
ἐξέλεξεν   vb 1st aor act ind 3rd pers sg   id.
ἐξελέξω   vb 1st aor mid ind 2nd pers sg   id.
ἐξελέσθαι   vb 2nd aor mid inf . . . . ἐξαιρέω
ἐξέλεσθε   vb 2nd aor mid impv 2nd pers pl   id.
ἐξελέσθωσαν   vb 2nd aor mid impv 3rd pers pl   id.
ἐξελεύσει   vb fut act ind 3rd pers sg . . . . ἐξέρχομαι
ἐξελεύσεσθαι   vb fut mid inf   id.
ἐξελεύσεσθε   vb fut mid ind 2nd pers pl   id.
ἐξελεύσεται   vb fut mid ind 3rd pers sg   id.
ἐξελεύσῃ   fut mid ind 2nd pers sg   id.
ἐξέλευσις   noun fem nom sg
ἐξελεύσομαι   vb fut mid ind 1st pers sg . . . . ἐξέρχομαι
ἐξελευσόμεθα   vb fut mid ind 1st pers pl   id.

ἐξελεύσονται vb fut mid ind 3rd pers pl . . . . . ἐξέρχομαι

ἐξελῇ vb fut mid ind 2nd pers sg . . . . ἐξαιρέω

ἐξεληλύθασιν vb perf act ind 3rd pers pl . . . . . ἐξέρχομαι

ἐξελήλυθεν vb perf act ind 3rd pers sg　　　　　id.

ἐξεληλυθότα vb perf act part neut nom and acc pl　　id.

ἐξεληλυθότων vb perf act part masc and neut gen pl　id.

ἐξεληλυθυίας vb perf act part fem gen sg　　　　id.

ἐξεληλυθώς vb perf act part masc nom sg　　　　id.

ἐξέληται vb 2nd aor mid subj 3rd pers sg . . . . ἐξαιρέω

ἐξέλθατε vb 1st aor act impv 2nd pers pl . . . . . ἐξέρχομαι

ἐξελθάτω vb 1st aor act impv 3rd pers sg　　　　id.

ἐξελθάτωσαν vb 1st aor act impv 3rd pers pl　　　id.

ἔξελθε vb 2nd aor act impv 2nd pers sg　　　　　id.

ἐξελθεῖν vb 2nd aor act inf　　　　　　　　　　id.

ἐξέλθετε vb 2nd aor act impv 2nd pers pl　　　　id.

ἐξελθέτω vb 2nd aor act impv 3rd pers sg　　　　id.

ἐξελθέτωσαν vb 2nd aor act impv 3rd pers pl　　　id.

ἐξέλθῃ vb 2nd aor act subj 3rd pers sg　　　　　id.

ἐξέλθῃς vb 2nd aor act subj 2nd pers sg　　　　id.

ἐξέλθητε vb 2nd aor act subj 2nd pers pl　　　　id.

ἐξέλθοι vb 2nd aor act opt 3rd pers sg　　　　　id.

ἐξελθόν vb 2nd aor act part neut nom and acc sg　　id.

ἐξελθόντας vb 2nd aor act part masc acc pl　　　id.

ἐξελθόντες vb 2nd aor act part masc nom pl　　　id.

ἐξελθόντος vb 2nd aor act part masc and neut gen sg　id.

ἐξελθόντων vb 2nd aor act part masc and neut gen pl　id.

ἐξελθοῦσα vb 2nd aor act part fem nom sg　　　　id.

ἐξέλθω vb 2nd aor act subj 1st pers sg　　　　　id.

ἐξέλθωμεν vb 2nd aor act subj 1st pers pl　　　　id.

ἐξελθών vb 2nd aor act part masc nom sg　　　　id.

ἐξέλθωσιν vb 2nd aor act subj 3rd pers pl　　　　id.

ἐξελίκμησεν vb 1st aor act ind 3rd pers sg . . . . . . ἐκλικμάω

ἐξέλιξεν vb 1st aor act ind 3rd pers sg . . . . ἐκλείχω

ἐξέλιπεν vb 2nd aor act ind 3rd pers sg . . . . ἐκλείπω

ἐξελίπομεν vb 2nd aor act ind 1st pers pl　　　　id.

ἐξέλιπον vb 2nd aor act ind 1st pers sg and 3rd pers pl　id.

ἐξελίποσαν vb 2nd aor act ind 3rd pers pl　　　　id.

ἐξελισσομένη vb pres m/p part fem nom sg . . . . . ἐξελίσσω

ἐξέλκῃς vb pres act subj 2nd pers sg . . . . ἐξέλκω

ἐξελκύσει vb fut act ind 3rd pers sg　　　　　　id.

ἐξελκύσῃς vb 1st aor act subj 2nd pers sg　　　　id.

ἐξελογίζοντο vb impf dep ind 3rd pers pl . . . . ἐκλογίζομαι

ἐξελοῦ vb 2nd aor mid impv 2nd pers sg . . . . ἐξαιρέω

ἐξελοῦμαι vb fut mid ind 1st pers sg　　　　　id.

ἐξελοῦνται vb fut mid ind 3rd pers pl　　　　　id.

ἐξελοῦσιν vb fut act ind 3rd pers pl　　　　　　id.

ἐξελύθη vb 1st aor pass ind 3rd pers sg . . . . ἐκλύω

ἐξελύθησαν vb 1st aor pass ind 3rd pers pl　　　id.

ἐξελυόμην vb impf m/p ind 1st pers sg　　　　　id.

ἐξέλυσαν vb 1st aor act ind 3rd pers pl　　　　　id.

ἐξέλυσεν vb 1st aor act ind 3rd pers sg　　　　　id.

ἐξέλωμαι vb 2nd aor mid subj 1st pers sg . . . . ἐξαιρέω

ἐξέλωνται vb 2nd aor mid subj 3rd pers pl . . . . . . ἐξαιρέω

ἐξεμαρτύρει vb impf act ind 3rd pers sg . . . . . ἐκμαρτυρέω

ἐξεμελίζετο vb impf m/p ind 3rd pers sg . . . . ἐκμελίζω

ἐξεμέλιζον vb impf act ind 3rd pers pl　　　　　id.

ἐξεμέσατε vb 1st aor act impv 2nd pers pl . . . . ἐξεμέω

ἐξεμέσει vb fut act ind 3rd pers sg　　　　　　id.

ἐξεμέσῃς vb 1st aor act subj 2nd pers sg　　　　id.

ἐξεμεσθήσεται vb fut pass ind 3rd pers sg　　　id.

ἐξεμοῦνται vb pres m/p ind 3rd pers pl　　　　　id.

ἐξεμυκτήρισαν vb 1st aor act ind 3rd pers pl　ἐκμυκτηρίζω

ἐξενέγκαι vb 1st aor act inf . . . . ἐκφέρω

ἐξενέγκας vb 1st aor act part masc nom sg　　　id.

ἐξενέγκασα vb 1st aor act part fem nom sg　　　id.

ἐξενέγκατε vb 1st aor act impv 2nd pers pl　　　id.

ἐξένεγκε vb 1st aor act impv 2nd pers sg　　　　id.

ἐξένευσεν vb 1st aor act ind 3rd pers sg . . . . ἐκνεύω

ἐξενεχθέντα vb 1st aor pass part

　　　neut nom and acc pl . . . . ἐκφέρω

ἐξενεχθῆναι vb 1st aor pass inf　　　　　　　id.

ἐξενεχθήσεσθε vb fut pass ind 2nd pers pl　　　id.

ἐξένηψεν vb 1st aor act ind 3rd pers sg . . . . ἐκνήφω

ἐξενολόγει vb impf act ind 3rd pers sg . . . . . . ξενολογέω

ἐξενολόγησα vb 1st aor act ind 1st pers sg　　　id.

ἐξενολόγησεν vb 1st aor act ind 3rd pers sg　　id.

ἐξενοτρόφει vb impf act ind 3rd pers sg . . . . . ξενοτροφέω

ἐξεπείρασαν vb 1st aor act ind 3rd pers pl . . . . . ἐκπειράζω

ἐξεπειράσασθε vb 1st aor mid ind 2nd pers pl　id.

ἐξέπεμψα vb 1st aor act ind 1st pers sg . . . . ἐκπέμπω

ἐξέπεμψαν vb 1st aor act ind 3rd pers pl　　　　id.

ἐξεπέρασεν vb 1st aor act ind 3rd pers sg . . . . ἐκπεράω

ἐξέπεσαν vb 1st aor act ind 3rd pers pl . . . . ἐκπίπτω

ἐξέπεσεν vb 1st aor act ind 3rd pers sg　　　　　id.

ἐξέπεσον vb 2nd aor act ind 3rd pers pl　　　　id.

ἐξεπέτασα vb 1st aor act ind 1st pers sg . . . . ἐκπετάζω

ἐξεπέτασαν vb 1st aor act ind 3rd pers pl　　　　id.

ἐξεπέτασεν vb 1st aor act ind 3rd pers sg　　　　id.

ἐξεπετάσθη vb 1st aor pass ind 3rd pers sg　　　id.

ἐξεπετάσθησαν vb 1st aor pass ind 3rd pers pl　id.

ἐξεπήδησαν vb 1st aor act ind 3rd pers pl . . . . . ἐκπηδάω

ἐξεπήδησεν vb 1st aor act ind 3rd pers sg　　　id.

ἐξεπήδων vb impf act ind 3rd pers pl　　　　　id.

ἐξεπίασεν vb 1st aor act ind 3rd pers sg . . . . ἐκπιάζω

ἐξέπιες vb 2nd aor act ind 2nd pers sg . . . . ἐκπίνω

ἐξεπίεσα vb 1st aor act ind 1st pers sg . . . . ἐκπιέζω

ἐξεπίκραναν vb 1st aor act ind 3rd pers pl . . . . ἐκπικραίνω

ἐξέπιον vb 2nd aor act ind 3rd pers pl . . . . ἐκπίνω

ἐξεπλάγησαν vb 2nd aor pass ind 3rd pers pl . . . . ἐκπλήσσω

ἐξεποίει vb impf act ind 3rd pers sg . . . . ἐκποιέω

ἐξεποίησεν vb 1st aor act ind 3rd pers sg　　　id.

ἐξεπολέμει vb impf act ind 3rd pers sg . . . . ἐκπολεμέω

ἐξεπολέμησαν vb 1st aor act ind 3rd pers pl　　id.

ἐξεπολιόρκουν vb impf act ind 3rd pers pl . . ἐκπολιορκέω

ἐξεπολίτευσεν   vb 1st aor act ind 3rd pers sg ..   ἐκπολιτεύω

ἐξεπορεύεσθε   vb impf dep ind 2nd pers pl ...   ἐκπορεύομαι

ἐξεπορεύετο   vb impf dep ind 3rd pers sg   id.

ἐξεπορευόμην   vb impf dep ind 1st pers sg   id.

ἐξεπορεύοντο   vb impf dep ind 3rd pers pl   id.

ἐξεπορεύου   vb impf dep ind 2nd pers sg   id.

ἐξεπόρνευσαν   vb 1st aor act ind 3rd pers pl ...   ἐκπορνεύω

ἐξεπόρνευσας   vb 1st aor act ind 2nd pers sg   id.

ἐξεπόρνευσεν   vb 1st aor act ind 3rd pers sg   id.

ἐξέπτησαν   vb 2nd aor pass ind 3rd pers pl ..... ἐκπέτομαι

ἐξεραυνήσατε   vb 1st aor act impv 2nd pers pl .. ἐξερευνάω

ἐξεργασάμενον   vb 1st aor mid part masc acc sg,

        neut nom and acc sg .... ἐξεργάζομαι

ἐξεργαστικόν   adj masc acc sg,

        neut nom and acc sg .... ἐξεργαστικός

ἐξερευγόμενα   vb pres dep part

        neut nom and acc pl .... ἐξερεύγομαι

ἐξερευνησάτω   vb 1st aor act impv 3rd pers sg .. ἐξερευνάω

ἐξερευνήσει   noun fem dat sg .... ἐξερεύνησις

ἐξερευνήσετε   vb fut act ind 2nd pers pl ...... ἐξερευνάω

ἐξερευνήσῃς   vb 1st aor act subj 2nd pers sg   id.

ἐξερευνήσω   vb 1st aor act subj 1st pers sg,

        fut act ind 1st pers sg   id.

ἐξερευνήσωσιν   vb 1st aor act subj 3rd pers pl   id.

ἐξερευνῶν   vb pres act part masc nom sg   id.

ἐξερευνῶντες   vb pres act part masc nom pl   id.

ἐξερεύξαιντο   vb 1st aor mid ind 3rd pers pl .. ἐξερεύγομαι

ἐξερεύξεται   vb fut mid ind 3rd pers pl   id.

ἐξερεύξονται   vb fut mid ind 3rd pers pl   id.

ἐξερημοῦντα   vb pres act part masc acc sg ...... ἐξερημόω

ἐξερημωθήσονται   vb fut pass ind 3rd pers pl   id.

ἐξερημῶν   vb pres act part masc nom sg   id.

ἐξερημῶσαι   vb 1st aor act inf   id.

ἐξερήμωσας   vb 1st aor act part masc nom sg   id.

ἐξερημώσει   vb fut act ind 3rd pers sg   id.

ἐξερημώσουσιν   vb fut act ind 3rd pers pl   id.

ἐξερημώσω   vb fut act ind 1st pers sg   id.

ἐξερριζώθη   vb 1st aor pass ind 3rd pers sg .... ἐκριζόω

ἐξερρίζωσεν   vb 1st aor act ind 3rd pers sg   id.

ἐξερριμμένα   vb perf m/p part neut nom and acc pl . ἐκρίπτω

ἐξερρίπτουν   vb impf act ind 3rd pers pl   id.

ἐξερρίφη   vb 2nd aor pass ind 3rd pers sg   id.

ἐξερρίφησαν   vb 2nd aor pass ind 3rd pers pl   id.

ἐξέρριψεν   vb 1st aor act ind 3rd pers sg   id.

ἐξερρύημεν   vb 2nd aor pass ind 1st pers pl .... ἐκρέω

ἐξερρύησαν   vb 2nd aor pass ind 3rd pers pl   id.

ἐξέρχεται   vb pres dep ind 3rd pers sg .... ἐξέρχομαι

ἐξέρχονται   vb pres dep ind 3rd pers pl   id.

ἐξέσπασα   vb 1st aor act ind 1st pers sg .... ἐκσπάω

ἐξέσπασεν   vb 1st aor act ind 3rd pers sg   id.

ἐξεσπασμένος   vb perf m/p part masc nom sg   id.

ἐξεστάθη   vb 1st aor pass ind 3rd pers sg .... ἐξίστημι

ἐξέσται   vb fut mid ind 3rd pers sg .... ἔξειμι

ἐξέστη   vb 2nd aor act ind 3rd pers sg .... ἐξίστημι

ἐξεστηκυῖα   vb perf act part fem nom sg   id.

ἐξέστημεν   vb 2nd aor act ind 1st pers pl   id.

ἐξέστην   vb 2nd aor act ind 1st pers sg   id.

ἐξέστησαν   vb 2nd aor act ind 3rd pers pl   id.

ἐξέστησας   vb 1st aor act ind 2nd pers sg   id.

ἐξέστησεν   vb 1st aor act ind 3rd pers sg   id.

ἔξεστιν   vb pres act ind 3rd pers sg .... ἔξειμι

ἐξεστραμμένη   vb perf m/p part fem nom sg .... ἐκστρέφω

ἐξεστρέψατε   vb 1st aor act ind 2nd pers pl   id.

ἐξεστώς   vb perf act part masc nom sg .... ἐξίστημι

ἐξέσυρεν   vb 1st aor act ind 3rd pers sg .... ἐκσύρω

ἐξέταζε   vb pres act impv 2nd pers sg .... ἐξετάζω

ἐξετάζει   vb pres act ind 3rd pers sg   id.

ἐξετάζετε   vb pres act ind 2nd pers pl   id.

ἐξεταζόμενος   vb pres m/p part masc nom sg   id.

ἐξετάθη   vb 1st aor pass ind 3rd pers sg .... ἐκτείνω

ἐξετάθησαν   vb 1st aor pass ind 3rd pers pl   id.

ἐξετάραξαν   vb 1st aor act ind 3rd pers pl ..... ἐκταράσσω

ἐξετάσει   vb fut act ind 3rd pers sg .... ἐξετάζω

ἐξετάσεως   noun fem gen sg .... ἐξέτασις

ἐξετάσῃς   vb 1st aor act subj 2nd pers sg .... ἐξετάζω

ἐξέτασις   noun fem nom sg

ἐξετασμοί   noun masc nom pl .... ἐξετασμός

ἐξετασμός   noun masc nom sg   id.

ἐξετασμῷ   noun masc dat sg   id.

ἐξεταστέον   verbal adj sg

ἐξετάσωσιν   vb 1st aor act subj 3rd pers pl ...... ἐξετάζω

ἐξετέθη   vb 1st aor pass ind 3rd pers sg .... ἐκτίθημι

ἐξέτεινα   vb 1st aor act ind 1st pers sg .... ἐκτείνω

ἐξέτειναν   vb 1st aor act ind 3rd pers pl   id.

ἐξέτεινας   vb 1st aor act ind 2nd pers sg   id.

ἐξέτεινεν   vb impf act ind 3rd pers sg,

        1st aor act ind 3rd pers sg   id.

ἐξέτεινον   vb impf act ind 1st pers sg   id.

ἐξετέλεσεν   vb 1st aor act ind 3rd pers sg .... ἐκτελέω

ἐξετεμε(ν)   vb 2nd aor act ind 3rd pers sg .... ἐκτέμνω

ἐξετηκόμην   vb impf m/p ind 1st pers sg .... ἐκτήκω

ἐξέτηξα   vb 1st aor act ind 1st pers sg   id.

ἐξέτηξας   vb 1st aor act ind 2nd pers sg   id.

ἐξέτηξεν   vb 1st aor act ind 3rd pers sg   id.

ἐξετίθετο   vb impf m/p ind 3rd pers sg .... ἐκτίθημι

ἐξέτιλεν   vb 1st aor act ind 3rd pers sg .... ἐκτίλλω

ἐξετίλη   vb 2nd aor pass ind 3rd pers sg   id.

ἐξετίναξα   vb 1st aor act ind 1st pers sg .... ἐκτινάσσω

ἐξετίναξαν   vb 1st aor act ind 3rd pers pl   id.

ἐξετίναξε(ν)   vb 1st aor act ind 3rd pers sg   id.

ἐξετινάχθην   vb 1st aor pass ind 1st pers sg   id.

ἐξετόπιζον   vb impf act ind 3rd pers pl .... ἐκτοπίζω

ἐξέτρεφον   vb impf act ind

        1st pers sg and 3rd pers pl .... ἐκτρέφω

ἐξετρίβησαν vb 2nd aor pass ind 3rd pers pl . . . . . ἐκτρίβω
ἐξέτριψα vb 1st aor act ind 1st pers sg   id.
ἐξέτριψαν vb 1st aor act ind 3rd pers pl   id.
ἐξέτριψας vb 1st aor act ind 2nd pers sg   id.
ἐξέτριψεν vb 1st aor act ind 3rd pers sg   id.
ἐξετυφλοῦντο vb impf m/p ind 3rd pers pl . . . . . ἐκτυφλόω
ἐξετύφλωσεν vb 1st aor act ind 3rd pers sg   id.
ἐξευμενίσωνται vb 1st aor mid subj
          3rd pers pl . . . . ἐξευμενίζομαι
ἐξεῦρεν vb 2nd aor act ind 3rd pers sg . . . . ἐξευρίσκω
ἐξεύρεσις noun fem nom sg
ἐξευρών vb 2nd aor act part masc nom sg . . . . . ἐξευρίσκω
ἐξεφάνθη vb 1st aor pass ind 3rd pers sg . . . . ἐκφαίνω
ἐξεφόβησαν vb 1st aor act ind 3rd pers pl . . . . ἐκφοβέω
ἐξεφόβησεν vb 1st aor act ind 3rd pers sg . . . .   id.
ἐξέφυγεν vb 2nd aor act ind 3rd pers sg . . . . ἐκφεύγω
ἐξεφύρθης vb 1st aor pass ind 2nd pers sg . . . . ἐκφύρω
ἐξεφύσησα vb 1st aor act ind 1st pers sg . . . . ἐκφυσάω
ἐξέχεα vb 1st aor act ind 1st pers sg . . . . ἐκχέω
ἐξέχεαν vb 1st aor act ind 3rd pers pl   id.
ἐξέχεας vb 1st aor act ind 2nd pers sg   id.
ἐξέχεεν vb impf act ind 3rd pers sg,
          1st aor act ind 3rd pers sg   id.
ἐξεχόλησεν vb 1st aor act ind 3rd pers sg . . . . ἐκχολάω
ἐξεχομένων vb pres m/p part gen pl . . . . ἐξέχω
ἐξέχον vb pres act part neut nom and acc sg   id.
ἐξέχοντες vb pres act part masc nom pl   id.
ἐξέχοντος vb pres act part masc and neut gen sg   id.
ἐξεχύθη vb 1st aor pass ind 3rd pers sg . . . . ἐκχέω
ἐξεχύθην vb 1st aor pass ind 1st pers sg   id.
ἐξεχύθησαν vb 1st aor pass ind 3rd pers pl   id.
ἐξέχων vb pres act part masc nom sg . . . . ἐξέχω
ἐξεχώρησεν vb 1st aor act ind 3rd pers sg . . . . . . ἐκχωρέω
ἐξεχώρισεν vb 1st aor act ind 3rd pers sg . . . . ἐκχωρίζω
ἐξέψυξεν vb 1st aor act ind 3rd pers sg . . . . ἐκψύχω
ἔξεως noun fem gen sg . . . . ἕξις
ἐξέωσεν vb 1st aor act ind 3rd pers sg . . . . ἐξωθέω
ἐξήγαγεν vb 2nd aor act ind 3rd pers sg . . . . ἐξάγω
ἐξήγαγες vb 2nd aor act ind 2nd pers sg   id.
ἐξηγάγετε vb 2nd aor act ind 2nd pers pl   id.
ἐξήγαγον vb 2nd aor act ind 1st pers sg and 3rd pers   id.
ἐξηγάγοσαν vb 2nd aor act ind 3rd pers pl   id.
ἐξήγγειλα vb 1st aor act ind 1st pers sg . . . . ἐξαγγέλλω
ἐξήγειρα vb 1st aor act ind 1st pers sg . . . . ἐξεγείρω
ἐξήγειρας vb 1st aor act ind 2nd pers sg   id.
ἐξήγειρεν vb impf act ind 3rd pers sg,
          1st aor act ind 3rd pers sg   id.
ἐξηγείρετο vb impf m/p ind 3rd pers sg   id.
ἐξηγειρόμην vb impf m/p ind 1st pers sg   id.
ἐξηγεῖτο vb impf dep ind 3rd pers sg . . . . ἐξηγέομαι
ἐξηγέρθη vb 1st aor pass ind 3rd pers sg . . . . ἐξεγείρω
ἐξηγέρθην vb 1st aor pass ind 1st pers sg   id.

ἐξηγέρθησαν vb 1st aor pass ind 3rd pers pl . . . . . ἐξεγείρω
ἐξηγήσασθαι vb 1st aor mid inf . . . . ἐξηγέομαι
ἐξηγήσατο vb 1st aor mid ind 3rd pers sg   id.
ἐξήγησιν noun fem acc sg . . . . ἐξήγησις
ἐξήγησις noun fem nom sg   id.
ἐξηγήσονται vb fut mid ind 3rd pers pl . . . . ἐξηγέομαι
ἐξηγηταῖς noun masc dat pl . . . . ἐξηγητής
ἐξηγητάς noun masc acc pl   id.
ἐξηγητής noun masc nom sg   id.
ἐξῆγον vb impf act ind 3rd pers pl . . . . ἐξάγω
ἐξήγοντο vb impf m/p ind 3rd pers pl   id.
ἐξηγόρευσαν vb 1st aor act ind 3rd pers pl . . . . ἐξαγορεύω
ἐξηγόρευσεν vb 1st aor act ind 3rd pers sg   id.
ἐξηγορίᾳ noun fem dat sg . . . . ἐξηγορία
ἐξηγορίαν noun fem acc sg   id.
ἐξηγούμενος vb pres dep part masc nom sg . . . . . ἐξηγέομαι
ἐξηγουμένου vb pres dep part masc and neut gen sg   id.
ἐξηγοῦντο vb impf dep ind 3rd pers pl   id.
ἐξηγριάνθη vb 1st aor pass ind 3rd pers sg . . . ἐξαγριαίνω
ἐξηκολούθησαν vb 1st aor act ind
          3rd pers pl . . . . ἐξακολουθέω
ἐξηκολούθησεν vb 1st aor act ind 3rd pers sg   id.
ἐξηκονήθη vb 1st aor pass ind 3rd pers sg . . . . . . ἐξακονάω
ἑξήκοντα indecl number
ἑξηκονταετοῦς adj gen sg . . . . ἑξηκονταετής
ἑξηκονταετῶν adj gen pl   id.
ἑξηκοστοῦ adj masc and neut gen sg . . . . ἑξηκοστός
ἑξηκοστῷ adj masc and neut dat sg   id.
ἐξηκριβάσατο vb 1st aor mid ind
          3rd pers sg . . . . ἐξακριβάζομαι
ἐξήλατο vb 1st aor mid ind 3rd pers sg . . . . ἐξάλλομαι
ἐξηλείφθησαν vb 1st aor pass ind 3rd pers pl . . . ἐξαλείφω
ἐξήλειψα vb 1st aor act ind 1st pers sg   id.
ἐξήλειψας vb 1st aor act ind 2nd pers sg   id.
ἐξήλειψεν vb 1st aor act ind 3rd pers sg   id.
ἐξῆλθαν vb 1st aor act ind 3rd pers pl . . . . ἐξέρχομαι
ἐξῆλθε see ἐξῆλθε(ν)
ἐξῆλθε(ν) vb 2nd aor act ind 3rd pers sg   id.
ἐξῆλθες vb 2nd aor act ind 2nd pers sg   id.
ἐξήλθετε vb 2nd aor act ind 2nd pers pl   id.
ἐξήλθομεν vb 2nd aor act ind 1st pers pl   id.
ἐξῆλθον vb 2nd aor act ind 1st pers sg and 3rd pers pl   id.
ἐξήλθοσαν vb 2nd aor act ind 3rd pers pl   id.
ἐξηλίασαν vb 1st aor act ind 3rd pers pl . . . . ἐξηλιάζω
ἐξηλιασμένων vb perf m/p part gen pl   id.
ἐξηλιάσωμεν vb 1st aor act subj 1st pers pl   id.
ἐξηλλαγμέναι vb perf m/p part fem nom pl . . . . ἐξαλλάσσω
ἐξήλλοντο vb impf dep ind 3rd pers pl . . . . ἐξάλλομαι
ἐξήμαρτεν vb 2nd aor act ind 3rd pers sg . . . . . ἐξαμαρτάνω
ἐξήμαρτες vb 2nd aor act ind 2nd pers sg   id.
ἐξημάρτομεν vb 2nd aor act ind 1st pers pl   id.
ἐξήμαρτον vb 2nd aor act ind 3rd pers pl   id.

ἐξημεροῖ vb pres act ind 3rd pers sg . . . . ἐξημερόω

ἐξήνεγκα vb 1st aor act ind 1st pers sg . . . . ἐκφέρω

ἐξήνεγκαν vb 1st aor act ind 3rd pers pl id.

ἐξήνεγκας vb 1st aor act ind 2nd pers sg id.

ἐξήνεγκεν vb 1st aor act ind 3rd pers sg id.

ἐξήνθησαν vb 1st aor act ind 3rd pers pl . . . . ἐξανθέω

ἐξήνθησεν vb 1st aor act ind 3rd pers sg id.

ἐξηπάτησεν vb 1st aor act ind 3rd pers sg . . . . . ἐξαπατάω

ἐξηπορήθην vb 1st aor pass ind 1st pers sg . . . . . ἐξαπορέω

ἐξήπται vb perf m/p ind 3rd pers sg . . . . ἐξάπτω

ἐξήρα vb 1st aor act ind 1st pers sg . . . . ἐξαίρω

ἐξήραμεν vb 1st aor act ind 1st pers pl id.

ἐξήραν vb 1st aor act ind 3rd pers pl id.

ἐξήρανας vb 1st aor act ind 2nd pers sg . . . . ξηραίνω

ἐξήρανεν vb 1st aor act ind 3rd pers sg id.

ἐξηράνθη vb 1st aor pass ind 3rd pers sg id.

ἐξηράνθην vb 1st aor pass ind 1st pers sg id.

ἐξηράνθησαν vb 1st aor pass ind 3rd pers pl id.

ἐξήρας vb 1st aor act ind 2nd pers sg . . . . ἐξαίρω

ἐξήρεν vb 1st aor act ind 3rd pers sg id.

ἐξηρευνήθη vb 1st aor pass ind 3rd pers sg . . . . ἐξερευνάω

ἐξηρεύνησαν vb 1st aor act ind 3rd pers pl id.

ἐξηρεύνησεν vb 1st aor act ind 3rd pers sg id.

ἐξηρεύνων vb impf act ind 3rd pers pl id.

ἐξηρεύξατο vb 1st aor mid ind 3rd pers sg . . . . ἐξερεύγομαι

ἐξηρημωμένας vb perf m/p part fem acc pl . . . . . ἐξερημόω

ἐξηρημωμένοις vb perf m/p part masc and neut dat pl id.

ἐξηρήμωσα vb 1st aor act ind 1st pers sg id.

ἐξηρήμωσεν vb 1st aor act ind 3rd pers sg id.

ἐξήρημωται vb perf m/p ind 3rd pers sg id.

ἐξήρησαι vb perf m/p ind 2nd pers sg . . . . ἐξαιρέω

ἐξήρθη vb 1st aor pass ind 3rd pers sg . . . . ἐξαίρω

ἐξήρθησαν vb 1st aor pass ind 3rd pers pl id.

ἐξήρθρουν vb impf act ind 3rd pers pl . . . . ἐξαρθρόω

ἐξηρίθμησα vb 1st aor act ind 1st pers sg . . . . . ἐξαριθμέω

ἐξηρίθμησαν vb 1st aor act ind 3rd pers pl id.

ἐξηρίθμησεν vb 1st aor act ind 3rd pers sg id.

ἐξηρμένους vb perf m/p part masc acc pl . . . . ἐξαίρω

ἐξήρον vb 2nd aor act ind 3rd pers pl id.

ἐξήροντο vb impf m/p ind 3rd pers pl id.

ἐξήρται vb perf m/p ind 3rd pers sg id.

ἐξηρτημέναι vb perf m/p part fem nom pl . . . . ἐξαρτάω

ἐξῆρχεν vb impf act ind 3rd pers sg . . . . ἐξάρχω

ἐξήρχετο vb impf m/p ind 3rd pers sg id.

ἐξῆρχον vb impf act ind 3rd pers pl id.

ἐξήρψεν vb 1st aor act ind 3rd pers sg . . . . ἐξέρπω

ἑξῆς adverb

ἐξησθενηκότας vb perf act part masc acc pl . . . ἐξασθενέω

ἐξησθένησαν vb 1st aor act ind 3rd pers pl id.

ἐξήτασας vb 1st aor act ind 2nd pers sg . . . . ἐξετάζω

ἐξήτασεν vb 1st aor act ind 3rd pers sg id.

ἐξήφθησαν vb 1st aor pass ind 3rd pers pl . . . . ἐξάπτω

ἐξηχεῖτο vb impf act ind 3rd pers sg . . . . ἐξηχέω

ἐξήχησαν vb 1st aor act ind 3rd pers pl id.

ἐξηχήσει vb fut act ind 3rd pers sg id.

ἐξήψαμεν vb 1st aor act ind 1st pers pl . . . . ἐξάπτω

ἐξῆψαν vb 1st aor act ind 3rd pers pl id.

ἐξῆψεν vb 1st aor act ind 3rd pers sg id.

ἐξικνούμενοι vb pres dep part masc nom pl . . . . ἐξικνέομαι

ἐξίλασαι vb 1st aor mid impv 2nd pers sg . . . ἐξιλάσκομαι

ἐξιλάσαι vb 1st aor act inf

          1st aor act opt 3rd pers sg id.

ἐξιλάσαντο vb 1st aor mid ind 3rd pers pl id.

ἐξιλάσασθαι vb 1st aor mid inf id.

ἐξιλασάσθω vb 1st aor mid impv 3rd pers sg id.

ἐξιλάσατο vb 1st aor mid ind 3rd pers sg id.

ἐξιλάσεσθε vb fut mid ind 2nd pers pl id.

ἐξιλάσεται vb fut mid ind 3rd pers sg id.

ἐξιλάσεως noun fem gen sg . . . . ἐξίλασις

ἐξιλάσθσθε vb 1st aor mid subj 2nd pers pl . . ἐξιλάσκομαι

ἐξιλασθήσεται vb fut pass ind 3rd pers sg id.

ἐξιλάσκεσθαι vb pres dep inf id.

ἐξιλάσκεσθε vb pres dep impv 2nd pers pl id.

ἐξιλάσκεται vb pres dep ind 3rd pers sg id.

ἐξιλασκόμενος vb pres dep part masc nom sg id.

ἐξίλασμα noun neut nom and acc sg

ἐξιλασμόν noun masc acc sg . . . . ἐξιλασμός

ἐξιλασμός noun masc nom sg id.

ἐξιλασμοῦ noun masc gen sg id.

ἐξιλασμῶν noun masc gen pl id.

ἐξιλάσομαι vb fut mid ind 1st pers sg . . . . . . ἐξιλάσκομαι

ἐξιλάσονται vb fut mid ind 3rd pers pl id.

ἐξιλάσωμαι vb 1st aor mid subj 1st pers sg id.

ἕξιν noun fem acc sg . . . . ἕξις

ἐξιόντες vb pres act part masc nom pl . . . . ἔξειμι

ἐξιόντι vb pres act part masc and neut dat sg id.

ἐξιόντων vb pres act part masc and neut gen pl id.

ἐξιππάσονται vb fut mid ind 3rd pers pl . . . . . ἐξιππάζομαι

ἐξίπτασθαι vb pres dep inf . . . . ἐξίπτομαι

ἕξις noun fem nom sg

ἐξισάζου vb pres m/p impv 2nd pers sg . . . . ἐξισάζω

ἐξισούμενοι vb pres m/p part masc nom pl . . . . ἐξισόω

ἐξισούμενον vb pres m/p part masc acc sg,

          neut nom and acc sg id.

ἐξιστάνειν vb pres act inf . . . . ἐξιστάνω

ἐξίσταντο vb impf m/p ind 3rd pers pl . . . . ἐξίστημι

ἐξίσταται vb pres m/p ind 3rd pers sg id.

ἐξίστατο vb impf m/p ind 3rd pers sg id.

ἐξιχνεύσει vb fut act ind 3rd pers sg . . . . ἐξιχνεύω

ἐξίχνευσεν vb 1st aor act ind 3rd pers sg id.

ἐξίχνευσον vb 1st aor act impv 2nd pers sg id.

ἐξιχνίασα vb 1st aor act ind 1st pers sg . . . . ἐξιχνιάζω

ἐξιχνιάσαι vb 1st aor act inf id.

ἐξιχνιάσαμεν vb 1st aor act ind 1st pers pl id.

ἐξιχνίασας vb 1st aor act ind 2nd pers sg	.....	ἐξιχνιάζω
ἐξιχνιάσατε vb 1st aor act impv 2nd pers pl		id.
ἐξιχνιάσει vb fut act ind 3rd pers sg		id.
ἐξιχνίασεν vb 1st aor act ind 3rd pers sg		id.
ἐξιχνιάσεται vb fut mid ind 3rd pers sg		id.
ἐξιχνιάσῃ vb 1st aor act subj 3rd pers sg		id.
ἐξιχνιασμοί noun masc nom pl	....	ἐξιχνιασμός
ἐξιχνίασον vb 1st aor act impv 2nd pers sg	....	ἐξιχνιάζω
ἐξιχνιάσω vb fut act ind 1st pers sg		id.
ἐξοδεύειν vb pres act inf	....	ἐξοδεύω
ἐξοδευθείς vb 1st aor pass part masc nom sg		id.
ἐξοδεύσαντες vb 1st aor act part masc nom pl		id.
ἐξοδεύσωσιν vb pres act subj 3rd pers pl		id.
ἐξοδίᾳ noun fem dat sg	....	ἐξοδία
ἐξοδίας noun fem gen sg and acc pl		id.
ἐξόδιον noun neut nom and acc sg		
ἐξοδίου noun neut gen sg	....	ἐξόδιον
ἔξοδοι noun fem nom pl	....	ἔξοδος
ἐξόδοις noun fem dat pl		id.
ἔξοδον noun fem acc sg		id.
ἔξοδος noun fem nom sg		id.
ἐξόδου noun fem gen sg		id.
ἐξόδους noun fem acc pl		id.
ἐξόδῳ noun fem dat sg		id.
ἐξόδων noun fem gen pl		id.
ἔξοικος adj masc and fem nom sg		
ἐξοίσει vb fut act ind 3rd pers sg	....	ἐκφέρω
ἐξοίσεις vb fut act ind 2nd pers sg		id.
ἐξοίσετε vb fut act ind 2nd pers pl		id.
ἐξοίσομεν vb fut act ind 1st pers pl		id.
ἐξοίσουσιν vb fut act ind 3rd pers pl		id.
ἐξοίσω vb fut act ind 1st pers sg		id.
ἐξολεθρεύεσθαι vb pres m/p inf	....	ἐξολεθρεύω
ἐξολεθρευθείη vb 1st aor pass opt 3rd pers sg		id.
ἐξολεθρευθῇ vb 1st aor pass subj 3rd pers sg		id.
ἐξολεθρευθῆναι vb 1st aor pass inf		id.
ἐξολεθρευθῆς vb 1st aor pass subj 2nd pers sg		id.
ἐξολεθρευθήσεται vb fut pass ind 3rd pers sg		id.
ἐξολεθρευθήσονται vb fut pass ind 3rd pers pl		id.
ἐξολεθρευθῆτε vb 1st aor pass subj 2nd pers pl		id.
ἐξολεθρευθῶσιν vb 1st aor pass subj 3rd pers pl		id.
ἐξολεθρεύματος noun neut gen sg	....	ἐξολέθρευμα
ἐξολεθρεύοντες vb pres act part		
masc and neut nom pl	....	ἐξολεθρεύω
ἐξολεθρεύοντι vb pres act part masc and neut dat sg		id.
ἐξολεθρεύσαι vb 1st aor act opt 3rd pers sg		id.
ἐξολεθρεῦσαι vb 1st aor act inf		id.
ἐξολεθρεύσας vb 1st aor act part masc nom sg		id.
ἐξολεθρεύσατε vb 1st aor act impv 2nd pers pl		id.
ἐξολεθρεύσει vb fut act ind 3rd pers sg		id.
ἐξολεθρεύσεις vb fut act ind 2nd pers sg		id.
ἐξολεθρεύσεως noun fem gen sg	....	ἐξολέθρευσις

ἐξολεθρεύσῃ vb 1st aor act subj 3rd pers sg	...	ἐξολεθρεύω
ἐξολεθρεύσῃς vb 1st aor act subj 2nd pers sg		id.
ἐξολέθρευσιν noun fem acc sg	....	ἐξολέθρευσις
Ἐξολέθρευσις pr noun fem nom sg		
ἐξολέθρευσον vb 1st aor act impv 2nd pers sg	.	ἐξολεθρεύω
ἐξολεθρεύσουσιν vb fut act ind 3rd pers pl		id.
ἐξολεθρεύσω vb 1st aor act subj 1st pers sg,		
fut act ind 1st pers sg		id.
ἐξολεθρεύσωμεν vb 1st aor act subj 1st pers pl		id.
ἐξολεθρεύσωσιν vb 1st aor act subj 3rd pers pl		id.
ἐξολεθρεύων vb pres act part masc nom sg		id.
ἐξολεῖται vb fut mid ind 3rd pers sg	....	ἐξόλλυμι
ἐξολῇ vb fut mid ind 2nd pers sg		id.
ἐξολλύει vb pres act ind 3rd pers sg	....	ἐξολλύω
ἐξόλλυσιν vb pres act ind 3rd pers pl	....	ἐξόλλυμι
ἐξολοθρευθήσονται vb fut pass ind		
3rd pers pl	....	ἐξολοθρεύω
ἐξομβρήσει vb fut act ind 3rd pers sg	....	ἐξομβρέω
ἔξομεν vb fut act ind 1st pers pl	....	ἔχω
ἐξόμνυμαι vb pres dep ind 1st pers sg		
ἐξόμνυσθαι vb pres dep inf	....	ἐξόμνυμαι
ἐξομοιοῦσθαι vb pres m/p inf	....	ἐξομοιόω
ἐξομολογεῖσθαι vb pres dep inf	....	ἐξομολογέομαι
ἐξομολογεῖσθε vb pres dep impv 2nd pers pl,		
pres dep ind 2nd pers pl		id.
ἐξομολογείσθωσαν vb pres dep impv 3rd pers pl		id.
ἐξομολογήσασθαι vb 1st aor mid inf		id.
ἐξομολογήσασθε vb 1st aor mid impv 2nd pers pl		id.
ἐξομολογησάσθωσαν vb 1st aor mid impv 3rd pers pl		id.
ἐξομολογήσει noun fem dat sg	....	ἐξομολόγησις
ἐξομολογήσεσιν noun fem dat pl		id.
ἐξομολογήσεται vb fut mid ind		
3rd pers sg	....	ἐξομολογέομαι
ἐξομολογήσεων noun fem gen pl	....	ἐξομολόγησις
ἐξομολογήσεως noun fem gen sg		id.
ἐξομολόγησιν noun fem acc sg		id.
ἐξομολόγησις noun fem nom sg		
ἐξομολογήσομαι vb fut mid ind		
1st pers sg	....	ἐξομολογέομαι
ἐξομολογησόμεθα vb fut mid ind 1st pers pl		id.
ἐξομολογήσονται vb fut mid ind 3rd pers pl		id.
ἐξομολογήσωνται vb 1st aor mid subj 3rd pers pl		id.
ἐξομολογοῦ vb pres dep impv 2nd pers sg		id.
ἐξομολογοῦμαι vb pres dep ind 1st pers sg		id.
ἐξομολογούμεθα vb pres dep ind 1st pers pl		id.
ἐξομολογουμένην vb pres dep part fem acc sg		id.
ἐξομολογούμενοι vb pres dep part masc nom pl		id.
ἐξομολογούμενος vb pres dep part masc nom sg		id.
ἐξομολογουμένων vb pres dep part gen pl		id.
ἐξομόσησθε vb 1st aor mid subj 2nd pers pl	.....	ἐξόμνυμι
ἐξομοῦμαι vb fut mid ind 1st pers sg		id.
ἐξόν vb pres act part neut nom and acc sg	....	ἔξειμι

ἐξόπισθεν	adverb and preposition	
ἐξοπλησίαν	noun fem acc sg	ἐξοπλησία
ἐξοπλίσατε	vb 1st aor act impv 2nd pers pl	ἐξοπλίζω
ἐξοπλίσησθε	vb 1st aor mid subj 2nd pers pl	id.
ἐξορκιῶ	vb fut act ind 1st pers sg	ἐξορκίζω
ἐξορύξαι	vb 1st aor act inf	ἐξορύσσω
ἐξουδένει	vb pres act impv 2nd pers sg	ἐξουδενέω
ἐξουδένημα	noun neut nom and acc sg	
ἐξουδένησεν	vb 1st aor act ind 3rd pers sg	ἐξουδενέω
ἐξουδενήσῃς	vb 1st aor act subj 2nd pers sg	id.
ἐξουδένουν	vb impf act ind 1st pers sg and 3rd pers pl	id.
ἐξουδενοῦντας	vb pres act part masc acc pl	id.
ἐξουδενοῦντες	vb pres act part masc nom pl	id.
ἐξουδενώθη	vb 1st aor pass ind 3rd pers sg	ἐξουδενόω
ἐξουδενωθήσονται	vb fut pass ind 3rd pers pl	id.
ἐξουδένωκα	vb perf act ind 1st pers sg	id.
ἐξουδενώκασιν	vb perf act ind 3rd pers pl	id.
ἐξουδενώματα	noun neut nom and acc pl	ἐξουδένωμα
ἐξουδενωμένα	vb pres m/p part	
neut nom and acc pl		ἐξουδενόω
ἐξουδενωμένη	vb pres m/p part fem nom sg	id.
ἐξουδενωμένον	vb pres m/p part masc acc sg,	
neut nom and acc sg		id.
ἐξουδενωμένος	vb pres m/p part masc nom sg	id.
ἐξουδενωμένους	vb pres m/p part masc acc pl	id.
ἐξουδένωνται	vb pres m/p ind 3rd pers pl	id.
ἐξουδένωσαν	vb 1st aor act ind 3rd pers pl	id.
ἐξουδένωσας	vb 1st aor act ind 2nd pers sg	id.
ἐξουδενώσας	vb 1st aor act part masc nom sg	id.
ἐξουδενώσει	noun fem dat sg	ἐξουδένωσις
ἐξουδενώσει	vb fut act ind 3rd pers sg	ἐξουδενόω
ἐξουδενώσεις	vb fut act ind 2nd pers sg	id.
ἐξουδένωσεν	vb 1st aor act ind 3rd pers sg	id.
ἐξουδενώσεως	noun fem gen sg	ἐξουδένωσις
ἐξουδένωσιν	noun fem acc sg	id.
ἐξουδένωσις	noun fem nom sg	id.
ἐξουδενώσουσιν	vb fut act ind 3rd pers pl	ἐξουδενόω
ἐξουδένωται	vb pres m/p subj 3rd pers sg	id.
ἐξουθενήκασιν	vb perf act ind 3rd pers pl	ἐξουθενέω
ἐξουθενήκατε	vb perf act ind 2nd pers pl	id.
ἐξουθενημένους	vb pres m/p part masc acc pl	id.
ἐξουθενημένῳ	vb pres m/p part masc and neut dat sg	id.
ἐξουθενήσῃς	vb 1st aor act subj 2nd pers sg	id.
ἐξουθενήσουσιν	vb fut act ind 3rd pers pl	id.
ἐξουθενοῦντες	vb pres act part masc nom pl	id.
ἐξουθενοῦσι	vb pres act part masc and neut dat pl	id.
ἐξουθενώθη	vb 1st aor pass ind 3rd pers sg	ἐξουθενόω
ἐξουθενῶν	vb pres act part masc nom sg	ἐξουθενέω
ἐξουθενώσει	vb fut act ind 3rd pers sg	ἐξουθενόω
ἐξουθένωσεν	vb 1st aor act ind 3rd pers sg	id.
ἐξουθενώσομεν	vb fut act ind 1st pers pl	id.
ἐξουσία	noun fem nom sg	

ἐξουσίᾳ	noun fem dat sg	ἐξουσία
ἐξουσιάζεται	vb pres m/p ind 3rd pers sg	ἐξουσιάζω
ἐξουσιάζῃ	vb pres m/p ind 2nd pers sg	id.
ἐξουσιάζονται	vb pres m/p ind 3rd pers pl	id.
ἐξουσιάζοντας	vb pres act part masc acc pl	id.
ἐξουσιάζοντος	vb pres act part masc and neut gen sg	id.
ἐξουσιαζόντων	vb pres act part masc and neut gen pl	id.
ἐξουσιάζουσιν	vb pres act ind 3rd pers pl	id.
ἐξουσιάζων	vb pres act part masc nom sg	id.
ἐξουσίαι	noun fem nom pl	ἐξουσία
ἐξουσίαις	noun fem dat pl	id.
ἐξουσίαν	noun fem acc sg	id.
ἐξουσίας	noun fem gen sg and acc pl	id.
ἐξουσιάσατο	vb 1st aor mid ind 3rd pers sg	ἐξουσιάζω
ἐξουσιάσει	vb fut act ind 3rd pers sg	id.
ἐξουσιάσεις	vb fut act ind 2nd pers sg	id.
ἐξουσίασεν	vb 1st aor act ind 3rd pers sg	id.
ἔξουσιν	vb fut act ind 3rd pers pl	ἔχω
ἐξουσιῶν	noun fem gen pl	ἐξουσία
ἐξοχῇ	noun fem dat sg	ἐξοχή
ἐξόχως	adverb	
ἐξύβριζεν	vb impf act ind 3rd pers sg	ἐξυβρίζω
ἐξυβρίζοντας	vb pres act part masc acc pl	id.
ἐξύβρισαν	vb 1st aor act part neut nom and acc sg	id.
ἐξύβρισας	vb 1st aor act part masc nom sg	id.
ἐξυλωμένα	vb perf m/p part neut nom and acc pl	ξυλόω
ἐξύλωσεν	vb 1st aor act ind 3rd pers sg	id.
ἐξύμνησεν	vb 1st aor act ind 3rd pers sg	ἐξυμνέω
ἐξυπνίσθη	vb 1st aor pass ind 3rd pers sg	ἐξυπνίζω
ἐξυπνισθήσονται	vb fut pass ind 3rd pers sg	id.
ἔξυπνος	adj masc and fem nom sg	
ἐξυπνώσεις	vb fut act ind 2nd pers sg	ἐξυπνόω
ἐξυρήθη	vb 1st aor pass ind 3rd pers sg	ξυράω
ἐξυρημένοι	vb perf m/p part masc nom pl	id.
ἐξυρημένους	vb perf m/p part masc acc pl	id.
ἐξύρησεν	vb 1st aor act ind 3rd pers pl	id.
ἐξυρήσατο	vb 1st aor mid ind 3rd pers sg	id.
ἐξύρησεν	vb 1st aor act ind 3rd pers sg	id.
ἐξύψου	vb pres m/p impv 2nd pers sg	ἐξυψόω
ἐξύψουν	vb impf act ind 3rd pers pl	id.
ἕξω	vb fut act ind 1st pers sg	ἔχω
ἔξω	adverb and preposition	
ἐξωδιάσθη	vb 1st aor pass ind 3rd pers sg	ἐξοδιάζω
ἔξωθεν	adverb and preposition	
ἐξώκειλεν	vb 2nd aor act ind 3rd pers sg	ἐξοκέλλω
ἐξωλεθρεύθη	vb 1st aor pass ind 3rd pers sg	ἐξολεθρεύω
ἐξωλεθρεύθησαν	vb 1st aor pass ind 3rd pers pl	id.
ἐξωλέθρευσα	vb 1st aor act ind 1st pers sg	id.
ἐξωλεθρεύσαμεν	vb 1st aor act ind 1st pers pl	id.
ἐξωλέθρευσεν	vb 1st aor act ind 3rd pers pl	id.
ἐξωλέθρευσας	vb 1st aor act ind 2nd pers sg	id.
ἐξωλεθρεύσατε	vb 1st aor act ind 2nd pers pl	ἐξολεθρεύω

ἐξωλέθρευσεν vb 1st aor act ind 3rd pers sg .. ἐξολεθρεύω

ἐξώμβρησεν vb 1st aor act ind 3rd pers sg ...... ἐξομβρέω

ἐξωμολογεῖτο vb impf dep ind 3rd pers sg . ἐξομολογέομαι

ἐξωμολογησάμην vb 1st aor mid ind 1st pers sg id.

ἐξωμολογήσαντο vb 1st aor mid ind 3rd pers pl id.

ἐξωμολογοῦντο vb impf dep ind 3rd pers pl id.

ἐξωπλισμένους vb perf m/p part masc acc pl .... ἐξοπλίζω

ἐξώρκισας vb 1st aor act ind 2nd pers sg .... ἐξορκίζω

ἐξώρμησαν vb 1st aor act ind 3rd pers pl .... ἐξορμάω

ἐξώρμησε(ν) vb 1st aor act ind 3rd pers sg id.

ἐξώρυξαν vb 1st aor act ind 3rd pers pl .... ἐξορύσσω

ἐξώρυξεν vb 1st aor act ind 3rd pers sg id.

ἐξῶσα vb 1st aor act ind 1st pers sg .... ἐξωθέω

ἐξῶσαι vb 1st aor act inf id.

ἔξωσαν vb 1st aor act ind 3rd pers pl id.

ἐξῶσαν see ἔξωσαν

ἐξώσατε vb 1st aor act impv 2nd pers pl id.

ἐξῶσεν vb 1st aor act ind 3rd pers sg id.

ἐξώσῃ vb 1st aor act subj 3rd pers sg id.

ἐξώσητε vb 1st aor act subj 2nd pers pl id.

ἐξωσθήσαν vb 1st aor pass ind 3rd pers pl id.

ἐξωσθήσονται vb fut pass ind 3rd pers pl id.

ἐξώσματα noun neut nom and acc pl .... ἔξωσμα

ἐξωσμένα vb pres m/p part neut nom and acc pl .... ἐξωθέω

ἐξωσμένη vb perf m/p part fem nom sg id.

ἐξωσμένην vb perf m/p part fem acc sg id.

ἐξωσμένοι vb perf m/p part masc nom pl id.

ἐξωσμένον vb 1st aor mid part masc acc sg,
    neut nom and acc sg id.

ἔξωσον vb 1st aor act impv 2nd pers sg id.

ἐξώσουσιν vb fut act ind 3rd pers pl id.

ἐξώσω vb 1st aor act subj 1st pers sg,
    fut act ind 1st pers sg id.

ἐξωτάτου superl adj masc and neut gen sg .... ἐξώτερος

ἐξωτέρᾳ adj fem dat sg id.

ἐξωτέραν adj fem acc sg id.

ἐξωτέρας adj fem gen sg id.

ἐξωτέρον adj masc acc sg, neut nom and acc sg id.

ἐξωτέρω adverb

ἐξωτέρῳ adj masc and neut dat sg .... ἐξώτερος

ἐξωτέρων adj gen pl id.

ἔοικεν vb perf act ind 3rd pers sg .... ἔοικα

ἑόρακα vb perf act ind 1st pers sg .... ὁράω

ἑόρακας vb perf act ind 2nd pers sg id.

ἑοράκασιν vb perf act ind 3rd pers pl id.

ἑοράκατε vb perf act ind 2nd pers pl id.

ἑόρακεν vb perf act ind 3rd pers sg id.

ἑόραται vb perf m/p ind 3rd pers sg id.

ἑόρταζε vb pres act impv 2nd pers sg .... ἑορτάζω

ἑορτάζειν vb pres act inf id.

ἑορτάζοντας vb pres act part masc acc pl id.

ἑορτάζοντες vb pres act part masc nom pl id.

ἑορτάζοντος vb pres act part masc and neut gen sg ἑορτάζω

ἑορταί noun fem nom pl .... ἑορτή

ἑορταῖς noun fem dat pl id.

ἑορτάς noun fem acc pl id.

ἑορτάσαι vb 1st aor act inf .... ἑορτάζω

ἑορτάσατε vb 1st aor act impv 2nd pers pl id.

ἑορτάσει vb fut act ind 3rd pers sg id.

ἑορτάσεις vb fut act ind 2nd pers sg id.

ἑορτάσετε vb fut act ind 2nd pers pl id.

ἑορτασμάτων noun neut gen pl .... ἑόρτασμα

ἑορτάσωσιν vb 1st aor act subj 3rd pers pl ..... ἑορτάζω

ἑορτή noun fem nom sg

ἑορτῇ noun fem dat sg .... ἑορτή

ἑορτήν noun fem acc sg id.

ἑορτῆς noun fem gen sg id.

ἑορτῶν noun fem gen pl id.

ἐπ᾽ see ἐπί

ἐπάγαγε vb 2nd aor act impv 2nd pers sg .... ἐπάγω

ἐπαγαγεῖν vb 2nd aor act inf id.

ἐπαγάγῃ vb 2nd aor act subj 3rd pers sg id.

ἐπαγάγῃς vb 2nd aor act subj 2nd pers sg id.

ἐπαγαγών vb 2nd aor act part masc nom sg id.

ἐπαγγειλάμενος vb 1st aor mid part
    masc nom sg .... ἐπαγγέλλω

ἐπαγγελίᾳ noun fem dat sg .... ἐπαγγελία

ἐπαγγελίαν noun fem acc sg id.

ἐπαγγελίας noun fem gen sg and acc pl id.

ἐπαγγέλλεται vb pres m/p ind 3rd pers sg ..... ἐπαγγέλλω

ἐπαγγελλομένη vb pres m/p part fem nom sg id.

ἐπαγγελλόμενος vb pres m/p part masc nom sg id.

ἐπαγγελλομένου vb pres m/p part masc and neut gen sg id.

ἐπάγει vb pres act ind 3rd pers sg .... ἐπάγω

ἐπάγη vb 2nd aor pass ind 3rd pers sg .... πήγνυμι

ἐπάγης vb 2nd aor pass ind 2nd pers sg id.

ἐπάγοντος vb pres act part masc and neut gen sg .... ἐπάγω

ἐπάγου vb pres m/p impv 2nd pers sg id.

ἐπάγουσα vb pres act part fem nom sg id.

ἐπάγουσιν vb pres act ind 3rd pers pl id.

ἐπάγω vb pres act ind 1st pers sg,
    pres act subj 1st pers sg id.

ἐπαγωγά adj neut nom and acc pl .... ἐπαγωγός

ἐπαγωγαί noun fem nom pl .... ἐπαγωγή

ἐπαγωγάς noun fem acc pl id.

ἐπαγωγῇ noun fem dat sg id.

ἐπαγωγήν noun fem acc sg id.

ἐπαγωγῆς noun fem gen sg id.

ἐπαγωγῶν noun fem gen pl id.

ἐπάγων vb pres act part masc nom sg .... ἐπάγω

ἐπᾴδοντι vb pres act part masc and neut dat sg ...... ἐπᾴδω

ἐπᾳδόντων vb pres act part masc and neut gen pl id.

ἐπαείδων vb pres act part masc nom sg .... ἐπαείδω

ἐπαιδεύθην vb 1st aor pass ind 1st pers sg .... παιδεύω

ἐπαιδεύθησαν vb 1st aor pass ind 3rd pers pl . . . παιδεύω
ἐπαίδευσαν vb 1st aor act ind 3rd pers pl id.
ἐπαίδευσας vb 1st aor act ind 2nd pers sg id.
ἐπαίδευσεν vb 1st aor act ind 3rd pers sg id.
ἔπαιζεν vb impf act ind 3rd pers sg . . . . παίζω
ἐπαίνει vb pres act impv 2nd pers sg . . . . ἐπαινέω
ἐπαινεῖ vb pres act ind 3rd pers sg id.
ἐπαινεῖν vb pres act inf id.
ἐπαινεῖσθαι vb pres m/p inf id.
ἐπαινεῖσθε vb pres m/p ind 2nd pers pl id.
ἐπαινεῖται vb pres m/p ind 3rd pers sg id.
ἐπαινέσατε vb 1st aor act impv 2nd pers pl id.
ἐπαινέσει vb fut act ind 3rd pers sg id.
ἐπαινέσῃς vb 1st aor act subj 2nd pers sg id.
ἐπαινεσθήσεται vb fut pass ind 3rd pers sg id.
ἐπαινεσθησόμεθα vb fut pass ind 1st pers pl id.
ἐπαινεσθήσονται vb fut pass ind 3rd pers pl id.
ἐπαινέσουσιν vb fut act ind 3rd pers pl id.
ἐπαινεστή adj fem nom sg . . . . ἐπαινεστός
ἐπαινέσω vb fut act ind 1st pers sg . . . . ἐπαινέω
ἔπαινον noun masc acc sg . . . . ἔπαινος
ἔπαινος noun masc nom sg id.
ἐπαινουμένῳ vb pres m/p part
    masc and neut dat sg . . . . ἐπαινέω
ἐπαινοῦντες vb pres act part masc nom pl id.
ἐπαίνους noun masc acc pl . . . . ἔπαινος
ἐπαίνῳ noun masc dat sg id.
ἐπαινῶν vb pres act part masc nom sg . . . . ἐπαινέω
ἔπαιξεν vb 1st aor act ind 3rd pers sg . . . . παίζω
ἐπαίρει vb pres act ind 3rd pers sg . . . . ἐπαίρω
ἐπαίρεσθαι vb pres m/p inf id.
ἐπαίρεσθε vb pres m/p impv 2nd pers pl id.
ἐπαίρεται vb pres m/p ind 3rd pers sg id.
ἐπαίρετε vb pres act impv 2nd pers pl id.
ἐπαιρέτω vb pres act impv 3rd pers sg id.
ἐπαίρῃ vb pres act subj 3rd pers sg id.
ἐπαιρόμενα vb pres m/p part neut nom and acc pl id.
ἐπαιρόμενον vb pres m/p part masc acc sg,
    neut nom and acc sg id.
ἐπαιρόμενος vb pres m/p part masc nom sg id.
ἐπαίρου vb pres m/p impv 2nd pers sg id.
ἔπαισα vb 1st aor act ind 1st pers sg . . . . παίζω
ἔπαισαν vb 1st aor act ind 3rd pers pl id.
ἔπαισας vb 1st aor act ind 2nd pers sg . . . . παίω
ἔπαισεν vb 1st aor act ind 3rd pers sg id.
ἐπαισχυνθῶ vb 1st aor pass subj 1st pers sg . . . . ἐπαισχύνω
ἐπαιτεῖν vb pres act inf . . . . ἐπαιτέω
ἐπαιτησάτωσαν vb 1st aor act impv 3rd pers pl id.
ἐπαιτήσεως noun fem gen sg . . . . ἐπαίτησις
ἐπαίτησις noun fem nom sg id.
ἐπακήκοεν vb perf act ind 3rd pers sg . . . . ἐπακούω
ἐπακολουθείτω vb pres act impv 3rd pers sg . ἐπακολουθέω

ἐπακολουθῆσαι vb 1st aor act inf . . . . ἐπακολουθέω
ἐπακολουθήσαντες vb 1st aor act part masc nom pl id.
ἐπακολουθήσατε vb 1st aor act impv 2nd pers pl id.
ἐπακολουθήσεις vb fut act ind 2nd pers sg id.
ἐπακολουθήσετε vb fut act ind 2nd pers pl id.
ἐπακολουθήσῃ vb 1st aor act subj 3rd pers sg id.
ἐπακούει vb pres act ind 3rd pers sg . . . . ἐπακούω
ἐπακούειν vb pres act inf id.
ἐπακούσαι vb 1st aor act opt 3rd pers sg id.
ἐπακούσαι vb 1st aor act inf id.
ἐπακούσαντι vb 1st aor act part masc and neut dat sg id.
ἐπακούσατε vb 1st aor act impv 2nd pers pl id.
ἐπακούσεται vb fut mid ind 3rd pers sg id.
ἐπακούσῃ vb 1st aor act subj 3rd pers sg id.
ἐπακούσομαι vb fut mid ind 1st pers sg id.
ἐπάκουσον vb 1st aor act impv 2nd pers sg id.
ἐπακουστός adj masc and fem nom sg id.
ἐπακρόασις noun fem nom sg
ἐπάλαιεν vb impf act ind 3rd pers sg . . . . παλαίω
ἐπαλαιώθη vb 1st aor pass ind 3rd pers sg . . . . παλαιόω
ἐπαλαιώθην vb 1st aor pass ind 1st pers sg id.
ἐπαλαιώθης vb 1st aor pass ind 2nd pers sg id.
ἐπαλαιώθησαν vb 1st aor pass ind 3rd pers pl id.
ἐπαλαίωσαν vb 1st aor act ind 3rd pers pl id.
ἐπαλαίωσεν vb 1st aor act ind 3rd pers sg id.
ἐπαλγέστερον comp adj neut nom and acc sg . . . . ἐπαλγής
ἐπαλλόμην vb impf dep ind 1st pers sg . . . . πάλλομαι
ἐπάλξεις noun fem nom and acc pl . . . . ἔπαλξις
ἐπάλξεων noun fem gen pl id.
ἐπάλξεως noun fem gen sg id.
ἐπαμῦναι vb 1st aor act inf . . . . ἐπαμύνω
ἐπαμύνονται vb pres m/p ind 3rd pers pl id.
ἐπάν particle
ἐπάναγε vb pres act impv 2nd pers sg . . . . ἐπανάγω
ἐπαναγόντων vb pres act part masc and neut gen pl id.
ἐπανάγων vb pres act part masc nom sg id.
ἐπανακαινίζων vb pres act part
    masc nom sg . . . . ἐπανακαινίζω
ἐπαναπαυομένων vb pres m/p part gen pl . . . . ἐπαναπαύω
ἐπαναπαύσεται vb fut mid ind 3rd pers sg id.
ἐπανάπαυσον vb 1st aor act impv 2nd pers sg id.
ἐπαναπέπουται vb perf m/p ind 3rd pers sg id.
ἐπανασταίη vb 2nd aor act opt 3rd pers sg . . . . ἐπανίστημι
ἐπαναστάσει noun fem dat sg . . . . ἐπανάστασις
ἐπαναστῇ vb 2nd aor act subj 3rd pers sg . . . . ἐπανίστημι
ἐπαναστῆναι vb 2nd aor act inf id.
ἐπαναστήσεται vb fut mid ind 3rd pers sg id.
ἐπαναστήσομαι vb fut mid ind 1st pers sg id.
ἐπαναστήσονται vb fut mid ind 3rd pers pl id.
ἐπαναστραφέν vb 2nd aor pass part
    neut nom and acc sg . . . . ἐπαναστρέφω
ἐπαναστραφήσεσθε vb fut pass ind 2nd pers pl id.

ἐπαναστραφήσεται vb fut pass ind	ἐπάξω vb fut act ind 1st pers sg . . . . ἐπάγω
3rd pers sg . . . . ἐπαναστρέφω	ἐπαοιδαῖς noun fem dat pl . . . . ἐπαοιδή
ἐπαναστραφήσῃ vb fut pass ind 2nd pers sg id.	ἐπαοιδήν noun fem acc sg id.
ἐπαναστραφήσομαι vb fut pass ind 1st pers sg id.	ἐπαοιδοί noun masc nom pl . . . . ἐπαοιδός
ἐπαναστρέφων vb pres act part masc nom sg id.	ἐπαοιδοῖς noun masc dat pl id.
ἐπαναστρέψας vb 1st aor act part masc nom sg id.	ἐπαοιδόν noun masc acc sg id.
ἐπαναστρέψει vb fut act ind 3rd pers sg id.	ἐπαοιδός noun masc nom sg id.
ἐπαναστρέψεις vb fut act ind 2nd pers sg id.	ἐπαοιδούς noun masc acc pl id.
ἐπανατρυγήσεις vb fut act ind 2nd pers sg . . ἐπανατρυγάω	ἐπαοιδῶν noun masc gen pl id.
ἐπαναχθέντας vb 1st aor pass part masc acc pl . . . ἐπανάγω	ἐπαπεσταλμένων vb perf m/p part gen pl . . . ἐπαποστέλλω
ἐπανδρῶσαι vb 1st aor act inf . . . . ἐπανδρόω	ἐπαπέστειλας vb 1st aor act ind 2nd pers sg id.
ἐπανελέσθαι vb 2nd aor mid inf . . . . ἐπαναιρέω	ἐπαποσταλήσεται vb fut pass ind 3rd pers sg id.
ἐπανελεύσεται vb fut mid ind 3rd pers sg . . . ἐπανέρχομαι	ἐπαποστεῖλαι vb 1st aor act inf id.
ἐπανελεύσομαι vb fut mid ind 1st pers sg id.	ἐπαποστείλω vb 1st aor act subj 1st pers sg id.
ἐπανελθόντος vb 2nd aor act part masc and neut gen sg id.	ἐπαποστελεῖ vb fut act ind 3rd pers sg id.
ἐπανελθών vb 2nd aor act part masc nom pl id.	ἐπαποστέλλω vb pres act ind 1st pers sg id.
ἐπανελόμενον vb 2nd aor mid part masc acc sg,	ἐπαποστελῶ vb fut act ind 1st pers sg id.
neut nom and acc sg . . . . ἐπαναιρέω	ἐπάραι vb 1st aor act opt 3rd pers sg . . . . ἐπαίρω
ἐπανεπαύετο vb impf m/p ind 3rd pers sg . . . . ἐπαναπαύω	ἐπάραι vb 1st aor act inf id.
ἐπανεπαύοντο vb impf m/p ind 3rd pers pl id.	ἐπάραντες vb 1st aor act part masc nom pl id.
ἐπανεπαύσαντο vb 1st aor mid ind 3rd pers pl id.	ἐπάρας vb 1st aor act part masc nom sg,
ἐπανεπαύσατο vb 1st aor mid ind 3rd pers sg id.	1st aor act ind 2nd pers sg id.
ἐπανέστη vb 2nd aor act ind 3rd pers sg . . . . . ἐπανίστημι	ἐπάρατε vb 1st aor act impv 2nd pers pl id.
ἐπανεστηκότων vb perf act part masc and neut gen pl id.	ἐπάρδων vb pres act part masc nom sg . . . . ἐπάρδω
ἐπανέστησαν vb 2nd aor act ind 3rd pers pl id.	ἐπάρῃ vb 1st aor act subj 3rd pers sg . . . . ἐπαίρω
ἐπανέστητε vb 2nd aor act ind 2nd pers pl id.	ἐπαρήγουσαν vb 1st aor act part fem acc sg . . . . . ἐπαρήγω
ἐπάνηκε vb pres act impv 2nd pers sg . . . . ἐπανήκω	ἐπάρῃς vb 1st aor act subj 2nd pers sg . . . . ἐπαίρω
ἐπανήξει vb fut act ind 3rd pers sg id.	ἐπαρθείς vb 1st aor pass part masc nom sg id.
ἐπανθήσει vb fut act ind 3rd pers sg . . . . ἐπανθέω	ἐπαρθέντα vb 1st aor pass part masc acc sg id.
ἐπανισταμένων vb pres m/p part gen pl . . . . . ἐπανίστημι	ἐπαρθέντες vb 1st aor pass part masc nom pl id.
ἐπανιστανόμενοι vb pres m/p part	ἐπαρθῆναι vb 1st aor pass inf id.
masc nom pl . . . . ἐπιανιστάνω	ἐπαρθήσεται vb fut pass ind 3rd pers sg id.
ἐπανιστανομένοις vb pres m/p part	ἐπαρθήσονται vb fut pass ind 3rd pers pl id.
masc and neut dat pl id.	ἐπάρθητε vb 1st aor pass impv 2nd pers pl id.
ἐπανιστανομένους vb pres m/p part masc acc pl id.	ἐπάρθητι vb 1st aor pass impv 2nd pers sg id.
ἐπανιστανομένων vb pres m/p part gen pl id.	ἐπαρκέσομεν vb fut act ind 1st pers pl . . . . ἐπαρκέω
ἐπανίστανται vb pres m/p ind 3rd pers pl . . . . . ἐπανίστημι	ἐπαρκέσουσιν vb fut act ind 3rd pers pl id.
ἐπανίστατο vb impf m/p ind 3rd pers sg id.	ἔπαρμα noun neut nom and acc sg
ἐπάνοδον noun fem acc sg . . . . ἐπάνοδος	ἐπάρξας vb 1st aor act part masc nom sg . . . . ἐπάρχω
ἐπάνοδος noun fem nom sg id.	ἐπαροιμίαζεν vb impf act ind 3rd pers sg . . . . παροιμιάζω
ἐπανορθῶσαι vb 1st aor act inf . . . . ἐπανορθόω	ἔπαρον vb 1st aor act impv 2nd pers sg . . . . ἐπαίρω
ἐπανορθώσει noun fem dat sg . . . . ἐπανόρθωσις	ἐπαρρησιάσατο vb 1st aor mid ind
ἐπανόρθωσιν noun fem acc sg id.	3rd pers sg . . . . παρρησιάζομαι
ἐπάνω adverb and preposition	ἐπάρσεις noun fem nom and acc pl . . . . ἔπαρσις
ἐπάνωθεν adverb and preposition	ἔπαρσιν noun fem acc sg id.
ἐπανωρθώθη vb 1st aor pass ind 3rd pers sg . . . . ἐπανορθόω	ἔπαρσις noun fem nom sg id.
ἐπάξαι vb 1st aor act inf . . . . ἐπάγω	ἐπαρυστῆρα noun masc acc sg . . . . ἐπαρυστήρ
ἐπάξει vb fut act ind 3rd pers sg id.	ἐπαρυστρίδας noun fem acc pl . . . . ἐπαρυστρίς
ἐπάξεις vb fut act ind 2nd pers sg id.	ἐπαρυστρίδες noun fem nom pl id.
ἐπάξεται vb fut mid ind 3rd pers sg id.	ἔπαρχοι noun masc nom pl . . . . ἔπαρχος
ἐπάξονται vb fut mid ind 3rd pers pl id.	ἐπάρχοις noun masc dat pl id.
ἐπάξουσι(ν) vb fut act ind 3rd pers pl id.	ἔπαρχον noun masc acc sg id.

ἔπαρχος noun masc nom sg
ἐπάρχου noun masc gen sg . . . . ἔπαρχος
ἐπάρχους noun masc acc pl   id.
ἐπάρχῳ noun masc dat sg   id.
ἐπᾶσαι vb 1st aor act inf . . . . ἐπάδω
ἔπασεν vb 1st aor act ind 3rd pers sg . . . . πάσσω
ἐπασθμαίνων vb pres act part masc nom sg . . . ἐπασθμαίνω
ἔπασχον vb impf act ind 3rd pers pl . . . . πάσχω
ἐπάταξα vb 1st aor act ind 1st pers sg . . . . πατάσσω
ἐπατάξαμεν vb 1st aor act ind 1st pers pl   id.
ἐπάταξαν vb 1st aor act ind 3rd pers pl   id.
ἐπάταξας vb 1st aor act ind 2nd pers sg   id.
ἐπατάξατε vb 1st aor act ind 2nd pers pl   id.
ἐπάταξε(ν) vb 1st aor act ind 3rd pers sg   id.
ἐπάτησαν vb 1st aor act ind 3rd pers pl . . . . πατέω
ἐπάτησεν vb 1st aor act ind 3rd pers sg   id.
ἐπατοῦσαν vb impf act ind 3rd pers pl   id.
Ἐπαύλεις pr noun fem nom and acc pl . . . . Ἔπαυλις
ἐπαύλεις noun fem nom and acc pl . . . . ἔπαυλις
ἐπαύλεσιν noun fem dat pl   id.
ἐπαύλεων noun fem gen pl   id.
ἐπαύλεως noun fem gen sg   id.
ἔπαυλιν noun fem acc sg   id.
ἔπαυλις noun fem nom sg   id.
ἐπαύξων vb pres act part masc nom sg . . . . ἐπαύξω
ἐπαύριον adverb
ἐπαύσαντο vb 1st aor mid ind 3rd pers pl . . . . παύω
ἐπαύσατο vb 1st aor mid ind 3rd pers sg   id.
ἐπαφῇ vb 2nd aor act subj 3rd pers sg . . . . ἐπαφίημι
ἐπαφήσεις vb fut act ind 2nd pers sg   id.
ἐπαφήσω vb fut act ind 1st pers sg   id.
ἐπαχθῇ vb 1st aor pass subj 3rd pers sg . . . . ἐπάγω
ἐπάχυνεν vb impf act ind 3rd pers sg,
        1st aor act ind 3rd pers sg . . . . παχύνω
ἐπαχύνθη vb 1st aor pass ind 3rd pers sg   id.
ἐπέβαινες vb impf act ind 2nd pers sg . . . . ἐπιβαίνω
ἐπέβαλεν vb 2nd aor act ind 3rd pers sg . . . . ἐπιβάλλω
ἐπέβαλον vb 2nd aor act ind 3rd pers pl   id.
ἐπεβάλοντο vb 2nd aor mid ind 3rd pers pl   id.
ἐπέβη vb 2nd aor act ind 3rd pers sg . . . . ἐπιβαίνω
ἐπέβης vb 2nd aor act ind 2nd pers sg   id.
ἐπέβησαν vb 2nd aor act ind 3rd pers pl   id.
ἐπέβητε vb 2nd aor act ind 2nd pers pl   id.
ἐπεβίβασαν vb 1st aor act ind 3rd pers pl . . . . . . ἐπιβιβάζω
ἐπεβίβασας vb 1st aor act ind 2nd pers sg   id.
ἐπεβίβασεν vb 1st aor act ind 3rd pers sg   id.
ἐπέβλεπον vb impf act ind
        1st pers sg and 3rd pers pl . . . . ἐπιβλέπω
ἐπέβλεψα vb 1st aor act ind 1st pers sg   id.
ἐπέβλεψαν vb 1st aor act ind 3rd pers pl   id.
ἐπέβλεψας vb 1st aor act ind 2nd pers sg   id.
ἐπεβλέψατε vb 1st aor act ind 2nd pers pl   id.

ἐπέβλεψεν vb 1st aor act ind 3rd pers sg . . . . . . ἐπιβλέπω
ἐπεβλήθη vb 1st aor pass ind 3rd pers sg . . . . . . ἐπιβάλλω
ἐπεγαμβρεύσατο vb 1st aor mid ind
        3rd pers sg . . . . ἐπιγαμβρεύω
ἐπεγγελάσῃς vb 1st aor act subj 2nd pers sg . . . ἐπεγγελάω
ἐπεγειρομένους vb pres m/p part masc acc pl . . . . ἐπεγείρω
ἐπεγειρομένων vb pres m/p part gen pl   id.
ἐπεγείρω vb pres act ind 1st pers sg   id.
ἐπεγέλων vb impf act ind 3rd pers pl . . . . ἐπιγελάω
ἐπεγερεῖ vb fut act ind 3rd pers sg . . . . ἐπεγείρω
ἐπεγερθῆναι vb 1st aor pass inf   id.
ἐπεγερθήσονται vb fut pass ind 3rd pers pl   id.
ἐπεγερῶ vb fut act ind 1st pers sg   id.
ἐπεγίνωσκον vb impf act ind 1st pers sg . . . . . ἐπιγινώσκω
ἐπέγνω vb 2nd aor act ind 3rd pers sg   id.
ἐπεγνωκόσι vb perf act part masc and neut dat pl   id.
ἐπεγνωκότες vb perf act part masc nom pl   id.
ἐπεγνωκότων vb perf act part masc and neut gen pl   id.
ἐπεγνωκώς vb perf act part masc nom sg   id.
ἐπέγνωμεν vb 2nd aor act ind 1st pers pl   id.
ἐπέγνων vb 2nd aor act ind 1st pers sg   id.
ἐπέγνωσαν vb 2nd aor act ind 3rd pers pl   id.
ἐπεγνώσθη vb 2nd aor pass ind 3rd pers sg   id.
ἐπεγνώσθησαν vb 2nd aor pass ind 3rd pers pl   id.
ἐπέγραψαν vb 1st aor act ind 3rd pers pl . . . . . . ἐπιγράφω
ἐπεδεήθης vb 1st aor pass ind 2nd pers sg . . . . ἐπιδέω
ἐπέδειξα vb 1st aor act ind 1st pers sg . . . . ἐπιδείκνύω
ἐπεδείξαντο vb 1st aor mid ind 3rd pers pl   id.
ἐπέδειξε(ν) vb 1st aor act ind 3rd pers sg   id.
ἐπεδέξαντο vb 1st aor mid ind 3rd pers pl . . . . . ἐπιδέχομαι
ἐπεδέξατο vb 1st aor mid ind 3rd pers sg   id.
ἐπεδήθην vb 1st aor pass ind 1st pers sg . . . . πεδάω
ἐπεδήθησαν vb 1st aor pass ind 3rd pers pl   id.
ἐπέδησαν vb 1st aor act ind 3rd pers pl . . . . ἐπιδέω
ἐπέδησεν vb 1st aor act ind 3rd pers sg   id.
ἐπεδίδου vb impf act ind 3rd pers sg . . . . ἐπιδίδωμι
ἐπεδόθη vb 1st aor pass ind 3rd pers sg   id.
ἐπέδραμεν vb 2nd aor act ind 3rd pers sg . . . . ἐπιτρέχω
ἐπέδραμον vb 2nd aor act ind 3rd pers pl   id.
ἐπεδράμοσαν vb 2nd aor act ind 3rd pers pl   id.
ἐπέδυ vb 2nd aor act ind 3rd pers sg . . . . ἐπιδύω
ἐπέδωκαν vb 1st aor act ind 3rd pers pl . . . . ἐπιδίδωμι
ἐπέδωκεν vb 1st aor act ind 3rd pers sg   id.
ἐπέζησεν vb 1st aor act ind 3rd pers sg . . . . ἐπιζάω
ἐπεζητήθη vb 1st aor pass ind 3rd pers sg . . . . ἐπιζητέω
ἐπεζήτησαν vb 1st aor act ind 3rd pers pl   id.
ἐπεζήτουν vb impf act ind 3rd pers pl   id.
ἐπεθέμεθα vb 2nd aor mid ind 2nd pers pl . . . . . . ἐπιτίθημι
ἐπέθεντο vb 2nd aor mid ind 3rd pers pl   id.
ἐπέθεσθε vb 2nd aor mid ind 2nd pers pl   id.
ἐπέθετο vb 2nd aor mid ind 3rd pers sg   id.
ἐπέθηκαν vb 1st aor act ind 3rd pers pl   id.

ἐπέθηκας vb 1st aor act ind 2nd pers sg . . . . ἐπιτίθημι

ἐπέθηκε(ν) vb 1st aor act ind 3rd pers sg   id.

ἐπέθου vb 2nd aor mid ind 2nd pers sg   id.

ἐπέθυεν vb impf act ind 3rd pers sg . . . . ἐπιθύω

ἐπεθύμησα vb 1st aor act ind 1st pers sg . . . . ἐπιθυμέω

ἐπεθύμησαν vb 1st aor act ind 3rd pers pl   id.

ἐπεθύμησας vb 1st aor act ind 2nd pers sg   id.

ἐπεθύμησε(ν) vb 1st aor act ind 3rd pers sg   id.

ἐπεθύμουν vb impf act ind 3rd pers pl   id.

ἐπεί conjunction

ἐπείγοντας vb pres act part masc acc pl . . . . ἐπείγω

ἐπείγουσιν vb pres act ind 3rd pers pl   id.

ἐπεῖδεν vb 2nd aor act ind 3rd pers sg . . . . ἐφοράω

ἐπεῖδες vb 2nd aor act ind 2nd pers sg   id.

ἐπειδή conjunction

ἐπεῖδον vb 2nd aor act ind 3rd pers pl . . . . ἐφοράω

ἐπείθετο vb impf m/p ind 3rd pers sg . . . . πείθω

ἐπειλημμένη vb perf m/p part fem nom sg . . . . ἐπιλαμβάνω

ἐπείνας vb 1st aor act ind 2nd pers sg . . . . πεινάω

ἐπείνασαν vb 1st aor act ind 3rd pers pl   id.

ἐπείνασεν vb 1st aor act ind 3rd pers sg   id.

ἐπείραζεν vb impf act ind 3rd pers sg . . . . πειράζω

ἐπειράθη vb 1st aor pass ind 3rd pers sg   id.

ἐπειράθημεν vb 1st aor pass ind 1st pers pl   id.

ἐπείρασα vb 1st aor act ind 1st pers sg   id.

ἐπείρασαν vb 1st aor act ind 3rd pers pl   id.

ἐπειράσατε vb 1st aor act ind 2nd pers pl   id.

ἐπείρασεν vb 1st aor act ind 3rd pers sg   id.

ἐπειράσθησαν vb 1st aor pass ind 3rd pers pl   id.

ἐπειρᾶτο vb impf m/p ind 3rd pers sg . . . . πειράω

ἐπειρῶντο vb impf m/p ind 3rd pers pl   id.

ἔπεισας vb 1st aor act ind 2nd pers sg . . . . πείθω

ἔπεισεν vb 1st aor act ind 3rd pers sg   id.

ἐπεισῆλθον vb 2nd aor act ind 3rd pers pl . . . ἐπεισέρχομαι

ἐπεισήνεγκεν vb 1st aor act ind 3rd pers sg . . . . . ἐπεισφέρω

ἐπείσθη vb 1st aor pass ind 3rd pers sg . . . . πείθω

ἐπείσθησαν vb 1st aor pass ind 3rd pers pl   id.

ἔπειτα adverb

ἐπεκάθισαν vb 1st aor act ind 3rd pers pl . . . . . . ἐπικαθίζω

ἐπεκάθισεν vb 1st aor act ind 3rd pers sg   id.

ἐπεκαλεῖτο vb impf m/p ind 3rd pers sg . . . . ἐπικαλέω

ἐπεκαλεσάμην vb 1st aor mid ind 1st pers sg   id.

ἐπεκάλεσαν vb 1st aor act ind 3rd pers pl   id.

ἐπεκαλέσαντο vb 1st aor mid ind 3rd pers pl   id.

ἐπεκαλέσατο vb 1st aor mid ind 3rd pers sg   id.

ἐπεκάλεσεν vb 1st aor act ind 3rd pers sg   id.

ἐπεκάλεσω vb 1st aor mid ind 2nd pers sg   id.

ἐπεκαλοῦντο vb impf m/p ind 3rd pers pl   id.

ἐπεκάλυπτον vb impf act ind 3rd pers pl . . . . . ἐπικαλύπτω

ἐπεκαλύφθησαν vb 1st aor pass ind 3rd pers pl   id.

ἐπεκάλυψαν vb 1st aor act ind 3rd pers pl   id.

ἐπεκάλυψεν vb 1st aor act ind 3rd pers sg   id.

ἐπέκεινα adverb

ἐπεκινοῦντο vb impf m/p ind 3rd pers pl . . . . ἐπικινέω

ἐπεκλήθη vb 1st aor pass ind 3rd pers sg . . . . . . ἐπικαλέω

ἐπεκλήθησαν vb 1st aor pass ind 3rd pers pl   id.

ἐπέκλυσας vb 1st aor act part masc nom sg . . . . . ἐπικλύζω

ἐπέκλυσεν vb 1st aor act ind 3rd pers sg   id.

ἐπεκοιμήθη vb 1st aor pass ind 3rd pers sg . . . . ἐπικοιμάω

ἐπεκράτει vb impf act ind 3rd pers sg . . . . ἐπικρατέω

ἐπεκράτησα vb 1st aor act ind 1st pers sg   id.

ἐπεκράτησαν vb 1st aor act ind 3rd pers pl   id.

ἐπεκράτησεν vb 1st aor act ind 3rd pers sg   id.

ἐπεκρατοῦσαν vb impf act ind 3rd pers pl   id.

ἐπέκρινεν vb 1st aor act ind 3rd pers sg,

           impf act ind 3rd pers sg . . . . ἐπικρίνω

ἐπεκρότησαν vb 1st aor act ind 3rd pers pl . . . . ἐπικροτέω

ἐπεκύλισαν vb 1st aor act ind 3rd pers pl . . . . . . ἐπικυλίω

ἐπεκχυθῶσιν vb 1st aor pass subj 3rd pers pl . . . . ἐπεκχέω

ἐπελάβετο vb 2nd aor mid ind 3rd pers sg . . . ἐπιλαμβάνω

ἐπελαβόμην vb 2nd aor mid ind 1st pers sg   id.

ἐπελάβοντο vb 2nd aor mid ind 3rd pers pl   id.

ἐπελάβου vb 2nd aor mid ind 2nd pers sg   id.

ἐπελάθεσθε vb 2nd aor mid ind 2nd pers pl . . . ἐπιλανθάνω

ἐπελάθετο vb 2nd aor mid ind 3rd pers sg   id.

ἐπελαθόμεθα vb 2nd aor mid ind 1st pers pl   id.

ἐπελαθόμην vb 2nd aor mid ind 1st pers sg   id.

ἐπελάθοντο vb 2nd aor mid ind 3rd pers pl   id.

ἐπελάθου vb 2nd aor mid ind 2nd pers sg   id.

ἐπελαμβάνετο vb impf m/p ind 3rd pers sg . . . ἐπιλαμβάνω

ἐπέλαμψεν vb 1st aor act ind 3rd pers sg . . . . ἐπιλάμπω

ἐπελανθάνετο vb impf m/p ind 3rd pers sg . . . ἐπιλανθάνω

ἐπελειώθη see ἐπελιώθη

ἐπελέκησαν vb 1st aor act ind 3rd pers pl . . . . . . πελεκάω

ἐπελέξαμεν vb 1st aor act ind 1st pers pl . . . . ἐπιλέγω

ἐπέλεξαν vb 1st aor act ind 3rd pers pl   id.

ἐπελέξατο vb 1st aor mid ind 3rd pers sg   id.

ἐπέλεξεν vb 1st aor act ind 3rd pers sg   id.

ἐπελεύσεσθαι vb fut mid inf . . . . ἐπέρχομαι

ἐπελεύσεται vb fut mid ind 3rd pers sg   id.

ἐπελεύσομαι vb fut mid ind 1st pers sg   id.

ἐπεληλύθει vb plpf act ind 3rd pers sg   id.

ἐπελήσθη vb 1st aor pass ind 3rd pers sg . . . . . ἐπιλανθάνω

ἐπελήσθην vb 1st aor pass ind 1st pers sg   id.

ἐπελήσθησαν vb 1st aor pass ind 3rd pers pl   id.

ἐπελθεῖν vb 2nd aor act inf . . . . ἐπέρχομαι

ἐπέλθῃ vb 2nd aor act subj 3rd pers sg   id.

ἐπέλθῃς vb 2nd aor act subj 2nd pers sg   id.

ἐπέλθοι vb 2nd aor act opt 3rd pers sg   id.

ἐπελθόν vb 2nd aor act part neut nom and acc sg   id.

ἐπελθόντα vb 2nd aor act part neut nom and acc pl   id.

ἐπελθόντες vb 2nd aor act part masc nom pl   id.

ἐπελθόντων vb 2nd aor act part masc and neut gen pl id.

ἐπελθοῦσαν vb 2nd aor act part fem acc sg   id.

ἐπελθούσῃ vb 2nd aor act part fem dat sg . . . . ἐπέρχομαι
ἐπελθούσης vb 2nd aor act part fem gen sg   id.
ἐπελθών vb 2nd aor act part masc nom sg   id.
ἐπελιώθη vb 1st aor pass ind 3rd pers sg . . . . πελιόομαι
ἐπελπιζέτω vb pres act impv 3rd pers sg . . . . ἐπελπίζω
ἐπεμαρτυράμην vb 1st aor mid ind

     1st pers sg . . . . ἐπιμαρτυρέω
ἐπεμαρτύρατο vb 1st aor mid ind 3rd pers sg   id.
ἐπεμαρτύρω vb 1st aor mid ind 2nd pers sg   id.
ἐπεμίγη vb 2nd aor pass ind 3rd pers sg . . . . . . ἐπιμίγνυμι
ἐπεμίγης vb 2nd aor pass ind 2nd pers sg   id.
ἐπεμνήσθησαν vb 1st aor pass ind

     3rd pers pl . . . . ἐπιμιμνήσκω
ἐπέμψαμεν vb 1st aor act ind 1st pers pl . . . . πέμπω
ἔπεμψαν vb 1st aor act ind 3rd pers pl   id.
ἔπεμψας vb 1st aor act ind 2nd pers sg   id.
ἔπεμψεν vb 1st aor act ind 3rd pers sg   id.
ἐπενδύτας noun masc acc pl . . . . ἐπενδύτης
ἐπενέγκαι vb 1st aor act inf . . . . ἐπιφέρω
ἐπενεγκεῖν vb 2nd aor act inf   id.
ἐπενέγκητε vb 1st aor act subj 2nd pers pl   id.
ἐπένευσαν vb 1st aor act ind 3rd pers pl . . . . ἐπινεύω
ἐπένευσεν vb 1st aor act ind 3rd pers sg   id.
ἐπενεχθέντος vb 1st aor pass part

     masc and neut gen sg . . . . ἐπιφέρω
ἐπένθει vb impf act ind 3rd pers sg . . . . πενθέω
ἐπενθήθησαν vb 1st aor pass ind 3rd pers pl   id.
ἐπένθησα vb 1st aor act ind 1st pers sg   id.
ἐπένθησαν vb 1st aor act ind 3rd pers pl   id.
ἐπένθησεν vb 1st aor act ind 3rd pers sg   id.
ἐπένθουν vb impf act ind 3rd pers pl   id.
ἐπενοήθη vb 1st aor pass ind 3rd pers sg . . . . ἐπινοέω
ἐπενόησεν vb 1st aor act ind 3rd pers sg   id.
ἐπεξένωται vb perf dep ind 3rd pers sg . . . . . ἐπιξενόομαι
ἐπεξέρχεται vb pres dep ind 3rd pers sg . . . . ἐπεξέρχομαι
ἐπεξῆλθες vb 2nd aor act ind 2nd pers sg   id.
ἐπέπεσαν vb 1st aor act ind 3rd pers pl . . . . ἐπιπίπτω
ἐπέπεσε(ν) vb 1st or 2nd aor act ind 3rd pers sg   id.
ἐπέπεσον vb 2nd aor act ind 3rd pers pl   id.
ἐπέπιπτεν vb impf act ind 3rd pers sg   id.
ἐπεπληροῦτο vb impf m/p ind 3rd pers sg . . . . . ἐπιπληρόω
ἐπεπλήρωτο vb plpf m/p ind 3rd pers sg . . . . πληρόω
ἐπεπόθησα vb 1st aor act ind 1st pers sg . . . . ἐπιποθέω
ἐπεπόθησεν vb 1st aor act ind 3rd pers sg   id.
ἐπεπόθουν vb impf act ind 3rd pers pl   id.
ἐπεποίθει vb plpf act ind 3rd pers sg . . . . πείθω
ἐπεποίθειν vb plpf act ind 1st pers sg   id.
ἐπεποίθεις vb plpf act ind 2nd pers sg   id.
ἐπεποίθεισαν vb plpf act ind 3rd pers pl   id.
ἐπεποίθησα vb 1st aor act ind 1st pers sg

     (from πέποιθα treated as a pres)   id.

ἐπεποίθησαν vb 1st aor act ind 3rd pers pl

     (from πέποιθα treated as a pres) . . . . πείθω
ἐπεπόλασεν vb 1st aor act ind 3rd pers sg . . . . ἐπιπολάζω
ἐπεπόνθεισαν vb plpf act ind 3rd pers pl . . . . πάσχω
ἐπερειδομένοις vb pres m/p part

     masc and neut dat pl . . . . ἐπερείδω
ἐπερίσσευσεν vb 1st aor act ind 3rd pers sg . . . περισσεύω
ἐπέρριφα vb 1st aor act ind 1st pers sg . . . . ἐπιρρίπτω
ἐπερρίφην vb 2nd aor pass ind 1st pers sg   id.
ἐπέρριψα vb 1st aor act ind 1st pers sg   id.
ἐπέρριψε(ν) vb 1st aor act ind 3rd pers sg   id.
ἐπερρώσθησαν vb 1st aor pass ind 3rd pers pl . . ἐπιρρωννύω
ἐπέρχεται vb pres dep ind 3rd pers sg . . . . ἐπέρχομαι
ἐπερχόμενα vb pres dep part neut nom and acc pl   id.
ἐπερχομένας vb pres dep part fem acc pl   id.
ἐπερχομένην vb pres dep part fem acc sg   id.
ἐπερχόμενον vb pres dep part masc acc sg,

     neut nom and acc sg   id.
ἐπερχομένων vb pres dep part gen pl   id.
ἐπέρχονται vb pres dep ind 3rd pers pl   id.
ἐπερωτᾷ vb pres act ind 3rd pers sg . . . . ἐπερωτάω
ἐπερωτᾶν vb pres act inf   id.
ἐπερωτᾷς vb pres act ind 2nd pers sg   id.
ἐπερωτηθείς vb 1st aor pass part masc nom sg   id.
ἐπερωτηθῇς vb 1st aor pass subj 2nd pers sg   id.
ἐπερώτημα noun neut nom and acc sg

ἐπερωτῆσαι vb 1st aor act inf . . . . ἐπερωτάω
ἐπερωτήσαντι vb 1st aor act part masc and neut dat sg   id.
ἐπερωτήσαντος vb 1st aor act part masc and neut gen sg   id.
ἐπερωτήσατε vb 1st aor act impv 2nd pers pl   id.
ἐπερωτήσῃ vb 1st aor act subj 3rd pers sg   id.
ἐπερώτησιν noun fem acc sg . . . . ἐπερώτησις
ἐπερώτησον vb 1st aor act impv 2nd pers sg   id.
ἐπερωτήσουσιν vb fut act ind 3rd pers pl   id.
ἐπερωτῶ vb pres act ind 1st pers sg   id.
ἐπερωτῶν vb pres act part masc nom sg   id.
ἐπερωτῶντος vb pres act part masc and neut gen sg   id.
ἐπερωτῶσιν vb pres act ind 3rd pers pl   id.
ἔπεσα vb 1st aor act ind 1st pers sg . . . . πίπτω
ἔπεσαν vb 1st aor act ind 3rd pers pl   id.
ἐπέσαξαν vb 1st aor act ind 3rd pers pl . . . . ἐπισάσσω
ἐπέσαξε(ν) vb 1st aor act ind 3rd pers sg   id.
ἔπεσας vb 1st aor act ind 2nd pers sg . . . . πίπτω
ἐπεσάσσετο vb impf m/p ind 3rd pers sg . . . . . ἐπισάσσω
ἔπεσε(ν) vb 2nd aor act ind 3rd pers sg . . . . πίπτω
ἐπέσεισεν vb 1st aor act ind 3rd pers sg . . . . ἐπισείω
ἐπεσήμηνα vb 1st aor mid ind 2nd pers sg . . . . ἐπισημαίνω
ἕπεσθαι vb pres dep inf . . . . ἕπομαι
ἐπεσιτίσαντο vb 1st aor mid ind 3rd pers pl . . . . ἐπισιτίζω
ἐπέσκαζεν vb impf act ind 3rd pers sg . . . . ἐπισκάζω
ἐπέσκεμμαι vb perf dep ind 1st pers sg . . . . . ἐπισκέπτομαι

ἐπεσκεμμένοι vb perf dep part masc nom pl . ἐπισκέπτομαι
ἐπεσκεμμένων vb perf dep part gen pl id.
ἐπεσκέπασας vb 1st aor act ind 2nd pers sg ... ἐπισκεπάζω
ἐπεσκέπη vb 2nd aor pass ind 3rd pers sg .... ἐπισκέπτομαι
ἐπεσκέπησαν vb 2nd aor pass ind 3rd pers pl id.
ἐπέσκεπται vb perf dep ind 3rd pers sg id.
ἐπεσκεύασεν vb 1st aor act ind 3rd pers sg ... ἐπισκευάζω
ἐπεσκεψάμεθα vb 1st aor mid ind
    1st pers pl .... ἐπισκέπτομαι
ἐπεσκεψάμην vb 1st aor mid ind 1st pers sg id.
ἐπεσκέψαντο vb 1st aor mid ind 3rd pers pl id.
ἐπεσκέψασθε vb 1st aor mid ind 2nd pers pl id.
ἐπεσκέψατο vb 1st aor mid ind 3rd pers sg id.
ἐπεσκέψω vb 1st aor mid ind 2nd pers sg id.
ἐπεσκίαζεν vb impf act ind 3rd pers sg .... ἐπισκιάζω
ἐπεσκίασας vb 1st aor act ind 2nd pers sg
ἔπεσον vb 2nd aor act ind 3rd pers pl .... πίπτω
ἐπεσπάσαντο vb 1st aor mid ind 3rd pers pl .... ἐπισπάω
ἐπεσπάσατο vb 1st aor mid ind 3rd pers sg id.
ἐπεσπούδαζον vb impf act ind 3rd pers pl ... ἐπισπουδάζω
ἐπεσπῶντο vb impf m/p ind 3rd pers pl .... ἐπισπάω
ἐπέσται vb fut mid ind 3rd pers sg .... ἔπειμι
ἐπεστάτουν vb impf act ind 3rd pers pl .... ἐπιστατέω
ἐπέστη vb 2nd aor act ind 3rd pers sg .... ἐφίστημι
ἐπέστην vb 2nd aor act ind 1st pers sg id.
ἐπεστήρικται vb perf m/p ind 3rd pers sg .... ἐπιστηρίζω
ἐπεστήρικτο vb plpf m/p ind 3rd pers sg id.
ἐπεστήρισας vb 1st aor act ind 2nd pers sg id.
ἐπεστηρίσατο vb 1st aor mid ind 3rd pers sg id.
ἐπεστήρισται vb perf mid ind 3rd pers sg id.
ἐπεστηρίχθη vb 1st aor pass ind 3rd pers sg id.
ἐπεστηρίχθην vb 1st aor pass ind 1st pers sg id.
ἐπέστησα vb 1st aor act ind 1st pers sg .... ἐφίστημι
ἐπέστησαν vb 1st aor act ind 3rd pers pl id.
ἐπέστησας vb 1st aor act ind 2nd pers sg id.
ἐπέστησεν vb 1st aor act ind 3rd pers sg id.
ἔπεστι vb pres act ind 3rd pers sg .... ἔπειμι
ἐπεστράτευσαν vb 1st aor act ind 3rd pers pl ἐπιστρατεύω
ἐπεστράτευσεν vb 1st aor act ind 3rd pers sg id.
ἐπεστρατοπέδευσαν vb 1st aor act ind
    3rd pers pl .... ἐπιστρατοπεδεύω
ἐπεστράφη vb 2nd aor pass ind 3rd pers sg .... ἐπιστρέφω
ἐπεστράφησαν vb 2nd aor pass ind 3rd pers pl id.
ἐπέστρεφεν vb impf act ind 3rd pers sg id.
ἐπέστρεφον vb impf act ind 3rd pers pl id.
ἐπεστρέφοντο vb impf m/p ind 3rd pers pl id.
ἐπέστρεψα vb 1st aor act ind 1st pers sg id.
ἐπεστρέψαμεν vb 1st aor act ind 1st pers pl id.
ἐπέστρεψαν vb 1st aor act ind 3rd pers pl id.
ἐπέστρεψας vb 1st aor act ind 2nd pers sg id.
ἐπεστρέψατε vb 1st aor act ind 2nd pers pl id.
ἐπέστρεψεν vb 1st aor act ind 3rd pers sg id.

ἐπέσχεν vb 2nd aor act ind 3rd pers sg .... ἐπέχω
ἐπέσχον vb 2nd aor act ind 1st pers sg id.
ἐπετάγη vb 2nd aor pass ind 3rd pers sg .... ἐπιτάσσω
ἐπέταντο vb 1st aor mid ind 3rd pers pl .... πέτομαι
ἐπέταξα vb 1st aor act ind 1st pers sg .... ἐπιτάσσω
ἐπέταξε(ν) vb 1st aor act ind 3rd pers sg id.
ἐπετάσθη vb 1st aor pass ind 3rd pers sg ..... πετάννυμι
ἐπετάσθησαν vb 1st aor pass ind 3rd pers pl id.
ἐπέτεινεν vb impf act ind 3rd pers sg .... ἐπιτείνω
ἐπέτεινον vb impf act ind 3rd pers pl id.
ἐπετέλει vb impf act ind 3rd pers sg .... ἐπιτελέω
ἐπετέλεσεν vb 1st aor act ind 3rd pers sg id.
ἐπετελέσθη vb 1st aor pass ind 3rd pers sg id.
ἐπετέτατο vb plpf m/p ind 3rd pers sg .... ἐπιτείνω
ἐπετήδευσαν vb 1st aor act ind 3rd pers pl .... ἐπιτηδεύω
ἐπετήδευσεν vb 1st aor act ind 3rd pers sg id.
ἐπετίθεντο vb impf m/p ind 3rd pers pl .... ἐπιτίθημι
ἐπετίθετο vb impf m/p ind 3rd pers sg id.
ἐπετίμησας vb 1st aor act ind 2nd pers sg ...... ἐπιτιμάω
ἐπετίμησεν vb 1st aor act ind 3rd pers sg id.
ἐπέτρεψα vb 1st aor act ind 1st pers sg ...... ἐπιτρέπω
ἐπετρέψατε vb 1st aor act ind 2nd pers pl id.
ἐπέτρεψεν vb 1st aor act ind 3rd pers sg id.
ἐπευθυμήσωσιν vb 1st aor act subj 3rd pers pl . ἐπευθυμέω
ἐπευκτή adj fem nom sg .... ἐπευκτός
ἐπεύχεσθαι vb pres dep inf .... ἐπεύχομαι
ἐπέφανεν vb 1st aor act ind 3rd pers sg .... ἐπιφαίνω
ἐπεφάνη vb 2nd aor pass ind 3rd pers sg id.
ἐπεφέρετο vb impf m/p ind 3rd pers sg .... ἐπιφέρω
ἐπεφύλλισας vb 1st aor act ind 2nd pers sg .... ἐπιφυλλίζω
ἐπεφώνησεν vb 1st aor act ind 3rd pers sg ...... ἐπιφωνέω
ἐπεχάρας vb 1st aor act ind 2nd pers sg .... ἐπιχαίρω
ἐπεχάρητε vb 2nd aor pass ind 2nd pers pl id.
ἔπεχε vb pres act impv 2nd pers sg .... ἐπέχω
ἐπέχεεν vb impf act ind 3rd pers sg .... ἐπιχέω
ἐπέχει vb pres act ind 3rd pers sg .... ἐπέχω
ἐπεχείρησαν vb 1st aor act ind 3rd pers pl ...... ἐπιχειρέω
ἐπεχείρησεν vb 1st aor act ind 3rd pers sg id.
ἐπεχείρουν vb impf act ind 3rd pers pl id.
ἐπέχοντας vb pres act part masc acc pl .... ἐπέχω
ἐπεχύθη vb 1st aor pass ind 3rd pers sg .... ἐπιχέω
ἐπέχων vb pres act part masc nom sg .... ἐπέχω
ἐπεχώρησεν vb 1st aor act ind 3rd pers sg ...... ἐπιχωρέω
ἐπέψαλλον vb impf act ind 3rd pers pl .... ἐπιψάλλω
ἔπεψαν vb 1st aor act ind 3rd pers pl .... πέσσω
ἔπεψεν vb 1st aor act ind 3rd pers sg id.
ἐπεψόφησας vb 1st aor act ind 2nd pers sg .... ἐπιψοφέω
ἔπη noun neut nom and acc pl .... ἔπος
ἐπήγαγε(ν) vb 2nd aor act ind 3rd pers sg .... ἐπάγω
ἐπήγαγες vb 2nd aor act ind 2nd pers sg id.
ἐπήγαγον vb 2nd aor act ind 1st pers sg and 3rd pers pl id.
ἐπηγγείλατο vb 1st aor mid ind 3rd pers sg .... ἐπαγγέλλω

ἐπηγγείλω	vb 1st aor mid ind 2nd pers sg	ἐπαγγέλλω
ἐπηγγελμένων	vb perf m/p part gen pl	id.
ἐπήγειρεν	vb impf act ind 3rd pers sg	ἐπαγείρω
ἐπηγμένην	vb perf m/p part fem acc sg	ἐπάγω
ἐπήκοα	adj neut nom and acc pl	ἐπήκοος
ἐπηκολούθει	vb impf act ind 3rd pers sg	ἐπακολουθέω
ἐπηκολούθησεν	vb 1st aor act ind 3rd pers sg	id.
ἐπήκουες	vb impf act ind 2nd pers sg	ἐπακούω
ἐπήκουσα	vb 1st aor act ind 1st pers sg	id.
ἐπήκουσαν	vb 1st aor act ind 3rd pers pl	id.
ἐπήκουσας	vb 1st aor act ind 2nd pers sg	id.
ἐπηκούσατε	vb 1st aor act ind 2nd pers pl	id.
ἐπήκουσε(ν)	vb 1st aor act ind 3rd pers sg	id.
ἐπηκούσθη	vb 1st aor pass ind 3rd pers sg	id.
ἐπῆλθε(ν)	vb 2nd aor act ind 3rd pers sg	ἐπέρχομαι
ἐπῆλθον	vb 2nd aor act ind 3rd pers pl	id.
ἐπήλπισα	vb 1st aor act ind 1st pers sg	ἐπελπίζω
ἐπήλπισας	vb 1st aor act ind 2nd pers sg	id.
ἐπήλπισεν	vb 1st aor act ind 3rd pers sg	id.
ἐπήλυτος	noun masc nom sg	
ἐπήνεγκαν	vb 1st aor act ind 3rd pers pl	ἐπιφέρω
ἐπήνεγκε(ν)	vb 1st aor act ind 3rd pers sg	id.
ἐπηνέθησαν	vb 1st aor pass ind 3rd pers pl	ἐπαινέω
ἐπήνεσα	vb 1st aor act ind 1st pers sg	id.
ἐπήνεσαν	vb 1st aor act ind 3rd pers pl	id.
ἐπήνεσε	vb 1st aor act ind 3rd pers sg	id.
ἔπηξαν	vb 1st aor act ind 3rd pers pl	πήγνυμι
ἔπηξεν	vb 1st aor act ind 3rd pers sg	id.
ἐπηξονοῦσαν	vb impf act ind 3rd pers pl	ἐπαξονέω
ἐπῆρα	vb 1st aor act ind 1st pers sg	ἐπαίρω
ἐπῆραν	vb 1st aor act ind 3rd pers pl	id.
ἐπήρατο	vb 1st aor mid ind 3rd pers sg	id.
ἐπηρείδετο	vb impf m/p ind 3rd pers sg	ἐπερείδω
ἐπῆρεν	vb 1st aor act ind 3rd pers sg	ἐπαίρω
ἐπήρετο	vb impf m/p ind 3rd pers sg	id.
ἐπήρθη	vb 1st aor pass ind 3rd pers sg	id.
ἐπήρθησαν	vb 1st aor pass ind 3rd pers pl	id.
ἐπηρμένοι	vb perf act part masc nom pl	id.
ἐπηρμένον	vb perf m/p part masc acc sg, neut nom and acc sg	id.
ἐπηρμένος	vb perf m/p part masc nom sg	id.
ἐπηρμένου	vb perf m/p part masc and neut gen sg	id.
ἐπηρμένους	vb perf m/p part masc acc pl	id.
ἐπηρμένων	vb perf m/p part gen pl	id.
ἐπήρχετο	vb impf dep ind 3rd pers sg	ἐπέρχομαι
ἐπήρωσεν	vb 1st aor act ind 3rd pers sg	πηρόω
ἐπηρώτησα	vb 1st aor act ind 1st pers sg	ἐπερωτάω
ἐπηρωτήσαμεν	vb 1st aor act ind 1st pers pl	id.
ἐπηρώτησαν	vb 1st aor act ind 3rd pers pl	id.
ἐπηρώτησας	vb 1st aor act ind 2nd pers sg	id.
ἐπηρώτησεν	vb 1st aor act ind 3rd pers sg	id.
ἐπηρωτῶμεν	vb impf act ind 1st pers pl	id.

ἐπηρώτων	vb impf act ind 3rd pers pl	ἐπερωτάω
ἐπῇσαν	vb impf act ind 3rd pers pl	ἔπειμι
ἐπῃσχύνθη	vb 1st aor pass ind 3rd pers sg	ἐπαισχύνω
ἐπῃσχύνθησαν	vb 1st aor pass ind 3rd pers pl	id.
ἐπί	preposition	
ἐπιβάθρας	noun fem acc pl	ἐπιβάθρα
ἐπιβαίνει	vb pres act ind 3rd pers sg	ἐπιβαίνω
ἐπιβαίνοντες	vb pres act part masc nom pl	id.
ἐπιβαίνοντι	vb pres act part masc and neut dat sg	id.
ἐπιβαίνουσιν	vb pres act ind 3rd pers pl	id.
ἐπιβαίνω	vb pres act ind 1st pers sg	id.
ἐπιβαίνων	vb pres act part masc nom sg	id.
ἐπίβαλε	vb 2nd aor act impv 2nd pers sg	ἐπιβάλλω
ἐπιβαλεῖ	vb fut act ind 3rd pers sg	id.
ἐπιβαλεῖν	vb 2nd aor act inf, fut act inf	id.
ἐπιβαλεῖς	vb fut act ind 2nd pers sg	id.
ἐπιβάλῃ	vb 2nd aor act subj 3rd pers sg	id.
ἐπιβάλῃς	vb 2nd aor act subj 2nd pers sg	id.
ἐπιβάλητε	vb 2nd aor act subj 2nd pers pl	id.
ἐπίβαλλε	vb pres act impv 2nd pers sg	id.
ἐπιβάλλει	vb pres act ind 3rd pers sg	id.
ἐπιβάλλετε	vb pres act ind 2nd pers pl	id.
ἐπιβαλλόμενον	vb pres m/p part masc acc sg, neut nom and acc sg	id.
ἐπιβαλλομένου	vb pres m/p part masc and neut gen sg	id.
ἐπιβάλλοντα	vb pres act part neut nom and acc pl	id.
ἐπιβάλλοντος	vb pres act part masc and neut gen sg	id.
ἐπιβαλλούσας	vb pres act part fem acc pl	id.
ἐπιβαλλούσης	vb pres act part fem gen sg	id.
ἐπιβαλοῦσιν	vb fut act ind 3rd pers pl	id.
ἐπιβάλω	vb 2nd aor act subj 1st pers sg	id.
ἐπιβαλῶ	vb fut act ind 1st pers sg	id.
ἐπιβαλών	vb 2nd aor act part masc nom sg	id.
ἐπιβάλωσι(ν)	vb 2nd aor act subj 3rd pers pl	id.
ἐπιβάσεως	noun fem gen sg	ἐπίβασις
ἐπίβασιν	noun fem acc sg	id.
ἐπίβασις	noun fem nom sg	id.
ἐπιβάται	noun masc nom pl	ἐπιβάτης
ἐπιβάτας	noun masc acc pl	id.
ἐπιβάτην	noun masc acc sg	id.
ἐπιβάτης	noun masc nom sg	id.
ἐπιβάτου	noun masc gen sg	id.
ἐπιβεβήκει	vb plpf act ind 3rd pers sg	ἐπιβαίνω
ἐπιβεβηκότα	vb perf act part neut nom and acc pl	id.
ἐπιβεβηκότες	vb perf act part masc nom pl	id.
ἐπιβεβηκότι	vb perf act part masc and neut dat sg	id.
ἐπιβεβηκυῖα	vb perf act part fem nom sg	id.
ἐπιβεβηκυίης	vb perf act part fem gen sg	id.
ἐπιβεβηκώς	vb perf act part masc nom sg	id.
ἐπιβέβληκας	vb perf act ind 2nd pers sg	ἐπιβάλλω
ἐπιβῇ	vb 2nd aor act subj 3rd pers sg	ἐπιβαίνω
ἐπίβηθι	vb 2nd aor act impv 2nd pers sg	id.

ἐπιβῆναι vb 2nd aor act inf . . . . ἐπιβαίνω
ἐπιβήσεται vb fut mid ind 3rd pers sg   id.
ἐπιβήσῃ vb 1st aor mid subj 2nd pers sg,
    fut mid ind 2nd pers sg   id.
ἐπιβήσομαι vb fut mid ind 1st pers sg   id.
ἐπιβήσονται vb fut mid ind 3rd pers pl   id.
ἐπίβητε vb 2nd aor act impv 2nd pers pl   id.
ἐπιβῆτε vb 2nd aor act subj 2nd pers pl   id.
ἐπιβιβᾷ vb pres act ind 3rd pers sg . . . . ἐπιβιβάω
ἐπιβιβᾷ vb fut act ind 3rd pers sg . . . . ἐπιβιβάζω
ἐπιβιβάσατε vb 1st aor act impv 2nd pers pl   id.
ἐπιβίβασον vb 1st aor act impv 2nd pers sg   id.
ἐπιβιβῶ vb fut act ind 1st pers sg   id.
ἐπιβιώσομεν vb fut act ind 1st pers pl . . . . ἐπιβιόω
ἐπιβλέπει vb pres act ind 3rd pers sg . . . . ἐπιβλέπω
ἐπιβλέπειν vb pres act inf   id.
ἐπιβλέπεις vb pres act ind 2nd pers sg   id.
ἐπιβλέπῃ vb pres act subj 3rd pers sg   id.
ἐπιβλεπόμενον vb pres m/p part masc acc sg
    neut nom and acc sg   id.
ἐπιβλέποντες vb pres act part masc nom pl   id.
ἐπιβλέπουσα vb pres act part fem nom sg   id.
ἐπιβλέπουσιν vb pres act ind 3rd pers pl   id.
ἐπιβλέπων vb pres act part masc nom sg   id.
ἐπιβλέψαι vb 1st aor act inf   id.
ἐπιβλέψας vb 1st aor act part masc nom sg   id.
ἐπιβλέψατε vb 1st aor act impv 2nd pers pl   id.
ἐπιβλεψάτω vb 1st aor act impv 3rd pers sg   id.
ἐπιβλέψεται vb fut mid ind 3rd pers sg   id.
ἐπιβλέψῃ vb 1st aor act subj 3rd pers sg,
    1st aor mid subj 2nd pers sg   id.
ἐπιβλέψῃς vb 1st aor act subj 2nd pers sg   id.
ἐπιβλέψομαι vb fut mid ind 1st pers sg   id.
ἐπίβλεψον vb 1st aor act impv 2nd pers sg   id.
ἐπιβλέψονται vb fut mid ind 3rd pers pl   id.
ἐπιβλέψω vb fut act ind 1st pers sg   id.
ἐπιβληθῇ vb 1st aor pass subj 3rd pers sg . . . . ἐπιβάλλω
ἐπιβληθήσεται vb fut pass ind 3rd pers sg   id.
ἐπιβλήματα noun neut nom and acc pl . . . . ἐπίβλημα
ἐπιβοᾶται vb pres m/p ind 3rd pers sg . . . . ἐπιβοάω
ἐπιβοηθεῖν vb pres act inf . . . . ἐπιβοηθέω
ἐπιβοηθοῦντας vb pres act part masc acc pl   id.
ἐπιβόλαια noun neut nom and acc pl . . . . ἐπιβόλαιον
ἐπιβολαίῳ noun neut dat sg   id.
ἐπιβολάς noun fem acc pl . . . . ἐπιβολή
ἐπιβολή noun fem nom sg   id.
ἐπιβουλάς noun fem acc pl . . . . ἐπιβουλή
ἐπιβουλεύειν vb pres act inf . . . . ἐπιβουλεύω
ἐπιβουλεύουσι vb pres act part masc and neut dat pl   id.
ἐπιβουλήν noun fem acc sg . . . . ἐπιβουλή
ἐπιβουλῆς noun fem gen sg   id.
ἐπίβουλοι adj masc and fem nom pl . . . . ἐπίβουλος

ἐπίβουλον adj acc sg, neut nom sg . . . . ἐπίβουλος
ἐπίβουλος adj masc and fem nom sg   id.
ἐπιβούλους adj masc and fem acc pl   id.
ἐπιβούλων adj gen pl   id.
ἐπιβούλων noun fem gen pl . . . . ἐπιβουλή
ἐπιβοῶντος vb pres act part masc and neut gen sg . ἐπιβοάω
ἐπιβρέξει vb fut act ind 3rd pers sg . . . . ἐπιβρέχω
ἐπιβρίθων vb pres act part masc nom sg . . . . ἐπιβρίθω
ἐπιβῶ vb 2nd aor act subj 1st pers sg . . . . ἐπιβαίνω
ἐπιγαμβρεύεται vb pres m/p ind 3rd pers sg . ἐπιγαμβρεύω
ἐπιγαμβρεῦσαι vb 1st aor act inf   id.
ἐπιγαμβρεύσασθε vb 1st aor mid ind 2nd pers pl   id.
ἐπιγάμβρευσον vb 1st aor act impv 2nd pers sg   id.
ἐπιγαμβρεύσω vb fut act ind 1st pers sg   id.
ἐπιγαμίας noun fem gen sg and acc pl . . . . ἐπιγαμία
ἐπιγελάσομαι vb fut mid ind 1st pers sg . . . . ἐπιγελάω
ἐπιγεμίζοντας vb pres act part masc acc pl . . . . . ἐπιγεμίζω
ἐπιγινομένοις vb pres dep part
    masc and neut dat pl . . . . ἐπιγίνομαι
ἐπιγινώσκειν vb pres act inf . . . . ἐπιγινώσκω
ἐπιγινώσκοντες vb pres act part masc nom pl   id.
ἐπιγινώσκω vb pres act ind 1st pers sg   id.
ἐπιγινώσκων vb pres act part masc nom sg   id.
ἐπιγνοῖ vb 2nd aor act subj 3rd pers sg   id.
ἐπιγνόντες vb 2nd aor act part masc nom pl   id.
ἐπιγνούς vb 2nd aor act part masc nom sg   id.
ἐπιγνοῦσα vb 2nd aor act part fem nom sg   id.
ἐπιγνῶ vb 2nd aor act subj 1st pers sg   id.
ἐπιγνῷ vb 2nd aor act subj 3rd pers sg   id.
ἐπίγνωθι vb 2nd aor act impv 2nd pers sg   id.
ἐπιγνῶμεν vb 2nd aor act subj 1st pers pl   id.
ἐπιγνώμονες adj masc and fem nom pl . . . . ἐπιγνώμων
ἐπιγνωμοσύνην noun fem acc sg . . . . ἐπιγνωμοσύνη
ἐπιγνώμων adj masc and fem nom sg,
    noun masc nom sg
ἐπιγνῶναι vb 2nd aor act inf . . . . ἐπιγινώσκω
ἐπιγνῷς vb 2nd aor act subj 2nd pers sg   id.
ἐπιγνώσεσθε vb fut mid ind 2nd pers pl   id.
ἐπιγνώσεται vb fut mid ind 3rd pers sg   id.
ἐπιγνώσεως noun fem gen sg . . . . ἐπίγνωσις
ἐπιγνώσῃ vb fut mid ind 2nd pers sg . . . . ἐπιγινώσκω
ἐπιγνωσθήσεται vb fut pass ind 3rd pers sg   id.
ἐπιγνωσθήσῃ vb fut pass ind 2nd pers sg   id.
ἐπίγνωσιν noun fem acc sg . . . . ἐπίγνωσις
ἐπίγνωσις noun fem nom sg   id.
ἐπιγνώσομαι vb fut mid ind 1st pers sg . . . . ἐπιγινώσκω
ἐπιγνώσονται vb fut mid ind 3rd pers pl   id.
ἐπίγνωστος adj masc and fem nom sg
ἐπιγνώτωσαν vb 2nd aor act impv 3rd pers pl . . ἐπιγινώσκω
ἐπιγονή noun fem nom sg
ἐπιγονῇ noun fem dat sg . . . . ἐπιγονή
ἐπιγονῆς noun fem gen sg   id.

ἐπιγράψει   vb fut act ind 3rd pers sg . . . . ἐπιγράφω
ἐπίγραψον   vb 1st aor act impv 2nd pers sg . . . . id.
ἔπιδε   vb 2nd aor act impv 2nd pers sg . . . . ἐφοράω
ἐπιδεδεγμενοις   vb perf dep part
        masc and neut dat pl . . . . ἐπιδέχομαι
ἐπιδεδεγμένους   vb perf dep part masc acc pl . . . . id.
ἐπιδεεῖς   adj masc and fem nom and acc pl . . . . ἐπιδεής
ἐπιδέεται   vb pres m/p ind 3rd pers sg . . . . ἐπιδέω
ἐπιδεής   adj masc and fem nom sg
ἐπιδεήσεις   vb fut act ind 2nd pers sg . . . . ἐπιδέω
ἐπιδεικνυμένην   vb pres m/p part fem acc sg . . . ἐπιδεικνύω
ἐπιδεικνύμενον   vb pres m/p part masc acc sg,
        neut nom and acc sg . . . . id.
ἐπιδείκνυμι   vb pres act ind 1st pers sg . . . . id.
ἐπιδεικνύναι   vb pres act inf . . . . id.
ἐπιδείκνυσθαι   vb pres m/p inf . . . . id.
ἐπιδεῖν   vb 2nd aor act inf . . . . ἐφοράω
ἐπιδεῖξαι   vb 1st aor act inf . . . . ἐπιδεικνύω
ἐπιδειξάμενος   vb 1st aor mid part masc nom sg   id.
ἐπιδείξασθαι   vb 1st aor mid inf . . . . id.
ἐπίδειξιν   noun fem acc sg . . . . ἐπίδειξις
ἐπιδειξώμεθα   vb 1st aor mid subj 1st pers pl . . . ἐπιδεικνύω
ἐπιδέκατα   noun neut nom and acc pl . . . . ἐπιδέκατον
ἐπιδέκατον   noun neut nom and acc sg . . . . id.
ἐπιδεκάτου   noun neut gen sg . . . . id.
ἐπιδεκάτων   noun neut gen pl . . . . id.
ἐπιδέξαι   vb 1st aor mid impv 2nd pers sg . . . . . ἐπιδέχομαι
ἐπιδεξαμένων   vb 1st aor mid part gen pl . . . . id.
ἐπιδέξασθαι   vb 1st aor mid inf . . . . id.
ἐπιδεξάσθω   vb 1st aor mid impv 3rd pers sg . . . . id.
ἐπιδέξεται   vb fut mid ind 3rd pers sg . . . . id.
ἐπιδέξιον   adj acc sg, neut nom sg . . . . ἐπιδέξιος
ἐπιδέξιος   adj masc and fem nom sg
ἐπιδέομαι   vb pres m/p ind 1st pers sg . . . . ἐπιδέω
ἐπιδεομένου   vb pres m/p part masc and neut gen sg   id.
ἐπιδεομένῳ   vb pres m/p part masc and neut dat sg   id.
ἐπιδεομένων   vb pres m/p part gen pl . . . . id.
ἐπίδετε   vb 2nd aor act impv 2nd pers pl . . . . ἐφοράω
ἐπίδῃ   vb 2nd aor act subj 3rd pers sg . . . . id.
ἐπίδηλον   adj acc sg, neut nom sg . . . . ἐπίδηλος
ἐπίδῃς   vb 2nd aor act subj 2nd pers sg . . . . ἐφοράω
ἐπιδήσεις   vb fut act ind 2nd pers sg . . . . ἐπιδέω
ἐπιδιδόντος   vb pres act part masc and neut gen sg   ἐπιδίδωμι
ἐπιδιδούς   vb pres act part masc nom sg   id.
ἐπιδιεῖλεν   vb 2nd aor act ind 3rd pers sg . . . . . . ἐπιδιαιρέω
ἐπιδιπλώσεις   vb fut act ind 2nd pers sg . . . . ἐπιδιπλόω
ἐπιδιώξαντα   vb 1st aor act part masc acc sg . . . . . ἐπιδιώκω
ἐπιδίωξον   vb 1st aor act impv 2nd pers sg . . . . id.
ἐπίδοι   vb 2nd aor act opt 2nd pers sg . . . . ἐπιδίδωμι
ἐπιδόντες   vb 2nd aor act part masc nom pl . . . . id.
ἐπίδοξος   adj masc and fem nom sg
ἐπιδόξως   adverb

ἐπίδοτε   vb 2nd aor act impv 2nd pers pl . . . . ἐπιδίδωμι
ἐπιδύνοντος   vb pres act part masc and neut gen sg .   ἐπιδύνω
ἐπιδύσεται   vb fut mid ind 3rd pers sg . . . . ἐπιδύω
ἐπιδών   vb 2nd aor act part masc nom sg . . . . ἐφοράω
ἐπιδῷς   vb 2nd aor act subj 2nd pers sg . . . . ἐπιδίδωμι
ἐπιδώσει   vb fut act ind 3rd pers sg   id.
ἐπιείκεια   noun fem nom sg
ἐπιεικείᾳ   noun fem dat sg . . . . ἐπιείκεια
ἐπιείκειαν   noun fem acc sg   id.
ἐπιεικείας   noun fem gen sg   id.
ἐπιεικεστέρας   comp adj fem gen sg . . . . ἐπιεικής
ἐπιεικέστερον   comp adj masc acc sg   id.
ἐπιεικεύσατο   vb 1st aor mid ind 3rd pers sg . ἐπιεικεύομαι
ἐπιεικέως   adverb
ἐπιεικής   adj masc and fem nom sg
ἐπιεικῶς   adverb
ἔπιεν   vb 2nd aor act ind 3rd pers sg . . . . πίνω
ἔπιες   vb 2nd aor act ind 2nd pers sg   id.
ἐπίετε   vb 2nd aor act ind 2nd pers pl   id.
ἐπιζεύξαντες   vb 1st aor act part masc nom pl . ἐπιζεύγνυμι
ἐπιζήμιον   noun neut nom and acc sg
ἐπιζήσας   vb 1st aor act part masc nom sg . . . . ἐπιζάω
ἐπιζητεῖ   vb pres act ind 3rd pers sg . . . . ἐπιζητέω
ἐπιζητεῖς   vb pres act ind 2nd pers sg   id.
ἐπιζητῆσαι   vb 1st aor act inf   id.
ἐπιζητήσατε   vb 1st aor act impv 2nd pers pl   id.
ἐπιζητήσομεν   vb fut act ind 1st pers pl   id.
ἐπιζήτησον   vb 1st aor act impv 2nd pers sg   id.
ἐπιζητήσουσιν   vb fut act ind 3rd pers pl   id.
ἐπιζητήσωμεν   vb 1st aor act subj 1st pers pl   id.
ἐπιζητήσωσιν   vb 1st aor act subj 3rd pers pl   id.
ἐπιζητουμένη   vb pres m/p part fem nom sg   id.
ἐπιζητούντων   vb pres act part masc and neut gen pl   id.
ἐπιθανατίων   adj gen pl . . . . ἐπιθανάτιος
ἐπιθεῖναι   vb 2nd aor act inf . . . . ἐπιτίθημι
ἐπιθείς   vb 2nd aor act part masc nom sg   id.
ἐπίθεμα   noun neut nom and acc sg
ἐπιθέματα   noun neut nom and acc pl . . . . ἐπίθεμα
ἐπιθέματι   noun neut dat sg   id.
ἐπιθέματος   noun neut gen sg   id.
ἐπιθεμάτων   noun neut gen pl   id.
ἐπιθέμενοι   vb 2nd aor mid part masc nom pl . . . . ἐπιτίθημι
ἐπιθεμένους   vb 2nd aor mid part masc acc pl   id.
ἐπιθέντες   vb 2nd aor act part masc nom pl   id.
ἐπίθες   vb 2nd aor act impv 2nd pers sg   id.
ἐπιθέσθαι   vb 2nd aor mid inf   id.
ἐπίθεσιν   noun fem acc sg . . . . ἐπίθεσις
ἐπίθετε   vb 2nd aor act impv 2nd pers pl . . . . ἐπιτίθημι
ἐπιθετωσαν   vb 2nd aor act impv 3rd pers pl   id.
ἐπιθεωρεῖτε   vb pres act impv 2nd pers pl . . . . ἐπιθεωρέω
ἐπιθῇ   vb 1st aor act subj 3rd pers sg . . . . ἐπιτίθημι
ἐπιθῇς   vb 1st aor act subj 2nd pers sg   id.

ἐπιθήσει vb fut act ind 3rd pers sg . . . . ἐπιτίθημι
ἐπιθήσειν vb fut act inf   id.
ἐπιθήσεις vb fut act ind 2nd pers sg   id.
ἐπιθήσετε vb fut act ind 2nd pers pl   id.
ἐπιθήσονται vb fut mid ind 3rd pers pl   id.
ἐπιθήσουσιν vb fut act ind 3rd pers pl   id.
ἐπιθήσω vb fut act ind 1st pers sg   id.
ἐπιθῆται vb 2nd aor mid subj 3rd pers sg   id.
ἐπιθῆτε vb 2nd aor act subj 2nd pers pl   id.
ἐπίθου vb 2nd aor mid impv 2nd pers sg   id.
ἐπιθύμει vb pres act impv 2nd pers sg . . . . ἐπιθυμέω
ἐπιθυμεῖ vb pres act ind 3rd pers sg   id.
ἐπιθυμεῖν vb pres act inf   id.
ἐπιθυμῇ vb pres act subj 3rd pers sg   id.
ἐπιθύμημα noun neut nom and acc sg
ἐπιθυμήμασι noun neut dat pl . . . . ἐπιθύμημα
ἐπιθυμήματα noun neut nom and acc pl   id.
ἐπιθυμήματος noun neut gen sg   id.
ἐπιθυμημάτων noun neut gen pl   id.
ἐπιθυμῆσαι vb 1st aor act inf . . . . ἐπιθυμέω
ἐπιθυμήσαντες vb 1st aor act part masc nom pl   id.
ἐπιθυμήσας vb 1st aor act part masc nom sg   id.
ἐπιθυμήσατε vb 1st aor act impv 2nd pers pl   id.
ἐπιθυμήσει vb fut act ind 3rd pers sg   id.
ἐπιθυμήσεις vb fut act ind 2nd pers sg   id.
ἐπιθυμήσῃ vb 1st aor act subj 3rd pers sg   id.
ἐπιθυμήσῃς vb 1st aor act subj 2nd pers sg   id.
ἐπιθυμήσητε vb 1st aor act subj 2nd pers pl   id.
ἐπιθυμητά adj neut nom and acc pl . . . . ἐπιθυμητός
ἐπιθυμηταί noun masc nom pl . . . . ἐπιθυμητής
ἐπιθυμητήν adj fem acc sg . . . . ἐπιθυμητός
ἐπιθυμητήν noun masc acc sg . . . . ἐπιθυμητής
ἐπιθυμητοῖς adj masc and neut dat pl . . . . ἐπιθυμητός
ἐπιθυμητόν adj masc acc sg, neut nom and acc sg   id.
ἐπιθυμητός adj masc nom sg   id.
ἐπιθυμητούς adj masc acc pl   id.
ἐπιθυμητῶν adj masc and neut gen pl   id.
ἐπιθυμία noun fem nom sg
ἐπιθυμίᾳ noun fem dat sg . . . . ἐπιθυμία
ἐπιθυμίαι noun fem nom pl   id.
ἐπιθυμίαις noun fem dat pl   id.
ἐπιθυμίαν noun fem acc sg   id.
ἐπιθυμίας noun fem gen sg and acc pl   id.
ἐπιθυμιῶν noun fem gen pl   id.
ἐπιθυμοῦντας vb pres act part masc acc pl . . . . . ἐπιθυμέω
ἐπιθυμοῦντες vb pres act part masc nom pl   id.
ἐπιθυμοῦσιν vb pres act ind 3rd pers pl   id.
ἐπιθύομεν vb pres act ind 1st pers pl . . . . ἐπιθύω
ἐπιθύοντας vb pres act part masc acc pl   id.
ἐπιθύουσιν vb pres act ind 3rd pers pl   id.
ἐπιθῦσαι vb 1st aor act inf   id.
ἐπιθῶ vb 2nd aor act subj 1st pers sg . . . . ἐπιτίθημι

ἐπιθώμεθα vb 2nd aor mid subj 1st pers pl . . . . . . ἐπιτίθημι
ἐπιθῶνται vb 2nd aor mid subj 3rd pers pl   id.
ἐπικαθήμενος vb pres m/p part masc nom sg . . ἐπικάθημαι
ἐπικαθημένου vb pres m/p part masc and neut gen sg   id.
ἐπικαθῆσθαι vb pres m/p inf   id.
ἐπικάθηται vb pres m/p ind 3rd pers sg   id.
ἐπικαθίσῃ vb 1st aor act subj 3rd pers sg . . . . ἐπικαθίζω
ἐπικαθιῶ vb fut act ind 1st pers sg   id.
ἐπικαινισθῆναι vb 1st aor pass inf . . . . ἐπικαινίζω
ἐπικαίροις adj dat pl . . . . ἐπίκαιρος
ἐπικαίρους adj masc and fem acc pl   id.
ἐπικαίρων adj gen pl   id.
ἐπικαλεῖσθαι vb pres m/p inf . . . . ἐπικαλέω
ἐπικαλεῖσθε vb pres m/p impv 2nd pers pl,
        pres m/p ind 2nd pers pl   id.
ἐπικαλεῖται vb pres m/p ind 3rd pers sg   id.
ἐπικάλεσαι vb 1st aor mid impv 2nd pers sg   id.
ἐπικαλεσαμένη vb 1st aor mid part fem nom sg   id.
ἐπικαλεσάμενοι vb 1st aor mid part masc nom pl   id.
ἐπικαλεσάμενος vb 1st aor mid part masc nom sg   id.
ἐπικαλεσαμένου vb 1st aor mid part
        masc and neut gen sg   id.
ἐπικαλέσασθαι vb 1st aor mid inf   id.
ἐπικαλέσασθε vb 1st aor mid impv 2nd pers pl   id.
ἐπικαλέσεσθε vb fut mid ind 2nd pers pl   id.
ἐπικαλέσεται vb fut mid ind 3rd pers sg   id.
ἐπικαλέσῃ vb 1st aor act subj 3rd pers sg   id.
ἐπικαλέσησθε vb 1st aor mid subj 2nd pers pl   id.
ἐπικαλέσηται vb 1st aor mid subj 3rd pers sg   id.
ἐπικαλέσομαι vb fut mid ind 1st pers sg   id.
ἐπικαλεσόμεθα vb fut mid ind 1st pers pl   id.
ἐπικαλέσονται vb fut mid ind 3rd pers pl   id.
ἐπικαλέσωμαι vb 1st aor mid subj 1st pers sg   id.
ἐπικαλεσώμεθα vb 1st aor mid subj 1st pers pl   id.
ἐπικαλέσωνται vb 1st aor mid subj 3rd pers pl   id.
ἐπικαλοῦ vb pres m/p impv 2nd pers sg   id.
ἐπικαλοῦμαι vb pres m/p ind 1st pers sg   id.
ἐπικαλουμένοις vb pres m/p part masc and neut dat pl   id.
ἐπικαλούμενος vb pres m/p part masc nom sg   id.
ἐπικαλουμένου vb pres m/p part masc and neut gen sg   id.
ἐπικαλουμένῳ vb pres m/p part masc and neut dat sg   id.
ἐπικαλοῦνται vb pres m/p ind 3rd pers pl   id.
ἐπικάλυμμα noun neut nom and acc sg
ἐπικαλύμματα noun neut nom and acc pl . . . . ἐπικάλυμμα
ἐπικαλύμματος noun neut gen sg   id.
ἐπικαλύπτουσαι vb pres act part fem nom pl . ἐπικαλύπτω
ἐπικαλύπτων vb pres act part masc nom sg   id.
ἐπικαλυψάτω vb 1st aor act impv 3rd pers sg   id.
ἐπικαλύψῃς vb 1st aor act subj 2nd pers sg   id.
ἐπικαλύψουσιν vb fut act ind 3rd pers pl   id.
ἐπικαρπολογούμενος vb pres m/p part
        masc nom sg . . . . ἐπικαρπολογέω

ἐπικαταλήμψεται vb fut mid ind

    3rd pers sg . . . . ἐπικαταλαμβάνω

ἐπικατάρασαι vb 1st aor mid impv

    2nd pers sg . . . . ἐπικαταράομαι

ἐπικαταράσομαι vb fut mid ind 1st pers sg   id.

ἐπικατάρατα adj neut nom and acc pl . . . . . ἐπικατάρατος

ἐπικατάρατοι adj masc and fem nom pl   id.

ἐπικατάρατον adj acc sg, neut nom sg   id.

ἐπικατάρατος adj masc and fem nom sg   id.

ἐπικαταρώμενον vb pres dep part masc acc sg,

    neut nom and acc sg . . . . ἐπικαταράομαι

ἐπικαταρωμένου vb pres dep part

    masc and neut gen sg   id.

ἐπικατηράσατο vb 1st aor mid ind 3rd pers sg   id.

ἐπικείμενα vb pres m/p part neut nom and acc pl . ἐπίκειμαι

ἐπικειμένου vb pres m/p part masc and neut gen sg   id.

ἐπικεῖσθαι vb pres m/p inf   id.

ἐπίκεισθε vb pres m/p ind 2nd pers pl   id.

ἐπίκειται vb pres m/p ind 3rd pers sg   id.

ἐπικεκαλυμμένος vb perf m/p part

    masc nom sg . . . . ἐπικαλύπτω

ἐπικεκλημένου vb perf m/p part

    masc and neut gen sg . . . . ἐπικαλέω

ἐπικέκληνται vb perf m/p ind 3rd pers pl   id.

ἐπικέκληται vb perf m/p ind 3rd pers sg   id.

ἐπικερδῆ adj masc and fem acc sg . . . . ἐπικερδής

ἐπικεχυμένου vb perf m/p part

    masc and neut gen sg . . . . ἐπιχέω

ἐπικίνδυνον adj acc sg, neut nom sg . . . . ἐπικίνδυνος

ἐπικληθῆναι vb 1st aor pass inf . . . . ἐπικαλέω

ἐπικληθήσεται vb fut pass ind 3rd pers sg   id.

ἐπικληθήσομαι vb fut pass ind 1st pers sg   id.

ἐπικλήσεως noun fem gen sg . . . . ἐπίκλησις

ἐπίκλητοι adj masc and fem nom pl . . . . ἐπίκλητος

ἐπίκλητος adj masc and fem nom sg   id.

ἐπικλῖναι vb 1st aor act inf . . . . ἐπικλίνω

ἐπίκλινον vb 1st aor act impv 2nd pers sg   id.

ἐπικλύζων vb pres act part masc nom sg . . . . ἐπικλύζω

ἐπικοιμηθήσεται vb fut pass ind 3rd pers sg . . . ἐπικοιμάω

ἐπικοινωνοῦσα vb pres act part fem nom sg . . ἐπικοινωνέω

ἐπικοινωνούσας vb pres act part fem acc pl   id.

ἐπικοπήν noun fem acc sg . . . . ἐπικοπή

ἐπικοσμηθῆναι vb 1st aor pass inf . . . . ἐπικοσμέω

ἐπικουρίας noun fem gen sg . . . . ἐπικουρία

ἐπικουφίζομαι vb pres dep ind 1st pers sg

ἐπίκρανεν vb 1st aor act ind 3rd pers sg . . . . πικραίνω

ἐπικράνθη vb 1st aor pass ind 3rd pers sg   id.

ἐπικράνθησαν vb 1st aor pass ind 3rd pers pl   id.

ἐπικραταιωθῇ vb 1st aor pass subj

    3rd pers sg . . . . ἐπικραταιόω

ἐπικρατεῖ vb pres act ind 3rd pers sg . . . . ἐπικρατέω

ἐπικράτεια noun fem nom sg

ἐπικράτειαν noun fem acc sg . . . . ἐπικράτεια

ἐπικρατείας noun fem gen sg and acc pl   id.

ἐπικρατεῖν vb pres act inf . . . . ἐπικρατέω

ἐπικρατῆσαι vb 1st aor act inf   id.

ἐπικρατήσας vb 1st aor act part masc nom sg   id.

ἐπικρατησάτωσαν vb 1st aor act impv 3rd pers pl   id.

ἐπικράτησιν noun fem acc sg . . . . ἐπικράτησις

ἐπικράτησον vb 1st aor act impv 2nd pers sg . ἐπικρατέω

ἐπικρατοῦντες vb pres act part masc nom pl   id.

ἐπικρατοῦντος vb pres act part masc and neut gen sg   id.

ἐπικρατούντων vb pres act part masc and neut gen pl   id.

ἐπικρατῶν vb pres act part masc nom sg   id.

ἐπικρεμάμενοι vb pres m/p part

    masc nom pl . . . . ἐπικρεμάννυμι

ἐπικρεμάμενος vb pres m/p part masc nom sg   id.

ἐπικριθεῖσαν vb 1st aor pass part fem acc sg . . . . . ἐπικρίνω

ἐπικροτεῖ vb pres act ind 3rd pers sg . . . . ἐπικροτέω

ἐπικροτήσει vb fut act ind 3rd pers sg   id.

ἐπικροτοῦντες vb pres act part masc nom pl   id.

ἐπικρούσει vb fut act ind 3rd pers sg . . . . ἐπικρούω

ἐπικτήτου adj gen sg . . . . ἐπίκτητος

ἐπίκυφον adj acc sg, neut nom sg . . . . ἐπίκυφος

ἐπιλαβεῖν vb 2nd aor act inf . . . . ἐπιλαμβάνω

ἐπιλαβέσθαι vb 2nd aor mid inf   id.

ἐπιλάβηται vb 2nd aor mid subj 3rd pers sg   id.

ἐπιλαβομένη vb 2nd aor mid part fem nom sg   id.

ἐπιλαβόμενοι vb 2nd aor mid part masc nom pl   id.

ἐπιλαβόμενος vb 2nd aor mid part masc nom sg   id.

ἐπιλαβομένου vb 2nd aor mid part masc and neut gen sg   id.

ἐπιλαβοῦ vb 2nd aor mid impv 2nd pers sg   id.

ἐπιλάβωνται vb 2nd aor mid subj 3rd pers pl   id.

ἐπιλαθέσθαι vb 2nd aor mid inf . . . . ἐπιλανθάνω

ἐπιλάθη vb 2nd aor act subj 3rd pers sg,

    2nd aor mid subj 2nd pers sg   id.

ἐπιλάθησθε vb 2nd aor mid subj 2nd pers pl   id.

ἐπιλάθηται vb 2nd aor mid subj 3rd pers sg   id.

ἐπιλάθοιτο vb 2nd aor mid opt 3rd pers sg   id.

ἐπιλάθου vb 2nd aor mid impv 2nd pers sg   id.

ἐπιλάθωμαι vb 2nd aor mid subj 1st pers sg   id.

ἐπιλάθωνται vb 2nd aor mid subj 3rd pers pl   id.

ἐπιλαμβάνεται vb pres m/p ind 3rd pers sg . . . ἐπιλαμβάνω

ἐπιλαμβανομένοις vb pres m/p part

    masc and neut dat pl   id.

ἐπιλαμβάνωνται vb pres m/p subj 3rd pers pl   id.

ἐπιλάμψει vb fut act ind 3rd pers sg . . . . ἐπιλάμπω

ἐπιλανθάνῃ vb pres m/p ind 2nd pers sg . . . . . ἐπιλανθάνω

ἐπιλανθανόμενα vb pres m/p part

    neut nom and acc pl   id.

ἐπιλανθανόμενοι vb pres m/p part masc nom pl   id.

ἐπιλανθανομένων vb pres m/p part gen pl   id.

ἐπιλανθάνου vb pres m/p impv 2nd pers sg   id.

ἐπίλεκτα adj neut nom and acc pl . . . . ἐπίλεκτος

ἐπίλεκτοι adj masc and fem nom pl . . . . ἐπίλεκτος
ἐπιλέκτοις adj dat pl id.
ἐπίλεκτος adj masc and fem nom sg id.
ἐπιλέκτους adj masc and fem acc pl id.
ἐπιλέκτων adj gen pl id.
ἐπιλελεγμέναις vb perf m/p part fem dat pl . . . . . . ἐπιλέγω
ἐπιλέλησθε vb perf m/p ind 2nd pers pl . . . . . ἐπιλανθάνω
ἐπιλελησμένη vb perf m/p part fem nom sg id.
ἐπιλελησμένῃ vb perf m/p part fem dat sg id.
ἐπιλέλησται vb perf m/p ind 3rd pers sg id.
ἐπιλελυπηκότα vb perf act part
     neut nom and acc pl . . . . ἐπιλυπέω
ἐπίλεξαι vb 1st aor mid impv 2nd pers sg . . . . ἐπιλέγω
ἐπιλεξάτωσαν vb 1st aor act impv 3rd pers pl id.
ἐπίλεξον vb 1st aor act impv 2nd pers sg id.
ἐπιλέξω vb fut act ind 1st pers sg,
     1st aor act subj 1st pers sg id.
ἐπιλημπτεύεσθαι vb pres m/p inf . . . . . . ἐπιλημπτεύομαι
ἐπιλημπτεύσασθε vb 1st aor mid impv 2nd pers pl id.
ἐπίλημπτον adj acc sg, neut nom sg . . . . ἐπίλημπτος
ἐπίλημπτος adj masc and fem nom sg id.
ἐπιλήμπτων adj gen pl id.
ἐπιλήμψεται vb fut mid ind 3rd pers sg . . . . . ἐπιλαμβάνω
ἐπιλήμψονται vb fut mid ind 3rd pers pl id.
ἐπιλήσεσθε vb fut mid ind 2nd pers pl . . . . ἐπιλανθάνω
ἐπιλήσεται vb fut mid ind 3rd pers sg id.
ἐπιλήσῃ vb fut mid ind 2nd pers sg id.
ἐπιλησθείη vb 1st aor pass opt 3rd pers sg id.
ἐπιλησθῇ vb 1st aor pass subj 3rd pers sg id.
ἐπιλησθῇς vb 1st aor pass subj 2nd pers sg id.
ἐπιλησθήσεται vb fut pass ind 3rd pers sg id.
ἐπιλησθήσονται vb fut pass ind 3rd pers pl id.
ἐπιλησμονήν noun fem nom sg . . . . ἐπιλησμονή
ἐπιλήσομαι vb fut mid ind 1st pers sg . . . . ἐπιλανθάνω
ἐπιλήσονται vb fut mid ind 3rd pers pl id.
ἐπιλογιζόμενος vb pres dep part
     masc nom sg . . . . ἐπιλογίζομαι
ἐπιλογίσασθαι vb 1st aor mid inf id.
ἐπιλογίσασθε vb 1st aor mid impv 2nd pers pl id.
ἐπίλοιπα adj neut nom and acc pl . . . . ἐπίλοιπος
ἐπίλοιποι adj masc and fem nom pl id.
ἐπιλοίποις adj dat pl id.
ἐπίλοιπον adj acc sg, neut nom sg id.
ἐπίλοιπος adj masc and fem nom sg id.
ἐπιλοίπους adj masc and fem acc pl id.
ἐπιλοίπῳ adj dat sg id.
ἐπιλοίπων adj gen pl id.
ἐπιλυπηθείς vb 1st aor pass part masc nom sg . . . ἐπιλυπέω
ἐπιλυπήσωμεν vb 1st aor act subj 1st pers pl id.
ἐπιμαινομένους vb pres dep part masc acc pl . ἐπιμαίνομαι
ἐπιμαρτύρασθε vb 1st aor mid impv
     2nd pers pl . . . . ἐπιμαρτυρέω

ἐπιμείγνυται vb pres m/p ind 3rd pers sg . . . . . ἐπιμίγνυμι
ἐπιμεῖναι vb 1st aor act inf . . . . ἐπιμένω
ἐπιμέλεια noun fem nom sg
ἐπιμελείᾳ noun fem dat sg . . . . ἐπιμέλεια
ἐπιμέλειαν noun fem acc sg id.
ἐπιμελείας noun fem gen sg and acc pl id.
ἐπιμέλεσθε vb pres dep ind 2nd pers pl . . . . ἐπιμέλομαι
ἐπιμελέστερον comp adverb . . . . ἐπιμελῶς
ἐπιμεληθῆναι vb 1st aor pass inf . . . . ἐπιμελέομαι
ἐπιμελήσεται vb fut mid ind 3rd pers sg id.
ἐπιμελοῦ vb pres dep impv 2nd pers sg id.
ἐπιμελοῦμαι vb pres dep ind 1st pers sg id.
ἐπιμελῶς adverb
ἐπιμήκης adj masc and fem nom sg
ἐπιμιγῆναι vb 2nd aor pass inf . . . . ἐπιμίγνυμι
ἐπίμικτοι adj masc and fem nom pl . . . . ἐπίμικτος
ἐπίμικτος adj masc and fem nom sg id.
ἐπιμίξ adverb
ἐπιμονή noun fem nom sg
ἐπίμοχθον adj acc sg, neut nom sg . . . . ἐπίμοχθος
ἐπιμύλιον noun neut nom and acc sg . . . . ἐπιμύλιον
ἐπιμυλίου noun neut gen sg id.
ἔπινεν vb impf act ind 3rd pers sg . . . . πίνω
ἔπινες vb impf act ind 2nd pers sg id.
ἐπίνετε vb impf act ind 2nd pers pl id.
ἐπινεύει vb pres act ind 3rd pers sg . . . . ἐπινεύω
ἐπινεύσαντος vb 1st aor act part masc and neut gen sg id.
ἐπινεφής noun masc nom sg
ἐπινίκια adj neut nom and acc pl . . . . ἐπινίκιος
ἐπινόει vb pres act impv 2nd pers sg . . . . ἐπινοέω
ἐπίνοια noun fem nom sg
ἐπινοίᾳ noun fem dat sg . . . . ἐπίνοια
ἐπίνοιαι noun fem nom pl id.
ἐπίνοιαν noun fem acc sg id.
ἐπινοίας noun fem gen sg and acc pl id.
ἔπινον vb impf act ind 3rd pers pl . . . . πίνω
ἐπινυστάξῃς vb 1st aor act subj 2nd pers sg . . ἐπινυστάζω
ἐπιξενωθείς vb 1st aor pass part masc nom sg . ἐπιξενόομαι
ἐπιξενωθήσεται vb fut pass ind 3rd pers sg id.
ἐπίομεν vb 2nd aor act ind 1st pers pl . . . . πίνω
ἔπιον vb 2nd aor act ind 1st pers sg and 3rd pers pl id.
ἐπιόντα vb pres act part masc acc sg . . . . ἔπειμι
ἐπιόντι vb pres act part masc and neut dat sg id.
ἐπιορκήσας vb 1st aor act part masc nom sg . . . . ἐπιορκέω
ἐπιορκία noun fem nom sg
ἐπίορκος adj masc and fem nom sg
ἐπιορκοῦσιν vb pres act ind 3rd pers pl . . . . ἐπιορκέω
ἐπίοσαν vb 2nd aor act ind 3rd pers pl . . . . πίνω
ἐπιοῦσα vb pres act part fem nom sg . . . . ἔπειμι
ἐπιπαρεγένετο vb 2nd aor mid ind
     3rd pers sg . . . . ἐπιπαραγίνομαι
ἐπιπέμπει vb pres act ind 3rd pers sg . . . . ἐπιπέμπω

ἐπίπεμπτον noun neut nom and acc sg

ἐπιπέμψαι vb 1st aor act inf . . . . ἐπιπέμπω

ἐπιπέμψας vb 1st aor act part masc nom sg　　id.

ἐπιπεπτώκασιν vb perf act ind 3rd pers pl . . . . . . ἐπιπίπτω

ἐπιπεπτώκει vb plpf act ind 3rd pers sg　　id.

ἐπιπέπτωκεν vb perf act ind 3rd pers sg　　id.

ἐπιπεσεῖν vb 2nd aor act inf　　id.

ἐπιπεσεῖται vb fut mid ind 3rd pers sg　　id.

ἐπιπέσῃ vb 2nd aor act subj 3rd pers sg,
　　　　fut mid ind 2nd pers sg　　id.

ἐπιπέσοι vb 2nd aor act opt 3rd pers sg　　id.

ἐπιπεσών vb 2nd aor act part masc nom sg　　id.

ἐπιπίπτει vb pres act ind 3rd pers sg　　id.

ἐπιπίπτετε vb pres act ind 2nd pers pl　　id.

ἐπιπίπτῃ vb pres act subj 3rd pers sg　　id.

ἐπιπίπτοντες vb pres act part masc nom pl　　id.

ἐπιπίπτων vb pres act part masc nom sg　　id.

ἐπιπλήξεως noun fem gen sg . . . . ἐπίπληξις

ἐπιποθεῖ vb pres act ind 3rd pers sg . . . . ἐπιποθέω

ἐπιποθεῖτε vb pres act ind 2nd pers pl　　id.

ἐπιποθῆσαι vb 1st aor act inf　　id.

ἐπιποθήσεις vb fut act ind 2nd pers sg　　id.

ἐπιποθήσῃς vb 1st aor act subj 2nd pers sg　　id.

ἐπιποθήσω vb fut act ind 1st pers sg　　id.

ἐπιπολαίως adverb

ἐπίπονον adj masc and fem acc sg . . . . ἐπίπονος

ἐπιπορεύεσθαι vb pres dep inf . . . . ἐπιπορεύομαι

ἐπιπορευομένη vb pres dep part fem nom sg　　id.

ἐπιπορευομένους vb pres dep part masc acc pl　　id.

ἐπιπορευσαμένη vb 1st aor mid part fem nom sg　　id.

ἐπιπροσθῶσιν vb 2nd aor act subj
　　　　3rd pers pl . . . . ἐπιπροστίθημι

ἔπιπτεν vb impf act ind 3rd pers sg . . . . πίπτω

ἔπιπτον vb impf act ind 3rd pers pl　　id.

ἐπιρρᾶναι vb 1st aor act inf . . . . ἐπιρραίνω

ἐπιρραντισθῇ vb 1st aor pass subj 3rd pers sg . ἐπιρραντίζω

ἐπιρρέων vb pres act part masc nom sg . . . . ἐπιρρέω

ἐπιρριπτοῦντες vb pres act part masc nom pl . . ἐπιρριπτέω

ἐπιρρίψει vb fut act ind 3rd pers sg . . . . ἐπιρρίπτω

ἐπιρρίψῃ vb 1st aor subj 3rd act pers sg　　id.

ἐπίρριψον vb 1st aor act impv 2nd pers sg　　id.

ἐπιρρίψουσιν vb fut act ind 3rd pers pl　　id.

ἐπιρρίψω vb fut act ind 1st pers sg　　id.

ἐπιρρωγολογούμενος vb pres m/p part
　　　　masc nom sg . . . . ἐπιρρωγολογέομαι

ἐπίσαγμα noun neut nom and acc sg

ἐπισάξατε vb 1st aor act impv 2nd pers pl . . . . . . ἐπισάσσω

ἐπίσαξον vb 1st aor act impv 2nd pers sg　　id.

ἐπισείει vb pres act ind 3rd pers sg . . . . ἐπισείω

ἐπισεσαγμένων vb perf m/p part gen pl . . . . ἐπισάσσω

ἐπισεσεικώς vb perf act part masc nom sg . . . . ἐπισείω

ἐπίσημα adj neut nom and acc pl . . . . ἐπίσημος

ἐπισημάνασθαι vb 1st aor mid inf . . . . ἐπισημαίνω

ἐπίσημον adj masc and fem acc sg . . . . ἐπίσημος

ἐπίσημος adj masc and fem nom sg　　id.

ἐπισήμῳ adj dat sg　　id.

ἐπισιτισμόν noun masc acc sg . . . . ἐπισιτισμός

ἐπισιτισμοῦ noun masc gen sg　　id.

ἐπισκεπέντες vb 2nd aor pass part
　　　　masc nom pl . . . . ἐπισκέπτομαι

ἐπισκεπῇ vb 2nd aor pass subj 3rd pers sg　　id.

ἐπισκεπῆναι vb 2nd aor pass inf　　id.

ἐπισκεπήσεται vb fut pass ind 3rd pers sg　　id.

ἐπισκεπήσῃ vb fut pass ind 2nd pers sg　　id.

ἐπισκεπήτω vb 2nd aor pass impv 3rd pers sg　　id.

ἐπισκέπτεσθαι vb pres dep inf　　id.

ἐπισκέπτεται vb pres dep ind 3rd pers sg　　id.

ἐπισκέπτῃ vb pres dep ind 2nd pers sg,
　　　　pres dep subj 2nd pers sg　　id.

ἐπισκέπτηται vb pres dep subj 3rd pers sg　　id.

ἐπισκεπτόμενος vb pres dep part masc nom sg　　id.

ἐπισκέπτου vb pres dep impv 2nd pers sg　　id.

ἐπισκέπτωμαι vb pres m/p subj 1st pers sg　　id.

ἐπισκέπτονται vb pres m/p subj 3rd pers pl　　id.

ἐπισκευάζῃ vb pres act subj 3rd pers sg . . . . . ἐπισκευάζω

ἐπισκευάσαι vb 1st aor act inf　　id.

ἐπισκευασθῆναι vb 1st aor pass inf　　id.

ἐπισκεφθῇ vb 1st aor pass subj 3rd pers sg . . . ἐπισκέπτομαι

ἐπισκεφθήσεται vb fut pass ind 3rd pers sg　　id.

ἐπίσκεψαι vb 1st aor mid impv 2nd pers sg　　id.

ἐπισκεψάμενοι vb 1st aor mid part masc nom pl　　id.

ἐπισκέψασθαι vb 1st aor mid inf　　id.

ἐπισκέψασθε vb 1st aor mid impv 2nd pers pl　　id.

ἐπισκεψάσθω vb 1st aor mid impv 3rd pers sg　　id.

ἐπισκέψεται vb fut mid ind 3rd pers sg　　id.

ἐπισκέψεως noun fem gen sg . . . . ἐπίσκεψις

ἐπισκέψῃ vb 1st aor act subj 3rd pers sg,
　　　　fut mid ind 2nd pers sg . . . . ἐπισκέπτομαι

ἐπισκέψηται vb 1st aor mid subj 3rd pers sg　　id.

ἐπίσκεψιν noun fem acc sg . . . . ἐπίσκεψις

ἐπίσκεψις noun fem nom sg　　id.

ἐπισκέψομαι vb fut mid ind 1st pers sg . . . . . ἐπισκέπτομαι

ἐπισκεψόμεθα vb fut mid ind 1st pers pl　　id.

ἐπισκέψωμαι vb 1st aor mid subj 1st pers sg　　id.

ἐπισκέψωνται vb 1st aor mid subj 3rd pers pl　　id.

ἐπισκιάζει vb pres act ind 3rd pers sg . . . . ἐπισκιάζω

ἐπισκιάσει vb fut act ind 3rd pers sg　　id.

ἐπισκοπεῖν vb pres act inf . . . . ἐπισκοπέω

ἐπισκοπεῖται vb pres m/p ind 3rd pers sg　　id.

ἐπισκοπή noun fem nom sg

ἐπισκοπῇ noun fem dat sg . . . . ἐπισκοπή

ἐπισκοπήν noun fem acc sg　　id.

ἐπισκοπῆς noun fem gen sg　　id.

ἐπίσκοποι noun masc nom pl . . . . ἐπίσκοπος ἐπισκόποις noun masc dat pl . . . . ἐπίσκοπος

ἐπίσκοπος noun masc nom sg id.

ἐπισκόπου noun masc gen sg id.

ἐπισκόπους noun masc acc pl id.

ἐπισκόπων noun masc gen pl id.

ἐπισκοπῶν vb pres act part masc nom sg . . . . . . ἐπισκοπέω

ἐπίσπασαι vb 1st aor mid impv 2nd pers sg . . . . . ἐπισπάω

ἐπισπασάμενοι vb 1st aor mid part masc nom pl id.

ἐπισπάσασθαι vb 1st aor mid inf id.

ἐπισπᾶσθαι vb pres m/p inf id.

ἐπισπᾶσθε vb pres m/p impv 2nd pers pl id.

ἐπίσπαστρον noun neut nom and acc sg

ἐπισπασώμεθα vb 1st aor mid subj 1st pers pl . . . . ἐπισπάω

ἐπισπεύδοντες vb pres act part masc nom pl . . . ἐπισπεύδω

ἐπισπεύδων vb pres act part masc nom sg id.

ἐπισπλαγχνιζόμενος vb pres m/p part

       masc nom sg . . . . ἐπισπλαγχνίζω

ἐπισπουδαζομένη vb pres m/p part

       fem nom sg . . . . ἐπισπουδάζω

ἐπισπουδαστής noun masc nom sg

ἐπισπώμενοι vb pres m/p part masc nom pl . . . . . . ἐπισπάω

ἐπίσταμαι vb pres dep ind 1st pers sg

ἐπισταμένη vb pres dep part fem nom sg . . . . . . ἐπίσταμαι

ἐπιστάμενοι vb pres dep part masc nom pl id.

ἐπιστάμενον vb pres dep part masc acc sg id.

ἐπιστάμενος vb pres dep part masc nom sg id.

ἐπισταμένου vb pres dep part masc and neut gen sg id.

ἐπισταμένους vb pres dep part masc acc pl id.

ἐπισταμένῳ vb pres dep part masc and neut dat sg id.

ἐπισταμένων vb pres dep part gen pl id.

ἐπίστανται vb pres dep ind 3rd pers pl id.

ἐπίστασαι vb pres dep ind 2nd pers sg id.

ἐπίστασθαι vb pres dep inf id.

ἐπίστασθε vb pres dep ind 2nd pers pl id.

ἐπίσταται vb pres dep ind 3rd pers sg id.

ἐπιστάται noun masc nom pl . . . . ἐπιστάτης

ἐπιστάτας noun masc acc pl id.

ἐπιστάτην noun masc acc sg id.

ἐπιστάτης noun masc gen sg id.

ἐπιστατῶν noun masc gen pl id.

ἐπιστεύθη vb 1st aor pass ind 3rd pers sg . . . . πιστεύω

ἐπίστευον vb impf act ind 1st pers sg and 3rd pers pl id.

ἐπίστευσα vb 1st aor act ind 1st pers sg id.

ἐπίστευσαν vb 1st aor act ind 3rd pers pl id.

ἐπιστεύσατε vb 1st aor act ind 2nd pers pl id.

ἐπίστευσεν vb 1st aor act ind 3rd pers sg id.

ἐπίστῃ vb pres dep ind 2nd pers sg,

       pres dep subj 2nd pers sg . . . . ἐπίσταμαι

ἐπίστηθι vb 2nd aor pass impv 2nd pers sg . . . . ἐφίστημι

ἐπιστήμη noun fem nom sg

ἐπιστήμῃ noun fem dat sg . . . . ἐπιστήμη

ἐπιστήμην noun fem acc sg id.

ἐπιστήμης noun fem gen sg . . . . ἐπιστήμη

ἐπιστήμονας adj masc and fem acc pl . . . . ἐπιστήμων

ἐπιστήμονες adj masc and fem nom pl id.

ἐπιστήμων adj masc and fem nom sg id.

ἐπιστήριγμα noun neut nom and acc sg

ἐπιστηριζομένη vb pres m/p part fem nom sg . . ἐπιστηρίζω

ἐπιστηρισθῇ vb 1st aor pass subj 3rd pers sg id.

ἐπιστηρίσομαι vb fut mid ind 1st pers sg id.

ἐπιστηριχθήσομαι vb fut pass ind 1st pers sg id.

ἐπιστηριῶ vb fut act ind 1st pers sg id.

ἐπιστῇς vb 2nd aor act subj 2nd pers sg . . . . ἐφίστημι

ἐπιστῆσαι vb 1st aor act inf id.

ἐπιστήσατε vb 1st aor act impv 2nd pers pl id.

ἐπιστήσει vb fut act ind 3rd pers sg id.

ἐπιστήσεις vb fut act ind 2nd pers sg id.

ἐπιστήσεται vb fut mid ind 3rd pers sg id.

ἐπιστήσῃς vb 1st aor act subj 2nd pers sg id.

ἐπίστησθε vb pres dep subj 2nd pers pl . . . . ἐπίσταμαι

ἐπιστήσομεν vb fut act ind 1st pers pl . . . . ἐφίστημι

ἐπίστησον vb 1st aor act impv 2nd pers sg id.

ἐπιστήσονται vb fut m/p ind 3rd pers pl id.

ἐπιστήσουσιν vb fut act ind 3rd pers pl id.

ἐπιστήσω vb fut act ind 1st pers sg id.

ἐπιστοιβάσῃς vb 1st aor act subj 2nd pers sg . . ἐπιστοιβάζω

ἐπιστοιβάσουσιν vb fut act ind 3rd pers pl id.

ἐπιστολαί noun fem nom pl . . . . ἐπιστολή

ἐπιστολαῖς noun fem dat pl id.

ἐπιστολάς noun fem acc pl id.

ἐπιστολή noun fem nom sg id.

ἐπιστολήν noun fem acc sg id.

ἐπιστολῆς noun fem gen sg id.

ἐπιστολῶν noun fem gen pl id.

ἐπιστοποίει vb impf act ind 3rd pers sg . . . . πιστοποιέω

ἐπιστοποίησας vb 1st aor act ind 2nd pers sg id.

ἐπίστου vb impf act ind 3rd pers sg . . . . πιστόω

ἐπιστρατείας noun fem gen sg and acc pl . . . . ἐπιστρατεία

ἐπιστρατεῦσαι vb 1st aor act inf . . . . ἐπιστρατεύω

ἐπιστρατεύσαντα vb 1st aor act part masc acc sg id.

ἐπιστράτηγον noun masc acc sg . . . . ἐπιστράτηγος

ἐπιστραφείς vb 2nd aor pass part masc nom sg . ἐπιστρέφω

ἐπιστραφέντες vb 2nd aor pass part masc nom pl id.

ἐπιστραφῇ vb 2nd aor pass subj 3rd pers sg id.

ἐπιστραφῆναι vb 2nd aor pass inf id.

ἐπιστραφῆς vb 2nd aor pass subj 2nd pers sg id.

ἐπιστραφήσεσθε vb fut pass ind 2nd pers pl id.

ἐπιστραφήσεται vb fut pass ind 3rd pers sg id.

ἐπιστραφήσῃ vb fut pass ind 2nd pers sg id.

ἐπιστραφήσομαι vb fut pass ind 1st pers sg id.

ἐπιστραφησόμεθα vb fut pass ind 1st pers pl id.

ἐπιστραφήσονται vb fut pass ind 3rd pers pl id.

ἐπιστράφητε vb 2nd aor pass impv 2nd pers pl id.

ἐπιστραφῆτε vb 2nd aor pass subj 2nd pers pl id.

ἐπιστράφητι vb 2nd aor pass impv 2nd pers sg . ἐπιστρέφω	ἐπισυνάγαγε vb 2nd aor act impv 2nd pers sg . ἐπισυνάγω
ἐπιστραφήτω vb 2nd aor pass impv 3rd pers sg id.	ἐπισυναγαγεῖν vb 2nd aor act inf id.
ἐπίστρεφε vb pres act impv 2nd pers sg id.	ἐπισυναγόμενος vb pres m/p part masc nom sg id.
ἐπιστρέφει vb pres act ind 3rd pers sg id.	ἐπισυναγωγήν noun fem acc sg . . . . ἐπισυναγωγή
ἐπιστρέφειν vb pres inf act id.	ἐπισυνάγων vb pres act part masc nom sg . . . . . ἐπισυνάγω
ἐπιστρέφεις vb pres act ind 2nd pers sg id.	ἐπισυνάξει vb fut act ind 3rd pers sg id.
ἐπιστρέφετε vb pres act ind 2nd pers pl id.	ἐπισυνάξω vb fut act ind 1st pers sg id.
ἐπιστρεφέτω vb pres act impv 3rd pers sg id.	ἐπισυναχθέντα vb 1st aor pass part neut nom and acc pl id.
ἐπιστρέφῃ vb pres act subj 3rd pers sg id.	ἐπισυναχθέντας vb 1st aor pass part masc acc pl id.
ἐπιστρέφομεν vb pres act ind 1st pers pl id.	ἐπισυναχθέντες vb 1st aor pass part masc nom pl id.
ἐπιστρέφον vb pres act part neut nom and acc sg id.	ἐπισυναχθῆναι vb 1st aor pass inf id.
ἐπιστρέφοντα vb pres act part masc acc sg id.	ἐπισυναχθήσονται vb fut pass ind 3rd pers pl id.
ἐπιστρέφονται vb pres m/p ind 3rd pers pl id.	ἐπισυνεσταμένη vb perf mid part fem dat sg . ἐπισυνίστημι
ἐπιστρέφοντας vb pres act part masc acc pl id.	ἐπισυνέστησαν vb 2nd aor act ind 3rd pers pl id.
ἐπιστρέφοντες vb pres act part masc nom pl id.	ἐπισυνέστησεν vb 2nd aor act ind 3rd pers sg id.
ἐπιστρέφοντος vb pres act part masc and neut gen sg id.	ἐπισυνέχοντας vb pres act part masc acc pl . . . ἐπισυνέχω
ἐπιστρέφου vb pres m/p impv 2nd pers sg id.	ἐπισυνήγαγεν vb 2nd aor act ind 3rd pers sg . . . ἐπισυνάγω
ἐπιστρέφουσα vb pres act part fem nom sg id.	ἐπισυνηγμένα vb perf m/p part neut nom and acc pl id.
ἐπιστρεφούσῃ vb pres act part fem dat sg id.	ἐπισυνηγμένην vb perf m/p part fem acc sg id.
ἐπιστρέφουσι(ν) vb pres act ind 3rd pers pl,	ἐπισυνηγμένοι vb perf m/p part masc nom pl id.
pres act part masc and neut dat pl id.	ἐπισυνηγμένοις vb perf m/p part masc and neut dat pl id.
ἐπιστρέφων vb pres act part masc nom sg id.	ἐπισυνήγοντο vb impf m/p ind 3rd pers pl id.
ἐπιστρέψαι vb 1st aor act inf id.	ἐπισυνῆκται vb perf m/p ind 3rd pers sg id.
ἐπιστρέψαντα vb 1st aor act part masc acc sg id.	ἐπισυνῆχθαι vb perf m/p inf id.
ἐπιστρέψαντες vb 1st aor act part masc nom pl id.	ἐπισυνήχθη vb 1st aor pass ind 3rd pers sg id.
ἐπιστρέψαντος vb 1st aor act part masc and neut gen sg id.	ἐπισυνήχθησαν vb 1st aor pass ind 3rd pers pl id.
ἐπιστρέψας vb 1st aor act part masc nom sg id.	ἐπισυστάντες vb 1st aor act part
ἐπιστρέψατε vb 1st aor act impv 2nd pers pl id.	masc nom pl . . . . ἐπισυνίστημι
ἐπιστρεψάτω vb 1st aor act impv 3rd pers sg id.	ἐπισυστάσει noun fem dat sg . . . . ἐπισύστασις
ἐπιστρεψάτωσαν vb 1st aor act impv 3rd pers pl id.	ἐπισυστάσεις noun fem nom and acc pl id.
ἐπιστρέψει vb fut act ind 3rd pers sg id.	ἐπισυστάσης vb 2nd aor act part fem gen sg . ἐπισυνίστημι
ἐπιστρέψεις vb fut act ind 2nd pers sg id.	ἐπισύστασις noun fem nom sg
ἐπιστρέψῃ vb 1st aor act subj 3rd pers sg,	ἐπισυστήσῃ vb fut mid ind 2nd pers sg . . . . . ἐπισυνίστημι
fut mid ind 2nd pers sg id.	ἐπισυστήσονται vb fut mid ind 3rd pers pl id.
ἐπιστρέψῃς vb 1st aor act subj 2nd pers sg id.	ἐπισυστήσω vb fut act ind 1st pers sg id.
ἐπιστρέψητε vb 1st aor act subj 2nd pers pl id.	ἐπισύστητε vb 2nd aor act impv 2nd pers pl id.
ἐπιστρέψομεν vb fut act ind 1st pers pl id.	ἐπισυστρέφεσθαι vb pres m/p inf . . . . ἐπισυστρέφω
ἐπίστρεψον vb 1st aor act impv 2nd pers sg,	ἐπισυστρέψαι vb 1st aor act inf id.
fut act part neut nom and acc sg id.	ἐπισυστῶμεν vb 2nd aor act subj 1st pers pl . ἐπισυνίστημι
ἐπιστρέψουσιν vb fut act ind 3rd pers pl id.	ἐπισφαλεῖς adj masc and fem nom and acc pl . . . ἐπισφαλής
ἐπιστρέψω vb 1st aor act subj 1st pers sg,	ἐπισφαλῶς adverb
fut act ind 1st pers sg id.	ἐπισφραγίζουσιν vb pres act ind 3rd pers pl . . ἐπισφραγίζω
ἐπιστρέψωμεν vb 1st aor act subj 1st pers pl id.	ἐπισφράγισαι vb 1st aor mid impv 2nd pers sg id.
ἐπιστρέψωσιν vb 1st aor act subj 3rd pers pl id.	ἐπίσχες vb 2nd aor act impv 2nd pers sg . . . . ἐπέχω
ἐπιστροφάς noun fem acc pl . . . . ἐπιστροφή	ἐπίσχης vb 2nd aor act subj 2nd pers sg id.
ἐπιστροφή noun fem nom sg id.	ἐπίσχυσον vb 1st aor act part neut nom and acc sg . ἐπισχύω
ἐπιστροφῇ noun fem dat sg id.	ἐπισχύων vb pres act part masc nom sg id.
ἐπιστροφήν noun fem acc sg id.	ἐπίσχω vb 2nd aor act subj 1st pers sg . . . . ἐπέχω
ἐπιστροφῆς noun fem gen sg id.	ἐπίσχωμεν vb 2nd aor act subj 1st pers pl id.
ἐπιστώθη vb 1st aor pass ind 3rd pers sg . . . . πιστόω	ἐπισχών vb 2nd aor act part masc nom sg id.
ἐπιστώθησαν vb 1st aor pass ind 3rd pers pl id.	ἐπιταγαῖς noun fem dat pl . . . . ἐπιταγή
ἐπιστῶνται vb pres m/p subj 3rd pers pl . . . . . ἐπίσταμαι	ἐπιταγῇ noun fem dat sg id.

ἐπιταγῇ vb 2nd aor pass subj 3rd pers sg ...... ἐπιτάσσω

ἐπιταγήν noun fem acc sg .... ἐπιταγή

ἐπιτάγμασι noun neut dat pl .... ἐπίταγμα

ἐπιτάξαντος vb 1st aor act part

    masc and neut gen sg .... ἐπιτάσσω

ἐπιτάξατε vb 1st aor act impv 2nd pers pl id.

ἐπιταξάτω vb 1st aor act impv 3rd pers sg id.

ἐπίταξον vb 1st aor act impv 2nd pers sg id.

ἐπιταράσσωνται vb 1st aor mid subj

    3rd pers pl .... ἐπιταράσσω

ἐπίτασιν noun fem acc sg .... ἐπίτασις

ἐπίτασις noun fem nom sg id.

ἐπιτάσσειν vb pres act inf .... ἐπιτάσσω

ἐπιτάσσων vb pres act part masc nom sg id.

ἐπιταφίου noun neut gen sg .... ἐπιτάφιον

ἐπιτείνεται vb pres m/p ind 3rd pers sg ..... ἐπιτείνω

ἐπιτεινόμενος vb pres m/p part masc nom sg id.

ἐπιτείνουσα vb pres act part fem nom sg id.

ἐπιτέλει vb pres act impv 2nd pers sg ...... ἐπιτελέω

ἐπιτελεῖ vb pres act ind 3rd pers sg id.

ἐπιτελεῖν vb pres act inf id.

ἐπιτελεῖτε vb pres act ind 2nd pers pl id.

ἐπιτελέσαι vb 1st aor act inf id.

ἐπιτελέσει vb fut act ind 3rd pers sg id.

ἐπιτελέσεις vb fut act ind 2nd pers sg id.

ἐπιτελεσθῇ vb 1st aor pass subj 3rd pers sg id.

ἐπιτελεσθῆναι vb 1st aor pass inf id.

ἐπιτελεσθήσεται vb fut pass ind 3rd pers sg id.

ἐπιτελεσθήτω vb 1st aor pass impv 3rd pers sg id.

ἐπιτέλεσον vb 1st aor act impv 2nd pers sg id.

ἐπιτελέσουσιν vb fut act ind 3rd pers pl id.

ἐπιτελέσω vb fut act ind 1st pers sg id.

ἐπιτελούμενον vb pres m/p part masc acc sg,

    neut nom and acc sg id.

ἐπιτελοῦντες vb pres act part masc nom pl id.

ἐπιτελοῦσαν vb pres act part fem acc sg id.

ἐπιτελῶν vb pres act part masc nom sg id.

ἐπιτεμεῖν vb fut act inf .... ἐπιτέμνω

ἐπιτερπῆ adj masc and fem acc sg .... ἐπιτερπής

ἐπιτέτακται vb perf m/p ind 3rd pers sg ...... ἐπιτάσσω

ἐπιτεύξεται vb fut mid ind 3rd pers sg ..... ἐπιτυγχάνω

ἐπιτήδεια adj neut nom and acc pl .... ἐπιτήδειος

ἐπιτήδειοι adj masc nom pl id.

ἐπιτήδειος adj masc nom sg id.

ἐπιτηδείῳ adj masc and neut dat sg id.

ἐπιτηδεύει vb pres act ind 3rd pers sg .... ἐπιτηδεύω

ἐπιτήδευμα noun neut nom and acc sg id.

ἐπιτηδεύμασι noun neut dat pl .... ἐπιτήδευμα

ἐπιτηδεύματα noun neut nom and acc pl id.

ἐπιτηδευμάτων noun neut gen pl id.

ἐπιτηδεύσεις vb fut act ind 2nd pers sg ...... ἐπιτηδεύω

ἐπιτηρεῖν vb pres act inf .... ἐπιτηρέω

ἐπιτιθέμενα vb pres m/p part neut nom and acc pl ἐπιτίθημι

ἐπιτιθέμενοι vb pres act part masc nom pl id.

ἐπιτίθεσθε vb pres m/p ind 2nd pers pl id.

ἐπιτιθῇς vb pres act subj 2nd pers sg id.

ἐπιτίθησιν vb pres act ind 3rd pers sg id.

ἐπιτιθοῦσαν vb pres act part fem acc sg .... ἐπιτιθέω

ἐπιτίμα vb pres act impv 2nd pers sg .... ἐπιτιμάω

ἐπιτιμηθείς vb 1st aor pass part masc nom sg id.

ἐπιτιμῆσαι vb 1st aor act opt 3rd pers sg id.

ἐπιτιμήσει noun fem dat sg .... ἐπιτίμησις

ἐπιτιμήσετε vb fut act ind 2nd pers pl .... ἐπιτιμάω

ἐπιτιμήσεως noun fem gen sg .... ἐπιτίμησις

ἐπιτιμήσῃς vb 1st aor act subj 2nd pers sg ..... ἐπιτιμάω

ἐπιτίμησιν noun fem acc sg .... ἐπιτίμησις

ἐπιτίμησις noun fem nom sg id.

ἐπιτίμησον vb 1st aor act impv 2nd pers sg ..... ἐπιτιμάω

ἐπιτιμίαν noun fem acc sg .... ἐπιτιμία

ἐπιτιμίοις noun neut dat pl .... ἐπιτίμιον

ἐπιτίμοις adj masc and neut dat pl .... ἐπίτιμος

ἐπιτομῆς noun fem gen sg .... ἐπιτομή

ἐπιτρέχων vb pres act part masc nom sg ...... ἐπιτρέχω

ἐπιτρέψαντες vb 1st aor act part masc nom pl ... ἐπιτρέπω

ἐπιτρέψειεν vb 1st aor act opt 3rd pers sg id.

ἐπιτροπήν noun fem acc sg .... ἐπιτροπή

ἐπίτροπον noun masc acc sg .... ἐπίτροπος

ἐπίτροπος noun masc nom sg id.

ἐπιτυγχάνων vb pres act part masc nom sg ... ἐπιτυγχάνω

ἐπιτυχίας noun fem gen sg .... ἐπιτυχία

ἐπιφαίνεσθαι vb pres m/p inf .... ἐπιφαίνω

ἐπιφᾶναι vb 1st aor act opt 3rd pers sg id.

ἐπιφᾶναι vb 1st aor act inf id.

ἐπιφάνας vb 1st aor act part masc nom sg id.

ἐπιφανείᾳ noun fem dat sg .... ἐπιφάνεια

ἐπιφάνειαν noun fem acc sg id.

ἐπιφανείας noun fem gen sg and acc pl id.

ἐπιφανείσης vb 2nd aor pass part fem gen sg ..... ἐπιφαίνω

ἐπιφανέντος vb 2nd aor pass part masc and neut gen sg id.

ἐπιφανές adj neut nom and acc sg .... ἐπιφανής

ἐπιφανέστατοι superl adj masc nom pl id.

ἐπιφανῆ adj masc and fem acc sg, neut nom and acc pl id.

Ἐπιφανῆ pr noun masc acc sg .... Ἐπιφανής

ἐπιφανῇ vb 2nd aor pass subj 3rd pers sg ...... ἐπιφαίνω

ἐπιφάνηθι vb 2nd aor pass impv 2nd pers sg id.

ἐπιφανῆναι vb 2nd aor pass inf id.

Ἐπιφανης pr noun masc nom sg

ἐπιφανής adj masc and fem nom sg

ἐπιφανήσεται vb fut pass ind 3rd pers sg ...... ἐπιφαίνω

ἐπίφανον vb 1st aor act impv 2nd pers sg id.

ἐπιφανοῦμαι vb fut mid ind 1st pers sg id.

ἐπιφανοῦς adj gen sg .... ἐπιφανής

Ἐπιφανοῦς pr noun masc gen sg .... Ἐπιφανής

ἐπιφαύσκει vb pres act ind 3rd pers sg .... ἐπιφαύσκω

ἐπιφαύσκεται	vb pres m/p ind 3rd pers sg	ἐπιφαύσκω
ἐπιφαύσκοντα	vb pres act part masc acc sg	id.
ἐπιφερούσας	vb pres act part fem acc pl	ἐπιφέρω
ἐπιφέρω	vb pres act ind 1st pers sg	id.
ἐπιφημίζει	vb pres act ind 3rd pers sg	ἐπιφημίζω
ἐπιφημίσηται	vb 2nd aor mid subj 3rd pers sg	id.
Επιφι	pr noun	
ἐπιφυλλίδα	noun fem acc sg	ἐπιφυλλίς
ἐπιφυλλίδες	noun fem nom pl	id.
ἐπιφυλλιεῖ	vb fut act ind 3rd pers sg	ἐπιφυλλίζω
ἐπιφυλλίς	noun fem nom sg	
ἐπιφύλλισον	vb 1st aor act impv 2nd pers sg . .	ἐπιουλλίζω
ἐπιφυόμενος	vb pres m/p part masc nom sg	ἐπιφύω
ἐπιφυτευομένη	vb pres m/p part fem nom sg . . .	ἐπιφυτεύω
ἐπιφωνήσαντες	vb 1st aor act part masc nom pl . .	ἐπιφωνέω
ἐπιφωνούντων	vb pres act part masc and neut gen pl	id.
ἐπίχαιρε	vb pres act impv 2nd pers sg	ἐπιχαίρω
ἐπιχαίρει	vb pres act ind 3rd pers sg	id.
ἐπιχαιρέτω	vb pres act impv 3rd pers sg	id.
ἐπιχαίροντες	vb pres act part masc nom pl	id.
ἐπιχαίρων	vb pres act part masc nom sg	id.
ἐπιχαρείησαν	vb 2nd aor pass opt 3rd pers pl	id.
ἐπιχαρεῖται	vb fut mid ind 3rd pers sg	id.
ἐπιχαρέντες	vb 2nd aor pass part masc nom pl	id.
ἐπιχαρῇ	vb 2nd aor pass subj 3rd pers sg	id.
ἐπιχαρής	adj masc and fem nom sg	
ἐπιχαρῆς	vb 2nd aor pass subj 2nd pers sg	ἐπιχαίρω
ἐπίχαρμα	noun neut nom and acc sg	
ἐπιχαρούμεθα	vb fut mid ind 1st pers pl	ἐπιχαίρω
ἐπιχαροῦνται	vb fut mid ind 3rd pers pl	id.
ἐπίχαρτος	adj masc and fem nom sg	
ἐπιχαρῶσιν	vb 2nd aor pass subj 3rd pers pl	ἐπιχαίρω
ἐπιχεεῖ	vb fut act ind 3rd pers sg	ἐπιχέω
ἐπιχεεῖς	vb fut act ind 2nd pers sg	id.
ἐπιχέετε	vb pres act ind 2nd pers pl	id.
ἐπίχειρα	noun neut nom and acc pl	ἐπίχειρον
ἐπιχειρεῖ	vb pres act ind 3rd pers sg	ἐπιχειρέω
ἐπιχειρεῖτε	vb pres act ind 2nd pers pl	id.
ἐπιχειρήμασι	noun neut dat pl	ἐπιχείρημα
ἐπιχειρήσας	vb 1st aor act part masc nom sg	ἐπιχειρέω
ἐπιχειρήσῃ	vb 1st aor act subj 3rd pers sg	id.
ἐπίχειρον	noun neut nom and acc sg	
ἐπιχειροῦντες	vb pres act part masc nom pl	ἐπιχειρέω
ἐπιχειροῦντι	vb pres act part masc and neut dat sg	id.
ἐπιχειροῦσι(ν)	vb pres act ind 3rd pers pl	id.
ἐπιχείρῳ	noun masc dat sg	ἐπίχειρον
ἐπιχεόντων	vb pres act part masc and neut gen pl . . .	ἐπιχέω
ἐπιχορηγῇ	vb pres act subj 3rd pers sg	ἐπιχορηγέω
ἐπιχυθῇ	vb 1st aor pass subj 3rd pers sg	ἐπιχέω
ἐπιχυθήσονται	vb fut pass ind 3rd pers pl	id.
ἐπιχύσεως	noun fem gen sg	ἐπίχυσις
ἐπιχωρηθῇ	vb 1st aor pass subj 3rd pers sg	ἐπιχωρέω
ἐπιχώρησιν	noun fem acc sg	ἐπιχώρησις
ἐπλαγίασαν	vb 1st aor act ind 3rd pers pl	πλαγιάζω
ἐπλανᾶτο	vb impf m/p ind 3rd pers sg	πλανάω
ἐπλανήθη	vb 1st aor pass ind 3rd pers sg	id.
ἐπλανήθημεν	vb 1st aor pass ind 1st pers pl	id.
ἐπλανήθην	vb 1st aor pass ind 1st pers sg	id.
ἐπλανήθησαν	vb 1st aor pass ind 3rd pers pl	id.
ἐπλάνησαν	vb 1st aor act ind 3rd pers pl	id.
ἐπλάνησας	vb 1st aor act ind 2nd pers sg	id.
ἐπλάνησεν	vb 1st aor act ind 3rd pers sg	id.
ἐπλανῶντο	vb impf m/p ind 3rd pers pl	id.
ἔπλασα	vb 1st aor act ind 1st pers sg	πλάσσω
ἔπλασεν	vb 1st aor act ind 3rd pers pl	id.
ἔπλασας	vb 1st aor act ind 2nd pers sg	id.
ἐπλάσατο	vb 1st aor mid ind 3rd pers sg	id.
ἔπλοσεν	vb 1st aor act ind 3rd pers sg	id.
ἐπλάσθη	vb 1st aor pass ind 3rd pers sg	id.
ἐπλάτυναν	vb 1st aor act ind 3rd pers pl	πλατύνω
ἐπλάτυνας	vb 1st aor act ind 2nd pers sg	id.
ἐπλάτυνεν	vb impf act ind 3rd pers sg,	
	1st aor act ind 3rd pers sg	id.
ἐπλατύνθη	vb 1st aor pass ind 3rd pers sg	id.
ἐπλατύνθησαν	vb 1st aor pass ind 3rd pers pl	id.
ἐπλεόνασαν	vb 1st aor act ind 3rd pers pl	πλεονάζω
ἐπλεόνασας	vb 1st aor act ind 2nd pers sg	id.
ἐπλεόνασεν	vb 1st aor act ind 3rd pers sg	id.
ἐπλεονάσθησαν	vb 1st aor pass ind 3rd pers pl	id.
ἔπλευσεν	vb 1st aor act ind 3rd pers sg	πλέω
ἐπλήγη	vb 2nd aor pass ind 3rd pers sg	πλήσσω
ἐπλήγην	vb 2nd aor pass ind 1st pers sg	id.
ἐπλήγησαν	vb 2nd aor pass ind 3rd pers pl	id.
ἐπλήθυνα	vb 1st aor act ind 1st pers sg	πληθύνω
ἐπληθύναμεν	vb 1st aor act ind 1st pers pl	id.
ἐπλήθυνεν	vb 1st aor act ind 3rd pers pl	id.
ἐπλήθυνας	vb 1st aor act ind 2nd pers sg	id.
ἐπληθύνατε	vb 1st aor act ind 2nd pers pl	id.
ἐπλήθυνεν	vb impf act ind 3rd pers sg,	
	1st aor act ind 3rd pers sg	id.
ἐπληθύνετο	vb impf m/p ind 3rd pers sg	id.
ἐπληθύνθη	vb 1st aor pass ind 3rd pers sg	id.
ἐπληθύνθης	vb 1st aor pass ind 2nd pers sg	id.
ἐπληθύνθησαν	vb 1st aor pass ind 3rd pers pl	id.
ἐπλήθυνον	vb impf act ind 3rd pers pl	id.
ἐπλημμέλησα	vb 1st aor act ind 1st pers sg	πλημμελέω
ἐπλημμελήσαμεν	vb 1st aor act ind 1st pers pl	id.
ἐπλημμέλησαν	vb 1st aor act ind 3rd pers pl	id.
ἐπλημμελήσατε	vb 1st aor act ind 2nd pers pl	id.
ἐπλημμελησεν	vb 1st aor act ind 3rd pers sg	id.
ἐπλήρου	vb impf act ind 3rd pers sg	πληρόω
ἐπληροφορήθη	vb 1st aor pass ind 3rd pers sg .	πληροφορέω
ἐπληρώθη	vb 1st aor pass ind 3rd pers sg	πληρόω
ἐπληρώθην	vb 1st aor pass ind 1st pers sg	id.

ἐπληρώθησαν   vb 1st aor pass ind 3rd pers pl ...... πληρόω
ἐπλήρωσα   vb 1st aor act ind 1st pers sg   id.
ἐπλήρωσαν   vb 1st aor act ind 3rd pers pl   id.
ἐπλήρωσας   vb 1st aor act ind 2nd pers sg   id.
ἐπληρώσατε   vb 1st aor act ind 2nd pers pl   id.
ἐπλήρωσεν   vb 1st aor act ind 3rd pers sg   id.
ἔπλησα   vb 1st aor act ind 1st pers sg .... πίμπλημι
ἐπλήσαμεν   vb 1st aor act ind 1st pers pl   id.
ἔπλησαν   vb 1st aor act ind 3rd pers pl   id.
ἔπλησας   vb 1st aor act ind 2nd pers sg   id.
ἔπλησε(ν)   vb 1st aor act ind 3rd pers sg   id.
ἐπλήσθη   vb 1st aor pass ind 3rd pers sg   id.
ἐπλήσθημεν   vb 1st aor pass ind 1st pers pl   id.
ἐπλήσθην   vb 1st aor pass ind 1st pers sg   id.
ἐπλήσθησαν   vb 1st aor pass ind 3rd pers pl   id.
ἐπλούτησαν   vb 1st aor act ind 3rd pers pl .... πλουτέω
ἐπλούτησεν   vb 1st aor act ind 3rd pers sg   id.
ἐπλούτισα   vb 1st aor act ind 1st pers sg .... πλουτίζω
ἐπλούτισας   vb 1st aor act ind 2nd pers sg   id.
ἐπλούτισεν   vb 1st aor act ind 3rd pers sg   id.
ἔπλυναν   vb 1st aor act ind 3rd pers pl .... πλύνω
ἐπλύναντο   vb 1st aor mid ind 3rd pers pl   id.
ἔπλυνεν   vb impf act ind 3rd pers sg,
    1st aor act ind 3rd pers sg   id.
ἐπνευματοφορεῖτο   vb impf m/p ind
    3rd pers sg .... πνευματοφορέω
ἔπνευσεν   vb 1st aor act ind 3rd pers sg .... πνέω
ἔπνιγεν   vb 1st aor act ind 3rd pers sg .... πνίγω
ἐποζέσει   vb fut act ind 3rd pers sg .... ἐπόζω
ἐποίει   vb impf act ind 3rd pers sg .... ποιέω
ἐποίεις   vb impf act ind 2nd pers sg   id.
ἐποιεῖτε   vb impf act ind 2nd pers pl   id.
ἐποιεῖτο   vb impf m/p ind 3rd pers sg   id.
ἐποιήθη   vb 1st aor pass ind 3rd pers sg   id.
ἐποίησα   vb 1st aor act ind 1st pers sg   id.
ἐποιήσαμεν   vb 1st aor act ind 1st pers pl   id.
ἐποίησαν   vb 1st aor act ind 3rd pers pl   id.
ἐποίησαν   see ἐποίησαν
ἐποιήσαντο   vb 1st aor mid ind 3rd pers pl   id.
ἐποίησας   vb 1st aor act ind 2nd pers sg   id.
ἐποιήσατε   vb 1st aor act ind 2nd pers pl   id.
ἐποιήσατο   vb 1st aor mid ind 3rd pers sg   id.
ἐποίησε(ν)   vb 1st aor act ind 3rd pers sg   id.
ἐποιήσω   vb 1st aor mid ind 2nd pers sg   id.
ἐποικίοις   noun neut dat pl .... ἐποίκιον
ἐποίμαινεν   vb impf act ind 3rd pers sg .... ποιμαίνω
ἐποίμαινον   vb impf act ind 1st pers sg   id.
ἐποίμανεν   vb 1st aor act ind 3rd pers sg   id.
ἐποίουν   vb impf act ind 1st pers sg and 3rd pers pl ... ποιέω
ἐποιοῦντο   vb impf m/p ind 3rd pers pl   id.
ἐποιοῦσαν   vb impf act ind 3rd pers pl   id.
ἐποίσει   vb fut act ind 3rd pers sg .... ἐπιφέρω

ἐποίσω   vb fut act ind 1st pers sg .... ἐπιφέρω
ἐπολέμει   vb impf act ind 3rd pers sg .... πολεμέω
ἐπολέμεις   vb impf act ind 2nd pers sg   id.
ἐπολέμησα   vb 1st aor act ind 1st pers sg   id.
ἐπολεμήσαμεν   vb 1st aor act ind 1st pers pl   id.
ἐπολέμησαν   vb 1st aor act ind 3rd pers pl   id.
ἐπολέμησε(ν)   vb 1st aor act ind 3rd pers sg   id.
ἐπολεμοτρόφει   vb impf act ind 3rd pers sg . πολεμοτροφέω
ἐπολέμουν   vb impf act ind 3rd pers pl .... πολεμέω
ἐπολέμωσεν   vb 1st aor act ind 3rd pers sg   id.
ἐπολιόρκει   vb impf act ind 3rd pers sg .... πολιορκέω
ἐπολιόρκησεν   vb 1st aor act ind 3rd pers sg   id.
ἐπολιόρκουν   vb impf act ind 3rd pers pl   id.
ἐπολυώρησας   vb 1st aor act ind 2nd pers sg .... πολυωρέω
ἐπονείδιστοι   adj masc and fem nom pl ..... ἐπονείδιστος
ἐπονείδιστος   adj masc and fem nom sg   id.
ἐπονειδίστους   adj masc and fem acc pl   id.
ἐπόνεσα   vb 1st aor act ind 1st pers sg .... πονέω
ἐπόνεσαν   vb 1st aor act ind 3rd pers pl   id.
ἐπονέσατε   vb 1st aor act ind 2nd pers pl   id.
ἐπόνεσεν   vb 1st aor act ind 3rd pers sg   id.
ἐπονηρεύοντο   vb impf dep ind 3rd pers pl .. πονηρεύομαι
ἐπονηρεύσαντο   vb 1st aor mid ind 3rd pers pl   id.
ἐπονηρεύσασθε   vb 1st aor mid ind 2nd pers pl   id.
ἐπονηρεύσατο   vb 1st aor mid ind 3rd pers sg   id.
ἐπονηρεύσω   vb 1st aor mid ind 2nd pers sg   id.
ἐπονομάζουσιν   vb pres act ind 3rd pers pl .... ἐπονομάζω
ἐπονομάσαι   vb 1st aor act inf   id.
ἐπονομάσας   vb 1st aor act part masc nom sg   id.
ἐπονομάσω   vb 1st aor act subj 1st pers sg   id.
ἐποξύνειν   vb pres act inf .... ἐποξύνω
ἔποπα   noun masc acc sg .... ἔποψ
ἔποπος   noun masc gen sg   id.
ἐπόπτην   noun masc acc sg .... ἐπόπτης
ἐπόπτης   noun masc nom sg   id.
ἐποπτική   adj fem nom sg .... ἐποπτικός
ἐπόπτου   noun masc gen sg .... ἐπόπτης
ἐποργισθήσεται   vb fut pass ind 3rd pers sg .. ἐποργίζομαι
ἐπορεύεσθε   vb impf dep ind 2nd pers pl ...... πορεύομαι
ἐπορεύετο   vb impf dep ind 3rd pers sg   id.
ἐπορεύθη   vb 1st aor pass ind 3rd pers sg   id.
ἐπορεύθημεν   vb 1st aor pass ind 1st pers pl   id.
ἐπορεύθην   vb 1st aor pass ind 1st pers sg   id.
ἐπορεύθης   vb 1st aor pass ind 2nd pers sg   id.
ἐπορεύθησαν   vb 1st aor pass ind 3rd pers pl   id.
ἐπορεύθητε   vb 1st aor pass ind 2nd pers pl   id.
ἐπορευόμεθα   vb impf dep ind 1st pers pl   id.
ἐπορευόμην   vb impf dep ind 1st pers sg   id.
ἐπορεύοντο   vb impf dep ind 3rd pers pl   id.
ἐπορεύου   vb impf dep ind 2nd pers sg   id.
ἐπόρθησεν   vb 1st aor act ind 3rd pers sg .... πορθέω
ἐπόρνευον   vb impf act ind 3rd pers pl .... πορνεύω

ἐπόρνευσαν vb 1st aor act ind 3rd pers pl . . . . . . πορνεύω

ἐπόρνευσας vb 1st aor act ind 2nd pers sg		id.

ἐπόρνευσεν vb 1st aor act ind 3rd pers sg		id.

ἐπόστρεψεν see ἐπέστρεψεν

ἐπότιζεν vb impf act ind 3rd pers sg . . . . ποτίζω

ἐποτίζετε vb impf act ind 2nd pers pl		id.

ἐπότιζον vb impf act ind 3rd pers pl		id.

ἐπότισα vb 1st aor act ind 1st pers sg		id.

ἐπότισαν vb 1st aor act ind 3rd pers pl		id.

ἐπότισας vb 1st aor act ind 2nd pers sg		id.

ἐπότισεν vb 1st aor act ind 3rd pers sg		id.

ἐποτρύνοντες vb pres act part masc nom pl . . . . . ἐποτρύνω

ἐποτρύνοντος vb pres act part masc and neut gen sg		id.

ἐπουράνιε adj masc and fem voc sg . . . . ἐπουράνιος

ἐπουράνιον adj acc sg, neut nom sg		id.

ἐπουρανίου adj gen sg		id.

ἐπόψεται vb fut mid ind 3rd pers sg . . . . ἐφοράω

ἐπόψῃ vb fut mid ind 2nd pers sg		id.

ἐπόψομαι vb fut mid ind 1st pers sg		id.

ἐπόψονται vb fut mid ind 3rd pers pl		id.

ἐπραγματευόμην vb impf dep ind

      1st pers sg . . . . πραγματεύομαι

ἐπραγματεύσατο vb 1st aor mid ind 3rd pers sg		id.

ἐπράθη vb 1st aor pass ind 3rd pers sg . . . . πιπράσκω

ἐπράθημεν vb 1st aor pass ind 1st pers pl		id.

ἐπράθησαν vb 1st aor pass ind 3rd pers pl		id.

ἐπράθητε vb 1st aor pass ind 2nd pers pl		id.

ἔπραξα vb 1st aor act ind 1st pers sg . . . . πράσσω

ἔπραξαν vb 1st aor act ind 3rd pers pl		id.

ἔπραξας vb 1st aor act ind 2nd pers sg		id.

ἔπραξεν vb 1st aor act ind 3rd pers sg		id.

ἔπρασσε vb impf act ind 3rd pers sg		id.

ἔπραττεν vb impf act ind 3rd pers sg . . . . πράττω

ἔπραττον vb impf act ind 3rd pers pl		id.

ἔπρεπεν vb impf act ind 3rd pers sg . . . . πρέπω

ἐπρίατο vb 1st aor mid ind 3rd pers sg . . . . πρίαμαι

ἔπριζον vb impf act ind 3rd pers pl . . . . πρίζω

ἐπρονομεύθησαν vb 1st aor pass ind

      3rd pers pl . . . . προνομεύω

ἐπρονομεύσαμεν vb 1st aor act ind 1st pers pl		id.

ἐπρονόμευσαν vb 1st aor act ind 3rd pers pl		id.

ἐπρονόμευσε(ν) vb 1st aor act ind 3rd pers sg		id.

ἐπροφήτευον vb impf act ind 3rd pers pl . . . . . . προφητεύω

ἐπροφήτευσα vb 1st aor act ind 1st pers sg		id.

ἐπροφήτευσαν vb 1st aor act ind 3rd pers pl		id.

ἐπροφήτευσας vb 1st aor act ind 2nd pers sg		id.

ἐπροφήτευσεν vb 1st aor act ind 3rd pers sg		id.

ἐπρωτοβάθρει vb impf act ind 3rd pers sg . . . πρωτοβαθρέω

ἑπτά indecl number

ἑπταετῆ adj masc and fem acc sg,

     neut nom and acc pl . . . . ἑπταετής

ἐπταίκασιν vb perf act ind 3rd pers pl . . . . πταίω

ἐπταικώς vb perf act part masc nom sg . . . . πταίω

ἔπταισαν vb 1st aor act ind 3rd pers pl		id.

ἔπταισεν vb 1st aor act ind 3rd pers sg		id.

ἑπτακαίδεκα indecl number

ἑπτακοιδέκατος adj masc nom sg

ἑπτακαιδεκάτῳ adj masc and neut dat sg . ἑπτακαιδέκατος

ἑπτάκι adverb . . . . ἑπτάκις

ἑπτάκις adverb

ἑπτακισχίλια adj neut nom and acc pl . . . . ἑπτακισχίλιοι

ἑπτακισχιλίαν adj fem acc sg . . . . ἑπτακισχίλιος

ἑπτακισχίλιοι adj masc nom pl

ἑπτακισχιλίους adj masc acc pl . . . . ἑπτακισχίλιοι

ἑπτακόσια adj neut nom and acc pl . . . . ἑπτακόσιοι

ἑπτακόσιαι adj fem nom pl		id.

ἑπτακόσιοι adj masc nom pl		id.

ἑπτακοσίους adj masc acc pl		id.

ἑπτάμηνον noun fem acc sg . . . . ἑπτάμηνος

ἑπταμήνῳ noun fem dat sg		id.

ἑπταμήτωρ noun fem nom sg

ἑπταπλάσια adj neut nom and acc pl . . . . . . ἑπταπλάσιος

ἑπταπλάσιον adj masc acc sg, neut nom and acc sg		id.

ἑπταπλασίονα adj neut nom and acc pl . . . . ἑπταπλασίων

ἑπταπλασίως adverb

ἑπτάπυργος adj masc and fem nom sg

ἐπτερνίκαμεν vb perf act ind 1st pers pl . . . . πτερνίζω

ἐπτέρνικεν vb perf act ind 3rd pers sg		id.

ἐπτέρνισεν vb 1st aor act ind 3rd pers sg		id.

ἔπτη vb 2nd aor mid ind 3rd pers sg . . . . πέτομαι

ἔπτηξαν vb 1st aor act ind 3rd pers pl . . . . πτήσσω

ἔπτηξεν vb 1st aor act ind 3rd pers sg		id.

ἐπτοεῖτο vb impf m/p ind 3rd pers sg . . . . πτοέω

ἐπτοήθη vb 1st aor pass ind 3rd pers sg		id.

ἐπτοήθησαν vb 1st aor pass ind 3rd pers pl		id.

ἐπτόηται vb perf m/p ind 3rd pers sg		id.

ἐπτωχεύσαμεν vb 1st aor act ind 1st pers pl . . . . . πτωχεύω

ἐπτώχευσαν vb 1st aor act ind 3rd pers pl		id.

ἐπτώχευσεν vb 1st aor act ind 3rd pers sg		id.

ἐπυνθάνετο vb impf dep ind 3rd pers sg . . . . . πυνθάνομαι

ἐπυνθανόμεθα vb impf dep ind 1st pers pl		id.

ἐπυρρώθησαν vb 1st aor pass ind 3rd pers pl . . . πυρρόομαι

ἐπύρωσας vb 1st aor act ind 2nd pers sg . . . . πυρόω

ἐπύροσεν vb 1st aor act ind 3rd pers sg		id.

ἐπώζεσεν vb 1st aor act ind 3rd pers sg . . . . ἐπόζω

ἐπώλει vb impf act ind 3rd pers sg . . . . πωλέω

ἐπώλουν vb impf act ind 3rd pers pl		id.

ἐπωμίδα noun fem acc sg . . . . ἐπωμίς

ἐπωμίδας noun fem acc pl		id.

ἐπωμίδες noun fem nom pl		id.

ἐπωμίδος noun fem gen sg		id.

ἐπωμίδων noun fem gen pl		id.

ἐπωνόμασαν vb 1st aor act ind 3rd pers pl . . . . . ἐπονομάζω

ἐπωνόμασεν vb 1st aor act ind 3rd pers sg		id.

ἐπωνομάσθη vb 1st aor pass ind 3rd pers sg . . . . ἐπονομάζω

ἐπωνύμοις noun fem dat pl . . . . ἐπώνυμος

ἐπώπιον see ἐνώπιον

ἐπώργισται vb perf dep ind 3rd pers sg . . . . . ἐποργίζομαι

ἐπωρύοντο vb impf dep ind 3rd pers pl . . . . . . ἐπωρύομαι

Εραηλ pr noun

ἐράσθητι vb 1st aor pass impv 2nd pers sg . . . . ἐράω

ἐρασταί noun masc nom pl . . . . ἐραστής

ἐρασταῖς noun masc dat pl   id.

ἐραστάς noun masc acc pl   id.

ἐραστής noun masc nom sg   id.

ἐραστῶν noun masc gen pl   id.

ἐραυνήσεις vb fut act ind 2nd pers sg . . . . ἐραυνάω

ἔργα noun neut nom and acc pl . . . . ἔργον

ἐργᾷ vb fut mid ind 2nd pers sg . . . . ἐργάζομαι

εργαβ translit

ἐργάζεσθαι vb pres dep inf . . . . ἐργάζομαι

ἐργάζεσθε vb pres dep impv 2nd pers pl,
          pres dep ind 2nd pers pl   id.

ἐργαζέσθω vb pres dep impv 3rd pers sg   id.

ἐργαζέσθωσαν vb pres dep impv 3rd pers pl   id.

ἐργάζεται vb pres dep ind 3rd pers sg   id.

ἐργάζῃ vb pres dep ind 2nd pers sg   id.

ἐργάζομαι vb pres dep ind 1st pers sg   id.

ἐργαζομένη vb pres dep part fem nom sg   id.

ἐργαζομένης vb pres dep part fem gen sg   id.

ἐργαζόμενοι vb pres dep part masc nom pl   id.

ἐργαζομένοις vb pres dep part masc and neut dat pl   id.

ἐργαζόμενον vb pres dep part masc acc sg,
          neut nom and acc sg   id.

ἐργαζόμενος vb pres dep part masc nom sg   id.

ἐργαζομένους vb pres dep part masc acc pl   id.

ἐργαζομένων vb pres dep part gen pl   id.

ἐργάζου vb pres dep impv 2nd pers sg   id.

ἐργαλεῖα noun neut nom and acc pl . . . . ἐργαλεῖον

ἔργασαι vb 1st aor mid impv 2nd pers sg . . . . . . ἐργάζομαι

ἐργασάμενος vb 1st aor mid part masc nom sg   id.

ἐργάσασθαι vb 1st aor mid inf   id.

ἐργάσασθε vb 1st aor mid impv 2nd pers pl   id.

ἐργάσησθε vb 1st aor mid subj 2nd pers pl   id.

ἐργάσηται vb 1st aor mid subj 3rd pers sg   id.

ἐργασθήσεται vb fut pass ind 3rd pers sg   id.

ἐργασία noun fem nom sg

ἐργασίᾳ noun fem dat sg . . . . ἐργασία

ἐργασίαι noun fem nom pl   id.

ἐργασίαν noun fem acc sg   id.

ἐργασίας noun fem gen sg and acc pl   id.

ἐργασίμη adj fem dat sg . . . . ἐργάσιμος

ἐργασίμῳ adj masc and neut dat sg   id.

ἐργάται noun masc nom pl . . . . ἐργάτης

ἐργᾶται vb fut mid ind 3rd pers sg . . . . ἐργάζομαι

ἐργατειῶν noun fem gen pl . . . . ἐργατεία

ἐργατεύεσθαι vb pres dep inf . . . . ἐργατεύομαι

ἐργάτης noun masc nom sg

ἐργάτις noun fem nom sg

ἐργάτου noun masc gen sg . . . . ἐργάτης

ἐργοδιῶκται noun masc nom pl . . . . ἐργοδιώκτης

ἐργοδιώκταις noun masc dat pl   id.

ἐργοδιώκτας noun masc acc pl   id.

ἐργοδιωκτοῦντες vb pres act part
          masc nom pl . . . . ἐργοδιωκτέω

ἐργοδιωκτῶν noun masc gen pl . . . . ἐργοδιώκτης

ἔργοις noun neut dat pl . . . . ἔργον

ἐργολαβίας noun fem gen sg and acc pl . . . . . ἐργολαβία

ἔργον noun neut nom and acc sg

ἔργου noun neut gen sg . . . . ἔργον

ἔργῳ noun neut dat sg   id.

ἔργων noun neut gen pl   id.

ἐργῶνται vb fut mid ind 3rd pers pl . . . . ἐργάζομαι

ἐρεᾶ adj fem acc sg, neut nom and acc pl . . . . ἐρεοῦς

Ερεβ pr noun

Ερεγαβα pr noun

ἐρεθίζει vb pres act ind 3rd pers sg . . . . ἐρεθίζω

ἐρεθίζειν vb pres act inf   id.

ἐρεθισθείς vb 1st aor pass part masc nom sg   id.

ἐρεθισθήσεται vb fut pass ind 3rd pers sg   id.

ἐρεθισμόν noun masc acc sg . . . . ἐρεθισμός

ἐρεθισμῷ noun masc dat sg   id.

ἐρεθιστής adj masc nom sg . . . . ἐρεθιστής

ἐρεῖ vb fut act ind 3rd pers sg . . . . εἶπον

ἐρείδει vb pres act ind 3rd pers sg . . . . ἐρείδω

ἐρείδεται vb pres m/p ind 3rd pers sg   id.

ἐρείδετε vb pres act ind 2nd pers pl   id.

ἐρειδέτω vb pres act impv 3rd pers sg   id.

ἐρειδόμενος vb pres m/p part masc nom sg   id.

ἐρείδονται vb pres m/p ind 3rd pers pl   id.

ἐρεῖς vb fut act ind 2nd pers sg . . . . εἶπον

ἐρείσαι vb 1st aor act opt 3rd pers sg . . . . ἐρείδω

ἐρείσει vb fut act ind 3rd pers sg   id.

ἔρεισμα noun neut nom and acc sg

ἐρεῖτε vb fut act ind 2nd pers pl . . . . εἶπον

Ερεμμων pr noun

ἐρεοῖς adj masc and neut dat pl . . . . ἐρεοῦς

ἐρεοῦ adj masc and neut gen sg   id.

ἐρεύγεται vb pres dep ind 3rd pers sg . . . . ἐρεύγομαι

ἐρευγόμενος vb pres dep part masc nom sg   id.

ἔρευνα noun fem nom sg

ἐρευνᾷ vb pres act ind 3rd pers sg . . . . ἐρευνάω

ἐρευνήσατε vb 1st aor act impv 2nd pers pl   id.

ἐρευνήσετε vb fut act ind 2nd pers pl   id.

ἐρευνήσουσιν vb fut act ind 3rd pers pl   id.

ἐρευνήσωσιν vb 1st aor act subj 3rd pers pl   id.

ἐρευνῶν vb pres act part masc nom sg   id.

ἐρεύξεται vb fut dep ind 3rd pers sg . . . . ἐρεύγομαι

Ερεω pr noun

ἐρεῷ adj masc and neut dat sg . . . . ἐρεοῦς

ἔρημα adj neut nom and acc pl . . . . ἔρημος

ἐρημίᾳ noun fem dat sg . . . . ἐρημία

ἐρημίαν noun fem acc sg   id.

ἐρημίας noun fem gen sg   id.

ἐρημικοῖς adj masc and neut dat pl . . . . ἐρημικός

ἐρημικῷ adj masc and neut dat sg   id.

ἐρημίτῃ noun masc dat sg . . . . ἐρημίτης

ἔρημοι adj masc and fem nom pl,

         noun fem nom pl . . . . ἔρημος

ἐρήμοις adj dat pl, noun fem dat pl   id.

ἔρημον adj acc sg and neut nom sg,

         noun fem acc sg   id.

ἔρημος adj masc and fem nom sg,

         noun fem nom sg   id.

ἐρήμου adj gen sg, noun fem gen sg   id.

ἐρημουμένη vb pres m/p part fem nom sg . . . . ἐρημόω

ἐρημοῦντα vb pres act part masc acc sg   id.

ἐρήμους adj masc and fem acc pl,

         noun fem acc pl . . . . ἔρημος

ἐρημοῦσα vb pres act part fem nom sg . . . . ἐρημόω

ἐρημοῦσιν vb pres act ind 3rd pers pl   id.

ἐρήμῳ adj dat sg, noun fem dat sg . . . . ἔρημος

ἐρημωθείς vb 1st aor pass part masc nom sg . . . . . . ἐρημόω

ἐρημωθῇ vb 1st aor pass subj 3rd pers sg   id.

ἐρημωθῆναι vb 1st aor pass inf   id.

ἐρημωθήσεται vb fut pass ind 3rd pers sg   id.

ἐρημωθήσῃ vb fut pass ind 2nd pers sg   id.

ἐρημωθήσονται vb fut pass ind 3rd pers pl   id.

ἐρημωθῶσιν vb 1st aor pass subj 3rd pers pl   id.

ἐρήμων adj gen pl, noun fem gen pl . . . . ἔρημος

ἐρημῶσαι vb 1st aor act inf . . . . ἐρημόω

ἐρημώσαντες vb 1st aor act part masc nom pl   id.

ἐρημώσει vb fut act ind 3rd pers sg   id.

ἐρημώσεων noun fem gen pl . . . . ἐρήμωσις

ἐρημώσεως noun fem gen sg   id.

ἐρήμωσιν noun fem acc sg   id.

ἐρήμωσις noun fem nom sg   id.

ἐρημώσουσιν vb fut act ind 3rd pers sg . . . . ἐρημόω

ἐρημώσω vb fut act ind 1st pers sg   id.

ἔρια noun neut nom and acc pl . . . . ἔριον

ἔριζε vb pres act impv 2nd pers sg . . . . ἐρίζω

ἐρίζεις vb pres act ind 2nd pers sg   id.

ἐρίζουσαι vb pres act part fem nom pl   id.

ἐρίθου noun fem gen sg . . . . ἐρίθος

ἐρικτά adj neut nom and acc pl . . . . ἐρικτός

ἔριον noun neut nom and acc sg

ἐρίου noun neut gen sg . . . . ἔριον

ἔρις noun fem nom sg

ἐρίσητε vb 1st aor act subj 2nd pers pl . . . . ἐρίζω

ἐρίφιον noun neut nom and acc sg

ἐρίφοις noun masc dat pl . . . . ἔριφος

ἔριφον noun masc acc sg   id.

ἔριφος noun masc nom sg   id.

ἐρίφους noun masc acc pl   id.

ἐρίφῳ noun masc dat sg   id.

ἐρίφων noun masc gen pl   id.

ἐρίων noun neut gen pl . . . . ἔριον

Ερμα pr noun

Ερμαθ pr noun

Ερμαν pr noun

ἑρμηνεία noun fem nom sg

ἑρμηνείαις noun fem dat pl . . . . ἑρμηνεία

ἑρμηνείαν noun fem acc sg   id.

ἑρμηνεύεται vb pres m/p ind 3rd pers sg . . . . . . ἑρμηνεύω

ἑρμηνευκέναι vb perf act inf   id.

ἑρμηνευτής noun masc nom sg

Ερμων pr noun

Ἑρμων pr noun masc nom sg

Ἑρμωνα pr noun masc acc sg . . . . Ἑρμων

Ερμωνι pr noun

Ερμωνιιμ pr noun

Ερσκ pr noun

ἐροῦμεν vb fut act ind 1st pers pl . . . . εἶπον

ἐροῦσιν vb fut act ind 3rd pers pl   id.

ἕρπει vb pres act ind 3rd pers sg . . . . ἕρπω

ἑρπετά noun neut nom and acc pl . . . . ερπετόν

ἑρπετοῖς noun neut dat pl   id.

ἑρπετόν noun neut nom and acc sg   id.

ἑρπετοῦ noun neut gen sg   id.

ἑρπετῷ noun neut dat sg   id.

ἑρπετῶν noun neut gen pl   id.

ἕρποντα vb pres act part neut nom and acc pl . . . . ἕρπω

ἕρποντι vb pres act part masc and neut dat sg   id.

ἑρπόντων vb pres act part masc and neut gen pl   id.

ἑρπούσης vb pres act part fem gen sg   id.

ἕρπουσι vb pres act part masc and neut dat pl   id.

ἐρρόβδιζεν vb impf act ind 3rd pers sg . . . . ῥαβδίζω

ἐρρόβδισεν vb 1st aor act ind 3rd pers sg   id.

ἐρράγη vb 2nd aor pass ind 3rd pers sg . . . . ῥήγνυμι

ἐρράγησαν vb 2nd aor pass ind 3rd pers pl   id.

ἔρρανεν vb 1st aor act ind 3rd pers sg . . . . ῥαίνω

ἐρραντίσθη vb 1st aor pass ind 3rd pers sg . . . . . . ῥαντίζω

ἐρράπιζεν vb impf act ind 3rd pers sg . . . . ῥαπίζω

ἐρράπιζον vb impf act ind 3rd pers pl   id.

ἐρράχθη vb 1st aor pass ind 3rd pers sg . . . . ῥάσσω

ἔρραψα vb 1st aor act ind 1st pers sg . . . . ῥάπτω

ἔρραψαν vb 1st aor act ind 3rd pers pl   id.

ἔρρεγχεν vb 1st aor act ind 3rd pers sg . . . . ῥέγχω

ἐρρέθη vb 1st aor pass ind 3rd pers sg . . . . εἶπον

ἐρρηκώς vb perf act part masc nom sg . . . . ῥήγνυμι

ἔρρηξαν vb 1st aor act ind 3rd pers pl   id.

ἔρρηξας vb 1st aor act ind 2nd pers sg   id.

ἔρρηξεν	vb 1st aor act ind 3rd pers sg	ῥήγνυμι
ἐρριζώθησαν	vb 1st aor pass ind 3rd pers pl	ῥιζόω
ἐρρίζωκεν	vb perf act ind 3rd pers sg	id.
ἐρριζωμένη	vb perf act part fem nom sg	id.
ἐρρίζωσα	vb 1st aor act ind 1st pers sg	id.
ἐρριμμένα	vb perf m/p part neut nom and acc pl	ῥίπτω
ἐρριμμένη	vb perf m/p part fem nom sg	id.
ἐρριμμένην	vb perf m/p part fem acc sg	id.
ἐρριμμένοι	vb perf m/p part masc nom pl	id.
ἐρριμμένον	vb perf m/p part masc acc sg,	
	neut nom and acc sg	id.
ἐρριμμένῳ	vb perf m/p part masc and neut dat sg	id.
ἐρρίπισεν	vb 1st aor act ind 3rd pers sg	ῥιπίζω
ἔρριπται	vb perf m/p ind 3rd pers sg	ῥίπτω
ἔρριπτεν	vb impf act ind 3rd pers sg	id.
ἔρριπτο	vb plpf m/p ind 3rd pers sg	id.
ἐρρίφη	vb 2nd aor pass ind 3rd pers sg	id.
ἐρρίφησαν	vb 2nd aor pass ind 3rd pers pl	id.
ἔρριψα	vb 1st aor act ind 1st pers sg	id.
ἔρριψαν	vb 1st aor act ind 3rd pers pl	id.
ἔρριψας	vb 1st aor act ind 2nd pers sg	id.
ἔρριψε(ν)	vb 1st aor act ind 3rd pers sg	id.
ἐρρύησαν	vb 1st aor act ind 3rd pers pl	ῥέω
ἐρρύθμισεν	vb 1st aor act ind 3rd pers sg	ῥυθμίζω
ἐρρυσάμην	vb 1st aor mid ind 1st pers sg	ῥύομαι
ἐρρύσαντο	vb 1st aor mid ind 3rd pers pl	id.
ἐρρύσασθε	vb 1st aor mid ind 2nd pers pl	id.
ἐρρύσατο	vb 1st aor mid ind 3rd pers sg	id.
ἐρρύσθη	vb 1st aor pass ind 3rd pers sg	id.
ἐρρύσθημεν	vb 1st aor pass ind 1st pers pl	id.
ἐρρύσθησαν	vb 1st aor pass ind 3rd pers pl	id.
ἐρρύσω	vb 1st aor mid ind 2nd pers sg	id.
ἐρρώγασιν	vb perf act ind 3rd pers pl	ῥήγνυμι
ἔρρωμαι	vb perf m/p ind 1st pers sg	ῥώννυμι
ἐρρώμεθα	vb perf m/p ind 1st pers pl	id.
ἐρρωμένων	vb perf m/p part gen pl	id.
ἐρρῶσθαι	vb perf m/p inf	id.
ἔρρωσθε	vb perf m/p impv 2nd pers pl	id.
ἐρύθημα	noun neut nom and acc sg	
ἐρυθήνας	vb 1st aor act part masc nom sg	ἐρυθαίνω
ἐρυθρά	adj neut nom and acc pl	ἐρυθρός
ἐρυθρᾷ	adj fem dat sg	id.
ἐρυθράν	adj fem acc sg	id.
ἐρυθρᾶς	adj fem gen sg	id.
ἐρυθριῶσα	vb pres act part fem nom sg	ἐρυθριάω
ἐρυμνότητι	noun fem dat sg	ἐρυμνότης
ἐρυμνῷ	adj masc and neut dat sg	ἐρυμνός
ἐρυσίβη	noun fem nom sg	
ἐρυσίβῃ	noun fem dat sg	ἐρυσίβη
ἔρχεσθαι	vb pres dep inf	ἔρχομαι
ἔρχεσθε	vb pres dep impv 2nd pers pl,	
	pres dep ind 2nd pers pl	id.

ἐρχέσθω	vb pres dep impv 3rd pers sg	ἔρχομαι
ἐρχέσθωσαν	vb pres dep impv 3rd pers pl	id.
ἔρχεται	vb pres dep ind 3rd pers sg	id.
ἔρχῃ	vb pres dep ind 2nd pers sg,	
	pres dep subj 2nd pers sg	id.
ἔρχησθε	vb pres dep subj 2nd pers pl	id.
ἔρχηται	vb pres dep subj 3rd pers sg	id.
Ερχι	pr noun	
ἔρχομαι	vb pres dep ind 1st pers sg	
ἐρχόμενα	vb pres dep part neut nom and acc pl	ἔρχομαι
ἐρχόμεναι	vb pres dep part fem nom pl	id.
ἐρχομένας	vb pres dep part fem acc pl	id.
ἐρχομένη	vb pres dep part fem nom sg	id.
ἐρχομένῃ	vb pres dep part fem dat sg	id.
ἐρχομένην	vb pres dep part fem acc sg	id.
ἐρχόμενοι	vb pres dep part masc nom pl	id.
ἐρχομένοις	vb pres dep part masc and neut dat pl	id.
ἐρχόμενον	vb pres dep part masc acc sg,	
	neut nom and acc sg	id.
ἐρχόμενος	vb pres dep part masc nom sg	id.
ἐρχομένους	vb pres dep part masc acc pl	id.
ἐρχομένῳ	vb pres dep part masc and neut dat sg	id.
ἐρχομένων	vb pres dep part gen pl	id.
ἔρχονται	vb pres dep ind 3rd pers pl	id.
ἔρχου	vb pres dep impv 2nd pers sg	id.
ἐρῶ	vb fut act ind 1st pers sg	εἶπον
ἐρωδιόν	noun masc acc sg	ἐρωδιός
ἐρωδιοῦ	noun masc gen sg	id.
Ερωμαφ	pr noun	
ἐρωμένη	vb pres m/p part fem dat sg	ἐράω
Ερωμωθ	pr noun	
ἔρως	noun masc nom sg	
ἐρωτᾷ	vb pres act ind 3rd pers sg,	
	pres act subj 3rd pers sg	ἐρωτάω
ἐρωτᾶν	vb pres act inf	id.
ἐρωτᾷς	vb pres act ind 2nd pers sg	id.
ἐρώτημα	noun neut nom and acc sg	
ἐρωτῆσαι	vb 1st aor act inf	ἐρωτάω
ἐρωτήσατε	vb 1st aor act impv 2nd pers pl	id.
ἐρωτήσεις	vb fut act ind 2nd pers sg	id.
ἐρωτήσῃ	vb 1st aor act subj 3rd pers sg	id.
ἐρώτησον	vb 1st aor act impv 2nd pers sg	id.
ἐρωτήσουσιν	vb fut act ind 3rd pers pl	id.
ἐρωτήσω	vb 1st aor act subj 1st pers sg,	
	fut act ind 1st pers sg	id.
ἐρωτήσωμεν	vb 1st aor act subj 1st pers pl	id.
ἐρωτήσωσι	vb 1st aor act subj 3rd pers pl	id.
ἔρωτι	noun masc dat sg	ἔρως
ἐρωτῶν	vb pres act part masc nom sg	ἐρωτάω
ἐρωτῶντες	vb pres act part masc nom pl	id.
ἐρωτῶσιν	vb pres act subj 3rd pers pl	id.
Εσαβανα	pr noun	

ἐσαββάτισεν vb 1st aor act ind 3rd pers sg .... σαββατίζω	ἐσημάνθη vb 1st aor pass ind 3rd pers sg .... σημαίνω
ἐσάθρωσαν vb 1st aor act ind 3rd pers pl .... σαθρόω	ἐσημειώθη vb 1st aor pass ind 3rd pers sg .... σημειόω
ἐσαλεύθη vb 1st aor pass ind 3rd pers sg .... σαλεύω	ἐσήμηνεν vb 1st aor act ind 3rd pers sg .... σημαίνω
ἐσαλεύθησαν vb 1st aor pass ind 3rd pers pl id.	Εσησσουαλ pr noun
ἐσαλεύοντο vb impf m/p ind 3rd pers pl id.	Εσθαμω pr noun
ἐσάλευσαν vb 1st aor act ind 3rd pers pl id.	Εσθαολ pr noun
ἐσάλευσεν vb 1st aor act ind 3rd pers sg id.	Εσθαωλαιοι pr noun masc nom pl
ἐσάλπιζον vb impf act ind 3rd pers pl .... σαλπίζω	Εσθεμω pr noun
ἐσάλπισαν vb 1st aor act ind 3rd pers pl id.	Εσθεμωη pr noun
ἐσάλπισεν vb 1st aor act ind 3rd pers sg id.	Εσθεμων pr noun
Εσαν pr noun	ἔσθενον vb impf act ind 3rd pers pl .... σθένω
ἐσάπησαν vb 1st aor act ind 3rd pers pl .... σήπω	ἔσθεται vb pres m/p ind 3rd pers sg .... ἔσθω
ἐσβέννυτο vb impf m/p ind 3rd pers sg .... σβέννυμι	ἔσθετε vb pres act impv 2nd pers pl,
ἔσβεσαν vb 1st aor act ind 3rd pers pl id.	pres act ind 2nd pers pl id.
ἔσβεσεν vb 1st aor act ind 3rd pers sg id.	Εσθηρ pr noun
ἐσβέσθη vb 1st aor pass ind 3rd pers sg id.	ἐσθήσεσιν noun fem dat pl .... ἔσθησις
ἐσβέσθησαν vb 1st aor pass ind 3rd pers pl id.	ἐσθῆτα noun fem acc sg .... ἐσθής
ἐσβεσμένοι vb perf m/p part masc nom pl id.	ἔσθητε vb pres act subj 2nd pers pl .... ἔσθω
ἐσβεσμένον vb perf m/p part neut nom and acc sg id.	ἐσθῆτι noun fem dat sg .... ἐσθής
Εσδρα pr noun masc voc sg and dat sg .... Εσδρας	Εσθιε pr noun
Εσδραν pr noun masc acc sg id.	ἐσθίει vb pres act ind 3rd pers sg .... ἐσθίω
Εσδρας pr noun masc nom sg id.	ἐσθίειν vb pres act inf id.
Εσδρηλων pr noun	ἐσθίεις vb pres act ind 2nd pers sg id.
Εσδρι pr noun	ἐσθίεσθαι vb pres m/p inf id.
Εσδριηλ pr noun	ἐσθιέτω vb pres act impv 3rd pers sg id.
Εσδρικαμ pr noun	ἐσθιέτωσαν vb pres act impv 3rd pers pl id.
Εσδριν pr noun masc acc sg .... Εσδρις	ἐσθιομενα vb pres m/p part neut nom and acc pl id.
Εσεβαν pr noun	ἐσθίον vb pres act part neut nom and acc sg id.
ἐσέβετο vb impf dep ind 3rd pers sg .... σέβομαι	ἐσθίοντα vb pres act part masc acc sg,
Εσεβιας pr noun	neut nom and acc pl id.
ἐσέβοντο vb impf dep ind 3rd pers pl .... σέβομαι	ἐσθίοντας vb pres act part masc acc pl id.
Εσεβων pr noun	ἐσθίοντες vb pres act part masc nom pl id.
Εσεβωνιτας pr noun masc acc pl .... Εσεβωνιτης	ἐσθιόντων vb pres act part masc and neut gen pl id.
Εσεδεκ pr noun	ἐσθίουσιν vb pres act ind 3rd pers pl,
ἔσει vb fut act ind 2nd pers sg .... εἰμί	pres act part masc and neut dat pl id.
ἐσείσθη vb 1st aor pass ind 3rd pers sg .... σείω	ἐσθίων vb pres act part masc nom sg id.
ἐσείσθησαν vb 1st aor pass ind 3rd pers pl id.	ἔσθοντες vb pres act part masc nom pl .... ἔσθω
Εσελια pr noun	ἔσθοντος vb pres act part masc and neut gen sg id.
Εσελιου pr noun masc gen sg .... Εσελιας	ἔσθουσαι vb pres act part fem nom pl id.
Εσελων pr noun	ἔσθουσαν vb pres act part fem acc sg id.
Εσεραηλ pr noun	ἔσθων vb pres act part masc nom sg id.
Εσερων pr noun	Εσι pr noun
ἔσεσθαι vb fut mid inf .... εἰμί	ἐσίγησα vb 1st aor act ind 1st pers sg .... σιγάω
ἔσεσθε vb fut mid ind 2nd pers pl id.	ἐσίγησαν vb 1st aor act ind 3rd pers pl id.
εσεφιν translit	ἐσίγησεν vb 1st aor act ind 3rd pers sg id.
ἔσῃ vb fut mid ind 2nd pers sg .... εἰμί	ἐσιτομέτρει vb impf act ind 3rd pers sg .... σιτομετρέω
Εσηλ pr noun	ἐσιώπησα vb 1st aor act ind 1st pers sg .... σιωπάω
Εσηλεββων pr noun	ἐσιώπησαν vb 1st aor act ind 3rd pers pl id.
ἐσήμαινον vb impf act ind 3rd pers pl .... σημαίνω	ἐσιώπησας vb 1st aor act ind 2nd pers sg id.
ἐσήμαναν vb 1st aor act ind 3rd pers pl id.	ἐσιώπησεν vb 1st aor act ind 3rd pers sg id.
ἐσήμανας vb 1st aor act ind 2nd pers sg id.	Εσκαμαν pr noun
ἐσήμανε(ν) vb 1st aor act ind 3rd pers sg id.	ἔσκαλλεν vb impf act ind 3rd pers sg .... σκάλλω

ἐσκέπασαν vb 1st aor act ind 3rd pers pl . . . . σκεπάζω

ἐσκέπασας vb 1st aor act ind 2nd pers sg   id.

ἐσκέπασεν vb 1st aor act ind 3rd pers sg   id.

ἐσκεπάσθη vb 1st aor pass ind 3rd pers sg   id.

ἐσκεύασα vb 1st aor act ind 1st pers sg . . . . σκευάζω

ἐσκευασμένον vb perf m/p part neut nom and acc sg   id.

ἐσκήνωσεν vb 1st aor act ind 3rd pers sg . . . . σκηνόω

ἐσκίαζον vb impf act ind 3rd pers pl . . . . σκιάζω

ἐσκίασαν vb 1st aor act ind 3rd pers pl   id.

ἐσκίασεν vb 1st aor act ind 3rd pers sg   id.

ἐσκιρτᾶτε vb impf act ind 2nd pers pl . . . . σκιρτάω

ἐσκίρτησαν vb 1st aor act ind 3rd pers pl   id.

ἐσκιρτήσατε vb 1st aor act ind 2nd pers pl   id.

ἐσκίρτων vb impf act ind 3rd pers pl   id.

ἐσκλήρυνα vb 1st aor act ind 1st pers sg . . . . σκληρύνω

ἐσκληρύναμεν vb 1st aor act ind 1st pers pl   id.

ἐσκλήρυναν vb 1st aor act ind 3rd pers pl   id.

ἐσκλήρυνας vb 1st aor act ind 2nd pers sg   id.

ἐσκλήρυνεν vb impf act ind 3rd pers sg,

                1st aor act ind 3rd pers sg   id.

ἐσκληρύνθη vb 1st aor pass ind 3rd pers sg   id.

ἐσκόρπισαν vb 1st aor act ind 3rd pers pl . . . . . . σκορπίζω

ἐσκόρπισεν vb 1st aor act ind 3rd pers sg   id.

ἐσκορπίσθη vb 1st aor pass ind 3rd pers sg   id.

ἐσκορπίσθησαν vb 1st aor pass ind 3rd pers pl   id.

ἐσκορπίσμεθα vb perf act ind 1st pers pl   id.

ἐσκορπισμέναι vb perf m/p part fem nom pl   id.

ἐσκότασαν vb 1st aor act ind 3rd pers pl . . . . σκοτάζω

ἐσκότασεν vb 1st aor act ind 3rd pers sg   id.

ἐσκοτισμένοι vb perf m/p part masc nom pl . . . . . σκοτίζω

ἐσκοτώθη vb 1st aor pass ind 3rd pers sg . . . . σκοτόω

ἐσκοτώθην vb 1st aor pass ind 1st pers sg   id.

ἐσκοτώθησαν vb 1st aor pass ind 3rd pers pl   id.

ἐσκότωται vb perf m/p ind 3rd pers sg   id.

ἐσκύλευσαν vb 1st aor act ind 3rd pers pl . . . . . . σκυλεύω

ἐσκύλευσας vb 1st aor act ind 2nd pers sg   id.

ἐσκύλευσεν vb 1st aor act ind 3rd pers sg   id.

ἐσμεν vb pres act ind 1st pers pl . . . . εἰμί

ἐσμέν vb pres act ind 1st pers pl   id.

ἐσμίκρυνας vb 1st aor act ind 2nd pers sg . . . . . . σμικρύνω

ἐσμίκρυνεν vb impf act ind 3rd pers sg,

                1st aor act ind 3rd pers sg   id.

ἐσμικρύνθη vb 1st aor pass ind 3rd pers sg   id.

ἐσμικρύνθημεν vb 1st aor pass ind 1st pers pl   id.

ἐσμικρύνθησαν vb 1st aor pass ind 3rd pers pl   id.

Εσοβα pr noun

ἔσομαι vb fut mid ind 1st pers sg . . . . εἰμί

ἐσόμεθα vb fut mid ind 1st pers pl   id.

ἐσόμενα vb fut mid part neut nom and acc pl   id.

ἐσομένην vb fut mid part fem acc sg   id.

ἐσομένης vb fut mid part fem gen sg   id.

ἐσόμενον vb fut mid part masc acc sg,

        neut nom and acc sg . . . . εἰμί

ἐσόμενος vb fut mid part masc nom sg   id.

ἐσομένου vb fut mid part masc and neut gen sg   id.

ἔσονται vb fut mid ind 3rd pers pl   id.

ἔσοπτρον noun neut nom and acc sg

ἐσοφισάμην vb 1st aor mid ind 1st pers sg . . . . σοφίζω

ἐσοφίσαντο vb 1st aor mid ind 3rd pers pl   id.

ἐσόφισας vb 1st aor act ind 2nd pers sg   id.

ἐσοφίσατο vb 1st aor mid ind 3rd pers sg   id.

ἐσοφίσθης vb 1st aor pass ind 2nd pers sg   id.

ἐσπανίσθη vb 1st aor pass ind 3rd pers sg . . . . σπανίζω

ἐσπανισμένους vb perf m/p part masc acc pl   id.

ἐσπαραγμέναι vb perf m/p part fem nom pl . . . σπαράσσω

ἐσπάραξεν vb 1st aor act ind 3rd pers sg   id.

ἐσπαράχθησαν vb 1st aor pass ind 3rd pers pl   id.

ἐσπαργανώθης vb 1st aor pass ind 2nd pers sg . σπαργανόω

ἐσπαργάνωσα vb 1st aor act ind 1st pers sg   id.

ἔσπαρκας vb perf act ind 2nd pers sg . . . . σπείρω

ἐσπαρμένη vb perf m/p part fem nom sg   id.

ἔσπασα vb 1st aor act ind 1st pers sg . . . . σπάω

ἐσπάσαντο vb 1st aor mid ind 3rd pers pl   id.

ἐσπάσατο vb 1st aor mid ind 3rd pers sg   id.

ἔσπασεν vb 1st aor act ind 3rd pers sg   id.

ἐσπασμένη vb perf m/p part fem nom sg   id.

ἐσπασμένην vb perf m/p part fem acc sg   id.

ἐσπασμένοι vb perf m/p part masc nom pl   id.

ἐσπασμένους vb perf m/p part masc acc pl   id.

ἐσπασμένων vb perf m/p part gen pl   id.

ἐσπατάλων vb impf act ind 3rd pers pl . . . . σπαταλάω

ἔσπειραν vb 1st aor act ind 3rd pers pl . . . . σπείρω

ἐσπείρατε vb 1st aor act ind 2nd pers pl   id.

ἔσπειρεν vb impf act ind 3rd pers sg,

        1st aor act ind 3rd pers sg   id.

ἐσπείσαμεν vb 1st aor act ind 1st pers pl . . . . σπένδω

ἔσπεισαν vb 1st aor act ind 3rd pers pl   id.

ἔσπεισεν vb 1st aor act ind 3rd pers sg   id.

ἔσπενδον vb impf act ind 3rd pers pl   id.

ἑσπέρα noun fem nom sg

ἑσπέρᾳ noun fem dat sg . . . . ἑσπέρα

ἑσπέραν noun fem acc sg   id.

ἑσπέρας noun fem gen sg   id.

ἑσπερινή adj fem nom sg . . . . ἑσπερινός

ἑσπερινῇ adj fem dat sg   id.

ἑσπερινήν adj fem acc sg   id.

ἑσπερινῆς adj fem gen sg   id.

ἑσπερινῷ adj masc and neut dat sg   id.

ἑσπερινῶν adj gen pl   id.

Ἕσπερον pr noun masc acc sg . . . . Ἕσπερος

ἕσπερον noun masc acc sg . . . . ἕσπερος

ἔσπευδεν vb impf act ind 3rd pers sg . . . . σπεύδω

ἐσπεύδετο vb impf m/p ind 3rd pers sg   id.

ἔσπευδον vb impf act ind 3rd pers pl . . . . σπεύδω	ἐστερήθην vb 1st aor pass ind 1st pers sg . . . . στερέω
ἔσπευσα vb 1st aor act ind 1st pers sg id.	ἐστερήθης vb 1st aor pass ind 2nd pers sg id.
ἔσπευσαν vb 1st aor act ind 3rd pers pl id.	ἐστερήθησαν vb 1st aor pass ind 3rd pers pl id.
ἔσπευσας vb 1st aor act ind 2nd pers sg id.	ἐστερημένος vb perf m/p part masc nom sg id.
ἔσπευσεν vb 1st aor act ind 3rd pers sg id.	ἐστέρηνται vb 1st aor mid ind 3rd pers pl id.
ἐσποδώσαντο vb 1st aor mid ind 3rd pers pl . . . . . σποδόω	ἐστερτσας vb 1st aor act ind 2nd pers sg id.
ἐσπούδακα vb perf act ind 1st pers sg . . . . σπουδάζω	ἐστερτσεν vb 1st aor act ind 3rd pers sg id.
ἐσπούδασα vb 1st aor act ind 1st pers sg id.	ἐστέρουν vb impf act ind 3rd pers pl id.
ἐσπούδασαν vb 1st aor act ind 3rd pers pl id.	ἐστεφάνωσαν vb 1st aor act ind 3rd pers pl . . . . . στεφανόω
ἐσπούδασας vb 1st aor act ind 2nd pers sg id.	ἐστεφανώσαντο vb 1st aor mid ind 3rd pers pl id.
ἐσπούδασεν vb 1st aor act ind 3rd pers sg id.	ἐστεφάνωσας vb 1st aor act ind 2nd pers sg id.
Εσραε pr noun	ἐστεφάνωσεν vb 1st aor act ind 3rd pers sg id.
Εσρι pr noun	ἔστη vb 2nd aor act ind 3rd pers sg . . . . ἵστημι
Εσρια pr noun	ἔστηκα vb perf act ind 1st pers sg id.
Εσριηλ pr noun	ἕστηκας vb perf act ind 2nd pers sg id.
Εσριηλι pr noun	ἑστήκατε vb perf act ind 2nd pers pl id.
Εσρικαμ pr noun	ἕστηκε(ν) vb perf act ind 3rd pers sg id.
Εσρωμ pr noun	ἑστήκει vb plpf act ind 3rd pers sg id.
Εσρων pr noun	ἑστήκεεν vb perf act ind 3rd pers sg id.
ἐστάθη vb 1st aor pass ind 3rd pers sg . . . . ἵστημι	ἑστηκότα vb perf act part masc acc sg,
ἐστάθησαν vb 1st aor pass ind 3rd pers pl id.	neut nom and acc pl id.
ἐσταθμωμένον vb 1st aor mid part masc acc sg,	ἑστηκότας vb perf act part masc acc pl id.
neut nom and acc sg . . . . σταθμόω	ἑστηκότες vb perf act part masc nom pl id.
ἔσται vb fut mid ind 3rd pers sg . . . . εἰμί	ἑστηκότι vb perf act part masc and neut dat sg id.
ἑστάκαμεν vb perf act ind 1st pers pl . . . . ἵστημι	ἑστηκότος vb perf act part masc and neut gen sg id.
ἐστάλαξεν vb 1st aor act ind 3rd pers sg . . . . σταλάζω	ἑστηκότον vb perf act part masc and neut gen pl id.
ἐσταλμέναι vb perf m/p part fem nom pl . . . . στέλλω	ἑστηκυῖα vb perf act part fem nom sg id.
ἐσταμένους vb perf m/p part masc acc pl . . . . ἵστημι	ἑστηκώς vb perf act part masc nom sg id.
ἑστάναι vb perf act inf id.	ἐστηλώθη vb 1st aor pass ind 3rd pers sg . . . . στηλόω
ἔσταξαν vb 1st aor act ind 3rd pers pl . . . . στάζω	ἐστηλομένοι vb perf m/p part masc nom pl id.
ἔσταξεν vb 1st aor act ind 3rd pers sg id.	ἐστηλωμένος vb perf m/p part masc nom sg id.
ἐστασίασαν vb 1st aor act ind 3rd pers pl . . . . . στασιάζω	ἐστήλωσαν vb 1st aor act ind 3rd pers pl id.
ἔσταται vb perf m/p ind 3rd pers sg . . . . ἵστημι	ἐστήλωσεν vb 1st aor act ind 3rd pers sg id.
ἐσταυρῶσθαι vb perf m/p inf . . . . σταυρόω	ἔστην vb 2nd aor act ind 1st pers sg . . . . ἵστημι
ἐστε vb pres act ind 2nd pers pl . . . . εἰμί	ἐστηριγμένα vb perf m/p part neut nom and acc pl . στηρίζω
ἐστέ vb pres act ind 2nd pers pl id.	ἐστηριγμέναι vb perf m/p part fem nom pl id.
ἐστεατωμένοι vb perf dep part masc nom pl . . στεατόομαι	ἐστηριγμένη vb perf m/p part fem nom sg id.
ἐστέγασαν vb 1st aor act ind 3rd pers pl . . . . στεγάζω	ἐστηριγμένος vb perf m/p part masc nom sg id.
ἐστείλαντο vb 1st aor mid ind 3rd pers pl . . . . στέλλω	ἐστήριζον vb impf act ind 3rd pers pl id.
ἐστείλατο vb 1st aor mid ind 3rd pers sg id.	ἐστήρικα vb perf act ind 1st pers sg id.
ἐστέναξα vb 1st aor act ind 1st pers sg . . . . στενάζω	ἐστήρικται vb perf m/p ind 3rd pers sg id.
ἐστέναξαν vb 1st aor act ind 3rd pers pl id.	ἐστήριξα vb 1st aor act ind 1st pers sg id.
ἐστέναξεν vb 1st aor act ind 3rd pers sg id.	ἐστήρισα vb 1st aor act ind 1st pers sg id.
ἐστενοχώρησεν vb 1st aor act ind 3rd pers sg . στενοχωρέω	ἐστήρισαι vb perf m/p ind 2nd pers sg id.
ἐστέρεσεν vb 1st aor act ind 3rd pers sg . . . . στερέω	ἐστηρίσατο vb 1st aor mid ind 3rd pers sg id.
ἐστερεώθη vb 1st aor pass ind 3rd pers sg . . . . . . στερεόω	ἐστήρισεν vb 1st aor act ind 3rd pers sg id.
ἐστερεώθησαν vb 1st aor pass ind 3rd pers pl id.	ἐστηρίσθαι vb perf m/p inf id.
ἐστερεωμένης vb perf m/p part fem gen sg id.	ἐστηρίσθη vb 1st aor pass ind 3rd pers sg id.
ἐστερέωσα vb 1st aor act ind 1st pers sg id.	ἐστηρισμένος vb perf m/p part masc nom sg id.
ἐστερέωσαν vb 1st aor act ind 3rd pers pl id.	ἐστήρισται vb perf m/p ind 3rd pers sg id.
ἐστερέωσεν vb 1st aor act ind 3rd pers sg id.	ἐστηρίχθην vb 1st aor pass ind 1st pers sg id.
ἐστερήθη vb 1st aor pass ind 3rd pers sg . . . . στερέω	ἔστησα vb 1st aor act ind 1st pers sg . . . . ἵστημι

ἐστήσαμεν vb 1st aor act ind 1st pers pl . . . . ἵστημι

ἔστησαν vb 1st aor act ind 3rd pers pl   id.

ἔστησας vb 1st aor act ind 2nd pers sg   id.

ἐστήσατε vb 1st aor act ind 2nd pers pl   id.

ἔστησε(ν) vb 1st aor act ind 3rd pers sg   id.

ἔστητε vb 2nd aor act ind 2nd pers pl   id.

ἐστι vb pres act ind 3rd pers sg . . . . εἰμί

ἔστι vb pres act ind 3rd pers sg   id.

ἐστί vb pres act ind 3rd pers sg   id.

ἐστία noun fem dat sg . . . . ἑστία

ἑστιατορία noun fem nom sg

ἑστιατορίαν noun fem acc sg . . . . ἑστιατορία

ἐστιβίζου vb impf m/p ind 2nd pers sg . . . . στιβίζω

ἔστιλβεν vb impf act ind 3rd pers sg . . . . στίλβω

ἐστιμίσατο vb 1st aor mid ind 3rd pers sg . . . . στιμίζω

ἐστιχισμέναι vb perf m/p part fem nom pl . . . . . . στιχίζω

ἐστοίβασεν vb 1st aor act ind 3rd pers sg . . . . . . στοιβάζω

ἐστοιβασμένη vb perf m/p part fem dat sg   id.

ἐστολίζετο vb impf m/p ind 3rd pers sg . . . . στολίζω

ἐστόλισεν vb 1st aor act ind 3rd pers sg   id.

ἐστολισμένοι vb perf m/p part masc nom pl   id.

ἐστολισμένος vb perf m/p part masc nom sg   id.

ἐστολισμένους vb perf m/p part masc acc pl   id.

ἐστραγγάληται vb perf dep ind

       3rd pers sg . . . . στραγγαλάομαι

ἐστραγγαλωμένος vb perf dep part

       masc nom sg . . . . στραγγαλόομαι

ἐστράτευσεν vb 1st aor act ind 3rd pers sg . . . . . στρατεύω

ἐστρατήγηται vb perf m/p ind 3rd pers sg . . . . . στρατηγέω

ἐστρατοπεδεύκει vb plpf act ind

       3rd pers sg . . . . στρατοπεδεύω

ἐστρατοπεδευκότα vb perf act part masc acc sg   id.

ἐστρατοπέδευσαν vb 1st aor act ind 3rd pers pl   id.

ἐστρατοπεδεύσατε vb 1st aor act ind 2nd pers pl   id.

ἐστρατοπέδευσεν vb 1st aor act ind 3rd pers sg   id.

ἐστράφη vb 2nd aor pass ind 3rd pers sg . . . . στρέφω

ἐστράφην vb 2nd aor pass ind 1st pers sg   id.

ἐστράφης vb 2nd aor pass ind 2nd pers sg   id.

ἐστράφησαν vb 2nd aor pass ind 3rd pers pl   id.

ἔστρεψαν vb 1st aor act ind 3rd pers pl   id.

ἔστρεψας vb 1st aor act ind 2nd pers sg   id.

ἔστρεψεν vb 1st aor act ind 3rd pers sg   id.

ἔστρωκα vb perf act ind 1st pers sg . . . . στρώννυμι

ἐστρωμέναι vb perf m/p part fem nom pl   id.

ἐστρωμένης vb perf m/p part fem gen sg   id.

ἔστρωσαν vb 1st aor act ind 3rd pers pl   id.

ἔστρωσεν vb 1st aor act ind 3rd pers sg   id.

ἔστρωται vb perf m/p ind 3rd pers sg   id.

ἐστύγνασαν vb 1st aor act ind 3rd pers pl . . . . . . στυγνάζω

ἔστω vb pres act impv 3rd pers sg . . . . εἰμί

ἑστώς vb perf act part masc nom sg . . . . ἵστημι

ἑστῶσα vb perf act part fem nom sg   id.

ἔστωσαν vb pres act impv 3rd pers pl . . . . εἰμί

ἑστῶτα vb perf act part masc acc sg,

       neut nom and acc pl . . . . ἵστημι

ἑστῶτας vb perf act part masc acc pl   id.

ἑστῶτες vb perf act part masc nom pl   id.

ἑστῶτος vb perf act part masc and neut gen sg   id.

ἑστώτων vb perf act part masc and neut gen pl   id.

ἔσυραν vb 1st aor act ind 3rd pers pl . . . . σύρω

ἐσύρισαν vb 1st aor act ind 3rd pers pl . . . . συρίζω

ἐσφαγμένος vb perf m/p part masc nom sg . . . . σφάζω

ἐσφαγμένου vb perf m/p part masc and neut gen sg   id.

ἐσφαγμένων vb perf m/p part gen pl   id.

ἔσφαζον vb impf act ind 3rd pers pl   id.

ἔσφαλεν vb 1st aor act ind 3rd pers sg . . . . σφάλλω

ἐσφάλησαν vb 2nd aor pass ind 3rd pers pl   id.

ἔσφαξαν vb 1st aor act ind 3rd pers pl . . . . σφάζω

ἔσφαξας vb 1st aor act ind 2nd pers sg   id.

ἔσφαξεν vb 1st aor act ind 3rd pers sg   id.

ἐσφενδόνησεν vb 1st aor act ind 3rd pers sg . . . σφενδονάω

ἐσφηνωμέναι vb perf m/p part fem nom pl . . . . σφηνόω

ἐσφήνωσεν vb 1st aor act ind 3rd pers sg   id.

ἔσφιγξαν vb 1st aor act ind 3rd pers pl . . . . σφίγγω

ἐσφραγισάμην vb 1st aor mid ind 1st pers sg . . . σφραγίζω

ἐσφράγισαν vb 1st aor act ind 3rd pers pl   id.

ἐσφράγιστο vb 1st aor mid ind 3rd pers pl   id.

ἐσφράγισας vb 1st aor act ind 2nd pers sg   id.

ἐσφράγιστο vb 1st aor mid ind 3rd pers sg   id.

ἐσφραγίσθη vb 1st aor pass ind 3rd pers sg   id.

ἐσφραγισμένα vb perf m/p part neut nom and acc pl   id.

ἐσφραγισμένη vb perf m/p part fem nom sg   id.

ἐσφραγισμένοι vb perf m/p part masc nom pl   id.

ἐσφραγισμένον vb perf m/p part masc acc sg,

       neut nom and acc sg   id.

ἐσφραγισμένου vb perf m/p part masc and neut gen sg   id.

ἐσφράγισται vb perf m/p ind 3rd pers sg   id.

ἐσφυροκόπησεν vb 1st aor act ind 3rd pers sg . σφυροκοπέω

ἐσχάρα noun fem nom sg

ἐσχάρα noun fem dat sg . . . . ἐσχάρα

ἐσχάραι noun fem nom pl   id.

ἐσχάραν noun fem acc sg   id.

ἐσχάρας noun fem gen sg   id.

ἐσχαρίτην noun masc acc sg . . . . ἐσχαρίτης

ἔσχατα adj neut nom and acc pl . . . . ἔσχατος

ἔσχαται adj fem nom pl   id.

ἐσχάταις adj fem dat pl   id.

ἐσχάτη adj fem nom sg   id.

ἐσχάτη adj fem dat sg   id.

ἐσχάτην adj fem acc sg   id.

ἐσχάτης adj fem gen sg   id.

ἐσχατίζοντας vb pres act part masc acc pl . . . . . ἐσχατίζω

ἐσχατογήρῳ adj dat sg . . . . ἐσχατογήρως

ἐσχατογήρως adj nom (and gen) sg

ἔσχατοι   adj masc nom pl .... ἔσχατος

ἐσχάτοις   adj masc and neut dat pl   id.

ἔσχατον   adj masc acc sg, neut nom and acc sg   id.

ἔσχατος   adj masc nom sg   id.

ἐσχάτου   adj masc and neut gen sg   id.

ἐσχάτους   adj masc acc pl   id.

ἐσχάτῳ   adj masc and neut dat sg   id.

ἐσχάτων   adj masc and neut gen pl   id.

ἐσχεδιάζομεν   vb impf act ind 1st pers pl ...... σχεδιάζω

ἔσχεν   vb 2nd aor act ind 3rd pers sg .... ἔχω

ἔσχες   vb 2nd aor act ind 2nd pers sg   id.

ἔσχηκεν   vb perf act ind 3rd pers sg   id.

ἐσχηκότα   vb perf act part masc acc sg   id.

ἐσχηκότες   vb perf act part masc nom pl   id.

ἐσχηκώς   vb perf act part masc nom sg   id.

ἐσχίζοντο   vb impf m/p ind 3rd pers pl .... σχίζω

ἔσχισεν   vb 1st aor act ind 3rd pers sg   id.

ἐσχίσθη   vb 1st aor pass ind 3rd pers sg   id.

ἐσχισμένοι   vb perf m/p part masc nom pl   id.

ἔσχομεν   vb 2nd aor act ind 1st pers pl .... ἔχω

ἔσχον   vb 2nd aor act ind 1st pers sg and 3rd pers pl   id.

ἔσχοσαν   vb 2nd aor act ind 3rd pers pl   id.

Εσχωλ   pr noun

ἔσω   adverb and preposition

ἔσῳζεν   vb impf act ind 3rd pers sg .... σῴζω

ἐσῴζετο   vb impf m/p ind 3rd pers sg   id.

Εσωθ   pr noun

ἔσωθεν   adverb

ἐσώθη   vb 1st aor pass ind 3rd pers sg .... σῴζω

ἐσώθην   vb 1st aor pass ind 1st pers sg   id.

ἐσώθησαν   vb 1st aor pass ind 3rd pers pl   id.

ἐσωματοποιήσατε   vb 1st aor act ind

     2nd pers pl .... σωματοποιέω

ἐσώρευσεν   vb 1st aor act ind 3rd pers sg .... σωρεύω

ἔσωσα   vb 1st aor act ind 1st pers sg .... σῴζω

ἔσωσαν   vb 1st aor act ind 3rd pers pl   id.

ἔσωσας   vb 1st aor act ind 2nd pers sg   id.

ἐσώσατε   vb 1st aor act ind 2nd pers pl   id.

ἔσωσε(ν)   vb 1st aor act ind 3rd pers sg   id.

ἐσώτατα   superl adj neut nom and acc pl .... ἐσώτατος

ἐσωτάτην   superl adj fem acc sg   id.

ἐσωτάτου   superl adj masc and neut gen sg   id.

ἐσωτέρα   comp adj neut nom and acc pl .... ἔσω

ἐσωτέρᾳ   comp adj fem dat sg   id.

ἐσωτέραν   comp adj fem acc sg   id.

ἐσωτέρας   comp adj fem gen sg   id.

ἐσώτερον   adverb and preposition

ἐσωτέρῳ   comp adj masc and neut dat sg .... ἔσω

ἐσωτέρων   comp adj masc and neut gen pl   id.

ἐτάζει   vb pres act ind 3rd pers sg .... ἐτάζω

ἐτάζων   vb pres act part masc nom sg   id.

ἑταίρας   noun fem gen sg .... ἑταίρα

ἐταιριζομένη   vb pres m/p part fem dat sg ...... ἑταιρίζω

ἑταῖροι   noun masc nom pl .... ἑταῖρος

ἑταίροις   noun masc dat pl   id.

ἑταῖρος   noun masc nom sg   id.

ἑταίρου   noun masc gen sg   id.

ἑταίρους   noun masc acc pl   id.

ἑταίρων   noun masc gen pl   id.

ἑταιρῶν   noun fem gen pl .... ἑταίρα

ἐτάκη   vb 2nd aor pass ind 3rd pers sg .... τήκω

ἐτάκην   vb 2nd aor pass ind 1st pers sg   id.

ἐτάκησαν   vb 2nd aor pass ind 3rd pers pl   id.

ἐταλαιπώρησα   vb 1st aor act ind 1st pers sg .. ταλαιπωρέω

ἐταλαιπωρήσαμεν   vb 1st aor act ind 1st pers pl   id.

ἐταλαιπώρησαν   vb 1st aor act ind 3rd pers pl   id.

ἐταλαιπώρησεν   vb 1st aor act ind 3rd pers sg   id.

ἐτάνυσαν   vb 1st aor act ind 3rd pers pl .... τανύω

ἔταξα   vb 1st aor act ind 1st pers sg .... τάσσω

ἔταξαν   vb 1st aor act ind 3rd pers pl   id.

ἐτάξαντο   vb 1st aor mid ind 3rd pers pl   id.

ἔταξες   vb 1st aor act ind 2nd pers sg   id.

ἐτάξατε   vb 1st aor act ind 2nd pers pl   id.

ἐτάξατο   vb 1st aor mid ind 3rd pers sg   id.

ἔταξεν   vb 1st aor act ind 3rd pers sg   id.

ἐταπείνου   vb impf act ind 3rd pers sg .... ταπεινόω

ἐταπεινούμην   vb impf m/p ind 1st pers sg   id.

ἐταπείνουν   vb impf act ind

     1st pers sg and 3rd pers pl   id.

ἐταπεινοφρόνουν   vb impf act ind

     1st pers sg .... ταπεινοφρονέω

ἐταπεινώθη   vb 1st aor pass ind 3rd pers sg ..... ταπεινόω

ἐταπεινώθην   vb 1st aor pass ind 1st pers sg   id.

ἐταπεινώθης   vb 1st aor pass ind 2nd pers sg   id.

ἐταπεινώθησαν   vb 1st aor pass ind 3rd pers pl   id.

ἐταπείνωσα   vb 1st aor act ind 1st pers sg   id.

ἐταπεινώσαμεν   vb 1st aor act ind 1st pers pl   id.

ἐταπείνωσαν   vb 1st aor act ind 3rd pers pl   id.

ἐταπείνωσας   vb 1st aor act ind 2nd pers sg   id.

ἐταπείνωσεν   vb 1st aor act ind 3rd pers sg   id.

ἐτάραξας   vb 1st aor act ind 2nd pers sg .... ταράσσω

ἐτάραξεν   vb 1st aor act ind 3rd pers sg   id.

ἐτάρασσες   vb impf act ind 2nd pers sg   id.

ἐταράσσετε   vb impf act ind 2nd pers pl   id.

ἐταράσσετο   vb impf m/p ind 3rd pers sg   id.

ἐτάρασσον   vb impf act ind 3rd pers pl   id.

ἐταράχθη   vb 1st aor pass ind 3rd pers sg   id.

ἐταράχθημεν   vb 1st aor pass ind 1st pers pl   id.

ἐταράχθην   vb 1st aor pass ind 1st pers sg   id.

ἐταράχθησαν   vb 1st aor pass ind 3rd pers pl   id.

ἐτάσαι   vb 1st aor act inf .... ἐτάζω

ἐτάσητε   vb 1st aor act subj 2nd pers pl   id.

ἐτασθήσονται   vb fut pass ind 3rd pers pl   id.

ἔτασιν   noun fem acc sg .... ἔτασις

ἔτασις noun fem nom sg

ἐτασμοῖς noun masc dat pl . . . . ἐτασμός

ἐτασμόν noun masc acc sg   id.

ἐτασμῶν noun masc gen pl   id.

ἔτασον vb 1st aor act impv 2nd pers sg . . . . ἐτάζω

ἐτάσω vb 1st aor act subj 1st pers sg   id.

ἐτάσωμεν vb 1st aor act subj 1st pers pl   id.

ἐτάφη vb 2nd aor pass ind 3rd pers sg . . . . θάπτω

ἐτάχυναν vb 1st aor act ind 3rd pers pl . . . . ταχύνω

ἐταχύνατε vb 1st aor act ind 2nd pers pl   id.

ἐτάχυνεν vb impf act ind 3rd pers sg,

           1st aor act ind 3rd pers sg   id.

Ετεβαθα pr noun

ἐτέθη vb 1st aor pass ind 3rd pers sg . . . . τίθημι

ἐτέθησαν vb 1st aor pass ind 3rd pers pl   id.

ἔτει noun neut dat sg . . . . ἔτος

ἐτείχισαν vb 1st aor act ind 3rd pers pl . . . . τειχίζω

ἔτεκεν vb 2nd aor act ind 3rd pers sg . . . . τίκτω

ἔτεκες vb 2nd aor act ind 2nd pers sg   id.

ἐτεκνοποίει vb impf act ind 3rd pers sg . . . . . . τεκνοποιέω

ἐτεκνοποίησαν vb 1st aor act ind 3rd pers pl

ἐτέκομεν vb 2nd aor act ind 1st pers pl . . . . τίκτω

ἔτεκον vb 2nd aor act ind 1st pers sg and 3rd pers pl   id.

ἐτέκταινον vb impf act ind 3rd pers pl . . . . τεκταίνω

ἐτελειώθη vb 1st aor pass ind 3rd pers sg . . . . τελειόω

ἐτελείωσαν vb 1st aor act ind 3rd pers pl   id.

ἐτελείωσεν vb 1st aor act ind 3rd pers sg   id.

ἐτέλεσαν vb 1st aor act ind 3rd pers pl . . . . τελέω

ἐτελέσθη vb 1st aor pass ind 3rd pers sg   id.

ἐτελέσθησαν vb 1st aor pass ind 3rd pers pl   id.

ἐτελεύτησα vb 1st aor act ind 1st pers sg . . . . . . τελευτάω

ἐτελεύτησαν vb 1st aor act ind 3rd pers pl   id.

ἐτελεύτησεν vb 1st aor act ind 3rd pers sg   id.

ἐτελωνεῖτο vb impf dep ind 3rd pers sg . . . . . . τελωνέομαι

ἔτεμνον vb impf act ind 3rd pers pl . . . . τέμνω

ἕτερα adj neut nom and acc pl . . . . ἕτερος

ἑτέρα adj fem nom sg   id.

ἑτέρᾳ adj fem dat sg   id.

ἕτεραι adj fem nom pl   id.

ἑτέραν adj fem acc sg   id.

ἑτέρας adj fem gen sg and acc pl   id.

ἑτεροζύγῳ adj dat sg . . . . ἑτερόζυγος

ἕτεροι adj masc nom pl . . . . ἕτερος

ἑτέροις adj masc and neut dat pl   id.

ἑτεροκλινῶς adverb

ἕτερον adj masc acc sg, neut nom and acc sg . . . . ἕτερος

ἕτερος adj masc nom sg   id.

ἑτέρου adj masc and neut gen sg   id.

ἑτέρους adj masc acc pl   id.

ἑτέρφθην vb 1st aor pass ind 1st pers sg . . . . τέρπω

ἑτέρῳ adj masc and neut dat sg . . . . ἕτερος

ἑτέρωθεν adverb

ἑτέρων adj gen pl . . . . ἕτερος

ἔτεσι noun neut dat pl . . . . ἔτος

ἐτέχθη vb 1st aor pass ind 3rd pers sg . . . . τίκτω

ἐτέχθην vb 1st aor pass ind 1st pers sg   id.

ἐτέχθης vb 1st aor pass ind 2nd pers sg   id.

ἐτέχθησαν vb 1st aor pass ind 3rd pers pl   id.

ἔτη noun neut nom and acc pl . . . . ἔτος

ἐτήκετο vb impf m/p ind 3rd pers sg . . . . τήκω

Ετηλ pr noun

ἐτήρει vb impf act ind 3rd pers sg . . . . τηρέω

ἐτήρησα vb 1st aor act ind 1st pers sg   id.

ἐτήρησαν vb 1st aor act ind 3rd pers pl   id.

ἐτήρησεν vb 1st aor act ind 3rd pers sg   id.

ἔτι adverb

ἐτίθει vb impf act ind 3rd pers sg . . . . τίθημι

ἐτίθεις vb impf act ind 2nd pers sg   id.

ἐτίθετο vb impf m/p ind 3rd pers sg   id.

ἔτικτεν vb impf act ind 3rd pers sg . . . . τίκτω

ἔτικτον vb impf act ind 3rd pers pl   id.

ἐτίλη vb 2nd aor pass ind 3rd pers sg . . . . τίλλω

ἔτιλλον vb impf act ind 1st pers sg   id.

ἐτίλλοσαν vb impf act ind 3rd pers pl   id.

ἐτιμήθησαν vb 1st aor pass ind 3rd pers pl . . . . τιμάω

ἐτίμησεν vb 1st aor act ind 3rd pers sg   id.

ἐτιμογράφησεν vb 1st aor act ind 3rd pers sg . τιμογραφέω

ἐτίμων vb impf act ind 3rd pers pl . . . . τιμάω

ἐτιμωρήσατο vb 1st aor mid ind 3rd pers sg . . . . . τιμωρέω

ἐτιμωρήσω vb 1st aor mid ind 2nd pers sg   id.

ἐτίτρωσκον vb impf act ind 3rd pers pl . . . . τιτρώσκω

ἐτμήθη vb 1st aor pass ind 3rd pers sg . . . . τέμνω

ἕτοιμα adj neut nom and acc pl . . . . ἕτοιμος

ἑτοίμαζε vb pres act impv 2nd pers sg . . . . ἑτοιμάζω

ἑτοιμάζειν vb pres act inf   id.

ἑτοιμάζεσθαι vb pres m/p inf   id.

ἑτοιμάζεσθε vb pres m/p impv 2nd pers pl   id.

ἑτοιμάζεται vb pres m/p ind 3rd pers sg   id.

ἑτοιμάζον vb pres act part neut nom and acc sg   id.

ἑτοιμάζονται vb pres m/p ind 3rd pers pl   id.

ἑτοιμάζοντες vb pres act part masc nom pl   id.

ἑτοιμάζοντι vb pres act part masc and neut dat sg   id.

ἑτοιμάζου vb pres m/p impv 2nd pers sg   id.

ἑτοιμάζουσιν vb pres act ind 3rd pers pl   id.

ἑτοιμάζω vb pres act ind 1st pers sg   id.

ἑτοιμάζων vb pres act part masc nom sg   id.

ἑτοίμασαι vb 1st aor mid impv 2nd pers sg   id.

ἑτοιμάσαι vb 1st aor act inf   id.

ἑτοιμάσας vb 1st aor act part masc nom sg   id.

ἑτοιμάσατε vb 1st aor act impv 2nd pers pl   id.

ἑτοιμασάτω vb 1st aor act impv 3rd pers sg   id.

ἑτοιμάσει vb fut act ind 3rd pers sg   id.

ἑτοιμάσεις vb fut act ind 2nd pers sg   id.

ἑτοιμάσῃ vb 1st aor act subj 3rd pers sg,

    fut mid ind 2nd pers sg . . . . ἑτοιμάζω

ἑτοιμασθέν vb 1st aor pass part neut nom and acc sg   id.

ἑτοιμασθῇ vb 1st aor pass subj 3rd pers sg   id.

ἑτοιμασθήσεται vb fut pass ind 3rd pers sg   id.

ἑτοιμασθήσονται vb fut pass ind 3rd pers pl   id.

ἑτοιμάσθητε vb 1st aor pass impv 2nd pers pl   id.

ἑτοιμάσθητι vb 1st aor pass impv 2nd pers sg   id.

ἑτοιμασία noun fem nom sg

ἑτοιμασίαν noun fem acc sg . . . . ἑτοιμασία

ἑτοιμασίας noun fem gen sg   id.

ἑτοίμασον vb 1st aor act impv 2nd pers sg . . . . . ἑτοιμάζω

ἑτοιμάσουσιν vb fut act ind 3rd pers pl   id.

ἑτοιμάσω vb fut act ind 1st pers sg   id.

ἑτοιμάσωμεν vb 1st aor act subj 1st pers pl   id.

ἑτοίμη adj fem nom sg . . . . ἕτοιμος

ἑτοίμην adj fem acc sg   id.

ἕτοιμοι adj masc nom pl   id.

ἕτοιμον adj masc acc sg, neut nom and acc sg   id.

ἕτοιμος adj masc nom sg   id.

ἑτοίμου adj masc and neut gen sg   id.

ἑτοίμους adj masc acc pl   id.

ἑτοίμῳ adj masc and neut dat sg   id.

ἑτοίμως adverb

ἐτόλμα vb impf act ind 3rd pers sg . . . . τολμάω

ἐτόλμησαν vb 1st aor act ind 3rd pers pl   id.

ἐτόλμησεν vb 1st aor act ind 3rd pers sg   id.

ἐτόξευσαν vb 1st aor act ind 3rd pers pl . . . . τοξεύω

ἐτόξευσεν vb 1st aor act ind 3rd pers sg   id.

ἔτος noun neut nom and acc sg

ἔτους noun neut gen sg . . . . ἔτος

ἐτράπησαν vb 2nd aor pass ind 3rd pers pl . . . . τρέπω

ἐτραυμάτισαν vb 1st aor act ind 3rd pers pl . . τραυματίζω

ἐτραυματίσθη vb 1st aor pass ind 3rd pers sg   id.

ἐτραυματίσθης vb 1st aor pass ind 2nd pers sg   id.

ἐτράφης vb 2nd aor pass ind 2nd pers sg . . . . τρέφω

ἐτραχηλίασεν vb 1st aor act ind 3rd pers sg . . . τραχηλιάω

ἐτρέπετο vb impf m/p ind 3rd pers sg . . . . τρέπω

ἔτρεφεν vb impf act ind 3rd pers sg . . . . τρέφω

ἐτρέφετο vb impf m/p ind 3rd pers sg   id.

ἐτρέφοντο vb impf m/p ind 3rd pers pl   id.

ἔτρεχεν vb impf act ind 3rd pers sg . . . . τρέχω

ἔτρεχον vb impf act ind 3rd pers pl   id.

ἐτρέψαντο vb 1st aor mid ind 3rd pers pl . . . . τρέπω

ἐτρέψατο vb 1st aor mid ind 3rd pers sg   id.

ἔτρεψε vb 1st aor act ind 3rd pers sg   id.

ἔτρησεν vb 1st aor act ind 3rd pers sg . . . . τετραίνω

ἔτριβον vb impf act ind 3rd pers pl . . . . τρίβω

ἐτρίσσευσαν vb 1st aor act ind 3rd pers pl . . . . τρισσεύω

ἐτρόμησαν vb 1st aor act ind 3rd pers pl . . . . τρομέω

ἐτροποῦτο vb impf m/p ind 3rd pers sg . . . . τροπόω

ἐτροπώθη vb 1st aor pass ind 3rd pers sg

ἐτροπώθησαν vb 1st aor pass ind 3rd pers pl . . . . . . τροπόω

ἐτροπώσατο vb 1st aor mid ind 3rd pers sg   id.

ἐτρόπωσεν vb 1st aor act ind 3rd pers sg   id.

ἐτροφοφόρησεν vb 1st aor act ind 3rd pers sg . τροφοφορέω

ἐτρύγησα vb 1st aor act ind 1st pers sg . . . . τρυγάω

ἐτρύγησαν vb 1st aor act ind 3rd pers pl   id.

ἐτρυγήσατε vb 1st aor act ind 2nd pers pl   id.

ἐτρύφησαν vb 1st aor act ind 3rd pers pl . . . . τρυφάω

ἐτρύχοντο vb impf m/p ind 3rd pers pl . . . . τρύχω

ἔτρωσε vb 1st aor act ind 3rd pers sg . . . . τιτρώσκω

ἐτύγχανεν vb impf act ind 3rd pers sg . . . . τυγχάνω

ἐτύγχανον vb impf act ind 3rd pers pl   id.

ἐτυλώθησαν vb 1st aor pass ind 3rd pers pl . . . . τυλόω

ἐτυμπάνιζεν vb impf act ind 3rd pers sg . . . . . τυμπανίζω

ἔτυπτε(ν) vb impf act ind 3rd pers sg . . . . τύπτω

ἔτυπτον vb impf act ind 3rd pers pl   id.

ἐτύπωσεν vb 1st aor act ind 3rd pers sg . . . . τυπόω

ἐτυρώθη vb 1st aor pass ind 3rd pers sg . . . . τυρόω

ἐτύρωσας vb 1st aor act ind 2nd pers sg   id.

ἐτυφλώθη vb 1st aor pass ind 3rd pers sg . . . . τυφλόω

ἐτυφλώθησαν vb 1st aor pass ind 3rd pers pl   id.

ἔτυχεν vb 2nd aor act ind 3rd pers sg . . . . τυγχάνω

ἐτύχομεν vb 2nd aor act ind 1st pers pl   id.

ἐτῶν noun neut gen pl . . . . ἔτος

εὖ adverb

εὐαγγέλια noun neut nom and acc pl . . . . εὐαγγέλιον

εὐαγγελία noun fem nom sg

εὐαγγελίαν noun fem acc sg . . . . εὐαγγελία

εὐαγγελίας noun fem gen sg   id.

εὐαγγελίζεσθε vb pres m/p impv 2nd pers pl . . . εὐαγγελίζω

εὐαγγελιζόμενοι vb pres m/p part masc nom pl   id.

εὐαγγελιζομένοις vb pres m/p part

    masc and neut dat pl   id.

εὐαγγελιζόμενος vb pres m/p part masc nom sg   id.

εὐαγγελιζομένου vb pres m/p part

    masc and neut gen sg   id.

εὐαγγελίζοντες vb pres act part masc nom pl   id.

εὐαγγελιῇ vb fut mid ind 2nd pers sg   id.

εὐαγγελιοῦνται vb fut mid ind 3rd pers pl   id.

εὐαγγελίσαι vb 1st aor mid ind 2nd pers sg   id.

εὐαγγελισάμενος vb 1st aor mid part masc nom sg   id.

εὐαγγελίσασθαι vb 1st aor mid inf   id.

εὐαγγελίσησθε vb 1st aor mid subj 2nd pers pl   id.

εὐαγγελισθήτω vb 1st aor pass impv 3rd pers sg   id.

εὐαγγελιῶ vb fut act ind 1st pers sg   id.

Ευαῖοι pr noun masc nom pl . . . . Ευαῖος

Ευαῖον pr noun masc acc sg   id.

Ευαῖος pr noun masc nom sg   id.

Ευαιου pr noun masc gen sg   id.

Ευαιους pr noun masc acc pl   id.

Ευαιῳ pr noun masc dat sg   id.

Ευαιων pr noun masc gen pl   id.

εὐάλωτος adj masc and fem nom sg

Ευαν pr noun fem acc sg . . . . Ευα

εὐανδρίας noun fem gen sg . . . . εὐανδρία

εὐαπάντητον adj acc sg, neut nom sg . . . . . . εὐαπάντητος

εὐαρέστει vb pres act impv 2nd pers sg . . . . . . εὐαρεστέω

εὐαρεστῆσαι vb 1st aor act inf								id.

εὐαρεστήσῃ vb 1st aor act subj 3rd pers sg								id.

εὐαρεστήσω vb fut act ind 1st pers sg								id.

εὐάρεστον adj acc sg, neut nom sg . . . . εὐάρεστος

εὐάρεστος adj masc and fem nom sg								id.

εὐαρμόστου adj gen sg . . . . εὐάρμοστος

εὖγε adverb and interjection

εὐγένειαν noun fem acc sg . . . . εὐγένεια

εὐγενείας noun fem gen sg								id.

εὐγενῆ adj masc and fem acc sg,

				neut nom and acc pl . . . . εὐγενής

εὐγενής adj masc and fem nom sg								id.

εὐγενίσας vb 1st aor act part masc nom sg . . . . εὐγενίζω

εὐγενῶς adverb

εὐγνωμοσύνην noun fem acc sg . . . . εὐγνωμοσύνη

εὔγνωστοι adj masc and fem nom pl . . . . εὔγνωστος

εὔγνωστος adj masc and fem nom sg								id.

εὐδία noun fem nom sg

εὐδοκεῖ vb pres act ind 3rd pers sg . . . . εὐδοκέω

εὐδοκήθη vb 1st aor pass ind 3rd pers sg								id.

εὐδόκησα vb 1st aor act ind 1st pers sg								id.

εὐδόκησαι vb 1st aor act inf								id.

εὐδόκησαν vb 1st aor act ind 3rd pers pl								id.

εὐδόκησας vb 1st aor act ind 2nd pers sg								id.

εὐδοκήσας vb 1st aor act part masc nom sg								id.

εὐδοκήσει vb fut act ind 3rd pers sg								id.

εὐδοκήσεις vb fut act ind 2nd pers sg								id.

εὐδόκησεν vb 1st aor act ind 3rd pers sg								id.

εὐδοκήσῃ vb 1st aor act subj 3rd pers sg								id.

εὐδοκήσῃς vb 1st aor act subj 2nd pers sg								id.

εὐδόκησον vb 1st aor act impv 2nd pers sg								id.

εὐδοκήσουσιν vb fut act ind 3rd pers pl								id.

εὐδοκήσω vb fut act ind 1st pers sg								id.

εὐδοκία noun fem nom sg

εὐδοκίᾳ noun fem dat sg . . . . εὐδοκία

εὐδοκίαις noun fem dat pl								id.

εὐδοκίαν noun fem acc sg								id.

εὐδοκίας noun fem gen sg and acc pl								id.

εὐδοκιμεῖται vb pres m/p ind 3rd pers sg . . . . . εὐδοκιμέω

εὐδοκιμηθήσεται vb fut pass ind 3rd pers sg								id.

εὐδόκιμοι adj masc and fem nom pl . . . . εὐδόκιμος

εὐδοκιμοῦν vb pres act part

				neut nom and acc sg . . . . εὐδοκιμέω

εὐδοκοῦμεν vb pres act ind 1st pers pl . . . . εὐδοκέω

εὐδοκοῦσι(ν) vb pres act ind 3rd pers pl								id.

εὐδοκῶ vb pres act ind 1st pers sg								id.

εὐδράνειαν noun fem acc sg . . . . εὐδράνεια

εὐειδεῖς adj masc and fem nom and acc pl . . . . εὐειδής

εὐεκτεῖν vb pres act inf . . . . εὐεκτέω

εὐέλπιδας adj masc and fem acc pl . . . . εὔελπις

εὐέλπιδες adj masc and fem nom pl								id.

εὔελπις adj masc nom sg								id.

εὐεξία noun fem nom sg

εὐεργεσίᾳ noun fem dat sg . . . . εὐεργεσία

εὐεργεσίαν noun fem acc sg								id.

εὐεργεσίας noun fem gen sg								id.

εὐεργεσιῶν noun fem gen pl								id.

εὐεργέταις noun masc dat pl . . . . εὐεργέτης

εὐεργέτας noun masc acc pl								id.

εὐεργετεῖν vb pres act inf . . . . εὐεργετέω

εὐεργετήθησαν vb 1st aor pass ind 3rd pers pl								id.

εὐεργετηθήσονται vb fut pass ind 3rd pers pl								id.

εὐεργετημάτων noun neut gen pl . . . . εὐεργέτημα

εὐεργετημένους vb perf m/p part masc acc pl . . . εὐεργετέω

εὐεργέτην noun masc acc sg . . . . εὐεργέτης

εὐεργετήσαντα vb 1st aor act part masc acc sg . . εὐεργετέω

εὐεργετήσαντι vb 1st aor act part

				masc and neut dat sg								id.

εὐεργετήσας vb 1st aor act part masc nom sg								id.

εὐεργετικόν adj masc acc sg,

				neut nom and acc sg . . . . εὐεργετικός

Ευεργετου pr noun masc gen sg . . . . Ευεργετης

εὐεργετοῦντι vb pres act part

				masc and neut dat sg . . . . εὐεργετέω

εὐεργετούντων vb pres act part

				masc and neut gen pl								id.

Ευζαι pr noun

εὔζωνοι adj masc and fem nom pl . . . . εὔζωνος

εὐζώνῳ adj dat sg								id.

εὐηγγελισάμην vb 1st aor mid ind

				1st pers sg . . . . εὐαγγελίζομαι

εὔηθες adj neut nom and acc sg . . . . εὐήθης

εὐήκοα adj neut nom and acc pl . . . . εὐήκοος

εὐήκοον adj masc acc sg, neut nom and acc sg								id.

εὐημερηκώς vb perf act part masc nom sg . . . . . . εὐημερέω

εὐημερησάντων vb 1st aor act part

				masc and neut gen pl								id.

εὐημερίᾳ noun fem dat sg . . . . εὐημερία

εὐημερίαις noun fem dat pl								id.

εὐημερίαν noun fem acc sg								id.

εὐημερίας noun fem gen sg and acc pl								id.

εὐημεροῦντες vb pres act part masc nom pl . . . . . εὐημερέω

εὐηργέτησεν vb 1st aor act ind 3rd pers sg . . . . εὐεργετέω

εὐηρέστει vb impf act ind 3rd pers sg . . . . εὐαρεστέω

εὐηρέστησα vb 1st aor act ind 1st pers sg								id.

εὐηρέστησαν vb 1st aor act ind 3rd pers pl								id.

εὐηρέστησεν vb 1st aor act ind 3rd pers sg								id.

εὐηρέστουν vb impf act ind 3rd pers pl								id.

εὐήχοις adj dat pl . . . . εὔηχος εὐήχων   adj gen pl . . . . εὐήχος

εὐθαλῆ   adj masc and fem acc sg,

      neut nom and acc pl . . . . εὐθαλής

εὐθαλῶν   vb pres act part masc nom sg . . . . εὐθαλέω

εὐθαρσεῖς   adj masc and fem nom and acc pl . . . . εὐθαρσής

εὐθαρσής   adj masc and fem nom sg   id.

εὐθαρσῶς   adverb

εὐθέα   adj neut nom and acc pl . . . . εὐθύς

εὐθεῖα   adj fem nom sg   id.

εὐθείᾳ   adj fem dat sg   id.

εὐθεῖαι   adj fem nom pl   id.

εὐθείαις   adj fem dat pl   id.

εὐθεῖαν   adj fem acc sg   id.

εὐθείας   adj fem gen sg   id.

εὐθεῖς   adj masc nom and acc pl   id.

εὐθείων   adj fem gen pl   id.

εὐθές   adj neut nom and acc sg . . . . εὐθής

εὐθέσι   adj masc and neut dat pl . . . . εὐθύς

εὔθετον   adj acc sg, neut nom sg . . . . εὔθετος

εὐθέτῳ   adj dat sg   id.

εὐθέως   adverb

εὐθῆ   adj masc and fem acc sg, neut nom and acc pl . . . εὐθής

εὐθηνῆσαι   vb 1st aor act inf . . . . εὐθηνέω

εὐθήνησαν   vb 1st aor act ind 3rd pers pl   id.

εὐθηνία   noun fem nom sg

εὐθηνίᾳ   noun fem dat sg . . . . εὐθηνία

εὐθηνίας   noun fem gen sg   id.

εὐθηνοῦν   vb pres act part neut nom and acc sg . . . . εὐθηνέω

εὐθηνοῦνται   vb pres m/p ind 3rd pers pl   id.

εὐθηνούντων   vb pres act part

      masc and neut gen pl   id.

εὐθηνοῦσα   vb pres act part fem nom sg   id.

εὐθηνοῦσαν   vb pres act part fem acc sg   id.

εὐθηνοῦσιν   vb pres act ind 3rd pers pl   id.

εὐθηνῶν   vb pres act part masc nom sg   id.

εὐθής   adj masc and fem nom sg

εὐθίκτως   adverb

εὐθοῦς   adj gen sg . . . . εὐθής

εὔθραυστα   adj neut nom and acc pl . . . . εὔθραυστος

εὐθύ   adj neut nom and acc sg . . . . εὐθύς

εὐθύθητα   see εὐθύτητα

εὔθυμοι   adj masc and fem nom pl . . . . εὔθυμος

εὐθῦναι   vb 1st aor act inf . . . . εὐθύνω

εὔθυναν   noun fem acc sg . . . . εὔθυνα

εὐθύνατε   vb 1st aor act impv 2nd pers pl . . . . εὐθύνω

εὐθυνεῖ   vb fut act ind 3rd pers sg   id.

εὐθυνεῖς   vb fut act ind 2nd pers sg   id.

εὐθύνεται   vb pres m/p ind 3rd pers sg   id.

εὐθύνῃ   vb pres act subj 3rd pers sg,

      1st aor act subj 3rd pers sg   id.

εὐθύνῃς   vb pres act subj 2nd pers sg,

      1st aor act subj 2nd pers sg   id.

εὐθύνθη   vb 1st aor pass ind 3rd pers sg . . . . εὐθύνω

εὔθυνον   vb 1st aor act impv 2nd pers sg   id.

εὐθύνοντας   vb pres act part masc acc pl   id.

εὐθύς   adverb

εὐθύτης   noun fem nom sg

εὐθύτητα   noun fem acc sg . . . . εὐθύτης

εὐθύτητας   noun fem acc pl   id.

εὐθύτητι   noun fem dat sg   id.

εὐθύτητος   noun fem gen sg   id.

Ευι   pr noun

Ευιλα   pr noun

Ευιλατ   pr noun

εὐιλατεύοντα   vb pres act part masc acc sg . . . . εὐιλατεύω

εὐιλατεῦσαι   vb 1st aor act inf   id.

εὐιλατεύσεις   vb fut act ind 2nd pers sg   id.

εὐίλατος   adj masc and fem nom sg

εὐιλάτου   adj gen sg . . . . εὐίλατος

Ευιλμαρωδαχ   pr noun

Ευιν   pr noun

εὐκαιρίᾳ   noun fem dat sg . . . . εὐκαιρία

εὐκαιρίαις   noun fem dat pl   id.

εὐκαιρίας   noun fem gen sg   id.

εὔκαιρον   adj acc sg, neut nom sg . . . . εὔκαιρος

εὐκαιροτάτους   superl adj masc acc pl   id.

εὐκαιροτάτῳ   superl adj masc and neut dat sg   id.

εὐκαίρως   adverb

εὐκατάλλακτον   adj acc sg, neut nom sg . . εὐκατάλλακτος

εὐκαταφρόνητον   adj acc sg,

      neut nom sg . . . . εὐκαταφρόνητος

εὐκαταφρόνητος   adj masc and fem nom sg   id.

εὐκίνητον   adj acc sg, neut nom sg . . . . εὐκίνητος

εὐκλεῆς   adj masc and fem nom sg

εὔκλεια   noun fem nom sg

εὐκλείας   noun fem gen sg . . . . εὔκλεια

εὐκληματοῦσα   vb pres act part fem nom sg . . εὐκληματέω

εὔκολοι   adj masc and fem nom pl . . . . εὔκολος

εὐκοπίαν   noun fem acc sg . . . . εὐκοπία

εὔκοπον   adj acc sg, neut nom sg . . . . εὔκοπος

εὐκοσμεῖν   vb pres act inf . . . . εὐκοσμέω

εὐκοσμίᾳ   noun fem dat sg . . . . εὐκοσμία

εὐκοσμίας   noun fem gen sg   id.

εὐκύκλου   adj gen sg . . . . εὔκυκλος

εὐλάβειαν   noun fem acc sg . . . . εὐλάβεια

εὐλαβείας   noun fem gen sg   id.

εὐλαβεῖς   adj masc and fem nom and acc pl . . . . . . εὐλαβής

εὐλαβεῖσθαι   vb pres dep inf . . . . εὐλαβέομαι

εὐλαβεῖσθε   vb pres dep impv 2nd pers pl   id.

εὐλαβείσθω   vb pres dep impv 3rd pers sg   id.

εὐλαβεῖτο   vb pres dep ind 3rd pers sg   id.

εὐλαβῇ   vb pres dep ind 2nd pers sg   id.

εὐλαβηθείς   vb 1st aor pass part masc nom sg   id.

εὐλαβηθεῖσα   vb 1st aor pass part fem nom sg   id.

εὐλαβήθη   vb 1st aor pass ind 3rd pers sg . . . . . εὐλαβέομαι

εὐλαβηθῇ   vb 1st aor pass subj 3rd pers sg   id.

εὐλαβήθην   vb 1st aor pass ind 1st pers sg   id.

εὐλαβηθῇς   vb 1st aor pass subj 2nd pers sg   id.

εὐλαβήθησαν   vb 1st aor pass ind 3rd pers pl   id.

εὐλαβηθήσεσθε   vb fut pass ind 2nd pers pl   id.

εὐλαβηθήσεται   vb fut pass ind 3rd pers sg   id.

εὐλαβηθήσῃ   vb fut pass ind 2nd pers sg   id.

εὐλαβηθήσονται   vb fut pass ind 3rd pers pl   id.

εὐλαβήθητε   vb 1st aor pass impv 2nd pers pl,
     1st aor pass ind 2nd pers pl   id.

εὐλαβής   adj masc and fem nom sg

εὐλαβοῦ   vb pres dep impv 2nd pers sg . . . . εὐλαβέομαι

εὐλαβοῦμαι   vb pres dep ind 1st pers sg   id.

εὐλαβουμένοις   vb pres dep part masc and neut dat pl   id.

εὐλαβούμενος   vb pres dep part masc nom sg   id.

εὐλαβουμένους   vb pres dep part masc acc pl   id.

εὐλαβουμένων   vb pres dep part gen pl   id.

εὐλαβούμην   vb impf dep ind 1st pers sg   id.

εὐλαβοῦνται   vb pres dep ind 3rd pers pl   id.

εὐλαβῶς   adverb

εὔλαλος   adj masc and fem nom sg

εὐλόγει   vb pres act impv 2nd pers sg . . . . εὐλογέω

εὐλογεῖ   vb pres act ind 3rd pers sg   id.

εὐλογεῖν   vb pres act inf   id.

εὐλογεῖς   vb pres act ind 2nd pers sg   id.

εὐλογεῖται   vb pres m/p ind 3rd pers sg   id.

εὐλογεῖτε   vb pres act impv 2nd pers pl,
     pres act ind 2nd pers pl   id.

εὐλογείτω   vb pres act impv 3rd pers sg   id.

εὐλογείτωσαν   vb pres act impv 3rd pers pl   id.

εὐλογῇ   vb pres act subj 3rd pers sg   id.

εὐλογηθείη   vb 1st aor pass opt 3rd pers sg   id.

εὐλογηθείητε   vb 1st aor pass opt 2nd pers pl   id.

εὐλογηθῆναι   vb 1st aor pass inf   id.

εὐλογήθησαν   vb 1st aor pass ind 3rd pers pl   id.

εὐλογηθήσεται   vb fut pass ind 3rd pers sg   id.

εὐλογηθήσονται   vb fut pass ind 3rd pers pl   id.

εὐλογήκαμεν   vb perf act ind 1st pers pl   id.

εὐλόγηκας   vb perf act ind 2nd pers sg   id.

εὐλογημένα   vb perf m/p part neut nom and acc pl   id.

εὐλογημέναι   vb perf m/p part fem nom pl   id.

εὐλογημένη   vb perf m/p part fem nom sg   id.

εὐλογημένοι   vb perf m/p part masc nom pl   id.

εὐλογημένον   vb perf m/p part masc acc sg,
     neut nom and acc sg   id.

εὐλογημένος   vb perf m/p part masc nom sg   id.

εὐλόγηνται   vb perf m/p ind 3rd pers pl   id.

εὐλόγησα   vb 1st aor act ind 1st pers sg   id.

εὐλογήσαι   vb 1st aor act opt 3rd pers sg   id.

εὐλογῆσαι   vb 1st aor act inf   id.

εὐλογήσαισαν   vb 1st aor act opt 3rd pers pl   id.

εὐλόγησαν   vb 1st aor act ind 3rd pers pl,
     1st aor act part neut nom and acc sg . . . . . . εὐλογέω

εὐλογήσαντες   vb 1st aor act part masc nom pl   id.

εὐλόγησας   vb 1st aor act ind 2nd pers sg   id.

εὐλογήσας   vb 1st aor act part masc nom sg   id.

εὐλογήσατε   vb 1st aor act impv 2nd pers pl   id.

εὐλογησάτωσαν   vb 1st aor act impv 3rd pers pl   id.

εὐλόγησε(ν)   vb 1st aor act ind 3rd pers sg   id.

εὐλογήσει   vb fut act ind 3rd pers sg   id.

εὐλογήσεις   vb fut act ind 2nd pers sg   id.

εὐλόγησεν   vb 1st aor act ind 3rd pers sg   id.

εὐλογήσετε   vb fut act ind 2nd pers pl   id.

εὐλογήσῃ   vb 1st aor act subj 3rd pers sg   id.

εὐλογήσῃς   vb 1st aor act subj 2nd pers sg   id.

εὐλογήσομεν   vb fut act ind 1st pers pl   id.

εὐλόγησον   vb 1st aor act impv 2nd pers sg   id.

εὐλογήσουσιν   vb fut act ind 3rd pers pl   id.

εὐλογήσω   vb 1st aor act subj 1st pers sg,
     fut act ind 1st pers sg   id.

εὐλογήσωσι   vb 1st aor act subj 3rd pers pl   id.

εὐλόγηται   vb perf m/p ind 3rd pers sg   id.

εὐλογητή   adj fem nom sg . . . . εὐλογητός

εὐλογητοί   adj masc nom pl   id.

εὐλογητόν   adj masc acc sg, neut nom and acc sg   id.

εὐλογητός   adj masc nom sg   id.

εὐλογία   noun fem nom sg

εὐλογία   noun fem dat sg . . . . εὐλογία

εὐλογίαι   noun fem nom pl   id.

εὐλογίαις   noun fem dat pl   id.

εὐλογίαν   noun fem acc sg   id.

εὐλογίας   noun fem gen sg   id.

εὐλογιστία   noun fem nom sg

εὐλογιστίας   noun fem gen sg . . . . εὐλογιστία

εὐλογοῦμεν   vb pres act ind 1st pers pl . . . . εὐλογέω

εὐλογουμένη   vb pres m/p part fem nom sg   id.

εὐλόγουν   vb impf act ind 3rd pers pl,
     pres act part neut nom and acc sg   id.

εὐλογοῦντα   vb pres act part masc acc sg   id.

εὐλογοῦνται   vb pres m/p ind 3rd pers pl   id.

εὐλογοῦντας   vb pres act part masc acc pl   id.

εὐλογοῦντες   vb pres act part masc nom pl   id.

εὐλογοῦσαν   vb pres act part fem acc sg   id.

εὐλογῶν   vb pres act part masc nom sg   id.

εὐλογῶσιν   vb pres act subj 3rd pers pl   id.

Ευμα   pr noun

εὐμαθῶς   adverb

εὐμεγέθεις   adj masc and fem nom and acc pl . . . . εὐμεγέθης

εὐμεγέθης   adj masc and fem nom sg   id.

εὐμελής   adj masc and fem nom sg

Εὐμενει   pr noun masc dat sg . . . . Εὐμενης

εὐμένειαν   noun fem acc sg . . . . εὐμένεια

εὐμενεῖς   adj masc and fem nom and acc pl . . . . εὐμενής εὐμενῶς adverb

εὐμετάβολος adj masc and fem nom sg

εὐμήκη adj masc and fem acc sg . . . . εὐμήκης

εὐμορφίαν noun fem acc sg . . . . εὐμορφία

εὐμορφίας noun fem gen sg   id.

εὐμόρφου adj gen sg . . . . εὔμορφος

εὐνοήσειν vb fut act inf . . . . εὐνοέω

εὐνοίᾳ noun fem dat sg . . . . εὔνοια

εὔνοιαν noun fem acc sg   id.

εὐνοίας noun fem gen sg and acc pl   id.

εὐνομίαν noun fem acc sg . . . . εὐνομία

εὐνοοῦντες vb pres act part masc nom pl . . . . εὐνοέω

εὐνοοῦσι vb pres act part masc and neut dat pl   id.

εὔνους adj masc and fem nom sg

εὐνοῦχοι noun masc nom pl . . . . εὐνοῦχος

εὐνούχοις noun masc dat pl   id.

εὐνοῦχον noun masc acc sg   id.

εὐνοῦχος noun masc nom sg   id.

εὐνούχου noun masc gen sg   id.

εὐνούχους noun masc acc pl   id.

εὐνούχῳ noun masc dat sg   id.

εὐνούχων noun masc gen pl   id.

εὔξαι vb
1st aor mid impv 2nd pers sg . . . . εὔχομαι

εὐξάμενος vb 1st aor mid part masc nom sg   id.

εὐξαμένου vb 1st aor mid part masc and neut gen sg id.

εὐξάμην vb 1st aor mid ind 1st pers sg   id.

εὔξαντο vb 1st aor mid ind 3rd pers pl   id.

εὔξασθαι vb 1st aor mid inf   id.

εὔξασθε vb 1st aor mid impv 2nd pers pl,
         1st aor mid ind 2nd pers pl   id.

εὔξεται vb fut mid ind 3rd pers sg   id.

εὔξῃ vb 1st aor mid subj 2nd pers sg,
      fut mid ind 2nd pers sg   id.

εὔξησθε vb 1st aor mid subj 2nd pers pl   id.

εὔξηται vb 1st aor mid subj 3rd pers sg   id.

εὔξομαι vb fut mid ind 1st pers sg   id.

εὔξονται vb fut mid ind 3rd pers pl   id.

εὔξω vb 1st aor mid ind 2nd pers sg   id.

εὔξωμαι vb 1st aor mid subj 1st pers sg   id.

εὔοδα adj neut nom and acc pl . . . . εὔοδος

εὐοδία noun fem nom sg

εὐοδίαι noun fem nom pl . . . . εὐοδία

εὐοδίαν noun fem acc sg   id.

εὔοδοι adj masc and fem nom pl . . . . εὔοδος

εὐοδοῖ vb pres act ind 3rd pers sg . . . . εὐοδόω

εὐοδοῖς vb pres act ind 2nd pers sg   id.

εὔοδος adj masc and fem nom sg

εὐοδούμενον vb pres m/p part masc acc sg,
            neut nom and acc sg . . . . εὐοδόω

εὐοδούμενος vb pres m/p part masc nom sg   id.

εὐοδουμένῳ vb pres m/p part masc and neut dat sg   id.

εὐοδοῦται vb pres m/p ind 3rd pers sg . . . . εὐοδόω

εὐοδωθείημεν vb 1st aor pass opt 1st pers pl   id.

εὐοδωθείητε vb 1st aor pass opt 2nd pers pl   id.

εὐοδώθη vb 1st aor pass ind 3rd pers sg   id.

εὐοδωθῇ vb 1st aor pass subj 3rd pers sg   id.

εὐοδωθήσεσθε vb fut pass ind 2nd pers pl   id.

εὐοδωθήσεται vb fut pass ind 3rd pers sg   id.

εὐοδωθήσῃ vb fut pass ind 2nd pers sg   id.

εὐοδωθήσονται vb fut pass ind 3rd pers pl   id.

εὐοδωθῶσιν vb 1st aor pass subj 3rd pers pl   id.

εὐόδωκεν vb perf act ind 3rd pers sg   id.

εὐόδως adverb

εὐόδωσα vb 1st aor act ind 1st pers sg . . . . εὐοδόω

εὐοδώσαι vb 1st aor act opt 3rd pers sg   id.

εὐοδώσαντα vb 1st aor act part masc acc sg   id.

εὐοδώσαντι vb 1st aor act part masc and neut dat sg id.

εὐοδώσει vb fut act ind 3rd pers sg   id.

εὐοδώσεις vb fut act ind 2nd pers sg   id.

εὐόδωσεν vb 1st aor act ind 3rd pers sg   id.

εὐοδώσῃ vb 1st aor act subj 3rd pers sg   id.

εὐόδωσον vb 1st aor act impv 2nd pers sg   id.

εὐοδώσω vb fut act ind 1st pers sg   id.

εὔοπτος adj masc and fem nom sg

εὐπαθοῦντες vb pres act part masc nom pl . . . . . . εὐπαθέω

εὐπαθῶν vb pres act part masc nom sg   id.

εὐπάρυφα adj neut nom and acc pl . . . . εὐπάρυφος

Εὐπάτορα pr noun masc acc sg . . . . Εὐπάτωρ

Εὐπάτωρ pr noun

εὐπειθείᾳ noun fem dat sg . . . . εὐπείθεια

εὐπείθειαν noun fem acc sg   id.

εὐπειθείας noun fem gen sg   id.

εὐπειθοῦντας vb pres act part masc acc pl . . . . . . εὐπειθέω

Εὐπόλεμον pr noun masc acc sg . . . . Εὐπόλεμος

Εὐπόλεμου pr noun masc gen sg   id.

εὐπορηθείς vb 1st aor pass part masc nom sg . . . . . εὐπορέω

εὐπορηθῇ vb 1st aor pass subj 3rd pers sg   id.

εὐπόρησεν vb 1st aor act ind 3rd pers sg   id.

εὐπραξίᾳ noun fem dat sg . . . . εὐπραξία

εὐπραξίαν noun fem acc sg   id.

εὐπρέπεια noun fem nom sg

εὐπρεπείᾳ noun fem dat sg . . . . εὐπρέπεια

εὐπρεπείαις noun fem dat pl   id.

εὐπρέπειαν noun fem acc sg   id.

εὐπρεπείας noun fem gen sg and acc pl . . . . εὐπρέπεια

εὐπρεπεῖς adj masc and fem nom and acc pl . . . . . εὐπρεπής

εὐπρεπεστέρα comp adj fem nom sg   id.

εὐπρεπῆ adj neut nom and acc pl   id.

εὐπρεπής adj masc and fem nom sg   id.

εὐπρεπῶς adverb

εὐπροσήγορα adj neut nom and acc pl . . . . εὐπροσήγορος

εὐπρόσωπος adj masc and fem nom sg

εὕραμεν vb 1st aor act ind 1st pers pl . . . . εὑρίσκω

εὗραν vb 1st aor act ind 3rd pers pl . . . . εὑρίσκω
εὗρε(ν) vb 2nd aor act ind 3rd pers sg   id.
εὑρέ vb 2nd aor act impv 2nd pers sg   id.
εὑρεθείη vb 1st aor pass opt 3rd pers sg   id.
εὑρεθείς vb 1st aor pass part masc nom sg   id.
εὑρεθεῖσαν vb 1st aor pass part fem acc sg   id.
εὑρεθείσας vb 1st aor pass part fem acc pl   id.
εὑρεθείσης vb 1st aor pass part fem gen sg   id.
εὑρεθεῖσι vb 1st aor pass part masc and neut dat pl   id.
εὑρεθέν vb 1st aor pass part neut nom and acc sg   id.
εὑρεθέντα vb 1st aor pass part masc acc sg,
          neut nom and acc pl   id.
εὑρεθέντας vb 1st aor pass part masc acc pl   id.
εὑρεθέντες vb 1st aor pass part masc nom pl   id.
εὑρεθέντι vb 1st aor pass part masc and neut dat sg id.
εὑρεθέντος vb 1st aor pass part masc and neut gen sg id.
εὑρέθη vb 1st aor pass ind 3rd pers sg   id.
εὑρεθῇ vb 1st aor pass subj 3rd pers sg   id.
εὑρέθην vb 1st aor pass ind 1st pers sg   id.
εὑρεθῆναι vb 1st aor pass inf   id.
εὑρέθης vb 1st aor pass ind 2nd pers sg   id.
εὑρέθησαν vb 1st aor pass ind 3rd pers pl   id.
εὑρεθήσεται vb fut pass ind 3rd pers sg   id.
εὑρεθήσομαι vb fut pass ind 1st pers sg   id.
εὑρεθήσονται vb fut pass ind 3rd pers pl   id.
εὑρεθήτω vb 1st aor pass impv 3rd pers sg   id.
εὑρεθῶσιν vb 1st aor pass subj 3rd pers pl   id.
εὑρεῖν vb 2nd aor act inf   id.
εὑρεῖς adj masc nom and acc pl . . . . εὐρύς
εὕρεμα noun neut nom and acc sg
εὗρεν vb 2nd aor act ind 3rd pers sg . . . . εὑρίσκω
εὗρες vb 2nd aor act ind 2nd pers sg   id.
εὕρεσις noun fem nom sg
εὕρετε vb 2nd aor act ind 2nd pers pl . . . . εὑρίσκω
εὑρετῇ adj fem dat sg . . . . εὑρετός
εὑρετής noun masc nom sg
εὑρέτωσαν vb 2nd aor act impv 3rd pers pl . . . . . . εὑρίσκω
εὕρῃ vb 2nd aor act subj 3rd pers sg   id.
εὕρηκα vb perf act ind 1st pers sg   id.
εὑρήκαμεν vb perf act ind 1st pers pl   id.
εὕρηκας vb perf act ind 2nd pers sg   id.
εὑρήκατε vb perf act ind 2nd pers pl   id.
εὕρηκεν vb perf act ind 3rd pers sg   id.
εὑρηκέναι vb perf act inf   id.
εὑρηκώς vb perf act part masc nom sg   id.
εὕρηνται vb perf m/p ind 3rd pers pl   id.
εὕρης vb 2nd aor act subj 2nd pers sg   id.
εὑρήσει vb fut act ind 3rd pers sg   id.
εὑρήσεις vb fut act ind 2nd pers sg   id.
εὑρήσετε vb fut act ind 2nd pers pl   id.
εὑρήσομεν vb fut act ind 1st pers pl   id.
εὑρήσουσιν vb fut act ind 3rd pers pl   id.

εὕρηται vb perf m/p ind 3rd pers sg . . . . εὑρίσκω
εὕρητε vb 2nd aor act subj 2nd pers pl   id.
εὑρίσκει vb pres act ind 3rd pers sg   id.
εὑρίσκειν vb pres act inf   id.
εὑρίσκεται vb pres m/p ind 3rd pers sg   id.
εὑρίσκετε vb pres act ind 2nd pers pl   id.
εὑρίσκετο vb impf m/p ind 3rd pers sg   id.
εὑρίσκῃ vb pres act subj 3rd pers sg   id.
εὑρίσκηται vb pres m/p subj 3rd pers sg   id.
εὑρίσκομεν vb pres act ind 1st pers pl   id.
εὑρισκόμενοι vb pres m/p part masc nom pl   id.
εὑρισκομένοις vb pres m/p part masc and neut dat pl id.
εὑρισκόμενος vb pres m/p part masc nom sg   id.
εὑρισκομένου vb pres m/p part masc and neut gen sg id.
εὑρίσκοντα vb pres act part masc acc sg   id.
εὑρίσκονται vb pres m/p ind 3rd pers pl   id.
εὑρίσκοντες vb pres act part masc nom pl   id.
εὑρίσκοντο vb impf m/p ind 3rd pers pl   id.
εὑρίσκοντος vb pres act part masc and neut gen sg id.
εὑρίσκουσα vb pres act part fem nom sg   id.
εὑρίσκουσι(ν) vb pres act part masc and neut dat pl id.
εὑρίσκουσιν vb pres act ind 3rd pers pl   id.
εὑρίσκω vb pres act ind 1st pers sg   id.
εὑρίσκων vb pres act part masc nom sg   id.
εὕροι vb 2nd aor act opt 3rd pers sg   id.
εὕροιμι vb 2nd aor act opt 1st pers sg   id.
εὕροις vb 2nd aor act opt 2nd pers sg   id.
εὕροισαν vb 2nd aor act opt 3rd pers pl   id.
εὕροιτε vb 2nd aor act opt 2nd pers pl   id.
εὕροιτο vb 2nd aor mid opt 3rd pers sg   id.
εὕρομεν vb 2nd aor act ind 1st pers pl   id.
εὗρον vb 2nd aor act ind 1st pers sg and 3rd pers pl id.
εὑρόντα vb 2nd aor act part masc acc sg   id.
εὑρόντες vb 2nd aor act part masc nom pl   id.
εὑρόντι vb 2nd aor act part masc and neut dat sg   id.
εὑρόντος vb 2nd aor act part masc and neut gen sg id.
εὖρος noun neut nom and acc sg
εὕροσαν vb 2nd aor act ind 3rd pers pl . . . . εὑρίσκω
εὔρους noun neut gen sg . . . . εὖρος
εὑροῦσα vb 2nd aor act part fem nom sg . . . . εὑρίσκω
εὑρούσαις vb 2nd aor act part fem dat pl   id.
εὔρυθμον adj acc sg, neut nom sg . . . . εὔρυθμος
Εὐρυχωρια pr noun fem nom sg
εὐρύχωροι adj masc and fem nom pl . . . . εὐρύχωρος
εὐρύχωρον adj acc sg, neut nom sg   id.
εὐρύχωρος adj masc and fem nom sg   id.
εὐρυχώρῳ adj dat sg   id.
εὕρω vb 2nd aor act subj 1st pers sg . . . . εὑρίσκω
εὕρωμεν vb 2nd aor act subj 1st pers pl   id.
εὑρών vb 2nd aor act part masc nom sg   id.
εὕρωσι(ν) vb 2nd aor act subj 3rd pers pl   id.
εὔρωστον adj acc sg, neut nom sg . . . . εὔρωστος

εὐρώστως adverb	
εὐρωτιῶν vb pres act part masc nom sg	εὐρωτιάω
εὐσεβεῖ adj dat sg	εὐσεβής
εὐσεβεῖ vb pres act ind 3rd pers sg	εὐσεβέω
εὐσέβεια noun fem nom sg	
εὐσεβείᾳ noun fem dat sg	εὐσέβεια
εὐσέβειαν noun fem acc sg	id.
εὐσεβείας noun fem gen sg	id.
εὐσεβεῖς adj masc and fem nom and acc pl	εὐσεβής
εὐσεβεῖτε vb pres act impv 2nd pers pl	εὐσεβέω
εὐσεβέσι adj dat pl	εὐσεβής
εὐσεβῆ adj neut nom and acc pl	id.
εὐσεβής adj masc and fem nom sg	id.
εὐσέβησαν vb 1st aor act ind 3rd pers pl	εὐσεβέω
εὐσεβήσουσι vb fut act ind 3rd pers pl	id.
εὐσεβοῦμεν vb pres act ind 1st pers pl	id.
εὐσεβούντων vb pres act part masc and neut gen pl	id.
εὐσεβοῦς adj gen sg	εὐσεβής
εὐσεβῶν adj gen pl	id.
εὐσήμῳ adj dat sg	εὔσημος
εὐσήμως adverb	
εὔσκιον adj acc sg, neut nom sg	εὔσκιος
εὔσπλαγχνος adj masc and fem nom sg	
εὐστάθεια noun fem nom sg	
εὐσταθείᾳ noun fem dat sg	εὐστάθεια
εὐστάθειαν noun fem acc sg	id.
εὐσταθείας noun fem gen sg	id.
εὐσταθεῖν vb pres act inf	εὐσταθέω
εὐσταθῆ adj neut nom and acc pl	εὐσταθής
εὐσταθήσειν vb fut act inf	εὐσταθέω
εὐστάθησεν vb 1st aor act ind 3rd pers sg	id.
εὐσταθοῦν adj neut nom and acc sg	εὐσταθής
εὐσταθοῦς adj gen sg	id.
εὔστοχοι adj masc and fem nom pl	εὔστοχος
εὐστόχως adverb	
εὐστροφίᾳ noun fem dat sg	εὐστροφία
εὐσυναλλάκτως adverb	
εὐσχημοσύνῃ noun fem dat sg	εὐσχημοσύνη
εὐσχήμων adj masc nom sg	
εὐτάκτει vb pres act impv 2nd pers sg	εὐτακτέω
εὐτάκτως adverb	
εὐταξίαν noun fem acc sg	εὐταξία
εὐτεκνίας noun fem gen sg	εὐτεκνία
εὐτελεῖ adj dat sg	εὐτελής
εὐτελεστέρα comp adj fem nom sg	id.
εὐτελῆ adj neut nom and acc pl	id.
εὐτελοῦς adj gen sg	id.
εὐτελῶς adverb	
εὔτηκτον adj acc sg, neut nom sg	εὔτηκτος
εὐτολμίας noun fem gen sg	εὐτολμία
εὐτονίας noun fem gen sg	εὐτονία
εὐτόνως adverb	

εὐτονώτερε comp adj masc voc sg	εὔτονος
εὐτονώτερον comp adj masc acc sg,	
neut nom and acc sg	id.
εὐτρέπιζε vb impf act ind 3rd pers sg	εὐτρεπίζω
εὐφημοῦντες vb pres act part masc nom pl	εὐφημέω
εὐφθάρτων adj gen pl	εὔφθαρτος
εὐφραίνει vb pres act ind 3rd pers sg	εὐφραίνω
εὐφραίνεσθαι vb pres m/p inf	id.
εὐφραίνεσθε vb pres m/p impv 2nd pers pl	id.
εὐφραινέσθω vb pres m/p impv 3rd pers sg	id.
εὐφραινέσθωσαν vb pres m/p impv 3rd pers pl	id.
εὐφραίνεται vb pres m/p ind 3rd pers sg	id.
εὐφραίνετο vb impf mid ind 3rd pers sg	id.
εὐφραίνηται vb pres m/p subj 3rd pers sg	id.
εὐφραινόμεθα vb pres m/p ind 1st pers pl	id.
εὐφραίνομεν vb pres act ind 1st pers pl	id.
εὐφραινομένη vb pres m/p part fem nom sg	id.
εὐφραινομένην vb pres m/p part fem acc sg	id.
εὐφραινομένης vb pres m/p part fem gen sg	id.
εὐφραινόμενοι vb pres m/p part masc nom pl	id.
εὐφραινόμενος vb pres m/p part masc nom sg	id.
εὐφραινομένους vb pres m/p part masc acc pl	id.
εὐφραινομένων vb pres m/p part gen pl	id.
εὐφραινόμην vb impf m/p ind 1st pers sg	id.
εὐφραίνοντα vb pres act part masc acc sg,	
neut nom and acc pl	id.
εὐφραίνονται vb pres m/p ind 3rd pers pl	id.
εὐφραίνοντο vb impf m/p ind 3rd pers pl	id.
εὐφραίνου vb pres m/p impv 2nd pers sg	id.
εὐφραίνουσιν vb pres act ind 3rd pers pl	id.
εὐφράναι vb 1st aor act opt 3rd pers sg	id.
εὐφράναι vb 1st aor act inf	id.
εὔφραναν vb 1st aor act ind 3rd pers pl	id.
εὔφρανας vb 1st aor act ind 2nd pers sg	id.
εὐφρανεῖ vb fut act ind 3rd pers sg	id.
εὐφρανεῖς vb fut act ind 2nd pers sg	id.
εὔφρανεν vb 1st aor act ind 3rd pers sg	id.
εὐφρανθείη vb 1st aor pass opt 3rd pers sg	id.
εὐφρανθείησαν vb 1st aor pass opt 3rd pers pl	id.
εὐφρανθείητε vb 1st aor pass opt 2nd pers pl	id.
εὐφρανθέντες vb 1st aor pass part masc nom pl	id.
εὐφράνθη vb 1st aor pass ind 3rd pers sg	id.
εὐφρανθῇ vb 1st aor pass subj 3rd pers sg	id.
εὐφράνθημεν vb 1st aor pass ind 1st pers pl	id.
εὐφράνθην vb 1st aor pass ind 1st pers sg	id.
εὐφρανθῆναι vb 1st aor pass inf	id.
εὐφρανθῆς vb 1st aor pass subj 2nd pers sg	id.
εὐφράνθησαν vb 1st aor pass ind 3rd pers pl	id.
εὐφρανθήσεσθε vb fut pass ind 2nd pers pl	id.
εὐφρανθήσεται vb fut pass ind 3rd pers sg	id.
εὐφρανθήσῃ vb fut pass ind 2nd pers sg	id.
εὐφρανθήσομαι vb fut pass ind 1st pers sg	id.

εὐφρανθησόμεθα vb fut pass ind 1st pers pl .... εὐφραίνω
εὐφρανθήσονται vb fut pass ind 3rd pers pl	id.
εὐφράνθητε vb 1st aor pass impv 2nd pers pl	id.
εὐφράνθητι vb 1st aor pass impv 2nd pers sg	id.
εὐφρανθήτω vb 1st aor pass impv 3rd pers sg	id.
εὐφρανθήτωσαν vb 1st aor pass impv 3rd pers pl	id.
εὐφρανθῶ vb 1st aor pass subj 1st pers sg	id.
εὐφρανθῶμεν vb 1st aor pass subj 1st pers pl	id.
εὐφρανθῶσιν vb 1st aor pass subj 3rd pers pl	id.
εὐφρανον vb 1st aor act impv 2nd pers sg	id.
εὐφρανοῦσιν vb fut act ind 3rd pers pl	id.
εὐφρανῶ vb fut act ind 1st pers sg	id.
Εὐφράτη pr noun masc dat sg .... Εὐφράτης
Εὐφράτην pr noun masc acc sg	id.
Εὐφράτης pr noun masc nom sg	id.
Εὐφράτου pr noun masc gen sg	id.
εὐφροσύναι noun fem nom pl .... εὐφροσύνη
εὐφροσύναις noun fem dat pl	id.
εὐφροσύνας noun fem acc pl	id.
εὐφροσύνη noun fem nom sg	id.
εὐφροσύνῃ noun fem dat sg	id.
εὐφροσύνην noun fem acc sg	id.
εὐφροσύνης noun fem gen sg	id.
εὐφρόσυνον adj masc and fem acc sg .... εὐφρόσυνος
εὐφροσύνους adj masc and fem acc pl	id.
εὐφυῆ adj masc and fem acc sg .... εὐφυής
εὐφυής adj masc and fem nom sg	id.
εὐχαί noun fem nom pl .... εὐχή
εὐχαῖς noun fem dat pl	id.
εὔχαρι adj neut nom and acc sg .... εὔχαρις
εὐχαριστήσαντες vb 1st aor act part
masc nom pl .... εὐχαριστέω
εὐχαριστήσωμεν vb 1st aor act subj 1st pers pl	id.
εὐχαριστίαν noun fem acc sg .... εὐχαριστία
εὐχαριστίας noun fem gen sg	id.
εὐχάριστος adj masc and fem nom sg
εὐχαριστοῦμεν vb pres act ind 1st pers pl .... εὐχαριστέω
εὐχαριστοῦντες vb pres act part masc nom pl	id.
εὐχάς noun fem acc pl .... εὐχή
εὐχερές adj neut nom and acc sg .... εὐχερής
εὐχερής adj masc and fem nom sg	id.
εὐχερῶς adverb
εὔχεσθαι vb pres dep inf .... εὔχομαι
εὐχή noun fem nom sg
εὐχήν noun fem acc sg .... εὐχή
εὐχῆς noun fem gen sg	id.
εὐχόμενοι vb pres dep part masc nom pl .... εὔχομαι
εὐχόμενον vb pres dep part masc acc sg,
neut nom and acc sg	id.
εὐχόμενος vb pres dep part masc nom sg	id.
εὐχομένῳ vb pres dep part masc and neut dat sg	id.
εὔχονται vb pres dep ind 3rd pers pl	id.

εὔχου vb pres dep impv 2nd pers sg .... εὔχομαι
εὐχρηστίας noun fem gen sg .... εὐχρηστία
εὔχρηστον adj acc sg, neut nom sg .... εὔχρηστος
εὐχῶν noun fem gen pl .... εὐχή
εὐψυχίᾳ noun fem dat sg .... εὐψυχία
εὐψυχίαν noun fem acc sg	id.
εὐψυχίας noun fem gen sg	id.
εὔψυχοι adj masc and fem nom pl .... εὔψυχος
εὔψυχος adj masc and fem nom sg	id.
εὐψύχως adverb
εὐωδεστάτοις superl adj masc and neut dat pl ..... εὐώδης
εὐωδία noun fem nom sg
εὐωδιάζων vb pres act part masc nom sg .... εὐωδιάζω
εὐωδίαν noun fem acc sg .... εὐωδία
εὐωδίας noun fem gen sg	id.
εὐωδιάσατε vb 1st aor act impv 2nd pers pl ..... εὐωδιάζω
εὐώδου vb impf act ind 3rd pers sg .... εὐοδόω
εὐώδους adj gen sg .... εὐώδης
εὐωδώθη vb 1st aor pass ind 3rd pers sg .... εὐοδόω
εὐώνυμα adj neut nom and acc pl .... εὐώνυμος
εὐώνυμος adj masc and fem nom sg	id.
εὐωνύμου adj gen sg	id.
εὐωνύμων adj gen pl	id.
εὐωχία noun fem nom sg
εὐωχίαν noun fem acc sg .... εὐωχία
εὐωχίας noun fem gen sg and acc pl	id.
εὐωχούμενος vb pres m/p part masc nom sg ...... εὐωχέω
εὐωχοῦντο vb impf act ind 3rd pers pl	id.
ἐφ᾽ see ἐπί
Εφααθ pr noun
ἐφάγαμεν vb 2nd aor act ind 1st pers pl .... ἐσθίω
ἔφαγε(ν) vb 2nd aor act ind 3rd pers sg	id.
ἔφαγες vb 2nd aor act ind 2nd pers sg	id.
ἐφάγετε vb 2nd aor act ind 2nd pers pl	id.
ἐφάγομεν vb 2nd aor act ind 1st pers pl	id.
ἔφαγον vb 2nd aor act ind 1st pers sg and 3rd pers pl
ἐφάγοσαν vb 2nd aor act ind 3rd pers pl	id.
εφαδανω translit
ἐφαίνετο vb impf m/p ind 3rd pers sg .... φαίνω
ἔφαινον vb impf act ind 3rd pers pl	id.
ἐφαίνοντο vb impf m/p ind 3rd pers pl	id.
ἐφαλεῖται vb fut act ind 3rd pers sg .... ἐφάλλομαι
ἐφαμαρτεῖν vb 2nd aor act inf .... ἐφαμαρτάνω
ἔφαναν vb 1st aor act ind 3rd pers pl .... φαίνω
ἐφάνη vb 2nd aor pass ind 3rd pers sg	id.
ἐφάνησαν vb 2nd aor pass ind 3rd pers pl	id.
ἐφάνητε vb 2nd aor pass ind 2nd pers pl	id.
ἐφάπτεσθαι vb pres m/p inf .... ἐφάπτω
ἐφαπτόμενοι vb pres m/p part masc nom pl	id.
ἐφαπτόμενος vb pres m/p part masc nom sg	id.
ἐφαρμακεύετο vb impf m/p ind 3rd pers sg .... φαρμακεύω
ἐφαρμόσαντες vb 1st aor act part masc nom pl .. ἐφαρμόζω

ἔφασαν   vb 2nd aor act ind 3rd pers pl . . . . φημί

ἐφάτνωσεν   vb 1st aor act ind 3rd pers sg . . . . φατνόω

ἐφαύλισα   vb 1st aor act ind 1st pers sg . . . . φαυλίζω

ἐφαυλίσαμεν   vb 1st aor act ind 1st pers pl   id.

ἐφαύλισαν   vb 1st aor act ind 3rd pers pl   id.

ἐφαύλισας   vb 1st aor act ind 2nd pers sg   id.

ἐφαύλισεν   vb 1st aor act ind 3rd pers sg   id.

ἐφείδετο   vb impf dep ind 3rd pers sg . . . . φείδομαι

ἐφείλκυσαν   vb 1st aor act ind 3rd pers pl . . . . ἐφέλκω

ἐφεισάμην   vb 1st aor mid ind 1st pers sg . . . . φείδομαι

ἐφείσαντο   vb 1st aor mid ind 3rd pers pl   id.

ἐφείσατο   vb 1st aor mid ind 3rd pers sg   id.

ἐφειστήκει   vb plpf act ind 3rd pers sg . . . . ἐφίστημι

ἐφείσω   vb 1st aor mid ind 2nd pers sg . . . . φείδομαι

ἐφέλκηται   vb pres m/p subj 3rd pers sg . . . . ἐφέλκω

ἐφελκόμενον   vb pres m/p part neut nom and acc sg   id.

ἐφέλκονται   vb pres m/p ind 3rd pers pl   id.

ἐφελκυσθεῖσα   vb 1st aor pass part fem nom sg . . . ἐφελκύω

ἐφέξει   vb fut act ind 3rd pers sg . . . . ἐπέχω

ἔφερεν   vb impf act ind 3rd pers sg . . . . φέρω

Εφερμεμ   pr noun

ἔφερον   vb impf act ind 3rd pers pl . . . . φέρω

ἐφέροσαν   vb impf act ind 3rd pers pl   id.

ἐφεσταμένη   vb perf mid part fem nom sg . . . . . . ἐφίστημι

ἐφέστηκα   vb perf act ind 1st pers sg   id.

ἐφέστηκεν   vb perf act ind 3rd pers sg   id.

ἐφεστηκόσι   vb perf act part masc and neut dat pl   id.

ἐφεστηκότων   vb perf act part masc and neut gen pl   id.

ἐφεστηκώς   vb perf act part masc nom sg   id.

ἐφεστός   vb perf act part neut nom and acc sg   id.

ἐφεστῶσαν   vb perf act part fem acc sg   id.

ἐφεστῶτα   vb perf act part masc acc sg   id.

ἐφεστῶτας   vb perf act part masc acc pl   id.

ἐφεστῶτι   vb perf act part masc and neut dat sg   id.

ἐφέτιον   adj masc acc sg, neut nom and acc sg . . . . . . ἐφέτιος

ἐφετίου   adj masc and neut gen sg   id.

ἔφευγον   vb impf act ind 3rd pers pl . . . . φεύγω

ἔφη   vb impf act ind 3rd pers sg . . . . φημί

ἐφηβεῖον   noun neut nom and acc sg

ἐφήβων   noun masc gen pl . . . . ἐφῆβος

ἐφήλατο   vb 2nd aor mid ind 3rd pers sg . . . . ἐφάλλομαι

ἔφηλος   adj masc and fem nom sg

ἐφημερία   noun fem nom sg

ἐφημερίαι   noun fem nom pl . . . . ἐφημερία

ἐφημερίαις   noun fem dat pl   id.

ἐφημερίαν   noun fem acc sg   id.

ἐφημερίας   noun fem acc pl   id.

ἐφημεριῶν   noun fem gen pl   id.

ἔφην   vb impf act ind 1st pers sg . . . . φημί

ἔφησεν   vb 1st aor act ind 3rd pers sg   id.

ἔφθακεν   vb perf act ind 3rd pers sg . . . . φθάνω

ἐφθάρη   vb 2nd aor pass ind 3rd pers sg . . . . φθείρω

ἐφθάρησαν   vb 2nd aor pass ind 3rd pers pl . . . . φθείρω

ἔφθασα   vb 1st aor act ind 1st pers sg . . . . φθάνω

ἔφθασαν   vb 1st aor act ind 3rd pers pl   id.

ἔφθασεν   vb 1st aor act ind 3rd pers sg   id.

ἐοθέγξατο   vb 1st aor mid ind 3rd pers sg . . . . . . φθέγγομαι

ἔοθειραν   vb 1st aor act ind 3rd pers pl . . . . φθείρω

ἔφθειρας   vb 1st aor act ind 2nd pers sg   id.

ἔφθειρεν   vb impf act ind 3rd pers sg,

     1st aor act ind 3rd pers sg   id.

ἐφθόν   adj masc acc sg, neut nom and acc sg . . . . ἐφθός

ἐφικτόν   adj masc acc sg, neut nom and acc sg . . . . . ἐφικτός

ἐφιλανθρώπησεν   vb 1st aor act ind

     3rd pers sg . . . . φιλανθρωπέω

ἐφίλει   vb impf act ind 3rd pers sg . . . . φιλέω

ἐφίλησα   vb 1st aor act ind 1st pers sg   id.

ἐφίλησεν   vb 1st aor act ind 3rd pers sg   id.

ἐφιλίασα   vb 1st aor act ind 1st pers sg . . . . φιλιάζω

ἐφιλίασας   vb 1st aor act ind 2nd pers sg   id.

ἐφιλίασεν   vb 1st aor act ind 3rd pers sg   id.

ἐφίμωσαν   vb 1st aor act ind 3rd pers pl . . . . φιμόω

ἔφιπποι   adj masc and fem nom pl . . . . ἔφιππος

ἔφιππος   adj masc and fem nom sg   id.

ἐφίπτονται   vb pres dep ind 3rd pers pl . . . . ἐφίπταμαι

ἔφισον   adj masc nom sg, neut nom and acc sg . . . . ἔφισος

ἔφισος   adj masc nom sg

ἐφίσταται   vb pres m/p ind 3rd pers sg . . . . ἐφίστημι

ἐφίστημι   vb pres act ind 1st pers sg   id.

ἐφλέγμανεν   vb 1st aor act ind 3rd pers sg . . . . . φλεγμαίνω

ἐφλόγισεν   vb 1st aor act ind 3rd pers sg . . . . φλογίζω

ἐφλογίσθη   vb 1st aor pass ind 3rd pers sg   id.

ἐφόβει   vb impf act ind 3rd pers sg . . . . φοβέω

ἐφοβεῖσθε   vb impf m/p ind 2nd pers pl   id.

ἐφοβεῖτο   vb impf m/p ind 3rd pers sg   id.

ἐφοβέρισεν   vb 1st aor act ind 3rd pers sg . . . . . . φοβερίζω

ἐφοβήθη   vb 1st aor pass ind 3rd pers sg . . . . φοβέω

ἐφοβήθημεν   vb 1st aor pass ind 1st pers pl   id.

ἐφοβήθην   vb 1st aor pass ind 1st pers sg   id.

ἐφοβήθης   vb 1st aor pass ind 2nd pers sg   id.

ἐφοβήθησαν   vb 1st aor pass ind 3rd pers pl   id.

ἐφοβήθητε   vb 1st aor pass ind 2nd pers pl   id.

ἐφόβου   vb impf m/p ind 2nd pers sg   id.

ἐφοβοῦντο   vb impf m/p ind 3rd pers pl   id.

ἐφοδεῦσαι   vb 1st aor act inf . . . . ἐφοδεύω

ἐφοδευσάτωσαν   vb 1st aor act impv 3rd pers pl   id.

ἐφοδεύων   vb pres act part masc nom sg   id.

ἐφοδιάσεις   vb fut act ind 2nd pers sg . . . . ἐφοδιάζω

ἐφόδιον   noun neut nom and acc sg

ἔφοδον   noun fem acc sg . . . . ἔφοδος

ἔφοδος   noun fem nom sg   id.

ἐφόδου   noun fem gen sg   id.

ἐφόδῳ   noun fem dat sg   id.

ἐφόνευσαν   vb 1st aor act ind 3rd pers pl . . . . φονεύω

ἐφόνευσας	vb 1st aor act ind 2nd pers sg	.... φονεύω
ἐφόνευσεν	vb 1st aor act ind 3rd pers sg	id.
ἐφονοκτονήθη	vb 1st aor pass ind 3rd pers sg	. φονοκτονέω
ἐφορᾷ	vb pres act ind 3rd pers sg	.... ἐφοράω
ἐφόρεσεν	vb 1st aor act ind 3rd pers sg	.... φορέω
ἐφόρτιζες	vb impf act ind 2nd pers sg	.... φορτίζω
ἐφορῶν	vb pres act part masc nom sg	.... ἐφοράω
ἐφορῶντες	vb pres act part masc nom pl	id.
ἐφορῶντος	vb pres act part masc and neut gen sg	id.
εφουδ	translit	
Εφρα	pr noun	
εφραθ	translit	
Εφραθ	pr noun	
Εφραθα	pr noun	
Εφραθαῖοι	pr noun masc nom pl	.... Εφραθαῖος
Εφραθι	pr noun	
Εφραθιτης	pr noun masc nom sg	
Εφραιμ	pr noun	
ἔφραξα	vb 1st aor act ind 1st pers sg	.... φράσσω
ἔφριξαν	vb 1st aor act ind 3rd pers pl	.... φρίσσω
ἔφριξεν	vb 1st aor act ind 3rd pers sg	id.
ἔφριττον	vb impf act ind 3rd pers pl	.... φρίττω
ἐφρόνησαν	vb 1st aor act ind 3rd pers pl	.... φρονέω
ἐφρόντιζεν	vb impf act ind 3rd pers sg	.... φροντίζω
ἐφρόντισα	vb 1st aor act ind 1st pers sg	id.
ἐφροντίσαμεν	vb 1st aor act ind 1st pers pl	id.
ἐφρουρεῖτο	vb impf m/p ind 3rd pers sg	.... φρουρέω
ἐφρούρωσε	vb 1st aor act ind 3rd pers sg	.... φρουρόω
ἐφρύαξαν	vb 1st aor act ind 3rd pers pl	.... φρυάσσω
Εφρων	pr noun	
ἐφύβριστος	adj masc and fem nom sg	
ἐφυγάδευσεν	vb 1st aor act ind 3rd pers sg	..... φυγαδεύω
ἔφυγαν	vb 1st aor act ind 3rd pers pl	.... φεύγω
ἔφυγε(ν)	vb 2nd aor act ind 3rd pers sg	id.
ἔφυγες	vb 2nd aor act ind 2nd pers sg	id.
ἔφυγον	vb 2nd aor act ind 1st pers sg and 3rd pers pl	id.
ἐφύγοσαν	vb 2nd aor act ind 3rd pers pl	id.
ἐφύλαξα	vb 1st aor act ind 1st pers sg	.... φυλάσσω
ἐφυλάξαμεν	vb 1st aor act ind 1st pers pl	id.
ἐφυλαξάμην	vb 1st aor mid ind 1st pers sg	id.
ἐφύλαξαν	vb 1st aor act ind 3rd pers pl	id.
ἐφυλάξαντο	vb 1st aor mid ind 3rd pers pl	id.
ἐφύλαξας	vb 1st aor act ind 2nd pers sg	id.
ἐφυλάξασθε	vb 1st aor mid ind 2nd pers pl	id.
ἐφυλάξατε	vb 1st aor act ind 2nd pers pl	id.
ἐφυλάξατο	vb 1st aor mid ind 3rd pers sg	id.
ἐφύλαξεν	vb 1st aor act ind 3rd pers sg	id.
ἐφύλασσεν	vb impf act ind 3rd pers sg	id.
ἐφυλάσσετο	vb impf m/p ind 3rd pers sg	id.
ἐφύλασσον	vb impf act ind 3rd pers pl	id.
ἐφυλάττετο	vb impf m/p ind 3rd pers sg	.... φυλάττω
ἐφυλάχθη	vb 1st aor pass ind 3rd pers sg	.... φυλάσσω

ἐφύοντο	vb impf m/p ind 3rd pers pl	.... φύω
ἐφύρασεν	vb 1st aor act ind 3rd pers sg	.... φυράω
ἐφύτευσα	vb 1st aor act ind 1st pers sg	.... φυτεύω
ἐφύτευσαν	vb 1st aor act ind 3rd pers pl	id.
ἐφύτευσας	vb 1st aor act ind 2nd pers sg	id.
ἐφυτεύσατε	vb 1st aor act ind 2nd pers pl	id.
ἐφύτευσεν	vb 1st aor act ind 3rd pers sg	id.
εφωδ	translit	
ἐφώδευσεν	vb 1st aor act ind 3rd pers sg	.... ἐφοδεύω
ἐφωδιάσθημεν	vb 1st aor pass ind 1st pers pl	.... ἐφοδιάζω
εφωθ	translit	
ἐφώνησαν	vb 1st aor act ind 3rd pers pl	.... φωνέω
ἐφώνησε(ν)	vb 1st aor act ind 3rd pers sg	id.
ἐφώνουν	vb impf act ind 3rd pers pl	id.
ἐφώτιζον	vb impf act ind 3rd pers pl	.... φωτίζω
ἐφώτισεν	vb 1st aor act ind 3rd pers sg	id.
ἐχαιρέτισαν	vb 1st aor act ind 3rd pers pl	..... χαιρετίζω
ἐχαιρέτισεν	vb 1st aor act ind 3rd pers sg	id.
ἐχάλασαν	vb 1st aor act ind 3rd pers pl	.... χαλάω
ἐχαλάσατε	vb 1st aor act ind 2nd pers pl	id.
ἐχαλέπαινεν	vb impf act ind 3rd pers sg	...... χαλεπαίνω
ἔχανεν	vb 2nd aor act ind 3rd pers sg	.... χαίνω
ἐχαράκωσα	vb 1st aor act ind 1st pers sg	.... χαρακόω
ἐχαράκωσεν	vb 1st aor act ind 3rd pers sg	id.
ἐχάραξαν	vb 1st aor act ind 3rd pers pl	.... χαράσσω
ἐχάραξεν	vb 1st aor act ind 3rd pers sg	id.
ἐχάρη	vb 2nd aor pass ind 3rd pers sg	.... χαίρω
ἐχάρημεν	vb 2nd aor pass ind 1st pers pl	id.
ἐχάρησαν	vb 2nd aor pass ind 3rd pers pl	id.
ἐχαρίζετο	vb impf dep ind 3rd pers sg	.... χαρίζομαι
ἐχαρισάμην	vb 1st aor mid ind 1st pers sg	id.
ἐχαρίσατο	vb 1st aor mid ind 3rd pers sg	id.
ἔχε	vb pres act impv 2nd pers sg	.... ἔχω
ἔχει	vb pres act ind 3rd pers sg	id.
ἔχειν	vb pres act inf	id.
ἐχειρώσαντο	vb 1st aor mid ind 3rd pers pl	.... χειρόω
ἔχεις	noun masc nom and acc pl	.... ἔχις
ἔχεις	vb pres act ind 2nd pers sg	.... ἔχω
Εχελα	pr noun	
ἐχέοντο	vb impf m/p ind 3rd pers pl	.... χέω
ἔχεσθαι	vb pres m/p inf	.... ἔχω
ἔχεται	vb pres m/p ind 3rd pers sg	id.
ἔχετε	vb pres act ind 2nd pers pl	id.
ἐχέτω	vb pres act impv 3rd pers sg	id.
ἔχῃ	vb pres act subj 3rd pers sg	id.
ἐχήρευσεν	vb 1st aor act ind 3rd pers sg	.... χηρεύω
ἔχῃς	vb pres act subj 2nd pers sg	.... ἔχω
ἔχητε	vb pres act subj 2nd pers pl	id.
ἐχθές	adverb	
ἔχθιστα	superl adj neut nom and acc pl	.... ἐχθρός
ἐχθίστη	superl adj fem dat sg	id.
ἔχθιστος	superl adj masc nom sg	id.

ἐχθίστων superl adj masc and neut gen pl . . . . ἐχθρός	ἐχόντων vb pres act part masc and neut gen pl . . . . ἔχω
ἔχθρα noun fem nom sg	ἐχόρευον vb impf act ind 3rd pers pl . . . . χορεύω
ἐχθρά adj fem nom sg . . . . ἐχθρός	ἐχορήγει vb impf act ind 3rd pers sg . . . . χορηγέω
ἔχθρᾳ noun fem dat sg . . . . ἔχθρα	ἐχορηγεῖτο vb impf m/p ind 3rd pers sg	id.
ἐχθραίνειν vb pres act inf . . . . ἐχθραίνω	ἐχορήγησαν vb 1st aor act ind 3rd pers pl	id.
ἐχθραίνετε vb pres act impv 2nd pers pl	id.	ἐχορήγησεν vb 1st aor act ind 3rd pers sg	id.
ἐχθραίνοντα vb pres act part masc acc sg	id.	ἐχορήγουν vb impf act ind 3rd pers pl	id.
ἐχθραίνοντας vb pres act part masc acc pl	id.	ἐχόρτασα vb 1st aor act ind 1st pers sg . . . . χορτάζω
ἐχθραίνοντες vb pres act part masc nom pl	id.	ἐχόρτασεν vb 1st aor act ind 3rd pers sg	id.
ἐχθραίνουσι(ν) vb pres act part masc and neut dat pl	id.	ἐχορτάσθησαν vb 1st aor pass ind 3rd pers pl	id.
ἐχθραίνων vb pres act part masc nom sg	id.	ἔχουσα vb pres act part fem nom sg . . . . ἔχω
ἔχθραν noun fem acc sg . . . . ἔχθρα	ἔχουσαι vb pres act part fem nom pl	id.
ἐχθράν adj fem acc sg . . . . ἐχθρος	ἔχουσαν vb pres act part fem acc sg	id.
ἔχθρας noun fem gen sg and acc pl . . . . ἔχθρα	ἐχούσας vb pres act part fem acc pl	id.
ἐχθρέ adj masc voc sg . . . . ἐχθρός	ἐχούσῃ vb pres act part fem dat sg	id.
ἐχθρεῦσαι vb 1st aor act inf . . . . ἐχθρεύω	ἐχούσης vb pres act part fem gen sg	id.
ἐχθρεύσουσιν vb fut act ind 3rd pers pl	id.	ἔχουσι(ν) vb pres act part masc and neut dat pl	id.
ἐχθρεύσω vb fut act ind 1st pers sg	id.	ἔχουσιν vb pres act ind 3rd pers pl	id.
Ἐχθρια pr noun fem nom sg	Εχραν pr noun
ἐχθροί adj masc nom pl . . . . ἐχθρός	ἐχρεμέτιζον vb impf act ind 3rd pers pl . . . . χρεμετίζω
ἐχθροῖς adj masc and neut dat pl	id.	ἐχρημάτισα vb 1st aor act ind 1st pers sg . . . . . χρηματίζω
ἐχθρόν adj masc acc sg, neut nom and acc sg	id.	ἐχρημάτισαν vb 1st aor act ind 3rd pers pl	id.
ἐχθρός adj masc nom sg	id.	ἐχρημάτισεν vb 1st aor act ind 3rd pers sg	id.
ἐχθροῦ adj masc and neut gen sg	id.	ἐχρησάμεθα vb 1st aor mid ind 1st pers pl . . . . χράω
ἐχθρούς adj masc acc pl	id.	ἔχρησαν vb 1st aor act ind 3rd pers pl	id.
ἐχθρῷ adj masc and neut dat sg	id.	ἐχρήσαντο vb 1st aor mid ind 3rd pers pl	id.
ἐχθρῶν adj gen pl	id.	ἔχρησας vb 1st aor act ind 2nd pers sg	id.
ἐχῖνοι noun masc nom pl . . . . ἐχῖνος	ἐχρήσατο vb 1st aor mid ind 3rd pers sg	id.
ἐχῖνος noun masc nom sg	id.	ἐχρήσω vb 1st aor mid ind 2nd pers sg	id.
ἐχίνους noun masc acc pl	id.	ἔχρισα vb 1st aor act ind 1st pers sg . . . . χρίω
Εχοζοβ pr noun	ἐχρίσαμεν vb 1st aor act ind 1st pers pl	id.
ἔχοιμ' see ἔχοιμι	ἔχρισαν vb 1st aor act ind 3rd pers pl	id.
ἔχοιμι vb pres act opt 1st pers sg . . . . ἔχω	ἐχρίσατο vb 1st aor mid ind 3rd pers sg	id.
ἔχομεν vb pres act ind 1st pers pl	id.	ἔχρισεν vb 1st aor act ind 3rd pers sg	id.
ἐχόμενα vb pres m/p part fem nom sg,	ἐχρίσθη vb 1st aor pass ind 3rd pers sg	id.
neut nom and acc pl	id.	ἐχρόνισα vb 1st aor act ind 1st pers sg . . . . χρονίζω
ἐχόμεναι vb pres m/p part fem nom pl	id.	ἐχρόνισαν vb 1st aor act ind 3rd pers pl	id.
ἐχομένας vb pres m/p part fem acc pl	id.	ἐχρόνισεν vb 1st aor act ind 3rd pers sg	id.
ἐχομένη vb pres m/p part fem nom sg	id.	ἐχρύσωσεν vb 1st aor act ind 3rd pers sg . . . . χρυσόω
ἐχομένῃ vb pres m/p part fem dat sg	id.	ἐχρῶντο vb impf dep ind 3rd pers pl . . . . χράομαι
ἐχομένην vb pres m/p part fem acc sg	id.	ἔχω vb pres act ind 1st pers sg
ἐχόμενοι vb pres m/p part masc nom pl	id.	ἐχώλαναν vb 1st aor act ind 3rd pers pl . . . . χωλαίνω
ἐχόμενον vb pres m/p part masc acc sg,	ἐχωλάνθη vb 1st aor pass ind 3rd pers sg	id.
neut nom and acc sg	id.	ἔχωμεν vb pres act subj 1st pers pl . . . . ἔχω
ἐχόμενος vb pres m/p part masc nom sg	id.	ἔχων vb pres act part masc nom sg	id.
ἐχομένως adverb	ἐχωνεύοντο vb impf m/p ind 3rd pers pl . . . . χωνεύω
ἔχον vb pres act part neut nom and acc sg . . . . ἔχω	ἐχώνευσαν vb 1st aor act ind 3rd pers pl	id.
ἔχοντα vb pres act part masc acc sg, neut nom and acc pl	id.	ἐχώνευσεν vb 1st aor act ind 3rd pers sg	id.
ἔχοντας vb pres act part masc acc pl	id.	ἔχωνται vb pres m/p subj 3rd pers pl . . . . ἔχω
ἔχοντες vb pres act part masc nom pl	id.	ἐχώρει vb impf act ind 3rd pers sg . . . . χωρέω
ἔχοντι vb pres act part masc and neut dat sg	id.	ἐχώρησεν vb 1st aor act ind 3rd pers sg	id.
ἔχοντος vb pres act part masc and neut gen sg	id.	ἐχώρισα vb 1st aor act ind 1st pers sg . . . . χωρίζω

ἐχώρισαν	vb 1st aor act ind 3rd pers pl	χωρίζω
ἐχωρίσθη	vb 1st aor pass ind 3rd pers sg	id.
ἐχωρίσθημεν	vb 1st aor pass ind 1st pers pl	id.
ἐχωρίσθησαν	vb 1st aor pass ind 3rd pers pl	id.
ἐχωροβάτησαν	vb 1st aor act ind 3rd pers pl . . .	χωροβατέω
Εχωχι	pr noun	
ἔψαλλεν	vb impf act ind 3rd pers sg	ψάλλω
ἔψαλλον	vb impf act ind 3rd pers pl	id.
ἔψε	vb pres act impv 2nd pers sg	ἕψω
ἔψεμα	noun neut nom and acc sg	
ἑψέματος	noun neut gen sg	ἕψεμα
ἔψετε	vb pres act impv 2nd pers pl	ἕψω
ἔψευσαι	vb perf dep ind 2nd pers sg	ψεύδομαι
ἐψευσάμεθα	vb 1st aor mid ind 1st pers pl	id.
ἐψευσάμην	vb 1st aor mid ind 1st pers sg	id.
ἐψεύσαντο	vb 1st aor mid ind 3rd pers pl	id.
ἐψεύσατο	vb 1st aor mid ind 3rd pers sg	id.
ἐψεύσω	vb 1st aor mid ind 2nd pers sg	id.
ἑψηθῇ	vb 1st aor pass subj 3rd pers sg	ἕψω
ἐψηλάφησεν	vb 1st aor act ind 3rd pers sg	ψηλαφάω
ἑψήματι	noun neut dat sg	ἕψεμα
ἑψήματος	noun neut gen sg	id.
ἑψήσατε	vb 1st aor act impv 2nd pers pl	ἕψω
ἑψήσεις	vb fut act ind 2nd pers sg	id.
ἑψήσουσιν	vb fut act ind 3rd pers pl	id.
ἔψητε	vb pres act subj 2nd pers pl	id.
ἐψιθύριζον	vb impf act ind 3rd pers pl	ψιθυρίζω
ἐψόγισεν	vb 1st aor act ind 3rd pers sg	ψογίζω
ἔψυξα	vb 1st aor act ind 1st pers sg	ψύχω
ἔψυξαν	vb 1st aor act ind 3rd pers pl	id.
ἔψυξεν	vb 1st aor act ind 3rd pers sg	id.
ἐψώμιζον	vb impf act ind 3rd pers pl	ψωμίζω

ἐψώμισα	vb 1st aor act ind 1st pers sg	ψωμίζω
ἐψώμισαν	vb 1st aor act ind 3rd pers pl	id.
ἐψώμισας	vb 1st aor act ind 2nd pers sg	id.
ἐψώμισεν	vb 1st aor act ind 3rd pers sg	id.
ἕω	noun fem acc sg	ἕως
Εωβης	pr noun	
ἑωθινή	adj fem nom sg	ἑωθινός
ἑωθινῇ	adj fem dat sg	id.
ἑωθινήν	adj fem acc sg	id.
ἑωθινῆς	adj fem gen sg	id.
ἑωθινός	adj masc nom sg	id.
ἕωλον	adj masc acc sg, neut nom and acc sg	ἕωλος
ἐῶντες	vb pres act part masc nom pl	ἐάω
ἑώρα	vb impf act ind 3rd pers sg	ὁράω
ἑώρακα	vb perf act ind 1st pers sg	id.
ἑωράκαμεν	vb perf act ind 1st pers pl	id.
ἑώρακαν	vb perf act ind 3rd pers pl	id.
ἑώρακας	vb perf act ind 2nd pers sg	id.
ἑωράκασιν	vb perf act ind 3rd pers pl	id.
ἑωράκατε	vb perf act ind 2nd pers pl	id.
ἑώρακε(ν)	vb perf act ind 3rd pers sg	id.
ἑωρακότας	vb perf act part masc acc pl	id.
ἑωρακότες	vb perf act part masc nom pl	id.
ἑωρακώς	vb perf act part masc nom sg	id.
ἑώραται	vb perf m/p ind 3rd pers sg	id.
ἑώρων	vb impf act ind 3rd pers pl	id.
ἕως	adverb, conjunction, preposition	
ἔωσαν	vb pres act part fem acc sg	ἐάω
ἑωσφόρον	noun masc acc sg	ἑωσφόρος
ἑωσφόρος	noun masc nom sg	id.
ἑωσφόρου	noun masc gen sg	id.

Z ζ

ζ΄	indecl number
Ζαβαδ	pr noun
Ζαβαδαιας	pr noun masc nom sg
Ζαβαδαίους	pr noun masc acc pl . . . . Ζαβαδαιοι
Ζαβαδια	pr noun
Ζαβαδιας	pr noun masc nom sg
Ζαβδαιος	pr noun
Ζαβδι	pr noun
Ζαβδια	pr noun
Ζαβδιας	pr noun masc nom sg
Ζαβδιηλ	pr noun
Ζαβδιου	pr noun
Ζαβδος	pr noun
Ζαβεδ	pr noun

Ζαβετ	pr noun
Ζαβου	pr noun
Ζαβουθ	pr noun
Ζαβουθαιθαν	pr noun
Ζαβουλων	pr noun
Ζαβουλωνιτης	pr noun masc nom sg
Ζαβουχαμ	pr noun
Ζαθοης	pr noun
Ζαθολθα	pr noun
Ζαθουα	pr noun
Ζαθουια	pr noun
ζαι	translit (Heb. letter: ז)
Ζαιθαν	pr noun
Ζαιρα	pr noun

Ζακαναϊμ pr noun	ζεύξατε vb 1st aor act impv 2nd pers pl . . . . ζευγνύω
Ζακχαῖον pr noun masc acc sg . . . . Ζακχαῖος	ζεῦξον vb 1st aor act impv 2nd pers sg id.
Ζακχου pr noun	Ζεχρι pr noun
Ζακχουρ pr noun	Ζεχωρα pr noun
ζακχω translit	ζέων vb pres act part masc nom sg . . . . ζέω
Ζαμαριας pr noun	ζῇ vb pres act ind 3rd pers sg,
Ζαμβινα pr noun	pres act subj 3rd pers sg . . . . ζάω
Ζαμβραμ pr noun	Ζηβ pr noun
Ζαμβρι pr noun	ζῆθι vb pres act impv 2nd pers sg . . . . ζάω
Ζαμβρις pr noun	ζήλει noun neut dat sg . . . . ζῆλος
Ζαμμα pr noun	ζηλοῖς vb pres act subj 2nd pers sg . . . . ζηλόω
Ζαμοθ pr noun	ζῆλον noun masc acc sg . . . . ζῆλος
Ζανω pr noun	ζῆλος noun masc nom sg
Ζανωακιμ pr noun	ζηλοτυπίας noun fem gen sg . . . . ζηλοτυπία
Ζαρα pr noun	ζήλου noun masc gen sg . . . . ζῆλος
Ζαραι pr noun	ζήλου vb pres m/p impv 2nd pers sg . . . . ζηλόω
Ζαραϊ pr noun	ζηλούντων vb pres act part masc and neut gen pl id.
Ζαραια pr noun	ζήλους noun masc acc pl . . . . ζῆλος
Ζαραιας pr noun masc nom sg	ζηλοῦτε vb pres act impv 2nd pers pl . . . . ζηλόω
Ζαραιου pr noun masc gen sg . . . . Ζαραιας	ζηλούτω vb pres act impv 3rd pers sg id.
Ζαρε pr noun	ζήλω noun masc dat sg . . . . ζῆλος
Ζαρετ pr noun	ζηλῶν vb pres act part masc nom sg . . . . ζηλόω
Ζαριον pr noun masc acc sg . . . . Ζαριος	ζηλῶσαι vb 1st aor act inf id.
Ζατου pr noun gen sg . . . . Ζατον	ζηλώσας vb 1st aor act part masc nom sg id.
Ζαφα pr noun	ζηλώσετε vb 1st aor act impv 2nd pers pl id.
Ζαφωιμ pr noun	ζηλώσει vb fut act ind 3rd pers sg id.
Ζαχαρια pr noun masc . . . . Ζαχαριας	ζηλώσεως noun fem gen sg . . . . ζήλωσις
Ζαχαρια pr noun masc nom sg	ζηλώσῃ vb 1st aor act subj 3rd pers sg . . . . ζηλόω
Ζαχαριαν pr noun masc acc sg . . . . Ζαχαριας	ζηλώσῃς vb 1st aor act subj 2nd pers sg id.
Ζαχαριας pr noun masc nom sg id.	ζήλωσον vb 1st aor act impv 2nd pers sg id.
Ζαχαριου pr noun masc gen sg id.	ζηλώσω vb fut act ind 1st pers sg id.
Ζαχουρ pr noun	ζηλωτήν adj fem acc sg . . . . ζηλωτός
Ζαχρι pr noun	ζηλωτής noun masc nom sg
Ζαχωρ pr noun	ζηλωτόν adj masc acc sg, neut nom and acc sg . . . . ζηλωτός
ζέαν noun fem acc sg . . . . ζέα	ζηλωτός adj masc nom sg id.
Ζεβεε pr noun	ζημία noun fem dat sg . . . . ζημία
Ζεβουλ pr noun	ζημίαν noun fem acc sg id.
Ζεθομ pr noun	ζημιουμένου vb pres m/p part masc and neut gen sg ζημιόω
Ζελφα pr noun fem nom sg	ζημιοῦν vb pres act inf id.
Ζελφαν pr noun fem acc sg . . . . Ζελφα	ζημιωθήσεται vb fut pass ind 3rd pers sg id.
Ζελφας pr noun fem gen sg id.	ζημιώσουσιν vb fut act ind 3rd pers pl id.
ζέμα noun neut nom and acc sg	ζῆν vb pres act inf . . . . ζάω
Ζεμβραν pr noun	ζῇς vb pres act ind 2nd pers sg,
Ζεμμα pr noun	pres act subj 2nd pers sg id.
Ζεμμαθ pr noun	ζῆσαι vb 1st aor act opt 3rd pers sg id.
Ζεμραν pr noun	ζῆσαι vb 1st aor act inf id.
ζέουσι vb pres act part masc and neut dat pl . . . . ζέω	ζήσαντες vb 1st aor act part masc nom pl id.
Ζερδαιας pr noun masc nom sg	ζήσατε vb 1st aor act impv 2nd pers pl id.
ζεύγη noun neut nom and acc pl . . . . ζεῦγος	ζησάτω vb 1st aor act impv 3rd pers sg id.
ζεῦγος noun neut nom and acc sg id.	ζησάτωσαν vb 1st aor act impv 3rd pers pl id.
ζεύγους noun neut gen sg id.	ζήσεις vb fut act ind 2nd pers sg id.
ζεύξας vb 1st aor act part masc nom sg . . . . ζευγνύω	ζήσεσθε vb fut mid ind 2nd pers pl id.

ζήσεται vb fut mid ind 3rd pers sg . . . . ζάω
ζήσετε vb fut act ind 2nd pers pl id.
ζήσῃ vb fut mid ind 2nd pers sg id.
ζήσῃς vb 1st aor act subj 2nd pers sg id.
ζήσηται vb 1st aor mid subj 3rd pers sg id.
ζήσητε vb 1st aor act subj 2nd pers pl id.
ζήσομαι vb fut mid ind 1st pers sg id.
ζησόμεθα vb fut mid ind 1st pers pl id.
ζῆσον vb 1st aor act impv 2nd pers sg id.
ζήσονται vb fut mid ind 3rd pers pl id.
ζῆτε vb pres act ind 2nd pers pl,
      pres act subj 2nd pers pl id.
ζήτει vb pres act impv 2nd pers sg . . . . ζητέω
ζητεῖ vb pres act ind 3rd pers sg id.
ζητεῖν vb pres act inf id.
ζητεῖς vb pres act ind 2nd pers sg id.
ζητεῖτε vb pres act ind 2nd pers pl id.
ζητηθείσης vb 1st aor pass part fem gen sg id.
ζητηθήσεται vb fut pass ind 3rd pers sg id.
ζητηθήσομαι vb fut pass ind 1st pers sg id.
ζητηθήσονται vb fut pass ind 3rd pers pl id.
ζητηθήτω vb 1st aor pass impv 3rd pers sg id.
ζητῇς vb pres act subj 2nd pers sg id.
ζητῆσαι vb 1st aor act inf id.
ζητήσαντας vb 1st aor act part masc acc pl id.
ζητήσατε vb 1st aor act impv 2nd pers pl id.
ζητησάτωσαν vb 1st aor act impv 3rd pers pl id.
ζητήσει vb fut act ind 3rd pers sg id.
ζητήσεις vb fut act ind 2nd pers sg id.
ζητήσετε vb fut act ind 2nd pers pl id.
ζητήσῃ vb 1st aor act subj 3rd pers sg id.
ζητήσῃς vb 1st aor act subj 2nd pers sg id.
ζητήσομεν vb fut act ind 1st pers pl id.
ζήτησον vb 1st aor act impv 2nd pers sg id.
ζητήσουσιν vb fut act ind 3rd pers pl id.
ζητήσω vb 1st aor act subj 1st pers sg,
      fut act ind 1st pers sg id.
ζητήσωσιν vb 1st aor act subj 3rd pers pl id.
ζητοῦμαι vb pres m/p ind 1st pers sg id.
ζητοῦμεν vb pres act ind 1st pers pl id.
ζητούμενος vb pres m/p part masc nom sg id.
ζητοῦν vb pres act part neut nom and acc sg id.
ζητοῦντας vb pres act part masc acc pl id.
ζητοῦντες vb pres act part masc nom pl id.
ζητοῦντι vb pres act part masc and neut dat sg id.
ζητοῦντος vb pres act part masc and neut gen sg id.
ζητούντων vb pres act part masc and neut gen pl id.
ζητοῦντων see ζητούντων
ζητοῦσα vb pres act part fem nom sg id.
ζητοῦσι(ν) vb pres act ind 3rd pers pl,
      pres act part masc and neut dat pl id.
ζήτω vb pres act impv 3rd pers sg . . . . ζάω

ζητῶ vb pres act ind 1st pers sg . . . . ζητέω
ζητῶν vb pres act part masc nom sg id.
ζιβύνας noun fem acc pl . . . . ζιβύνη
ζιβύνην noun fem acc sg id.
Ζιζα pr noun
Ζιφ pr noun
Ζιφαῖοι pr noun masc nom pl . . . . Ζιφαῖος
Ζιφαιους pr noun masc acc pl id.
Ζογορ pr noun
Ζογορα pr noun
Ζομζομμιν pr noun
Ζοροβαβελ pr noun
Ζουε pr noun
Ζουζα pr noun
Ζουκαμ pr noun
Ζουκαν pr noun
ζυγά noun neut nom and acc pl . . . . ζυγόν
ζυγοί noun masc nom pl . . . . ζυγός
ζυγοῖς noun dat pl id.
ζυγόν noun masc acc sg id.
ζυγός noun masc nom sg id.
ζυγοῦ noun gen sg id.
ζυγῷ noun dat sg id.
ζῦθον noun masc acc sg . . . . ζῦθος
ζύμη noun fem nom sg
ζύμῃ noun fem dat sg . . . . ζύμη
ζύμην noun fem acc sg id.
ζυμίταις noun masc dat pl . . . . ζυμίτης
ζυμωθῆναι vb 1st aor pass inf . . . . ζυμόω
ζυμωτόν adj masc acc sg, neut nom and acc sg . . . . ζυμωτός
ζῶ vb pres act ind 1st pers sg . . . . ζάω
ζῷα noun neut nom and acc pl . . . . ζῷον
Ζωαθ pr noun
ζωάς noun fem acc pl . . . . ζωή
ζωγραφεῖν vb pres act inf . . . . ζωγραφέω
ζωγραφῆσαι vb 1st aor act inf id.
ζωγραφίαν noun fem acc sg . . . . ζωγραφία
ζωγρείαν noun fem acc sg . . . . ζωγρεία
ζωγρῆσαι vb 1st aor act inf . . . . ζωγρέω
ζωγρήσατε vb 1st aor act impv 2nd pers pl id.
ζωγρήσετε vb fut act ind 2nd pers pl id.
ζωγρίαν noun fem acc sg . . . . ζωγρία
Ζωελεθ pr noun
Ζωη pr noun fem nom sg
ζωή noun fem nom sg
ζωῇ noun fem dat sg . . . . ζωή
ζωήν noun fem acc sg id.
ζωῆς noun fem gen sg id.
ζῶμεν vb pres act ind 1st pers pl,
      pres act subj 1st pers pl . . . . ζάω
ζωμόν noun masc acc sg . . . . ζωμός
ζωμός noun masc nom sg

ζῶν vb pres act part masc nom sg,

    neut nom and acc sg . . . . ζάω

ζώναις noun fem dat pl . . . . ζωνή

ζώνας noun fem acc pl   id.

ζώνη noun fem nom sg   id.

ζώνῃ noun fem dat sg   id.

ζώνην noun fem acc sg   id.

ζώνης noun fem gen sg   id.

ζῶντα vb pres act part masc acc sg,

    neut nom and acc pl . . . . ζάω

ζῶντας vb pres act part masc acc pl   id.

ζῶντες vb pres act part masc nom pl   id.

ζῶντι vb pres act part masc and neut dat sg   id.

ζῶντος vb pres act part masc and neut gen sg   id.

ζώντων vb pres act part masc and neut gen pl   id.

Ζωοβ pr noun

ζωογονεῖ vb pres act ind 3rd pers sg . . . . ζωογονέω

ζωογονεῖτε vb pres act ind 2nd pers sg   id.

ζωογονήσει vb fut act ind 3rd pers sg   id.

ζωογονήσωσιν vb 1st aor act subj 3rd pers pl   id.

ζωογονούντων vb pres act part masc and neut gen pl   id.

ζῴοις noun neut dat pl . . . . ζῷον

ζῷον noun neut nom and acc sg

ζωοποιεῖς vb pres act ind 2nd pers sg . . . . ζωοποιέω

ζωοποιῆσαι vb 1st aor act inf   id.

ζωοποιήσει vb fut act ind 3rd pers sg . . . . ζωοποιέω

ζωοποίησιν noun fem acc sg . . . . ζωοποίησις

ζῴου noun neut gen sg . . . . ζῷον

ζώπυρα noun neut nom and acc pl . . . . ζώπυρον

ζῶσα vb pres act part fem nom sg . . . . ζάω

ζῶσαι vb pres act part fem nom pl   id.

ζῶσαι vb 1st aor mid impv 2nd pers sg . . . . ζώννυμι

ζῶσαν vb pres act part fem acc sg . . . . ζάω

ζώσαντες vb 1st aor act part masc nom pl . . . . . . ζώννυμι

Ζωσαρα pr noun fem nom sg

Ζωσαραν pr noun fem acc sg . . . . Ζωσαρα

ζώσασθε vb 1st aor mid impv 2nd pers pl . . . . ζώννυμι

ζώσεις vb fut act ind 2nd pers sg   id.

ζώσεται vb fut mid ind 3rd pers sg   id.

ζώσῃ vb pres act part fem dat sg . . . . ζάω

ζώσῃ vb fut mid ind 2nd pers sg . . . . ζώννυμι

ζώσης vb pres act part fem gen sg . . . . ζάω

ζῶσιν noun fem acc sg . . . . ζῶσις

ζῶσιν vb pres act ind 3rd pers pl,

    pres act subj 3rd pers pl . . . . ζάω

ζωσῶν vb pres act part fem gen pl   id.

ζωτικόν adj masc acc sg, neut nom and acc sg . . . . . ζωτικός

ζῴῳ noun neut dat sg . . . . ζῷον

ζῴων noun neut gen pl   id.

ζωώσεις vb fut act ind 2nd pers sg . . . . ζωόω

Η η

η translit (Heb. letter: ה)

η΄ indecl number

ἡ art fem nom sg . . . . ὁ

ἥ rel pron fem nom sg . . . . ὅς

ἤ particle

ἦ adverb

ᾗ rel pron fem dat sg . . . . ὅς

ᾖ vb pres act subj 3rd pers sg . . . . εἰμί

ἠβούλεσθε vb impf dep ind 2nd pers pl . . . . βούλομαι

ἠβούλετο vb impf dep ind 3rd pers sg   id.

ἠβουλήθην vb 1st aor pass ind 1st pers sg   id.

ἠβουλόμεθα vb impf mid ind 1st pers pl   id.

ἠβούλοντο vb impf dep ind 3rd pers pl   id.

ἤγαγεν vb 2nd aor act ind 3rd pers sg . . . . ἄγω

ἤγαγες vb 2nd aor act ind 2nd pers sg   id.

ἤγαγον vb 2nd aor act ind 1st pers sg and 3rd pers pl   id.

ἠγάγοσαν vb 2nd aor act ind 3rd pers pl   id.

ἠγαθοποίησεν vb 1st aor act ind 3rd pers sg . . ἀγαθοποιέω

ἠγάθυνας vb 1st aor act ind 2nd pers sg . . . . ἀγαθύνω

ἠγάθυνεν vb 1st aor act ind 3rd pers sg   id.

ἠγαθύνθη vb 1st aor pass ind 3rd pers sg   id.

ἠγαλλιασαμεθα vb 1st aor mid ind

    1st pers pl . . . . ἀγαλλιάομαι

ἠγαλλιάσαντο vb 1st aor mid ind 3rd pers pl   id.

ἠγαλλιάσατο vb 1st aor mid ind 3rd pers sg   id.

ἠγαλλίασεν vb 1st aor act ind 3rd pers sg   id.

ἠγαλλιώμεθα vb impf dep ind 1st pers pl   id.

ἠγανάκτησαν vb 1st aor act ind 3rd pers pl . . . . ἀγανακτέω

ἠγανάκτουν vb impf act ind 3rd pers pl   id.

ἠγάπα vb impf act ind 3rd pers sg . . . . ἀγαπάω

ἠγαπήθη vb 1st aor pass ind 3rd pers sg   id.

ἠγαπήθης vb 1st aor pass ind 2nd pers sg   id.

ἠγάπηκα vb perf act ind 1st pers sg   id.

ἠγαπήκαμεν vb perf act ind 1st pers pl   id.

ἠγάπηκας vb perf act ind 2nd pers sg   id.

ἠγαπήκει vb plpf act ind 3rd pers sg   id.

ἠγαπήκειν vb plpf act ind 1st pers sg   id.

ἠγάπηκεν vb perf act ind 3rd pers sg   id.

ἠγαπημένα vb perf m/p part neut nom and acc pl   id.

ἠγαπημένε vb perf m/p part masc voc sg   id.

ἠγαπημένη vb perf m/p part fem nom sg   id.

ἠγαπημένῃ vb perf m/p part fem dat sg   id.

ἠγαπημένην vb perf m/p part fem acc sg	. . . . ἀγαπάω	
ἠγαπημένης vb perf m/p part fem gen sg	id.	
ἠγαπημένοι vb perf m/p part masc nom pl	id.	
ἠγαπημένον vb perf m/p part masc acc sg,		
neut nom and acc sg	id.	
ἠγαπημένος vb perf m/p part masc nom sg	id.	
ἠγαπημένου vb perf m/p part masc and neut gen sg	id.	
ἠγαπημένῳ vb perf m/p part masc and neut dat sg	id.	
ἠγαπημένων vb perf m/p part gen pl	id.	
ἠγάπησα vb 1st aor act ind 1st pers sg	id.	
ἠγάπησαν vb 1st aor act ind 3rd pers pl	id.	
ἠγάπησας vb 1st aor act ind 2nd pers sg	id.	
ἠγάπησε(ν) vb 1st aor act ind 3rd pers sg	id.	
ἠγάπων vb impf act ind 3rd pers pl	id.	
ἠγαυριῶντο vb impf m/p ind 3rd pers pl	. . . . ἀγαυριάω	
ἤγγιζεν vb impf act ind 3rd pers sg	. . . . ἐγγίζω	
ἠγγίκασιν vb perf act ind 3rd pers pl	id.	
ἤγγικεν vb perf act ind 3rd pers sg	id.	
ἤγγισα vb 1st aor act ind 1st pers sg	id.	
ἤγγισαν vb 1st aor act ind 3rd pers pl	id.	
ἤγγισας vb 1st aor act ind 2nd pers sg	id.	
ἠγγίσατε vb 1st aor act ind 2nd pers pl	id.	
ἤγγισεν vb 1st aor act ind 3rd pers sg	id.	
ἤγειρα vb 1st aor act ind 1st pers sg	. . . . ἐγείρω	
ἤγειραν vb 1st aor act ind 3rd pers pl	id.	
ἤγειρε(ν) vb impf act ind 3rd pers sg,		
1st aor act ind 3rd pers sg	id.	
ἡγεῖσθαι vb pres dep inf	. . . . ἡγέομαι	
ἡγεῖσθε vb pres dep ind 2nd pers pl	id.	
ἡγείσθω vb pres dep impv 3rd pers sg	id.	
ἡγεῖται vb pres dep ind 3rd pers sg	id.	
ἡγεῖτο vb impf dep ind 3rd pers sg	id.	
ἡγεμόνα noun masc acc sg	. . . . ἡγεμών	
ἡγεμόνας noun masc acc pl	id.	
ἡγεμόνες noun masc nom pl	id.	
ἡγεμονία noun fem nom sg		
ἡγεμονίαις noun fem dat pl	. . . . ἡγεμονία	
ἡγεμονίαν noun fem acc sg	id.	
ἡγεμονίας noun fem gen sg	id.	
ἡγεμονίδην noun masc acc sg	. . . . ἡγεμονίδης	
ἡγεμονικάς adj fem acc pl	. . . . ἡγεμονικός	
ἡγεμονικῷ adj masc and neut dat sg		
ἡγεμόνων noun masc gen pl	. . . . ἡγεμών	
ἡγεμόσι noun masc dat pl	id.	
ἡγεμών noun masc nom sg	id.	
ἦγεν vb impf act ind 3rd pers sg	. . . . ἄγω	
ἠγέρθη vb 1st aor pass ind 3rd pers sg	. . . . ἐγείρω	
ἠγέρθησαν vb 1st aor pass ind 3rd pers pl	id.	
ἤγετο vb impf m/p ind 3rd pers sg	. . . . ἄγω	
ἥγημα noun neut nom and acc sg		
ἥγημαι vb perf dep ind 1st pers sg	. . . . ἡγέομαι	
ἥγησαι vb perf dep ind 2nd pers sg	id.	
ἡγησάμεθα vb 1st aor mid ind 1st pers pl	. . . . ἡγέομαι	
ἡγησάμενοι vb 1st aor mid part masc nom pl	id.	
ἡγησάμην vb 1st aor mid ind 1st pers sg	id.	
ἡγήσατο vb 1st aor mid ind 3rd pers sg	id.	
ἡγήσεται vb fut mid ind 3rd pers sg	id.	
ἡγήσεως noun fem gen sg	. . . . ἥγησις	
ἥγησιν noun fem acc sg	id.	
ἡγήσω vb 1st aor mid ind 2nd pers sg	. . . . ἡγέομαι	
ἥγηται vb perf dep ind 3rd pers sg	id.	
ἡγητέον verbal adj sg		
ἡγίακα vb perf act ind 1st pers sg	. . . . ἁγιάζω	
ἡγίακεν vb perf act ind 3rd pers sg	id.	
ἡγίασα vb 1st aor act ind 1st pers sg	id.	
ἡγίασαν vb 1st aor act ind 3rd pers pl	id.	
ἡγίασας vb 1st aor act ind 2nd pers sg	id.	
ἡγιάσατε vb 1st aor act ind 2nd pers pl	id.	
ἡγίασεν vb 1st aor act ind 3rd pers sg	id.	
ἡγιάσθη vb 1st aor pass ind 3rd pers sg	id.	
ἡγιάσθης vb 1st aor pass ind 2nd pers sg	id.	
ἡγιάσθησαν vb 1st aor pass ind 3rd pers pl	id.	
ἡγιασμένα vb perf m/p part neut nom and acc pl	id.	
ἡγιασμένας vb perf m/p part fem acc pl	id.	
ἡγιασμένης vb perf m/p part fem gen sg	id.	
ἡγιασμένοι vb perf m/p part masc nom pl	id.	
ἡγιασμένοις vb perf m/p part masc and neut dat pl	id.	
ἡγιασμένον vb perf m/p part masc acc sg,		
neut nom and acc sg	id.	
ἡγιασμένου vb perf m/p part masc and neut gen sg	id.	
ἡγιασμένους vb perf m/p part masc acc pl	id.	
ἡγιασμένων vb perf m/p part gen pl	id.	
ἡγμένων vb perf m/p part gen pl	. . . . ἄγω	
ἡγνίκαμεν vb perf act ind 1st pers pl	. . . . ἁγνίζω	
ἡγνίσαμεν vb 1st aor act ind 1st pers pl	id.	
ἥγνισαν vb 1st aor act ind 3rd pers pl	id.	
ἡγνίσαντο vb 1st aor mid ind 3rd pers pl	id.	
ἡγνίσθη vb 1st aor pass ind 3rd pers sg	id.	
ἡγνίσθησαν vb 1st aor pass ind 3rd pers pl	id.	
ἡγνισμένα vb perf m/p part neut nom and acc pl	id.	
ἠγνόηκα vb perf act ind 1st pers sg	. . . . ἀγνοέω	
ἠγνοήκαμεν vb perf act ind 1st pers pl	id.	
ἠγνόηκας vb perf act ind 2nd pers sg	id.	
ἠγνοηκός vb perf act part masc and neut gen sg	id.	
ἠγνοημένων vb perf m/p part gen pl	id.	
ἠγνοήσαμεν vb 1st aor act ind 1st pers pl	id.	
ἠγνόησεν vb 1st aor act ind 3rd pers sg	id.	
ἠγνόουν vb impf act ind 1st pers sg	id.	
ἦγον vb impf act ind 3rd pers pl	. . . . ἄγω	
ἤγοντο vb impf m/p ind 3rd pers pl	id.	
ἠγόραζον vb impf act ind		
1st pers sg and 3rd pers pl	. . . . ἀγοράζω	
ἠγορασμένα vb perf m/p part neut nom and acc pl	id.	
ἡγουμένη vb pres dep part fem nom sg	. . . . ἡγέομαι	

ἡγουμένην vb pres dep part fem acc sg . . . . ἡγέομαι	ἡδίστου superl adj masc and neut gen sg . . . . ἡδύς
ἡγούμενοι vb pres dep part masc nom pl	id.	ἡδίστῳ superl adj masc and neut dat sg	id.
ἡγουμένοις vb pres dep part masc and neut dat pl	id.	ἠδολέσχει vb impf act ind 3rd pers sg . . . . ἀδολεσχέω
ἡγούμενον vb pres dep part masc acc sg	ἠδολέσχησα vb 1st aor act ind 1st pers sg	id.
neut nom and acc sg	id.	ἠδολέσχουν vb impf act ind 1st pers sg and 3rd pers pl	id.
ἡγούμενος vb pres dep part masc nom sg	id.	ἡδοναῖς noun fem dat pl . . . . ἡδονή
ἡγουμένου vb pres dep part masc and neut gen sg	id.	ἡδονάς noun fem acc pl	id.
ἡγουμένους vb pres dep part masc acc pl	id.	ἡδονή noun fem nom sg	id.
ἡγουμένῳ vb pres dep part masc and neut dat sg	id.	ἡδονῇ noun fem dat sg	id.
ἡγουμένων vb pres dep part gen pl	id.	ἡδονήν noun fem acc sg	id.
ἡγοῦντο vb impf dep ind 3rd pers pl	id.	ἡδονῆς noun fem gen sg	id.
ἠγρύπνεις vb impf act ind 2nd pers sg . . . . ἀγρυπνέω	ἡδονῶν noun fem gen pl	id.
ἠγρύπνησα vb 1st aor act ind 1st pers sg	id.	ἡδρασμένη vb perf m/p part fem nom sg . . . . ἑδράζω
ἠγρύπνησε(ν) vb 1st aor act ind 3rd pers sg	id.	ἡδρυμμένα vb perf m/p part neut nom and acc pl . . . ἁδρύνω
ἠγχιστεύθησαν vb 1st aor pass ind 3rd pers pl . ἀγχιστεύω	ἡδρύνθη vb 1st aor pass ind 3rd pers sg	id.
ἠγωνίζοντο vb impf dep ind 3rd pers pl . . . . . . ἀγωνίζομαι	ἡδρύνθησαν vb 1st aor pass ind 3rd pers pl	id.
ἠγωνίσατο vb 1st aor mid ind 3rd pers sg	id.	ἡδύ adj neut nom and acc sg . . . . ἡδύς
Ηδαδ pr noun	ἥδυναν vb 1st aor act ind 3rd pers pl . . . . ἡδύνω
Ηδαις pr noun	ἠδύναντο vb impf dep ind 3rd pers pl . . . . δύναμαι
Ηδαν pr noun	ἠδυνάσθη vb 1st aor pass ind 3rd pers sg	id.
ἠδάφισαν vb 1st aor act ind 3rd pers pl . . . . ἐδαφίζω	ἠδυνάσθην vb 1st aor pass ind 1st pers sg	id.
ἥδε dem pron fem nom sg . . . . ὅδε	ἠδυνάσθης vb 1st aor pass ind 2nd pers sg	id.
ἡδεῖ adj masc and neut dat sg . . . . ἡδύς	ἠδυνάσθησαν vb 1st aor pass ind 3rd pers pl	id.
ᾔδει vb plpf act ind 3rd pers sg . . . . οἶδα	ἠδύνατο vb impf dep ind 3rd pers sg	id.
ἡδεῖα adj fem nom sg . . . . ἡδύς	ἠδυνήθη vb 1st aor pass ind 3rd pers sg	id.
ἡδείας adj fem gen sg	id.	ἠδυνήθημεν vb 1st aor pass ind 1st pers pl	id.
ᾔδειμεν vb plpf act ind 1st pers pl . . . . οἶδα	ἠδυνήθην vb 1st aor pass ind 1st pers sg	id.
ᾔδειν vb plpf act ind 1st pers sg	id.	ἠδυνήθης vb 1st aor pass ind 2nd pers sg	id.
ᾔδεις vb plpf act ind 2nd pers sg	id.	ἠδυνήθησαν vb 1st aor pass ind 3rd pers pl	id.
ᾔδεισαν vb plpf act ind 3rd pers pl	id.	ἠδυνθείη vb 1st aor pass opt 3rd pers sg . . . . ἡδύνω
ᾔδειτε vb plpf act ind 2nd pers pl	id.	ἡδύνθη vb 1st aor pass ind 3rd pers sg	id.
ᾐδέσατο vb 1st aor mid ind 3rd pers sg . . . . αἰδέομαι	ἡδύνθης vb 1st aor pass ind 2nd pers sg	id.
ἥδεσθε vb pres dep ind 2nd pers pl . . . . ἥδομαι	ἡδύνθησαν vb 1st aor pass ind 3rd pers pl	id.
ᾐδέσθης vb 1st aor pass ind 2nd pers sg . . . . αἰδέομαι	ἡδύνουσιν vb pres act ind 3rd pers pl	id.
ἥδεται vb pres dep ind 3rd pers sg . . . . ἥδομαι	ἡδυπαθείας noun fem gen sg . . . . ἡδυπάθεια
ἡδέων adj masc and neut gen pl . . . . ἡδύς	ἡδύς adj masc nom sg
ἡδέως adverb	ἡδύσματα noun neut nom and acc pl . . . . ἥδυσμα
ἤδη adverb	ἡδύσματος noun neut gen sg	id.
ἠδικηκός vb perf act part neut nom and acc sg . . . . . ἀδικέω	ἡδυσμάτων noun neut gen pl	id.
ἠδικηκότι vb perf act part masc and neut dat sg	id.	ἡδυσμοῦ noun masc gen sg . . . . ἡδυσμός
ἠδικηκότος vb perf act part masc and neut gen sg	id.	ἡδυφώνου adj gen sg . . . . ἡδύφωνος
ἠδικημένοι vb perf m/p part masc nom pl	id.	ηδω translit
ἠδικημένου vb perf m/p part masc and neut gen sg	id.	Ηζιρ pr noun
ἠδίκησα vb 1st aor act ind 1st pers sg	id.	ηθ translit (Heb. letter: ח)
ἠδικήσαμεν vb 1st aor act ind 1st pers pl	id.	Ηθαμ pr noun
ἠδίκησαν vb 1st aor act ind 3rd pers pl	id.	ἤθελε(ν) vb impf act ind 3rd pers sg . . . . θέλω
ἠδίκησας vb 1st aor act ind 2nd pers sg	id.	ἠθέληκα vb perf act ind 1st pers sg	id.
ἠδίκησεν vb 1st aor act ind 3rd pers sg	id.	ἠθέλησα vb 1st aor act ind 1st pers sg	id.
ἠδίκηται vb perf m/p ind 3rd pers sg	id.	ἠθέλησαν vb 1st aor act ind 3rd pers pl	id.
ἠδίκουν vb impf act ind 3rd pers pl	id.	ἠθέλησας vb 1st aor act ind 2nd pers sg	id.
Ηδιν pr noun	ἠθελήσατε vb 1st aor act ind 2nd pers pl	id.
ἥδιον comp adverb . . . . ἡδέως	ἠθέλησεν vb 1st aor act ind 3rd pers sg	id.

ἤθελον vb impf act ind 1st pers sg and 3rd pers pl . . . . . θέλω

ἠθέτηκα vb perf act ind 1st pers sg . . . . ἀθετέω

ἠθετήκασιν vb perf act ind 3rd pers pl   id.

ἠθέτησαν vb 1st aor act ind 3rd pers pl   id.

ἠθέτησας vb 1st aor act ind 2nd pers sg   id.

ἠθέτησεν vb 1st aor act ind 3rd pers sg   id.

ἠθέτουν vb impf act ind 3rd pers pl   id.

ἤθη noun neut nom and acc pl . . . . ἦθος

Ηθιρ pr noun

ἠθλοθέτει vb impf act ind 3rd pers sg . . . . ἀθλοθετέω

ἠθολογήσαιμι vb 1st aor act opt 1st pers sg . . . . ἠθολογέω

ἦθος noun neut nom and acc sg

ἠθροίζοντο vb impf m/p ind 3rd pers pl . . . . ἀθροίζω

ἤθροισεν vb 1st aor act ind 3rd pers sg   id.

ἠθροίσθη vb 1st aor pass ind 3rd pers sg   id.

ἠθροίσθησαν vb 1st aor pass ind 3rd pers pl   id.

ἠθύμει vb impf act ind 3rd pers sg . . . . ἀθυμέω

ἠθύμησεν vb 1st aor act ind 3rd pers sg   id.

ἠθῶν noun neut gen pl . . . . ἦθος

ἠθῴωμαι vb perf m/p ind 1st pers sg . . . . ἀθῳόω

Ἤιδειν see ᾔδειν

ἤκαμεν vb perf act ind 1st pers pl . . . . ἥκω

ἥκασι(ν) vb perf act ind 3rd pers pl   id.

ἠκαταστάτησαν vb 1st aor act ind

          3rd pers pl . . . . ἀκαταστατέω

ἥκατε vb perf act ind 2nd pers pl . . . . ἥκω

ἧκε vb pres act impv 2nd pers sg   id.

ἧκε(ν) vb impf act ind 3rd pers sg   id.

ἥκει vb pres act ind 3rd pers sg   id.

ἥκειν vb pres act inf   id.

ἥκεις vb pres act ind 2nd pers sg   id.

ἥκετε vb pres act impv 2nd pers pl   id.

ἠκηδίασεν vb 1st aor act ind 3rd pers sg . . . . ἀκηδιάω

ᾐκίζοντο vb impf act ind 3rd pers pl . . . . αἰκίζομαι

ᾐκισμένοις vb perf dep part masc and neut dat pl   id.

ᾐκισμένους vb perf dep part masc acc pl   id.

ἠκολούθει vb impf act ind 3rd pers sg . . . . ἀκολουθέω

ἠκολουθηκότων vb perf act part masc and neut gen pl   id.

ἠκολούθησαν vb 1st aor act ind 3rd pers pl   id.

ἠκολούθησεν vb 1st aor act ind 3rd pers sg   id.

ἠκολούθουν vb impf act ind 3rd pers pl   id.

ἥκομεν vb pres act ind 1st pers pl . . . . ἥκω

ἠκονημένα vb perf m/p part neut nom and acc pl . . . ἀκονάω

ἠκονημένον vb perf m/p part masc acc sg,

          neut nom and acc sg   id.

ἠκόνησαν vb 1st aor act ind 3rd pers pl   id.

ἥκοντα vb pres act part masc acc sg . . . . ἥκω

ἥκοντας vb pres act part masc acc pl   id.

ἥκοντες vb pres act part masc nom pl   id.

ἠκόντιζε(ν) vb impf act ind 3rd pers sg . . . . ἀκοντίζω

ἥκοντος vb pres act part masc and neut gen sg . . . . ἥκω

ἠκούετο vb impf m/p ind 3rd pers sg . . . . ἀκούω

ἤκουον vb impf act ind 1st pers sg and 3rd pers pl . . . ἀκούω

ἤκουσα vb 1st aor act ind 1st pers sg   id.

ἠκούσαμεν vb 1st aor act ind 1st pers pl   id.

ἤκουσαν vb 1st aor act ind 3rd pers pl   id.

ἤκουσας vb 1st aor act ind 2nd pers sg   id.

ἠκούσατε vb 1st aor act ind 2nd pers pl   id.

ἤκουσε(ν) vb 1st aor act ind 3rd pers sg   id.

ἠκούσθη vb 1st aor pass ind 3rd pers sg   id.

ἠκούσθησαν vb 1st aor pass ind 3rd pers pl   id.

ἠκουσιάσαντο vb 1st aor mid ind

          3rd pers pl . . . . ἑκουσιάζομαι

ἠκουσιάσθησαν vb 1st aor pass ind 3rd pers pl   id.

ἤκουσται vb perf m/p ind 3rd pers sg . . . . ἀκούω

ἠκούτισας vb 1st aor act ind 2nd pers sg . . . . . . ἀκουτίζω

ἠκούτισεν vb 1st aor act ind 3rd pers sg   id.

ἠκριβάσθη vb 1st aor pass ind 3rd pers sg . . . . . . ἀκριβάζω

ἦκται vb perf m/p ind 3rd pers sg . . . . ἄγω

ἠκύρωσε(ν) vb 1st aor act ind 3rd pers sg . . . . ἀκυρόω

ἥκω vb pres act ind 1st pers sg

ἥκων vb pres act part masc nom sg . . . . ἥκω

Ηλα pr noun

ἠλάλαξαν vb 1st aor act ind 3rd pers pl . . . . ἀλαλάζω

ἠλάλαξεν vb 1st aor act ind 3rd pers sg   id.

Ηλαμ pr noun

Ηλαμ-ααρ pr noun

Ηλαμαῖοι pr noun

Ηλαμ-αρ pr noun

Ηλας pr noun

Ηλασα pr noun

ἥλατο vb 1st aor mid ind 3rd pers sg . . . . ἅλλομαι

ἠλαττόνησεν vb 1st aor act ind 3rd pers sg . . . . ἐλαττονέω

ἠλαττονοῦτο vb impf m/p ind 3rd pers sg . . . . . ἐλαττονόω

ἠλαττώθη vb 1st aor pass ind 3rd pers sg . . . . ἐλαττόω

ἠλαττώθημεν vb 1st aor pass ind 1st pers pl   id.

ἠλαττώθησαν vb 1st aor pass ind 3rd pers pl   id.

ἠλάττωσας vb 1st aor act ind 2nd pers sg   id.

ἠλαύνοντο vb impf m/p ind 3rd pers pl . . . . ἐλαύνω

ἤλγησαν vb 1st aor act ind 3rd pers pl . . . . ἀλγέω

ἤλεγξεν vb 1st aor act ind 3rd pers sg . . . . ἐλέγχω

ἠλεημένη vb perf m/p part fem nom sg . . . . ἐλεέω

ἠλεημένην vb perf m/p part fem acc sg   id.

ἠλέησαν vb 1st aor act ind 3rd pers pl   id.

ἠλέησας vb 1st aor act ind 2nd pers sg   id.

ἠλέησεν vb 1st aor act ind 3rd pers sg   id.

ἠλειμμένοι vb perf mid part masc nom pl . . . . ἀλείφω

ἠλειψάμην vb 1st aor mid ind 1st pers sg   id.

ἤλειψας vb 1st aor act ind 2nd pers sg   id.

ἠλείψατε vb 1st aor act ind 2nd pers pl   id.

ἠλείψατο vb 1st aor mid ind 3rd pers sg   id.

ἠλέκτρου noun neut gen sg . . . . ἤλεκτρον

ἤληθον vb impf act ind 3rd pers pl . . . . ἀλήθω

ἦλθα vb 1st aor act ind 1st pers sg . . . . ἔρχομαι ἤλθαμεν vb 1st aor act ind 1st pers pl . . . . ἔρχομαι

ἤλθαν vb 1st aor act ind 3rd pers pl   id.

ἤλθατε vb 1st aor act ind 2nd pers pl   id.

ἦλθε(ν) vb 2nd aor act ind 3rd pers sg   id.

ἦλθες vb 2nd aor act ind 2nd pers sg   id.

ἤλθετε vb 2nd aor act ind 2nd pers pl   id.

ἤλθομεν vb 2nd aor act ind 1st pers pl   id.

ἦλθον vb 2nd aor act ind 1st pers sg and 3rd pers pl   id.

ἤλθοσαν vb 2nd aor act ind 3rd pers pl   id.

Ηλι pr noun

Ηλια pr noun

Ηλιαθα pr noun

Ηλιαμ pr noun

Ηλιαν pr noun masc acc sg . . . . Ηλιας

Ηλιας pr noun masc nom sg

ἡλιασθέντων vb 1st aor pass part

          masc and neut gen pl . . . . ἡλιάζομαι

ἡλικία noun fem nom sg

ἡλικίᾳ noun fem dat sg . . . . ἡλικία

ἡλικίαν noun fem acc sg   id.

ἡλικίας noun fem gen sg and acc pl   id.

ἡλικιώτης noun masc nom sg

Ἡλιοδωρον pr noun masc acc sg . . . . Ἡλιοδωρος

Ἡλιοδωρος pr noun masc nom sg   id.

Ἡλιοδωρῳ pr noun masc dat sg   id.

ἥλιον noun masc acc sg . . . . ἥλιος

ἥλιος noun masc nom sg   id.

Ηλιου pr noun

Ηλιου pr noun masc gen sg . . . . Ηλιας

Ἡλιου pr noun masc gen sg . . . . Ἡλιος

ἡλίου noun masc gen sg . . . . ἥλιος

ἡλισγημένη vb perf m/p part fem nom sg . . . . ἁλισγέω

ἡλισγημένους vb perf m/p part masc acc pl   id.

ἡλισγήσαμεν vb 1st aor act ind 1st pers pl   id.

ἡλίσθης vb 1st aor pass ind 2nd pers sg . . . . ἁλίζω

ἡλισμένον vb perf m/p part masc acc sg   id.

ἡλίῳ noun masc dat sg . . . . ἥλιος

Ηλκανα pr noun

ἤλλαξαν vb 1st aor act ind 3rd pers pl . . . . ἀλλάσσω

ἠλλάξαντο vb 1st aor mid ind 3rd pers pl   id.

ἠλλάξατο vb 1st aor mid ind 3rd pers sg   id.

ἤλλαξεν vb 1st aor act ind 3rd pers sg   id.

ἠλλοιώθη vb 1st aor pass ind 3rd pers sg . . . . ἀλλοιόω

ἠλλοιώθησαν vb 1st aor pass ind 3rd pers pl   id.

ἠλλοίωμαι vb perf m/p ind 1st pers sg   id.

ἠλλοιωμένον vb perf m/p part masc acc sg,

          neut nom and acc sg   id.

ἠλλοίωσαν vb 1st aor act ind 3rd pers pl   id.

ἠλλοίωσεν vb 1st aor act ind 3rd pers sg   id.

ἡλλόμην vb impf dep ind 1st pers sg . . . . ἅλλομαι

ἠλλοτριοῦντο vb impf m/p ind 3rd pers pl . . . . ἀλλοτριόω

ἠλλοτριοῦτο vb impf m/p ind 3rd pers sg

ἠλλοτριώθη vb 1st aor pass ind 3rd pers sg . . . . ἀλλοτριόω

ἡλόησεν vb 1st aor act ind 3rd pers sg . . . . ἀλοάω

ἧλοι noun masc nom pl . . . . ἧλος

ἥλοις noun masc dat pl   id.

ἥλους noun masc acc pl   id.

ἠλπίζομεν vb impf act ind 1st pers pl . . . . ἐλπίζω

ἤλπισα vb 1st aor act ind 1st pers sg   id.

ἠλπίσαμεν vb 1st aor act ind 1st pers pl   id.

ἤλπισαν vb 1st aor act ind 3rd pers pl   id.

ἤλπισαν see ἤλπισαν

ἤλπισας vb 1st aor act ind 2nd pers sg   id.

ἠλπίσατε vb 1st aor act ind 2nd pers pl   id.

ἤλπισεν vb 1st aor act ind 3rd pers sg   id.

ἥλων noun masc gen pl . . . . ἧλος

Ηλωνμαωνενιμ pr noun

Ημαξαβουν pr noun

Ημαξ pr noun

ἡμάρτανον vb impf act ind 3rd pers pl . . . . ἁμαρτάνω

ἥμαρτεν vb 2nd aor act ind 3rd pers sg   id.

ἥμαρτες vb 2nd aor act ind 2nd pers sg   id.

ἡμάρτετε vb 2nd aor act ind 2nd pers pl   id.

ἡμάρτηκα vb perf act ind 1st pers sg   id.

ἡμαρτήκαμεν vb perf act ind 1st pers pl   id.

ἡμάρτηκας vb perf act ind 2nd pers sg   id.

ἡμαρτήκατε vb perf act ind 2nd pers pl   id.

ἡμάρτηκεν vb perf act ind 3rd pers sg   id.

ἡμαρτηκόσι vb perf act part masc and neut dat pl   id.

ἡμαρτηκότων vb perf act part masc and neut gen pl   id.

ἡμαρτηκώς vb perf act part masc nom sg   id.

ἡμαρτήσαμεν vb 1st aor act ind 1st pers pl   id.

ἡμάρτομεν vb 2nd aor act ind 1st pers pl   id.

ἥμαρτον vb 2nd aor act ind 1st pers sg and 3rd pers pl id.

ἡμάρτοσαν vb 2nd aor act ind 3rd pers pl   id.

ἡμᾶς pers pron 2nd pers acc pl . . . . ἐγώ

Ημασοραϊμ pr noun

ἠμαυρώθησαν vb 1st aor pass ind 3rd pers pl . . . ἀμαυρόω

ἠμβλύνθησαν vb 1st aor pass ind 3rd pers pl . . . . . ἀμβλύνω

ἠμβλυωπουν vb impf act ind 3rd pers pl . . . . . . ἀμβλυωπέω

ἤμεθα vb impf mid ind 1st pers pl . . . . εἰμί

ἡμεῖς pers pron 1st pers nom pl . . . . ἐγώ

ἠμέλησα vb 1st aor act ind 1st pers sg . . . . ἀμελέω

ἠμέλησας vb 1st aor act ind 2nd pers sg   id.

ἤμελλεν vb impf act ind 3rd pers sg . . . . μέλλω

ἠμελξας vb 1st aor act ind 2nd pers sg . . . . ἀμέλγω

ἦμεν vb impf act ind 1st pers pl . . . . εἰμί

ἥμερα adj neut nom and acc pl . . . . ἥμερος

ἡμέρα noun fem nom sg

ἡμέρᾳ noun fem dat sg . . . . ἡμέρα

ἡμέραι noun fem nom pl   id.

ἡμέραις noun fem dat pl   id.

Ἡμεραν pr noun fem acc sg . . . . Ἡμερα

ἡμέραν noun fem acc sg . . . . ἡμέρα

ἡμέρας noun fem gen sg and acc pl . . . . ἡμέρα	Ηναδδα pr noun
ἥμερον adj acc sg, neut nom sg . . . . ἥμερος	Ηναϊμ pr noun
ἡμεροῦτο vb impf dep ind 3rd pers sg . . . . ἡμερόομαι	Ηναν pr noun
ἡμερῶν noun fem gen pl . . . . ἡμέρα	Ηναγαδδι pr noun
ἡμέτερα adj neut nom and acc pl . . . . ἡμέτερος	Ηναγαννιμ pr noun
ἡμετέρᾳ adj fem dat sg id.	ἠνδραγάθησεν vb 1st aor act ind 3rd pers sg . . ἀνδραγαθέω
ἡμετέραν adj fem acc sg id.	ἤνεγκα vb 1st aor act ind 1st pers sg . . . . φέρω
ἡμετέρας adj fem gen sg id.	ἠνέγκαμεν vb 1st aor act ind 1st pers pl id.
ἡμέτεροι adj masc nom pl id.	ἤνεγκαν vb 1st aor act ind 3rd pers pl id.
ἡμετέροις adj masc and neut dat pl id.	ἠνέγκατε vb 1st aor act ind 2nd pers pl id.
ἡμέτερον adj masc acc sg, neut nom and acc sg id.	ἤνεγκε(ν) vb 1st aor act ind 3rd pers sg id.
ἡμέτερος adj masc nom sg id.	ἠνείχοντο vb impf m/p ind 3rd pers pl . . . . ἀνέχω
ἡμετέρους adj masc acc pl id.	ἤνεσα vb 1st aor act ind 1st pers sg . . . . αἰνέω
ἡμετέρων adj gen pl id.	ἤνεσαν vb 1st aor act ind 3rd pers pl id.
ἤμην vb impf mid ind 1st pers sg . . . . εἰμί	ἤνεσας vb 1st aor act ind 2nd pers sg id.
Ημι pr noun	ἠνέσατε vb 1st aor act ind 2nd pers pl id.
ἡμίεφθον adj acc sg, neut nom sg . . . . ἡμίεφθος	ἤνεσεν vb 1st aor act ind 3rd pers sg id.
ἡμιθανής adj masc and fem nom sg	ἠνέχθη vb 1st aor pass ind 3rd pers sg . . . . φέρω
ἡμίθνητος adj masc and fem nom sg	ἠνέχθησαν vb 1st aor pass ind 3rd pers pl id.
Ημιμ pr noun	ἠνεχύραζες vb impf act ind 2nd pers sg . . . . . . ἐνεχυράζω
ἡμῖν pers pron 1st pers dat pl . . . . ἐγώ	ἠνεχύρασαν vb 1st aor act ind 3rd pers pl id.
ἡμίονοι noun masc nom pl . . . . ἡμίονος	ἠνεωγμένα vb perf m/p part neut nom and acc pl . . . ἀνοίγω
ἡμίονον noun masc or fem acc sg id.	ἠνεωγμένους vb perf m/p part masc acc pl id.
ἡμίονος noun masc nom sg id.	ἠνέῳξεν vb 1st aor act ind 3rd pers sg id.
ἡμιόνου noun masc gen sg id.	ἠνεῴχθησαν vb 1st aor pass ind 3rd pers pl id.
ἡμιόνους noun masc or fem acc pl id.	ἤνθηκεν vb perf act ind 3rd pers sg . . . . ἀνθέω
ἡμιόνων noun masc gen pl id.	ἤνθησαν vb 1st aor act ind 3rd pers pl id.
ἡμίσει adj masc and neut dat sg . . . . ἥμισυς	ἤνθησεν vb 1st aor act ind 3rd pers sg id.
ἡμίσεις adj masc nom and acc pl id.	Ηνια pr noun
ἡμίσεσι adj masc and neut dat pl id.	ἡνίαι noun fem nom pl . . . . ἡνία
ἡμίσευμα noun neut nom and acc sg	ἡνίκα adverb
ἡμισεύματος noun neut gen sg . . . . ἡμίσευμα	ἡνιόχῳ noun masc dat sg . . . . ἡνίοχος
ἡμισεύσωσιν vb 1st aor act subj 3rd pers pl . . . . . ἡμισεύω	ἡνιῶν noun fem gen pl . . . . ἡνία
ἡμίσους adj masc and neut gen sg . . . . ἥμισυς	ἠνοίγετο vb impf m/p ind 3rd pers sg . . . . ἀνοίγω
ἥμισυ adj neut nom and acc sg id.	ἠνοιγμένα vb perf m/p part neut nom and acc pl id.
ἡμμένον vb perf dep part neut nom and acc sg . . . . ἅπτομαι	ἤνοιγον vb impf act ind 3rd pers pl id.
ἠμυνάμην vb 1st aor mid ind 1st pers sg . . . . ἀμύνω	ἤνοιξα vb 1st aor act ind 1st pers sg id.
ἠμύναντο vb 1st aor mid ind 3rd pers pl id.	ἠνοίξαμεν vb 1st aor act ind 1st pers pl id.
ἠμύνατο vb 1st aor mid ind 3rd pers sg id.	ἤνοιξαν vb 1st aor act ind 3rd pers pl id.
ἠμφίασα vb 1st aor act ind 1st pers sg . . . . ἀμφιάζω	ἤνοιξας vb 1st aor act ind 2nd pers sg id.
ἠμφιασάμην vb 1st aor mid ind 1st pers sg id.	ἠνοίξατε vb 1st aor act ind 2nd pers pl id.
ἠμφιέσαντο vb 1st aor mid ind 3rd pers pl . . . . . ἀμφιέννυμι	ἤνοιξεν vb 1st aor act ind 3rd pers sg id.
ἠμωδίασαν vb 1st aor act ind 3rd pers pl . . . . αἱμωδιάω	ἠνοίχθη vb 1st aor pass ind 3rd pers sg id.
ἡμῶν pers pron 1st pers gen pl . . . . ἐγώ	ἠνοίχθησαν vb 1st aor pass ind 3rd pers pl id.
ἥν rel pron fem acc sg . . . . ὅς	ἠνόμησα vb 1st aor act ind 1st pers sg . . . . ἀνομέω
ἦν vb impf act ind 3rd pers sg . . . . εἰμί	ἠνομήσαμεν vb 1st aor act ind 1st pers pl id.
ἠνάγκαζεν vb impf act ind 3rd pers sg . . . . ἀναγκάζω	ἠνόμησαν vb 1st aor act ind 3rd pers pl id.
ἠναγκάζετο vb impf m/p ind 3rd pers sg id.	ἠνόμησας vb 1st aor act ind 2nd pers sg id.
ἠναγκάζοντο vb impf m/p ind 3rd pers pl id.	ἠνομήσατε vb 1st aor act ind 2nd pers pl id.
ἠνάγκασαν vb 1st aor act ind 3rd pers pl id.	ἠνόμησεν vb 1st aor act ind 3rd pers sg id.
ἠναγκασμένη vb perf m/p part fem nom sg id.	ἠνομοῦσαν vb impf act ind 3rd pers pl id.
Ηναδαδ pr noun	ἤνουν vb impf act ind 3rd pers pl . . . . αἰνέω

Ηνρεμμων pr noun
ἤντλησεν vb 1st aor act ind 3rd pers sg . . . . ἀντλέω
ἤντλουν vb impf act ind 3rd pers pl   id.
ἠνυπνιασάμην vb 1st aor mid ind
      1st pers sg . . . . ἐνυπνιάζομαι
ἠνυπνιάσθη vb 1st aor pass ind 3rd pers sg   id.
ἠνυπνιάσθην vb 1st aor pass ind 1st pers sg   id.
ἤνυστρον noun neut nom and acc sg
ἠνωτίσαντο vb 1st aor mid ind 3rd pers pl . . . . ἐνωτίζομαι
ἠνωτίσασθε vb 1st aor mid ind 2nd pers pl   id.
ἠνωχλήθην vb 1st aor pass ind 1st pers sg . . . . . . ἐνοχλέω
ἥξει vb fut act ind 3rd pers sg . . . . ἥκω
ἥξεις vb fut act ind 2nd pers sg   id.
ἥξετε vb fut act ind 2nd pers pl   id.
ἠξίου vb impf act ind 3rd pers sg . . . . ἀξιόω
ἠξίουν vb impf act ind 1st pers sg and 3rd pers pl   id.
ἠξιώθην vb 1st aor pass ind 1st pers sg   id.
ἠξίωσα vb 1st aor act ind 1st pers sg   id.
ἠξιώσαμεν vb 1st aor act ind 1st pers pl   id.
ἠξίωσαν vb 1st aor act ind 3rd pers pl   id.
ἠξίωσε(ν) vb 1st aor act ind 3rd pers sg   id.
ἠξίωται vb perf m/p ind 3rd pers sg   id.
ἥξομεν vb fut act ind 1st pers pl . . . . ἥκω
ἥξουσι(ν) vb fut act ind 3rd pers pl   id.
ἥξω vb fut act ind 1st pers sg   id.
ἥξων vb fut act part masc nom sg   id.
ἡπαλύνθη vb 1st aor pass ind 3rd pers sg . . . . ἀπαλύνω
ἡπαλύνθησαν vb 1st aor pass ind 3rd pers pl   id.
ἧπαρ noun neut nom and acc sg
ἥπατα noun neut nom and acc pl . . . . ἧπαρ
ἠπάτα vb impf act ind 3rd pers sg . . . . ἀπατάω
ἠπατήθη vb 1st aor pass ind 3rd pers sg   id.
ἠπατήθην vb 1st aor pass ind 1st pers sg   id.
ἠπάτησαν vb 1st aor act ind 3rd pers pl   id.
ἠπάτησας vb 1st aor act ind 2nd pers sg   id.
ἠπάτησεν vb 1st aor act ind 3rd pers sg   id.
ἥπατι noun neut dat sg . . . . ἧπαρ
ἥπατος noun neut gen sg   id.
ἡπατοσκοπήσασθαι vb 1st aor mid inf . . . . ἡπατοσκοπέω
ἤπειγεν vb impf act ind 3rd pers sg . . . . ἐπείγω
ἠπειθήσαμεν vb 1st aor act ind 1st pers pl . . . . ἀπειθέω
ἠπείθησαν vb 1st aor act ind 3rd pers pl   id.
ἠπειθήσατε vb 1st aor act ind 2nd pers pl   id.
ἠπείθησεν vb 1st aor act ind 3rd pers sg   id.
ἤπερ comp conjunction
ἠπιότητος noun fem gen sg . . . . ἠπιότης
ἠπιστάμην vb impf dep ind 1st pers sg . . . . ἐπίσταμαι
ἠπίσταντο vb impf dep ind 3rd pers pl   id.
ἠπίστω vb impf dep ind 2nd pers sg   id.
ἠπόρει vb impf act ind 3rd pers sg . . . . ἀπορέω
ἠπορεῖτο vb impf m/p ind 3rd pers sg   id.
ἧπται vb perf dep ind 3rd pers sg . . . . ἅπτομαι

ἥπτετο vb impf dep ind 3rd pers sg . . . . ἅπτομαι
ἥπτοντο vb impf dep ind 3rd pers pl   id.
Ηρ pr noun
Ηρα pr noun
ἦρα vb 1st aor act ind 1st pers sg . . . . αἴρω
Ηραε pr noun
Ηρακλεους pr noun
Ηραμ pr noun
ἦραν vb 1st aor act ind 3rd pers pl . . . . αἴρω
ἦρας vb 1st aor act ind 2nd pers sg   id.
ἠράσθη vb 1st aor pass ind 3rd pers sg . . . . ἐράω
ἠράσω vb 1st aor mid ind 2nd pers sg . . . . ἀράομαι
ἠργάζετο vb impf dep ind 3rd pers sg . . . . ἐργάζομαι
ἠργάζοντο vb impf dep ind 3rd pers pl   id.
ἠργασάμην vb 1st aor mid ind 1st pers sg   id.
ἠργάσαντο vb 1st aor mid ind 3rd pers pl   id.
ἤργει vb impf act ind 3rd pers sg . . . . ἀργέω
ἤργησαν vb 1st aor act ind 3rd pers pl   id.
ἤργησεν vb 1st aor act ind 3rd pers sg   id.
ἦργμαι vb perf m/p ind 1st pers sg . . . . ἄρχω
ἠρδαλωμένῳ vb pres m/p part
      masc and neut dat sg . . . . ἀρδαλόω
ἤρεισεν vb 1st aor act ind 3rd pers sg . . . . ἐρείδω
ἠρεῖτο vb impf m/p ind 3rd pers sg . . . . αἱρέω
Ηρεμ pr noun
ἠρεμάζων vb pres act part masc nom sg . . . . ἠρεμάζω
ἦρεν vb 1st aor act ind 3rd pers sg . . . . αἴρω
ἤρεσαν vb 1st aor act ind 3rd pers pl . . . . ἀρέσκω
ἤρεσε(ν) vb 1st aor act ind 3rd pers sg   id.
ἡρέτικα vb perf act ind 1st pers sg . . . . αἱρετίζω
ἡρέτικεν vb perf act ind 3rd pers sg   id.
ἡρέτισα vb 1st aor act ind 1st pers sg   id.
ἡρετισάμεθα vb 1st aor mid ind 1st pers pl   id.
ἡρετισάμην vb 1st aor mid ind 1st pers sg   id.
ἡρέτισαν vb 1st aor act ind 3rd pers pl   id.
ἡρετίσαντο vb 1st aor mid ind 3rd pers pl   id.
ἡρετίσατο vb 1st aor mid ind 3rd pers sg   id.
ἡρέτισεν vb 1st aor act ind 3rd pers sg   id.
ἡρετίσω vb 1st aor mid ind 2nd pers sg   id.
ἠρεύνα vb impf act ind 3rd pers sg . . . . ἐρευνάω
ἠρεύνησαν vb 1st aor act ind 3rd pers pl   id.
ἠρεύνησας vb 1st aor act ind 2nd pers sg   id.
ἠρεύνησεν vb 1st aor act ind 3rd pers sg   id.
ἤρευνων vb impf act ind 3rd pers pl   id.
ἠρημώθη vb 1st aor pass ind 3rd pers sg . . . . ἐρημόω
ἠρημώθην vb 1st aor pass ind 1st pers sg   id.
ἠρημωκότας vb perf act part masc acc pl   id.
ἠρημωμέναις vb perf m/p part fem dat pl   id.
ἠρημωμένας vb perf m/p part fem acc pl   id.
ἠρημωμένη vb perf m/p part fem nom sg   id.
ἠρημωμένην vb perf m/p part fem acc sg   id.
ἠρημωμένης vb perf m/p part fem gen sg   id.

ἠρημωμένον vb perf m/p part masc acc sg,

     neut nom and acc sg . . . . ἐρημόω

ἠρημωμένων vb perf m/p part gen pl   id.

ἠρήμωσα vb 1st aor act ind 1st pers sg   id.

ἠρήμωσαν vb 1st aor act ind 3rd pers pl   id.

ἠρημώσατε vb 1st aor act ind 2nd pers pl   id.

ἠρήμωσεν vb 1st aor act ind 3rd pers sg   id.

ἠρήμωται vb 1st aor mid ind 3rd pers sg   id.

ἤρθη vb 1st aor pass ind 3rd pers sg . . . . αἴρω

ἤρθησαν vb 1st aor pass ind 3rd pers pl   id.

ἠριθεύετο vb impf dep ind 3rd pers sg . . . . ἐριθεύομαι

ἠριθμήθησαν vb 1st aor pass ind 3rd pers pl . . . . . ἀριθμέω

ἠρίθμησαν vb 1st aor act ind 3rd pers pl   id.

ἠρίθμησας vb 1st aor act ind 2nd pers sg   id.

ἠρίθμησεν vb 1st aor act ind 3rd pers sg   id.

ἠρίθμηται vb perf m/p ind 3rd pers sg   id.

ἠρίστα vb perf act ind 3rd pers sg . . . . ἀριστάω

ἤρκεν vb perf act ind 3rd pers pl . . . . αἴρω

ἤρκεσεν vb 1st aor act ind 3rd pers sg . . . . ἀρκέω

ἠρκέσθη vb 1st aor pass ind 3rd pers sg   id.

ἤρκται vb perf m/p ind 3rd pers sg . . . . ἄρχω

ἡρμηνευμένην vb perf m/p part fem acc sg . . . . . ἑρμηνεύω

ἥρμοσαν vb 1st aor act ind 3rd pers pl . . . . ἁρμόζω

ἡρμοσμένοις vb perf m/p part masc and neut dat pl   id.

ἡρμοσμένῳ vb perf m/p part masc and neut dat sg   id.

ἠρνήσατο vb 1st aor mid ind 3rd pers sg . . . . . . ἀρνέομαι

ἠρνοῦντο vb impf dep ind 3rd pers pl   id.

ἦρξαι vb 1st aor act inf . . . . ἄρχω

ἠρξάμην vb 1st aor mid ind 1st pers sg   id.

ἦρξαν vb 1st aor act ind 3rd pers pl   id.

ἤρξαντο vb 1st aor mid ind 3rd pers pl   id.

ἦρξας vb 1st aor act ind 2nd pers sg   id.

ἤρξατο vb 1st aor mid ind 3rd pers sg   id.

ἦρξεν vb 1st aor act ind 3rd pers sg   id.

ἦρξω vb 1st aor mid ind 2nd pers sg   id.

ἦρον vb impf act ind 3rd pers pl . . . . αἴρω

ἤροσαν vb impf act ind 3rd pers pl   id.

ἠροτρία vb impf act ind 3rd pers sg . . . . ἀροτριάω

ἠροτριάσατε vb 1st aor act ind 2nd pers pl   id.

ἡρπάγη vb 2nd aor pass ind 3rd pers sg . . . . ἁρπάζω

ἥρπακεν vb perf act ind 3rd pers sg   id.

ἥρπασα vb 1st aor act ind 1st pers sg   id.

ἥρπασαν vb 1st aor act ind 3rd pers pl   id.

ἥρπασεν vb 1st aor act ind 3rd pers sg   id.

ἡρπασμένον vb perf m/p part masc acc sg,

     neut nom and acc sg   id.

ἡρπασμένος vb perf m/p part masc nom sg   id.

ἠρρώστει vb impf act ind 3rd pers sg . . . . ἀρρωστέω

ἠρρώστησε(ν) vb 1st aor act ind 3rd pers sg   id.

ἦρται vb perf m/p ind 3rd pers sg . . . . αἴρω

ἠρυθρίων vb impf act ind 1st pers sg . . . . ἐρυθριάω

ἠρυθροδανωμένα vb perf m/p part

     neut nom and acc pl . . . . ἐρυθροδανόω

ἤρχετο vb impf dep ind 3rd pers sg . . . . ἔρχομαι

ἠρχιτεκτόνησεν vb 1st aor act ind

     3rd pers sg . . . . ἀρχιτεκτονέω

ἠρχόμην vb impf m/p ind 1st pers sg . . . . ἔρχομαι

ἤρχοντο vb impf m/p ind 3rd pers pl   id.

ἤρχου vb impf m/p ind 2nd pers sg   id.

Ηρων pr noun

ἠρώτα vb impf act ind 3rd pers sg . . . . ἐρωτάω

ἠρωτήθη vb 1st aor pass ind 3rd pers sg   id.

ἠρωτημένος vb perf m/p part masc nom sg   id.

ἠρώτησα vb 1st aor act ind 1st pers sg   id.

ἠρωτήσαμεν vb 1st aor act ind 1st pers pl   id.

ἠρώτησαν vb 1st aor act ind 3rd pers pl   id.

ἠρώτησας vb 1st aor act ind 2nd pers sg   id.

ἠρώτησεν vb 1st aor act ind 3rd pers sg   id.

ἠρώτων vb impf act ind 1st pers sg and 3rd pers pl   id.

Ἡρώων pr noun masc gen pl . . . . ἥρως

ἧς rel pron fem gen sg . . . . ὅς

ἧς vb impf act ind 2nd pers sg . . . . εἰμί

ᾖς vb pres act subj 2nd pers sg   id.

Ησαιαν pr noun masc acc sg . . . . Ησαιας

Ησαιας pr noun masc nom sg   id.

Ησαιου pr noun masc gen sg   id.

Ησαμ pr noun

Ησαμαθιμ pr noun

ἦσαν vb impf act ind 3rd pers pl . . . . εἰμί

ᾖσαν vb 1st aor act ind 3rd pers pl . . . . ᾄδω

Ησαρεϊ pr noun

Ησαυ pr noun

ἠσεβήκασιν vb perf act ind 3rd pers pl . . . . ἀσεβέω

ἠσεβηκότων vb perf act part masc and neut gen pl   id.

ἠσέβησα vb 1st aor act ind 1st pers sg   id.

ἠσεβήσαμεν vb 1st aor act ind 1st pers pl   id.

ἠσέβησαν vb 1st aor act ind 3rd pers pl   id.

ἠσέβησας vb 1st aor act ind 2nd pers sg   id.

ἠσεβήσατε vb 1st aor act ind 2nd pers pl   id.

ἠσέβησεν vb 1st aor act ind 3rd pers sg   id.

ἠσέβουν vb impf act ind 3rd pers pl   id.

ᾖσεν vb 1st aor act ind 3rd pers sg . . . . ᾄδω

Ησεραι pr noun

ἦσθα vb impf act ind 2nd pers sg . . . . εἰμί

ᾐσθάνοντο vb impf dep ind 3rd pers pl . . . . . . αἰσθάνομαι

ἠσθένει vb impf act ind 3rd pers sg . . . . ἀσθενέω

ἠσθενηκός vb perf act part neut nom and acc sg   id.

ἠσθένησα vb 1st aor act ind 1st pers sg   id.

ἠσθένησαν vb 1st aor act ind 3rd pers pl   id.

ἠσθένησας vb 1st aor act ind 2nd pers sg   id.

ἠσθενήσατε vb 1st aor act ind 2nd pers pl   id.

ἠσθένησεν vb 1st aor act ind 3rd pers sg   id.

ἤσθετο vb 2nd aor mid ind 3rd pers sg

    (but *see* ἤσθετο) . . . . ἤδομαι

ἤσθετο vb 2nd aor mid ind 3rd pers sg . . . . αἰσθάνομαι

ἤσθιε(ν) vb impf act ind 3rd pers sg . . . . ἐσθίω

ἠσθίετε vb impf act ind 2nd pers pl   id.

ἠσθίομεν vb impf act ind 1st pers pl   id.

ἤσθιον vb impf act ind 1st pers sg and 3rd pers pl   id.

ἤσθοντο vb 2nd aor mid ind 3rd pers pl . . . . . αἰσθάνομαι

ἤσθοσαν vb 2nd aor act ind 3rd pers pl . . . . ἐσθίω

ἠσμένισαν vb 1st aor act ind 3rd pers pl . . . . ασμενίζω

ἠσπάσαντο vb 1st aor mid ind 3rd pers pl . . . . ἀσπάζομαι

ἠσπάσατο vb 1st aor mid ind 3rd pers sg   id.

ἡσσόνων adj gen pl . . . . ἥσσων

ἥσσων adj masc and fem nom sg   id.

ἡστινοσοῦν rel pron fem sg . . . . ὁστισοῦν

Ησυηλος pr noun

ἠσυνθέτηκα vb perf act ind 1st pers sg . . . . ἀσυνθετέω

ἠσυνθετήκατε vb perf act ind 2nd pers pl   id.

ἠσυνθετήσαμεν vb 1st aor act ind 1st pers pl   d.

ἠσυνθέτησαν vb 1st aor act ind 3rd pers pl   d.

ἡσυχάζει vb pres act ind 3rd pers sg . . . . ἡσυχάζω

ἡσυχάζεται vb pres m/p ind 3rd pers sg   d.

ἡσυχάζετε vb pres act impv 2nd pers pl,

       pres act ind 2nd pers pl   d.

ἡσυχάζοντα vb pres act part masc acc sg   id.

ἡσυχάζοντας vb pres act part masc acc pl   id.

ἡσυχάζουσα vb pres act part fem nom sg   id.

ἡσυχάζουσιν vb pres act ind 3rd pers pl   id.

ἡσύχασα vb 1st aor act ind 1st pers sg   id.

ἡσυχάσαι vb 1st aor act inf   id.

ἡσυχάσαν vb 1st aor act ind 3rd pers pl   id.

ἡσυχάσει vb fut act ind 3rd pers sg   id.

ἡσυχάσεις vb fut act ind 2nd pers sg   id.

ἡσύχασεν vb 1st aor act ind 3rd pers sg   id.

ἡσυχάσῃ vb 1st aor act subj 3rd pers sg   id.

ἡσύχασον vb 1st aor act impv 2nd pers sg   id.

ἡσυχῇ adverb

ἡσυχία noun fem nom sg

ἡσυχίᾳ noun fem dat sg . . . . ἡσυχία

ἡσυχίαν noun fem acc sg   id.

ἡσυχίας noun fem gen sg and acc pl   id.

ἡσύχιον adj acc sg, neut nom sg . . . . ἡσύχιος

ἡσύχου adj gen sg . . . . ἥσυχος

ἡσύχῳ adj dat sg   id.

ἠσφαλισάμην vb 1st aor mid ind 1st pers sg . . . . ἀσφαλίζω

ἠσφαλίσατο vb 1st aor mid ind 3rd pers sg   id.

ἠσχάτισεν vb 1st aor act ind 3rd pers sg . . . . ἐσχατίζω

ἤσχυμμαι vb perf m/p ind 1st pers sg . . . . αἰσχύνω

ἤσχυναν vb 1st aor act ind 3rd pers pl   id.

ἠσχύνετο vb impf m/p ind 3rd pers sg   id.

ἠσχύνθη vb 1st aor pass ind 3rd pers sg   id.

ἠσχύνθημεν vb 1st aor pass ind 1st pers pl   id.

ἠσχύνθην vb 1st aor pass ind 1st pers sg . . . . αἰσχύνω

ἠσχύνθησαν vb 1st aor pass ind 3rd pers pl   id.

ἠσχυνόμην vb impf m/p ind 1st pers sg   id.

ἠσχύνοντο vb impf m/p ind 3rd pers pl   id.

ἤσχυνται vb perf m/p ind 3rd pers sg   id.

Ηταμ pr noun

ἤτασεν vb 1st aor act ind 3rd pers sg . . . . ἐτάζω

ἠτάσθη vb 1st aor pass ind 3rd pers sg   id.

ἦτε vb impf act ind 2nd pers pl . . . . εἰμί

ἠτεκνώθησαν vb 1st aor pass ind 3rd pers pl . . . . . ἀτεκνόω

ἠτέκνωμαι vb perf m/p ind 1st pers sg   id.

ἠτεκνωμένη vb perf m/p part fem nom sg   id.

ἠτεκνώσατε vb 1st aor act ind 2nd pers pl   id.

ἠτέκνωσεν vb 1st aor act ind 3rd pers sg   id.

ᾔτησα vb 1st aor act ind 1st pers sg . . . . αἰτέω

ᾔτησαι vb 1st aor mid ind 2nd pers sg   id.

ᾐτησάμην vb 1st aor mid ind 1st pers sg   id.

ᾔτησαν vb 1st aor act ind 3rd pers pl   id.

ᾐτήσαντο vb 1st aor mid ind 3rd pers pl   id.

ᾔτησας vb 1st aor act ind 2nd pers sg   id.

ᾐτήσατο vb 1st aor mid ind 3rd pers sg   id.

ᾔτησεν vb 1st aor act ind 3rd pers sg   id.

ᾐτήσω vb 1st aor mid ind 2nd pers sg   id.

ἠτίμασαν vb 1st aor act ind 3rd pers pl . . . . ἀτιμάζω

ἠτίμασεν vb 1st aor act ind 3rd pers sg   id.

ἠτιμάσθη vb 1st aor pass ind 3rd pers sg   id.

ἠτιμάσθην vb 1st aor pass ind 1st pers sg   id.

ἠτιμάσθησαν vb 1st aor pass ind 3rd pers pl   id.

ἠτιμασμένοι vb perf m/p part masc nom pl   id.

ἠτιμώθη vb 1st aor pass ind 3rd pers sg . . . . ἀτιμόω

ἠτιμωμένη vb perf m/p part fem nom sg   id.

ἠτιμωμένοι vb perf m/p part masc nom pl   id.

ἠτιμωμένον vb perf m/p part masc acc sg,

      neut nom and acc sg   id.

ἠτιμωμένος vb perf m/p part masc nom sg   id.

ἠτίμωσας vb 1st aor act ind 2nd pers sg   id.

ἠτίμωσεν vb 1st aor act ind 3rd pers sg   id.

ἥτις rel pron fem nom sg . . . . ὅστις

ἤτοι conjunction

ἡτοίμαζεν vb impf act ind 3rd pers sg . . . . ἑτοιμάζω

ἡτοίμακα vb perf act ind 1st pers sg   id.

ἡτοιμάκαμεν vb perf act ind 1st pers pl   id.

ἡτοίμακεν vb perf act ind 3rd pers sg   id.

ἡτοιμακέναι vb perf act inf   id.

ἡτοίμασα vb 1st aor act ind 1st pers sg   id.

ἡτοίμασαν vb 1st aor act ind 3rd pers pl   id.

ἡτοιμάσαντο vb 1st aor mid ind 3rd pers pl   id.

ἡτοίμασας vb 1st aor act ind 2nd pers sg   id.

ἡτοιμάσατο vb 1st aor mid ind 3rd pers sg   id.

ἡτοίμασεν vb 1st aor act ind 3rd pers sg   id.

ἡτοιμάσθαι vb perf m/p inf   id.

ἡτοιμάσθη vb 1st aor pass ind 3rd pers sg   id.

ἡτοιμάσθην vb 1st aor pass ind 1st pers sg . . . . . ἑτοιμάζω
ἡτοιμάσθησαν vb 1st aor pass ind 3rd pers pl id.
ἡτοιμασμένη vb perf m/p part fem nom sg id.
ἡτοιμασμένον vb perf m/p part masc acc sg,
    neut nom and acc sg id.
ἡτοίμασται vb perf m/p ind 3rd pers sg id.
ἡτοίμαστο vb plpf m/p ind 3rd pers sg id.
ἡτοίμησεν vb 1st aor act ind 3rd pers sg id.
ἡτοῦμεν vb impf act ind 1st pers pl . . . . αἰτέω
ἡττᾶσθε vb pres m/p impv 2nd pers pl . . . . ἡττάω
ἡττηθείς vb 1st aor pass part masc nom sg id.
ἡττηθέντες vb 1st aor pass part masc nom pl id.
ἡττήθη vb 1st aor pass ind 3rd pers sg id.
ἡττηθῇ vb 1st aor pass subj 3rd pers sg id.
ἡττήθησαν vb 1st aor pass ind 3rd pers pl id.
ἡττηθήσεσθε vb fut pass ind 2nd pers pl id.
ἡττηθήσεται vb fut pass ind 3rd pers sg id.
ἡττηθήσονται vb fut pass ind 3rd pers pl id.
ἥττημα noun neut nom and acc sg
ἡττήσεις vb fut act ind 2nd pers sg . . . . ἡττάω
ἡττήσωσι vb 1st aor act subj 3rd pers pl id.
ἧττον adj neut nom and acc sg . . . . ἥττων
ἥττονα adj masc and fem acc sg id.
ἥττονες adj masc and fem nom pl id.
ἥττονι adj dat sg id.
ἡττώμενος vb pres m/p part masc nom sg . . . . ἡττάω
ἥττων adj masc and fem nom sg
ἤτω vb pres act impv 3rd pers sg . . . . εἰμί
ηὔγει vb impf act ind 3rd pers sg . . . . αὐγέω
ηὐγμένος vb perf dep part masc nom sg . . . . εὔχομαι
ηὐγμένου vb perf dep part masc and neut gen sg id.
ηὐδόκησας vb 1st aor act ind 2nd pers sg . . . . εὐδοκέω
ηὐδόκουν vb impf act ind 1st pers sg id.
ηὐθύνθη vb 1st aor pass ind 3rd pers sg . . . . εὐθύνω
ηὐλίζετο vb impf m/p ind 3rd pers sg . . . . αὐλίζω
ηὐλιζόμην vb impf m/p ind 1st pers sg id.
ηὐλίζοντο vb impf m/p ind 3rd pers pl id.
ηὐλίσθη vb 1st aor pass ind 3rd pers sg id.
ηὐλίσθην vb 1st aor pass ind 1st pers sg id.
ηὐλίσθησαν vb 1st aor pass ind 3rd pers pl id.
ηὐλόγηκα vb perf act ind 1st pers sg . . . . εὐλογέω
ηὐλόγηκας vb perf act ind 2nd pers sg id.
ηὐλογημένον vb perf m/p part neut nom and acc sg id.
ηὐλογημένος vb perf m/p part masc nom sg id.
ηὐλόγησα vb 1st aor act ind 1st pers sg id.
ηὐλόγησαν vb 1st aor act ind 3rd pers pl id.
ηὐλόγησεν vb 1st aor act ind 3rd pers sg id.
ηὐλόγουν vb impf act ind 3rd pers pl id.
ηὐξάμην vb 1st aor mid ind 1st pers sg . . . . εὔχομαι
ηὔξατο vb 1st aor mid ind 3rd pers sg id.
ηὐξήθη vb 1st aor pass ind 3rd pers sg . . . . αὐξάνω
ηὐξήθησαν vb 1st aor pass ind 3rd pers pl id.

ηὐξημένος vb perf m/p part masc nom sg . . . . αὐξάνω
ηὔξησεν vb 1st aor act ind 3rd pers sg id.
ηὔξω vb 1st aor mid ind 2nd pers sg . . . . εὔχομαι
ηὑρέθη vb 1st aor pass ind 3rd pers sg . . . . εὑρίσκω
ηὑρέθησαν vb 1st aor pass ind 3rd pers pl id.
ηὑρίσκετο vb impf m/p ind 3rd pers sg id.
ηὕρισκον vb impf act ind 3rd pers pl id.
ηὐτομόλησα vb 1st aor act ind 1st pers sg . . . . . αὐτομολέω
ηὐτομόλησαν vb 1st aor act ind 3rd pers pl id.
ηὐφραίνεσθε vb impf m/p ind 2nd pers pl . . . . . εὐφραίνω
ηὔφραναν vb 1st aor act ind 3rd pers pl id.
ηὔφρανας vb 1st aor act ind 2nd pers sg id.
ηὔφρανεν vb 1st aor act ind 3rd pers sg id.
ηὐφράνθη vb 1st aor pass ind 3rd pers sg id.
ηὐφράνθημεν vb 1st aor pass ind 1st pers pl id.
ηὐφράνθην vb 1st aor pass ind 1st pers sg id.
ηὐφράνθησαν vb 1st aor pass ind 3rd pers pl id.
ηὐχαρίστουν vb impf act ind 3rd pers pl . . . . . εὐχαριστέω
ηὔχετο vb impf dep ind 3rd pers sg . . . . εὔχομαι
ηὔχοντο vb impf dep ind 3rd pers pl id.
Ηφαδ pr noun
ἠφάνισαν vb 1st aor act ind 3rd pers pl . . . . ἀφανίζω
ἠφάνισεν vb 1st aor act ind 3rd pers sg id.
ἠφανίσθη vb 1st aor pass ind 3rd pers sg id.
ἠφανίσθησαν vb 1st aor pass ind 3rd pers pl id.
ἠφανισμέναι vb perf m/p part fem nom pl id.
ἠφανισμένας vb perf m/p part fem acc pl id.
ἠφανισμένη vb perf m/p part fem nom sg id.
ἠφανισμένην vb perf mid part fem acc sg id.
ἠφανισμένοι vb perf mid part masc nom pl id.
ἠφανισμένοις vb perf m/p part masc and neut dat pl id.
ἠφανισμένον vb perf m/p part masc acc sg,
    neut nom and acc sg id.
ἠφανισμένος vb perf m/p part masc nom sg id.
ἠφάνισται vb perf m/p ind 3rd pers sg id.
ἠφίεις vb impf act ind 2nd pers sg . . . . ἀφίημι
ἠφρονεύσαντο vb 1st aor mid ind
    3rd pers pl . . . . ἀφρονεύομαι
Ηχα pr noun
ἤχει vb impf act ind 3rd pers sg . . . . ἠχέω
ἠχεῖν vb pres act inf id.
ἠχῆσαι vb 1st aor act inf id.
ἤχησαν vb 1st aor act ind 3rd pers pl id.
ἠχήσατε vb 1st aor act impv 2nd pers pl id.
ἠχήσει vb fut act ind 3rd pers sg id.
ἤχησεν vb 1st aor act ind 3rd pers sg id.
ἠχήσουσιν vb fut act ind 3rd pers pl id.
ἤχθη vb 1st aor pass ind 3rd pers sg . . . . ἄγω
ἤχθησαν vb 1st aor pass ind 3rd pers pl id.
ἤχθραναν vb 1st aor act ind 3rd pers pl . . . . ἐχθραίνω
ἠχμαλωτεύθη vb 1st aor pass ind 3rd pers sg . αἰχμαλωτεύω
ἠχμαλωτεύθησαν vb 1st aor pass ind 3rd pers pl id.

ἠχμαλωτευμένοι   vb perf m/p part

     masc nom pl . . . . αἰχμαλωτεύω

ἠχμαλώτευσαν   vb 1st aor act ind 3rd pers pl   id.

ἠχμαλώτευσας   vb 1st aor act ind 2nd pers sg   id.

ἠχμαλωτεύσατε   vb 1st aor act ind 2nd pers pl   id.

ἠχμαλώτευσεν   vb 1st aor act ind 3rd pers sg   id.

ἠχμαλώτευται   vb perf m/p ind 3rd pers sg   id.

ἠχμαλωτίκασιν   vb perf act ind 3rd pers pl . . αἰχμαλωτίζω

ἠχμαλώτισαν   vb 1st aor act ind 3rd pers pl   id.

ἠχμαλώτισεν   vb 1st aor act ind 3rd pers sg   id.

ἠχμαλωτίσθην   vb 1st aor pass ind 1st pers sg   id.

ἦχοι   noun masc nom pl . . . . ἦχος

ἦχον   noun masc acc sg   id.

ἦχον   vb impf act ind 3rd pers pl . . . . ἠχέω

ἦχος   noun masc nom sg

ἤχου   noun masc gen sg . . . . ἦχος

ἠχοῦντι   vb pres act part masc and neut dat sg . . . . ἠχέω

ἤχους   noun masc acc pl . . . . ἦχος

ἠχοῦς   noun fem gen sg . . . . ἠχώ

ἠχοῦσαν   vb pres act part fem acc sg . . . . ἠχέω

ἠχούσης   vb pres act part fem gen sg   id.

ἠχρείωκαν   vb perf act ind 3rd pers pl . . . . ἀχρειόω

ἠχρεώθησαν   vb 1st aor pass ind 3rd pers pl   id.

ἠχώ   noun fem nom sg

ἤχῳ   noun masc dat sg . . . . ἦχος

ἠχῶν   vb pres act part masc nom sg . . . . ἠχέω

ἡψάμην   vb 1st aor mid ind 1st pers sg . . . . ἅπτομαι

ἧψαν   vb 1st aor act ind 3rd pers pl . . . . ἅπτω

ἥψαντο   vb 1st aor mid ind 3rd pers pl . . . . ἅπτομαι

ἥψατο   vb 1st aor mid ind 3rd pers sg   id.

ἡψήθη   vb 1st aor pass ind 3rd pers sg . . . . ἕψω

ἡψημένον   vb 1st aor mid part neut nom and acc sg   id.

ἡψημένων   vb pres m/p part gen pl   id.

ἡψήσαμεν   vb 1st aor act ind 1st pers pl   id.

ἥψησαν   vb 1st aor act ind 3rd pers pl   id.

ἥψησεν   vb 1st aor act ind 3rd pers sg   id.

ἥψηται   vb perf dep ind 3rd pers sg   id.

ἥψουον   vb impf act ind 3rd pers pl . . . . ἑψέω

Θ θ

θ′   indecl number

Θααθ   pr noun

θααλα   translit

Θααναχ   pr noun

Θαβασων   pr noun

Θαβωθ   pr noun

Θαβωρ   pr noun

Θαγλαθφαλνασαρ   pr noun

Θαγλαθφελλασαρ   pr noun

Θαεν   pr noun

Θαεσθεν   pr noun

θαιηλαθα   translit

Θαιλαμ   pr noun

Θαιμαν   pr noun

Θαιμανίτη   pr noun masc dat sg . . . . Θαιμανίτης

Θαιμανιτης   pr noun masc nom sg   id.

Θαιμανιτιδος   pr noun fem gen sg . . . . Θαιμανιτις

Θαιμανων   pr noun masc gen pl . . . . Θαιμεν

Θακουαθ   pr noun

Θαλαβιν   pr noun

θαλάμοις   noun masc dat pl . . . . θάλαμος

θάλασσα   noun fem nom sg

θάλασσαι   noun fem nom pl . . . . θάλασσα

θαλάσσαις   noun fem dat pl   id

θάλασσαν   noun fem acc sg   id

θαλάσσας   noun fem acc pl   id

θαλάσση   noun fem dat sg   id

θαλάσσης   noun fem gen sg . . . . θάλασσα

θαλασσίαν   adj fem acc sg . . . . θαλάσσιος

θαλασσῶν   noun fem gen pl . . . . θάλασσα

Θαλε   pr noun

θάλλει   vb pres act ind 3rd pers sg . . . . θάλλω

θάλλον   vb pres act part neut nom and acc sg   id.

θάλλουσα   vb pres act part fem nom sg   id.

θαλλῶν   noun masc gen pl . . . . θαλλός

θάλπη   vb pres act subj 3rd pers sg . . . . θάλπω

θαλπιωθ   translit

θάλπουσα   vb pres act part fem nom sg . . . . θάλπω

Θαλχα   pr noun

θάλψει   vb fut act ind 3rd pers sg . . . . θάλπω

Θαμανα   pr noun

Θαμαρ   pr noun

Θαμασι   pr noun

θαμβεῖσθαι   vb pres m/p inf . . . . θαμβέω

θάμβοι   noun masc nom pl . . . . θάμβος

θάμβος   noun neut nom and acc sg   id.

θαμβούμενοι   vb pres m/p part masc nom pl . . . . θαμβέω

θαμβουμένους   vb pres m/p part masc acc pl   id.

θάμβους   noun neut gen sg . . . . θάμβος

Θαμμους   pr noun

Θαμνα   pr noun

Θαμναθα   pr noun

Θαμναθαιου   pr noun masc gen sg . . . . Θαμναθαιος

Θαμναθαρες   pr noun

Θαμναθασαχαρα pr noun

Θαμνασαραχ pr noun

Θαμνι pr noun

Θανα pr noun

Θανααχ pr noun

Θαναεμεθ pr noun

Θανακ pr noun

θάνατε noun masc voc sg . . . . θάνατος

θανατηφόροι adj masc and fem nom pl . . . . . θανατηφόρος

θανατηφόρον adj acc sg, neut nom sg   id.

θανατηφόρος adj masc and fem nom sg   id.

θανατοῖ vb pres act ind 3rd pers sg,

      pres act subj 3rd pers sg . . . . θανατόω

θάνατον noun masc acc sg . . . . θάνατος

θάνατος noun masc nom sg   id.

θανάτου noun masc gen sg   id.

θανατούμεθα vb pres m/p ind 1st pers pl . . . . θανατόω

θανατουμένων vb pres m/p part gen pl   id.

θανατοῦν vb pres act inf   id.

θανατοῦντας vb pres act part masc acc pl   id.

θανατοῦντες vb pres act part masc nom pl   id.

θανατοῦσαι vb pres act part fem nom pl   id.

θανατούσθω vb pres m/p impv 3rd pers sg   id.

θανατούσθωσαν vb pres m/p impv 3rd pers pl   id.

θανατοῦσιν vb pres act ind 3rd pers pl   id.

θανατοῦτε vb pres act impv 2nd pers pl   id.

θανάτῳ noun masc dat sg . . . . θάνατος

θανατωθήσεται vb fut pass ind 3rd pers sg . . . . . . θανατόω

θανατωθήσῃ vb fut pass ind 2nd pers sg   id.

θανατωθήτω vb 1st aor pass impv 3rd pers sg   id.

θανατῶσαι vb 1st aor act inf   id.

θανατώσατε vb 1st aor act impv 2nd pers pl   id.

θανατώσει vb fut act ind 3rd pers sg   id.

θανατώσειν vb fut act inf   id.

θανατώσεις vb fut act ind 2nd pers sg   id.

θανατώσεως noun fem gen sg . . . . θανάτωσις

θανατώσῃ vb 1st aor act subj 3rd pers sg . . . . θανατόω

θανατώσητε vb 1st aor act subj 2nd pers pl   id.

θανατώσομεν vb fut act ind 1st pers pl   id.

θανάτωσον vb 1st aor act impv 2nd pers sg   id.

θανατώσουσιν vb 1st aor act subj 3rd pers pl   id.

θανατώσω vb fut act ind 1st pers sg   id.

θανατώσωσιν vb 1st aor act subj 3rd pers pl   id.

θανεῖν vb 2nd aor act inf . . . . θνήσκω

θανεῖται vb fut mid ind 3rd pers sg   id.

Θανεμαθ pr noun

Θανθαναι pr noun

θαννουριμ translit

θάνοιεν vb 2nd aor act opt 3rd pers pl . . . . θνήσκω

θανόντα vb 2nd aor act part masc acc sg   id.

θανόντας vb 2nd aor act part masc acc pl   id.

θανόντος vb 2nd aor act part masc and neut gen sg   id.

Θαπους pr noun

θάπτει vb pres act ind 3rd pers sg . . . . θάπτω

θάπτειν vb pres act inf   id.

θάπτεται vb pres m/p ind 3rd pers sg   id.

θάπτοντα vb pres act part masc acc sg   id.

θάπτοντες vb pres act part masc nom pl   id.

θαπτόντων vb pres act part masc and neut gen pl   id.

θάπτουσιν vb pres act ind 3rd pers pl   id.

θάπτω vb pres act ind 1st pers sg   id.

θάπτων vb pres act part masc nom sg   id.

Θαρα pr noun

Θαραβα pr noun

Θαραβααμ pr noun

Θαρακα pr noun

Θαραλα pr noun

θαραφιν translit

Θαραχ pr noun

Θαργαθιιμ pr noun

Θαργαλ pr noun

Θαρεηλα pr noun

Θαρθακ pr noun

Θαρθαν pr noun

Θαρρα pr noun

θαρραλέοι adj masc nom pl . . . . θαρραλέος

θαρραλέως adverb

θάρρει vb pres act impv 2nd pers sg . . . . θαρρέω

θαρροῦσα vb pres act part fem nom sg . . . . θαρσέω

Θαρσα pr noun

θάρσει noun neut dat sg . . . . θάρσος

θάρσει vb pres act impv 2nd pers sg . . . . θαρσέω

θαρσεῖ vb pres act ind 3rd pers sg   id.

θαρσεῖτε vb pres act impv 2nd pers pl,

      pres act ind 2nd pers pl   id.

Θαρσεου pr noun masc gen sg . . . . Θαρσεας

θαρσήσατε vb 1st aor act impv 2nd pers pl . . . . θαρσέω

θάρσησον vb 1st aor act impv 2nd pers sg   id.

Θαρσιλα pr noun

θαρσις translit

Θαροις pr noun

θάρσος noun neut nom and acc sg

θάρσυνον vb 1st aor act impv 2nd pers sg . . . . θαρσύνω

Θαρχνα pr noun

Θασιρι pr noun

Θασμους pr noun

Θασοβαν pr noun

Θασσι pr noun

θᾶττον comp adj neut nom and acc sg . . . . ταχύς

θαυ translit (Heb. letter: ת)

θαῦμα noun neut nom and acc sg

θαύμαζε vb pres act impv 2nd pers sg . . . . θαυμάζω

θαυμάζει vb pres act ind 3rd pers sg   id.

θαυμάζετε vb pres act impv 2nd pers pl   id.

θαυμάζομεν vb pres act ind 1st pers pl . . . . θαυμάζω		
θαυμαζόμενον vb pres m/p part masc acc sg,		
neut nom and acc sg	id.	
θαυμάζοντας vb pres act part masc acc pl	id.	
θαυμάζοντες vb pres act part masc nom pl	id.	
θαυμάζω vb pres act ind 1st pers sg	id.	
θαυμάσαι vb 1st aor act inf	id.	
θαυμασάντων vb 1st aor act part masc and neut gen pl	id.	
θαυμάσας vb 1st aor act part masc nom sg	id.	
θαυμάσατε vb 1st aor act impv 2nd pers pl	id.	
θαυμάσει vb fut act ind 3rd pers sg	id.	
θαυμάσειας vb 1st aor act opt 2nd pers sg	id.	
θαυμάσεις vb fut act ind 2nd pers sg	d.	
θαυμάσετε vb fut act ind 2nd pers pl	d.	
θαυμάσῃς vb 1st aor act subj 2nd pers sg	d.	
θαυμασθέντες vb 1st aor pass part masc nom pl	d.	
θαυμασθῆναι vb 1st aor pass inf	d.	
θαυμασθήσεσθε vb fut pass ind 2nd pers pl	d.	
θαυμασθήσεται vb fut pass ind 3rd pers sg	d.	
θαυμασθήσομαι vb fut pass ind 1st pers sg	d.	
θαυμάσια adj neut nom and acc pl . . . . θαυμάσιος		
θαυμασίοις adj masc and neut dat pl	id.	
θαυμάσιον adj masc acc sg, neut nom and acc sg	id.	
θαυμασίων adj gen pl	id.	
θαυμασιώτατον superl adj masc nom sg	id.	
θαυμασμοῦ noun masc gen sg . . . . θαυμασμός		
θαυμασμῷ noun masc dat sg	id.	
θαυμασόμεθα vb fut mid ind 1st pers pl . . . . θαυμάζω		
θαυμάσονται vb fut mid ind 3rd pers pl	id.	
θαυμάσουσιν vb fut act ind 3rd pers pl	id.	
θαυμαστά adj neut nom and acc pl . . . . θαυμαστός		
θαυμαστάς adj fem acc pl	id.	
θαυμαστή adj fem nom sg	id.	
θαυμαστῇ adj fem dat sg	id.	
θαυμαστήν adj fem acc sg	id.	
θαυμαστῆς adj fem gen sg	id.	
θαυμαστοί adj masc nom pl	id.	
θαυμαστόν adj masc acc sg, neut nom and acc sg	id.	
θαυμαστός adj masc nom sg	id.	
θαυμαστοῦ adj masc and neut gen sg	id.	
θαυμαστῶν adj gen pl	id.	
θαυμαστῶς adverb		
θαυμάστωσον vb 1st aor act impv 2nd pers sg . θαυμαστόω		
Θαφεθ pr noun		
Θαφθωθ pr noun		
Θαχχια pr noun		
θάψαι vb 1st aor act inf . . . . θάπτω		
θάψας vb 1st aor act part masc nom sg	id.	
θάψατε vb 1st aor act impv 2nd pers pl	id.	
θάψει vb fut act ind 3rd pers sg	id.	
θάψεις vb fut act ind 2nd pers sg	id.	
θάψετε vb fut act ind 2nd pers pl	id.	

θάψῃ vb 1st aor act subj 3rd pers sg . . . . θάπτω		
θάψῃς vb 1st aor act subj 2nd pers sg	id.	
θάψον vb 1st aor act impv 2nd pers sg	id.	
θάψουσιν vb fut act ind 3rd pers pl	id.	
θάψω vb 1st aor act subj 1st pers sg,		
fut act ind 1st pers sg	id.	
θάψωμεν vb 1st aor act subj 1st pers pl	id.	
θάψωσιν vb 1st aor act subj 3rd pers pl	id.	
θέαν noun fem acc sg . . . . θέα		
θέας noun fem gen sg	id.	
θεασάμενοι vb 1st aor mid part masc nom pl . . . . . θεάομαι		
θεάσασθαι vb 1st aor mid inf	id.	
θεάσασθε vb 1st aor mid impv 2nd pers pl	id.	
Θεβες pr noun		
Θεδμορ pr noun		
θεε translit		
θεέ noun masc voc sg . . . . θεός		
θεεβουλαθω translit		
Θεησους pr noun		
Θεθηρ pr noun		
θεία adj fem nom sg . . . . θεῖος		
θεῖα adj neut nom and acc pl	id.	
θείᾳ adj fem dat sg	id.	
θείαν adj fem acc sg	id.	
θείας adj fem gen sg	id.	
θείη vb 2nd aor act opt 3rd pers sg . . . . τίθημι		
θεϊμ translit		
θεῖναι vb 2nd aor act inf . . . . τίθημι		
θεῖον adj masc acc sg, neut nom and acc sg . . . . θεῖος		
θεῖος adj masc nom sg	id.	
θειότητος noun fem gen sg . . . . θειότης		
θείου adj masc and neut gen sg . . . . θεῖος		
θείους adj masc acc pl	id.	
θείς vb 2nd aor act part masc nom sg . . . . τίθημι		
θεῖσα vb 2nd aor act part fem nom sg	id.	
θείῳ adj masc and neut dat sg . . . . θεῖος		
θείῳ noun neut dat sg . . . . θεῖον		
θείων adj gen pl . . . . θεῖος		
θεκελ translit		
Θεκεμινα pr noun fem nom sg		
Θεκεμινας pr noun fem gen sg . . . . Θεκεμινα		
Θεκουε pr noun		
Θεκουμ pr noun		
Θεκω pr noun		
Θεκωε pr noun		
Θεκωι pr noun		
Θεκωιν pr noun		
Θεκωίτης pr noun masc nom sg		
Θεκωῖτις pr noun fem nom sg		
Θελαμιν pr noun		
Θελαρησα pr noun		
θέλε vb pres act impv 2nd pers sg . . . . θέλω		

θέλει vb pres act ind 3rd pers sg . . . . θέλω
θέλειν vb pres act inf   id.
θέλεις vb pres act ind 2nd pers sg   id.
Θελερσας pr noun
θέλετε vb pres act ind 2nd pers pl . . . . θέλω
θέλῃ vb pres act subj 3rd pers sg   id.
θέλημα noun neut nom and acc sg
θελήμασι noun neut dat pl . . . . θέλημα
θελήματα noun neut nom and acc pl   id.
θελήματι noun neut dat sg   id.
θελήματος noun neut gen sg   id.
θέλῃς vb pres act subj 2nd pers sg . . . . θέλω
θελήσει noun fem dat sg . . . . θέλησις
θελήσει vb fut act ind 3rd pers sg . . . . θέλω
θελήσεις vb fut act ind 2nd pers sg   id.
θελήσεως noun fem gen sg . . . . θέλησις
θελήσῃ vb 1st aor act subj 3rd pers sg . . . . θέλω
θελήσῃς vb 1st aor act subj 2nd pers sg   id.
θέλησιν noun fem acc sg . . . . θέλησις
θέλησις noun fem nom sg   id.
θελήσουσιν vb fut act ind 3rd pers pl . . . . θέλω
θελήσω vb 1st aor act subj 1st pers sg,
         fut act ind 1st pers sg   id.
θελήσωσιν vb 1st aor act subj 3rd pers pl   id.
θελητάς noun masc acc pl . . . . θελητής
θέλητε vb pres act subj 2nd pers pl . . . . θέλω
θελητή adj fem nom sg . . . . θελητός
θελητήν noun fem acc sg . . . . θελητής
θελητής noun masc nom sg   id.
θελητόν adj masc acc sg, neut nom and acc sg . . . . θελητός
Θελμελεθ pr noun
θέλοιεν vb pres act opt 3rd pers pl . . . . θέλω
θέλοντα vb pres act part neut nom and acc pl   id.
θέλοντας vb pres act part masc acc pl   id.
θέλοντες vb pres act part masc nom pl   id.
θέλοντος vb pres act part masc and neut gen sg   id.
θελόντων vb pres act part masc and neut gen pl   id.
θελούσῃ vb pres act part fem dat sg   id.
θέλουσιν vb pres act ind 3rd pers pl   id.
θέλω vb pres act ind 1st pers sg   id.
θέλων vb pres act part masc nom sg   id.
θέμα noun neut nom and acc sg
Θεμα pr noun
Θεμαδ pr noun
θέματα noun neut nom and acc pl . . . . θέμα
θέματι noun neut dat sg   id.
θεμέλια noun neut nom and acc pl . . . . θεμέλιον
θεμέλιοι noun masc nom pl . . . . θεμέλιος
θεμέλιον noun masc acc sg   id.
θεμέλιον noun neut nom and acc sg
θεμέλιος noun masc nom sg
θεμελίου noun neut gen sg . . . . θεμέλιον

θεμελιοῦν vb pres act inf . . . . θεμελιόω
θεμελίους noun masc acc pl . . . . θεμέλιος
θεμελιοῦσθαι vb pres m/p inf . . . . θεμελιόω
θεμελιοῦτε vb pres act ind 2nd pers pl   id.
θεμελίων noun neut gen pl . . . . θεμέλιον
θεμελιῶν vb pres act part masc nom sg . . . . θεμελιόω
θεμελιώσαντα vb 1st aor act part masc acc sg   id.
θεμελιώσει noun fem dat sg . . . . θεμελίωσις
θεμελιώσει vb fut act ind 3rd pers sg . . . . θεμελιόω
θεμελιώσω vb fut act ind 1st pers sg   id.
θέμενος vb 2nd aor mid part masc nom sg . . . . τίθημι
θεμένου vb 2nd aor mid part masc and neut gen sg   id.
θέμις noun fem nom sg
θεμιτόν adj masc acc sg, neut nom and acc sg . . . . . θεμιτός
Θεμμων pr noun
Θενναχ pr noun
θεννουριμ translit
θέντες vb 2nd aor act part masc nom pl . . . . τίθημι
Θεοδοτον pr noun masc acc sg . . . . Θεοδοτος
Θεόδοτος pr noun masc nom sg   id.
θεοί noun masc nom pl . . . . θεός
θεοῖς noun masc dat pl   id.
θεοκτίστου adj gen sg . . . . θεόκτιστος
θεομαχεῖν vb pres act inf . . . . θεομαχέω
θεόν noun masc acc sg . . . . θεός
θεός noun masc nom sg   id.
θεοσέβεια noun fem nom sg
θεοσέβειαν noun fem acc sg . . . . θεοσέβεια
θεοσεβείας noun fem gen sg   id.
θεοσεβεῖς adj masc and fem nom and acc pl . . . . . θεοσεβής
θεοσεβής adj masc and fem nom sg   id.
θεοσεβοῦς adj gen sg   id.
θεοτόκου adj masc and fem gen sg . . . . θεοτόκος
θεοῦ noun masc gen sg . . . . θεός
θεούς noun masc acc pl   id.
Θεους pr noun masc acc pl . . . . Θεος
Θερα pr noun
Θεραν pr noun . . . . Θερα
θεράπαινα noun fem nom sg
θεράπαιναι noun fem nom pl . . . . θεράπαινα
θεραπαίναις noun fem dat pl   id.
θεραπαίνης noun fem gen sg   id.
θεραπεία noun fem nom sg
θεραπείαν noun fem acc sg . . . . θεραπεία
θεραπείας noun fem gen sg   id.
θεραπεύειν vb pres act inf . . . . θεραπεύω
θεραπεύετε vb pres act impv 2nd pers pl   id.
θεραπευθῆναι vb 1st aor pass inf   id.
θεραπεύοντας vb pres act part masc acc pl   id.
θεραπεύοντες vb pres act part masc nom pl   id.
θεραπεύοντι vb pres act part masc and neut dat sg   id.
θεραπεύου vb pres m/p impv 2nd pers sg   id.

θεραπεύουσα vb pres act part fem nom sg . . . . . . θεραπεύω

θεραπεύουσι(ν) vb pres act ind 3rd pers pl,
      pres act part masc and neut dat pl   id.

θεραπεύσουσιν vb fut act ind 3rd pers pl   id.

θεραπεύων vb pres act part masc nom sg   id.

θεράποντα noun masc acc sg . . . . θεράπων

θεράποντας noun masc acc pl   id.

θεράποντες noun masc nom pl   d.

θεράποντι noun masc dat sg   d.

θεράποντος noun masc gen sg   id.

θεραπόντων noun masc gen pl   d.

θεράπουσι noun masc dat pl   id.

θεράπων noun masc nom sg   id.

θεραφιν translit

Θεργαμα pr noun

Θερεε pr noun

θέρει noun neut dat sg . . . . θέρος

θερίζειν vb pres act inf . . . . θερίζω

θερίζητε vb pres act subj 2nd pers pl   ic.

θεριζόμενος vb pres m/p part masc nom sg   ιc.

θερίζοντας vb pres act part masc acc pl   ic.

θερίζοντος vb pres act part masc and neut gen sg   ic.

θεριζόντων vb pres act part masc and neut gen pl   id.

θερίζουσι vb pres act part masc and neut dat pl   id.

θερίζων vb pres act part masc nom sg   id.

θερίζωσιν vb pres act subj 3rd pers pl   id

θερινῆς adj fem gen sg . . . . θερινός

θερινόν adj masc acc sg, neut nom and acc sg   id.

θερινῷ adj masc and neut dat sg   id.

θεριοῦσιν vb fut act ind 3rd pers pl . . . . θερίζω

θερίσαντες vb 1st aor act part masc nom pl   id.

θερίσατε vb 1st aor act impv 2nd pers pl   id.

θερίσει vb fut act ind 3rd pers sg   id.

θερίσῃς vb 1st aor act subj 2nd pers sg   id.

θερισθῇ vb 1st aor pass subj 3rd pers sg   id.

θερισμόν noun masc acc sg . . . . θερισμός

θερισμός noun masc nom sg   id.

θερισμοῦ noun masc gen sg   id.

θερισμῷ noun masc dat sg   id.

θερισταῖς noun masc dat pl . . . . θεριστής

θεριστάς noun masc acc pl   id.

θέριστρα noun neut nom and acc pl . . . . θέριστρον

θέριστρον noun neut nom and acc sg   id.

Θερμα pr noun

Θερμαι pr noun

θερμαινόμενον vb pres m/p part masc acc sg,
      neut nom and acc sg . . . . θερμαίνω

θερμανθείς vb 1st aor pass part masc nom sg   id.

θερμανθῇ vb 1st aor pass subj 3rd pers sg   id.

θερμανθήσεται vb fut pass ind 3rd pers sg   id.

θέρμανον vb 1st aor act impv 2nd pers sg   id.

θερμασίᾳ noun fem dat sg . . . . θερμασία

θερμασίαν noun fem acc sg . . . . θερμασία

θερμάστρεις noun fem nom and acc pl . . . . . . θέρμαστρις

Θερμελεθ pr noun

θέρμη noun fem nom sg

θερμή adj fem nom sg . . . . θερμός

θέρμῃ adj fem dat sg . . . . θερμός

θέρμην adj fem acc sg   id.

θέρμης adj fem gen sg   id.

θερμόν adj masc acc sg, neut nom and acc sg . . . . . . θερμός

θερμότητος noun fem gen sg . . . . θερμότης

θερμούς adj masc acc pl . . . . θερμός

θέρος noun neut nom and acc sg

θέρους noun neut gen sg . . . . θέρος

Θερσα pr noun

θές vb 2nd aor act impv 2nd pers sg . . . . τίθημι

Θεσβίτην pr noun masc acc sg . . . . Θεσβίτης

Θεσβίτης pr noun masc nom sg   id.

Θεσβίτου pr noun masc gen sg   id.

Θεσβων pr noun

θέσει noun fem dat sg . . . . θέσις

θέσεις noun fem nom and acc pl   id.

θέσθαι vb 2nd aor mid inf . . . . τίθημι

θέσθε vb 2nd aor mid impv 2nd pers pl   id.

θέσθω vb 2nd aor mid impv 3rd pers sg   id.

θέσιν noun fem acc sg . . . . θέσις

θέσις noun fem nom sg   id.

θεσμόν noun masc acc sg . . . . θεσμός

θεσμούς noun masc acc pl   id.

θεσμῶν noun masc gen pl   id.

Θεσσαμυς pr noun

θέτε vb 2nd aor act impv 2nd pers pl . . . . τίθημι

θεῷ noun masc dat sg . . . . θεός

θεῶν noun masc gen pl   id.

θεώρει vb pres act impv 2nd pers sg . . . . θεωρέω

θεωρεῖ vb pres act ind 3rd pers sg   id.

θεωρεῖν vb pres act inf   id.

θεωρεῖς vb pres act ind 2nd pers sg   id.

θεωρεῖσθαι vb pres m/p inf   id.

θεωρεῖται vb pres m/p ind 3rd pers sg   id.

θεωρεῖτε vb pres act impv 2nd pers pl   id.

θεωρῆσαι vb 1st aor act inf   id.

θεωρήσαντες vb 1st aor act part masc nom pl   id.

θεωρήσασα vb 1st aor act part fem nom sg   id.

θεωρητόν adj masc acc sg, neut nom and acc sg . . θεωρητός

θεωρία noun fem nom sg

θεωρίαν noun fem acc sg . . . . θεωρία

θεωρουμένης vb pres m/p part fem gen sg . . . . θεωρέω

θεωρούμενον vb pres m/p part masc acc sg,
      neut nom and acc sg   id.

θεωρούμενος vb pres m/p part masc nom sg   id.

θεωροῦντες vb pres act part masc nom pl   id.

θεωρούς noun masc acc pl . . . . θεωρός

θεωροῦσα vb pres act part fem nom sg . . . . θεωρέω	θηρεύσαισαν vb 1st aor act opt 3rd pers pl . . . . . . θηρεύω
θεωροῦσι(ν) vb pres act ind 3rd pers pl,	θηρεύσας vb 1st aor act part masc nom sg id.
pres act part masc and neut dat pl id.	θηρεύσει vb fut act ind 3rd pers sg id.
θεωρῶν vb pres act part masc nom sg id.	θηρεύσεις vb fut act ind 2nd pers sg id.
θῇ vb 2nd aor act subj 3rd pers sg . . . . τίθημι	θηρεύσῃ vb 1st aor act subj 3rd pers sg id.
Θηβης pr noun	θήρευσον vb 1st aor act impv 2nd pers sg id.
Θηζια pr noun	θηρεύσουσιν vb fut act ind 3rd pers pl id.
θῆκαι noun fem nom pl . . . . θήκη	θηρευτάς noun masc acc pl . . . . θηρευτής
θήκας noun fem acc pl id.	θηρευτής noun masc nom sg id.
θήκης noun fem gen sg id.	θηρευτῶν noun masc gen pl id.
θηλάζει vb pres act ind 3rd pers sg . . . . θηλάζω	θηρία noun neut nom and acc pl . . . . θηρίον
θηλάζον vb pres act part neut nom and acc sg id.	Θηρια pr noun
θηλάζοντα vb pres act part masc acc sg,	θηριάλωτον adj acc sg, neut nom sg . . . . θηριάλωτος
neut nom and acc pl id.	θηριαλώτου adj gen sg id.
θηλάζοντος vb pres act part masc and neut gen sg id.	θηριόβρωτος adj masc and fem nom sg . . . . . θηριόβρωτος
θηλαζόντων vb pres act part masc and neut gen pl id.	θηρίοις noun neut dat pl . . . . θηρίον
θηλαζούσας vb pres act part fem acc pl id.	θηρίον noun neut nom and acc sg id.
θηλάζων vb pres act part masc nom sg id.	θηρίου noun neut gen sg id.
θηλάσαι vb 1st aor act inf id.	θηρίῳ noun neut dat sg id.
θηλάσασαν vb 1st aor act part fem acc sg id.	θηριώδει adj dat sg . . . . θηριώδης
θηλάσει vb fut act ind 3rd pers sg id.	θηριωδέστατε superl adj masc voc sg id.
θηλάσειεν vb 1st aor act opt 3rd pers sg id.	θηριωδῶς adverb
θηλάσεις vb fut act ind 2nd pers sg id.	θηρίων noun neut gen pl . . . . θηρίον
θηλάσητε vb 1st aor act subj 2nd pers pl id.	θηρός noun masc gen sg . . . . θήρ
θήλασον vb 1st aor act impv 2nd pers sg id.	θηρσί noun masc dat pl id.
θήλεια adj fem nom sg . . . . θῆλυς	θῆς vb 2nd aor act subj 2nd pers sg . . . . τίθημι
θηλείᾳ adj fem dat sg id.	θησαυρίζει vb pres act ind 3rd pers sg . . . . θησαυρίζω
θήλειαι adj fem nom pl id.	θησαυρίζεις vb pres act ind 2nd pers sg id.
θηλείαις adj fem dat pl id.	θησαυρίζεται vb pres m/p ind 3rd pers sg id.
θήλειαν adj fem acc sg id.	θησαυρίζοντες vb pres act part masc nom pl id.
θηλείας adj fem gen sg id.	θησαυρίζουσιν vb pres act ind 3rd pers pl id.
θῆλυ adj neut nom and acc sg id.	θησαυρίζων vb pres act part masc nom sg id.
θηλυκοῦ adj masc and neut gen sg . . . . θηλυκός	θησαυρίσαι vb 1st aor act inf id.
θηλυμανεῖς adj masc and fem nom and acc pl . . θηλυμανής	θησαυρίσματα noun neut nom and acc pl . . . . θησαύρισμα
θῆλυν adj masc acc sg . . . . θῆλυς	θησαυροί noun masc nom pl . . . . θησαυρός
Θημα pr noun	θησαυροῖς noun masc dat pl id.
Θημαρ pr noun	θησαυρόν noun masc acc sg id.
Θηνασα pr noun	θησαυρός noun masc nom sg id.
θήρα noun fem nom sg	θησαυροῦ noun masc gen sg id.
θήρᾳ noun fem dat sg . . . . θήρα	θησαυρούς noun masc acc pl id.
θήραν noun fem acc sg id.	θησαυροφύλακι noun masc dat sg . . . . . . θησαυροφύλαξ
θήρας noun fem gen sg id.	θησαυρῷ noun masc dat sg . . . . θησαυρός
θήρας noun fem acc pl id.	θησαυρῶν noun masc gen pl id.
θῆρες noun masc nom pl . . . . θήρ	θήσει vb fut act ind 3rd pers sg . . . . τίθημι
θηρευθήσονται vb fut pass ind 3rd pers pl . . . . θηρεύω	θήσειν vb fut act inf id.
θήρευμα noun neut nom and acc sg	θήσεις vb fut act ind 2nd pers sg id.
θηρεύματα noun neut nom and acc pl . . . . θήρευμα	θήσεσθαι vb fut mid inf id.
θηρευόμενα vb pres m/p part neut nom and acc pl . . θηρεύω	θήσεται vb fut mid ind 3rd pers sg id.
θηρευόμενοι vb pres m/p part masc nom pl id.	θήσετε vb fut act ind 2nd pers pl id.
θηρεύοντες vb pres act part masc nom pl id.	θήσῃ vb fut mid ind 2nd pers sg id.
θηρευόντων vb pres act part masc and neut gen pl id.	θῆσθε vb 2nd aor mid subj 2nd pers pl id.
θηρεῦσαι vb 1st aor act inf id.	θήσομαι vb fut mid ind 1st pers sg id.

θήσονται vb fut mid ind 3rd pers pl . . . . τίθημι	θλίψεως noun fem gen sg . . . . θλῖψις
θήσουσιν vb fut act ind 3rd pers pl id.	θλίψῃ vb 1st aor act subj 3rd pers sg . . . . θλίβω
θήσω vb fut act ind 1st pers sg id.	θλίψῃς vb 1st aor act subj 2nd pers sg id.
θῆται vb 2nd aor mid subj 3rd pers sg id.	θλίψητε vb 1st aor act subj 2nd pers pl id.
θίασον noun masc acc sg . . . . θίασος	θλίψιν noun fem acc sg . . . . θλῖψις
θιάσου noun masc gen sg id.	θλῖψις noun fem nom sg id.
θίβει noun fem dat sg . . . . θῖβις	θλίψωσιν vb 1st aor act subj 3rd pers pl . . . . θλίβω
θῖβιν noun fem acc sg id.	θνησιμαῖα adj neut nom and acc pl . . . . θνησιμαῖος
θιγεῖν vb 2nd aor act inf . . . . θιγγάνω	θνησιμαίοις adj masc and neut dat pl id.
Θιε pr noun	θνησιμαῖον adj masc acc sg, neut nom and acc sg id.
Θιλων pr noun	θνησιμαίου adj masc and neut gen sg id.
Θιμαθ pr noun	θνησιμαίων adj gen pl id.
θιμωνιά noun fem nom sg	θνητῇ adj fem dat sg . . . . θνητός
θιμωνιάν noun fem acc sg . . . . θημωνιά	θνητόν adj masc acc sg, neut nom and acc sg id.
θιμωνιάς noun fem acc pl id.	θνητός adj masc nom sg id.
θῖνας noun fem acc sg . . . . θίς	θνητοῦ adj masc and neut gen sg id.
θινῶν noun masc gen pl id.	θνητῷ adj masc and neut dat sg id.
Θιρας pr noun	θνητῶν adj gen pl id.
Θισβης pr noun fem gen sg . . . . Θισβη	Θοαδα pr noun
θλαδίαν noun masc acc sg . . . . θλαδίας	Θοβελ pr noun
θλαδίας noun masc nom sg d.	θοῖναν noun fem acc sg . . . . θοίνα
θλάσμασι noun neut dat pl . . . . θλάσμα	Θοκανου pr noun masc gen sg . . . . Θοκανος
θλάσον vb 1st aor act impv 2nd pers sg . . . . θλάω	Θοκε pr noun
θλάσω vb fut act ind 1st pers sg id.	Θοκκαν pr noun
θλιβέντων vb 2nd aor pass part masc and neut gen pl . θλίβω	θολερᾷ adj fem dat sg . . . . θολερός
θλίβεσθαι vb pres m/p inf id.	Θολμαι pr noun
θλιβέτω vb pres act impv 3rd pers sg id.	Θολμι pr noun
θλιβῆναι vb 2nd aor pass inf id.	Θολμιν pr noun
θλιβήσεται vb fut pass ind 3rd pers sg id.	Θομοι pr noun
θλίβομαι vb pres m/p ind 1st pers sg id.	Θοου pr noun
θλιβόμενον vb pres m/p part masc acc sg,	Θοργαμα pr noun
neut nom and acc sg id.	θορυβηθήσονται vb fut pass ind 3rd pers pl . . . . . θορυβέω
θλίβοντα vb pres act part masc acc sg id.	θορυβήσαντες vb 1st aor act part masc nom pl id.
θλίβοντας vb pres act part masc acc pl id.	θόρυβον noun masc acc sg . . . . θόρυβος
θλίβοντες vb pres act part masc nom pl id.	θόρυβος noun masc nom sg id.
θλίβοντος vb pres act part masc and neut gen sg id.	θορύβου noun masc gen sg id.
θλιβόντων vb pres act part masc and neut gen pl id.	θορύβων noun masc gen pl id.
θλίβουσιν vb pres act ind 3rd pers pl id.	θοῦ vb 2nd aor mid impv 2nd pers sg . . . . τίθημι
θλιβουσῶν vb pres act part fem gen pl id.	Θουλαδ pr noun
θλίβωμαι vb pres m/p subj 1st pers sg id.	θραελ translit
θλίβων vb pres act part masc nom sg id.	Θρακῶν pr noun masc gen pl . . . . Θραξ
θλιμμόν noun masc acc sg . . . . θλιμμός	θράσει noun neut dat sg . . . . θράσος
θλῖψαι vb 1st aor act inf . . . . θλίβω	θρασεῖα adj fem nom sg . . . . θρασύς
θλίψαντες vb 1st aor act part masc nom pl id.	θρασείᾳ adj fem dat sg id.
θλιψάντων vb 1st aor act part masc and neut gen pl id.	θρασεῖς adj masc nom and acc pl id.
θλίψει noun fem dat sg . . . . θλῖψις	θράσος noun neut nom and acc sg
θλίψει vb fut act ind 3rd pers sg . . . . θλίβω	θράσους noun neut gen sg . . . . θράσος
θλίψεις noun fem nom and acc pl . . . . θλῖψις	θρασύ adj neut nom and acc sg . . . . θρασύς
θλίψεις vb fut act ind 2nd pers sg . . . . θλίβω	θρασυκάρδιος adj masc and fem nom sg
θλίψεσιν noun fem dat pl . . . . θλῖψις	θρασύν adj masc acc sg . . . . θρασύς
θλίψετε vb fut act ind 2nd pers pl . . . . θλίβω	θρασυνθείς vb 1st aor pass part masc nom sg . . . . θρασύνω
θλίψεων noun fem gen pl . . . . θλῖψις	θρασυνθέντες vb 1st aor pass part masc nom pl id.

θρασύς   adj masc nom sg

θραύειν   vb pres act inf . . . . θραύω

θραύεσθε   vb pres m/p ind 2nd pers pl   id.

θραῦσαι   vb 1st aor act inf   id.

θραύσει   noun fem dat sg . . . . θραῦσις

θραύσει   vb fut act ind 3rd pers sg . . . . θραύω

θραύσεις   vb fut act ind 2nd pers sg   id.

θραυσθῇ   vb 1st aor pass subj 3rd pers sg   id.

θραυσθήσεται   vb fut pass ind 3rd pers sg   id.

θραῦσις   noun fem nom sg

θραῦσμα   noun neut nom and acc sg

θραύσματος   noun neut gen sg . . . . θραῦσμα

θραυσμός   noun masc nom sg

θραῦσον   vb 1st aor act impv 2nd pers sg . . . . θραύω

θρεπτή   noun fem nom sg

θρέψαι   vb 1st aor act inf . . . . τρέφω

θρέψαντι   vb 1st aor act part masc and neut dat sg   id.

θρέψει   vb fut act ind 3rd pers sg   id.

θρηνεῖν   vb pres act inf . . . . θρηνέω

θρηνεῖτε   vb pres act impv 2nd pers pl,
           pres act ind 2nd pers pl   id.

θρηνείτω   vb pres act impv 3rd pers sg   id.

θρηνηθήσεται   vb fut pass ind 3rd pers sg   id.

θρήνημα   noun neut nom and acc sg

θρηνήσατε   vb 1st aor act impv 2nd pers pl . . . . θρηνέω

θρηνήσει   vb fut act ind 3rd pers sg   id.

θρηνήσεις   vb fut act ind 2nd pers sg   id.

θρηνήσον   vb 1st aor act impv 2nd pers sg   id.

θρηνήσουσιν   vb fut act ind 3rd pers pl   id.

θρήνοις   noun masc dat pl . . . . θρῆνος

θρῆνον   noun masc acc sg   id.

θρῆνος   noun masc nom sg   id.

θρήνου   noun masc gen sg   id.

θρηνουμένων   vb pres m/p part gen pl . . . . θρηνέω

θρηνούντων   vb pres act part masc and neut gen pl   id.

θρηνοῦσα   vb pres act part fem nom sg   id.

θρηνοῦσαι   vb pres act part fem nom pl   id.

θρηνούσας   vb pres act part fem acc pl   id.

θρήνῳ   noun masc dat sg . . . . θρῆνος

θρήνων   noun masc gen pl   id.

θρησκεία   noun fem nom sg

θρησκείᾳ   noun fem dat sg . . . . θρησκεία

θρησκείας   noun fem gen sg   id.

θρίξ   noun fem nom sg

θριξίν   noun fem dat pl . . . . θρίξ

θρόνοι   noun masc nom pl . . . . θρόνος

θρόνοις   noun masc dat pl   id.

θρόνον   noun masc acc sg   id.

θρόνος   noun masc nom sg   id.

θρόνου   noun masc gen sg   id.

θρόνους   noun masc acc pl   id.

θρόνῳ   noun masc dat sg   id.

θρόνων   noun masc gen pl . . . . θρόνος

θροῦς   noun masc nom sg

θρυληθείην   vb 1st aor pass opt 1st pers sg . . . . θρυλέω

θρύλημα   noun neut nom and acc sg

θρυλουμένην   vb pres m/p part fem acc sg . . . . θρυλέω

θύγατερ   noun fem voc sg . . . . θυγάτηρ

θυγατέρα   noun fem acc sg   id.

θυγατέρας   noun fem acc pl   id.

θυγατέρες   noun fem nom pl   id.

θυγατέρων   noun fem gen pl   id.

θυγάτηρ   noun fem nom sg   id.

θυγατράσιν   noun fem dat pl   id.

θυγατρί   noun fem dat sg   id.

θυγατρός   noun fem gen sg   id.

θύει   vb pres act ind 3rd pers sg . . . . θύω

θύειν   vb pres act inf   id.

θύελλα   noun fem nom sg

θύεσθαι   vb pres m/p inf . . . . θύω

θυΐα   noun fem dat sg . . . . θυΐα

θυΐσκαι   noun fem nom pl . . . . θυΐσκη

θυΐσκας   see θυΐσκας

θυΐσκας   noun fem acc pl   id.

θυΐσκην   noun fem acc sg   id.

θυισκῶν   noun fem gen pl   id.

θυλάκια   noun neut nom and acc pl . . . . θυλάκιον

θυλάκοις   noun masc dat pl . . . . θύλακος

θῦμα   noun neut nom and acc sg

θύματα   noun neut nom and acc pl . . . . θῦμα

θυμάτων   noun neut gen pl

θυμηρέστερος   comp adj masc nom sg . . . . θυμήρης

θυμιαθῆναι   vb 1st aor pass inf . . . . θυμιάω

θυμιαθήτω   vb 1st aor pass impv 3rd pers sg   id.

θυμίαμα   noun neut nom and acc sg

θυμιάμασι   noun neut dat pl . . . . θυμίαμα

θυμιάματα   noun neut nom and acc pl   id.

θυμιάματι   noun neut dat sg   id.

θυμιάματος   noun neut gen sg   id.

θυμιαμάτων   noun neut gen pl   id.

θυμιᾶν   vb pres act inf . . . . θυμιάω

θυμιάσαι   vb 1st aor act inf   id.

θυμιάσει   vb fut act ind 3rd pers sg   id.

θυμιάσετε   vb fut act ind 2nd pers pl   id.

θυμιατήριον   noun neut nom and acc sg

θυμιατηρίῳ   noun neut dat sg . . . . θυμιατήριον

θυμιῶμεν   vb pres act ind 1st pers pl . . . . θυμιάω

θυμιῶντα   vb pres act part masc acc sg   id.

θυμιῶντας   vb pres act part masc acc pl   id.

θυμιῶντες   vb pres act part masc nom pl   id.

θυμιῶσαι   vb pres act part fem nom pl   id.

θυμιῶσιν   vb pres act ind 3rd pers pl   id.

θυμοῖ   vb pres m/p ind 2nd pers sg . . . . θυμόω

θυμοῖς   noun masc dat pl . . . . θυμός

θυμόν noun masc acc sg	. . . .	θιμός
θυμός noun masc nom sg		id.
θυμοῦ noun masc gen sg		id.
θυμούμενος vb pres m/p part masc nom sg	. . . . . .	θυμόω
θυμούς noun masc acc pl	. . . .	θυμός
θυμοῦσθαι vb pres m/p inf	. . . .	θυμόω
θυμῷ noun masc dat sg	. . . .	θυμός
θυμώδει adj dat sg	. . . .	θυμώδης
θυμώδεις adj masc and fem nom and acc pl		id.
θυμώδης adj masc and fem nom sg		d.
θυμώδους adj gen sg		d.
θυμωθείς vb 1st aor pass part masc nom sg	. . . .	θυμόω
θυμωθέντα vb 1st aor pass part masc acc sg		id.
θυμωθῇ vb 1st aor pass subj 3rd pers sg		id.
θυμωθῆναι vb 1st aor pass inf		id.
θυμωθῆς vb 1st aor pass subj 2nd pers sg		id.
θυμωθήσεσθαι vb fut pass inf		id.
θυμωθήσεται vb fut pass ind 3rd pers sg		ic.
θυμωθήσομαι vb fut pass ind 1st pers sg		ic.
θυμώθητι vb 1st aor pass impv 2nd pers sg		id.
θύοντες vb pres act part masc nom pl	. . . .	θύω
θύοντι vb pres act part masc and neut dat sg		id.
θύοντος vb pres act part masc and neut gen sg		id
θυόντων vb pres act part masc and neut gen pl		id.
θύρα noun fem nom sg		
θύρᾳ noun fem dat sg	. . . .	θύρα
θύραι noun fem nom pl		id.
θύραις noun fem dat pl		id.
θύραν noun fem acc sg		id.
θύρας noun fem gen sg and acc pl		id
θυρεοί noun masc nom pl	. . . .	θυρεός
θυρεῖς noun masc dat pl		id.
θυρεόν noun masc acc sg		id.
θυρεός noun masc nom sg		id.
θυρεοῦ noun masc gen sg		id.
θυρεούς noun masc acc pl		id.
θυρεοφόροι noun masc nom pl	. . . .	θυρεοφόρος
θυρεῷ noun masc dat sg	. . . .	θυρεός
θυρίδα noun fem acc sg	. . . .	θυρίς
θυρίδας noun fem acc pl		id.
θυρίδες noun fem nom pl		id.
θυρίδι noun fem dat sg		id.
θυρίδος noun fem gen sg		id.
θυρίδων noun fem gen pl		id.
θυρίσιν noun fem dat pl		id.
θύρσους noun masc acc pl	. . . .	θύρσος
θύρωμα noun neut nom and acc sg		
θυρώμασι noun neut dat pl	. . . .	θύρωμα
θυρώματα noun neut nom and acc pl		d.
θυρώματι noun neut dat sg		id.
θυρώματος noun neut gen sg		id.
θυρωμάτων noun neut gen pl		id.

θυρῶν noun fem gen pl	. . . .	θύρα
θυρωροί noun masc nom pl	. . . .	θυρωρός
θυρωροῖς noun masc dat pl		id.
θυρωρός noun masc or fem nom sg		id.
θυρωρῶν noun masc gen pl		id.
θῦσαι vb 1st aor act inf	. . . .	θύω
θύσαντες vb 1st aor act part masc nom pl		id.
θύσας vb 1st aor act part masc nom sg		id.
θύσατε vb 1st aor act impv 2nd pers pl		id.
θυσάτωσαν vb 1st aor act impv 3rd pers pl		id.
θύσει vb fut act ind 3rd pers sg		id
θύσεις vb fut act ind 2nd pers sg		id.
θύσετε vb fut act ind 2nd pers pl		id.
θύσῃς vb 1st aor act subj 2nd pers sg		id.
θύσητε vb 1st aor act subj 2nd pers pl		id.
θυσία noun fem nom sg		
θυσίᾳ noun fem dat sg	. . . .	θυσία
θυσιάζειν vb pres act inf	. . . .	θυσιάζω
θυσιάζῃ vb pres act subj 3rd pers sg		id.
θυσιάζομεν vb pres act ind 1st pers pl		id.
θυσιαζομένων vb pres m/p part gen pl		id.
θυσιάζοντες vb pres act part masc nom pl		id.
θυσιάζοντι vb pres act part masc and neut dat sg		id.
θυσιαζόντων vb pres act part masc and neut gen pl		id.
θυσιάζουσιν vb pres act ind 3rd pers pl		id.
θυσιάζων vb pres act part masc nom sg		id.
θυσίαι noun fem nom pl	. . . .	θυσία
θυσίαις noun fem dat pl		id.
θυσίαν noun fem acc sg		id.
θυσίας noun fem gen sg and acc pl		id.
θυσιάσαι vb 1st aor act inf	. . . .	θυσιάζω
θυσιάσετε vb fut act ind 2nd pers pl		id.
θυσίασμα noun neut nom and acc sg		
θυσιάσματα noun neut nom and acc pl	. . . .	θυσίασμα
θυσιάσματος noun neut gen sg		id.
θυσιασμάτων noun neut gen pl		id.
θυσιάσουσιν vb fut act ind 3rd pers pl	. . . .	θυσιάζω
θυσιαστήρια noun neut nom and acc pl	. . .	θυσιαστήριον
θυσιαστήριον noun neut nom and acc sg		id.
θυσιαστηρίου noun neut gen sg		id.
θυσιαστηρίῳ noun neut dat sg		id.
θυσιαστηρίων noun neut gen pl		id.
θυσιάσωσιν vb 1st aor act subj 3rd pers pl	. . . . . .	θυσιάζω
θυσιῶν noun fem gen pl	. . . .	θυσία
θύσομεν vb fut act ind 1st pers pl	. . . .	θύω
θῦσον vb 1st aor act impv 2nd pers sg		id.
θύσουσιν vb fut act ind 3rd pers pl		id.
θύσω vb fut act ind 1st pers sg		id.
θύσωμεν vb 1st aor act subj 1st pers pl		id.
θύσωσι(ν) vb 1st aor act subj 3rd pers pl		id.
θύω vb pres act ind 1st pers sg		id.
θύων vb pres act part masc nom sg		id.

θῶ   vb 2nd aor act subj 1st pers sg .... τίθημι

Θωα   pr noun

θωδαθα   translit

Θωλα   pr noun

Θωλαϊ   pr noun

θῶμεν   vb 2nd aor act subj 1st pers pl .... τίθημι

θῶνται   vb 2nd aor mid subj 3rd pers pl   id.

θώρακα   noun masc acc sg .... θώραξ

θώρακας   noun masc acc pl   id.

θώρακες   noun masc nom pl   id.

θωρακισμούς   noun masc acc pl .... θωρακισμός

θώρακος   noun masc gen sg .... θώραξ

θώραξι   noun masc dat pl   id.

θῶσιν   vb 2nd aor act subj 3rd pers pl .... τίθημι

Ι ι

ι΄   indecl number

ια΄   indecl number

Ιααιμ   pr noun

Ιααλων   pr noun

ιααρ   translit

Ιαβας   pr noun

Ιαβες   pr noun

Ιαβι   pr noun

Ιαβιν   pr noun

Ιαβις   pr noun

Ιαβνη   pr noun

Ιαβνηλ   pr noun

Ιαβοκ   pr noun

Ιαγουρ   pr noun

Ιαδα   pr noun

Ιαδαε   pr noun

Ιαδαι   pr noun

Ιαδδαι   pr noun

Ιαδηλα   pr noun

Ιαδια   pr noun

Ιαδιας   pr noun

Ιαδιηλ   pr noun

Ιαδινος   pr noun

Ιαδου   pr noun

Ιαζηλ   pr noun

Ιαζηρ   pr noun

Ιαζια   pr noun

Ιαζιζ   pr noun

Ιαζιηλ   pr noun

Ιαηλ   pr noun

Ιαθ   pr noun

Ιαθαν   pr noun

ἰάθη   vb 1st aor pass ind 3rd pers sg .... ἰάομαι

ἰάθημεν   vb 1st aor pass ind 1st pers pl   id.

ἰαθῆναι   vb 1st aor pass inf   id.

ἰάθησαν   vb 1st aor pass ind 3rd pers pl   id.

ἰαθήσεσθε   vb fut pass ind 2nd pers pl   id.

ἰαθήσεται   vb fut pass ind 3rd pers sg   id.

ἰαθήσομαι   vb fut pass ind 1st pers sg   id.

Ιαϊηλ   pr noun

Ιαϊρ   pr noun

Ιαϊρου   pr noun masc gen sg .... Ιαϊρος

Ιαις   pr noun

Ιακαβα   pr noun

ιακανα   translit

Ιακαρεηλ   pr noun

Ιακεφζηβ   pr noun

Ιακεφζηφ   pr noun

Ιακιμ   pr noun

Ιακουβος   pr noun

Ιακωβ   pr noun

Ιαλ   pr noun

Ιαλλεληλ   pr noun

Ιαλων   pr noun

ἴαμα   noun neut nom and acc sg

ἴαμαι   vb perf dep ind 1st pers sg .... ἰάομαι

ἰάματα   noun neut nom and acc pl .... ἴαμα

Ιαμβρι   pr noun

Ιαμεθ   pr noun

ιαμιβιν   translit

ιαμιν   translit

Ιαμιν   pr noun

Ιαμινι   pr noun

Ιαμνεια   pr noun fem dat sg .... Ιαμνεια

Ιαμνειαν   pr noun fem acc sg   id.

Ιαμνειας   pr noun fem gen sg   id.

Ιαμνιταις   pr noun masc dat pl .... Ιαμνιτης

Ιαμουν   pr noun

Ιαμουνι   pr noun

Ιανα   pr noun

Ιαναθα   pr noun

Ιανι   pr noun

Ιανουε   pr noun

Ιανουμ   pr noun

Ιανουου   pr noun

Ιανωκα   pr noun

Ιανωχ   pr noun

Ιαους   pr noun

Ιϲρασια pr noun

Ιαραχ pr noun

Ιορβααλ pr noun

Ιορβαλ pr noun

Ιαρεδ pr noun

Ιαριβ pr noun

Ιαριβι pr noun

Ιαριηλ pr noun

Ιαρικαμ pr noun

Ιαριμ pr noun

Ιαριμουθ pr noun

Ιαριμωθ pr noun

Ιαριν pr noun

Ιαριων pr noun

Ιαρμωθ pr noun

Ιασα pr noun

ἴασαι vb 1st aor mid impv 2nd pers sg . . . . ἰάομαι

ἰασάμην vb 1st aor mid ind 1st pers sg   id.

Ιασαν pr noun

ἰάσαντο vb 1st aor mid ind 3rd pers pl . . . . ἰάομαι

ἰάσασθαι vb 1st aor mid inf   id.

ἰάσατο vb 1st aor mid ind 3rd pers sg   id.

ἰάσει noun fem dat sg . . . . ἴασις

ἰάσεται vb fut mid ind 3rd pers sg . . . . ἰάομαι

ἰάσεως noun fem gen sg . . . . ἴασις

ἰάσηται vb 1st aor mid subj 3rd pers sg . . . . ἰάομαι

Ιασιηλ pr noun

ἴασιν noun fem acc sg . . . . ἴασις

ἴασις noun fem nom sg   id.

Ιασιο pr noun

Ιασολ pr noun

ἰάσομαι vb fut mid ind 1st pers sg . . . . ἰάομαι

Ἰασονα pr noun masc acc sg . . . . Ἰασων

Ἰασονος pr noun masc gen sg   id.

Ιασουβ pr noun

Ιασουβι pr noun

Ιασουβος pr noun

Ιασουια pr noun

ἴασπιν noun fem acc sg . . . . ἴασπις

ἴασπις noun fem nom sg   id

Ιασσα pr noun

Ιασσιβ pr noun

ἰάσω vb fut act ind 1st pers sg . . . . ἰάομαι

Ἰασων pr noun masc nom sg

Ἰασωνα pr noun masc acc sg . . . . Ἰασων

Ἰασωνος pr noun masc gen sg   id.

ἰᾶται vb pres dep ind 3rd pers sg . . . . ἰάομαι

ἰαται noun masc nom pl . . . . ἰατής

ἰατρεία noun fem nom sg

ἰατρεῖα noun neut nom and acc pl . . . . ἰατρεῖον

ἰατρευθῆναι vb 1st aor pass inf . . . . ἰατρεύω

ἰατρεύθης vb 1st aor pass ind 2nd pers sg   id.

ἰατρευόμενον vb pres m/p part masc acc sg,

    neut nom and acc sg . . . . ἰατρεύω

ἰατρεύσομεν vb 1st aor act ind 1st pers pl   id.

ἰατρεύσω vb 1st aor act subj 1st pers sg,

    fut act ind 1st pers sg   id.

ἰατροί noun masc nom pl . . . . ἰατρός

ἰατρόν noun masc acc sg   id.

ἰατρός noun masc nom sg   id.

ἰατροῦ noun masc gen sg   id.

ἰατρούς noun masc acc pl   id.

ἰατρῷ noun masc dat sg   id.

Ιαφαγαι pr noun

Ιαφαλητ pr noun

Ιαφεθ pr noun

Ιαχαν pr noun

Ιαχιν pr noun

Ιαχινι pr noun

Ιαχιραν pr noun

Ιαχιρανι pr noun

Ιαχουμ pr noun

Ιαως pr noun

ιβ΄ indecl number

Ιβααρ pr noun

Ιβαναα pr noun

ἴβεις noun fem nom and acc pl . . . . ἴβις

ἴβιν noun fem acc sg   id.

ιγ΄ indecl number

Ιγααλ pr noun

Ιγαβης pr noun

ιγλααμ translit

ἰγνύαις noun fem dat pl . . . . ἰγνύα

ιδ΄ indecl number

Ιδαερ pr noun

Ιδαι pr noun

ἰδέ vb 2nd aor act impv 2nd pers sg . . . . ὁράω

Ιδεαδαλεα pr noun

ἰδέαι noun fem nom pl . . . . ἰδέα

ἰδέαις noun fem dat pl   id.

ἰδέαν noun fem acc sg   id.

Ιδεδι pr noun

Ιδεϊα pr noun

ἰδεῖν vb 2nd aor act inf . . . . ὁράω

ἴδετε vb 2nd aor act impv 2nd pers pl   id.

ἰδέτω vb 2nd aor act impv 3rd pers sg   id.

ἰδέτωσαν vb 2nd aor act impv 3rd pers pl   id.

ἴδῃ vb 2nd aor act subj 3rd pers sg   id.

ἴδῃς vb 2nd aor act subj 2nd pers sg   id.

ἴδητε vb 2nd aor act subj 2nd pers pl   id.

Ιδια pr noun

ἴδια adj neut nom and acc pl . . . . ἴδιος

ἰδία adj fem nom sg   id.

ἰδίᾳ adj fem dat sg   id.

ἰδίαις adj fem dat pl . . . . ἴδιος

ἰδίαν adj fem acc sg   id.

ἰδίας adj fem gen sg   id.

Ιδιηλ pr noun

Ιδιθουν pr noun

Ιδιθων pr noun

ἰδιόγραφος adj masc and fem nom sg

ἰδίοις adj masc and neut dat pl . . . . ἴδιος

ἴδιον adj masc acc sg, neut nom and acc sg   id.

ἰδιοποιεῖτο vb impf m/p ind 3rd pers sg . . . . ἰδιοποιέω

ἴδιος adj masc nom sg

ἰδιότητα noun fem acc sg . . . . ἰδιότης

ἰδίου adj masc and neut gen sg . . . . ἴδιος

ἰδίους adj masc acc pl   id.

ἰδίῳ adj masc and neut dat sg   id.

ἰδίων adj gen pl   id.

ἰδιῶται noun masc nom pl . . . . ἰδιώτης

ἰδιωτικά adj neut nom and acc pl . . . . ἰδιωτικός

ἰδιωτικῶν adj gen pl   id.

ἴδοι vb 2nd aor act opt 3rd pers sg . . . . ὁράω

ἴδοιμεν vb 2nd aor act opt 1st pers pl   id.

ἴδοιμι vb 2nd aor act opt 1st pers sg   id.

ἴδοις vb 2nd aor act opt 2nd pers sg   id.

ἴδοισαν vb 2nd aor act opt 3rd pers pl   id.

ἰδόντα vb 2nd aor act part masc acc sg   id.

ἰδόντας vb 2nd aor act part masc acc pl   id.

ἰδόντες vb 2nd aor act part masc nom pl   id.

ἰδόντι vb 2nd aor act part masc and neut dat sg   id.

ιδού see ἰδού

ἰδού interjection

ἰδοῦ vb 2nd aor mid impv 2nd pers sg . . . . ὁράω

Ιδουα pr noun

Ιδουδ pr noun

Ιδουηλον pr noun masc acc sg . . . . Ιδουηλος

Ιδουιας pr noun

Ιδουμα pr noun

Ιδουμαια pr noun fem nom sg

Ιδουμαια pr noun fem dat sg . . . . Ιδουμαια

Ιδουμαιαν pr noun fem acc sg   id.

Ιδουμαιας pr noun fem gen sg   id.

Ιδουμαῖοι pr noun masc nom pl . . . . Ιδουμαῖος

Ιδουμαῖον pr noun masc acc sg   id.

Ιδουμαῖος pr noun masc nom sg   id.

Ιδουμαιων pr noun masc gen pl   id.

Ιδουραμ pr noun

ἰδοῦσα vb 2nd aor act part fem nom sg . . . . ὁράω

ἰδρυμένη vb perf m/p part fem nom sg . . . . ἱδρύω

ἱδρῶν vb pres act part masc nom sg . . . . ἱδρόω

ἱδρῶτι noun masc dat sg . . . . ἱδρώς

ἱδρῶτος noun masc gen sg   id.

ἴδω vb 2nd aor act subj 1st pers sg . . . . ὁράω

ἴδωμεν vb 2nd aor act subj 1st pers pl   id.

ἰδών vb 2nd aor act part masc nom sg . . . . ὁράω

ἴδωσιν vb 2nd aor act subj 3rd pers pl   id.

ιε΄ indecl number

Ιεαλη pr noun

Ιεασι pr noun

Ιεβααρ pr noun

Ιεβαθα pr noun

Ιεβασαμ pr noun

Ιεβλααμ pr noun

Ιεβοσθε pr noun

Ιεβους pr noun

Ιεβουσαι pr noun

Ιεβουσαῖοι pr noun masc nom pl . . . . Ιεβουσαῖος

Ιεβουσαῖον pr noun masc acc sg   id.

Ιεβουσαῖος pr noun masc nom sg   id.

Ιεβουσαιου pr noun masc gen sg   id.

Ιεβουσαιους pr noun masc acc pl   id.

Ιεβουσαιων pr noun masc gen pl   id.

Ιεβουσι pr noun

Ιεγεβαλ pr noun

Ιεγλομ pr noun

Ιεδαια pr noun

Ιεδαιος pr noun

Ιεδδου pr noun

Ιεδδουα pr noun

Ιεδδουραν pr noun

Ιεδεϊου pr noun

Ιεδια pr noun

Ιεδιδα pr noun

Ιεδιηλ pr noun

Ιεδιου pr noun

Ιεδλαφ pr noun

Ιεδουα pr noun

Ιεεθ pr noun

Ιεζαβελ pr noun

Ιεζεβουθ pr noun

Ιεζεκιηλ pr noun

Ιεζερ pr noun

Ιεζηλου pr noun masc gen sg . . . . Ἰεζηλος

Ιεζιας pr noun masc nom sg

Ιεζιηλ pr noun

Ιεζιχαρ pr noun

Ιεζλια pr noun

Ιεζονιαν pr noun masc acc sg . . . . Ιεζονιας

Ιεζονιας pr noun masc nom sg   id.

Ιεζραελ pr noun

Ιεζραηλ pr noun

Ιεζραηλιτη pr noun masc dat sg . . . . Ιεζραηλιτης

Ιεζραηλιτην pr noun masc acc sg   id.

Ιεζραηλιτης pr noun masc nom sg   id.

Ιεζραηλιτιδι pr noun fem dat sg . . . . Ιεζραηλιτις

Ιεζραηλιτιδος pr noun fem gen sg   id.

Ιεζραηλῖτις pr noun fem nom sg

Ιεζραηλιτου pr noun masc gen sg . . . . Ιεζραηλίτης

Ιεζρια pr noun

Ιεζριηλος pr noun

Ιεηλα pr noun

Ιεηλι pr noun

Ιεηλου pr noun masc gen sg . . . . 'Ιεηλος

Ιεθ pr noun

Ιεθεβααλ pr noun

Ιεθεμα pr noun

Ιεθερ pr noun

Ιεθερααμ pr noun

Ιεθερμαθ pr noun

Ιεθετ pr noun

Ιεθηρι pr noun

Ιεθθαρ pr noun

Ιεθθι pr noun

Ιεθθορ pr noun

Ιεθισαιος pr noun masc nom sg

Ιεθλα pr noun

Ιεθνουηλ pr noun

Ιεθραμ pr noun

Ιεθραν pr noun

Ιεθρι pr noun

Ιεκδααμ pr noun

Ιεκεμια pr noun

Ιεκθιηλ pr noun

Ιεκμααμ pr noun

Ιεκμον pr noun

Ιεκναμ pr noun

Ιεκοναμ pr noun

Ιεκταν pr noun

Ιελδαθ pr noun

Ιεμαϊν pr noun

Ιεμενι pr noun

Ιεμηρ pr noun

Ιεμιναιος pr noun masc nom sg

Ιεμιναιου pr noun masc gen sg . . . . Ιεμιναιος

Ιεμινι pr noun

Ιεμλα pr noun

Ιεμνα pr noun

Ιεμνααν pr noun

Ιεμναι pr noun

Ιεμολοχ pr noun

Ιεμου pr noun

Ιεμουαε pr noun

Ιεμουηλ pr noun

Ιεξαν pr noun

Ιεουηλ pr noun

Ιεουλ pr noun

Ιεους pr noun

ἱερά adj fem nom sg, neut nom and acc pl . . . . ἱερός

ἱέρακα noun masc acc sg . . . . ἱέραξ

Ιερακων pr noun

Ιεραμηλι pr noun

Ιεραμι pr noun

Ιεραμωθ pr noun

ἱεράν adj fem acc sg . . . . ἱερος

ἱέραξ noun masc nom sg

ἱεράς adj fem acc pl . . . . ἱερός

ἱεράς adj fem gen sg   id.

ἱερατεία noun fem nom sg

ἱερατείαν noun fem acc sg . . . . ἱερατεία

ἱερατείας noun fem gen sg and acc pl   id.

ἱερατειῶν noun fem gen pl   id.

ἱερατεύειν vb pres act inf . . . . ἱερατεύω

ἱεράτευμα noun neut nom and acc sg

ἱερατεύουσιν vb pres act ind 3rd pers pl . . . . ἱερατεύω

ἱερατεύσει vb fut act ind 3rd pers sg   id.

ἱεράτευσεν vb 1st aor act ind 3rd pers sg   id.

ἱερατεύσοντας vb fut act part masc acc pl   id.

ἱερατεύσουσιν vb fut act ind 3rd pers pl   id.

ἱερατεύωσιν vb pres act subj 3rd pers pl   id.

ἱερατικαῖς adj fem dat pl . . . . ἱερατικός

ἱερατικάς adj fem acc pl   id.

ἱερατικήν adj fem acc sg   id.

ἱερέα noun masc acc sg . . . . ἱερεύς

ἱερεῖ noun masc dat sg   id.

ἱερείαν noun fem acc sg . . . . ἱερεία

ἱερεῖς noun masc nom and acc pl . . . . ἱερεύς

Ιερεμεηλ pr noun

Ιερεμια pr noun masc voc and dat sg . . . . Ιερεμιας

Ιερεμιαν pr noun masc acc sg   id.

Ιερεμιας pr noun masc nom sg   id.

Ιερεμιν pr noun

Ιερεμιου pr noun masc gen sg . . . . Ιερεμιας

Ιερεμωθ pr noun

ἱερεῦ noun masc voc sg . . . . ἱερεύς

ἱερεύς noun masc nom sg   id.

ἱερεῦσι noun masc dat pl   id.

Ιερεχου pr noun masc gen sg . . . . Ιερεχος

ἱερέων noun masc gen pl . . . . ἱερεύς

ἱερέως noun masc gen sg   id.

Ιεριηλ pr noun

Ιεριμ pr noun

Ιεριμουθ pr noun

Ιεριμωθ pr noun

Ιεριχω pr noun

Ιεριωθ pr noun

Ιερκααν pr noun

Ιερμας pr noun

Ιερμια pr noun

Ιερμιας pr noun

Ιερμουθ pr noun

Ιεροβααλ pr noun
Ιεροβεαμ pr noun
Ιεροβοαμ pr noun
ἱερόδουλοι noun masc nom pl . . . . ἱερόδουλος
ἱεροδούλοις noun masc dat pl   id.
ἱεροδούλων noun masc gen pl   id.
ἱεροί adj masc nom pl . . . . ἱερός
ἱεροῖς adj masc and neut dat pl   id.
ἱερόν adj masc acc sg, neut nom and acc sg   id.
ἱεροπρεπής adj masc and fem nom sg
ἱεροπρεποῦς adj gen sg . . . . ἱεροπρεπής
ἱερός adj masc nom sg
Ιεροσολυμα pr noun neut nom and acc pl
Ιεροσολυμῖται pr noun masc nom pl . . . . . Ιεροσολυμιτης
Ιεροσολυμιτας pr noun masc acc pl   id.
Ιεροσολυμιτης pr noun masc nom sg   id.
Ιεροσολυμοις pr noun neut dat pl . . . . Ιεροσολυμα
Ιεροσολυμων pr noun neut gen pl   id.
ἱεροστάταις noun masc dat pl . . . . ἱεροστάτης
ἱεροσυλεῖν vb pres act inf . . . . ἱεροσυλέω
ἱεροσυλημάτων noun masc gen pl . . . . ἱεροσύλημα
ἱεροσυλίας noun fem gen sg . . . . ἱεροσυλία
ἱερόσυλον noun masc acc sg . . . . ἱερόσυλος
ἱεροῦ adj masc and neut gen sg . . . . ἱερός
ἱερουργίαν noun fem acc sg . . . . ἱερουργία
ἱερούς adj masc acc pl . . . . ἱερός
Ιερουσα pr noun
Ιερουσαλημ pr noun
ἱεροψάλται noun masc nom pl . . . . ἱεροψάλτης
ἱεροψάλταις noun masc dat pl   id.
ἱεροψαλτῶν noun masc gen pl   id.
ἱερόψυχε adj masc and fem voc sg . . . . ἱερόψυχος
Ιερφαηλ pr noun
ἱερῷ adj masc and neut dat sg . . . . ἱερός
ἱερώματα noun neut nom and acc pl . . . . ἱέρωμα
ἱερῶν adj gen pl . . . . ἱερός
Ἱερωνυμος pr noun masc nom sg
ἱερωσύνη noun fem nom sg
ἱερωσύνην noun fem acc sg . . . . ἱερωσύνη
ἱερωσύνης noun fem gen sg   id.
Ιεσβακασα pr noun
Ιεσβι pr noun
Ιεσβοαμ pr noun
Ιεσβοκ pr noun
Ιεσδρι pr noun
Ιεσεβααλ pr noun
Ιεσερ pr noun
Ιεσερι pr noun
Ιεσι pr noun
Ιεσια pr noun
Ιεσιας pr noun
Ιεσιηλ pr noun

Ιεσμεγα pr noun
Ιεσου pr noun
Ιεσουα pr noun
Ιεσουι pr noun
Ιεσραε pr noun
Ιεσσαι pr noun
Ιεσσαιμουν pr noun
Ιεσσια pr noun
Ιεσσιβαθ pr noun
Ιεσσιου pr noun
Ιεσσιου pr noun masc gen sg . . . . Ιεσσιας
Ιεσφα pr noun
Ιεσχα pr noun
Ιεταμαρου pr noun
Ιετεβα pr noun
Ιετουρ pr noun
Ιεττα pr noun
Ιεττουρ pr noun
Ιεφερια pr noun
Ιεφθα pr noun
Ιεφθαε pr noun
Ιεφθαηλ pr noun
Ιεφθαμαι pr noun
Ιεφιες pr noun
Ιεφοννη pr noun
Ιεχεμιαν pr noun masc acc sg . . . . Ιεχεμιας
Ιεχθαηλ pr noun
Ιεχονια-ασιρ pr noun
Ιεχονιαν pr noun masc acc sg . . . . Ιεχονιας
Ιεχονιας pr noun masc nom sg   id.
Ιεχονιου pr noun masc gen sg   id.
Ιεων pr noun
ιζ΄ indecl number
ιη΄ indecl number
Ιηου pr noun
Ιηουλ pr noun
Ἰησοῖ pr noun masc dat sg . . . . Ἰησοῦς
Ιησου pr noun
Ιησου pr noun masc gen sg and dat sg . . . . Ιησοῦς
Ιησουε pr noun
Ἰησοῦν pr noun masc acc sg . . . . Ἰησοῦς
Ιησουνι pr noun
Ἰησοῦς pr noun masc nom sg
ιθ΄ indecl number
Ιθακ pr noun
Ιθαμαρ pr noun
ἴθι vb pres act impv 2nd pers sg . . . . εἶμι
Ιθναζιφ pr noun
Ιια pr noun
Ιιηλ pr noun
Ικακ pr noun
Ικαμ pr noun

ἱκανά adj neut nom and acc pl . . . . ἱκανός

ἱκανή adj fem nom sg   id.

ἱκανήν adj fem acc sg   id.

ἱκανοί adj masc nom pl   id.

ἱκανόν adj masc acc sg, neut nom and acc sg   d.

ἱκανός adj masc nom sg   d.

ἱκανοῦ adj masc and neut gen sg   d.

ἱκανούμενος vb pres m/p part masc nom sg . . . . ἱκανόω

ἱκανούς adj masc acc pl . . . . ἱκανός

ἱκανούσθω vb pres m/p impv 3rd pers sg . . . . ἱκανόω

ἱκανοῦται vb pres m/p ind 3rd pers sg   id.

ἱκανωθῆναι vb 1st aor pass inf   id.

ἱκανώθησαν vb 1st aor pass ind 3rd pers pl   id.

ἱκανῶν adj gen pl . . . . ἱκανός

ἱκανῶς adverb

ἱκάνωσον vb 1st aor act impv 2nd pers sg . . . . ἱκανόω

Ικασμων pr noun

Ικεμιας pr noun masc nom sg

ἱκέται noun masc nom pl . . . . ἱκέτης

ἱκετείαν noun fem acc sg . . . . ἱκετεία

ἱκετεύει vb pres act ind 3rd pers sg . . . . ἱκετεύω

ἱκέτευον vb impf act ind 1st pers sg and 3rd pers pl   id.

ἱκετεύοντες vb pres act part masc nom pl   id.

ἱκετεύουσα vb pres act part fem nom sg   id.

ἱκετευσάντων vb 1st aor act part masc and neut gen pl   id.

ἱκέτευσον vb 1st aor act impv 2nd pers sg   id.

ἱκέτην noun masc acc sg . . . . ἱκέτης

ἱκετηρίᾳ adj fem dat sg . . . . ἱκετήριος

ἱκετηρίας adj fem gen sg   id.

ἱκετῶν noun masc gen pl . . . . ἱκέτης

ἱκμάδα noun fem acc sg . . . . ἱκμάς

ἴκτερον noun masc acc sg . . . . ἴκτερος

ἴκτερος noun masc nom sg   id.

ἱκτέρῳ noun masc dat sg   id.

ἱκτῖνα noun masc acc sg . . . . ἱκτίν

Ικωκ pr noun

ἱλαραῖς adj fem dat pl . . . . ἱλαρός

ἱλαρόν adj masc acc sg, neut nom and acc sg   id.

ἱλαρότητα noun fem acc sg . . . . ἱλαρότης

ἱλαρότητι noun fem dat sg   id.

ἱλαρότητος noun fem gen sg   id.

ἱλαρῦναι vb 1st aor act inf . . . . ἱλαρύνω

ἱλαρύνει vb pres act ind 3rd pers sg   id.

ἱλαρῶς adverb

ἱλαρώσει vb fut act ind 3rd pers sg . . . . ἱλαρόω

ἱλαρώσῃς vb 1st aor act subj 2nd pers sg   id

ἱλάρωσον vb 1st aor act impv 2nd pers sg   id.

ἴλας noun fem acc pl . . . . ἴλη

ἱλάσεται vb fut mid ind 3rd pers sg . . . . ἱλάσκομαι

ἱλάσῃ vb fut mid ind 2nd pers sg   id.

ἱλάσθη vb 1st aor pass ind 3rd pers sg   id.

ἱλασθῆναι vb 1st aor pass inf   id.

ἱλάσθης vb 1st aor pass ind 2nd pers sg . . . . ἱλάσκομαι

ἱλάσθητι vb 1st aor pass impv 2nd pers sg   id.

ἱλασμοί noun masc nom pl . . . . ἱλασμός

ἱλασμόν noun masc acc sg   id.

ἱλασμός noun masc nom sg   id.

ἱλασμοῦ noun masc gen sg   id.

ἱλαστήριον noun neut nom and acc sg

ἱλαστήριον see ἱλαστήριον

ἱλαστηρίου noun neut gen sg   id.

ἱλάτευσον vb 1st aor act impv 2nd pers sg . . . . ἱλατεύω

ἵλεω adj gen sg . . . . ἵλεως

ἵλεως adj masc and fem nom sg   id.

ἵλεως adverb

Ιλιαδουν pr noun

Ιλουθωθ pr noun

ἰλύν noun fem acc sg . . . . ἰλύς

ἰλύος noun fem gen sg   id.

Ιμαλκουε pr noun

Ιμανα pr noun

ἱμάντες noun masc nom pl . . . . ἱμάς

ἱμάντι noun masc dat sg   id.

ἱμάντωσις noun fem nom sg

Ιμαρη pr noun

ἱμάς noun masc nom sg

ἱμᾶσι noun masc dat pl . . . . ἱμάς

ἱμάτια noun neut nom and acc pl . . . . ἱμάτιον

ἱματίοις noun neut dat pl   id.

ἱμάτιον noun neut nom and acc sg   id.

ἱματίου noun neut gen sg   id.

ἱματιοφύλακος noun masc gen sg . . . . ἱματιοφύλαξ

ἱματισμόν noun masc acc sg . . . . ἱματισμός

ἱματισμοῦ noun masc gen sg   id.

ἱματισμῷ noun masc dat sg   id.

ἱματίῳ noun neut dat sg . . . . ἱμάτιον

ἱματίων noun neut gen pl   id.

ιν translit

ἵν᾽ see ἵνα

ἵνα adverb and conjunction

Ιναηλ pr noun

ἰνδάλμασι noun masc dat pl . . . . ἴνδαλμα

ἰνδάλματα noun masc acc sg   id.

Ἰνδικήν pr noun fem acc sg . . . . Ἰνδική

Ἰνδικῆς pr noun fem gen sg   id.

Ἰνδος pr noun masc nom sg

ἰξευτοῦ noun masc gen sg . . . . ἰξευτής

ἰοβόλων adj gen pl . . . . ἰοβόλος

Ιοδδους pr noun

Ιοδομ pr noun

Ιοθορ pr noun

Ιοιδα pr noun

Ιοκομ pr noun

ἰόν noun masc acc sg . . . . ἰός

Ιοππη pr noun fem dat sg . . . . Ιοππη
Ιοππην pr noun fem acc sg   id.
Ιοππης pr noun fem gen sg   id.
Ιοππῖται pr noun masc nom pl . . . . Ιοππιτης
Ιοππιτῶν pr noun masc gen pl   id.
Ιορδανη pr noun masc dat sg . . . . Ιορδανης
Ιορδανην pr noun masc acc sg   id.
Ιορδανης pr noun masc nom sg   id.
Ιορδανου pr noun masc gen sg   id.
ἰός noun masc nom sg
Ιου pr noun
ἰοῦ noun masc gen sg . . . . ἰός
Ιουαχ pr noun
Ιουβαλ pr noun
Ιουδα pr noun
Ιουδα pr noun masc dat sg . . . . Ιουδας
Ιουδαια pr noun fem nom sg . . . . Ιουδαια
Ιουδαιᾳ pr noun fem dat sg   id.
Ιουδαιαν pr noun fem acc sg   id.
Ιουδαιας pr noun fem gen sg   id.
ιουδαίζον vb impf act ind 3rd pers pl . . . . ἰουδαίζω
Ιουδαϊκῆς adj fem gen sg . . . . Ιουδαϊκός
Ιουδαῖοι pr noun masc nom pl . . . . Ιουδαῖος
Ιουδαιοις pr noun masc dat pl   id.
Ιουδαῖον pr noun masc acc sg   id.
Ιουδαῖος pr noun masc nom sg   id.
Ιουδαιου pr noun masc gen sg   id.
Ιουδαιους pr noun masc acc pl   id.
Ιουδαϊσμον pr noun masc acc sg . . . . Ιουδαϊσμος
Ιουδαϊσμοῦ pr noun masc gen sg   id.
Ιουδαϊσμῷ pr noun masc dat sg   id.
Ιουδαϊστι adverb
Ιουδαιῳ pr noun masc dat sg . . . . Ιουδαῖος
Ιουδαιων pr noun masc gen pl   id.
Ιουδαν pr noun masc acc sg . . . . Ιουδας
Ιουδας pr noun masc nom sg
Ιουδιας pr noun
Ιουδιθ pr noun
Ιουδιν pr noun
Ιουδου pr noun masc gen sg . . . . Ιουδας
Ιουηλ pr noun
Ιουθ pr noun
Ιουρι pr noun
ἰούς noun masc acc pl . . . . ἰός
ἰοῦται vb pres dep ind 3rd pers sg . . . . ἰόομαι
ἱππαζόμενοι vb pres dep part masc nom pl . . . . ἱππάζομαι
ἱππαζομένους vb pres dep part masc acc pl   id.
ἱππάρχαι noun masc nom pl . . . . ἱππάρχης
ἱππασία noun fem nom sg
ἱππασίας noun fem gen sg . . . . ἱππασία
ἱππάσονται vb fut mid ind 3rd pers pl . . . . ἱππάζομαι
ἱππεῖς noun masc nom and acc pl . . . . ἱππεύς

ἱππεύοντας vb pres act part masc acc pl . . . . ἱππεύω
ἱππευόντων vb pres act part masc and neut gen pl   id.
ἱππεύς noun masc nom sg
ἵππευσεν vb 1st aor act ind 3rd pers sg . . . . ἱππεύω
ἱππεῦσι noun masc dat pl . . . . ἱππεύς
ἱππέων noun masc gen pl   id.
ἱππέως noun masc gen sg   id.
ἱππικαῖς adj fem dat pl . . . . ἱππικός
ἱππικάς adj fem acc pl   id.
ἱππόδρομον noun masc acc sg . . . . ἱππόδρομος
ἱπποδρόμου noun masc gen sg   id.
ἱπποδρόμῳ noun masc dat sg   id.
ἵπποι noun masc or fem nom pl . . . . ἵππος
ἵπποις noun masc or fem dat pl   id.
ἵππον noun masc or fem acc sg   id.
ἵππος noun masc or fem nom sg   id.
ἵππου noun masc or fem gen sg   id.
ἵππους noun masc or fem acc pl   id.
ἵππῳ noun masc or fem dat sg   id.
ἵππων noun masc or fem gen pl   id.
ιρ translit
Ιρα pr noun
Ιρααμ pr noun
Ιραμ pr noun
Ιραμαηλ pr noun
Ιραμεηλ pr noun
Ιρας pr noun
ἵρεως noun fem gen sg . . . . ἶρις
ἴσα adj neut nom and acc pl . . . . ἴσος
ἴσα adverb
Ισαακ pr noun
Ισαβια pr noun
Ισαδεκ pr noun
Ισαθι pr noun
Ισαι pr noun
Ισαια pr noun
Ισακιῳ pr noun masc dat sg . . . . Ισακιος
Ισαμαρι pr noun
ισανα translit
Ισανα pr noun
ἰσαστέρους adj masc acc pl . . . . ἰσάστερος
Ισβααλ pr noun
Ισβακωμ pr noun
Ισδαηλ pr noun
Ισεϊ pr noun
Ισεμιηλ pr noun
Ισεριηλ pr noun
ἴση adj fem nom sg . . . . ἴσος
ἰσηγορεῖσθαι vb pres dep inf . . . . ἰσηγορέομαι
ἴσθι vb pres act impv 2nd pers sg . . . . εἰμί
Ισια pr noun
Ισμαηλ pr noun

Ισμαηλῖται pr noun masc nom pl . . . . Ισμαηλίτης
Ισμαηλιταις pr noun masc dat pl   id.
Ισμαηλιτης pr noun masc nom sg   id.
Ισμαηλιτῶν pr noun masc gen pl   id.
Ισμαηλος pr noun
Ισθαμ pr noun
Ισεβααμ pr noun
ἰσεδυναμεῖ vb pres act ind 3rd pers sg . . . . . . ἰσοδυναμέω
ἰσοδύναμον adj masc acc sg,
          neut nom and acc sg . . . . ἰσοδύναμος
ἰσόθεα adj neut nom and acc pl . . . . ἰσόθεος
ἴσοι adj masc nom pl . . . . ἴσος
ἰσομοίρους adj masc acc pl . . . . ἰσόμοιρος
ἴσον adj masc acc sg, neut nom and acc sg . . . . ἴσος
ἰσονομεῖν vb pres act inf . . . . ἰσονομέω
ἰσόπεδον adj acc sg, neut nom sg . . . . ἰσόπεδος
ἰσοπολίτας noun masc acc pl . . . . ἰσοπολίτης
ἰσοπολίτιδος adj fem gen sg . . . . ἰσοπολῖτις
ἴσος adj masc nom sg
ἰσότητα noun fem acc sg . . . . ἰσότης
ἰσότητι noun fem dat sg   id.
ἴσου adj masc and neut gen sg . . . . ἴσος
Ισουα pr noun
Ισουι pr noun
ἴσους adj masc acc pl . . . . ἴσος
ἰσόψυχε adj masc voc sg . . . . ἰσόψυχος
Ισραηλ pr noun
Ισραηλῖται pr noun masc nom pl . . . . Ισραηλιτης
Ισραηλιτη pr noun masc dat sg   id.
Ισραηλιτης pr noun masc nom sg   id.
Ισραηλίτιδος adj fem gen sg . . . . Ισραηλῖτις
Ισραηλῖτιν adj fem acc sg   id.
Ισραηλιτου pr noun masc gen sg . . . . Ισραηλιτης
Ισσααρ pr noun
Ισσαρι pr noun
Ισσαχαρ pr noun
Ισσιηρ pr noun
ἰσταίη vb pres act opt 3rd pers sg . . . . ἵστημι
Ισταλκουρου pr noun masc gen sg . . . . Ισταλκουρος
ἰστάνειν vb pres act inf . . . . ἵστημι
ἵστανται vb pres m/p ind 3rd pers pl   id.
ἵστασθε vb pres m/p impv 2nd pers pl   id.
ἵσταται vb pres m/p ind 3rd pers sg   id.
ἵστατε vb pres act ind 2nd pers pl   id.
ἵστατο vb impf m/p ind 3rd pers sg   id.
ἵστε vb perf act ind 2nd pers pl . . . . οἶδα
ἵστημι vb pres act ind 1st pers sg
ἰστία noun neut nom and acc pl . . . . ἱστίον
ἰστίοις noun neut dat pl   id.
ἰστίων noun neut gen pl   id.
ἰστόν noun masc acc sg . . . . ἱστός

ἰστορηθέντα vb 1st aor pass part
          neut nom and acc pl . . . . ἱστορέω
ἱστόρηται vb perf m/p ind 3rd pers sg   id.
ἰστορίαν noun fem acc sg . . . . ἱστορία
ἰστορίας noun fem gen sg   id.
ἰστοριῶν noun fem gen pl   id.
ἱστορουμένων vb pres m/p part gen pl . . . . ἱστορέω
ἰστός noun masc nom sg
ἰστούς noun masc acc pl . . . . ἱστός
Ιστωβ pr noun
ἰστῶν noun masc gen pl . . . . ἱστός
ἰστῶν vb pres act part masc nom sg . . . . ἵστημι
ἰστῶσιν vb pres act subj 3rd pers pl   id.
Ισφαν pr noun
ἰσχίων noun neut gen pl . . . . ἰσχίον
ἰσχνόφωνος adj masc and fem nom sg
ἴσχυε vb pres act impv 2nd pers sg . . . . ἰσχύω
ἰσχύει vb pres act ind 3rd pers sg   id.
ἰσχύειν vb pres act inf   id.
ἴσχυεν vb impf act ind 3rd pers sg   id.
ἰσχύετε vb pres act impv 2nd pers pl   id.
ἰσχύι noun fem dat sg . . . . ἰσχύς
ἰσχυκός vb perf act part neut nom and acc sg . . . . ἰσχύω
ἰσχυκότες vb perf act part masc nom pl   id.
ἰσχύν noun fem acc sg . . . . ἰσχύς
ἰσχύομεν vb pres act ind 1st pers pl . . . . ἰσχύω
ἴσχυον vb impf act ind 3rd pers pl   id.
ἰσχύοντα vb pres act part masc acc sg   id.
ἰσχύοντας vb pres act part masc acc pl   id.
ἰσχύοντες vb pres act part masc nom pl   id.
ἰσχύοντι vb pres act part masc and neut dat sg   id.
ἰσχύοντος vb pres act part masc and neut gen sg   id.
ἰσχύος noun fem gen sg . . . . ἰσχύς
ἰσχύουσαν vb pres act part fem acc sg . . . . ἰσχύω
ἰσχύουσι vb pres act part masc and neut dat pl   id.
ἰσχυρά adj fem nom sg, neut nom and acc pl . . . . . ἰσχυρός
ἰσχυρᾷ adj fem dat sg   id.
ἰσχυραί adj fem nom pl   id.
ἰσχυράν adj fem acc sg   id.
ἰσχυράς adj fem acc pl   id.
ἰσχυράς adj fem gen sg   id.
ἰσχυροί adj masc nom pl   id.
ἰσχυροῖς adj masc and neut dat pl   id.
ἰσχυρόν adj masc acc sg, neut nom and acc sg   id.
ἰσχυρός adj masc nom sg   id.
ἰσχυροτάτους superl adj masc acc pl   id.
ἰσχυρότερα comp adj fem nom sg,
          neut nom and acc pl   id.
ἰσχυρότεραι comp adj fem nom pl   id.
ἰσχυρότεροι comp adj masc nom pl   id.
ἰσχυρότερον comp adj masc acc sg, neut nom and acc sg   id.
ἰσχυρότερος comp adj masc nom sg   id.

ἰσχυροτέρους comp adj masc acc pl . . . . ἰσχυρός
ἰσχυροτέρῳ comp adj masc and neut dat sg   id.
ἰσχυροῦ adj masc and neut gen sg   id.
ἰσχυρούς adj masc acc pl   id.
ἰσχυρῷ adj masc and neut dat sg   id.
ἰσχυρῶν adj gen pl   id.
ἰσχυρῶς adverb
ἰσχύρωσαν vb 1st aor act ind 3rd pers pl . . . . ἰσχυρόω
Ἰσχυς pr noun masc nom sg
ἰσχύς noun fem nom sg
ἴσχυσα vb 1st aor act ind 1st pers sg . . . . ἰσχύω
ἰσχῦσαι vb 1st aor act inf   id.
ἰσχύσαμεν vb 1st aor act ind 1st pers pl   id.
ἴσχυσαν vb 1st aor act ind 3rd pers pl,
                1st aor act part neut nom and acc sg id.
ἰσχύσαντες vb 1st aor act part masc nom pl   id.
ἴσχυσας vb 1st aor act ind 2nd pers sg,
                1st aor act part masc nom sg   id.
ἰσχύσατε vb 1st aor act impv 2nd pers pl   id.
ἰσχυσάτωσαν vb 1st aor act impv 3rd pers pl   id.
ἰσχύσει vb fut act ind 3rd pers sg   id.
ἰσχύσεις vb fut act ind 2nd pers sg   id.
ἴσχυσεν vb 1st aor act ind 3rd pers sg   id.
ἰσχύσεσιν noun fem dat pl . . . . ἰσχύς
ἰσχύσῃ vb 1st aor act subj 3rd pers sg . . . . ἰσχύω
ἰσχύσητε vb 1st aor act subj 2nd pers pl   id.
ἰσχύσομεν vb fut mid ind 1st pers pl   id.
ἰσχύσουσιν vb fut act ind 3rd pers pl   id.
ἰσχύω vb pres act ind 1st pers sg   id.
ἰσχύων noun fem gen pl . . . . ἰσχύς
ἰσχύων vb pres act part masc nom sg . . . . ἰσχύω
ἴσῳ adj masc and neut dat sg . . . . ἴσος
ἰσωθήσεται vb fut pass ind 3rd pers sg . . . . ἰσόω
ἴσων adj gen pl . . . . ἴσος
ἴσως adverb
Ἰταβύριον pr noun neut nom and acc sg
ἰταβύριον noun neut nom and acc sg
ἰταμία noun fem nom sg
ἰταμίας noun fem gen sg . . . . ἰταμία
ἰταμός adj masc nom sg
Ιταν pr noun
ἰτέα noun fem nom sg
ἰτέαις noun fem dat pl . . . . ἰτέα
ἰτέας noun fem gen sg and acc pl   id.
Ιτουραιων pr noun masc gen pl . . . . Ιτουραιος
ἴτω vb pres act impv 3rd pers sg . . . . εἰμι
ις΄ indecl number
Ιφινα pr noun
ἰχθύας noun masc acc pl . . . . ἰχθύς
ἰχθύες noun masc nom pl   id.
ἰχθυηράν adj fem acc sg . . . . ἰχθυηρός
ἰχθύν noun masc acc sg . . . . ἰχθύς

ἰχθύος noun masc gen sg . . . . ἰχθύς
ἰχθύς noun masc nom sg   id.
ἰχθῦς noun masc acc pl   id.
ἰχθύων noun masc gen pl   id.
ἴχνει noun neut dat sg . . . . ἴχνος
ἴχνεσι noun neut dat pl   id.
ἴχνευον vb impf act ind 1st pers sg . . . . ἰχνεύω
ἰχνευόντων vb pres act part masc and neut gen pl   id.
ἰχνευτής noun masc nom sg
ἴχνη noun neut nom and acc pl . . . . ἴχνος
ἴχνος noun neut nom and acc sg   id.
ἴχνους noun neut gen sg   id.
ἰχῶρα noun masc acc sg . . . . ἰχώρ
ἰχῶρος noun masc gen sg   id.
ἰχώρων noun masc gen pl   id.
Ιωα pr noun
Ιωαα pr noun
Ιωαβ pr noun
Ιωαδ pr noun
Ιωαδα pr noun
Ιωαδαε pr noun
Ιωαδεν pr noun
Ιωαδιν pr noun
Ιωαζαε pr noun
Ιωαζαρ pr noun
Ιωαθαμ pr noun
Ιωαθαν pr noun
Ιωακιμ pr noun
Ιωαναν pr noun
Ιωανας pr noun
Ιωανης pr noun masc nom sg
Ιωαννη pr noun
Ιωαννην pr noun masc acc sg . . . . Ιωαννης
Ιωαννης pr noun masc nom sg   id.
Ιωαννου pr noun masc gen sg   id.
Ιωανου pr noun masc gen sg . . . . Ιωανας
Ιωαριβ pr noun
Ιωαριμ pr noun
Ιωας pr noun
Ιωασαρ pr noun
Ιωαχ pr noun
Ιωαχα pr noun
Ιωαχαζ pr noun
Ιωαχαλ pr noun
Ιωαχας pr noun
Ιωβ pr noun
Ιωβαβ pr noun
Ιωβελ pr noun
Ιωβηλ pr noun
Ιωδα pr noun
Ιωδαε pr noun
Ιωδαν pr noun

Ιωδανος pr noun

Ιωδιηλ pr noun

Ιωζαβαδ pr noun

Ιωζαβαθ pr noun

Ιωζαβδος pr noun

Ιαζαβεδ pr noun

Ιωηλ pr noun

ιωθ translit (Heb. letter: ')

ἰωθήτω vb 1st aor pass impv 3rd pers sg . . . . ἰάομαι

Ιωιαδα pr noun

Ιωιαριβ pr noun

Ιωκαν pr noun

Ιωμαν pr noun

ἰώμενοι vb pres dep part masc nom pl . . . . ἰάομαι

ἰώμενον vb pres dep part masc acc sg,
         neut nom and acc sg   id.

ἰώμενος vb pres dep part masc nom sg   id.

Ιων pr noun

Ιωνα pr noun

Ιωναδαβ pr noun

Ιωναθαμ pr noun

Ιωναθαν pr noun

Ιωναθας pr noun

Ιωναθη pr noun

Ιωναθην pr noun masc acc sg . . . . Ιωναθης

Ιωναθης pr noun masc nom sg   id.

Ιωναθου pr noun masc gen sg   id.

Ιωναν pr noun masc acc sg . . . . Ιωνας

Ιωνας pr noun masc nom sg   id.

ἰῶνται vb pres dep ind 3rd pers pl . . . . ἰάομαι

ἰῶντο vb impf dep ind 3rd pers pl   id.

Ιωρα pr noun

Ιωραμ pr noun

Ιωρεε pr noun

Ιωριβ pr noun

Ιωριβον pr noun masc acc sg . . . . Ιωριβος

Ιωριβος pr noun masc nom sg

Ιωσαβδος pr noun

Ιωσαβεε pr noun

Ιωσαβεθ pr noun

Ιωσαδακ pr noun

Ιωσαιας pr noun masc nom sg

Ιωσαφατ pr noun

Ιωσαφιου pr noun masc gen sg . . . . Ιωσαφιας

Ιωσεδεκ pr noun

Ιωσεφια pr noun

Ιωσηπον pr noun masc acc sg . . . . Ιωσηπος

Ιωσηπος pr noun masc nom sg

Ιωσηφ pr noun

Ιωσια pr noun

Ιωσιαν pr noun masc acc sg . . . . Ιωσιας

Ιωσιας pr noun masc nom sg   id.

Ιωσιου pr noun masc gen sg   id.

Ιωσφη pr noun

Ιωυαν pr noun

Ιωυκαμ pr noun

Ιωφαλητ pr noun

Ιωχα pr noun

Ιωχαβεδ pr noun

Ιωχαβηδ pr noun

Ιωχηλ pr noun

Κ κ

κ΄ indecl number

κα΄ indecl number

Καααθ pr noun

Κααει pr noun

Κααείτης pr noun masc nom sg

Καβοσαηλ pr noun

Καβεσεηλ pr noun

κάβου noun masc gen sg . . . . κάβος

Καβσαϊμ pr noun

Καβσεηλ pr noun

κἀγώ = καὶ ἐγώ

Καδες pr noun

καδημιμ translit

Καδημωθ pr noun

Καδης pr noun

καδησιμ translit

κάδιον noun neut nom and acc sg

καδίῳ noun neut dat sg . . . . κάδιον

Καδμιηλ pr noun

Καδμιηλου pr noun masc gen sg . . . . Καδμιηλος

κάδου noun masc gen sg . . . . κάδος

καῆναι vb 2nd aor pass inf . . . . καίω

καήσεται vb fut pass ind 3rd pers sg   id.

καήσονται vb fut pass ind 3rd pers pl   id.

κάηται vb 2nd aor mid subj 3rd pers sg   id.

καθ' see κατά

καθά adverb

καθαγιάσει vb fut act ind 3rd pers sg . . . . καθαγιάζω

καθαγιασθῇ vb 1st aor pass subj 3rd pers sg   id.

καθαγίασον vb 1st aor act impv 2nd pers sg   id.

καθαιρεθῇ vb 1st aor pass subj 3rd pers sg . . . . . καθαιρέω
καθαιρεθήσεται vb fut pass ind 3rd pers sg id.
καθαιρεθήσονται vb fut pass ind 3rd pers pl id.
καθαιρεθῶσιν vb 1st aor pass subj 3rd pers pl id.
καθαιρεῖν vb pres act inf id.
καθαιρεῖτε vb pres act ind 2nd pers pl id.
καθαιρέσει noun fem dat sg . . . . καθαίρεσις
καθαίρεσιν noun fem acc sg id.
καθαίρεται vb pres m/p ind 3rd pers sg . . . . καθαιρέω
καθαιροῦντα vb pres act part masc acc sg id.
καθαιροῦντες vb pres act part masc nom pl id.
καθαιροῦσιν vb pres act ind 3rd pers pl id.
καθαιρῶ vb pres act ind 1st pers sg id.
καθαιρῶν vb pres act part masc nom sg id.
καθάπερ adverb
καθαρά adj fem nom sg, neut nom and acc pl . . . . . καθαρός
καθαρᾷ adj fem dat sg id.
καθαραί adj fem nom pl id.
καθαραῖς adj fem dat pl id.
καθαράν adj fem acc sg id.
καθαρᾶς adj fem gen sg id.
καθαριεῖ vb fut act ind 3rd pers sg . . . . καθαρίζω
καθαριεῖς vb fut act ind 2nd pers sg id.
καθαρίζει vb pres act ind 3rd pers sg id.
καθαριζόμενοι vb pres m/p part masc nom pl id.
καθαριζόμενον vb pres m/p part masc acc sg,
  neut nom and acc sg id.
καθαριζομένου vb pres m/p part masc and neut gen sg id.
καθαρίζων vb pres act part masc nom sg id.
καθαριότητα noun fem acc sg . . . . καθαριότης
καθαριότητι noun fem dat sg id.
καθαριότητος noun fem gen sg id.
καθαριοῦσιν vb fut act ind 3rd pers pl . . . . καθαρίζω
καθαρίσαι vb 1st aor act inf id.
καθαρίσαντες vb 1st aor act part masc nom pl id.
καθαρίσασθε vb 1st aor mid impv 2nd pers pl id.
καθαρίσατε vb 1st aor act impv 2nd pers pl id.
καθαρίσει vb fut act ind 3rd pers sg id.
καθαρίσῃ vb 1st aor act subj 3rd pers sg id.
καθαρισθείς vb 1st aor pass part masc nom sg id.
καθαρισθέντα vb 1st aor pass part masc acc sg id.
καθαρισθέντος vb 1st aor pass part masc and neut gen sg id.
καθαρισθῇ vb 1st aor pass subj 3rd pers sg id.
καθαρισθῆναι vb 1st aor pass inf id.
καθαρισθῆς vb 1st aor pass subj 2nd pers sg id.
καθαρισθήσεσθε vb fut pass ind 2nd pers pl id.
καθαρισθήσεται vb fut pass ind 3rd pers sg id.
καθαρισθήσῃ vb fut pass ind 2nd pers sg id.
καθαρισθήσομαι vb fut pass ind 1st pers sg id.
καθαρισθῆτε vb 1st aor pass subj 2nd pers pl id.
καθαρίσθητι vb 1st aor pass impv 2nd pers sg id.
καθαρισμόν noun masc acc sg . . . . καθαρισμός

καθαρισμός noun masc nom sg
καθαρισμοῦ noun masc gen sg . . . . καθαρισμός
καθαρισμῷ noun masc dat sg id.
καθάρισον vb 1st aor act impv 2nd pers sg . . . . . καθαρίζω
καθαριῶ vb fut act ind 1st pers sg id.
καθαροί adj masc nom pl . . . . καθαρός
καθαρόν adj masc acc sg, neut nom and acc sg id.
καθαρός adj masc nom sg id.
καθαρότητα noun fem acc sg . . . . καθαρότης
καθαροῦ adj masc and neut gen sg . . . . καθαρός
καθαρούς adj masc acc pl id.
καθάρσει noun fem dat sg . . . . κάθαρσις
καθάρσεως noun fem gen sg id.
κάθαρσιν noun fem acc sg id.
καθάρσιον noun neut nom and acc sg
καθαρῷ adj masc and neut dat sg . . . . καθαρός
καθαρῶν adj gen pl id.
καθεδεῖται vb fut mid ind 3rd pers sg . . . . καθέζομαι
καθεδοῦνται vb fut mid ind 3rd pers pl id.
καθέδρα noun fem nom sg
καθέδρᾳ noun fem dat sg . . . . καθέδρα
καθέδραν noun fem acc sg id.
καθέδρας noun fem gen sg and acc pl id.
καθεῖλαν vb 1st aor act ind 3rd pers pl . . . . καθαιρέω
καθεῖλεν vb 2nd aor act ind 3rd pers sg id.
καθεῖλες vb 2nd aor act ind 2nd pers sg id.
καθεῖλον vb 2nd aor act ind 3rd pers pl id.
καθείλοσαν vb 2nd aor act ind 3rd pers pl id.
καθεῖς = καθ᾽ εἷς
καθειστήκεισαν vb plpf act ind 3rd pers pl . . . . καθίστημι
καθελεῖ vb fut act ind 3rd pers sg . . . . καθαιρέω
καθελεῖν vb 2nd aor act inf id.
καθελεῖς vb fut act ind 2nd pers sg id.
καθελεῖτε vb fut act ind 2nd pers pl id.
καθέλῃς vb 2nd aor act subj 2nd pers sg id.
καθελόντες vb 2nd aor act part masc nom pl id.
καθελόντος vb 2nd aor act part masc and neut gen sg id.
καθελοῦσιν vb fut act ind 3rd pers pl id.
καθέλω vb 2nd aor act subj 1st pers sg id.
καθελῶ vb fut act ind 1st pers sg id.
κάθεμα noun neut nom and acc sg
καθένα number masc acc sg . . . . καθεῖς
καθέξει vb fut act ind 3rd pers sg . . . . κατέχω
καθέξουσι(ν) vb fut act ind 3rd pers pl id.
κάθες vb 2nd aor act impv 2nd pers sg . . . . καθίημι
καθεσθείς vb 1st aor pass part masc nom sg . . . . καθέζομαι
καθεσθήσεται vb fut pass ind 3rd pers sg id.
καθεστάκαμεν vb perf act ind 1st pers pl . . . . . καθίστημι
καθεσταμένοι vb perf m/p part masc nom pl id.
καθεσταμένος vb perf m/p part masc nom sg id.
καθεσταμένων vb perf m/p part gen pl id.
καθεστάναι vb perf act inf id.

καθέστηκαν vb perf act ind 3rd pers pl . . . . . . καθίστημι
καθέστηκας vb perf act ind 2nd pers sg   id.
καθεστήκασιν vb perf act ind 3rd pers pl   id.
καθέστηκε(ν) vb perf act ind 3rd pers sg   id.
καθεστηκός vb perf act part neut nom and acc sg   id.
καθεστηκότος vb perf act part masc and neut gen sg   id.
καθεστηκυίης vb perf act part fem gen sg   id.
καθεστηκώς vb perf act part masc nom sg   id.
καθεστώς vb perf act part masc nom sg   id.
καθεστῶτα vb perf act part neut nom and acc pl   id.
καθεστῶτας vb perf act part masc acc pl   id.
καθεστῶτες vb perf act part masc nom pl   id.
καθεστῶτι vb perf act part masc and neut dat sg   id.
καθεστῶτος vb perf act part masc and neut gen sg   id.
καθεστώτων vb perf act part masc and neut gen pl   d.
κάθευδε vb pres act impv 2nd pers sg . . . . καθεύδω
καθεύδει vb pres act ind 3rd pers sg   d.
καθεύδειν vb pres act inf   d.
καθεύδεις vb pres act ind 2nd pers sg   d.
καθεύδης vb pres act subj 2nd pers sg   d.
καθεύδοντα vb pres act part masc acc sg   d.
καθεύδοντας vb pres act part masc acc pl   d.
καθεύδοντες vb pres act part masc nom pl   d.
καθευδόντων vb pres act part masc and neut gen pl   d.
καθεύδω vb pres act ind 1st pers sg   d.
καθεύδων vb pres act part masc nom sg   d.
κάθη vb pres m/p subj 2nd pers sg . . . . κάθημαι
καθηγεμόνα noun masc acc sg . . . . καθηγεμων
καθηγιασμένον vb perf m/p part masc acc sg,
          neut nom and acc sg . . . . καθαγιάζω
καθηγιασμένου vb perf m/p part masc and neut gen sg   ic.
καθηγιασμένων vb perf m/p part gen pl   ic.
καθήκει vb pres act ind 3rd pers sg . . . . καθήκω
καθήκειν vb pres act inf   ic.
καθῆκεν vb 1st aor act ind 3rd pers sg . . . . καθίημι
καθῆκον vb pres act part neut nom and acc sg . . . . . καθήκω
καθήκοντα vb pres act part neut nom and acc pl   id.
καθήκοντας vb pres act part masc acc pl   id.
καθηκούσαις vb pres act part fem dat pl   id.
καθηκούσαν vb pres act part fem acc sg   id.
καθηκούσας vb pres act part fem acc pl   id.
καθήλωσον vb 1st aor act impv 2nd pers sg . . . . . . καθηλόω
κάθημαι vb pres m/p ind 1st pers sg
καθήμεθα vb pres m/p ind 1st pers pl . . . . κάθημαι
καθήμεναι vb pres m/p part fem nom pl   id.
καθημένη vb pres m/p part fem nom sg   id.
καθημένην vb pres m/p part fem acc sg   id.
καθημένης vb pres m/p part fem gen sg   id.
καθήμενοι vb pres m/p part masc nom pl   id.
καθημένοις vb pres m/p part masc and neut dat pl   id.
καθήμενον vb pres m/p part masc acc sg,
          neut nom and acc sg   id.

καθήμενος vb pres m/p part masc nom sg . . . . . . κάθημαι
καθημένου vb pres m/p part masc and neut gen sg   id.
καθημένους vb pres m/p part masc acc pl   id.
καθημένων vb pres m/p part gen pl   id.
καθημερινήν adj fem acc sg . . . . καθημερινός
κάθηνται vb pres m/p ind 3rd pers pl . . . . κάθημαι
καθῃρέθη vb 1st aor pass ind 3rd pers sg . . . . . . καθαιρεω
καθῃρέθης vb 1st aor pass ind 2nd pers sg   id.
καθῃρημενα vb perf m/p part neut nom and acc pl   id.
καθῃρημενας vb perf m/p part fem acc pl   id.
καθῃρημένους vb perf m/p part masc acc pl   id.
καθῃρημένων vb perf m/p part gen pl   id.
καθήρητο vb impf m/p ind 3rd pers sg   ic.
κάθησαι vb pres m/p ind 2nd pers sg . . . . κάθημαι
καθήσεσθε vb fut mid ind 2nd pers pl   id.
καθήσεται vb fut mid ind 3rd pers sg   id.
καθήσῃ vb fut mid ind 2nd pers sg   id.
καθῆσθαι vb pres m/p inf   id.
κάθησθε vb pres m/p ind 2nd pers pl   id.
κάθησο vb pres m/p impv 2nd pers sg   id.
καθήσομαι vb fut mid ind 1st pers sg   id.
καθήσονται vb fut mid ind 3rd pers pl   id.
κάθηται vb pres m/p ind 3rd pers sg   id.
κάθιδρος adj masc and fem nom sg
καθιδρυμένων vb perf m/p part gen pl . . . . καθιδρύω
καθιδρύσαντες vb 1st aor act part masc nom pl   id.
καθίδρυσεν vb 1st aor act ind 3rd pers sg   id.
καθιεῖ vb fut act ind 3rd pers sg . . . . καθίζω
καθιεῖς vb fut act ind 2nd pers sg   id.
καθιεῖται vb fut mid ind 3rd pers sg   id.
καθίεται vb fut mid ind 3rd pers sg . . . . κάθημαι
καθιζάνει vb pres act ind 3rd pers sg . . . . καθιζάνω
καθιζάνων vb pres act part masc nom sg   id.
καθίξετε vb fut act ind 2nd pers pl . . . . καθικνέομαι
καθίομαι vb fut mid ind 1st pers sg . . . . καθίζω
καθιοῦνται vb fut mid ind 3rd pers pl   id.
καθιπτάμενα vb perf dep part
          neut nom and acc pl . . . . καθίπταμαι
κάθισαι vb 1st aor mid impv 2nd pers sg . . . . καθίζω
καθίσαι vb 1st aor act inf   id.
καθίσαντες vb 1st aor act part masc nom pl   id.
καθίσας vb 1st aor act part masc nom sg   id.
καθίσατε vb 1st aor act impv 2nd pers pl   id.
καθισάτω vb 1st aor act impv 3rd pers sg   id.
καθίσει vb fut act ind 3rd pers sg   id.
καθίσεται vb fut mid ind 3rd pers sg   id.
καθίσῃ vb 1st aor act subj 3rd pers sg   id.
καθίσῃς vb 1st aor act subj 2nd pers sg   id.
καθίσητε vb 1st aor act subj 2nd pers pl   id.
κάθισιν noun fem acc sg . . . . κάθισις
καθίσομαι vb fut mid ind 1st pers sg . . . . καθίζω
κάθισον vb 1st aor act impv 2nd pers sg   id.

καθιστᾷ vb pres act ind 3rd pers sg . . . . καθιστάω
καθιστάναι vb pres act inf . . . . καθίστημι
καθιστάντες vb pres act part masc nom pl   id.
καθίσταται vb pres pass ind 3rd pers sg   id.
καθίστημι vb pres act ind 1st pers sg   id.
καθιστῶν vb pres act part masc nom sg   id.
καθίσω vb fut act ind 1st pers sg . . . . καθίζω
καθίσωμεν vb 1st aor act subj 1st pers pl   id.
καθιῶ vb fut act ind 1st pers sg   id.
καθό adverb
καθοδηγήσας vb 1st aor act part masc nom sg . . καθοδηγέω
καθοδηγήσω vb fut act ind 1st pers sg   id.
καθοδηγῶν vb pres act part masc nom sg   id.
κάθοδος noun fem nom sg
καθόδους noun fem acc pl . . . . κάθοδος
Καθοηλ pr noun
καθόλου adverb
καθομολογήσηται vb 1st aor mid subj
          3rd pers sg . . . . καθομολογέω
καθοπλίσας vb 1st aor act part masc nom sg . . . καθοπλίζω
καθόπλισον vb 1st aor act impv 2nd pers sg   id.
καθοπλισώμεθα vb 1st aor mid subj 1st pers pl   id.
καθορᾷ vb pres act ind 3rd pers sg . . . . καθοράω
καθορᾷς vb pres act ind 2nd pers sg   id.
καθόρμια noun neut nom and acc pl . . . . καθόρμιον
καθορῶν vb pres act part masc nom sg . . . . καθοράω
καθότι adverb and conjunction
κάθου vb pres m/p impv 2nd pers sg . . . . κάθημαι
Καθουα pr noun
καθυβρίζει vb pres act ind 3rd pers sg . . . . καθυβρίζω
καθυβρίσαι vb 1st aor act inf   id.
καθυβρίσουσιν vb fut act ind 3rd pers pl   id.
καθυμνοῦντες vb pres act part masc nom pl . . . . καθυμνέω
καθύπερθε adverb
καθυπνῶ vb pres act ind 1st pers sg . . . . καθυπνόω
καθυστερῆσαι vb 1st aor act inf . . . . καθυστερέω
καθυστερήσει vb fut act ind 3rd pers sg   id.
καθυστερήσεις vb fut act ind 2nd pers sg   id.
καθυφανεῖς vb fut act ind 2nd pers sg . . . . καθυφαίνω
καθυφασμένων vb perf m/p part gen pl   id.
καθωμολογήσατο vb 1st aor mid ind
          3rd pers sg . . . . καθομολογέω
καθωπλικώς vb perf act part masc nom sg . . . . . καθοπλίζω
καθωπλίσαντο vb 1st aor mid ind 3rd pers pl   id.
καθωπλισμένης vb perf m/p part fem gen sg   id.
καθωπλισμένοι vb perf m/p part masc nom pl   id.
καθωπλισμένος vb perf m/p part masc nom sg   id.
καθώς adverb and conjunction
καί adverb and conjunction
Καιβαισελεηλ pr noun
καίεται vb pres m/p ind 3rd pers sg . . . . καίω
καίετε vb pres act ind 2nd pers pl   id.

Καιν pr noun
Καινα pr noun
καινά adj neut nom and acc pl . . . . καινός
Καιναῖον pr noun masc acc sg . . . . Καιναῖος
Καιναιους pr noun masc acc pl   id.
Καιναν pr noun
καινή adj fem nom sg . . . . καινός
Καινῆ pr noun fem dat sg . . . . Καινή
καινήν adj fem acc sg . . . . καινός
Καινην pr noun fem acc sg . . . . Καινή
καινῆς adj fem gen sg . . . . καινός
καινιεῖ vb fut act ind 3rd pers sg . . . . καινίζω
καινίζει vb pres act ind 3rd pers sg   id.
καινίζειν vb pres act inf   id.
καινιοῦσιν vb fut act ind 3rd pers pl   id.
καινοί adj masc nom pl . . . . καινός
καινοῖς adj masc and neut dat pl   id.
καινόν adj masc acc sg, neut nom and acc sg   id.
καινός adj masc nom sg   id.
καινότητος noun fem gen sg . . . . καινότης
καινοῦ adj masc and neut gen sg . . . . καινός
καινουργέ adj masc voc sg . . . . καινουργός
καινούς adj masc acc pl . . . . καινός
καινῷ adj masc and neut dat sg   id.
καιόμενα vb pres m/p part neut nom and acc pl . . . . . . καίω
καιόμεναι vb pres m/p part fem nom pl   id.
καιομένη vb pres m/p part fem nom sg   id.
καιομένην vb pres m/p part fem acc sg   id.
καιομένης vb pres m/p part fem gen sg   id.
καιομένοις vb pres m/p part masc and neut dat pl   id.
καιόμενον vb pres m/p part masc acc sg,
          neut nom and acc sg   id.
καιόμενος vb pres m/p part masc nom sg   id.
καιομένου vb pres m/p part masc and neut gen sg   id.
καιομένῳ vb pres m/p part masc and neut dat sg   id.
καιομένων vb pres m/p part gen pl   id.
καίοντες vb pres act part masc nom pl   id.
καίουσι(ν) vb pres act ind 3rd pers pl   id.
καίπερ conjunction
καίριον adj masc acc sg, neut nom and acc sg . . . . . καίριος
καιροί noun masc nom pl . . . . καιρός
καιροῖς noun masc dat pl   id.
καιρόν noun masc acc sg   id.
καιρός noun masc nom sg   id.
καιροῦ noun masc gen sg   id.
καιρούς noun masc acc pl   id.
καιρῷ noun masc dat sg   id.
καιρῶν noun masc gen pl   id.
καίτοι conjunction
κακά adj neut nom and acc pl . . . . κακός
κακαί adj fem nom pl   id.
κακάς adj fem acc pl   id.

κἀκεῖ = καὶ ἐκεῖ

κἀκεῖνοι = καὶ ἐκεῖνος

κἀκείνοις = καὶ ἐκείνοις

κἀκείνου = καὶ ἐκείνου

κακή adj fem nom sg . . . . κακός

κακῇ adj fem dat sg   id.

κακήν adj fem acc sg   id.

κακῆς adj fem gen sg   id.

κακία noun fem nom sg

κακίᾳ noun fem dat sg . . . . κακία

κακίαι noun fem nom pl   id.

κακίαις noun fem dat pl   id.

κακίαν noun fem acc sg   id.

κακίας noun fem gen sg and acc pl   id.

κακισθείς vb 1st aor pass part masc nom sg . . . . κακίζω

κακιῶν noun fem gen pl . . . . κακία

κακοηθεία noun fem dat sg . . . . κακοήθεια

κακοήθειαν noun fem acc sg   id.

κακοηθείας noun fem gen sg and acc pl   id.

κακοήθη adj neut nom and acc pl . . . . κακοήθης

κακοήθης adj masc and fem nom sg   id.

κακοί adj masc nom pl . . . . κακός

κακοῖς adj masc and neut dat pl   id.

κακολογήσεις vb fut act ind 2nd pers sg . . . . . . κακολογέω

κακολογοῦντες vb pres act part masc nom pl   id.

κακολογοῦντος vb pres act part masc and neut gen sg   id.

κακολογῶν vb pres act part masc nom sg   id.

κακόμοχθος adj masc and fem nom sg

κακόν adj masc acc sg, neut nom and acc sg . . . . κακός

κακοπάθειαν noun fem acc sg . . . . κακοπάθεια

κακοπαθείας noun fem gen sg and acc pl   id.

κακοποιεῖ vb pres act ind 3rd pers sg . . . . κακοποιέω

κακοποιεῖν vb pres act inf   id.

κακοποιῆσαι vb 1st aor act inf   id.

κακοποιήσει vb fut act ind 3rd pers sg   id.

κακοποιήσητε vb 1st aor act subj 2nd pers pl   id.

κακοποίησιν noun fem acc sg . . . . κακοποίησις

κακοποιήσω vb fut act ind 1st pers sg . . . . κακοποιέω

κακοποιήσωσιν vb 1st aor act subj 3rd pers pl   id.

κακοποιοῖς adj masc and neut dat pl . . . . κακοποιός

κακοποιός adj masc and fem nom sg   id.

κακοποιοῦσα vb pres act part fem nom sg . . . . κακοποιέω

κακοποιῶν vb pres act part masc nom sg   id.

κακοπραγία noun fem nom sg

κακός adj masc nom sg

κακοτεχνήσωμεν vb 1st aor act subj

     1st pers pl . . . . κακοτεχνέομαι

κακότεχνον adj acc sg, neut nom sg . . . . κακότεχνος

κακότεχνος adj masc and fem nom sg   id.

κακοτέχνων adj gen pl   id.

κακοῦ adj masc and neut gen sg . . . . κακός

κακούμενος vb pres m/p part masc nom sg . . . . κακόω

κακοῦν vb pres act inf . . . . κακόω

κακοῦντας vb pres act part masc acc pl   id.

κακοῦντες vb pres act part masc nom pl   id.

κακούντων vb pres act part masc and neut gen pl   id.

κακουργία noun fem nom sg

κακουργίαν noun fem acc sg . . . . κακουργία

κακουργίας noun fem gen sg   id.

κακούργοις adj dat pl . . . . κακοῦργος

κακούργου adj gen sg   id.

κακούργους adj masc and fem acc pl   id.

κακούργῳ adj dat sg   id.

κακούς adj masc acc pl . . . . κακός

κακόφρονι adj dat sg . . . . κακόφρων

κακοφροσύνη noun fem nom sg

κακόφρων adj masc and fem nom sg

κακῷ adj masc and neut dat sg . . . . κακός

κακωθῆναι vb 1st aor pass inf . . . . κακόω

κακωθήσεται vb fut pass ind 3rd pers sg   id.

κακωθήσομαι vb fut pass ind 1st pers sg   id.

κακῶν adj gen pl . . . . κακός

κακῶς adverb

κακώσαι vb 1st aor act opt 3rd pers sg . . . . κακόω

κακῶσαι vb 1st aor act inf   id.

κακώσαντες vb 1st aor act part masc nom pl   id.

κακώσατε vb 1st aor act impv 2nd pers pl   id.

κακώσει noun fem dat sg . . . . κάκωσις

κακώσει vb fut act ind 3rd pers sg . . . . κακόω

κακώσεις vb fut act ind 2nd pers sg   id.

κακώσετε vb fut act ind 2nd pers pl   id.

κακώσεως noun fem gen sg . . . . κάκωσις

κακώσῃ vb 1st aor act subj 3rd pers sg . . . . κακόω

κακώσῃς vb 1st aor act subj 2nd pers sg   id.

κακώσητε vb 1st aor act subj 2nd pers pl   id.

κάκωσιν noun fem acc sg . . . . κάκωσις

κάκωσις noun fem nom sg

κακώσομεν vb fut act ind 1st pers pl . . . . κακόω

κακώσουσιν vb fut act ind 3rd pers pl   id.

κακώσωσιν vb 1st aor act subj 3rd pers pl   id.

καλά adj neut nom and acc pl . . . . καλός

καλαβώτης noun masc nom sg

κάλαθος noun masc nom sg

καλάθους noun masc acc pl . . . . κάλαθος

καλαί adj fem nom pl . . . . καλός

καλαμᾶσθε vb pres dep ind 2nd pers pl . . . . . καλαμάομαι

καλάμη noun fem nom sg

καλάμῃ noun fem dat sg . . . . καλάμη

καλάμην noun fem acc sg   id.

καλάμης noun fem gen sg   id.

καλαμήσασθαι vb 1st aor mid inf . . . . καλαμάομαι

καλαμήσηται vb 1st aor mid subj 3rd pers sg   id.

καλαμήσονται vb fut mid ind 3rd pers pl   id.

καλαμίνη adj fem nom sg . . . . καλάμινος

καλαμίνην adj fem acc sg . . . . καλάμινος
καλαμίσκοι noun masc nom pl . . . . καλαμίσκος
καλαμίσκοις noun masc dat pl   id.
καλαμίσκους noun masc acc pl   id.
καλαμίσκῳ noun masc dat sg   id.
καλαμίσκων noun masc gen pl   id.
κάλαμον noun masc acc sg . . . . κάλαμος
κάλαμος noun masc nom sg   id.
καλάμου noun masc gen sg   id.
καλάμους noun masc acc pl   id.
Καλαμω pr noun
καλάμῳ noun masc dat sg . . . . κάλαμος
καλαμώμενος vb pres dep part masc nom sg . καλαμάομαι
καλαμῶνται vb pres dep ind 3rd pers pl   id.
καλάς adj fem acc pl . . . . καλός
καλέ adj masc voc sg   id.
καλεῖ vb pres act ind 3rd pers sg . . . . καλέω
καλεῖν vb pres act inf   id.
καλεῖσθαι vb pres m/p inf   id.
καλεῖται vb pres m/p ind 3rd pers sg   id.
καλεῖτε vb pres act impv 2nd pers pl,
              pres act ind 2nd pers pl   id.
καλέσαι vb 1st aor act inf,
              1st aor act opt 3rd pers sg   id.
καλέσας vb 1st aor act part masc nom sg   id.
καλέσατε vb 1st aor act impv 2nd pers pl   id.
καλεσάτω vb 1st aor act impv 3rd pers sg   id.
καλέσει vb fut act ind 3rd pers sg   id.
καλέσεις vb fut act ind 2nd pers sg   id.
καλέσετε vb fut act ind 2nd pers pl   id.
καλέσῃ vb 1st aor act subj 3rd pers sg   id.
κάλεσον vb 1st aor act impv 2nd pers sg   id.
καλέσουσιν vb fut act ind 3rd pers pl   id.
καλέσω vb 1st aor act subj 1st pers sg,
              fut act ind 1st pers sg   id.
καλέσωμεν vb 1st aor act subj 1st pers pl   id.
καλέσωσιν vb 1st aor act subj 3rd pers pl   id.
καλή adj fem nom sg . . . . καλός
καλήν adj fem acc sg   id.
καλῆς adj fem gen sg   id.
Καλιτα pr noun
Καλιτας pr noun
Καλλαι pr noun
κάλλει noun neut dat sg . . . . κάλλος
κάλλιον comp adj neut nom and acc sg . . . . καλός
καλλίονα comp adj neut nom and acc pl   id.
καλλίπαις noun fem nom sg
Καλλισθενην pr noun masc acc sg . . . . Καλλισθενης
κάλλιστα superl adj neut nom and acc pl . . . . καλός
καλλίστας superl adj fem acc pl   id.
καλλίστῃ superl adj fem dat sg   id.
καλλίστην superl adj fem acc sg   id.

καλλίστης superl adj fem gen sg . . . . καλός
κάλλιστοι superl adj masc nom pl   id.
καλλίστοις superl adj masc and neut dat pl   id.
κάλλιστον superl adj masc acc sg, neut nom and acc sg id.
κάλλιστος superl adj masc nom sg   id.
καλλίστων superl adj gen pl   id.
καλλονή noun fem nom sg
καλλονῇ noun fem dat sg . . . . καλλονή
καλλονήν noun fem acc sg   id.
καλλονῆς noun fem gen sg   id.
Καλλος pr noun neut nom and acc sg
κάλλος noun neut nom and acc sg
κάλλους noun neut gen sg . . . . κάλλος
κάλλυνθρα noun neut nom and acc pl . . . . κάλλυνθρον
καλοί adj masc nom pl . . . . καλός
καλοῖς adj masc and neut dat pl   id.
καλοκάγαθία noun fem dat sg . . . . καλοκάγαθία
καλοκάγαθίαν noun fem acc sg   id.
καλοκάγαθίας noun fem gen sg   id.
καλόν adj masc acc sg, neut nom and acc sg . . . . καλός
καλός adj masc nom sg   id.
καλοῦ adj masc and neut gen sg   id.
καλούμενον vb pres m/p part masc acc sg,
              neut nom and acc sg . . . . καλέω
καλούμενος vb pres m/p part masc nom sg   id.
καλουμένου vb pres m/p part masc and neut gen sg   id.
καλουμένους vb pres m/p part masc acc pl   id.
καλοῦνται vb pres m/p ind 3rd pers pl   id.
καλοῦντος vb pres act part masc and neut gen sg   id.
κάλους noun masc acc pl . . . . κάλος
καλούς adj masc acc pl . . . . καλός
καλοῦσιν vb pres act ind 3rd pers pl . . . . καλέω
κάλπην noun fem acc sg . . . . κάλπη
κάλυμμα noun neut nom and acc sg
καλύμματα noun neut nom and acc pl . . . . κάλυμμα
καλύμματι noun neut dat sg   id.
κάλυξιν noun fem dat pl . . . . κάλυξ
καλύπτει vb pres act ind 3rd pers sg . . . . καλύπτω
καλύπτειν vb pres act inf   id.
καλύπτεσθαι vb pres m/p inf   id.
καλύπτῃ vb pres act subj 3rd pers sg   id.
καλυπτῆρα noun masc acc sg . . . . καλυπτήρ
καλύπτοντες vb pres act part masc nom pl . . . . . . καλύπτω
καλύπτουσιν vb pres act ind 3rd pers pl   id.
καλύπτων vb pres act part masc nom sg   id.
καλυφθήσεται vb fut pass ind 3rd pers sg   id.
καλύψαι vb 1st aor act inf   id.
καλύψατε vb 1st aor act impv 2nd pers pl   id.
καλύψει vb fut act ind 3rd pers sg   id.
καλύψεις vb fut act ind 2nd pers sg   id.
καλύψεως noun fem gen sg . . . . κάλυψις
καλύψῃ vb 1st aor act subj 3rd pers sg . . . . καλύπτω

καλύψης vb 1st aor act subj 2nd pers sg . . . . καλύπτω
κάλυψον vb 1st aor act impv 2nd pers sg   id.
καλύψουσιν vb fut act ind 3rd pers pl   id.
καλύψω vb fut act ind 1st pers sg   id.
καλῶ vb pres act ind 1st pers sg . . . . καλέω
καλῷ adj masc and neut dat sg . . . . καλός
καλώδια noun neut nom and acc pl . . . . καλώδιον
καλωδίοις noun neut dat pl   id.
καλῶν adj gen pl . . . . καλός
καλῶν vb pres act part masc nom sg . . . . καλέω
καλῶς adverb
καμάκων noun masc gen pl . . . . κάμαξ
καμάραν noun fem acc sg . . . . καμάρα
κάμέ = καὶ ἐμέ
κάμηλοι noun masc or fem nom pl . . . . κάμηλος
καμήλοις noun masc or fem dat pl   id.
κάμηλον noun masc or fem acc sg   id.
καμηλοπάρδαλιν noun fem acc sg . . . . . καμηλοπάρδαλις
καμήλου noun masc or fem gen sg . . . . κάμηλος
καμήλους noun masc or fem acc pl   id.
καμήλων noun masc or fem gen pl   id.
Καμιν pr noun
καμιναίας noun fem gen sg . . . . καμιναία
κάμινον noun masc or fem acc sg . . . . κάμινος
κάμινος noun masc or fem nom sg   id.
καμίνου noun masc or fem gen sg   id.
καμίνῳ noun masc or fem dat sg   id.
καμμύσαι vb 1st aor act inf . . . . καμμύω
καμμύσει vb fut act ind 3rd pers sg   id.
καμμύων vb pres act part masc nom sg   id.
κάμνειν vb pres act inf . . . . κάμνω
κάμνων vb pres act part masc nom sg   id.
κάμοί = καὶ ἐμοί
κάμοῦ = καὶ ἐμοῦ
Καμουηλ pr noun
κάμπη noun fem nom sg
κάμπης noun fem gen sg . . . . κάμπη
καμπῆς noun fem gen sg . . . . καμπή
κάμπτων vb pres act part masc nom sg . . . . κάμπτω
καμπύλαι adj fem nom pl . . . . καμπύλος
καμφθῆναι vb 1st aor pass inf . . . . κάμπτω
κάμψαντες vb 1st aor act part masc nom pl   id.
κάμψας vb 1st aor act part masc nom sg   id.
κάμψει vb fut act ind 3rd pers sg   id.
κάμψεις vb fut act ind 2nd pers sg   id.
κάμψῃ vb 1st aor act subj 3rd pers sg   id.
κάμψῃς vb 1st aor act subj 2nd pers sg   id.
κάμψον vb 1st aor act impv 2nd pers sg   id.
κάμψουσιν vb fut act ind 3rd pers sg   id.
καμών vb 2nd aor act part masc nom sg . . . . κάμνω
κἄν = καὶ ἄν
Κανα pr noun

κανᾶ noun neut nom and acc pl . . . . κανοῦν
Κανααθ pr noun
Καναθ pr noun
Κανθαν pr noun
κάνθαρος noun masc nom sg
κανθῶν noun masc gen pl . . . . κανθός
κανόνα noun masc acc sg . . . . κανών
κανόνι noun masc dat sg   id.
κανόνος noun masc gen sg   id.
κανοῦ noun neut gen sg . . . . κανοῦν
κανοῦν noun neut nom and acc sg   id.
κανῷ noun neut dat sg   id.
κάπηλοι noun masc nom pl . . . . κάπηλος
κάπηλος noun masc nom sg   id.
Καπιρα pr noun
καπνιζομένη vb pres m/p part fem nom sg . . . . . . καπνίζω
καπνιζόμενον vb pres m/p part masc acc sg,
        neut nom and acc sg   id.
καπνιζόμενος vb pres m/p part masc nom sg   id.
καπνιζομένων vb pres m/p part gen pl   id.
καπνίζον vb pres act part neut nom and acc sg   id.
καπνίζονται vb pres m/p ind 3rd pers pl   id.
καπνίσαι vb 1st aor act inf   id.
καπνίσεις vb fut act ind 2nd pers sg   id.
καπνισθήσονται vb fut pass ind 3rd pers pl   id.
κάπνισον vb 1st aor act impv 2nd pers sg   id.
καπνόν noun masc acc sg . . . . καπνος
καπνός noun masc nom sg   id.
καπνοῦ noun masc gen sg   id.
καπνῷ noun masc dat sg   id.
Καππαδοκες pr noun
Καππαδοκιας pr noun fem gen sg . . . . Καππαδοκια
κάππαρις noun fem nom sg
κάπτειν vb pres act inf . . . . κάπτω
Καραβασιων pr noun
Καρανα pr noun
καρασιμ translit
Καραφα pr noun
καρδία noun fem nom sg
καρδίᾳ noun fem dat sg . . . . καρδία
καρδίαι noun fem nom pl   id.
καρδίαις noun fem dat pl   id.
καρδίαν noun fem acc sg   id.
καρδίας noun fem gen sg and acc pl   id.
καρδιῶν noun fem gen pl   id.
Καρεμ pr noun
Καρηε pr noun
Καριαθαιμ pr noun
Καριαθαρβοκ pr noun
Καριαθαρβοκσεφερ pr noun
Καριαθαρβοξεφερ pr noun
Καριαθβαελ pr noun

Καριαθιαριμ pr noun

Καριαθιαριν pr noun

Καριαθιαριος pr noun

Καριαθσωφαρ pr noun

Καριαν pr noun fem acc sg . . . . Καρια

Καριωθ pr noun

Καρκαρ pr noun

Καρμηλια pr noun fem dat sg . . . . Καρμηλια

Καρμηλιας pr noun fem gen sg   id.

Καρμηλιον pr noun neut nom and acc sg

Καρμηλιος pr noun masc nom sg

Καρμηλιου pr noun masc gen sg . . . . Καρμηλιος

Καρμηλον pr noun masc acc sg . . . . Καρμηλος

Καρμηλος pr noun masc nom sg   id.

Καρμηλου pr noun masc gen sg   id.

Καρμηλω pr noun masc dat sg   id.

Καρναιν pr noun

Καρνιον pr noun neut nom and acc sg

καρπασίνοις noun masc dat pl . . . . καρπάσινος

καρπίζεσθαι vb pres dep inf . . . . καρπίζομαι

κάρπιμον adj acc sg, neut nom sg . . . . κάρπιμος

καρπόβρωτον noun masc acc sg . . . . καρπόβρωτος

καρποί noun masc nom pl . . . . καρπός

καρπόν noun masc acc sg   id.

καρπός noun masc nom sg   id.

καρποῦ noun masc gen sg   id.

καρπούς noun masc acc pl   id.

καρποῦσθαι vb pres m/p inf . . . . καρπόω

καρποφόρα adj neut nom and acc pl . . . . καρποφόρος

καρποφορήσει vb fut act ind 3rd pers sg . . . . . καρποφορέω

καρποφόρον adj masc and fem acc sg . . . . . . καρποφόρος

καρποφοροῦντα vb pres act part

          neut nom and acc pl . . . . καρποφορέω

καρπῷ noun masc dat sg . . . . καρπός

κάρπωμα noun neut nom and acc sg

καρπώμασι noun neut dat pl . . . . κάρπωμα

καρπώματα noun neut nom and acc pl   id.

καρπώματος noun neut gen sg   id.

καρπωμάτων noun neut gen pl   id.

καρπῶν noun masc gen pl . . . . καρπός

καρπῶσαι vb 1st aor act inf . . . . καρπόω

καρπώσεων noun fem gen pl . . . . κάρπωσις

καρπώσεως noun fem gen sg   id.

κάρπωσιν noun fem acc sg   id.

κάρπωσις noun fem nom sg   id.

καρπωτόν adj acc sg, neut nom sg . . . . καρπωτός

καρπωτός adj masc and fem nom sg   id.

καρτάλλοις noun masc dat pl . . . . κάρταλλος

κάρταλλον noun masc acc sg   id.

καρτάλλῳ noun masc dat sg   id.

καρτερᾶς adj fem gen sg . . . . καρτερός

καρτέρει vb pres act impv 2nd pers sg . . . . καρτερέω

καρτερήσαντος vb 1st aor act part

          masc and neut gen sg . . . . καρτερέω

καρτερήσεις vb fut act ind 2nd pers sg   id.

καρτερήσῃ vb 1st aor act subj 3rd pers sg   id.

καρτέρησον vb 1st aor act impv 2nd pers sg   id.

καρτερία noun fem nom sg

καρτερίαν noun fem acc sg . . . . καρτερία

καρτερίας noun fem gen sg   id.

καρτεροί adj masc nom pl . . . . καρτερός

καρτεροῖς adj masc and neut dat pl   id.

καρτερός adj masc nom sg   id.

καρτεροψυχίαν noun fem acc sg . . . . καρτεροψυχία

καρτερῶν vb pres act part masc nom sg . . . . . . καρτερέω

καρτερῶς adverb

κάρυα noun neut nom and acc pl . . . . κάρυον

καρύας noun fem gen sg and acc pl . . . . καρύα

καρύϊνην adj fem acc sg . . . . καρύϊνος

καρυΐσκους noun masc acc pl . . . . καρυΐσκος

καρυωτά adj neut nom and acc pl . . . . καρυωτός

κάρφος noun neut nom and acc sg

Καρχηδονα pr noun fem acc sg . . . . Καρχηδων

Καρχηδονιοι adj masc nom pl . . . . Καρχηδονιος

Καρχηδονος pr noun fem gen sg . . . . Καρχηδων

καρωθῶσιν vb 1st aor pass subj 3rd pers pl . . . . καρόω

Κασεριν pr noun

κασία noun fem nom sg

Κασιαν pr noun fem acc sg . . . . Κασια

κασίας noun fem gen sg . . . . κασία

Κασιμ pr noun

Κασπιν pr noun

κασσιτέρινον adj masc acc sg,

          neut nom and acc sg . . . . κασσιτέρινος

κασσίτερον noun masc acc sg . . . . κασσίτερος

κασσίτερος noun masc nom sg   id.

κασσιτέρου noun masc gen sg   id.

κασσιτέρῳ noun masc dat sg   id.

Κασων pr noun

κατ᾽ see κατά

κατά adverb and preposition

Κατααθ pr noun

καταβαίνει vb pres act ind 3rd pers sg . . . . καταβαίνω

καταβαίνειν vb pres act inf   id.

καταβαίνετε vb pres act impv 2nd pers pl   id.

καταβαινέτω vb pres act impv 3rd pers sg   id.

καταβαῖνον vb pres act part neut nom and acc sg   id.

καταβαίνοντα vb pres act part masc acc sg,

          neut nom and acc pl   id.

καταβαίνοντας vb pres act part masc acc pl   id.

καταβαίνοντες vb pres act part masc nom pl   id.

καταβαίνοντος vb pres act part masc and neut gen sg id.

καταβαινόντων vb pres act part masc and neut gen pl id.

καταβαίνουσα vb pres act part fem nom sg   id.

καταβαινούσης vb pres act part fem gen sg ... καταβαίνω
καταβαίνουσι(ν) vb pres act ind 3rd pers pl,
    pres act part masc and neut dat pl   id.
καταβαινουσῶν vb pres act part fem gen pl   id.
καταβαίνω vb pres act ind 1st pers sg   id.
καταβαίνων vb pres act part masc nom sg   id.
κατάβαλε vb 2nd aor act impv 2nd pers sg ... καταβάλλω
καταβαλεῖ vb fut act ind 3rd pers sg   id.
καταβαλεῖν vb 2nd aor act inf   id.
καταβαλεῖς vb fut act ind 2nd pers sg   id.
καταβαλεῖτε vb fut act ind 2nd pers pl   id.
καταβάλῃ vb 2nd aor act subj 3rd pers sg   id.
καταβάλῃς vb 2nd aor act subj 2nd pers sg   id.
καταβάλλει vb pres act ind 3rd pers sg   id.
καταβάλλεσθαι vb pres m/p inf   id.
καταβάλλομεν vb pres act ind 1st pers pl   id.
καταβαλλόμενος vb pres m/p part masc nom sg   id.
καταβάλλων vb pres act part masc nom sg   id.
καταβαλοῦσι(ν) vb fut act ind 3rd pers pl   id.
καταβαλῶ vb fut act ind 1st pers sg   id.
καταβάν vb 2nd aor act part
    neut nom and acc sg .... καταβαίνω
καταβάντες vb 2nd aor act part masc nom pl   id.
καταβαρυνθῶμεν vb 1st aor pass subj
    1st pers pl .... καταβαρύνω
καταβαρυνόμενοι vb pres m/p part masc nom pl   id.
καταβάς vb 2nd aor act part masc nom sg ..... καταβαίνω
καταβᾶσα vb 2nd aor act part fem nom sg   id.
καταβάσει noun fem dat sg .... κατάβασις
καταβάσεως noun fem gen sg   id.
κατάβασιν noun fem acc sg   id.
καταβάσιον adj acc sg, neut nom sg .... καταβάσιος
κατάβασις noun fem nom sg
καταβέβηκεν vb perf act ind 3rd pers sg ..... καταβαίνω
καταβεβηκέναι vb perf act inf   id
καταβέβληκεν vb perf act ind 3rd pers sg .... καταβάλλω
καταβεβλημένη vb perf m/p part fem nom sg   id.
καταβῇ vb 2nd aor act subj 3rd pers sg ...... καταβαίνω
κατάβηθι vb 2nd aor act impv 2nd pers sg   id.
καταβῆναι vb 2nd aor act inf   id.
καταβῇς vb 2nd aor act subj 2nd pers sg   id.
καταβήσει vb fut mid ind 2nd pers sg   id
καταβήσεσθε vb fut mid ind 2nd pers pl   id.
καταβήσεται vb fut mid ind 3rd pers sg   id.
καταβήσῃ vb fut mid ind 2nd pers sg   id.
καταβήσομαι vb fut mid ind 1st pers sg   id.
καταβησόμεθα vb fut mid ind 1st pers pl   id.
καταβήσονται vb fut mid ind 3rd pers pl   id.
κατάβητε vb 2nd aor act impv 2nd pers pl   id.
καταβήτω vb 2nd aor act impv 3rd pers sg   id.
καταβήτωσαν vb 2nd aor act impv 3rd pers pl   id.

καταβιβάσθητι vb 1st aor pass impv
    2nd pers sg .... καταβιβάζω
καταβιβάσουσιν vb fut act ind 3rd pers pl   id.
καταβιβάσω vb fut act ind 1st pers sg   id.
καταβίου vb pres act impv 2nd pers sg .... καταβιόω
καταβλάπτοντος vb pres act part
    masc and neut gen sg .... καταβλάπτω
καταβληθείς vb 1st aor pass part masc nom sg   καταβάλλω
καταβοήσεται vb fut mid ind 3rd pers sg .... καταβοάω
καταβοήσῃ vb 1st aor act subj 3rd pers sg   id.
καταβόησις noun fem nom sg
καταβοήσωσι vb 1st aor act subj 3rd pers pl ... καταβοάω
καταβολῆς noun fem gen sg .... καταβολή
καταβοσκῆσαι vb 1st aor act inf .... κάταβόσκω
καταβοσκήσῃ vb 1st aor act subj 3rd pers sg   id.
καταβοώντων vb pres act part
    masc and neut gen pl .... καταβοάω
καταβρωθῇ vb 1st aor pass subj 3rd pers sg . καταβιβρώσκω
καταβρωθῆναι vb 1st aor pass inf   id.
καταβρωθήτω vb 1st aor pass impv 3rd pers sg   id.
κατάβρωμα noun neut nom and acc sg
καταβρώσει noun fem dat sg .... κατάβρωσις
κατάβρωσιν noun fem acc sg   id.
καταβῶ vb 2nd aor act subj 1st pers sg .... καταβαίνω
καταβῶμεν vb 2nd aor act subj 1st pers pl   id.
κατάγαγε vb 2nd aor act impv 2nd pers sg .... κατάγω
καταγαγεῖν vb 2nd aor act inf   id.
καταγάγετε vb 2nd aor act impv 2nd pers pl   id.
καταγαγέτωσαν vb 2nd aor act impv 3rd pers pl   id.
καταγαγόντες vb 2nd aor act part masc nom pl   id.
καταγαγόντι vb 2nd aor act part masc and neut dat sg   id.
καταγαγών vb 2nd aor act part masc nom sg   id.
κατάγαια adj neut nom and acc pl .... κατάγαιος
καταγαίοις adj dat pl   id.
καταγγέλλοντα vb pres act part masc acc sg .. καταγγέλλω
καταγεγραμμέναι vb perf m/p part
    fem nom pl .... καταγράφω
καταγεγραμμένοι vb perf m/p part masc nom pl   id.
καταγεγραμμένων vb perf m/p part gen pl   id.
κατάγει vb pres act ind 3rd pers sg .... κατάγω
κατάγεις vb pres act ind 2nd pers sg   id.
καταγέλα vb pres act impv 2nd pers sg .... καταγελάω
καταγελᾷ vb pres act ind 3rd pers sg   id.
καταγελασάτωσαν vb 1st aor act impv 3rd pers pl   id.
καταγελάσεται vb fut mid ind 3rd pers sg   id.
καταγελάσετε vb fut act ind 2nd pers pl   id.
καταγελάσῃ vb fut mid ind 2nd pers sg   id.
καταγελασθήσονται vb fut pass ind 3rd pers pl   id.
καταγελασθῶμεν vb 1st aor pass subj 1st pers pl   id.
καταγελάσονται vb fut mid ind 3rd pers pl   id.
καταγέλαστον adj acc sg, neut nom sg .... καταγέλαστος
καταγελᾶται vb pres m/p ind 3rd pers sg ..... καταγελάω

καταγελώμενοι   vb pres m/p part masc nom pl   .. καταγελάω
καταγελῶν   vb pres act part masc nom sg   id.
καταγελῶντα   vb pres act part masc acc sg   id.
καταγελῶνται   vb pres m/p ind 3rd pers pl   id.
καταγελῶντες   vb pres act part masc nom pl   id.
κατάγελως   noun masc nom sg
καταγέλωτα   noun masc acc sg   ....   κατάγελως
καταγέλωτι   noun masc dat sg
καταγηράσητε   vb 1st aor act subj 2nd pers pl   .. καταγηράω
καταγίνομαι   vb pres dep ind 1st pers sg
καταγινόμενοι   vb pres dep part
     masc nom pl . . . . καταγίνομαι
καταγνώσεται   vb fut mid ind 3rd pers sg   ... καταγινώσκω
καταγνωσθήσεται   vb fut pass ind 3rd pers sg   id.
καταγνῶσιν   vb 2nd aor act subj 3rd pers pl   id.
κατάγνωσις   noun fem nom sg
καταγογγύζουσιν   vb pres act ind
     3rd pers pl . . . . καταγογγύζω
καταγομένῳ   vb pres m/p part masc and neut dat sg   . κατάγω
κατάγουσαι   vb pres act part fem nom pl   id.
κατάγουσιν   vb pres act ind 3rd pers pl   id.
καταγραφείς   vb 2nd aor pass part masc nom sg   . καταγράφω
κατάγραψον   vb 1st aor act impv 2nd pers sg   id.
καταγράψω   vb fut act ind 1st pers sg   id.
καταδεδεμένα   vb perf m/p part
     neut nom and acc pl . . . . καταδέω
καταδέδεται   vb perf m/p ind 3rd pers sg   id.
καταδεδικασμένος   vb perf m/p part
     masc nom sg . . . . καταδικάζω
καταδεδυνάστευνται   vb perf m/p ind
     3rd pers sg . . . . καταδυναστεύω
καταδείξας   vb 1st aor act part masc nom sg   . καταδείκνυμι
καταδεξάσθωσαν   vb 1st aor mid impv
     3rd pers pl . . . . καταδέχομαι
καταδεσμεύσει   vb fut act ind 3rd pers sg   ... καταδεσμεύω
καταδεσμεύσῃς   vb 1st aor act subj 2nd pers sg   id.
καταδέσμους   noun masc acc pl . . . . καταδέσμος
καταδεχόμενος   vb pres dep part
     masc nom sg . . . . καταδέχομαι
καταδῆσαι   vb 1st aor act inf . . . . καταδέω
κατάδησον   vb 1st aor act impv 2nd pers sg   id.
καταδήσω   vb fut act ind 1st pers sg   id.
καταδιείλαντο   vb 2nd aor mid ind
     3rd pers pl . . . . καταδιαιρέω
καταδίελε   vb 2nd aor act impv 2nd pers sg   id.
καταδιέλεσθε   vb 2nd aor mid impv 2nd pers pl   id.
καταδιελόντι   vb 2nd aor act part masc and neut dat sg   id.
καταδικαζομένη   vb pres m/p part
     fem nom sg . . . . καταδικάζω
καταδικάζων   vb pres act part masc nom sg   id.
καταδικάσαι   vb 1st aor act inf   id.
καταδικάσεται   vb fut mid ind 3rd pers sg   id.

καταδικάσῃς   vb 1st aor act subj 2nd pers sg   .. καταδικάζω
καταδικάσηται   vb 1st aor mid subj 3rd pers sg   id.
καταδικάσητε   vb 1st aor act subj 2nd pers pl   id.
καταδικάσονται   vb fut mid ind 3rd pers pl   id.
καταδικάσωμεν   vb 1st aor act subj 1st pers pl   id.
καταδίκης   noun fem gen sg . . . . καταδίκη
καταδίωκε   vb pres act impv 2nd pers sg . . . . . . καταδιώκω
καταδιώκει   vb pres act ind 3rd pers sg   id.
καταδιώκειν   vb pres act inf   id.
καταδιώκεις   vb pres act ind 2nd pers sg   id.
καταδιώκοντες   vb pres act part masc nom pl   id.
καταδιωκόντων   vb pres act part masc and neut gen pl   id.
καταδιώκων   vb pres act part masc nom sg   id.
καταδιώξαι   vb 1st aor act opt 3rd pers sg   id.
καταδιώξαντας   vb 1st aor act part masc acc pl   id.
καταδιώξατε   vb 1st aor act impv 2nd pers pl   id.
καταδιώξεις   vb fut act ind 2nd pers sg   id.
καταδιώξεται   vb fut mid ind 3rd pers sg   id.
καταδιώξῃς   vb 1st aor act subj 2nd pers sg   id.
καταδίωξον   vb 1st aor act impv 2nd pers sg   id.
καταδιώξονται   vb fut mid ind 3rd pers pl   id.
καταδιώξω   vb 1st aor act subj 1st pers sg,
     fut act ind 1st pers sg   id.
καταδολεσχήσει   vb fut act ind 3rd pers sg   . καταδολεσχέω
καταδουλουμένους   vb pres m/p part
     masc acc pl . . . . καταδουλόω
καταδουλοῦνται   vb pres m/p ind 3rd pers pl   id.
καταδουλοῦσθαι   vb pres m/p inf   id.
καταδουλωσάμενον   vb 1st aor mid part masc acc sg,
     neut nom and acc sg   id.
καταδουλωσαμένων   vb 1st aor mid part gen pl   id.
καταδουλώσω   vb fut act ind 1st pers sg   id.
καταδρομάς   noun fem acc pl . . . . καταδρομή
καταδυναστεία   noun fem nom sg
καταδυναστείᾳ   noun fem dat sg . . . . καταδυναστεία
καταδυναστείαν   noun fem acc sg   id.
καταδυναστείας   noun fem gen sg   id.
καταδυναστεύει   vb pres act ind
     3rd pers sg . . . . καταδυναστεύω
καταδυναστεύειν   vb pres act inf   id.
καταδυναστεύετε   vb pres act impv 2nd pers pl   id.
καταδυναστευθῆναι   vb 1st aor pass inf   id.
καταδυναστεύομεν   vb pres act ind 1st pers pl   id.
καταδυναστεύόμεναι   vb pres m/p part fem nom pl   id.
καταδυναστεύοντας   vb pres act part masc acc pl   id.
καταδυναστεύοντες   vb pres act part masc nom pl   id.
καταδυναστεύουσαι   vb pres act part fem nom pl   id.
καταδυναστεῦσαι   vb 1st aor act inf   id.
καταδυναστεύσαντες   vb 1st aor act part masc nom pl   id.
καταδυναστεύσας   vb 1st aor act part masc nom sg   id.
καταδυναστεύσῃ   vb 1st aor act subj 3rd pers sg   id.
καταδυναστεύσητε   vb 1st aor act subj 2nd pers pl   id.

καταδυναστεύσουσιν vb fut act ind	
3rd pers pl . . . . καταδυναστεύω	
καταδυναστεύσωμεν vb 1st aor act subj 1st pers pl	id.
καταδύσει vb fut act ind 3rd pers sg . . . . καταδύω	
καταδύσεις noun fem nom and acc pl . . . . . . κατάδυσις	
καταδύσεται vb fut mid ind 3rd pers sg . . . . καταδύω	
καταδύσωσιν vb 1st aor act subj 3rd pers pl	id.
καταθέσθαι vb 2nd aor mid inf . . . . κατατίθημι	
καταθλάσαι vb 1st aor act inf . . . . κεταθλάω	
κατάθου vb 2nd aor mid impv 2nd pers sg . . . . κατατίθημι	
καταθύμια adj neut nom and acc pl . . . . καταθύμ_ος	
καταθύμιον adj masc acc sg, neut nom and acc sg	d.
καταιγίδι noun fem dat sg . . . . κατανίς	
καταιγίδος noun fem gen sg	d.
καταιγίδων noun fem gen pl	d.
καταιγίς noun fem nom sg	d.
καταιδεσθέντες vb 1st aor pass part	
masc nom pl . . . . καταιδέομαι	
καταικίζεις vb pres act ind 2nd pers sg . . . . . . καταικίζω	
καταικιζόμενος vb pres m/p part masc nom sg	id.
καταικιζομένους vb pres m/p part masc acc pl	id.
καταικίσας vb 1st aor act part masc nom sg	id.
καταικισθείς vb 1st aor pass part masc nom sg	id.
καταισχύνει vb pres act ind 3rd pers sg . . . . . καταισχύνω	
καταισχύνετε vb pres act ind 2nd pers pl	id.
καταισχύνη vb pres act subj 3rd pers sg	id.
καταισχύνης vb pres act subj 2nd pers sg	id.
καταισχύνητε vb pres act subj 2nd pers pl	id.
καταισχυνθείην vb 1st aor pass opt 1st pers sg	id.
καταισχυνθείησαν vb 1st aor pass opt 3rd pers pl	id.
καταισχυνθῇ vb 1st aor pass subj 3rd pers sg	id.
καταισχυνθῇς vb 1st aor pass subj 2nd pers sg	id.
καταισχυνθήσεται vb fut pass ind 3rd pers sg	id.
καταισχυνθήσῃ vb fut pass ind 2nd pers sg	id.
καταισχυνθήσονται vb fut pass ind 3rd pers pl	id.
καταισχυνθήτωσαν vb 1st aor pass impv 3rd pers pl	id.
καταισχυνθῶσιν vb 1st aor pass subj 3rd pers pl	id.
καταισχυνόμενοι vb pres m/p part masc nom pl	id.
καταισχύνουσα vb pres act part fem nom sg	id.
καταισχυνῶ vb fut act ind 1st pers sg	id.
καταισχύνων vb pres act part masc nom sg	id.
κατακαήσεται vb fut pass ind 3rd pers sg . . . . . . κατακαίω	
κατακαήσονται vb fut pass ind 3rd pers pl	id.
κατακαίειν vb pres act inf	id.
κατακαίεται vb pres m/p ind 3rd pers sg	id.
κατακαίουσιν vb pres act ind 3rd pers pl	id.
κατακαίων vb pres act part masc nom sg	id.
κατακάλυμμα noun neut nom and acc sg	
κατακαλύπτον vb pres act part	
neut nom and acc sg . . . . κατακαλύπτω	
κατακαλύψαι vb 1st aor act inf	id.
κατακαλύψει vb fut act ind 3rd pers sg	id.

κατακαλύψεις vb fut act ind 2nd pers sg . . κατακαλύπτω	
κατακαλύψῃ vb 1st aor act subj 3rd pers sg	id.
κατακαλύψομαι vb fut mid ind 1st pers sg	id.
κατακαλύψουσιν vb fut act ind 3rd pers pl	id.
κατακαλύψω vb fut act ind 1st pers sg	id.
κατακαμπτόμενος vb pres m/p part	
masc nom sg . . . . κατακάμπτω	
κατάκαρπος adj masc and fem nom sg	
κατακάρπως adverb	
κατακάρπωσιν noun fem acc sg . . . . κατακάρπωσις	
κατακαυεῇ vb 1st aor pass subj 3rd pers sg . . . . . κατακαίω	
κατακαυεῇς vb 1st aor pass subj 2nd pers sg	id.
κατακαυεῇσεται vb fut pass ind 3rd pers sg	id.
κατακαυθήσονται vb fut pass ind 3rd pers pl	id.
κατακαυθήτω vb 1st aor pass impv 3rd pers sg	id
κατάκαυμα noun neut nom and acc sg	
κατακαύματι noun neut dat sg . . . . κατάκαυμα	
κατακαύματος noun neut gen sg	
κατακαύσαι vb 1st aor act opt 3rd pers sg . . . . . κατακαίω	
κατακαῦσαι vb 1st aor act inf	id.
κατακαύσει vb fut act ind 3rd pers sg	id.
κατακαύσεις vb fut act ind 2nd pers sg	id.
κατακαύσετε vb fut act ind 2nd pers pl	id.
κατακαύσομεν vb fut act ind 1st pers pl	id.
κατακαύσουσιν vb fut act ind 3rd pers pl	id.
κατακαύσομεν vb 1st aor act subj 1st pers pl	id.
κατακαυχησονται vb fut mid ind	
3rd pers pl . . . . κατακαυχάομαι	
κατάκεισαι vb pres m/p ind 2nd pers sg . . . . . κατάκειμαι	
κατακείσῃ vb fut mid ind 2nd pers sg	id.
κατακεκαλυμμένα vb perf m/p part	
neut nom and acc pl . . . . κατακαλύπτω	
κατακεκαλυμμένη vb perf m/p part fem nom sg	id.
κατακέκαυται vb perf m/p ind 1st pers sg . . . . . κατακαίω	
κατακεκαυμένα vb perf m/p part neut nom and acc pl	id.
κατακεκαυμένας vb perf m/p part fem acc pl	id.
κατακεκαυμένη vb perf m/p part fem nom sg	id.
κατακεκαυμένης vb perf m/p part fem gen sg	id.
κατακεκαυμένοι vb perf m/p part masc nom pl	id.
κατακεκαυμένον vb perf m/p part masc acc sg,	
neut nom and acc sg	id.
κατακεκαυμένος vb perf m/p part masc nom sg	id.
κατακεκαυμένων vb perf m/p part gen pl	id.
κατακεκεντημένοι vb perf m/p part	
masc nom pl . . . . κατακεντέω	
κατακεκλεισμένους vb perf m/p part	
masc acc pl . . . . κατακλείω	
κατακεκομμένην vb perf m/p part fem acc sg . . κατακόπτω	
κατακεκομμένους vb perf m/p part masc acc pl	id.
κατακεκρυμμένος vb perf m/p part	
masc nom sg . . . . κατακρύπτω	
κατακενοῦν vb pres act inf . . . . κατακενόω	

κατακέντει vb pres act impv 2nd pers sg . . . . . κατακεντέω
κατακεχαλκωμένα vb perf m/p part
 neut nom and acc pl . . . . καταχαλκόω
κατακεχρυσωμένους vb perf m/p part
 masc acc pl . . . . καταχρυσόω
κατακλεισθείς vb 1st aor pass part
 masc nom sg . . . . κατακλείω
κατακλεισθέντες vb 1st aor pass part masc nom pl id.
κατάκλειστοι adj masc and fem nom pl . . . κατάκλειστος
κατακλείστους adj masc acc pl id.
κατακληροδοτῇ vb pres act subj
 3rd pers sg . . . . κατακληροδοτέω
κατακληροδοτῆσαι vb 1st aor act inf id.
κατακληρονομεῖ vb pres act ind
 3rd pers sg . . . . κατακληρονομέω
κατακληρονομεῖν vb pres act inf id.
κατακληρονομεῖς vb pres act ind 2nd pers sg id.
κατακληρονομήθητι vb 1st aor pass impv 2nd pers sg id.
κατακληρονομῆσαι vb 1st aor act inf id.
κατακληρονομήσαντας vb 1st aor act part
 masc acc pl id.
κατακληρονομήσαντες vb 1st aor act part
 masc nom pl id.
κατακληρονομήσατε vb 1st aor act impv 2nd pers pl id.
κατακληρονομήσει vb fut act ind 3rd pers sg id.
κατακληρονομήσεις vb fut act ind 2nd pers sg id.
κατακληρονομήσετε vb fut act ind 2nd pers pl id.
κατακληρονομήσῃ vb 1st aor act subj 3rd pers sg id.
κατακληρονομήσῃς vb 1st aor act subj 2nd pers sg id.
κατακληρονομήσητε vb 1st aor act subj 2nd pers pl id.
κατακληρονομήσομεν vb fut act ind 1st pers pl id.
κατακληρονόμησον vb 1st aor act impv 2nd pers sg id.
κατακληρονομήσουσιν vb fut act ind 3rd pers pl id.
κατακληρονομήσω vb fut act ind 1st pers sg id.
κατακληρονομῶν vb pres act part masc nom sg id.
κατακληροῦται vb pres m/p ind 3rd pers sg . κατακληρόω
κατακληρώσηται vb 1st aor mid subj 3rd pers sg id.
κατακλιθείς vb 1st aor pass part masc nom sg . . κατακλίνω
κατακλιθῇ vb 1st aor pass subj 3rd pers sg id.
κατακλιθῶμεν vb 1st aor pass subj 1st pers pl id.
κατακλινομένην vb pres m/p part fem acc sg id.
κατάκλιτα noun neut nom and acc pl . . . . κατάκλιτον
κατακλυζομένην vb pres m/p part fem acc sg . . κατακλύζω
κατακλύζοντα vb pres act part masc acc sg
κατακλύζοντι vb pres act part masc and neut dat sg id.
κατακλύζοντος vb pres act part masc and neut gen sg id.
κατακλύζων vb pres act part masc nom sg id.
κατακλύσει vb fut act ind 3rd pers sg id.
κατακλυσθήσονται vb fut pass ind 3rd pers pl id.
κατακλυσμόν noun masc acc sg . . . . κατακλυσμός
κατακλυσμός noun masc nom sg id.
κατακλυσμοῦ noun masc gen sg id.

κατακλυσμῷ noun masc dat sg . . . . κατακλυσμός
κατακολουθεῖν vb pres act inf . . . . κατακολουθέω
κατακολουθῆσαι vb 1st aor act inf id.
κατακολουθήσαντες vb 1st aor act part masc nom pl id.
κατακολουθήσῃς vb 1st aor act subj 2nd pers sg id.
κατακολουθῶν vb pres act part masc nom sg id.
κατάκοποι adj masc and fem nom pl . . . . κατάκοπος
κατάκοπον adj acc sg, neut nom sg id.
κατακόπων adj gen pl id.
κατακοπῶν noun fem gen pl . . . . κατακοπή
κατακόψει vb fut act ind 3rd pers sg . . . . κατακόπτω
κατακόψεις vb fut act ind 2nd pers sg id.
κατακόψουσιν vb fut act ind 3rd pers pl id.
κατακόψω vb fut act ind 1st pers sg id.
κατακρατεῖ vb pres act ind 3rd pers sg . . . . . . κατακρατέω
κατακρατεῖτε vb pres act ind 2nd pers pl id.
κατακρατῆσαι vb 1st aor act inf id.
κατακρατήσας vb 1st aor act part masc nom sg id.
κατακράτησον vb 1st aor act impv 2nd pers sg id.
κατακρατοῦντες vb pres act part masc nom pl id.
κατακρημνίσαντα vb 1st aor act part
 masc acc sg . . . . κατακρημνίζω
κατακρημνισθῆναι vb 1st aor pass inf id.
κατακρῖναι vb 1st aor act inf . . . . κατακρίνω
κατακρινεῖ vb fut act ind 3rd pers sg id.
κατακρινῶ vb fut act ind 1st pers sg id.
κατακρίνων vb pres act part masc nom sg id.
κατακροτήσατε vb 1st aor act impv
 2nd pers pl . . . . κατακροτέω
κατακρύβηθι vb 2nd aor pass impv
 2nd pers sg . . . . κατακρύπτω
κατακρυβῆναι vb 2nd aor pass inf id.
κατακρύψαι vb 1st aor act inf id.
κατακρύψεις vb fut act ind 2nd pers sg id.
κατάκρυψον vb 1st aor act impv 2nd pers sg id.
κατακρύψουσιν vb fut act ind 3rd pers pl id.
κατακτεῖναι vb 1st aor act inf . . . . κατακτείνω
κατακτείνας vb 1st aor act part masc nom sg id.
κατακτήσεσθαι vb fut mid inf . . . . κατακτάομαι
κατακτήσωμαι vb 1st aor mid subj 1st pers sg id.
κατακυλισθησόμεθα vb fut pass ind
 1st pers pl . . . . κατακυλίω
κατακυλιῶ vb fut act ind 1st pers sg id.
κατακυρίευε vb pres act impv 2nd pers sg . . κατακυριεύω
κατακυριεύειν vb pres act inf id.
κατακυριευθῇ vb 1st aor pass subj 3rd pers sg id.
κατακυριεῦσαι vb 1st aor act inf id.
κατακυριεύσατε vb 1st aor act impv 2nd pers pl id.
κατακυριευσάτω vb 1st aor act impv 3rd pers sg id.
κατακυριεύσει vb fut act ind 3rd pers sg id.
κατακυριεύσητε vb 1st aor act subj 2nd pers pl id.
κατακυριεύσουσιν vb fut act ind 3rd pers pl id.

κατακυριεύσω   vb fut act ind 1st pers sg .... κατακυριεύω

κατακυριεύσωσιν   vb 1st aor act subj 3rd pers pl   id.

καταλαβέσθαι   vb 2nd aor mid inf ...... καταλαμβάνω

καταλάβετε   vb 2nd aor act impv 2nd pers pl   id.

καταλαβέτωσαν   vb 2nd aor act impv 3rd pers pl   id.

καταλάβῃ   vb 2nd aor act subj 3rd pers sg   id.

καταλάβῃς   vb 2nd aor act subj 2nd pers sg   id.

καταλάβοι   vb 2nd aor act opt 3rd pers sg   id.

καταλαβόμενοι   vb 2nd aor mid part masc nom pl   id.

καταλαβοῦσαν   vb 2nd aor act part fem acc sg   id.

καταλάβω   vb 2nd aor act subj 1st pers sg   id.

καταλαβώμεθα   vb 2nd aor mid subj 1st pers pl   id.

καταλάβωσιν   vb 2nd aor act subj 3rd pers pl   id.

καταλαλεῖν   vb pres act inf .... καταλαλέω

καταλαλεῖτε   vb pres act ind 2nd pers pl   id.

καταλαλῆσαι   vb 1st aor act inf   id.

καταλαλήσουσιν   vb fut act ind 3rd pers pl   id.

καταλαλιᾶς   noun fem gen sg .... καταλαλιά

καταλαλοῦντα   vb pres act part masc acc sg ... καταλαλέω

καταλαμβανομένης   vb pres m/p part
     fem gen sg .... καταλαμβάνω

καταλαμβανομένου   vb pres m/p part
     masc and neut gen sg   id.

καταλαμβάνονται   vb pres m/p ind 3rd pers pl   id.

καταλαμβάνων   vb pres act part masc nom sg   id.

καταλεανεῖ   vb fut act ind 3rd pers sg ...... καταλεαίνω

καταλέγων   vb pres act part masc nom sg ...... καταλέγω

κατάλειμμα   noun neut nom and acc sg

καταλείμματα   noun neut nom and acc pl .... κατάλειμμα

καταλείπει   vb pres act ind 3rd pers sg .... καταλείπω

καταλειπόμενα   vb pres m/p part neut nom and acc pl   id.

καταλειπόμενοι   vb pres m/p part masc nom pl   id.

καταλειπόμενος   vb pres m/p part masc nom sg   id.

καταλειπομένων   vb pres m/p part gen pl   id.

καταλείποντες   vb pres act part masc nom pl   id.

καταλείπουσιν   vb pres act ind 3rd pers pl   id.

καταλειφθείς   vb 1st aor pass part masc nom sg   id.

καταλειφθεῖσαι   vb 1st aor pass part fem nom pl   id.

καταλειφθεῖσαν   vb 1st aor pass part fem acc sg   id.

καταλειφθείσας   vb 1st aor pass part fem acc pl   id.

καταλειφθείσῃ   vb 1st aor pass part fem dat sg   id.

καταλειφθεῖσι   vb 1st aor pass part masc and neut dat pl   id.

καταλειφθέν   vb 1st aor pass part neut nom and acc sg   id.

καταλειφθέντα   vb 1st aor pass part masc acc sg   id.

καταλειφθέντας   vb 1st aor pass part masc acc pl   id.

καταλειφθέντες   vb 1st aor pass part masc nom pl   id.

καταλειφθέντι   vb 1st aor pass part masc and neut dat sg   id.

καταλειφθέντος   vb 1st aor pass part
     masc and neut gen sg   id.

καταλειφθέντων   vb 1st aor pass part
     masc and neut gen pl   id.

καταλειφθῇ   vb 1st aor pass subj 3rd pers sg   id.

καταλειφθῆναι   vb 1st aor pass inf .... καταλείπω

καταλειφθήσεσθε   vb fut pass ind 2nd pers pl   id.

καταλειφθήσεται   vb fut pass ind 3rd pers sg   id.

καταλειφθήσῃ   vb fut pass ind 2nd pers sg   id.

καταλειφθήσονται   vb fut pass ind 3rd pers pl   id.

καταλειφθῆτε   vb 1st aor pass subj 2nd pers pl   id.

καταλειφθῶσιν   vb 1st aor pass subj 3rd pers pl   id.

καταλείψει   vb fut act ind 3rd pers sg   id.

καταλείψεις   vb fut act ind 2nd pers sg   id.

καταλείψετε   vb fut act ind 2nd pers pl   id.

καταλείψῃς   vb 1st aor act subj 2nd pers sg   id.

κατάλειψιν   noun fem acc sg .... κατάλειψις

καταλείψουσιν   vb fut act ind 3rd pers pl ..... καταλείπω

καταλείψω   vb fut act ind 1st pers sg   id.

καταλελειμμένα   vb perf m/p part neut nom and acc pl   id.

καταλελειμμένη   vb perf m/p part fem nom sg   id.

καταλελειμμένην   vb perf m/p part fem acc sg   id.

καταλελειμμένοι   vb perf m/p part masc nom pl   id.

καταλελειμμένοις   vb perf m/p part
     masc and neut dat pl   id.

καταλελειμμένον   vb perf m/p part masc acc sg,
     neut nom and acc sg   id.

καταλελειμμένος   vb perf m/p part masc nom sg   id.

καταλελειμμένους   vb perf m/p part masc acc pl   id.

καταλελειμμένων   vb perf m/p part gen pl   id.

καταλέλειπται   vb perf m/p ind 3rd pers sg   id.

καταλελεῖφθαι   vb perf m/p inf   id.

καταλελοίπατε   vb perf act ind 2nd pers pl   id.

καταλελοιπότα   vb perf act part masc acc sg   id.

καταλελοιπότες   vb perf act part masc nom pl   id.

καταλελοιπώς   vb perf act part masc nom sg   id.

καταλελύκαμεν   vb perf act ind 1st pers pl ...... καταλύω

καταλέσας   vb 1st aor act part masc nom sg ..... καταλέω

καταληγούσης   vb pres act part fem gen sg ..... καταλήγω

καταλημφθῇ   vb 1st aor pass subj
     3rd pers sg .... καταλαμβάνω

καταλημφθήσονται   vb fut pass ind 3rd pers pl   id.

καταλήμψεσθε   vb fut mid ind 2nd pers pl   id.

καταλήμψεται   vb fut mid ind 3rd pers sg   id.

καταλήμψῃ   vb fut mid ind 2nd pers sg   id.

κατάλημψιν   noun fem acc sg .... κατάλημψις

καταλήμψομαι   vb fut mid ind 1st pers sg .. καταλαμβάνω

καταλήμψονται   vb fut mid ind 3rd pers pl   id.

καταλήξαντες   vb 1st aor act part masc nom pl .. καταλήγω

καταλήξαντος   vb 1st aor act part masc and neut gen sg   id.

καταληφθήσεται   vb fut pass ind
     3rd pers sg .... καταλαμβάνω

καταληφθῶσι   vb 1st aor pass subj 3rd pers pl   id.

καταλιθοβολῆσαι   vb 1st aor act inf ..... καταλιθοβολέω

καταλιθοβολήσουσιν   vb fut act ind 3rd pers pl   id.

κατάλιθον   adj acc sg, neut nom sg .... κατάλιθος

καταλιμπάνει   vb pres act ind 3rd pers sg ... καταλιμπάνω

καταλιμπάνειν vb pres act inf . . . . καταλιμπάνω
καταλιμπάνουσιν vb pres act ind 3rd pers pl id.
καταλιπεῖν vb 2nd aor act inf . . . . καταλείπω
καταλίπετε vb 2nd aor act impv 2nd pers pl id.
καταλιπέτω vb 2nd aor act impv 3rd pers sg id.
καταλίπῃ vb 2nd aor act subj 3rd pers sg id.
καταλίπητε vb 2nd aor act subj 2nd pers pl id.
καταλιπόντας vb 2nd aor act part masc acc pl id.
καταλιπόντες vb 2nd aor act part masc nom pl id.
καταλιπόντων vb 2nd aor act part
    masc and neut gen pl id.
καταλιποῦσα vb 2nd aor act part fem nom sg id.
καταλίπωμεν vb 2nd aor act subj 1st pers pl id.
καταλιπών vb 2nd aor act part masc nom sg id.
καταλίπωσιν vb 2nd aor act subj 3rd pers pl id.
καταλλαγείη vb 2nd aor act opt 3rd pers sg . καταλλάσσω
καταλλαγῇ noun fem dat sg . . . . καταλλαγή
καταλλαγῆναι vb 2nd aor act inf . . . . καταλλάσσω
καταλλαγῆς noun fem gen sg . . . . καταλλαγή
καταλλαγήσεται vb fut mid ind 3rd pers sg . καταλλάσσω
κατάλοιπα adj neut nom and acc pl . . . . κατάλοιπος
κατάλοιποι adj masc and fem nom pl id.
καταλοίποις adj dat pl id.
κατάλοιπον adj acc sg, neut nom sg id.
κατάλοιπος adj masc and fem nom sg id.
καταλοίπου adj gen sg id.
καταλοίπους adj masc and fem acc pl id.
καταλοίπῳ adj dat sg id.
καταλοίπων adj gen pl id.
καταλοχίαις noun fem dat pl . . . . καταλοχία
καταλοχισμοῖς noun masc dat pl . . . . καταλοχισμός
καταλοχισμός noun masc nom sg id.
καταλοχισμῷ noun masc dat sg id.
καταλύεσθαι vb pres m/p inf . . . . καταλύω
καταλυθῆναι vb 1st aor pass inf id.
κατάλυμα noun neut nom and acc sg
καταλύματα noun neut nom and acc pl . . . . κατάλυμα
καταλύματι noun neut dat sg id.
καταλυμάτων noun neut gen pl id.
καταλυομένας vb pres m/p part fem acc pl . . . . . . καταλύω
καταλύοντας vb pres act part masc acc pl id.
καταλύοντες vb pres act part masc nom pl id.
καταλύοντι vb pres act part masc and neut dat sg id.
καταλυόντων vb pres act part masc and neut gen pl id.
καταλύουσα vb pres act part fem nom sg id.
καταλύουσιν vb pres act ind 3rd pers pl id.
καταλῦσαι vb 1st aor act inf id.
καταλύσας vb 1st aor act part masc nom sg id.
καταλύσασα vb 1st aor act part fem nom sg id.
καταλύσατε vb 1st aor act impv 2nd pers pl id.
καταλύσει vb fut act ind 3rd pers sg id.

καταλύσῃ vb 1st aor act subj 3rd pers sg,
    fut mid ind 2nd pers sg . . . . καταλύω
καταλύσῃς vb 1st aor act subj 2nd pers sg id.
κατάλυσιν noun fem acc sg . . . . κατάλυσις
κατάλυσις noun fem nom sg id.
κατάλυσομεν vb fut act ind 1st pers pl . . . . καταλύω
κατάλυσον vb 1st aor act impv 2nd pers sg id.
καταλύσουσιν vb fut act ind 3rd pers pl id.
καταλύσω vb fut act ind 1st pers sg id.
καταλύτου noun masc gen sg . . . . καταλύτης
καταλύω vb pres act ind 1st pers sg
καταλύων vb pres act part masc nom sg . . . . καταλύω
κατάμαθε vb 2nd aor act impv 2nd pers sg . καταμανθάνω
καταμαθεῖν vb 2nd aor act inf id.
καταμάνθανε vb pres act impv 2nd pers sg id.
καταμανθάνων vb pres act part masc nom sg id.
καταμαρτυρήσαντες vb 1st aor act part
    masc nom pl . . . . καταμαρτυρέω
καταμαρτυρησάτωσαν vb 1st aor act impv 3rd pers pl id.
καταμαρτυρήσομεν vb fut act ind 1st pers pl id.
καταμαρτυρήσουσιν vb fut act ind 3rd pers pl id.
καταμαρτυρῶν vb pres act part masc nom sg id.
καταμείνῃ vb 1st aor act subj 3rd pers sg . . . . . . καταμένω
καταμεμεστωμένης vb perf m/p part
    fem gen sg . . . . καταμεστόω
καταμεμιγμένα vb perf m/p part
    neut nom and acc pl . . . . καταμίγνυμι
καταμεριεῖτε vb fut act ind 2nd pers pl . . . . . . καταμερίζω
καταμερίζει vb pres act ind 3rd pers sg id.
καταμερίσαι vb 1st aor act inf id.
καταμερίσει vb fut act ind 3rd pers sg id.
καταμερισθῶσιν vb 1st aor pass subj 3rd pers pl id.
καταμερισμός noun masc nom sg
καταμετρεῖσθαι vb pres m/p inf . . . . καταμετρέω
καταμετρηθήσεται vb fut pass ind 3rd pers sg id.
καταμετρήσετε vb fut act ind 2nd pers pl id.
καταμηνίων adj gen pl . . . . καταμήνιος
καταμνησθείς vb 1st aor pass part
    masc nom sg . . . . καταμιμνήσκω
καταμωκήσεται vb fut mid ind
    3rd pers sg . . . . καταμωκάομαι
καταμωκήσονται vb fut mid ind 3rd pers pl id.
καταμωκώμενοι vb pres dep part masc nom pl id.
καταναγκάζοντες vb pres act part
    masc nom pl . . . . καταναγκάζω
Καταναθ pr noun
καταναλισκόμενοι vb pres m/p part
    masc nom pl . . . . καταναλίσκω
κατανάλισκον vb impf act ind 3rd pers pl,
    pres act part neut nom and acc sg id.
καταναλώθη vb 1st aor pass ind 3rd pers sg id.
καταναλωθήσεται vb fut pass ind 3rd pers sg id.

καταναλῶσαι vb 1st aor act inf . . . . καταναλίσκω

καταναλώσει vb fut act ind 3rd pers sg   id.

καταναλώσεν vb 1st aor act ind 3rd pers sg   id.

καταναλώσῃ vb 1st aor act subj 3rd pers sg   id.

καταναλώσουσιν vb fut act ind 3rd pers pl   id.

κατανένυγμαι vb perf m/p ind 1st pers sg . . . . κατανύσσω

κατανενυγμένη vb perf m/p part fem nom sg   id.

κατανενυγμένοι vb perf m/p part masc nom pl   id.

κατανενυγμένον vb perf m/p part masc acc sg,

      neut nom and acc sg   id.

κατανενυγμένος vb perf m/p part masc nom sg   id.

κατανίστασθε vb pres m/p ind 2nd pers pl . . κατανίστημι

κατανοεῖ vb pres act ind 3rd pers sg . . . . κατανοέω

κατανοεῖς vb pres act ind 2nd pers sg   id.

κατανοῆσαι vb 1st aor act inf   id.

κατανοήσας vb 1st aor act part masc nom sg   id.

κατανοήσατε vb 1st aor act impv 2nd pers pl   id.

κατανοήσεις vb fut act ind 2nd pers sg   id.

κατανοήσετε vb fut act ind 2nd pers pl   id.

κατανοήσεως noun fem gen sg . . . . κατανόησις

κατανοήσω vb fut act ind 1st pers sg . . . . κατανοέω

κατανοοῦντες vb pres act part masc nom pl   id.

κατανοοῦσιν vb pres act ind 3rd pers pl   id.

κατανοῶν vb pres act part masc nom sg   id.

κατάντημα noun neut nom and acc sg

καταντήσαντας vb 1st aor act part masc acc pl . . καταντάω

καταντήσαντος vb 1st aor act part

      masc and neut gen sg   id.

καταντησάτωσαν vb 1st aor act impv 3rd pers pl   id.

καταντλούμενος vb pres m/p part

      masc nom sg . . . . καταντλέω

κατανυγῆναι vb 1st aor act inf . . . . κατανύσσω

κατανυγήσεται vb fut pass ind 3rd pers sg   id.

κατανυγήσῃ vb fut pass ind 2nd pers sg   id.

κατανύγητε vb 2nd aor pass impv 2nd pers pl   id.

κατανυγῶ vb 2nd aor pass subj 1st pers sg   id.

κατανύειν vb pres act inf . . . . κατανύω

κατανύξεως noun fem gen sg . . . . κατάνυξις

κατανυχθέντος vb 1st aor pass part

      masc and neut gen sg . . . . κατανύσσω

καταξανῶ vb fut act ind 1st pers sg . . . . καταξαίνω

κατάξας vb 1st aor act part masc nom sg . . . . . . κατάγνυμι

κατάξει vb fut act ind 3rd pers sg . . . . κατάγω

κατάξεις vb fut act ind 2nd pers sg   id.

κατάξετε vb fut act ind 2nd pers pl   id.

καταξηρανεῖ vb fut act ind 3rd pers sg . . . . . καταξηραίνω

κατάξηρος adj masc and fem nom sg

καταξίαν adj fem acc sg . . . . κατάξιος

καταξιῶσαι vb 1st aor act inf . . . . καταξιόω

καταξιωσάντων vb 1st aor act part

      masc and neut gen pl   id.

καταξίωσον vb 1st aor act impv 2nd pers sg   id.

κάταξον vb 1st aor act impv 2nd pers sg . . . . . κατάγνυμι

κατάξουσιν vb fut act ind 3rd pers pl . . . . κατάγω

κατάξω vb fut act ind 1st pers sg   id.

καταπαίξεται vb fut act ind 3rd pers sg . . . . . καταπαίζω

καταπαλαῖσαι vb 1st aor act inf . . . . καταπαλαίω

κατάπασαι vb 1st aor mid impv 2nd pers sg . . καταπάσσω

καταπασάμενοι vb 1st aor mid part masc nom pl   id.

καταπάσαντες vb 1st aor act part masc nom pl   id.

καταπάσασθε vb 1st aor mid impv 2nd pers pl   id.

καταπατεῖν vb pres act inf . . . . καταπατέω

καταπατηθήσεσθε vb fut pass ind 2nd pers pl   id.

καταπατηθήσεται vb fut pass ind 3rd pers sg   id.

καταπάτημα noun neut nom and acc sg

καταπατήματος noun neut gen sg . . . . καταπάτημα

καταπατῆσαι vb 1st aor act opt 3rd pers sg . . . . καταπατέω

καταπατήσατε vb 1st aor act impv 2nd pers pl   id.

καταπατήσει vb fut act ind 3rd pers sg   id.

καταπατήσεις vb fut act ind 2nd pers sg   id.

καταπατήσετε vb fut act ind 2nd pers pl   id.

καταπατήσῃ vb 1st aor act subj 3rd pers sg   id.

καταπάτησιν noun fem acc sg . . . . καταπάτησις

καταπατήσουσιν vb fut act ind 3rd pers pl . . . . καταπατέω

καταπατήσω vb fut act ind 1st pers sg   id.

καταπατήσωσιν vb 1st aor act subj 3rd pers pl   id.

καταπατούμενον vb pres m/p part masc acc sg,

      neut nom and acc sg   id.

καταπατοῦν vb pres act part neut nom and acc sg   id.

καταπατοῦνται vb pres m/p ind 3rd pers pl   id.

καταπατοῦντας vb pres act part masc acc pl   id.

καταπατοῦντες vb pres act part masc nom pl   id.

καταπατούντων vb pres act part masc and neut gen pl id.

καταπατοῦσαι vb pres act part fem nom pl   id.

καταπατοῦσιν vb pres act ind 3rd pers pl   id.

καταπατῶν vb pres act part masc nom sg   id.

καταπαύματος noun neut gen sg . . . . κατάπαυμα

καταπαυομένης vb pres m/p part fem gen sg . . καταπαύω

καταπαῦσαι vb 1st aor act inf   id.

καταπαύσασθαι vb 1st aor mid inf   id.

καταπαύσει noun fem dat sg . . . . κατάπαυσις

καταπαύσει vb fut act ind 3rd pers sg . . . . καταπαύω

καταπαύσεις vb fut act ind 2nd pers sg   id.

καταπαύσεως noun fem gen sg . . . . κατάπαυσις

καταπαύσῃ vb 1st aor act subj 3rd pers sg . . . . καταπαύω

κατάπαυσιν noun fem acc sg . . . . κατάπαυσις

κατάπαυσις noun fem nom sg   id.

κατάπαυσον vb 1st aor act impv 2nd pers sg . . . καταπαύω

καταπαύσουσιν vb fut act ind 3rd pers pl   id.

καταπαύσω vb 1st aor act subj 1st pers sg,

      fut act ind 1st pers sg   id.

καταπαύσωμεν vb 1st aor act subj 1st pers pl   id.

καταπαύσωσιν vb 1st aor act subj 3rd pers pl   id.

καταπέλται noun masc nom pl . . . . καταπέλτης

καταπέλτας noun masc acc pl . . . . καταπέλτης

καταπέλτῃ noun masc dat sg   id.

καταπέλτην noun masc acc sg   id.

καταπεπατημένης vb pres m/p part

    fem gen sg . . . . καταπατέω

καταπεπατημένον vb perf m/p part masc acc sg,

    neut nom and acc sg   id.

καταπεπάτηνται vb perf m/p ind 3rd pers pl   id.

καταπεπελματωμένα vb perf dep part

    neut nom and acc pl . . . . καταπελματόομαι

καταπεπληγμένοι vb perf m/p part

    masc nom pl . . . . καταπλήσσω

καταπεπτωκότων vb perf act part

    masc and neut gen pl . . . . καταπίπτω

καταπέσῃ vb 2nd aor act subj 3rd pers sg   id.

καταπεσών vb 2nd aor act part masc nom sg   id.

καταπετασθῇ vb 1st aor pass subj

    3rd pers sg . . . . καταπετάννυμι

καταπέτασμα noun neut nom and acc sg

καταπετάσματα noun neut nom and acc pl . . καταπέτασμα

καταπετάσματι noun neut dat sg   id.

καταπετάσματος noun neut gen sg   id.

καταπιεῖν vb 2nd aor act inf . . . . καταπίνω

καταπίεται vb fut mid ind 3rd pers sg   id.

καταπιέτω vb 2nd aor act impv 3rd pers sg   id.

καταπίῃ vb 2nd aor act subj 3rd pers sg   id.

κατάπικροι adj masc and fem nom pl . . . . κατάπικρος

καταπίνειν vb pres act inf . . . . καταπίνω

καταπίνοντες vb pres act part masc nom pl   id.

καταπίοι vb 2nd aor act opt 3rd pers sg   id.

καταπίονται vb fut mid ind 3rd pers pl   id.

καταπίπτετε vb pres act ind 2nd pers pl . . . . . καταπίπτω

καταπίπτοντας vb pres act part masc acc pl   id.

καταπίπτων vb pres act part masc nom sg   id.

καταπιστεύετε vb pres act ind 2nd pers pl . . καταπιστεύω

καταπίω vb 2nd aor act subj 1st pers sg . . . . καταπίνω

καταπίωμεν vb 2nd aor act subj 1st pers pl   id.

καταπίωσιν vb 2nd aor act subj 3rd pers pl   id.

καταπλαγείησαν vb 2nd aor pass opt

    3rd pers pl . . . . καταπλήσσω

καταπλαγείς vb 2nd aor pass part masc nom sg   id.

καταπλαγέντας vb 2nd aor pass part masc acc pl   id.

καταπλαγέντος vb 2nd aor pass part

    masc and neut gen sg   id.

καταπλαγῆναι vb 2nd aor pass inf   id.

κατάπλασαι vb 1st aor mid impv

    2nd pers sg . . . . καταπλάσσω

καταπλάσσει vb pres act ind 3rd pers sg   id.

καταπληγμός noun masc nom sg

καταπλήξει noun fem dat sg . . . . κατάπληξις

καταπλήσσεις vb pres act ind 2nd pers sg . . . καταπλήσσω

καταπλησσέτω vb pres act impv 3rd pers sg   id.

κατάπλῳ noun masc dat sg . . . . κατάπλους

καταποθῇ vb 2nd aor pass subj 3rd pers sg . . . . . καταπίνω

καταπολεμεῖτε vb pres act ind 2nd pers pl . . καταπολεμέω

κατάπονον adj acc sg, neut nom sg . . . . κατάπονος

καταπονούμεθα vb pres m/p ind 1st pers pl . . . καταπονέω

καταπονουμένοις vb pres m/p part

    masc and neut dat pl   id.

καταποντίζεις vb pres act ind 2nd pers sg . . καταποντίζω

καταποντιοῦσιν vb fut act ind 3rd pers pl   id.

καταποντισάτω vb 1st aor act impv 3rd pers sg   id.

καταποντισμοῦ noun masc gen sg . . . . . . καταποντισμός

καταπόντισον vb 1st aor act impv

    2nd pers sg . . . . καταποντίζω

καταποντιῶ vb fut act ind 1st pers sg   id.

καταπορευομένοις vb pres dep part

    masc and neut dat pl . . . . καταπορεύομαι

καταπραΰνει vb pres act ind 3rd pers sg . . . . καταπραΰνω

καταπραΰνεις vb pres act ind 2nd pers sg   id.

καταπραΰνῃς vb 1st aor act subj 2nd pers sg,

    pres act subj 2nd pers sg   id.

καταπρίσῃ vb 1st aor act subj 3rd pers sg . . . . . . καταπρίω

καταπροδιδούς vb pres act part

    masc nom sg   καταπροδίδωμι

καταπτήξει vb fut act ind 3rd pers sg . . . . . . καταπτήσσω

καταπτήσσει vb pres act ind 3rd pers sg   id.

κατάπτωμα noun neut nom and acc sg

καταπτώσει noun fem dat sg . . . . κατάπτωσις

κατάρα noun fem nom sg

κατάρᾳ noun fem dat sg . . . . κατάρα

καταραθείη vb 1st aor pass opt 3rd pers sg . . . καταράομαι

κατάραι noun fem nom pl . . . . κατάρα

κατάραις noun fem dat pl   id.

καταράκτην noun masc acc sg . . . . καταρράκτης

κατάραν noun fem acc sg . . . . κατάρα

κατάρας noun fem gen sg and acc pl   id.

καταράσαι vb 1st aor mid impv 2nd pers sg . . καταράομαι

καταρᾶσαι see κατάρασαι

καταράσαιτο vb 1st aor mid opt 3rd pers sg   id.

καταρασάμενον vb 1st aor mid part masc acc sg   id.

καταράσασθαι vb 1st aor mid inf   id.

καταράσασθε vb 1st aor mid impv 2nd pers pl   id.

καταράσει noun fem dat sg . . . . κατάρασις

καταράσῃ vb 1st aor mid subj 2nd pers sg,

    fut mid ind 2nd pers sg . . . . καταράομαι

καταράσηται vb 1st aor mid subj 3rd pers sg   id.

καταρᾶσθαι vb pres dep inf   id.

καταρᾶσθε vb pres dep impv 2nd pers pl   id.

καταράσθω vb pres dep impv 3rd pers sg   id.

κατάρασιν noun fem acc sg . . . . κατάρασις

καταράσομαι vb fut mid ind 1st pers sg . . . . . καταράομαι

καταράσονται vb fut mid ind 3rd pers pl   id.

καταράσσειν vb pres act inf . . . . καταράσσω καταράσωμαι vb 1st aor mid subj 1st pers sg . καταράομαι

καταράσωνται vb 1st aor mid subj 3rd pers pl   id.

καταρᾶται vb pres dep ind 3rd pers sg   id.

κατάρατον adj acc sg, neut nom sg . . . . κατάρατος

καταράτου adj gen sg   id.

καταραχθήσεται vb fut pass ind 3rd pers sg . . καταράσσω

καταργηθῆναι vb 1st aor pass inf . . . . καταργέω

καταργῆσαι vb 1st aor act inf   id.

καταριθμουμένῳ vb pres m/p part

     masc and neut dat sg . . . . καταριθμέω

καταριθμοῦνται vb pres m/p ind 3rd pers pl   id.

κατάρξαι vb 1st aor act inf . . . . κατάρχω

καταρξάμενος vb 1st aor mid part masc nom sg   id.

κατάρξει vb fut act ind 3rd pers sg   id.

κατάρξω vb fut act ind 1st pers sg   id.

καταρράκται noun masc nom pl . . . . καταρράκτης

καταρράκτας noun masc acc pl   id.

καταρράκτην noun masc acc sg   id.

καταρράκτου noun masc gen sg   id.

καταρρακτῶν noun masc gen pl   id.

καταρρεῖν vb pres act inf . . . . καταρρέω

καταρρήγνυνται vb pres m/p ind

     3rd pers sg . . . . καταρρήγνυμι

καταρριπτομένων vb pres m/p part gen pl . . . καταρρίπτω

κατάρρυτον adj acc sg, neut nom sg . . . . κατάρρυτος

καταρτιζόμενος vb pres m/p part masc nom sg . καταρτίζω

καταρτιζομένου vb pres m/p part masc and neut gen sg   id.

κατάρτισαι vb 1st aor mid impv 2nd pers sg   id.

καταρτίσασθαι vb 1st aor mid inf   id.

καταρτισθῇ vb 1st aor pass subj 3rd pers sg   id.

καταρτισθῶσιν vb 1st aor pass subj 3rd pers pl   id.

κατάρχεις vb pres act ind 2nd pers sg . . . . κατάρχω

καταρχομένου vb pres m/p part masc and neut gen sg   id.

κατάρχων vb pres act part masc nom sg   id.

καταρώμενοι vb pres dep part masc nom pl . . . καταράομαι

καταρωμένοις vb pres dep part masc and neut dat pl   id.

καταρώμενος vb pres dep part masc nom sg   id.

καταρωμένου vb pres dep part masc and neut gen sg   id.

καταρωμένους vb pres dep part masc acc pl   id.

κατασβέσει vb fut act ind 3rd pers sg . . . . . κατασβέννυμι

κατασείοντες vb pres act part masc nom pl . . . . . κατασείω

Κατασεμ pr noun

κατασῆσαι vb 1st aor act inf . . . . κατασείω

κατασιωπήσω vb 1st aor act subj 1st pers sg . . κατασιωπάω

κατασκάπτει vb pres act ind 3rd pers sg . . . . κατασκάπτω

κατασκάπτειν vb pres act inf   id.

κατασκαπτόμενον vb pres m/p part masc acc sg,

     neut nom and acc sg   id.

κατασκάπτονται vb pres m/p ind 3rd pers pl   id.

κατασκαφήσεται vb fut pass ind 3rd pers sg   id.

κατασκάψατε vb 1st aor act impv 2nd pers pl   id.

κατασκάψει vb fut act ind 3rd pers sg   id.

κατασκάψετε vb fut act ind 2nd pers pl . . . . κατασκάπτω

κατασκάψουσιν vb fut act ind 3rd pers pl   id.

κατασκάψω vb fut act ind 1st pers sg   id.

κατασκευάζει vb pres act ind 3rd pers sg . . . κατασκευάζω

κατασκευάζειν vb pres act inf   id.

κατασκευάζοντες vb pres act part masc nom pl   id.

κατασκευάζουσιν vb pres act ind 3rd pers pl   id.

κατασκευαῖς noun fem dat pl . . . . κατασκευή

κατασκευάς noun fem acc pl   id.

κατασκευάσαι vb 1st aor act inf . . . . κατασκευάζω

κατασκευάσας vb 1st aor act part masc nom sg   id.

κατασκευασθέντα vb 1st aor pass part

     neut nom and acc pl   id.

κατασκευασθέντος vb 1st aor pass

     part masc and neut gen sg   id.

κατασκευασθῇ vb 1st aor pass subj 3rd pers sg   id

κατασκευάσματα noun neut

     nom and acc pl . . . . κατασκεύασμα

κατασκευάσματι noun neut dat sg   id.

κατασκευή noun fem nom sg

κατασκευήν noun fem acc sg . . . . κατασκευη

κατασκευῆς noun fem gen sg   id.

κατασκεψάμενοι vb 1st aor mid part

     masc nom pl . . . . κατασκέπτομαι

κατασκεψαμένων vb 1st aor mid part gen pl   id.

κατασκέψασθαι vb 1st aor mid inf   id.

κατασκέψασθε vb 1st aor mid impv 2nd pers pl   id.

κατασκέψασθωσαν vb 1st aor mid impv 3rd pers pl   id.

κατασκέψεται vb fut mid ind 3rd pers sg   id.

κατασκηνοῖ vb pres act ind 3rd pers sg . . . . . κατασκηνόω

κατασκήνου vb pres act impv 2nd pers sg   id.

κατασκηνοῦν vb pres act inf   id.

κατασκηνοῦντα vb pres act part masc acc sg   id.

κατασκηνοῦντας vb pres act part masc acc pl   id.

κατασκηνοῦντι vb pres act part masc and neut dat sg   id.

κατασκηνῶν vb pres act part masc nom sg   id.

κατασκηνώσαι vb 1st aor act opt 3rd pers sg   id.

κατασκηνῶσαι vb 1st aor act inf   id.

κατασκηνώσας vb 1st aor act part masc nom sg   id.

κατασκηνώσει vb fut act ind 3rd pers sg   id.

κατασκηνώσεις vb fut act ind 2nd pers sg   id.

κατασκηνωσεως noun fem gen sg . . . . . . κατασκήνωσις

κατασκήνωσιν noun fem acc sg   id.

κατασκήνωσις noun fem nom sg   id.

κατασκήνωσον vb 1st aor act impv

     2nd pers sg . . . . κατασκηνόω

κατασκηνώσουσι(ν) vb fut act ind 3rd pers pl   id.

κατασκηνώσω vb 1st aor act subj 1st pers sg,

     fut act ind 1st pers sg   id.

κατάσκιον adj acc sg, neut nom sg . . . . κατάσκιος

κατασκίου adj gen sg   id.

κατασκίων adj gen pl   id.

κατασκοπεύοντας vb pres act part

    masc acc pl . . . . κατασκοπεύω

κατασκοπεῦσαι vb 1st aor act inf   id.

κατασκοπεύσαντας vb 1st aor act part masc acc pl   id.

κατασκοπεύσαντες vb 1st aor act part masc nom pl   id.

κατασκοπεύσασι vb 1st aor act part

    masc and neut dat pl   id.

κατασκοπῆσαι vb 1st aor act inf . . . . κατασκοπέω

κατασκοπήσωσιν vb 1st aor act subj 3rd pers pl   id.

κατάσκοποι noun masc nom pl . . . . κατάσκοπος

κατάσκοπος noun masc nom sg   id.

κατασκόπους noun masc acc pl   id.

κατασοφίσασθαι vb 1st aor mid inf . . . . . κατασοφίζομαι

κατασοφισώμεθα vb 1st aor mid subj 1st pers pl   id.

κατασπᾷ vb pres act ind 3rd pers sg . . . . κατασπάω

κατασπαρήσονται vb fut pass ind

    3rd pers pl . . . . κατασπείρω

κατασπάσαι vb 1st aor act inf . . . . κατασπάω

κατάσπασον vb 1st aor act impv 2nd pers sg   id.

κατασπάσω vb fut act ind 1st pers sg   id.

κατασπαταλᾷ vb pres act ind 3rd pers sg . κατασπαταλάω

κατασπαταλῶντες vb pres act part masc nom pl   id.

κατασπερεῖς vb fut act ind 2nd pers sg . . . . . . κατασπείρω

κατασπεύδει vb pres act ind 3rd pers sg . . . . . κατασπεύδω

κατασπευδομένη vb pres m/p part fem nom sg   id.

κατασπεύδοντας vb pres act part masc acc pl   id.

κατασπεύδουσα vb pres act part fem nom sg   id.

κατασπεῦσαι vb 1st aor act inf   id.

κατασπεύσατε vb 1st aor act impv 2nd pers pl   id.

κατασπευσάτω vb 1st aor act impv 3rd pers sg   id.

κατάσπευσον vb 1st aor act impv 2nd pers sg   id.

κατασπουδασθῶ vb 1st aor pass subj

    1st pers sg . . . . κατασπουδάζομαι

κατασπῶντες vb pres act part masc nom pl . . . . κατασπάω

κατα0τταθέντα vb 1st aor pass part masc acc sg . καθίστημι

κατασταθέντα vb 1st aor pass part masc acc sg . καθίστημι

κατασταθέντες vb 1st aor pass part masc nom pl   id.

κατασταθῆναι vb 1st aor pass inf   id.

κατασταθήσεσθαι vb fut pass inf   id.

κατασταθήσεται vb fut pass ind 3rd pers sg   id.

κατασταθήσονται vb fut pass ind 3rd pers pl   id.

κατασταθῶσιν vb 1st aor pass subj 3rd pers pl   id.

καταστάντες vb 1st aor act part masc nom pl   id.

καταστάς vb 1st aor act part masc nom sg   id.

καταστᾶσα vb 1st aor act part fem nom sg   id.

καταστασιάσασι vb 1st aor act part

    masc and neut dat pl . . . . καταστασιάζω

κατάστασιν noun fem acc sg . . . . κατάστασις

καταστεῖλαι vb 1st aor act inf . . . . καταστέλλω

καταστείλας vb 1st aor act part masc nom sg   id.

κατάστεμα noun neut nom and acc sg

καταστενάζοντες vb pres act part

    masc nom pl . . . . κατασπτενάζω

    masc nom pl . . . . καταστενάζω

καταστεναζόντων vb perf act part

    masc and neut gen pl . . . . καταστενάζω

καταστενάξεις vb fut act ind 2nd pers sg   id.

καταστέναξον vb 1st aor act impv 2nd pers sg   id.

καταστῇ vb 2nd aor act subj 3rd pers sg . . . . . . καθίστημι

καταστήσαι vb 1st aor act opt 3rd pers sg   id.

καταστῆσαι vb 1st aor act inf   id.

καταστήσαντος vb 1st aor act part

    masc and neut gen sg   id.

καταστήσας vb 1st aor act part masc nom sg   id.

καταστήσασα vb 1st aor act part fem nom sg   id.

καταστήσατε vb 1st aor act impv 2nd pers pl   id.

καταστησάτω vb 1st aor act impv 3rd pers sg   id.

καταστήσει vb fut act ind 3rd pers sg   id.

καταστήσειν vb fut act inf   id.

καταστήσεις vb fut act ind 2nd pers sg   id.

καταστήσεται vb fut mid ind 3rd pers sg   id.

καταστήσετε vb fut act ind 2nd pers pl   id.

καταστήσῃ vb 1st aor act subj 3rd pers sg   id.

καταστήσῃς vb 1st aor act subj 2nd pers sg   id.

κατάστησον vb 1st aor act impv 2nd pers sg   id.

καταστήσουσιν vb fut act ind 3rd pers pl   id.

καταστήσω vb fut act ind 1st pers sg   id.

κατάστητε vb 2nd aor act impv 2nd pers pl,

    2nd aor act subj 2nd pers pl   id.

καταστολήν noun fem acc sg . . . . καταστολή

καταστραγγιεῖ vb fut act ind 3rd pers sg . καταστραγγίζω

καταστραφήσεται vb fut pass ind 3rd pers sg . καταστρέφω

καταστρέφεται vb pres m/p ind 3rd pers sg   id.

καταστρέφων vb pres act part masc nom sg   id.

καταστρέψαι vb 1st aor act inf   id.

καταστρέψας vb 1st aor act part masc nom sg   id.

καταστρέψει vb fut act ind 3rd pers sg   id.

καταστρέψῃ vb 1st aor act subj 3rd pers sg   id.

καταστρέψω vb fut act ind 1st pers sg   id.

καταστροφή noun fem nom sg

καταστροφήν noun fem acc sg . . . . καταστροφή

καταστροφῆς noun fem gen sg   id.

καταστρωθῆναι vb 1st aor pass inf . . . . . καταστρώννυμι

καταστρωθήσονται vb fut pass ind 3rd pers pl   id.

καταστρωννύων vb pres act part

    masc nom sg . . . . καταστρωννύω

καταστρῶσαι vb 1st aor act inf . . . . καταστρώννυμι

καταστρώσατε vb 1st aor act impv 2nd pers pl   id.

κατασυριεῖ vb fut act ind 3rd pers sg . . . . κατασύρω

κατασύρων vb pres act part masc nom sg   id.

κατασφάζειν vb pres act inf . . . . κατασφάζω

κατασφάξαι vb 1st aor act inf   id.

κατασφάξουσιν vb fut act ind 3rd pers pl   id.

κατασφραγίζει vb pres act ind 3rd pers sg . κατασφραγίζω

κάτασχε vb 2nd aor act impv 2nd pers sg . . . . κατέχω

κατασχεθήσεσθε vb fut pass ind 2nd pers pl   id.

κατασχεθήτω vb 1st aor pass impv 3rd pers sg ... κατέχω

κατασχεῖν vb 2nd aor act inf   id.

κατασχέσει noun fem dat sg .... κατάσχεσις

κατασχέσεσιν noun fem dat pl   id.

κατασχέσεως noun fem gen sg   id.

κατάσχεσιν noun fem acc sg   id.

κατάσχεσις noun fem nom sg   id.

κατάσχῃς vb 2nd aor act subj 2nd pers sg .... κατέχω

κατασχίσαντες vb 1st aor act part

     masc nom pl .... κατασχίζω

κατάσχωμεν vb 1st aor act subj 1st pers pl .... κατέχω

κατατάξουσιν vb fut act ind 3rd pers pl .... κατατάσσω

κατατάσσων vb pres act part masc nom sg   id.

κατατεινόμενος vb pres m/p part masc nom sg . κατατείνω

κατατεμοῦσιν vb fut act ind 3rd pers pl ...... κατατέμνω

κατατενεῖ vb fut act ind 3rd pers sg .... κατατείνω

κατατενεῖς vb fut act ind 2nd pers sg   id.

κατατέρπου vb pres m/p impv 2nd pers sg .... κατατέρπω

κατατέτακται vb perf m/p ind 3rd pers sg ... κατατάσσω

κατατετμημένοι vb perf m/p part masc nom pl . κατατέμνω

κατατήξεις vb fut act ind 2nd pers sg .... κατατήκω

κατατίθεσθαι vb pres m/p inf .... κατατίθημι

κατατολμήσαντας vb 1st aor act part

     masc acc pl .... κατατολμάω

κατατοξευθήσεται vb fut pass ind

     3rd pers sg .... κατατοξεύω

κατατοξεῦσαι vb 1st aor act inf   id.

κατατοξεύσει vb fut act ind 3rd pers sg   id.

κατατοξεύσουσιν vb fut act ind 3rd pers pl   id.

κατατρέχοντες vb pres act part masc nom pl ... κατατρέχω

κατατρέχοντος vb pres act part masc and neut gen sg   id.

κατατρέχουσιν vb pres act ind 3rd pers pl   id.

κατατριβῶσιν vb 2nd aor pass subj 3rd pers pl . κατατρίβω

κατατρίψει vb fut act ind 3rd pers sg   id.

κατατρύφησον vb 1st aor act impv

     2nd pers sg .... κατατρυφάω

κατατρυφήσουσιν vb fut act ind 3rd pers pl   id.

κατατρώγει vb pres act ind 3rd pers sg .... κατατρώγω

κατατύχωσιν vb 2nd aor act subj 3rd pers pl . κατατυγχάνω

καταυγάζειν vb pres act inf .... καταυγάζω

κατάφαγε vb 2nd aor act impv 2nd pers sg ...... κατεσθίω

καταφαγεῖν vb 2nd aor act inf   id.

καταφάγεσαι vb fut mid ind 2nd pers sg   id.

καταφάγεται vb fut mid ind 3rd pers sg   id.

καταφαγέτω vb 2nd aor act impv 3rd pers sg   id.

καταφάγῃ vb 2nd aor act subj 3rd pers sg   id.

καταφάγοι vb 2nd aor act opt 3rd pers sg   id.

καταφάγοισαν vb 2nd aor act opt 3rd pers pl   id.

καταφάγονται vb fut mid ind 3rd pers pl   id.

καταφάγωσιν vb 2nd aor act subj 3rd pers pl   id.

καταφερομένη vb pres m/p part fem nom sg .... καταφέρω

καταφερομένην vb pres m/p part fem acc sg   id.

καταφερόμενον vb pres m/p part

     neut nom and acc sg .... καταφέρω

καταφερομένου vb pres m/p part masc and neut gen sg   id.

καταφερούς adj gen sg .... καταφερής

καταφεύξεσθε vb fut mid ind 2nd pers pl ..... καταφεύγω

καταφεύξεται vb fut mid ind 3rd pers sg   id.

καταφεύξονται vb fut mid ind 3rd pers pl   id.

καταφθαρήσεται vb fut pass ind 3rd pers sg .. καταφθείρω

καταφθαρήσῃ vb fut pass ind 2nd pers sg   id.

καταφθαρήσονται vb fut pass ind 3rd pers pl   id.

καταφθεῖραι vb 1st aor act inf   id.

καταφθείρατε vb 1st aor act impv 2nd pers pl   id.

καταφθείρει vb pres act ind 3rd pers sg   id.

καταφθείρῃ vb pres act subj 3rd pers sg   id.

καταφθειρομένην vb pres m/p part fem acc sg   id.

καταφθείρω vb pres act ind 1st pers sg   id.

καταφθερῶ vb fut act ind 1st pers sg   id.

καταφθορά noun fem nom sg

καταφθοράν noun fem acc sg .... καταφθορά

καταφθορᾶς noun fem gen sg   id.

καταφιλῆσαι vb 1st aor act inf .... καταφιλέω

καταφιλήσας vb 1st aor act part masc nom sg   id.

καταφιλήσει vb fut act ind 3rd pers sg   id.

καταφιλήσω vb fut act ind 1st pers sg   id.

καταφλέγον vb pres act part neut

     nom and acc sg .... καταφλέγω

καταφλέγοντες vb pres act part masc nom pl   id.

καταφλέξῃ vb 1st aor act subj 3rd pers sg   id.

κατάφοβοι adj masc and fem nom pl .... κατάφοβος

καταφορᾷ noun fem dat sg .... καταφορά

καταφρασσόμενοι vb pres m/p part

     masc nom pl .... καταφράσσω

καταφρόνει vb pres act impv 2nd pers sg .... καταφρονέω

καταφρονεῖ vb pres act ind 3rd pers sg   id.

καταφρονεῖσθαι vb pres m/p inf   id.

καταφρονηθήσεται vb fut pass ind 3rd pers sg   id.

καταφρονηθῶμεν vb 1st aor pass subj 1st pers pl   id.

καταφρονήσαντες vb 1st aor act part masc nom pl   id.

καταφρονήσει vb fut act ind 3rd pers sg   id.

καταφρονήσεις vb fut act ind 2nd pers sg   id.

καταφρονήσῃς vb 1st aor act subj 2nd pers sg   id.

καταφρόνησιν noun fem acc sg .... καταφρόνησις

καταφρονηταί noun masc nom pl .... καταφρονητής

καταφρονητής noun masc nom sg   id.

καταφρονουμενου vb pres m/p part

     masc and neut gen sg .... καταφρονέω

καταφρονοῦντας vb pres act part masc acc pl   id.

καταφρονοῦντες vb pres act part masc nom pl   id.

καταφρονούντων vb pres act part masc and neut gen pl   id.

καταφρονῶν vb pres act part masc nom sg   id.

καταφυγεῖν vb 2nd aor act inf .... καταφεύγω

καταφυγή noun fem nom sg

καταφύγη vb 2nd aor act subj 3rd pers sg . . . . . καταφεύγω
καταφυγήν noun fem acc sg . . . . καταφυγή
καταφυγῆς noun fem gen sg id.
καταφυγοῦσα vb 2nd aor act part fem nom sg . . καταφεύγω
καταφυγῶν noun fem gen pl . . . . καταφυγή
καταφυτεύειν vb pres act inf . . . . καταφυτεύω
καταφυτεύεσθαι vb pres m/p inf id.
καταφυτεύσας vb 1st aor act part masc nom sg id.
καταφυτεύσετε vb fut act ind 2nd pers pl id.
καταφύτευσιν noun fem acc sg . . . . καταφύτευσις
καταφύτευσον vb 1st aor act impv

      2nd pers sg . . . . καταφυτεύω
καταφυτεύσουσιν vb fut act ind 3rd pers pl id.
καταφυτεύσω vb fut act ind 1st pers sg id.
καταχαροῦμαι vb fut mid ind 1st pers sg . . . . . καταχαίρω
καταχέει vb pres act ind 3rd pers sg . . . . καταχέω
καταχεῖν vb pres act inf id.
καταχθείησαν vb 1st aor pass opt 3rd pers pl . . . . . κατάγω
καταχθέντες vb 1st aor pass part masc nom pl id.
κατάχρεῳ adj dat sg . . . . κατάχρεος
καταχρίσας vb 1st aor act part masc nom sg . . . καταχρίω
καταχρύσεα translit
καταχρυσώσεις vb fut act ind 2nd pers sg . . καταχρυσόω
καταχρωμένων vb pres dep part gen pl . . . . . καταχράομαι
καταχρῶνται vb pres dep ind 3rd pers pl id.
κατάχυσις noun fem nom sg
καταχωρίσαι vb 1st aor act inf . . . . καταχωρίζω
καταχώσουσιν vb fut act ind 3rd pers pl . . . . καταχώννυμι
καταψευδόμενον vb pres m/p part masc acc sg,

      neut nom and acc sg . . . . καταψεύδω
καταψευσμόν noun masc acc sg . . . . καταψευσμός
καταψύξατε vb 1st aor act impv 2nd pers pl . . . καταψύχω
κατέαξαν vb 1st aor act ind 3rd pers pl . . . . . . κατάγνυμι
κατεάχθη vb 1st aor pass ind 3rd pers sg . . . . κατάγω
κατέβαινεν vb impf act ind 3rd pers sg . . . . . . καταβαίνω
κατέβαινον vb impf act ind 3rd pers pl id.
κατέβαλε(ν) vb 2nd aor act ind 3rd pers sg . . . καταβάλλω
κατέβαλες vb 2nd aor act ind 2nd pers sg id.
κατέβαλον vb 2nd aor act ind 3rd pers pl id.
κατεβαρύνετο vb impf m/p ind 3rd pers sg . . καταβαρύνω
κατέβη vb 2nd aor act ind 3rd pers sg . . . . καταβαίνω
κατέβημεν vb 2nd aor act ind 1st pers pl id.
κατέβην vb 2nd aor act ind 1st pers sg id.
κατέβης vb 2nd aor act ind 2nd pers sg id.
κατέβησαν vb 2nd aor act ind 3rd pers pl id.
κατεβιάζετο vb impf m/p ind 3rd pers sg . . . . . καταβιάζω
κατεβιάζοντο vb impf m/p ind 3rd pers pl id.
κατεβίβαζον vb impf act ind 1st pers sg . . . . . καταβιβάζω
κατεβίβασας vb 1st aor act ind 2nd pers sg id.
κατεβίβασεν vb 1st aor act ind 3rd pers sg id.
κατέβλεψαν vb 1st aor act ind 3rd pers pl . . . . . καταβλέπω
κατεβόησαν vb 1st aor act ind 3rd pers pl . . . . καταβοάω

κατεβρώθησαν vb 1st aor pass ind

      3rd pers pl . . . . καταβιβρώσκω
κατεγέλασαν vb 1st aor act ind 3rd pers pl . . . . καταγελάω
κατεγέλασεν vb 1st aor act ind 3rd pers sg id.
κατεγέλων vb impf act ind 3rd pers pl id.
κατεγινόμην vb impf dep ind 1st pers sg . . . . καταγίνομαι
κατεγίνοντο vb impf dep ind 3rd pers pl id.
κατέγνω vb 2nd aor act ind 3rd pers sg . . . . καταγινώσκω
κατεγράφη vb 2nd aor pass ind 3rd pers sg . . . . καταγράφω
κατέγραψαν vb 1st aor act ind 3rd pers pl id.
κατέγραψας vb 1st aor act ind 2nd pers sg id.
κατέγραψεν vb 1st aor act ind 3rd pers sg id.
κατεγχειρουμένοις vb pres m/p part

      masc and neut dat pl . . . . κατεγχειρέω
κατεδαμάσατε vb 1st aor act ind 2nd pers pl . καταδαμάζω
κατεδαπανήθημεν vb 1st aor pass ind

      1st pers pl . . . . καταδαπανάομαι
κατεδέετο vb impf m/p ind 3rd pers sg . . . . καταδέω
κατεδεήθης vb 1st aor pass ind 2nd pers sg id.
κατεδέθη vb 1st aor pass ind 3rd pers sg id.
κατέδειξεν vb 1st aor act ind 3rd pers sg . . . καταδείκνυμι
κατέδεσθε vb fut mid ind 2nd pers pl . . . . κατεσθίω
κατέδεται vb fut mid ind 3rd pers sg id.
κατεδήσατε vb 1st aor act ind 2nd pers pl . . . . καταδέω
κατεδήσατο vb 1st aor act mid ind 3rd pers sg id.
κατεδίωκον vb impf act ind 3rd pers pl . . . . καταδιώκω
κατεδίωξαν vb 1st aor act ind 3rd pers pl id.
κατεδίωξας vb 1st aor act ind 2nd pers sg id.
κατεδίωξεν vb 1st aor act ind 3rd pers sg id.
κατεδιώχθητε vb 1st aor pass ind 2nd pers pl id.
κατέδονται vb fut mid ind 3rd pers pl . . . . κατεσθίω
κατεδουλοῦντο vb impf m/p ind 3rd pers pl . . καταδουλόω
κατεδουλώσαντο vb 1st aor mid ind 3rd pers pl id.
κατεδουλώσατο vb 1st aor mid ind 3rd pers sg id.
κατέδραμεν vb 2nd aor act ind 3rd pers sg . . . . κατατρέχω
κατέδραμον vb 2nd aor act ind 3rd pers pl id.
κατεδυνάστευον vb impf act ind

      3rd pers pl . . . . καταδυναστεύω
κατεδυνάστευσα vb 1st aor act ind 1st pers sg id.
κατεδυνάστευσαν vb 1st aor act ind 3rd pers pl id.
κατεδυνάστευσας vb 1st aor act ind 2nd pers sg id.
κατεδυνάστευσεν vb 1st aor act ind 3rd pers sg id.
κατέδυσαν vb 1st aor act ind 3rd pers pl . . . . καταδύω
κατεθάρσησεν vb 1st aor act ind 3rd pers sg . . καταθαρσέω
κατέθεντο vb 2nd aor mid ind 3rd pers pl . . . . κατατίθημι
κατέθηκεν vb 2nd aor act ind 3rd pers sg id.
κατέθλασα vb 1st aor act ind 1st pers sg . . . . . . καταθλάω
κατειλημμένα vb perf m/p part

      neut nom and acc pl . . . . καταλαμβάνω
κατειλημμένη vb perf m/p part fem nom sg id.
κατειλημμένοις vb perf m/p part

      masc and neut dat pl id.

κατείπαντες vb 1st aor act part masc nom pl . . . . κατεῖπον
κατειργάσασθε vb 1st aor mid ind
    2nd pers pl . . . . κατεργάζομαι
κατειργάσατο vb 1st aor mid ind 3rd pers sg id.
κατειργάσθη vb 1st aor pass ind 3rd pers sg id.
κατειργασμένης vb perf dep part fem gen sg id.
κατειργάσω vb 1st aor mid ind 2nd pers sg id.
κατεκάησαν vb 2nd aor pass ind 3rd pers pl . . . . κατακαίω
κατεκαίετο vb impf m/p ind 3rd pers sg id.
κατέκαιον vb impf act ind 3rd pers pl id.
κατεκάλυπτον vb impf act ind 3rd pers pl . . κατακαλύπτω
κατεκαλύφθη vb 1st aor pass ind 3rd pers sg id.
κατεκάλυψα vb 1st aor act ind 1st pers sg id.
κατεκαλύψατο vb 1st aor mid ind 3rd pers sg id.
κατεκάλυψεν vb 1st aor act ind 3rd pers sg id.
κατεκάμφθην vb 1st aor pass ind 1st pers sg . κατακάμπτω
κατέκαμψαν vb 1st aor act ind 3rd pers pl id.
κατέκαυσα vb 1st aor act ind 1st pers sg . . . . . . κατακαίω
κατέκαυσαν vb 1st aor act ind 3rd pers pl id.
κατέκαυσας vb 1st aor act ind 2nd pers sg id.
κατέκαυσεν vb 1st aor act ind 3rd pers sg id.
κατεκαυχᾶσθε vb impf dep ind
    2nd pers pl . . . . κατακαυχάομαι
κατεκαυχῶντο vb impf dep ind 3rd pers pl id.
κατέκειτο vb impf m/p ind 3rd pers sg . . . . . . κατάκειμαι
κατεκέντησαν vb 1st aor act ind 3rd pers pl . . κατακεντέω
κατεκένωσεν vb 1st aor act ind 3rd pers sg . . . . κατακενόω
κατεκλάσθη vb 1st aor pass ind 3rd pers sg . . . . κατακλάω
κατέκλεισεν vb 1st aor act ind 3rd pers sg . . . . κατακλείω
κατεκλείσθη vb 1st aor pass ind 3rd pers sg id.
κατεκληρονομήθης vb 1st aor pass ind
    2nd pers sg . . . . κατακληρονομέω
κατεκληρονόμησα vb 1st aor act ind 1st pers sg id.
κατεκληρονόμησαν vb 1st aor act ind 3rd pers pl id.
κατεκληρονομήσατε vb 1st aor act ind 2nd pers pl id.
κατεκληρονόμησεν vb 1st aor act ind 3rd pers sg id.
κατεκλίθη vb 1st aor pass ind 3rd pers sg . . . . . κατακλίνω
κατέκλινεν vb impf act ind 3rd pers sg id.
κατέκλυσεν vb 1st aor act ind 3rd pers sg . . . . . κατακλύζω
κατεκλύσθησαν vb 1st aor pass ind 3rd pers pl id.
κατεκονδυλίζετε vb impf act ind
    2nd pers pl . . . . κατακονδυλίζω
κατεκόπησαν vb 1st aor act ind 3rd pers pl . . . κατακόπτω
κατέκοπτον vb impf act ind 3rd pers pl id.
κατεκόσμησαν vb 1st aor act ind 3rd pers pl . . κατακοσμέω
κατεκόσμησεν vb 1st aor act ind 3rd pers sg id.
κατέκοψαν vb 1st aor act ind 3rd pers pl . . . . . . κατακόπτω
κατέκοψε(ν) vb 1st aor act ind 3rd pers sg id.
κατεκρατήθη vb 1st aor pass ind 3rd pers sg . . κατακρατέω
κατεκρατήθησαν vb 1st aor pass ind 3rd pers pl id.
κατεκράτησαν vb 1st aor act ind 3rd pers pl id.
κατεκρατήσατε vb 1st aor act ind 2nd pers pl id.

κατεκράτησεν vb 1st aor act ind 3rd pers sg . . κατακρατέω
κατεκρημνιζον vb impf act ind 3rd pers pl . κατακρημνίζω
κατεκρήμνισεν vb 1st aor act ind 3rd pers sg id.
κατέκριναν vb 1st aor act ind 3rd pers pl . . . . . κατακρίνω
κατέκρινας vb 1st aor act ind 2nd pers sg id.
κατεκρίνατε vb 1st aor act ind 2nd pers pl id.
κατέκρινεν vb 1st aor act ind 3rd pers sg id.
κατέκρουσεν vb 1st aor act ind 3rd pers sg . . . κατακρούω
κατεκρύβησαν vb 2nd aor pass ind
    3rd pers pl . . . . κατακρύπτω
κατέκρυψαν vb 1st aor act ind 3rd pers pl id.
κατέκρυψας vb 1st aor act ind 2nd pers sg id.
κατέκρυψεν vb 1st aor act ind 3rd pers sg id.
κατεκυλίσθη vb 1st aor pass ind 3rd pers sg . . . κατακυλίω
κατεκυρίευσαν vb 1st aor act ind
    3rd pers pl . . . . κατακυριεύω
κατεκυριεύσατε vb 1st aor act ind 2nd pers pl id.
κατέκυψαν vb 1st aor act ind 3rd pers pl . . . . . . κατακύπτω
κατέλαβεν vb 2nd aor act ind 3rd pers sg . . καταλαμβάνω
κατέλαβες vb 2nd aor act ind 2nd pers sg id.
κατελάβεσθε vb 2nd aor mid ind 2nd pers pl id.
κατελάβετο vb 2nd aor mid ind 3rd pers sg id.
κατελάβομεν vb 2nd aor act ind 1st pers pl id.
κατελαβόμην vb 2nd aor mid ind 1st pers sg id.
κατέλαβον vb 2nd aor act ind 3rd pers pl id.
κατελάβοντο vb 2nd aor mid ind 3rd pers pl id.
κατελάβοσαν vb 2nd aor act ind 3rd pers pl id.
κατελάλει vb impf act ind 3rd pers sg . . . . καταλαλέω
κατελάλεις vb impf act ind 2nd pers sg id.
κατελαλήσαμεν vb 1st aor act ind 1st pers pl id.
κατελάλησαν vb 1st aor act ind 3rd pers pl id.
κατελάλουν vb impf act ind 3rd pers pl id.
κατελάμπετο vb impf m/p ind 3rd pers sg . . . . καταλάμπω
κατελεήσατε vb 1st aor act impv 2nd pers pl . . . . κατελεέω
κατελείφθη vb 1st aor pass ind 3rd pers sg . . . . καταλείπω
κατελείφθημεν vb 1st aor pass ind 1st pers pl id.
κατελείφθην vb 1st aor pass ind 1st pers sg id.
κατελείφθησαν vb 1st aor pass ind 3rd pers pl id.
κατελήμφθη vb 1st aor pass ind 3rd pers sg . καταλαμβάνω
κατελθόντας vb 2nd aor act part masc acc pl . . κατέρχομαι
κατελθόντες vb 2nd aor act part masc nom pl id.
κατελθοῦσα vb 2nd aor act part fem nom sg id.
κατέλιπεν vb 2nd aor act ind 3rd pers sg . . . . . . καταλείπω
κατέλιπες vb 2nd aor act ind 2nd pers sg id.
κατελίπομεν vb 2nd aor act ind 1st pers pl id.
κατέλιπον vb 2nd aor act ind 1st pers sg and 3rd pers pl id.
κατελίποσαν vb 2nd aor act ind 3rd pers pl id.
κατελογίσθη vb 1st aor pass ind
    3rd pers sg . . . . καταλογίζομαι
κατελογίσθης vb 1st aor pass ind 2nd pers sg id.
κατέλυεν vb impf act ind 3rd pers sg . . . . καταλύω
κατελύθης vb 1st aor pass ind 2nd pers sg id.

κατέλυον vb impf act ind 3rd pers pl . . . . καταλύω
κατέλυσαν vb 1st aor act ind 3rd pers pl   id.
κατέλυσας vb 1st aor act ind 2nd pers sg   id.
κατέλυσε(ν) vb 1st aor act ind 3rd pers sg   id.
κατέμαθον vb 2nd aor act ind 1st pers sg . . . καταμανθάνω
κατεμάνθανεν vb impf act ind 3rd pers sg   id.
κατεμαρτύρησαν vb 1st aor act ind

    3rd pers pl . . . . καταμαρτυρέω
κατεμβλέψαι vb 1st aor act inf . . . . καταμβλέπω
κατεμείναμεν vb 1st aor act ind 1st pers pl . . . . . καταμένω
κατέμειναν vb 1st aor act ind 3rd pers pl   id.
κατέμεινεν vb 1st aor act ind 3rd pers sg   id.
κατεμερίσαντο vb 1st aor mid ind 3rd pers pl . καταμερίζω
κατεμέρισεν vb 1st aor act ind 3rd pers sg   id.
κατεμετρήθη vb 1st aor pass ind 3rd pers sg . . καταμετρέω
κατεμήνυσε vb 1st aor act ind 3rd pers sg . . . . καταμηνύω
κατέναντι adverb and preposition
κατεναντίον adverb and preposition
κατενέγκη vb 1st aor act subj 3rd pers sg . . . . καταφέρω
κατένεγκον vb 1st aor act impv 2nd pers sg   id.
κατενεμήσατο vb 1st aor mid ind 3rd pers sg . . . κατανέμω
κατενόησα vb 1st aor act ind 1st pers sg . . . . κατανοέω
κατενόησαν vb 1st aor act ind 3rd pers pl   id.
κατενόησεν vb 1st aor act ind 3rd pers sg   id.
κατενόουν vb impf act ind 1st pers sg and 3rd pers pl   id.
κατενοοῦσαν vb impf act ind 3rd pers pl   id.
κατεντευκτήν noun masc acc sg . . . . κατεντευκτής
κατενύγη vb 2nd aor pass ind 3rd pers sg . . . . . κατανύσσω
κατενύγην vb 2nd aor pass ind 1st pers sg   id.
κατενύγησαν vb 2nd aor pass ind 3rd pers pl   id.
κατενύχθη vb 1st aor pass ind 3rd pers sg   id.
κατενύχθησαν vb 1st aor pass ind 3rd pers pl   id.
κατενώπιον preposition
κατενωτίσαντο vb 1st aor mid ind

    3rd pers pl . . . . κατανωτίζομαι
κατέξανεν vb 1st aor act ind 3rd pers sg . . . . . . καταξαίνω
κατεξήρανεν vb 1st aor act ind 3rd pers sg . . καταξηραίνω
κατεξυσμένη vb perf m/p part fem nom sg . . . . . . καταξύω
κατέπαιζον vb impf act ind 3rd pers pl . . . . καταπαίζω
κατεπανουργεύσαντο vb 1st aor mid ind

    3rd pers pl . . . . καταπανουργεύομαι
κατεπάσατο vb 1st aor mid ind 3rd pers sg . . . καταπάσσω
κατεπάτεις vb impf act ind 2nd pers sg . . . . . . καταπατέω
κατεπατεῖτε vb impf act ind 2nd pers pl   id.
κατεπατήθη vb 1st aor pass ind 3rd pers sg   id.
κατεπάτησα vb 1st aor act ind 1st pers sg   id.
κατεπατήσαμεν vb 1st aor act ind 1st pers pl   id.
κατεπάτησαν vb 1st aor act ind 3rd pers pl   id.
κατεπάτησεν vb 1st aor act ind 3rd pers sg   id.
κατεπάτουν vb impf act ind 3rd pers pl   id.
κατεπατοῦσαν vb impf act ind 3rd pers pl   id.
κατέπαυον vb impf act ind 3rd pers pl . . . . καταπαύω

κατέπαυσαν vb 1st aor act ind 3rd pers pl . . . . . καταπαύω
κατέπαυσας vb 1st aor act ind 2nd pers sg   id.
κατέπαυσεν vb 1st aor act ind 3rd pers sg   id.
κατεπείγων vb pres act part masc nom sg . . . . . . κατεπείγω
κατεπείρασεν vb 1st aor act ind 3rd pers sg . καταπειράζω
κατεπέκυψεν vb 1st aor act ind 3rd pers sg . . κατεπικύπτω
κατεπένθησαν vb 1st aor act ind 3rd pers pl . . καταπενθέω
κατέπεσον vb 2nd aor act ind 3rd pers pl . . . . . καταπίπτω
κατεπήδησεν vb 1st aor act ind 3rd pers sg . . . καταπηδάω
κατέπηξαν vb 1st aor act ind 3rd pers pl . . . καταπήγνυμι
κατέπιεν vb 2nd aor act ind 3rd pers sg . . . . καταπίνω
κατεπίθυμος adj masc and fem nom sg
κατεπίομεν vb 2nd aor act ind 1st pers pl . . . . . καταπίνω
κατέπιον vb 2nd aor act ind 3rd pers pl   id.
κατεπλάγησαν vb 2nd aor pass ind

    3rd pers pl . . . . καταπλήσσω
κατεπόθη vb 1st aor pass ind 3rd pers sg . . . . . . καταπίνω
κατεπόθησαν vb 1st aor pass ind 3rd pers pl   id.
κατεπόντισεν vb 1st aor act ind 3rd pers sg . καταποντίζω
κατεπράυνεν vb 1st aor act ind 3rd pers sg . . καταπραΰνω
κατεπρονόμευσαν vb 1st aor act ind

    3rd pers pl . . . . καταπρονομεύω
κατέπτηκεν vb perf act ind 3rd pers sg . . . . . καταπτήσσω
κάτεργα noun neut nom and acc pl . . . . κάτεργον
κατεργᾷ vb fut mid ind 2nd pers sg . . . . κατεργάζομαι
κατεργάζεσθαι vb pres dep inf   id.
κατεργάζεται vb pres dep ind 3rd pers sg   id.
κατεργάζονται vb pres dep ind 3rd pers pl   id.
κατεργασθήσεσθε vb fut pass ind 2nd pers pl   id.
κατεργασίας noun fem gen sg . . . . κατεργασία
κάτεργον noun neut nom and acc sg
κατερραγμένους vb perf m/p part

    masc acc pl . . . . καταρρήγνυμι
κατέρραξαν vb 1st aor act ind 3rd pers pl . . . καταρράσσω
κατέρραξας vb 1st aor act ind 2nd pers sg   id.
κατέρραξεν vb 1st aor act ind 3rd pers sg   id.
κατέρρει vb pres act ind 3rd pers sg . . . . καταρρέω
κατερρεῖτο vb impf m/p ind 3rd pers sg   id.
κατέρριψεν vb 1st aor act ind 3rd pers sg . . . . καταρρίπτω
κατερρόμβευσεν vb 1st aor act ind

    3rd pers sg . . . . καταρομβεύω
κατερρύηκεν vb perf act ind 3rd pers sg . . . . καταρρέω
κατερρωγότας vb perf act part masc acc pl . καταρρήγνυμι
κατέσβεσεν vb 1st aor act ind 3rd pers sg . . κατασβέννυμι
κατέσησαν vb 1st aor act ind 3rd pers pl . . . . . . κατασείω
κατέσθετε vb pres act ind 2nd pers pl . . . . κατέσθω
κατέσθη vb pres act subj 3rd pers sg   id.
κατεσθίει vb pres act ind 3rd pers sg . . . . κατεσθίω
κατεσθίειν vb pres act inf   id.
κατεσθιέτωσαν vb pres act impv 3rd pers pl   id.
κατεσθίοντας vb pres act part masc acc pl   id.
κατεσθίοντες vb pres act part masc nom pl   id.

κατεσθίουσα vb pres act part fem nom sg ...... κατεσθίω

κατεσθιούσης vb pres act part fem gen sg   id.

κατεσθίουσιν vb pres act ind 3rd pers pl   id.

κατεσθίων vb pres act part masc nom sg   id.

κατεσθόντων vb pres act part

    masc and neut gen pl .... κατέσθω

κατέσθουσα vb pres act part fem nom sg   id.

κατέσθων vb pres act part masc nom sg   id.

κατεσιώπησεν vb 1st aor act ind 3rd pers sg .. κατασιωπάω

κατεσιώπων vb impf act ind 3rd pers pl   id.

κατεσκαμμένα vb perf m/p part

    neut nom and acc pl .... κατασκάπτω

κατεσκαμμέναι vb perf m/p part fem nom pl   id.

κατεσκαμμένον vb perf m/p part neut nom and acc sg   id.

κατεσκάφη vb 2nd aor pass ind 3rd pers sg   id.

κατεσκάφησαν vb 2nd aor pass ind 3rd pers pl   id.

κατέσκαψαν vb 1st aor act ind 3rd pers pl   id.

κατέσκαψεν vb 1st aor act ind 3rd pers sg   id.

κατεσκέδασεν vb 1st aor act ind

    3rd pers sg .... κατασκεδάζω

κατεσκεύαζον vb impf act ind 3rd pers pl ... κατασκευάζω

κατεσκεύασα vb 1st aor act ind 1st pers sg   id.

κατεσκεύασας vb 1st aor act ind 2nd pers sg   id.

κατεσκεύασεν vb 1st aor act ind 3rd pers sg   id.

κατεσκευασμένα vb perf m/p part neut nom and acc pl id.

κατεσκεύασται vb perf m/p ind 3rd pers sg   id.

κατεσκεψάμεθα vb 1st aor mid ind

    1st pers pl .... κατασκέπτομαι

κατεσκεψάμην vb 1st aor mid ind 1st pers sg   id.

κατεσκέψαντο vb 1st aor mid ind 3rd pers pl   id.

κατεσκέψασθε vb 1st aor mid ind 2nd pers pl   id.

κατεσκήνουν vb impf act ind 1st pers sg

    and 3rd pers pl .... κατασκηνόω

κατεσκήνωσα vb 1st aor act ind 1st pers sg   id.

κατεσκήνωσαν vb 1st aor act ind 3rd pers pl   id.

κατεσκήνωσας vb 1st aor act ind 2nd pers sg   id.

κατεσκήνωσεν vb 1st aor act ind 3rd pers sg   id.

κατεσκόπευεν vb impf act ind 3rd pers sg ... κατασκοπεύω

κατεσκόπευσαν vb 1st aor act ind 3rd pers pl   id.

κατεσμικρύνθη vb 1st aor pass ind

    3rd pers sg .... κατασμικρύνω

κατεσοφίσατο vb 1st aor mid ind

    3rd pers sg .... κατασοφίζομαι

κατέσπασα vb 1st aor act ind 1st pers sg ...... κατασπάω

κατέσπασαν vb 1st aor act ind 3rd pers pl   id.

κατέσπασεν vb 1st aor act ind 3rd pers sg   id.

κατεσπάσθη vb 1st aor pass ind 3rd pers sg   id.

κατεσπείροντο vb impf m/p ind 3rd pers pl .. κατασπείρω

κατέσπευδεν vb impf act ind 3rd pers sg ..... κατασπεύδω

κατέσπευδον vb impf act ind 3rd pers pl   id.

κατέσπευσαν vb 1st aor act ind 3rd pers pl   id.

κατέσπευσεν vb 1st aor act ind 3rd pers sg   id.

κατεστάθη vb 1st aor pass ind 3rd pers sg ..... καθίστημι

κατεστάθην vb 1st aor pass ind 1st pers sg   id.

κατέστακα vb perf act ind 1st pers sg   id.

κατεστεμμένοι vb perf mid part masc nom pl .. καταστέφω

κατεστέναξαν vb 1st aor act ind 3rd pers pl . καταστενάζω

κατέστη vb 2nd aor act ind 3rd pers sg ...... καθίστημι

κατεστηρίχθαι vb perf m/p inf .... καταστηρίζω

κατέστησα vb 1st aor act ind 1st pers sg ...... καθίστημι

κατέστησαν vb 1st aor act ind 3rd pers pl   id.

κατέστησας vb 1st aor act ind 2nd pers sg   id.

κατέστησε(ν) vb 1st aor act ind 3rd pers sg   id.

κατεστραμμένη vb perf m/p part fem nom sg . καταστρέφω

κατεστραμμένης vb perf m/p part fem gen sg   id.

κατέστραπται vb perf m/p ind 3rd pers sg   id.

κατεστρατοπέδευσαν vb 1st aor act ind

    3rd pers pl .... καταστρατοπεδεύω

κατεστρατοπέδευσεν vb 1st aor act ind 3rd pers sg   id.

κατεστράφη vb 2nd aor pass ind 3rd pers sg .. καταστρέφω

κατέστρεψα vb 1st aor act ind 1st pers sg   id.

κατέστρεψας vb 1st aor act ind 2nd pers sg   id.

κατέστρεψε(ν) vb 1st aor act ind 3rd pers sg   id.

κατέστρωσαν vb 1st aor act ind

    3rd pers pl .... καταστρώννυμι

κατέστρωσεν vb 1st aor act ind 3rd pers sg   id.

κατέσυρα vb 1st aor act ind 1st pers sg .... κατασύρω

κατεσφάγησαν vb 2nd aor pass ind 3rd pers pl   κατασφάζω

κατέσφαζον vb impf act ind 3rd pers pl   id.

κατέσφαξαν vb 1st aor act ind 3rd pers pl   id.

κατέσφαξεν vb 1st aor act ind 3rd pers sg   id.

κατεσφραγίσθη vb 1st aor pass ind

    3rd pers sg .... κατασφραγίζω

κατεσχέθη vb 1st aor pass ind 3rd pers sg .... κατέχω

κατέσχεν vb 2nd aor act ind 3rd pers sg   id.

κατέσχον vb 2nd aor act ind 1st pers sg

    and 3rd pers pl   id.

κατέσχοσαν vb 2nd aor act ind 3rd pers pl   id.

κατέταξας vb 1st aor act ind 2nd pers sg ..... κατατάσσω

κατετέμνοντο vb impf m/p ind 3rd pers pl .... κατατέμνω

κατέτιλα vb 1st aor act ind 3rd pers sg ...... κατατίλλω

κατετιτρώσκετο vb impf m/p ind

    3rd pers sg .... κατατιτρώσκω

κατετόλμησεν vb 1st aor act ind 3rd pers sg . κατατολμάω

κατετόξευσαν vb 1st aor act ind 3rd pers pl .. κατατοξεύω

κατετρίβη vb 2nd aor pass ind 3rd pers sg ..... κατατρίβω

κατευθικτήσας vb 1st aor act part

    masc nom sg .... κατευθικτέω

κατεύθυνα vb 1st aor act ind 1st pers sg ...... κατευθύνω

κατευθύναι vb 1st aor act opt 3rd pers sg   id.

κατευθῦναι vb 1st aor act inf   id.

κατεύθυναν vb 1st aor act ind 3rd pers pl   id.

κατευθύναντος vb 1st aor act part masc and neut gen sg id.

κατευθύνατε vb 1st aor act impv 2nd pers pl   id.

κατεύθυνε vb pres act impv 2nd pers sg ..... κατευθύνω

κατευθύνει vb pres act ind 3rd pers sg   id.

κατευθυνεῖ vb fut act ind 3rd pers sg   id.

κατευθύνειν vb pres act inf   id.

κατευθυνεῖς vb fut act ind 2nd pers sg   id.

κατεύθυνεν vb impf act ind 3rd pers sg,

       1st aor act ind 3rd pers sg   id.

κατευθύνεται vb pres m/p ind 3rd pers sg   id.

κατευθύνῃ vb 1st aor act subj 3rd pers sg,

       pres act subj 3rd pers sg   id.

κατευθυνθείησαν vb 1st aor pass opt 3rd pers pl   id.

κατευθύνθη vb 1st aor pass ind 3rd pers sg   id.

κατευθυνθήσεται vb fut pass ind 3rd pers sg   id.

κατευθυνθήτω vb 1st aor pass impv 3rd pers sg   id.

κατευθυνομένην vb pres m/p part fem acc sg   id.

κατεύθυνον vb 1st aor act impv 2nd pers sg   id.

κατευθύνονται vb pres m/p ind 3rd pers pl   id.

κατευθύνοντας vb pres act part masc acc pl   id.

κατευθύνοντος vb pres act part masc and neut gen sg   id.

κατευθυνόντων vb pres act part masc and neut gen pl   id.

κατευθύνουσα vb pres act part fem nom sg   id.

κατευθυνούσης vb pres act part fem gen sg   id.

κατευθυνοῦσιν vb fut act ind 3rd pers pl   id.

κατευθύνων vb pres act part masc nom sg   id.

κατευθύνωσιν vb 1st aor act subj 3rd pers pl,

       pres act subj 3rd pers pl   id.

κατευλόγει vb impf act ind 3rd pers sg ...... κατευλογέω

κατευλόγησεν vb 1st aor act ind 3rd pers sg   id.

κατευξάμενος vb 1st aor mid

       part masc nom sg .... κατεύχομαι

κατευοδοῖ vb pres act ind 3rd pers sg .... κατευοδόω

κατευοδοῦ vb pres act impv 2nd pers sg   id.

κατευοδουμένῳ vb pres m/p part masc and neut dat sg   id.

κατευοδοῦνται vb pres m/p ind 3rd pers pl   id.

κατευοδώθη vb 1st aor pass ind 3rd pers sg   id.

κατευοδωθήσεται vb fut pass ind 3rd pers sg   id.

κατευοδώσει vb fut act ind 3rd pers sg   id.

κατευφημήσαντες vb 1st aor act part

       masc nom pl .... κατευφημέω

κατεύχεσθαι vb pres dep inf .... κατεύχομαι

κατέφαγε(ν) vb 2nd aor act ind 3rd pers sg ..... κατεσθίω

κατέφαγον vb 2nd aor act ind 3rd pers pl   id.

κατεφάγοσαν vb 2nd aor act ind 3rd pers pl   id.

κατεφάνη vb 2nd aor pass ind 3rd pers sg .... καταφαίνω

κατεφέρετο vb impf m/p ind 3rd pers sg ...... καταφέρω

κατεφθάρησαν vb 2nd aor pass ind

       3rd pers pl .... καταφθείρω

κατεφθάρκατε vb perf act ind 2nd pers pl   id.

κατεφθαρκότας vb perf act part masc acc pl   id.

κατεφθαρμένη vb perf m/p part fem nom sg   id.

κατέφθασεν vb 1st aor act ind 3rd pers sg .... καταφθάνω

κατέφθειραν vb 1st aor act ind 3rd pers pl .... καταφθείρω

κατέφθειρε(ν) vb impf act ind 3rd pers sg,

       1st aor act ind 3rd pers sg .... καταφθείρω

κατεφθείρετο vb impf m/p ind 3rd pers sg   id.

κατεφίλησαν vb 1st aor act ind 3rd pers pl .... καταφιλέω

κατεφίλησεν vb 1st aor act ind 3rd pers sg   id.

κατεφίλουν vb impf act ind 3rd pers pl   id.

κατέφλεγεν vb impf act ind 3rd pers sg ...... καταφλέγω

κατέφλεξας vb 1st aor act ind 2nd pers sg   id.

κατέφλεξεν vb 1st aor act ind 3rd pers sg   id.

κατεφλόγισεν vb 1st aor act ind 3rd pers sg . καταφλογίζω

κατεφρονεῖτο vb impf m/p ind 3rd pers sg ... καταφρονέω

κατεφρόνησαν vb 1st aor act ind 3rd pers pl   id.

κατεφρόνησας vb 1st aor act ind 2nd pers sg   id.

κατεφρόνησεν vb 1st aor act ind 3rd pers sg   id.

κατεφρόνουν vb impf act ind 3rd pers pl   id.

κατέφυγα vb 1st aor act ind 1st pers sg ...... καταφεύγω

κατέφυγεν vb 2nd aor act ind 3rd pers sg   id.

κατεφύγομεν vb 2nd aor act ind 1st pers pl   id.

κατέφυγον vb 2nd aor act ind 1st pers sg   id.

κατεφύγοσαν vb 2nd aor act ind 3rd pers pl   id.

κατεφύτευσα vb 1st aor act ind 1st pers sg ... καταφυτεύω

κατεφύτευσας vb 1st aor act ind 2nd pers sg   id.

κατεφύτευσεν vb 1st aor act ind 3rd pers sg   id.

κατεχάλασεν vb 1st aor act ind 3rd pers sg ... καταχαλάω

κατέχεας vb 1st aor act ind 2nd pers sg .... καταχέω

κατέχεεν vb impf act ind 3rd pers sg   id.

κατέχει vb pres act ind 3rd pers sg .... κατέχω

κατέχεον vb impf act ind 3rd pers pl .... καταχέω

κατέχετε vb pres act ind 2nd pers pl .... κατέχω

κατεχόμενος vb pres m/p part masc nom sg   id.

κατέχοντα vb pres act part masc acc sg   id.

κατέχονται vb pres m/p ind 3rd pers pl   id.

κατέχοντες vb pres act part masc nom pl   id.

κατεχρήσαντο vb 1st aor mid ind

       3rd pers pl .... καταχράομαι

κατέχρισεν vb 1st aor act ind 3rd pers sg ...... καταχρίω

κατεχρύσωσαν vb 1st aor act ind 3rd pers pl . καταχρυσόω

κατεχρύσωσεν vb 1st aor act ind 3rd pers sg   id.

κατέχων vb pres act part masc nom sg ...... κατέχω

κατεχωρίσθη vb 1st aor pass ind 3rd pers sg .. καταχωρίζω

κατήγαγεν vb 2nd aor act ind 3rd pers sg .... κατάγω

κατήγαγες vb 2nd aor act ind 2nd pers sg   id.

κατήγαγον vb 2nd aor act ind 1st pers sg

       and 3rd pers pl   id.

κατήγγελλεν vb impf act ind 3rd pers sg ..... καταγγέλλω

κατηγορημένων vb perf m/p part gen pl ...... κατηγορέω

κατηγόρησαν vb 1st aor act ind 3rd pers pl   id.

κατηγόρησεν vb 1st aor act ind 3rd pers sg   id.

κατηγορήσουσιν vb fut act ind 3rd pers pl   id.

κατήγορος noun masc nom sg

κατηγορούμενος vb pres m/p part

       masc nom sg .... κατηγορέω

κατήκιζον vb impf act ind 3rd pers pl . . . . καταικίζω

κατηκόντισεν vb 1st aor act ind 3rd pers sg . κατακοντίζω

κατήλεσεν vb 1st aor act ind 3rd pers sg . . . . καταλέω

κατήλθον vb 2nd aor act ind 1st pers sg

    and 3rd pers pl . . . . κατέρχομαι

κατήλλαξεν vb 1st aor act ind 3rd pers sg . . . καταλλάσσω

κατήνεγκαν vb 1st aor act ind 3rd pers pl . . . . . . καταφέρω

κατήνεγκεν vb 1st aor act ind 3rd pers sg   id.

κατηνέχθη vb 1st aor pass ind 3rd pers sg   id.

κατήντησεν vb 1st aor act ind 3rd pers sg . . . . . καταντάω

κατηξιώθησαν vb 1st aor pass ind 3rd pers pl . . . καταξιόω

κατηραμένην vb perf dep part fem acc sg . . . . καταράομαι

κατηραμένον vb perf dep part masc acc sg,

    neut nom and acc sg   id.

κατηρασάμην vb 1st aor mid ind 1st pers sg   id.

κατηράσαντο vb 1st aor mid ind 3rd pers pl   id.

κατηράσατο vb 1st aor mid ind 3rd pers sg   id.

κατηράσω vb 1st aor mid ind 2nd pers sg   id.

κατήργησαν vb 1st aor act ind 3rd pers pl . . . . . . καταργέω

κατηργυρωμένοι vb perf m/p part

    masc nom pl . . . . καταργυρόω

κατηριθμημένοι vb perf m/p part

    masc nom pl . . . . καταριθμέω

κατῆρξαν vb 1st aor act ind 3rd pers pl . . . . κατάρχω

κατήρξατο vb 1st aor mid ind 3rd pers sg   id.

κατηρτίσαντο vb 1st aor mid ind 3rd pers pl . . . καταρτίζω

κατηρτίσατο vb 1st aor mid ind 3rd pers sg   id.

κατηρτισμένη vb perf m/p part fem nom sg   id.

κατηρτισμένοι vb perf m/p part masc nom pl   id.

κατηρτίσω vb 1st aor mid ind 2nd pers sg   id.

κατηρῶντο vb impf dep ind 3rd pers pl . . . . . . καταράομαι

κατήσθιεν vb impf act ind 3rd pers sg . . . . κατεσθίω

κατησφαλίσαντο vb 1st aor mid ind

    3rd pers pl . . . . κατασφαλίζω

κατησφαλισμένοι vb perf m/p part

    masc nom pl   id.

κατησχυμμένος vb perf m/p part

    masc nom sg . . . . καταισχύνω

κατήσχυνας vb 1st aor act ind 2nd pers sg   id.

κατησχύνατε vb 1st aor act ind 2nd pers pl   id.

κατήσχυνεν vb impf act ind 3rd pers sg   id.

κατησχύνθη vb 1st aor pass ind 3rd pers sg   id.

κατησχύνθημεν vb 1st aor pass ind 1st pers pl   id.

κατησχύνθης vb 1st aor pass ind 2nd pers sg   id.

κατησχύνθησαν vb 1st aor pass ind 3rd pers pl   id.

κατήσχυνται vb perf m/p ind 3rd pers pl   id.

κατηύγαζεν vb impf act ind 3rd pers sg . . . . . . καταυγάζω

κατηύθυναν vb 1st aor act ind 3rd pers pl . . . . . κατευθύνω

κατηύθυνας vb 1st aor act ind 2nd pers sg   id.

κατηύθυνεν vb 1st aor act ind 3rd pers sg   id.

κατηφῆ adj neut nom and acc pl . . . . κατηφής

κατήχθη vb 1st aor pass ind 3rd pers sg . . . . κατάγω

κατήχθησαν vb 1st aor pass ind 3rd pers pl . . . . . . κατάγω

κάτιδε vb 2nd aor act impv 2nd pers sg . . . . καθοράω

κατιδεῖν vb 2nd aor act inf   id.

κατίσχυε vb pres act impv 2nd pers sg . . . . κατισχύω

κατίσχυε vb pres act ind 3rd pers sg   id.

κατίσχυεν vb impf act ind 3rd pers sg   id.

κατισχύετε vb pres act impv 2nd pers pl,

    pres act ind 2nd pers pl   id.

κατισχυέτω vb pres act impv 3rd pers sg   id.

κατισχυέτωσαν vb pres act impv 3rd pers pl   id.

κατίσχυον vb impf act ind 3rd pers pl   id.

κατισχύοντες vb pres act part masc nom pl   id.

κατισχυόντων vb pres act part masc and neut gen pl id.

κατισχύουσιν vb pres act ind 3rd pers pl   id.

κατίσχυσα vb 1st aor act ind 1st pers sg   id.

κατισχύσαι vb 1st aor act opt 3rd pers sg   id.

κατισχῦσαι vb 1st aor act inf   id.

κατίσχυσαν vb 1st aor act ind 3rd pers pl,

    1st aor act part neut nom and acc sg   id.

κατισχύσαντας vb 1st aor act part masc acc pl   id.

κατισχύσας vb 1st aor act part masc nom sg   id.

κατισχύσατε vb 1st aor act impv 2nd pers pl   id.

κατισχυσάτω vb 1st aor act impv 3rd pers sg   id.

κατίσχυσε(ν) vb 1st aor act ind 3rd pers sg   id.

κατισχύσει vb fut act ind 3rd pers sg   id.

κατισχύσῃ vb 1st aor act subj 3rd pers sg   id.

κατισχύσητε vb 1st aor act subj 2nd pers pl   id.

κατισχύσον vb 1st aor act impv 2nd pers sg   id.

κατισχύσουσι(ν) vb fut act ind 3rd pers pl   id.

κατισχύσω vb fut act ind 1st pers sg   id.

κατισχύσωσιν vb 1st aor act subj 3rd pers pl   id.

κατισχύων vb pres act part masc nom sg   id.

κατίωσεν vb 1st aor act ind 3rd pers sg . . . . κατιόω

κατοίκει vb pres act impv 2nd pers sg . . . . κατοικέω

κατοικεῖ vb pres act ind 3rd pers sg   id.

κατοικεῖν vb pres act inf   id.

κατοικεῖς vb pres act ind 2nd pers sg   id.

κατοικεῖσθαι vb pres m/p inf   id.

κατοικεῖται vb pres m/p ind 3rd pers sg   id.

κατοικεῖτε vb pres act impv 2nd pers pl,

    pres act ind 2nd pers pl   id.

κατοικείτω vb pres act impv 3rd pers sg   id.

κατοικείτωσαν vb pres act impv 3rd pers pl   id.

κατοικεσίας noun fem gen sg . . . . κατοικεσία

κατοικηθῇ vb 1st aor pass subj 3rd pers sg . . . . . κατοικέω

κατοικηθῇς vb 1st aor pass subj 2nd pers sg   id.

κατοικηθήσεται vb fut pass ind 3rd pers sg   id.

κατοικηθήσῃ vb fut pass ind 2nd pers sg   id.

κατοικηθησομένας vb fut pass part fem acc pl   id.

κατοικηθήσονται vb fut pass ind 3rd pers pl   id.

κατοικηθῶσιν vb 1st aor pass subj 3rd pers pl   id.

κατοικῆσαι vb 1st aor act inf   id.

κατοικήσαντα vb 1st aor act part masc acc sg . . . κατοικέω
κατοικήσαντες vb 1st aor act part masc nom pl id.
κατοικήσας vb 1st aor act part masc nom sg id.
κατοικήσατε vb 1st aor act impv 2nd pers pl id.
κατοικησάτω vb 1st aor act impv 3rd pers sg id.
κατοικήσει noun fem dat sg . . . . κατοίκησις
κατοικήσει vb fut act ind 3rd pers sg . . . . κατοικέω
κατοικήσεις vb fut act ind 2nd pers sg id.
κατοικήσετε vb fut act ind 2nd pers pl id.
κατοικήσεως noun fem gen sg . . . . κατοίκησις
κατοικήσῃ vb 1st aor act subj 3rd pers sg,
  fut mid ind 2nd pers sg . . . . κατοικέω
κατοικήσῃς vb 1st aor act subj 2nd pers sg id.
κατοικήσητε vb 1st aor act subj 2nd pers pl id.
κατοίκησις noun fem nom sg
κατοικήσομεν vb fut act ind 1st pers pl . . . . . . κατοικέω
κατοίκησον vb 1st aor act impv 2nd pers sg id.
κατοικήσουσιν vb fut act ind 3rd pers pl id.
κατοικήσω vb 1st aor act subj 1st pers sg,
  fut act ind 1st pers sg id.
κατοικήσωσιν vb 1st aor act subj 3rd pers pl id.
κατοικητήριον noun neut nom and acc sg
κατοικητηρίου noun neut gen sg . . . . κατοικητήριον
κατοικητηρίῳ noun neut dat sg id.
κατοικία noun fem nom sg
κατοικίᾳ noun fem dat sg . . . . κατοικία
κατοικίαι noun fem nom pl id.
κατοικίαις noun fem dat pl id.
κατοικίαν noun fem acc sg id.
κατοικίας noun fem gen sg and acc pl id.
κατοικιεῖ vb fut act ind 3rd pers sg . . . . κατοικίζω
κατοικιεῖς vb fut act ind 2nd pers sg id.
κατοικίζει vb pres act ind 3rd pers sg id.
κατοικίζων vb pres act part masc nom sg id.
κατοικίσαι vb 1st aor act inf id.
κατοικισθῆναι vb 1st aor pass inf id.
κατοικισθήσεται vb fut pass ind 3rd pers sg id.
κατοίκισον vb 1st aor act impv 2nd pers sg id.
κατοικίσω vb fut act ind 1st pers sg id.
κατοικιῶ vb fut act ind 1st pers sg id.
κατοικιῶν noun fem gen pl . . . . κατοικία
κάτοικοι noun masc nom pl . . . . κάτοικος
κατοικούμεναι vb pres m/p part fem nom pl . . . . κατοικέω
κατοικουμένας vb pres m/p part fem acc pl id.
κατοικουμένη vb pres m/p part fem nom sg id.
κατοικουμένην vb pres m/p part fem acc sg id.
κατοικουμένης vb pres m/p part fem gen sg id.
κατοικούμενον vb pres m/p part masc acc sg,
  neut nom and acc sg id.
κατοικοῦν vb pres act part neut nom and acc sg id.
κατοικοῦντα vb pres act part masc acc sg,
  neut nom and acc pl id.

κατοικοῦντας vb pres act part masc acc pl . . . . . κατοικέω
κατοικοῦντες vb pres act part masc nom pl id.
κατοικοῦντι vb pres act part masc and neut dat sg id.
κατοικοῦντος vb pres act part masc and neut gen sg id.
κατοικούντων vb pres act part masc and neut gen pl id.
κατοικοῦσα vb pres act part fem nom sg id.
κατοικούσῃ vb pres act part fem dat sg id.
κατοικοῦσι(ν) vb pres act ind 3rd pers pl,
  pres act part masc and neut dat pl id.
κατοικτίρας vb 1st aor act part masc nom sg . . κατοικτείρω
κατοικτίρωμεν vb 1st aor act subj 1st pers pl id.
κατοικῶ vb pres act ind 1st pers sg . . . . κατοικέω
κατοίκων noun masc gen pl . . . . κάτοικος
κατοικῶν vb pres act part masc nom sg . . . . κατοικέω
κατοικῶσιν vb pres act subj 3rd pers pl id.
κατοινωμένος vb pres m/p part masc nom sg . . . . κατοινόω
κατόπισθεν adverb and preposition
κατοπίσω preposition
κατοπτεύοντος vb pres act part
  masc and neut gen sg . . . . κατοπτεύω
κατόπτρων noun neut gen pl . . . . κάτοπτρον
κατορθοῖ vb pres act ind 3rd pers sg . . . . κατορθόω
κατορθούντων vb pres act part masc and neut gen pl id.
κατορθοῦσι vb pres act part masc and neut dat pl id.
κατορθωθήτω vb 1st aor pass impv 3rd pers sg id.
κατορθῶν vb pres act part masc nom sg id.
κατορθῶσαι vb 1st aor act inf id.
κατορθώσασθαι vb 1st aor mid inf id.
κατορθώσατε vb 1st aor act impv 2nd pers pl id.
κατορθώσει vb fut act ind 3rd pers sg id.
κατορθώσεις vb fut act ind 2nd pers sg id.
κατορθώσῃ vb 1st aor act subj 3rd pers sg id.
κατόρθωσιν noun fem acc sg . . . . κατόρθωσις
κατόρθωσις noun fem nom sg
Κατόρθωσις pr noun fem nom sg
κατορθώσω vb fut act ind 1st pers sg . . . . κατορθόω
κατορυγῶσιν vb 2nd aor pass subj 3rd pers pl . κατορύσσω
κατορύξουσιν vb fut act ind 3rd pers pl id.
κατοχεύσεις vb fut act ind 2nd pers sg . . . . κατοχεύω
κατόχιμοι adj masc nom pl . . . . κατόχιμος
κάτοχοι adj masc and fem nom pl . . . . κάτοχος
 Καττάθ pr noun
κάτω adverb
κατώδυνοι adj masc and fem nom pl . . . . κατώδυνος
κατώδυνος adj masc and fem nom sg id.
κατωδυνωμένην vb perf m/p part fem acc sg . . . κατοδυνάω
κατωδυνωμένων vb perf m/p part gen pl id.
κατωδύνων vb impf act ind 3rd pers pl id.
κάτωθεν adverb
κατῴκει vb impf act ind 3rd pers sg . . . . κατοικέω
κατῴκεις vb impf act ind 2nd pers sg id.
κατῳκεῖτε vb impf act ind 2nd pers pl id.

κατῳκεῖτο vb impf m/p ind 3rd pers sg	κατοικέω	καύσω vb fut act ind 1st pers sg	καίω
κατῴκηκα vb perf act ind 1st pers sg	id.	καύσων noun masc nom sg	
κατῴκησα vb 1st aor act ind 1st pers sg	id.	καύσων noun masc acc sg	καύσων
κατῳκήσαμεν vb 1st aor act ind 1st pers pl	id.	καύσωνος noun masc gen sg	id.
κατῴκησαν vb 1st aor act ind 3rd pers pl	id.	καυτηρίοις noun neut dat pl	καυτήριον
κατῳκήσατε vb 1st aor act ind 2nd pers pl	id.	καυχᾶσθαι vb pres dep inf	καυχάομαι
κατῴκησεν vb 1st aor act ind 3rd pers sg	id.	καυχᾶσθε vb pres dep impv 2nd pers pl	id.
κατῴκισα vb 1st aor act ind 1st pers sg	κατοικίζω	καυχάσθω vb pres dep impv 3rd pers sg	id.
κατῴκισαν vb 1st aor act ind 3rd pers pl	id.	καύχημα noun neut nom and acc sg	
κατῴκισας vb 1st aor act ind 2nd pers sg	id.	καυχήματος noun neut gen sg	καύχημα
κατῴκισεν vb 1st aor act ind 3rd pers sg	id.	καυχήσασθαι vb 1st aor mid inf	καυχάομαι
κατῳκίσθη vb 1st aor pass ind 3rd pers sg	id.	καυχήσεται vb fut mid ind 3rd pers sg	id.
κατῳκίσθημεν vb 1st aor pass ind 1st pers pl	id.	καυχήσεως noun fem gen sg	καύχησις
κατῳκίσθησαν vb 1st aor pass ind 3rd pers pl	id.	καυχήση vb 1st aor act subj 3rd pers sg	καυχάομαι
κατῳκίσθητε vb 1st aor pass ind 2nd pers pl	id.	καυχήσηται vb 1st aor mid subj 3rd pers sg	id.
κατῴκισται vb perf m/p ind 3rd pers sg	id.	καύχησιν noun fem acc sg	καύχησις
κατῳκοδομημέναις vb perf mid part		καυχήσονται vb fut mid ind 3rd pers pl	καυχάομαι
fem dat pl	κατοικοδομέω	καυχήσωνται vb 1st aor mid subj 3rd pers pl	id.
κατῴκουν vb impf act ind 3rd pers pl	κατοικέω	καυχῶ vb pres dep impv 2nd pers sg	id.
κατωρθούμην vb 1st aor mid ind 1st pers sg	κατορθόω	καυχώμενοι vb pres dep part masc nom pl	id.
κατωρθοῦτο vb impf act ind 3rd pers sg	id.	καυχώμενος vb pres dep part masc nom sg	id.
κατωρθώθη vb 1st aor pass ind 3rd pers sg	id.	Καφαν pr noun	
κατώρθωσαν vb 1st aor act ind 3rd pers pl	id.	Καφηραμμιν pr noun	
κατώρθωσεν vb 1st aor act ind 3rd pers sg	id.	Καφθοριιμ pr noun	
κατωρύγη vb 2nd aor pass ind 3rd pers sg	κατορύσσω	Καφιρα pr noun	
κατώρυξα vb 1st aor act ind 1st pers sg	id.	καφουρη translit	
κατώρυξαν vb 1st aor act ind 3rd pers pl	id.	καψάκη noun masc dat sg	καψάκης
κατωρχήσαντο vb 1st aor mid ind		καψάκην noun masc acc sg	id.
3rd pers pl	κατορχεομαι	καψάκης noun masc nom sg	id.
κατώτατα superl adj neut nom and acc pl	κατώτατος	κβ΄ indecl number	
κατωτάτοις superl adj masc and neut dat pl	id.	Κεαφ pr noun	
κατωτάτου superl adj masc and neut gen sg	id.	Κεβλααμ pr noun	
κατωτάτω superl adverb	κάτω	κέγχρον noun masc acc sg	κέγχρος
κατωτάτῳ superl adj masc and neut dat sg	κατώτατος	Κεδαμωθ pr noun	
κατώτερον preposition	κάτω	Κεδελ pr noun	
καυθήσεται vb fut pass ind 3rd pers sg	καίω	Κεδεμ pr noun	
καυθήσονται vb fut pass ind 3rd pers pl	id.	Κεδες pr noun	
καυλόν noun masc acc sg	καυλός	Κεδημωθ pr noun	
καυλός noun masc nom sg	id.	Κεδμα pr noun	
καῦμα noun neut nom and acc sg		Κεδμωναιους pr noun masc acc pl	Κεδμωναιος
καύματι noun neut dat sg	καῦμα	κέδρινα adj neut nom and acc pl	κέδρινος
καύματος noun neut gen sg	id.	κέδριναι adj fem nom pl	id.
καῦσαι vb 1st aor act inf	καίω	κεδρίνην adj fem acc sg	id.
καύσαντες vb 1st aor act part masc nom pl	id.	κεδρίνοις adj masc and neut dat pl	id.
καύσει vb fut act ind 3rd pers sg	id.	κέδρινον adj masc acc sg, neut nom and acc sg	id.
καύσετε vb fut act ind 2nd pers pl	id.	κεδρίνῳ adj masc and neut dat sg	id.
καύσεως noun fem gen sg	καῦσις	κεδρίνων adj gen pl	id.
καῦσιν noun fem acc sg	id.	κέδροι noun fem nom pl	κέδρος
καύσουσιν vb fut act ind 3rd pers pl	καίω	κέδροις noun fem dat pl	id.
καυστικαῖς adj fem dat pl	καυστικός	κέδρον noun fem acc sg	id.
καυστικώτερον comp adj masc acc sg,		κέδρος noun fem nom sg	id.
neut nom and acc sg	id.	κέδρου noun fem gen sg	id.

κέδρους noun fem acc pl . . . . κέδρος
κέδρῳ noun fem dat sg   id.
κέδρων noun fem gen pl   id.
Κεδρών pr noun
Κεζιβ pr noun
Κεϊλα pr noun
Κεϊλαμ pr noun
κεῖμαι vb pres m/p ind 1st pers sg
κείμενα vb pres m/p part neut nom and acc pl . . . . κεῖμαι
κειμένης vb pres m/p part fem gen sg   id.
κείμενοι vb pres m/p part masc nom pl   id.
κειμένοις vb pres m/p part masc and neut dat pl   id.
κείμενον vb pres m/p part masc acc sg,
    neut nom and acc sg   id.
κείμενος vb pres m/p part masc nom sg   id.
κειμένου vb pres m/p part masc and neut gen sg   id.
κειμένους vb pres m/p part masc acc pl   id.
κειμένῳ vb pres m/p part masc and neut dat sg   id.
κειμένων vb pres m/p part gen pl   id.
κεῖνται vb pres m/p ind 3rd pers pl   id.
κεῖραι vb 1st aor act inf,
    1st aor mid impv 2nd pers sg . . . . κείρω
κείρει vb pres act ind 3rd pers sg   id.
κείρειν vb pres act inf   id.
κείρεσθαι vb pres m/p inf   id.
κείρῃς vb 1st aor act subj 2nd pers sg,
    pres act subj 2nd pers sg   id.
κειρίαις noun fem dat pl . . . . κειρία
κειρόμενος vb pres m/p part masc nom sg . . . . κείρω
κείροντας vb pres act part masc acc pl   id.
κείροντες vb pres act part masc nom pl   id.
κείροντος vb pres act part masc and neut gen sg   id.
κείρουσι(ν) vb pres act ind 3rd pers pl,
    pres act part masc and neut dat pl   id.
κεῖσθαι vb pres m/p inf . . . . κεῖμαι
κεῖται vb pres m/p ind 3rd pers sg   id.
κεκαθαρισμένον vb perf m/p part masc acc sg . . καθαρίζω
κεκαθαρισμένον vb perf m/p part neut nom and acc sg   id.
κεκαθαρισμένῳ vb perf m/p part masc and neut dat sg   id.
κεκαθάρισται vb perf m/p ind 3rd pers sg   id.
κεκάκωκας vb perf act ind 2nd pers sg . . . . κακόω
κεκακῶσθαι vb perf m/p inf   id.
κεκαλλωπισμένα vb perf m/p part
    neut nom and acc pl . . . . καλλωπίζω
κεκαλλωπισμέναι vb perf m/p part fem nom pl   id.
κεκαλλωπισμένη vb perf m/p part fem nom sg   id.
κεκάλυφεν vb perf act ind 3rd pers sg . . . . καλύπτω
κεκαρμένους vb perf m/p part masc acc pl . . . . κείρω
κεκαρμένων vb perf m/p part gen pl   id.
κεκατηραμένος vb perf dep part
    masc nom sg . . . . καταράομαι
κεκατήρανται vb perf dep ind 3rd pers pl   id.

κεκερασμένου vb perf m/p part
    masc and neut gen sg . . . . κεράννυμι
κεκηλίδωσαι vb perf dep ind 2nd pers sg . . . . . κηλιδόομαι
κεκλείκασιν vb perf act ind 3rd pers pl . . . . κλείω
κέκλεινται vb perf m/p ind 3rd pers pl   id.
κεκλεισμένη vb perf m/p part fem nom sg   id.
κεκλεισμένος vb perf m/p part masc nom sg   id.
κεκλεισμένῳ vb perf m/p part masc and neut dat sg   id.
κεκλεμμένον vb perf m/p part neut nom and acc sg . κλέπτω
κέκληκα vb perf act ind 1st pers sg . . . . καλέω
κέκληκας vb perf act ind 2nd pers sg   id.
κεκλήκατε vb perf act ind 2nd pers pl   id.
κέκληκεν vb perf act ind 3rd pers sg   id.
κέκλημαι vb perf m/p ind 1st pers sg   id.
κεκλημένοι vb perf m/p part masc nom pl   id.
κεκλημένον vb perf m/p part masc acc sg   id.
κεκλημένων vb perf m/p part gen pl   id.
κεκλήσεται vb fut perf m/p ind 3rd pers sg   id.
κεκλήσθω vb perf m/p impv 3rd pers sg   id.
κέκληται vb perf m/p ind 3rd pers sg   id.
κέκλικεν vb perf act ind 3rd pers sg . . . . κλίνω
κεκλικυῖα vb perf act part fem nom sg   id.
κεκλικώς vb perf act part masc nom sg   id.
κεκλιμένῳ vb perf m/p part masc and neut dat sg   id.
κεκλωσμένη vb perf m/p part fem dat sg . . . . κλώθω
κεκλωσμένην vb perf m/p part fem acc sg   id.
κεκλωσμένης vb perf m/p part fem gen sg   id.
κεκλωσμένον vb perf m/p part neut nom and acc sg   id.
κεκλωσμένου vb perf m/p part masc and neut gen sg   id.
κεκλωσμένῳ vb perf m/p part masc and neut dat sg   id.
κεκμηκότων vb perf act part masc and neut gen pl . . . κάμνω
κεκμηκώς vb perf act part masc nom sg   id.
κεκοιμημένοι vb perf m/p part masc nom pl . . . . . . κοιμάω
κεκοίμησαι vb perf m/p ind 2nd pers sg   id.
κεκοίμηται vb perf m/p ind 3rd pers sg   id.
κεκοιμισμένον vb perf m/p part masc acc sg,
    neut nom and acc sg . . . . κοιμίζω
κεκολαμμένα vb perf m/p part
    neut nom and acc pl . . . . κολάπτω
κεκολαμμένη vb perf m/p part fem nom sg   id.
κεκολαμμένῃ vb perf m/p part fem dat sg   id.
κεκολαμμένης vb perf m/p part fem gen sg   id.
κεκόλληκα vb perf act ind 1st pers sg . . . . κολλάω
κεκόλληνται vb perf m/p ind 3rd pers pl   id.
κεκόλληται vb perf m/p ind 3rd pers sg   id.
κεκόμισαι vb perf m/p ind 2nd pers sg . . . . κομίζω
κεκομίσμεθα vb perf m/p ind 1st pers pl   id.
κεκομμένον vb perf m/p part neut nom and acc sg . . . κόπτω
κεκομμένου vb perf m/p part masc and neut gen sg   id.
κεκομμένῳ vb perf m/p part masc and neut dat sg   id.
κεκονιαμένοις vb perf m/p part
    masc and neut dat pl . . . . κονιάω

κεκόπακεν vb perf act ind 3rd pers sg . . . . κοπάζω

κεκοπανισμένου vb perf m/p part

   masc and neut gen sg . . . . κοπανίζω

κεκοπίακας vb perf act ind 2nd pers sg . . . . κοπιάω

κεκοπωμένοι vb perf m/p part masc nom pl . . . . κοπόω

κεκοσμημένα vb perf m/p part neut nom and acc pl . κοσμέω

κεκοσμημένη vb perf m/p part fem nom sg   id.

κεκοσμημένῃ vb perf m/p part fem dat sg   id.

κεκοσμημένον vb perf m/p part neut nom and acc sg   id.

κεκοσμημένος vb perf m/p part masc nom sg   id.

κέκραγα vb perf act ind 1st pers sg . . . . κράζω

κεκράγασιν vb perf act ind 3rd pers pl   id.

κέκραγεν vb perf act ind 3rd pers sg   id.

κεκραγέναι vb perf act inf   id.

κεκραγέτωσαν vb perf act impv 3rd pers pl   id.

κεκραγότων vb perf act part masc and neut gen pl   id.

κεκραγώς vb perf act part masc nom sg   id.

κεκραιπαληκώς vb perf act part masc nom sg . . κραιπαλάω

κεκράξαι vb 1st aor act inf . . . . κράζω

κεκράξαντες vb 1st aor act part masc nom pl   id.

κεκράξατε vb 1st aor act impv 2nd pers pl   id.

κεκράξεσθε vb fut perf m/p ind 2nd pers pl   id.

κεκράξεται vb fut perf m/p ind 3rd pers sg   id.

κεκράξῃ vb fut perf m/p ind 2nd pers sg   id.

κεκράξομαι vb fut perf m/p ind 1st pers sg   id.

κέκραξον vb 1st aor act impv 2nd pers sg   id.

κεκράξονται vb fut perf m/p ind 3rd pers pl   id.

κεκραταίωνται vb perf m/p ind 3rd pers pl . . . . κραταιόω

κεκρατήκαμεν vb perf act ind 1st pers pl . . . . κρατέω

κεκρατήκει vb plpf act ind 3rd pers sg   id.

κεκρατηκέναι vb perf act inf   id.

κεκρατημένος vb perf m/p part masc nom sg   id.

κεκρίκασιν vb perf act ind 3rd pers pl . . . . κρίνω

κέκρικεν vb perf act ind 3rd pers sg   id.

κεκριμένα vb perf m/p part neut nom and acc pl   id.

κεκριμένον vb perf m/p part masc acc sg   id.

κεκριμένων vb perf m/p part gen pl   id.

κέκριται vb perf m/p ind 3rd pers sg   id.

κεκρυμμένα vb perf m/p part neut nom and acc pl . . κρύπτω

κεκρυμμένη vb perf m/p part fem nom sg   id.

κεκρυμμένην vb perf m/p part fem acc sg   id.

κεκρυμμένοι vb perf m/p part masc nom pl   id.

κεκρυμμένος vb perf m/p part masc nom sg   id.

κεκρυμμένων vb perf m/p part gen pl   id.

κεκρυμμένως adverb

κέκρυπται vb perf m/p ind 3rd pers sg . . . . κρύπτω

κέκτημαι vb perf dep ind 1st pers sg . . . . κτάομαι

κεκτήμεθα vb perf dep ind 1st pers pl   id.

κεκτημένοις vb perf dep part masc and neut dat pl   id.

κεκτημένον vb perf dep part masc acc sg   id.

κεκτημένος vb perf dep part masc nom sg   id.

κεκτημένῳ vb perf dep part masc and neut dat sg   id.

κεκτημένων vb perf dep part gen pl . . . . κτάομαι

κέκτηται vb perf dep ind 3rd pers sg   id.

Κελεζ pr noun

κελευόντων vb pres act part masc and neut gen pl . . κελεύω

κελεύσας vb 1st aor act part masc nom sg   id.

κελευσθέντες vb 1st aor pass part masc nom pl   id.

κελεύσματος noun neut gen sg . . . . κέλευσμα

κελεύων vb pres act part masc nom sg . . . . κελεύω

κενά adj neut nom and acc pl . . . . κενός

κεναί adj fem nom pl   id.

κενάς adj fem acc pl   id.

Κενδεβαῖον pr noun masc acc sg . . . . Κενδεβαῖος

Κενδεβαῖος pr noun masc nom sg   id.

Κενεζ pr noun

Κενεζαῖος pr noun masc nom sg

Κενεζαιου pr noun masc gen sg . . . . Κενεζαῖος

Κενεζαιους pr noun masc acc pl   id.

Κενεζι pr noun

Κενερεθ pr noun

Κενερωθ pr noun

κενεῶνα noun masc acc sg . . . . κενεών

κενεῶνας noun masc acc pl   id.

κενή adj fem nom sg . . . . κενός

κενῇ adj fem dat sg   id.

κενήν adj fem acc sg   id.

κενῆς adj fem gen sg   id.

κενοδοξήσωμεν vb 1st aor act subj 1st pers pl . . κενοδοξέω

κενοδοξίᾳ noun fem dat sg . . . . κενοδοξία

κενοδοξίαν noun fem acc sg   id.

κενοδοξίας noun fem gen sg   id.

κενοδοξῶν vb pres act part masc nom sg . . . . . . κενοδοξέω

κενοί adj masc nom pl . . . . κενός

κενοῖς adj masc and neut dat pl   id.

κενολογοῦντας vb pres act part masc acc pl . . . κενολογέω

κενόν adj masc acc sg, neut nom and acc sg . . . . κενός

κενός adj masc nom sg   id.

κενοτάφια noun neut nom and acc pl . . . . κενοτάφιον

κενούς adj masc acc pl . . . . κενός

κεντοῦσι vb pres act ind 3rd pers pl . . . . κεντέω

κέντρον noun neut nom and acc sg

κέντρου noun neut gen sg . . . . κέντρον

κέντρῳ noun neut dat sg   id.

κενῷ adj masc and neut dat sg . . . . κενός

κενῶς adverb

κεπφωθείς vb 1st aor pass part masc nom sg . . . . κεπφόομαι

κεραμεῖ noun masc dat sg . . . . κεραμεύς

κεραμεῖς noun masc nom and acc pl   id.

κεραμεύς noun masc nom sg   id.

κεραμέως noun masc gen sg   id.

κεραμικοῦ adj masc and neut gen sg . . . . κεραμικός

κεράμιον noun neut nom and acc sg

κεραμίου noun neut gen sg . . . . κεράμιον κεράμου noun masc gen sg . . . . κέραμος

κεραννύντες vb pres act part masc nom pl . . . . . κεράννυμι

κέρας noun neut nom and acc sg

κεράσας vb 1st aor act part masc nom sg . . . . . . κεράννυμι

κερασθείς vb 1st aor pass part masc nom sg id.

κέρασι noun neut dat pl . . . . κέρας

κέρασμα noun neut nom and acc sg

κεράσματος noun neut gen sg . . . . κέρασμα

κεράστου noun masc gen sg . . . . κεράστης

κέρατα noun neut nom and acc pl . . . . κέρας

κέρατι noun neut dat sg id.

κερατιεῖ vb fut act ind 3rd pers sg . . . . κερατίζω

κερατιεῖς vb fut act ind 2nd pers sg id.

κερατίζοντα vb pres act part masc acc sg id.

κερατίναι noun fem nom pl . . . . κερατίνη

κερατίναις noun fem dat pl id.

κερατίνας noun fem acc pl id.

κερατίνη noun fem dat sg id.

κερατίνης noun fem gen sg id.

κερατιοῦμεν vb fut act ind 1st pers pl . . . . κερατίζω

κερατίσῃ vb 1st aor act subj 3rd pers sg id.

κερατιστής noun masc nom sg

κεράτων noun neut gen pl . . . . κέρας

κεραυνούς noun masc acc pl . . . . κεραυνός

κεραυνῶν noun masc gen pl id.

κεραυνώσει vb fut act ind 3rd pers sg . . . . κεραυνόω

κερεῖς vb fut act ind 2nd pers sg . . . . κείρω

κέρκον noun fem acc sg . . . . κέρκος

κέρκου noun fem gen sg id.

κέρκων noun fem gen pl id.

κερκώπων noun masc gen pl . . . . κέρκωψ

Κερωε pr noun

Κεσιων pr noun

κεφαλαί noun fem nom pl . . . . κεφαλή

κεφάλαια noun neut nom and acc pl . . . . κεφάλαιον

κεφάλαιον noun neut nom and acc sg id.

κεφαλαῖς noun fem dat pl . . . . κεφαλή

κεφαλαίωσον vb 1st aor act impv 2nd pers sg . . κεφαλαιόω

κεφαλάς noun fem acc pl . . . . κεφαλή

κεφαλή noun fem nom sg id.

κεφαλῇ noun fem dat sg id.

κεφαλήν noun fem acc sg id.

κεφαλῆς noun fem gen sg id.

κεφαλίδα noun fem acc sg . . . . κεφαλίς

κεφαλίδας noun fem acc pl id.

κεφαλίδες noun fem nom pl id.

κεφαλίδι noun fem dat sg id.

κεφαλίδος noun fem gen sg id.

κεφαλίδων noun fem gen pl id.

κεφαλίς noun fem nom sg id.

κεφαλῶν noun fem gen pl . . . . κεφαλή

Κεφιρα pr noun

κεφφουρε translit

κεφφουρη noun neut nom and acc pl . . . . κεφφουρης

Κεχαρ pr noun

κεχαρισμένης vb perf dep part fem gen sg . . . . χαρίζομαι

κεχάρισται vb perf dep ind 3rd pers sg id.

κεχαριτωμένῳ vb perf dep part

    masc and neut dat sg . . . . χαριτόομαι

κεχερσωμένη vb perf dep part fem nom sg . . . . χερσόομαι

κεχορηγημένοι vb perf m/p part masc nom pl . . . . χορηγέω

κεχρηματικέναι vb perf act inf . . . . χρηματίζω

κεχρημένον vb perf dep part masc acc sg,

    neut nom and acc sg . . . . χράομαι

κέχρηται vb perf dep ind 3rd pers sg id.

κέχρικα vb perf act ind 1st pers sg . . . . χρίω

κέχρικεν vb perf act ind 3rd pers sg id.

κεχρισμένα vb perf m/p part neut nom and acc pl id.

κεχρισμένος vb perf m/p part masc nom sg id.

κέχρισται vb perf m/p ind 3rd pers sg id.

κεχρόνικεν vb perf act ind 3rd pers sg . . . . χρονίζω

κεχρυσωμένων vb perf m/p part gen pl . . . . χρυσόω

κεχυμένῳ vb perf m/p part masc and neut dat sg . . . . χέω

κέχυται vb perf m/p ind 3rd pers sg id.

κεχωματισμένας vb perf m/p part fem acc pl . . . χωματίζω

κεχωρισμένος vb perf m/p part masc nom sg . . . . . . χωρίζω

κεχωρισμένων vb perf m/p part gen pl id.

Κηδαρ pr noun

κηδείαν noun fem acc sg . . . . κηδεία

κηδείας noun fem acc pl id.

κηδεμόνα noun masc acc sg . . . . κηδεμών

κηδεμονίαν noun fem acc sg . . . . κηδεμονία

κηδεμονίας noun fem gen sg id.

Κηδες pr noun

κηλῖδα noun fem acc sg . . . . κηλίς

κηλιδωθήσονται vb fut pass ind 3rd pers pl . . κηλιδόομαι

κημῷ noun masc dat sg . . . . κημός

κήποις noun masc dat pl . . . . κῆπος

κῆπον noun masc acc sg id.

κῆπος noun masc nom sg id.

κήπου noun masc gen sg id.

κήπους noun masc acc pl id.

κήπῳ noun masc dat sg id.

κήπων noun masc gen pl id.

Κηραος pr noun

Κηρας pr noun

κηρία noun neut nom and acc pl . . . . κηρίον

κηρίοις noun neut dat pl id.

κηρίον noun neut nom and acc sg id.

κηρογονίας noun fem gen sg . . . . κηρογονία

κηρός noun masc nom sg

κήρυγμα noun neut nom and acc sg

κηρύγματος noun neut gen sg . . . . κήρυγμα

κήρυκος noun masc gen sg . . . . κῆρυξ

κῆρυξ noun masc nom sg
κηρύξαι vb 1st aor act inf . . . . κηρύσσω
κηρύξατε vb 1st aor act impv 2nd pers pl id.
κηρυξάτωσαν vb 1st aor act impv 3rd pers pl id.
κηρύξεις vb fut act ind 2nd pers sg id.
κήρυξον vb 1st aor act impv 2nd pers sg id.
κήρυσσε vb pres act impv 2nd pers sg id.
κηρύσσεται vb pres m/p ind 3rd pers sg id.
κηρυσσέτω vb pres act impv 3rd pers sg id.
κηρύσσοντας vb pres act part masc acc pl id.
Κηταβ pr noun
κήτει noun neut dat sg . . . . κῆτος
κήτη noun neut nom and acc pl id.
κῆτος noun neut nom and acc sg id.
κήτους noun neut gen sg id.
κητῶν noun neut gen pl id.
κθ΄ indecl number
κίβδηλα adj neut nom and acc pl . . . . κίβδηλος
κίβδηλον adj masc acc sg, neut nom and acc sg id.
κιβωτόν noun fem acc sg . . . . κιβωτός
κιβωτός noun fem nom sg id.
κιβωτοῦ noun fem gen sg id.
κιβωτούς noun fem acc pl id.
κιβωτῷ noun fem dat sg id.
κιδάρεις noun fem nom and acc pl . . . . κίδαρις
κιδάρεως noun fem gen sg id.
κίδαριν noun fem acc sg id.
κιθάρα noun fem nom sg
κιθάρᾳ noun fem dat sg . . . . κιθάρα
κιθάραις noun fem dat pl id.
κιθάραν noun fem acc sg id.
κιθάρας noun fem gen sg and acc pl id.
κιθάρισον vb 1st aor act impv 2nd pers sg . . . . . . κιθαρίζω
Κιλαν pr noun
Κιλικια pr noun fem dat sg . . . . Κιλικια
Κιλικιαν pr noun fem acc sg id.
Κιλικιας pr noun fem gen sg id.
Κινα pr noun
Κιναιοι pr noun masc nom pl . . . . Κιναῖος
Κιναῖον pr noun masc acc sg id.
Κιναῖος pr noun masc nom sg id.
Κιναιου pr noun masc gen sg id.
Κιναν pr noun
κινδυνεύει vb pres act ind 3rd pers sg . . . . κινδυνεύω
κινδυνεύειν vb pres act inf id.
κινδυνεύσει vb fut act ind 3rd pers sg id.
κινδυνεύσουσιν vb fut act ind 3rd pers pl id.
κινδυνεύσω vb fut act ind 1st pers sg id.
κίνδυνοι noun masc nom pl . . . . κίνδυνος
κίνδυνον noun masc acc sg id.
κίνδυνος noun masc nom sg id.
κινδύνους noun masc acc pl id.

κινδύνῳ noun masc dat sg . . . . κίνδυνος
κινδύνων noun masc gen pl id.
κινεῖν vb pres act inf . . . . κινέω
κινεῖσθαι vb pres m/p inf id.
κινηθῇ vb 1st aor pass subj 3rd pers sg id.
κινηθῇς vb 1st aor pass subj 2nd pers sg id.
κινηθήσεται vb fut pass ind 3rd pers sg id.
κινηθήσονται vb fut pass ind 3rd pers pl id.
κινηθῶσιν vb 1st aor pass subj 3rd pers pl id.
κίνημα noun neut nom and acc sg
κινήματα noun neut nom and acc pl . . . . κίνημα
κινῆσαι vb 1st aor act inf . . . . κινέω
κινήσας vb 1st aor act part masc nom sg id.
κινήσατε vb 1st aor act impv 2nd pers pl id.
κινήσάτω vb 1st aor act impv 3rd pers sg id.
κινήσει noun fem dat sg . . . . κίνησις
κινήσει vb fut act ind 3rd pers sg . . . . κινέω
κινήσεις noun fem nom and acc pl . . . . κίνησις
κινήσεως noun fem gen sg id.
κίνησιν noun fem acc sg id.
κινήσουσιν vb fut act ind 3rd pers pl . . . . κινέω
κινήσω vb fut act ind 1st pers sg id.
κινητικώτερον comp adj masc acc sg,
    neut nom and acc sg . . . . κινητικός
κιννάμωμον noun neut nom and acc sg
κινναμώμου noun neut gen sg . . . . κιννάμωμον
κινναμώμῳ noun neut dat sg id.
κινούμενα vb pres m/p part neut nom and acc pl . . . . κινέω
κινουμένη vb pres m/p part fem nom sg id.
κινουμένης vb pres m/p part fem gen sg id.
κινούμενοι vb pres m/p part masc nom pl id.
κινουμένοις vb pres m/p part masc and neut dat pl id.
κινούμενον vb pres m/p part masc acc sg,
    neut nom and acc sg id.
κινουμένων vb pres m/p part fem gen pl id.
κινοῦνται vb pres m/p ind 3rd pers pl id.
κινύρα noun fem nom sg
κινύρᾳ noun fem dat sg . . . . κινύρα
κινύραι noun fem nom pl id.
κινύραις noun fem dat pl id.
κινύραν noun fem acc sg id.
κινύρας noun fem gen sg and acc pl id.
κίονας noun masc acc pl . . . . κίων
κιόνων noun masc gen pl id.
Κιραδας pr noun
Κιραμας pr noun
Κιρας pr noun
Κις pr noun
Κισαι pr noun
Κισαιου pr noun masc gen sg . . . . Κισαιας
κισσούς noun masc acc pl . . . . κισσός
κισσοφύλλῳ noun neut dat sg . . . . κισσόφυλλον

Κισων pr noun

Κιτιαιων pr noun masc gen pl . . . . Κιτιαιοι

Κιτιεῖς pr noun masc nom and acc pl

Κιτιεων pr noun masc gen pl . . . . Κιτιεῖς

Κιτιοι pr noun masc nom pl

κιχρᾷ vb pres act ind 3rd pers sg . . . . κιχράω

κιχρῶ vb pres act ind 1st pers sg id.

κιχρῶν vb pres act part masc nom sg id.

κλάδοι noun masc nom pl . . . . κλάδος

κλάδοις noun masc dat pl id.

κλάδον noun masc acc sg id.

κλάδους noun masc acc pl id.

κλάδων noun masc gen pl id.

κλαίει vb pres act ind 3rd pers sg . . . . κλαίω

κλαίειν vb pres act inf id.

κλαίεις vb pres act ind 2nd pers sg id.

κλαίετε vb pres act impv 2nd pers pl,

      pres act ind 2nd pers pl id.

κλαῖον vb pres act part neut nom and acc sg id.

κλαίοντες vb pres act part masc nom pl id.

κλαιόντων vb pres act part masc and neut gen pl id.

κλαίουσα vb pres act part fem nom sg id.

κλαίουσιν vb pres act ind 3rd pers pl id.

κλαίω vb pres act ind 1st pers sg id.

κλαίων vb pres act part masc nom sg id.

κλαπῇ vb 2nd aor pass subj 3rd pers sg . . . . κλέπτω

κλασθῇ vb 1st aor pass subj 3rd pers sg . . . . κλάω

κλάσμα noun neut nom and acc sg

κλάσματα noun neut nom and acc pl . . . . κλάσμα

κλάσματι noun neut dat sg id.

κλασμάτων noun neut gen pl id.

κλαυθμοί noun masc nom pl . . . . κλαυθμός

κλαυθμόν noun masc acc sg id.

κλαυθμός noun masc nom sg id.

κλαυθμοῦ noun masc gen sg id.

κλαυθμῷ noun masc dat sg id.

Κλαυθμων pr noun masc nom sg

Κλαυθμῶνα pr noun masc acc sg . . . . Κλαυθμών

Κλαυθμῶνες pr noun masc nom pl id.

κλαυθμῶνος noun masc gen sg . . . . κλαυθμών

κλαῦσαι vb 1st aor act inf . . . . κλαίω

κλαύσατε vb 1st aor act impv 2nd pers pl id.

κλαύσεται vb fut mid ind 3rd pers sg id.

κλαύσητε vb 1st aor act subj 2nd pers pl id.

κλαυσθῇς vb 1st aor pass subj 2nd pers sg id.

κλαυσθήσονται vb fut pass ind 3rd pers pl id.

κλαύσομαι vb fut mid ind 1st pers sg id.

κλαῦσον vb 1st aor act impv 2nd pers sg id.

κλαύσονται vb fut mid ind 3rd pers pl id.

κλαύσωμεν vb 1st aor act subj 1st pers pl id.

κλεῖδα noun fem acc sg . . . . κλείς

κλεῖδας noun fem acc pl id.

κλειδός noun fem gen sg . . . . κλείς

κλειδῶν noun fem gen pl id.

κλειέσθωσαν vb pres m/p impv 3rd pers pl . . . . κλείω

κλεῖθρα noun neut nom and acc pl . . . . κλεῖθρον

κλείθροις noun neut dat pl id.

κλείθρου noun neut gen sg id.

κλείσας vb 1st aor act part masc nom sg . . . . κλείω

κλείσατε vb 1st aor act impv 2nd pers pl id.

κλείσει vb fut act ind 3rd pers sg id.

κλείσῃ vb 1st aor act subj 3rd pers sg id.

κλεισθῇ vb 1st aor pass subj 3rd pers sg id.

κλεισθήσονται vb fut pass ind 3rd pers pl id.

κλεῖσον vb 1st aor act impv 2nd pers sg id.

κλείσουσιν vb fut act ind 3rd pers pl id.

κλείσωμεν vb 1st aor act subj 1st pers pl id.

κλέμμα noun neut nom and acc sg

κλέμματα noun neut nom and acc pl . . . . κλέμμα

κλέμματος noun neut gen sg id.

Κλεοπατρα pr noun fem nom sg

Κλεοπατραν pr noun fem acc sg . . . . Κλεοπατρα

Κλεοπατρας pr noun fem gen sg id.

κλέος noun neut nom and acc sg

κλέπται noun masc nom pl . . . . κλέπτης

κλέπτει vb pres act ind 3rd pers sg . . . . κλέπτω

κλέπτειν vb pres act inf id.

κλέπτετε vb pres act ind 2nd pers pl id.

κλέπτῃ noun masc dat sg . . . . κλέπτης

κλέπτην noun masc acc sg id.

κλέπτης noun masc nom sg id.

κλέπτοντας vb pres act part masc acc pl . . . . κλέπτω

κλέπτου noun masc gen sg . . . . κλέπτης

κλέπτων vb pres act part masc nom sg . . . . κλέπτω

κλεπτῶν noun masc gen pl . . . . κλέπτης

κλέψαιμεν vb 1st aor act opt 1st pers pl . . . . κλέπτω

κλέψαντες vb 1st aor act part masc nom pl id.

κλέψας vb 1st aor act part masc nom sg id.

κλέψεις vb fut act ind 2nd pers sg id.

κλέψετε vb fut act ind 2nd pers pl id.

κλέψῃ vb 1st aor act subj 3rd pers sg id.

κλεψιμαῖον adj masc acc sg,

      neut nom and acc sg . . . . κλεψιμαῖος

κλέψω vb fut act ind 1st pers sg . . . . κλέπτω

κληδονιζόμενος vb pres m/p part masc nom sg . κληδονίζω

κληδονισμῶν noun masc gen pl . . . . κληδονισμός

κληδόνων noun fem gen pl . . . . κληδών

κληθείησαν vb 1st aor pass opt 3rd pers pl . . . . καλέω

κληθεῖσα vb 1st aor pass part fem nom sg id.

κληθέν vb 1st aor pass part neut nom and acc sg id.

κληθέντες vb 1st aor pass part masc nom pl id.

κληθῇ vb 1st aor pass subj 3rd pers sg id.

κληθῆναι vb 1st aor pass inf id.

κληθῇς vb 1st aor pass subj 2nd pers sg id.

κληθήσεσθε vb fut pass ind 2nd pers pl . . . . καλέω
κληθήσεται vb fut pass ind 3rd pers sg   id.
κληθήση vb fut pass ind 2nd pers sg   id.
κληθήσονται vb fut pass ind 3rd pers pl   id.
κληθήτω vb 1st aor pass impv 3rd pers sg   id.
κλῆμα noun neut nom and acc sg
κλήματα noun neut nom and acc pl . . . . κλῆμα
κληματίδα noun fem acc sg . . . . κληματίς
κληματίδας noun fem acc pl   id.
κληματίς noun fem nom sg   id.
κλημάτων noun neut gen pl . . . . κλῆμα
κληροδοσίᾳ noun fem dat sg . . . . κληροδοσία
κληροδοσίαν noun fem acc sg   id.
κληροδοσίας noun fem gen sg   id.
κληροδοτήσητε vb 1st aor act subj 2nd pers pl κληροδοτέω
κλῆροι noun masc nom pl . . . . κλῆρος
κλήροις noun masc dat pl   id.
κλῆρον noun masc acc sg   id.
κληρονόμει vb pres act impv 2nd pers sg . . . . κληρονομέω
κληρονομεῖν vb pres act inf   id.
κληρονομεῖτε vb pres act ind 2nd pers pl   id.
κληρονομείτωσαν vb pres act impv 3rd pers pl   id.
κληρονομῆσαι vb 1st aor act inf   id.
κληρονομήσαισαν vb 1st aor act opt 3rd pers pl   id.
κληρονομήσασι vb 1st aor act part masc and neut dat pl id.
κληρονομήσατε vb 1st aor act impv 2nd pers pl   id.
κληρονομησάτω vb 1st aor act impv 3rd pers sg   id.
κληρονομήσει vb fut act ind 3rd pers sg   id
κληρονομήσεις vb fut act ind 2nd pers sg   id.
κληρονομήσετε vb fut act ind 2nd pers pl   id.
κληρονομήση vb 1st aor act subj 3rd pers sg   id.
κληρονομήσης vb 1st aor act subj 2nd pers sg   id.
κληρονομήσητε vb 1st aor act subj 2nd pers pl   id.
κληρονομήσομεν vb fut act ind 1st pers pl   id.
κληρονομήσουσι(ν) vb fut act ind 3rd pers pl   id.
κληρονομήσω vb fut act ind 1st pers sg   id.
κληρονομήσωμεν vb 1st aor act subj 1st pers pl   id.
κληρονομήσωσιν vb 1st aor act subj 3rd pers pl   id.
κληρονομία noun fem nom sg
κληρονομίᾳ noun fem dat sg . . . . κληρονομία
κληρονομίαι noun fem nom pl   id.
κληρονομίαν noun fem acc sg   id.
κληρονομίας noun fem gen sg and acc pl   id.
κληρονόμοις noun masc dat pl . . . . κληρονόμος
κληρονόμον noun masc acc sg   id.
κληρονόμος noun masc nom sg   id.
κληρονόμου noun masc gen sg   id.
κληρονόμους noun masc acc pl   id.
κληρονομούσης vb pres act part fem gen sg . . κληρονομέω
κλῆρος noun masc nom sg
κλήρου noun masc gen sg . . . . κλῆρος
κλήρους noun masc acc pl   id.

κληροῦται vb pres m/p ind 3rd pers sg . . . . κληρόω
κλήρῳ noun masc dat sg . . . . κλῆρος
κλήρων noun masc gen pl   id.
κληρώσῃ vb 1st aor mid subj 2nd pers sg . . . . κληρόω
κληρωτί adverb
κλήσεσιν noun fem dat pl . . . . κλῆσις
κλήσεως noun fem gen sg   id.
κλῆσιν noun fem acc sg   id.
κληταί adj fem nom pl . . . . κλητός
κλητάς adj fem acc pl   id.
κλητέον verbal adj sg
κλητή adj fem nom sg . . . . κλητός
κλητήν adj fem acc sg   id.
κλητοί adj masc nom pl   id.
κλητούς adj masc acc pl   id.
κλίβανοι noun masc nom pl . . . . κλίβανος
κλιβάνοις noun masc dat pl   id.
κλίβανον noun masc acc sg   id.
κλίβανος noun masc nom sg   id.
κλιβάνῳ noun masc dat sg   id.
κλιθῇ vb 1st aor pass subj 3rd pers sg . . . . κλίνω
κλιθήσεται vb fut pass ind 3rd pers sg   id.
κλίμα noun neut nom and acc sg
κλίμακας noun fem acc pl . . . . κλίμαξ
κλίμακος noun fem gen sg   id.
κλιμακτῆρες noun masc nom pl . . . . κλιμακτήρ
κλιμακτῆρσι noun masc dat pl   id.
κλιμάκων noun fem gen pl . . . . κλίμαξ
κλίμαξ noun fem nom sg
κλῖναι noun fem nom pl . . . . κλίνη
κλῖναι vb 1st aor act inf . . . . κλίνω
κλίνας noun fem acc pl . . . . κλίνη
κλίνατε vb 1st aor act impv 2nd pers pl . . . . κλίνω
κλινεῖ vb fut act ind 3rd pers sg   id.
κλίνη noun fem nom sg
κλίνη noun fem dat sg . . . . κλίνη
κλίνῃ vb pres act subj 3rd pers sg,
        1st aor act subj 3rd pers sg . . . . κλίνω
κλίνην noun fem acc sg . . . . κλίνη
κλίνης noun fem gen sg   id.
κλίνης vb pres act subj 2nd pers sg . . . . κλίνω
κλίνον vb pres act part neut nom and acc sg,
        1st aor act impv 2nd pers sg   id.
κλίνοντας vb pres act part masc acc pl   id.
κλινοῦσιν vb fut act ind 3rd pers pl   id.
κλίνω vb pres act ind 1st pers sg   id.
κλινῶ vb fut act ind 1st pers sg   id.
κλινῶν noun fem gen pl . . . . κλίνη
κλισίαις noun fem dat pl . . . . κλισία
κλίτει noun neut dat sg . . . . κλίτος
κλίτεσι noun neut dat pl   id.
κλίτη noun neut nom and acc pl   id.

κλίτος noun neut nom and acc sg

κλίτους noun neut gen sg . . . . κλίτος

κλιτῶν noun neut gen pl id.

κλοιοί noun masc nom pl . . . . κλοιός

κλοιόν noun masc acc sg id.

κλοιοῦ noun masc gen sg id.

κλοιούς noun masc acc pl id.

κλοιῷ noun masc dat sg id.

κλοιῶν noun masc gen pl id.

κλοπαῖς noun fem dat pl . . . . κλοπή

κλοπή noun fem nom sg id.

κλοπῇ noun fem dat sg id.

κλοπῆς noun fem gen sg id.

κλύδων noun masc nom sg

κλύδωνα noun masc acc sg . . . . κλύδων

κλύδωνας noun masc acc pl id.

κλύδωνι noun masc dat sg id.

κλυδωνισθήσονται vb fut pass ind

3rd pers pl . . . . κλυδωνίζομαι

κλύδωνος noun masc gen sg . . . . κλύδων

κλώμενος vb pres m/p part masc nom sg . . . . κλάω

κλῶνες noun masc nom pl . . . . κλών

κλῶσμα noun neut nom and acc sg

κλωστόν adj masc acc sg, neut nom and acc sg . . . . κλωστός

κνῆμαι noun fem nom pl . . . . κνήμη

κνήμαις noun fem dat pl id.

κνήμας noun fem acc pl id.

κνήμην noun fem acc sg id.

κνημῖδες noun fem nom pl . . . . κνημίς

κνήφη noun fem dat sg . . . . κνήφη

κνίδη noun fem nom sg

Κνιδον pr noun fem acc sg . . . . Κνιδος

κνίζων vb pres act part masc nom sg . . . . κνίζω

κνώδαλα noun neut nom and acc pl . . . . κνώδαλον

κνωδάλων noun neut gen pl id.

κοθωνοι translit

κοῖλα adj neut nom and acc pl . . . . κοῖλος

κοιλάδα noun fem acc sg . . . . κοιλάς

κοιλάδας noun fem acc pl id.

κοιλάδες noun fem nom pl id.

κοιλάδι noun fem dat sg id.

κοιλάδος noun fem gen sg id.

κοιλάδων noun fem gen pl id.

Κοιλας pr noun

κοιλάς noun fem nom sg

κοιλάσιν noun fem dat pl . . . . κοιλάς

κοιλάσματι noun neut dat sg . . . . κοίλασμα

κοίλη adj fem nom sg . . . . κοῖλος

Κοιλη pr noun fem dat sg . . . . Κοίλη

κοίλην adj fem acc sg . . . . κοῖλος

Κοιλην pr noun fem acc sg . . . . Κοιλη

Κοιλης pr noun fem gen sg id.

κοιλία noun fem nom sg

κοιλίᾳ noun fem dat sg . . . . κοιλία

κοιλίαι noun fem nom pl id.

κοιλίαν noun fem acc sg id.

κοιλίας noun fem gen sg and acc pl id.

κοῖλον adj masc acc sg, neut nom and acc sg . . . . . . κοῖλος

κοιλοστάθμοις noun masc dat pl . . . . κοιλόσταθμος

κοιλότητος noun fem gen sg . . . . κοιλότης

κοιλώματα noun neut nom and acc pl . . . . κοίλωμα

κοιλώματι noun neut dat sg id.

κοιλώματος noun neut gen sg id.

κοιλωμάτων noun neut gen pl id.

κοιμᾷ vb pres m/p ind 2nd pers sg . . . . κοιμάω

κοιμᾶσθαι vb pres m/p inf id.

κοιμᾶται vb pres m/p ind 3rd pers sg id.

κοιμηθείς vb 1st aor pass part masc nom sg id.

κοιμηθέντα vb 1st aor pass part masc acc sg id.

κοιμηθῇ vb 1st aor pass subj 3rd pers sg id.

κοιμηθῆναι vb 1st aor pass inf id.

κοιμηθήσεσθε vb fut pass ind 2nd pers pl id.

κοιμηθήσεται vb fut pass ind 3rd pers sg id.

κοιμηθήσῃ vb fut pass ind 2nd pers sg id.

κοιμηθήσομαι vb fut pass ind 1st pers sg id.

κοιμηθήσονται vb fut pass ind 3rd pers pl id.

κοιμηθῆτε vb 1st aor pass subj 2nd pers pl id.

κοιμήθητι vb 1st aor pass impv 2nd pers sg id.

κοιμηθήτω vb 1st aor pass impv 3rd pers sg id.

κοιμηθῶ vb 1st aor pass subj 1st pers sg id.

κοιμηθῶμεν vb 1st aor pass subj 1st pers pl id.

κοιμηθῶσιν vb 1st aor pass subj 3rd pers pl id.

κοιμήσει noun fem dat sg . . . . κοίμησις

κοιμήσεως noun fem gen sg id.

κοιμίζων vb pres act part masc nom sg . . . . κοιμίζω

κοιμίσας vb 1st aor act part masc nom sg id.

κοιμώμενοι vb pres m/p part masc nom pl . . . . κοιμάω

κοιμωμένοις vb pres m/p part masc and neut dat pl id.

κοιμώμενον vb pres m/p part masc acc sg,

neut nom and acc sg id.

κοιμώμενος vb pres m/p part masc nom sg id.

κοιμωμένους vb pres m/p part masc acc pl id.

κοιμῶνται vb pres m/p ind 3rd pers pl id.

κοινά adj neut nom and acc pl . . . . κοινός

κοινῇ adj fem dat sg id.

κοινήν adj fem acc sg id.

κοινῆς adj fem gen sg id.

κοινολογησόμενον vb fut mid part

masc acc sg . . . . κοινολογέομαι

κοινολογίαν noun fem acc sg . . . . κοινολογία

κοινόν adj masc acc sg, neut nom and acc sg . . . . . . κοινός

κοινοῦ adj masc and neut gen sg id.

Κοιντος pr noun masc nom sg

κοινῷ adj masc and neut dat sg . . . . κοινός κοινώνει vb pres act impv 2nd pers sg . . . . κοινωνέω

κοινωνεῖ vb pres act ind 3rd pers sg   id.

κοινωνεῖν vb pres act inf   id.

κοινωνήσας vb 1st aor act part masc nom sg   id.

κοινωνήσει vb fut act ind 3rd pers sg   id.

κοινώνησον vb 1st aor act impv 2nd pers sg   id.

κοινωνήσοντες vb fut act part masc nom pl   id.

κοινωνία noun fem dat sg . . . . κοινωνία

κοινωνίαν noun fem acc sg   id.

κοινωνίας noun fem gen sg   id.

κοινωνοί noun masc or fem nom pl . . . . κοινωνός

κοινωνόν noun masc or fem acc sg   id.

κοινωνός noun masc or fem nom sg   id.

κοινωνοῦ noun masc or fem gen sg   id.

κοινωνούς noun masc or fem acc pl   id.

κοινωνῶν vb pres act part masc nom sg . . . . κοινωνέω

κοινῶς adverb

κοιτάζεις vb pres act ind 2nd pers sg . . . . κοιτάζω

κοιτάζηται vb pres m/p subj 3rd pers sg   id.

κοιταζόμενος vb pres m/p part masc nom sg   id.

κοιταζομένους vb pres m/p part masc acc pl   id.

κοιταζόντων vb pres act part masc and neut gen pl   id.

κοίταις noun fem dat pl . . . . κοίτη

κοίτας noun fem acc pl   id.

κοιτασθήσεται vb fut pass ind 3rd pers sg . . . . . . κοιτάζω

κοιτασθήσονται vb fut pass ind 3rd pers pl   id.

κοιτασίαν noun fem acc sg . . . . κοιτασία

κοίτη noun fem nom sg

κοίτῃ noun fem dat sg . . . . κοίτη

κοίτην noun fem acc sg   id.

κοίτης noun fem gen sg   id.

κοιτῶν noun fem gen pl   id.

κοιτῶνα noun masc acc sg . . . . κοιτών

κοιτῶνι noun masc dat sg   id.

κοιτῶνος noun masc gen sg   id.

κοιτώνων noun masc gen pl   id.

κόκκινα adj neut nom and acc pl . . . . κόκκινος

κόκκινον adj masc acc sg, neut nom and acc sg   id.

κοκκίνου adj masc and neut gen sg   id.

κοκκίνῳ adj masc and neut dat sg   id.

κόκκῳ noun masc dat sg . . . . κόκκος

κόκκων noun masc gen pl   id.

κολαβρισθείησαν vb 1st aor pass opt

     3rd pers pl . . . . κολαβρίζομαι

κολάζειν vb pres act inf . . . . κολάζω

κολάζεται vb pres m/p ind 3rd pers sg   id.

κολαζόμενοι vb pres m/p part masc nom pl   id.

κολάζοντα vb pres act part masc acc sg   id.

κολάζων vb pres act part masc nom sg   id.

κολακεύει vb pres act ind 3rd pers sg . . . . κολακεύω

κολακεύων vb pres act part masc nom sg   id.

κολακεύωσιν vb pres act subj 3rd pers pl   id.

κολάσαι vb 1st aor act inf . . . . κολάζω

κολάσασθαι vb 1st aor mid inf   id.

κολασάτω vb 1st aor act impv 3rd pers sg   id.

κολάσεσιν noun fem dat pl . . . . κόλασις

κολάσεων noun fem gen pl   id.

κολάσεως noun fem gen sg   id.

κολάσῃς vb 1st aor act subj 2nd pers sg . . . . κολάζω

κολασθείς vb 1st aor pass part masc nom sg   id.

κολασθέντων vb 1st aor pass part masc and neut gen pl   id.

κολασθῆναι vb 1st aor pass inf   id.

κολασθήσεται vb fut pass ind 3rd pers sg   id.

κολασθήσονται vb fut pass ind 3rd pers pl   id.

κολασθῶσιν vb 1st aor pass subj 3rd pers pl   id.

κόλασιν noun fem acc sg . . . . κόλασις

κολεόν noun masc acc sg . . . . κολεός

κολεοῦ noun masc gen sg   id.

κολεῷ noun masc dat sg   id.

κολλᾶται vb pres m/p ind 3rd pers sg . . . . κολλάω

κόλλῃ noun fem dat sg . . . . κόλλη

κολληθείη vb 1st aor pass opt 3rd pers sg . . . . κολλάω

κολληθήσεται vb fut pass ind 3rd pers sg   id.

κολληθήσῃ vb fut pass ind 2nd pers sg   id.

κολληθήσονται vb fut pass ind 3rd pers pl   id.

κολλήθητι vb 1st aor pass impv 2nd pers sg   id.

κολλύρια noun neut nom and acc pl . . . . κολλύριον

κολλυρίδα noun fem acc sg . . . . κολλυρίς

κολλυρίδας noun fem acc pl   id.

κολλυρισάτω vb 1st aor act impv 3rd pers sg . . κολλυρίζω

κολλώμενος vb pres m/p part masc nom sg . . . . κολλάω

κολλῶνται vb pres m/p ind 3rd pers pl   id.

κολοβόκερκον adj masc acc sg,

     neut nom and acc sg . . . . κολοβόκερκος

κολοβόριν adj masc nom sg

κολοβόρριν see κολοβόριν

κολοβοῦσιν vb pres act ind 3rd pers pl . . . . κολοβόω

κολόκυνθαν noun fem acc sg . . . . κολόκυνθα

κολοκύνθη noun fem dat sg   id.

κολοκύνθης noun fem gen sg   id.

κόλπον noun masc acc sg . . . . κόλπος

κόλπου noun masc gen sg   id.

κόλπους noun masc acc pl   id.

κόλπῳ noun masc dat sg   id.

κόλπωμα noun neut nom and acc sg

κολυμβήθρα noun fem nom sg

κολυμβήθραν noun fem acc sg . . . . κολυμβήθρα

κολυμβήθρας noun fem gen sg and acc pl   id.

κόμαι noun fem nom pl . . . . κόμη

κόμας noun fem acc pl   id.

κόμην noun fem acc sg   id.

κόμης noun fem gen sg   id.

κομιδῆ noun fem dat sg . . . . κομιδή

κομίζου vb pres m/p impv 2nd pers sg . . . . κομίζω

κομίζουσιν vb pres act ind 3rd pers pl .... κομίζω	κοπιάσεις vb fut act ind 2nd pers sg .... κοπιάω
κομιοῦμαι vb fut mid ind 1st pers sg id.	κοπιάσῃ vb 1st aor act subj 3rd pers sg id.
κομιοῦνται vb fut mid ind 3rd pers pl id.	κοπιάσουσιν vb fut act ind 3rd pers pl id.
κομιοῦντας vb fut act part masc acc pl id.	κοπιᾶτε vb pres act impv 2nd pers sg id.
κόμισαι vb 1st aor mid impv 2nd pers sg id.	κοπιῶ vb pres act ind 1st pers sg id.
κομίσαι vb 1st aor act inf id.	κοπιῶν vb pres act part masc nom sg id.
κομίσας vb 1st aor act part masc nom sg id.	κοπιῶντας vb pres act part masc acc pl id.
κομίσασθαι vb 1st aor mid inf id.	κοπιῶντι vb pres act part masc and neut dat sg id.
κομισάσθωσαν vb 1st aor mid impv 3rd pers pl id.	κοπιώντων vb pres act part masc and neut gen pl id.
κομίσεται vb fut mid ind 3rd pers sg id.	κόποι noun masc nom pl .... κόπος
κομίσῃ vb 1st aor act subj 3rd pers sg id.	κόποις noun masc dat pl id.
κομίσωμαι vb 1st aor mid subj 1st pers sg id.	κόπον noun masc acc sg id.
κόμμα noun neut nom and acc sg	κόπος noun masc nom sg id.
κόμποις noun masc dat pl .... κόμπος	κόπου noun masc gen sg id.
κόμπῳ noun masc dat sg id.	κόπους noun masc acc pl id.
κόνδυ noun neut nom and acc sg	κόπρια noun neut nom and acc pl .... κόπριον
κονδυλίζοντας vb pres act part masc acc pl ... κονδυλίζω	κοπρία noun fem nom sg
κονδυλισμούς noun masc acc pl .... κονδυλισμός	κοπρίας noun fem gen sg .... κοπρία
κόνει noun fem dat sg .... κόνις	κοπρίων noun neut gen pl .... κόπριον
κονία noun fem nom sg	κοπριῶν noun fem gen pl .... κοπρία
κονίᾳ noun fem dat sg .... κονία	κόπρον noun fem acc sg .... κόπρος
κονίαμα noun neut nom and acc sg	κόπρος noun fem nom sg id.
κονιάματος noun neut gen sg .... κονίαμα	κόπρου noun fem gen sg id.
κονίαν noun fem acc sg .... κονία	κόπρῳ noun fem dat sg id.
κονίας noun fem gen sg id.	κόπτειν vb pres act inf .... κόπτω
κονιάσεις vb fut act ind 2nd pers sg .... κονιάω	κόπτεσθε vb pres m/p impv 2nd pers pl,
κονιορτόν noun masc acc sg .... κονιορτός	pres m/p ind 2nd pers pl id.
κονιορτός noun masc nom sg id.	κόπτετε vb pres act impv 2nd pers pl id.
κονιορτοῦ noun masc gen sg id.	κοπτόμενοι vb pres m/p part masc nom pl id.
κονιορτῶν noun masc gen pl id.	κόπτονται vb pres m/p ind 3rd pers pl id.
κοντοῖς noun masc dat pl .... κοντός	κόπτοντες vb pres act part masc nom pl id.
κοντός noun masc nom sg id.	κόπτοντος vb pres act part masc and neut gen sg id.
κονύζης noun fem gen sg .... κόνυζα	κόπτουσιν vb pres act ind 3rd pers pl id.
κοπανίζον vb pres act part neut nom and acc sg .. κοπανίζω	κόπτων vb pres act part masc nom sg id.
κοπάσαι vb 1st aor act inf .... κοπάζω	κόπῳ noun masc dat sg .... κόπος
κοπάσει vb fut act ind 3rd pers sg id.	κόπων noun masc gen pl id.
κοπάσῃ vb 1st aor act subj 3rd pers sg id.	κοπώσει vb fut act ind 3rd pers sg .... κοπόω
κόπασον vb 1st aor act impv 2nd pers sg id.	κόπωσις noun fem nom sg
κοπάσουσιν vb fut act ind 3rd pers pl id.	κόραι noun fem nom pl .... κόρη
κοπάσω vb 1st aor act subj 1st pers sg,	κόραις noun fem dat pl id.
fut act ind 1st pers sg id.	κόρακα noun masc acc sg .... κόραξ
κοπετόν noun masc acc sg .... κοπετός	κόρακες noun masc nom pl id.
κοπετός noun masc nom sg id.	κόρακι noun masc dat sg id.
κοπετοῦ noun masc gen sg id.	κοράκων noun masc gen pl id.
κοπετῷ noun masc dat sg id.	κόραν noun fem acc sg .... κόρη
κοπήν noun fem acc sg .... κοπή	κόραξ noun masc nom sg
κοπῆς noun fem gen sg id.	κόραξι noun masc dat pl .... κόραξ
κοπῆς vb 2nd aor pass subj 2nd pers sg .... κόπτω	κόρας noun fem acc pl .... κόρη
κοπήσονται vb fut pass ind 3rd pers pl id.	κοράσια noun neut nom and acc pl .... κοράσιον
κοπήτω vb 1st aor act impv 3rd pers sg id.	κορασίοις noun neut dat pl id.
κοπιᾶσαι vb 1st aor act inf .... κοπιάω	κοράσιον noun neut nom and acc sg id.
κοπιάσει vb fut act ind 3rd pers sg id.	κορασίου noun neut gen sg id.

κορασίων noun neut gen pl . . . . κοράσιον	κοτύλης noun fem gen sg . . . . κοτύλη
Κορε pr noun	κοτυλῶν noun fem gen pl id.
Κορεΐμ pr noun	Κουε pr noun
κόρην noun fem acc sg . . . . κόρη	Κουθα pr noun
κόρης noun fem gen sg id.	Κουλον pr noun
κορήσουσιν vb fut act ind 3rd pers pl . . . . κορέω	κουρᾷ noun fem dat sg . . . . κουρά
Κορινθιου pr noun masc gen sg . . . . Κορινθιος	κουρᾶς noun fem gen sg id.
κόριον noun neut nom and acc sg	κουρέα noun masc acc sg . . . . κουρεύς
κορίου noun neut gen sg . . . . κόριον	κουρέως noun masc gen sg id.
Κορῖται pr noun masc nom pl . . . . Κορίτης	κουρῶν noun fem gen pl . . . . κουρά
Κοριτη pr noun masc dat sg . . . . Κοριτη	κούφη adj fem nom sg . . . . κοῦφος
κόροι noun masc nom pl . . . . κόρος	κούφης adj fem gen sg id.
κόρον noun masc acc sg id.	κουφιεῖς vb fut act ind 2nd pers sg . . . . κουφίζω
κόρου noun masc gen sg id.	κουφίζεται vb pres m/p ind 3rd pers sg id.
κόρους noun masc acc pl id.	κουφίζουσα vb pres act part fem nom sg id.
κόρυθα noun fem acc sg . . . . κόρυς	κουφιοῦσιν vb fut act ind 3rd pers pl id.
κορύνην noun fem acc sg . . . . κορύνη	κουφίσῃ vb 1st aor act subj 3rd pers sg id.
κορυφαῖς noun fem dat pl . . . . κορυφή	κουφισθῆναι vb aor pass inf id.
κορυφάς noun fem acc pl id.	κούφισον vb 1st 1st aor act impv 2nd pers sg id.
κορυφή noun fem nom sg id.	κοῦφοι adj masc nom pl . . . . κοῦφος
κορυφῇ noun fem dat sg id.	κούφοις adj masc and neut dat pl id.
κορυφήν noun fem acc sg id.	κοῦφον adj masc acc sg, neut nom and acc sg id.
κορυφῆς noun fem gen sg id.	κοῦφος adj masc nom sg id.
κορυφῶν noun fem gen pl id.	κουφότεροι comp adj masc nom pl id.
κόρων noun masc gen pl . . . . κόρος	κούφως adverb
κορῶναι noun fem nom pl . . . . κορώνη	κοφίνῳ noun masc dat sg . . . . κόφινος
κορώνη noun fem nom sg id.	κόχλαξ noun masc nom sg
κοσκίνου noun neut gen sg . . . . κόσκινον	κόχλαξι noun neut masc pl . . . . κόχλαξ
κοσμῆσαι vb 1st aor act inf . . . . κοσμέω	κόψαι vb 1st aor act inf . . . . κόπτω
κοσμήσει vb fut act ind 3rd pers sg id.	κόψασθαι vb 1st aor mid inf id.
κοσμήσειν vb fut act inf id.	κόψασθε vb 1st aor mid impv 2nd pers pl id.
κοσμήσῃ vb 1st aor mid subj 2nd pers sg id.	κόψατε vb 1st aor act impv 2nd pers pl id.
κόσμησον vb 1st aor act impv 2nd pers sg id.	κοψάτωσαν vb 1st aor act impv 3rd pers pl id.
κόσμιον noun neut nom and acc sg	κόψει vb fut act ind 3rd pers sg id.
κόσμον noun masc acc sg . . . . κόσμος	κόψεις vb fut act ind 2nd pers sg id.
κοσμοπληθεῖ adj dat sg . . . . κοσμοπληθής	κόψεσθε vb fut mid ind 2nd pers pl id.
κοσμοποιίας noun fem gen sg . . . . κοσμοποιία	κόψεται vb fut mid ind 3rd pers sg id.
κόσμος noun masc nom sg	κόψησθε vb 1st aor mid subj 2nd pers pl id.
κόσμου noun masc gen sg . . . . κόσμος	κόψομεν vb fut act ind 1st pers pl id.
κοσμούμενα vb pres m/p part neut nom and acc pl . . κοσμέω	κόψονται vb fut mid ind 3rd pers pl id.
κοσμοῦντες vb pres act part masc nom pl id.	κόψωνται vb 1st aor mid subj 3rd pers pl id.
κόσμους noun masc acc pl . . . . κόσμος	κόψωσιν vb 1st aor act subj 3rd pers pl id.
κοσμοῦσι vb pres act ind 3rd pers pl . . . . κοσμέω	κραδαίνων vb pres act part masc nom sg . . . . κραδαίνω
κοσμοφοροῦσα vb pres act part fem nom sg . . κοσμοφορέω	κραδάνας vb 1st aor act part masc nom sg id.
κόσμῳ noun masc dat sg . . . . κόσμος	κράζειν vb pres act inf . . . . κράζω
κόσμων noun masc gen pl id.	κράζεις vb pres act ind 2nd pers sg id.
κόσυμβοι noun masc nom pl . . . . κόσυμβος	κραζόντων vb pres act part masc and neut gen pl id.
κοσύμβους noun masc acc pl id.	κράζουσα vb pres act part fem nom sg id.
κοσυμβωτόν adj masc acc sg,	κράζων vb pres act part masc nom sg id.
neut nom and acc sg . . . . κοσυμβωτός	κραιπαλήσατε vb 1st aor act ind 2nd pers pl . . . κραιπαλάω
κοτύλαι noun fem nom pl . . . . κοτύλη	κραιπαλῶν vb pres act part masc nom sg id.
κοτύλην noun fem acc sg id.	κρᾶμα noun neut nom and acc sg

κρανίον noun neut nom and acc sg
κράσπεδα noun neut nom and acc pl .... κράσπεδον
κρασπέδοις noun neut dat pl   id.
κρασπέδου noun neut gen sg   id.
κρασπέδων noun neut gen pl   id.
κραταιά adj fem nom sg .... κραταιός
κραταιᾷ adj fem dat sg   id.
κραταιάν adj fem acc sg   id.
κραταιᾶς adj fem gen sg   id.
κραταιοί adj masc nom pl   id.
κραταιοῖς adj masc and neut dat pl   id.
κραταιόν adj masc acc sg, neut nom and acc sg   id.
κραταιός adj masc nom sg   id.
κραταιότερον comp adj masc acc sg,
        neut nom and acc sg   id.
κραταιότητι noun fem dat sg .... κραταιότης
κραταιοῦ adj masc and neut gen sg .... κραταιός
κραταιοῦ vb pres m/p impv 2nd pers sg .... κραταιόω
κραταιοῦντας vb pres act part masc acc pl   id.
κραταιούς adj masc acc pl .... κραταιός
κραταιοῦσθε vb pres m/p impv 2nd pers pl ..... κραταιόω
κραταιούσθω vb pres m/p impv 3rd pers sg   id.
κραταιούσθωσαν vb pres m/p impv 3rd pers pl   id.
κραταιοῦται vb pres m/p ind 3rd pers sg   id.
κραταιῷ adj masc and neut dat sg .... κραταιός
κραταιωθῇ vb 1st aor pass subj 3rd pers sg ..... κραταιόω
κραταιώθητε vb 1st aor pass impv 2nd pers pl   id.
κραταιωθήτω vb 1st aor pass impv 3rd pers sg   id.
κραταιωθῶμεν vb 1st aor pass subj 1st pers pl   id.
κραταιωθῶσιν vb 1st aor pass subj 3rd pers pl   id.
κραταίωμα noun neut nom and acc sg
κραταιῶν adj gen pl .... κραταιός
κραταιῶς adverb
κραταιῶσαι vb 1st aor act inf .... κραταιόω
κραταιώσει vb fut act ind 3rd pers sg   id.
κραταιώσητε vb 1st aor act subj 2nd pers pl   id.
κραταίωσιν noun fem acc sg .... κραταίωσις
κραταίωσις noun fem nom sg   id.
κραταιώσομεν vb fut act ind 1st pers pl .... κραταιόω
κραταίωσον vb 1st aor act impv 2nd pers sg   id.
κράτει noun neut dat sg .... κράτος
κρατεῖ vb pres act ind 3rd pers sg .... κρατέω
κρατεῖν vb pres act inf   id.
κρατεῖς vb pres act ind 2nd pers sg   id.
κρατεῖται vb pres m/p ind 3rd pers sg   id.
κράτη noun neut nom and acc pl .... κράτος
κρατηθείσης vb 1st aor pass part fem gen sg ...... κρατέω
κρατήρ noun masc nom sg
κρατῆρα noun masc acc sg .... κρατήρ
κρατῆρας noun masc acc pl   id.
κρατῆρες noun masc nom pl   id.
κρατῆσαι vb 1st aor act inf .... κρατέω

κρατήσαντας vb 1st aor act part masc acc pl ...... κρατέω
κρατήσας vb 1st aor act part masc nom sg   id.
κρατήσει vb fut act ind 3rd pers sg   id.
κρατήσῃ vb 1st aor act subj 3rd pers sg,
        fut mid ind 2nd pers sg   id.
κράτησις noun fem nom sg
κράτησον vb 1st aor act impv 2nd pers sg .... κρατέω
κρατήσουσιν vb fut act ind 3rd pers pl   id.
κρατήσω vb fut act ind 1st pers sg   id.
κρατήσωμεν vb 1st aor act subj 1st pers pl   id.
κρατήσωσιν vb 1st aor act subj 3rd pers pl   id.
Κρατητα pr noun masc acc sg .... Κρατης
κράτιστα superl adj neut nom and acc pl .... κρείσσων
κρατίσταις superl adj fem dat pl   id.
κρατίστας superl adj fem acc pl   id.
κρατίστη superl adj fem nom sg   id.
κρατίστοις superl adj masc and neut dat pl   id.
κράτιστον superl adj masc acc sg,
        neut nom and acc sg   id.
κρατίστους superl adj masc acc pl   id.
κράτος noun neut nom and acc sg
κρατούμενα vb pres m/p part neut nom and acc pl .. κρατέω
κρατουμένων vb pres m/p part gen pl   id.
κρατοῦντα vb pres act part masc acc sg   id.
κρατοῦντας vb pres act part masc acc pl   id.
κρατοῦντες vb pres act part masc nom pl   id.
κρατοῦντι vb pres act part masc and neut dat sg   id.
κρατούντων vb pres act part masc and neut gen pl id.
κράτους noun neut gen sg .... κράτος
κρατοῦσα vb pres act part fem nom sg .... κρατέω
κρατοῦσι vb pres act ind 3rd pers pl   id.
κρατυνθέν vb 1st aor pass part
        neut nom and acc sg .... κρατύνω
κρατῶν vb pres act part masc nom sg .... κρατέω
κραυγή noun fem nom sg
κραυγῇ noun fem dat sg .... κραυγή
κραυγήν noun fem acc sg   id.
κραυγῆς noun fem gen sg   id.
κρέα noun neut nom and acc pl .... κρέας
κρεάγρα noun fem nom sg
κρεάγρᾳ noun fem dat sg .... κρεάγρα
κρεάγρας noun fem acc pl   id.
κρεαγρῶν noun fem gen pl   id.
κρέας noun neut nom and acc sg
κρεῖσσον adj neut nom and acc sg .... κρείσσων
κρείσσους adj masc and fem nom and acc pl   id.
κρείσσω adj neut nom and acc pl   id.
κρείσσων adj masc and fem nom sg   id.
κρεῖττον adj neut nom and acc sg .... κρείττων
κρείττονι adj dat sg   id.
κρείττω adj masc and fem acc sg, neut nom and acc pl id.
κρείττων adj masc and fem nom sg

κρεμάζων   vb pres act part masc nom sg . . . . κρεμάζω

κρεμαμένη   vb pres m/p part fem nom sg . . . . κρεμάω

κρεμάμενοι   vb pres m/p part masc nom pl   id.

κρεμάμενον   vb pres m/p part masc acc sg   id.

κρεμάμενος   vb pres m/p part masc nom sg   id.

κρέμανται   vb pres m/p ind 3rd pers pl   id.

κρεμάσαι   vb 1st aor act inf   id.

κρεμάσαντες   vb 1st aor act part masc nom pl   id.

κρεμάσατε   vb 1st aor act impv 2nd pers pl   id.

κρεμάσει   vb fut act ind 3rd pers sg   id.

κρεμάσητε   vb 1st aor act subj 2nd pers pl   id.

κρεμασθῆναι   vb 1st aor pass inf   id.

κρεμασθήτω   vb 1st aor pass impv 3rd pers sg   id.

κρεμαστά   adj neut nom and acc pl . . . . κρεμαστός

κρεμαστόν   adj masc acc sg, neut nom and acc sg   id.

κρεμάσω   vb fut act ind 1st pers sg . . . . κρεμάζω

κρέμαται   vb pres m/p ind 3rd pers sg . . . . κρεμάω

κρεῶν   noun neut gen pl . . . . κρέας

κρημνοῦ   noun masc gen sg . . . . κρημνός

κρήνας   noun fem acc pl . . . . κρήνη

κρήνην   noun fem acc sg   id.

κρήνης   noun fem gen sg   id.

κρηπῖδα   noun fem acc sg . . . . κρηπίς

κρηπῖδος   noun fem gen sg   id.

κρηπίδων   noun fem gen pl   id.

Κρῆτας   pr noun masc acc pl . . . . Κρῆτες

Κρῆτες   pr noun masc nom pl   id.

Κρητη   pr noun fem nom sg

Κρητης   pr noun fem gen sg . . . . Κρητη

Κρητῶν   pr noun gen pl . . . . Κρῆτες

κριθαί   noun fem nom pl . . . . κριθή

κριθάς   noun fem acc pl   id.

κριθή   noun fem nom sg   id.

κριθῇ   noun fem dat sg   id.

κριθῇ   vb 1st aor pass subj 3rd pers sg . . . . κρίνω

κριθήν   noun fem acc sg . . . . κριθή

κριθῆναι   vb 1st aor pass inf . . . . κρίνω

κριθῆς   noun fem gen sg . . . . κριθή

κριθήσεται   vb fut pass ind 3rd pers sg . . . . κρίνω

κριθήσομαι   vb fut pass ind 1st pers sg   id.

κριθησόμενος   vb fut pass part masc nom sg   id.

κρίθητε   vb 1st aor pass impv 2nd pers pl   id.

κρίθητι   vb 1st aor pass impv 2nd pers sg   id.

κριθήτωσαν   vb 1st aor pass impv 3rd pers pl   id.

κρίθινον   adj masc acc sg, neut nom and acc sg . . . . κρίθινος

κριθίνου   adj masc and neut gen sg   id.

κριθίνους   adj masc acc pl   id.

κριθῶμεν   vb 1st aor pass subj 1st pers pl . . . . κρίνω

κριθῶν   noun fem gen pl . . . . κριθή

κρίκοι   noun masc nom pl . . . . κρίκος

κρίκοις   noun masc dat pl   id.

κρίκον   noun masc acc sg   id.

κρίκους   noun masc acc pl . . . . κρίκος

κρίμα   noun neut nom and acc sg

κρίμασι   noun neut dat pl . . . . κρίμα

κρίματα   noun neut nom and acc pl   id.

κρίματι   noun neut dat sg   id.

κρίματος   noun neut gen sg   id.

κριμάτων   noun neut gen pl   id.

κρίνα   noun neut nom and acc pl . . . . κρίνον

κρίναι   vb 1st aor act opt 3rd pers sg . . . . κρίνω

κρῖναι   vb 1st aor act inf   id.

κρίνας   vb 1st aor act part masc nom sg   id.

κρίνατε   vb 1st aor act impv 2nd pers pl   id.

κρινάτω   vb 1st aor act impv 3rd pers sg   id.

κρῖνε   vb pres act impv 2nd pers sg   id.

κρίνει   vb pres act ind 3rd pers sg   id.

κρινεῖ   vb fut act ind 3rd pers sg   id.

κρίνειν   vb pres act inf   id.

κρίνεις   vb pres act ind 2nd pers sg   id.

κρινεῖς   vb fut act ind 2nd pers sg   id.

κρίνεσθαι   vb pres m/p inf   id.

κρίνεται   vb pres m/p ind 3rd pers sg   id.

κρίνετε   vb pres act ind 2nd pers pl

κρίνῃ   vb pres act subj 3rd pers sg,
     1st aor act subj 3rd pers sg   id.

κρίνῃς   vb pres act subj 2nd pers sg,
     1st aor act subj 2nd pers sg   id.

κρίνηται   vb pres m/p subj 3rd pers sg,
     1st aor mid subj 3rd pers sg   id.

κρίνοις   noun neut dat pl . . . . κρίνον

κρίνομαι   vb pres m/p ind 1st pers sg . . . . κρίνω

κρίνομεν   vb pres act ind 1st pers pl   id.

κρινόμενοι   vb pres m/p part masc nom pl   id.

κρινόμενος   vb pres m/p part masc nom sg   id.

κρινομένου   vb pres m/p part masc and neut gen sg   id.

κρινομένων   vb pres m/p part gen pl   id.

κρίνον   noun neut nom and acc sg

κρῖνον   vb 1st aor act impv 2nd pers sg . . . . κρίνω

κρίνοντες   vb pres act part masc nom pl   id.

κρίνοντος   vb pres act part masc and neut gen sg   id.

κρινόντων   vb pres act part masc and neut gen pl   id.

κρίνου   noun neut gen sg . . . . κρίνον

κρινοῦσι(ν)   vb fut act ind 3rd pers pl . . . . κρίνω

κρίνω   vb pres act ind 1st pers sg,
     1st aor act subj 1st pers sg   id.

κρινῶ   vb fut act ind 1st pers sg   id.

κρίνων   vb pres act part masc nom sg   id.

κρίνωσιν   vb 1st aor act subj 3rd pers pl   id.

κριοί   noun masc nom pl . . . . κριός

κριοῖς   noun masc dat pl   id.

κριόν   noun masc acc sg   id.

κριός   noun masc nom sg   id.

κριοῦ   noun masc gen sg   id.

κριούς noun masc acc pl	. . . .	κριός
κρίσει noun fem dat sg	. . . .	κρίσις
κρίσεις noun fem nom and acc pl		id.
κρίσεων noun fem gen pl		id.
κρίσεως noun fem gen sg		id.
κρίσιν noun fem acc sg		id.
κρίσις noun fem nom sg		id.
κριταί noun masc nom pl	. . . .	κριτής
κριταῖς noun masc dat pl		id.
κριτάς noun masc acc pl		id.
κριτήν noun masc acc sg		id.
κριτήριον noun neut nom and acc sg		
κριτηρίου noun neut gen sg	. . . .	κριτήριον
κριτής noun masc nom sg		
κριτοῦ noun masc gen sg	. . . .	κριτής
κριτῶν noun masc gen pl		id.
κριῷ noun masc dat sg	. . . .	κριός
κριῶν noun masc gen pl		id.
κρόκη noun fem nom sg		
κρόκη noun fem dat sg	. . . .	κρόκη
κρόκην noun fem acc sg		id.
κρόκης noun fem gen sg		id.
κροκόδειλος noun masc nom sg		
κρόκος noun masc nom sg		
κρόκῳ noun masc dat sg	. . . .	κρόκος
κρόμμυα noun neut nom and acc pl	. . . .	κρόμμυον
κροσσούς noun masc acc pl	. . . .	κροσός
κροσσωτά adj neut nom and acc pl	. . . .	κροσσωτός
κροσσωτοῖς adj masc and neut dat pl		id.
κροτάφοις noun masc dat pl	. . . .	κρόταφος
κρόταφον noun masc acc sg		id.
κροτάφῳ noun masc dat sg		id.
κροτάφων noun masc gen pl		id.
κροτήσατε vb 1st aor act impv 2nd pers pl	. . . .	κροτέω
κροτήσει vb fut act ind 3rd pers sg		id.
κρότησον vb 1st aor act impv 2nd pers sg		id.
κροτήσουσιν vb fut act ind 3rd pers pl		id.
κροτήσω vb fut act ind 1st pers sg		id.
κρούει vb pres act ind 3rd pers sg	. . . .	κρούω
κρουνηδόν adverb		
κρούοντες vb pres act part masc nom pl	. . . .	κρούω
κρυβῇ adverb		
κρύβηθι vb 2nd aor pass impv 2nd pers sg	. . . .	κρύπτω
κρυβῆναι vb 2nd aor pass inf		id.
κρυβήσεσθε vb fut pass ind 2nd pers pl		id.
κρυβήσεται vb fut pass ind 3rd pers sg		id.
κρυβήσομαι vb fut pass ind 1st pers sg		id.
κρυβήσονται vb fut pass ind 3rd pers pl		id.
κρυβόμενος vb 2nd aor pass part masc nom sg		id.
κρυβῶ vb 2nd aor pass subj 1st pers sg		id.
κρυπτά adj neut nom and acc pl	. . . .	κρυπτός
κρυπταί adj fem nom pl		id.

κρυπτάς adj fem acc pl	. . . .	κρυπτός
κρύπτει vb pres act ind 3rd pers sg	. . . .	κρύπτω
κρύπτειν vb pres act inf		id.
κρύπτεσθε vb pres m/p impv 2nd pers pl		id.
κρύπτεται vb pres m/p ind 3rd pers sg		id.
κρύπτῃ vb pres m/p ind 2nd pers sg		id.
κρυπτήν adj fem acc sg	. . . .	κρυπτός
κρυπτομένης vb pres m/p part fem gen sg	. . . .	κρύπτω
κρυπτόμενοι vb pres m/p part masc nom pl		id.
κρυπτόν adj masc acc sg, neut nom and acc sg	. . . .	κρυπτός
κρυπτῷ adj masc and neut dat sg		id.
κρύπτων vb pres act part masc nom sg	. . . .	κρύπτω
κρυπτῶν adj gen pl	. . . .	κρυπτός
κρυπτῶς adverb		
κρυσταλλοειδές adj neut nom and acc sg		κρυσταλλοειδής
κρύσταλλον noun masc acc sg	. . . .	κρύσταλλος
κρύσταλλος noun masc nom sg		id.
κρυστάλλου noun masc gen sg		id.
κρυφαία adj fem dat sg	. . . .	κρυφαῖος
κρυφαίοις adj masc and neut dat pl		id.
κρυφαίως adverb		
κρυφῇ adverb		
κρύφια adj neut nom and acc pl	. . . .	κρύφιος
κρύφιε adj masc voc sg		id.
κρυφίοις adj masc and neut dat pl		id.
κρύφιος adj masc nom sg		id.
κρυφίων adj gen pl		id.
κρύφοις noun masc dat pl	. . . .	κρύφος
κρύφους noun masc acc pl		id.
κρύψαι vb 1st aor act inf	. . . .	κρύπτω
κρύψας vb 1st aor act part masc nom sg		id.
κρύψει vb fut act ind 3rd pers sg		id.
κρύψῃ vb 1st aor act subj 3rd pers sg,		
fut mid ind 2nd pers sg		id.
κρύψῃς vb 1st aor act subj 2nd pers sg		id.
κρύψητε vb 1st aor act subj 2nd pers pl		id.
κρύψον vb 1st aor act impv 2nd pers sg		id.
κρύψουσιν vb fut act ind 3rd pers pl		id.
κρύψω vb 1st aor act subj 1st pers sg,		
fut act ind 1st pers sg		id.
κρύψωμεν vb 1st aor act subj 1st pers pl		id.
κτᾶσαι vb pres dep ind 2nd pers sg	. . . .	κτάομαι
κτᾶσθαι vb pres dep inf		id.
κτᾶται vb pres dep ind 3rd pers sg		id.
κτεῖναι vb 1st aor act inf	. . . .	κτείνω
κτεῖνε vb pres act impv 2nd pers sg		id.
κτεινομένους vb pres m/p part masc acc pl		id.
κτηθήσονται vb fut pass ind 3rd pers pl	. . . .	κτάομαι
κτῆμα noun neut nom and acc sg		
κτήματα noun neut nom and acc pl	. . . .	κτῆμα
κτημάτων noun neut gen pl		id.
κτήνει noun neut dat sg	. . . .	κτῆνος

κτήνεσι noun neut dat pl	. . . .	κτῆνος
κτήνη noun neut nom and acc pl		id.
κτῆνος noun neut nom and acc sg		id.
κτηνοτρόφοι adj masc and fem nom pl	. . . . .	κτηνοτρόφος
κτηνοτρόφος adj masc and fem nom sg		id.
κτηνοτρόφων adj gen pl		id.
κτήνους noun neut gen sg	. . . .	κτῆνος
κτηνώδης adj masc and fem nom sg		
κτηνῶν noun neut gen pl	. . . .	κτῆνος
κτῆσαι vb 1st aor mid impv 2nd pers sg	. . . .	κτάομαι
κτησάμενοι vb 1st aor mid part masc nom pl		id.
κτησάμενον vb 1st aor mid part masc acc sg		id.
κτησαμένῳ vb 1st aor mid part masc and neut dat sg		id.
κτήσασθαι vb 1st aor mid inf		id.
κτήσασθε vb 1st aor mid impv 2nd pers pl		id.
κτήσει noun fem dat sg	. . . .	κτῆσις
κτήσεις noun fem nom and acc pl		id.
κτήσεσθε vb fut mid ind 2nd pers pl	. . . .	κτάομαι
κτήσεται vb fut mid ind 3rd pers sg		id.
κτήσεων noun fem gen pl	. . . .	κτῆσις
κτήσεως noun fem gen sg		id.
κτήσῃ vb 1st aor mid subj 2nd pers sg,		
fut mid ind 2nd pers sg	. . . .	κτάομαι
κτήσηται vb 1st aor mid subj 3rd pers sg		id.
κτήσιν noun fem acc sg	. . . .	κτῆσις
κτῆσις noun fem nom sg		id.
κτήσομαι vb fut mid ind 1st pers sg	. . . .	κτάομαι
κτήσονται vb fut mid ind 3rd pers pl		id.
κτησώμεθα vb 1st aor mid subj 1st pers pl		id.
κτιζόμενος vb pres m/p part masc nom sg	. . . .	κτίζω
κτίζοντι vb pres act part masc and neut dat sg		id.
κτίζω vb pres act ind 1st pers sg		id.
κτίζων vb pres act part masc nom sg		id.
κτίσαι vb 1st aor act inf		id.
κτίσαντα vb 1st aor act part masc acc sg		id.
κτίσαντι vb 1st aor act part masc and neut dat sg		id.
κτίσαντος vb 1st aor act part masc and neut gen sg		id.
κτίσας vb 1st aor act part masc nom sg		id.
κτίσασα vb 1st aor act part fem nom sg		id.
κτίσει noun fem dat sg	. . . .	κτίσις
κτίσεις noun fem nom and acc pl		id.
κτίσεως noun fem gen sg		id.
κτισθέντα vb 1st aor pass part masc acc sg	. . . .	κτίζω
κτισθῆναι vb 1st aor pass inf		id.
κτισθήσονται vb fut pass ind 3rd pers pl		id.
κτίσιν noun fem acc sg	. . . .	κτίσις
κτίσις noun fem nom sg		id.
κτίσμα noun neut nom and acc sg		
κτίσμασι noun neut dat pl	. . . .	κτίσμα
κτίσματι noun neut dat sg		id
κτισμάτων noun neut gen pl		id.
κτίσον vb 1st aor act impv 2nd pers sg	. . . .	κτίζω
κτίστα noun masc voc sg	. . . .	κτίστης
κτίστῃ noun masc dat sg		id.
κτίστην noun masc acc sg		id.
κτίστης noun masc nom sg		id.
κτύπος noun masc nom sg		
κτώμενος vb pres dep part masc nom sg	. . . .	κτάομαι
κτωμένου vb pres dep part masc and neut gen sg		id.
κτωμένων vb pres dep part gen pl		id.
κυάθους noun masc acc pl	. . . .	κύαθος
κύαμον noun masc acc sg	. . . .	κύαμος
Κυαμωνος pr noun masc gen sg	. . . .	Κυαμων
κυβερνᾶν vb pres act inf	. . . .	κυβερνάω
κυβερνηθεῖσα vb 1st aor pass part fem nom sg		id.
κυβερνήσασα vb 1st aor act part fem nom sg		id.
κυβερνήσεως noun fem gen sg	. . . .	κυβέρνησις
κυβέρνησιν noun fem acc sg		id.
κυβέρνησις noun fem nom sg		id.
κυβερνῆται noun masc nom pl	. . . .	κυβερνήτης
κυβερνήτης noun masc nom sg		id.
κυβερνῶσιν vb pres act ind 3rd pers pl	. . . .	κυβερνάω
κύβοις noun masc dat pl	. . . .	κύβος
κύβον noun masc acc sg		id.
Κυδιως pr noun		
κυδοιμῶν noun masc gen pl	. . . .	κυδοιμός
κῦδος noun neut nom and acc sg		
κύησιν noun fem acc sg	. . . .	κύησις
κύθραν noun fem acc sg	. . . .	κύθρα
κυθρόποδες noun masc nom pl	. . . .	κυθρόπους
κυκλόθεν adverb and preposition		
κυκλοῖ vb pres act ind 3rd pers sg	. . . .	κυκλόω
κύκλον noun masc acc sg	. . . .	κύκλος
κυκλούμενον vb pres m/p part masc acc sg,		
neut nom and acc sg	. . . .	κυκλόω
κυκλοῦν vb pres act inf		id.
κυκλοῦντα vb pres act part masc acc sg		id.
κυκλοῦντες vb pres act part masc nom pl		id.
κύκλους noun masc acc pl	. . . .	κύκλος
κυκλοῦσα vb pres act part fem nom sg	. . . .	κυκλόω
κυκλοῦσαν vb pres act part fem acc sg		id.
κυκλοῦσιν vb pres act ind 3rd pers pl		id.
κύκλῳ noun masc dat sg	. . . .	κύκλος
κύκλωμα noun neut nom and acc sg		
κυκλώματα noun neut nom and acc pl	. . . .	κύκλωμα
κυκλώματος noun neut gen sg		id.
κυκλῶν vb pres act part masc nom sg	. . . .	κυκλόω
κυκλῶσαι vb 1st aor act inf		id.
κυκλώσαντα vb 1st aor act part masc acc sg		id.
κυκλώσαντες vb 1st aor act part masc nom pl		id.
κυκλωσάντων vb 1st aor act part masc and neut gen pl		id.
κυκλώσατε vb 1st aor act impv 2nd pers pl		id.
κυκλώσει noun fem dat sg	. . . .	κύκλωσις
κυκλώσει vb fut act ind 3rd pers sg	. . . .	κυκλόω

κυκλώσῃ vb 1st aor act subj 3rd pers sg . . . . κυκλόω	κυπαρίσσου noun fem gen sg . . . . κυπάρισσος
κυκλώσουσιν vb fut act ind 3rd pers pl id.	κυπαρίσσῳ noun fem dat sg id.
κυκλώσω vb fut act ind 1st pers sg id.	κυπαρίσσων noun fem gen pl id.
κύκνειοι adj masc nom pl . . . . κύκνειος	Κυπριαρχης pr noun masc nom sg
κύκνον noun masc acc sg . . . . κύκνος	κυπρίζουσιν vb pres act ind 3rd pers pl . . . . κυπρίζω
κυλίει vb pres act ind 3rd pers sg . . . . κυλίω	κυπρισμός noun masc nom sg
κυλίεται vb pres m/p ind 3rd pers sg id.	Κυπριων pr noun masc gen pl . . . . Κυπριοι
κυλικεῖον noun neut nom and acc sg	κύπροι noun fem nom pl . . . . κύπρος
κυλίκιον noun neut nom and acc sg	Κυπρον pr noun fem acc sg . . . . Κυπρος
κυλιομένη vb pres m/p part fem nom sg . . . . κυλίω	Κυπρου noun fem gen sg . . . . κύπρος
κυλίονται vb pres m/p ind 3rd pers pl id.	κύπτον vb pres act part neut nom and acc sg . . . . κύπτω
κυλίσατε vb 1st aor act impv 2nd pers pl id.	Κυρηναιου pr noun masc gen sg . . . . Κυρηναιος
κυλισθήσεται vb fut pass ind 3rd pers sg id.	Κυρηνην pr noun fem acc sg . . . . Κυρηνη
κυλίω vb pres act ind 1st pers sg id.	κύρια adj neut nom and acc pl . . . . κύριος
κυλίων vb pres act part masc nom sg id.	κυρία noun fem nom sg
κῦμα noun neut nom and acc sg	κυρίᾳ noun fem dat sg . . . . κυρία
κυμαινόμενον vb pres m/p part masc acc sg,	κυρίαν noun fem acc sg id.
neut nom and acc sg . . . . κυμαίνω	κυρίας noun fem gen sg id.
κυμαίνουσα vb pres act part fem nom sg id.	κύριε noun masc voc sg . . . . κύριος
κυμαινούσης vb pres act part fem gen sg id.	κυριεία noun fem nom sg
κυμαίνουσιν vb pres act ind 3rd pers pl id.	κυριείᾳ noun fem dat sg . . . . κυριεία
κύμασι noun neut dat pl . . . . κῦμα	κυριείαν noun fem acc sg id.
κύματα noun neut nom and acc pl id.	κυριείας noun fem gen sg id.
κυμάτια noun neut nom and acc pl . . . . κυμάτιον	κυριεύει vb pres act ind 3rd pers sg . . . . κυριεύω
κυμάτιον noun neut nom and acc sg id.	κυριεύειν vb pres act inf id.
κυμάτων noun neut gen pl . . . . κῦμα	κυριεύεις vb pres act ind 2nd pers sg id.
κύμβαλα noun neut nom and acc pl . . . . κύμβαλον	κυριευθησόμεθα vb fut pass ind 1st pers pl id.
κυμβαλίζοντες vb pres act part masc nom pl . . . κυμβαλίζω	κυριευθήσονται vb fut pass ind 3rd pers pl id.
κυμβάλοις noun neut dat pl . . . . κύμβαλον	κυριεύοντα vb pres act part masc acc sg id.
κύμινον noun neut nom and acc sg	κυριεύοντες vb pres act part masc nom pl id.
κύνα noun masc acc sg . . . . κύων	κυριεύουσα vb pres act part fem nom sg id.
κύνας noun masc acc pl id.	κυριεύουσιν vb pres act ind 3rd pers pl id.
κύνες noun masc nom pl id.	κυριεῦσαι vb 1st aor act inf id.
κυνηγεῖν vb pres act inf . . . . κυνηγέω	κυριεύσαντες vb 1st aor act part masc nom pl id.
κυνήγια noun neut nom and acc pl . . . . κυνήγιον	κυριεύσει vb fut act ind 3rd pers sg id.
κυνηγός noun masc nom sg	κυριεύσεις vb fut act ind 2nd pers sg id.
κυνί noun masc dat sg . . . . κύων	κυριεύσῃ vb 1st aor act subj 3rd pers sg id.
κυνικός adj masc nom sg	κυριεύσομεν vb fut act ind 1st pers pl id.
κυνόμυια noun fem nom sg	κυριεύσουσιν vb fut act ind 3rd pers pl id.
κυνόμυιαν noun fem acc sg . . . . κυνόμυια	κυριεύων vb pres act part masc nom sg id.
κυνομυίης noun fem gen sg id.	κύριοι noun masc nom pl . . . . κύριος
κυνός noun masc or fem gen sg . . . . κύων	κυρίοις noun masc dat pl id.
κυνῶν noun masc or fem gen pl id.	κύριον noun masc acc sg id.
κύουσιν vb pres act ind 3rd pers pl . . . . κύω	κύριος noun masc nom sg id.
κυοφορίαι noun fem nom pl . . . . κυοφορία	κύριου see κυρίου
κυοφορίαις noun fem dat pl id.	κυρίου noun masc gen sg id.
κυοφορούσης vb pres act part fem gen sg . . . . . . κυοφορέω	κυρίους noun masc acc pl id.
κυπαρίσσινα adj neut nom and acc pl . . . . . κυπαρίσσινος	κυρίῳ noun masc dat sg id.
κυπαρισσίνων adj gen pl id.	κυρίων noun masc gen pl id.
κυπάρισσοι noun fem nom pl . . . . κυπάρισσος	κυριωτάτη superl adj fem nom sg id.
κυπάρισσον noun fem acc sg id.	Κύρος pr noun masc nom sg
κυπάρισσος noun fem nom sg	Κυρου pr noun masc gen sg . . . . Κῦρος

κυρτός   adj masc nom sg

Κυρῳ   pr noun masc dat sg . . . . Κῦρος

κυρωθήσεται   vb fut pass ind 3rd pers sg . . . . κυρόω

κύτος   noun neut nom and acc sg

κύφοντα   vb pres act part masc acc sg . . . . κύφω

κύψαντες   vb 1st aor act part masc nom pl . . . . κύπτω

κύψας   vb 1st aor act part masc nom sg   id.

κύψει   vb fut act ind 3rd pers sg   id.

κυψέλην   noun fem acc sg . . . . κυψέλη

κύψον   vb 1st aor act impv 2nd pers sg . . . . κύπτω

κύων   noun masc nom sg

Κῶ   pr noun

κώδια   noun neut nom and acc pl . . . . κώδιον

κωδίων   noun neut gen pl   id.

κώδων   noun masc nom sg

κώδωνα   noun masc acc sg . . . . κώδων

κώδωνας   noun masc acc pl   id.

κώδωσι   noun masc dat pl   id.

κώθων   noun masc nom sg

κώθωνα   noun masc acc sg . . . . κώθων

κωκυτόν   noun masc acc sg . . . . κωκυτός

κῶλα   noun neut nom and acc pl . . . . κῶλον

Κωλα   pr noun

Κωλαδαμ   pr noun

κωλέαν   noun fem acc sg . . . . κωλέα

Κωλια   pr noun

Κωλιος   pr noun

Κωλιτας   pr noun

κώλυε   vb pres act impv 2nd pers sg . . . . κωλύω

κωλύει   vb pres act ind 3rd pers sg   id.

κωλύειν   vb pres act inf   id.

κωλυθῇ   vb 1st aor pass subj 3rd pers sg   id.

κωλυθήσεται   vb fut pass ind 3rd pers sg   id.

κωλύματι   noun neut dat sg . . . . κώλυμα

κωλυόμενος   vb pres m/p part masc nom sg . . . . κωλύω

κωλυόντων   vb pres act part masc and neut gen pl   id.

κωλύου   vb pres m/p impv 2nd pers sg   id.

κωλῦσαι   vb 1st aor act inf   id.

κωλύσει   vb fut act ind 3rd pers sg . . . . κωλύω

κωλύσῃ   vb 1st aor act subj 3rd pers sg,
     fut mid ind 2nd pers sg   id.

κωλύσῃς   vb 1st aor act subj 2nd pers sg   id.

κώλυσον   vb 1st aor act impv 2nd pers sg   id.

κωλύσω   vb 1st aor act subj 1st pers sg,
     fut act ind 1st pers sg   id.

κωλύσων   vb fut act part masc nom sg   id.

κωλυτικῶν   adj gen pl . . . . κωλυτικός

κωλύων   vb pres act part masc nom sg . . . . κωλύω

κῶμαι   noun fem nom pl . . . . κώμη

κώμαις   noun fem dat pl   id.

κωμάρχας   noun masc acc pl . . . . κωμάρχης

κώμας   noun fem acc pl . . . . κώμη

κώμην   noun fem acc sg   id.

κώμης   noun fem gen sg   id.

κώμους   noun masc acc pl . . . . κῶμος

κώμων   noun masc gen pl   id.

κωμῶν   noun fem gen pl . . . . κώμη

Κωνα   pr noun

κωνώπιον   noun neut nom and acc sg

κωνωπίῳ   noun neut dat sg . . . . κωνώπιον

κώπας   noun fem acc pl . . . . κώπη

κωπηλάται   noun masc nom pl . . . . κωπηλάτης

Κωρη   pr noun

Κως   pr noun

κωφ   translit (Heb. letter: ק)

κωφά   adj neut nom and acc pl . . . . κωφός

κωφεύετε   vb pres act ind 2nd pers pl . . . . κωφεύω

κωφεῦσαι   vb 1st aor act inf   id.

κωφεύσατε   vb 1st aor act impv 2nd pers pl   id.

κώφευσον   vb 1st aor act impv 2nd pers sg   id.

κωφεύσω   vb fut act ind 1st pers sg   id.

κωφῆς   adj fem gen sg . . . . κωφός

κωφοί   adj masc nom pl   id.

κωφόν   adj masc acc sg, neut nom and acc sg   id.

κωφός   adj masc nom sg   id.

κωφῶν   adj gen pl   id.

Λ λ

Λααδ   pr noun

Λααδα   pr noun

Λααδαν   pr noun

Λαβαν   pr noun

Λαβανα   pr noun

Λαβαναθ   pr noun

Λαβανω   pr noun

λαβδ   translit (Heb. letter: ל)

Λαβδων   pr noun

λαβέ   vb 2nd aor act impv 2nd pers sg . . . . λαμβάνω

λαβεῖν   vb 2nd aor act inf   id.

Λαβεκ   pr noun

λάβετε   vb 2nd aor act impv 2nd pers pl . . . . λαμβάνω

λαβέτω   vb 2nd aor act impv 3rd pers sg   id.

λαβέτωσαν   vb 2nd aor act impv 3rd pers pl   id.

λάβῃ   vb 2nd aor act subj 3rd pers sg   id.

λαβήν noun fem acc sg . . . . λαβή

λάβῃς vb 2nd aor act subj 2nd pers sg . . . . λαμβάνω

λάβητε vb 2nd aor act subj 2nd pers pl   id.

λαβίδας noun fem acc pl . . . . λαβίς

λαβίδες noun fem nom pl   id.

λαβίδι noun fem dat sg   id.

Λαβιιμ pr noun

λάβοι vb 2nd aor act opt 3rd pers sg . . . . λαμβάνω

λαβόμενος vb 2nd aor mid part masc nom sg   id.

λαβόντα vb 2nd aor act part masc acc sg   id.

λαβόντας vb 2nd aor act part masc acc pl   id.

λαβόντες vb 2nd aor act part masc nom pl   id.

λαβόντος vb 2nd aor act part masc and neut gen sg   id.

λαβοῦσα vb 2nd aor act part fem nom sg   id.

λάβρος adj masc and fem nom sg

λαβροτάτῳ superl adj masc and neut dat sg . . . . λάβρος

λάβρῳ adj dat sg   id.

λάβω vb 2nd aor act subj 1st pers sg . . . . λαμβάνω

Λαβωεμαθ pr noun

Λαβωθ pr noun

λάβωμεν vb 2nd aor act subj 1st pers pl . . . . λαμβάνω

λαβών vb 2nd aor act part masc nom sg   id.

Λαβως pr noun

λάβωσιν vb 2nd aor act subj 3rd pers pl . . . . λαμβάνω

λάγανα noun neut nom and acc pl . . . . λάγανον

λάγανον noun neut nom and acc sg   id.

λαγόνας noun fem acc pl . . . . λαγών

Λαδαβαρ pr noun

Λαδαν pr noun

Λαηλ pr noun

λαθεῖν vb 2nd aor act inf . . . . λανθάνω

λάθῃ vb 2nd aor act subj 3rd pers sg   id.

λαθόντες vb 2nd aor act part masc nom pl   id.

λάθρᾳ adverb

λαθραῖον adj acc sg, neut nom sg . . . . λαθραῖος

λαθραίως adverb

λάθριος adj masc and fem nom sg

λαίλαπι noun fem dat sg . . . . λαῖλαψ

λαίλαπος noun fem gen sg   id.

λαῖλαψ noun fem nom sg   id.

λαιμαργία noun fem nom sg

Λαις pr noun

Λαισα pr noun

λακάνη noun fem dat sg . . . . λακάνη

Λακεδαιμονιους pr noun masc acc pl . . . . Λακεδαιμονιος

Λακεϊ pr noun

λάκκοι noun masc nom pl . . . . λάκκος

λάκκοις noun masc dat pl   id.

λάκκον noun masc acc sg   id.

λάκκος noun masc nom sg   id.

λάκκου noun masc gen sg   id.

Λακκουνος pr noun

λάκκους noun masc acc pl . . . . λάκκος

λάκκῳ noun masc dat sg   id.

λάκκων noun masc gen pl   id.

Λακου pr noun gen sg masc . . . . Λακος

λακωνικά adj neut nom and acc pl . . . . λακωνικός

λάλει vb pres act impv 2nd pers sg . . . . λαλέω

λαλεῖ vb pres act ind 3rd pers sg   id.

λαλεῖν vb pres act inf   id.

λαλεῖς vb pres act ind 2nd pers sg   id.

λαλεῖτε vb pres act impv 2nd pers pl,
        pres act ind 2nd pers pl   id.

λαλείτω vb pres act impv 3rd pers sg   id.

λαληθέν vb 1st aor pass part neut nom and acc sg   id.

λαληθέντων vb 1st aor pass part masc and neut gen pl   id.

λαληθῇ vb 1st aor pass subj 3rd pers sg   id.

λαληθήσεται vb fut pass ind 3rd pers sg   id.

λάλημα noun neut nom and acc sg

λαλήσαι vb 1st aor act opt 3rd pers sg . . . . λαλέω

λαλῆσαι vb 1st aor act inf   id.

λαλῆσαν vb 1st aor act part neut nom and acc sg   id.

λαλήσαντες vb 1st aor act part masc nom pl   id.

λαλήσαντι vb 1st aor act part masc and neut dat sg   id.

λαλήσαντος vb 1st aor act part masc and neut gen sg   id.

λαλήσας vb 1st aor act part masc nom sg   id.

λαλήσασι vb 1st aor act part masc and neut dat pl   id.

λαλήσατε vb 1st aor act impv 2nd pers pl   id.

λαλησάτω vb 1st aor act impv 3rd pers sg   id.

λαλησάτωσαν vb 1st aor act impv 3rd pers pl   id.

λαλήσει vb fut act ind 3rd pers sg   id.

λαλήσειν vb fut act inf   id.

λαλήσεις vb fut act ind 2nd pers sg   id.

λαλήσῃ vb 1st aor act subj 3rd pers sg   id.

λαλήσῃς vb 1st aor act subj 2nd pers sg   id.

λαλήσητε vb 1st aor act subj 2nd pers pl   id.

λαλήσομεν vb fut act ind 1st pers pl   id.

λάλησον vb 1st aor act impv 2nd pers sg,
        fut act part neut nom and acc sg   id.

λαλήσουσιν vb fut act ind 3rd pers pl   id.

λαλήσω vb 1st aor act subj 1st pers sg,
        fut act ind 1st pers sg   id.

λαλήσωμεν vb 1st aor act subj 1st pers pl   id.

λαλήσωσιν vb 1st aor act subj 3rd pers pl   id.

λαλητόν noun masc acc sg . . . . λαλητός

λαλιά noun fem nom sg

λαλιᾷ noun fem dat sg . . . . λαλιά

λαλιαί noun fem nom pl   id.

λαλιάν noun fem acc sg   id.

λαλιᾶς noun fem gen sg and acc pl   id.

λαλοῦν vb pres act part neut nom and acc sg . . . . λαλέω

λαλοῦντα vb pres act part masc acc sg,
        neut nom and acc pl   id.

λαλοῦντας vb pres act part masc acc pl   id.

λαλοῦντες vb pres act part masc nom pl . . . . λαλέω

λαλοῦντι vb pres act part masc and neut dat sg   id.

λαλοῦντος vb pres act part masc and neut gen sg   id.

λαλούντων vb pres act part masc and neut gen pl   id.

λαλοῦσα vb pres act part fem nom sg   id.

λαλοῦσαι vb pres act part fem nom pl   id.

λαλούσης vb pres act part fem gen sg   id.

λαλοῦσιν vb pres act ind 3rd pers pl   id.

λαλῶ vb pres act ind 1st pers sg   id.

λαλῶν vb pres act part masc nom sg   id.

λαλῶσι vb pres act subj 3rd pers pl   id.

Λαμας pr noun

λάμβανε vb pres act impv 2nd pers sg . . . . λαμβάνω

λαμβάνει vb pres act ind 3rd pers sg   id.

λαμβάνειν vb pres act inf   id.

λαμβάνετε vb pres act ind 2nd pers pl   id.

λαμβάνῃ vb pres act subj 3rd pers sg   id.

λαμβάνοντα vb pres act part masc acc sg,
            neut nom and acc pl   id.

λαμβάνοντας vb pres act part masc acc pl   id.

λαμβάνοντες vb pres act part masc nom pl   id.

λαμβάνοντος vb pres act part masc and neut gen sg   id.

λαμβάνουσα vb pres act part fem nom sg   id.

λαμβάνουσιν vb pres act ind 3rd pers pl   id.

λαμβάνω vb pres act ind 1st pers sg   id.

λαμβάνων vb pres act part masc nom sg   id.

λαμβάνωσιν vb pres act subj 3rd pers pl   id.

Λαμεχ pr noun

λαμπάδα noun fem acc sg . . . . λαμπάς

λαμπάδας noun fem acc pl   id.

λαμπάδες noun fem nom pl   id.

λαμπάδια noun neut nom and acc pl . . . . λαμπάδιον

λαμπάδιον noun neut nom and acc sg   id.

λαμπαδίου noun neut gen sg   id.

λαμπάδος noun fem gen sg . . . . λαμπάς

λαμπάδων noun fem gen pl   id.

λαμπάς noun fem nom sg   id.

λαμπάσιν noun fem dat pl   id.

λαμπήναις noun fem dat pl . . . . λαμπήνη

λαμπήνῃ noun fem dat sg   id.

λαμπηνικάς adj fem acc pl . . . . λαμπηνικός

λαμπηνῶν noun fem gen pl . . . . λαμπήνη

λάμπουσιν vb pres act ind 3rd pers pl . . . . λάμπω

λαμπρά adj fem nom sg, neut nom and acc pl . . . . . λαμπρός

λαμπρόν adj masc acc sg, neut nom and acc sg   id.

λαμπρότης noun fem nom sg

λαμπρότησιν noun fem dat pl . . . . λαμπρότης

λαμπρότητα noun fem acc sg   id.

λαμπρότητι noun fem dat sg   id.

λαμπρότητος noun fem gen sg   id.

λαμπρῷ adj masc and neut dat sg . . . . λαμπρός

λαμπτήρ noun masc nom sg

λαμπτῆρα noun masc acc sg . . . . λαμπτήρ

λάμψει vb fut act ind 3rd pers sg . . . . λάμπω

λάμψιν noun fem acc sg . . . . λάμψις

λάμψουσιν vb fut act ind 3rd pers pl . . . . λάμπω

Λανακ pr noun

λανθάνειν vb pres act inf . . . . λανθάνω

λάξ adverb

λάξευσον vb 1st aor act impv 2nd pers sg . . . . λαξεύω

λαξεύσωμεν vb 1st aor act subj 1st pers pl   id.

λαξευτήν adj fem acc sg . . . . λαξευτός

λαξευτηρίῳ noun neut dat sg . . . . λαξευτήριον

λαογραφίαν noun fem acc sg . . . . λαογραφία

λαοί noun masc nom pl . . . . λαός

λαοῖς noun masc dat pl   id.

λαόν noun masc acc sg   id.

λαός noun masc nom sg   id.

Λαος-μου pr noun . . . . λαός-ἐγω

λαοῦ noun masc gen sg . . . . λαός

λαούς noun masc acc pl   id.

λαπιστής noun masc nom sg

λάρον noun masc acc sg . . . . λάρος

λάρυγγι noun masc dat sg . . . . λάρυγξ

λάρυγγος noun masc gen sg   id.

λάρυγξ noun masc nom sg   id.

Λασα pr noun

Λασενδακ pr noun

Λασθενει pr noun masc dat sg . . . . Λασθενης

λατομεῖται vb pres m/p ind 3rd pers sg . . . . λατομέω

λατομῆσαι vb 1st aor act inf   id.

λατομήσῃ vb 1st aor act subj 3rd pers sg   id.

λατομητούς adj masc acc pl . . . . λατομητός

λατόμοις noun masc dat pl . . . . λατόμος

λατόμους noun masc acc pl   id.

λατόμων noun masc gen pl   id.

Λατουσιιμ pr noun

λατρεία noun fem nom sg

λατρείᾳ noun fem dat sg . . . . λατρεία

λατρείαν noun fem acc sg   id.

λατρείας noun fem gen sg   id.

λατρεύειν vb pres act inf . . . . λατρεύω

λατρεύεις vb pres act ind 2nd pers sg   id.

λατρεύετε vb pres act impv 2nd pers pl,
            pres act ind 2nd pers pl   id.

λατρεύομεν vb pres act ind 1st pers pl   id.

λατρεύοντες vb pres act part masc nom pl   id.

λατρεύουσα vb pres act part fem nom sg   id.

λατρεύουσιν vb pres act ind 3rd pers pl   id.

λατρεῦσαι vb 1st aor act inf   id.

λατρεύσατε vb 1st aor act impv 2nd pers pl   id.

λατρεύσει vb fut act ind 3rd pers sg   id.

λατρεύσεις vb fut act ind 2nd pers sg   id.

λατρεύσετε vb fut act ind 2nd pers pl   id.

λατρεύσῃ vb 1st aor act subj 3rd pers sg . . . . λατρεύω

λατρεύσῃς vb 1st aor act subj 2nd pers sg id.

λατρεύσητε vb 1st aor act subj 2nd pers pl id.

λατρεύσομεν vb fut act ind 1st pers pl id.

λατρεύσουσιν vb fut act ind 3rd pers pl id.

λατρεύσω vb fut act ind 1st pers sg id.

λατρεύσωμεν vb 1st aor act subj 1st pers pl id.

λατρεύσωσι(ν) vb 1st aor act subj 3rd pers pl id.

λατρευτόν adj masc acc sg, neut nom and acc sg λατρευτός

λάτρις noun fem nom sg

Λαφιδωθ pr noun

λάφυρα noun neut nom and acc pl . . . . λάφυρον

λαφύρων noun neut gen pl id.

λάχανα noun neut nom and acc pl . . . . λάχανον

λαχανείας noun fem gen sg . . . . λαχανεία

λαχάνων noun neut gen pl . . . . λάχανον

Λαχης pr noun

Λαχις pr noun

λαψάντων vb 1st aor act part masc and neut gen pl . . . λάπτω

λάψασι vb 1st aor act part masc and neut dat pl id.

λάψῃ vb 1st aor act subj 3rd pers sg id.

λαῷ noun masc dat sg . . . . λαός

λαῶν noun masc gen pl id.

λέαινα noun fem nom sg

λεαίνης noun fem gen sg . . . . λέαινα

λεανῶ vb fut act ind 1st pers sg . . . . λεαίνω

Λεασαμυς pr noun

Λεβ pr noun

λέβης noun masc nom sg

λέβησι noun masc dat pl . . . . λέβης

λέβητα noun masc acc sg id.

λέβητας noun masc acc pl id.

λέβητες noun masc nom pl id.

λέβητι noun masc dat sg id.

λέβητος noun masc gen sg id.

λεβήτων noun masc gen pl id.

Λεβνα pr noun

Λεβωνα pr noun

λέγε vb pres act impv 2nd pers sg . . . . λέγω

λέγει vb pres act ind 3rd pers sg id.

λέγειν vb pres act inf id.

λέγεις vb pres act ind 2nd pers sg id.

λέγεσθαι vb pres m/p inf id.

λεγέσθω vb pres m/p impv 3rd pers sg id.

λέγεται vb pres m/p ind 3rd pers sg id.

λέγετε vb pres act impv 2nd pers pl,
pres act ind 2nd pers pl id.

λεγέτω vb pres act impv 3rd pers sg id.

λεγέτωσαν vb pres act impv 3rd pers pl id.

λέγῃ vb pres act subj 3rd pers sg id.

λέγῃς vb pres act subj 2nd pers sg id.

λέγητε vb pres act subj 2nd pers pl id.

λεγόμενα vb pres m/p part neut nom and acc pl . . . . . . λέγω

λεγομένη vb pres m/p part fem nom sg id.

λεγομένην vb pres m/p part fem acc sg id.

λεγόμενοι vb pres m/p part masc nom pl id.

λεγομένοις vb pres m/p part masc and neut dat pl id.

λεγόμενον vb pres m/p part masc acc sg,
neut nom and acc sg id.

λεγόμενος vb pres m/p part masc nom sg id.

λεγομένους vb pres m/p part masc acc pl id.

λεγομένῳ vb pres m/p part masc and neut dat sg id.

λεγομένων vb pres m/p part gen pl id.

λέγον vb pres act part neut nom and acc sg id.

λέγοντα vb pres act part masc acc sg id.

λέγοντας vb pres act part masc acc pl id.

λέγοντες vb pres act part masc nom pl id.

λέγοντι vb pres act part masc and neut dat sg id.

λέγοντος vb pres act part masc and neut gen sg id.

λεγόντων vb pres act part masc and neut gen pl id.

λέγουσα vb pres act part fem nom sg id.

λέγουσαι vb pres act part fem nom pl id.

λέγουσαν vb pres act part fem acc sg id.

λεγούσης vb pres act part fem gen sg id.

λέγουσι(ν) vb pres act ind 3rd pers pl id.

λέγω vb pres act ind 1st pers sg id.

λέγων vb pres act part masc nom sg id.

λέγωσιν vb pres act subj 3rd pers pl id.

Λεεμι pr noun

λεηλατεῖν vb pres act inf . . . . λεηλατέω

λεῖα adj neut nom and acc pl . . . . λεῖος

Λεια pr noun fem nom and dat sg

Λειαν pr noun fem acc sg . . . . Λεια

λείας adj fem gen sg . . . . λεῖος

Λειας pr noun fem gen sg . . . . Λεια

λείμματος noun neut gen sg . . . . λεῖμμα

λείξουσιν vb fut act ind 3rd pers pl . . . . λείχω

λεῖος adj masc nom sg

λείους adj masc acc pl . . . . λεῖος

λείπεται vb pres m/p ind 3rd pers sg . . . . λείπω

λειπόμενοι vb pres m/p part masc nom pl id.

λειπομένοις vb pres m/p part masc and neut dat pl id.

λειποτακτήσητε vb 1st aor act subj
2nd pers pl . . . . λειποτακτέω

λείπουσαν vb pres act part fem acc sg . . . . λείπω

λειτουργεῖν vb pres act inf . . . . λειτουργέω

λειτουργείτωσαν vb pres act impv 3rd pers pl id.

λειτουργήματα noun neut nom and acc pl . . λειτούργημα

λειτουργῆσαι vb 1st aor act inf . . . . λειτουργέω

λειτουργήσατε vb 1st aor act impv 2nd pers pl id.

λειτουργήσει vb fut act ind 3rd pers sg id.

λειτουργήσετε vb fut act ind 2nd pers pl id.

λειτουργησίμων adj gen pl . . . . λειτουργήσιμος

λειτουργήσουσιν vb fut act ind 3rd pers pl . . . λειτουργέω λειτουργία noun fem nom sg

λειτουργία noun fem dat sg . . . . λειτουργία

λειτουργίαν noun fem acc sg   id.

λειτουργίας noun fem gen sg and acc pl

λειτουργικά adj neut nom and acc pl . . . . . λειτουργικός

λειτουργικάς adj fem acc pl   id.

λειτουργιῶν noun fem gen pl . . . . λειτουργία

λειτουργοί noun masc nom pl . . . . λειτουργός

λειτουργοῖς noun masc dat pl   id.

λειτουργός noun masc nom sg   id.

λειτουργοῦντας vb pres act part masc acc pl . . λειτουργέω

λειτουργοῦντες vb pres act part masc nom pl   id.

λειτουργούς noun masc acc pl . . . . λειτουργός

λειτουργοῦσα vb pres act part fem nom sg . . . . λειτουργέω

λειτουργοῦσαν vb pres act part fem acc sg   id.

λειτουργοῦσι(ν) vb pres act ind 3rd pers pl,
            pres act part masc and neut dat pl   id.

λειτουργῶν noun masc gen pl . . . . λειτουργός

λειτουργῶν vb pres act part masc nom sg . . . . λειτουργέω

λεκάνη noun fem nom sg

λεκάνη noun fem dat sg . . . . λεκάνη

λελάληκα vb perf act ind 1st pers sg . . . . λαλέω

λελάληκας vb perf act ind 2nd pers sg   id.

λελαλήκασιν vb perf act ind 3rd pers pl   id.

λελαλήκατε vb perf act ind 2nd pers pl   id.

λελάληκεν vb perf act ind 3rd pers sg   id.

λελάληται vb perf m/p ind 3rd pers sg   id.

λελαξευμέναι vb perf m/p part fem nom pl . . . . λαξεύω

λελαξευμένον vb perf m/p part masc acc sg,
            neut nom and acc sg   id.

λελαξευμένου vb pres m/p part
            masc and neut gen sg   id.

λελαξευμένων vb perf m/p part gen pl   id.

λελατομημένους vb perf m/p part masc acc pl . . . λατομέω

λελειμμένος vb perf m/p part masc nom sg . . . . λείπω

λελεπρωμένος vb perf dep part masc nom sg . . . λεπρόομαι

λελευκανθισμένη vb perf m/p part
            fem nom sg . . . . λευκανθίζω

λέληθεν vb perf act ind 3rd pers sg . . . . λανθάνω

λεληθότως adverb

λελιβανωμένου vb perf m/p part
            masc and neut gen sg . . . . λιβανόω

λελιθοβόληται vb perf m/p ind 3rd pers sg . . . . λιθοβολέω

λελικμημένα vb perf m/p part neut nom and acc pl . λικμάω

λελογίσμεθα vb perf dep ind 1st pers pl . . . . . . λογίζομαι

λελόγισται vb perf dep ind 3rd pers sg

λελογχώς vb perf act part masc nom sg . . . . λαγχάνω

λελουσμέναι vb perf m/p part fem nom pl . . . . λούω

λελυμένη vb perf m/p part fem nom sg . . . . λύω

λελυμένους vb perf m/p part masc acc pl   id.

λελυμένων vb perf m/p part gen pl   id.

λελύπημαι vb perf m/p ind 1st pers sg . . . . λυπέω

λελύπησαι vb perf m/p ind 2nd pers sg . . . . λυπέω

λελύπηται vb perf m/p ind 3rd pers sg   id.

λέλυται vb perf m/p ind 3rd pers sg . . . . λύω

λελυτρωμένοι vb perf m/p part masc nom pl . . . . . . λυτρόω

λελυτρωμένοις vb perf m/p part masc and neut dat pl   id.

λελυτρωμένον vb perf m/p part masc acc sg,
            neut nom and acc sg   id.

λελύτρωται vb perf m/p ind 3rd pers sg   id.

Λεμνα pr noun

Λεμωνα pr noun

λέξεων noun fem gen pl . . . . λέξις

λέξεως noun fem gen sg   id.

λέξιν noun fem acc sg   id.

λέξις noun fem nom sg   id.

λέοντα noun masc acc sg . . . . λέων

λέοντας noun masc acc pl   id.

λέοντες noun masc nom pl   id.

λεοντηδον adverb

λέοντι noun masc dat sg . . . . λέων

λέοντος noun masc gen sg   id.

λεόντων noun masc gen pl   id.

λέουσι noun masc dat pl   id.

λεπίδας noun fem acc pl . . . . λεπίς

λεπίδες noun fem nom pl   id.

λεπίσαι vb 1st aor act inf . . . . λεπίζω

λεπίσματα noun neut nom and acc pl . . . . λέπισμα

λέπρα noun fem nom sg

λεπρᾷ vb pres act ind 3rd pers sg . . . . λεπράω

λέπρας noun fem gen sg . . . . λέπρα

λεπροί adj masc nom pl . . . . λεπρός

λεπρόν adj masc acc sg, neut nom and acc sg   id.

λεπρός adj masc nom sg   id.

λεπροῦ adj masc and neut gen sg   id.

λεπρῶσα vb pres act part fem nom sg . . . . λεπράω

λεπτά adj neut nom and acc pl . . . . λεπτός

λεπταί adj fem nom pl   id.

λεπτή adj fem nom sg   id.

λεπτήν adj fem acc sg   id.

λεπτῆς adj fem gen sg   id.

λεπτοί adj masc nom pl   id.

λεπτόν adj masc acc sg, neut nom and acc sg   id.

λεπτοτάτον superl adj gen pl   id.

λεπτότερον comp adj masc acc sg, neut nom and acc sg id.

λεπτύνει vb pres act ind 3rd pers sg . . . . λεπτύνω

λεπτυνεῖ vb fut act ind 3rd pers sg   id.

λεπτυνεῖς vb fut act ind 2nd pers sg   id.

λεπτῦνον vb pres act part neut nom and acc sg   id.

λεπτυνοῦσιν vb fut act ind 3rd pers pl   id.

λεπτυνῶ vb fut act ind 1st pers sg   id.

λέπυρον noun neut nom and acc sg

λέσχαι noun fem nom pl . . . . λέσχη

Λευι pr noun

Λευιν pr noun masc acc sg .... Λευις

Λευις pr noun

Λευῖται pr noun masc nom pl .... Λευίτης

Λευιταις pr noun masc dat pl   id.

Λευιτας pr noun masc acc pl   id.

Λευιτης pr noun masc nom sg   id.

λευίτης see Λευίτης

Λευιτου pr noun masc gen sg   id.

Λευιτῶν pr noun masc gen pl   id.

λευκά adj neut nom and acc pl .... λευκός

λευκαθίζοντα vb pres act part

       neut nom and acc pl .... λευκαθίζω

λευκαίνουσα vb pres act part fem nom sg ..... λευκαίνω

λευκανθήσομαι vb fut pass ind 1st pers sg   id.

λευκανῶ vb fut act ind 1st pers sg   id.

λευκή adj fem nom sg .... λευκός

λευκῇ adj fem dat sg   id.

λεύκην noun fem acc sg .... λεύκη

λευκήν adj fem acc sg .... λευκός

λεύκης adj fem gen sg .... λεύκη

Λευκιος pr noun masc nom sg

λευκοί adj masc nom pl .... λευκός

λευκόν adj masc acc sg, neut nom and acc sg   id.

λευκός adj masc nom sg   id.

λευκότητος noun fem gen sg .... λευκότης

λευκώμασιν noun neut dat pl .... λεύκωμα

λευκώματα noun neut nom and acc pl   id.

λευκωμάτων noun neut gen pl   id.

λεχθέντα vb 1st aor pass part neut nom and acc pl .... λέγω

Λεχι pr noun

λεχώ noun fem nom sg

λέων noun masc nom sg

λεωπετρίαν noun fem acc sg .... λεωπετρία

λήγειν vb pres act inf .... λήγω

λήγοντος vb pres act part masc and neut gen sg   id.

ληγόντων vb pres act part masc and neut gen pl   id.

λήθη noun fem nom sg

λήθη noun fem dat sg .... λήθη

λήθην noun fem acc sg   id.

λήθης noun fem gen sg   id.

λῆμμα noun neut nom and acc sg

λήμματα noun neut nom and acc pl .... λῆμμα

λήμματος noun neut gen sg   id.

λημμάτων noun neut gen pl   id.

λημφθέντα vb 1st aor pass part

       neut nom and acc pl .... λαμβάνω

λημφθέντας vb 1st aor pass part masc acc pl   id.

λημφθῆναι vb 1st aor pass inf   id.

λημφθήσεται vb fut pass ind 3rd pers sg   id.

λημφθήσονται vb fut pass ind 3rd pers pl   id.

λημφθήτω vb 1st aor pass impv 3rd pers sg   id.

λήμψεις noun fem nom and acc pl .... λῆμψις

λήμψεσθαι vb fut mid inf .... λαμβάνω

λήμψεσθε vb fut mid ind 2nd pers pl   id.

λήμψεται vb fut mid ind 3rd pers sg   id.

λήμψεως noun fem gen sg .... λῆμψις

λήμψῃ vb fut mid ind 2nd pers sg .... λαμβάνω

λῆμψις noun fem nom sg

λήμψομαι vb fut mid ind 1st pers sg .... λαμβάνω

λημψόμεθα vb fut mid ind 1st pers pl   id.

λημψόμενον vb fut mid part masc acc sg,

       neut nom and acc sg   id.

λημψόμενος vb fut mid part masc nom sg   id.

λήμψονται vb fut mid ind 3rd pers pl   id.

ληνοί noun fem nom pl .... ληνός

ληνοῖς noun fem dat pl   id.

ληνόν noun fem acc sg   id.

ληνός noun fem nom sg   id.

ληνοῦ noun fem gen sg   id.

ληνούς noun fem acc pl   id.

ληνῷ noun fem dat sg   id.

ληνῶν noun fem gen pl   id.

λῆρον noun masc acc sg .... λῆρος

ληρῶδες adj masc and fem nom and acc sg ...... ληρώδης

λήσεται vb fut mid ind 3rd pers sg .... λανθάνω

λησταί noun masc nom pl .... λῃστής

ληστάς noun masc acc pl   id.

ληστεύειν vb pres act inf .... λῃστεύω

λῃστῇ noun masc dat sg .... λῃστής

λῃστήρια noun neut nom and acc pl .... λῃστήριον

λῃστήριον noun neut nom and acc sg   id.

λῃστής noun masc nom sg

λῃστῶν noun masc gen pl .... λῃστής

Ληχα pr noun

λήψεσθε vb fut mid ind 2nd pers pl .... λαμβάνω

λήψεται vb fut mid ind 3rd pers sg   id.

λήψῃ vb fut mid ind 2nd pers sg   id.

λίαν adverb

λίβα noun masc acc sg .... λίψ

λίβανον noun masc acc sg .... λίβανος

Λιβανον pr noun masc acc sg .... Λιβανος

Λιβανος pr noun masc nom sg   id.

λιβάνου noun masc gen sg .... λίβανος

Λιβανου pr noun masc gen sg .... Λιβανος

Λιβανῳ pr noun masc dat sg   id.

λιβάνῳ noun masc dat sg .... λίβανος

λιβανωτοῦ noun masc gen sg .... λιβανωτός

λιβί noun masc dat sg .... λίψ

λιβός noun masc gen sg   id.

Λιβυες pr noun masc nom pl .... Λιβυς

Λιβυων pr noun masc gen pl   id.

λιγύριον noun neut nom and acc sg

λιθάζων vb pres act part masc nom sg .... λιθάζω

λίθινα adj neut nom and acc pl .... λίθινος

λίθιναι adj fem nom pl	λίθινος
λιθίνας adj fem acc pl	id.
λιθίνην adj fem acc sg	id.
λίθινοι adj masc nom pl	id.
λιθίνοις adj masc and neut dat pl	id.
λιθίνους adj masc acc pl	id.
λιθίνων adj gen pl	id.
λιθοβόλα noun neut nom and acc pl	λιθοβόλον
λιθοβολείτω vb pres act impv 3rd pers sg	λιθοβολέω
λιθοβοληθήσεται vb fut pass ind 3rd pers sg	id.
λιθοβοληθησόμεθα vb fut pass ind 1st pers pl	id.
λιθοβοληθήσονται vb fut pass ind 3rd pers pl	id.
λιθοβολῆσαι vb 1st aor act inf	id.
λιθοβολήσατε vb 1st aor act impv 2nd pers pl	id.
λιθοβολησάτωσαν vb 1st aor act impv 3rd pers pl	id.
λιθοβολήσετε vb fut act ind 2nd pers pl	id.
λιθοβόλησον vb 1st aor act impv 2nd pers sg	id.
λιθοβολήσουσιν vb fut act ind 3rd pers pl	id.
λίθοι noun masc nom pl	λίθος
λίθοις noun masc dat pl	id.
λίθον noun masc acc sg	id.
λίθος noun masc nom sg	id.
λιθόστρωτον adj acc sg, neut nom sg	λιθόστρωτος
λιθοστρώτου adj gen sg	id.
λίθου noun masc gen sg	λίθος
λιθουργῆσαι vb 1st aor act inf	λιθουργέω
λιθουργικά adj neut nom and acc pl	λιθουργικός
λιθουργικῆς adj fem gen sg	id.
λιθουργοῦ noun masc gen sg	λιθουργός
λίθους noun masc acc pl	λίθος
λίθῳ noun masc dat sg	id.
λιθώδεσι adj dat pl	λιθώδης
λίθων noun masc gen pl	λίθος
λίκμα vb pres act impv 2nd pers sg	λικμάω
λικμᾷ vb pres act ind 3rd pers sg	id.
λικμᾶται vb pres m/p ind 3rd pers sg	id.
λικμηθέντες vb 1st aor pass part masc nom pl	id.
λικμήσας vb 1st aor act part masc nom sg	id.
λικμήσει vb fut act ind 3rd pers sg	id.
λικμήσεις vb fut act ind 2nd pers sg	id.
λικμήσω vb fut act ind 1st pers sg	id.
λικμήτωρ noun masc nom sg	
λικμῶ vb fut act ind 1st pers sg	λικμίζω
λικμῷ noun masc dat sg	λικμός
λικμωμένους vb pres m/p part masc acc pl	λικμάω
λικμώντων vb pres act part masc and neut gen pl	id.
λιμένα noun masc acc sg	λιμήν
λιμένος noun masc gen sg	id.
λιμένων noun masc gen pl	id.
λίμναι noun fem nom pl	λίμνη
λίμνας noun fem acc pl	id.
λίμνην noun fem acc sg	id.

λιμοκτονήσει vb fut act ind 3rd pers sg	λιμοκτονέω
λιμέν noun masc acc sg	λιμός
λιμός noun masc (or fem) nom sg	id.
λιμοῦ noun masc gen sg	id.
λιμῷ noun masc dat sg	id.
λιμώξουσιν vb fut act ind 3rd pers pl	λιμώσσω
λινᾶ adj neut nom and acc pl	λινοῦς
λινᾶς adj fem acc pl	id.
λινῇ adj fem dat sg	id.
λινῆν adj fem acc sg	id.
λινοῖς adj masc and neut dat pl	id.
λινοκαλάμη noun fem dat sg	λινοκαλάμη
λίνον noun neut nom and acc sg	
λινοῦν adj masc acc sg, neut nom and acc sg	λινοῦς
λιπαίνει vb pres act ind 3rd pers sg	λιπαίνω
λιπανάτω vb 2nd aor act impv 3rd pers sg	id.
λίπανον vb 1st aor act impv 2nd pers sg	id.
λιπαρᾷ adj fem dat sg	λιπαρός
λιπαρόν adj masc acc sg, neut nom and acc sg	id.
λιπαρός adj masc nom sg	id.
λιπάσματα noun neut nom and acc pl	λίπασμα
λιποθυμεῖν vb pres act inf	λιποθυμέω
λίσσομαι vb pres dep ind 1st pers sg	
λιτανεία noun fem nom sg	
λιτανείαν noun fem acc sg	λιτανεία
λιτανείας noun fem gen sg	id.
λιτανεύσουσιν vb fut act ind 3rd pers pl	λιτανεύω
λιτοί adj masc nom pl	λιτός
λιχήν noun masc nom sg	
λιχῆνας noun masc acc pl	λιχήν
λιχνείας noun fem gen sg	λιχνεία
λίψ noun masc nom sg	
Λοβενα pr noun	
Λοβενι pr noun	
Λοβνα pr noun	
λοβόν noun masc acc sg	λοβός
Λοβον pr noun	
λοβούς noun masc acc pl	λοβός
Λοβωημαθ pr noun	
λόγε noun masc voc sg	λόγος
λογεῖον noun neut nom and acc sg	
λογείου noun neut gen sg	λογεῖον
λογείῳ noun neut dat sg	id.
λόγια noun neut nom and acc pl	λόγιον
λογιεῖται vb fut mid ind 3rd pers sg	λογίζομαι
λογίζεσθαι vb pres dep inf	id.
λογίζεσθε vb pres dep impv 2nd pers pl,	
pres dep ind 2nd pers pl	id.
λογιζέσθω vb pres dep impv 3rd pers sg	id.
λογίζεται vb pres dep ind 3rd pers sg	id.
λογίζῃ vb pres dep subj 2nd pers sg	id.
λογίζομαι vb pres dep ind 1st pers sg	id.

λογιζόμενοι vb pres dep part masc nom pl . . . . . . λογίζομαι

λογιζόμενον vb pres dep part masc acc sg,

     neut nom and acc sg   id.

λογιζόμενος vb pres dep part masc nom sg   id.

λογιζομένους vb pres dep part masc acc pl   id.

λογιζομένων vb pres dep part gen pl   id.

λογίζονται vb pres dep ind 3rd pers pl   id.

λογιῇ vb fut mid ind 2nd pers sg   id.

λόγιον noun neut nom and acc sg

λογιοῦμαι vb fut mid ind 1st pers sg . . . . λογίζομαι

λογιούμεθα vb fut mid ind 1st pers pl   id.

λογιοῦνται vb fut mid ind 3rd pers pl   id.

λογισάμενοι vb 1st aor mid part masc nom pl   id.

λογισάμενος vb 1st aor mid part masc nom sg   id.

λογίσησθε vb 1st aor mid subj 2nd pers pl   id.

λογίσηται vb 1st aor mid subj 3rd pers sg   id.

λογισθείη vb 1st aor pass opt 3rd pers sg   id.

λογισθέν vb 1st aor pass part neut nom and acc sg   id.

λογισθῆναι vb 1st aor pass inf   id.

λογισθήσεσθε vb fut pass ind 2nd pers pl   id.

λογισθήσεται vb fut pass ind 3rd pers sg   id.

λογισθήσονται vb fut pass ind 3rd pers pl   id.

λογισθήτωσαν vb 1st aor pass impv 3rd pers pl   id.

λογισμέ noun masc voc sg . . . . λογισμός

λογισμοί noun masc nom pl   id.

λογισμόν noun masc acc sg   id.

λογισμός noun masc nom sg   id.

λογισμοῦ noun masc gen sg   id.

λογισμούς noun masc acc pl   id.

λογισμῷ noun masc dat sg   id.

λογισμῶν noun masc gen pl   id.

λογιστοῦ noun masc gen sg . . . . λογιστής

λογισώμεθα vb 1st aor mid subj 1st pers pl . . . . . λογίζομαι

λογίων noun neut gen pl . . . . λόγιον

λόγοι noun masc nom pl . . . . λόγος

λόγοις noun masc dat pl   id.

λόγον noun masc acc sg   id.

λόγος noun masc nom sg   id.

λόγου noun masc gen sg   id.

λόγους noun masc acc pl   id.

λόγχαι noun fem nom pl . . . . λόγχη

λόγχαις noun fem dat pl   id.

λόγχας noun fem acc pl   id.

λόγχη noun fem nom sg   id.

λογχῶν noun fem gen pl   id.

λόγῳ noun masc dat sg . . . . λόγος

λόγων noun masc gen pl   id.

Λοδ pr noun

Λοζων pr noun

λοιδορεῖσθε vb pres m/p ind 2nd pers pl . . . . λοιδορέω

λοιδόρησις noun fem nom sg

λοιδορίαι noun fem nom pl . . . . λοιδορία

λοιδορίαν noun fem acc sg . . . . λοιδορία

λοιδορίας noun fem gen sg and acc pl   id.

λοίδορος adj masc and fem nom sg

λοιδόρου vb pres m/p impv 2nd pers sg . . . . λοιδορέω

λοιδοροῦντες vb pres act part masc nom pl   id.

λοιδορῶνται vb pres m/p subj 3rd pers pl   id.

λοιμεύηται vb pres dep subj 3rd pers sg . . . . . λοιμεύομαι

λοιμήν adj fem acc sg . . . . λοιμός

λοιμοί adj or noun masc nom pl   id.

λοιμοῖς noun masc dat pl   id.

λοιμόν adj masc acc sg, neut nom and acc sg   id.

λοιμόν noun masc acc sg   id.

λοιμός adj masc nom sg   id.

λοιμότητι noun fem dat sg . . . . λοιμότης

λοιμοῦ adj masc and neut gen sg . . . . λοιμός

λοιμούς noun masc acc pl   id.

λοιμῷ adj masc and neut dat sg   id.

λοιμῶν adj or noun gen pl   id.

λοιπά adj neut nom and acc pl . . . . λοιπός

λοιπαί adj fem nom pl   id.

λοιπαῖς adj fem dat pl   id.

λοιπάς adj fem acc pl   id.

λοιπή adj fem nom sg   id.

λοιπήν adj fem acc sg   id.

λοιποί adj masc nom pl   id.

λοιποῖς adj masc and neut dat pl   id.

λοιπόν adj masc acc sg, neut nom and acc sg   id.

λοιπός adj masc nom sg   id.

λοιπῷ adj masc and neut dat sg   id.

λοιπῶν adj gen pl   id.

Λομνα pr noun

Λομναν pr noun fem acc sg . . . . Λομνα

Λουδ pr noun

Λουδιιμ pr noun

Λουζα pr noun

Λουιθ pr noun

Λουκαμ pr noun

λουομένην vb pres m/p part fem acc sg . . . . λούω

λοῦσαι vb 1st aor act inf,

     1st aor mid impv 2nd pers sg   id.

Λουσαμηνχα pr noun

λούσασθαι vb 1st aor mid inf . . . . λούω

λούσασθε vb 1st aor mid impv 2nd pers pl   id.

λούσεις vb fut act ind 2nd pers sg   id.

λούσεται vb fut mid ind 3rd pers sg   id.

λούσῃ vb fut mid ind 2nd pers sg   id.

λούσηται vb 1st aor mid subj 3rd pers sg   id.

λούσομαι vb fut mid ind 1st pers sg   id.

λούσονται vb fut mid ind 3rd pers pl   id.

λούσω vb fut act ind 1st pers sg   id.

λούσωμαι vb 1st aor mid subj 1st pers sg   id.

λουτῆρα noun masc acc sg . . . . λουτήρ λουτῆρας   noun masc acc pl   . . . . λουτήρ

λουτῆρες   noun masc nom pl   id.

λουτήρων   noun masc gen pl   id.

λουτροῦ   noun neut gen sg . . . . λουτρόν

λουτρῷ   noun neut dat sg   id.

λοφιάν   noun fem acc sg   . . . . λοφιά

λοφιᾶς   noun fem gen sg   id.

λοχευομένων   vb pres m/p part gen pl   . . . . λοχεύω

λοχεύονται   vb pres m/p ind 3rd pers pl   id.

λοχῶν   noun masc gen pl   . . . . λόχος

Λοωμιμ   pr noun

Λυδδα   pr noun

Λυδιαν   pr noun fem acc sg   . . . . Λυδια

Λυδοι   pr noun masc nom pl   . . . . Λυδος

λῦε   vb pres act impv 2nd pers sg   . . . . λύω

λύει   vb pres act ind 3rd pers sg   id.

λυθέντες   vb 1st aor pass part masc nom pl   id.

λυθήσονται   vb fut pass ind 3rd pers pl   id.

λυθρώδει   adj dat sg   . . . . λυθρώδης

Λυκιαν   pr noun fem acc sg   . . . . Λυκία

λύκοι   noun masc nom pl   . . . . λύκος

λύκος   noun masc nom sg   id.

λύκους   noun masc acc pl   id.

λυμαίνεται   vb pres m/p ind 3rd pers sg   . . . . λυμαίνω

λυμαίνοιτο   vb pres m/p opt 3rd pers sg   id.

λυμαινόμενος   vb pres m/p part masc nom sg   id.

λυμαινομένου   vb pres m/p part masc and neut gen sg   id.

λυμανεῖται   vb fut mid ind 3rd pers sg   id.

λυμανοῦνται   vb fut mid ind 3rd pers pl   id.

λυμεών   noun masc nom sg

λυμήνῃ   vb 2nd aor mid subj 2nd pers sg   . . . . λυμαίνω

λύουσα   vb pres act part fem nom sg   . . . . λύω

λύπαις   noun fem dat pl . . . . λύπη

λύπας   noun fem acc pl   id.

λυπεῖ   vb pres act ind 3rd pers sg   . . . . λυπέω

λυπεῖσθαι   vb pres m/p inf   id.

λυπεῖσθε   vb pres m/p impv 2nd pers pl   id.

λυπεῖται   vb pres m/p ind 3rd pers sg   id.

λύπη   noun fem nom sg

λύπη   noun fem dat sg   . . . . λύπη

λυπηθείς   vb 1st aor pass part masc nom sg   . . . . λυπέω

λυπηθήσεσθε   vb fut pass ind 2nd pers pl   id.

λυπηθήσεται   vb fut pass ind 3rd pers sg   id.

λυπηθήσῃ   vb fut pass ind 2nd pers sg   id.

λυπηθήσονται   vb fut pass ind 3rd pers pl   id.

λυπήθητε   vb 1st aor pass impv 2nd pers pl   id.

λύπην   noun fem acc sg   . . . . λύπη

λυπηρά   adj fem nom sg   . . . . λυπηρός

λυπηράν   adj fem acc sg   id.

λυπηρόν   adj masc acc sg, neut nom and acc sg   id.

λυπηρός   adj masc nom sg   id.

λυπηροῦ   adj masc and neut gen sg   id.

λύπης   noun fem gen sg   . . . . λύπη

λυπήσει   vb fut act ind 3rd pers sg   . . . . λυπέω

λυπήσῃς   vb 1st aor act subj 2nd pers sg   id.

λυπήσω   vb fut act ind 1st pers sg   id.

λυποῦ   vb pres m/p impv 2nd pers sg   id.

λυπουμένη   vb pres m/p part fem nom sg   id.

λυπούμενος   vb pres m/p part masc nom sg   id.

λυποῦντες   vb pres act part masc nom pl   id.

λυπῶν   noun fem gen pl   . . . . λύπη

λῦσαι   vb 1st aor act inf,

        1st aor mid impv 2nd pers sg   . . . . λύω

λύσαντες   vb 1st aor act part masc nom pl   id.

λύσας   vb 1st aor act part masc nom sg   id.

λύσατε   vb 1st aor act impv 2nd pers pl   id.

λύσει   vb fut act ind 3rd pers sg   id.

λύσεις   noun fem nom and acc pl   . . . . λύσις

Λυσια   pr noun masc dat sg   . . . . Λυσιας

Λυσιαν   pr noun masc acc sg   id.

Λυσιας   pr noun masc nom sg   id.

Λυσιμαχον   pr noun masc acc sg   . . . . Λυσιμαχος

Λυσιμαχου   pr noun masc gen sg   id.

λύσιν   noun fem acc sg   . . . . λύσις

Λυσιου   pr noun masc gen sg   . . . . Λυσιας

λύσις   noun fem nom sg

λυσιτελεῖ   vb pres act ind 3rd pers sg   . . . . λυσιτελέω

λυσιτέλειαν   noun fem acc sg   . . . . λυσιτέλεια

λυσιτελής   adj masc and fem nom sg

λυσιτελήσει   vb fut act ind 3rd pers sg   . . . . . . λυσιτελέω

λύσουσιν   vb fut act ind 3rd pers pl   . . . . λύω

λύτρα   noun neut nom and acc pl   . . . . λύτρον

λύτροις   noun neut dat pl   id.

λύτρον   noun neut nom and acc sg   id.

λύτρου   noun neut gen sg   id.

λυτρούμενον   vb pres m/p part masc acc sg,

        neut nom and acc sg   . . . . λυτρόω

λυτρούμενος   vb pres m/p part masc nom sg   id.

λυτρουμένου   vb pres m/p part masc and neut gen sg   id.

λυτρουμένῳ   vb pres m/p part masc and neut dat sg   id.

λυτροῦται   vb pres m/p ind 3rd pers sg   id.

λύτρῳ   noun neut dat sg   . . . . λύτρον

λυτρωθῇ   vb 1st aor pass subj 3rd pers sg   . . . . λυτρόω

λυτρωθήσεσθε   vb fut pass ind 2nd pers pl   id.

λυτρωθήσεται   vb fut pass ind 3rd pers sg   id.

λύτρων   noun neut gen pl   . . . . λύτρον

λυτρῶνας   noun masc acc pl   . . . . λυτρών

λύτρωσαι   vb 1st aor mid impv 2nd pers sg   . . . . λυτρόω

λυτρωσάμενος   vb 1st aor mid part masc nom sg   id.

λυτρωσαμένου   vb 1st aor mid part

        masc and neut gen sg   id.

λυτρώσασθαι   vb 1st aor mid inf   id.

λυτρωσάσθω   vb 1st aor mid impv 3rd pers sg   id.

λυτρώσεται vb fut mid ind 3rd pers sg . . . . λυτρόω
λυτρώσεως noun fem gen sg . . . . λύτρωσις
λυτρώσῃ vb fut mid ind 2nd pers sg . . . . λυτρόω
λυτρώσηται vb 1st aor mid subj 3rd pers sg   id.
λύτρωσιν noun fem acc sg . . . . λύτρωσις
λύτρωσις noun fem nom sg   id.
λυτρώσομαι vb fut mid ind 1st pers sg . . . . λυτρόω
λυτρωτά noun masc voc sg . . . . λυτρωτής
λυτρῶται vb pres m/p subj 3rd pers sg . . . . λυτρόω
λυτρωταί noun masc nom pl . . . . λυτρωτής
λυτρωτής noun masc nom sg   id.
λυχνία noun fem nom sg
λυχνίᾳ noun fem dat sg . . . . λυχνία
λυχνίαν noun fem acc sg   id.
λυχνίας noun fem gen sg and acc pl   id.
λυχνιῶν noun fem gen pl   id.
λύχνοι noun masc nom pl . . . . λύχνος

λυχνοί see λύχνοι
λύχνοις noun masc dat pl . . . . λύχνος
λύχνον noun masc acc sg   id.
λύχνος noun masc nom sg   id.
λύχνου noun masc gen sg   id.
λύχνους noun masc acc pl   id.
(λύχνους noun neut gen sg OG: Dan 5 title   id.)
λύχνων noun masc gen pl   id.
λύων vb pres act part masc nom sg . . . . λύω
Λωδαβαρ pr noun
Λωθασουβος pr noun
λῶμα noun neut nom and acc sg
λώματος noun neut gen sg . . . . λῶμα
λωποδυτήσῃ vb 1st aor act subj 3rd pers sg . . . . λωποδυτέω
Λωτ pr noun
Λωταν pr noun

Μ μ

μά particle
Μααζια pr noun
Μααθ pr noun
Μααλα pr noun
Μααλαθ pr noun
Μααλλων pr noun
Μααλων pr noun
Μααν pr noun
Μααναιμ pr noun
Μααναιν pr noun
Μααvι pr noun
Μααραγαβε pr noun
Μαας pr noun
Μαασα pr noun
Μαασαι pr noun
Μαασαια pr noun
Μαασαιαν pr noun masc acc sg . . . . Μαασαιας
Μαασαιου pr noun masc gen sg   id.
Μαασηα pr noun
Μαασια pr noun
Μαασιαν pr noun masc acc sg . . . . Μαασιας
Μαασιας pr noun masc nom sg   id.
Μαασμαν pr noun
Μααταρωθορεχ pr noun
Μααχα pr noun
Μααχαν pr noun fem acc sg . . . . Μααχα
Μααχατι pr noun
Μααχως pr noun
Μαβασαμ pr noun

Μαβσαν pr noun
Μαβσαρ pr noun
Μαγαδαγαδ pr noun
Μαγαρωθ pr noun
Μαγαφης pr noun
Μαγδαλγαδ pr noun
Μαγδαλιηλ pr noun
Μαγδαν pr noun fem acc sg . . . . Μαγδα
Μαγδω pr noun
Μαγδωλον pr noun masc acc sg . . . . Μάγδωλος
Μαγδωλου pr noun masc gen sg   id.
Μαγδωλῳ pr noun masc dat sg   id.
Μαγδων pr noun
Μαγεβως pr noun
Μαγεδδαους pr noun
Μαγεδδω pr noun
Μαγεδδων pr noun
Μαγεδω pr noun
Μαγεδων pr noun
μαγειρεῖα noun neut nom and acc pl . . . . μαγειρεῖον
μαγειρείων noun neut gen pl   id.
μαγειρίσσας noun fem acc pl . . . . μαγείρισσα
μάγειρος noun masc nom sg
μαγείρῳ noun masc dat sg . . . . μάγειρος
μαγικῆς adj fem gen sg . . . . μαγικός
μαγίς noun fem nom sg
μάγοι noun masc nom pl . . . . μάγος
μάγον noun masc acc sg   id.
μάγους noun masc acc pl   id.

Μαγωγ pr noun

μάγων noun masc gen pl . . . . μάγος

Μαδαι pr noun

Μαδαν pr noun

Μαδβαριτιδι pr noun fem dat sg . . . . Μαδβαρῖτις

Μαδβαρῖτις pr noun fem nom sg . . . . id.

Μαδεβηνα pr noun

μαδήσῃ vb 1st aor act subj 3rd pers sg . . . . μαδάω

Μαδιαμ pr noun

Μαδιαν pr noun

Μαδιανιτη pr noun masc dat sg . . . . Μαδιανιτης

Μαδιανιτιδι adj fem dat sg . . . . Μαδιανῖτις

Μαδιανιτιδος adj fem gen sg . . . . id.

Μαδιανῖτιν adj fem acc sg . . . . id.

Μαδιανιτῶν pr noun masc gen pl . . . . Μαδιανίτης

Μαδιηναιοι pr noun masc nom pl . . . . Μαδιηναῖος

Μαδιηναιοις pr noun masc dat pl . . . . id.

μαδῶν vb pres act part masc nom sg . . . . μαδάω

Μαδων pr noun

Μαεβερ pr noun

Μαελα pr noun

μαελεθ translit

Μαελεθ pr noun

μάζαν noun fem acc sg . . . . μάζα

Μαζαρ pr noun

μάζας noun fem acc pl . . . . μάζα

Μαζιτιας pr noun masc nom sg

μαζουρωθ translit

Μαηλων pr noun

Μαηρος pr noun

Μαθαθα pr noun

Μαθαθια pr noun

Μαθαν pr noun

Μαθαναι pr noun

Μαθανι pr noun

Μαθανια pr noun

μάθε vb 2nd aor act impv 2nd pers sg . . . . μανθάνω

μαθεῖν vb 2nd aor act inf . . . . id.

μάθετε vb 2nd aor act impv 2nd pers pl . . . . id.

μάθη vb 2nd aor act subj 3rd pers sg . . . . id.

μαθήματα noun neut nom and acc pl . . . . μάθημα

μάθῃς vb 2nd aor act subj 2nd pers sg . . . . μανθάνω

μαθήσεσθε vb fut mid ind 2nd pers pl . . . . id.

μαθήσῃ vb fut mid ind 2nd pers sg . . . . id.

μαθήσομαι vb fut mid ind 1st pers sg . . . . id.

μαθήσονται vb fut mid ind 3rd pers pl . . . . id.

μάθητε vb 2nd aor act subj 2nd pers pl . . . . id.

Μαθθαναι pr noun

Μαθθανιαν pr noun masc acc sg . . . . Μαθθανιας

Μαθθανιας pr noun masc nom sg . . . . id.

μαθόντες vb 2nd aor act part masc nom pl . . . . . . μανθάνω

Μαθουσαλα pr noun

μάθω vb 2nd aor act subj 1st pers sg . . . . μανθάνω

μάθωμεν vb 2nd aor act subj 1st pers pl . . . . id.

μαθών vb 2nd aor act part masc nom sg . . . . id.

μάθωσιν vb 2nd aor act subj 3rd pers pl . . . . id.

μαῖα noun fem nom sg

μαῖαι noun fem nom pl . . . . μαῖα

μαίαις noun fem dat pl . . . . id.

Μαιανι pr noun

Μαιαννας pr noun

μαίας noun fem acc pl . . . . μαῖα

Μαιδαβα pr noun

Μαιζοοβ pr noun

Μαιηλ pr noun

μαιμάσσει vb pres act ind 3rd pers sg . . . . μαιμάσσω

Μαιναμ pr noun

μαινομένῳ vb pres dep part masc and neut dat sg . μαίνομαι

μαιοῦσθε vb pres dep ind 2nd pers pl . . . . μαιόομαι

Μαισα pr noun

Μαισαλωθ pr noun

Μαιτεβεηλ pr noun

μαιωθήσονται vb fut pass ind 3rd pers pl . . . . . . μαιόομαι

Μακαλωθ pr noun

Μακαλων pr noun

μακαρία adj fem nom sg . . . . μακάριος

μακάριαι adj fem nom pl . . . . id.

μακαριεῖ vb fut act ind 3rd pers sg . . . . μακαρίζω

μακάριζε vb pres act impv 2nd pers sg . . . . id.

μακαρίζει vb pres act ind 3rd pers sg . . . . id.

μακαρίζομεν vb pres act ind 1st pers pl . . . . id.

μακαρίζοντες vb pres act part masc nom pl . . . . id.

μακαρίζουσιν vb pres act ind 3rd pers pl . . . . id.

μακαρίζω vb pres act ind 1st pers sg . . . . id.

μακάριοι adj masc nom pl . . . . μακάριος

μακάριον adj masc acc sg, neut nom and acc sg . . . . . . id.

μακάριος adj masc nom sg . . . . id.

μακαριότητα noun fem acc sg . . . . μακαριότης

μακαρίου adj masc and neut gen sg . . . . μακάριος

μακαριοῦμεν vb fut act ind 1st pers pl . . . . μακαρίζω

μακαρίους adj masc acc pl . . . . μακάριος

μακαριοῦσιν vb fut act ind 3rd pers pl . . . . μακαρίζω

μακαρίσαι vb 1st aor act opt 3rd pers sg . . . . id.

μακαρίσαιμ' see μακαρίσαιμι

μακαρίσαιμι vb 1st aor act opt 1st pers sg . . . . id.

μακαρισθήσομαι vb fut pass ind 1st pers sg . . . . id.

μακαριστόν adj masc acc sg,

        neut nom and acc sg . . . . μακαριστός

μακαριστός adj masc nom sg . . . . id.

μακαρίως adverb

Μακεδ pr noun

Μακεδονα pr noun masc acc sg . . . . Μακεδων

Μακεδονας pr noun masc acc pl . . . . id.

Μακεδοσι pr noun masc dat pl . . . . id.

Μακεδων pr noun masc nom sg

Μακελλαθ pr noun

Μακελλωθ pr noun

Μακενια pr noun

Μακενιας pr noun masc nom sg

Μακηδα pr noun

Μακηδαν pr noun

Μακηλωθ pr noun

Μακκαβαιον pr noun masc acc sg .... Μακκαβαιος

Μακκαβαιος pr noun masc nom sg   id.

Μακκαβαιω pr noun masc dat sg   id.

μακρᾷ adj fem dat sg .... μακρός

μακράν adj fem acc sg   id.

μακράν adverb

μακράς adj fem acc pl .... μακρός

μακρᾶς adj fem gen sg   id.

μακρόβιοι adj masc and fem nom pl .... μακρόβιος

μακρόβιον adj acc sg, neut nom sg   id.

μακροβίωσις noun fem nom sg

μακροημερεύσει vb fut act ind 3rd pers sg . μακροημερεύω

μακροημερεύσετε vb fut act ind 2nd pers pl   id.

μακροημερεύσητε vb 1st aor act subj 2nd pers pl   id.

μακροημέρευσιν noun fem acc sg ..... μακροημέρευσις

μακροημέρευσις noun fem nom sg   id.

μακροήμεροι adj masc and fem nom pl ..... μακροήμερος

μακρόθεν adverb

μακροθυμεῖ vb pres act ind 3rd pers sg ...... μακροθυμέω

μακροθυμήσατε vb 1st aor act impv 2nd pers pl   id.

μακροθυμήσῃ vb 1st aor act subj 3rd pers sg   id.

μακροθύμησον vb 1st aor act impv 2nd pers sg   id.

μακροθυμήσω vb 1st aor act subj 1st pers sg   id.

μακροθυμίᾳ noun fem dat sg .... μακροθυμία

μακροθυμίαν noun fem acc sg   id.

μακρόθυμος adj masc nom sg

μακροθυμῶν adj gen pl .... μακρόθυμος

μακρόν adj masc acc sg, neut nom and acc sg ...... μακρός

μακρός adj masc nom sg   id.

μακρότερα comp adj neut nom and acc pl   id.

μακροτέρα comp adj fem nom sg   id.

μακρότερον comp adj masc acc sg,
            neut nom and acc sg   id.

μακρότερον adverb

μακρότης noun fem nom sg

μακρότητα noun fem acc sg .... μακρότης

μακρότητος noun fem gen sg   id.

μακρούς adj masc acc pl .... μακρός

μακροχρόνιος adj masc and fem nom sg

μακροχρονίσῃ vb 1st aor act subj
            3rd pers sg .... μακροχρονίζω

μακροχρονίσωσιν vb 1st aor act subj 3rd pers pl   id.

μακρύμμασι noun neut dat pl .... μάκρυμμα

μακρύναι vb 1st aor act opt 3rd pers sg .... μακρύνω

μακρῦναι vb 1st aor act inf .... μακρύνω

μακρυνεῖ vb fut act ind 3rd pers sg   id.

μακρυνεῖς vb fut act ind 2nd pers sg   id.

μακρύνης see μακρύνης

μακρύνῃς vb pres act subj 2nd pers sg,
            1st aor act subj 2nd pers sg   id.

μακρυνθείη vb 1st aor pass opt 3rd pers sg   id.

μακρυνθῆναι vb 1st aor pass inf   id.

μακρυνθήσεται vb fut pass ind 3rd pers sg   id.

μακρυνθήσονται vb fut pass ind 3rd pers pl   id.

μάκρυνον vb 1st aor act impv 2nd pers sg   id.

μακρύνοντες vb pres act part masc nom pl   id.

μακρῷ adj masc and neut dat sg .... μακρός

μακρῶν adj gen pl   id.

Μακρων pr noun

Μακχι pr noun

Μαλ pr noun

μάλα adverb

Μαλα pr noun

μάλαγμα noun neut nom and acc sg

μαλακή adj fem nom sg .... μαλακός

μαλακία noun fem nom sg

μαλακίᾳ noun fem dat sg .... μαλακία

μαλακίαις noun fem dat pl   id.

μαλακίαν noun fem acc sg   id.

μαλακίας noun fem gen sg   id.

μαλακισθείς vb 1st aor pass part
            masc nom sg .... μαλακίζομαι

μαλακισθῆναι vb 1st aor pass inf   id.

μαλακίσθητι vb 1st aor pass impv 2nd pers sg   id.

μαλακοί adj masc nom pl .... μαλακός

μαλακοψυχήσαντας vb 1st aor act part
            masc acc pl .... μαλακοψυχέω

μαλακῶς adverb

Μαλαχ pr noun

Μαλελεηλ pr noun

Μαλελ ηλ pr noun

Μαλεχεθ pr noun

Μαλησεαρ pr noun

μάλιστα superl adverb .... μάλα

Μαλληθι pr noun

μᾶλλον adverb

Μαλλω pr noun

Μαλλωτας pr noun masc acc pl .... Μαλλωτης

Μαλουχ pr noun

Μαλτανναιος pr noun

Μαλχια pr noun

Μαλωχ pr noun

Μαμβρη pr noun

Μαμδαι pr noun

μάμμη noun fem nom sg

Μαμνιταναιμος pr noun

Μαμουχος pr noun
Μαμφιν pr noun
μαν translit
Μαν pr noun
μαναα translit
μανααν translit
Μαναεμ pr noun
Μαναημ pr noun
Μαναθι pr noun
Μαναϊμ pr noun
Μανασση pr noun
Μανασσηας pr noun
Μανασσης pr noun masc nom sg
Μαναχαθ pr noun
Μαναχαθι pr noun
μάνδρα noun fem nom sg
μάνδρᾳ noun fem dat sg . . . . μάνδρα
μανδραγόραι noun masc nom pl . . . . μανδραγόρας
μανδραγόρας noun masc acc pl   id.
μανδραγόρου noun masc gen sg   id.
μανδραγορῶν noun masc gen pl   id.
μάνδραι noun fem nom pl . . . . μάνδρα
μάνδραις noun fem dat pl   id.
μάνδρας noun fem gen sg and acc pl   id.
μανδρῶν noun fem gen pl   id.
μανδύαν noun masc acc sg . . . . μανδύας
μανδύας noun masc nom sg and acc pl   id.
μανδύου noun masc gen sg   id.
μανδυῶν noun masc gen pl   id.
μανη translit
μανῆναι vb 2nd aor pass inf . . . . μαίνομαι
Μανης pr noun
μανῇς vb 2nd aor pass subj 2nd pers sg . . . . μαίνομαι
μανήσονται vb fut pass ind 3rd pers pl   id.
Μανθαναιν pr noun
μάνθανε vb pres act impv 2nd pers sg . . . . μανθάνω
μανθάνειν vb pres act inf   id.
μανθάνετε vb pres act impv 2nd pers pl   id.
Μανθανιας pr noun masc nom sg
Μανθανιου pr noun masc gen sg . . . . Μανθανιας
μανθάνομεν vb pres act ind 1st pers pl . . . . μανθάνω
μανθανόντων vb pres act part masc and neut gen pl   id.
Μανι pr noun
μανία noun fem nom sg
μανιάκην noun masc acc sg . . . . μανιάκης
μανιάκης noun masc nom sg   id.
μανίαν noun fem acc sg . . . . μανία
μανίας noun fem acc pl   id.
Μανιος pr noun masc nom sg
μανιῶδες adj neut nom and acc pl . . . . μανιώδης
μαννα translit
Μανοχω pr noun

μαντεία noun fem nom sg
μαντεῖα noun neut nom and acc pl . . . . μαντεῖον
μαντεῖαι noun fem nom pl . . . . μαντεία
μαντείαν noun fem acc sg   id.
μαντείας noun fem gen sg and acc pl   id.
μαντεῖον noun neut nom and acc sg
μάντεις noun masc nom and acc pl . . . . μάντις
μαντειῶν noun fem gen pl . . . . μαντεία
μαντεύεσθαι vb pres dep inf . . . . μαντεύομαι
μαντευόμενοι vb pres dep part masc nom pl   id.
μαντευόμενος vb pres dep part masc nom sg   id.
μαντευομένων vb pres dep part gen pl   id.
μάντευσαι vb 1st aor mid impv 2nd pers sg   id.
μαντεύσασθαι vb 1st aor mid inf   id.
μαντεύσησθε vb 1st aor mid subj 2nd pers pl   id.
μάντιν noun masc acc sg . . . . μάντις
Μανωε pr noun
Μαουδα pr noun
Μαουεκ pr noun
Μαραγελλα pr noun
Μαραια pr noun
Μαραιωθ pr noun
Μαραλα pr noun
μαράναι vb 1st aor act opt 3rd pers sg . . . . μαραίνω
μαρανθῆναι vb 1st aor pass inf   id.
Μαρδοχαϊκῆς adj fem gen sg . . . . Μαρδοχαικος
Μαρδοχαῖον pr noun masc acc sg . . . . Μαρδοχαῖος
Μαρδοχαῖος pr noun masc nom sg   id.
Μαρδοχαιου pr noun masc gen sg   id.
Μαρδοχαιω pr noun masc dat sg   id.
Μαρεθ pr noun
Μαρερωθ pr noun
Μαρησα pr noun
Μαρι pr noun
Μαριαμ pr noun
Μαριας pr noun fem gen sg . . . . Μαρια
Μαριβααλ pr noun
Μαριηλ pr noun
Μαριμωθ pr noun
Μαρισα pr noun masc nom sg
Μαρισαν pr noun fem acc sg . . . . Μαρισα
Μαρισης pr noun fem gen sg   id.
Μαριωθ pr noun
Μαρμα pr noun
μαρμάρινοι adj masc nom pl . . . . μαρμάρινος
μαρμάρου noun fem gen sg . . . . μάρμαρος
Μαρμασιμε pr noun
Μαρμηνα pr noun
Μαρμωθι pr noun
Μαρρων pr noun
μαρσίππιον noun neut nom and acc sg
μαρσιππίου noun neut gen sg . . . . μαρσίππιον

μαρσιππίῳ noun neut dat sg . . . . μαρσίππιον
μαρσίπποις noun masc dat pl . . . . μάρσιππος
μάρσιππον noun masc acc sg id.
μαρσίππου noun masc gen sg id.
μαρσίππους noun masc acc pl id.
μαρσίππῳ noun masc dat sg id.
μάρτυρα noun masc acc sg . . . . μάρτυς
μάρτυρας noun masc acc pl id.
μαρτύρασθαι vb 1st aor mid inf . . . . μαρτυρέω
μαρτυρεῖ vb pres act ind 3rd pers sg id.
μάρτυρες noun masc nom pl . . . . μάρτυς
μαρτυρῆσαι vb 1st aor act inf . . . . μαρτυρέω
μαρτυρήσει vb fut act ind 3rd pers sg id.
μαρτυρήσω vb 1st aor act subj 1st pers sg,
        fut act ind 1st pers sg id.
μάρτυρι noun masc dat sg . . . . μάρτυς
μαρτύρια noun neut nom and acc pl . . . . μαρτύριον
μαρτυρία noun fem nom sg
μαρτυρίαν noun fem acc sg . . . . μαρτυρία
μαρτυρίας noun fem gen sg id.
μαρτυρίοις noun neut dat pl . . . . μαρτύριον
μαρτύριον noun neut nom and acc sg id.
μαρτυρίου noun neut gen sg id.
μαρτυρίῳ noun neut dat sg id.
μαρτυρίων noun neut gen pl id.
μαρτυρόμεθα vb pres dep ind 1st pers pl . . . . . μαρτύρομαι
μαρτυροῦμεν vb pres act ind 1st pers pl . . . . μαρτυρέω
μαρτυροῦσα vb pres act part fem nom sg id.
μαρτύρων noun masc gen pl . . . . μάρτυς
μάρτυς noun masc nom sg id.
μάρτυσι noun masc dat pl id.
μαρυκᾶται vb pres dep ind 3rd pers sg . . . . . . μαρυκάομαι
Μαρωδαχ pr noun
Μαρωδαχβαλαδαν pr noun
Μαρωζ pr noun
Μαρωθ pr noun
Μαρων pr noun
Μασα pr noun
Μασαια pr noun
Μασαιας pr noun masc nom sg
Μασαλ pr noun
Μασαλαμι pr noun
μασανα translit
Μασβακ pr noun
Μασεζεβηλ pr noun
Μασεκ pr noun
Μασεκκας pr noun fem gen sg . . . . Μασεκκα
Μασελμωθ pr noun
Μασεμαννη pr noun
μασενα translit
Μασερεμ pr noun
Μασερεφωθμαιμ pr noun

Μασερων pr noun
Μασηα pr noun
Μασηας pr noun
Μασιας pr noun
Μασμα pr noun
μασμαρωθ translit
μασομελ translit
Μασσαλημ pr noun
Μασσαμ pr noun
Μασση pr noun
Μασσημα pr noun
Μασσηφα pr noun
Μασσηφαθ pr noun
Μασσιας pr noun masc nom sg
Μασσουρουθ pr noun
Μασσωχ pr noun
μάστιγα noun fem acc sg . . . . μάστιξ
μάστιγας noun fem acc pl id.
μάστιγες noun fem nom pl id.
μάστιγι noun fem dat sg id.
μάστιγξι(ν) noun fem dat pl id.
μαστιγοῖ vb pres act ind 3rd pers sg . . . . μαστιγόω
μαστιγοῖς vb pres act ind 2nd pers sg id.
μάστιγος noun fem gen sg . . . . μάστιξ
μαστιγούμενος vb pres m/p part masc nom sg . . . μαστιγόω
μαστιγουμένου vb pres m/p part
      masc and neut gen sg id.
μαστιγωθείς vb 1st aor pass part masc nom sg id.
μαστιγωθῇς vb 1st aor pass subj 2nd pers sg id.
μαστιγωθήσονται vb fut pass ind 3rd pers pl id.
μαστίγων noun fem gen pl . . . . μάστιξ
μαστιγῶσαι vb 1st aor act inf . . . . μαστιγόω
μαστιγώσει vb fut act ind 3rd pers sg id.
μαστιγώσουσι(ν) vb fut act ind 3rd pers pl id.
μαστιζόμενον vb pres m/p part masc acc sg,
      neut nom and acc sg . . . . μαστίζω
μάστιξ noun fem nom sg
μαστίξαι vb 1st aor act inf . . . . μαστίζω
μάστιξιν noun fem dat pl . . . . μάστιξ
μαστοί noun masc nom pl . . . . μαστός
μαστοῦ noun masc gen sg id.
μαστούς noun masc acc pl id.
μαστῶν noun masc gen pl id.
Μασφα pr noun
Μασφαρ pr noun
Μασφαραθ pr noun
Μασφασσατ pr noun
Μασφε pr noun
μάταια adj neut nom and acc pl . . . . μάταιος
ματαία adj fem nom sg id.
ματαίᾳ adj fem dat sg id.
μάταιαι adj fem nom pl id.

ματαίαν adj fem acc sg	. . . .	μάταιος
ματαίας adj fem acc pl		id.
μάταιοι adj masc (and fem) nom pl		id.
ματαίοις adj masc and neut dat pl		id.
μάταιον adj masc acc sg, neut nom and acc sg		id.
μάταιος adj masc nom sg		id.
ματαιότης noun fem nom sg		
ματαιότητα noun fem acc sg	. . . .	ματαιότης
ματαιότητας noun fem acc pl		id.
ματαιότητες noun fem nom pl		id.
ματαιότητι noun fem dat sg		id.
ματαιότητος noun fem gen sg		id.
ματαιοτήτων noun fem gen pl		id.
ματαίους adj masc acc pl	. . . .	μάταιος
ματαιοῦσιν vb pres act ind 3rd pers pl	. . . .	ματαιόω
ματαιόφρονες noun masc nom pl	. . . .	ματαιόφρων
ματαίῳ adj masc and neut dat sg	. . . .	μάταιος
ματαιωθήσεται vb fut pass ind 3rd pers sg	. . . . . .	ματαιόω
ματαίων adj gen pl	. . . .	μάταιος
ματαίως adverb		
Ματανιας pr noun masc nom sg		
Ματεκκα pr noun		
μάτην adverb		
Ματθαν pr noun		
Ματραιθ pr noun		
Ματταθια pr noun		
Ματταθιαν pr noun masc acc sg	. . . .	Ματταθιας
Ματταθιας pr noun masc nom sg		id.
Ματταθιου pr noun masc gen sg		id.
Ματταρι pr noun		
Μαφα pr noun		
Μαφεκαδ pr noun		
Μαχαβανναι pr noun		
Μαχαβηνα pr noun		
Μαχαδ pr noun		
Μαχαθι pr noun		
μάχαι noun fem nom pl	. . . .	μάχη
μάχαιρα noun fem nom sg		
μαχαίρα noun fem dat sg	. . . .	μάχαιρα
μάχαιραι noun fem nom pl		id.
μαχαίραις noun fem dat pl		id.
μάχαιραν noun fem acc sg		id.
μαχαίρας noun fem gen sg and acc pl		id.
μαχαίρῃ noun fem dat sg		id.
μαχαίρης noun fem gen sg		id.
μαχαιρῶν noun fem gen pl		id.
μάχαις noun fem dat pl	. . . .	μάχη
Μαχαμας pr noun		
Μαχαναρεθ pr noun		
Μαχανια pr noun		
Μαχαριμ pr noun		
μάχας noun fem acc pl	. . . .	μαχη

Μαχατι pr noun		
Μαχεμας pr noun		
Μαχες pr noun		
μάχεσθαι vb pres dep inf	. . . .	μάχομαι
μάχη noun fem nom sg		
μάχῃ noun fem dat sg	. . . .	μάχη
μάχην noun fem acc sg		id.
μάχης noun fem gen sg		id.
μαχηταί noun masc nom pl	. . . .	μαχητής
μαχηταῖς noun masc dat pl		id.
μαχητάς noun masc acc pl		id.
μαχητήν noun masc acc sg		id.
μαχητής noun masc nom sg		id.
μαχητοῦ noun masc gen sg		id.
μαχητῶν noun masc gen pl		id.
μάχιμοι adj masc and fem nom pl	. . . .	μάχιμος
μαχίμου adj gen sg		id.
μαχίμους adj masc and fem acc pl		id.
μαχίμων adj gen pl		id.
μαχιρ translit		
Μαχιρ pr noun		
Μαχιρι pr noun		
μαχμα translit		
Μαχμας pr noun		
Μαχναδαβου pr noun		
μαχόμενος vb pres dep part masc nom sg	. . . .	μάχομαι
μαχομένους vb pres dep part masc acc pl		id.
μαχομένων vb pres dep part gen pl		id.
Μαχω pr noun		
μάχωνται vb pres dep subj 3rd pers pl	. . . .	μάχομαι
Μαψαρ pr noun		
Μαωζ pr noun		
μαωζιν translit		
Μαων pr noun		
Μαωνιμ pr noun		
Μαωρ pr noun		
με pers pron acc sg	. . . .	ἐγώ
Μεαζωθ pr noun		
Μεαμιν pr noun		
Μεβααρ pr noun		
μέγα adj neut nom and acc sg	. . . .	μέγας
μεγάλα adj neut nom and acc pl		id.
Μεγαλα pr noun		
μεγάλαι adj fem nom pl	. . . .	μέγας
μεγάλαις adj fem dat pl		id.
μεγάλας adj fem acc pl		id.
μεγαλαυχεῖν vb pres act inf	. . . .	μεγαλαυχέω
μεγαλαυχῆσαι vb 1st aor act inf		id.
μεγαλαυχίας noun fem gen sg	. . . .	μεγαλαυχία
μεγαλεῖα adj neut nom and acc pl	. . . .	μεγαλεῖος
μεγαλεῖον adj masc acc sg, neut nom and acc sg		id.
μεγαλειότης noun fem nom sg		

μεγαλειότητα noun fem acc sg . . . . μεγαλειότης

μεγαλείῳ adj masc and neut dat sg . . . . μεγαλεῖος

μεγάλη adj fem nom sg . . . . μέγας

μεγάλῃ adj fem dat sg   id.

μεγάλην adj fem acc sg   id.

μεγάλης adj fem gen sg   id.

μεγαλόδοξος adj masc and fem nom sg

μεγαλοδόξως adverb

μεγάλοι adj masc nom pl . . . . μέγας

μεγάλοις adj masc and neut dat pl   id.

μεγαλοκράτωρ noun masc nom sg

μεγαλομεροῦς adj gen sg . . . . μεγαλομερής

μεγαλομερῶς adverb

μεγαλοπρεπεῖ adj dat sg . . . . μεγαλοπρεπής

μεγαλοπρέπεια noun fem nom sg

μεγαλοπρεπείᾳ noun fem dat sg . . . . μεγαλοπρέπεια

μεγαλοπρέπειαν noun fem acc sg   id.

μεγαλοπρεπείας noun fem gen sg   id.

μεγαλοπρεπεστάτην superl adj fem acc sg . μεγαλοπρεπής

μεγαλοπρεπής adj masc and fem nom sg   id.

μεγαλοπρεποῦς adj gen sg   id.

μεγαλοπρεπῶς adverb

μεγαλοπτέρυγος adj masc and fem nom sg

μεγαλορήμονα adj neut nom and acc pl . . . μεγαλορρήμων

μεγαλορημοσύνη noun fem nom sg . . . μεγαλορρημοσύνη

μεγαλορρημονήσῃς vb 1st aor act subj

           2nd pers sg . . . . μεγαλορρημονέω

μεγαλορρήμονι adj dat sg . . . . μεγαλορρήμων

μεγαλορρημονοῦντες vb pres act part

           masc nom pl . . . . μεγαλορρημονέω

μεγαλορρημοσύνη noun fem nom sg

μεγαλοσάρκους adj masc and fem acc pl . . μεγαλόσαρκος

μεγαλοσθενοῦς adj gen sg . . . . μεγαλοσθενής

μεγαλοσύνην noun fem acc sg . . . . μεγαλοσύνη

μεγάλου adj masc and neut gen sg . . . . μέγας

μεγάλους adj masc acc pl   id.

μεγαλοφρονοῦντα vb pres act part

           masc acc sg . . . . μεγαλοφρονέω

μεγαλόφρων noun masc nom sg

μεγαλόψυχοι adj masc and fem nom pl . . . . . μεγαλόψυχος

μεγαλοψύχως adverb

μεγαλύναι vb 1st aor act opt 3rd pers sg . . . . μεγαλύνω

μεγαλῦναι vb 1st aor act inf   id.

μεγαλύνας vb 1st aor act part masc nom sg   id.

μεγαλύνατε vb 1st aor act impv 2nd pers pl   id.

μεγαλύνει vb pres act ind 3rd pers sg . . . . μεγαλύνω

μεγαλυνεῖ vb fut act ind 3rd pers sg   id.

μεγαλύνεσθε vb pres m/p impv 2nd pers pl,

           pres m/p ind 2nd pers pl   id.

μεγαλύνῃ vb 1st aor act subj 3rd pers sg,

           pres act subj 3rd pers sg   id.

μεγαλύνηται vb 1st aor mid subj 3rd pers sg,

           pres m/p subj 3rd pers sg . . . . μεγαλύνω

μεγαλυνθείη vb 1st aor pass opt 3rd pers sg   id.

μεγαλυνθείης vb 1st aor pass opt 2nd pers sg   id.

μεγαλυνθέν vb 1st aor pass part neut nom and acc sg   id.

μεγαλυνθήσεται vb fut pass ind 3rd pers sg   id.

μεγαλυνθήσομαι vb fut pass ind 1st pers sg   id.

μεγαλυνθησόμεθα vb fut pass ind 1st pers pl   id.

μεγαλυνθήτω vb 1st aor pass impv 3rd pers sg   id.

μεγαλυνόμενος vb pres m/p part masc nom sg   id.

μεγαλύνονται vb pres m/p ind 3rd pers pl   id.

μεγαλυνοῦμεν vb fut act ind 1st pers pl   id.

μεγαλυνῶ vb fut act ind 1st pers sg   id.

μεγαλύνωμεν vb 1st aor act subj 1st pers pl,

           pres act subj 1st pers pl   id.

μεγαλύνων vb pres act part masc nom sg   id.

μεγάλῳ adj masc and neut dat sg . . . . μέγας

μεγαλώματος noun neut gen sg . . . . μεγάλωμα

μεγάλων adj gen pl . . . . μέγας

μεγαλώνυμος adj masc and fem nom sg

μεγάλως adverb

μεγαλωστί adverb

μεγαλωσύνη noun fem nom sg

μεγαλωσύνην noun fem acc sg . . . . μεγαλωσύνη

μεγαλωσύνης noun fem gen sg   id.

μέγαν adj masc acc sg . . . . μέγας

μέγας adj masc nom sg   id.

Μεγεδδω pr noun

Μεγεδιηλ pr noun

μεγέθει noun neut dat sg . . . . μέγεθος

μέγεθος noun neut nom and acc sg   id.

μεγέθους noun neut gen sg   id.

μεγιστάν noun masc nom sg

μεγιστάνας noun masc acc pl . . . . μεγιστάν

μεγιστάνες noun masc nom pl   id.

μεγιστάνι noun masc dat sg   id.

μεγιστάνων noun masc gen pl   id.

μεγίστας superl adj fem acc pl . . . . μέγας

μεγιστᾶσι noun masc dat pl . . . . μεγιστάν

μέγιστε superl adj masc voc sg . . . . μέγας

μεγίστη superl adj fem nom sg   id.

μεγίστην superl adj fem acc sg   id.

μεγίστης superl adj fem gen sg   id.

μέγιστον superl adj masc acc sg, neut nom and acc sg   id.

μέγιστος superl adj masc nom sg   id.

μεγίστου superl adj masc and neut gen sg   id.

μεγίστῳ superl adj masc and neut dat sg   id.

μεγίστων superl adj gen pl   id.

Μεδεβηνα pr noun

Μεεδδα pr noun

Μεελεφ pr noun

Μεηρα pr noun

Μεηταβηλ pr noun

Μεθ pr noun

μεθ' see μετά

μέθαις noun fem dat pl . . . . μέθη

μεθαρμοζόμενα vb pres m/p part

    neut nom and acc pl . . . . μεθαρμόζω

μεθαχαβιν translit

μεθερμηνεῦσαι vb 1st aor act inf . . . . μεθερμηνεύω

μέθη noun fem nom sg

μέθη noun fem dat sg . . . . μέθη

μέθην noun fem acc sg   id.

μέθης noun fem gen sg   id.

μεθιστᾷ vb pres act ind 3rd pers sg . . . . μεθίστημι

μεθισταμένους vb pres m/p part masc acc pl   id.

μεθιστᾶν vb pres act part neut nom and acc sg id.

μεθίσταντο vb impf m/p ind 3rd pers pl   id.

μεθιστῶν vb pres act part masc nom sg   id.

μεθιστῶσιν vb pres act subj 3rd pers pl   id.

Μεθλα pr noun

μεθόδων noun fem gen pl . . . . μέθοδος

μεθόριον noun neut nom and acc sg

μεθύοντες vb pres act part masc nom pl . . . . μεθύω

μεθύουσα vb pres act part fem nom sg   id.

μεθύουσαν vb pres act part fem acc sg   id.

μεθύσατε vb 1st aor act impv 2nd pers pl   id.

μεθύσει vb fut act ind 3rd pers sg   id.

μεθύσῃ vb 1st aor act subj 3rd pers sg   id.

μεθυσθήσεται vb fut pass ind 3rd pers sg   id.

μεθυσθήσῃ vb fut pass ind 2nd pers sg   id.

μεθυσθήσονται vb fut pass ind 3rd pers pl   id.

μεθύσθητε vb 1st aor pass impv 2nd pers pl   id.

μεθύσκει vb pres act ind 3rd pers sg . . . . μεθύσκω

μεθύσκεσθε vb pres m/p impv 2nd pers pl   id.

μεθύσκον vb pres act part neut nom and acc sg id.

μεθύσκοντα vb pres act part masc acc sg   id.

μεθύσκονται vb pres m/p ind 3rd pers pl   id.

μεθύσκων vb pres act part masc nom sg   id.

μεθύσμα noun neut nom and acc sg

μεθύσματι noun neut dat sg . . . . μέθυσμα

μέθυσον vb 1st aor act impv 2nd pers sg . . . . μεθύω

μέθυσος adj masc and fem nom sg

μεθύσου adj gen sg . . . . μέθυσος

μεθύσω vb fut act ind 1st pers sg . . . . μεθύω

μεθύων vb pres act part masc nom sg   id.

μεθώδευσεν vb 1st aor act ind 3rd pers sg . . . . . . μεθοδεύω

μεθωεσιμ translit

μεῖγμα noun neut nom and acc sg

μείγνυται vb pres m/p ind 3rd pers sg . . . . μείγνυμι

Μεϊδα pr noun

μειδιάσει vb fut act ind 3rd pers sg . . . . μειδιάω

μεῖζον comp adj neut nom and acc sg . . . . μέγας

μείζονα comp adj masc and fem acc sg,

    neut nom and acc pl . . . . μέγας

μείζονας comp adj masc and fem acc pl   id.

μείζονι comp adj masc and fem dat sg   id.

μείζονος comp adj gen sg   id.

μείζω comp adj masc and fem acc sg   id.

μείζων comp adj masc and fem nom sg   id.

μεῖναι vb 1st aor act inf . . . . μένω

μείναντες vb 1st aor act part masc nom pl   id.

μεινάτω vb 1st aor act impv 3rd pers sg   id.

μείνῃ vb 1st aor act subj 3rd pers sg   id.

μείνῃς vb 1st aor act subj 2nd pers sg   id.

μεῖνον vb 1st aor act impv 2nd pers sg   id.

Μεΐνωμ pr noun

μείνωμεν vb 1st aor act subj 1st pers pl . . . . μένω

μείνωσιν vb 1st aor act subj 3rd pers pl   id.

μειούμενος vb pres m/p part masc nom sg . . . . μειόω

μείρακες noun masc nom pl . . . . μεῖραξ

μειράκια noun neut nom and acc pl . . . . μειράκιον

μειρακίου noun neut gen sg   id.

μειρακίσκοι noun masc nom pl . . . . μειρακίσκος

μειρακίσκος noun masc nom sg   id.

μειρακίων noun neut gen pl . . . . μειράκιον

μείχθητε vb 1st aor pass impv 2nd pers pl . . . . μίγνυμι

Μεκεδω pr noun

μέλαθρα noun neut nom and acc pl . . . . μέλαθρον

μέλαθρον noun neut nom and acc sg   id.

μέλαινα adj fem nom sg . . . . μέλας

μέλανες adj masc nom pl   id.

μελάνθιον noun neut nom and acc sg

μελανία noun fem dat sg . . . . μελανία

μελέα adj fem nom sg . . . . μέλεος

μέλει noun neut dat sg . . . . μέλος

μέλει vb pres act ind 3rd pers sg . . . . μέλω

μέλεσι noun neut dat pl . . . . μέλος

μελέτα vb pres act impv 2nd pers sg . . . . μελετάω

μελετᾷ vb pres act ind 3rd pers sg   id.

μελετᾶν vb pres act inf   id.

μελέτας noun fem acc pl . . . . μελέτη

μελέτη noun fem nom sg   id.

μελέτῃ noun fem dat sg   id.

μελετήσει vb fut act ind 3rd pers sg . . . . μελετάω

μελετήσεις vb fut act ind 2nd pers sg   id.

μελετήσω vb fut act ind 1st pers sg   id.

μελετῶν vb pres act part masc nom sg   id.

μελετῶσιν vb pres act ind 3rd pers pl   id.

μέλη noun neut nom and acc pl . . . . μέλος

μέλῃ vb pres act subj 3rd pers sg . . . . μέλω

μέλι noun neut nom and acc sg

μελιοῦσιν vb fut act ind 3rd pers pl . . . . μελίζω

μελισάτωσαν vb 1st aor act impv 3rd pers pl   id.

μέλισσα noun fem nom sg

μέλισσαι	noun fem nom pl	μέλισσα
μέλισσαν	noun fem acc sg	id.
μελίσσῃ	noun fem dat sg	id.
μελισσῶν	noun fem gen pl	id.
μελισσῶνα	noun masc acc sg	μελισσών
μελισσῶνος	noun masc gen sg	id.
μέλιτι	noun neut dat sg	μέλι
μέλιτος	noun neut gen sg	id.
μέλλει	vb pres act ind 3rd pers sg	μέλλω
μέλλειν	vb pres act inf	id.
μέλλεις	vb pres act ind 2nd pers sg	id.
μέλλετε	vb pres act ind 2nd pers pl	id.
μέλλῃ	vb pres act subj 3rd pers sg	id.
Μελληθι	pr noun	
μέλλης	vb pres act subj 2nd pers sg	μέλλω
μέλλοντα	vb pres act part neut nom and acc pl	id.
μέλλοντας	vb pres act part masc acc pl	id.
μέλλοντες	vb pres act part masc nom pl	id.
μέλλοντος	vb pres act part masc and neut gen sg	id.
μελλόντων	vb pres act part masc and neut gen pl	id.
μέλλουσαν	vb pres act part fem acc sg	id.
μέλλουσιν	vb pres act ind 3rd pers pl	id.
μέλλω	vb pres act ind 1st pers sg	id.
μέλλων	vb pres act part masc nom sg	id.
μελον	translit	
μέλος	noun neut nom and acc sg	
Μελχα	pr noun	
Μελχαμ	pr noun	
Μελχας	pr noun fem gen sg	Μελχα
Μελχηλ	pr noun	
Μελχια	pr noun	
Μελχιας	pr noun masc nom sg	
Μελχιηλ	pr noun	
Μελχιηλι	pr noun	
Μελχιου	pr noun masc gen sg	Μελχιας
Μελχιραμ	pr noun	
Μελχισα	pr noun	
Μελχισεδεκ	pr noun	
Μελχισουε	pr noun	
Μελχολ	pr noun	
Μελχομ	pr noun	
μελῳδίαι	noun fem nom pl	μελῳδία
μελῳδόν	adj masc and fem acc sg	μελῳδός
μεμάθηκεν	vb perf act ind 3rd pers sg	μανθάνω
μεμαθηκέναι	vb perf act inf	id.
μεμαθηκότες	vb perf act part masc nom pl	id.
μεμακρυγκότων	vb perf act part masc and neut gen pl	μακρύνω
μεμακρυμμένου	vb perf m/p part masc and neut gen sg	id.
μεμαλάκισται	vb perf dep ind 3rd pers sg . . .	μαλακίζομαι
μεμαστιγωμένον	vb perf m/p part masc acc sg . .	μαστιγόω

μεμαστιγωμένος	vb perf m/p part masc nom sg . .	μαστιγόω
μεμαστίγωνται	vb perf m/p ind 3rd pers pl	id.
μεμαστίγωσαι	vb perf m/p ind 2nd pers sg	id.
μεματαίωμαι	vb perf m/p ind 1st pers sg	ματαιόω
μεματαίωται	vb perf m/p ind 3rd pers sg	id.
Μεμβρα	pr noun	
μεμεγάλυνται	vb perf m/p ind 3rd pers pl	μεγαλύνω
μεμεθυσμένῳ	vb perf m/p part masc and neut dat sg . .	μεθύω
μεμελαθρωμέναι	vb perf m/p part fem nom pl . . .	μελαθρόω
μεμελανωμένη	vb perf dep part fem nom sg . .	μελανόομαι
μεμελανωμένοι	vb perf dep part masc nom pl	id.
μεμενηκότας	vb perf act part masc acc pl	μένω
μεμερισμένη	vb perf m/p part fem nom sg	μερίζω
μεμερισμένην	vb perf m/p part fem acc sg	id.
μεμεστωμένος	vb perf dep part masc nom sg . . .	μεστόομαι
μεμεστωμένους	vb perf dep part masc acc pl	id.
μεμέτρηται	vb perf m/p ind 3rd pers sg	μετρέω
μεμήνασιν	vb perf act ind 3rd pers pl	μαίνομαι
μεμηχανευμένας	vb perf dep part	
fem acc pl		μηχανεύομαι
μεμηχανευμένων	vb perf dep part gen pl	id.
μεμηχανημένων	vb perf dep part gen pl . . .	μηχανάομαι
μεμιαμμένη	vb perf m/p part fem nom sg	μιαίνω
μεμιαμμένον	vb perf m/p part masc acc sg,	
neut nom and acc sg		id.
μεμιαμμένος	vb perf m/p part masc nom sg	id.
μεμιαμμένων	vb perf m/p part gen pl	id.
μεμίανσαι	vb perf m/p ind 2nd pers sg	id.
μεμίανται	vb perf m/p ind 3rd pers pl	id.
μεμιγμένον	vb perf m/p part masc acc sg,	
neut nom and acc sg		μίγνυμι
μεμίσηκα	vb perf act ind 1st pers sg	μισέω
μεμισήκαμεν	vb perf act ind 1st pers pl	id.
μεμίσηκας	vb perf act ind 2nd pers sg	id.
μεμισημένην	vb perf m/p part fem acc sg	id.
μεμίσθωμαι	vb perf dep ind 1st pers sg	μισθόομαι
μεμίσθωνται	vb perf dep ind 3rd pers pl	id.
Μεμμιος	pr noun masc nom sg	
μεμνημένοι	vb perf m/p part masc nom pl	μιμνήσκω
μεμνημένοις	vb perf m/p part masc and neut dat pl	id.
μεμνημένους	vb perf m/p part masc acc pl	id.
μέμνησαι	vb perf m/p ind 2nd pers sg	id.
μεμνηστευμένη	vb perf dep part fem nom sg .	μνηστεύομαι
μεμνηστευμένην	vb perf dep part fem acc sg	id.
μεμνήστευται	vb perf dep ind 3rd pers sg	id.
μέμνηται	vb perf m/p ind 3rd pers sg	μιμνήσκω
μεμολυμμένα	vb perf m/p part	
neut nom and acc pl		μολύνω
μεμολυμμέναι	vb perf m/p part fem nom pl	id.
μεμολυσμένη	vb perf m/p part fem nom sg	id.
μεμολυσμένος	vb perf m/p part masc nom sg	id.

μεμυαλωμένα vb perf m/p part

    neut nom and acc pl . . . . μυαλόω

μεμυημένοις vb perf dep part masc and neut dat pl . μυέομαι

Μεμφεως pr noun fem gen sg . . . . Μεμφις

Μεμφιβοσθε pr noun

Μεμφιν pr noun fem acc sg . . . . Μεμφις

Μεμφις pr noun fem nom sg

μεμψάμενος vb 1st aor mid part masc nom sg . . . μέμφομαι

μέμψεται vb fut mid ind 3rd pers sg   id.

μέμψῃ vb 1st aor mid subj 2nd pers sg,

    fut mid ind 2nd pers sg   id.

μέμψιν noun fem acc sg . . . . μέμψις

μέμψις noun fem nom sg   id.

μεμωκημένα vb perf dep part

    neut nom and acc pl . . . . μωκάομαι

μεμωμημένη vb perf dep part fem nom sg . . . . . . μωμάομαι

μέν particle

μένε vb pres act impv 2nd pers sg . . . . μένω

μένει vb pres act ind 3rd pers sg   id.

μενεῖ vb fut act ind 3rd pers sg   id.

μένειν vb pres act inf   id.

μένεις vb pres act ind 2nd pers sg   id.

μενεῖς vb fut act ind 2nd pers sg   id.

Μενελαον pr noun masc acc sg . . . . Μενελαος

Μενελαος pr noun masc nom sg   id.

Μενελαου pr noun masc gen sg   id.

Μενεσθεως pr noun masc gen sg . . . . Μενεσθευς

μένετε vb pres act ind 2nd pers pl . . . . μένω

μενέτω vb pres act impv 3rd pers sg   id.

μένομεν vb pres act ind 1st pers pl   id.

μένοντα vb pres act part masc acc sg   id.

μένοντες vb pres act part masc nom pl   id.

μένουσα vb pres act part fem nom sg   id.

μένουσιν vb pres act ind 3rd pers pl   id.

μενοῦσιν vb fut act ind 3rd pers pl   id.

μέντοι particle

μέντοιγε particle

μενῶ vb fut act ind 1st pers sg . . . . μένω

μένων vb pres act part masc nom sg   id.

Μεραθων pr noun

Μεραμωθ pr noun

Μεραρι pr noun

Μεργαβ pr noun

μέρει noun neut dat sg . . . . μέρος

μέρεσι noun neut dat pl   id.

μέρη noun neut nom and acc pl   id.

Μεριβααλ pr noun

μερίδα noun fem acc sg . . . . μερίς

μεριδάρχην noun fem acc sg . . . . μεριδάρχης

μεριδαρχιαν noun fem acc sg . . . . μεριδαρχία

μεριδαρχίας noun fem acc pl   id.

μερίδας noun fem acc pl . . . . μερίς

μερίδες noun fem nom pl . . . . μερίς

μερίδι noun fem dat sg   id.

μερίδος noun fem gen sg   id.

μερίδων noun fem gen pl   id.

μεριεῖ vb fut act ind 3rd pers sg . . . . μερίζω

μεριεῖς vb fut act ind 2nd pers sg   id.

μερίζειν vb pres act inf   id.

μερίζεται vb pres m/p ind 3rd pers sg   id.

μερίζουσιν vb pres act ind 3rd pers pl   id.

μέριμνα noun fem nom sg

μέριμναι noun fem nom pl . . . . μέριμνα

μέριμναν noun fem acc sg   id.

μερίμνας noun fem acc pl   id.

μεριμνάτωσαν vb pres act impv 3rd pers pl . . . . . μεριμνάω

μερίμνῃ noun fem dat sg . . . . μέριμνα

μερίμνης noun fem gen sg   id.

μεριμνήσει vb fut act ind 3rd pers sg . . . . μεριμνάω

μεριμνήσω vb fut act ind 1st pers sg   id.

μεριμνῶμεν vb pres act subj 1st pers pl   id.

μεριμνῶντες vb pres act part masc nom pl   id.

μεριμνῶντι vb pres act part masc and neut dat sg   id.

Μεριμωθ pr noun

μεριοῦνται vb fut mid ind 3rd pers pl . . . . μερίζω

μερίς noun fem nom sg

μερίσαντες vb 1st aor act part masc nom pl . . . . . . μερίζω

μερίσατε vb 1st aor act impv 2nd pers pl   id.

μερισθεῖσα vb 1st aor pass part fem nom sg   id.

μερισθήσεσθε vb fut pass ind 2nd pers pl   id.

μερισθήσεται vb fut pass ind 3rd pers sg   id.

μερισμοῖς noun masc dat pl . . . . μερισμός

μερισμῷ noun masc dat sg   id.

μέρισον vb 1st aor act impv 2nd pers sg . . . . μερίζω

μερίσω vb 1st aor act subj 1st pers sg   id.

μεριτεύονται vb pres dep ind 3rd pers pl . . . . μεριτεύομαι

μεριῶ vb fut act ind 1st pers sg . . . . μερίζω

Μεροβ pr noun

μέρος noun neut nom and acc sg

μέρους noun neut gen sg . . . . μέρος

Μερρα pr noun

Μερραν pr noun

μερῶν noun neut gen pl . . . . μέρος

μέσα adj neut nom and acc pl . . . . μέσος

μεσαζούσης vb pres act part fem gen sg . . . . μεσάζω

μέσακλον noun neut nom and acc sg

μέσας adj fem acc pl . . . . μέσος

μέσῃ adj fem dat sg   id.

Μεσημα pr noun

μεσημβρία noun fem nom sg

μεσημβρίᾳ noun fem dat sg . . . . μεσημβρία

μεσημβρίαν noun fem acc sg   id.

μεσημβρίας noun fem gen sg   id.

μεσημβρινῇ adj fem dat sg . . . . μεσημβρινός μεσημβρινόν adj masc acc sg,

    neut nom and acc sg . . . . μεσημβρινός

μεσημβρινοῦ adj masc and neut gen sg   id.

μέσην adj fem acc sg . . . . μέσος

μέσης adj fem gen sg   id.

μεσθααλ translit

μεσίτης noun masc nom sg

μεσογείου adj gen sg . . . . μεσόγειος

μέσοι adj masc nom pl . . . . μέσος

Μεσολαμον pr noun masc acc sg . . . . Μεσολαμος

Μεσολλαμ pr noun

μέσον adj masc acc sg, neut nom and acc sg . . . . μέσος

μεσονύκτιον noun neut nom and acc sg

μεσονυκτίου noun neut gen sg . . . . μεσονύκτιον

μεσονυκτίῳ noun neut dat sg   id.

μεσοπόρφυρα adj neut nom and acc pl . . . . μεσοπόρφυρος

μεσοπορφύρου adj masc gen sg   id.

Μεσοποταμια pr noun fem dat sg . . . . Μεσοποταμια

Μεσοποταμιαν pr noun fem acc sg   id.

Μεσοποταμιας pr noun fem gen sg   id.

μέσος adj masc nom sg

μεσότητα noun fem acc sg . . . . μεσότης

μέσου adj masc and neut gen sg . . . . μέσος

Μεσουλαμ pr noun

μεσοῦντος vb pres act part masc and neut gen sg . . . . μεσόω

μέσους adj masc acc pl . . . . μέσος

μεσούσης vb pres act part fem gen sg . . . . μεσόω

Μεσραιμ pr noun

Μεσσααμ pr noun

μεσσαβ translit

Μεσσαρα pr noun

μεστή adj fem nom sg . . . . μεστός

μεστόν adj masc acc sg, neut nom and acc sg   id.

μεστός adj masc nom sg   id.

Μεστραιμ pr noun

μέσῳ adj masc and neut dat sg . . . . μέσος

Μεσωζεβηλ pr noun

μέσων adj gen pl . . . . μέσος

μετ᾽ see μετά

μετά preposition

μεταβαίνειν vb pres act inf . . . . μεταβαίνω

μεταβαίνουσα vb pres act part fem nom sg   id.

μεταβαλεῖ vb fut act ind 3rd pers sg . . . . μεταβάλλω

μεταβάλῃ vb 2nd aor act subj 3rd pers sg   id.

μεταβάλλει vb pres act ind 3rd pers sg   id.

μεταβαλλόμενον vb pres m/p part masc acc sg   id.

μεταβαλοίμεθα vb 2nd aor mid opt 1st pers pl,

    fut mid opt 1st pers pl   id.

μεταβαλόμενοι vb 2nd aor mid part masc nom pl   id.

μεταβαλόντων vb 2nd aor act part masc and neut gen pl id.

μεταβαλοῦσα vb 2nd aor act part fem nom sg   id.

μεταβαλοῦσιν vb fut act ind 3rd pers pl   id.

μεταβαλών vb 2nd aor act part masc nom sg . . . μεταβάλλω

μεταβεβηκέναι vb perf act inf . . . . μεταβαίνω

μεταβεβληκυῖαν vb perf act part fem acc sg . . . μεταβάλλω

μεταβηχας translit

μεταβολαῖς noun fem dat pl . . . . μεταβολή

μεταβολάς noun fem acc pl   id.

μεταβολῇ noun fem dat sg   id.

μεταβολῆς noun fem gen sg   id.

μεταβολίας noun fem gen sg . . . . μεταβολία

μεταβόλοι noun masc nom pl . . . . μεταβόλος

μεταβόλων noun masc gen pl   id.

μεταγενέστερος comp adj masc nom sg . . . . . μεταγενής

μεταγενομένοις vb 2nd aor mid part

    masc and neut dat pl . . . . μεταγίνομαι

μεταγενομένους vb 2nd aor mid part masc acc pl   id.

μετάγεται vb pres m/p ind 3rd pers sg . . . . μετάγω

μεταδιαιτηθέντες vb 1st aor pass part

    masc nom pl . . . . μεταδιαιτέω

μεταδιδόασιν vb pres act ind 3rd pers pl . . . . . μεταδίδωμι

μεταδιδόντος vb pres act part masc and neut gen sg   id.

μεταδίδωμι vb pres act ind 1st pers sg   id.

μεταδιώκειν vb pres act inf . . . . μεταδιώκω

μεταδόντος vb 2nd aor act part

    masc and neut gen sg . . . . μεταδίδωμι

μεταθεῖναι vb 2nd aor act inf . . . . μετατίθημι

μεταθέμενον vb 2nd aor mid part masc acc sg,

    neut nom and acc sg   id.

μετάθες vb 2nd aor act impv 2nd pers sg   id.

μεταθέσει noun fem dat sg . . . . μετάθεσις

μεταθῇς vb 2nd aor act subj 2nd pers sg . . . . . . μετατίθημι

μεταθήσω vb fut act ind 1st pers sg   id.

μέταιρε vb pres act impv 2nd pers sg . . . . μεταίρω

μεταιτίους adj masc and fem acc pl . . . . μεταίτιος

μετακαλέσαι vb 1st aor act inf . . . . μετακαλέω

μετακινηθήσονται vb fut pass ind 3rd pers pl . μετακινέω

μετακινήσει vb fut act ind 3rd pers sg   id.

μετακινήσεις vb fut act ind 2nd pers sg   id.

μετακινήσουσιν vb fut act ind 3rd pers pl   id.

μετακινήσω vb fut act ind 1st pers sg   id.

μετακινουμένη vb pres m/p part fem nom sg   id.

μετακομίσοντας vb fut act part masc acc pl . . μετακομίζω

μεταλαβόντες vb 2nd aor act part

    masc nom pl . . . . μεταλαμβάνω

μεταλαβοῦσαι vb 2nd aor act inf   id.

μεταλαβών vb 2nd aor act part masc nom sg   id.

μεταλαμβάνων vb pres act part masc nom sg   id.

μεταλήμψεσθαι vb fut mid inf   id.

μεταλλάξαι vb 1st aor act inf . . . . μεταλλάσσω

μεταλλάξαντος vb 1st aor act part

    masc and neut gen sg   id.

μεταλλάσσοντας vb pres act part masc acc pl   id.

μεταλλεύει vb pres act ind 3rd pers sg . . . . μεταλλεύω

μεταλλευομένη vb pres m/p part fem nom sg .. μεταλλεύω
μεταλλεύσεις vb fut act ind 2nd pers sg id.
μετάλλων noun neut gen pl .... μέταλλον
μεταμέλεια noun fem nom sg
μεταμελείᾳ noun fem dat sg .... μεταμέλεια
μεταμεληθείς vb 1st aor pass part masc nom sg . μεταμελέω
μεταμεληθέντες vb 1st aor pass part masc nom pl id.
μεταμεληθῇς vb 1st aor pass subj 2nd pers sg id.
μεταμεληθήσεσθε vb fut pass ind 2nd pers pl id.
μεταμεληθήσεται vb fut pass ind 3rd pers sg id.
μεταμεληθήσῃ vb fut pass ind 2nd pers sg id.
μεταμελήσῃ vb 1st aor act subj 3rd pers sg id.
μετάμελον noun masc acc sg .... μετάμελος
μετάμελος noun masc nom sg id.
μεταμελοῦ vb pres m/p impv 2nd pers sg ...... μεταμελέω
μεταμεμέλημαι vb perf mid ind 1st pers sg id.
μεταναστεύου vb pres m/p impv 2nd pers sg μεταναστεύω
μεταναστεύσαι vb 1st aor act opt 3rd pers sg id.
μεταναστεύσω vb 1st aor act subj 1st pers sg id.
μεταναστήσεις vb fut act ind 2nd pers sg .... μετανίστημι
μεταναστήτωσαν vb 2nd aor act impv 3rd pers pl id.
μετανόει vb pres act impv 2nd pers sg .... μετανοέω
μετανοεῖν vb pres act inf id.
μετανοῆσαι vb 1st aor act inf id.
μετανοήσατε vb 1st aor act impv 2nd pers pl id.
μετανοήσει vb fut act ind 3rd pers sg id.
μετανόησον vb 1st aor act impv 2nd pers sg id.
μετανοήσω vb fut act ind 1st pers sg id.
μετάνοιαν noun fem acc sg .... μετάνοια
μετανοίας noun fem gen sg id.
μετανοοῦντες vb pres act part masc nom pl ..... μετανοέω
μετανοούντων vb pres act part masc and neut gen pl id.
μετανοοῦσιν vb pres act ind 3rd pers pl id.
μετανοῶν vb pres act part masc nom sg id.
μετάξαι vb 1st aor act inf .... μετάγω
μεταξύ adverb
μεταπαιδεύεται vb pres m/p ind 3rd pers sg . μεταπαιδεύω
μεταπεῖσαι vb 1st aor act inf .... μεταπείθω
μεταπέμψομαι vb fut mid ind 1st pers sg .. μεταπέμπομαι
μεταπεσεῖσθαι vb fut mid inf .... μεταπίπτω
μεταπέσῃ vb 2nd aor act subj 3rd pers sg id.
μετασκευάζων vb pres act part masc nom sg . μετασκευάζω
μεταστάντος vb 2nd aor act part
　　masc and neut gen sg .... μεθίστημι
μεταστῇ vb 2nd aor act subj 3rd pers sg id.
μεταστῆσαι vb 1st aor act inf id.
μεταστήσας vb 1st aor act part masc nom sg id.
μεταστήσεις vb fut act ind 2nd pers sg id.
μεταστήσεσθαι vb fut mid inf id.
μεταστήσεται vb fut mid ind 3rd pers sg id.
μετάστησον vb 1st aor act impv 2nd pers sg id.
μεταστήσουσιν vb fut act ind 3rd pers pl id.

μεταστήσω vb fut act ind 1st pers sg .... μεθίστημι
μετάστητε vb 2nd aor act impv 2nd pers pl id.
μεταστραφήσεται vb fut pass ind 3rd pers sg . μεταστρέφω
μεταστραφήσονται vb fut pass ind 3rd pers pl id.
μεταστρέφει vb pres act ind 3rd pers sg id.
μεταστρεφόμενος vb pres m/p part masc nom sg id.
μεταστρέφοντας vb pres act part masc acc pl id.
μεταστρέφω vb pres act ind 1st pers sg id.
μεταστρέφων vb pres act part masc nom sg id.
μεταστρέψαι vb 1st aor act inf id.
μεταστρέψω vb fut act ind 1st pers sg id.
μεταστροφή noun fem nom sg
μετασχεῖν vb 2nd aor act inf .... μετέχω
μετάσχετε vb 2nd aor act impv 2nd pers pl id.
μετασχέτω vb 2nd aor act impv 3rd pers sg id.
μετασχηματιζόμενος vb pres m/p part
　　masc nom sg .... μετασχηματίζω
μετάσχωσι vb 2nd aor act subj 3rd pers pl .... μετέχω
μετατεθήσεται vb fut pass ind 3rd pers sg .... μετατίθημι
μετατιθείς vb pres act part masc nom sg id.
μετατιθέμενος vb pres m/p part masc nom sg id.
μετατιθέντες vb pres act part masc nom pl id.
μετατίθεσθαι vb pres m/p inf id.
μετατρέψαι vb 1st aor act inf .... μετατρέπω
μεταφέρειν vb pres act inf .... μεταφέρω
μετάφρασιν noun fem acc sg .... μετάφρασις
μετάφρενα noun neut nom and acc pl .... μετάφρενον
μεταφρένοις noun neut dat pl id.
μεταφρένων noun neut gen pl id.
μεταχέων vb pres act part masc nom sg .... μεταχέω
μεταχθέντες vb 1st aor pass part masc nom pl ..... μετάγω
μεταχθῇ vb 1st aor pass subj 3rd pers sg id.
μετέβαινεν vb impf act ind 3rd pers sg ...... μεταβαίνω
μετέβαλεν vb 2nd aor act ind 3rd pers sg ..... μεταβάλλω
μετεβάλλετο vb impf m/p ind 3rd pers sg id.
μετεδίδου vb impf act ind 3rd pers sg ...... μεταδίδωμι
μετέδωκα vb 1st aor act ind 1st pers sg id.
μετέδωκεν vb 1st aor act ind 3rd pers sg id.
μετέθηκεν vb 1st aor act ind 3rd pers sg ..... μετατίθημι
μετεῖχον vb impf act ind 3rd pers pl .... μετέχω
μετεκάλεσα vb 1st aor act ind 1st pers sg .... μετακαλέω
μετεκίνησεν vb 1st aor act ind 3rd pers sg .... μετακινέω
μετεκιρνᾶτο vb impf dep ind 3rd pers sg .. μετακιρνάομαι
μετέλαβεν vb 2nd aor act ind 3rd pers sg .... μεταλαμβάνω
μετελάβετε vb 2nd aor act ind 2nd pers pl id.
μετέλαβον vb 2nd aor act ind 3rd pers pl id.
μετελεύσεται vb fut mid ind 3rd pers sg ..... μετέρχομαι
μετελθεῖν vb 2nd aor act inf id.
μετελθέτω vb 2nd aor pass impv 3rd pers sg id.
μετέλθω vb 2nd aor act subj 1st pers sg id.
μετεμελήθη vb 1st aor pass ind 3rd pers sg .... μεταμελέω
μετεμέλοντο vb impf m/p ind 3rd pers pl id.

μετενέγκωμεν vb 1st aor act subj 1st pers pl .... μεταφέρω
μετενόησα vb 1st aor act ind 1st pers sg ...... μετανοέω
μετενόησεν vb 1st aor act ind 3rd pers sg   id.
μετέπειτα adverb
μετεπέμψατο vb 1st aor mid ind

       3rd pers sg .... μεταπέμπομαι
μετέπεσεν vb 2nd aor act ind 3rd pers sg ..... μεταπίπτω
μετεστάθη vb 1st aor pass ind 3rd pers sg ..... μεθίστημι
μετεστάθησαν vb 1st aor pass ind 3rd pers pl   id.
μετέστησαν vb 1st aor act ind 3rd pers pl   id.
μετέστησε(ν) vb 1st aor act ind 3rd pers sg   id.
μετεστράφη vb 2nd aor pass ind 3rd pers sg .. μεταστρέφω
μετεστράφησαν vb 2nd aor pass ind 3rd pers pl   id.
μετέστρεψεν vb 1st aor act ind 3rd pers sg   id.
μετέσχεν vb 2nd aor act ind 3rd pers sg .... μετέχω
μετεσχηκότας vb perf act part masc acc pl   id.
μετετέθη vb 1st aor pass ind 3rd pers sg ...... μετατίθημι
μετετράπη vb 2nd aor pass ind 3rd pers sg .... μετατρέπω
μετετρέπετο vb impf m/p ind 3rd pers sg   id.
μετέτρεψεν vb 1st aor act ind 3rd pers sg   id.
μετέχειν vb pres act inf .... μετέχω
μετέχοντες vb pres act part masc nom pl   id.
μετέωρα adj neut nom and acc pl .... μετέωρος
μετεωρίζεσθαι vb pres m/p inf .... μετεωρίζω
μετεωρίζου vb pres m/p impv 2nd pers sg   id.
μετεωρισθέντα vb 1st aor pass part neut nom and acc pl   id.
μετεωρισθῇς vb 1st aor pass subj 2nd pers sg   id.
μετεωρισθήσεται vb fut pass ind 3rd pers sg   id.
μετεωρισμοί noun masc nom pl .... μετεωρισμός
μετεωρισμοῖς noun masc dat pl   id.
μετεωρισμόν noun masc acc sg   id.
μετεωρισμούς noun masc acc pl   id.
μετέωροι adj masc and fem nom pl .... μετέωρος
μετέωρον adj acc sg, neut nom sg   id.
μετέωρος adj masc and fem nom sg   id.
μετεώρου adj gen sg   id.
μετεώρῳ adj dat sg   id.
μετεώρων adj gen pl   id.
μετήγαγεν vb 2nd aor act ind 3rd pers sg .... μετάγω
μετήγαγες vb 2nd aor act ind 2nd pers sg   id.
μετῆλθεν vb 2nd aor act ind 3rd pers sg ...... μετέρχομαι
μετήλλαξεν vb 1st aor act ind 3rd pers sg ... μεταλλάσσω
μετηλλαχότος vb perf act part masc and neut gen sg   id.
μετῆρας vb 1st aor act ind 2nd pers sg .... μεταίρω
μετῆρεν vb 1st aor act ind 3rd pers sg   id.
μετήχθησαν vb 1st aor pass ind 3rd pers pl ...... μετάγω
μετοικεσία noun fem nom sg
μετοικεσίᾳ noun fem dat sg .... μετοικεσία
μετοικεσίαν noun fem acc sg   id.
μετοικεσίας noun fem gen sg   id.
μετοικίᾳ noun fem dat sg .... μετοικία
μετοικίαν noun fem acc sg   id.

μετοικίας noun fem gen sg .... μετοικία
μετοικιοῦσιν vb fut act ind 3rd pers pl .... μετοικίζω
μετοικίσαι vb 1st aor act inf   id.
μετοικιῶ vb fut act ind 1st pers sg   id.
μέτοικον noun masc acc sg .... μέτοικος
μετουσίαν noun fem acc sg .... μετουσία
μετοχή noun fem nom sg
μετοχῇ noun fem dat sg .... μετοχή
μέτοχοι adj masc nom pl .... μέτοχος
μέτοχον noun masc acc sg   id.
μέτοχος noun masc nom sg   id.
μέτοχος adj masc nom sg   id.
μετόχους adj masc acc pl   id.
μέτρα noun neut nom and acc pl .... μέτρον
μετρήσαντες vb 1st aor act part masc nom pl ..... μετρέω
μετρήσει noun fem dat sg ....μέτρησις
μετρήσεις vb fut act ind 2nd pers sg .... μετρέω
μετρηταί noun masc nom pl .... μετρητής
μετρητάς noun masc acc pl   id.
μετρητῶν noun masc gen pl   id.
μετριάζων vb pres act part masc nom sg .... μετριάζω
μέτριον adj masc acc sg, neut nom and acc sg ..... μέτριος
μετρίῳ adj masc and neut dat sg   id.
μετρίως adverb
μέτροις noun neut dat pl .... μέτρον
μέτρον noun neut nom and acc sg   id.
μέτρου noun neut gen sg   id.
μέτρῳ noun neut dat sg   id.
μέτρων noun neut gen pl   id.
μετῴκηκας vb perf act ind 2nd pers sg .... μετοικέω
μετῴκισα vb 1st aor act ind 1st pers sg .... μετοικίζω
μετῴκισαν vb 1st aor act ind 3rd pers pl   id.
μετῴκισεν vb 1st aor act ind 3rd pers sg   id.
μετῳκίσθη vb 1st aor pass ind 3rd pers sg   id.
μέτωπα noun neut nom and acc pl .... μέτωπον
μέτωπον noun neut nom and acc sg   id.
μετώπου noun neut gen sg   id.
μετώπῳ noun neut dat sg   id.
Μεφααθ pr noun
μέχρι adverb and preposition
μέχρις see μέχρι
μεχωνωθ translit
μή adverb and conjunction
Μηδαβα pr noun
μηδαμόθεν adverb
μηδαμῶς adverb
μηδέ conjunction
μηδείς adj masc nom sg
μηδεμία adj fem nom sg .... μηδείς
μηδεμιᾶς adj fem gen sg   id.
μηδέν adj neut nom and acc sg   id.
μηδένα adj masc acc sg   id.

μηδενί adj masc and neut dat sg . . . . μηδείς
μηδενός adj masc and neut gen sg   id.
μηδέποτε adverb
Μηδια pr noun fem dat sg . . . . Μηδια
Μηδιαν pr noun fem acc sg   id.
Μηδιας pr noun fem gen sg   id.
Μηδικῆς pr noun fem gen sg . . . . Μηδικη
Μῆδοι pr noun masc nom pl . . . . Μῆδος
Μῆδοις pr noun masc dat pl   id.
Μῆδος pr noun masc nom sg   id.
Μηδους pr noun masc acc pl   id.
Μηδων pr noun masc gen pl   id.
μηθείς adj masc nom sg
μηθέν adj neut nom and acc sg . . . . μηθείς
μηθενός adj masc and neut gen sg   id.
μηθετέρῳ adj masc and neut dat sg . . . . μηθέτερος
μήκει noun neut dat sg . . . . μῆκος
μηκέτι adverb
μῆκος noun neut nom and acc sg
μήκους noun neut gen sg . . . . μῆκος
μηκύνω vb pres act ind 1st pers sg
μηκύνωσιν vb pres act subj 3rd pers pl . . . . μηκύνω
μῆλα noun neut nom and acc pl . . . . μῆλον
μήλοις noun neut dat pl   id.
μῆλον noun neut nom and acc sg   id.
μηλωτῇ noun fem dat sg . . . . μηλωτή
μηλωτήν noun fem acc sg   id.
μημ translit (Heb. letter: מ)
μήν noun masc nom sg
μήν particle
μῆνα noun masc acc sg . . . . μήν
μῆνας noun masc acc pl   id.
μῆνες noun masc nom pl   id.
μηνί noun masc dat sg   id.
μηνιαίου adj masc and neut gen sg . . . . μηνιαῖος
μηνιαίου adj masc and neut gen sg   id.
μηνίαμα noun neut nom and acc sg
μηνιάσῃς vb 1st aor act subj 2nd pers sg . . . . μηνιάω
μηνιεῖ vb fut act ind 3rd pers sg . . . . μηνίω
μηνιεῖς vb fut act ind 2nd pers sg   id.
μῆνιν noun fem acc sg . . . . μῆνις
μῆνις noun fem nom sg   id.
μηνίσας vb 1st aor act part masc nom sg . . . . μηνίω
μηνίσεως noun fem gen sg . . . . μῆνις
μηνίσῃς vb 1st aor act subj 2nd pers sg . . . . μηνίω
μηνίσκους noun masc acc pl . . . . μηνίσκος
μηνίσκων noun masc gen pl   id.
μηνιῶ vb fut act ind 1st pers sg . . . . μηνίω
μηνός noun masc gen sg . . . . μήν
μηνύειν vb pres act inf . . . . μηνύω
μηνυθέντες vb 1st aor pass part masc nom pl   id.
μηνυθέντων vb 1st aor pass part masc nom sg   id.

μηνύων vb pres act part masc nom sg . . . . μηνύω
μηνῶν noun masc gen pl . . . . μήν
μήποτε adverb and particle
μήπως adverb
μηρίων noun neut gen pl . . . . μηρίον
μηροί noun masc nom pl . . . . μηρός
μηροῖς noun masc dat pl   id.
μηρὸν noun masc acc sg   id.
μηρός noun masc nom sg   id.
μηροῦ noun masc gen sg   id.
μηρούς noun masc acc pl   id.
μηρυκισμόν noun masc acc sg . . . . μηρυκισμός
μηρυομένη vb pres dep part fem nom sg . . . . μηρύομαι
μηρῷ noun masc dat sg . . . . μηρός
Μηρωζ pr noun
μηρῶν noun masc gen pl . . . . μηρός
μησί noun masc dat pl . . . . μήν
μήτε conjunction
μῆτερ noun fem voc sg . . . . μήτηρ
μητέρα noun fem acc sg   id.
μητέρας noun fem acc pl   id.
μητέρες noun fem nom pl   id.
μητέρων noun fem gen pl   id.
μήτηρ noun fem nom sg   id.
μήτι adverb
μήτρα noun fem nom sg
μήτρᾳ noun fem dat sg . . . . μήτρα
μήτραν noun fem acc sg   id.
μήτρας noun fem gen sg   id.
μητράσιν noun fem dat pl . . . . μήτηρ
μητρί noun fem dat sg   id.
μητροπόλεσιν noun fem dat pl . . . . μητρόπολις
μητροπόλεων noun fem gen pl   id.
μητρόπολιν noun fem acc sg   id.
μητρόπολις noun fem nom sg   id.
μητρός noun fem gen sg . . . . μήτηρ
μητρῴας adj fem gen sg . . . . μητρῷος
μηχαναῖς noun fem dat pl . . . . μηχανή
μηχανάς noun fem acc pl   id.
μηχανᾶσθαι vb pres dep inf . . . . μηχανάομαι
μηχανήμασι noun neut dat pl . . . . μηχάνημα
μηχανήματα noun neut nom and acc pl   id.
μηχανήν noun fem acc sg . . . . μηχανή
μηχανώμενοι vb pres dep part masc nom pl . . . μηχανάομαι
μηχανῶν noun fem gen pl . . . . μηχανή
μία adj fem nom sg . . . . εἷς
μιᾷ adj fem dat sg   id.
μιαίνειν vb pres act inf . . . . μιαίνω
μιαίνεσθε vb pres m/p impv 2nd pers pl,
          pres m/p ind 2nd pers pl   id.
μιαινομένη vb pres m/p part fem nom sg   id.
μιαίνωνται vb pres m/p subj 3rd pers pl   id.

μιαιφονίαν noun fem acc sg . . . . μιαιφονία

μιαιφόνον adj acc sg, neut nom sg . . . . μιαιφόνος

μιαιφόνους adj masc and fem acc pl   id.

Μιαμιν pr noun

Μιαμινος pr noun

μίαν adj fem acc sg . . . . εἷς

μιᾶναι vb 1st aor act inf . . . . μιαίνω

μιάνατε vb 1st aor act impv 2nd pers pl   id.

μιανεῖ vb fut act ind 3rd pers sg   id.

μιανεῖς vb fut act ind 2nd pers sg   id.

μιανεῖτε vb fut act ind 2nd pers pl   id.

μιάνῃ vb 1st aor act subj 3rd pers sg   id.

μιανθῇ vb 1st aor pass subj 3rd pers sg   id.

μιανθῆναι vb 1st aor pass inf   id.

μιανθήσεσθε vb fut pass ind 2nd pers pl   id.

μιανθήσεται vb fut pass ind 3rd pers sg   id.

μιανθήσονται vb fut pass ind 3rd pers pl   id.

μιανθῶσιν vb 1st aor pass subj 3rd pers pl   id.

μιανοῦσι(ν) vb fut act ind 3rd pers pl   id.

μιάνσει noun fem dat sg . . . . μίανσις

μιανῶ vb fut act ind 1st pers sg . . . . μιαίνω

μιαρά adj fem nom sg . . . . μιαρός

μιαραῖς adj fem dat pl   id.

μιαροί adj masc nom pl   id.

μιαρός adj masc nom sg   id.

μιαροῦ adj masc and neut gen sg   id.

μιαροφαγῆσαι vb 1st aor act inf . . . . μιαροφαγέω

μιαροφαγήσαιεν vb 1st aor act opt 3rd pers pl   id.

μιαροφαγήσαιμεν vb 1st aor act opt 1st pers pl   id.

μιαροφαγίᾳ noun fem dat sg . . . . μιαροφαγία

μιαροφαγίαν noun fem acc sg   id.

μιαροφαγίας noun fem gen sg   id.

μιαροφαγοῦμεν vb pres act ind 1st pers pl . . . μιαροφαγέω

μιαροφαγοῦντα vb pres act part masc acc sg   id.

μιαρῶν adj gen pl . . . . μιαρός

μιαρώτατε superl adj masc voc sg   id.

μιᾶς adj fem gen sg . . . . εἷς

μίασμα noun neut nom and acc sg

μιάσματα noun neut nom and acc pl . . . . μίασμα

μιασμάτων noun neut gen pl   id.

μιασμός noun masc nom sg

μιασμοῦ noun masc gen sg . . . . μιασμός

Μιθραδατη pr noun masc dat sg . . . . Μιθραδατης

Μιθραδατης pr noun masc nom sg   id.

Μιθραδατου pr noun masc gen sg   id.

Μιθριδατη see Μιθραδατη

Μιι pr noun

μικρά adj fem nom sg, neut nom and acc pl . . . . μικρός

μικρᾷ adj fem dat sg   id.

μικραί adj fem nom pl   id.

μικράν adj fem acc sg   id.

μικράς adj fem acc pl   id.

μικρᾶς adj fem gen sg . . . . μικρός

μικροῖς adj masc and neut dat pl   id.

μικρολόγῳ adj masc and neut dat sg . . . . μικρολόγος

μικρόν adj masc acc sg, neut nom and acc sg . . . . . . μικρός

μικρός adj masc nom sg   id.

μικρότατος superl adj masc nom sg   id.

μικρότερος comp adj masc nom sg   id.

μικρότης noun fem nom sg

μικρότητι noun fem dat sg . . . . μικρότης

μικροῦ adj masc and neut gen sg . . . . μικρός

μικρούς adj masc acc pl   id.

μικρῷ adj masc and neut dat sg   id.

μικρῶς adverb

Μιλητου pr noun fem gen sg . . . . Μιλητος

μίλτῳ noun fem dat sg . . . . μίλτος

μιμεῖται vb pres dep ind 3rd pers sg . . . . μιμέομαι

μίμημα noun neut nom and acc sg

μιμήσασθε vb 1st aor mid impv 2nd pers pl . . . . . μιμέομαι

μιμησώμεθα vb 1st aor mid subj 1st pers pl   id.

μιμνήσκεσθε vb pres m/p impv 2nd pers pl . . . . . μιμνήσκω

μιμνήσκῃ vb pres m/p ind 2nd pers sg   id.

μιμνήσκομαι vb pres m/p ind 1st pers sg   id.

μιμνησκόμεθα vb pres m/p ind 1st pers pl   id.

μιμνησκόμενοι vb pres m/p part masc nom pl   id.

μιμνήσκου vb pres m/p impv 2nd pers sg   id.

μιμοῦνται vb pres dep ind 3rd pers pl . . . . μιμέομαι

Μιναῖος pr noun masc nom sg

Μιναιους pr noun masc acc pl . . . . Μιναῖος

Μιναιων pr noun masc gen pl   id.

Μιρων pr noun

Μισα pr noun

Μισαβια pr noun

Μισαδαι pr noun

Μισαηλ pr noun

μισάνθρωπε adj masc and fem voc sg . . . . . . μισάνθρωπος

μισάρετε adj masc voc sg . . . . μισάρετος

Μισαχ pr noun

μίσγουσι(ν) vb pres act ind 3rd pers pl . . . . μίσγω

μίσει noun neut dat sg . . . . μῖσος

μισεῖ vb pres act ind 3rd pers sg . . . . μισέω

μισεῖν vb pres act inf   id.

μισεῖς vb pres act ind 2nd pers sg   id.

μισεῖται vb pres m/p ind 3rd pers sg   id.

μισεῖτε vb pres act ind 2nd pers pl   id.

μισηθείς vb 1st aor pass part masc nom sg   id.

μισηθῇ vb 1st aor pass subj 3rd pers sg   id.

μισηθῆναι vb 1st aor pass inf   id.

μισηθῇς vb 1st aor pass subj 2nd pers sg   id.

μισηθήσεται vb fut pass ind 3rd pers sg   id.

μισῆσαι vb 1st aor act inf   id.

μισήσας vb 1st aor act part masc nom sg   id.

μισήσει vb fut act ind 3rd pers sg   id.

μισήσεις vb fut act ind 2nd pers sg . . . . μισέω

μισήση vb 1st aor act subj 3rd pers sg   id.

μισήσης vb 1st aor act subj 2nd pers sg   id.

μίσησον vb 1st aor act impv 2nd pers sg   id.

μισήσουσιν vb fut act ind 3rd pers pl   id.

μισητά adj neut nom and acc pl . . . . μισητός

μισητή adj fem nom sg   id.

μισητόν adj masc acc sg, neut nom and acc sg   id.

μισητός adj masc nom sg   id.

μίσθιον noun masc acc sg . . . . μίσθιος

μισθίου noun masc gen sg   id.

μισθόν noun masc acc sg . . . . μισθός

Μισθος pr noun masc nom sg   id.

μισθός noun masc nom sg   id.

μισθοῦ noun masc gen sg   id.

μισθούμενοι vb pres dep part masc nom pl . . . . μισθόομαι

μισθούς noun masc acc pl . . . . μισθός

μισθῷ noun masc dat sg   id.

μίσθωμα noun neut nom and acc sg

μισθώματα noun neut nom and acc pl . . . . μίσθωμα

μισθώματος noun neut gen sg   id.

μισθωμάτων noun neut gen pl   id.

μισθωσάμενοι vb 1st aor mid part masc nom pl . μισθόομαι

μισθώσασθαι vb 1st aor mid inf   id.

μισθωταί noun masc nom pl . . . . μισθωτής

μισθωτέ adj masc voc sg . . . . μισθωτός

μισθωτοί adj masc nom pl   id.

μισθωτός adj masc nom sg   id.

μισθωτοῦ adj masc and neut gen sg   id.

μισθωτῷ adj masc and neut dat sg   id.

μισοξενίαν noun fem acc sg . . . . μισοξενία

μισοπονηρῆσαι vb 1st aor act inf . . . . μισοπονηρέω

μισοπονηρήσαντες vb 1st aor act part masc nom pl   id.

μισοπονηρίαν noun fem acc sg . . . . μισοπονηρία

μισοπόνηρον adj acc sg, neut nom sg . . . . . . μισοπόνηρος

μῖσος noun neut nom and acc sg

μισοῦμαι vb pres m/p ind 1st pers sg . . . . μισέω

μισουμένη vb pres m/p part fem nom sg   id.

μισουμένη vb pres m/p part fem dat sg   id.

μισουμένης vb pres m/p part fem gen sg   id.

μισουμένῳ vb pres m/p part masc and neut dat sg   id.

μισοῦντα vb pres act part masc acc sg   id.

μισοῦντας vb pres act part masc acc pl   id.

μισοῦντες vb pres act part masc nom pl   id.

μισούντων vb pres act part masc and neut gen pl   id.

μίσους noun neut gen sg . . . . μῖσος

μισοῦσα vb pres act part fem nom sg . . . . μισέω

μισοῦσαν vb pres act part fem acc sg   id.

μισοῦσι(ν) vb pres act ind 3rd pers pl,
            pres act part masc and neut dat pl   id.

μίσυβρι noun masc dat sg . . . . μίσυβρις

μισῶν vb pres act part masc nom sg . . . . μισέω

Μισωρ pr noun

μισῶσιν vb pres act subj 3rd pers pl . . . . μισέω

μίτρα noun fem dat sg . . . . μίτρα

μίτραν noun fem acc sg   id.

μίτρας noun fem gen sg and acc pl   id.

Μιφιθιμ pr noun

Μιχα pr noun

Μιχαηλ pr noun

Μιχαηλου pr noun masc gen sg . . . . Μιχαηλος

Μιχαια pr noun

Μιχαιαν pr noun masc acc sg . . . . Μιχαιας

Μιχαιας pr noun masc nom sg   id.

Μιχαιου pr noun masc gen sg   id.

Μιχας pr noun

μίχθητε vb 1st aor pass impv 2nd pers pl . . . . μίγνυμι

Μιχια pr noun

Μιχολ pr noun

μνᾶ noun fem nom sg

μναῖ noun fem nom pl . . . . μνᾶ

μνᾶς noun fem acc pl   id.

μνεία noun fem nom sg

μνείᾳ noun fem dat sg . . . . μνεία

μνείαν noun fem acc sg   id.

μνῆμα noun neut nom and acc sg

μνήμασι noun neut dat pl . . . . μνῆμα

Μνημασι pr noun neut dat pl   id.

μνήματα noun neut nom and acc pl   id.

μνήματι noun neut dat sg   id.

μνήματος noun neut gen sg   id.

μνημάτων noun neut gen pl   id.

μνημείοις noun neut dat pl . . . . μνημεῖον

μνημεῖον noun neut nom and acc sg   id.

μνημείου noun neut gen sg   id.

μνημείῳ noun neut dat sg   id.

μνημείων noun neut gen pl   id.

μνήμη noun fem nom sg

μνήμῃ noun fem dat sg . . . . μνήμη

μνήμην noun fem acc sg   id.

μνήμης noun fem gen sg   id.

μνημόνευε vb pres act impv 2nd pers sg . . . . . . μνημονεύω

μνημονεύει vb pres act ind 3rd pers sg   id.

μνημονεύειν vb pres act inf   id.

μνημονεύετε vb pres act impv 2nd pers pl   id.

μνημονεύοντες vb pres act part masc nom pl   id.

μνημονευόντων vb pres act part masc and neut gen pl   id.

μνημονεύουσιν vb pres act ind 3rd pers pl   id.

μνημονευσάτω vb 1st aor act impv 3rd pers sg   id.

μνημονεύσει vb fut act ind 3rd pers sg   id.

μνημονεύσω vb fut act ind 1st pers sg   id.

μνημονεύω vb pres act ind 1st pers sg   id.

μνημονεύων vb pres act part masc nom sg   id.

μνημόσυνα noun neut nom and acc pl . . . . μνημόσυνον

μνημόσυνον noun neut nom and acc sg

μνημοσύνου noun neut gen sg . . . . μνημόσυνον

μνημῶν noun fem gen pl . . . . μνήμη

μνησθείη vb 1st aor pass opt 3rd pers sg . . . . μιμνήσκω

μνησθείς vb 1st aor pass part masc nom sg   id.

μνησθεῖσα vb 1st aor pass part fem nom sg   id.

μνησθῇ vb 1st aor pass subj 3rd pers sg   id.

μνησθῆναι vb 1st aor pass inf   id.

μνησθῇς vb 1st aor pass subj 2nd pers sg   id.

μνησθήσεσθε vb fut pass ind 2nd pers pl   id.

μνησθήσεται vb fut pass ind 3rd pers sg   id.

μνησθήση vb fut pass ind 2nd pers sg   id.

μνησθήσομαι vb fut pass ind 1st pers sg   id.

μνησθήσονται vb fut pass ind 3rd pers pl   id.

μνήσθητε vb 1st aor pass impv 2nd pers pl   id.

μνησθῆτε vb 1st aor pass subj 2nd pers pl   id.

μνήσθητι vb 1st aor pass impv 2nd pers sg   id.

μνησθῶ vb 1st aor pass subj 1st pers sg   id.

μνησθῶσιν vb 1st aor pass subj 3rd pers pl   id.

μνησικακεῖ vb pres act ind 3rd pers sg . . . . . . μνησικακέω

μνησικακεῖτε vb pres act ind 2nd pers pl   id.

μνησικακείτω vb pres act impv 3rd pers sg   id.

μνησικακήση vb 1st aor act subj 3rd pers sg   id.

μνησικάκων adj gen pl . . . . μνησίκακος

μνηστευομένοις vb pres dep part

　　　　masc and neut dat pl . . . . μνηστεύομαι

μνηστεύσομαι vb fut mid ind 1st pers sg   id.

μνηστευσόμεθα vb fut mid ind 1st pers pl   id.

μνῶν noun fem gen pl . . . . μνᾶ

μογιλάλων adj gen pl . . . . μογίλαλος

μόγις adverb

Μοζε pr noun

μοι pers pron dat sg . . . . ἐγώ

μοιχαλίδα noun fem acc sg . . . . μοιχαλίς

μοιχαλίδας noun fem acc pl   id.

μοιχαλίδες noun fem nom pl   id.

μοιχαλίδος noun fem gen sg   id.

μοιχαλίν noun fem acc sg   id.

μοιχᾶσθε vb pres dep ind 2nd pers pl . . . . μοιχάομαι

μοιχεία noun fem nom sg

μοιχείαν noun fem acc sg . . . . μοιχεία

μοιχευομένη vb pres m/p part fem nom sg . . . . . . μοιχεύω

μοιχεύοντες vb pres act part masc nom pl   id.

μοιχεύουσιν vb pres act ind 3rd pers pl   id.

μοιχεύσεις vb fut act ind 2nd pers sg   id.

μοιχεύσηται vb 1st aor mid subj 3rd pers sg   id.

μοιχεύσουσιν vb fut act ind 3rd pers pl   id.

μοιχεύων vb pres act part masc nom sg   id.

μοιχεύωσιν vb pres act subj 3rd pers pl   id.

μοιχόν noun masc acc sg . . . . μοιχός

μοιχός noun masc nom sg   id.

μοιχοῦ noun masc gen sg   id.

μοιχωμένη vb pres dep part fem nom sg . . . . . . μοιχάομαι

μοιχωμένους vb pres dep part masc acc pl   id.

μοιχῶν noun masc gen pl . . . . μοιχός

μοιχῶνται vb pres dep ind 3rd pers pl . . . . μοιχάομαι

μόλιβον noun masc acc sg . . . . μόλιβος

μόλιβος noun masc nom sg   id.

μολίβου noun masc gen sg   id.

μολίβῳ noun masc dat sg   id.

μόλις adverb

Μολλαθ pr noun

Μολοχ pr noun

μολόχη noun fem nom sg

μόλυβον noun masc acc sg . . . . μόλιβος

μολῦναι vb 1st aor act inf . . . . μολύνω

μολύνει vb pres act ind 3rd pers sg   id.

μολυνθῇς vb 1st aor pass subj 2nd pers sg   id.

μολυνθήσεται vb fut pass ind 3rd pers sg   id.

μολυνθήσονται vb fut pass ind 3rd pers pl   id.

μολύνσεως noun fem gen sg . . . . μόλυνσις

μολυνῶ vb fut act ind 1st pers sg . . . . μολύνω

μολυσμός noun masc nom sg

μολυσμοῦ noun masc gen sg . . . . μολυσμός

μολυσμῷ noun masc dat sg   id.

Μολχολ pr noun

Μομδιος pr noun

μονάζον vb pres act part neut nom and acc sg . . . . . μονάζω

μόναρχε noun masc voc sg . . . . μόναρχος

μόνας adj fem acc pl . . . . μόνος

μόνη adj fem nom sg   id.

μόνῃ adj fem dat sg   id.

μόνην adj fem acc sg   id.

μονήν noun fem acc sg . . . . μονή

μόνης adj fem gen sg . . . . μόνος

Μονι pr noun

μόνιμον adj masc acc sg, neut nom and acc sg . . . . μόνιμος

μονίμων adj gen pl   id.

μονιός adj masc nom sg

μονογενεῖς adj masc and fem nom and acc pl . . . μονογενής

μονογενές adj neut nom and acc sg   id.

μονογενή see μονογενῆ

μονογενῆ adj masc and fem acc sg   id.

μονογενής adj masc and fem nom sg   id.

μονόζωνοι noun masc nom pl . . . . μονόζωνος

μονοζώνοις noun masc dat pl   id.

μονόζωνον noun masc acc sg   id.

μονόζωνος noun masc nom sg   id.

μονοζώνους noun masc acc pl   id.

μονοημέρου adj gen sg . . . . μονοήμερος

μόνοι adj masc nom pl . . . . μόνος

μόνοις adj masc and neut dat pl   id.

μονόκερως noun masc nom sg

μονοκέρωτος noun masc gen sg . . . . μονόκερως μονοκερώτων noun masc gen pl . . . . μονόκερως

μονομαχήσομεν vb fut act ind 1st pers pl . . . . μονομαχέω

μόνον adj masc acc sg, neut nom and acc sg . . . . μόνος

μόνον adverb

μόνορχις noun masc nom sg

μόνος adj masc nom sg

μονοτρόπους adj masc acc pl . . . . μονότροπος

μόνου adj masc and neut gen sg . . . . μόνος

μονοφαγία noun fem nom sg

μονοφάγος noun masc nom sg

μόνῳ adj masc and neut dat sg . . . . μόνος

μόνων adj gen pl   id.

μονώσει noun fem dat sg . . . . μόνωσις

μονωτάτη superl adj fem nom sg . . . . μόνος

μονώτατοι superl adj masc nom pl   id.

μονώτατον superl adj masc acc sg, neut nom and acc sg   id.

μονώτατος superl adj masc nom sg   id.

Μοοδι pr noun

Μοολαμ pr noun

Μοολι pr noun

Μοοραι pr noun

Μοορε pr noun

Μοοσσιας pr noun masc nom sg

Μοουλαθι pr noun

Μοοχα pr noun

μόρου noun masc gen sg . . . . μόρος

μορφή noun fem nom sg

μορφήν noun fem acc sg . . . . μορφή

μορφῆς noun fem gen sg   id.

μόρῳ noun masc dat sg . . . . μόρος

μόρων noun neut gen pl . . . . μόρον

Μοσερι pr noun

Μοσοαθ pr noun

Μοσολαμωθ pr noun

Μοσολλαμ pr noun

Μοσολλαμια pr noun

Μοσολλαμος pr noun

Μοσοχ pr noun

μοσφαθαιμ translit

μοσχάρια noun neut nom and acc pl . . . . μοσχάριον

μοσχάριον noun neut nom and acc sg   id.

μοσχευμάτων noun neut gen pl . . . . μόσχευμα

μόσχοι noun masc nom pl . . . . μόσχος

μόσχοις noun masc dat pl   id.

μόσχον noun masc acc sg   id.

μόσχος noun masc nom sg   id.

μόσχου noun masc gen sg   id.

μόσχους noun masc acc pl   id.

μόσχῳ noun masc dat sg   id.

μόσχων noun masc gen pl   id.

Μοσωβαβ pr noun

μοτώσει vb fut act ind 3rd pers sg . . . . μοτόω

μου pers pron gen sg . . . . ἐγώ

μοῦ see μου

Μουσι pr noun

μουσικά noun neut nom and acc pl

μουσικῶν adj gen pl . . . . μουσικός

Μουχαιος pr noun masc nom sg

Μοχατι pr noun

μοχθεῖ vb pres act ind 3rd pers sg . . . . μοχθέω

μοχθεῖς vb pres act ind 2nd pers sg   id.

μοχθεῖτε vb pres act ind 2nd pers pl   id.

μοχθῇ vb pres act subj 3rd pers sg   id.

μοχθηρά adj fem nom sg,

            neut nom and acc pl . . . . μοχθηρός

μοχθήσῃ vb 1st aor act subj 3rd pers sg . . . . μοχθέω

μόχθοι noun masc nom pl . . . . μόχθος

μόχθοις noun masc dat pl   id.

μόχθον noun masc acc sg   id.

μόχθος noun masc nom sg   id.

μόχθου noun masc gen sg   id.

μόχθους noun masc acc pl   id.

μοχθῶ vb pres act ind 1st pers sg . . . . μοχθέω

μόχθῳ noun masc dat sg . . . . μόχθος

μόχθων noun masc gen pl   id.

μοχλοί noun masc nom pl . . . . μοχλός

μοχλοῖς noun masc dat pl   id.

μοχλόν noun masc acc sg   id.

μοχλός noun masc nom sg   id.

μοχλούς noun masc acc pl   id.

μοχλῷ noun masc dat sg   id.

μοχλῶν noun masc gen pl   id.

Μοχμουρ pr noun

Μοχοραθι pr noun

Μοωχα pr noun

μύας noun masc acc pl . . . . μῦς

μυγαλῆ noun fem nom sg

μυελόν noun masc acc sg . . . . μυελός

μυελός noun masc nom sg   id.

μυελοῦ noun masc gen sg   id.

μύες noun masc nom pl . . . . μῦς

μυθολόγοι noun masc nom pl . . . . μυθολόγος

μῦθος noun masc nom sg

μυῖαι noun fem nom pl . . . . μυῖα

μυίαις noun fem dat pl   id.

μυῖαν noun fem acc sg   id.

μυιῶν noun fem gen pl   id.

μυκτήρ noun masc nom sg

μυκτῆρα noun masc acc sg . . . . μυκτήρ

μυκτῆρας noun masc acc pl   id.

μυκτῆρι noun masc dat sg   id.

μυκτηρίζει vb pres act ind 3rd pers sg . . . . μυκτηρίζω

μυκτηρίζεται vb pres m/p ind 3rd pers sg   id.

μυκτηριζόμενος vb pres m/p part masc nom sg   id.

μυκτηρίζοντες vb pres act part masc nom pl . . . μυκτηρίζω	μυρσίνης noun fem gen sg . . . . μυρσίνη
μυκτηρίσῃ vb 1st aor act subj 3rd pers sg	id.	Μυρσινῶνι pr noun masc dat sg . . . . Μυρσινων
μυκτηρισμόν noun masc acc sg . . . . μυκτηρισμός	Μυρσινῶνος pr noun masc gen sg	id.
μυκτηρισμός noun masc nom sg	id.	μύρῳ noun neut dat sg . . . . μύρον
μυκτηρισμῷ noun masc dat sg	id.	μύρων noun neut gen pl	id.
μυκτῆρσι noun masc dat pl . . . . μυκτήρ	μῦς noun masc nom sg
μυκτήρων noun masc gen pl	id.	Μυσαρχην pr noun masc acc sg . . . . Μυσαρχης
μύλαι noun fem nom pl . . . . μύλη	μυσερόν adj masc acc sg, neut nom and acc sg . . . . μυσερός
μύλαις noun fem dat pl	id.	μύσος noun neut nom and acc sg
μύλας noun fem acc pl	id.	μύσους noun neut gen sg . . . . μύσος
μύλον noun masc acc sg . . . . μύλος	μύστακα noun masc acc sg . . . . μύσταξ
μύλου noun masc gen sg	id.	μύστας noun masc acc pl . . . . μύστης
μύλῳ noun masc dat sg	id.	μυστήρια noun neut nom and acc pl . . . . μυστήριον
μύλωνος see μυλῶνος	μυστήριον noun neut nom and acc sg	id.
μυλῶνος noun masc gen sg . . . . μυλών	μυστηρίου noun neut gen sg	id.
Μυνδον pr noun masc acc sg . . . . Μύνδος	μυστικῶς adverb
μυξωτήρων noun masc gen pl . . . . μυξωτήρ	μύστις noun fem nom sg
μύρα noun neut nom and acc pl . . . . μύρον	μυχός noun masc nom sg
μυρεψικά adj neut nom and acc pl . . . . μυρεψικός	μυχῶν noun masc gen pl . . . . μυχός
μυρεψικόν adj masc acc sg, neut nom and acc sg	id.	μυῶν noun masc gen pl . . . . μῦς
μυρεψικοῦ adj masc and neut gen sg	id.	Μωαβ pr noun
μυρεψοί noun masc nom pl . . . . μυρεψός	Μωαβι pr noun
μυρεψός noun masc nom sg	id.	Μωαβῖται pr noun masc nom pl . . . . Μωαβίτης
μυρεψοῦ noun masc gen sg	id.	Μωαβιταις pr noun masc dat pl	id.
μυρεψούς noun masc acc pl	id.	Μωαβιτης pr noun masc nom sg	id.
μυρεψῶν noun masc gen pl	id.	Μωαβιτιδας pr noun fem acc pl . . . . Μωαβῖτις
μύρια adj neut nom and acc pl . . . . μύριοι	Μωαβιτιδι pr noun fem dat sg	id.
μυριάδας noun fem acc pl . . . . μυριάς	Μωαβιτιδος pr noun fem gen sg	id.
μυριάδες noun fem nom pl	id.	Μωαβῖτιν pr noun fem acc sg	id.
μυριάδων noun fem gen pl	id.	Μωαβῖτις pr noun fem nom sg	id.
μύριαι adj fem nom pl . . . . μύριοι	Μωαβιτῶν pr noun masc gen pl . . . . Μωαβίτης
μυρίας adj fem acc pl	id.	Μωδαδ pr noun
μυριάς noun fem nom sg	Μωδεϊν pr noun
μυριάσι(ν) noun fem dat pl . . . . μυριάς	Μωεθ pr noun
μυρίοις adj masc and neut dat pl . . . . μύριοι	μωκός noun masc nom sg
μυριοπλάσιον adj acc sg, neut acc sg . . . . . μυριοπλάσιος	Μωλα pr noun
μυριοπλασίως adverb	Μωλαδα pr noun
μυριότητι noun fem dat sg . . . . μυριότης	Μωλιδ pr noun
μυρίους adj masc acc pl . . . . μύριοι	μώλωπα noun masc acc sg . . . . μώλωψ
μυρισμῷ noun masc dat sg . . . . μυρισμός	μώλωπες noun masc nom pl	id.
μυρίων adj gen pl . . . . μύριοι	μώλωπι noun masc dat sg	id.
μύρμηκα noun masc acc sg . . . . μύρμηξ	μώλωπος noun masc gen sg	id.
μύρμηκες noun masc nom pl	id.	μώλωψ noun masc nom sg	id.
μυρμηκιῶντα vb pres act part	μωμησαμένους vb 1st aor mid part masc acc pl . . μωμάομαι
neut nom and acc pl . . . . μυρμηκιάω	μωμήσεται vb fut mid ind 3rd pers sg	id.
μυρμηκολέων noun masc nom sg	μωμητά adj neut nom and acc pl . . . . μωμητός
μυροβρεχῆ adj masc and fem acc sg . . . . . . μυροβραχής	μῶμον noun masc acc sg . . . . μῶμος
μύροις noun neut dat pl . . . . μύρον	μῶμος noun masc nom sg	id.
μύρον noun neut nom and acc sg	id.	μωρά adj neut nom and acc pl . . . . μωρός
μύρου noun neut gen sg	id.	Μωραδ pr noun
μυρσίνη noun fem nom sg	Μωραθιτης pr noun masc nom sg
μυρσίνην noun fem acc sg . . . . μυρσίνη	μωρανθῇς vb 1st aor pass subj 2nd pers sg . . . . . . μωραίνω

μωρανθήσεται vb fut pass ind 3rd pers sg . . . . μωραίνω

Μωρασθι pr noun

μωρεύων vb pres act part masc nom sg . . . . μωρεύω

Μωρηδ pr noun

μωρίαν noun fem acc sg . . . . μωρία

μωροί adj masc nom pl . . . . μωρός

μωρόν adj masc acc sg, neut nom and acc sg   id.

μωρός adj masc nom sg   id.

μωροῦ adj masc and neut gen sg   id.

μωρῷ adj masc and neut dat sg   id.

μωρῶν adj gen pl   id.

Μωσα pr noun

Μωσῆ pr noun

Μωυσεῖ pr noun masc dat sg . . . . Μωυσῆς

Μωυσεας pr noun masc gen sg   id.

Μωυσῆ pr noun masc voc and gen sg   id.

Μωυσῆ pr noun masc dat sg   id.

Μωυσῆν pr noun masc acc sg   id.

Μωυσῆς pr noun masc nom sg   id.

Μωφααθ pr noun

Μωφαζ pr noun

Μωφαθ pr noun

Μωχα pr noun

N ν

Νααθ pr noun

Νααθος pr noun

Νααλιηλ pr noun

Νααλωλ pr noun

Νααμα pr noun

Ναανα pr noun

Νααναν pr noun

Νααραι pr noun

Νααραν pr noun

Ναας pr noun

Ναασσων pr noun

Ναβααλ pr noun

Ναβαδ pr noun

Ναβαι pr noun

Ναβαιωθ pr noun

Ναβαλ pr noun

Ναβαριας pr noun

Ναβατ pr noun

Ναβαταιοις pr noun masc dat pl . . . . Ναβαταιοι

Ναβαταιους pr noun masc acc pl   id.

Ναβαυ pr noun

Ναβδεηλ pr noun

Ναβεθ pr noun

Ναβι pr noun

Ναβι-ααρ pr noun

νάβλα noun fem nom sg

νάβλαις noun fem dat pl . . . . νάβλα

νάβλας noun fem acc pl   id.

Ναβου pr noun

Ναβουζαρδαν pr noun

Ναβουθαι pr noun

Ναβουσαρις pr noun

Ναβουσαχαρ pr noun

Ναβουχοδονοσορ pr noun

Ναβωθ pr noun

Ναβωκ pr noun

Ναγαργασνεσερ pr noun

Ναγε pr noun

Ναγεβ pr noun

Ναγεδ pr noun

Ναδαβ pr noun

Ναδαβαθ pr noun

Ναδαβαιων pr noun masc gen pl . . . . Ναδαβαιος

Ναεθ pr noun

Ναεμανι pr noun

ναζιρ translit

ναζιραιοι noun masc nom pl . . . . ναζιραιος

ναζιραιον noun masc acc sg   id.

ναζιραιος noun masc nom sg   id.

ναζιραιους adj masc acc pl   id.

Ναημ pr noun

Ναθαν pr noun

Ναθαναηλ pr noun

Ναθαναηλος pr noun

Ναθανιας pr noun masc nom sg

Ναθανιου pr noun masc gen sg . . . . Ναθανιας

ναθιναιοι translit

ναθινιμ translit

ναθινιν translit

ναί adverb and particle

Ναϊ pr noun

Ναιδ pr noun

Ναϊδος pr noun

Ναιμαν pr noun

ναίων vb pres act part masc nom sg . . . . ναίω

Νακαν pr noun

Νακεβ pr noun

νακκαριμ translit

νάματος noun neut gen sg . . . . νᾶμα

Ναμβρα pr noun fem nom sg

Ναμβραν pr noun fem acc sg . . . . Ναμβρα

Ναμεσσι pr noun

Ναμεσσιου pr noun masc gen sg . . . . Ναμεσσιας

Ναμνα pr noun

Ναμουηλ pr noun

Ναμουηλι pr noun

Ναναιας pr noun fem gen sg . . . . Ναναια

Ναναιου pr noun masc gen sg . . . . Ναναιος

ναόν noun masc acc sg . . . . ναός

ναός noun masc nom sg   id.

ναοῦ noun masc gen sg   id.

Ναουμ pr noun

ναούς noun masc acc pl . . . . ναός

νάπαι noun fem nom pl . . . . νάπη

νάπαις noun fem dat pl   id.

νάπας noun fem acc pl   id.

νάπη noun fem dat sg   id.

νάπην noun fem acc sg   id.

νάπης noun fem gen sg   id.

Ναργαλασαρ pr noun

νάρδος noun fem nom sg

νάρδων noun fem gen pl . . . . νάρδος

ναρκήσει vb fut act ind 3rd pers sg . . . . ναρκάω

Νασαραχ pr noun

Νασβας pr noun

Νασι pr noun

νασιβ translit

Νασιβ pr noun

νασιφ translit

Νασουε pr noun

Ναταϊμ pr noun

Ναυαθ pr noun

Ναυη pr noun

ναῦλον noun neut nom and acc sg

ναῦν noun fem acc sg . . . . ναῦς

ναῦς noun fem nom sg, nom and acc pl   id.

ναυσίν noun fem dat pl   id.

ναυτικοί adj masc nom pl . . . . ναυτικός

ναυτικούς adj masc acc pl   id.

Ναφαγ pr noun

Ναφεδδωρ pr noun

Ναφεκ pr noun

Ναφες pr noun

Ναφετα pr noun

νάφθαν noun fem acc sg . . . . νάφθα

Ναφθω pr noun

Ναφισαιων pr noun masc gen pl . . . . Ναφισαιος

Ναφισι pr noun

Ναφισων pr noun

Ναφλαζων pr noun

ναχαλ translit

Ναχαλιγαας pr noun

Ναχαλιγαιας pr noun

Ναχεθ pr noun

Ναχεμ pr noun

Ναχοθ pr noun

Ναχωρ pr noun

ναῷ noun masc dat sg . . . . ναός

νέα adj neut nom and acc pl . . . . νέος

νεάζειν vb pres act inf . . . . νεάζω

νέαν adj fem acc sg . . . . νέος

νεανίᾳ noun masc dat sg . . . . νεανίας

νεανίαι noun masc nom pl   id.

νεανίαις noun masc dat pl   id.

νεανίαν noun masc acc sg   id.

νεανίας noun masc nom sg and acc pl   id.

νεάνιδα noun fem acc sg . . . . νεᾶνις

νεάνιδας noun fem acc pl   id.

νεάνιδες noun fem nom pl   id.

νεάνιδι noun fem dat sg   id.

νεάνιδος noun fem gen sg   id.

νεανίδων noun fem gen pl   id.

νεανικῆς adj fem gen sg . . . . νεανικός

νεᾶνιν noun fem acc sg . . . . νεᾶνις

νεανίου noun masc gen sg . . . . νεανίας

νεᾶνις noun fem nom sg

νεάνισιν noun fem dat pl . . . . νεᾶνις

νεανίσκε noun masc voc sg . . . . νεανίσκος

νεανίσκοι noun masc nom pl   id.

νεανίσκοις noun masc dat pl   id.

νεανίσκον noun masc acc sg   id.

νεανίσκος noun masc nom sg   id.

νεανίσκου noun masc gen sg   id.

νεανίσκους noun masc acc pl   id.

νεανίσκῳ noun masc dat sg   id.

νεανίσκων noun masc gen pl   id.

νεανιῶν noun masc gen pl . . . . νεανίας

νεβελ translit

Νεβελ pr noun

Νεβριμ pr noun

νεβροί noun masc nom pl . . . . νεβρός

νεβρῷ noun masc dat sg   id.

Νεβρωδ pr noun

Νεβσαν pr noun

νεελασα translit

Νεεμιαν pr noun masc acc sg . . . . Νεεμιας

Νεεμιας pr noun masc nom sg   id.

Νεεμιου pr noun masc gen sg   id.

Νεεσθαν pr noun

νεεσσαραν translit

νεζερ translit

νεῖκος noun neut nom and acc sg

νείκους noun neut gen sg .... νεῖκος

νεκρά adj fem nom sg, neut nom and acc pl .... νεκρός

νεκράς adj fem acc pl   id.

νεκρᾶς adj fem gen sg   id.

νεκροί adj masc nom pl   id.

νεκροῖς adj masc dat pl   id.

νεκρόν adj masc acc sg, neut nom and acc sg   id.

νεκρός adj masc nom sg   id.

νεκροῦ adj masc gen sg   id.

νεκρούς adj masc acc pl   id.

νεκρῷ adj masc dat sg   id.

νεκρῶν adj masc gen pl   id.

Νεκωδα pr noun

Νεκωδαν pr noun

Νελαμιτην pr noun masc acc sg .... Νελαμιτης

νεμέσθωσαν vb pres m/p impv 3rd pers pl .... νέμω

νεμήσει vb fut act ind 3rd pers sg   id.

νεμήσεται vb fut mid ind 3rd pers sg   id.

νεμήσονται vb fut mid ind 3rd pers pl   id.

νέμηται vb pres m/p subj 3rd pers sg   id.

νεμόμενοι vb pres m/p part masc nom pl   id.

Νεμρα pr noun

Νεμριμ pr noun

νέμων vb pres act part masc nom sg .... νέμω

νενευροκοπημένης vb perf m/p part

     fem gen sg .... νευροκοπέω

νενησμένα vb perf m/p part neut nom and acc pl ..... νήθω

νενησμένης vb perf m/p part fem gen sg   id.

νενησμένου vb perf m/p part masc and neut gen sg   id.

νενηστεύκατε vb perf act ind 2nd pers pl .... νηστεύω

νενικῆσθαι vb perf m/p inf .... νικάω

νένιπται vb perf m/p ind 3rd pers sg .... νίπτω

νενουθέτησαι vb perf m/p ind 2nd pers sg ..... νουθετέω

νεογνά adj neut nom and acc pl .... νεογνός

νέοι adj masc nom pl .... νέος

νέοις adj masc and neut dat pl   id.

νεοκτίστους adj masc acc pl .... νεόκτιστος

νεομηνία noun fem nom sg

νεομηνίᾳ noun fem dat sg .... νεομηνία

νεομηνίαις noun fem dat pl   id.

νεομηνίας noun fem gen sg and acc pl   id.

νέον adj masc acc sg, neut nom and acc sg .... νέος

νέος adj masc nom sg   id.

νεοσσιά noun fem nom sg

νεοσσοί noun masc nom pl .... νεοσσός

νεοσσοῖς noun masc dat pl   id.

νεοσσόν noun masc acc sg   id.

νεοσσός noun masc nom sg   id.

νεοσσούς noun masc acc pl   id.

νεοσσῶν noun masc gen pl   id.

νεότης noun fem nom sg

νεότησιν noun fem dat pl .... νεότης

νεότητα noun fem acc sg .... νεότης

νεότητι noun fem dat sg   id.

νεότητος noun fem gen sg   id.

νεοττῶν noun masc gen pl .... νεοττός

νέου adj masc and neut gen sg ..... νέος

νέους adj masc acc pl   id.

νεόφυτα adj neut nom and acc pl .... νεόφυτος

νεόφυτον adj acc sg, neut nom sg   id.

Νεσεραχ pr noun

Νεσθα pr noun

Νεσιβ pr noun

νεσσα translit

Νετεβας pr noun

Νετουφατ pr noun

Νετωφα pr noun

Νετωφαθι pr noun

Νετωφαθίτης pr noun masc nom sg

Νετωφατι pr noun

νευέτω vb pres act impv 3rd pers sg .... νεύω

νεύμασι noun neut dat pl .... νεῦμα

νεύματι noun neut dat sg   id.

νεῦρα noun neut nom and acc pl .... νεῦρον

νευραῖς noun fem dat pl .... νευρά

νευράς noun fem acc pl   id.

νευρέαις noun fem dat pl   νευρέα

νευρέας noun fem gen sg and acc pl   id.

νεύροις noun neut dat pl .... νεῦρον

νευροκοπήσεις vb fut act ind 2nd pers sg .... νευροκοπέω

νευροκοπήσουσιν vb fut act ind 3rd pers pl   id.

νεῦρον noun neut nom and acc sg

νεύρου noun neut gen sg .... νεῦρον

νεύρων noun neut gen pl   id.

νεύσῃ vb 1st aor act subj 3rd pers sg .... νεύω

νεφέλαι noun fem nom pl .... νεφέλη

νεφέλαις noun fem dat pl   id.

νεφέλας noun fem acc pl   id.

νεφέλη noun fem nom sg   id.

νεφέλῃ noun fem dat sg   id.

νεφέλην noun fem acc sg   id.

νεφέλης noun fem gen sg   id.

νεφελῶν noun fem gen pl   id.

νέφη noun neut nom and acc pl .... νέφος

νεφθαι translit

Νεφθαλι pr noun

Νεφθαλιμ pr noun

Νεφθαλιμ pr noun

νεφθαρ translit

νέφος noun neut nom and acc sg

νέφους noun neut gen sg .... νέφος

νεφροί noun masc nom pl .... νεφρός

νεφροῖς noun masc dat pl   id.

νεφρούς noun masc acc pl   id.

νεφρῶν noun masc gen pl . . . . νεφρός

νεφῶν noun neut gen pl . . . . νέφος

Νεφωσασιμ pr noun

Νεχαω pr noun

νεχωθα translit

νεώ noun masc acc and gen sg . . . . νεώς

νέῳ adj masc and neut dat sg . . . . νέος

νεώματα noun neut nom and acc pl . . . . νέωμα

νέων adj gen pl . . . . νέος

νεώς noun masc nom sg

νεώσατε vb 1st aor act impv 2nd pers pl . . . . νεόω

νεωστί adverb

νεώτατος superl adj masc nom sg . . . . νέος

νεωτέρα comp adj fem nom sg,

               neut nom and acc pl   id.

νεωτέρᾳ comp adj fem dat sg   id.

νεωτέραις comp adj fem dat pl   id.

νεωτέραν comp adj fem acc sg   id.

νεωτέρας comp adj fem gen sg   id.

νεωτερικῆς adj fem gen sg . . . . νεωτερικός

νεωτερίσαντες vb 1st aor act part masc nom pl . . νεωτερίζω

νεώτεροι comp adj masc nom pl . . . . νέος

νεώτερον comp adj masc acc sg, neut nom and acc sg   id.

νεώτερος comp adj masc nom sg   id.

νεωτέρου comp adj masc and neut gen sg   id.

νεωτέρους comp adj masc acc pl   id.

νεωτέρῳ comp adj masc and neut dat sg   id.

νεωτέρων comp adj gen pl   id.

νή particle

νήθειν vb pres act inf . . . . νήθω

νηί noun fem dat sg . . . . ναῦς

νηκτά adj neut nom and acc pl . . . . νηκτός

νηός noun fem gen sg . . . . ναῦς

νήπια adj neut nom and acc pl . . . . νήπιος

νήπιοι adj masc nom pl   id.

νηπίοις adj masc and neut dat pl   id.

νηπιοκτόνου adj gen sg . . . . νηπιοκτόνος

νήπιον adj masc acc sg, neut nom and acc sg . . . . . . νήπιος

νήπιος adj masc nom sg   id.

νηπιότητος noun fem gen sg . . . . νηπιότης

νηπίου adj masc and neut gen sg . . . . νήπιος

νηπίους adj masc acc pl   id.

νηπίων adj gen pl   id.

Νηρ pr noun

Νηριγελ pr noun

Νηριου pr noun masc gen sg . . . . Νηριας

νῆσοι noun fem nom pl . . . . νῆσος

νήσοις noun fem dat pl   id.

νήσους noun fem acc pl   id.

νηστεία noun fem nom sg

νηστείᾳ noun fem dat sg . . . . νηστεία

νηστείαις noun fem dat pl   id.

νηστείαν noun fem acc sg . . . . νηστεία

νηστείας noun fem gen sg   id.

νηστειῶν noun fem gen pl   id.

νηστεύετε vb pres act ind 2nd pers pl . . . . νηστεύω

νηστεύουσιν vb pres act ind 3rd pers pl   id.

νηστευσασῶν vb 1st aor act part fem gen pl   id.

νηστεύσατε vb 1st aor act impv 2nd pers pl   id.

νηστεύσητε vb 1st aor act subj 2nd pers pl   id.

νηστεύσωσιν vb 1st aor act subj 3rd pers pl   id.

νηστεύω vb pres act ind 1st pers sg   id.

νηστεύων vb pres act part masc nom sg   id.

νῆστις noun fem nom sg

νηστόν adj masc acc sg, neut nom and acc sg . . . . . . νηστός

νήσῳ noun fem dat sg . . . . νῆσος

νήσων noun fem gen pl   id.

νήχεται vb pres dep ind 3rd pers sg . . . . νήχομαι

νηῶν noun fem gen pl . . . . ναῦς

νικᾷ vb pres act ind 3rd pers sg . . . . νικάω

Νικανορα pr noun masc acc sg . . . . Νικανωρ

Νικανορι pr noun masc dat sg   id.

Νικανορος pr noun masc gen sg   id.

Νικανωρ pr noun masc nom sg   id.

νίκη noun fem nom sg

νίκην noun fem acc sg . . . . νίκη

νίκης noun fem gen sg   id.

νικῆσαι vb 1st aor act inf . . . . νικάω

νικήσαντες vb 1st aor act part masc nom pl   id.

νικήσαντος vb 1st aor act part masc and neut gen sg   id.

νικήσασα vb 1st aor act part fem nom sg   id.

νικήσασιν vb 1st aor act part masc dat pl   id.

νικήσῃ vb 1st aor act subj 3rd pers sg   id.

νικήσῃς vb 1st aor act subj 2nd pers sg   id.

νικήσωσιν vb 1st aor act subj 3rd pers pl   id.

νῖκος noun neut nom and acc sg

νικώμενον vb pres m/p part masc acc sg,

               neut nom and acc sg . . . . νικάω

Νινευη pr noun

Νινευητῶν pr noun masc gen pl . . . . Νινευήτης

νίπτεσθαι vb pres m/p inf . . . . νίπτω

νίπτωνται vb pres m/p subj 3rd pers pl   id.

Νισα pr noun

Νισαν pr noun

Νισια pr noun

Νισω pr noun

νίτρῳ noun neut dat sg . . . . νίτρον

νιφετοί noun masc nom pl . . . . νιφετός

νιφετός noun masc nom sg   id.

νιφήσεται vb fut pass ind 3rd pers sg . . . . νίπτω

Νιφις pr noun

νίψαι vb 1st aor act inf,

               1st aor act opt 3rd pers sg . . . . νίπτω

νιψάμενος vb 1st aor mid part masc nom sg   id.

νίψασθαι vb 1st aor mid inf . . . . νίπτω

νίψασθε vb 1st aor mid impv 2nd pers pl id.

νιψάτωσαν vb 1st aor act impv 3rd pers pl id.

νίψεται vb fut mid ind 3rd pers sg id.

νίψομαι vb fut mid ind 1st pers sg id.

νίψονται vb fut mid ind 3rd pers pl id.

Νοεβα pr noun

νόει vb pres act impv 2nd pers sg . . . . νοέω

Νοεμα pr noun

Νοεμαν pr noun

Νοεμανι pr noun

νοερόν adj masc acc sg, neut nom and acc sg . . . . . . νοερός

νοερῶν adj gen pl id.

νόημα noun neut nom and acc sg

νοημάτων noun neut gen pl . . . . νόημα

νοήμονες adj masc and fem nom pl . . . . νοήμων

νοήμονι adj dat sg id.

νοήμων adj masc and fem nom sg id.

νοῆσαι vb 1st aor act opt 3rd pers sg . . . . νοέω

νοῆσαι vb 1st aor act inf id.

νοήσαντες vb 1st aor act part masc nom pl id.

νοήσας vb 1st aor act part masc nom sg id.

νοήσατε vb 1st aor act impv 2nd pers pl id.

νοησάτωσαν vb 1st aor act impv 3rd pers pl id.

νοήσει vb fut act ind 3rd pers sg id.

νοήσῃ vb 1st aor act subj 3rd pers sg id.

νόησον vb 1st aor act impv 2nd pers sg id.

νοήσουσιν vb fut act ind 3rd pers pl id.

νοητῶς adverb

νοθεύων vb pres act part masc nom sg . . . . νοθεύω

νόθων adj gen pl . . . . νόθος

νόθως adverb

νομάδες noun masc or fem nom pl . . . . νομάς

νομάδων noun masc or fem gen pl id.

νομαί noun fem nom pl . . . . νομή

νομαῖς noun fem dat pl id.

νομάς noun fem acc pl id.

Νομβα pr noun

νόμε noun masc voc sg . . . . νόμος

Νομεε pr noun

νομή noun fem nom sg

νομῇ noun fem dat sg . . . . νομή

νομήν noun fem acc sg id.

νομῆς noun fem gen sg id.

νομίζομεν vb pres act ind 1st pers pl . . . . νομίζω

νομιζομένων vb pres m/p part gen pl id.

νομίζοντες vb pres act part masc nom pl id.

νομικός adj masc nom sg

νόμιμα adj neut nom and acc pl . . . . νόμιμος

νομίμοις adj masc and neut dat pl id.

νόμιμον adj masc acc sg, neut nom and acc sg id.

νομίμου adj masc and neut gen sg id.

νομίμους adj masc acc pl . . . . νόμιμος

νομίμων adj gen pl id.

νομίμως adverb

νομίσαντες vb 1st aor act part masc nom pl . . . . νομίζω

νομίσας vb 1st aor act part masc nom sg id.

νομίσειεν vb 1st aor act opt 3rd pers sg id.

νομίσῃς vb 1st aor act subj 2nd pers sg id.

νομίσητε vb 1st aor act subj 2nd pers pl id.

νόμισμα noun neut nom and acc sg

νομιστέον verbal adj sg

νομοθεσίας noun fem gen sg . . . . νομοθεσία

νομοθέσμως adverb

νομοθετηθῇ vb 1st aor pass subj 3rd pers sg . . . νομοθετέω

νομοθέτην noun masc acc sg . . . . νομοθέτης

νομοθετῆσαι vb 1st aor act inf . . . . νομοθετέω

νομοθετήσαντα vb 1st aor act part masc acc sg,
    neut nom and acc pl id.

νομοθετήσει vb fut act ind 3rd pers sg id.

νομοθέτησον vb 1st aor act impv 2nd pers sg id.

νομοθετῶν vb pres act part masc nom sg id.

νόμοι noun masc nom pl . . . . νόμος

νόμοις noun masc dat pl id.

νόμον noun masc acc sg id.

νομόν noun masc acc sg . . . . νομός

νόμος noun masc nom sg

νόμός noun masc nom sg

νόμου noun masc gen sg . . . . νόμος

νόμους noun masc acc pl id.

νομούς noun masc acc pl . . . . νομός

νομοφύλαξ noun fem nom sg

νόμῳ noun masc dat sg . . . . νόμος

νόμων noun masc gen pl id.

νομῶν noun masc gen pl . . . . νομός

Νοο pr noun

Νοοζα pr noun

Νοομ pr noun

Νοομα pr noun

Νοομμα pr noun

νοός noun masc gen sg . . . . νοῦς

νοσερῷ adj masc and neut dat sg . . . . νοσερός

νόσον noun fem acc sg . . . . νόσος

νόσος noun fem nom sg id.

νόσου noun fem gen sg id.

νόσους noun fem acc pl id.

νοσούσης vb pres act part fem gen sg . . . . νοσέω

νοσσεύοντα vb pres act part neut nom and acc pl . . νοσσεύω

νοσσεύουσαι vb pres act part fem nom pl id.

νοσσία noun neut nom and acc pl . . . . νοσσίον

νοσσιᾷ noun fem dat sg . . . . νοσσιά

νοσσιαί noun fem nom pl id.

νοσσιάν noun fem acc sg id.

νοσσιάς noun fem acc pl id.

νοσσιᾶς noun fem gen sg . . . . νοσσιά

νοσσοποιήσουσιν vb fut act ind 3rd pers pl . . νοσσοποιέω

νοσφισάμενος vb 1st aor mid part

        masc nom sg . . . . νοσφίζομαι

νόσῳ noun fem dat sg . . . . νόσος

νότε noun masc voc sg . . . . νότος

νότον noun masc acc sg   id.

νότος noun masc nom sg   id.

νότου noun masc gen sg   id.

νότῳ noun masc dat sg   id.

Νουα pr noun

νουθεσίαν noun fem acc sg . . . . νουθεσία

νουθετεῖς vb pres act ind 2nd pers sg . . . . νουθετέω

νουθετῇ vb pres act subj 3rd pers sg   id.

νουθετηθέντες vb 1st aor pass part masc nom pl   id.

νουθέτημα noun neut nom and acc sg

νουθετήσει vb fut act ind 3rd pers sg . . . . νουθετέω

νουθέτησιν noun fem acc sg . . . . νουθέτησις

νουθετοῦ vb pres m/p impv 2nd pers sg . . . . νουθετέω

νουθετούμενοι vb pres m/p part masc nom pl   id.

νουθετούμενος vb pres m/p part masc nom sg   id.

νουθετοῦσιν vb pres act ind 3rd pers pl   id.

νουθετῶν vb pres act part masc nom sg   id.

Νουμ pr noun

νουμηνία noun fem nom sg

νουμηνίᾳ noun fem dat sg . . . . νουμηνία

νουμηνίαι noun fem nom pl   id.

νουμηνίαις noun fem dat pl   id.

νουμηνίας noun fem gen sg and acc pl   id.

Νουμηνιον pr noun masc acc sg . . . . Νουμηνιος

Νουμηνιος pr noun masc nom sg   id.

νουμηνιῶν noun fem gen pl . . . . νουμηνία

νουν translit (Heb. letter: ‏נ‎)

νοῦν noun masc acc sg . . . . νοῦς

νοῦς noun masc nom sg   id.

νύκτα noun fem acc sg . . . . νύξ

νύκτας noun fem acc pl   id.

νυκτερίδα noun fem acc sg . . . . νυκτερίς

νυκτερίδες noun fem nom pl   id.

νυκτερινάς adj fem acc pl . . . . νυκτερινός

νυκτερινή adj fem nom sg   id.

νυκτερινῇ adj fem dat sg   id.

νυκτερινόν adj masc acc sg, neut nom and acc sg   id.

νυκτερινοῦ adj masc and neut gen sg   id.

νυκτερίσιν noun fem dat pl . . . . νυκτερίς

νύκτες noun fem nom pl . . . . νύξ

νυκτί noun fem dat sg   id.

νυκτικόρακα noun masc acc sg . . . . νυκτικόραξ

νυκτικόραξ noun masc nom sg   id.

νυκτός noun fem gen sg . . . . νύξ

νυκτῶν noun fem gen pl   id.

νύκτωρ adverb

νυμφαγωγός adj masc and fem nom sg

νυμφαγωγῷ adj dat sg . . . . νυμφαγωγός

νύμφαι noun fem nom pl . . . . νύμφη

νύμφαις noun fem dat pl   id.

νύμφας noun fem acc pl   id.

νυμφεύσεως noun fem gen sg . . . . νύμφευσις

νύμφη noun fem nom sg

νύμφῃ noun fem dat sg . . . . νύμφη

νύμφην noun fem acc sg   id.

νύμφης noun fem gen sg   id.

νυμφίον noun masc acc sg . . . . νυμφίος

νυμφίος noun masc nom sg   id.

νυμφίου noun masc gen sg   id.

νυμφίῳ noun masc dat sg   id.

νυμφῶνα noun masc acc sg . . . . νυμφών

νυμφῶνι noun masc dat sg   id.

νυμφῶσι noun masc dat pl   id.

νῦν adverb

νυνί adverb

νύξ noun fem nom sg

νυξίν noun fem dat pl . . . . νύξ

νύσσων vb pres act part masc nom sg . . . . νύσσω

νυσταγμάτων noun neut gen pl . . . . νύσταγμα

νυσταγμόν noun masc acc sg . . . . νυσταγμός

νυσταγμός noun masc nom sg   id.

νυστάζεις vb pres act ind 2nd pers sg . . . . νυστάζω

νυστάζοντας vb pres act part masc acc pl   id.

νυστάζοντι vb pres act part masc and neut dat sg   id.

νυστάζω vb pres act ind 1st pers sg   id.

νυστάξαι vb 1st aor act inf   id.

νυστάξει vb fut act ind 3rd pers sg   id.

νυστάξῃ vb 1st aor act subj 3rd pers sg   id.

νυστάξουσιν vb fut act ind 3rd pers pl   id.

Νωα pr noun

Νωαδια pr noun

Νωβαι pr noun

Νωδαβ pr noun

Νωε pr noun

Νωεμιν pr noun

νωθροῖς adj masc and neut dat pl . . . . νωθρός

νωθροκάρδιος adj masc and fem nom sg

νωθρός adj masc nom sg

νωθρότητα noun fem acc sg . . . . νωθρότης

νωκηδ translit

Νωμα pr noun

Νωμαν pr noun

νῶτα noun neut nom and acc pl . . . . νῶτον

νῶτοι noun masc nom pl . . . . νῶτος

νώτοις noun masc dat pl   id.

νῶτον noun masc acc sg   id.

νῶτος noun masc nom sg   id.

νώτου noun neut gen sg   id.

νωτοφόρων adj gen pl . . . . νωτοφόρος

Ξ ξ

ξανθῆς adj fem gen sg . . . . ξανθός
ξανθίζουσα vb pres act part fem nom sg . . . . ξανθίζω
Ξανθικοῦ pr noun masc gen sg . . . . Ξανθικός
ξένας adj fem acc pl . . . . ξένος
ξένη adj fem nom sg   id.
ξένῃ adj fem dat sg   id.
ξένην adj fem acc sg   id.
ξένης adj fem gen sg   id.
ξένια noun neut nom and acc pl . . . . ξένιον
ξενιεῖς vb fut act ind 2nd pers sg . . . . ξενίζω
ξενιζούσαις vb pres act part fem dat pl   id.
ξενίζουσαν vb pres act part fem acc sg   id.
ξενίοις noun neut dat pl . . . . ξένιον
Ξενίου pr noun masc gen sg . . . . Ξένιος
ξενισμός noun masc nom sg
ξενιτείας noun fem gen sg . . . . ξενιτεία
ξένοι adj masc nom pl . . . . ξένος
ξένοις adj masc and neut dat pl   id.
ξένον adj masc acc sg, neut nom and acc sg   id.
ξένος adj masc nom sg   id.
ξένους adj masc acc pl   id.
ξένῳ adj masc and neut dat sg   id.
ξένων adj gen pl   id.
Ξέρξου pr noun masc gen sg . . . . Ξέρξης
ξεστῷ adj masc and neut dat sg . . . . ξεστός
ξηρά adj fem nom sg, neut nom and acc pl . . . . ξηρός
ξηραίνεται vb pres m/p ind 3rd pers sg . . . . ξηραίνω
ξηραινόμενος vb pres m/p part masc nom sg   id.
ξηραίνων vb pres act part masc nom sg   id.
ξηράν adj fem acc sg . . . . ξηρός
ξηρανεῖ vb fut act ind 3rd pers sg . . . . ξηραίνω
ξηρανθείη vb 1st aor pass opt 3rd pers sg   id.
ξηρανθῆναι vb 1st aor pass inf   id.
ξηρανθήσεται vb fut pass ind 3rd pers sg   id.
ξηρανθήσονται vb fut pass ind 3rd pers pl   id.
ξηρανῶ vb fut act ind 1st pers sg   id.
ξηρᾶς adj fem gen sg . . . . ξηρός
ξηρασία noun fem nom sg
ξηρασίᾳ noun fem dat sg . . . . ξηρασία
ξηρασίας noun fem gen sg   id.
ξηρόν adj masc acc sg, neut nom and acc sg . . . . ξηρός
ξηρός adj masc nom sg   id.
ξηροῦ adj masc and neut gen sg   id.
ξηρούς adj masc acc pl   id.
ξίφει noun neut dat sg . . . . ξίφος

ξίφεσι noun neut dat pl   ξίφος
ξιφηφόρον adj acc sg, neut nom sg . . . . ξιφηφόρος
ξίφος noun neut nom and acc sg
ξίφους noun neut gen sg . . . . ξίφος
ξιφῶν noun neut gen pl   id.
ξύῃ vb pres act subj 3rd pers sg . . . . ξύω
ξύλα noun neut nom and acc pl . . . . ξύλον
ξυλάρια noun neut nom and acc pl . . . . ξυλάριον
ξύλινα adj neut nom and acc pl . . . . ξύλινος
ξυλίνη adj fem nom sg   id.
ξυλίνην adj fem acc sg   id.
ξύλινοι adj masc nom pl   id.
ξυλίνοις adj masc and neut dat pl   id.
ξύλινον adj masc acc sg, neut nom and acc sg   id.
ξύλινος adj masc nom sg   id.
ξυλίνου adj masc and neut gen sg   id.
ξυλίνους adj masc acc pl   id.
ξυλίνῳ adj masc and neut dat sg   id.
ξυλίνων adj gen pl   id.
ξύλοις noun neut dat pl . . . . ξύλον
ξυλοκόποι noun masc nom pl . . . . ξυλοκόπος
ξυλοκόπος noun masc nom sg   id.
ξυλοκόπου noun masc gen sg   id.
ξυλοκόπους noun masc acc pl   id.
ξύλον noun neut nom and acc sg
ξύλου noun neut gen sg . . . . ξύλον
ξυλοφορίας noun fem gen sg . . . . ξυλοφορία
ξυλοφόρων adj gen pl . . . . ξυλοφόρος
ξύλῳ noun neut dat sg . . . . ξύλον
ξύλων noun neut gen pl   id.
ξυρηθῆναι vb 1st aor pass inf . . . . ξυράω
ξυρηθήσεσθε vb fut pass ind 2nd pers pl   id.
ξυρηθήσεται vb fut pass ind 3rd pers sg   id.
ξύρησαι vb 1st aor mid impv 2nd pers sg   id.
ξυρήσασθαι vb 1st aor mid inf   id.
ξυρήσει vb fut act ind 3rd pers sg   id.
ξυρήσεις vb fut act ind 2nd pers sg   id.
ξυρήσεται vb fut mid ind 3rd pers sg   id.
ξύρησιν noun fem acc sg . . . . ξύρησις
ξυρήσονται vb fut mid ind 3rd pers pl . . . . ξυράω
ξυρήσωμαι vb 1st aor mid subj 1st pers sg   id.
ξυρόν noun neut nom and acc sg
ξυρῷ noun neut dat sg . . . . ξυρόν
ξυστοῦ adj masc and neut gen sg . . . . ξυστός
ξυστούς adj masc acc pl   id.

ξυστῶν adj gen pl . . . . ξυστός

ξύων vb pres act part masc nom sg . . . . ξύω

O o

ὁ art masc nom sg

ὅ rel pron neut nom and acc sg . . . . ὅς

Οβα pr noun

Οββια pr noun

Οβδια pr noun

ὀβελίσκοι noun masc nom pl . . . . ὀβελίσκος

ὀβελίσκους noun masc acc pl   id.

ὄβολοι see ὀβολοί

ὀβολοί noun masc nom pl . . . . ὀβολός

ὀβολός noun masc nom sg   id.

ὀβολοῦ noun masc gen sg   id.

ὀβολούς noun masc acc pl   id.

ὀγδόη adj fem nom sg . . . . ὄγδοος

ὀγδόῃ adj fem dat sg   id.

ὀγδοήκοντα indecl number

ὀγδοηκοστοῦ adj masc and neut gen sg . . . . . ὀγδοηκοστός

ὀγδόης adj fem gen sg . . . . ὄγδοος

ὄγδοον adj masc acc sg, neut nom and acc sg   id.

ὄγδοος adj masc nom sg   id.

ὀγδόου adj masc and neut gen sg   id.

ὀγδόῳ adj masc and neut dat sg   id.

Ογοθολια pr noun

ὅδε dem pron masc nom sg

ὁδηγῆσαι vb 1st aor act inf . . . . ὁδηγέω

ὁδηγήσει vb fut act ind 3rd pers sg   id.

ὁδηγήσεις vb fut act ind 2nd pers sg   id.

ὁδήγησον vb 1st aor act impv 2nd pers sg   id.

ὁδηγοί noun masc nom pl . . . . ὁδηγός

ὁδηγόν noun masc acc sg   id.

ὁδηγός noun masc nom sg   id.

ὁδηγῶν vb pres act part masc nom sg . . . . ὁδηγέω

ὁδοί noun fem nom pl . . . . ὁδός

ὁδοιπορίαν noun fem acc sg . . . . ὁδοιπορία

ὁδοιπορίας noun fem gen sg and acc pl   id.

ὁδοιπόροι noun masc nom pl . . . . ὁδοιπόρος

ὁδοιπόρον noun masc acc sg   id.

ὁδοιπόρος noun masc nom sg   id.

ὁδοιπόρῳ noun masc dat sg   id.

ὁδοιπόρων noun masc gen pl   id.

ὁδοῖς noun fem dat pl . . . . ὁδός

Οδολλαμ pr noun

Οδολλαμιτην pr noun masc acc sg . . . . Οδολλαμιτης

Οδολλαμιτης pr noun masc nom sg   id.

Οδολλαμιτου pr noun masc gen sg   id.

Οδομ pr noun

Οδομηρα pr noun

ὀδόν noun fem acc sg . . . . ὁδός

ὀδόντα noun masc acc sg . . . . ὀδούς

ὀδόντας noun masc acc pl   id.

ὀδόντες noun masc nom pl   id.

ὀδόντος noun masc gen sg   id.

ὀδόντων noun masc gen pl   id.

ὁδοποιήσατε vb 1st aor act impv 2nd pers pl . . . . ὁδοποιέω

Οδορρα pr noun

ὁδός noun fem nom sg

ὁδοῦ noun fem gen sg . . . . ὁδός

Οδουια pr noun

Οδουιας pr noun masc nom sg

ὁδούς noun fem acc pl . . . . ὁδός

ὀδούς noun masc nom sg

ὀδοῦσι noun masc dat pl . . . . ὀδούς

ὀδυνᾷ vb pres act ind 3rd pers sg . . . . ὀδυνάω

ὀδύναι noun fem nom pl . . . . ὀδύνη

ὀδύναις noun fem dat pl   id.

ὀδύνας noun fem acc pl   id.

ὀδυνᾶται vb pres m/p ind 3rd pers sg . . . . ὀδυνάω

ὀδύνη noun fem nom sg

ὀδύνῃ noun fem dat sg . . . . ὀδύνη

ὀδυνηθήσεται vb fut pass ind 3rd pers sg . . . . ὀδυνάω

ὀδυνηθήσονται vb fut pass ind 3rd pers pl   id.

ὀδύνην noun fem acc sg . . . . ὀδύνη

ὀδυνηρά adj fem nom sg . . . . ὀδυνηρός

ὀδυνηρᾷ adj fem dat sg   id.

ὀδυνηράν adj fem acc sg   id.

ὀδυνηρᾶς adj fem gen sg   id.

ὀδύνης noun fem gen sg . . . . ὀδύνη

ὀδυνωμένην vb pres m/p part fem acc sg . . . . ὀδυνάω

ὀδυνώμενοι vb pres m/p part masc nom pl   id.

ὀδυνωμένοις vb pres m/p part masc and neut dat pl   id.

ὀδυνῶν noun fem gen pl . . . . ὀδύνη

ὀδυρμοῦ noun masc gen sg . . . . ὀδυρμός

ὀδυρμῶν noun masc gen pl   id.

ὀδυρομένου vb pres dep part

   masc and neut gen sg . . . . ὀδύρομαι

ὁδῷ noun fem dat sg . . . . ὁδός

ὁδῶν noun fem gen pl   id.

Οζα pr noun

Οζαζα pr noun

Οζαζιας pr noun masc nom sg

Οζαν pr noun

Οζι   pr noun

Οζια   pr noun masc gen/dat sg . . . . Οζιας

Οζια   pr noun

Οζιαν   pr noun masc acc sg . . . . Οζιας

Οζιας   pr noun masc nom sg

Οζιβ   pr noun

Οζιζα   pr noun

Οζιηλ   pr noun

Οζιηλις   pr noun

Οζιου   pr noun masc gen sg . . . . Οζιας

ὄζοις   noun masc dat pl . . . . ὄζος

Οζομ   pr noun

Οζουζ   pr noun

Οζριηλ   pr noun

Οθαλι   pr noun

ὅθεν   adverb

Οθομ   pr noun

ὀθόνια   noun neut nom and acc pl . . . . ὀθόνιον

Οθονιας   pr noun masc nom sg

οἱ   art masc nom pl . . . . ὁ

οἵ   rel pron masc nom pl . . . . ὅς

οἵα   rel pron fem nom sg . . . . οἷος

οἷα   rel pron neut nom and acc pl . . . . id.

οἴακας   noun masc acc pl . . . . οἴαξ

οἰακίζει   vb pres act ind 3rd pers sg . . . . οἰακίζω

οἵας   adj fem gen sg and acc pl . . . . οἷος

οἶδ’   see οἶδα

οἶδα   vb perf act ind 1st pers sg . . . . οἶδα

οἴδαμεν   vb perf act ind 1st pers pl . . . . id.

οἶδας   vb perf act ind 2nd pers sg . . . . id.

οἴδασιν   vb perf act ind 3rd pers pl . . . . id.

οἴδατε   vb perf act ind 2nd pers pl . . . . id.

οἴδε   dem pron masc nom pl . . . . ὅδε

οἶδε(ν)   vb perf act ind 3rd pers sg . . . . οἶδα

οἴει   vb pres dep ind 2nd pers sg . . . . οἴομαι

οἴεται   vb pres dep ind 3rd pers sg . . . . id.

οἴη   vb pres dep ind 2nd pers sg . . . . id.

οἴκει   vb pres act impv 2nd pers sg . . . . οἰκέω

οἰκεία   adj fem nom sg . . . . οἰκεῖος

οἰκεῖα   adj neut nom and acc pl . . . . id.

οἰκεῖαι   adj fem nom pl . . . . id.

οἰκεῖν   vb pres act inf . . . . οἰκέω

οἰκεῖοι   adj masc nom pl . . . . οἰκεῖος

οἰκείοις   adj masc and neut dat pl . . . . id.

οἰκεῖον   adj masc acc sg, neut nom and acc sg . . . . . id.

οἰκεῖος   adj masc nom sg . . . . id.

οἰκειότητα   noun fem acc sg . . . . οἰκειότης

οἰκείου   adj masc and neut gen sg . . . . οἰκεῖος

οἰκείους   adj masc acc pl . . . . id.

οἰκείτωσαν   vb pres act impv 3rd pers pl . . . . οἰκέω

οἰκείῳ   adj masc and neut dat sg . . . . οἰκεῖος

οἰκειωθησόμενα   vb fut pass part

       neut nom and acc pl . . . . οἰκειόω

οἰκείων   adj gen pl . . . . οἰκεῖος

οἰκέται   noun masc nom pl . . . . οἰκέτης

οἰκέταις   noun masc dat pl   id.

οἰκέτας   noun masc acc pl   id.

οἰκέτῃ   noun masc dat sg   id.

οἰκέτην   noun masc acc sg   id.

οἰκέτης   noun masc nom sg   id.

οἰκετικην   noun fem acc sg . . . . οἰκετικός

οἰκέτιν   noun fem acc sg . . . . οἰκέτις

οἰκέτις   noun fem nom sg   id.

οἰκετου   noun masc gen sg . . . . οἰκέτης

οἰκετῶν   noun masc gen pl   id.

οἴκημα   noun neut nom and acc sg

οἰκῆσαι   vb 1st aor act inf . . . . οἰκέω

οἰκήσατε   vb 1st aor act impv 2nd pers pl   id.

οἰκήσει   vb fut act ind 3rd pers sg   id.

οἰκήσεις   noun fem nom and acc pl . . . . οἴκησις

οἰκήσεις   vb fut act ind 2nd pers sg . . . . οἰκέω

οἰκήσετε   vb fut act ind 2nd pers pl   id.

οἰκήσεως   noun fem gen sg . . . . οἴκησις

οἴκησιν   noun fem acc sg   id.

οἰκήσομεν   vb fut act ind 1st pers pl . . . . οἰκέω

οἴκησον   vb 1st aor act impv 2nd pers sg   id.

οἰκήσουσιν   vb fut act ind 3rd pers pl   id.

οἰκητήν   adj fem acc sg . . . . οἰκητός

οἰκητήριον   noun neut nom and acc sg

οἰκητόν   adj masc acc sg, neut nom and acc sg . . . . . οἰκητός

οἰκήτορας   noun masc acc pl . . . . οἰκήτωρ

οἰκήτορες   noun masc nom pl   id.

οἰκητός   adj masc nom sg

οἰκία   noun fem nom sg

οἰκίᾳ   noun fem dat sg . . . . οἰκία

οἰκίαι   noun fem nom pl   id.

οἰκίαις   noun fem dat pl   id.

οἰκίαν   noun fem acc sg   id.

οἰκίας   noun fem gen sg and acc pl   id.

οἰκίδιον   noun neut nom and acc sg

οἰκιδίων   noun neut gen pl . . . . οἰκίδιον

οἰκισθησεται   vb fut pass ind 3rd pers sg . . . . οἰκίζω

οἰκιῶν   noun fem gen pl . . . . οἰκία

οἰκογενεῖς   adj masc and fem nom and acc pl . . . . οἰκογενής

οἰκογενέσι   adj dat pl   id.

οἰκογενής   adj masc and fem nom sg   id.

οἰκογενοῦς   adj masc and fem gen sg   id.

οἰκοδομεῖ   vb pres act ind 3rd pers sg . . . . οἰκοδομέω

οἰκοδομεῖν   vb pres act inf   id.

οἰκοδομεῖς   vb pres act ind 2nd pers sg   id.

οἰκοδομεῖσθαι   vb pres m/p inf   id.

οἰκοδομεῖται   vb pres m/p ind 3rd pers sg   id.

οἰκοδομεῖτε   vb pres act ind 2nd pers pl   id.

οἰκοδομείτω vb pres act impv 3rd pers sg	.....	οἰκοδομέω
οἰκοδομείτωσαν vb pres act impv 3rd pers pl		id.
οἰκοδομή noun fem nom sg		
οἰκοδομῇ noun fem dat sg	....	οἰκοδομή
οἰκοδομηθῇ vb 1st aor pass subj 3rd pers sg	...	οἰκοδομέω
οἰκοδομηθῆναι vb 1st aor pass inf		id.
οἰκοδομηθῆς vb 1st aor pass subj 2nd pers sg		id.
οἰκοδομηθήσεσθε vb fut pass ind 2nd pers pl		id.
οἰκοδομηθήσεται vb fut pass ind 3rd pers sg		id.
οἰκοδομηθήσῃ vb fut pass ind 2nd pers sg		id.
οἰκοδομηθήσονται vb fut pass ind 3rd pers pl		id.
οἰκοδομηθήτω vb 1st aor pass impv 3rd pers sg		id.
οἰκοδομήν noun fem acc sg	....	οἰκοδομή
οἰκοδομῆς noun fem gen sg		id.
οἰκοδομῆσαι vb 1st aor act inf	....	οἰκοδομέω
οἰκοδομήσαντες vb 1st aor act part masc nom pl		id.
οἰκοδομήσας vb 1st aor act part masc nom sg		id.
οἰκοδομήσατε vb 1st aor act impv 2nd pers pl		id.
οἰκοδομησάτω vb 1st aor act impv 3rd pers sg		id.
οἰκοδομήσει vb fut act ind 3rd pers sg		id.
οἰκοδομήσεις vb fut act ind 2nd pers sg		id.
οἰκοδομήσετε vb fut act ind 2nd pers pl		id.
οἰκοδομήσῃ vb 1st aor act subj 3rd pers sg,		
fut mid ind 2nd pers sg		id.
οἰκοδομήσῃς vb 1st aor act subj 2nd pers sg		id.
οἰκοδομήσητε vb 1st aor act subj 2nd pers pl		id.
οἰκοδομήσομεν vb fut act ind 1st pers pl		id.
οἰκοδόμησον vb 1st aor act impv 2nd pers sg		id.
οἰκοδομήσουσιν vb fut act ind 3rd pers pl		id.
οἰκοδομήσω vb fut act ind 1st pers sg		id.
οἰκοδομήσωμεν vb 1st aor act subj 1st pers pl		id.
οἰκοδομήσωσιν vb 1st aor act subj 3rd pers pl		id.
οἰκοδόμοι noun masc nom pl	....	οἰκοδόμος
οἰκοδόμοις noun masc dat pl		id.
οἰκοδόμος noun masc nom sg		id.
οἰκοδομοῦμεν vb pres act ind 1st pers pl	......	οἰκοδομέω
οἰκοδομουμένη vb pres m/p part fem nom sg		id.
οἰκοδομούμενον vb pres m/p part masc acc sg,		
neut nom and acc sg		id.
οἰκοδομούμενος vb pres m/p part masc nom sg		id.
οἰκοδομοῦντας vb pres act part masc acc pl		id.
οἰκοδομοῦντες vb pres act part masc nom pl		id.
οἰκοδομούντων vb pres act part masc and neut gen pl		id.
οἰκοδόμους noun masc acc pl	....	οἰκοδόμος
οἰκοδομοῦσι(ν) pres act ind 3rd pers pl,		
vb pres act part masc and neut dat pl	...	οἰκοδομέω
οἰκοδομῶ vb pres act ind 1st pers sg		id.
οἰκοδόμων noun masc gen pl	....	οἰκοδόμος
οἰκοδομῶν vb pres act part masc nom sg	......	οἰκοδομέω
οἶκοι noun masc nom pl	....	οἶκος
οἴκοις noun masc dat pl		id.
οἶκον noun masc acc sg		id.

οἰκονομήσει vb fut act ind 3rd pers sg	....	οἰκονομέω
οἰκονομήσων vb fut act part masc nom sg		id.
οἰκονομίαν noun fem acc sg	....	οἰκονομία
οἰκονομίας noun fem gen sg		id.
οἰκονόμοι noun masc nom pl	....	οἰκονόμος
οἰκονόμοις noun masc dat pl		id.
οἰκονόμον noun masc acc sg		id.
οἰκονόμος noun masc nom sg		id.
οἰκονόμου noun masc gen sg		id.
οἰκονομουμένων vb pres m/p part gen pl	.....	οἰκονομέω
οἰκονόμους noun masc acc pl	....	οἰκονόμος
οἰκόπεδα noun neut nom and acc pl	....	οἰκόπεδον
οἰκοπέδῳ noun neut dat sg		id.
οἰκοπέδων noun neut gen pl		id.
οἶκος noun masc nom sg		
Οἶκος pr noun masc nom sg	....	οἶκος
οἴκου noun masc gen sg		id.
οἴκου see οἴκου		
οἰκοῦμεν vb pres act ind 1st pers pl	....	οἰκέω
οἰκούμενα vb pres m/p part neut nom and acc pl		id.
οἰκουμένη vb pres m/p part fem nom sg		id.
οἰκουμένῃ vb pres m/p part fem dat sg		id.
οἰκουμένην vb pres m/p part fem acc sg		id.
οἰκουμένης vb pres m/p part fem gen sg		id.
οἰκοῦντας vb pres act part masc acc pl		id.
οἰκοῦντες vb pres act part masc nom pl		id.
οἰκοῦντι vb pres act part masc and neut dat sg		id.
οἰκοῦντος vb pres act part masc and neut gen sg		id.
οἰκούντων vb pres act part masc and neut gen pl		id.
οἴκους noun masc acc pl	....	οἶκος
οἰκούσαις vb pres act part fem dat pl	....	οἰκέω
οἰκοῦσι(ν) vb pres act ind 3rd pers pl,		
pres act part masc and neut dat pl		id.
οἰκτῖραι vb 1st aor act inf	....	οἰκτείρω
οἰκτίρει vb pres act ind 3rd pers sg		id.
οἰκτίρημα noun neut nom and acc sg		
οἰκτιρήσαι vb 1st aor act opt 3rd pers sg	....	οἰκτείρω
οἰκτιρῆσαι vb 1st aor act inf		id.
οἰκτίρησας vb 1st aor act ind 2nd pers sg		id.
οἰκτιρήσει vb fut act ind 3rd pers sg		id.
οἰκτιρήσεις vb fut act ind 2nd pers sg		id.
οἰκτίρησεν vb 1st aor act ind 3rd pers sg		id.
οἰκτιρήσῃ vb 1st aor act subj 3rd pers sg		id.
οἰκτιρήσῃς vb 1st aor act subj 2nd pers sg		id.
οἰκτίρησον vb 1st aor act impv 2nd pers sg		id.
οἰκτιρήσουσιν vb fut act ind 3rd pers pl		id.
οἰκτιρήσω vb fut act ind 1st pers sg		id.
οἰκτιρμοί noun masc nom pl	....	οἰκτιρμός
οἰκτιρμοῖς noun masc dat pl		id.
οἰκτιρμόν noun masc acc sg		id.
οἰκτιρμόνων adj gen pl	....	οἰκτίρμων
οἰκτιρμός noun masc nom sg		

οἰκτιρμοῦ noun masc gen sg	. . . .	οἰκτιρμός
οἰκτιρμούς noun masc acc pl		id.
οἰκτιρμῷ noun masc dat sg		id.
οἰκτίρμων adj masc and fem nom sg		
οἰκτιρμῶν noun masc gen pl	. . . .	οἰκτιρμός
οἰκτίρομαι vb pres m/p ind 1st pers sg	. . . .	οἰκτείρω
οἰκτίρουσιν vb pres act ind 3rd pers pl		id.
οἰκτίρω vb pres act subj 1st pers sg		id.
οἰκτίρων vb pres act part masc nom sg		id.
οἰκτίστῳ superl adj masc and neut dat sg	. . . .	οἰκτρός
οἶκτον noun masc acc sg	. . . .	οἶκτος
οἴκτου noun masc gen sg		id.
οἰκτρά adj fem nom sg	. . . .	οἰκτρός
οἰκτρόν adj masc acc sg, neut nom and acc sg		id.
οἰκτροτάτην superl adj fem acc sg		id.
οἰκῶ vb pres act ind 1st pers sg	. . . .	οἰκέω
οἴκῳ noun masc dat sg	. . . .	οἶκος
οἴκων noun masc gen pl		id.
οἰκῶν vb pres act part masc nom sg	. . . .	οἰκέω
οἶμαι vb pres dep ind 1st pers sg	. . . .	οἴομαι
οἴμμοι interjection		
οἰμωγήν noun fem acc sg	. . . .	οἰμωγή
οἰμώξεις vb fut act ind 2nd pers sg	. . . .	οἰμώζω
οἴνοις noun masc dat pl	. . . .	οἶνος
οἶνον noun masc acc sg		id.
οἰνοπότει vb pres act impv 2nd pers sg	. . . . .	οἰνοποτέω
οἰνοπότης noun neut nom and acc sg		
οἶνος noun masc nom sg		
οἴνου noun masc gen sg	. . . .	οἶνος
οἴνους noun masc acc pl		id.
οἰνοφλυγεῖ vb pres act ind 3rd pers sg	. . . . .	οἰνοφλυγέω
οἰνοχόας adj fem acc pl	. . . .	οἰνοχόος
οἰνοχοῆσαι vb 1st aor act inf	. . . .	οἰνοχοέω
οἰνοχόον noun masc acc sg	. . . .	οἰνοχόος
οἰνοχόος noun masc nom sg		id.
οἰνοχόους noun masc acc pl		id.
οἰνοχοῶν noun masc gen pl		id.
οἴνῳ noun masc dat sg	. . . .	οἶνος
οἴνων noun masc gen pl		id.
οἰόμενοι vb pres dep part masc nom pl	. . . .	οἴομαι
οἰόμενος vb pres dep part masc nom sg		id.
οἶον adj masc acc sg, neut nom and acc sg	. . . .	οἶος
οἶος adj masc nom sg		id.
οἷς rel pron masc and neut dat pl	. . . .	ὅς
οἴσει vb fut act ind 3rd pers sg	. . . .	φέρω
οἴσεις vb fut act ind 2nd pers sg		id.
οἴσετε vb fut act ind 2nd pers pl		id.
οἶσθα vb perf act ind 2nd pers sg	. . . .	οἶδα
οἴσομεν vb fut act ind 1st pers pl	. . . .	φέρω
οἴσουσιν vb fut act ind 3rd pers pl		id.
οἰστρηλασίαν noun fem acc sg	. . . .	οἰστρηλασία
οἶστρον noun masc acc sg	. . . .	οἶστρος

οἴστρων noun masc gen pl	. . . .	οἶστρος
οἴσω vb fut act ind 1st pers sg	. . . .	φέρω
οἵτινες rel pron masc nom pl	. . . .	ὅστις
οιφι translit		
οἰχήσεται vb fut mid ind 3rd pers sg	. . . .	οἴχομαι
οἰωνιεῖσθε vb fut mid ind 2nd pers pl	. . . . .	οἰωνίζομαι
οἰωνιεῖται vb fut mid ind 3rd pers sg		id.
οἰωνίζεται vb pres dep ind 3rd pers sg		id.
οἰωνίζετο vb impf dep ind 3rd pers sg		id.
οἰωνιζόμενος vb pres dep part masc nom sg		id.
οἰωνίζοντο vb impf dep ind 3rd pers pl		id.
οἰωνισάμην vb 1st aor mid ind 1st pers sg		id.
οἰωνίσαντο vb 1st aor mid ind 3rd pers pl		id.
οἰώνισμα noun neut nom and acc sg		
οἰωνίσματα noun neut nom and acc pl	. . . .	οἰώνισμα
οἰωνισμάτων noun neut gen pl		id.
οἰωνισμοί noun masc nom pl	. . . .	οἰωνισμός
οἰωνισμός noun masc nom sg		id.
οἰωνισμῷ noun masc dat sg		id.
οἰωνοβρώτους adj masc acc pl	. . . .	οἰωνόβρωτος
οἰωνοῖς noun masc dat pl	. . . .	οἰωνός
Οκινα pr noun		
ὀκλακώς vb perf act part masc nom sg	. . . .	ὀκλάζω
ὄκνει vb pres act impv 2nd pers sg	. . . .	ὀκνέω
ὀκνεῖτε vb pres act impv 2nd pers pl		id.
ὀκνηρά adj neut nom and acc pl	. . . .	ὀκνηρός
ὀκνηρέ adj masc voc sg		id.
ὀκνηρίαις noun fem dat pl	. . . .	ὀκνηρία
ὀκνηροί adj masc nom pl	. . . .	ὀκνηρός
ὀκνηρόν adj masc acc sg, neut nom and acc sg		id.
ὀκνηρός adj masc nom sg		id.
ὀκνηροῦ adj masc and neut gen sg		id.
ὀκνηρούς adj masc acc pl		id.
ὀκνησάτω vb 1st aor act impv 3rd pers sg	. . . .	ὀκνέω
ὀκνήσῃς vb 1st aor act subj 2nd pers sg		id.
ὀκνήσητε vb 1st aor act subj 2nd pers pl		id.
ὀκτακισχίλια adj neut nom and acc pl	. . . .	ὀκτακισχίλιοι
ὀκτακισχιλία adj fem nom sg	. . . .	ὀκτακισχιλίος
ὀκτακισχίλιοι adj masc nom pl		
ὀκτακισχιλίους adj masc acc pl	. . . .	ὀκτακισχίλιοι
ὀκτακόσια adj neut nom and acc pl	. . . .	ὀκτακόσιοι
ὀκτακόσιαι adj fem nom pl		id.
ὀκτακοσίαις adj fem dat pl		id.
ὀκτακόσιοι adj masc nom pl		id.
ὀκτακοσίους adj masc acc pl		id.
ὀκταπήχεσι adj dat pl	. . . .	ὀκτάπηχυς
ὀκτώ indecl number		
ὀκτωκαίδεκα indecl number		
ὀκτωκαιδεκάτη adj fem dat sg	. . . .	ὀκτωκαιδέκατος
ὀκτωκαιδέκατος adj masc nom sg		id.
ὀκτωκαιδεκάτου adj masc and neut gen sg		id.
ὀκτωκαιδεκάτῳ adj masc and neut dat sg		id.

ὄλβος noun masc nom sg

Ολδαν pr noun

ὀλεθρευθήσεται vb fut pass ind 3rd pers sg . . . . ὀλεθρεύω

ὀλεθρεύοντα vb pres act part masc acc sg id.

ὀλεθρεῦσαι vb 1st aor act inf id.

ὀλεθρεύσει vb fut act ind 3rd pers sg id.

ὀλεθρεύσεις vb fut act ind 2nd pers sg id.

ὀλεθρεύσητε vb 1st aor act subj 2nd pers pl id.

ὀλεθρεύσουσιν vb fut act ind 3rd pers pl id.

ὀλεθρεύσω vb fut act ind 1st pers sg id.

ὀλεθρεύων vb pres act part masc nom sg id.

ὀλεθρίαν noun fem acc sg . . . . ὀλεθρία

ὀλεθρίας adj fem gen sg . . . . ὀλέθριος

ὀλεθρίας noun fem gen sg . . . . ὀλεθρία

ὀλέθριον adj masc acc sg, neut nom and acc sg . . . ὀλέθριος

ὄλεθρον noun masc acc sg . . . . ὄλεθρος

ὄλεθρος noun masc nom sg id.

ὀλέθρου noun masc gen sg id.

ὀλεθροφόρον adj masc and fem acc sg . . . . . ὀλεθροφόρος

ὀλέθρῳ noun masc dat sg . . . . ὄλεθρος

ὀλεῖ vb fut act ind 3rd pers sg . . . . ὄλλυμι

ὀλεῖται vb fut mid ind 3rd pers sg id.

ὀλέκει vb pres act ind 3rd pers sg . . . . ὀλέκω

ὀλέκεις vb pres act ind 2nd pers sg id.

ὀλέκομαι vb pres m/p ind 1st pers sg id.

ὀλέσαισαν vb 1st aor act opt 3rd pers pl . . . . ὄλλυμι

ὀλέσητε vb 1st aor act subj 2nd pers pl id.

ὅλη adj fem nom sg . . . . ὅλος

ὅλῃ adj fem dat sg id.

ὅλην adj fem acc sg id.

ὅλης adj fem gen sg id.

ὀλίγα adj neut nom and acc pl . . . . ὀλίγος

ὀλίγαι adj fem nom pl id.

ὀλίγας adj fem acc pl id.

ὀλίγη adj fem nom sg id.

ὀλιγόβιος adj masc and fem nom sg

ὀλίγοι adj masc nom pl . . . . ὀλίγος

ὀλίγοις adj masc and neut dat pl id.

ὀλίγον adj masc acc sg, neut nom and acc sg id.

ὀλίγος adj masc nom sg id.

ὀλιγοστοί adj masc and fem nom pl . . . . ὀλιγοστός

ὀλιγοστόν adj acc sg, neut nom sg id.

ὀλιγοστός adj masc and fem nom sg id.

ὀλιγοστούς adj masc and fem acc pl id.

ὀλιγοστῷ adj dat sg id.

ὀλιγότητα noun fem acc sg . . . . ὀλιγότης

ὀλίγου adj masc and neut gen sg . . . . ὀλίγος

ὀλίγους adj masc acc pl id.

ὀλιγοχρόνιος adj masc and fem nom sg

ὀλιγοψυχήσῃς vb 1st aor act subj 2nd pers sg . ὀλιγοψυχέω

ὀλιγοψυχίαν noun fem acc sg . . . . ὀλιγοψυχία

ὀλιγοψυχίας noun fem gen sg id.

ὀλιγόψυχοι adj masc and fem nom pl . . . . ὀλιγόψυχος

ὀλιγοψύχοις adj dat pl id.

ὀλιγόψυχον adj acc sg, neut nom sg id.

ὀλιγόψυχος adj masc and fem nom sg id.

ὀλιγοψυχοῦντες vb pres act part

    masc nom pl . . . . ὀλιγοψυχέω

ὀλίγῳ adj masc and neut dat sg . . . . ὀλίγος

ὀλιγωθήσεται vb fut pass ind 3rd pers sg . . . . ὀλιγόω

ὀλιγωθήτω vb 1st aor pass impv 3rd pers sg id.

ὀλίγων adj gen pl . . . . ὀλίγος

ὀλιγώρει vb pres act impv 2nd pers sg . . . . ὀλιγωρέω

ὀλιγωρήσει vb fut act ind 3rd pers sg . . . . ὀλιγωρέω

ὀλιγώσεις vb fut act ind 2nd pers sg . . . . ὀλιγόω

ὀλιγώσῃς vb 1st aor act subj 2nd pers sg

ὀλισθάνειν vb pres act inf . . . . ὀλισθάνω

ὀλισθάνων vb pres act part masc nom sg id.

ὀλίσθημα noun neut nom and acc sg

ὀλισθήμασι noun neut dat pl . . . . ὀλίσθημα

ὀλισθήματος noun neut gen sg id.

ὀλίσθης vb 1st aor act subj 2nd pers sg . . . . ὀλισθάνω

ὀλισθήσουσιν vb fut act ind 3rd pers pl id.

ὀλισθρήμασι noun neut dat pl . . . . ὀλίσθρημα

ὁλκεῖα noun neut nom and acc pl . . . . ὁλκεῖον

ὁλκή noun fem nom sg

ὁλκήν noun fem acc sg . . . . ὁλκή

ὁλκῆς noun fem gen sg id.

ὀλλύντα vb pres act part masc acc sg . . . . ὄλλυμι

ὄλλυνται vb pres m/p ind 3rd pers pl id.

ὄλλυται vb pres m/p ind 3rd pers sg id.

ὅλοις adj masc and neut dat pl . . . . ὅλος

ὁλοκαρπούμενον vb pres dep part masc acc sg,

    neut nom and acc sg . . . . ὁλοκαρπόομαι

ὁλοκαρπωθήσονται vb fut pass ind 3rd pers pl id.

ὁλοκάρπωμα noun neut nom and acc sg

ὁλοκαρπώσεις noun fem nom and acc pl . . . . ὁλοκάρπωσις

ὁλοκαρπώσεως noun fem gen sg id.

ὁλοκάρπωσιν noun fem acc sg id.

ὁλόκαυτος adj masc and fem nom sg

ὁλοκαύτωμα noun neut nom and acc sg

ὁλοκαυτώμασι noun neut dat pl . . . . ὁλοκαύτωμα

ὁλοκαυτώματα noun neut nom and acc pl id.

ὁλοκαυτώματος noun neut gen sg id.

ὁλοκαυτωμάτων noun neut gen pl id.

ὁλοκαυτώσεις noun fem nom and acc pl . . . . ὁλοκαύτωσις

ὁλοκαυτώσεως noun fem gen sg id.

ὁλοκαύτωσιν noun fem acc sg id.

ὁλοκαύτωσις noun fem nom sg id.

ὁλόκληρον adj acc sg, neut nom sg . . . . ὁλόκληρος

ὁλόκληρος adj masc and fem nom sg id.

ὁλοκλήρου adj gen sg id.

ὁλοκλήρους adj masc and fem acc pl id.

ὁλοκλήρων adj gen pl id.

ὀλολυγμός noun masc nom sg
ὀλολύζετε vb pres act impv 2nd pers pl . . . . ὀλολύζω
ὀλολύξατε vb 1st aor act impv 2nd pers pl   id.
ὀλολύξάτω vb 1st aor act impv 3rd pers sg   id.
ὀλολύξει vb fut act ind 3rd pers sg   id.
ὀλολύξετε vb fut act ind 2nd pers pl   id.
ὀλόλυξον vb 1st aor act impv 2nd pers sg   id.
ὀλολύξουσιν vb fut act ind 3rd pers pl   id.
ὅλον adj masc acc sg, neut nom and acc sg . . . . ὅλος
ὁλοπόρφυρον adj acc sg, neut nom sg . . . . . . ὁλοπόρφυρος
ὁλορριζεί adverb
ὁλόρριζοι adj masc and fem nom pl . . . . ὁλόρριζος
ὅλος adj masc nom sg
ὁλοσφύρητον adj acc sg, neut nom sg . . . . . . ὁλοσφυρητος
ὁλοσχερῆ adj masc and fem acc sg . . . . ὁλοσχερής
ὁλοσχερῶς adverb
ὅλου adj masc and neut gen sg . . . . ὅλος
ὀλοῦνται vb fut mid ind 3rd pers pl . . . . ὄλλυμι
Ολοφερνη pr noun masc voc sg . . . . Ολοφερνης
Ολοφερνη pr noun masc dat sg   id.
Ολοφερνην pr noun masc acc sg   id.
Ολοφερνης pr noun masc nom sg   id.
Ολοφερνου pr noun masc gen sg   id.
ὀλοφυρομένων vb pres dep part gen pl . . . . . . ὀλοφύρομαι
Ὀλυμπιου pr noun masc gen sg . . . . Ὀλυμπιος
ὀλύνθους noun masc acc pl . . . . ὄλυνθος
ὀλύρα noun fem nom sg
ὄλυραν see ὀλύραν
ὀλύραν noun fem acc sg . . . . ὀλύρα
ὀλυρίτης noun masc nom sg
ὅλῳ adj masc and neut dat sg . . . . ὅλος
ὀλωλότων vb perf act part masc and neut gen pl . . . . ὄλλυμι
ὅλων adj gen pl . . . . ὅλος
ὁμαλίσῃ vb 1st aor act subj 3rd pers sg . . . . ὁμαλίζω
ὁμαλισμόν noun masc acc sg . . . . ὁμαλισμός
ὁμαλιῶ vb fut act ind 1st pers sg . . . . ὁμαλίζω
Ομαχαθι pr noun
ὀμβρήματα noun neut nom and acc pl . . . . ὄμβρημα
ὄμβροις noun masc dat pl . . . . ὄμβρος
ὄμβρος noun masc nom sg   id.
ὄμβρῳ noun masc dat sg   id.
ὀμείρονται vb pres dep ind 3rd pers pl . . . . ὀμείρομαι
ὀμεῖσθε vb fut mid ind 2nd pers pl . . . . ὄμνυμι
ὀμεῖται vb fut mid ind 3rd pers sg   id.
ὀμῇ vb fut mid ind 2nd pers sg   id.
ὄμηρα noun neut nom and acc pl . . . . ὄμηρος
ὁμίλει vb pres act impv 2nd pers sg . . . . ὁμιλέω
ὁμιλεῖτε vb pres act impv 2nd pers pl   id.
ὁμιλείτω vb pres act impv 3rd pers sg   id.
ὁμιλήσαντες vb 1st aor act part masc nom pl   id.
ὁμιλήσει vb fut act ind 3rd pers sg   id.
ὁμιλίᾳ noun fem dat sg . . . . ὁμιλία

ὁμιλίαν noun fem acc sg . . . . ὁμιλία
ὁμιλίας noun fem gen sg   id.
ὁμιλοῦντες vb pres act part masc acc pl . . . . ὁμιλέω
ὁμίχλη noun fem nom sg
ὁμίχλῃ noun fem dat sg . . . . ὁμίχλη
ὁμίχλην noun fem acc sg   id.
ὁμίχλης noun fem gen sg   id.
ὄμμα noun neut nom and acc sg
Ομμαιους pr noun masc acc pl . . . . Ομμαιος
ὄμμασι noun neut dat pl . . . . ὄμμα
ὄμματα noun neut nom and acc pl   id.
ὀμμάτων noun neut gen pl   id.
Ομμιν pr noun
Ομμωθ pr noun
ὀμνύει vb pres act ind 3rd pers sg . . . . ὄμνυμι
ὀμνύειν vb pres act inf   id.
ὀμνύετε vb pres act impv 2nd pers pl,
     pres act ind 2nd pers pl   id.
ὀμνυμένων vb pres m/p part gen pl   id.
ὀμνύοντας vb pres act part masc acc pl   id.
ὀμνύοντες vb pres act part masc nom pl   id.
ὀμνύοντος vb pres act part masc and neut gen sg   id.
ὀμνύουσαι vb pres act part fem nom pl   id.
ὀμνύουσιν vb pres act ind 3rd pers pl   id.
ὀμνύω vb pres act ind 1st pers sg   id.
ὀμνύων vb pres act part masc nom sg   id.
ὁμοεθνεῖς adj masc and fem nom and acc pl . . . . . ὁμοεθνής
ὁμοεθνῇ adj masc and fem acc sg   id.
ὁμοεθνῶν adj gen pl   id.
ὁμοζηλία noun fem nom sg
ὁμοθυμαδόν adverb
ὅμοια adj neut nom and acc pl . . . . ὅμοιος
ὁμοία adj fem nom sg   id.
ὁμοίᾳ adj fem dat sg   id.
ὅμοιαι adj fem nom pl   id.
ὁμοίαν adj fem acc sg   id.
ὅμοιοι adj masc nom pl   id.
ὅμοιον adj masc acc sg, neut nom and acc sg   id.
ὁμοιοπαθεῖς adj masc and fem nom and acc pl   ὁμοιοπαθής
ὁμοιοπαθῆ adj masc and fem acc sg   id.
ὅμοιος adj masc nom sg
ὁμοιότητα noun fem acc sg . . . . ὁμοιότης
ὁμοίῳ adj masc and neut dat sg . . . . ὅμοιος
ὁμοιωθήσεται vb fut pass ind 3rd pers sg . . . . ὁμοιόω
ὁμοιωθήσομαι vb fut pass ind 1st pers sg   id.
ὁμοιωθησόμεθα vb fut pass ind 1st pers pl   id.
ὁμοιωθήσονται vb fut pass ind 3rd pers pl   id.
ὁμοιώθητι vb 1st aor pass impv 2nd pers sg   id.
ὁμοιωθῶμεν vb 1st aor pass subj 1st pers pl   id.
ὁμοίωμα noun neut nom and acc sg
ὁμοιώματα noun neut nom and acc pl . . . . ὁμοίωμα
ὁμοιώματι noun neut dat sg   id.

ὁμοιώματος noun neut gen sg . . . . ὁμοίωμα

ὁμοίων adj gen pl . . . . ὅμοιος

ὁμοίως adverb

ὁμοιῶσαι vb 1st aor act inf . . . . ὁμοιόω

ὁμοιώσεως noun fem gen sg . . . . ὁμοίωσις

ὁμοίωσιν noun fem acc sg id.

ὁμοίωσις noun fem nom sg id.

ὁμοιώσω vb fut act ind 1st pers sg . . . . ὁμοιόω

ὁμολογεῖν vb pres act inf . . . . ὁμολογέω

ὁμολογῆσαι vb 1st aor act inf id.

ὁμολογήσαντες vb 1st aor act part masc nom pl id.

ὁμολόγησον vb 1st aor act impv 2nd pers sg . . . . ὁμολογέω

ὁμολογήσω vb fut act ind 1st pers sg . . . . ὁμολογέω

ὁμολογίαις noun fem dat pl . . . . ὁμολογία

ὁμολογίαν noun fem acc sg id.

ὁμολογίας noun fem gen sg and acc pl id.

ὁμολογουμένως adverb

ὁμολογοῦντες vb pres act part masc nom pl . . . . ὁμολογέω

ὁμολόγους adj masc acc pl . . . . ὁμόλογος

ὁμολογῶ vb pres act ind 1st pers sg . . . . ὁμολογέω

ὁμολόγως adverb

ὁμομήτριον adj masc acc sg,

        neut nom and acc sg . . . . ὁμομήτριος

ὁμόνοια noun fem nom sg

ὁμονοίᾳ noun fem dat sg . . . . ὁμόνοια

ὁμόνοιαν noun fem acc sg id.

ὁμονοοῦντας vb pres act part masc acc pl . . . . . . ὁμονοέω

ὁμονοοῦντες vb pres act part masc nom pl id.

ὁμονοούντων vb pres act part masc and neut gen pl id.

ὁμοπατρία adj fem nom sg . . . . ὁμοπάτριος

ὅμορα adj neut nom and acc pl . . . . ὅμορος

ὁμοροῦντας vb pres act part masc acc pl . . . . ὁμορέω

ὁμοροῦντες vb pres act part masc nom pl id.

ὁμόρους adj masc acc pl . . . . ὅμορος

ὁμορούσας vb pres act part fem acc pl . . . . ὁμορέω

ὀμόσαι vb 1st aor act inf . . . . ὄμνυμι

ὀμόσαντες vb 1st aor act part masc nom pl id.

ὀμόσατε vb 1st aor act impv 2nd pers pl id.

ὀμοσάτω vb 1st aor act impv 3rd pers sg id.

ὀμόσῃ vb 1st aor act subj 3rd pers sg id.

ὄμοσον vb 1st aor act impv 2nd pers sg id.

ὁμοσπόνδους adj masc and fem acc pl . . . . . . ὁμόσπονδος

ὀμόσω vb fut act ind 1st pers sg . . . . ὄμνυμι

ὁμοῦ adverb

ὀμοῦμαι vb fut mid ind 1st pers sg . . . . ὄμνυμι

ὀμοῦνται vb fut mid ind 3rd pers pl id.

Ομουσι pr noun

ὁμοφύλους adj masc and fem acc pl . . . . ὁμόφυλος

ὁμοψήφου adj gen sg . . . . ὁμόψηφος

ὁμόψυχον adj acc sg, neut nom sg . . . . ὁμόψυχος

ὄμφακα noun fem acc sg . . . . ὄμφαξ

ὀμφακίζουσα vb pres act part fem nom sg . . . . . . ὀμφακίζω

ὀμφαλόν noun masc acc sg . . . . ὀμφαλός

ὀμφαλός noun masc nom sg id.

ὀμφαλοῦ noun masc gen sg id.

ὄμφαξ noun fem nom sg

ὀμώμοκα vb perf act ind 1st pers sg . . . . ὄμνυμι

ὀμωμόκαμεν vb perf act ind 1st pers pl id.

ὀμώμοκεν vb perf act ind 3rd pers sg id.

ὅμως conjunction

ὅν rel pron masc acc sg . . . . ὅς

ὄν vb pres act part neut nom and acc sg . . . . εἰμί

ὄναγροι noun masc nom pl . . . . ὄναγρος

ὀνάγρων noun masc gen pl id.

ὀνείδει noun neut dat sg . . . . ὄνειδος

ὀνείδη noun neut nom and acc pl id.

ὀνειδιεῖ vb fut act ind 3rd pers sg . . . . ὀνειδίζω

ὀνείδιζε vb pres act impv 2nd pers sg id.

ὀνειδίζει vb pres act ind 3rd pers sg id.

ὀνειδίζειν vb pres act inf id.

ὀνειδιζόμενος vb pres m/p part masc nom sg id.

ὀνειδίζοντος vb pres act part masc and neut gen sg id.

ὀνειδιζόντων vb pres act part masc and neut gen pl id.

ὀνειδίζουσαν vb pres act part fem acc sg id.

ὀνειδίζουσι vb pres act ind 3rd pers pl id.

ὀνειδίζων vb pres act part masc nom sg id.

ὀνειδίσαι vb 1st aor act inf id.

ὀνειδίσας vb 1st aor act part masc nom sg id.

ὀνειδίσει vb fut act ind 3rd pers sg id.

ὀνειδίσῃ vb 1st aor act subj 3rd pers sg id.

ὀνειδισθῆναι vb 1st aor pass inf id.

ὀνειδισθήσονται vb fut pass ind 3rd pers pl id.

ὀνείδισμα noun neut nom and acc sg

ὀνειδισμοί noun masc nom pl . . . . ὀνειδισμός

ὀνειδισμόν noun masc acc sg id.

ὀνειδισμός noun masc nom sg id.

ὀνειδισμοῦ noun masc gen sg id.

ὀνειδισμούς noun masc acc pl id.

ὀνειδισμῷ noun masc dat sg id.

ὀνειδισμῶν noun masc gen pl id.

ὀνειδίσωσιν vb 1st aor act subj 3rd pers pl . . . . . . ὀνειδίζω

ὄνειδος noun neut nom and acc sg

ὀνείδους noun neut gen sg . . . . ὄνειδος

ὄνειροι noun masc nom pl . . . . ὄνειρος

ὄνειρον noun masc acc sg id.

ὀνείρῳ noun masc dat sg id.

ὀνείρων noun masc gen pl id.

ὀνήσεται vb fut mid ind 3rd pers sg . . . . ὀνίνημι

ὄνησιν noun fem acc sg . . . . ὄνησις

Ονια pr noun masc dat sg . . . . Ονιας

Ονιαν pr noun masc acc sg id.

Ονιας pr noun masc nom sg id.

Ονιου pr noun masc gen sg id.

Οννάμ pr noun

ὄνοι	noun masc or fem nom pl	ὄνος
ὄνοις	noun masc or fem dat pl	id.
ὀνοκένταυροι	noun masc nom pl	ὀνοκένταυρος
ὀνοκενταύροις	noun masc dat pl	id.
Ονομ	pr noun	
ὄνομα	noun neut nom and acc sg	
ὀνομάζει	vb pres act ind 3rd pers sg	ὀνομάζω
ὀνομάζετε	vb pres act impv 2nd pers pl	id.
ὀνομάζομεν	vb pres act ind 1st pers pl	id.
ὀνομαζομένην	vb pres m/p part fem acc sg	id.
ὀνομάζουσιν	vb pres act ind 3rd pers pl	id.
ὀνομάζων	vb pres act part masc nom sg	id.
ὀνομάσαι	vb 1st aor act inf	id.
ὀνομάσας	vb 1st aor act part masc nom sg	id.
ὀνομάσει	vb fut act ind 3rd pers sg	id.
ὀνομάσῃ	vb 1st aor act subj 3rd pers sg	id.
ὀνομασθῆναι	vb 1st aor pass inf	id.
ὀνομασθήσεται	vb fut pass ind 3rd pers sg	id.
ὀνόμασι	noun neut dat pl	ὄνομα
ὀνομασίᾳ	noun fem dat sg	ὀνομασία
ὀνομαστή	adj fem nom sg	ὀνομαστός
ὀνομαστοί	adj masc nom pl	id.
ὀνομαστόν	adj masc acc sg, neut nom and acc sg	id.
ὀνομαστός	adj masc nom sg	id.
ὀνομαστούς	adj masc acc pl	id.
ὀνομαστῶν	adj gen pl	id.
ὀνομάσω	vb fut act ind 1st pers sg	ὀνομάζω
ὀνόματα	noun neut nom and acc pl	ὄνομα
ὀνόματι	noun neut dat sg	id.
ὀνοματογραφία	noun fem nom sg	
ὀνοματογραφίαν	noun fem acc sg	ὀνοματογραφία
ὀνόματος	noun neut gen sg	ὄνομα
ὀνομάτων	noun neut gen pl	id.
ὄνον	noun masc or fem acc sg	ὄνος
ὄνος	noun masc or fem nom sg	id.
ὄνου	noun masc or fem gen sg	id.
ὄνους	noun masc or fem acc pl	id.
ὄντα	vb pres act part masc acc sg, neut nom and acc pl	εἰμί
ὄντας	vb pres act part masc acc pl	id.
ὄντες	vb pres act part masc nom pl	id.
ὄντι	vb pres act part masc and neut dat sg	id.
ὀντιναοῦν	rel pron masc acc sg	ὁστισοῦν
ὀντινοῦν	rel pron masc acc sg	id.
ὄντος	vb pres act part masc and neut gen sg	εἰμί
ὄντων	vb pres act part masc and neut gen pl	id.
ὄντως	adverb	
ὄνυξ	noun masc nom sg	
ὄνυξι	noun masc dat pl	ὄνυξ
ὄνυχα	noun masc acc sg	id.
ὄνυχας	noun masc acc pl	id.
ὄνυχες	noun masc nom pl	id.
ὄνυχι	noun masc dat sg	ὄνυξ
ὀνυχίζει	vb pres act ind 3rd pers sg	ὀνυχίζω
ὀνυχίζον	vb pres act part neut nom and acc sg	id.
ὀνυχιζόντων	vb pres act part masc and neut gen pl	id.
ὀνύχιον	noun neut nom and acc sg	
ὀνυχιστῆρας	noun masc acc pl	ὀνυχιστήρ
ὀνύχων	noun masc gen pl	ὄνυξ
ὄνῳ	noun masc or fem dat sg	ὄνος
ὄνων	noun masc or fem gen pl	id.
ὄξει	noun neut dat sg	ὄξος
ὀξεῖ	adj masc and neut dat sg	ὀξύς
ὀξεῖα	adj fem nom sg	id.
ὀξεῖαν	adj fem acc sg	id.
ὀξεῖς	adj masc nom and acc pl	id.
ὀξέσι	adj masc and neut dat pl	id.
ὀξέως	adverb	
ὄξος	noun neut nom and acc sg	
ὀξύ	adj neut nom and acc sg	ὀξύς
ὀξυγράφου	adj masc and neut gen sg	ὀξυγράφος
ὀξύθυμος	adj masc and fem nom sg	
ὀξύν	adj masc acc sg	ὀξύς
ὀξῦναι	vb 1st aor act inf	ὀξύνω
ὀξύνει	vb pres act ind 3rd pers sg	id.
ὀξυνεῖ	vb fut act ind 3rd pers sg	id.
ὀξυνθῇ	vb 1st aor pass subj 3rd pers sg	id.
ὀξύνου	vb pres m/p impv 2nd pers sg	id.
ὀξύς	adj masc nom sg	
ὀξύτεροι	comp adj masc nom pl	ὀξύς
ὀξύτητος	noun fem gen sg	ὀξύτης
Οολ	pr noun	
Οολα	pr noun	
Οολαν	pr noun fem acc sg	Οολα
Οολι	pr noun	
Οολιβα	pr noun	
Οολιβαν	pr noun fem acc sg	Οολιβα
ὀπαῖς	noun fem dat pl	ὀπή
ὀπάς	noun fem acc pl	id.
ὅπερ	rel pron neut nom and acc sg	ὅσπερ
ὀπήν	noun fem acc sg	ὀπή
ὀπηνίκα	adverb	
ὀπῆς	noun fem gen sg	ὀπή
ὀπήτιον	noun neut nom and acc sg	
ὀπητίῳ	noun neut dat sg	ὀπήτιον
ὄπισθε	see ὄπισθεν	
ὄπισθεν	adverb and preposition	
ὀπίσθια	adj neut nom and acc pl	ὀπίσθιος
ὀπισθίου	adj masc and neut gen sg	id.
ὀπισθίῳ	adj masc and neut dat sg	id.
ὀπισθίων	adj gen pl	id.
ὀπισθίως	adverb	
ὀπισθότονος	adj masc and fem nom sg	
ὀπισθοφανές	adj neut nom and acc sg	ὀπισθοφανής

ὀπισθοφανῶς adverb

ὀπίσω adverb and preposition

ὅπλα noun neut nom and acc pl . . . . ὅπλον

ὁπλαῖς noun fem dat pl . . . . ὁπλή

ὁπλάς noun fem acc pl id.

ὁπλήν noun fem acc sg id.

ὁπλῆς noun fem gen sg id.

ὁπλίτης noun masc nom sg

ὁπλοδότησεν vb 1st aor act ind 3rd pers sg . . . . ὁπλοδοτέω

ὁπλοθήκας noun fem acc pl . . . . ὁπλοθήκη

ὅπλοις noun neut dat pl . . . . ὅπλον

ὁπλολογήσαντες vb 1st aor act part

masc nom pl . . . . ὁπλολογέω

ὁπλομάχοι noun masc nom pl . . . . ὁπλομάχος

ὁπλομάχῳ noun masc dat sg id.

ὅπλον noun neut nom and acc sg

ὁπλοποιήσει vb fut act ind 3rd pers sg . . . . ὁπλοποιέω

ὅπλου noun neut gen sg . . . . ὅπλον

ὁπλοφόρων adj gen pl . . . . ὁπλοφόρος

ὅπλῳ noun neut dat sg . . . . ὅπλον

ὅπλων noun neut gen pl id.

ὁπλῶν noun fem gen pl . . . . ὁπλή

ὁποίας adj fem gen sg . . . . ὁποῖος

ὁπόταν conjunction

ὁπότε adverb

ὅπου adverb and particle

ὀπτά adj neut nom and acc pl . . . . ὀπτός

ὀπτάζῃ vb pres dep ind 2nd pers sg . . . . ὀπτάζομαι

ὀπτασίᾳ noun fem dat sg . . . . ὀπτασία

ὀπτασίαν noun fem acc sg id.

ὀπτασίας noun fem gen sg id.

ὀπτῆσαι vb 1st aor act inf . . . . ὀπτάω

ὀπτήσαντες vb 1st aor act part masc nom pl id.

ὀπτήσας vb 1st aor act part masc nom sg id.

ὀπτήσεις vb fut act ind 2nd pers sg id.

ὀπτήσωμεν vb 1st aor act subj 1st pers pl id.

ὀπῶν noun fem gen pl . . . . ὀπή

ὀπώραν noun fem acc sg . . . . ὀπώρα

ὀπωροφυλάκιον noun neut nom and acc sg

ὅπως conjunction

ὅρα vb pres act impv 2nd pers sg . . . . ὁράω

ὁρᾷ vb pres act ind 3rd pers sg id.

ὁραθῇ vb 1st aor pass subj 3rd pers sg id.

ὁραθῆναι vb 1st aor pass inf id.

ὁραθήσεται vb fut pass ind 3rd pers sg id.

ὅραμα noun neut nom and acc sg

ὁράμασι noun neut dat pl . . . . ὅραμα

ὁράματα noun neut nom and acc pl id.

ὁράματι noun neut dat sg id.

ὁράματος noun neut gen sg id.

ὁραμάτων noun neut gen pl id.

ὁρᾶν vb pres act inf . . . . ὁράω

ὁρᾶς see ὁρᾷς

ὁρᾷς vb pres act ind 2nd pers sg . . . . ὁράω

ὁράσει noun fem dat sg . . . . ὅρασις

ὁράσεις noun fem nom and acc pl id.

ὁράσεσιν noun fem dat pl id.

ὁράσεως noun fem gen sg id.

ὅρασιν noun fem acc sg id.

ὅρασις noun fem nom sg id.

ὁρᾶτε vb pres act ind 2nd pers pl,

pres act impv 2nd pers pl . . . . ὁράω

ὁρατῆς noun masc nom sg

ὁρατικόν adj masc acc sg, neut nom and acc sg . . ὁρατικός

ὁρατοί adj masc nom pl . . . . ὁρατός

ὁρατόν adj masc acc sg, neut nom and acc sg id.

ὀργαί noun fem nom pl . . . . ὀργή

ὀργαῖς noun fem dat pl id.

ὄργανα noun neut nom and acc pl . . . . ὄργανον

ὀργανικῶν adj gen pl . . . . ὀργανικός

ὀργάνοις noun neut dat pl . . . . ὄργανον

ὄργανον noun neut nom and acc sg id.

ὀργάνου noun neut gen sg id.

ὀργάνῳ noun neut dat sg id.

ὀργάνων noun neut gen pl id.

ὀργάς noun fem acc pl . . . . ὀργή

ὀργή noun fem nom sg id.

ὀργῇ noun fem dat sg id.

ὀργήν noun fem acc sg id.

ὀργῆς noun fem gen sg id.

ὀργίζεσθε vb pres m/p impv 2nd pers pl . . . . ὀργίζω

ὀργιζέσθωσαν vb pres m/p impv 3rd pers pl id.

ὀργίζῃ vb pres m/p ind 2nd pers sg id.

ὀργίζομαι vb pres m/p ind 1st pers sg id.

ὀργιζόμενος vb pres m/p part masc nom sg id.

ὀργίζου vb pres m/p impv 2nd pers sg id.

ὀργίλος adj masc nom sg

ὀργίλου adj gen sg . . . . ὀργίλος

ὀργίλῳ adj masc and neut dat sg id.

ὀργίλων adj gen pl id.

ὀργίλως adverb

ὀργισθείς vb 1st aor pass part masc nom sg . . . . ὀργίζω

ὀργισθῇ vb 1st aor pass subj 3rd pers sg id.

ὀργισθῆναι vb 1st aor pass inf id.

ὀργισθῇς vb 1st aor pass subj 2nd pers sg id.

ὀργισθήσεται vb fut pass ind 3rd pers sg id.

ὀργισθήσῃ vb fut pass ind 2nd pers sg id.

ὀργισθήσομαι vb fut pass ind 1st pers sg id.

ὀργισθήτω vb 1st aor pass impv 3rd pers sg id.

ὄρει noun neut dat sg . . . . ὄρος

ὀρεινή noun fem nom sg

ὀρεινῇ noun fem dat sg . . . . ὀρεινή

ὀρεινήν noun fem acc sg id.

ὀρεινῆς noun fem gen sg id.

ὀρεινόν   adj masc acc sg, neut nom and acc sg ..... ὀρεινός
ὀρέξεων   noun fem gen pl .... ὄρεξις
ὀρέξεως   noun fem gen sg .... id.
ὄρεξιν   noun fem acc sg .... id.
ὄρεξις   noun fem nom sg .... id.
ὄρεσι   noun neut dat pl .... ὄρος
Ορεχ   pr noun
ὀρέων   noun neut gen pl .... ὄρος
Ορη   pr noun
ὄρη   noun neut nom and acc pl .... ὄρος
ὀρθά   adj neut nom and acc pl .... ὀρθός
ὀρθαί   adj fem nom pl .... id.
ὀρθαῖς   adj fem dat pl .... id.
ὀρθάς   adj fem acc pl .... id.
ὀρθή   adj fem nom sg .... id.
ὀρθῇ   adj fem dat sg .... id.
ὄρθιον   adj masc acc sg, neut nom and acc sg .... ὄρθιος
ὀρθοί   adj masc nom pl .... ὀρθός
ὀρθόν   adj masc acc sg, neut nom and acc sg   ic.
ὀρθός   adj masc nom sg   ic.
ὀρθοτομεῖ   vb pres act ind 3rd pers sg .... ὀρθοτομέω
ὀρθοτομῇ   vb pres act subj 3rd pers sg   ic.
ὀρθοῦ   adj masc and neut gen sg .... ὀρθός
ὀρθούς   adj masc acc pl .... id.
ὀρθριεῖς   vb fut act ind 2nd pers sg .... ὀρθρίζω
ὀρθριεῖτε   vb fut act ind 2nd pers pl   id.
ὄρθριζε   vb pres act impv 2nd pers sg   id.
ὀρθρίζει   vb pres act ind 3rd pers sg   id.
ὀρθρίζειν   vb pres act inf   id.
ὀρθρίζοντες   vb pres act part masc nom pl   id.
ὀρθρίζουσιν   vb pres act ind 3rd pers pl   id.
ὀρθρίζω   vb pres act ind 1st pers sg   id.
ὀρθρίζων   vb pres act part masc nom sg   id.
ὀρθρινή   adj fem nom sg .... ὀρθρινός
ὀρθρινῶν   adj gen pl   id.
ὄρθριος   adj masc nom sg
ὀρθριοῦσι   vb fut act ind 3rd pers pl .... ὀρθρίζω
ὀρθρίσαι   vb 1st aor act inf   id.
ὀρθρίσαντες   vb 1st aor act part masc nom pl   id.
ὀρθρίσας   vb 1st aor act part masc nom sg   id.
ὀρθρίσατε   vb 1st aor act impv 2nd pers pl   id.
ὀρθρίσεις   vb fut act ind 2nd pers sg   id.
ὄρθρισον   vb 1st aor act impv 2nd pers sg   id.
ὀρθρίσωμεν   vb 1st aor act subj 1st pers pl   id.
ὄρθροις   noun masc dat pl .... ὄρθρος
ὄρθρον   noun masc acc sg   id.
ὄρθρος   noun masc nom sg   id.
ὄρθρου   noun masc gen sg   id.
ὀρθωθῇ   vb 1st aor pass subj 3rd pers sg .... ὀρθόω
ὀρθωθήσεται   vb fut pass ind 3rd pers sg   id.
ὀρθῶν   adj gen pl .... ὀρθός
ὀρθῶς   adverb

ὀρθώσει   vb fut act ind 3rd pers sg .... ὀρθόω
Ὀρθωσιαν   pr noun fem acc sg .... Ὀρθωσία
ὅρια   noun neut nom and acc pl .... ὅριον
ὁριεῖ   vb fut act ind 3rd pers sg .... ὁρίζω
ὁρίζει   vb pres act ind 3rd pers sg   id.
ὁρίοις   noun neut dat pl .... ὅριον
ὅριον   noun neut nom and acc sg   id.
ὁρίου   noun neut gen sg   id.
ὁρισάμενοι   vb 1st aor mid part masc nom pl .... ὁρίζω
ὁρισάμενος   vb 1st aor mid part masc nom sg   id.
ὁρίσηται   vb 1st aor mid subj 3rd pers sg   id.
ὁρισμοί   noun masc nom pl .... ὁρισμός
ὁρισμόν   noun masc acc sg   id.
ὁρισμός   noun masc nom sg   id.
ὁρισμοῦ   noun masc gen sg   id.
ὁρισμούς   noun masc acc pl   id.
ὁρισμῷ   noun masc dat sg   id.
ὁρίῳ   noun neut dat sg .... ὅριον
ὁρίων   noun neut gen pl   id.
ὁρκιεῖ   vb fut act ind 3rd pers sg .... ὁρκίζω
ὁρκίζειν   vb pres act inf   id.
ὁρκίζομεν   vb pres act ind 1st pers pl   id.
ὁρκίζω   vb pres act ind 1st pers sg   id.
ὁρκίσας   vb 1st aor act part masc nom sg   id.
ὁρκισθείς   vb 1st aor pass part masc nom sg   id.
ὁρκισμόν   noun masc acc sg .... ὁρκισμός
ὁρκισμοῦ   noun masc gen sg   id.
ὅρκοις   noun masc dat pl .... ὅρκος
ὅρκον   noun masc acc sg   id.
Ὅρκος   pr noun masc nom sg
ὅρκος   noun masc nom sg
ὅρκου   noun masc gen sg .... ὅρκος
ὅρκους   noun masc acc pl   id.
ὅρκῳ   noun masc dat sg   id.
ὁρκωμοσία   noun fem nom sg
ὁρκωμοσίαν   noun fem acc sg .... ὁρκωμοσία
ὅρκων   noun masc gen pl .... ὅρκος
ὁρμάς   noun fem acc pl .... ὁρμή
ὁρμή   noun fem nom sg   id.
ὁρμῇ   noun fem dat sg   id.
ὅρμημα   noun neut nom and acc sg
ὁρμήματα   noun neut nom and acc pl .... ὅρμημα
ὁρμήματι   noun neut dat sg   id.
ὁρμήν   noun fem acc sg .... ὁρμή
ὁρμῆς   noun fem gen sg   id.
ὁρμησάντων   vb 1st aor act part masc and neut gen pl . ὁρμάω
ὁρμήσας   vb 1st aor act part masc nom sg   id.
ὁρμήσουσιν   vb fut act ind 3rd pers pl   id.
ὁρμίσκοι   noun masc nom pl .... ὁρμίσκος
ὁρμίσκοις   noun masc dat pl   id.
ὅρμισκον   noun masc acc sg   id.
ὁρμίσκος   noun masc nom sg

ὁρμίσκῳ noun masc dat sg . . . . ὁρμίσκος
ὁρμίσκων noun masc gen pl   id.
ὅρμον noun masc acc sg . . . . ὅρμος
ὅρμων noun masc gen pl   id.
ὁρμῶσιν vb pres act ind 3rd pers pl . . . . ὁρμάω
Ορνα pr noun masc nom sg
Ορναν pr noun masc acc sg . . . . Ορνα
ὄρνεα noun neut nom and acc pl . . . . ὄρνεον
ὀρνέοις noun neut dat pl   id.
ὄρνεον noun neut nom and acc sg   id.
ὀρνέου noun neut gen sg   id.
ὀρνέῳ noun neut dat sg   id.
ὀρνέων noun neut gen pl   id.
Ορνια pr noun
ὀρνίθια noun neut nom and acc pl . . . . ὀρνίθιον
ὀρνίθιον noun neut nom and acc sg   id.
ὀρνιθίου noun neut gen sg   id.
ὀρνιθίῳ noun neut dat sg   id.
ὀρνιθοσκοπήσεσθε vb fut mid ind
              2nd pers pl . . . . ὀρνιθοσκοπέομαι
ὀρνίθων noun masc gen pl . . . . ὄρνις
Ορνιου pr noun
ὄρον noun masc acc sg . . . . ὄρος
ὄρος noun neut nom and acc sg
ὄρους noun neut gen sg . . . . ὄρος
ὀρόφοις noun masc dat pl . . . . ὄροφος
ὀροφοιτοῦντα vb pres act part
              neut nom and acc pl . . . . ὀροφοιτόω
ὀροφώματα noun neut nom and acc pl . . . . ὀρόφωμα
ὀρτυγομήτρα noun fem nom sg
ὀρτυγομήτραν noun fem acc sg . . . . ὀρτυγομήτρα
ὄρυγα noun masc acc sg . . . . ὄρυξ
ὀρυγῇ vb 2nd aor pass subj 3rd pers sg . . . . ὀρύσσω
ὀρύξας vb 1st aor act part masc nom sg   id.
ὀρύξεις vb fut act ind 2nd pers sg   id.
ὄρυξον vb 1st aor act impv 2nd pers sg   id.
ὀρύσσει vb pres act ind 3rd pers sg   id.
ὀρύσσοντες vb pres act part masc nom pl   id.
ὀρύσσω vb pres act ind 1st pers sg   id.
ὀρύσσων vb pres act part masc nom sg   id.
Ορφα pr noun
ὀρφανά adj neut nom and acc pl . . . . ὀρφανός
ὀρφανείαν noun fem acc sg . . . . ὀρφανία
ὀρφανίᾳ noun fem dat sg   id.
ὀρφανοί adj masc nom pl . . . . ὀρφανός
ὀρφανοῖς adj masc and neut dat pl   id.
ὀρφανόν adj masc acc sg, neut nom and acc sg   id.
ὀρφανός adj masc nom sg   id.
ὀρφανοῦ adj masc and neut gen sg   id.
ὀρφανούς adj masc acc pl   id.
ὀρφανῷ adj masc and neut dat sg   id.
ὀρφανῶν adj gen pl   id.

ὀρχήσασθαι vb 1st aor mid inf . . . . ὀρχέομαι
ὀρχήσομαι vb fut mid ind 1st pers sg   id.
ὀρχήσονται vb fut mid ind 3rd pers pl   id.
ὀρχούμενον vb pres dep part masc acc sg   id.
ὀρχουμένων vb pres dep part gen pl   id.
ὀρῶ vb pres act ind 1st pers sg . . . . ὁράω
ὁρώμενος vb pres m/p part masc nom sg   id.
ὁρωμένων vb pres m/p part gen pl   id.
ὁρῶν vb pres act part masc nom sg   id.
ὁρῶντα vb pres act part masc acc sg   id.
ὁρῶντας vb pres act part masc acc pl   id.
ὁρῶντες vb pres act part masc nom pl   id.
ὁρῶντος vb pres act part masc and neut gen sg   id.
ὁρώντων vb pres act part masc and neut gen pl   id.
ὁρῶσα vb pres act part fem nom sg   id.
ὁρῶσαν vb pres act part fem acc sg   id.
ὁρῶσιν vb pres act ind 3rd pers pl   id.
ὅς rel pron masc nom sg
ὅσα adj neut nom and acc pl . . . . ὅσος
ὅσαι adj fem nom pl   id.
ὅσας adj fem acc pl   id.
ὅση adj fem nom sg   id.
ὅσια adj neut nom and acc pl . . . . ὅσιος
ὁσία adj fem nom sg   id.
ὁσίας adj fem gen sg and acc pl   id.
ὅσιοι adj masc nom pl   id.
ὁσίοις adj masc and neut dat pl   id.
ὅσιον adj masc acc sg, neut nom and acc sg   id.
ὅσιος adj masc nom sg   id.
ὁσιότητα noun fem acc sg . . . . ὁσιότης
ὁσιότητι noun fem dat sg   id.
ὁσιότητος noun fem gen sg   id.
ὁσίου adj masc and neut gen sg . . . . ὅσιος
ὁσίους adj masc acc pl   id.
ὁσίῳ adj masc and neut dat sg   id.
ὁσιωθήσῃ vb fut pass ind 2nd pers sg . . . . ὁσιόω
ὁσιωθήσονται vb fut pass ind 3rd pers pl   id.
ὁσίων adj gen pl . . . . ὅσιος
ὁσίως adverb
ὀσμή noun fem nom sg
ὀσμῇ noun fem dat sg . . . . ὀσμή
ὀσμήν noun fem acc sg   id.
ὀσμῆς noun fem gen sg   id.
ὅσοι adj masc nom pl . . . . ὅσος
ὅσοις adj masc and neut dat pl   id.
Οσομ pr noun
ὅσον adj masc acc sg, neut nom and acc sg . . . . ὅσος
ὀσπρίων noun neut gen pl . . . . ὄσπριον
Οσσα pr noun
ὀστᾶ noun neut nom and acc pl . . . . ὀστέον
ὀστέα noun neut nom and acc pl   id.
ὀστέοις noun neut dat pl   id.

ὀστέου   noun neut gen sg . . . . ὀστέον
ὀστέων   noun neut gen pl   id.
ὅστις   rel pron masc nom sg
ὀστοῦν   noun neut nom and acc sg . . . . ὀστέον
ὀστράκινα   adj neut nom and acc pl . . . . ὀστράκινος
ὀστράκινον   adj masc acc sg, neut nom and acc sg   id.
ὀστρακίνου   adj masc and neut gen sg   id.
ὀστρακίνους   adj masc acc pl   id.
ὀστρακίνῳ   adj masc and neut dat sg   id.
ὄστρακον   noun neut nom and acc sg
ὀστράκου   noun neut gen sg . . . . ὄστρακον
ὀστράκῳ   noun neut dat sg   id.
ὀστρακώδει   adj dat sg . . . . ὀστρακώδης
ὀστῶν   noun neut gen pl . . . . ὀστέον
ὀσφύν   noun fem acc sg . . . . ὀσφύς
ὀσφραίνεσθαι   vb pres dep inf . . . . ὀσφραίνομαι
ὀσφραίνεται   vb pres dep ind 3rd pers sg   id.
ὀσφρανθείη   vb 1st aor pass opt 3rd pers sg   id.
ὀσφρανθῇ   vb 1st aor pass subj 3rd pers sg   id.
ὀσφρανθῆναι   vb 1st aor pass inf   id.
ὀσφρανθήσεται   vb fut pass ind 3rd pers sg   id.
ὀσφρανθήσονται   vb fut pass ind 3rd pers pl   id.
ὀσφρανθῶ   vb 1st aor pass subj 1st pers sg   id.
ὀσφρανθῶσιν   vb 1st aor pass subj 3rd pers pl   id.
ὀσφρασία   noun fem nom sg
ὀσφύας   noun fem acc pl . . . . ὀσφύς
ὀσφύες   noun fem nom pl   id.
ὀσφύι   noun fem dat sg   id.
ὀσφύν   noun fem acc sg   id.
ὀσφύος   noun fem gen sg   id.
ὀσφύς   noun fem nom sg   id.
ὅσῳ   adj masc and neut dat sg . . . . ὅσος
ὅσων   adj gen pl   id.
ὅταν   adverb
ὅτε   adverb
ὅτι   conjunction
ὁτιοῦν   rel pron neut nom and acc sg . . . . ὅστισοῦν
ὅτου   rel pron masc and neut gen sg . . . . ὅστις
οὐ   adverb and particle
οὔ   adverb
οὗ   rel pron gen sg . . . . ὅς
Οὐαι   pr noun
οὐαί   interjection
ουαυ   translit (Heb. letter: ו)
Ουαφρη   pr noun
Ουβαλ   pr noun
Ουγαυα   pr noun
οὐδ'   see οὐδέ
Ουδαδαν   pr noun
οὐδαμοῦ   adverb
οὐδαμῶς   adverb
Ουδαν   pr noun

οὐδέ   conjunction and particle
οὐδείς   adj masc nom sg
οὐδεῖς   see οὐδείς
οὐδεμία   adj fem nom sg . . . . οὐδείς
οὐδεμιᾷ   adj fem dat sg   id.
οὐδεμίαν   adj fem acc sg   id.
οὐδέν   adj neut nom and acc sg   id.
οὐδένα   adj masc acc sg, neut nom and acc pl   id.
οὐδενί   adj masc and neut dat sg   id.
οὐδενός   adj masc and neut gen sg   id.
οὐδέποτε   adverb
οὐδέπω   adverb
Ουδια   pr noun
Ουδουια   pr noun
Ουεσβι   pr noun
Ουηλ   pr noun
οὐθείς   adj masc nom sg
οὐθέν   adj neut nom and acc sg . . . . οὐθείς
οὐθενί   adj masc and neut dat sg   id.
οὐθενός   adj masc and neut gen sg   id.
Ουθι   pr noun
Ουιεχωα   pr noun
οὐκ   see οὐ
οὐκ   see οὐ
Ουκαν   pr noun
οὐκέτι   adverb and conjunction
Οὐκ-ἠλεημένη   pr noun nom sg . . . . οὐ+ἐλεέω
Οὐκ-ἠλεημενην   pr noun acc sg   id.
Ουλ   pr noun
Ουλαι   pr noun
Ουλαιμαραδαχ   pr noun
Ουλαμ   pr noun
Ουλαμαις   pr noun
Ουλαμλευς   pr noun
Οὐ-λαος-μου   pr noun nom sg . . . . οὐ+λαός+ἐγω
Οὐ-λαῷ-μου   pr noun dat sg   id.
οὐλή   noun fem nom sg
οὐλῇ   noun fem dat sg . . . . οὐλή
οὐλῆς   noun fem gen sg   id.
οὖν   particle
οὖπερ   adverb
οὔπω   adverb
Ουρ   pr noun
οὐρά   noun fem nom sg
οὐράγει   vb pres act impv 2nd pers sg . . . . οὐραγέω
οὐραγίαν   noun fem acc sg . . . . οὐραγία
οὐραγοῦντες   vb pres act part masc nom pl . . . . . . οὐραγέω
οὐράν   noun fem acc sg . . . . οὐρά
οὐρανέ   noun masc voc sg . . . . οὐρανός
οὐράνιον   adj acc sg, neut nom sg . . . . οὐράνιος
οὐρανίου   adj masc and neut gen sg   id.
οὐρανίους   adj masc acc pl   id.

οὐρανίῳ adj dat sg . . . . οὐράνιος				

οὐρανίῳ adj dat sg . . . . οὐράνιος
οὐρανίων adj gen pl   id.
οὐρανόθεν adverb
οὐρανοί noun masc nom pl . . . . οὐρανός
οὐρανοῖς noun masc dat pl   id.
οὐρανόν noun masc acc sg   id.
οὐρανός noun masc nom sg   id.
οὐρανοῦ noun masc gen sg   id.
οὐρανούς noun masc acc pl   id.
οὐρανῷ noun masc dat sg   id.
οὐρανῶν noun masc gen pl   id.
οὐρᾶς noun fem gen sg . . . . οὐρά
Ουρι pr noun
Ουρια pr noun
Ουρια pr noun masc dat sg . . . . Ουριας
Ουριαν pr noun masc acc sg   id.
Ουριας pr noun masc nom sg   id.
Ουριας pr noun
Ουριηλ pr noun
οὔριον adj masc acc sg, neut nom and acc sg . . . . . . οὔριος
Ουριου pr noun masc gen sg . . . . Ουριας
οὖρον noun neut nom and acc sg
οὐροῦντα vb pres act part masc acc sg . . . . οὐρέω
οὐρῶν noun fem gen pl . . . . οὐρά
οὕς rel pron masc acc pl . . . . ὅς
οὖς noun neut nom and acc sg
Ουσα pr noun
οὖσα vb pres act part fem nom sg . . . . εἰμί
Ουσαθι pr noun
οὖσαι vb pres act part fem nom pl . . . . εἰμί
οὖσαν vb pres act part fem acc sg   id.
οὔσας vb pres act part fem acc pl   id.
οὔσῃ vb pres act part fem dat sg   id.
οὔσης vb pres act part fem gen sg   id.
οὖσι vb pres act part masc and neut dat pl   id.
οὐσίαν noun fem acc sg . . . . οὐσία
οὐσῶν vb pres act part fem gen pl . . . . εἰμί
Ουτα pr noun
οὔτε conjunction
οὗτοι dem pron masc nom pl . . . . οὗτος
οὗτος dem pron masc nom sg   id.
οὕτω see οὕτως
οὕτως adverb
Ουφι pr noun
Ουφιρ pr noun
οὐχ see οὐ
οὐχί see οὐ
Οφαρ pr noun
ὄφει noun masc dat sg . . . . ὄφις
ὀφείλει vb pres act ind 3rd pers sg . . . . ὀφείλω
ὀφειλέσει vb fut act ind 3rd pers sg   id.
ὀφείλετε vb pres act ind 2nd pers pl   id.

ὀφείλημα noun neut nom and acc sg
ὀφειλήσειν vb fut act inf . . . . ὀφείλω
ὀφειλήσῃς vb 1st aor act subj 2nd pers sg   id.
ὀφειλήσουσιν vb fut act ind 3rd pers pl   id.
ὀφείλομεν vb pres act ind 1st pers pl   id.
ὀφειλομένης vb pres m/p part fem gen sg   id.
ὀφειλομένους vb pres m/p part masc acc pl   id.
ὀφείλοντα vb pres act part masc acc sg   id.
ὀφείλοντος vb pres act part masc and neut gen sg   id.
ὀφείλων vb pres act part masc nom sg   id.
ὄφεις noun masc nom and acc pl . . . . ὄφις
ὄφελον vb 2nd aor act part neut nom and acc sg . . . . ὀφείλω
ὄφελος noun neut nom and acc sg
Οφερ pr noun
Οφερι pr noun
ὄφεων noun masc gen pl . . . . ὄφις
ὄφεως noun masc gen sg   id.
ὀφθαλμοί noun masc nom pl . . . . ὀφθαλμός
ὀφθαλμοῖς noun masc dat pl   id.
ὀφθαλμόν noun masc acc sg   id.
ὀφθαλμός noun masc nom sg   id.
ὀφθαλμοῦ noun masc gen sg   id.
ὀφθαλμούς noun masc acc pl   id.
ὀφθαλμοφανῶς adverb
ὀφθαλμῷ noun masc dat sg . . . . ὀφθαλμός
ὀφθαλμῶν noun masc gen pl   id.
ὀφθείς vb 1st aor pass part masc nom sg . . . . ὁράω
ὀφθεῖσαν vb 1st aor pass part fem acc sg   id.
ὀφθέντα vb 1st aor pass part masc acc sg   id.
ὀφθέντι vb 1st aor pass part masc and neut dat sg   id.
ὀφθέντος vb 1st aor pass part masc and neut gen sg   id.
ὀφθῇ vb 1st aor pass subj 3rd pers sg   id.
ὀφθῆναι vb 1st aor pass inf   id.
ὀφθῇς vb 1st aor pass subj 2nd pers sg   id.
ὀφθήσεται vb fut pass ind 3rd pers sg   id.
ὀφθήσῃ vb fut pass ind 2nd pers sg   id.
ὀφθήσομαι vb fut pass ind 1st pers sg   id.
ὄφθητι vb 1st aor pass impv 2nd pers sg   id.
ὀφθήτω vb 1st aor pass impv 3rd pers sg   id.
ὀφθήτωσαν vb 1st aor pass impv 3rd pers pl   id.
ὀφθῶμεν vb 1st aor pass subj 1st pers pl   id.
Οφιμιν pr noun
ὄφιν noun masc acc sg . . . . ὄφις
ὀφιόδηκτον adj acc sg, neut nom sg . . . . ὀφιόδηκτος
ὀφιομάχην noun masc acc sg . . . . ὀφιομάχης
ὄφις noun masc nom sg
Οφλα pr noun
ὄφλησιν noun fem acc sg . . . . ὄφλησις
Οφνι pr noun
ὀφρύας noun fem acc pl . . . . ὀφρύς
ὀχείαν noun fem acc sg . . . . ὀχεία
Οχιηλος pr noun

ὀχλαγωγήσῃς	vb 1st aor act subj 2nd pers sg . . . ὀχλαγωγέω	ὀχυρωμάτιον	noun neut nom and acc sg
ὀχλεῖ	vb pres act ind 3rd pers sg . . . . ὀχλέω	ὀχυρώματος	noun neut gen sg . . . . ὀχύρωμα
ὀχλῇ	vb pres act subj 3rd pers sg id.	ὀχυρωμάτων	noun neut gen pl id.
ὀχληθῇ	vb 1st aor pass subj 3rd pers sg id.	ὀχυρῶν	adj gen pl . . . . ὀχυρός
ὄχλοι	noun masc nom pl . . . . ὄχλος	ὀχυρῶσαι	vb 1st aor act inf . . . . ὀχυρόω
ὄχλοις	noun masc dat pl id.	ὀχυρώσασα	vb 1st aor act part fem nom sg id.
ὄχλον	noun masc acc sg id.	ὀχυρώσεως	noun fem gen sg . . . . ὀχύρωσις
ὄχλος	noun masc nom sg id.	ὀχυρώσῃ	vb 1st aor act subj 3rd pers sg . . . . ὀχυρόω
ὄχλου	noun masc gen sg id.	ὀχύρωσιν	noun fem acc sg . . . . ὀχύρωσις
ὄχλους	noun masc acc pl id.	Οχχοφφα	pr noun
ὄχλῳ	noun masc dat sg id.	ὄψα	noun neut nom and acc pl . . . . ὄψον
ὄχλων	noun masc gen pl id.	ὀψάρια	noun neut nom and acc pl . . . . ὀψάριον
Οχοζαθ	pr noun	ὀψέ	adverb
Οχοζια	pr noun	ὄψει	noun fem dat sg . . . . ὄψις
Οχοζια	pr noun masc dat sg . . . . Οχοζιας	ὄψει	vb fut mid ind 2nd pers sg . . . . ὁράω
Οχοζιαν	pr noun masc acc sg id.	ὄψεις	noun fem nom and acc pl . . . . ὄψις
Οχοζιας	pr noun masc nom sg id.	ὄψεσθαι	vb fut mid inf . . . . ὁράω
Οχοζιου	pr noun masc gen sg id.	ὄψεσθε	vb fut mid ind 2nd pers pl id.
ὀχυρά	adj fem nom sg, neut nom and acc pl . . . . ὀχυρός	ὄψεται	vb fut mid ind 3rd pers sg id.
ὀχυραί	adj fem nom pl id.	ὄψεως	noun fem gen sg . . . . ὄψις
ὀχυραῖς	adj fem dat pl id.	ὄψῃ	vb fut mid ind 2nd pers sg . . . . ὁράω
ὀχυράν	adj fem acc sg id.	ὀψία	noun fem nom sg
ὀχυράς	adj fem acc pl id.	Οψιβα	pr noun
ὀχυρᾶς	adj fem gen sg id.	ὄψιμα	adj neut nom and acc pl . . . . ὄψιμος
ὀχυροί	adj masc nom pl id.	ὄψιμον	adj acc sg, neut nom sg id.
ὀχυροῖς	adj masc and neut dat pl id.	ὄψιμος	adj masc and fem nom sg id.
ὀχυρόν	adj masc acc sg, neut nom and acc sg id.	ὄψιν	noun fem acc sg . . . . ὄψις
ὀχυρός	adj masc nom sg id.	ὄψις	noun fem nom sg id.
ὀχυρούς	adj masc acc pl id.	ὀψίσῃ	vb 1st aor act subj 3rd pers sg . . . . ὀψίζω
ὀχυροῦσιν	vb pres act ind 3rd pers pl . . . . ὀχυρόω	ὄψομαι	vb fut mid ind 1st pers sg . . . . ὁράω
ὀχυρῷ	adj masc and neut dat sg . . . . ὀχυρός	ὀψόμεθα	vb fut mid ind 1st pers pl id.
ὀχύρωμα	noun neut nom and acc sg	ὄψονται	vb fut mid ind 3rd pers pl id.
ὀχυρώμασι	noun neut dat pl . . . . ὀχύρωμα	ὀψοποιημάτων	noun neut gen pl . . . . ὀψοποίημα
ὀχυρώματα	noun neut nom and acc pl id.	ὄψος	noun neut nom and acc sg
ὀχυρώματι	noun neut dat sg id.	ὀψώνια	noun neut nom and acc pl . . . . ὀψώνιον

Π π

παγγέωργος	noun masc nom sg	παγίδος	noun fem gen sg . . . . παγίς
παγείς	vb 2nd aor pass part masc nom sg . . . . πήγνυμι	παγίδων	noun fem gen pl id.
παγεῖσα	vb 2nd aor pass part fem nom sg id.	παγίς	noun fem nom sg id.
παγετῷ	noun masc dat sg . . . . παγετός	παγκρατῆ	adj masc and fem acc sg . . . . παγκρατής
παγήσεται	vb fut pass ind 3rd pers sg . . . . πήγνυμι	πάγοι	noun masc nom pl . . . . πάγος
παγίδα	noun fem acc sg . . . . παγίς	πάγος	noun masc nom sg id.
παγίδας	noun fem acc pl id.	πάγους	noun masc acc pl id.
παγίδες	noun fem nom pl id.	Παθαια	pr noun
παγιδεύεις	vb pres act ind 2nd pers sg . . . . παγιδεύω	Παθαιος	pr noun
παγιδεύονται	vb pres m/p ind 3rd pers pl id.	παθεῖν	vb 2nd aor act inf . . . . πάσχω
παγίδι	noun fem dat sg . . . . παγίς	παθεινούς	noun masc acc pl . . . . παθεινός

πάθεσι noun neut dat pl . . . . πάθος	παιδεύσει vb fut act ind 3rd pers sg . . . . παιδεύω
πάθη noun neut nom and acc pl id.	παιδεύσῃς vb 1st aor act subj 2nd pers sg id.
παθοκράτειαν noun fem acc sg . . . . παθοκράτεια	παίδευσον vb 1st aor act impv 2nd pers sg id.
παθοκρατείαν see παθοκράτειαν	παιδεύσουσιν vb fut act ind 3rd pers pl id.
παθοκρατεῖσθαι vb pres dep inf . . . . παθοκρατέομαι	παιδεύσω vb fut act ind 1st pers sg id.
πάθος noun neut nom and acc sg	παιδεύσωσιν vb 1st aor act subj 3rd pers pl id.
Παθουρη pr noun	παιδευτά noun masc voc sg . . . . παιδευτής
Παθουρης pr noun	παιδευτής noun masc nom sg id.
πάθους noun neut gen sg . . . . πάθος	παιδεύων vb pres act part masc nom sg . . . . παιδεύω
παθών vb 2nd aor act part masc nom sg . . . . πάσχω	παιδί noun masc dat sg . . . . παῖς
παθῶν noun neut gen pl . . . . πάθος	παιδία noun neut nom and acc pl . . . . παιδίον
πάθωσιν vb 2nd aor act subj 3rd pers pl . . . . πάσχω	παιδίοις noun neut dat pl id.
παιάνων noun masc gen pl . . . . παιάν	παιδίον noun neut nom and acc sg
παίγνια noun neut nom and acc pl . . . . παίγνιον	παιδίου noun neut gen sg . . . . παιδίον
παιγνία noun fem nom sg	παιδίσκαι noun fem nom pl . . . . παιδίσκη
παιγνίαις noun fem dat pl . . . . παιγνία	παιδίσκας noun fem acc pl id.
παιγνίοις noun neut dat pl . . . . παίγνιον	παιδίσκη noun fem nom sg id.
παίγνιον noun neut nom and acc sg id.	παιδίσκῃ noun fem dat sg id.
παῖδα noun masc or fem acc sg . . . . παῖς	παιδίσκην noun fem acc sg id.
παιδάρια noun neut nom and acc pl . . . . παιδάριον	παιδίσκης noun fem gen sg id.
παιδαρίοις noun neut dat pl id.	παιδισκῶν noun fem gen pl id.
παιδάριον noun neut nom and acc sg id.	παιδίῳ noun neut dat sg . . . . παιδίον
παιδαρίου noun neut gen sg id.	παιδίων noun neut gen pl id.
παιδαρίῳ noun neut dat sg id.	παιδοποιήσασθαι vb 1st aor mid inf . . . . παιδοποιέω
παιδαρίων noun neut gen pl id.	παιδοποιία noun fem nom sg
παῖδας noun masc acc pl . . . . παῖς	παιδός noun masc or fem gen sg . . . . παῖς
παιδεία noun fem nom sg	παίδων noun masc or fem gen pl id.
παιδείᾳ noun fem dat sg . . . . παιδεία	παῖζε vb pres act impv 2nd pers sg . . . . παίζω
παιδεῖαι noun fem nom pl id.	παίζειν vb pres act inf id.
παιδείαν noun fem acc sg id.	παίζοντα vb pres act part masc acc sg id.
παιδείας noun fem gen sg and acc pl id.	παίζοντες vb pres act part masc nom pl id.
παῖδες noun masc nom pl . . . . παῖς	παιζόντων vb pres act part masc and neut gen pl id.
παίδευε vb pres act impv 2nd pers sg . . . . παιδεύω	παίζουσαι vb pres act part fem nom pl id.
παιδεύει vb pres act ind 3rd pers sg id.	παίζων vb pres act part masc nom sg id.
παιδεύειν vb pres act inf id.	παιξάτω vb 1st aor act impv 3rd pers sg id.
παιδεύεσθαι vb pres m/p inf id.	παιξάτωσαν vb 1st aor act impv 3rd pers pl id.
παιδεύεσθε vb pres m/p impv 2nd pers pl id.	παίξῃ vb fut mid ind 2nd pers sg id.
παιδεύεται vb pres m/p ind 3rd pers sg id.	παίξομαι vb fut mid ind 1st pers sg id.
παιδευθέντες vb 1st aor pass part masc nom pl id.	παίοντα vb pres act part masc acc sg . . . . παίω
παιδευθῇ vb 1st aor pass subj 3rd pers sg id.	παίοντι vb pres act part masc and neut dat sg id.
παιδευθήσεσθε vb fut pass ind 2nd pers pl id.	παίοντος vb pres act part masc and neut gen sg id.
παιδευθήσεται vb fut pass ind 3rd pers sg id.	παῖς noun masc or fem nom sg
παιδευθήσῃ vb fut pass ind 2nd pers sg id.	παίσαντα vb 1st aor act part masc acc sg . . . . παίζω
παιδευθησόμεθα vb fut pass ind 1st pers pl id.	παίσῃ vb 1st aor act subj 3rd pers sg id.
παιδευθήσονται vb fut pass ind 3rd pers pl id.	παισί noun masc or fem dat pl . . . . παῖς
παιδεύθητε vb 1st aor pass impv 2nd pers pl id.	παίω vb pres act ind 1st pers sg
παιδευθῆτε vb 1st aor pass subj 2nd pers pl id.	παίων vb pres act part masc nom sg . . . . παίω
παιδευόμενοι vb pres m/p part masc nom pl id.	παλάθας noun fem acc pl . . . . παλάθη
παιδευόμενος vb pres m/p part masc nom sg id.	παλάθην noun fem acc sg id.
παιδεύοντος vb pres act part masc and neut gen sg id.	παλάθης noun fem gen sg id.
παιδεύσαι vb 1st aor act opt 3rd pers sg id.	πάλαι adverb
παιδεῦσαι vb 1st aor act inf id.	παλαιά adj neut nom and acc pl . . . . παλαιός

παλαιᾶς adj fem gen sg	....	παλαιός
παλαίειν vb pres act inf	....	παλαίω
παλαιόν adj masc acc sg, neut nom and acc sg	....	παλαιός
παλαιός adj masc nom sg		id.
παλαιοτέροις comp adj masc and neut dat pl		id.
παλαιοτέρων comp adj gen pl		id.
παλαιοῦ adj masc and neut gen sg		id.
παλαιουμένη vb pres act part fem nom sg	....	παλαιόω
παλαιούς adj masc acc pl	....	παλαιός
παλαιοῦται vb pres m/p ind 3rd pers sg	....	παλαιόω
παλαιστάς noun fem acc pl	....	παλαιστή
παλαιστήν noun fem acc sg		id.
παλαιστής noun masc nom sg		
παλαιστῆς noun fem gen sg	....	παλαιστή
παλαιστοῦ noun masc gen sg	....	παλαιστής
παλαίστρη noun fem dat sg	....	παλαίστρα
παλαιωθῇ vb 1st aor pass subj 3rd pers sg	...	παλαιόω
παλαιωθήσεσθε vb fut pass ind 2nd pers pl		id.
παλαιωθήσεται vb fut pass ind 3rd pers sg		id.
παλαιωθήσονται vb fut pass ind 3rd pers pl		id.
παλαιώθητι vb 1st aor pass impv 2nd pers sg		id.
παλαιώμασι noun masc dat pl	....	παλαίωμα
παλαιώματα noun neut nom and acc pl		id.
παλαιῶν adj gen pl	....	παλαιός
παλαιῶν vb pres act part masc nom sg	....	παλαιόω
παλαιώσει vb fut act ind 3rd pers sg		id.
παλαίωσιν vb 2nd aor act subj 3rd pers pl	....	παλαιόω
παλαιώσουσιν vb fut act ind 3rd pers pl	....	παλαιόω
πάλιν adverb		
παλλακαί noun fem nom pl	....	παλλακή
παλλακάς noun fem acc pl		id.
παλλακή noun fem nom sg		id.
παλλακῇ noun fem dat sg		id.
παλλακήν noun fem acc sg		id.
παλλακῆς noun fem gen sg		id.
παλλακίδων noun fem gen pl	....	παλλακίς
παλλακῶν noun fem gen pl	....	παλλακή
παμβασιλεῖ noun masc dat sg	....	παμβασιλεύς
παμβότανον noun neut nom and acc sg		
παμμειγέσι adj dat pl	....	παμμιγής
παμμελέσι adj dat pl	....	παμμελής
παμμιαρώτατος superl adj masc nom sg	......	παμμιαρός
παμμιγῆ adj masc and fem acc sg	....	παμμιγης
παμπληθεῖς adj masc and fem nom and acc pl	..	παμπληθής
παμποίκιλοι adj masc and fem nom pl	.....	παμποίκιλος
παμπονήρου adj gen sg	....	παμπόνηρος
πάμφυλα adj neut nom and acc pl	....	πάμφυλος
Παμφυλιαν pr noun fem acc sg	....	Παμφυλια
πάμφυλον noun masc acc sg	....	πάμφυλος
παμφύλων adj gen pl		id.
πᾶν adj neut nom and acc sg (also: πᾶν = πάντα)	....	πᾶς
παναγιε adj masc and fem voc sg	....	παναγιος

πανάγιος adj masc and fem nom sg		
πάνδεινον adj acc sg, neut nom sg	....	πάνδεινος
πανδημεί adverb		
πάνδημον adj acc sg, neut nom sg	....	πάνδημος
πανεθνεί adverb		
πανεπίσκοπον adj acc sg, neut nom sg	....	πανεπίσκοπος
πανηγύρεις noun fem nom and acc pl	....	πανήγυρις
πανηγύρεσιν noun fem dat pl		id.
πανηγύρεως noun fem gen sg		id.
πανηγυρίσατε vb 1st aor act impv 2nd pers pl	.	πανηγυρίζω
πανηγυρισμόν noun masc acc sg	....	πανηγυρισμός
πάνθ' see παντί		
πανθήρ noun masc nom sg		
πανόδυρτον adj acc sg, neut nom sg	....	πανόδυρτος
πανόδυρτος adj masc and fem nom sg		id.
πανοικία noun fem nom sg		
πανοικίᾳ noun fem dat sg	....	πανοικία
πανοικίαν noun fem acc sg		id.
πανοπλίᾳ noun fem dat sg	....	πανοπλία
πανοπλίαις noun fem dat pl		id.
πανοπλίαν noun fem acc sg		id.
πανοπλίας noun fem gen sg and acc pl		id.
πανουργεύμασι noun neut dat pl	....	πανούργευμα
πανουργεύματα noun neut nom and acc pl		id.
πανουργεύσεται vb 1st aor mid subj 3rd pers sg	....	πανουργεύω
πανουργία noun fem nom sg		
πανουργίαν noun fem acc sg	....	πανουργία
πανουργίας noun fem gen sg		id.
πανοῦργοι adj masc and fem nom pl	....	πανοῦργος
πανοῦργον adj acc sg, neut nom sg		id.
πανοῦργος adj masc and fem nom sg		id.
πανουργότερος comp adj masc nom sg		id.
πανούργων adj gen pl		id.
πάνσοφος adj masc and fem nom sg		
πανσόφῳ adj dat sg	....	πάνσοφος
πάντα adj masc acc sg, neut nom and acc pl	....	πᾶς
πάντας adj masc acc pl		id.
πανταχῇ adverb		
πανταχῆ adverb		
πανταχόθεν adverb		
πανταχοῦ adverb		
παντελῆ adj masc and fem acc sg	....	παντελής
παντελῶς adverb		
παντεπόπτης adj masc nom sg		
πάντες adj masc nom pl	....	πᾶς
παντευχίας noun fem acc pl	....	παντευχία
πάντη adverb		
παντί adj masc and neut dat sg	....	πᾶς
παντοδαπά adj neut nom and acc pl	....	παντοδαπός
παντοδύναμον adj acc sg, neut nom sg	....	παντοδύναμος
παντοδύναμος adj masc and fem nom sg		

πάντοθεν adverb

παντοῖα adj neut nom and acc pl . . . . παντοῖος

παντοίοις adj masc and neut dat pl id.

παντοίους adj masc acc pl id.

παντοίων adj gen pl id.

παντοκράτορα noun masc acc sg . . . . παντοκράτωρ

παντοκράτορι noun masc dat sg id.

παντοκράτορος noun masc gen sg id.

παντοκράτωρ noun masc nom sg id.

παντός adj masc and neut gen sg . . . . πᾶς

πάντοτε adverb

παντοτρόφῳ adj fem dat sg . . . . παντοτρόφος

παντοφαγία noun fem nom sg

πάντων adj masc and neut gen pl . . . . πᾶς

πάντως adverb

πάνυ adverb

πανυπέρτατον adj masc acc sg,

       neut nom and acc sg . . . . πανυπέρτατος

πάππος noun masc nom sg

πάπυρον noun masc acc sg . . . . πάπυρος

πάπυρος noun masc nom sg id.

παπύρου noun masc gen sg id.

παρ' see παρά

παρά preposition

παραβαίνειν vb pres act inf . . . . παραβαίνω

παραβαίνετε vb pres act ind 2nd pers pl id.

παραβαίνοντας vb pres act part masc acc pl id.

παραβαίνοντες vb pres act part masc nom pl id.

παραβαίνουσιν vb pres act ind 3rd pers pl id.

παραβαίνων vb pres act part masc nom sg id.

παραβαίνωσι vb pres act subj 3rd pers pl id.

παράβαλε vb 2nd aor act impv 2nd pers sg . . . παραβάλλω

παραβαλεῖς vb fut act ind 2nd pers sg id.

παραβαλεῖτε vb fut act ind 2nd pers pl id.

παράβαλλε vb pres act impv 2nd pers sg id.

παραβάλλοντες vb pres act part masc nom pl id.

παραβάσεις noun fem nom and acc pl . . . . παράβασις

παραβᾶσι vb 2nd aor act part

      masc and neut dat pl . . . . παραβαίνω

παραβασιλεύετε vb pres act ind

      2nd pers pl . . . . παραβασιλεύω

παράβασιν noun fem acc sg . . . . παράβασις

παραβέβηκας vb perf act ind 2nd pers sg . . . . . παραβαίνω

παραβεβηκότας vb perf act part masc acc pl id.

παραβεβηκότων vb perf act part

      masc and neut gen pl id.

παραβεβλημένος vb perf m/p part

      masc nom sg . . . . παραβάλλω

παραβῇ vb 2nd aor act subj 3rd pers sg . . . . παραβαίνω

παραβῆναι vb 2nd aor act inf id.

παραβήσῃ vb fut mid ind 2nd pers sg id.

παραβησόμεθα vb fut mid ind 1st pers pl id.

παραβήσονται vb fut mid ind 3rd pers pl . . . . . παραβαίνω

παραβῆτε vb 2nd aor act subj 2nd pers pl id.

παραβιασάμενοι vb 1st aor mid part

      masc nom pl . . . . παραβιάζομαι

παραβιβάζων vb pres act part masc nom sg . . . παραβιβάζω

παραβίβασον vb 1st aor act impv 2nd pers sg id.

παραβιῶνται vb pres m/p subj 3rd pers pl . . . . . . παραβιάω

παράβλεπε vb pres act impv 2nd pers sg . . . . . παραβλέπω

παραβολαί noun fem nom pl . . . . παραβολή

παραβολαῖς noun fem dat pl id.

παραβολάς noun fem acc pl id.

παραβολή noun fem nom sg id.

παραβολῇ noun fem dat sg id.

παραβολήν noun fem acc sg id.

παραβολῶν noun fem gen pl id.

παραβῶσιν vb 2nd aor act subj 3rd pers pl . . . . . παραβαίνω

παράγαγε vb 2nd aor act impv 2nd pers sg . . . . παράγω

παραγαγεῖν vb 2nd aor act inf id.

παραγγείλας vb 1st aor act part masc nom sg . παραγγέλλω

παραγγείλατε vb 1st aor act impv 2nd pers pl id.

παραγγέλλεται vb pres m/p ind 3rd pers sg id.

παραγγέλματος noun neut gen sg . . . . παράγγελμα

παραγέγονα vb perf act ind 1st pers sg . . . . . παραγίνομαι

παραγέγονας vb perf act ind 2nd pers sg id.

παραγεγόνασιν vb perf act ind 3rd pers pl id.

παραγεγόνατε vb perf act ind 2nd pers pl id.

παραγέγονεν vb perf act ind 3rd pers sg id.

παραγεγονότας vb perf act part masc acc pl id.

παραγεγονότων vb perf act part masc and neut gen pl id.

παράγειν vb pres act inf . . . . παράγω

παραγενέσθαι vb 2nd aor mid inf . . . . παραγίνομαι

παραγένεσθε vb 2nd aor mid impv 2nd pers pl id.

παραγενηθείς vb 1st aor pass part masc nom sg id.

παραγενηθέντα vb 1st aor pass part neut nom and acc pl id.

παραγενηθέντες vb 1st aor pass part masc nom pl id.

παραγενηθῆναι vb 1st aor pass inf id.

παραγενήθητε vb 1st aor pass impv 2nd pers pl id.

παραγενηθήτωσαν vb 1st aor pass impv 3rd pers pl id.

παραγένηται vb 2nd aor mid subj 3rd pers sg id.

παραγενόμεναι vb 2nd aor mid part fem nom pl id.

παραγενόμενοι vb 2nd aor mid part masc nom pl id.

παραγενόμενος vb 2nd aor mid part masc nom sg id.

παραγενομένων vb 2nd aor mid part gen pl id.

παραγένωνται vb 2nd aor mid subj 3rd pers pl id.

παραγίνεσθαι vb pres dep inf id.

παραγίνεσθε vb pres dep impv 2nd pers pl id.

παραγίνεται vb pres dep ind 3rd pers sg id.

παραγίνῃ vb pres dep subj 2nd pers sg id.

παραγίνομαι vb pres dep ind 1st pers sg id.

παραγινομένης vb pres dep part fem gen sg id.

παραγινόμενοι vb pres dep part masc nom pl id.

παραγινομένοις vb pres dep part masc and neut dat pl id.

παραγινόμενον vb pres dep part	παραδοθήσεται vb fut pass ind 3rd pers sg . . . παραδίδωμι
masc acc sg . . . . παραγίνομαι	παραδοθήση vb fut pass ind 2nd pers sg id.
παραγινόμενος vb pres dep part masc nom sg id.	παραδοθήσονται vb fut pass ind 3rd pers pl id.
παραγινομένου vb pres dep part masc and neut gen sg id.	παραδοθήτωσαν vb 1st aor pass impv 3rd pers pl id.
παραγινομένους vb pres dep part masc acc pl id.	παραδοῖ vb 2nd aor act opt 3rd pers sg id.
παραγινομένων vb pres dep part gen pl id.	παράδοξα adj neut nom and acc pl . . . . παράδοξος
παραγίνονται vb pres dep ind 3rd pers pl id.	παραδοξάζοντα vb pres act part masc acc sg . παραδοξάζω
παραγίνου vb pres dep impv 2nd pers sg id.	παραδοξάσει vb fut act ind 3rd pers sg id.
παράγοντες vb pres act part masc nom pl . . . . παράγω	παραδοξάσω vb fut act ind 1st pers sg id.
παράγουσιν vb pres act ind 3rd pers pl id.	παράδοξον adj acc sg, neut nom sg . . . . παράδοξος
παραδεδομένους vb perf m/p part	παραδοξότατον superl adj masc acc sg,
masc acc pl . . . . παραδίδωμι	neut nom and acc sg id.
παραδέδονται vb perf m/p ind 3rd pers pl id.	παραδόξῳ adj dat sg id.
παραδέδωκα vb perf act ind 1st pers sg id.	παραδόξως adverb
παραδέδωκεν vb perf act ind 3rd pers sg id.	παράδος vb 2nd aor act impv 2nd pers sg . . . . . παραδίδωμι
παράδειγμα noun neut nom and acc sg	παραδόσει noun fem dat sg . . . . παράδοσις
παραδειγματισθῆναι vb 1st aor pass	παράδοτε vb 2nd aor act impv 2nd pers pl . . . . παραδίδωμι
inf . . . . παραδειγματίζω	παραδοῦναι vb 2nd aor act inf id.
παραδειγματισθήσεσθε vb fut pass ind 2nd pers pl id.	παραδρομαῖς noun fem dat pl . . . . παραδρομή
παραδειγματισμόν noun masc acc sg παραδειγματισμός	παραδρομῆς noun fem gen sg id.
παραδειγματισμῶν noun masc gen pl id.	παραδῶ vb 2nd aor act subj 1st and 3rd pers sg . παραδίδωμι
παραδειγμάτισον vb 1st aor act impv	παραδώη vb 2nd aor act opt 3rd pers sg id.
2nd pers sg . . . . παραδειγματίζω	παραδῷς vb 2nd aor act subj 2nd pers sg id.
παραδείγματος noun neut gen sg . . . . παράδειγμα	παραδώσει vb fut act ind 3rd pers sg id.
παραδείξατε vb 1st aor act impv 2nd pers pl . παραδεικνύω	παραδώσειν vb fut act inf id.
παράδειξον vb 1st aor act impv 2nd pers sg id.	παραδώσεις vb fut act ind 2nd pers sg id.
παραδείξω vb 1st aor act subj 1st pers sg,	παραδῶσιν vb 2nd aor act subj 3rd pers pl id.
fut act ind 1st pers sg id.	παραδώσομεν vb fut act ind 1st pers pl id.
παράδεισοι noun masc nom pl . . . . παράδεισος	παραδώσουσιν vb fut act ind 3rd pers pl id.
παράδεισον noun masc acc sg id.	παραδώσω vb fut act ind 1st pers sg id.
παράδεισος noun masc nom sg id.	παραδῶτε vb 2nd aor act subj 2nd pers pl id.
παραδείσου noun masc gen sg id.	παραζήλου vb pres act impv 2nd pers sg . . . . . παραζηλόω
παραδείσους noun masc acc pl id.	παραζηλώσει vb fut act ind 3rd pers sg id.
παραδείσῳ noun masc dat sg id.	παραζηλώσω vb 1st aor act subj 1st pers sg,
παραδειχθέν vb 1st aor pass part	fut act ind 1st pers sg id.
neut nom and acc sg . . . . παραδεικνύω	παραζώνην noun fem acc sg . . . . παραζώνη
παραδεξάμενος vb 1st aor mid part	παραθαλασσίαν adj fem acc sg . . . . παραθαλάσσιος
masc nom sg . . . . παραδέχομαι	παραθαλασσίας adj fem gen sg id.
παραδέξη vb fut mid ind 2nd pers sg id.	παραθαλασσίους adj fem acc pl id.
παραδέχεται vb pres dep ind 3rd pers sg id.	παράθεμα noun neut nom and acc sg
παραδιδομένη vb pres m/p part fem nom sg . . παραδίδωμι	παραθέματος noun neut gen sg . . . . παράθεμα
παραδιδόναι vb pres act inf id.	παράθες vb 2nd aor act impv 2nd pers sg . . . . . παρατίθημι
παραδίδοσθαι vb pres m/p inf id.	παραθέσει noun fem dat sg . . . . παράθεσις
παραδίδοται vb pres m/p ind 3rd pers sg id.	παραθέσεις noun fem nom and acc pl id.
παραδιδούς vb pres act part masc nom sg id.	παραθέσεως noun fem gen sg id.
παραδίδωμι vb pres act ind 1st pers sg id.	παραθέσθαι vb 2nd aor mid inf . . . . παρατίθημι
παραδιδῷς vb pres act subj 2nd pers sg id.	παράθεσιν noun fem acc sg . . . . παράθεσις
παραδίδωσιν vb pres act ind 3rd pers sg id.	παράθεσις noun fem nom sg id.
παραδοθέντα vb 1st aor pass part masc acc sg id.	παράθετε vb 2nd aor act impv 2nd pers pl . . . . παρατίθημι
παραδοθῇ vb 1st aor pass subj 3rd pers sg id.	παραθήκη noun fem dat sg . . . . παραθήκη
παραδοθῆναι vb 1st aor pass inf id.	παραθήκην noun fem acc sg id.
παραδοθήσεσθε vb fut pass ind 2nd pers pl id.	παραθήσει vb fut act ind 3rd pers sg . . . . παρατίθημι

παραθήσεις vb fut act ind 2nd pers sg	. . . . . .	παρατίθημι
παραθήσομαι vb fut mid ind 1st pers sg		id.
παραθήσομεν vb fut act ind 1st pers pl		id.
παραθήσω vb fut act ind 1st pers sg		id.
παραθλίψατε vb 1st aor act impv 2nd pers pl	. .	παραθλίβω
παραινέσαντος vb 1st aor act part		
masc and neut gen sg	. . . .	παραινέω
παραινέσας vb 1st aor act part masc nom sg		id.
παραίνεσις noun fem nom sg		
παραιτεῖσθαι vb pres m/p inf	. . . .	παραιτέω
παραιτησάμενοι vb 1st aor mid part masc nom pl		id.
παραιτήσασθαι vb 1st aor mid inf		id.
παραίτιος adj masc and fem nom sg		
παραιτούμενος vb pres m/p part masc nom sg	. .	παραιτέω
παρακαθεύδοντες vb pres act part		
masc nom pl	. . . .	παρακαθεύδω
παρακαθήμενοι vb pres m/p part		
masc nom pl	. . . .	παρακάθημαι
παρακάλει vb pres act impv 2nd pers sg	. . . . .	παρακαλέω
παρακαλεῖν vb pres act inf		id.
παρακαλεῖσθαι vb pres m/p inf		id.
παρακαλεῖται vb pres m/p ind 3rd pers sg		id.
παρακαλεῖτε vb pres act impv 2nd pers pl,		
pres act ind 2nd pers pl		id.
παρακαλέσαι vb 1st aor act inf		id.
παρακαλέσαντες vb 1st aor act part masc nom pl		id.
παρακαλέσας vb 1st aor act part masc nom sg		id.
παρακαλέσατε vb 1st aor act impv 2nd pers pl		id.
παρακαλέσει vb fut act ind 3rd pers sg		id.
παρακαλέσεις vb fut act ind 2nd pers sg		id.
παρακαλέσετε vb fut act ind 2nd pers pl		id.
παρακαλέσῃ vb 1st aor act subj 3rd pers sg		id.
παρακάλεσον vb 1st aor act impv 2nd pers sg		id.
παρακαλέσοντα vb fut act part masc acc sg		id.
παρακαλέσουσιν vb fut act ind 3rd pers pl		id.
παρακαλέσω vb fut act ind 1st pers sg		id.
παρακαλέσωσι vb 1st aor act subj 3rd pers pl		id.
παρακαλούμενος vb pres m/p part masc nom sg		id.
παρακαλοῦντας vb pres act part masc acc pl		id.
παρακαλοῦντες vb pres act part masc nom pl		id.
παρακαλοῦντος vb pres act part masc and neut gen sg		id.
παρακαλοῦσα vb pres act part fem nom sg		id.
παρακαλύμματι noun neut dat sg	. . . .	παρακάλυμμα
παρακαλύπτεσθε vb pres m/p impv		
2nd pers pl	. . . .	παρακαλύπτω
παρακαλῶ vb pres act ind 1st pers sg	. . . .	παρακαλέω
παρακαλῶν vb pres act part masc nom sg		id.
παρακαταθεμένοις vb 2nd aor mid part		
masc and neut dat pl	. . . .	παρακατατίθημι
παρακαταθήκας noun fem acc pl	. . . .	παρακαταθήκη
παρακαταθήκῃ noun fem dat sg		id.
παρακαταθήκης noun fem gen sg		id.

παρακαταστραθέντα vb 1st aor pass part		
neut nom and acc pl	. . . .	παρακαθίστημι
παρακείμεθα vb pres m/p ind 1st pers pl	. . . . .	παράκειμαι
παρακείμενα vb pres m/p part		
neut nom and acc pl		id.
παρακειμένην vb pres m/p part fem acc sg		id.
παρακειμένης vb pres m/p part fem gen sg		id.
παρακείμενοι vb pres m/p part masc nom pl		id.
παρακειμένους vb pres m/p part masc acc pl		id.
παράκεινται vb pres m/p ind 3rd pers pl		id.
παρακέκλημαι vb perf m/p ind 1st pers sg	. . . .	παρακλίνω
παρακεκλημένοι vb perf m/p part		
masc nom pl	. . . .	παρακαλέω
παρακέκλησθε vb perf m/p ind 2nd pers pl		id.
παρακελεύομαι vb pres m/p ind 1st pers sg	. .	παρακελεύω
παρακληθείς vb 1st aor pass part masc nom sg		παρακαλέω
παρακληθέντες vb 1st aor pass part masc nom pl		id.
παρακληθῇ vb 1st aor pass subj 3rd pers sg		id.
παρακληθῆναι vb 1st aor pass inf		id.
παρακληθῇς vb 1st aor pass subj 2nd pers sg		id.
παρακληθήσεσθε vb fut pass ind 2nd pers pl		id.
παρακληθήσεται vb fut pass ind 3rd pers sg		id.
παρακληθήσονται vb fut pass ind 3rd pers pl		id.
παρακλήθητι vb 1st aor pass impv 2nd pers sg		id.
παρακλήσει noun fem dat sg	. . . .	παράκλησις
παρακλήσεις noun fem nom and acc pl		id.
παρακλήσεως noun fem gen sg		id.
παράκλησιν noun fem acc sg		id.
παράκλησις noun fem nom sg		id.
παρακλητικούς adj masc acc pl	. . . .	παρακλητικός
παρακλήτορες noun masc nom pl	. . . .	παρακλήτωρ
παρακμάσῃ vb 1st aor act subj 3rd pers sg	. . .	παρακμάζω
παράκοιτοι noun fem nom pl	. . . .	παράκοιτος
παρακολουθήσειν vb fut act inf	. . . .	παρακολουθέω
παρακολουθοῦντα vb pres act part masc acc sg		id.
παρακομίζειν vb pres act inf	. . . .	παρακομίζω
παρακομίζοντα vb pres act part masc acc sg		id.
παρακομίζοντας vb pres act part masc acc pl		id.
παρακομιζόντων vb pres act part masc and neut gen pl		id.
παρακομίσαντες vb 1st aor act part masc nom pl		id.
παρακούεις vb pres act ind 2nd pers sg	. . . .	παρακούω
παρακούουσιν vb pres act ind 3rd pers pl		id.
παρακούσῃς vb 1st aor act subj 2nd pers sg		id.
παρακύπτει vb pres act ind 3rd pers sg	. . . .	παρακύπτω
παρακυπτομένας vb pres m/p part fem acc pl		id.
παρακύπτουσα vb pres act part fem nom sg		id.
παρακύπτων vb pres act part masc nom sg		id.
παρακύψας vb 1st aor act part masc nom sg		id.
παράλαβε vb 2nd aor act impv 2nd pers sg	.	παραλαμβάνω
παραλαβεῖν vb 2nd aor act inf		id.
παραλαβόντες vb 2nd aor act part masc nom pl		id.
παραλαβόντος vb 2nd aor act part masc and neut gen sg		id.

παραλάβω vb 2nd aor act subj 1st pers sg . . παραλαμβάνω
παραλαβών vb 2nd aor act part masc nom sg   d.
παραλαλοῦντος vb pres act part
      masc and neut gen sg . . . . παραλαλέω
παραλείπουσαι vb pres act part fem nom pl . . . παραλείπω
παραλελυμένα vb perf m/p part
      neut nom and acc pl . . . . παραλύω
παραλελυμένον vb perf m/p part masc acc sg,
      neut nom and acc sg   id.
παραλελυμένους vb perf m/p part masc acc pl   id.
παραλημφθεῖσαν vb 1st aor pass part
      fem acc sg . . . . παραλαμβάνω
παραλήμψεται vb fut mid ind 3rd pers sg   id.
παραλήμψομαι vb fut mid ind 1st pers sg   id.
παραλημψόμενος vb fut mid part masc nom sg   id.
παραλήμψονται vb fut mid ind 3rd pers pl   id.
παραλήψεται vb fut mid ind 3rd pers sg   id.
παραλήψονται vb fut mid ind 3rd pers pl   id.
παραλίᾳ adj fem dat sg . . . . παράλιος
παραλίαν adj fem acc sg   id.
παραλίαν adverb
παραλίαν noun fem acc sg . . . . παραλία
παραλίας adj fem gen sg . . . . παράλιος
παραλίας noun fem gen sg . . . . παραλία
παράλιον adj masc acc sg, neut nom and acc sg . . παράλιος
παράλιος adj masc nom sg   ic.
παραλίους adj masc acc pl   ic.
παραλιπεῖν vb 2nd aor act inf . . . . παραλείπω
παραλλαγῇ noun fem dat sg . . . . παραλλαγή
παραλλάξαι vb 1st aor act inf . . . . παραλλάσσω
παραλλάξεως noun fem gen sg . . . . παράλλαξις
παράλλαξον vb 1st aor act impv 2nd pers sg . παραλλάσσω
παραλλάσσον vb pres act part neut nom and acc sg   id.
παραλλάσσουσιν vb pres act ind 3rd pers pl   id.
παραλογιζέσθω vb pres dep impv
      3rd pers sg . . . . παραλογίζομαι
παραλογισαμένων vb 1st aor mid part gen pl   id.
παραλογισμοί noun masc nom pl . . . . παραλογισμός
παραλογισμοῖς noun masc dat pl   id.
παραλογισμῷ noun masc dat sg   id.
παραλυθήσονται vb fut pass ind 3rd pers pl . . . . παραλύω
παραλῦσαι vb 1st aor act inf   id.
παραλύσει vb fut act ind 3rd pers sg   id.
παράλυσιν noun fem acc sg . . . . παράλυσις
παραλύω vb pres act ind 1st pers sg
παραμείνῃ vb 1st aor act subj 3rd pers sg . . . . . παραμένω
παραμένει vb pres act ind 3rd pers sg   id.
παραμένουσιν vb pres act ind 3rd pers pl   id.
παραμενῶ vb fut act ind 1st pers sg   id.
παραμυθία noun fem nom sg
παραμυθίαν noun fem acc sg . . . . παραμυθία
παραμύθιον noun neut nom and acc sg

παραμυθούμενος vb pres dep part
      masc nom sg . . . . παραμυθέομαι
παραναγνούς vb 2nd aor act part
      masc nom sg . . . . παραναγινώσκω
παραναγνωσθέντος vb 1st aor pass part
      masc and neut gen sg   id.
παρανέκλινας vb 1st aor act ind
      2nd pers sg . . . . παρανακλίνω
παρανηλώμεθα vb perf m/p ind 1st pers pl . . παραναλίσκω
παράνομα adj neut nom and acc pl . . . . παράνομος
παρανομεῖν vb pres act inf . . . . παρανομέω
παρανομεῖς vb pres act ind 2nd pers sg   id.
παρανομεῖτε vb pres act impv 2nd pers pl   id.
παρανομήσασι vb 1st aor act part masc and neut dat pl   id.
παρανομία noun fem nom sg
παρανομίᾳ noun fem dat sg . . . . παρανομία
παρανομίαι noun fem nom pl   id.
παρανομίαις noun fem dat pl   id.
παρανομίαν noun fem acc sg   id.
παρανομίας noun fem gen sg and acc pl   id.
παράνομοι adj masc and fem nom pl . . . . παράνομος
παρανόμοις adj dat pl   id.
παράνομον adj acc sg, neut nom sg   id.
παράνομος adj masc and fem nom sg   id.
παρανόμου adj gen sg   id.
παρανομοῦντος vb pres act part
      masc and neut gen sg . . . . παρανομέω
παρανομούντων vb pres act part
      masc and neut gen pl   id.
παρανόμους adj masc and fem acc pl . . . . παράνομος
παρανομούσης vb pres act part fem gen sg . . . . παρανομέω
παρανομοῦσιν vb pres act ind 3rd pers pl   id.
παρανόμῳ adj dat sg . . . . παράνομος
παρανόμων adj gen pl   id.
παρανόμως adverb
παραξιφίδι noun fem dat sg . . . . παραξιφίς
παράπαν adverb
παραπέμποντας vb pres act part masc acc pl . . . παραπέμπω
παραπέμψας vb 1st aor act part masc nom sg   id.
παραπέπτωκας vb perf act ind 2nd pers sg . . . . παραπίπτω
παραπεσάτω vb 1st aor act impv 3rd pers sg   id.
παραπεσεῖν vb 2nd aor act inf   id.
παραπέσητε vb 2nd aor act subj 2nd pers pl   id.
παραπετάσματα noun neut nom and acc pl . παραπέτασμα
παραπικραίνειν vb pres act inf . . . . παραπικραίνω
παραπικραίνοντα vb pres act part masc acc sg   id.
παραπικραίνοντας vb pres act part masc acc pl   id.
παραπικραίνοντες vb pres act part masc nom pl   id.
παραπικραίνουσα vb pres act part fem nom sg   id.
παραπικραίνων vb pres act part masc nom sg   id.
παραπικρᾶναι vb 1st aor act inf   id.
παραπικράναντες vb 1st aor act part masc nom pl   id.

παραπικρασμῷ noun masc dat sg . . . . παραπικρασμός
παραπίπτοντας vb pres act part masc acc pl . . . παραπίπτω
παράπληκτος adj masc and fem nom sg
παραπληξίᾳ noun fem dat sg . . . . παραπληξία
παράπλου noun masc gen sg . . . . παράπλους
παραπομπῆς noun fem gen sg . . . . παραπομπή
παραπορεύεσθε vb pres dep impv
       2nd pers pl . . . . παραπορεύομαι
παραπορεύεσθε vb pres dep ind 2nd pers pl   id.
παραπορεύέσθωσαν vb pres dep impv 3rd pers pl id.
παραπορεύεται vb pres dep ind 3rd pers sg   id.
παραπορευόμεθα vb pres dep ind 1st pers sg   id.
παραπορευομένης vb pres dep part fem gen sg   id.
παραπορευόμενοι vb pres dep part masc nom pl   id.
παραπορευομένοις vb pres dep part
      masc and neut dat pl   id.
παραπορευόμενον vb pres dep part masc acc sg,
      neut nom and acc sg   id.
παραπορευόμενος vb pres dep part masc nom sg id.
παραπορευομένους vb pres dep part masc acc pl id.
παραπορευομένων vb pres dep part gen pl   id.
παραπορεύσῃ vb fut mid ind 2nd pers sg   id.
παραπορεύωνται vb pres dep subj 3rd pers pl   id.
παράπτωμα noun neut nom and acc sg
παραπτώμασι noun neut dat pl . . . . παράπτωμα
παραπτώματα noun neut nom and acc pl   id.
παραπτώματι noun neut dat sg   id.
παραπτώματος noun neut gen sg   id.
παραπτωμάτων noun neut gen pl   id.
παραπτώσει noun fem dat sg . . . . παράπτωσις
παραρρέον vb pres act part neut nom and acc sg . παραρρέω
παραρριπτεῖσθαι vb pres mid inf . . . . παραρριπτέω
παράρριψον vb 1st aor act impv 2nd pers sg   id.
παραρρυῇς vb pres act subj 2nd pers sg . . . . παραρρέω
παραρρύματα noun neut nom and acc pl . . . . . παάρρυμα
παρασήμῳ adj dat sg . . . . παράσημος
παρασιωπᾷ vb pres act ind 3rd pers sg . . . . . παρασιωπάω
παρασιωπηθήσεται vb fut pass ind 3rd pers sg   id.
παρασιωπήσεται vb fut mid ind 3rd pers pl   id.
παρασιωπήσῃ vb 1st aor act subj 3rd pers sg,
      fut mid ind 2nd pers sg   id.
παρασιωπήσῃς vb 1st aor act subj 2nd pers sg   id.
παρασιωπήσομαι vb fut mid ind 1st pers sg   id.
παρασιωπήσονται vb fut mid ind 3rd pers pl   id.
παρασκευάζει vb pres act ind 3rd pers sg . . παρασκευάζω
παρασκευάζειν vb pres act inf   id.
παρασκευάζεται vb pres m/p ind 3rd pers sg   id.
παρασκευάζετε vb pres act ind 2nd pers pl   id.
παρασκευαζόμενα vb pres m/p part
      neut nom and acc pl   id.
παρασκευάζοντι vb pres act part masc and neut dat sg id.
παρασκευάζου vb pres m/p impv 2nd pers sg   id.

παρασκευάσαι vb 1st aor act inf . . . . παρασκευάζω
παρασκευάσασθαι vb 1st aor mid inf   id.
παρασκευάσασθε vb 1st aor mid impv 2nd pers pl id.
παρασκευάσατε vb 1st aor act impv 2nd pers pl id.
παρασκευάσῃ vb fut mid ind 2nd pers sg   id.
παρασκευασθέντα vb 1st aor pass part
      neut nom and acc sg   id.
παρασκευήν noun fem acc sg . . . . παρασκευή
παραστάντες vb 2nd aor act part masc nom pl . . παρίστημι
παραστάς vb 2nd aor act part masc nom sg   id.
παράστασιν noun fem acc sg . . . . παράστασις
παράστηθι vb 2nd aor act impv 2nd pers sg . . . παρίστημι
παραστήκοντες vb perf act part masc nom pl   id.
παραστῆναι vb 2nd aor act inf   id.
παραστῆσαι vb 1st aor act inf   id.
παραστήσας vb 1st aor act part masc nom sg   id.
παραστήσεται vb fut mid ind 3rd pers sg   id.
παραστήσομαι vb fut mid ind 1st pers sg   id.
παραστήσονται vb fut mid ind 3rd pers pl   id.
παραστήσω vb fut act ind 1st pers sg   id.
παρασυνεβλήθη vb 1st aor pass ind
      3rd pers sg . . . . παρασυμβάλλω
παρασχέσθαι vb 2nd aor mid inf . . . . παρέχω
παρατάξαι vb 1st aor mid impv 2nd pers sg . . παρατάσσω
παραταξαμένους vb 1st aor mid part masc acc pl id.
παρατάξασθαι vb 1st aor mid inf   id.
παρατάξασθε vb 1st aor mid impv 2nd pers pl   id.
παρατάξει noun fem dat sg . . . . παράταξις
παρατάξεται vb fut mid ind 3rd pers sg . . . . . παρατάσσω
παρατάξεων noun fem gen pl . . . . παράταξις
παρατάξεως noun fem gen sg   id.
παρατάξῃ vb fut mid ind 2nd pers sg . . . . παρατάσσω
παρατάξηται vb 1st aor mid subj 3rd pers sg   id.
παράταξιν noun fem acc sg . . . . παράταξις
παράταξις noun fem nom sg   id.
παρατάξονται vb fut mid ind 3rd pers pl . . . . παρατάσσω
παραταξώμεθα vb 1st aor mid subj 1st pers pl   id.
παρατάσσεται vb pres m/p ind 3rd pers sg   id.
παρατασσόμενοι vb pres m/p part masc nom pl   id.
παρατασσόμενος vb pres m/p part masc nom sg   id.
παρατάσσονται vb pres m/p ind 3rd pers pl   id.
παρατεθέντα vb 1st aor pass part
      neut nom and acc pl . . . . παρατίθημι
παρατεθέρμανται vb perf m/p ind
      3rd pers pl . . . . παραθερμαίνω
παρατεθῆναι vb 1st aor pass inf . . . . παρατίθημι
παράτεινον vb 1st aor act impv 2nd pers sg . . . . παρατείνω
παρατεῖνον vb pres act part neut nom and acc sg id.
παρατείνοντα vb pres act part neut nom and acc pl id.
παρατείνουσαν vb pres act part fem acc sg   id.
παρατενεῖ vb fut act ind 3rd pers sg   id.
παρατέταγμαι vb perf m/p ind 1st pers sg . . . . παρατάσσω

παρατέτακται   vb perf m/p ind 3rd pers sg   . . .   παρατάσσω

παρατηρεῖν   vb pres act inf . . . . παρατηρέω

παρατηρήσεται   vb fut mid ind 3rd pers sg   d.

παρατηρήσῃ   vb 1st aor mid subj 2nd pers sg   d.

παρατηροῦντες   vb pres act part masc nom pl   d.

παρατιθέασιν   vb pres act ind 3rd pers pl   . . . .   παρατίθημι

παρατίθεμαι   vb pres m/p ind 1st pers sg   d.

παρατιθέμενα   vb pres m/p part neut nom and acc pl   d.

παρατίθεται   vb pres m/p ind 3rd pers sg   d.

παρατρέχειν   vb pres act inf . . . . παρατρέχω

παρατρέχοντα   vb pres act part masc acc sg   d.

παρατρέχοντες   vb pres act part masc nom pl   d.

παρατρεχόντων   vb pres act part masc and neut gen pl   d.

παρατρέχουσα   vb pres act part fem nom sg   d.

παρατρέχουσιν   vb pres act ind 3rd pers pl   d.

παραυτίκα   adverb

παράφρονας   noun masc acc pl . . . . παράφρων

παραφρονήσει   noun fem dat sg . . . . παραφρόνησις

παραφρονοῦντα   vb pres act part masc acc sg   .   παραφρονέω

παραφυάδας   noun fem acc pl . . . . παραφυάς

παραφυάδες   noun fem nom pl   id.

παραφυάσιν   noun fem dat pl   id.

παραχρῆμα   adverb

παραχωρήσαντες   vb 1st aor act part

     masc nom pl . . . . παραχωρέω

παραχωρήσειν   vb fut act inf   id.

παρδάλεις   noun fem nom and acc pl . . . . παρδαλις

παρδάλεοι   adj masc nom pl . . . . παρδάλεος

παρδάλεων   noun fem gen pl . . . . παρδαλις

πάρδαλιν   noun fem acc sg   id.

πάρδαλις   noun fem nom sg   id.

παρεβαίνετε   vb impf act ind 2nd pers pl . . . . . . παραβαίνω

παρέβαλεν   vb 2nd aor act ind 3rd pers sg   . . . .   παραβάλλω

παρέβαλλον   vb impf act ind 1st pers sg   id.

παρέβη   vb 2nd aor act ind 3rd pers sg . . . . παραβαίνω

παρέβημεν   vb 2nd aor act ind 1st pers pl   id.

παρέβην   vb 2nd aor act ind 1st pers sg   id.

παρέβησαν   vb 2nd aor act ind 3rd pers pl   id.

παρέβητε   vb 2nd aor act ind 2nd pers pl   id.

παρεβιάζοντο   vb impf dep ind 3rd pers pl   .   παραβιάζομαι

παρεβιάσαντο   vb 1st aor mid ind 3rd pers pl   id.

παρεβιάσατο   vb 1st aor mid ind 3rd pers sg   id.

παρεβίβασεν   vb 1st aor act ind 3rd pers sg   . . .   παραβιβάζω

παρέβλεψεν   vb 1st aor act ind 3rd pers sg   . . . . .   παραβλέπω

παρεγένετο   vb 2nd aor mid ind 3rd pers sg   . .   παραγίνομαι

παρεγενήθη   vb 1st aor pass ind 3rd pers sg   id.

παρεγενήθησαν   vb 1st aor pass ind 3rd pers pl   id.

παρεγενήθητε   vb 1st aor pass ind 2nd pers pl   id.

παρεγενόμην   vb 2nd aor mid ind 1st pers sg   id.

παρεγένοντο   vb 2nd aor mid ind 3rd pers pl   id.

παρεγένου   vb 2nd aor mid ind 2nd pers sg   id.

παρεγίνετο   vb impf dep ind 3rd pers sg   id.

παρεγίνοντο   vb impf dep ind 3rd pers pl . . . . παραγίνομαι

παρεδειγμάτισαν   vb 1st aor act ind

     3rd pers pl . . . . παραδειγματίζω

παρέδειξα   vb 1st aor act ind 1st pers sg . . . . . παραδεικνύω

παρεδίδοντο   vb impf m/p ind 3rd pers pl   . . . .   παραδίδωμι

παρεδόθη   vb 1st aor pass ind 3rd pers sg   id.

παρεδόθημεν   vb 1st aor pass ind 1st pers pl   id.

παρεδόθην   vb 1st aor pass ind 1st pers sg   id.

παρεδόθησαν   vb 1st aor pass ind 3rd pers pl   id.

παρεδόθητε   vb 1st aor pass ind 2nd pers pl   id.

παρεδόξασας   vb 1st aor act ind 2nd pers sg   . .   παραδοξάζω

παρεδόξασεν   vb 1st aor act ind 3rd pers sg   id.

παρεδρεύει   vb pres act ind 3rd pers sg   . . . . . .   παρεδρεύω

πάρεδρον   noun masc acc sg . . . . πάρεδρος

παρέδωκα   vb 1st aor act ind 1st pers sg . . . . . παραδίδωμι

παρεδώκαμεν   vb 1st aor act ind 1st pers pl   id.

παρέδωκαν   vb 1st aor act ind 3rd pers pl   id.

παρέδωκας   vb 1st aor act ind 2nd pers sg   id.

παρέδωκεν   vb 1st aor act ind 3rd pers sg   id.

παρέζευξεν   vb 1st aor act ind 3rd pers pl   . .   παραζεύγνυμι

παρεζήλωσαν   vb 1st aor act ind 3rd pers pl   . . .   παραζηλόω

παρεζήλωσεν   vb 1st aor act ind 3rd pers sg   id.

παρεθάρσυνον   vb impf act ind 3rd pers pl   .   παραθαρσύνω

παρεθέμην   vb 2nd aor mid ind 1st pers sg   . . . .   παρατίθημι

παρέθεντο   vb 2nd aor mid ind 3rd pers pl   id.

παρέθετο   vb 2nd aor mid ind 3rd pers sg   id.

παρέθηκαν   vb 1st aor act ind 3rd pers pl   id.

παρέθηκεν   vb 1st aor act ind 3rd pers sg   id.

πάρει   vb pres act ind 2nd pers sg . . . . πάρειμι

παρείθησαν   vb 1st aor pass ind 3rd pers pl . . . . . . παρίημι

παρείλατο   vb 1st aor mid ind 3rd pers sg . . . . . . παραιρέω

παρείλημμαι   vb perf m/p ind 1st pers sg . . . παραλαμβάνω

παρεῖμαι   vb perf m/p ind 1st pers sg . . . . παρίημι

παρείμεθα   vb perf m/p ind 1st pers pl   id.

παρειμέναι   vb perf m/p part fem nom pl   id.

παρειμέναις   vb perf m/p part fem dat pl   id.

παρειμένη   vb perf m/p part fem nom sg   id.

παρειμένη   vb perf m/p part fem dat sg   id.

παρειμένος   vb perf m/p part masc nom sg   id.

παρειμένους   vb perf m/p part masc acc pl   id.

πάρειμι   vb pres act ind 1st pers sg

παρεῖναι   vb pres act inf . . . . πάρειμι

παρείσθωσαν   vb perf m/p impv 3rd pers pl . . . . . . παρίημι

πάρεισιν   vb pres act ind 3rd pers pl . . . . πάρειμι

παρεισπορευόμενοι   vb pres dep part

     masc nom pl . . . . παρεισπορεύομαι

παρειστήκει   vb plpf act ind 3rd pers sg . . . . παρίστημι

παρειστήκεισαν   vb plpf act ind 3rd pers pl   id.

παρεκάθισαν   vb 1st aor act ind 3rd pers pl   . . .   παρακαθίζω

παρεκάλει   vb impf act ind 3rd pers sg . . . . παρακαλέω

παρεκάλεσα   vb 1st aor act ind 1st pers sg   id.

παρεκάλεσαν vb 1st aor act ind 3rd pers pl . . . παρακαλέω
παρεκάλεσας vb 1st aor act ind 2nd pers sg   id.
παρεκάλεσε(ν) vb 1st aor act ind 3rd pers sg   id.
παρεκάλουν vb impf act ind 3rd pers pl   id.
παρεκάλυπτον vb impf act ind 3rd pers pl . παρακαλύπτω
παρεκατέθετο vb 2nd aor mid ind
     3rd pers sg . . . . παρακάθημαι
παρεκατετιθέμην vb impf m/p ind
     1st pers sg . . . . παρακατατίθημι
παρεκέλευεν vb impf act ind 3rd pers sg . . . . . παρακελεύω
παρέκλεισεν vb 1st aor act ind 3rd pers sg . . . . παρακλείω
παρεκλήθη vb 1st aor pass ind 3rd pers sg . . . . παρακαλέω
παρεκλήθην vb 1st aor pass ind 1st pers sg   id.
παρεκλήθης vb 1st aor pass ind 2nd pers sg   id.
παρεκλήθησαν vb 1st aor pass ind 3rd pers pl   id.
παρεκομίζετο vb impf m/p ind 3rd pers sg . . . παρακομίζω
παρεκρούσατο vb 1st aor mid ind 3rd pers sg . παρακρούω
παρεκτεῖνον vb pres act part neut
     nom and acc sg . . . . παρεκτείνω
παρεκτείνου vb pres m/p impv 2nd pers sg   id.
παρέκυψεν vb 1st aor act ind 3rd pers sg . . . . . παρακύπτω
παρέλαβε(ν) vb 2nd aor act ind 3rd pers sg . παραλαμβάνω
παρέλαβες vb 2nd aor act ind 2nd pers sg   id.
παρελεύσεσθε vb fut mid ind 2nd pers pl . . . . παρέρχομαι
παρελεύσεται vb fut mid ind 3rd pers sg   id.
παρελεύσῃ vb fut mid ind 2nd pers sg   id.
παρελεύσομαι vb fut mid ind 1st pers sg   id.
παρελευσόμεθα vb fut mid ind 1st pers pl   id.
παρελεύσονται vb fut mid ind 3rd pers pl   id.
παρεληλυθότα vb perf act part neut nom and acc pl   id.
παρεληλυθότας vb perf act part masc acc pl   id.
παρέλθατε vb 1st aor act impv 2nd pers pl   id.
παρελθάτω vb 1st aor act impv 3rd pers sg   id.
πάρελθε vb 2nd aor act impv 2nd pers sg   id.
παρελθεῖν vb 2nd aor act inf   id.
παρελθέτω vb 2nd aor act impv 3rd pers sg   id.
παρελθέτωσαν vb 2nd aor act impv 3rd pers pl   id.
παρέλθῃ vb 2nd aor act subj 3rd pers sg   id.
παρέλθῃς vb 2nd aor act subj 2nd pers sg   id.
παρέλθοι vb 2nd aor act opt 3rd pers sg   id.
παρελθόν vb 2nd aor act part neut nom and acc sg   id.
παρελθόντες vb 2nd aor act part masc nom pl   id.
παρελθόντων vb 2nd aor act part masc and neut gen pl   id.
παρέλθω vb 2nd aor act subj 1st pers sg   id.
παρέλθωμεν vb 2nd aor act subj 1st pers pl   id.
παρελθών vb 2nd aor act part masc nom sg   id.
παρέλιπον vb 2nd aor act ind 3rd pers pl . . . . . παραλείπω
παρελκύσει vb fut act ind 3rd pers sg . . . . παρέλκω
παρελκύσῃς vb 1st aor act subj 2nd pers sg   id.
παρέλκυσις noun fem nom sg
παρελογίσαντο vb 1st aor mid ind
     3rd pers pl . . . . παραλογίζομαι

παρελογίσασθε vb 1st aor mid ind
     2nd pers pl . . . . παραλογίζομαι
παρελογίσατο vb 1st aor mid ind 3rd pers sg   id.
παρελογίσω vb 1st aor mid ind 2nd pers sg   id.
παρέλυεν vb impf act ind 3rd pers sg . . . . παραλύω
παρελύθη vb 1st aor pass ind 3rd pers sg   id.
παρελύθησαν vb 1st aor pass ind 3rd pers pl   id.
παρελύοντο vb impf m/p ind 3rd pers pl   id.
παρέλυσεν vb 1st aor act ind 3rd pers sg   id.
παρέμβαλε vb 2nd aor act impv 2nd pers sg . . . παρεμβάλλω
παρεμβαλεῖ vb fut act ind 3rd pers sg   id.
παρεμβαλεῖν vb 2nd aor act inf   id.
παρεμβάλετε vb 2nd aor act impv 2nd pers pl   id.
παρεμβαλέτωσαν vb 2nd aor act impv 3rd pers pl   id.
παρεμβάλῃ vb 2nd aor act subj 3rd pers sg   id.
παρεμβάλητε vb 2nd aor act subj 2nd pers pl   id.
παρεμβάλλει vb pres act ind 3rd pers sg   id.
παρεμβάλλειν vb pres act inf   id.
παρεμβάλλομεν vb pres act ind 1st pers pl   id.
παρεμβάλλοντες vb pres act part masc nom pl   id.
παρεμβάλλου vb pres m/p impv 2nd pers sg   id.
παρεμβάλλουσαι vb pres act part fem nom pl   id.
παρεμβάλλουσιν vb pres act ind 3rd pers pl   id.
παρεμβαλοῦμεν vb fut act ind 1st pers pl   id.
παρεμβαλοῦσιν vb fut act ind 3rd pers pl   id.
παρεμβαλῶ vb fut act ind 1st pers sg   id.
παρεμβεβλήκασι vb perf act ind 3rd pers pl   id.
παρεμβεβλήκει vb plpf act ind 3rd pers sg   id.
παρεμβεβλήκεισαν vb plpf act ind 3rd pers pl   id.
παρεμβεβληκότας vb perf act part masc acc pl   id.
παρεμβεβληκότες vb perf act part masc nom pl   id.
παρεμβεβληκυῖαν vb perf act part fem acc sg   id.
παρεμβεβληκώς vb perf act part masc nom sg   id.
Παρεμβολαι pr noun fem nom pl . . . . παρεμβολή
παρεμβολαί noun fem nom pl   id.
παρεμβολαῖς noun fem dat pl   id.
παρεμβολάς noun fem acc pl   id.
Παρεμβολη pr noun fem nom sg   id.
παρεμβολή noun fem nom sg   id.
παρεμβολῇ noun fem dat sg   id.
παρεμβολήν noun fem acc sg   id.
παρεμβολῆς noun fem gen sg   id.
παρεμβολῶν noun fem gen pl   id.
παρέμεινεν vb 1st aor act ind 3rd pers sg . . . . παραμένω
παρέμενεν vb impf act ind 3rd pers sg   id.
παρεμπίπτει vb pres act ind 3rd pers sg . . . . . . παρεμπίπτω
παρενέβαλε(ν) vb 2nd aor act ind 3rd pers sg . παρεμβάλλω
παρενέβαλλον vb impf act ind 3rd pers pl   id.
παρενεβάλομεν vb 2nd aor act ind 1st pers pl   id.
παρενέβαλον vb 2nd aor act ind 3rd pers pl   id.
παρενεβάλοσαν vb 2nd aor act ind 3rd pers pl   id.
παρενοχλεῖν vb pres act inf . . . . παρενοχλέω

παρενοχλείτω vb pres act impv 3rd pers sg . . . παρενοχλέω

παρενοχληθήσεται vb fut pass ind 3rd pers sg   id.

παρενοχλῆσαι vb 1st aor act inf   id.

παρενοχλήσει vb fut act ind 3rd pers sg   id.

παρενοχλῶν vb pres act part masc nom sg   id.

παρενώχλησεν vb 1st aor act ind 3rd pers sg   id.

πάρεξ preposition

παρέξει vb fut act ind 3rd pers sg . . . . παρέχω

παρεξέλιπεν vb 2nd aor act ind 3rd pers sg . . . παρεκλείπω

παρεξεστηκώς vb perf act part masc nom sg . παρεξίστημι

παρεξόμεθα vb fut mid ind 1st pers pl . . . . παρέχω

παρεξόμενος vb fut mid part masc nom sg   id.

παρέπεσεν vb 1st aor act ind 3rd pers sg . . . . . παραπίπτω

παρέπεσον vb 2nd aor act ind 3rd pers pl   id.

παρεπήδησεν vb 1st aor act ind 3rd pers sg . . . παραπηδάω

παρεπιδεικνύς vb pres act part

     masc nom sg . . . . παρεπιδείκνυμι

παρεπίδημος adj masc and fem nom sg

παρεπίκρανα vb 1st aor act ind 1st pers sg . παραπικραίνω

παρεπίκραναν vb 1st aor act ind 3rd pers pl   id.

παρεπίκρανας vb 1st aor act ind 2nd pers sg   id.

παρεπίκρανε vb 1st aor act ind 3rd pers sg   id.

παρεπορεύετο vb impf dep ind

     3rd pers sg . . . . παραπορεύομαι

παρεπορεύθημεν vb 1st aor pass ind 1st pers pl   id.

παρεπορεύοντο vb impf dep ind 3rd pers pl   id.

πάρεργος adj masc and fem nom sg

παρέρριψαν vb 1st aor act ind 3rd pers pl . . . . παραρρίπτω

παρερχομένους vb pres dep part masc acc pl   παρέρχομαι

πάρες vb 2nd aor act impv 2nd pers sg . . . . παρίημι

παρέσει vb fut mid ind 2nd pers sg . . . . πάρειμι

παρέση vb fut mid ind 2nd pers sg   id.

παρεσιώπα vb impf act ind 3rd pers sg . . . . . παρασιωπάω

παρεσιωπήσατε vb 1st aor act ind 2nd pers pl   id.

παρεσιώπησεν vb 1st aor act ind 3rd pers sg   id.

παρεσκευάσαντο vb 1st aor mid ind

     3rd pers pl . . . . παρασκευάζω

παρεσκευασμένη vb perf m/p part fem nom sg   id.

παρεσκευασμένοι vb perf m/p part masc nom pl   id.

πάρεσμεν vb pres act ind 1st pers pl . . . . πάρειμι

παρέσται vb fut m/p ind 3rd pers sg   id.

παρεστάναι vb perf act inf . . . . παρίστημι

παρέστη vb 2nd aor act ind 3rd pers sg   id.

παρέστηκαν vb perf act ind 3rd pers pl   id.

παρεστήκασιν vb perf act ind 3rd pers pl   id.

παρέστηκεν vb perf act ind 3rd pers sg   id.

παρεστηκέναι vb perf act inf   id.

παρεστηκόσι vb perf act part masc and neut dat pl   id.

παρεστηκότας vb perf act part masc acc pl   id.

παρεστηκότες vb perf act part masc nom pl   id.

παρεστηκότος vb perf act part masc and neut gen sg   id.

παρεστηκότων vb perf act part masc and neut gen pl   id.

παρεστηκυῖα vb perf act part fem nom sg . . . . . παρίστημι

παρεστηκυῖαι vb perf act part fem nom pl   id.

παρεστηκώς vb perf act part masc nom sg   id.

παρέστην vb 2nd aor act ind 1st pers sg   id.

παρέστησαν vb 2nd aor act ind 3rd pers pl   id.

παρέστησεν vb 1st aor act ind 3rd pers sg   id.

πάρεστιν vb pres act ind 3rd pers sg . . . . πάρειμι

παρεστῶτας vb perf act part masc acc pl . . . . . . παρίστημι

παρεστῶτες vb perf act part masc nom pl   id.

παρέσχες vb 2nd aor act ind 2nd pers sg . . . . παρέχω

παρέσχον vb 2nd aor act ind 3rd pers pl   id.

παρέσχου vb 2nd aor mid ind 2nd pers sg   id.

παρετάξαντο vb 1st aor mid ind 3rd pers pl . . παρατάσσω

παρετάξατο vb 1st aor mid ind 3rd pers sg   id.

παρετάσσετο vb impf m/p ind 3rd pers sg   id.

παρετάσσοντο vb impf m/p ind 3rd pers pl   id.

παρετέθη vb 1st aor pass ind 3rd pers sg . . . . . παρατίθημι

παρέτεινον vb 1st aor act ind 3rd pers pl . . . . . . παρατείνω

παρετήρησαν vb 1st aor act ind 3rd pers pl . . . . παρατηρέω

παρετηροῦσαν vb impf act ind 3rd pers pl   id.

παρεφέρετο vb impf m/p ind 3rd pers sg . . . . . . παραφέρω

παρέφερον vb impf act ind 3rd pers pl   id.

παρέχει vb pres act ind 3rd pers sg . . . . παρέχω

παρέχειν vb pres act inf   id.

παρέχετε vb pres act ind 2nd pers pl   id.

παρεχούσης vb pres act part fem gen sg   id.

παρέχουσι vb pres act ind 3rd pers pl   id.

παρέχων vb pres act part masc nom sg   id.

παρέχωσιν vb pres act subj 3rd pers pl   id.

παρεωραμένος vb perf m/p part masc nom sg . . . παροράω

παρεωραμένῳ vb pres m/p part masc and neut dat sg   id.

παρῇ vb pres act subj 3rd pers sg . . . . πάρειμι

παρήγαγεν vb 2nd aor act ind 3rd pers sg . . . . παράγω

παρήγγειλε(ν) vb 1st aor act ind 3rd pers sg . . παραγγέλλω

παρηγγελμέναις vb perf m/p part fem dat pl   id.

παρῆγεν vb impf act ind 3rd pers sg . . . . παράγω

παρῆγον vb impf act ind 3rd pers pl   id.

παρηγορεῖν vb pres act inf . . . . παρηγορέω

παρηγορίαις noun fem dat pl . . . . παρηγορία

παρηγορίαν noun fem acc sg   id.

παρῆκαν vb 1st aor act ind 3rd pers pl . . . . παρίημι

παρήκουσα vb 1st aor act ind 1st pers sg . . . . . . παρακούω

παρήκουσαν vb 1st aor act ind 3rd pers pl   id.

παρηκούσατε vb 1st aor act ind 2nd pers pl   id.

παρῆλθαν vb 1st aor act ind 3rd pers pl . . . . . . παρέρχομαι

παρῆλθεν vb 2nd aor act ind 3rd pers sg   id.

παρῆλθες vb 2nd aor act ind 2nd pers sg   id.

παρήλθετε vb 2nd aor act ind 2nd pers pl   id.

παρήλθομεν vb 2nd aor act ind 1st pers pl   id.

παρῆλθον vb 2nd aor act ind 1st pers sg and 3rd pers pl   id.

παρήλθοσαν vb 2nd aor act ind 3rd pers pl   id.

παρηλλαγμένα vb perf m/p part

    neut nom and acc pl . . . . παραλλάσσω

παρηλλαγμένον vb perf m/p part masc acc sg   id.

παρῆν vb impf act ind 3rd pers sg . . . . πάρειμι

παρήνεγκαν vb 1st aor act ind 3rd pers pl . . . . . . παραφέρω

παρήνει vb impf act ind 3rd pers sg . . . . παραινέω

παρηνόμουν vb impf act ind 3rd pers pl . . . . . . παρανομέω

παρηνώχλησα vb 1st aor act ind 1st pers sg . . παρενοχλέω

παρηνώχλησαν vb 1st aor act ind 3rd pers pl   id.

παρηνώχλησας vb 1st aor act ind 2nd pers sg   id.

παρηνώχλησεν vb 1st aor act ind 3rd pers sg   id.

παρηρίθμησεν vb 1st aor act ind 3rd pers sg . . παραριθμέω

παρῇς vb pres act subj 2nd pers sg . . . . πάρειμι

παρῆσαν vb impf act ind 3rd pers pl   id.

παρήσει vb fut act ind 3rd pers sg . . . . παρίημι

παρήσομεν vb fut act ind 1st pers pl   id.

παρήσω vb fut act ind 1st pers sg   id.

παρῃτεῖτο vb impf m/p ind 3rd pers sg . . . . παραιτέω

παρῃτήσατο vb 1st aor mid ind 3rd pers sg   id.

παρῄτηται vb perf m/p ind 3rd pers sg   id.

παρήχθη vb 1st aor pass ind 3rd pers sg . . . . παράγω

παρθένια noun neut nom and acc pl . . . . παρθένια

παρθενίᾳ noun fem dat sg . . . . παρθενία

παρθενίας noun fem gen sg   id.

παρθενικά adj neut nom and acc pl . . . . παρθενικός

παρθενικόν adj masc acc sg   id.

παρθένοι noun fem nom pl . . . . παρθένος

παρθένον noun fem acc sg   id.

παρθένος noun fem nom sg   id.

παρθένου noun fem gen sg   id.

παρθένους noun fem acc pl   id.

παρθένῳ noun fem dat sg   id.

παρθένων noun fem gen pl   id.

πάριδε vb 2nd aor act impv 2nd pers sg . . . . παροράω

παριδεῖν vb 2nd aor act inf   id.

παρίδῃ vb 2nd aor act subj 3rd pers sg   id.

παρίδῃς vb 2nd aor act subj 2nd pers sg   id.

παριδόντα vb 2nd aor act part masc acc sg   id.

παριδών vb 2nd aor act part masc nom sg   id.

παρίνοις adj masc and neut dat pl . . . . πάρινος

παρίνου noun neut gen sg   id.

πάριον noun masc acc sg . . . . πάριος

παριόντας vb pres act part masc acc pl . . . . πάρειμι

παριόντων vb pres act part masc and neut gen pl   id.

παριστάμενος vb pres m/p part masc nom sg . . παρίστημι

παρίστασθαι vb pres m/p inf   id.

παριστάσθω vb pres m/p impv 3rd pers sg   id.

παριστῶσα vb pres act part fem nom sg . . . . . . παριστάω

παροδεύοντος vb pres act part

    masc and neut gen sg . . . . παροδεύω

παροδεύσαντες vb 1st aor act part masc nom pl   id.

παροδευσάτω vb 1st aor act impv 3rd pers sg   id.

παροδεύσῃ vb 1st aor act subj 3rd pers sg . . . . . . παροδεύω

παροδεύσω vb 1st aor act subj 1st pers sg,

    fut act ind 1st pers sg   id.

παρόδοις noun fem dat pl . . . . πάροδος

πάροδον noun fem (or masc) acc sg   id.

πάροδος noun fem nom sg   id.

παρόδῳ noun fem (or masc) dat sg   id.

πάροικε vb 2nd aor act impv 2nd pers sg . . . . . . παροικέω

παροίκει vb pres act impv 2nd pers sg   id.

παροικεῖ vb pres act ind 3rd pers sg   id.

παροικεῖν vb pres act inf   id.

παροικεῖς vb pres act ind 2nd pers sg   id.

παροικεσίας noun fem gen sg . . . . παροικεσία

παροικῆσαι vb 1st aor act inf . . . . παροικέω

παροικήσει noun fem dat sg . . . . παροίκησις

παροικήσει vb fut act ind 3rd pers sg . . . . παροικέω

παροικήσεις vb fut act ind 2nd pers sg   id.

παροικήσεως noun fem gen sg . . . . παροίκησις

παροικήσῃ vb 1st aor act subj 3rd pers sg . . . . . . παροικέω

παροικήσῃς vb 1st aor act subj 2nd pers sg   id.

παροικήσουσιν vb fut act ind 3rd pers pl   id.

παροικήσω vb fut act ind 1st pers sg   id.

παροικία noun fem nom sg

παροικίᾳ noun fem dat sg . . . . παροικία

παροικίαις noun fem dat pl   id.

παροικίαν noun fem acc sg   id.

παροικίας noun fem gen sg   id.

παροικιῶν noun fem gen pl   id.

πάροικοι adj masc and fem nom pl . . . . πάροικος

πάροικον adj acc sg, neut nom sg   id.

πάροικος adj masc and fem nom sg   id.

παροίκου adj gen sg   id.

παροικοῦντα vb pres act part masc acc sg . . . . . . παροικέω

παροικοῦντας vb pres act part masc acc pl   id.

παροικοῦντες vb pres act part masc nom pl   id.

παροικούντων vb pres act part masc and neut gen pl   id.

παροίκους adj masc and fem acc pl . . . . πάροικος

παροικοῦσι vb pres act part masc and neut dat pl . παροικέω

παροικῶ vb pres act ind 1st pers sg   id.

παροίκῳ adj dat sg . . . . πάροικος

παροίκων adj gen pl   id.

παροικῶν vb pres act part masc nom sg . . . . παροικέω

παροιμίαι noun fem nom pl . . . . παροιμία

παροιμίαις noun fem dat pl   id.

παροιμίαν noun fem acc sg   id.

παροιμίας noun fem gen sg and acc pl   id.

παροιμιῶν noun fem gen pl   id.

παροινήσουσιν vb fut act ind 3rd pers pl . . . . . . παροινέω

παροίστρησεν vb 1st aor act ind 3rd pers sg . . παροιστράω

παροιστρήσουσι vb fut act ind 3rd pers pl   id.

παροιστρῶσα vb pres act part fem nom sg   id.

παρόν vb pres act part neut nom and acc sg . . . . πάρειμι

παρόντα	vb pres act part masc acc sg	πάρειμι	παρρησίαν	noun fem acc sg	παρρησία
παρόντας	vb pres act part masc acc pl	id.	παρρησίας	noun fem gen sg	id.
παρόντες	vb pres act part masc nom pl	id.	παρρησιάзεται	vb fut mid	
παρόντος	vb pres act part masc and neut gen sg	id.	ird 3rd pers sg	παρρησιάζομαι
παρόντων	vb pres act part masc and neut gen pl	id.	παρρησιαзθήσῃ	vb fut pass ind 2nd pers sg	id.
παροξῦναι	vb 1st aor act inf	παροξύνω	παρρησιάзομαι	vb fut mid ind 1st pers sg	id.
παροξύναντες	vb 1st aor act part masc nom pl	id.	παρώδευσεν	vb 1st aor act ind 3rd pers sg	παροδεύω
παροξυνάντων	vb 1st aor act part masc and neut gen pl	id.	παρῴκει	vb impf act ind 3rd pers sg	παροικέω
παρόξυνε	vb pres act impv 2nd pers sg	id.	παρῳκήκασιν	vb perf act ind 3rd pers pl	id.
παροξύνει	vb pres act ind 3rd pers sg	id.	παρῴκησα	vb 1st aor act ind 1st pers sg	id.
παροξυνεῖ	vb pres act ind 3rd pers sg	id.	παρῳκήσομεν	vb 1st aor act ind 1st pers pl	id.
παροξύνῃ	vb pres m/p ind 2nd pers sg	id.	παρῴκησαν	vb 1st aor act ind 3rd pers pl	id.
παροξυνθείς	vb 1st aor pass part masc nom sg	id.	παρῴκησας	vb 1st aor act ind 2nd pers sg	id.
παροξυνθῇς	vb 1st aor pass subj 2nd pers sg	id.	παρῴκησεν	vb 1st aor act ind 3rd pers sg	id.
παροξυνθήσεται	vb fut pass ind 3rd pers sg	id.	παρῳκοῦσαν	vb impf act ind 3rd pers pl	id.
παροξύνοντες	vb pres act part masc nom pl	id.	παρωμίδας	noun fem acc pl	παρωμίς
παροξύνουσα	vb pres act part fem nom sg	id.	παρωξύναμεν	vb 1st aor act ind 1st pers pl	παροξύνω
παροξυνοῦσιν	vb fut act ind 3rd pers pl	id.	παρώξυναν	vb 1st aor act ind 3rd pers pl	id.
παροξυνῶ	vb fut act ind 1st pers sg	id.	παρώξυνας	vb 1st aor act ind 2nd pers sg	id.
παροξύνων	vb pres act part masc nom sg	id.	παρωξύνατε	vb 1st aor act ind 2nd pers pl	id.
παροξυσμῷ	noun masc dat sg	παροξυσμός	παρώξυνεν	vb 1st aor act ind 3rd pers sg	id.
παροραθήσεσθαι	vb fut pass inf	παροράω	παρωξύνθη	vb 1st aor pass ind 3rd pers sg	id.
παρορᾷς	vb pres act ind 2nd pers sg	id.	παρωξύνθην	vb 1st aor pass ind 1st pers sg	id.
παρόρασις	noun fem nom sg		παρώργισα	vb 1st aor act ind 1st pers sg	παροργίζω
παροργίζειν	vb pres act inf	παροργίζω	παρώργισαν	vb 1st aor act ind 3rd pers pl	id.
παροργίζετε	vb pres act impv 2nd pers pl	id.	παρώργισας	vb 1st aor act ind 2nd pers sg	id.
παροργίζητε	vb pres act subj 2nd pers pl	id.	παρωργίσατε	vb 1st aor act ind 2nd pers pl	id.
παροργίζοντες	vb pres act part masc nom pl	id.	παρώργισεν	vb 1st aor act ind 3rd pers sg	id.
παροργίζουσιν	vb pres act ind 3rd pers pl	id.	παρωργισμένην	vb perf m/p part fem acc sg	id.
παροργίζων	vb pres act part masc nom sg	id.	παρώσας	vb 1st aor act part masc nom sg	παρωθέω
παροργιοῦσιν	vb fut act ind 3rd pers pl	id.	πᾶς	adj masc nom sg	
παροργίσαι	vb 1st aor act inf	id.	πᾶσα	adj fem nom sg	πᾶς
παροργίσῃς	vb 1st aor act subj 2nd pers sg	id.	πᾶσαι	adj fem nom pl	id.
παροργισθήσεται	vb fut pass ind 3rd pers sg	id.	πάσαις	adj fem dat pl	id.
παροργίσματα	noun neut nom and acc pl	παρόργισμα	πάσαις	see πάσαις	
παροργισμάτων	noun masc gen pl	id.	πασάμεναι	vb 1st aor mid part fem nom pl	πάσσω
παροργισμοῦ	noun masc gen sg	παροργισμός	πᾶσαν	adj fem acc sg	πᾶς
παροργισμούς	noun masc acc pl	id.	πάσας	adj fem acc pl	id.
παροργισμῷ	noun masc dat sg	id.	πασάτω	vb 1st aor act impv 3rd pers sg	πάσσω
παροργίσωσιν	vb 1st aor act subj 3rd pers pl	παροργίζω	πάσῃ	adj fem dat sg	πᾶς
παροργιῶ	vb fut act ind 1st pers sg	id.	πάσης	adj fem gen sg	id.
παρορμῆσαι	vb 1st aor act inf	παρορμάω	πᾶσι	adj masc and neut dat pl	id.
παρορμήσειεν	vb 1st aor act opt 3rd pers sg	id.	πάσσαλοι	noun masc nom pl	πάσσαλος
παρορῶ	vb pres act ind 1st pers sg	παροράω	πασσάλοις	noun masc dat pl	id.
Παροσωμ	pr noun		πάσσαλον	noun masc acc sg	id.
παροῦσα	vb pres act part fem nom sg	πάρειμι	πάσσαλος	noun masc nom sg	id.
παροῦσαν	vb pres act part fem acc sg	id.	πασσάλου	noun masc gen sg	id.
παροῦσι	vb pres act part masc and neut dat pl	id.	πασσάλους	noun masc acc pl	id.
παρουσία	noun fem nom sg		πασσάλῳ	noun masc dat sg	id.
παρουσίαν	noun fem acc sg	παρουσία	πάσσει	vb pres act ind 3rd pers sg	πάσσω
παρόψεται	vb fut mid ind 3rd pers sg	παροράω	πάσσοντος	vb pres act part masc and neut gen sg	id.
παρρησίᾳ	noun fem dat sg	παρρησία	πάσσων	vb pres act part masc nom sg	id.

παστόν noun masc acc sg	. . . .	παστός
παστοῦ noun masc gen sg		id.
παστούς noun masc acc pl		id.
παστοφόρια noun neut nom and acc pl	. . . . .	παστοφόριον
παστοφορίοις noun neut dat pl		id.
παστοφόριον noun neut nom and acc sg		id.
παστοφορίου noun neut gen sg		id.
παστοφορίων noun neut gen pl		id.
παστῷ noun masc dat sg	. . . .	παστός
πασχα translit		
πάσχα see πασχα		
πάσχομεν vb pres act ind 1st pers pl	. . . .	πάσχω
πάσχοντες vb pres act part masc nom pl		id.
πάσχουσιν vb pres act ind 3rd pers pl		id.
πάσχω vb pres act ind 1st pers sg		id.
πάσχων vb pres act part masc nom sg		id.
Πασχωρ pr noun		
πασῶν adj fem gen pl	. . . .	πᾶς
πατάξαι vb 1st aor act inf	. . . .	πατάσσω
πατάξαντα vb 1st aor act part masc acc sg		id.
πατάξαντας vb 1st aor act part masc acc pl		id.
πατάξαντες vb 1st aor act part masc nom pl		id.
πατάξαντι vb 1st aor act part masc and neut dat sg		id.
πατάξαντος vb 1st aor act part masc and neut gen sg		id.
παταξάντων vb 1st aor act part masc and neut gen pl		id.
πατάξας vb 1st aor act part masc nom sg		id.
πατάξατε vb 1st aor act impv 2nd pers pl		id.
πατάξει vb fut act ind 3rd pers sg		id.
πατάξεις vb fut act ind 2nd pers sg		id.
πατάξετε vb fut act ind 2nd pers pl		id.
πατάξῃ vb 1st aor act subj 3rd pers sg, fut mid ind 2nd pers sg		id.
πατάξῃς vb 1st aor act subj 2nd pers sg		id.
πατάξητε vb 1st aor act subj 2nd pers pl		id.
πατάξομεν vb fut act ind 1st pers pl		id.
πάταξον vb 1st aor act impv 2nd pers sg		id.
πατάξουσιν vb fut act ind 3rd pers pl		id.
πατάξω vb 1st aor act subj 1st pers sg, fut act ind 1st pers sg		id.
πατάξωμεν vb 1st aor act subj 1st pers pl		id.
πατάξωσιν vb 1st aor act subj 3rd pers pl		id.
πατάσσειν vb pres act inf		id.
παταχρα translit		
παταχρον translit		
πατεῖ vb pres act ind 3rd pers sg	. . . .	πατέω
πατεῖν vb pres act inf		id.
πατεῖτε vb pres act impv 2nd pers pl		id.
πάτερ noun masc voc sg	. . . .	πατήρ
πατέρα noun masc acc sg		id.
πατέρας noun masc acc pl		id.
πατέρες noun masc nom pl		id.
πατέρων noun masc gen pl		id.
πάτημα noun neut nom and acc sg		
πατήματα noun neut nom and acc pl	. . . .	πάτημα
πατήρ noun masc nom sg		
πατῆσαι vb 1st aor act inf	. . . .	πατέω
πατησάτω vb 1st aor act impv 3rd pers sg		id.
πατήσῃ vb 1st aor act subj 3rd pers sg		id.
πατήσουσιν vb fut act ind 3rd pers pl		id.
πατητοῦ adj masc and neut gen sg	. . . .	πατητός
πατοῦντα vb pres act part neut nom and acc pl	. . . . . .	πατέω
πατοῦντας vb pres act part masc acc pl		id.
πατοῦντες vb pres act part masc nom pl		id.
πατοῦσιν vb pres act ind 3rd pers pl		id.
πατράδελφος noun masc nom sg		
πατραδέλφου noun masc gen sg	. . . .	πατράδελφος
πατράσι noun masc dat pl	. . . .	πατήρ
πατρί noun masc dat sg		id.
πατριά noun fem nom sg		
πατριᾷ noun fem dat sg	. . . .	πατριά
πατριαί noun fem nom pl		id.
πατριάν noun fem acc sg		id.
πατριάρχαι noun masc nom pl	. . . .	πατριάρχης
πατριάρχας noun masc acc pl		id.
πατριαρχῶν noun masc gen pl		id.
πατριάς noun fem acc pl	. . . .	πατριά
πατριᾶς noun fem gen sg		id.
πατρίδα noun fem acc sg	. . . .	πατρίς
πατρίδι noun fem dat sg		id.
πατρίδος noun fem gen sg		id.
πατρική adj fem nom sg	. . . .	πατρικός
πατρικήν adj fem acc sg		id.
πατρικῆς adj fem gen sg		id.
πατρικοῖς adj masc and neut dat pl		id.
πατρικόν adj masc acc sg, neut nom and acc sg		id.
πατρικούς adj masc acc pl		id.
πατρικῷ adj masc and neut dat sg		id.
πατρικῶν adj gen pl		id.
πάτριον adj acc sg, neut nom sg	. . . .	πάτριος
πάτριος adj masc and fem nom sg		id.
πατρίους adj masc and fem acc pl		id.
πατρίῳ adj dat sg		id.
πατρίων adj gen pl		id.
πατριῶν noun fem gen pl	. . . .	πατριά
Πατρόκλου pr noun masc gen sg	. . . .	Πατροκλος
πατρός noun masc gen sg	. . . .	πατήρ
Πατροσωνιμ pr noun		
πατρῴαν adj fem acc sg	. . . .	πατρῷος
πατρῷον adj masc acc sg, neut nom and acc sg		id.
πατρῴου adj masc and neut gen sg		id.
πατρῴους adj masc (and fem) acc pl		id.
παύει vb pres act ind 3rd pers sg	. . . .	παύω
παῦλαν noun fem acc sg	. . . .	παῦλα
παύομαι vb pres m/p ind 1st pers sg	. . . .	παύω

παῦσαι vb 1st aor mid impv 2nd pers sg	. . . .	παύω
παυσαμένου vb 1st aor mid part masc and neut gen sg		id.
παύσασθαι vb 1st aor mid inf		id.
παύσασθε vb 1st aor mid impv 2nd pers pl		id.
παυσάσθω vb 1st aor mid impv 3rd pers sg		id.
παυσάσθωσαν vb 1st aor mid impv 3rd pers pl		id.
παύσει vb fut act ind 3rd pers sg		id.
παύσεις vb fut act ind 2nd pers sg		id.
παύσεται vb fut mid ind 3rd pers sg		id.
παύσῃ vb 1st aor act subj 3rd pers sg,		
fut mid ind 2nd pers sg		id.
παύσηται vb 1st aor mid subj 3rd pers sg		id.
παῦσιν noun fem acc sg	. . . .	παύσις
παύσομαι vb fut mid ind 1st pers sg	. . . .	παύω
παῦσον vb 1st aor act impv 2nd pers sg		id.
παύσονται vb fut mid ind 3rd pers pl		id.
παύσω vb fut act ind 1st pers sg		id.
παυσώμεθα vb 1st aor mid subj 1st pers pl		id.
παύσωνται vb 1st aor mid subj 3rd pers pl		id.
πάχει noun neut dat sg	. . . .	πάχος
παχεῖ adj masc and neut dat sg	. . . .	παχύς
παχεῖς adj neut nom and acc pl		id.
παχέος adj masc and neut gen sg		id.
πάχη noun neut nom and acc pl	. . . .	πάχος
πάχναι noun fem nom pl	. . . .	πάχνη
πάχνη noun fem nom sg		id.
πάχνῃ noun fem dat sg		id.
πάχνην noun fem acc sg		id.
πάχος noun neut nom and acc sg		
παχύ adj neut nom and acc sg	. . . .	παχύς
παχυνθῇ vb 1st aor pass subj 3rd pers sg	. . . .	παχύνω
παχυτέρα comp adj fem acc sg	. . . .	παχύς
παχύτερος comp adj masc nom sg		id.
Παχων pr noun		
πέδαι noun fem nom pl	. . . .	πέδη
πέδαις noun fem dat pl		id.
πέδας noun fem acc pl		id.
πεδήσαντας vb 1st aor act part masc acc pl	. . . .	πεδάω
πεδήσας vb 1st aor act part masc nom sg		id.
πεδῆται noun masc nom pl	. . . .	πεδήτης
πεδία noun neut nom and acc pl	. . . .	πεδίον
Πεδιας pr noun masc nom sg		
πεδίλοις noun neut dat pl	. . . .	πέδιλον
πεδινή adj fem nom sg	. . . .	πεδινός
πεδινῇ adj fem dat sg		id.
πεδινήν adj fem acc sg		id.
πεδινῆς adj fem gen sg		id.
πεδινοῦ adj masc and neut gen sg		id.
πεδίοις noun neut dat pl	. . . .	πεδίον
πεδίον noun neut nom and acc sg		id.
πεδίου noun neut gen sg		id.
πεδίῳ noun neut dat sg		id.

πεδίον noun neut gen pl	. . . .	πεδίον
πεζῇ adj fem dat sg	. . . .	πεζός
πεζικαῖς adj fem dat pl	. . . .	πεζικός
πεζικάς adj fem acc pl		id.
πεζική adj fem nom sg		id.
πεζοί adj masc nom pl	. . . .	πεζός
πεζοῖς adj masc and neut dat pl		id.
πεζομαχίαν noun fem acc sg	. . . .	πεζομαχία
πεζούς adj masc acc pl	. . . .	πεζός
πεζῶν adj gen pl		id.
πειθαρχῇ vb pres act subj 3rd pers sg	. . . .	πειθαρχέω
πειθαρχήσουσιν vb fut act ind 3rd pers pl		id.
πειθαρχοῦσιν vb pres act ind 3rd pers pl		id.
πείθεσθαι vb pres m/p inf	. . . .	πείθω
πείθεσθε vb pres m/p impv 2nd pers pl		id.
πείθονται vb pres m/p ind 3rd pers pl		id.
πεινᾷ vb pres act ind 3rd pers sg	. . . .	πεινάω
πεινάσει vb fut act ind 3rd pers sg		id.
πεινάσετε vb fut act ind 2nd pers pl		id.
πεινάσητε vb 1st aor act subj 2nd pers pl		id.
πεινάσουσιν vb fut act ind 3rd pers pl		id.
πεινάσω vb 1st aor act subj 1st pers sg		id.
πεινάσωμεν vb 1st aor act subj 1st pers pl		id.
πεινάσωσιν vb 1st aor act subj 3rd pers pl		id.
πεινῶμεν vb pres act ind 1st pers pl		id.
πεινῶν vb pres act part masc nom sg		id.
πεινῶντας vb pres act part masc acc pl		id.
πεινῶντες vb pres act part masc nom pl		id.
πεινῶντι vb pres act part masc and neut dat sg		id.
πεινώντων vb pres act part masc and neut gen pl		id.
πεινῶσα vb pres act part fem nom sg		id.
πεινῶσαν vb pres act part fem acc sg		id.
πεινώσας vb pres act part fem acc pl		id.
πεινῶσι(ν) vb pres act ind 3rd pers pl,		
pres act part masc and neut dat pl		id.
πεῖρα noun fem nom sg		
πείρᾳ noun fem dat sg	. . . .	πεῖρα
πείραζε vb pres act impv 2nd pers sg	. . . .	πειράζω
πειράζει vb pres act ind 3rd pers sg		id.
πειράζειν vb pres act inf		id.
πειράζετε vb pres act ind 2nd pers pl		id.
πειράζουσι(ν) vb pres act ind 3rd pers pl,		
pres act part masc and neut dat pl		id.
πειράζων vb pres act part masc nom sg		id.
πεῖραν noun fem acc sg	. . . .	πεῖρα
πειράσαι vb 1st aor act inf	. . . .	πειράζω
πειράσει vb fut act ind 3rd pers sg		id.
πειράσῃ vb 1st aor act subj 3rd pers sg		id.
πειρασθεῖσα vb 1st aor pass part fem nom sg		id.
πειρασθῶσι vb 1st aor pass subj 3rd pers pl		id.
πειρασμόν noun masc acc sg	. . . .	πειρασμός
πειρασμός noun masc nom sg		

πειρασμοῦ noun masc gen sg . . . . πειρασμός		πέμματι noun neut dat sg . . . . πέμμα
πειρασμούς noun masc acc pl	id.	πέμπει vb pres act ind 3rd pers sg . . . . πέμπω
πειρασμῷ noun masc dat sg	id.	πέμπταις adj fem dat pl . . . . πέμπτος
Πειρασμῷ pr noun masc dat sg . . . . Πειρασμός		πέμπτη adj fem nom sg	id.
πειράσομαι vb fut mid ind 1st pers sg . . . . πειράω		πέμπτῃ adj fem dat sg	id.
πειρασόμεθα vb fut mid ind 1st pers pl	id.	πέμπτης adj fem gen sg	id.
πείρασον vb 1st aor act impv 2nd pers sg . . . . . . πειράζω		πέμπτον adj masc acc sg, neut nom and acc sg	id.
πειράσουσιν vb fut act ind 3rd pers pl	id.	πέμπτος adj masc nom sg	id.
πειράσω vb 1st aor act subj 1st pers sg,		πέμπτου adj masc and neut gen sg	id.
fut act ind 1st pers sg	id.	πέμπτῳ adj masc and neut dat sg	id.
πειράσωμεν vb 1st aor act subj 1st pers pl	id.	πεμφθείς vb 1st aor pass part masc nom sg . . . . πέμπω
πειραταῖς noun masc dat pl . . . . πειρατής		πεμφθέντες vb 1st aor pass part masc nom pl	id.
πειρατεύσει vb fut act ind 3rd pers sg . . . . πειρατεύω		πεμφθήτω vb 1st aor pass impv 3rd pers sg	id.
πειρατήρια noun neut nom and acc pl . . . . . . πειρατήριον		πέμψαι vb 1st aor act inf	id.
πειρατήριον noun neut nom and acc sg	id.	πέμψασα vb 1st aor act part fem nom sg	id.
πειρατηρίου noun neut gen sg	id.	πέμψατε vb 1st aor act impv 2nd pers pl	id.
πειρατοῦ noun masc gen sg . . . . πειρατής		πεμψάτω vb 1st aor act impv 3rd pers sg	id.
πειρατῶν noun masc gen pl	id.	πέμψειν vb fut act inf	id.
πεῖσαι vb 1st aor act inf . . . . πείθω		πέμψον vb 1st aor act impv 2nd pers sg	id.
πείσαιμ' see πείσαιμι		πενηθείς vb 1st aor pass part masc nom sg . . . . πενέω
πείσαιμι vb 1st aor act opt 1st pers sg	id.	πένης noun masc nom sg	
πείσει vb fut act ind 3rd pers sg	id.	πένησι noun masc dat pl . . . . πένης
πείσειεν vb 1st aor act opt 3rd pers sg	id.	πένητα noun masc acc sg	id.
πείσειν vb fut act inf	id.	πένηται vb pres dep subj 3rd pers sg . . . . πένομαι
πείσεται vb fut mid ind 3rd pers sg	id.	πένητας noun masc acc pl . . . . πένης
πεισθείημεν vb 1st aor pass opt 1st pers pl	id.	πένητες noun masc nom pl	id.
πεισθείης vb 1st aor pass opt 2nd pers sg	id.	πένητι noun masc dat sg	id.
πεισθείς vb 1st aor pass part masc nom sg	id.	πένητος noun masc gen sg	id.
πεισθέντας vb 1st aor pass part masc acc pl	id.	πενήτων noun masc gen pl	id.
πεισθῇς vb 1st aor pass subj 2nd pers sg	id.	πένθει noun neut dat sg . . . . πένθος
πείσθητι vb 1st aor pass impv 2nd pers sg	id.	πενθεῖ vb pres act ind 3rd pers sg . . . . πενθέω
πεῖσον vb 1st aor act impv 2nd pers sg	id.	πενθεῖς vb pres act ind 2nd pers sg	id.
πείσονται vb fut mid ind 3rd pers pl	id.	πενθεῖτε vb pres act impv 2nd pers pl,	
πείσω vb fut act ind 1st pers sg	id.	pres act ind 2nd pers pl	id.
πελάγει noun neut dat sg . . . . πέλαγος		πενθείτω vb pres act impv 3rd pers sg	id.
πέλαγος noun neut nom and acc sg	id.	πενθερά noun fem nom sg	
πέλας adverb		πενθερᾷ noun fem dat sg . . . . πενθερά
πέλειοι adj masc nom pl . . . . πέλειος		πενθεράν noun fem acc sg	id.
πελεκᾶνα noun masc acc sg . . . . πελεκάν		πενθερᾶς noun fem gen sg	id.
πελεκᾶνι noun masc dat sg	id.	πενθερόν noun masc acc sg . . . . πενθερός
πελέκει noun masc dat sg . . . . πέλεκυς		πενθερός noun masc nom sg	id.
πελεκητῶν adj gen pl . . . . πελεκητός		πενθεροῦ noun masc gen sg	id.
πέλεκυν noun masc acc sg . . . . πέλεκυς		πενθερούς noun masc acc pl	id.
πέλεκυς noun masc nom sg	id.	πένθη noun neut nom and acc pl . . . . πένθος
πέλματα noun neut nom and acc pl . . . . πέλμα		πενθῆσαι vb 1st aor act inf . . . . πενθέω
πέλται noun fem nom pl . . . . πέλτη		πενθήσει vb fut act ind 3rd pers sg	id.
πέλταις noun fem dat pl	id.	πενθήσῃς vb 1st aor act subj 2nd pers sg	id.
πέλτας noun fem acc pl	id.	πενθήσον vb 1st aor act impv 2nd pers sg	id.
πελτασταί noun masc nom pl . . . . πελταστής		πενθήσουσιν vb fut act ind 3rd pers pl	id.
πέλυξ noun masc nom sg		πενθικά adj neut nom and acc pl . . . . πενθικός
πέμμα noun neut nom and acc sg		πενθικοῖς adj masc and neut dat pl	id.
πέμματα noun neut nom and acc pl . . . . πέμμα		Πενθος pr noun neut nom and acc sg	

πένθος noun neut nom and acc sg

πενθοῦντας vb pres act part masc acc pl .... πενθέω

πενθοῦντος vb pres act part masc and neut gen sg id.

πενθούντων vb pres act part masc and neut gen pl id.

πένθους noun neut gen sg .... πένθος

πενθοῦσα vb pres act part fem nom sg .... πενθέω

πενθοῦσιν vb pres act ind 3rd pers pl id.

πενθῶν vb pres act part masc nom sg id.

πενία noun fem nom sg

πενίᾳ noun fem dat sg .... πενία

πενίαν noun fem acc sg id.

πενίας noun fem gen sg id.

πενιχροῖς adj masc and neut dat pl .... πενιχρός

πενιχροῦ adj masc and neut gen sg id.

πενιχρῷ adj masc and neut dat sg id.

πενόμενος vb pres dep part masc nom sg .... πένομαι

πενταετηρικοῦ adj masc and neut gen sg .. πενταετηρικός

πενταετοῦς adj gen sg .... πενταετής

πεντάκις adverb

πεντακισχίλια adj neut nom and acc pl .. πεντακισχίλιοι

πεντακισχίλιαι adj fem nom pl id.

πεντακισχιλίαν adj fem acc sg .... πεντακισχίλιος

πεντακισχιλίας adj fem acc pl .... πεντακισχίλιοι

πεντακισχιλίους adj masc acc pl id.

πεντακισχιλίων adj gen pl id.

πεντακόσια adj neut nom and acc pl .... πεντακόσιοι

πεντακοσία adj fem nom sg id.

πεντακόσιαι adj fem nom pl id.

πεντακόσιοι adj masc nom pl id.

πεντακοσίοις adj masc and neut dat pl id.

πεντακοσίους adj masc acc pl id.

πεντακοσίων adj gen pl id.

πεντάπηχυν noun masc acc sg .... πεντάπηχυς

πενταπλᾶς adj fem acc pl .... πενταπλοῦς

πενταπλασίως adverb

Πενταπολεως pr noun fem gen sg .... Πενταπολις

πέντε indecl number

πεντεκαίδεκα indecl number

πεντεκαιδεκάτῃ adj fem dat sg .... πεντεκαιδέκατος

πεντεκαιδεκάτην adj fem acc sg id.

πεντεκαιδέκατος adj masc nom sg id.

πεντεκαιδεκάτῳ adj masc and neut dat sg id.

πεντεκαιεικοσαετοῦς noun masc

    gen sg .... πεντεκαιεικοσαετός

πεντήκοντα indecl number

πεντηκονταετοῦς adj masc and neut

    gen sg .... πεντηκονταετής

πεντηκόνταρχον noun masc acc sg .... πεντηκόνταρχος

πεντηκόνταρχος noun masc nom sg id.

πεντηκοντάρχους noun masc acc pl id.

πεντηκοστῇ adj fem dat sg .... πεντηκοστός

πεντηκοστήν adj fem acc sg id.

πεντηκοστόν adj masc acc sg,

    neut nom and acc sg .... πεντηκοστός

πεντηκοστοῦ adj masc and neut gen sg id.

πεντηκοστῷ adj masc and neut dat sg id.

πεπαιδευμένης vb perf m/p part fem gen sg ..... παιδεύω

πεπαιδευμένος vb perf m/p part masc nom sg id.

πεπαιδευμένῳ vb perf m/p part masc and neut dat sg id.

πέπαικας vb perf act ind 2nd pers sg .... παίω

πέπαικεν vb perf act ind 3rd pers sg id.

πεπαλαιωμένα vb perf m/p part

    neut nom and acc pl .... παλαιόω

πεπαλαιωμένε vb perf m/p part masc voc sg id.

πεπαλαίωνται vb perf m/p ind 3rd pers pl id.

πεπαλαίωται vb perf m/p ind 3rd pers sg id.

πεπασμένα vb perf m/p part neut nom and acc pl .... πάσσω

πέπαυται vb perf m/p ind 3rd pers sg .... παύω

πεπεδημένοι vb perf m/p part masc nom pl .... πεδάω

πεπεδημένους vb perf m/p part masc acc pl id.

πεπεδημένων vb perf m/p part gen pl id.

πεπείραμαι vb perf m/p ind 1st pers sg .... πειράζω

πέπειροι noun masc nom pl .... πέπειρος

πέπεισμαι vb perf m/p ind 1st pers sg .... πείθω

πεπεισμένοι vb perf m/p part masc nom pl id.

πεπεμμενην vb perf m/p part fem acc sg .... πέσσω

πεπήγασιν vb perf act ind 3rd pers pl .... πήγνυμι

πέπηγεν vb perf act ind 3rd pers sg id.

πεπηγός vb perf act part neut nom and acc sg id.

πεπηγώς vb perf act part masc nom sg id.

πεπιστευκόσιν vb perf act ind 3rd pers pl .... πιστεύω

πεπιστευκότας vb perf act part masc acc pl id.

πεπιστευκώς vb perf act part masc nom sg id.

πεπιστευμένα vb perf m/p part neut nom and acc pl id.

πεπλάνηκα vb perf act ind 1st pers sg .... πλανάω

πεπλάνημαι vb perf m/p ind 1st pers sg id.

πεπλανημένη vb perf m/p part fem dat sg id.

πεπλανημένοι vb perf m/p part masc nom pl id.

πεπλανημένον vb perf m/p part masc acc sg id.

πεπλανημένος vb perf m/p part masc nom sg id.

πεπλάνηται vb perf m/p ind 3rd pers sg id.

πεπλασμένον vb perf m/p part masc acc sg ...... πλάσσω

πεπλεγμένα vb perf m/p part neut nom and acc pl .... πλέκω

πεπλήγασιν vb perf act ind 3rd pers pl .... πλήσσω

πεπληγότος vb perf act part masc and neut gen sg id.

πεπληγυία vb perf act part fem dat sg id.

πεπληγυῖαν vb perf act part fem acc sg id.

πεπληγώς vb perf act part masc nom sg id.

πεπληθυμμένη vb perf m/p part fem nom sg ..... πληθύνω

πεπληθυμμένοι vb perf m/p part masc nom pl id.

πεπλήθυνται vb perf m/p ind 3rd pers pl id.

πεπλήρωκεν vb perf act ind 3rd pers sg .... πληρόω

πεπληρωκώς vb perf act part masc nom sg id.

πεπληρωμέναι vb perf m/p part fem nom pl id.

πεπληρωμένη vb perf m/p part fem nom sg . . . . πληρόω	πεπόνθασιν vb perf act ind 3rd pers pl . . . . πάσχω
πεπληρωμένην vb perf m/p part fem acc sg id.	πεπόρευμαι vb perf dep ind 1st pers sg . . . . πορεύομαι
πεπληρωμένοι vb perf m/p part masc nom pl id.	πεπορευμένοι vb perf dep part masc nom pl id.
πεπληρωμένος vb perf m/p part masc nom sg id.	πεπορευμένος vb perf dep part masc nom sg id.
πεπληρωμένους vb perf m/p part masc acc pl id.	πεπορευμένων vb perf dep part gen pl id.
πεπλήρωνται vb perf m/p ind 3rd pers pl id.	πεπόρευνται vb perf dep ind 3rd pers pl id.
πεπληρῶσθαι vb perf m/p inf id.	πεπόρευσαι vb perf dep ind 2nd pers sg id.
πεπλούτηκα vb perf act ind 1st pers sg . . . . πλουτέω	πεπόρευσθε vb perf dep ind 2nd pers pl id.
πεπλουτήκαμεν vb perf act ind 1st pers pl id.	πεπόρευται vb perf dep ind 3rd pers sg id.
πεποίηκα vb perf act ind 1st pers sg . . . . ποιέω	πεπορνεύκασιν vb perf act ind 3rd pers pl . . . . . . πορνεύω
πεποίηκας vb perf act ind 2nd pers sg id.	πεπότικεν vb perf act ind 3rd pers sg . . . . ποτίζω
πεποιήκασιν vb perf act ind 3rd pers pl id.	πέπρακα vb perf act ind 1st pers sg . . . . πιπράσκω
πεποιήκατε vb perf act ind 2nd pers pl id.	πέπρακαν vb perf act ind 3rd pers pl id.
πεποιήκεισαν vb plpf act ind 3rd pers pl id.	πέπρακεν vb perf act ind 3rd pers sg id.
πεποίηκεν vb perf act ind 3rd pers sg id.	πεπρακώς vb perf act part masc nom sg id.
πεποιηκέναι vb perf act inf id.	πεπραμένους vb perf m/p part masc acc pl id.
πεποιηκότας vb perf act part masc acc pl id.	πέπρασαι vb perf m/p ind 2nd pers sg id.
πεποιηκότες vb perf act part masc nom pl id.	πεπραχέναι vb perf act inf . . . . πράσσω
πεποιηκυῖα vb perf act part neut nom and acc pl id.	πεπρησμένην vb perf m/p part fem acc sg . . . . πρήθω
πεποιηκώς vb perf act part masc nom sg id.	πεπρονομευμένος vb perf m/p part
πεποιημένα vb perf m/p part neut nom and acc pl id.	masc nom sg . . . . προνομεύω
πεποιημέναι vb perf m/p part fem nom pl id.	πέπτωκα vb perf act ind 1st pers sg . . . . πίπτω
πεποιημένον vb perf m/p part masc acc sg,	πέπτωκας vb perf act ind 2nd pers sg id.
neut nom and acc sg id.	πεπτώκασι(ν) vb perf act ind 3rd pers pl id.
πεποιημένῳ vb perf m/p part masc and neut dat sg id.	πέπτωκεν vb perf act ind 3rd pers sg id.
πεποίηται vb perf m/p ind 3rd pers sg id.	πεπτωκέναι vb perf act inf id.
πέποιθα vb perf act ind 1st pers sg . . . . πείθω	πεπτωκός vb perf act part neut nom and acc sg id.
πεποίθαμεν vb perf act ind 1st pers pl id.	πεπτωκότα vb perf act part neut nom and acc pl id.
πέποιθαν vb perf act ind 3rd pers pl id.	πεπτωκότας vb perf act part masc acc pl id.
πέποιθας vb perf act ind 2nd pers sg id.	πεπτωκότες vb perf act part masc nom pl id.
πεποίθασιν vb perf act ind 3rd pers pl id.	πεπτωκότων vb perf act part masc and neut gen pl id.
πεποίθατε vb perf act impv 2nd pers pl,	πεπτωκυῖα vb perf act part fem nom sg id.
perf act ind 2nd pers pl id.	πεπτωκυῖαν vb perf act part fem acc sg id.
πέποιθεν vb perf act ind 3rd pers sg id.	πεπτωκώς vb perf act part masc nom sg id.
πεποιθέναι vb perf act inf id.	πεπυκασμένων vb perf m/p part gen pl . . . . πυκάζω
πεποιθέτω vb perf act impv 3rd pers sg id.	πεπυρωμένα vb perf m/p part neut nom and acc pl . . . πυρόω
πεποίθησις noun fem nom sg	πεπυρωμένης vb perf m/p part fem gen sg id.
πεποιθόσι vb perf act part masc and neut dat pl . . . . . πείθω	πεπυρωμένοι vb perf m/p part masc nom pl id.
πεποιθότα vb perf act part masc acc sg id.	πεπυρωμένον vb perf m/p part masc acc sg,
πεποιθότας vb perf act part masc acc pl id.	neut nom and acc sg id.
πεποιθότες vb perf act part masc nom pl id.	πεπυρωμένος vb perf m/p part masc nom sg id.
πεποιθότων vb perf act part masc and neut gen pl id.	πέπωκα vb perf act ind 1st pers sg . . . . πίνω
πεποιθότως adverb	πέπωκας vb perf act ind 2nd pers sg id.
πεποιθυῖα vb perf act part fem nom sg . . . . πείθω	πεπώκει vb plpf act ind 3rd pers sg id.
πεποιθυῖαι vb perf act part fem nom pl id.	πέπωκεν vb perf act ind 3rd pers sg id.
πεποιθώς vb perf act part masc nom sg id.	πεπώρωνται vb perf m/p ind 3rd pers pl . . . . πωρόω
πεποικιλμένη vb perf m/p part fem nom sg . . . . . ποικίλλω	πέρα adverb and preposition
πεπολιόρκημαι vb perf m/p ind 1st pers sg . . . . πολιορκέω	πέραν adverb and preposition
πέπομφα vb perf act ind 1st pers sg . . . . πέμπω	περάνῃ vb 1st aor act subj 3rd pers sg . . . . περαίνω
πεπόμφατε vb perf act ind 2nd pers pl id.	περανθέντος vb 1st aor pass part masc and neut gen sg id.
πέπονας noun masc acc pl . . . . πέπων	περανοῦσιν vb fut act ind 3rd pers pl id.
πεπονηρεῦσθαι vb perf dep inf . . . . πονηρεύομαι	πέρας noun neut nom and acc sg

πέρασι noun neut dat pl . . . . πέρας

περασμός noun masc nom sg

πέρατα noun neut nom and acc pl . . . . πέρας

περάτῃ noun masc dat sg . . . . περάτης

πέρατι noun neut dat sg . . . . πέρας

πέρατος noun neut gen sg   id.

περάτων noun neut gen pl   id.

πέρδιξ noun fem nom sg

περί preposition

περιαγαγόντες vb 2nd aor act part masc nom pl . . περιάγω

περιαγαγών vb 2nd aor act part masc nom sg   id.

περιαγκωνίσαντες vb 1st aor act part

          masc nom pl . . . . περιαγκωνίζω

περιαιρεθήσεται vb fut pass ind 3rd pers sg . . . . περιαιρέω

περιαιρεθήσονται vb fut pass ind 3rd pers pl   id.

περιαιρεῖται vb pres m/p ind 3rd pers sg   id.

περιαντλουμένη vb pres m/p part fem nom sg   περιαντλέω

περιάξει vb fut act ind 3rd pers sg . . . . περιάγω

περιάργυρα adj neut nom and acc pl . . . . . . περιάργυρος

περιάργυροι adj masc nom pl   id.

περιαργύρων adj gen pl   id.

περιαστράπτοντες vb pres act part

          masc nom pl . . . . περιαστράπτω

περίβαλε vb 2nd aor act impv 2nd pers sg . . . . . περιβάλλω

περιβαλεῖ vb fut act ind 3rd pers sg   id.

περιβαλεῖν vb 2nd aor act inf   id.

περιβαλεῖς vb fut act ind 2nd pers sg   id.

περιβαλεῖται vb fut mid ind 3rd pers sg   id.

περιβαλέσθαι vb 2nd aor mid inf   id.

περιβαλέσθω vb 2nd aor mid impv 3rd pers sg   id.

περιβαλέσθωσαν vb 2nd aor mid impv 3rd pers pl   id.

περιβάλῃ vb 2nd aor act subj 3rd pers sg,

          2nd aor mid subj 2nd pers sg   id.

περιβάλλει vb pres act ind 3rd pers sg   id.

περιβάλλεσθαι vb pres m/p inf   id.

περιβάλλεσθε vb pres m/p ind 2nd pers pl   id.

περιβάλλεται vb pres m/p ind 3rd pers sg   id.

περιβάλληται vb pres m/p subj 3rd pers sg   id.

περιβαλλομένη vb pres m/p part fem nom sg   id.

περιβαλλομένου vb pres m/p part masc and neut gen sg   id.

περιβάλλοντι vb pres act part masc and neut dat sg   id.

περιβάλλουσιν vb pres act ind 3rd pers pl   id.

περιβαλόμενοι vb 2nd aor mid part masc nom pl   id.

περιβαλοῦ vb 2nd aor mid impv 2nd pers sg   id.

περιβαλούμεθα vb fut mid ind 1st pers pl   id.

περιβαλῶ vb fut act ind 1st pers sg   id.

περιβάλωνται vb 2nd aor mid subj 3rd pers pl   id.

περιβεβιωκότες vb perf act part masc nom pl . . . . περιβιόω

περιβεβλημένη vb perf m/p part fem nom sg . . . περιβάλλω

περιβεβλημένοι vb perf m/p part masc nom pl   id.

περιβεβλημένον vb perf m/p part masc acc sg   id.

περιβεβλημένος vb perf m/p part masc nom sg   id.

περιβεβλημένου vb perf m/p part

          masc and neut gen sg . . . . περιβάλλω

περιβεβλημένους vb perf m/p part masc acc pl   id.

περιβεβλημένῳ vb perf m/p part masc and neut dat sg   id.

περιβεβλημένων vb perf m/p part gen pl   id.

περιβλεπομένη vb pres m/p part fem nom sg . . . περιβλέπω

περιβλέπου vb pres m/p impv 2nd pers sg   id.

περίβλεπτος adj masc and fem nom sg

περιβλέψαι vb 1st aor mid impv 2nd pers sg . . . περιβλέπω

περιβλεψόμενος vb 1st aor mid part masc nom sg   id.

περιβλέψαντες vb 1st aor act part masc nom pl   id.

περιβλέψεται vb fut mid ind 3rd pers sg   id.

περιβλέψῃς vb 1st aor act subj 2nd pers sg   id.

περιβληθέντες vb 1st aor pass part masc nom pl περιβάλλω

περίβλημα noun neut nom and acc sg

περιβόητον adj masc acc sg,

          neut nom and acc sg . . . . περιβόητος

περιβόλαια noun neut nom and acc pl . . . . περιβόλαιον

περιβόλαιον noun neut nom and acc sg   id.

περιβολαίων noun neut gen pl   id.

περιβολῇ noun fem dat sg . . . . περιβολή

περιβολήν noun fem acc sg   id.

περιβόλοις noun masc dat pl . . . . περίβολος

περίβολον noun masc acc sg   id.

περίβολος noun masc nom sg   id.

περιβόλου noun masc gen sg   id.

περιβόλῳ noun masc dat sg   id.

περιβόλων noun masc gen pl   id.

περιγενηθεῖσαν vb 1st aor pass part

          fem acc sg . . . . περιγίνομαι

περιδειπνῆσαι vb 1st aor act inf . . . . περιδειπνέω

περιδείπνῳ noun neut dat sg . . . . περίδειπνον

περιδέξια noun neut nom and acc pl . . . . περιδέξιον

περιδέξιον noun neut nom and acc sg   id.

περιδράμετε vb 2nd aor act impv 2nd pers pl . . . . περιτρέχω

περιδραμοῦνται vb fut mid ind 3rd pers pl   id.

περιέβαλε(ν) vb 2nd aor act ind 3rd pers sg . . . . περιβάλλω

περιέβαλες vb 2nd aor act ind 2nd pers sg   id.

περιεβάλεσθε vb 2nd aor mid ind 2nd pers pl   id.

περιεβάλετο vb 2nd aor mid ind 3rd pers sg   id.

περιέβαλλον vb impf act ind 3rd pers pl   id.

περιέβαλον vb 2nd aor act ind

          1st pers sg and 3rd pers pl   id.

περιεβάλοντο vb 2nd aor mid ind 3rd pers pl   id.

περιεβλέπετο vb impf m/p ind 3rd pers sg . . . . . περιβλέπω

περιεβλέψατο vb 1st aor mid ind 3rd pers sg   id.

περιεγένοντο vb 2nd aor mid ind 3rd pers pl . . περιγίνομαι

περιέδησεν vb 1st aor act ind 3rd pers sg . . . . περιδέω

περιεδίπλωσε vb 1st aor act ind 3rd pers sg . . . . περιδιπλόω

περιέδυσαν vb 1st aor act ind 3rd pers pl . . . . . . περιδύω

περιεζώσαντο vb 1st aor mid ind 3rd pers pl . . περιζώννυμι

περιέζωσας vb 1st aor act ind 2nd pers sg   id.

περιεζώσατο vb 1st aor mid ind 3rd pers sg ... περιζώννυμι

περιέζωσεν vb 1st aor act ind 3rd pers sg id.

περιεζωσμέναι vb perf m/p part fem nom pl id.

περιεζωσμένη vb perf m/p part fem nom sg id.

περιεζωσμένην vb perf m/p part fem acc sg id.

περιεζωσμένοι vb perf m/p part masc nom pl id.

περιεζωσμένον vb perf m/p part masc acc sg,
    neut nom and acc sg id.

περιεζωσμένος vb perf m/p part masc nom sg id.

περιεζωσμένου vb perf m/p part
    masc and neut gen sg id.

περιέθεσαν vb 2nd aor act ind 3rd pers sg ..... περιτίθημι

περιέθετο vb 2nd aor mid ind 3rd pers sg id.

περιέθηκα vb 1st aor act ind 1st pers sg id.

περιέθηκαν vb 1st aor act ind 3rd pers pl id.

περιέθηκας vb 1st aor act ind 2nd pers sg id.

περιέθηκεν vb 1st aor act ind 3rd pers sg id.

περιείλαντο vb 1st aor mid ind 3rd pers pl ..... περιαιρέω

περιείλατο vb 1st aor mid ind 3rd pers sg id.

περιεῖλεν vb 2nd aor act ind 3rd pers sg id.

περιειληφυῖα vb perf act part fem nom sg ... περιλαμβάνω

περιεῖλον vb 2nd aor act ind 3rd pers pl ...... περιαιρέω

περιεῖχεν vb impf act ind 3rd pers sg .... περιέχω

περιειχόμην vb impf m/p ind 1st pers sg id.

περιεκάθαρεν vb 1st aor act ind 3rd pers sg . περικαθαίρω

περιεκάθηντο vb impf m/p ind 3rd pers pl .. περικάθημαι

περιεκάθητο vb impf m/p ind 3rd pers sg id.

περιεκάθισαν vb 1st aor act ind 3rd pers pl .... περικαθίζω

περιεκάθισεν vb 1st aor act ind 3rd pers sg id.

περιέκαιεν vb impf act ind 3rd pers sg .... περικαίω

περιεκάλυπτον vb impf act ind 3rd pers pl .. περικαλύπτω

περιεκέχυτο vb plpf m/p ind 3rd pers sg .... περιχέω

περιέκλασεν vb 1st aor act ind 3rd pers sg ..... περικλάω

περιεκλύσατο vb 1st aor mid ind 3rd pers sg ... περικλύζω

περιέκλων vb impf act ind 3rd pers pl .... περικλάω

περιεκόμπουν vb impf act ind 3rd pers pl .... περικομπέω

περιεκράτησε(ν) vb 1st aor act ind 3rd pers sg περικρατέω

περιεκτικώταται superl adj fem nom pl ..... περιεκτικός

περιεκύκλου vb impf act ind 3rd pers sg ..... περικυκλόω

περιεκύκλωσαν vb 1st aor act ind 3rd pers pl id.

περιεκύκλωσε vb 1st aor act ind 3rd pers sg id.

περιέλαβεν vb 2nd aor act ind 3rd pers sg ... περιλαμβάνω

περίελε vb 2nd aor act impv 2nd pers sg .... περιαιρέω

περιελεῖ vb fut act ind 3rd pers sg id.

περιελεῖν vb 2nd aor act inf id.

περιελεῖς vb fut act ind 2nd pers sg id.

περιέλεσθε vb 2nd aor mid impv 2nd pers pl id.

περιέλετε vb 2nd aor act impv 2nd pers pl id.

περιελέτω vb 2nd aor act impv 3rd pers sg id.

περιελεύσεται vb fut mid ind 3rd pers sg .... περιέρχομαι

περιελεύσονται vb fut mid ind 3rd pers pl id.

περιέλη vb 2nd aor act subj 3rd pers sg .... περιαιρέω

περιέλῃς vb 2nd aor act subj 2nd pers sg id.

περιελθεῖν vb 2nd aor act inf .... περιέρχομαι

περιελθοῦσα vb 2nd aor act part fem nom sg id.

περιελθών vb 2nd aor act part masc nom sg id.

περιελομένη vb 2nd aor mid part fem nom sg ... περιαιρέω

περιελόμενος vb 2nd aor mid part masc nom sg id.

περιελοῦ vb 2nd aor mid impv 2nd pers sg id.

περιελοῦνται vb fut mid ind 3rd pers pl id.

περιελῶ vb fut act ind 1st pers sg id.

περιελών vb 2nd aor act part masc nom sg id.

περιενέγκασαν vb 1st aor act part fem acc sg ... περιφέρω

περιέξυσεν vb 1st aor act ind 3rd pers sg .... περιξύω

περιεπάτει vb impf act ind 3rd pers sg .... περιπατέω

περιεπάτησα vb 1st aor act ind 1st pers sg id.

περιεπάτησαν vb 1st aor act ind 3rd pers pl id.

περιεπάτησας vb 1st aor act ind 2nd pers sg id.

περιεπατοῦμεν vb impf act ind 1st pers pl id.

περιεπάτουν vb impf act ind
    1st pers sg and 3rd pers pl id.

περιέπεσεν vb 2nd aor act ind 3rd pers sg ..... περιπίπτω

περιέπεσον vb 2nd aor act ind 1st pers sg id.

περιεπλάκησαν vb 2nd aor pass ind 3rd pers pl . περιπλέκω

περιέπλεκεν vb impf act ind 3rd pers sg id.

περιεποιησάμην vb 1st aor mid ind 1st pers sg .. περιποιέω

περιεποιήσαντο vb 1st aor mid ind 3rd pers pl id.

περιεποιήσατο vb 1st aor mid ind 3rd pers sg id.

περιεποιοῦντο vb impf m/p ind 3rd pers pl id.

περιεργάζου vb pres dep impv 2nd pers sg . περιεργάζομαι

περιεργίας noun fem gen sg .... περιεργία

περιερραντίσθη vb 1st aor pass ind
    3rd pers sg .... περιρραντίζω

περιέρρεον vb impf act ind 3rd pers pl .... περιρρέω

περιέρχεται vb pres dep ind 3rd pers sg ... περιέρχομαι

περιερχομένη vb pres dep part fem nom sg id.

περιέσπασεν vb 1st aor act ind 3rd pers sg ..... περισπάω

περιέστειλες vb 2nd aor act ind 2nd pers sg .. περιστέλλω

περιεστηκόσι vb perf act part
    masc and neut dat pl .... περιίστημι

περίεστιν vb pres act ind 3rd pers sg .... περίειμι

περιεστώς vb perf act part masc nom sg .... περιίστημι

περιεστῶτες vb perf act part masc nom pl id.

περιέσχεν vb 2nd aor act ind 3rd pers sg .... περιέχω

περιέσχον vb 2nd aor act ind 3rd pers pl id.

περιετείχισεν vb 1st aor act ind 3rd pers sg .. περιτειχίζω

περιετέμεμεν vb 2nd aor act ind 3rd pers sg ...... περιτέμνω

περιετέμετο vb 2nd aor mid ind 3rd pers sg id.

περιετέμον vb 2nd aor act ind 3rd pers pl id.

περιετέμοντο vb 2nd aor mid ind 3rd pers pl id.

περιετίθετο vb impf m/p ind 3rd pers sg ...... περιτίθημι

περιετμήθη vb 1st aor pass ind 3rd pers sg ...... περιτέμνω

περιεφέροσαν vb impf act ind 3rd pers pl ...... περιφέρω

περιέφραξας vb 1st aor act ind 2nd pers sg . . . περιφράσσω

περιεφρόνει vb impf act ind 3rd pers sg . . . . . . περιφρονέω

περιεφύτευσεν vb 1st aor act ind 3rd pers sg . . περιφυτεύω

περιεχαράκωσαν vb 1st aor act

       ind 3rd pers pl . . . . περιχαρακόω

περιέχει vb pres act ind 3rd pers sg . . . . περιέχω

περιέχεον vb impf act ind 3rd pers pl . . . . περιχέω

περιεχόμενα vb pres m/p part neut nom and acc pl . . περιέχω

περιεχόμενοι vb pres m/p part masc nom pl . . . . id.

περιεχόμενος vb pres m/p part masc nom sg . . . . id.

περιεχόντας vb pres act part masc acc pl . . . . id.

περιέχουσαι vb pres act part fem nom pl . . . . id.

περιέχουσαν vb pres act part fem acc sg . . . . id.

περιεχούσης vb pres act part fem gen sg . . . . id.

περιέχουσιν vb pres act ind 3rd pers pl . . . . id.

περιεχουσῶν vb pres act part fem gen pl . . . . id.

περιεχρύσωσεν vb 1st aor act ind 3rd pers sg . περιχρυσόω

περιεχύθη vb 1st aor pass ind 3rd pers sg . . . . περιχέω

περίζωμα noun neut nom and acc sg

περιζώματα noun neut nom and acc pl . . . . περίζωμα

περιζώννυνται vb pres m/p ind 3rd pers sg . . . . περιζωννύω

περιζωννύων vb pres act part masc nom sg . . . . id.

περίζωσαι vb 1st aor mid impv 2nd pers sg . . . . id.

περιζώσασθε vb 1st aor mid impv 2nd pers pl . . . . id.

περιζώσῃ vb fut mid ind 2nd pers sg . . . . id.

περιζώσονται vb fut mid ind 3rd pers pl . . . . id.

περιήγαγεν vb 2nd aor act ind 3rd pers sg . . . . περιάγω

περιήγαγον vb 2nd aor act ind 1st pers sg . . . . id.

περιήειν vb impf act ind 1st pers sg . . . . περίειμι

περιῆλθον vb 2nd aor act ind 1st pers sg . . . . . περιέρχομαι

περιήλθοσαν vb 2nd aor act ind 3rd pers pl . . . . id.

περιηργυρωμένα vb perf m/p part

       neut nom and acc pl . . . . περιαργυρόω

περιηργυρωμέναι vb perf m/p part fem nom pl . . . . id.

περιηργυρωμένοι vb perf m/p part masc nom pl . . . . . . id.

περιηργύρωσεν vb 1st aor act ind 3rd pers sg . . . . id.

περιηρεῖτο vb impf m/p ind 3rd pers sg . . . . περιαιρέω

περιῆψαν vb 1st aor act ind 3rd pers pl . . . . περιάπτω

περιθεῖναι vb 2nd aor act inf . . . . περιτίθημι

περιθείς vb 2nd aor act part masc nom sg . . . . id.

περίθεμα noun neut nom and acc sg

περιθεμάτων noun neut gen pl . . . . περίθεμα

περιθέμεναι vb 2nd aor mid part fem nom pl . . . περιτίθημι

περιθέμενος vb 2nd aor mid part masc nom sg . . . . id.

περιθέσθαι vb 2nd aor mid inf . . . . id.

περιθέσθω vb 2nd aor mid impv 3rd pers sg . . . . id.

περιθήσει vb fut act ind 3rd pers sg . . . . id.

περιθήσεις vb fut act ind 2nd pers sg . . . . id.

περιθήσεται vb fut mid ind 3rd pers sg . . . . id.

περιθήσετε vb fut act ind 2nd pers pl . . . . id.

περιθήσῃ vb fut mid ind 2nd pers sg . . . . id.

περιθήσουσιν vb fut act ind 3rd pers pl . . . . id.

περιθήσω vb fut act ind 1st pers sg . . . . περιτίθημι

περίθου vb 2nd aor mid impv 2nd pers sg . . . . id.

περιιπτάμενα vb pres dep part

       neut nom and acc pl . . . . περιίπταμαι

περιισταμένου vb pres m/p part

       masc and neut gen sg . . . . περιίστημι

περικαθαίρων vb pres act part masc nom sg . περικαθαίρω

περικαθαριεῖ vb fut act ind 3rd pers sg . . . . περικαθαρίζω

περικαθαριεῖτε vb fut act ind 2nd pers pl . . . . id.

περικάθαρμα noun neut nom and acc sg

περικάθηνται vb pres m/p ind 3rd pers pl . . . περικάθημαι

περικαθῆσθαι vb pres m/p inf . . . . id.

περικάθηται vb pres m/p ind 3rd pers sg . . . . id.

περικαθιεῖς vb fut act ind 2nd pers sg . . . . περικαθίζω

περικαθίσαι vb 1st aor act inf . . . . id.

περικαθίσαντες vb 1st aor act part masc nom pl . . . . . . id.

περικαθίσῃς vb 1st aor act subj 2nd pers sg . . . . id.

περικαλύπτειν vb pres act inf . . . . περικαλύπτω

περικαλύψαι vb 1st aor act inf . . . . id.

περικατάλημπτος adj masc and fem

       nom sg . . . . περικατάληπτος

περικείμενα vb pres m/p part

       neut nom and acc pl . . . . περίκειμαι

περικείμενον vb pres m/p part masc acc sg . . . . id.

περίκεινται vb pres m/p ind 3rd pers pl . . . . id.

περικειρόμενον vb pres m/p part masc acc sg . . . περικείρω

περικεκαλυμμένα vb perf m/p part

       neut nom and acc pl . . . . περικαλύπτω

περικεκαρμένον vb perf m/p part masc acc sg . . . περικείρω

περικεκοσμημέναι vb perf m/p part

       fem nom pl . . . . περικοσμέω

περικεκυκλωμένα vb perf m/p part

       neut nom and acc pl . . . . περικυκλόω

περικεκυκλωμένας vb perf m/p part fem acc pl . . . . . . id.

περικεφαλαία noun fem nom sg

περικεφαλαῖαι noun fem nom pl . . . . περικεφαλαία

περικεφαλαίαις noun fem dat pl . . . . id.

περικεφαλαίαν noun fem acc sg . . . . id.

περικεφαλαίας noun fem gen sg and acc pl . . . . id.

περικεχαλασμένων vb perf m/p part gen pl . . . περιχαλάω

περικεχρυσωμένα vb perf m/p part

       neut nom and acc pl . . . . περιχρυσόω

περικεχυμένος vb perf m/p part masc nom sg . . . . . περιχέω

περικλασθήσονται vb fut pass ind 3rd pers pl . . περικλάω

περικλύσασθαι vb 1st aor mid inf . . . . περικλύζω

περικλῶντες vb pres act part masc nom pl . . . . . . περικλάω

περικνημῖσι noun fem dat pl . . . . περικνημίς

περικρατεῖ vb pres act ind 3rd pers sg . . . . περικρατέω

περικρατήσειεν vb 1st aor act opt 3rd pers sg . . . . id.

περικρατοῦσιν vb pres act ind 3rd pers pl . . . . id.

περικύκλω adverb

περικυκλωθήσεται vb fut pass ind 3rd pers sg περικυκλόω

περικυκλώσουσιν vb fut act ind 3rd pers pl .. περικυκλόω
περιλαβεῖν vb 2nd aor act inf .... περιλαμβάνω
περιλάβετε vb 2nd aor act impv 2nd pers pl   id.
περιλάβῃ vb 2nd aor act subj 3rd pers sg   id.
περιλαβών vb 2nd aor act part masc nom sg   id.
περιλακιζομένας vb pres m/p part fem acc pl .. περιλακίζω
περιλαμβάνων vb pres act part masc nom sg . περιλαμβάνω
περιλειπόμενοι vb pres m/p part masc nom pl ... περιλείπω
περιλειπόμενον vb pres m/p part masc acc sg,
                neut nom and acc sg   id.
περιλελειμμένα vb perf m/p part neut nom and acc pl   id.
περιλημφθήσονται vb fut pass ind
                3rd pers pl .... περιλαμβάνω
περιλήμψεται vb fut mid ind 3rd pers sg   id.
περιλήμψεως noun fem gen sg .... περίλημψις
περιλοίποις adj dat pl .... περίλοιπος
περιλοίπους adj masc and fem acc pl   id.
περίλυπος adj masc and fem nom sg
περιλύσαντες vb 1st aor act part masc nom pl .... περιλύω
περιμενοῦσιν vb fut act ind 3rd pers pl .... περιμένω
περιμένω vb pres act ind 1st pers sg   id.
περίμετρον noun neut nom and acc sg
περιμέτρῳ noun neut dat sg .... περίμετρον
περινίψασθαι vb 1st aor mid inf .... περινίπτω
περιοδεῦσαι vb 1st aor act inf .... περιοδεύω
περιοδεύσατε vb 1st aor act impv 2nd pers pl   id.
περιόδῳ noun fem dat sg .... περίοδος
περίοικα adj neut nom and acc pl .... περίοικος
περιοικοδομήσει vb fut act ind 3rd pers sg . περιοικοδομέω
περιοικοδομήσουσιν vb fut act ind 3rd pers pl   id.
περίοικον adj acc sg, neut nom sg .... περίοικος
περιοίκου adj gen sg   id.
περιοίκους adj masc and fem acc pl   id.
περιοίκῳ adj masc and neut dat sg   id.
περιόν vb pres act part neut nom and acc sg ...... περίειμι
περιόντες vb pres act part masc nom pl   id.
περιόντος vb pres act part masc and neut gen sg   id.
περιονυχιεῖς vb fut act ind 2nd pers sg ...... περιονυχίζω
περιοῦσαν vb pres act part fem acc sg .... περίειμι
περιουσιασμόν noun masc acc sg ...... περιουσιασμός
περιουσιασμούς noun masc acc pl   id.
περιούσιον adj acc sg, neut nom sg .... περιούσιος
περιούσιος adj masc and fem nom sg   id.
περιοχή noun fem nom sg
περιοχῇ noun fem dat sg .... περιοχή
περιοχήν noun fem acc sg   id.
περιοχῆς noun fem gen sg   id.
περιπαθῶς adverb
περιπάτει vb pres act impv 2nd pers sg .... περιπατέω
περιπατεῖς vb pres act ind 2nd pers sg   id.
περιπατῇς vb pres act subj 2nd pers sg   id.
περιπατήσαισαν vb 1st aor act opt 3rd pers pl   id.

περιπατήσας vb 1st aor act part masc nom sg .. περιπατέω
περιπατήσει vb fut act ind 3rd pers sg   id.
περιπατήσεις vb fut act ind 2nd pers sg   id.
περιπατήσῃ vb 1st aor act subj 3rd pers sg   id.
περιπατήσουσιν vb fut act ind 3rd pers pl   id.
περίπατοι noun masc nom pl .... περίπατος
περιπάτοις noun masc dat pl   id.
περίπατον noun masc acc sg   id.
περίπατος noun masc nom sg   id.
περιπάτου noun masc gen sg   id.
περιπατοῦντας vb pres act part masc acc pl ... περιπατέω
περιπατοῦντος vb pres act part masc and neut gen sg   id.
περιπατούντων vb pres act part masc and neut gen pl   id.
περιπατοῦσαν vb pres act part fem acc sg   id.
περιπατοῦσιν vb pres act ind 3rd pers pl   id.
περιπατῶ vb pres act ind 1st pers sg   id.
περιπατῶν vb pres act part masc nom sg   id.
περιπεπλεγμένη vb perf m/p part fem nom sg .. περιπλέκω
περιπεπλεγμένοι vb perf m/p part masc nom pl   id.
περιπεπληγμένον vb perf m/p part masc acc sg   id.
περιπεποίημαι vb perf m/p ind 1st pers sg ..... περιποιέω
περιπεσεῖν vb 2nd aor act inf .... περιπίπτω
περιπεσεῖσθε vb fut mid ind 2nd pers pl   id.
περιπεσόντα vb 2nd aor act part masc acc sg   id.
περιπεσών vb 2nd aor act part masc nom sg   id.
περιπεφραγμέναι vb perf m/p part
                fem nom pl .... περιφράσσω
περιπεφραγμένην vb perf m/p part fem acc sg   id.
περιπίπτει vb pres act ind 3rd pers sg .... περιπίπτω
περιπίπτειν vb pres act inf   id.
περιπλεκομένη vb pres m/p part fem nom sg ... περιπλέκω
περιπλεκόμενοι vb pres m/p part masc nom pl   id.
περιπλέκων vb pres act part masc nom sg   id.
περιποιεῖσθε vb pres m/p impv 2nd pers pl ..... περιποιέω
περιποιεῖται vb pres m/p ind 3rd pers sg   id.
περιποίησαι vb 1st aor mid impv 2nd pers sg   id.
περιποιῆσαι vb 1st aor act inf   id.
περιποιησάμενος vb 1st aor mid part masc nom sg   id.
περιποιήσαντι vb 1st aor act part masc and neut dat sg   id.
περιποιήσασθαι vb 1st aor mid inf   id.
περιποιήσασθε vb 1st aor mid impv 2nd pers pl   id.
περιποιήσεσθε vb fut mid ind 2nd pers pl   id.
περιποιήσεται vb fut mid ind 3rd pers sg   id.
περιποιήσετε vb fut act ind 2nd pers pl   id.
περιποιήσῃ vb fut mid ind 2nd pers sg   id.
περιποίησιν noun fem acc sg .... περιποίησις
περιποιησόμεθα vb fut mid ind 1st pers pl ..... περιποιέω
περιποιήσονται vb fut mid ind 3rd pers pl   id.
περιποιησώμεθα vb 1st aor mid subj 1st pers pl   id.
περιπόλια noun neut nom and acc pl .... περιπόλιον
περιπορεύεται vb pres dep ind 3rd pers sg . περιπορεύομαι
περιπόρφυρα adj neut nom and acc pl ..... περιπόρφυρος

περίπτερα adj neut nom and acc pl . . . . περίπτερος
περίπτερον adj acc sg, neut nom sg id.
περιπτώματι noun neut dat sg . . . . περίπτωμα
περιρραίνων vb pres act part masc nom sg . . περιρραίνω
περιρρανεῖ vb fut act ind 3rd pers sg id.
περιρρανεῖς vb fut act ind 2nd pers sg id.
περιρρήξας vb 1st aor act part masc nom sg περιρρήγνυμι
περισεσιαλωμένους vb perf m/p part
     masc acc pl . . . . περισιαλόω
περισκελές adj neut nom and acc sg . . . . περισκελής
περισκελῆ adj neut nom and acc pl id.
περισκυθίσαντας vb 1st aor act part
     masc acc pl . . . . περισκυθίζω
περισπᾷ vb pres act ind 3rd pers sg . . . . περισπάω
περισπᾶσθαι vb pres m/p inf id.
περισπασμόν noun masc acc sg . . . . περισπασμός
περισπασμός noun masc nom sg id.
περισπασμοῦ noun masc gen sg id.
περισπασμῷ noun masc dat sg id.
περισπόρια noun neut nom and acc pl . . . . . περισπόριον
περισπωμένῳ vb pres m/p part
     masc and neut dat sg . . . . περισπάω
περισσά adj neut nom and acc pl . . . . περισσός
περισσάς adj fem acc pl id.
περισσεία noun fem nom sg
περισσεύει vb pres act ind 3rd pers sg . . . . περισσεύω
περισσεύματος noun neut gen sg . . . . περίσσευμα
περισσεύσῃ vb 1st aor act subj 3rd pers sg . . . περισσεύω
περισσεύσῃς vb 1st aor act subj 2nd pers sg id.
περισσεύων vb pres act part masc nom sg id.
περισσή adj fem nom sg . . . . περισσός
περισσοί adj masc nom pl id.
περισσοῖς adj masc and neut dat pl id.
περισσόν adj masc acc sg, neut nom and acc sg id.
περισσόν adverb
περισσός adj masc nom sg
περισσοτέρα comp adj neut nom and acc pl . . . . . περισσός
περισσοῦ adj masc and neut gen sg id.
περισσῶς adverb
περισταλῆς vb 2nd aor pass subj 2nd pers sg . . περιστέλλω
περιστάντες vb 2nd aor act part masc nom pl . . περιίστημι
περίστασιν noun fem acc sg . . . . περίστασις
περίστασις noun fem nom sg id.
περιστείλῃς vb 1st aor act subj 2nd pers sg . . . περιστέλλω
περίστειλον vb 1st aor act impv 2nd pers sg id.
περιστελεῖ vb fut act ind 3rd pers sg id.
περιστερά noun fem nom sg
περιστεραί noun fem nom pl . . . . περιστερά
περιστεράν noun fem acc sg id.
περιστερᾶς noun fem gen sg id.
περιστερῶν noun fem gen pl id.
περιστήθιον noun neut nom and acc sg

περίστησον vb 1st aor act impv 2nd pers sg . . . . περιίστημι
περιστήσωσιν vb 1st aor act subj 3rd pers pl id.
περιστολῇ noun fem dat sg . . . . περιστολή
περιστολήν noun fem acc sg id.
περιστόμιον noun neut nom and acc sg
περιστομίου noun neut gen sg . . . . περιστόμιον
περιστραφέντα vb 2nd aor pass part
     neut nom and acc pl . . . . περιστρέφω
περιστραφήσεται vb fut pass ind 3rd pers sg id.
περιστροφή noun fem dat sg . . . . περιστροφή
περίστυλα noun neut nom and acc pl . . . . περίστυλον
περίστυλοις noun neut dat pl id.
περίστυλον noun neut nom and acc sg id.
περιστύλου noun neut gen sg id.
περιστύλῳ noun neut dat sg id.
περισύραντες vb 1st aor act part masc nom pl . . . περισύρω
περισύρων vb pres act part masc nom sg id.
περισχίζοντος vb pres act part
     masc and neut gen sg . . . . περισχίζω
περισχιζούσης vb pres act part fem gen sg id.
περίτειχος noun neut nom and acc sg
περίτεμε vb 2nd aor act impv 2nd pers sg . . . . περιτέμνω
περιτεμεῖ vb fut act ind 3rd pers sg id.
περιτεμεῖς vb fut act ind 2nd pers sg id.
περιτεμεῖσθε vb fut mid ind 2nd pers pl id.
περιτέμεσθε vb 2nd aor mid impv 2nd pers pl id.
περιτέμνεσθαι vb pres m/p inf id.
περιτετειχισμένα vb perf m/p part
     neut nom and acc pl . . . . περιτειχίζω
περιτετμηκότας vb perf act part masc acc pl . . . . περιτέμνω
περιτετμηκυῖαι vb perf act part fem nom pl id.
περιτετμηκυίας vb perf act part fem acc pl id.
περιτετμημένον vb perf m/p part
     neut nom and acc sg id.
περιτετμημένους vb perf m/p part masc acc pl id.
περιτέτμηνται vb perf m/p ind 3rd pers pl id.
περιτιθείς vb pres act part masc nom sg . . . . . . περιτίθημι
περιτμηθέντες vb 1st aor pass part masc nom pl . περιτέμνω
περιτμηθῆναι vb 1st aor pass inf id.
περιτμηθήσεσθε vb fut pass ind 2nd pers pl id.
περιτμηθήσεται vb fut pass ind 3rd pers sg id.
περιτμήθητε vb 1st aor pass impv 2nd pers pl id.
περιτομή noun fem dat sg . . . . περιτομή
περιτομῆς noun fem gen sg id.
περιτρέψει vb fut act ind 3rd pers sg . . . . περιτρέπω
περιφανῶς adverb
περιφέρει vb pres act ind 3rd pers sg . . . . περιφέρω
περιφέρεις noun fem nom sg
περιφερές adj neut nom and acc sg . . . . περιφερής
περιφέρεται vb pres m/p ind 3rd pers sg . . . . . . περιφέρω
περιφοράν noun fem acc sg . . . . περιφορά
περιφράξαι vb 1st aor act inf . . . . περιφράσσω

περιφράξας vb 1st aor act part masc nom sg .. περιφράσσω

περίφραξον vb 1st aor act impv 2nd pers sg id.

περίφρονες noun masc nom pl . . . . περίφρων

περιφρονῆσαι vb 1st aor act inf . . . . περιφρονέω

περιχαλκώσεις vb fut act ind 2nd pers sg . . . . περιχαλκόω

περιχαράκωσον vb 1st aor act impv

        2nd pers sg . . . . περιχαρακόω

περιχαρεῖς adj masc and fem nom and acc pl . . . περιχαρής

περίχρυσα adj neut nom and acc pl . . . . περίχρυσος

περίχρυσοι adj masc and fem nom pl id.

περιχρύσων adj gen pl id.

περιχυθέντα vb 1st aor pass part masc acc sg . . . . . περιχέω

περίχωρα adj neut nom and acc pl . . . . περίχωρος

περίχωρον adj acc sg, neut nom sg id.

περίχωρος adj masc and fem nom sg id.

περιχώρου adj gen sg id.

περιχώρους adj masc and fem acc pl id.

περιχώρῳ adj dat sg id.

περιχώρων adj gen pl id.

περίψημα noun neut nom and acc sg

περιψύχων vb pres act part masc nom sg . . . . περιψύχω

περιωδεύκαμεν vb perf act ind 1st pers pl . . . . περιοδεύω

περιώδευσαν vb 1st aor act ind 3rd pers pl id.

περιῳκοδόμημαι vb perf m/p ind

        1st pers sg . . . . περιοικοδομέω

περιῳκοδόμησαν vb 1st aor act ind 3rd pers pl id.

περκαζούσης vb pres act part fem gen sg . . . . περκάζω

περκάσει vb fut act ind 3rd pers sg id.

Περσαι pr noun masc nom pl . . . . Περσης

Περσαις pr noun masc dat pl id.

Περσας pr noun masc acc pl id.

Περσεα pr noun

Περσεπολιν pr noun fem acc sg . . . . Περσεπολις

Περσης pr noun masc nom sg

Περσιδα pr noun fem acc sg . . . . Περσις

Περσιδι pr noun fem dat sg id.

Περσιδος pr noun fem gen sg id.

Περσικην pr noun fem acc sg . . . . Περσικη

Περσου pr noun masc gen sg . . . . Περσης

Περσῶν pr noun masc gen pl id.

πέσατε vb 1st aor act impv 2nd pers pl . . . . πίπτω

πεσεῖν vb 2nd aor act inf id.

πεσεῖσθε vb fut mid ind 2nd pers pl id.

πεσεῖται vb fut mid ind 3rd pers sg id.

πεσέτω vb 2nd aor act impv 3rd pers sg id.

πεσέτωσαν vb 2nd aor act impv 3rd pers pl id.

πέσῃ vb 2nd aor act subj 3rd pers sg id.

πεσῇ vb fut mid ind 2nd pers sg id.

πέσῃς vb 2nd aor act subj 2nd pers sg id.

πέσητε vb 2nd aor act subj 2nd pers pl id.

πέσοι vb 2nd aor act opt 3rd pers sg id.

πεσόντα vb 2nd aor act part masc acc sg id.

πεσόντες vb 2nd aor act part masc nom pl . . . . πίπτω

πεσοῦμαι vb fut mid ind 1st pers sg id.

πεσούμεθα vb fut mid ind 1st pers pl id.

πεσοῦνται vb fut mid ind 3rd pers pl id.

πεσοῦσα vb 2nd aor act part fem nom sg id.

πεσοῦσαν vb 2nd aor act part fem acc sg id.

πέσσετε vb pres act impv 2nd pers pl . . . . πέσσω

πέσσητε vb pres act subj 2nd pers pl id.

πεσσούσας vb pres act part fem acc pl id.

πέσσουσιν vb pres act ind 3rd pers pl id.

πέσω vb 2nd aor act subj 1st pers sg . . . . πίπτω

πεσών vb 2nd aor act part masc nom sg id.

πέσωσιν vb 2nd aor act subj 3rd pers pl id.

πέταλα noun neut nom and acc pl . . . . πέταλον

πέταλον noun neut nom and acc sg id.

πέτανται vb pres dep ind 3rd pers pl . . . . πέταμαι

πέτασθαι vb pres dep inf id.

πετασθήσομαι vb fut pass ind 1st pers sg id.

πετασθήσονται vb fut pass ind 3rd pers pl id.

πέτασον noun masc acc sg . . . . πέτασος

πέταται vb pres dep ind 3rd pers sg . . . . πέταμαι

πετεινά noun neut nom and acc pl . . . . πετεινόν

πετεινοῖς noun neut dat pl id.

πετεινόν noun neut nom and acc sg id.

πετεινοῦ noun neut gen sg id.

πετεινῷ noun neut dat sg id.

πετεινῶν noun neut gen pl id.

πέτευρον noun neut nom and acc sg

Πετεφρη pr noun masc dat sg . . . . Πετεφρης

Πετεφρης pr noun masc nom sg id.

πετόμενα vb pres dep part neut nom and acc pl . . . . πέτομαι

πετόμενοι vb pres dep part masc nom pl id.

πετόμενον vb pres dep part masc acc sg id.

πετόμενος vb pres dep part masc nom sg id.

πετομένου vb pres dep part masc and neut gen sg id.

πετομένων vb pres dep part gen pl id.

πέτονται vb pres dep ind 3rd pers pl id.

Πετρα pr noun fem nom sg

πέτρα noun fem nom sg

πέτρᾳ noun fem dat sg . . . . πέτρα

πέτραι noun fem nom pl id.

πέτραις noun fem dat pl id.

πέτραν noun fem acc sg id.

Πετραν pr noun fem acc sg . . . . Πετρα

Πετρας pr noun fem gen sg id.

πέτρας noun fem gen sg and acc pl . . . . πέτρα

πετρίνας adj fem acc pl . . . . πέτρινος

πετροβόλοις noun masc dat pl . . . . πετροβόλος

πετροβόλον noun masc acc sg

πετροβόλου noun masc gen sg id.

πετροβόλους adj masc acc pl id.

πέτρους noun masc acc pl . . . . πέτρος

πετρῶν noun masc gen pl	. . . .	πέτρος
πεύκη noun fem dat sg	. . . .	πεύκη
πεύκινα adj neut nom and acc pl	. . . .	πεύκινος
πευκίναις adj fem dat pl		id.
πευκίνοις adj masc and neut dat pl		id.
πευκίνων adj gen pl		id.
πεφατνωμένα vb perf mid part neut nom and acc pl	.	φατνόω
πεφαυλισμένοι vb perf mid part masc nom pl	. . . .	φαυλίζω
πεφαυλισμένος vb perf mid part masc nom sg		id.
πέφευγα vb perf act ind 1st pers sg	. . . .	φεύγω
πέφευγας vb perf act ind 2nd pers sg		id.
πεφεύγασιν vb perf act ind 3rd pers pl		id.
πέφευγεν vb perf act ind 3rd pers sg		id.
πεφευγότα vb perf act part neut nom and acc pl		id.
πεφευγότων vb perf act part masc and neut gen pl		id.
πεφθήσεται vb fut pass ind 3rd pers sg	. . . .	πέσσω
πεφθήσονται vb fut pass ind 3rd pers pl		id.
πεφιλοπονημένων vb perf mid part gen pl	. . . .	φιλοπονέω
πεφόβησθε vb perf mid ind 2nd pers pl	. . . .	φοβέω
πεφόνευκεν vb perf act ind 3rd pers sg	. . . .	φονεύω
πεφονευμένης vb perf mid part fem gen sg		id.
πεφόνευται vb perf mid ind 3rd pers sg		id.
πεφραγμένη vb perf mid part fem nom sg	. . . .	ὁράσσω
πεφραγμένον vb perf mid part neut nom and acc sg		id.
πεφρενωμένος vb perf mid part masc nom sg	. . .	φρενόομαι
πεφρυαγμένου vb perf mid part		
masc and neut gen sg	. . . .	φρυάζω
πεφρυγμένα vb perf mid part neut nom and acc pl	. . .	φρύγω
πεφυγαδευκότες vb perf act part masc nom pl	. . .	φυγαδεύω
πεφυγαδευκότων vb perf act part		
masc and neut gen pl		id.
πέφυκεν vb perf act ind 3rd pers sg	. . . .	φύω
πεφυκότα vb perf act part neut nom and acc pl		id.
πεφυλαγμένα vb perf mid part		
neut nom and acc pl	. . . .	φυλάσσω
πεφυλαγμένην vb perf mid part fem acc sg		id.
πεφυλαγμένοι vb perf mid part masc nom pl		id.
πεφύλακα vb perf act ind 1st pers sg		id.
πεφύλακται vb perf mid ind 3rd pers sg		id.
πεφύλαξαι vb perf m/p ind 2nd pers sg		id.
πεφυραμένη vb perf m/p part fem nom sg	. . . .	φυράω
πεφυραμένην vb perf m/p part fem acc sg		id.
πεφυραμένης vb perf m/p part fem gen sg		id.
πεφυραμένους vb perf m/p part masc acc pl		id.
πέφυρμαι vb perf dep ind 1st pers sg	. . . .	φύρομαι
πεφύρμεναι vb perf dep part fem nom pl		id.
πεφυρμένη vb perf dep part fem nom sg		id.
πεφυρμένην vb perf dep part fem acc sg		id.
πεφυρμένον vb perf dep part masc acc sg		id.
πεφυρμένος vb perf dep part masc nom sg		id.
πεφύτευκαν vb perf act ind 3rd pers pl	. . . .	φυτεύω
πεφυτευμένη vb perf m/p part fem nom sg		id.
πεφυτευμένοι vb perf m/p part masc nom pl	. . . . . .	φυτεύω
πεφυτευμένον vb perf m/p part masc acc sg,		
neut nom and acc sg		id.
πέψιν noun fem acc sg	. . . .	πέψις
πέψουσι(ν) vb fut act ind 3rd pers pl	. . . .	πέσσω
πηγαί noun fem nom pl	. . . .	πηγή
πηγάς noun fem acc pl		id.
Πηγή pr noun fem nom sg	. . . .	Πηγη
πηγή noun fem nom sg		
πηγῇ noun fem dat sg	. . . .	πηγή
Πηγήν pr noun fem acc sg	. . . .	Πηγη
πηγήν noun fem acc sg	. . . .	πηγή
πηγῆς noun fem gen sg		id.
πῆγμα noun neut nom and acc sg		
πηγῶν noun fem gen pl	. . . .	πηγή
πηδαλιουχῶν vb pres act part masc nom sg	. .	πηδαλιουχέω
πηδᾶν vb pres act inf	. . . .	πηδάω
πηδῶν vb pres act part masc nom sg		id.
πηλίκαις interr pron fem dat pl	. . . .	πηλίκος
πηλίκον interr pron neut nom and acc sg		id.
πηλίνας adj fem acc pl	. . . .	πήλινος
πήλινον adj masc acc sg, neut nom and acc sg		id.
πήλινος adj masc nom sg		id.
πηλίνῳ adj masc and neut dat sg		id.
πηλόν noun masc acc sg	. . . .	πηλός
πηλός noun masc nom sg		id.
πηλοῦ noun masc gen sg		id.
πηλουργός noun masc nom sg		
πηλῷ noun masc dat sg	. . . .	πηλός
πήξας vb 1st aor act part masc nom sg	. . . .	πήγνυμι
πήξει vb fut act ind 3rd pers sg		id.
πήξεως noun fem gen sg	. . . .	πῆξις
πῆξον vb 1st aor act impv 2nd pers sg	. . . .	πήγνυμι
πήξουσιν vb fut act ind 3rd pers pl		id.
πήραν noun fem acc sg	. . . .	πήρα
πήρας noun fem gen sg		id.
πήχει noun masc dat sg	. . . .	πῆχυς
πήχεις adj masc nom and acc pl		id.
πήχεος noun masc gen sg		id.
πήχεσι noun masc dat pl		id.
πήχεων noun masc gen pl		id.
πῆχυν noun masc acc sg		id.
πῆχυς noun masc nom sg		id.
πηχῶν noun masc gen pl		id.
πιαίνει vb pres act ind 3rd pers sg	. . . .	πιαίνω
πιαίνεται vb pres m/p ind 3rd pers sg		id.
πιανάτω vb 1st aor act impv 3rd pers sg		id.
πιανεῖ vb fut act ind 3rd pers sg		id.
πιανθήσεται vb fut pass ind 3rd pers sg		id.
πιανθήσονται vb fut pass ind 3rd pers pl		id.
πιάσατε vb 1st aor act impv 2nd pers pl	. . . .	πιάζω
πιασθήσεται vb fut pass ind 3rd pers sg		id.

πίε   vb 2nd aor act impv 2nd pers sg . . . . πίνω

πιεῖν   vb 2nd aor act inf   id.

πιέσαι   vb fut mid ind 2nd pers sg   id.

πιέσεις   vb fut act ind 2nd pers sg . . . . πιέζω

πίεσθε   vb 2nd aor mid impv 2nd pers pl,

     fut mid ind 2nd pers pl . . . . πίνω

πίεται   vb fut mid ind 3rd pers sg   id.

πίετε   vb 2nd aor act impv 2nd pers pl   id.

πιέτω   vb 2nd aor act impv 3rd pers sg   id.

πιέτωσαν   vb 2nd aor act impv 3rd pers pl   id.

πίῃ   vb 1st aor act subj 3rd pers sg   id.

πίῃς   vb 2nd aor act subj 2nd pers sg   id.

πίητε   vb 2nd aor act subj 2nd pers pl   id.

πιθήκων   noun masc gen pl . . . . πίθηκος

πίθος   noun masc nom sg

Πιθωμ   pr noun

πικρά   adj fem nom sg, neut nom and acc pl . . . . πικρός

πικραί   adj fem nom pl   id.

πικραινομένη   vb pres m/p part fem nom sg . . . . . πικραίνω

πικράν   adj fem acc sg . . . . πικρός

Πικραν   pr noun fem acc sg . . . . Πικρα

πικρᾶναι   vb 1st aor act inf . . . . πικραίνω

πικράνας   vb 1st aor act part masc nom sg   id.

πικρανθῇ   vb 1st aor pass subj 3rd pers sg   id.

πικρανθῇς   vb 1st aor pass subj 2nd pers sg   id.

πικρανθήσονται   vb fut pass ind 3rd pers pl   id.

πίκρανον   vb 1st aor act impv 2nd pers sg   id.

πικράς   adj fem acc pl . . . . πικρός

πικρᾶς   adj fem gen sg   id.

πικρασμῷ   noun masc dat sg . . . . πικρασμός

Πικρία   pr noun fem nom sg

πικρία   noun fem nom sg

πικρίᾳ   noun fem dat sg . . . . πικρία

Πικριαις   pr noun fem dat pl   id.

πικρίαν   noun fem acc sg   id.

πικρίας   noun fem gen sg and acc pl   id.

πικρίδων   noun fem gen pl . . . . πικρίς

πικροί   adj masc nom pl . . . . πικρός

πικρόν   adj masc acc sg, neut nom and acc sg   id.

πικρός   adj masc nom sg   id.

πικρότερον   comp adj masc acc sg, neut nom and acc sg   id.

πικροτέρων   comp adj gen pl   id.

πικροῦ   adj masc and neut gen sg   id.

πικρῷ   adj masc and neut dat sg   id.

πικρῶν   adj gen pl   id.

πικρῶς   adverb

πίμπλησιν   vb pres act ind 3rd pers sg . . . . πίμπλημι

πίμπληται   vb pres m/p subj 3rd pers sg   id.

πιμπλῶν   vb pres act part masc nom sg   id.

πῖνε   vb pres act impv 2nd pers sg . . . . πίνω

πίνει   vb pres act ind 3rd pers sg   id.

πίνειν   vb pres act inf   id.

πίνεται   vb pres m/p ind 3rd pers sg . . . . πίνω

πίνετε   vb pres act ind 2nd pers pl   id.

πινέτωσαν   vb pres act impv 3rd pers pl   id.

πίνῃς   vb pres act subj 2nd pers sg   id.

πιννίνου   noun masc gen sg . . . . πίννινος

πινόμενος   vb pres m/p part masc nom sg . . . . πίνω

πίνοντα   vb pres act part neut nom and acc pl   id.

πίνοντας   vb pres act part masc acc pl   id.

πίνοντες   vb pres act part masc nom pl   id.

πινόντων   vb pres act part masc and neut gen pl   id.

πίνουσαι   vb pres act part fem nom pl   id.

πίνουσιν   vb pres act ind 3rd pers pl   id.

πίνων   vb pres act part masc nom sg   id.

πίνωσιν   vb pres act subj 3rd pers pl   id.

πίομαι   vb fut mid ind 1st pers sg   id.

πιόμεθα   vb fut mid ind 1st pers pl   id.

πίον   vb 2nd aor act part neut nom and acc sg   id.

πίονα   adj masc and fem acc sg,

     neut nom and acc pl . . . . πίων

πίονας   adj masc and fem acc pl   id.

πίονες   adj masc and fem nom pl   id.

πίονι   adj dat sg   id.

πίονται   vb fut mid ind 3rd pers pl . . . . πίνω

πιόντες   vb 2nd aor act part masc nom pl   id.

πιόνων   adj gen pl . . . . πίων

πίοσι   adj dat pl   id.

πιότης   noun fem nom sg

πιότητα   noun fem acc sg . . . . πιότης

πιότητος   noun fem gen sg   id.

πιοῦσα   vb 2nd aor act part fem nom sg . . . . πίνω

πίπτει   vb pres act ind 3rd pers sg . . . . πίπτω

πίπτετε   vb pres act ind 2nd pers pl   id.

πῖπτον   vb pres act part neut nom and acc sg   id.

πίπτοντα   vb pres act part masc acc sg   id.

πίπτοντας   vb pres act part masc acc pl   id.

πίπτοντες   vb pres act part masc nom pl   id.

πιπτόντων   vb pres act part masc and neut gen pl   id.

πίπτουσα   vb pres act part fem nom sg   id.

πίπτουσιν   vb pres act ind 3rd pers pl   id.

πίπτω   vb pres act ind 1st pers sg   id.

πίπτων   vb pres act part masc nom sg   id.

πίσσα   noun fem nom sg

πίσσαν   noun fem acc sg . . . . πίσσα

πίσσης   noun fem gen sg   id.

πιστά   adj neut nom and acc pl . . . . πιστός

πισταί   adj fem nom pl   id.

πιστάς   adj fem acc pl   id.

πίστει   noun fem dat sg . . . . πίστις

πίστεις   noun fem nom and acc pl   id.

πίστεσιν   noun fem dat pl   id.

πίστευε   vb pres act impv 2nd pers sg . . . . πιστεύω

πιστεύει   vb pres act ind 3rd pers sg   id.

πιστεύεις vb pres act ind 2nd pers sg . . . . πιστεύω

πιστεύετε vb pres act ind 2nd pers pl id.

πιστευέτω vb pres act impv 3rd pers sg id.

πιστευθείς vb 1st aor pass part masc nom sg id.

πιστευθέντων vb 1st aor pass part masc and neut gen pl id.

πιστευθήσονται vb fut pass ind 3rd pers pl id.

πιστεύοντας vb pres act part masc acc pl id.

πιστεύοντες vb pres act part masc nom pl id.

πιστεύουσιν vb pres act ind 3rd pers pl id.

πιστεύσαντες vb 1st aor act part masc nom pl id.

πιστεύσατε vb 1st aor act impv 2nd pers pl id.

πιστεύσει vb fut act ind 3rd pers sg id.

πιστεύσεις vb fut act ind 2nd pers sg id.

πιστεύσῃ vb 1st aor act subj 3rd pers sg id.

πιστεύσῃς vb 1st aor act subj 2nd pers sg id.

πιστεύσητε vb 1st aor act subj 2nd pers pl id.

πίστευσον vb 1st aor act impv 2nd pers sg id.

πιστεύσουσιν vb fut act ind 3rd pers pl id.

πιστεύσωσιν vb 1st aor act subj 3rd pers pl id.

πιστεύω vb pres act ind 1st pers sg id.

πιστεύων vb pres act part masc nom sg id.

πίστεως noun fem gen sg . . . . πίστις

πιστή adj fem nom sg . . . . πιστός

πιστήν adj fem acc sg id.

πίστιν noun fem acc sg . . . . πίστις

πίστις noun fem nom sg id.

πιστοί adj masc nom pl . . . . πιστός

πιστόν adj masc acc sg, neut nom and acc sg id.

πιστός adj masc nom sg id.

πιστότερος comp adj masc nom sg id.

πιστοῦ adj masc and neut gen sg id.

πιστούς adj masc acc pl id.

πιστῷ adj masc and neut dat sg id.

πιστωθῆναι vb 1st aor pass inf . . . . πιστόω

πιστωθήσεται vb fut pass ind 3rd pers sg id.

πιστώθητι vb 1st aor pass impv 2nd pers sg id.

πιστωθήτω vb 1st aor pass impv 3rd pers sg id.

πιστῶν adj gen pl . . . . πιστός

πιστῶς adverb

πιστώσαι vb 1st aor act opt 3rd pers sg . . . . πιστόω

πιστώσαντος vb 1st aor act part masc and neut gen sg id.

πίστωσον vb 1st aor act impv 2nd pers sg id.

πιστώσω vb fut act ind 1st pers sg id.

πίτυες noun fem nom pl . . . . πίτυς

πίτυρα noun neut nom and acc pl . . . . πίτυρον

πίτυς noun fem nom sg

πίω vb 2nd aor act subj 1st pers sg . . . . πίνω

πίωμεν vb 2nd aor act subj 1st pers pl id.

πίων adj masc and fem nom sg

πίωσιν vb 2nd aor act subj 3rd pers pl . . . . πίνω

πλάγια adj neut nom and acc pl . . . . πλάγιος

πλαγίας adj fem gen sg and acc pl id.

πλαγιάσῃ vb 1st aor act subj 3rd pers sg . . . . πλαγιάζω

πλάγιοι adj masc nom pl . . . . πλάγιος

πλαγίῳ adj masc and neut dat sg id.

πλαγίων adj gen pl id.

πλάκας noun fem acc pl . . . . πλάξ

πλακείς vb 2nd aor pass part masc nom sg . . . . πλέκω

πλάκες noun fem nom pl . . . . πλάξ

πλακῶν noun fem gen pl id.

πλάνα vb pres act impv 2nd pers sg . . . . πλανάω

πλανᾷ vb pres act ind 3rd pers sg id.

πλάναι noun fem nom pl . . . . πλάνη

πλανᾶσθαι vb pres m/p inf . . . . πλανάω

πλανᾶται vb pres m/p ind 3rd pers sg,
                     pres m/p subj 3rd pers sg id.

πλάνῃ noun fem dat sg . . . . πλάνη

πλανηθεῖσαν vb 1st aor pass opt 3rd pers pl . . . . . πλανάω

πλανηθείς vb 1st aor pass part masc nom sg id.

πλανηθέντες vb 1st aor pass part masc nom pl id.

πλανηθῇ vb 1st aor pass subj 3rd pers sg id.

πλανηθῆναι vb 1st aor pass inf id.

πλανηθήσεται vb fut pass ind 3rd pers sg id.

πλανηθήσῃ vb fut pass ind 2nd pers sg id.

πλανήθητε vb 1st aor pass impv 2nd pers pl id.

πλανηθῆτε vb 1st aor pass subj 2nd pers pl id.

πλανηθῶσιν vb 1st aor pass subj 3rd pers pl id.

πλάνης noun fem gen sg . . . . πλάνη

πλανῆσαι vb 1st aor act inf . . . . πλανάω

πλανησάντων vb 1st aor act part
                     masc and neut gen pl id.

πλανήσει noun fem dat sg . . . . πλάνησις

πλανήσει vb fut act ind 3rd pers sg . . . . πλανάω

πλανήσεις vb fut act ind 2nd pers sg id.

πλανήσεως noun fem gen sg . . . . πλάνησις

πλάνησιν noun fem acc sg id.

πλάνησις noun fem nom sg id.

πλανήσουσιν vb fut act ind 3rd pers pl . . . . πλανάω

πλανήσωσιν vb 1st aor act subj 3rd pers pl id.

πλάνηται noun masc nom pl . . . . πλανήτης

πλανῆτις noun fem nom sg

πλάνοις noun masc dat pl . . . . πλάνος

πλάνος noun masc nom sg id.

πλανῶ vb pres act ind 1st pers sg,
                     pres m/p impv 2nd pers sg . . . . πλανάω

πλανώμενα vb pres m/p part neut nom and acc pl id.

πλανώμενοι vb pres m/p part masc nom pl id.

πλανωμένοις vb pres m/p part masc and neut dat pl id.

πλανώμενον vb pres m/p part masc acc sg,
                     neut nom and acc sg id.

πλανώμενος vb pres m/p part masc nom sg id.

πλανωμένων vb pres m/p part gen pl id.

πλανῶν vb pres act part masc nom sg id.

πλανῶνται vb pres m/p ind 3rd pers pl id.

πλανῶντας	vb pres act part masc acc pl	πλανάω
πλανῶντες	vb pres act part masc nom pl	id.
πλανώντων	vb pres act part masc and neut gen pl	id.
πλανῶσιν	vb pres act ind 3rd pers pl	id.
πλαξίν	noun fem dat pl	πλάξ
πλάσαι	vb 1st aor act inf	πλάσσω
πλάσαντα	vb 1st aor act part masc acc sg	id.
πλάσαντι	vb 1st aor act part masc and neut dat sg	id.
πλάσας	vb 1st aor act part masc nom sg	id.
πλασθέντες	vb 1st aor pass part masc nom pl	id.
πλασθῆναι	vb 1st aor pass inf	id.
πλασθήσονται	vb fut pass ind 3rd pers pl	id.
πλάσμα	noun neut nom and acc sg	
πλάσματος	noun neut gen sg	πλάσμα
πλάσσει	vb pres act ind 3rd pers sg	πλάσσω
πλάσσοντες	vb pres act part masc nom pl	id.
πλάσσω	vb pres act ind 1st pers sg	id.
πλάσσων	vb pres act part masc nom sg	id.
πλάστιγγι	noun fem dat sg	πλάστιγξ
πλαστίγγων	noun fem gen pl	
πλάτανος	noun fem nom sg	
πλατάνου	noun fem gen sg	πλάτανος
πλάτει	adj masc and neut dat sg	πλατύς
πλατεῖα	adj fem nom sg	id.
πλατεῖα	noun fem nom pl	πλατεῖα
πλατείᾳ	adj fem dat sg	πλατύς
πλατεῖαι	adj fem nom pl	id.
πλατεῖαι	noun fem nom pl	πλατεῖα
πλατείαις	adj fem dat pl	πλατύς
πλατεῖαν	adj fem acc sg	id.
πλατείας	adj fem gen sg and acc pl	id.
πλατείας	noun fem gen sg and acc pl	πλατεῖα
πλατεῖς	adj masc nom and acc pl	πλατύς
πλατειῶν	adj gen pl	id.
πλατέος	adj masc and neut gen sg	id.
πλάτη	noun neut nom and acc pl	πλάτος
πλάτος	noun neut nom and acc sg	id.
πλάτους	noun neut gen sg	id.
πλατύ	adj neut nom and acc sg	πλατύς
πλατύναι	vb 1st aor act opt 3rd pers sg	πλατύνω
πλατυνθῇ	vb 1st aor pass subj 3rd pers sg	id.
πλατυνθήσεται	vb fut pass ind 3rd pers sg	id.
πλάτυνον	vb 1st aor act impv 2nd pers sg	id.
πλατύνου	vb pres m/p impv 2nd pers sg	id.
πλατύνω	vb pres act ind 1st pers sg,	
	pres act subj 1st pers sg	id.
πλατυσμόν	noun masc acc sg	πλατυσμός
πλατυσμῷ	noun masc dat sg	id.
Πλειαδα	pr noun fem acc sg	Πλειας
Πλειαδος	pr noun fem gen sg	id.
πλεῖν	vb pres act inf	πλέω
πλεῖον	comp adj neut nom and acc sg	πολύς

πλείονα	comp adj masc and fem acc sg,	
	neut nom and acc pl	πολύς
πλείονας	comp adj masc and fem acc pl	id.
πλείονες	comp adj masc and fem nom pl	id.
πλείονι	comp adj dat sg	id.
πλείονος	comp adj gen sg	id.
πλειόνων	comp adj gen pl	id.
πλείοσι	comp adj dat pl	id.
πλείους	comp adj masc and fem nom and acc pl	id.
πλεῖστα	superl adj neut nom and acc pl	id.
πλείσταις	superl adj fem dat pl	id.
πλειστάκις	adverb	
πλείστας	superl adj fem acc pl	πολύς
πλείστη	superl adj fem dat sg	id.
πλείστην	superl adj fem acc sg	id.
πλεῖστοι	superl adj masc nom pl	id.
πλείστοις	superl adj masc and neut dat pl	id.
πλεῖστον	superl adj masc acc sg, neut nom and acc sg	id.
πλείστῳ	superl adj masc and neut dat sg	id.
πλείω	comp adj neut nom and acc pl	id.
πλείων	comp adj masc nom sg	id.
πλέον	comp adj neut nom and acc sg	id.
πλέονα	comp adj neut nom and acc pl	id.
πλεονάζει	vb pres act ind 3rd pers sg	πλεονάζω
πλεονάζειν	vb pres act inf	id.
πλεονάζον	vb pres act part neut nom and acc sg	id.
πλεονάζοντες	vb pres act part masc nom pl	id.
πλεοναζόντων	vb pres act part masc and neut gen pl	id.
πλεοναζούσῃ	vb pres act part fem dat sg	id.
πλεοναζούσης	vb pres act part fem gen sg	id.
πλεονάζων	vb pres act part masc nom sg	id.
πλεονάκις	adverb	
πλεονάσαι	vb 1st aor act inf	πλεονάζω
πλεονάσεις	vb fut act ind 2nd pers sg	id.
πλεόνασμα	noun neut nom and acc sg	
πλεονασμόν	noun masc acc sg	πλεονασμός
πλεονασμῶν	noun masc gen pl	id.
πλεοναστόν	adj masc acc sg,	
	neut nom and acc sg	πλεοναστός
πλεονάσω	vb fut act ind 1st pers sg	πλεονάζω
πλεονάσωσιν	vb 1st aor act subj 3rd pers pl	id.
πλεονέκτου	noun masc gen sg	πλεονέκτης
πλεονεκτούντων	vb pres act part	
	masc and neut gen pl	πλεονεκτέω
πλεονεκτῶν	vb pres act part masc nom sg	id.
πλεονεκτῶσιν	vb pres act subj 3rd pers pl	id.
πλεονεξίᾳ	noun fem dat sg	πλεονεξία
πλεονεξίαν	noun fem acc sg	id.
πλεονεξίας	noun fem gen sg and acc pl	id.
πλέοντες	vb pres act part masc nom pl	πλέω
πλεόντων	vb pres act part masc and neut gen pl	id.
πλευρά	noun fem nom sg	

πλευρά noun neut nom and acc pl . . . . πλευρόν
πλευρᾷ noun fem dat sg . . . . πλευρά
πλευραί noun fem nom pl id.
πλευραῖς noun fem dat pl id.
πλευράν noun fem acc sg id.
πλευράς noun fem acc pl id.
πλευρᾶς noun fem gen sg id.
πλευροῖς noun neut dat pl . . . . πλευρόν
πλευρόν noun neut nom and acc sg id.
πλευροῦ noun neut gen sg id.
πλευρῶν noun fem gen pl . . . . πλευρά
πλεῦσαι vb 1st aor act inf . . . . πλέω
πληγαί noun fem nom pl . . . . πληγή
πληγαῖς noun fem dat pl id.
πληγάς noun fem acc pl id.
πληγείς vb 2nd aor pass part masc nom sg . . . . πλήσσω
πληγέντες vb 2nd aor pass part masc nom pl id.
πληγή noun fem nom sg
πληγῇ noun fem dat sg . . . . πληγή
πληγήν noun fem acc sg id.
πληγῆς noun fem gen sg id.
πληγήσεσθε vb fut pass ind 2nd pers pl . . . . πλήσσω
πληγήσεται vb fut pass ind 3rd pers sg id.
πληγῆτε vb 2nd aor pass subj 2nd pers pl id.
πληγῶν noun fem gen pl . . . . πληγή
πλήθει noun neut dat sg . . . . πλῆθος
πλήθεσι noun neut dat pl id.
πλήθη noun neut nom and acc pl id.
πλῆθος noun neut nom and acc sg id.
πλήθους noun neut gen sg id.
πληθύν noun fem acc sg . . . . πληθύς
πληθύναι vb 1st aor act opt 3rd pers sg . . . . πληθύνω
πληθῦναι vb 1st aor act inf id.
πληθύνας vb 1st aor act part masc nom sg id.
πληθύνατε vb 1st aor act impv 2nd pers pl id.
πληθύνει vb pres act ind 3rd pers sg id.
πληθυνεῖ vb fut act ind 3rd pers sg id.
πληθυνεῖτε vb fut act ind 2nd pers pl id.
πληθύνεσθε vb pres m/p impv 2nd pers pl,
        pres m/p ind 2nd pers pl id.
πληθυνέσθωσαν vb pres mid impv 3rd pers pl id.
πληθύνεται vb pres m/p ind 3rd pers sg id.
πληθύνῃ vb pres act subj 3rd pers sg,
        1st aor act subj 3rd pers sg id.
πληθύνῃς vb pres act subj 2nd pers sg,
        1st aor act subj 2nd pers sg id.
πληθύνητε vb pres act subj 2nd pers pl,
        1st aor act subj 2nd pers pl id.
πληθυνθείη vb 1st aor pass opt 3rd pers sg id.
πληθυνθείησαν vb 1st aor pass opt 3rd pers pl id.
πληθυνθέντος vb 1st aor pass part masc and neut gen sg id.
πληθυνθέντων vb 1st aor pass part masc and neut gen pl id.

πληθυνθῇ vb 1st aor pass subj 3rd pers sg . . . . πληθύνω
πληθυνθῆναι vb 1st aor pass inf id.
πληθυνθήσεται vb fut pass ind 3rd pers sg id.
πληθυνθήσονται vb fut pass ind 3rd pers pl id.
πληθυνθῆτε vb 1st aor pass subj 2nd pers pl id.
πληθυνθῶσιν vb 1st aor pass subj 3rd pers pl id.
πλήθυνον vb 1st aor act impv 2nd pers sg id.
πληθύνοντα vb pres act part masc acc sg,
        neut nom and acc pl id.
πληθύνοντες vb pres act part masc nom pl id.
πληθύνου vb pres m/p impv 2nd pers sg id.
πληθύνουσα vb pres act part fem nom sg id.
πληθυνοῦσι vb fut act ind 3rd pers pl id.
πληθύνουσιν vb pres act ind 3rd pers pl id.
πληθύνω vb pres act ind 1st pers sg,
        pres act subj 1st pers sg,
        1st aor act subj 1st pers sg id.
πληθυνῶ vb fut act ind 1st pers sg id.
πληθύνων vb pres act part masc nom sg id.
πληθύνωσιν vb pres act subj 3rd pers pl,
        1st aor act subj 3rd pers pl id.
πληθύουσα vb pres act part fem nom sg id.
πληθῶν noun neut gen pl . . . . πλῆθος
πλημμέλεια noun fem nom sg
πλημμελείᾳ noun fem dat sg . . . . πλημμέλεια
πλημμέλειαι noun fem nom pl id.
πλημμελείαις noun fem dat pl id.
πλημμέλειαν noun fem acc sg id.
πλημμελείας noun fem gen sg and acc pl id.
πλημμέλημα noun neut nom and acc sg
πλημμελής adj masc and fem nom sg
πλημμελήσατε vb 1st aor act impv 2nd pers pl . πλημμελέω
πλημμελήσει vb fut act ind 3rd pers sg id.
πλημμελήσεως noun fem gen sg . . . . πλημμέλησις
πλημμελήσῃ vb 1st aor act subj 3rd pers sg . . . . πλημμελέω
πλημμελήσῃς vb 1st aor act subj 2nd pers sg id.
πλημμέλησιν noun fem acc sg . . . . πλημμέλησις
πλημμελήσουσιν vb fut act ind 3rd pers pl . . . . πλημμελέω
πλημμελήσωσιν vb 1st aor act subj 3rd pers pl id.
πλήμμυρα noun fem nom sg
πλήν adverb, conjunction, and preposition
πλήρει adj dat sg . . . . πλήρης
πλήρεις adj masc and fem nom and acc pl id.
πλῆρες adj neut nom and acc sg id.
πλήρη adj masc and fem acc sg, neut nom and acc pl id.
πλήρης adj masc and fem nom sg id.
πληρουμένων vb pres m/p part gen pl . . . . πληρόω
πληροῦν vb pres act inf id.
πληροῦντας vb pres act part masc acc pl id.
πληροῦντες vb pres act part masc nom pl id.
πληροῦντος vb pres act part masc and neut gen sg id.
πλήρους adj gen sg . . . . πλήρης

πληροῦσθαι vb pres m/p inf . . . . πληρόω
πληροῦτε vb pres act ind 2nd pers pl   id.
πληρῶ vb fut act ind 1st pers sg   id.
πληρωθείς vb 1st aor pass part masc nom sg   id.
πληρωθέν vb 1st aor pass part neut nom and acc sg   id.
πληρωθῇ vb 1st aor pass subj 3rd pers sg   id.
πληρωθῆναι vb 1st aor pass inf   id.
πληρωθήσεται vb fut pass ind 3rd pers sg   id.
πληρωθήτω vb 1st aor pass impv 3rd pers sg   id.
πληρωθῶσιν vb 1st aor pass subj 3rd pers pl   id.
πλήρωμα noun neut nom and acc sg
πληρώματα noun neut nom and acc pl . . . . πλήρωμα
πληρώματι noun neut dat sg
πληρῶσαι vb 1st aor act opt 3rd pers sg . . . . πληρόω
πληρῶσαι vb 1st aor act inf   id.
πληρώσατε vb 1st aor act impv 2nd pers pl   id.
πληρώσει noun fem dat sg . . . . πλήρωσις
πληρώσει vb fut act ind 3rd pers sg . . . . πληρόω
πληρώσεις vb fut act ind 2nd pers sg   id.
πληρώσεως noun fem gen sg . . . . πλήρωσις
πληρώσῃ vb 1st aor act subj 3rd pers sg . . . . πληρόω
πλήρωσιν noun fem acc sg . . . . πλήρωσις
πλήρωσον vb 1st aor act impv 2nd pers sg . . . . πληρόω
πληρώσουσιν vb fut act ind 3rd pers sg   id.
πληρώσω vb fut act ind 1st pers sg   id.
πλήσατε vb 1st aor act impv 2nd pers pl . . . . πίμπλημι
πλήσει vb fut act ind 3rd pers sg   id.
πλησθείς vb 1st aor pass part masc nom sg   id.
πλησθῇ vb 1st aor pass subj 3rd pers sg   id.
πλησθῆναι vb 1st aor pass inf   id.
πλησθῇς vb 1st aor pass subj 2nd pers sg   id.
πλησθήσεσθε vb fut pass ind 2nd pers pl   id.
πλησθήσεται vb fut pass ind 3rd pers sg   id.
πλησθήσῃ vb fut pass ind 2nd pers sg   id.
πλησθησόμεθα vb fut pass ind 1st pers pl   id.
πλησθήσονται vb fut pass ind 3rd pers pl   id.
πλησθῶμεν vb 1st aor pass subj 1st pers pl   id.
πλησθῶσιν vb 1st aor pass subj 3rd pers pl   id.
πλησιαζόντων vb pres act part
     masc and neut gen pl . . . . πλησιάζω
πλησιέστερον comp adverb . . . . πλησίον
πλησίοι noun masc nom pl . . . . πλησίος
πλησίον adverb and preposition
πλησμονή noun fem nom sg
πλησμονῇ noun fem dat sg . . . . πλησμονή
πλησμονήν noun fem acc sg   id.
πλησμονῆς noun fem gen sg   id.
πλῆσον vb 1st aor act impv 2nd pers sg . . . . πίμπλημι
πλήσουσιν vb fut act ind 3rd pers pl   id.
πλήσσουσι vb pres act ind 3rd pers pl . . . . πλήσσω
πλήσω vb fut act ind 1st pers sg . . . . πίμπλημι

πλήσωμεν vb 1st aor act subj 1st pers pl . . . . πίμπλημι
πλινθεία noun fem dat sg . . . . πλινθεία
πλινθείας noun fem gen sg   id.
πλινθείου noun neut gen sg . . . . πλινθεῖον
πλινθεύσωμεν vb 1st aor act subj 1st pers pl . . . . πλινθεύω
πλίνθοι noun fem nom pl . . . . πλίνθος
πλίνθοις noun fem dat pl   id.
πλίνθον noun fem acc sg   id.
πλίνθος noun fem nom sg   id.
πλίνθου noun fem gen sg   id.
πλινθουργίαν noun fem acc sg . . . . πλινθουργία
πλίνθους noun fem acc pl . . . . πλίνθος
πλίνθῳ noun fem dat sg   id.
πλοῖα noun neut nom and acc pl . . . . πλοῖον
πλοίοις noun neut dat pl   id.
πλοῖον noun neut nom and acc sg   id.
πλοίου noun neut gen sg   id.
πλοίῳ noun neut dat sg   id.
πλοίων noun neut gen pl   id.
πλοκάμους noun masc acc pl . . . . πλόκαμος
πλοκῆς noun fem gen sg . . . . πλοκή
πλόκιον noun neut nom and acc sg
πλοῦν noun masc acc sg . . . . πλοῦς
πλουσία adj fem nom sg . . . . πλούσιος
πλούσιαι adj fem nom pl   id.
πλουσίας adj fem acc pl   id.
πλούσιοι adj masc nom pl   id.
πλούσιον adj masc acc sg, neut nom and acc sg   id.
πλούσιος adj masc nom sg   id.
πλουσίου adj masc and neut gen sg   id.
πλουσίους adj masc acc pl   id.
πλουσίῳ adj masc and neut dat sg   id.
πλουσίων adj gen pl   id.
πλουσιώτερον comp adj masc acc sg,
     neut nom and acc sg   id.
πλουσιωτέρῳ comp adj masc and neut dat sg   id.
πλουτεῖν vb pres act inf . . . . πλουτέω
πλουτῆσαι vb 1st aor act inf   id.
πλουτήσει vb fut act ind 3rd pers sg   id.
πλουτήσῃ vb 1st aor act subj 3rd pers sg   id.
πλουτιεῖν vb fut act inf . . . . πλουτίζω
πλουτίζει vb pres act ind 3rd pers sg   id.
πλουτίζοντες vb pres act part masc nom pl   id.
πλουτίζουσιν vb pres act ind 3rd pers pl   id.
πλουτίσαι vb 1st aor act inf   id.
πλουτισθῇ vb 1st aor pass subj 3rd pers sg   id.
πλουτισθήσεται vb fut pass ind 3rd pers sg   id.
πλοῦτον noun masc acc sg . . . . πλοῦτος
πλοῦτος noun masc (and neut) nom sg   id.
πλούτου noun masc gen sg   id.
πλουτοῦντας vb pres act part masc acc pl . . . . πλουτέω
πλούτῳ noun masc dat sg . . . . πλοῦτος

πλουτῶν vb pres act part masc nom sg . . . . πλουτέω	
πλυθῆναι vb 1st aor pass inf . . . . πλύνω	
πλυθήσεται vb fut pass ind 3rd pers sg	id.
πλυνάμενος vb 1st aor mid part masc nom sg	id.
πλυνάτωσαν vb 1st aor act impv 3rd pers pl	id.
πλυνεῖ vb fut act ind 3rd pers sg	id.
πλύνειν vb pres act inf	id.
πλυνεῖς vb fut act ind 2nd pers sg	id.
πλυνεῖσθε vb fut mid ind 2nd pers pl	id.
πλύνῃ vb pres act subj 3rd pers sg,	
1st aor act subj 3rd pers sg	id.
πλῦνον vb 1st aor act impv 2nd pers sg	id.
πλυνόντων vb pres act part masc and neut gen pl	id.
πλυνοῦσιν vb fut act ind 3rd pers pl	id.
πλωτήν adj fem acc sg . . . . πλωτός	
πλωτόν adj masc acc sg, neut nom and acc sg	id.
πνεῖ vb pres act ind 3rd pers sg . . . . πνέω	
πνεῦμα see πνεῦμα	
πνεῦμα noun neut nom and acc sg	id.
πνεύματα noun neut nom and acc pl	id.
πνεύματι noun neut dat sg	id.
πνεύματος noun neut gen sg	id.
πνευματοφόροι noun masc nom pl . . . . . . πνευματοφόρος	
πνευματοφόρος noun masc nom sg	id.
πνευμάτων noun neut gen pl . . . . πνεῦμα	
πνεύμονος noun masc gen sg . . . . πνεύμων	
πνεύσει vb fut act ind 3rd pers sg . . . . πνέω	
πνεύσεται vb fut mid ind 3rd pers sg	id.
πνέων vb pres act part masc nom sg	id.
πνίγει vb pres act ind 3rd pers sg . . . . πνίγω	
πνιγμοῦ noun masc gen sg . . . . πνιγμός	
πνοή noun fem nom sg	
πνοῇ noun fem dat sg . . . . πνοή	
πνοήν noun fem acc sg	id.
πνοῆς noun fem gen sg	id.
πόα noun fem nom sg	
πόαν noun fem acc sg . . . . πόα	
πόδα noun masc acc sg . . . . πούς	
ποδάγραις noun fem dat pl . . . . ποδάγρα	
πόδας noun masc acc pl . . . . πούς	
πόδες noun masc nom pl	id.
ποδήρη adj masc and fem acc sg,	
neut nom and acc pl . . . . ποδήρης	
ποδήρους adj gen sg	id.
ποδί noun masc dat sg . . . . πούς	
ποδιστῆρας noun masc acc pl . . . . ποδιστήρ	
ποδός noun masc gen sg . . . . πούς	
ποδῶν noun masc gen pl	id.
ποθεῖ vb pres act ind 3rd pers sg . . . . ποθέω	
ποθεινή adj fem nom sg . . . . ποθεινός	
ποθεινοτέρα comp adj fem nom sg	id.
ποθεινοτέραν comp adj fem acc sg	id.

πόθεν adverb and preposition	
ποθήσατε vb 1st aor act impv 2nd pers pl . . . . ποθέω	
ποθουμένην vb pres m/p part fem acc sg	id.
ποθοῦντες vb pres act part masc nom pl	id.
ποθοῦσα vb pres act part fem nom sg	id.
ποθοῦσιν vb pres act ind 3rd pers pl	id.
ποία adj fem nom sg . . . . ποῖος	
ποίᾳ adj fem dat sg	id.
ποίας adj fem gen sg	id.
ποίει vb pres act impv 2nd pers sg . . . . ποιέω	
ποιεῖ vb pres act ind 3rd pers sg	id.
ποιεῖν vb pres act inf	id.
ποιεῖς vb pres act ind 2nd pers sg	id.
ποιεῖσθαι vb pres m/p inf	id.
ποιεῖται vb pres m/p ind 3rd pers sg	id.
ποιεῖτε vb pres act impv 2nd pers pl,	
pres act ind 2nd pers pl	id.
ποιείτω vb pres act impv 3rd pers sg	id.
ποιείτωσαν vb pres act impv 3rd pers pl	id.
ποιῇ vb pres act subj 3rd pers sg	id.
ποιηθῇ vb 1st aor pass subj 3rd pers sg	id.
ποιηθήσεται vb fut pass ind 3rd pers sg	id.
ποιηθησόμενον vb fut pass part neut nom and acc sg	id.
ποιηθήσονται vb fut pass ind 3rd pers pl	id.
ποίημα noun neut nom and acc sg	
ποιήμασι noun neut dat pl . . . . ποίημα	
ποιήματα noun neut nom and acc pl	id.
ποιήματι noun neut dat sg	id.
ποιήματος noun neut gen sg	id.
ποιῇς vb pres act subj 2nd pers sg . . . . ποιέω	
ποιήσαι vb 1st aor mid impv 2nd pers sg	id.
ποιήσαι vb 1st aor act opt 3rd pers sg	id.
ποιήσαι vb 1st aor act inf	id.
ποιήσαισαν vb 1st aor act opt 3rd pers pl	id.
ποιησάμενοι vb 1st aor mid part masc nom pl	id.
ποιησάμενος vb 1st aor mid part masc nom sg	id.
ποιησαμένου vb 1st aor mid part masc and neut gen sg	id.
ποιῆσαν vb 1st aor act part neut nom and acc sg	id.
ποιήσαντα vb 1st aor act part masc acc sg	id.
ποιήσαντας vb 1st aor act part masc acc pl	id.
ποιήσαντες vb 1st aor act part masc nom pl	id.
ποιήσαντι vb 1st aor act part masc and neut dat sg	id.
ποιήσαντος vb 1st aor act part masc and neut gen sg	id.
ποιησάντων vb 1st aor act part masc and neut gen pl	id.
ποιήσας vb 1st aor act part masc nom sg	id.
ποιήσασα vb 1st aor act part fem nom sg	id.
ποιήσασθαι vb 1st aor mid inf	id.
ποιήσασθε vb 1st aor mid impv 2nd pers pl	id.
ποιήσατε vb 1st aor act impv 2nd pers pl	id.
ποιησάτω vb 1st aor act impv 3rd pers sg	id.
ποιησάτωσαν vb 1st aor act impv 3rd pers pl	id.
ποιήσει noun fem dat sg . . . . ποίησις	

ποιήσει vb fut act ind 3rd pers sg	. . . .	ποιέω
ποιήσειν vb fut act inf		id.
ποιήσεις vb fut act ind 2nd pers sg		id.
ποιήσεται vb fut mid ind 3rd pers sg		id.
ποιήσετε vb fut act ind 2nd pers pl		id.
ποιήσεως noun fem gen sg	. . . .	ποίησις
ποιήσῃ vb 1st aor act subj 3rd pers sg,		
fut mid ind 2nd pers sg	. . . .	ποιέω
ποιήσῃς vb 1st aor act subj 2nd pers sg		id.
ποιήσηται vb 1st aor mid subj 3rd pers sg		id.
ποιήσητε vb 1st aor act subj 2nd pers pl		id.
ποίησιν noun fem acc sg	. . . .	ποίησις
ποίησις noun fem nom sg		id.
ποιήσομαι vb fut mid ind 1st pers sg	. . . .	ποιέω
ποιήσομεν vb fut act ind 1st pers pl		id.
ποίησον vb 1st aor act impv 2nd pers sg		id.
ποιήσονται vb fut mid ind 3rd pers pl		id.
ποιήσουσι(ν) vb fut act ind 3rd pers pl		id.
ποιήσω vb 1st aor act subj 1st pers sg,		
fut act ind 1st pers sg		id.
ποιήσωμεν vb 1st aor act subj 1st pers pl		id.
ποιήσωσιν vb 1st aor act subj 3rd pers pl		id.
ποιητάς noun masc acc pl	. . . .	ποιητής
ποιῆτε vb pres act subj 2nd pers pl	. . . .	ποιέω
ποικίλα adj neut nom and acc pl	. . . .	ποικίλος
ποικίλαις adj fem dat pl		id.
ποικίλας adj fem acc pl		id.
ποικίλη adj fem nom sg		id.
ποικίλην adj fem acc sg		id.
ποικιλία noun fem nom sg		
ποικιλίᾳ noun fem dat sg	. . . .	ποικιλία
ποικιλίαν noun fem acc sg		id.
ποικιλίας noun fem gen sg and acc pl		id.
ποικίλματα noun neut nom and acc pl	. . . .	ποίκιλμα
ποικίλοι adj masc nom pl	. . . .	ποικίλος
ποικίλοις adj masc and neut dat pl		id.
ποικίλον adj masc acc sg, neut nom and acc sg		id.
ποικίλους adj masc acc pl		id.
ποικιλτά adj neut nom and acc pl	. . . .	ποικιλτός
ποικιλτικά adj neut nom and acc pl	. . . .	ποικιλτικός
ποικιλτικήν adj fem acc sg		id.
ποικιλτοῦ noun masc gen sg	. . . .	ποικιλτής
ποικιλτῶν noun masc gen pl		id.
ποικίλων adj gen pl	. . . .	ποικίλος
ποικίλως adverb		
ποίμαινε vb pres act impv 2nd pers sg	. . . .	ποιμαίνω
ποιμαίνει vb pres act ind 3rd pers sg		id.
ποιμαίνειν vb pres act inf		id.
ποιμαίνεις vb pres act ind 2nd pers sg		id.
ποιμαίνετε vb pres act impv 2nd pers pl		id.
ποιμαίνοντας vb pres act part masc acc pl		id.
ποιμαίνοντες vb pres act part masc nom pl		id.

ποιμαίνοντι vb pres act part		
masc and neut dat sg	. . . .	ποιμαίνω
ποιμαίνουσαι vb pres act part fem nom pl		id.
ποιμαίνουσιν vb pres act ind 3rd pers pl		id.
ποιμαίνων vb pres act part masc nom sg		id.
ποιμανεῖ vb fut act ind 3rd pers sg		id.
ποιμανεῖς vb fut act ind 2nd pers sg		id.
ποιμανθήσῃ vb fut pass ind 2nd pers sg		id.
ποίμανον vb 1st aor act impv 2nd pers sg		id.
ποιμανοῦσιν vb fut act ind 3rd pers pl		id.
ποιμανῶ vb fut act ind 1st pers sg		id.
ποιμένα noun masc acc sg	. . . .	ποιμήν
ποιμένας noun masc acc pl		id.
ποιμένες noun masc nom pl		id.
ποιμένι noun masc dat sg		id.
ποιμενικά adj neut nom and acc pl	. . . .	ποιμενικός
ποιμενικῷ adj masc and neut dat sg		id.
ποιμένος noun masc gen sg	. . . .	ποιμήν
ποιμένων noun masc gen pl		id.
ποιμέσι noun masc dat pl		id.
ποιμήν noun masc nom sg		id.
ποίμνης noun fem gen sg	. . . .	ποίμνη
ποίμνια noun neut nom and acc pl	. . . .	ποίμνιον
ποιμνίοις noun neut dat pl		id.
ποίμνιον noun neut nom and acc sg		id.
ποιμνίου noun neut gen sg		id.
ποιμνίῳ noun neut dat sg		id.
ποιμνίων noun neut gen pl		id.
ποίοις adj masc and neut dat pl	. . . .	ποῖος
ποῖον adj masc acc sg, neut nom and acc sg		id.
ποῖος adj masc nom sg		id.
ποίου adj masc and neut gen sg		id.
ποιοῦμεν vb pres act ind 1st pers pl	. . . .	ποιέω
ποιούμενοι vb pres m/p part masc nom pl		id.
ποιούμενος vb pres m/p part masc nom sg		id.
ποιουμένου vb pres m/p part masc and neut gen sg		id.
ποιουμένῳ vb pres m/p part masc and neut dat sg		id.
ποιουμένων vb pres m/p part gen pl		id.
ποιοῦν vb pres act part neut nom and acc sg		id.
ποιοῦντα vb pres act part masc acc sg,		
neut nom and acc pl		id.
ποιοῦντας vb pres act part masc acc pl		id.
ποιοῦντες vb pres act part masc nom pl		id.
ποιοῦντι vb pres act part masc and neut dat sg		id.
ποιοῦντος vb pres act part masc and neut gen sg		id.
ποιούντων vb pres act part masc and neut gen pl		id.
ποιοῦσα vb pres act part fem nom sg		id.
ποιοῦσαι vb pres act part fem nom pl		id.
ποιούσαις vb pres act part fem dat pl		id.
ποιοῦσαν vb pres act part fem acc sg		id.
ποιοῦσι(ν) vb pres act ind 3rd pers pl,		
pres act part masc and neut dat pl		id.

ποιῶ vb pres act ind 1st pers sg,

    pres act subj 1st pers sg . . . . ποιέω

ποίῳ adj masc and neut dat sg . . . . πoῖος

ποιῶν vb pres act part masc nom sg . . . . ποιέω

ποιῶσιν vb pres act subj 3rd pers pl id.

πόκον noun masc acc sg . . . . πόκος

πόκου noun masc gen sg id.

πόκῳ noun masc dat sg id.

πόκων noun masc gen pl id.

πόλει noun fem dat sg . . . . πόλις

πόλεις noun fem nom and acc pl id.

πολέμει vb pres act impv 2nd pers sg . . . . πολεμέω

πολεμεῖ vb pres act ind 3rd pers sg id.

πολεμεῖν vb pres act inf id.

πολεμεῖτε vb pres act ind 2nd pers pl id.

πολεμῇ vb pres act subj 3rd pers sg id.

πολεμηθήσεται vb fut pass ind 3rd pers sg id.

πολεμῆσαι vb 1st aor act inf id.

πολεμήσατε vb 1st aor act impv 2nd pers pl id.

πολεμήσει vb fut act ind 3rd pers sg id.

πολεμήσεις vb fut act ind 2nd pers sg id.

πολεμήσετε vb fut act ind 2nd pers pl id.

πολεμήσῃ vb 1st aor act subj 3rd pers sg id.

πολεμήσομεν vb fut act ind 1st pers pl id.

πολέμησον vb 1st aor act impv 2nd pers sg id.

πολεμήσουσιν vb fut act ind 3rd pers pl id.

πολεμήσω vb fut act ind 1st pers sg id.

πολεμήσωμεν vb 1st aor act subj 1st pers pl id.

πολεμήσωσιν vb 1st aor act subj 3rd pers pl id.

πολεμίαν adj fem acc sg . . . . πολέμιος

πολέμιε adj masc voc sg id.

πολεμικά adj neut nom and acc pl . . . . πολεμικός

πολεμικαῖς adj fem dat pl id.

πολεμική adj fem nom sg id.

πολεμικοῖς adj masc and neut dat pl id.

πολεμικόν adj masc acc sg, neut nom and acc sg id.

πολέμιοι adj masc nom pl . . . . πολέμιος

πολεμίοις adj masc and neut dat pl id.

πολέμιον adj masc acc sg, neut nom and acc sg id.

πολέμιος adj masc nom sg id.

πολεμίου adj masc and neut gen sg id.

πολεμίους adj masc acc pl id.

πολεμισταί noun masc nom pl . . . . πολεμιστής

πολεμισταῖς noun masc dat pl id.

πολεμιστάς noun masc acc pl id.

πολεμιστήν noun masc acc sg id.

πολεμιστής noun masc nom sg id.

πολεμιστοῦ noun masc gen sg id.

πολεμιστῶν noun masc gen pl id.

πολεμίων adj gen pl . . . . πολέμιος

πόλεμοι noun masc nom pl . . . . πόλεμος

πολέμοις noun masc dat pl id.

πόλεμον noun masc acc sg . . . . πόλεμος

πόλεμος noun masc nom sg id.

πολεμοτροφεῖν vb pres act inf . . . . πολεμοτροφέω

πολεμοτροφοῦσιν vb pres act ind 3rd pers pl id.

πολέμου noun masc gen sg . . . . πόλεμος

πολεμοῦμεν vb pres act ind 1st pers pl . . . . πολεμέω

πολεμουμένη vb pres m/p part fem nom sg id.

πολεμουμένοις vb pres m/p part masc and neut dat pl id.

πολεμοῦντα vb pres act part masc acc sg id.

πολεμοῦντας vb pres act part masc acc pl id.

πολεμοῦντες vb pres act part masc nom pl id.

πολεμοῦντος vb pres act part masc and neut gen sg id.

πολεμούντων vb pres act part masc and neut gen pl id.

πολέμους noun masc acc pl . . . . πόλεμος

πολεμοῦσι(ν) vb pres act ind 3rd pers pl,

    pres act part masc and neut dat pl . . . . πολεμέω

πολέμῳ noun masc dat sg . . . . πόλεμος

πολέμων noun masc gen pl id.

πολεμῶν vb pres act part masc nom sg . . . . πολεμέω

πόλεσι(ν) noun fem dat pl . . . . πόλις

πόλεων noun fem gen pl id.

πόλεως noun fem gen sg id.

πολιά noun fem nom sg

πολιᾷ noun fem dat sg . . . . πολιά

πολιαί noun fem nom pl id.

πολιαῖς noun fem dat pl id.

πολιάν noun fem acc sg id.

πολιάς noun fem acc pl id.

πολιάς noun fem gen sg id.

Πολιν pr noun fem acc sg . . . . Πολις

πόλιν noun fem acc sg . . . . πόλις

πολιορκῆσαι vb 1st aor act inf . . . . πολιορκέω

πολιορκήσει noun fem dat sg . . . . πολιόρκησις

πολιορκήσουσιν vb fut act ind 3rd pers pl . . . . πολιορκέω

πολιορκία noun fem nom sg

πολιορκίᾳ noun fem dat sg . . . . πολιορκία

πολιορκίαν noun fem acc sg id.

πολιορκίας noun fem acc pl id.

πολιορκουμένη vb pres m/p part fem nom sg . . πολιορκέω

πολιορκοῦντα vb pres act part masc acc sg id.

πολιορκοῦντας vb pres act part masc acc pl id.

πολιορκοῦντες vb pres act part masc nom pl id.

πολιορκούντων vb pres act part masc and neut gen pl id.

πολιορκοῦσιν vb pres act ind 3rd pers pl id.

πολιοῦ adj masc and neut gen sg . . . . πολιός

Πολις pr noun fem nom sg

πόλις noun fem nom sg

Πόλις-ασεδεκ pr noun

πολίταις noun masc dat pl . . . . πολίτης

πολίτας noun masc acc pl id.

πολιτείαν noun fem acc sg . . . . πολιτεία

πολιτείας noun fem gen sg and acc pl id.

πολιτεύεσθαι vb pres m/p inf . . . . πολιτεύω
πολίτευμα noun neut nom and acc sg
πολιτευόμενοι vb pres m/p part masc nom pl . . . πολιτεύω
πολιτευόμενος vb pres m/p part masc nom sg   id.
πολιτευομένους vb pres m/p part masc acc pl   id.
πολίτην noun masc acc sg . . . . πολίτης
πολιτῶν noun masc gen pl   id.
πολιῶν noun fem gen pl . . . . πολιά
πολλά adj neut nom and acc pl . . . . πολύς
πολλαί adj fem nom pl   id.
πολλαῖς adj fem dat pl   id.
πολλάκις adverb
πολλάς adj fem acc pl . . . . πολύς
πολλαχόθεν adverb
πολλαχῶς adverb
πολλή adj fem nom sg . . . . πολύς
πολλῇ adj fem dat sg   id.
πολλήν adj fem acc sg   id.
πολλῆς adj fem gen sg   id.
πολλοί adj masc nom pl   id.
πολλοῖς adj masc and neut dat pl   id.
πολλοστός adj masc nom sg
πολλοῦ adj masc and neut gen sg . . . . πολύς
πολλούς adj masc acc pl   id.
πολλῷ adj masc and neut dat sg   id.
πολλῶν adj gen pl   id.
πολύ adj neut nom and acc sg   id.
πολύ see πολύς
Πολυανδριον pr noun neut nom and acc sg
πολυάνδριον noun neut nom and acc sg
πολυανδρίῳ noun neut dat sg . . . . πολυάνδριον
πολύγονον adj acc sg, neut nom sg . . . . πολύγονος
πολυγονώτεραι comp adj fem nom pl   id.
πολύδακρυν adj masc and fem acc sg . . . . πολύδακρυς
πολυέλεε adj masc and fem voc sg . . . . πολυέλεος
πολυέλεος adj masc and fem nom sg   id.
πολυετές adj gen sg . . . . πολυετής
πολυημερεύσητε vb 1st aor act subj
           2nd pers pl . . . . πολυημερεύω
πολυήμεροι adj masc and fem nom pl . . . . πολυήμερος
πολυήμερος adj masc and fem nom sg   id.
πολύθρηνος adj masc and fem nom sg
πολυκέφαλον adj masc and fem acc sg . . . . . πολυκέφαλος
πολυλογίας noun fem gen sg . . . . πολυλογία
πολυμερές adj neut nom and acc sg . . . . πολυμερής
πολύν adj masc acc sg . . . . πολύς
πολυοδίαις noun fem dat pl . . . . πολυοδία
πολύορκος adj masc and fem nom sg
πολυόρκου adj gen sg . . . . πολύορκος
πολυοχλίαν noun fem acc sg . . . . πολυοχλία
πολυοχλίας noun fem gen sg   id.
πολύπαις noun fem nom sg

πολυπειρία noun fem nom sg
πολυπειρίαν noun fem acc sg . . . . πολυπειρία
πολύπειρος adj masc and fem nom sg
πολυπλάσια adj neut nom and acc pl . . . . . πολυπλάσιος
πολυπλασιασθῆτε vb 1st aor pass subj
           2nd pers pl . . . . πολυπλασιάζω
πολυπληθεῖ vb pres act ind 3rd pers sg . . . . . πολυπληθέω
πολυπλήθειαν noun fem acc sg . . . . πολυπλήθεια
πολυπληθεῖτε vb pres act ind 2nd pers pl . . . . πολυπληθέω
πολυπληθυνῶ vb fut act ind 1st pers sg . . . . . πολυπληθύνω
πολυπλόκοις adj dat pl . . . . πολύπλοκος
πολύπλοκον adj acc sg, neut nom sg   id.
πολύπλοκος adj masc and fem nom sg   id.
πολυπλόκων adj gen pl   id.
πολυπραγμονεῖν vb pres act inf . . . . πολυπραγμονέω
πολυρῆμον adj neut nom and acc sg . . . . πολυρρήμων
πολύς adj masc nom sg
πολυτελεῖ adj dat sg . . . . πολυτελής
πολυτελεῖς adj masc and fem nom and acc pl   id.
πολυτελές adj neut nom and acc sg   id.
πολυτελέσι adj dat pl   id.
πολυτελῆ adj masc and fem acc sg   id.
πολυτελοῦς adj gen sg   id.
πολυτελῶν adj gen pl   id.
πολυτόκα adj neut nom and acc pl . . . . πολυτόκος
πολυτρόποις adj dat pl . . . . πολυτρόπος
πολυτροπωτάτη superl adj fem nom sg   id.
πολυτροπωτέρων comp adj gen pl   id.
πολυφρόντιδα noun masc acc sg . . . . πολυφροντίς
πολυχρονιεῖτε vb fut act ind 2nd pers pl . . . . πολυχρονίζω
πολυχρόνιοι adj masc and fem nom pl . . . . . πολυχρόνιος
πολυχρόνιον adj acc sg, neut nom sg   id.
πολυχρόνιος adj masc and fem nom sg   id.
πολυχρονίους adj masc and fem acc pl   id.
πολυχρονίῳ adj dat sg   id.
πολυωρήσει vb fut act ind 3rd pers sg . . . . πολυωρέω
πολυωρήσεις vb fut act ind 2nd pers sg   id.
πόμα noun neut nom and acc sg
πόμασι noun neut dat pl . . . . πόμα
πόματος noun neut gen sg   id.
πομπεύει vb pres act ind 3rd pers sg . . . . πομπεύω
πομπεύειν vb pres act inf   id.
πονεῖ vb pres act ind 3rd pers sg . . . . πονέω
πονεῖν vb pres act inf   id.
πονεῖτε vb pres act ind 2nd pers pl   id.
πονέσει vb fut act ind 3rd pers sg   id.
πονέσουσιν vb fut act ind 3rd pers pl   id.
πονηρά adj fem nom sg, neut nom and acc pl . . . . . πονηρός
πονηρᾷ adj fem dat sg   id.
πονηραί adj fem nom pl   id.
πονηράν adj fem acc sg   id.
πονηράς adj fem acc pl   id.

πονηρᾶς adj fem gen sg . . . . πονηρός

πονηρεύεσθαι vb pres dep inf . . . . πονηρεύομαι

πονηρεύεσθε vb pres dep ind 2nd pers pl   id.

πονηρευόμενοι vb pres dep part masc nom pl   id.

πονηρευομένοις vb pres dep part masc and neut dat pl   id.

πονηρευόμενος vb pres dep part masc nom sg   id.

πονηρευομένους vb pres dep part masc acc pl   id.

πονηρευομένων vb pres dep part gen pl   id.

πονηρεύονται vb pres dep ind 3rd pers pl   id.

πονηρεύσεται vb fut mid ind 3rd pers sg   id.

πονηρεύσησθε vb 1st aor mid subj 2nd pers pl   id.

πονηρεύσηται vb 1st aor mid subj 3rd pers sg   id.

πονηρία noun fem nom sg

πονηρίᾳ noun fem dat sg . . . . πονηρία

πονηρίαι noun fem nom pl   id.

πονηρίαις noun fem dat pl   id.

πονηρίαν noun fem acc sg   id.

πονηρίας noun fem gen sg and acc pl   id.

πονηριῶν noun fem gen pl   id.

πονηροί adj masc nom pl . . . . πονηρός

πονηροῖς adj masc and neut dat pl   id.

πονηρόν adj masc acc sg, neut nom and acc sg   id.

πονηρός adj masc nom sg   id.

πονηροτάτῳ superl adj masc and neut dat sg   id.

πονηρότερον comp adj masc acc sg, neut nom and acc sg id.

πονηρότερος comp adj masc nom sg   id.

πονηροῦ adj masc and neut gen sg   id.

πονηρούς adj masc acc pl   id.

πονηρῷ adj masc and neut dat sg   id.

πονηρῶν adj gen pl   id.

πόνοι noun masc nom pl . . . . πόνος

πόνοις noun masc dat pl   id.

πόνον noun masc acc sg   id.

πόνος noun masc nom sg   id.

πόνου noun masc gen sg   id.

πονούντων vb pres act part masc and neut gen pl . . . . πονέω

πόνους noun masc acc pl . . . . πόνος

ποντοβρόχους adj masc and fem acc pl . . . . . ποντόβροχος

ποντοπορούσης vb pres act part fem gen sg . . ποντοπορέω

πόντῳ noun masc dat sg . . . . πόντος

πονῶ vb pres act ind 1st pers sg . . . . πονέω

πόνῳ noun masc dat sg . . . . πόνος

πόνων noun masc gen pl   id.

πονῶν vb pres act part masc nom sg . . . . πονέω

πορεία noun fem nom sg

πορεῖα noun neut nom and acc pl . . . . πορεῖον

πορείᾳ noun fem dat sg . . . . πορεία

πορεῖαι noun fem nom pl   id.

πορείαν noun fem acc sg   id.

πορείας noun fem gen sg and acc pl   id.

πορεύεσθαι vb pres dep inf . . . . πορεύομαι

πορεύεσθε vb pres dep impv 2nd pers pl,

　　　pres dep ind 2nd pers pl . . . . πορεύομαι

πορευέσθω vb pres dep impv 3rd pers sg   id.

πορευέσθωσαν vb pres dep impv 3rd pers pl   id.

πορεύεται vb pres dep ind 3rd pers sg   id.

πορεύῃ vb pres dep ind 2nd pers sg,

　　　pres dep subj 2nd pers sg   id.

πορεύησθε vb pres dep subj 2nd pers pl   id.

πορεύηται vb pres dep subj 3rd pers sg   id.

πορευθείς vb 1st aor pass part masc nom sg   id.

πορευθεῖσα vb 1st aor pass part fem nom sg   id.

πορευθεῖσαι vb 1st aor pass part fem nom pl   id.

πορευθεῖσιν vb 1st aor pass part masc and neut dat pl id.

πορευθέντα vb 1st aor pass part masc acc sg   id.

πορευθέντας vb 1st aor pass part masc acc pl   id.

πορευθέντες vb 1st aor pass part masc nom pl   id.

πορευθέντι vb 1st aor pass part masc and neut dat sg   id.

πορευθέντων vb 1st aor pass part masc and neut gen pl id.

πορευθῇ vb 1st aor pass subj 3rd pers sg   id.

πορευθῆναι vb 1st aor pass inf   id.

πορευθῇς vb 1st aor pass subj 2nd pers sg   id.

πορευθήσῃ vb fut pass ind 2nd pers sg   id.

πορεύθητε vb 1st aor pass impv 2nd pers pl   id.

πορευθῆτε vb 1st aor pass subj 2nd pers pl   id.

πορεύθητι vb 1st aor pass impv 2nd pers sg   id.

πορευθήτω vb 1st aor pass impv 3rd pers sg   id.

πορευθῶ vb 1st aor pass subj 1st pers sg   id.

πορευθῶμεν vb 1st aor pass subj 1st pers pl   id.

πορευθῶσιν vb 1st aor pass subj 3rd pers pl   id.

πορεύομαι vb pres dep ind 1st pers sg   id.

πορευόμεθα vb pres dep ind 1st pers pl   id.

πορευόμενα vb pres dep part neut nom and acc pl   id.

πορευομένη vb pres dep part fem nom sg   id.

πορευόμενοι vb pres dep part masc nom pl   id.

πορευομένοις vb pres dep part masc and neut dat pl id.

πορευόμενον vb pres dep part masc acc sg,

　　　neut nom and acc sg   id.

πορευόμενος vb pres dep part masc nom sg   id.

πορευομένου vb pres dep part masc and neut gen sg id.

πορευομένους vb pres dep part masc acc pl   id.

πορευομένῳ vb pres dep part masc and neut dat sg   id.

πορευομένων vb pres dep part gen pl   id.

πορεύονται vb pres dep ind 3rd pers pl   id.

πορεύου vb pres dep impv 2nd pers sg   id.

πορεύσεσθε vb fut mid ind 2nd pers pl   id.

πορεύσεται vb fut mid ind 3rd pers sg   id.

πορεύσεως noun fem gen sg . . . . πόρευσις

πορεύσῃ vb 1st aor mid subj 2nd pers sg,

　　　fut mid ind 2nd pers sg . . . . πορεύομαι

πορεύσομαι vb fut mid ind 1st pers sg   id.

πορευσόμεθα vb fut mid ind 1st pers pl   id.

πορεύσονται vb fut mid ind 3rd pers pl   id.

πορευσώμεθα	vb 1st aor mid subj 1st pers pl . . .	πορεύομαι
πορευτήν	adj fem acc sg	πορευτός
πορευτόν	adj masc acc sg, neut nom and acc sg	id.
πορεύωνται	vb pres dep subj 3rd pers pl	πορεύομαι
πορθεῖς	vb pres act ind 2nd pers sg	πορθέω
πορίζειν	vb pres act inf	πορίζω
πορισμοῦ	noun masc gen sg	πορισμός
πορισμῶν	noun masc gen pl	id.
πόρναι	noun fem nom pl	πόρνη
πόρναις	noun fem dat pl	id.
πόρνας	noun fem acc pl	id.
πορνεία	noun fem nom sg	
πορνεῖα	noun neut nom and acc pl	πορνεῖον
πορνείᾳ	noun fem dat sg	πορνεία
πορνεῖαι	noun fem nom pl	id.
πορνείαις	noun fem dat pl	id.
πορνείαν	noun fem acc sg	id.
πορνείας	noun fem gen sg	id.
πορνεῖον	noun neut nom and acc sg	
πορνεύοντα	vb pres act part masc acc sg	πορνεύω
πορνεύοντες	vb pres act part masc nom pl	id.
πορνεύουσι	vb pres act part masc and neut dat pl	id.
πορνεῦσαι	vb 1st aor act inf	id.
πορνεύσει	vb fut act ind 3rd pers sg	id.
πορνεύσῃς	vb 1st aor act subj 2nd pers sg	id.
πορνεύων	vb pres act part masc nom sg	id.
πορνεύωσιν	vb pres act subj 3rd pers pl	id.
πόρνη	noun fem nom sg	
πόρνῃ	noun fem dat sg	πόρνη
πόρνην	noun fem acc sg	id.
πόρνης	noun fem gen sg	id.
πορνικόν	adj masc acc sg, neut nom and acc sg . .	πορνικός
πορνοκόπος	adj masc nom sg	
πόρνος	noun masc nom sg	
πόρνῳ	noun masc dat sg	πόρνος
πορνῶν	noun fem gen pl	πόρνη
πόρπην	noun fem acc sg	πόρπη
πόρρω	adverb	
πόρρωθεν	adverb	
πορφύρα	noun fem nom sg	
πορφυρᾶ	adj fem nom sg	πορφυροῦς
πορφύρᾳ	noun fem dat sg	πορφύρα
πορφύραν	noun fem acc sg	id.
πορφύρας	noun fem gen sg	id.
πορφυρίδων	noun fem gen pl	πορφυρίς
πορφυρίωνα	noun masc acc sg	πορφυρίων
πορφυροῖς	adj masc and neut dat pl	πορφυροῦς
πορφυροῦν	adj masc acc sg, neut nom and acc sg	id.
πορφυρῶν	adj gen pl	id.
πόσα	adj neut nom and acc pl	πόσος
πόσαι	adj fem nom pl	id.
πόσαις	adj fem dat pl	id.

ποσάκις	adverb	
ποσαπλῶς	adverb	
ποσαχῶς	adverb	
πόση	adj fem nom sg	πόσος
πόσης	adj fem gen sg	id.
ποσί	noun masc dat pl	πούς
Ποσιδώνιον	pr noun masc acc sg	Ποσιδώνιος
πόσιν	noun fem acc sg	πόσις
πόσον	adj masc acc sg, neut nom and acc sg	πόσος
πόσῳ	adj masc and neut dat sg	id.
ποτ'	see ποτέ	
ποτά	noun neut nom and acc pl	ποτόν
ποταμοί	noun masc nom pl	ποταμός
ποταμοῖς	noun masc dat pl	id.
ποταμόν	noun masc acc sg	id.
ποταμός	noun masc nom sg	id.
ποταμοῦ	noun masc gen sg	id.
ποταμούς	noun masc acc pl	id.
ποταμῷ	noun masc dat sg	id.
ποταμῶν	noun masc gen pl	id.
ποταπῷ	adj masc and neut dat sg	ποταπός
ποτε	see ποτέ	
πότε	interr adverb	
ποτέ	encl particle	
πότερον	adverb	
πότημα	noun neut nom and acc sg	
ποτήρια	noun neut nom and acc pl	ποτήριον
ποτήριον	noun neut nom and acc sg	id.
ποτηρίου	noun neut gen sg	id.
ποτιεῖ	vb fut act ind 3rd pers sg	ποτίζω
ποτιεῖς	vb fut act ind 2nd pers sg	id.
ποτιεῖτε	vb fut act ind 2nd pers pl	id.
πότιζε	vb pres act impv 2nd pers sg	id.
ποτίζειν	vb pres act inf	id.
ποτιζομένη	vb pres m/p part fem nom sg	id.
ποτίζων	vb pres act part masc nom sg	id.
ποτίζωσιν	vb pres act subj 3rd pers pl	id.
ποτιοῦμεν	vb fut act ind 1st pers pl	id.
ποτιοῦσιν	vb fut act ind 3rd pers pl	id.
ποτίσαι	vb 1st aor act inf	id.
ποτίσαντες	vb 1st aor act part masc nom pl	id.
ποτίσας	vb 1st aor act part masc nom sg	id.
ποτίσει	vb fut act ind 3rd pers sg	id.
ποτισθήσεται	vb fut pass ind 3rd pers sg	id.
πότισον	vb 1st aor act impv 2nd pers sg	id.
ποτιστήριον	noun neut nom and acc sg	
ποτιστηρίων	noun neut gen pl	ποτιστήριον
ποτίσωμεν	vb 1st aor act subj 1st pers pl	ποτίζω
ποτιῶ	vb fut act ind 1st pers sg	id.
πότοι	noun masc nom pl	πότος
πότον	noun masc acc sg	id.
ποτόν	noun neut nom and acc sg	

πότος noun masc nom sg		
πότου noun masc gen sg	. . . .	πότος
πότῳ noun masc dat sg		id.
ποτῷ noun neut dat sg	. . . .	ποτόν
που see ποῦ		
ποῦ adverb		
πούς noun masc nom sg		
πρᾶγμα noun neut nom and acc sg		
πράγμασι noun neut dat pl	. . . .	πρᾶγμα
πράγματα noun neut nom and acc pl		id.
πραγματεία noun fem nom sg		
πραγματείᾳ noun fem dat sg	. . . .	πραγματεία
πραγματείαις noun fem dat pl		id.
πραγματείαν noun fem acc sg		id.
πραγματείας noun fem gen sg and acc pl		id.
πράγματι noun neut dat sg	. . . .	πρᾶγμα
πραγματικοῖς adj masc and neut dat pl	. . . . .	πραγματικός
πράγματος noun neut gen sg	. . . .	πρᾶγμα
πραγμάτων noun neut gen pl		id.
πραεία adj fem dat sg	. . . .	πραΰς
πραεῖς adj masc nom and acc pl		id.
πραέων adj gen pl		id.
πραθέντα vb 1st aor pass part masc acc sg	. . . . . .	πιπράσκω
πραθῇ vb 1st aor pass subj 3rd pers sg		id.
πραθῆναι vb 1st aor pass inf		id.
πραθήσεσθε vb fut pass ind 2nd pers pl		id.
πραθήσεται vb fut pass ind 3rd pers sg		id.
πραθήσονται vb fut pass ind 3rd pers pl		id.
πραθήτω vb 1st aor pass impv 3rd pers sg		id.
πράκτορες noun masc nom pl	. . . .	πράκτωρ
πρᾶξαι vb 1st aor act inf	. . . .	πράσσω
πράξας vb 1st aor act part masc nom sg		id.
πράξασαν vb 1st aor act part fem acc sg		id.
πράξει noun fem dat sg	. . . .	πρᾶξις
πράξεις noun fem nom and acc pl		id.
πράξεις vb fut act ind 2nd pers sg	. . . .	πράσσω
πράξεσι noun fem dat pl	. . . .	πρᾶξις
πράξεων noun fem gen pl		id.
πράξεως noun fem gen sg		id.
πράξῃ vb 1st aor act subj 3rd pers sg	. . . .	πράσσω
πράξῃς vb 1st aor act subj 2nd pers sg		id.
πρᾶξιν noun fem acc sg	. . . .	πρᾶξις
πρᾶξις noun fem nom sg		id.
πράξω vb 1st aor act subj 1st pers sg	. . . .	πράσσω
πρᾶον adj masc acc sg, neut nom and acc sg	. . . .	πρᾶος
πραότης noun fem nom sg		
πράσα noun neut nom and acc pl	. . . .	πράσον
πράσει noun fem dat sg	. . . .	πρᾶσις
πράσεων noun fem gen pl		id.
πράσεως noun fem gen sg		id.
πρασιάν noun fem acc sg	. . . .	πρασιά
πρᾶσιν noun fem acc sg	. . . .	πρᾶσις

πράσινος noun masc nom sg		
πρᾶσις noun fem nom sg		
πράσσε vb pres act impv 2nd pers sg	. . . .	πράσσω
πράσσει vb pres act ind 3rd pers sg		id.
πράσσειν vb pres act inf		id.
πράσσῃς vb pres act subj 2nd pers sg		id.
πράσσοντας vb pres act part masc acc pl		id.
πράσσουσιν vb pres act ind 3rd pers pl		id.
πράσσων vb pres act part masc nom sg		id.
πρατήν adj fem acc sg	. . . .	πρατός
πράττειν vb pres act inf	. . . .	πράττω
πράττων vb pres act part masc nom sg		id.
πραΰθυμος adj masc and fem nom sg		
πραΰν adj masc acc sg	. . . .	πραΰς
πραῦναι vb 1st aor act inf	. . . .	πραΰνω
πραΰνει vb pres act ind 3rd pers sg		id.
πραΰς adj masc nom sg		
πραΰτης noun fem nom sg		
πραΰτητα noun fem acc sg	. . . .	πραΰτης
πραΰτητι noun fem dat sg		id.
πραΰτητος noun fem gen sg		id.
πραχθέν vb 1st aor pass part neut nom and acc sg	. .	πράσσω
πρέπει vb pres act ind 3rd pers sg	. . . .	πρέπω
πρέπον vb pres act part neut nom and acc sg		id.
πρέποντα vb pres act part masc acc sg		id.
πρεπόντως adverb		
πρεπούσαις vb pres act part fem dat pl	. . . .	πρέπω
πρεσβεῖα noun neut nom and acc pl	. . . .	πρεσβεῖον
πρεσβείαν noun fem acc sg	. . . .	πρεσβεία
πρεσβεῖον noun neut nom and acc sg		
πρεσβείου noun neut gen sg	. . . .	πρεσβεῖον
πρέσβεις noun masc nom and acc acc pl	. . . .	πρέσβυς
πρεσβείῳ noun neut dat sg	. . . .	πρεσβεῖον
πρεσβευταί noun masc nom pl	. . . .	πρεσβευτής
πρεσβευταῖς noun masc dat pl		id.
πρεσβευτάς noun masc acc pl		id.
πρέσβυς noun masc nom sg		
πρεσβῦτα noun masc voc sg	. . . .	πρεσβύτης
πρεσβῦται noun masc nom pl		id.
πρεσβύτας noun masc acc pl		id.
πρεσβύτατον superl adj masc acc sg,		
neut nom and acc sg	. . . .	πρέσβυς
πρεσβυτέρα comp adj fem nom sg		id.
πρεσβύτεραι comp adj fem nom pl		id.
πρεσβυτέραν comp adj fem acc sg		id.
πρεσβυτέρας comp adj fem acc pl		id.
πρεσβύτερε comp adj masc voc sg		id.
πρεσβύτεροι comp adj masc nom pl		id.
πρεσβυτέροις comp adj masc and neut dat pl		id.
πρεσβύτερον comp adj masc acc sg,		
neut nom and acc sg		id.
πρεσβύτερος comp adj masc nom sg		id.

πρεσβυτέρου comp adj masc and neut gen sg .... πρέσβυς
πρεσβυτέρους comp adj masc acc pl id.
πρεσβυτέρῳ comp adj masc and neut dat sg id.
πρεσβυτέρων comp adj gen pl id.
πρεσβύτην noun masc acc sg .... πρεσβύτης
πρεσβύτης noun masc nom sg id.
πρεσβῦτι noun fem voc sg .... πρεσβῦτις
πρεσβύτου noun masc gen sg .... πρεσβύτης
πρηνέα adj masc acc sg .... πρηνής
πρηνεῖς adj masc and fem nom and acc pl id.
πρῆσαι vb 1st aor act inf .... πρήθω
πρησθήσεται vb fut pass ind 3rd pers sg id.
πρίασθαι vb 1st aor mid inf .... πρίαμαι
πρίασθε vb 1st aor mid impv 2nd pers pl id.
πρίν adverb and preposition
πρῖνον noun fem acc sg .... πρῖνος
πρίονι noun masc dat sg .... πρίων
πρίονος noun masc gen sg id.
πρίοσι noun masc dat pl id.
πρῖσαι vb 1st aor act inf .... πρίω
πριστηροειδεῖς adj masc and fem
      nom and acc pl .... πριστηροειδής
πρίων noun masc nom sg
πρό preposition
προάγοντος vb pres act part masc and neut gen sg .. προάγω
προάγουσαι vb pres act part fem nom pl id.
προαιρέσει noun fem dat sg .... προαίρεσις
προαιρέσεις noun fem nom and acc pl id.
προαιρέσεως noun fem gen sg id.
προαίρεσιν noun fem acc sg id.
προαίρεσις noun fem nom sg id.
προαιρῇ vb pres act subj 3rd pers sg .... προαιρέω
προαιρούμεθα vb pres m/p ind 1st pers pl id.
προαιρουμένους vb pres m/p part masc acc pl id.
προαιροῦνται vb pres m/p ind 3rd pers pl id.
προαιρῶνται vb pres m/p subj 3rd pers pl id.
προαλής adj masc and fem nom sg
προαναμέλποντες vb pres act part
      masc nom pl .... προαναμέλπω
προανατάξωμαι vb 1st aor mid subj
      1st pers sg .... προανατάσσω
προανατέλλοντα vb pres act part
      neut nom and acc pl .... προανατέλλομαι
προάξει vb fut act ind 3rd pers sg .... προάγω
προαπαγγείλῃς vb 1st aor act subj
      2nd pers sg .... προαπαγγέλλω
προαποδεδειγμένων vb perf m/p part
      gen pl .... προαποδείκνυμι
προαποθανόντας vb 2nd aor act part
      masc acc pl .... προαποθνήσκω
προασπίζει vb pres act ind 3rd pers sg .... προασπίζω
προασπίζοντα vb pres act part masc acc sg id.

προασπίσαιμεν vb 1st aor act opt 1st pers pl ... προασπίζω
προάστεια noun neut nom and acc pl ...... προάστειον
προαχθείς vb 1st aor pass part masc nom sg .... προάγω
προαχθέντες vb 1st aor pass part masc nom pl id.
προβαίνοντα vb pres act part masc acc sg ...... προβαίνω
προβαίνουσα vb pres act part fem nom sg id.
προβαίνουσαι vb pres act part fem nom pl id.
προβαινούσης vb pres act part fem gen sg id.
προβαίνων vb pres act part masc nom sg id.
προβάλετε vb 2nd aor act impv 2nd pers pl ..... προβάλλω
προβάλλομαι vb pres m/p ind 1st pers sg id.
προβαλλομένοις vb pres m/p part masc and neut dat pl id.
προβάλλουσιν vb pres act ind 3rd pers pl id.
προβαλοῦ vb 2nd aor mid impv 2nd pers sg id.
προβαλῶ vb fut act ind 1st pers sg id.
προβαλών vb 2nd aor act part masc nom sg id.
προβασανισθέντι vb 1st aor pass part
      masc and neut dat sg .... προβασανίζω
προβασανισθέντων vb 1st aor pass part
      masc and neut gen pl id.
προβασκάνιον noun neut nom and acc sg
πρόβατα noun neut nom and acc pl .... πρόβατον
προβατικήν adj fem acc sg .... προβατικός
προβατικῆς adj fem gen sg id.
προβάτοις noun neut dat pl .... πρόβατον
πρόβατον noun neut nom and acc sg id.
προβάτου noun neut gen sg id.
προβάτῳ noun neut dat sg id.
προβάτων noun neut gen pl id.
προβέβηκα vb perf act ind 1st pers sg .... προβαίνω
προβέβηκας vb perf act ind 2nd pers sg id.
προβεβήκει vb plpf act ind 3rd pers sg id.
προβεβηκότες vb perf act part masc nom pl id.
προβεβηκότος vb perf act part masc and neut gen sg id.
προβεβηκώς vb perf act part masc nom sg id.
προβῇ vb 2nd aor act subj 3rd pers sg id.
προβιβάσαι vb 1st aor act inf .... προβιβάζω
προβιβάσεις vb fut act ind 2nd pers sg id.
προβλέπει vb pres act ind 3rd pers sg .... προβλέπω
πρόβλημα noun neut nom and acc sg
προβλήματα noun neut nom and acc pl ...... πρόβλημα
προβλῆτες noun masc nom pl .... προβλής
προγεγονότα vb perf act part
      neut nom and acc pl .... προγίνομαι
προγεγονότων vb perf act part masc and neut gen pl id.
προγεγονώς vb perf act part masc nom sg id.
προγεγραμμένοι vb perf m/p part masc nom pl .. προγράφω
προγινώσκει vb pres act ind 3rd pers sg ..... προγινώσκω
προγνώσει noun fem dat sg .... πρόγνωσις
προγνωσθῆναι vb 1st aor pass inf .... προγινώσκω
πρόγνωσιν noun fem acc sg .... πρόγνωσις
προγονικήν adj fem acc sg .... προγονικός

προγονικῆς adj fem gen sg . . . . προγονικός
πρόγονοι noun masc nom pl . . . . πρόγονος
προγόνοις noun masc dat pl id.
προγόνους noun masc acc pl id.
προγόνων noun masc gen pl id.
προγραφήτωσαν vb 2nd aor pass impv
　　　　　3rd pers pl . . . . προγράφω
προδεδηλωμένην vb perf m/p part fem acc sg . . . προδηλόω
πρόδηλον adj acc sg, neut nom sg . . . . πρόδηλος
πρόδηλος adj masc and fem nom sg id.
προδίδωμι vb pres act ind 1st pers sg
προδίδωσιν vb pres act ind 3rd pers sg . . . . . . προδίδωμι
προδοσία noun fem nom sg
προδοσίᾳ noun fem dat sg . . . . προδοσία
προδότας noun masc acc pl . . . . προδότης
προδότην noun masc acc sg id.
προδότης noun masc nom sg id.
προδράμωμεν vb 2nd aor act subj 1st pers pl . . . . προστρέχω
προδραμών vb 2nd aor act part masc nom sg id.
πρόδρομοι adj masc and fem nom pl . . . . πρόδρομος
πρόδρομος adj masc and fem nom sg id.
προδρόμους adj masc and fem acc pl id.
προδώσων vb fut act part masc nom sg . . . . προδίδωμι
προέβαλεν vb 2nd aor act ind 3rd pers sg . . . . . . προβάλλω
προεβάλου vb 2nd aor mid ind 2nd pers sg id.
προεγνώσθη vb 1st aor pass ind 3rd pers sg . . . προγινώσκω
προεθέμην vb 2nd aor mid ind 1st pers sg . . . . . . προτίθημι
προέθεντο vb 2nd aor mid ind 3rd pers pl id.
προέθεσαν vb 1st aor act ind 3rd pers pl id.
προέθετο vb 2nd aor mid ind 3rd pers sg id.
προεθήκαμεν vb 1st aor act ind 1st pers pl id.
προέθηκεν vb 1st aor act ind 3rd pers sg id.
προεθυμήθην vb 1st aor pass ind 1st pers sg . προθυμέομαι
προεθυμήθησαν vb 1st aor pass ind 3rd pers pl id.
προεῖδες vb 2nd aor act ind 2nd pers sg . . . . προοράω
προεῖδον vb 2nd aor act ind 3rd pers pl id.
προειδυίας vb perf act part fem acc pl id.
προείλαντο vb 1st aor mid ind 3rd pers pl . . . . . . προαιρέω
προείλατο vb 1st aor mid ind 3rd pers sg id.
προειλόμην vb 2nd aor mid ind 1st pers sg id.
προείλω vb 1st aor mid ind 2nd pers sg id.
προειρήκαμεν vb perf act ind 1st pers pl . . . . προερέω
προειρημένας vb perf m/p part fem acc pl id.
προειρημένοις vb perf m/p part
　　　　　masc and neut dat pl id.
προειρημένον vb perf m/p part masc acc sg,
　　　　　neut nom and acc sg id.
προειρημένος vb perf m/p part masc nom sg id.
προειρημένους vb perf m/p part masc acc pl id.
προειρημένῳ vb perf m/p part masc and neut dat sg id.
προειρημένων vb perf m/p part gen pl id.
προεκάθητο vb impf m/p ind 3rd pers sg . . . . . προκάθημαι

προέκρινα vb 1st aor act ind 1st pers sg . . . . . . προκρίνω
προελέσθαι vb 2nd aor mid inf . . . . προαιρέω
προελεύσεται vb fut mid ind 3rd pers sg . . . . προέρχομαι
προελθεῖν vb 2nd aor act inf id.
προελθέτω vb 2nd aor act impv 3rd pers sg id.
προελοῦσα vb 2nd aor act part fem nom sg . . . . προαιρέω
προεμάχησεν vb 1st aor act ind 3rd pers sg . . . . προμαχέω
προέμενοι vb 2nd aor mid part masc nom pl . . . . . . προΐημι
προεμήνυσαν vb 1st aor act ind 3rd pers pl . . . προμηνύω
προενόησεν vb 1st aor act ind 3rd pers sg . . . . . . προνοέω
προεξαπέστειλεν vb 1st aor act ind
　　　　　3rd pers sg . . . . προεξαποστέλλω
προεξήνεγκεν vb 1st aor act ind 3rd pers sg . . . προεκφέρω
προεπορεύετο vb impf dep ind 3rd pers sg . προπορεύομαι
προεπορεύοντο vb impf dep ind 3rd pers pl id.
προέσθαι vb 2nd aor mid inf . . . . προΐημι
προεστήκασιν vb perf act ind 3rd pers pl . . . . προΐστημι
προεστηκόσι vb perf act part masc and neut dat pl id.
προεστηκότα vb perf act part masc acc sg id.
προεστηκότας vb perf act part masc acc pl id.
προεστηκότος vb perf act part masc and neut gen sg id.
προέστην vb 2nd aor act ind 1st pers sg id.
προεστώς vb perf act part masc nom sg id.
προέτεινεν vb impf act ind 3rd pers sg,
　　　　　1st aor act ind 3rd pers sg . . . . προτείνω
προετοιμάσει vb fut act ind 3rd pers sg . . . προετοιμάζω
προετρέπετο vb impf m/p ind 3rd pers sg . . . προτρέπω
προετρέψατο vb 1st aor mid ind 3rd pers sg id.
προεφέροντο vb impf m/p ind 3rd pers pl . . . . . . προφέρω
προεφήτευσεν vb 1st aor act ind 3rd pers sg . . . προφητεύω
προέφθακεν vb perf act ind 3rd pers sg . . . . . . προφθάνω
προέφθασα vb 1st aor act ind 1st pers sg id.
προέφθασαν vb 1st aor act ind 3rd pers pl id.
προέφθασας vb 1st aor act ind 2nd pers sg id.
προέφθασεν vb 1st aor act ind 3rd pers sg id.
πρόῃ vb pres act subj 3rd pers sg . . . . πρόειμι
προηγεῖται vb pres dep ind 3rd pers sg . . . . . προηγέομαι
προῆγεν vb impf act ind 3rd pers sg . . . . προάγω
προηγησαμένου vb 1st aor mid part
　　　　　masc and neut gen sg . . . . προηγέομαι
προῆγον vb impf act ind 3rd pers pl . . . . προάγω
προηγορήσαντες vb 1st aor act part
　　　　　masc nom pl . . . . προηγορέω
προήγορον noun masc acc sg . . . . προήγορος
προήγορος noun masc nom sg id.
προηγούμενοι vb pres dep part masc nom pl . . προηγέομαι
προηγούμενος vb pres dep part masc nom sg id.
προηγουμένους vb pres dep part masc acc pl id.
προηγουμένῳ vb pres dep part masc and neut dat sg id.
προηγουμένων vb pres dep part gen pl id.
προηγωνίζετο vb impf dep ind 3rd pers sg προαγωνίζομαι
προῄδει vb plpf act ind 3rd pers sg . . . . πρόοιδα

προηδικημένοι vb perf m/p part masc nom pl .. προαδικέω
προήκων vb pres act part masc nom sg . . . . προήκω
προῆλθεν vb 2nd aor act ind 3rd pers sg . . . . . προέρχομαι
προῆλθον vb 2nd aor act ind 3rd pers pl   id.
προήνεγκεν vb 1st aor act ind 3rd pers sg . . . . . . προφέρω
προήσεται vb fut mid ind 3rd pers sg . . . . προΐημι
προήσομαι vb fut mid ind 1st pers sg   id.
προητοίμασας vb 1st aor act ind 2nd pers sg . προετοιμάζω
προήχθη vb 1st aor pass ind 3rd pers sg . . . . προάγω
προήχθημεν vb 1st aor pass ind 1st pers pl   id.
προθέντων vb 1st aor act part
            masc and neut gen pl . . . . προτίθημι
προθέσεις noun fem nom and acc pl . . . . πρόθεσις
προθέσεως noun fem gen sg   id.
πρόθεσιν noun fem acc sg   id.
προθήσεις vb fut act ind 2nd pers sg . . . . προτίθημι
προθήσεται vb fut mid ind 3rd pers sg   id.
προθυμηθέντα vb 1st aor pass part
            masc acc sg . . . . προθυμέομαι
προθυμηθέντων vb 1st aor pass part
            masc and neut gen pl   id.
προθυμηθῆναι vb 1st aor pass inf   id.
προθυμίας noun fem gen sg . . . . προθυμία
πρόθυμον adj acc sg, neut nom sg . . . . πρόθυμος
πρόθυμος adj masc and fem nom sg   id.
προθυμοτέρους comp adj masc acc pl   id.
προθυμούμενος vb pres m/p part masc nom sg .. προθυμέω
προθύμους adj masc and fem acc pl . . . . πρόθυμος
προθύμως adverb
πρόθυρα noun neut nom and acc pl . . . . πρόθυρον
προθύροις noun neut dat pl   id.
πρόθυρον noun neut nom and acc sg   id.
προθύρου noun neut gen sg   id.
προθύρων noun neut gen pl   id.
προΐεμαι vb pres m/p ind 1st pers sg . . . . προΐημι
προϊέμενον vb pres m/p part masc acc sg   id.
προΐεντο vb 2nd aor act ind 3rd pers pl   id.
προΐῃ vb pres m/p ind 2nd pers sg   id.
πρόιμα adj neut nom and acc pl . . . . πρόιμος
πρόιμον adj acc sg, neut nom sg   id.
πρόιμος adj masc and fem nom sg   id.
προκαθηγουμένων vb pres dep part
            gen pl . . . . προκαθηγέομαι
προκαθήμενοι vb pres m/p part masc nom pl .. προκάθημαι
προκαθημένων vb pres m/p part gen pl   id.
προκαθίσας vb 1st aor act part masc nom sg . . . προκαθίζω
προκακωθέντα vb 1st aor pass part masc acc sg .. προκακόω
προκαλούμενος vb pres m/p part masc nom sg .. προκαλέω
προκαταλαβέσθαι vb 2nd aor mid inf . προκαταλαμβάνω
προκαταλαβέτωσαν vb 2nd aor act impv 3rd pers pl   id.
προκαταλάβῃ vb 2nd aor act subj 3rd pers sg   id.
προκαταλάβηται vb 2nd aor mid subj 3rd pers sg   id.

προκαταλαβοῦ vb 2nd aor mid impv
            2nd pers sg . . . . προκαταλαμβάνω
προκαταλάβωμαι vb 2nd aor mid subj 1st pers sg   id.
προκαταλάβωνται vb 2nd aor mid subj 3rd pers pl   id.
προκαταλαμβάνεσθαι vb pres m/p inf   id.
προκαταλήμψη vb fut mid ind 2nd pers sg   id.
προκατασκευαζομένους vb pres m/p part
            masc acc pl . . . . προκατασκευάζω
προκατείλημπται vb perf m/p ind
            3rd pers sg . . . . προκαταλαμβάνω
προκατελάβετο vb 2nd aor mid ind 3rd pers sg   id.
προκατελάβοντο vb 2nd aor mid ind 3rd pers pl   id.
προκατεσκιρωμένης vb perf dep part
            fem gen sg . . . . προκατασκιρρόομαι
προκείμενα vb pres m/p part
            neut nom and acc pl . . . . πρόκειμαι
προκειμένας vb pres m/p part fem acc pl   id.
προκειμένην vb pres m/p part fem acc sg   id.
προκείμενον vb pres m/p part masc acc sg,
            neut nom and acc sg   id.
προκειμένους vb pres m/p part masc acc pl   id.
προκειμένων vb pres m/p part gen pl   id.
πρόκειται vb pres m/p ind 3rd pers sg   id.
προκεχάλασται vb perf m/p ind 3rd pers sg . . . προχαλάω
προκοπή noun fem nom sg
προκοπήν noun fem acc sg . . . . προκοπή
πρόκρημνον adj acc sg, neut nom sg . . . . πρόκρημνος
προκυνήσουσιν vb fut act ind 3rd pers pl . . . . . προσκυνέω
προλέγων vb pres act part masc nom sg . . . . προλέγω
προλημφθείς vb 1st aor pass part
            masc nom sg . . . . προλαμβάνω
προλήνιον noun neut nom and acc sg
πρόλοβον noun masc acc sg . . . . πρόλοβος
προμαχῶνας noun masc acc pl . . . . προμαχών
προμαχῶνες noun masc nom pl   id.
προνοεῖ vb pres act ind 3rd pers sg . . . . προνοέω
προνοηθῇ vb 1st aor pass subj 3rd pers sg   id.
προνοηθῆναι vb 1st aor pass inf   id.
προνοήθητι vb 1st aor pass impv 2nd pers sg   id.
πρόνοια noun fem nom sg
προνοίᾳ noun neut dat sg . . . . πρόνοια
πρόνοιαν noun fem acc sg   id.
προνοίας noun fem gen sg   id.
προνομευθήσεται vb fut pass ind 3rd pers sg .. προνομεύω
προνομεύοντας vb pres act part masc acc pl   id.
προνομεύοντες vb pres act part masc nom pl   id.
προνομευόντων vb pres act part masc and neut gen pl id.
προνομεύουσιν vb pres act ind 3rd pers pl   id.
προνομεῦσαι vb 1st aor act inf   id.
προνομεύσαντας vb 1st aor act part masc acc pl   id.
προνομευσάντων vb 1st aor act part
            masc and neut gen pl   id.

προνομεύσει vb fut act ind 3rd pers sg ...... προνομεύω

προνομεύσεις vb fut act ind 2nd pers sg id.

προνόμευσον vb 1st aor act impv 2nd pers sg id.

προνομεύσουσιν vb fut act ind 3rd pers pl id.

προνομεύσω vb fut act ind 2nd pers sg id.

προνομεύσωσιν vb 1st aor act subj 3rd pers pl id.

προνομή noun fem dat sg .... προνομή

προνομήν noun fem acc sg id.

προνομῆς noun fem gen sg id.

προνοοῦ vb pres m/p impv 2nd pers sg .... προνοέω

προνοούμενοι vb pres m/p part masc nom pl id.

προνοοῦσιν vb pres act ind 3rd pers pl id.

προνουμηνιῶν noun fem gen pl .... προνουμηνία

προοδηγόν noun masc acc sg .... προοδηγός

προοίμιον noun neut nom and acc sg

προοιμίῳ noun neut dat sg .... προοίμιον

πρόπαπποι noun masc nom pl .... πρόπαππος

προπάτωρ noun masc nom sg

προπέμπειν vb pres act inf .... προπέμπω

προπέμπωσιν vb pres act subj 3rd pers pl id.

προπέμψαντες vb 1st aor act part masc nom pl id.

προπέμψουσιν vb fut act ind 3rd pers pl id.

προπέμψωσιν vb 1st aor act subj 3rd pers pl id.

προπεπραγμένα vb perf m/p part

    neut nom and acc pl .... προπράσσω

προπεπτωκότα vb perf act part masc acc sg .... προπίπτω

προπεπτωκότας vb perf act part masc acc pl id.

προπεπτωκότων vb perf act part masc and neut gen pl id.

προπεπτωκώς vb perf act part masc nom sg id.

προπεσοῦνται vb fut mid ind 3rd pers pl id.

προπετής adj masc and fem nom sg

προπετοῦς adj gen sg .... προπετής

προπομπήν noun fem acc sg .... προπομπή

προπορεύεσθε vb pres dep impv

    2nd pers pl .... προπορεύομαι

προπορεύεται vb pres dep ind 3rd pers sg id.

προπορευόμενα vb pres dep part neut nom and acc pl id.

προπορευομένη vb pres dep part fem nom sg id.

προπορευομένης vb pres dep part fem gen sg id.

προπορευομένοις vb pres dep part masc and neut dat pl id.

προπορευόμενος vb pres dep part masc nom sg id.

προπορεύονται vb pres dep ind 3rd pers pl id.

προπορεύου vb pres dep impv 2nd pers sg id.

προπορεύσεται vb fut mid ind 3rd pers sg id.

προπορεύσῃ vb fut mid ind 2nd pers sg id.

προπορεύσομαι vb fut mid ind 1st pers sg id.

προπορεύσονται vb fut mid ind 3rd pers pl id.

προπραχθέντα vb aor pass part

    neut nom and acc pl .... προπράσσω

προπτύσας vb 1st aor act part masc nom sg ...... προπτύω

προπτώσεως noun fem gen sg .... πρόπτωσις

πρόπτωσιν noun fem acc sg id.

πρόπυλα noun neut nom and acc pl .... πρόπυλον

πρός preposition

προσαββάτου noun neut gen sg .... προσάββατον

προσαββάτων noun neut gen pl id.

προσάγαγε vb 2nd aor act impv 2nd pers sg ...... προσάγω

προσαγαγεῖν vb 2nd aor act inf id.

προσαγάγετε vb 2nd aor act impv 2nd pers pl id.

προσαγάγῃ vb 2nd aor act subj 3rd pers sg id.

προσαγάγῃς vb 2nd aor act subj 2nd pers sg id.

προσαγάγητε vb 2nd aor act subj 2nd pers pl id.

προσαγαγόντες vb 2nd aor act part masc nom pl id.

προσαγάγου vb 2nd aor mid impv 2nd pers sg id.

προσαγγεῖλαι vb 1st aor act inf .... προσαγγέλλω

προσαγγελέντος vb 2nd aor pass part

    masc and neut gen sg id.

προσαγγελῇ vb 1st aor pass subj 3rd pers sg id.

πρόσαγε vb pres act impv 2nd pers sg .... προσάγω

προσάγει vb pres act ind 3rd pers sg id.

προσάγειν vb pres act inf id.

προσαγειόχασιν vb perf act ind 3rd pers pl id.

προσάγεται vb pres m/p ind 3rd pers sg id.

προσάγομεν vb pres act ind 1st pers pl id.

προσάγοντα vb pres act part masc acc sg id.

προσάγοντας vb pres act part masc acc pl id.

προσάγοντες vb pres act part masc nom pl id.

προσαγόντον vb pres act part masc and neut gen pl id.

προσαγορευθέντος vb 1st aor pass part

    masc and neut gen sg .... προσαγορεύω

προσαγορευόμενος vb pres m/p part masc nom sg id.

προσαγορεύουσιν vb pres act ind 3rd pers pl id.

προσαγορεύσεις vb fut act ind 2nd pers sg id.

προσάγουσιν vb pres act ind 3rd pers pl .... προσάγω

προσάγων vb pres act part masc nom sg id.

προσαιτήσουσιν vb fut act ind 3rd pers pl .... προσαιτέω

προσαναβαίνει vb pres act ind 3rd pers sg . προσαναβαίνω

προσαναβάντες vb 2nd aor act part masc nom pl id.

προσαναβάσεως noun fem gen sg ...... προσανάβασις

προσαναβῆναι vb 2nd aor act inf .... προσαναβαίνω

προσαναβήσεται vb fut mid ind 3rd pers sg id.

προσαναλεξάμενος vb 1st aor mid part

    masc nom sg .... προσαναλέγω

προσαναπαύσομαι vb fut mid ind

    1st pers sg .... προσαναπαύω

προσαναπληρώσωσιν vb 1st aor act subj

    3rd pers pl .... προσαναπληρόω

προσανατρέψουσιν vb fut act ind

    3rd pers pl .... προσανατρέπω

προσαναφέρουσιν vb pres act ind

    3rd pers pl .... προσαναφέρω

προσανέβησαν vb 2nd aor act ind

    3rd pers pl .... προσαναβαίνω

προσανενεχθῆναι vb 1st aor pass inf ...... προσαναφέρω

προσανοικοδομηθήσεται vb fut pass ind

   3rd pers sg . . . . προσανοικοδομέω

προσανοίσω vb fut act ind 1st pers sg . . . . . . προσαναφέρω

προσάξει vb fut act ind 3rd pers sg . . . . προσάγω

προσάξεις vb fut act ind 2nd pers sg   id.

προσάξετε vb fut act ind 2nd pers pl   id.

προσάξομεν vb fut act ind 1st pers pl   id.

προσάξουσιν vb fut act ind 3rd pers pl   id.

προσάξω vb fut act ind 1st pers sg   id.

προσαποθανεῖται vb fut mid ind

   3rd pers sg . . . . προσαποθνήσκω

προσαπολέσαι vb 1st aor act inf . . . . προσαπόλλυμι

προσαποστείλας vb 1st aor act part

   masc nom sg . . . . προσαποστέλλω

προσαπωθεῖται vb pres m/p ind 3rd pers sg . . προσαπωθέω

προσαρτίως adverb

προσαχθήσεται vb fut pass ind 3rd pers sg . . . . . . προσάγω

προσβαίνοντας vb pres act part masc acc pl . . . προσβαίνω

προσβαίνουσι vb pres act part masc and neut dat pl   id.

προσβάλλων vb pres act part masc nom sg . . . προσβάλλω

προσβαλόντες vb 2nd aor act part masc nom pl   id.

προσβαλών vb 2nd aor act part masc nom sg   id.

προσβάσεως noun fem gen sg . . . . πρόσβασις

πρόσβασιν noun fem acc sg   id.

πρόσβασις noun fem nom sg   id.

προσβῆναι vb 2nd aor act inf . . . . προσβαίνω

προσβλητόν adj masc acc sg,

   neut nom and acc sg . . . . προσβλητός

προσβολάς noun fem acc pl . . . . προσβολή

προσβολῆς noun fem gen sg   id.

προσγεγενημένων vb perf dep part gen pl . . . προσγίνομαι

προσγεγραμμένων vb perf m/p part gen pl . . . . προσγράφω

προσγελάσεται vb fut mid ind 3rd pers sg . . . . προσγελάω

προσγελάσῃ vb 1st aor act subj 3rd pers sg   id.

προσγελῶν vb pres act part masc nom sg   id.

προσγένηται vb 2nd aor mid subj

   3rd pers sg . . . . προσγίνομαι

προσγενόμενος vb 2nd aor mid part masc nom sg   id.

προσδεηθήσεται vb fut pass ind 3rd pers sg . . . . . προσδέω

προσδεθῇς vb 1st aor pass subj 2nd pers sg   id.

προσδεκτά adj neut nom and acc pl . . . . προσδεκτός

προσδεκτοί adj masc nom pl   id.

πρόσδεξαι vb 1st aor mid impv 2nd pers sg . . προσδέχομαι

προσδέξασθαι vb 1st aor mid inf   id.

προσδέξασθε vb 1st aor mid impv 2nd pers pl   id.

προσδέξεσθε vb fut mid ind 2nd pers pl   id.

προσδέξεται vb fut mid ind 3rd pers sg   id.

προσδέξῃ vb fut mid ind 2nd pers sg   id.

προσδέξομαι vb fut mid ind 1st pers sg   id.

προσδέξονται vb fut mid ind 3rd pers pl   id.

προσδεόμενος vb pres m/p part masc nom sg . . . . . προσδέω

προσδεομένου vb pres m/p part masc and neut gen sg   id.

προσδεχθείημεν vb 1st aor pass opt

   1st pers pl . . . . προσδέχομαι

προσδεχομένη vb pres dep part fem nom sg   id.

προσδεχόμενοι vb pres dep part masc nom pl   id.

προσδεχόμενος vb pres dep part masc nom sg   id.

προσδέχονται vb pres dep ind 3rd pers pl   id.

προσδέχου vb pres dep impv 2nd pers sg   id.

προσδιδόναι vb pres act inf . . . . προσδίδωμι

προσδοκᾶν vb pres act inf . . . . προσδοκάω

προσδοκάσθω vb pres m/p impv 3rd pers sg   id.

προσδοκία noun fem nom sg

προσδοκίαν noun fem acc sg . . . . προσδοκία

προσδοκίας noun fem gen sg   id.

προσδοκῶμεν vb pres act subj 1st pers pl . . . . . προσδοκάω

προσδοκῶντα vb pres act part neut nom and acc pl   id.

προσδοκῶντας vb pres act part masc acc pl   id.

προσδοκώντων vb pres act part masc and neut gen pl   id.

προσδοκῶσιν vb pres act subj 3rd pers pl   id.

προσδόντες vb 2nd aor act part masc nom pl . . προσδίδωμι

προσδραμόντες vb 2nd aor act part

   masc nom pl . . . . προστρέχω

προσδραμοῦσα vb 2nd aor act part fem nom sg   id.

προσδραμών vb 2nd aor act part masc nom sg   id.

προσέβαλεν vb 2nd aor act ind 3rd pers sg . . . προσβάλλω

προσέβαλλον vb impf act ind 3rd pers pl   id.

προσέβαλον vb 2nd aor act ind 3rd pers pl   id.

προσέβη vb 2nd aor act ind 3rd pers sg . . . . . . προσβαίνω

προσεγγιεῖ vb fut act ind 3rd pers sg . . . . προσεγγίζω

προσεγγίζων vb pres act part masc nom sg   id.

προσεγγίσαι vb 1st aor act inf   id.

προσεγγίσας vb 1st aor act part masc nom sg   id.

προσεγγίσητε vb 1st aor act subj 2nd pers pl   id.

προσεδεήθη vb 1st aor pass ind 3rd pers sg . . . . . . προσδέω

προσεδέξαντο vb 1st aor mid ind 3rd pers pl . προσδέχομαι

προσεδέξατο vb 1st aor mid ind 3rd pers sg   id.

προσεδέχθη vb 1st aor pass ind 3rd pers sg   id.

προσεδεχόμην vb impf dep ind 1st pers sg   id.

προσεδέχοντο vb impf dep ind 3rd pers pl   id.

προσέδησαν vb 1st aor act ind 3rd pers pl . . . . . . προσδέω

προσεδίδου vb impf act ind 3rd pers sg . . . . . . προσδίδωμι

προσεδόκα vb impf act ind 3rd pers sg . . . . . . προσδοκάω

προσεδόκησεν vb 1st aor act ind 3rd pers sg   id.

προσεδοκῶμεν vb impf act ind 1st pers pl   id.

προσεδόκων vb impf act ind 1st pers sg   id.

προσέδραμεν vb 2nd aor act ind 3rd pers sg . . . προστρέχω

προσεδρείας noun fem gen sg and acc pl . . . . . προσεδρεία

προσέδωκεν vb 1st aor act ind 3rd pers sg . . . . προσδίδωμι

προσέθεντο vb 2nd aor mid ind 3rd pers pl . . . προστίθημι

προσέθετο vb 2nd aor mid ind 3rd pers sg   id.

προσέθηκα vb 1st aor act ind 1st pers sg   id.

προσέθηκαν vb 1st aor act ind 3rd pers pl   id.

προσέθηκας vb 1st aor act ind 2nd pers sg   id.

προσέθηκε(ν) vb 1st aor act ind 3rd pers sg ... προστίθημι
προσέθλιψεν vb 1st aor act ind 3rd pers sg .... προσθλίβω
προσεῖδον vb 2nd aor act ind 3rd pers pl .... προσοράω
προσείληφεν vb perf act ind 3rd pers sg ... προσλαμβάνω
προσεῖπας vb 1st aor act ind 2nd pers sg ...... προσεῖπον
προσεῖπεν vb 2nd aor act ind 3rd pers sg   id.
προσείχετε vb impf act ind 2nd pers pl .... προσέχω
προσεκαλέσαντο vb 1st aor mid ind

    3rd pers pl .... προσκαλέω
προσεκαλέσατο vb 1st aor mid ind 3rd pers sg   id.
προσεκαλούμην vb impf m/p ind 1st pers sg   id.
προσεκαλοῦντο vb impf m/p ind 3rd pers pl   id.
προσεκαρτέρουν vb impf act ind

    3rd pers pl .... προσκαρτερέω
προσεκέκλιτο vb plpf mid ind 3rd pers sg ..... προσκλίνω
προσεκλήθη vb 1st aor pass ind 3rd pers sg .... προσκαλέω
προσεκλήθησαν vb 1st aor pass ind 3rd pers pl   id.
προσεκολλήθη vb 1st aor pass ind 3rd pers sg   προσκολλάω
προσεκολλήθησαν vb 1st aor pass ind 3rd pers pl   id.
προσέκοπτεν vb impf act ind 3rd pers sg ...... προσκόπτω
προσέκοψεν vb 1st aor act ind 3rd pers sg   id.
προσέκρουεν vb impf act ind 3rd pers sg ..... προσκρούω
προσεκύνει vb impf act ind 3rd pers sg ...... προσκυνέω
προσεκύνησα vb 1st aor act ind 1st pers sg   id.
προσεκύνησαν vb 1st aor act ind 3rd pers pl   id.
προσεκύνησε(ν) vb 1st aor act ind 3rd pers sg   id.
προσεκύνουν vb impf act ind 3rd pers pl   id.
προσελάβετο vb 2nd aor mid ind

    3rd pers sg .... προσλαμβάνω
προσελάβου vb 2nd aor mid ind 2nd pers sg
προσελεύσεται vb fut mid ind 3rd pers sg .. προσέρχομαι
προσελεύσῃ vb fut mid ind 2nd pers sg   id.
προσελεύσονται vb fut mid ind 3rd pers pl   id.
προσέλθατε vb 1st aor act impv 2nd pers pl   id.
πρόσελθε vb 2nd aor act impv 2nd pers sg   id.
προσελθεῖν vb 2nd aor act inf   id.
προσέλθετε vb 2nd aor act impv 2nd pers pl   id.
προσέλθῃ vb 2nd aor act subj 3rd pers sg   id.
προσέλθῃς vb 2nd aor act subj 2nd pers sg   id.
προσέλθητε vb 2nd aor act subj 2nd pers pl   id.
προσελθόντες vb 2nd aor act part masc nom pl   id.
προσελθόντι vb 2nd aor act part masc and neut dat sg id.
προσελθόντος vb 2nd aor act part masc and neut gen sg id.
προσελθοῦσα vb 2nd aor act part fem nom sg   id.
προσελθοῦσαι vb 2nd aor act part fem nom pl   id.
προσέλθωμεν vb 2nd aor act subj 1st pers pl   id.
προσελθών vb 2nd aor act part masc nom sg   id.
προσέλθωσιν vb 2nd aor act subj 3rd pers pl   id.
προσελογίσθην vb 1st aor pass ind

    1st pers sg .... προσλογίζομαι
προσελογίσθης vb 1st aor pass ind 2nd pers sg   id.

προσεμειδίασεν vb 1st aor act ind

    3rd pers sg .... προσμειδιάω
προσέμειναν vb 1st aor act ind 3rd pers pl ..... προσμένω
προσέμεινεν vb 1st aor act ind 3rd pers sg   id.
προσεμπρήσῃ vb 1st aor act subj

    3rd pers sg .... προσεμπίμπρημι
προσενεβριμήσατο vb 1st aor mid ind

    3rd pers sg .... προσεμβριμάομαι
προσενέγκαι vb 1st aor act inf .... προσφέρω
προσενεγκάμενοι vb 1st aor mid part masc nom pl   id.
προσενεγκάμενος vb 1st aor mid part masc nom sg   id.
προσενέγκασθαι vb 1st aor mid inf   id.
προσένεγκε vb 2nd aor act impv 2nd pers sg   id.
προσενεγκεῖν vb 2nd aor act inf   id.
προσενέγκῃ vb 1st aor act subj 3rd pers sg   id.
προσενέγκῃς vb 1st aor act subj 2nd pers sg   id.
προσενέγκητε vb 1st aor act subj 2nd pers pl   id.
προσενέγκωσιν vb 1st aor act subj 3rd pers pl   id.
προσενέχεσθαι vb pres dep inf .... προσενέχομαι
προσενεχθῆναι vb 1st aor pass inf .... προσφέρω
προσενηνόχαμεν vb perf act ind 1st pers pl   id.
προσενόησα vb 1st aor act ind 1st pers sg ..... προσνοέω
προσενόησεν vb 1st aor act ind 3rd pers sg   id.
προσενόουν vb impf act ind 1st pers sg   id.
προσέξει vb fut act ind 3rd pers sg .... προσέχω
προσεξέκαυσαν vb 1st aor act ind 3rd pers pl . προσεκκαίω
προσεξηγησάμενος vb 1st aor mid part

    masc nom sg .... προσεξηγέομαι
προσέξουσιν vb fut act ind 3rd pers pl .... προσέχω
προσέπασεν vb 1st aor act ind 3rd pers sg .... προσπάσσω
προσέπεσεν vb 1st aor act ind 3rd pers sg ..... προσπίπτω
προσεπετίμησαν vb 1st aor act ind

    3rd pers pl .... προσεπιτιμάω
προσεπικατέτεινον vb impf act ind

    3rd pers pl .... προσεπικατατείνω
προσέπιπτεν vb impf act ind 3rd pers sg ...... προσπίπτω
προσεποιεῖτο vb impf m/p ind 3rd pers sg ..... προσποιέω
προσεποιήσαντο vb 1st aor mid ind 3rd pers pl   id.
προσεποιήσατο vb 1st aor mid ind 3rd pers sg   id.
προσεπύρωσαν vb 1st aor act ind 3rd pers pl ... προσπυρόω
προσέρρανεν vb 1st aor act ind 3rd pers sg .... προσραίνω
προσέρχεσθαι vb pres dep inf .... προσέρχομαι
προσέρχῃ vb pres dep ind 2nd pers sg,

    pres dep subj 2nd pers sg   id.
προσεσημαμμένων vb perf m/p part gen pl ... προσημαίνω
προσέσχεν vb 2nd aor act ind 3rd pers sg ...... προσέχω
προσέσχες vb 2nd aor act ind 2nd pers sg   id.
προσέσχετε vb 2nd aor act ind 2nd pers pl   id.
προσέσχον vb 2nd aor act ind 3rd pers pl   id.
προσετάγη vb 2nd aor pass ind 3rd pers sg ... προστάσσω
προσέταξα vb 1st aor act ind 1st pers sg   id.
προσέταξαν vb 1st aor act ind 3rd pers pl   id.

προσέταξας vb 1st aor act ind 2nd pers sg . . . . προστάσσω
προσέταξεν vb 1st aor act ind 3rd pers sg   id.
προσετέθη vb 1st aor pass ind 3rd pers sg . . . . προστίθημι
προσετέθην vb 1st aor pass ind 1st pers sg   id.
προσετέθης vb 1st aor pass ind 2nd pers sg   id.
προσετέθησαν vb 1st aor pass ind 3rd pers pl   id.
προσέτι adverb
πρόσευξαι vb 1st aor mid impv 2nd pers sg . . προσεύχομαι
προσευξάμενοι vb 1st aor mid part masc nom pl   id.
προσευξάμην vb 1st aor mid ind 1st pers sg   id.
προσεύξασθαι vb 1st aor mid inf   id.
προσεύξασθε vb 1st aor mid impv 2nd pers pl,
            1st aor mid ind 2nd pers pl   id.
προσεύξατο vb 1st aor mid ind 3rd pers sg   id.
προσεύξεται vb fut mid ind 3rd pers sg   id.
προσεύξομαι vb fut mid ind 1st pers sg   id.
προσεύξονται vb fut mid ind 3rd pers pl   id.
προσευξώμεθα vb 1st aor mid subj 1st pers pl   id.
προσεύξωνται vb 1st aor mid subj 3rd pers pl   id.
προσευχαῖς noun fem dat pl . . . . προσευχή
προσευχάς noun fem acc pl   id.
προσεύχεσθαι vb pres dep inf . . . . προσεύχομαι
προσεύχεται vb pres dep ind 3rd pers sg   id.
προσευχή noun fem nom sg
προσευχῇ noun fem dat sg . . . . προσευχή
προσευχήν noun fem acc sg   id.
προσευχῆς noun fem gen sg   id.
προσεύχομαι vb pres dep ind 1st pers sg
προσευχομένη vb pres dep part fem nom sg . προσεύχομαι
προσευχόμενοι vb pres dep part masc nom pl   id.
προσευχόμενος vb pres dep part masc nom sg   id.
προσευχομένου vb pres dep part masc and neut gen sg   id.
προσευχόμην vb impf dep ind 1st pers sg   id.
προσεύχου vb pres dep impv 2nd pers sg   id.
προσεύχωνται vb pres dep subj 3rd pers pl   id.
προσεφάνησαν vb 2nd aor pass ind 3rd pers pl . προσφαίνω
προσέφερεν vb impf act ind 3rd pers sg . . . . προσφέρω
προσέφερον vb impf act ind 3rd pers pl   id.
προσέχαιρεν vb impf act ind 3rd pers sg . . . . . . προσχαίρω
πρόσεχε vb pres act impv 2nd pers sg . . . . προσέχω
προσέχεαν vb 1st aor act ind 3rd pers pl . . . . προσχέω
προσέχεεν vb impf act ind 3rd pers sg   id.
προσέχει vb pres act ind 3rd pers sg . . . . προσέχω
προσέχειν vb pres act inf   id.
προσέχεις vb pres act ind 2nd pers sg   id.
προσέχεον vb impf act ind 3rd pers pl . . . . προσχέω
προσέχετε vb pres act impv 2nd pers pl,
            pres act ind 2nd pers pl . . . . προσέχω
προσεχέτω vb pres act impv 3rd pers sg   id.
προσεχέτωσαν vb pres act impv 3rd pers pl   id.
προσέχητε vb pres act subj 2nd pers pl   id.
προσέχον vb pres act part neut nom and acc sg   id.

προσέχοντα vb pres act part neut nom and acc pl . . προσέχω
προσέχοντες vb pres act part masc nom pl   id.
προσέχοντος vb pres act part masc and neut gen sg   id.
προσεχόντως adverb
προσέχων vb pres act part masc nom sg . . . . προσέχω
προσεχώρησαν vb 1st aor act ind 3rd pers pl . . . προσχωρέω
προσεχωρήσατε vb 1st aor act ind 2nd pers pl   id.
προσέῳξεν vb 1st aor act ind 3rd pers sg . . . . προσοίγνυμι
προσήγαγε(ν) vb 2nd aor act ind 3rd pers sg . . . . . προσάγω
προσηγάγετε vb 2nd aor act ind 2nd pers pl   id.
προσηγάγετο vb 2nd aor mid ind 3rd pers sg   id.
προσηγαγόμην vb 2nd aor mid ind 1st pers sg   id.
προσήγαγον vb 2nd aor act ind
            1st pers sg and 3rd pers pl   id.
προσήγγειλαν vb 1st aor act ind 3rd pers pl . προσαγγέλλω
προσήγγειλεν vb 1st aor act ind 3rd pers sg   id.
προσήγγιζον vb impf act ind 3rd pers pl . . . . . προσεγγίζω
προσήγγισαν vb 1st aor act ind 3rd pers pl   id.
προσήγγισε(ν) vb 1st aor act ind 3rd pers sg   id.
προσῆγεν vb impf act ind 3rd pers sg . . . . προσάγω
προσῆγον vb impf act ind 3rd pers pl   id.
προσήγοντο vb impf m/p ind 3rd pers pl   id.
προσηγόρευνται vb perf m/p ind
            3rd pers pl . . . . προσαγορεύω
προσηγόρευσαν vb 1st aor act ind 3rd pers pl   id.
προσήδρευεν vb impf act ind 3rd pers sg . . . . . προσεδρεύω
προσήκειν vb pres act inf . . . . προσήκω
προσῆκον vb pres act part neut nom and acc sg   id.
προσηκόντως adverb
προσήλθατε vb 1st aor act ind 2nd pers pl . . . προσέρχομαι
προσῆλθε(ν) vb 2nd aor act ind 3rd pers sg   id.
προσῆλθες vb 2nd aor act ind 2nd pers sg   id.
προσήλθετε vb 2nd aor act ind 2nd pers pl   id.
προσήλθομεν vb 2nd aor act ind 1st pers pl   id.
προσῆλθον vb 2nd aor act ind
            1st pers sg and 3rd pers pl   id.
προσήλθοσαν vb 2nd aor act ind 3rd pers pl   id.
προσηλυτευόντων vb pres act part
            masc and neut gen pl . . . . προσηλυτεύω
προσήλυτοι noun masc nom pl . . . . προσήλυτος
προσηλύτοις noun masc dat pl   id.
προσήλυτον noun masc acc sg   id.
προσήλυτος noun masc nom sg   id.
προσηλύτου noun masc gen sg   id.
προσηλύτους noun masc acc pl   id.
προσηλύτῳ noun masc dat sg   id.
προσηλύτων noun masc gen pl   id.
προσηλωμένοι vb perf m/p part masc nom pl . . . . προσηλόω
προσημαινομένου vb pres m/p part
            masc and neut gen sg . . . . προσημαίνω
προσημανθεῖσαν vb 1st aor pass part fem acc sg   id.

προσημειουμένους vb pres m/p part

    masc acc pl . . . . προσημειόω

προσηνέγκαμεν vb 1st aor act ind 1st pers pl . . . προσφέρω

προσήνεγκαν vb 1st aor act ind 3rd pers pl   id.

προσηνέγκαντο vb 1st aor mid ind 3rd pers pl   id.

προσηνέγκατε vb 1st aor act ind 2nd pers pl   id.

προσηνέγκατο vb 1st aor mid ind 3rd pers sg   id.

προσήνεγκεν vb 1st aor act ind 3rd pers sg   id.

προσηνές adj neut nom and acc sg . . . . προσηνής

προσηνέχθη vb 1st aor pass ind 3rd pers sg . . . . . προσφέρω

προσηνέχθησαν vb 1st aor pass ind 3rd pers pl   id.

προσηξίωσαν vb 1st aor act ind 3rd pers pl . . . . προσαξιόω

προσηρυθρίων vb impf act ind 1st pers sg . . προσερυθριάω

προσηυξάμεθα vb 1st aor mid ind

    1st pers pl . . . . προσεύχομαι

προσηυξάμην vb 1st aor mid ind 1st pers sg   id.

προσηύξατο vb 1st aor mid ind 3rd pers sg   id.

προσηύξω vb 1st aor mid ind 2nd pers sg   id.

προσηύχετο vb impf dep ind 3rd pers sg   id.

προσήχθη vb 1st aor pass ind 3rd pers sg . . . . προσάγω

προσθείη vb 2nd aor act opt 3rd pers sg . . . . . . προστίθημι

προσθεῖναι vb 2nd aor act inf   id.

προσθείς vb 2nd aor act part masc nom sg   id.

προσθεῖσα vb 2nd aor act part fem nom sg   id.

πρόσθεμα noun neut nom and acc sg

προσθέμενοι vb 2nd aor mid part masc nom pl   προστίθημι

προσθέμενος vb 2nd aor mid part masc nom sg   id.

πρόσθες vb 2nd aor act impv 2nd pers sg   id.

πρόσθεσις noun fem nom sg

προσθέτω vb 2nd aor mid impv 3rd pers sg . . . προστίθημι

προσθῇ vb 2nd aor act subj 3rd pers sg   id.

προσθῇς vb 2nd aor act subj 2nd pers sg   id.

προσθήσει vb fut act ind 3rd pers sg   id.

προσθήσεις vb fut act ind 2nd pers sg   id.

προσθήσεσθε vb fut mid ind 2nd pers pl   id.

προσθήσετε vb fut act ind 2nd pers pl   id.

προσθήσῃ vb fut mid ind 2nd pers sg   id.

προσθῆσθε vb 2nd aor mid subj 2nd pers pl   id.

προσθήσομεν vb fut act ind 1st pers pl   id.

προσθήσουσιν vb fut act ind 3rd pers pl   id.

προσθήσω vb fut act ind 1st pers sg   id.

προσθήσωσιν vb 2nd aor act subj 3rd pers pl   id.

προσθῆτε vb 2nd aor act subj 2nd pers pl   id.

προσθῶ vb 2nd aor act subj 1st pers sg   id.

προσθώμεθα vb 2nd aor mid subj 1st pers pl   id.

προσθῶμεν vb 2nd aor act subj 1st pers pl   id.

προσθῶσιν vb 2nd aor act subj 3rd pers pl   id.

προσιδεῖν vb 2nd aor act inf . . . . προσοράω

προσιόντα vb pres act part masc acc sg . . . . πρόσειμι

προσιόντας vb pres act part masc acc pl   id.

προσιόντες vb pres act part masc nom pl   id.

πρόσκαιρον adj masc and fem acc sg . . . . πρόσκαιρος

προσκαίρου adj gen sg . . . . πρόσκαιρος

προσκαλεσάμενος vb 1st aor mid part

    masc nom sg . . . . προσκαλέω

προσκαλεσαμένου vb 1st aor mid part

    masc and neut gen sg   id.

προσκαλέσεται vb fut mid ind 3rd pers sg   id.

προσκαλουμένη vb pres m/p part fem nom sg   id.

προσκαλούμενος vb pres m/p part masc nom sg   id.

προσκαρτερήσαντες vb 1st aor act part

    masc nom pl . . . . προσκαρτερέω

προσκαρτερῶ vb pres act ind 1st pers sg   id.

προσκατέλιπον vb 2nd aor act ind

    3rd pers pl . . . . προσκαταλείπω

προσκατέστησαν vb 1st aor act ind

    3rd pers pl . . . . προσκαθίστημι

προσκαυθῇ vb 1st aor pass subj 3rd pers sg . . . . . προσκαίω

πρόσκαυμα noun neut nom and acc sg

προσκειμένας vb pres m/p part fem acc pl . . . πρόσκειμαι

προσκείμενοι vb pres m/p part masc nom pl   id.

προσκειμένοις vb pres m/p part

    masc and neut dat pl   id.

προσκείμενος vb pres m/p part masc nom sg   id.

προσκειμένους vb pres m/p part masc acc pl   id.

προσκειμένῳ vb pres m/p part masc and neut dat sg   id.

προσκειμένων vb pres m/p part gen pl   id.

πρόσκεισαι vb pres m/p ind 2nd pers sg   id.

προσκεῖσθαι vb pres m/p inf   id.

πρόσκειται vb pres m/p ind 3rd pers sg   id.

προσκέκλιται vb perf m/p ind 3rd pers sg . . . . προσκαλέω

προσκεκυνηκασιν vb perf act ind 3rd pers pl . . προσκυνέω

προσκεφάλαια noun neut nom and acc pl . προσκεφάλαιον

προσκεφάλαιον noun neut nom and acc sg   id.

προσκήνιον noun neut nom and acc sg

προσκληθείς vb 1st aor pass part masc nom sg . προσκαλέω

πρόσκλησιν noun fem acc sg . . . . πρόσκλησις

προσκολλᾶσθαι vb pres m/p inf . . . . προσκολλάω

προσκολληθήσεσθε vb fut pass ind 2nd pers pl   id.

προσκολληθήσεται vb fut pass ind 3rd pers sg   id.

προσκολληθήσονται vb fut pass ind 3rd pers pl   id.

προσκολλήθητι vb 1st aor pass impv 2nd pers sg   id.

προσκολλήσαι vb 1st aor act opt 3rd pers sg   id.

προσκολλήσω vb fut act ind 1st pers sg   id.

προσκολλώμενοι vb pres m/p part masc nom pl   id.

πρόσκομμα noun neut nom and acc sg

προσκόμματα noun neut nom and acc pl . . . . . . πρόσκομμα

προσκόμματι noun neut dat sg   id.

προσκόμματος noun neut gen sg   id.

προσκόπτῃ vb pres act subj 3rd pers sg . . . . προσκόπτω

προσκόπτουσιν vb pres act ind 3rd pers pl   id.

προσκόψαι vb 1st aor act inf   id.

προσκόψει vb fut act ind 3rd pers sg   id.

προσκόψῃ vb 1st aor act subj 3rd pers sg,

    fut mid ind 2nd pers sg . . . . προσκόπτω

προσκόψῃς vb 1st aor act subj 2nd pers sg   id.

προσκόψουσι vb fut act ind 3rd pers pl   id.

προσκρούσει vb fut act ind 3rd pers sg . . . . . . προσκρούω

προσκυνεῖ vb pres act ind 3rd pers sg . . . . προσκυνέω

προσκυνεῖν vb pres act inf   id.

προσκυνεῖς vb pres act ind 2nd pers sg   id.

προσκυνεῖτε vb pres act impv 2nd pers pl,

    pres act ind 2nd pers pl   id.

προσκυνῆσαι vb 1st aor act inf   id.

προσκυνήσαντες vb 1st aor act part masc nom pl   id.

προσκυνησάντων vb 1st aor act part

    masc and neut gen pl   id.

προσκυνήσας vb 1st aor act part masc nom sg   id.

προσκυνήσατε vb 1st aor act impv 2nd pers pl   id.

προσκυνησάτωσαν vb 1st aor act impv 3rd pers pl   id.

προσκυνήσει noun fem dat sg . . . . προσκύνησις

προσκυνήσει vb fut act ind 3rd pers sg . . . . . . προσκυνέω

προσκυνήσεις vb fut act ind 2nd pers sg   id.

προσκυνήσετε vb fut act ind 2nd pers pl   id.

προσκυνήσεων noun fem gen sg . . . . προσκύνησις

προσκυνήσῃ vb 1st aor act subj 3rd pers sg . . . . προσκυνέω

προσκυνήσῃς vb 1st aor act subj 2nd pers sg   id.

προσκυνήσητε vb 1st aor act subj 2nd pers pl   id.

προσκυνήσομεν vb fut act ind 1st pers pl   id.

προσκύνησον vb 1st aor act impv 2nd pers sg   id.

προσκυνήσουσιν vb fut act ind 3rd pers pl   id.

προσκυνήσω vb 1st aor act subj 1st pers sg,

    fut act ind 1st pers sg   id.

προσκυνήσωμεν vb 1st aor act subj 1st pers pl   id.

προσκυνήσωσι(ν) vb 1st aor act subj 3rd pers pl   id.

προσκυνοῦμεν vb pres act ind 1st pers pl   id.

προσκυνούμενον vb pres m/p part masc acc sg   id.

προσκυνοῦντας vb pres act part masc acc pl   id.

προσκυνοῦντες vb pres act part masc nom pl   id.

προσκυνοῦντος vb pres act part masc and neut gen sg   id.

προσκυνοῦσι(ν) vb pres act ind 3rd pers pl   id.

προσκυνῶν vb pres act part masc nom sg   id.

προσκυροῦσαν vb pres act part fem acc sg . . . . προσκυρέω

προσκύψασα vb 1st aor act part fem nom sg . . . προσκύπτω

προσλαβόμενοι vb 2nd aor mid part

    masc nom pl . . . . προσλαμβάνω

προσλαλήσει vb fut act ind 3rd pers sg . . . . . . προσλαλέω

προσλαλῶν vb pres act part masc nom sg   id.

προσλαμβανόμενοι vb pres m/p part

    masc nom pl . . . . προσλαμβάνω

προσλογιεῖται vb fut mid ind 3rd pers sg . προσλογίζομαι

προσλογίζεται vb pres dep ind 3rd pers sg   id.

προσλογίζου vb pres dep impv 2nd pers sg   id.

προσμαρτυρησάντων vb 1st aor act part

    masc and neut gen pl . . . . προσμαρτυρέω

προσμείγνυται vb pres m/p ind 3rd pers sg . . προσμείγνυμι

προσμειξάντων vb 1st aor act part masc and neut gen pl   id.

προσμενοῦσιν vb fut act ind 3rd pers pl . . . . . . προσμένω

προσμενῶ vb fut act ind 1st pers sg   id.

προσνέμομεν vb pres act ind 1st pers pl . . . . . . προσνέμω

προσνοήσει vb fut act ind 3rd pers sg . . . . προσνοέω

προσνοήσω vb fut act ind 1st pers sg   id.

προσνοῶν vb pres act part masc nom sg   id.

πρόσοδος noun fem nom sg

προσόδου noun fem gen sg . . . . πρόσοδος

προσόδους noun fem acc pl   id.

προσοδυρόμενοι vb pres dep part

    masc nom pl . . . . προσοδύρομαι

προσόδων noun fem gen pl . . . . πρόσοδος

προσοίσει vb fut act ind 3rd pers sg . . . . προσφέρω

προσοίσεις vb fut act ind 2nd pers sg   id.

προσοίσεσθαι vb fut mid inf   id.

προσοίσετε vb fut act ind 2nd pers pl   id.

προσοίσουσι(ν) vb fut act ind 3rd pers pl   id.

προσοίσω vb fut act ind 1st pers sg   id.

προσονομάσαι vb 1st aor act inf . . . . προσονομάζω

προσοχή noun fem nom sg

προσοχῆς noun fem gen sg . . . . προσοχή

προσοχθιεῖ vb fut act ind 3rd pers sg . . . . . . προσοχθίζω

προσοχθιεῖς vb fut act ind 2nd pers sg   id.

προσοχθιεῖτε vb fut act ind 2nd pers pl   id.

προσοχθίσῃ vb 1st aor act subj 3rd pers sg   id.

προσοχθίσῃς vb 1st aor act subj 2nd pers sg   id.

προσόχθισμα noun neut nom and acc sg

προσοχθίσματα noun neut nom and acc pl . . προσόχθισμα

προσοχθίσματι noun neut dat sg   id.

προσοχθισμάτων noun neut gen pl   id.

πρόσοψιν noun fem acc sg . . . . πρόσοψις

πρόσοψις noun fem nom sg   id.

πρόσπαιζε vb pres act impv 2nd pers sg . . . . . . προσπαίζω

προσπαίζουσιν vb pres act ind 3rd pers pl   id.

προσπαρακαλέσαντες vb 1st aor act part

    masc nom pl . . . . προσπαρακαλέω

προσπεσεῖν vb 2nd aor act inf . . . . προσπίπτω

προσπέσῃς vb 1st aor act subj 2nd pers sg   id.

προσπεσόν vb 2nd aor act part neut nom and acc sg   id.

προσπεσόντες vb 2nd aor act part masc nom pl   id.

προσπεσόντος vb 2nd aor act part masc and neut gen sg   id.

προσπεσόντων vb 2nd aor act part masc and neut gen pl   id.

προσπέσωμεν vb 2nd aor act subj 1st pers pl   id.

πρόσπιπτε vb pres act impv 2nd pers sg   id.

προσπίπτοντα vb pres act part neut nom and acc pl   id.

προσποιῶν vb pres act part masc nom sg . . . . . . προσποιέω

προσπορεύεσθαι vb pres dep inf . . . . προσπορεύομαι

προσπορεύεσθε vb pres dep ind 2nd pers pl   id.

προσπορευέσθωσαν vb pres dep impv 3rd pers pl   id.

προσπορεύῃ vb pres mid ind 2nd pers sg,	
pres mid subj 2nd pers sg ...... προσπορεύομαι	
προσπορευομένοις vb pres dep part	
masc and neut dat pl	id.
προσπορευόμενον vb pres dep part masc acc sg	id.
προσπορευόμενος vb pres dep part masc nom sg	id.
προσπορευομένων vb pres dep part gen pl	id.
προσπορεύωνται vb pres dep subj 3rd pers pl	id.
προσρανεῖ vb fut act ind 3rd pers sg .... προσραίνω	
προσσιελίσῃ vb 1st aor act subj 3rd pers sg .. προσσιελίζω	
προσταγεῖσι vb 2nd aor pass part	
masc and neut dat pl .... προστάσσω	
προσταγέν vb 2nd aor pass part neut nom and acc sg	id.
προσταγήν noun fem acc sg .... προσταγή	
πρόσταγμα noun neut nom and acc sg	
προστάγμασι noun neut dat pl .... πρόσταγμα	
προστάγματα noun neut nom and acc pl	id.
προστάγματι noun neut dat sg	id.
προστάγματος noun neut gen sg	id.
προσταγμάτων noun neut gen pl	id.
προστάδα noun fem acc sg .... προστάς	
προστάξαι vb 1st aor act inf,	
1st aor act opt 3rd pers sg .... προστάσσω	
προστάξαντος vb 1st aor act part	
masc and neut gen sg	id.
προστάξας vb 1st aor act part masc nom sg	id.
προσταξάτω vb 1st aor act impv 3rd pers sg	id.
προστάξει vb fut act ind 3rd pers sg	id.
πρόσταξον vb 1st aor act impv 2nd pers sg	id.
προσταράξῃς vb 1st aor act subj	
2nd pers sg .... προσταράσσω	
προστάσσεις vb pres act ind 2nd pers sg ..... προστάσσω	
προστάσσοντα vb pres act part masc acc sg	id.
προστάσσων vb pres act part masc nom sg	id.
προστάται noun masc nom pl .... προστάτης	
προστάτας noun masc acc pl	id.
προστατεῖν vb pres act inf .... προστατέω	
προστάτῃ noun masc dat sg .... προστάτης	
προστάτης noun masc nom sg	id.
προστατῆσαι vb 1st aor act inf .... προστατέω	
προστάττειν vb pres act inf .... προστάττω	
προστατῶν noun masc gen pl .... προστάτης	
προσταχθέντα vb 1st aor pass part	
neut nom and acc pl .... προστάσσω	
προστεθείη vb 1st aor pass opt 3rd pers sg .... προστίθημι	
προστεθείκαμεν vb perf act ind 1st pers pl	id.
προστέθεικας vb perf act ind 2nd pers sg	id.
προστεθειμένοις vb perf m/p part masc and neut dat pl	id.
προστεθείς vb 1st aor pass part masc nom sg	id.
προστέθειται vb perf m/p ind 3rd pers sg	id.
προστεθέντας vb 1st aor pass part masc acc pl	id.
προστεθέντες vb 1st aor pass part masc nom pl	id.
προστεθῇ vb 1st aor pass subj 3rd pers sg .... προστίθημι	
προστεθήσεσθε vb fut pass ind 2nd pers pl	id.
προστεθήσεται vb fut pass ind 3rd pers sg	id.
προστεθήσῃ vb fut pass ind 2nd pers sg	id.
προστεθήσομαι vb fut pass ind 1st pers sg	id.
προστεθήσονται vb fut pass ind 3rd pers pl	id.
προστεθῆτε vb 1st aor pass subj 2nd pers pl	id.
προστέθητι vb 1st aor pass impv 2nd pers sg	id.
προστεθήτω vb 1st aor pass impv 3rd pers sg	id.
προστεθήτωσαν vb 1st aor pass impv 3rd pers pl	id.
προστεταγμένα vb perf m/p part	
neut nom and acc pl .... προστάσσω	
προστεταγμένον vb perf m/p part neut nom and acc sg	id.
προστέτακται vb perf m/p ind 3rd pers sg	id.
προστέτοχα vb perf act ind 1st pers sg	id.
προστετόχαμεν vb perf act ind 1st pers pl	id.
προστετοχώς vb perf act part masc nom sg	id.
πρόστητε vb 2nd aor act impv 2nd pers pl ..... προΐστημι	
προστιθείς vb pres act part masc nom sg ..... προστίθημι	
προστίθεμαι vb pres m/p ind 1st pers sg	id.
προστιθεμένοις vb pres m/p part masc and neut dat pl	id.
προστιθεμένων vb pres m/p part gen pl	id.
προστιθέντες vb pres act part masc nom pl	id.
προστίθεσθε vb pres m/p ind 2nd pers pl	id.
προστίθετε vb pres act ind 2nd pers pl	id.
προστίθημι vb pres act ind 1st pers sg	id.
προστίθησιν vb pres act ind 3rd pers sg	id.
πρόστιμα noun neut nom and acc pl .... πρόστιμον	
προσυνεσταλμένην vb perf m/p part	
fem acc sg .... προσυστέλλομαι	
προσυπομνήσας vb pres act part	
masc nom sg .... προσυπομιμνήσκω	
προσυψῶσαι vb 1st aor act inf .... προσυψόω	
πρόσφατοι adj masc and fem nom pl .... πρόσφατος	
πρόσφατον adj acc sg, neut nom sg	id.
πρόσφατος adj masc and fem nom sg	id.
προσφάτως adverb	
πρόσφερε vb pres act impv 2nd pers sg .... προσφέρω	
προσφέρει vb pres act ind 3rd pers sg	id.
προσφέρειν vb pres act inf	id.
προσφέρεται vb pres m/p ind 3rd pers sg	id.
προσφέρετε vb pres act impv 2nd pers pl	id.
προσφέρῃ vb pres act subj 3rd pers sg	id.
προσφέρῃς vb pres act subj 2nd pers sg	id.
προσφέρητε vb pres act subj 2nd pers pl	id.
προσφέρομεν vb pres act ind 1st pers pl	id.
προσφερόμενα vb pres m/p part neut nom and acc pl	id.
προσφερομένην vb pres m/p part fem acc sg	id.
προσφερόμενον vb pres m/p part neut nom and acc sg	id.
προσφερομένου vb pres m/p part masc and neut gen sg	id.
προσφερομένων vb pres m/p part gen pl	id.
προσφέρονται vb pres m/p ind 3rd pers pl	id.

προσφέροντας vb pres act part masc acc pl ..... προσφέρω
προσφέροντες vb pres act part masc nom pl   id.
προσφέροντι vb pres act part masc and neut dat sg   id.
προσφέροντος vb pres act part masc and neut gen sg   id.
προσφερόντων vb pres act part masc and neut gen pl   id.
προσφέρουσιν vb pres act ind 3rd pers pl   id.
προσφέρων vb pres act part masc nom sg   id.
προσφέρωνται vb pres m/p subj 3rd pers pl   id.
προσφέρωσιν vb pres act subj 3rd pers pl   id.
προσφιλές adj neut nom and acc sg .... προσφιλής
προσφιλῆ adj masc and fem acc sg   id.
προσφορά noun fem nom sg
προσφορᾷ noun fem dat sg .... προσφορά
προσφοραῖς noun fem dat pl   id.
προσφοράν noun fem acc sg   id.
προσφοράς noun fem acc pl   id.
προσφορᾶς noun fem gen sg   id.
προσφυέντος vb 2nd aor pass part
          masc and neut gen sg .... προσφύω
προσφωνηθῆναι vb 1st aor pass inf .... προσφωνέω
προσφωνῆσαι vb 1st aor act inf   id.
προσφωνησάτω vb 1st aor act impv 3rd pers sg   id.
προσχεεῖ vb fut act ind 3rd pers sg .... προσχέω
προσχέειν vb pres act inf   id.
προσχεεῖς vb fut act ind 2nd pers sg   id.
προσχέοντι vb pres act part masc and neut dat sg   id.
προσχεοῦσιν vb fut act ind 3rd pers pl   id.
πρόσχες vb 2nd aor act impv 2nd pers sg   id.
προσχῇς vb 2nd aor act subj 2nd pers sg   id.
προσχρησάμενοι vb 1st aor mid part
          masc nom pl .... προσχράω
πρόσχωμα noun neut nom and acc sg
προσχωρῆσαι vb 1st aor act inf .... προσχωρέω
προσώζεσαν vb 1st aor act ind 3rd pers pl .... προσόζω
προσωθοῦσιν vb pres act ind 3rd pers pl ...... προσωθέω
πρόσωπα noun neut nom and acc pl .... πρόσωπον
προσωπεῖα noun neut nom and acc pl .... προσωπεῖον
προσώποις noun neut dat pl .... πρόσωπον
πρόσωπον noun neut nom and acc sg   id.
προσώπου noun neut gen sg   id.
προσώπῳ noun neut dat sg   id.
προσώπων noun neut gen pl   id.
προσώχθικα vb perf act ind 1st pers sg ...... προσοχθίζω
προσώχθισα vb 1st aor act ind 1st pers sg   id.
προσώχθισαν vb 1st aor act ind 3rd pers pl   id.
προσώχθισεν vb 1st aor act ind 3rd pers sg   id.
προσωχθίσθη vb 1st aor pass ind 3rd pers sg   id.
προσωχύρωσεν vb 1st aor act ind 3rd pers sg . προσοχυρόω
προτεθειμένων vb perf m/p part gen pl .... προτίθημι
προτεθέντος vb 1st aor pass part masc and neut gen sg id.
προτεθερισμένα vb perf m/p part
          neut nom and acc pl .... προθερίζω

προτείναντα vb 1st aor act part masc acc sg .... προτείνω
προτείναντες vb 1st aor act part masc nom pl   id.
προτείνας vb 1st aor act part masc nom sg   id.
προτείνουσαι vb pres act part fem nom pl   id.
προτείχισμα noun neut nom and acc sg
προτειχίσματι noun neut dat sg .... προτείχισμα
προτειχίσματος noun neut gen sg   id.
πρότερα comp adj neut nom and acc pl .... πρότερος
προτέρα comp adj fem nom sg   id.
προτέρᾳ comp adj fem dat sg   id.
πρότεραι comp adj fem nom pl   id.
προτέραις comp adj fem dat pl   id.
προτέραν comp adj fem acc sg   id.
προτέρας comp adj fem gen sg and acc pl   id.
προτέρημα noun neut nom and acc sg
πρότεροι comp adj masc nom pl .... πρότερος
προτέροις comp adj masc and neut dat pl   id.
πρότερον comp adj masc acc sg, neut nom and acc sg id.
πρότερον adverb
πρότερος comp adj masc nom sg
προτέρου comp adj masc and neut gen sg ...... πρότερος
προτέρους comp adj masc acc pl   id.
προτέρων comp adj gen pl   id.
προτεταγμένοις vb perf m/p part
          masc and neut dat pl .... προτάσσω
προτετιμημένη vb perf m/p part fem dat sg ..... προτιμάω
προτιμῶν vb pres act part masc nom sg   id.
προτομαί noun fem nom pl .... προτομή
προτομήν noun fem acc sg   id.
προτρέχοντας vb pres act part masc acc pl ..... προτρέχω
προτρεψαμένης vb 1st aor mid part fem gen sg .. προτρέπω
προϋπῆρχεν vb impf act ind 3rd pers sg ...... προϋπάρχω
προϋποτεταγμένων vb perf dep part
          gen pl .... προϋποτάσσομαι
προυφάνησαν vb 1st aor act ind 3rd pers pl .. προφαίνομαι
προϋφεστῶτος vb perf act part
          masc and neut gen sg .... προϋφίστημι
προφανῶς adverb
προφάσεις noun fem nom and acc pl .... πρόφασις
προφασίζεσθαι vb pres m/p inf .... προφασίζω
προφασίζεται vb pres m/p ind 3rd pers sg   id.
πρόφασιν noun fem acc sg .... πρόφασις
προφασιστικούς adj masc acc pl .... προφασιστικός
προφέρει vb pres act ind 3rd pers sg .... προφέρω
προφερόμενοι vb pres m/p part masc nom pl   id.
προφερόμενος vb pres m/p part masc nom sg   id.
προφῆται noun masc nom pl .... προφήτης
προφήταις noun masc dat pl   id.
προφήτας noun masc acc pl   id.
προφητεία noun fem nom sg
προφητείᾳ noun fem dat sg .... προφητεία
προφητεῖαι noun fem nom pl   id.

προφητείαις   noun fem dat pl .... προφητεία
προφητείαν   noun fem acc sg   id.
προφητείας   noun fem gen sg and acc pl   d.
προφήτευε   vb pres act impv 2nd pers sg ..... προφητεύω
προφητεύει   vb pres act ind 3rd pers sg   id.
προφητεύειν   vb pres act inf   id.
προφητεύεις   vb pres act ind 2nd pers sg   id.
προφητεύοντας   vb pres act part masc acc pl   id.
προφητεύοντες   vb pres act part masc nom pl   id.
προφητεύοντι   vb pres act part masc and neut dat sg   id.
προφητεύοντος   vb pres act part masc and neut gen sg   id.
προφητευόντων   vb pres act part masc and neut gen pl   id.
προφητευούσας   vb pres act part fem acc pl   id.
προφητεύουσιν   vb pres act ind 3rd pers pl,
      pres act part masc and neut dat pl   id.
προφητεῦσαι   vb 1st aor act inf   id.
προφητεύσαντα   vb 1st aor act part masc acc sg   id.
προφητεύσαντες   vb 1st aor act part masc nom pl   id.
προφητεύσας   vb 1st aor act part masc nom sg   id.
προφητεύσει   vb fut act ind 3rd pers sg   id.
προφητεύσεις   vb fut act ind 2nd pers sg   id.
προφητεύσῃ   vb 1st aor act subj 3rd pers sg   id.
προφητεύσῃς   vb 1st aor act subj 2nd pers sg   id.
προφητεύσητε   vb 1st aor act subj 2nd pers pl   id.
προφήτευσον   vb 1st aor act impv 2nd pers sg   id.
προφητεύσουσιν   vb fut act ind 3rd pers pl   id.
προφητεύων   vb pres act part masc nom sg   id.
προφήτη   noun masc dat sg .... προφήτης
προφήτην   noun masc acc sg   id.
προφήτης   noun masc nom sg   id.
προφῆτιν   noun fem acc sg .... προφῆτις
προφῆτις   noun fem nom sg   id.
προφήτου   noun masc gen sg .... προφήτης
προφητῶν   noun masc gen pl   id.
προφθάσει   vb fut act ind 3rd pers sg .... προφθάνω
πρόφθασον   vb 1st aor act impv 2nd pers sg   id.
προφθάσωμεν   vb 1st aor act subj 1st pers pl   id.
προφύλακας   noun masc acc pl .... προφύλαξ
προφυλακάς   noun fem acc pl .... προφυλακή
προφυλακή   noun fem nom sg   id.
προφυλακῇ   noun fem dat sg   id.
προφυλακήν   noun fem acc sg   id.
προφυλακῆς   noun fem gen sg   id.
προφυλάξομαι   vb fut mid ind 1st pers sg ... προφυλάσσω
προχείρισαι   vb 1st aor mid impv 2nd pers sg .. προχειρίζω
προχειρισάμενος   vb 1st aor mid part
      masc nom sg   id.
προχειρίσασθε   vb 1st aor mid impv 2nd pers pl   id.
προχειρισθέντες   vb 1st aor pass part masc nom pl   id.
πρόχειρος   adj masc and fem nom sg
προχωρημάτων   noun neut gen pl .... προχώρημα
προῶμαι   vb 1st aor mid subj 1st pers sg .... προίημι

προωρώμην   vb impf m/p ind 1st pers sg .... προοράω
πρυτάνεις   noun masc nom and acc pl .... πρύτανις
πρώην   adverb
πρῴην   see πρώην
πρωΐ   adverb
πρωΐα   adj fem dat sg .... πρώιος
πρωΐαν   adj fem acc sg   id.
πρωΐας   adj fem gen sg and acc pl   id.
πρωΐθεν   adverb .... πρωΐθεν
πρωϊνή   adj fem nom sg .... πρωϊνός
πρωϊνῇ   adj fem dat sg   id.
πρωϊνήν   adj fem acc sg   id.
πρωϊνῆς   adj fem gen sg   id.
πρωϊνόν   adj masc acc sg, neut nom and acc sg   id.
πρωϊνοῦ   adj masc and neut gen sg   id.
πρωρεῖς   noun masc nom and acc pl .... πρωρεύς
πρωρεύς   noun masc nom sg   id.
πρώσωπον   see πρόσωπον
πρῶτα   superl adj neut nom and acc pl .... πρῶτος
πρωταγωνισταί   noun masc nom pl ...... πρωταγωνιστής
πρωταγωνιστής   noun masc nom sg   id.
πρῶται   superl adj fem nom pl .... πρῶτος
πρώταις   superl adj fem dat pl   id.
πρώταρχον   adj masc acc sg,
      neut nom and acc sg .... πρώταρχος
πρώτας   superl adj fem acc pl .... πρῶτος
πρωτεύειν   vb pres act inf .... πρωτεύω
πρωτεύοντα   vb pres act part masc acc sg   id.
πρωτευόντων   vb pres act part masc and neut gen pl   id.
πρώτη   superl adj fem nom sg .... πρῶτος
πρώτῃ   superl adj fem dat sg   id.
πρώτην   superl adj fem acc sg   id.
πρώτης   superl adj fem gen sg   id.
πρωτοβλήσει   vb fut act ind 3rd pers sg ..... πρωτοβολέω
πρωτογενές   adj neut nom and acc sg .... πρωτογενής
πρωτογενήματα   noun neut nom and acc pl .. πρωτογένημα
πρωτογενήματος   noun neut gen sg   id.
πρωτογενημάτων   noun neut gen pl   id.
πρωτόγονα   adj neut nom and acc pl .... πρωτόγονος
πρωτογόνῳ   adj dat sg   id.
πρῶτοι   superl adj masc nom pl .... πρῶτος
πρώτοις   superl adj masc and neut dat pl   id.
πρωτοκλίσια   noun neut nom and acc pl .... πρωτοκλίσιον
πρωτοκουρίας   noun fem acc pl .... πρωτοκουρία
πρωτολογία   noun fem dat sg .... πρωτολογία
πρῶτον   superl adj masc acc sg, neut nom and acc sg . πρῶτος
πρῶτον   adverb
πρωτόπλαστον   adj acc sg, neut nom sg .... πρωτόπλαστος
πρωτοπλάστου   adj gen sg   id.
πρῶτος   superl adj masc nom sg
πρωτοστάτης   noun masc nom sg
πρωτότοκα   adj neut nom and acc pl .... πρωτότοκος

πρωτοτοκεῦσαι vb 1st aor act inf . . . . πρωτοτοκεύω	πτηξάτω vb 1st aor act impv 3rd pers sg . . . . πτήσσω
πρωτοτόκια noun neut nom and acc pl . . . . . πρωτοτόκιον	πτήξητε vb 1st aor pass impv 2nd pers pl id.
πρωτοτόκοις adj dat pl . . . . πρωτότοκος	πτίλος adj masc nom sg
πρωτότοκον adj acc sg, neut nom sg id.	πτόη noun fem nom sg
πρωτότοκος adj masc and fem nom sg id.	πτοηθείην vb 1st aor pass opt 1st pers sg . . . . πτοέω
πρωτοτόκος see πρωτότοκος	πτοηθείησαν vb 1st aor pass opt 3rd pers pl id.
πρωτοτόκου adj gen sg id.	πτοηθῇς vb 1st aor pass subj 2nd pers sg id.
πρωτοτοκούσας vb pres act part masc acc pl . . πρωτοτοκέω	πτοηθήσεται vb fut pass ind 3rd pers sg id.
πρωτοτοκούσης vb pres act part fem gen sg id.	πτοηθήσῃ vb fut pass ind 2nd pers sg id.
πρωτοτόκῳ adj dat sg . . . . πρωτότοκος	πτοηθήσομαι vb fut pass ind 1st pers sg id.
πρωτοτόκων adj gen pl id.	πτοηθήσονται vb fut pass ind 3rd pers pl id.
πρώτου superl adj masc and neut gen sg . . . . πρῶτος	πτοηθῆτε vb 1st aor pass subj 2nd pers pl id.
πρώτους superl adj masc acc pl id.	πτοηθῶσιν vb 1st aor pass subj 3rd pers pl id.
πρώτῳ superl adj masc and neut dat sg id.	πτόην noun fem acc sg . . . . πτόη
πρώτων superl adj gen pl id.	πτοήσει vb fut act ind 3rd pers sg . . . . πτοέω
πταίει vb pres act ind 3rd pers sg . . . . πταίω	πτόησιν noun fem acc sg . . . . πτόησις
πταῖσαι vb 1st aor act inf id.	πτοήσω vb fut act ind 1st pers sg . . . . πτοέω
πταίσῃ vb 1st aor act subj 3rd pers sg id.	Πτολεμαεῖς pr noun masc nom pl
πταίσῃς vb 1st aor act subj 2nd pers sg id.	Πτολεμαιδα pr noun fem acc sg . . . . Πτολεμαΐς
πταῖσμα noun neut nom and acc sg	Πτολεμαιδι pr noun fem dat sg id.
πταρμῷ noun masc dat sg . . . . πταρμός	Πτολεμαιδος pr noun fem gen sg id.
πτερά noun neut nom and acc pl . . . . πτερόν	Πτολεμαϊκῶν adj gen pl . . . . Πτολεμαϊκος
πτέρναι noun fem nom pl . . . . πτέρνα	Πτολεμαιον pr noun masc acc sg . . . . Πτολεμαιος
πτέρναις noun fem dat pl id.	Πτολεμαιος pr noun masc nom sg id.
πτέρναν noun fem acc sg id.	Πτολεμαιου pr noun masc gen sg id.
πτέρνας noun fem acc pl id.	Πτολεμαιῳ pr noun masc dat sg id.
πτέρνη noun fem dat sg id.	πτοοῦνται vb pres m/p ind 3rd pers pl . . . . πτοέω
πτέρνης noun fem gen sg id.	πτύελον noun masc acc sg . . . . πτύελος
πτέρνης noun fem gen sg . . . . πτέρνα	πτύξιν noun fem acc sg . . . . πτύξις
πτερνιεῖ vb fut act ind 3rd pers sg . . . . πτερνίζω	πτύσῃς vb 1st aor act subj 2nd pers sg . . . . πτύω
πτερνίζετε vb pres act ind 2nd pers pl id.	πτυχαί noun fem nom pl . . . . πτυχή
πτερνισμόν noun masc acc sg . . . . πτερνισμός	πτύων vb pres act part masc nom sg . . . . πτύω
πτερνισμῷ noun masc dat sg id.	πτῶμα noun neut nom and acc sg
πτεροῖς noun neut dat pl . . . . πτερόν	πτώματα noun neut nom and acc pl . . . . πτῶμα
πτεροφυήσουσιν vb fut act ind 3rd pers pl . . . . πτεροφυέω	πτώματι noun neut dat sg id.
πτέρυγας noun fem acc pl . . . . πτέρυξ	πτώματος noun neut gen sg id.
πτέρυγες noun fem nom pl id.	πτώσει noun fem dat sg . . . . πτῶσις
πτερύγια noun neut nom and acc pl . . . . πτερυγίον	πτώσεως noun fem gen sg id.
πτερυγίον noun neut nom and acc sg id.	πτῶσιν noun fem acc sg id.
πτερυγίου noun neut gen sg id.	πτῶσις noun fem nom sg id.
πτερυγίων noun neut gen pl id.	πτωχεία noun fem nom sg
πτέρυγος noun fem gen sg . . . . πτέρυξ	πτωχεία noun fem dat sg . . . . πτωχεία
πτερύγων noun fem gen pl id.	πτωχείαν noun fem acc sg id.
πτέρυξ noun fem nom sg id.	πτωχείας noun fem gen sg id.
πτέρυξιν noun fem dat pl id.	πτωχεῦσαι vb 1st aor act inf . . . . πτωχεύω
πτερυσσόμεναι vb pres dep part fem nom pl . πτερύσσομαι	πτωχεύσει vb fut act ind 3rd pers sg id.
πτερυσσομένων vb pres dep part gen pl id.	πτωχίζει vb pres act ind 3rd pers sg . . . . πτωχίζω
πτερωτά adj neut nom and acc pl . . . . πτερωτός	πτωχοί noun masc nom pl . . . . πτωχός
πτερωτοί adj masc nom pl id.	πτωχοῖς noun masc dat pl id.
πτερωτοῖς adj masc and neut dat pl id.	πτωχόν noun masc acc sg id.
πτερωτόν adj masc acc sg, neut nom and acc sg id.	πτωχός noun masc nom sg id.
πτερωτοῦ adj masc and neut gen sg id.	πτωχοῦ noun masc gen sg id.

πτωχούς noun masc acc pl . . . . πτωχός
πτωχῷ noun masc dat sg   id.
πτωχῶν noun masc gen pl   id.
πύγαργον noun masc acc sg . . . . πύγαργος
πυγμαῖς noun fem dat pl . . . . πυγμή
πυγμῇ noun fem dat sg   id.
πυθέσθαι vb 2nd aor mid inf . . . . πυνθάνομαι
πυθμένα noun masc acc sg . . . . πυθμήν
πυθμένες noun masc nom pl   id.
πυθμένι noun masc dat sg   id.
πυθομένου vb 2nd aor mid part
       masc and neut gen sg . . . . πυνθάνομαι
πυκάζουσα vb pres act part fem nom sg . . . . πυκάζω
πυκάζουσιν vb pres act ind 3rd pers pl   id.
πυκάσῃ vb 1st aor act subj 3rd pers sg   id.
πυκνοτάτης superl adj fem gen sg . . . . πυκνός
πυκνότερον comp adj masc acc sg,
       neut nom and acc sg   id.
πυκνότερον comp adverb
πυκνοτέρῳ comp adj masc and neut dat sg . . . . πυκνός
πυκνῷ adj masc and neut dat sg   id.
πύλαι noun fem nom pl . . . . πύλη
πύλαις noun fem dat pl   id.
πύλας noun fem acc pl   id.
πύλη noun fem nom sg   id.
πύλῃ noun fem dat sg   id.
πύλην noun fem acc sg   id.
πύλης noun fem gen sg   id.
πυλών noun masc nom sg
πυλῶν noun fem gen pl . . . . πύλη
πυλῶνα noun masc acc sg . . . . πυλών
πυλῶνας noun masc acc pl   id.
πυλῶνι noun masc dat sg   id.
πυλῶνος noun masc gen sg   id.
πυλωροί noun masc nom pl . . . . πυλωρός
πυλωροῖς noun masc dat pl   id.
πυλωρός noun masc nom sg   id.
πυλωρούς noun masc acc pl   id.
πυλωρῶν noun masc gen pl   id.
πυλῶσι noun masc dat pl . . . . πυλών
πυνθάνεσθαι vb pres dep inf . . . . πυνθάνομαι
πυνθανόμενοι vb pres dep part masc nom pl   id.
πυνθανομένου vb pres dep part masc and neut gen sg   id.
πυξία noun neut nom and acc pl . . . . πυξίον
πυξίον noun neut nom and acc sg   id.
πυξίου noun neut gen sg   id.
πύξον noun fem acc sg . . . . πύξος
πῦρ noun neut nom and acc sg
πυρά noun fem nom sg
πυρᾷ noun fem dat sg . . . . πυρά
πυραμίδας noun fem acc pl . . . . πυραμίς
πυράς noun fem acc pl . . . . πυρά

πυρᾶς noun fem gen sg . . . . πυρά
πυργοβάρεις noun fem nom and acc pl . . . . . πυργόβαρις
πυργοβάρεσιν noun fem dat pl   id.
πύργοι noun masc nom pl . . . . πύργος
πύργοις noun masc dat pl   id.
πύργον noun masc acc sg   id.
πύργος noun masc nom sg   id.
πύργου noun masc gen sg   id.
πύργους noun masc acc pl   id.
πύργῳ noun masc dat sg   id.
πύργων noun masc gen pl   id.
πυρεῖα noun neut nom and acc pl . . . . πυρεῖον
πυρεῖον noun neut nom and acc sg   id.
πυρείου noun neut gen sg   id.
πυρείων noun neut gen pl   id.
πυρετῷ noun masc dat sg . . . . πυρετός
πυρί noun neut dat sg . . . . πῦρ
πυρίκαυστοι adj masc and fem nom pl . . . . . πυρίκαυστος
πυρίκαυστος adj masc and fem nom sg   id.
πυρίνων adj gen pl . . . . πύρινος
πυριφλεγῆ adj masc and fem acc sg . . . . πυριφλεγής
πυριφλεγής adj masc and fem nom sg   id.
πυροβόλα adj neut nom and acc pl . . . . πυροβόλος
πυροί noun masc nom pl . . . . πυρός
πυρόν noun masc acc sg   id.
πυρόπνουν adj masc and fem acc sg . . . . πυρόπνους
πυρός noun neut gen sg . . . . πῦρ
πυρός noun masc nom sg
πυροῦ noun masc gen sg . . . . πυρός
πυρούς noun masc acc pl   id.
πυροῦται vb pres m/p ind 3rd pers sg . . . . πυρόω
πυροῦτε vb pres act impv 2nd pers pl   id.
πυροφόρος adj masc and fem nom sg
πυρπνόον adj masc acc sg, neut nom and acc sg . . πυρπνόος
πυρπολούμενος vb pres m/p part masc nom sg . . πυρπολέω
πυρρά adj neut nom and acc pl . . . . πυρρός
πυρράκης noun masc nom sg
πυρράν adj fem acc sg . . . . πυρρός
πυρρᾶς adj fem gen sg   id.
πυρρίζουσα vb pres act part fem nom sg . . . . πυρρίζω
πυρριζούσας vb pres act part fem acc pl   id.
πυρροί adj masc nom pl . . . . πυρρός
πυρρόν adj masc acc sg, neut nom and acc sg   id.
πυρρός adj masc nom sg   id.
πυρροῦ adj masc and neut gen sg   id.
πυρσεύει vb pres act ind 3rd pers sg . . . . πυρσεύω
πυρσεύσαισαν vb 1st aor act opt 3rd pers pl   id.
πυρσόν noun masc acc sg . . . . πυρσός
πυρσός noun masc nom sg   id.
πυρφόρου adj gen sg . . . . πυρφόρος
πυρώδεις adj masc and fem nom and acc pl . . . . . . πυρώδης
πυρωθείς vb 1st aor pass part masc nom sg . . . . πυρόω

πυρωθέντες	vb 1st aor pass part masc nom pl	. . . . πυρόω	πωλεῖν	vb pres act inf	. . . . πωλέω
πυρωθῶσιν	vb 1st aor pass subj 3rd pers pl	id.	πωλεῖτε	vb pres act ind 2nd pers pl	id.
πυρῶν	noun masc gen pl	. . . . πυρός	πῶλον	noun masc acc sg	. . . . πῶλος
πυρῶσαι	vb 1st aor act inf	. . . . πυρόω	πῶλος	noun masc nom sg	id.
πυρώσαντες	vb 1st aor act part masc nom pl	id.	πωλουμένους	vb pres m/p part masc acc pl	. . . . πωλέω
πυρώσει	noun fem dat sg	. . . . πύρωσις	πωλοῦντα	vb pres act part masc acc sg	id.
πύρωσις	noun fem nom sg	id.	πωλοῦντες	vb pres act part masc nom pl	id.
πύρωσον	vb 1st aor act impv 2nd pers sg	. . . . πυρόω	πώλους	noun masc acc pl	. . . . πῶλος
πυρώσω	vb fut act ind 1st pers sg	id.	πωλοῦσα	vb pres act part fem nom sg	. . . . πωλέω
πώγων	noun masc nom sg		πωλῶν	vb pres act part masc nom sg	id.
πώγωνα	noun masc acc sg	. . . . πώγων	πωλῶσιν	vb pres act subj 3rd pers pl	id.
πώγωνας	noun masc acc pl	id.	πώποτε	adverb	
πώγωνι	noun masc dat sg	id.	πως	particle	
πώγωνος	noun masc gen sg	id.	πῶς	interr adverb	

Ρ ρ

Ραα	pr noun		Ραγουηλ	pr noun	
Ρααβ	pr noun		Ραγουηλου	pr noun masc gen sg	. . . . Ραγουηλος
Ρααβια	pr noun		Ῥαγων	pr noun masc gen pl	. . . . Ῥαγοι
Ρααβιας	pr noun masc nom sg		ῥαγῶσιν	vb 2nd aor pass subj 3rd pers pl	. . . . ῥήγνυμι
Ρααια	pr noun		ῥαδάμνοις	noun masc dat pl	. . . . ῥάδαμνος
Ραασσων	pr noun		ῥάδαμνος	noun masc nom sg	id.
Ρααυ	pr noun		Ραδδαι	pr noun	
Ραβα	pr noun		ῥάδιον	adj masc acc sg, neut nom and acc sg	. . . . . . ῥάδιος
Ραβαμαγ	pr noun		Ραεμ	pr noun	
Ραββα	pr noun		Ραεμμαθ	pr noun	
Ραββαθ	pr noun		Ραζις	pr noun	
Ραββωθ	pr noun		Ραθαμα	pr noun	
ῥαβδίζων	vb pres act part masc nom sg	. . . . ῥαβδίζω	Ραθαμιν	pr noun	
ῥάβδοι	noun fem nom pl	. . . . ῥάβδος	ραθμ	translit	
ῥάβδοις	noun fem dat pl	id.	ῥαθύμει	vb pres act impv 2nd pers sg	. . . . ῥαθυμέω
ῥάβδον	noun fem acc sg	id.	ῥαθυμεῖτε	vb pres act ind 2nd pers pl	id.
ῥάβδος	noun fem nom sg	id.	ῥαθυμίας	noun fem gen sg	. . . . ῥαθυμία
ῥάβδου	noun fem gen sg	id.	ῥαθυμούντων	vb pres act part	
ῥάβδους	noun fem acc pl	id.		masc and neut gen pl	. . . . ῥαθυμέω
ῥάβδῳ	noun fem dat sg	id.	ῥαθυμῶν	vb pres act part masc nom sg	id.
ῥάβδων	noun fem gen pl	id.	Ραια	pr noun	
Ῥαγα	pr noun		Ραιφαν	pr noun	
ῥαγάδα	noun fem acc sg	. . . . ῥαγάς	ῥάκη	noun neut nom and acc pl	. . . . ῥάκος
Ῥαγας	pr noun		ῥάκος	noun neut nom and acc sg	id.
Ραγαυ	pr noun		ῥακώδη	noun neut nom and acc pl	. . . . ῥακώδης
Ραγεμ	pr noun		Ραμ	pr noun	
Ραγη	pr noun		Ραμα	pr noun	
ῥαγῇ	vb 2nd aor pass subj 3rd pers sg	. . . . ῥήγνυμι	Ραμαθ	pr noun	
ῥαγήσεται	vb fut pass ind 3rd pers sg	id.	Ραμεν	pr noun	
Ραγμα	pr noun		Ραμεσσαι	pr noun	
ῥάγμασι	noun neut dat pl	. . . . ῥάγμα	Ραμεσση	pr noun	
Ραγοις	pr noun masc dat pl	. . . . Ῥαγοι	Ραμια	pr noun	

ῥάμμα noun neut nom and acc sg	Ραφιδιν pr noun
Ραμμαθ pr noun	Ραφις pr noun
Ραμμω pr noun	Ραφου pr noun
ῥάμνον noun fem acc sg . . . . ῥάμνος	Ραφων pr noun
ῥάμνος noun fem nom sg id.	Ραχηλ pr noun
ῥάμνου noun fem gen sg id.	ῥάχις noun fem nom sg
ῥάμνῳ noun fem dat sg id.	ῥάψαι vb 1st aor act inf . . . . ῥάπτω
Ραμνων pr noun	Ραψακην pr noun masc acc sg . . . . Ραψακης
Ραμωθ pr noun	Ραψακης pr noun masc nom sg id.
Ρανα pr noun	Ραψακου pr noun masc gen sg id.
ῥανάτωσαν vb 2nd aor act impv 3rd pers pl . . . . ῥαίνω	Ραωβ pr noun
ῥανεῖ vb fut act ind 3rd pers sg id.	Ραωμ pr noun
ῥανεῖς vb fut act ind 2nd pers sg id.	Ρεβεκκα pr noun
ῥανίς noun fem nom sg	Ρεβεκκαν pr noun fem acc sg . . . . Ρεβεκκα
ῥαντά adj neut nom and acc pl . . . . ῥαντός	Ρεβεκκας pr noun fem gen sg id.
ῥαντάς adj fem acc pl id.	Ρεβες pr noun
ῥαντιεῖς vb fut act ind 2nd pers sg . . . . ῥαντίζω	Ρεγμα pr noun
ῥαντισθῇ vb 1st aor pass subj 3rd pers sg id.	ῥέγχεις vb pres act ind 2nd pers sg . . . . ῥέγχω
ῥαντισμοῦ noun masc gen sg . . . . ῥαντισμός	Ρεελιας pr noun
ῥαντοί adj masc nom pl . . . . ῥαντός	ῥέῃ vb pres act subj 3rd pers sg . . . . ῥέω
ῥαντόν adj masc acc sg, neut nom and acc sg	Ρεηα pr noun
ῥαντούς adj masc acc pl id.	Ρεημα pr noun
ῥανῶ vb fut act ind 1st pers sg . . . . ῥαίνω	Ρεηρωθ pr noun
ῥάξει vb fut act ind 3rd pers sg . . . . ῥάσσω	ῥείτω vb pres act impv 3rd pers sg . . . . ῥέω
ῥάξον vb 1st aor act impv 2nd pers sg id.	Ρεκεμ pr noun
ῥάξουσιν vb fut act ind 3rd pers pl id.	Ρεκκαθ pr noun
ῥάξω vb fut act ind 1st pers sg id.	Ρεκομ pr noun
Ραουμ pr noun	Ρεκχα pr noun
Ραουμος pr noun masc nom sg	Ρεμαθ pr noun
Ραουμῳ pr noun masc dat sg . . . . Ραουμος	ῥεμβασμός noun masc nom sg
ῥαπίζων vb pres act part masc nom sg . . . . ῥαπίζω	ῥέμβεται vb pres m/p ind 3rd pers sg . . . . ῥέμβω
ῥαπίσματα noun neut nom and acc pl . . . . ῥάπισμα	ῥέμβευσον vb 1st aor act impv 2nd pers sg . . . . . . ῥεμβεύω
ῥαπτά adj neut nom and acc pl . . . . ῥαπτός	Ρεμμαθ pr noun
Ραρα pr noun	Ρεμμαν pr noun
Ρασεφ pr noun	Ρεμμας pr noun
Ρασια pr noun	Ρεμμωθ pr noun
Ρασιμ pr noun	Ρεμμων pr noun
Ρασσις pr noun	Ρεμμωνα pr noun
ῥάσσω vb pres act ind 1st pers sg	Ρεμνα pr noun
Ρασων pr noun	Ρεναθ pr noun
Ραφα pr noun	Ρεννα pr noun
Ραφαηλ pr noun	ῥέον vb pres act part neut nom and acc sg . . . . ῥέω
Ραφαια pr noun	Ρεουμ pr noun
Ραφαϊμ pr noun	ῥέουσα vb pres act part fem nom sg . . . . ῥέω
Ραφαϊν pr noun	ῥέουσαν vb pres act part fem acc sg id.
Ραφακα pr noun	ῥεούσης vb pres act part fem gen sg id.
Ραφες pr noun	ῥεριμμένος vb perf m/p part masc nom sg . . . . ῥίπτω
Ραφη pr noun	Ρεσφα pr noun
Ραφι pr noun	ῥεύματος noun neut gen sg . . . . ῥεῦμα
Ῥαφιαν pr noun fem acc sg . . . . Ῥαφια	ῥευσάτωσαν vb 1st aor act impv 3rd pers pl . . . . ῥέω
ῥαφιδευτά adj neut nom and acc pl . . . . ῥαφιδευτός	ῥέων vb pres act part masc nom sg id.
ῥαφιδευτοῦ noun masc gen sg . . . . ῥαφιδευτής	ῥήγματα noun neut nom and acc pl . . . . ῥῆγμα

ρήγνυται   vb pres m/p ind 3rd pers sg   . . . .   ρήγνυμι
ρηθείσης   vb 1st aor pass part fem gen sg   . . . .   εἶπον
ρηθεῖσι   vb 1st aor pass part masc and neut dat pl   id.
ρηθέντα   vb 1st aor pass part neut nom and acc pl   id.
ρηθέντων   vb 1st aor pass part masc and neut gen pl   id.
ρηθῆναι   vb 1st aor pass inf   id.
ρηθήσεται   vb fut pass ind 3rd pers sg   id.
ρηθησομένοις   vb fut pass part masc and neut dat pl   id.
Ρηι   pr noun
ρῆμα   noun neut nom and acc sg
ρήμασι   noun neut dat pl   . . . .   ρῆμα
ρήματα   noun neut nom and acc pl   id.
ρήματι   noun neut dat sg   id.
ρήματος   noun neut gen sg   id.
ρημάτων   noun neut gen pl   id.
Ρημωθ   pr noun
ρῆξαι   vb 1st aor act inf   . . . .   ρήγνυμι
ρήξαντες   vb 1st aor act part masc nom pl   id.
ρήξας   vb 1st aor act part masc nom sg   id.
ρηξάτω   vb 1st aor act impv 3rd pers sg   id.
ρηξάτωσαν   vb 1st aor act impv 3rd pers pl   id.
ρήξει   vb fut act ind 3rd pers sg   id.
ρῆξον   vb 1st aor act impv 2nd pers sg   id.
ρήξω   vb fut act ind 1st pers sg   id.
ρης   translit (Heb. letter: ר)
Ρησαιου   pr noun masc gen sg   . . . .   Ρησαιας
ρήσει   noun fem dat sg   . . . .   ρῆσις
ρήσεις   noun fem nom and acc pl   id.
ρήσεις   vb fut act ind 2nd pers sg   . . . .   ρέω
ρῆσιν   noun fem acc sg   . . . .   ρῆσις
ρήσσω   vb pres act ind 1st pers sg
Ρησφαρα   pr noun
ρητίνη   noun fem nom sg
ρητίνην   noun fem acc sg   . . . .   ρητίνη
ρητίνης   noun fem gen sg   id.
ρητόν   adj masc acc sg, neut nom and acc sg   . . . .   ρητός
Ρηφα   pr noun
Ρηχα   pr noun
Ρηχαβ   pr noun
Ριβα   pr noun
Ριβαι   pr noun
ρίγει   noun neut dat sg   . . . .   ρῖγος
ρῖγος   noun neut nom and acc sg   id.
ρίζα   noun fem nom sg
ρίζαι   noun fem nom pl   . . . .   ρίζα
ρίζαν   noun fem acc sg   id.
ρίζας   noun fem acc pl   id.
ρίζης   noun fem gen sg   id.
ριζωθῇ   vb 1st aor pass subj 3rd pers sg   . . . .   ριζόω
ρίζωμα   noun neut nom and acc sg
ριζώματα   noun neut nom and acc pl   . . . .   ρίζωμα
ριζῶν   noun fem gen pl   . . . .   ρίζα

ρῖνα   noun fem acc sg   . . . .   ρίς
ρῖνας   noun fem acc pl   id.
ρῖνες   noun fem nom pl   id.
ρινί   noun fem dat sg   id.
Ῥινοκορουρων   pr noun gen pl   . . . .   Ῥινοκορουρα
ρινός   noun fem gen sg   . . . .   ρίς
ριπιστά   adj neut nom and acc pl   . . . .   ριπιστός
ριπτοῦμεν   vb pres act ind 1st pers pl   . . . .   ριπτέω
ριπτοῦντος   vb pres act part masc and neut gen sg   id.
ρίπτω   vb pres act ind 1st pers sg
ρισίν   noun fem dat pl   . . . .   ρίς
Ρισων   pr noun
Ριφαθ   pr noun
ριφείς   vb 2nd aor pass part masc nom sg   . . . .   ρίπτω
ριφέντα   vb 2nd aor pass part masc acc sg   id.
ριφῇ   vb 2nd aor pass subj 3rd pers sg   id.
ριφῆναι   vb 2nd aor pass inf   id.
ριφήσεται   vb fut pass ind 3rd pers sg   id.
ριφήσῃ   vb fut pass ind 2nd pers sg   id.
ριφήσονται   vb fut pass ind 3rd pers pl   id.
ρίψαντες   vb 1st aor act part masc nom pl   id.
ρίψατε   vb 1st aor act impv 2nd pers pl   id.
ρίψει   vb fut act ind 3rd pers sg   id.
ρίψεις   vb fut act ind 2nd pers sg   id.
ρῖψον   vb 1st aor act impv 2nd pers sg   id.
ρίψωμεν   vb 1st aor act subj 1st pers pl   id.
ρόα   noun fem nom sg
ρόα   noun fem dat sg   . . . .   ρόα
ρόαι   noun fem nom pl   id.
ροαί   see ρόαι
ρόακος   noun fem gen sg   . . . .   ρόαξ
ρόαν   noun fem acc sg   . . . .   ρόα
ρόας   noun fem gen sg and acc pl   id.
Ροβε   pr noun
Ροβοαμ   pr noun
Ροβοκ   pr noun
ρόδα   noun neut nom and acc pl   . . . .   ρόδον
Ῥοδιοι   pr noun masc nom pl
Ῥοδιων   pr noun masc gen pl   . . . .   Ῥοδιοι
Ροδοκος   pr noun masc nom sg
Ῥοδον   pr noun acc sg   . . . .   Ῥοδος
ρόδον   noun neut nom and acc sg
ρόδου   noun neut gen sg   . . . .   ρόδον
ροδοφόρον   adj masc and fem acc sg   . . . .   ροδοφόρος
ρόδων   noun neut gen pl   . . . .   ρόδον
ροῖζος   noun masc nom sg
ροίζου   noun masc gen sg   . . . .   ροῖζος
ροιζοῦντος   vb pres act part masc and neut gen sg   . .   ροιζέω
ροίζῳ   noun masc dat sg   . . . .   ροῖζος
Ροϊμου   pr noun masc gen sg   . . . .   Ροϊμος
ροίσκοις   noun masc dat pl   . . . .   ροίσκος
ροίσκον   noun masc acc sg   id.

ῥοΐσκος   noun masc nom sg
ῥοΐσκους   noun masc acc pl . . . .   ῥοΐσκος
ῥοΐσκων   noun masc gen pl   id.
Ροκομ   pr noun
Ρομελια   pr noun
Ρομελιου   pr noun masc gen sg . . . .   Ρομελιας
Ρομμα   pr noun
ῥομφαία   noun fem nom sg
ῥομφαίᾳ   noun fem dat sg . . . .   ῥομφαία
ῥομφαῖαι   noun fem nom pl   id.
ῥομφαίαν   noun fem acc sg   id.
ῥομφαίας   noun fem gen sg and acc pl   id.
ῥομφαιῶν   noun fem gen pl   id.
Ροολλαμ   pr noun
ῥόπαλον   noun neut nom and acc sg
ῥοπή   noun fem nom sg
ῥοπῇ   noun fem dat sg . . . .   ῥοπή
ῥοπήν   noun fem acc sg   id.
ῥοποπῶλαι   noun masc nom pl . . . .   ῥωποπώλης
Ρουβην   pr noun
Ρουβηνι   pr noun
Ρουθ   pr noun
Ρουμα   pr noun
ῥοῦν   noun masc acc sg . . . .   ῥοῦς
Ροωβ   pr noun
Ροωβωθ   pr noun
ῥοῶν   noun fem gen pl . . . .   ῥόα
ῥοῶνος   noun masc gen sg . . . .   ῥοών
Ρωως   pr noun
ῥύδην   adverb
ῥύεται   vb pres dep ind 3rd pers sg . . . .   ῥύομαι
ῥυήσεται   vb fut mid ind 3rd pers sg . . . .   ῥέω
ῥυήσονται   vb fut mid ind 3rd pers pl   id.
ῥυθμοί   noun masc nom pl . . . .   ῥυθμός
ῥυθμόν   noun masc acc sg   id.
ῥυθμός   noun masc nom sg   id.
ῥυθμοῦ   noun masc gen sg   id.
ῥῦμαι   noun fem nom pl . . . .   ῥύμη
ῥύμαις   noun fem dat pl   id.
ῥυόμενοι   vb pres dep part masc nom pl . . . .   ῥύομαι
ῥυομένοις   vb pres dep part masc and neut dat pl   id.
ῥυόμενος   vb pres dep part masc nom sg   id.
ῥυπαρά   adj neut nom and acc pl . . . .   ῥυπαρός
ῥύπον   noun masc acc sg . . . .   ῥύπος

ῥύπου   noun masc gen sg . . . .   ῥύπος
ῥύπῳ   noun masc dat sg   id.
ῥῦσαι   vb 1st aor mid impv 2nd pers sg . . . .   ῥύομαι
ῥύσαιτο   vb 1st aor mid opt 3rd pers sg   id.
ῥυσάμενον   vb 1st aor mid part masc acc sg   id.
ῥυσάμενος   vb 1st aor mid part masc nom sg   id.
ῥυσαμένου   vb 1st aor mid part masc and neut gen sg   id.
ῥύσασθαι   vb 1st aor mid inf   id.
ῥύσασθε   vb 1st aor mid impv 2nd pers pl   id.
ῥυσάσθω   vb 1st aor mid impv 3rd pers sg   id.
ῥύσει   noun fem dat sg . . . .   ῥύσις
ῥύσεται   vb fut mid ind 3rd pers sg . . . .   ῥύομαι
ῥύσεως   noun fem gen sg . . . .   ῥύσις
ῥύσῃ   vb fut mid ind 2nd pers sg . . . .   ῥύομαι
ῥύσηται   vb 1st aor mid subj 3rd pers sg   id.
ῥυσθείην   vb 1st aor pass opt 1st pers sg   id.
ῥυσθέντας   vb 1st aor pass part masc acc pl   id.
ῥυσθήσῃ   vb fut pass ind 2nd pers sg   id.
ῥυσθήσομαι   vb fut pass ind 1st pers sg   id.
ῥυσθῶσιν   vb 1st aor pass subj 3rd pers pl   id.
ῥύσιν   noun fem acc sg . . . .   ῥύσις
ῥύσις   noun fem nom sg   id.
ῥύσομαι   vb fut mid ind 1st pers sg . . . .   ῥύομαι
ῥύσονται   vb fut mid ind 3rd pers pl   id.
ῥύστης   noun masc nom sg
ῥύσωνται   vb 1st aor mid subj 3rd pers pl . . . .   ῥύομαι
ῥῶγας   noun masc acc pl . . . .   ῥώξ
Ρωγελλιμ   pr noun
ῥῶγες   noun fem nom pl . . . .   ῥώξ
Ρωγηλ   pr noun
Ρωκεϊμ   pr noun
Ῥωμαῖοι   pr noun masc nom pl . . . .   Ῥωμαῖοι
Ῥωμαιοις   pr noun masc dat pl   id.
Ῥωμαιους   pr noun masc acc pl   id.
Ῥωμαιων   pr noun masc gen pl   id.
ῥωμαλέοι   adj masc nom pl . . . .   ῥωμαλέος
Ρωμεμθι-αδ   pr noun
Ῥωμη   pr noun fem dat sg . . . .   Ῥωμη
ῥώμῃ   noun fem dat sg . . . .   ῥώμη
Ῥωμην   pr noun fem acc sg . . . .   Ῥωμη
Ῥωμης   pr noun fem gen sg   id.
ῥώξ   noun masc or fem nom sg
Ρως   pr noun
Ρωσαι   pr noun

Σ σ

ς′ indecl number

σά poss pron 2nd pers neut nom and acc pl . . . . σός

Σααρ pr noun

Σααρημ pr noun

Σααρια pr noun

Σααρις pr noun

Σαβα pr noun

Σαβαθα pr noun

Σαβαθαι pr noun

Σαβαθος pr noun

Σαβαϊμ pr noun

Σαβακαθα pr noun

Σαβανια pr noun

Σαβανναιους pr noun

Σαβαννου pr noun gen sg . . . . Σαβαννος

Σαβαου pr noun

Σαβατ pr noun

Σαβατια pr noun

σαβαχα translit

σαβαωθ translit

Σαββαιας pr noun

σάββασιν noun neut dat pl . . . . σάββατον

σάββατα noun neut nom and acc pl   id.

Σαββαταιος pr noun

σαββατιεῖ vb fut act ind 3rd pers sg . . . . σαββατίζω

σαββατιεῖτε vb fut act ind 2nd pers pl   id.

σαββατίζειν vb pres act inf   id.

σαββατίσαι vb 1st aor act inf,

       1st aor act opt 3rd pers sg   id.

σαββάτοις noun neut dat pl . . . . σάββατον

σάββατον noun neut nom and acc sg   id.

σαββάτου noun neut gen sg   id.

σαββάτῳ noun neut dat sg   id.

σαββάτων noun neut gen pl   id.

Σαβεε pr noun

σαβεκ translit

Σαβερ pr noun

Σαβευ pr noun

Σαβηβα pr noun

σαβι translit

Σαβι pr noun

Σαβια pr noun

Σαβιν pr noun

Σαβουδ pr noun

Σαβχια pr noun

Σαβων pr noun . . . . Σαβαι

Σαγαφ pr noun

σαγῇ noun fem dat sg . . . . σαγή

σαγῆναι noun fem nom pl . . . . σαγήνη

σαγήναις noun fem dat pl   id.

σαγήνας noun fem acc pl   id.

σαγήνῃ noun fem dat sg   id.

σαγηνῶν noun fem gen pl   id.

σάγματα noun neut nom and acc pl . . . . σάγμα

Σαδαιεμ pr noun

Σαδδαι pr noun

Σαδδουκ pr noun

Σαδδουκου pr noun gen sg . . . . Σαδδουκος

σαδη translit (Heb. letter: צ)

σαδημωθ translit

σαδηρωθ translit

Σαδουχ pr noun

Σαδωκ pr noun

Σαδωμ pr noun

Σαεμηρων pr noun

Σαθαρβουζανα pr noun

Σαθουρ pr noun

Σαθραβουζάνῃ pr noun masc dat sg . . . . . Σαθραβουζανης

Σαθραβουζανης pr noun masc nom sg   id.

σαθρόν adj masc acc sg, neut nom and acc sg . . . . . . σαθρός

σαθρότερον comp adj masc acc sg,

            neut nom and acc sg   id.

Σαιζα pr noun

Σαιν pr noun fem acc sg . . . . Σαις

σαῖς poss pron 2nd pers fem dat pl . . . . σός

Σακαριμ pr noun

σάκκοις noun masc dat pl . . . . σάκκος

σάκκον noun masc acc sg   id.

σάκκος noun masc nom sg   id.

σάκκου noun masc gen sg   id.

σάκκους noun masc acc pl   id.

σάκκῳ noun masc dat sg   id.

σάκκων noun masc gen pl   id.

Σακχαρωνα pr noun

Σαλα pr noun

Σαλαβιν pr noun

Σαλαβωνι pr noun

Σαλαβωνιτης pr noun masc nom sg

Σαλαδ pr noun

Σαλαθιηλ pr noun

Σαλαμαν pr noun

Σαλαμανασαρ pr noun

Σαλαμανασσαρ pr noun

Σαλαμι pr noun

Σαλαμια pr noun

Σαλαμιηλ pr noun

σαλαμιν translit		
Σαλαμιν pr noun		
Σαλεμ pr noun		
σαλεύηται vb pres m/p subj 3rd pers sg	. . . .	σαλευω
σαλευθῇ vb 1st aor pass subj 3rd pers sg	id.	
σαλευθῆναι vb 1st aor pass inf	id.	
σαλευθῇς vb 1st aor pass subj 2nd pers sg	id.	
σαλευθήσεται vb fut pass ind 3rd pers sg	id.	
σαλευθησόμεθα vb fut pass ind 1st pers pl	id.	
σαλευθήσονται vb fut pass ind 3rd pers pl	id.	
σαλευθήτω vb 1st aor pass impv 3rd pers sg	id.	
σαλευθήτωσαν vb 1st aor pass impv 3rd pers pl	id.	
σαλευθῶ vb 1st aor pass subj 1st pers sg	id.	
σαλευθῶσιν vb 1st aor pass subj 3rd pers pl	id.	
σαλευόμενα vb pres m/p part neut nom and acc pl	id.	
σαλευόμενοι vb pres m/p part masc nom pl	id.	
σαλευόμενον vb pres m/p part masc acc sg,		
neut nom and acc sg	id.	
σαλευόμενος vb pres m/p part masc nom sg	id.	
σαλεύονται vb pres m/p ind 3rd pers pl	id.	
σαλεύσαι vb 1st aor act opt 3rd pers sg	id.	
σαλεύσαι vb 1st aor act inf	id.	
σαλεύσει vb fut act ind 3rd pers sg	id.	
σαλεύων vb pres act part masc nom sg	id.	
Σαλεφ pr noun		
Σαλη pr noun		
Σαλημ pr noun		
Σαλημου pr noun gen sg	. . . .	Σαλημ•ς
Σαλθας pr noun		
Σαλθι pr noun		
Σαλι pr noun		
Σαλιμ pr noun		
Σαλιμουθ pr noun		
Σαλισα pr noun		
Σαλλαι pr noun		
Σαλλουμος pr noun		
Σαλμαα pr noun		
Σαλμαν pr noun		
Σαλμανα pr noun		
Σαλμων pr noun		
σάλον noun masc acc sg	. . . .	σάλcς
σάλος noun masc nom sg	ic.	
σάλου noun masc gen sg	ic.	
Σαλουια pr noun		
Σαλουμ pr noun		
Σαλπααδ pr noun		
σάλπιγγα noun fem acc sg	. . . .	σάλπιγξ
σάλπιγγας noun fem acc pl	ic.	
σάλπιγγες noun fem nom pl	ic.	
σάλπιγγι noun fem dat sg	ic.	
σάλπιγγος noun fem gen sg	ic.	
σαλπίγγων noun fem gen pl	ic.	

σάλπιγξ noun fem nom sg		
σάλπιγξι(ν) noun fem dat pl	. . . .	σάλπιγξ
σαλπιεῖ vb fut act ind 3rd pers sg	. . . . . .	σαλπίζω
σαλπιεῖτε vb fut act ind 2nd pers pl	id.	
σαλπίζει vb pres act ind 3rd pers sg	id.	
σαλπίζειν vb pres act inf	id.	
σαλπίζοντες vb pres act part masc nom pl	id.	
σαλπίζουσαι vb pres act part fem nom pl	id.	
σαλπίζων vb pres act part masc nom sg	id.	
σαλπιοῦσιν vb fut act ind 3rd pers pl	id.	
σαλπίσατε vb 1st aor act impv 2nd pers pl	id.	
σαλπίσεις vb fut act ind 2nd pers sg	id.	
σαλπίσῃ vb 1st aor act subj 3rd pers sg	id.	
σαλπίσητε vb 1st aor act subj 2nd pers pl	id.	
σαλπίσωσιν vb 1st aor act subj 3rd pers pl	id.	
σαλπιῶ vb fut act ind 1st pers sg	id.	
Σαλω pr noun		
σάλῳ noun masc dat sg	. . . .	σάλος
Σαλωμ pr noun		
Σαλωμιθ pr noun		
Σαλωμωθ pr noun		
Σαλωμων pr noun masc nom sg [also: indecl]		
Σαλωμῶντα pr noun masc acc sg	. . . .	σαλωμών
Σαλωμῶντος noun masc gen sg	id.	
Σαμα pr noun		
Σαμαα pr noun		
Σαμαγωθ pr noun		
Σαμαε pr noun		
Σαμαθ pr noun		
Σαμαθιιμ pr noun		
Σαμαϊ pr noun		
Σαμαια pr noun		
Σαμαια pr noun masc dat sg	. . . .	Σαμαιας
Σαμαιαν pr noun masc acc sg	id.	
Σαμαιας pr noun masc nom sg	id.	
Σαμαιος pr noun		
Σαμαιου pr noun masc gen sg	. . . .	Σαμαιας
Σαμαλα pr noun		
Σαμαλαι pr noun		
Σαμαραθ pr noun		
Σαμαραῖον pr noun masc acc sg	. . . .	Σαμαραῖος
Σαμαραν pr noun		
Σαμαρανι pr noun		
Σαμαρεια pr noun fem nom sg	. . . .	Σαμαρεια
Σαμαρειᾳ pr noun fem dat sg	id.	
Σαμαρειαν pr noun fem acc sg	id.	
Σαμαρειας pr noun fem gen sg	id.	
Σαμαρι pr noun		
Σαμαρια pr noun fem nom sg		
Σαμαριαν pr noun fem acc sg	. . . .	Σαμαρια
Σαμαρῖται pr noun masc nom pl	. . . .	Σαμαρίτης
Σαμαριτιδος pr noun fem gen sg	. . . .	Σαμαριτις

Σαμαρῖτιν pr noun fem acc sg . . . . Σαμαρῖτις	Σαουλ pr noun
Σαματος pr noun	Σαουλι pr noun
Σαμαχια pr noun masc nom sg	Σαουρ pr noun
Σαμαωθ pr noun	σαπήσεται vb fut pass ind 3rd pers sg . . . . σήπω
Σαμβρι pr noun	σαπρία noun fem nom sg
σαμβύκης noun fem gen sg . . . . σαμβύκη	σαπρίᾳ noun fem dat sg . . . . σαπρία
Σαμεγαρ pr noun	σαπρίαν noun fem acc sg id.
Σαμερι pr noun	σαπρίας noun fem gen sg id.
Σαμες pr noun	σαπριοῦσιν vb fut act ind 3rd pers pl . . . . σαπρίζω
Σαμηρ pr noun	σάπφειρον noun fem acc sg . . . . σάπφειρος
Σαμι pr noun	σάπφειρος noun fem nom sg id.
Σαμια pr noun	σαπφείρου noun fem gen sg id.
Σαμιρ pr noun	σαπφείρῳ noun fem dat sg id.
Σαμμα pr noun	Σαπφιν pr noun
Σαμμαυς pr noun	σαπῶσιν vb 2nd aor pass subj 3rd pers pl . . . . σήπω
Σαμμους pr noun	Σαρα pr noun
Σαμμωθ pr noun	Σαραα pr noun
Σαμον pr noun acc sg . . . . Σάμος	σαράβαρα noun neut nom and acc pl
Σαμου pr noun	σαραβάροις noun neut dat pl . . . . σαράβαρα
Σαμουε pr noun	Σαραβια pr noun
Σαμουηλ pr noun	Σαραβιας pr noun masc nom sg
Σαμουι pr noun	Σαραδ pr noun
Σαμουιας pr noun masc nom sg	Σαραδα pr noun
Σαμς pr noun	Σαραθ pr noun
Σαμσαι pr noun	Σαραθαιοι pr noun masc nom pl
Σαμσαιος pr noun masc nom sg	Σαραθι pr noun
Σαμσαιῳ pr noun masc dat sg . . . . Σαμσαιος	Σαραια pr noun
Σαμσαρια pr noun	Σαραια pr noun masc dat sg . . . . Σαραιας
σαμχ translit (Heb letter: ס)	Σαραιαν pr noun masc acc sg id.
Σαμψάμη pr noun . . . . Σαμψάμης	Σαραιας pr noun masc nom sg id.
Σαμψων pr noun	Σαραιου pr noun masc gen sg id.
Σαν pr noun	Σαραν pr noun fem acc sg . . . . Σαρα
Σαναα pr noun	Σαρας pr noun fem gen sg id.
Σαναας pr noun	Σαρασαδαι pr noun
Σαναβαλλατ pr noun	Σαρασαρ pr noun
Σαναβασσαρος pr noun masc nom sg	Σαραφ pr noun
Σαναβασσαρου pr noun masc gen sg . . . . Σαναβασσαρος	Σαραφι pr noun
Σαναβασσαρῳ pr noun masc dat sg id.	Σαρβαχα pr noun
σανδάλια noun neut nom and acc pl . . . . σανδάλιον	Σαργαριμ pr noun
σανδάλιον noun neut nom and acc sg id.	σάρδιον noun neut nom and acc sg
Σανεσαρ pr noun	σαρδίου noun neut gen sg . . . . σάρδιον
Σανι pr noun	Σαρεδ pr noun
σανίδα noun fem acc sg . . . . σανίς	Σαρεδι pr noun
σανίδος noun fem gen sg id.	Σαρεθ pr noun
σανιδώματι noun neut dat sg . . . . σανίδωμα	Σαρεπτα pr noun
σανίδων noun fem gen pl . . . . σανίς	Σαρεπτων pr noun fem gen pl . . . . Σαρεπτα
σανιδωτόν adj masc acc sg, neut nom and acc sg σανιδωτός	Σαρια pr noun
Σανιρ pr noun	Σαριδ pr noun
Σανιωρ pr noun	Σαριρα pr noun
Σανσαννα pr noun	Σαριχ pr noun
Σαου pr noun	σάρκα noun fem acc sg . . . . σάρξ
Σαουια pr noun	σάρκας noun fem acc pl id.

σάρκες noun fem nom pl	. . . .	σάρξ
σαρκί noun fem dat sg		id.
σαρκίνη adj fem nom sg	. . . .	σάρκινος
σαρκίνην adj fem acc sg		id.
σάρκινοι adj masc nom pl		id.
σάρκινον adj masc acc sg, neut nom and acc sg		id.
σαρκός noun fem gen sg	. . . .	σάρξ
σαρκοφαγεῖν vb pres act inf	. . . .	σαρκοφαγέω
σαρκοφαγίαν noun fem acc sg	. . . .	σαρκοφαγία
σαρκῶν noun fem gen pl	. . . .	σάρξ
σάρξ noun fem nom sg		id.
σαρξί(ν) noun fem dat pl		id.
Σαρου pr noun		
Σαρουια pr noun		
Σαρουιας pr noun masc gen sg	. . . .	Σαρουια
Σαρουιας pr noun masc nom sg		
Σαρρα pr noun fem nom sg		
Σαρραν pr noun fem acc sg	. . . .	Σαρρα
Σαρρας pr noun fem gen sg		id.
Σαρρας pr noun		
Σαρσαθαιος pr noun		
Σαρσουσιν pr noun		
Σαρωθιε pr noun		
Σαρων pr noun		
Σαρωνιτης pr noun masc		
σάς poss pron 2nd pers fem acc pl	. . . .	σός
Σασαβασαρ pr noun		
Σασιμα pr noun		
σάτα noun neut nom and acc pl	. . . .	σάτον
σαταν translit		
σατανᾶν noun masc acc sg	. . . .	σατανᾶς
Σατι pr noun		
Σατραις pr noun		
σατράπαι noun masc nom pl	. . . .	σατράπης
σατράπαις noun masc dat pl		id.
σατράπας noun masc acc pl		id.
σατραπείαις noun fem dat pl	. . . .	σατραπεία
σατραπείας noun fem acc pl		id.
σατράπην noun masc acc sg	. . . .	σατράπης
σατραπίαι noun fem nom pl	. . . .	σατραπία
σατραπῶν noun masc gen pl	. . . .	σατράπης
Σαττιν pr noun		
Σαυα pr noun		
Σαυας pr noun		
Σαυη pr noun		
Σαυναν pr noun		
Σαυνις pr noun		
σαύρα noun fem nom sg		
σαυτῇ dem pron fem dat sg	. . . .	σεαυτοῦ
σαυτοῦ refl pron masc and neut gen sg		id.
σαυτῷ refl pron masc and neut dat sg		id.
Σαυχαιων pr noun masc gen pl	. . . .	Σαυχαιος

Σαυχιτης pr noun masc nom sg		
Σαφ pr noun		
Σαφαθ pr noun		
Σαφαμ pr noun		
Σαφαν pr noun		
Σαφανια pr noun		
Σαφαρ pr noun		
Σαφαραθ pr noun		
Σαφατ pr noun		
Σαφατια pr noun		
Σαφατιας pr noun masc nom sg		
Σαφατιου pr noun masc gen sg	. . . .	Σαφατιας
Σαφεκ pr noun		
σαφές adj neut nom and acc sg	. . . .	σαφής
σαφέστερον comp adj neut nom and acc sg		id.
Σαφθαβηθαεμεκ pr noun		
Σαφθαιβαιθμε pr noun		
Σαφι pr noun		
Σαφιρ pr noun		
Σαφου pr noun		
Σαφυθι pr noun		
Σαφφαν pr noun		
σαφφωθ translit		
Σαφφωθ pr noun		
Σαφων pr noun		
Σαφωνι pr noun		
σαφῶς adverb		
Σαχανια pr noun		
Σαχαρ pr noun		
Σαχερδονος pr noun masc		
σαχωλ translit		
Σαων-εσβι-εμωηδ pr noun		
Σαωχω pr noun		
σβεννύντι vb pres act part masc and neut dat sg	. .	σβέννυμι
σβέννυται vb pres m/p ind 3rd pers sg		id.
σβέσαι vb 1st aor act inf		id.
σβέσας vb 1st aor act part masc nom sg		id.
σβέσει vb fut act ind 3rd pers sg		id.
σβέσης vb 1st aor act subj 2nd pers sg		id.
σβεσθέντος vb 1st aor pass part masc and neut gen sg		id.
σβεσθῇ vb 1st aor pass subj 3rd pers sg		id.
σβεσθῆναι vb 1st aor pass inf		id.
σβεσθήσεται vb fut pass ind 3rd pers sg		id.
σβέσον vb 1st aor act impv 2nd pers sg		id.
σβέσουσιν vb fut act ind 3rd pers pl		id.
σβεστικῆς adj fem gen sg	. . . .	σβεστικός
σβέσων vb fut act part masc nom sg	. . . .	σβέννυμι
σε pers pron 2nd pers sg acc sg	. . . .	σύ
σεαυτῇ refl pron fem dat sg	. . . .	σεαυτοῦ
σεαυτήν refl pron fem acc sg		id.
σεαυτῆς refl pron fem gen sg		id.
σεαυτόν refl pron masc acc sg		id.

σεαυτοῦ refl pron masc and neut gen sg . . . . σεαυτοῦ

σεαυτῷ refl pron masc and neut dat sg   id.

Σεβαμα pr noun

Σεβανι pr noun

Σεβανια pr noun

σέβασμα noun neut nom and acc sg

σεβάσματα noun neut nom and acc pl . . . . σέβασμα

σεβασμάτων noun neut gen pl   id.

Σεβεγων pr noun

Σεβεε pr noun

σέβειν vb pres act inf . . . . σέβω

Σεβεκαθα pr noun

σέβεσθαι vb pres dep inf . . . . σέβομαι

σέβεσθε vb pres dep ind 2nd pers pl   id.

σέβεται vb pres dep ind 3rd pers sg   id.

Σεβημα pr noun

σέβησθε vb pres dep subj 2nd pers pl . . . . σέβομαι

Σεβια pr noun

σέβομαι vb pres dep ind 1st pers sg

σεβόμενοι vb pres dep part masc nom pl . . . . σέβομαι

σεβομένοις vb pres dep part masc and neut dat pl   id.

σέβονται vb pres dep ind 3rd pers pl   id.

Σεβοχα pr noun

Σεβραιμ pr noun

Σεβωιμ pr noun

Σεβωιν pr noun

σέβωνται vb pres dep subj 3rd pers pl . . . . σέβομαι

Σεγουβ pr noun

Σεδδαδα pr noun

Σεδδουκ pr noun

Σεδεκια pr noun

Σεδεκια pr noun masc nom, voc or dat sg . . . . Σεδεκιας

Σεδεκιαν pr noun masc acc sg   id.

Σεδεκιας pr noun masc nom sg   id.

Σεδεκιου pr noun masc gen sg   id.

Σεδεκιου pr noun

Σεδεμ pr noun

Σεδιουρ pr noun

Σεδραχ pr noun

Σεηρα pr noun

Σεθεννακ pr noun

σείεται vb pres m/p ind 3rd pers sg . . . . σείω

σείομαι vb pres m/p ind 1st pers sg   id.

σειραῖς noun fem dat pl . . . . σειρά

Σεῖραμ pr noun

σειράς noun fem acc pl . . . . σειρά

σειρῆνες noun fem nom pl . . . . σειρήν

σειρήνιοι adj masc and fem nom pl . . . . σειρήνιος

σειρήνων noun fem gen pl . . . . σειρήν

σειρομάσταις noun masc dat pl . . . . σειρομάστης

σειρομάστας noun masc acc pl   id.

σειρομάστην noun masc acc sg   id.

Σεϊρωθα pr noun

σεισθήσεται vb fut pass ind 3rd pers sg . . . . σείω

σεισθήσονται vb fut pass ind 3rd pers pl   id.

σείσθητι vb 2nd aor pass impv 2nd pers sg   id.

σεισθῶσιν vb 1st aor pass subj 3rd pers pl   id.

σείσματι noun neut dat sg . . . . σεῖσμα

σεισμόν noun masc acc sg . . . . σεισμός

σεισμός noun masc nom sg   id.

σεισμοῦ noun masc gen sg   id.

σείσω vb fut act ind 1st pers sg . . . . σείω

σείω vb pres act ind 1st pers sg   id.

σείων vb pres act part masc nom sg   id.

Σεκελα pr noun

Σεκελακ pr noun

Σεκλαγ pr noun

Σελαθι pr noun

Σελεϊ pr noun

Σελεϊμ pr noun

Σελεμι pr noun

Σελεμια pr noun

Σελεμιας pr noun masc nom sg

Σελεμιου pr noun masc gen sg . . . . Σελεμιας

Σελευκειας pr noun fem gen sg . . . . Σελευκεια

Σελευκον pr noun masc acc sg . . . . Σελευκος

Σελευκος pr noun masc nom sg   id.

Σελευκου pr noun masc gen sg   id.

Σελευκῳ pr noun masc dat sg   id.

Σελεφ pr noun

Σεληκ pr noun

Σεληκαν pr noun

σελήνη noun fem nom sg

σελήνη noun fem dat sg . . . . σελήνη

σελήνην noun fem acc sg   id.

σελήνης noun fem gen sg   id.

σελίδας noun fem acc pl . . . . σελίς

Σελλα pr noun

Σελλημ pr noun

Σελλημι pr noun

Σελλης pr noun

Σελλησα pr noun

Σελλουμ pr noun

Σελμανα pr noun

Σελμων pr noun

Σελμωνα pr noun

Σελνα pr noun

Σελχα pr noun

Σελωμ pr noun

Σεμαα pr noun

Σεμαι pr noun

Σεμεϊ pr noun

Σεμεια pr noun

Σεμειας pr noun

Σεμεϊου pr noun masc gen sg .... Σεμεΐας
Σεμεΐς pr noun
Σεμειων pr noun
Σεμελιου pr noun masc gen sg .... Σεμελιας
Σεμερων pr noun
Σεμεων pr noun
Σεμηρ pr noun
σεμιδάλεως noun fem gen sg .... σεμίδαλις
σεμίδαλιν noun fem acc sg   id.
σεμίδαλις noun fem nom sg   id.
Σεμιρα pr noun
Σεμιραμωθ pr noun
Σεμιων pr noun
Σεμμα pr noun
Σεμμηρ pr noun
σεμνά adj neut nom and acc pl .... σεμνός
σεμναί adj fem nom pl   id.
σεμνή adj fem nom sg   id.
σεμνήν adj fem acc sg   id.
σεμνῆς adj fem gen sg   id.
σεμνολογήσας vb 1st aor act ind 2nd pers sg .. σεμνολογέω
σεμνόν adj masc acc sg, neut nom and acc sg ...... σεμνός
σεμνοτάτης superl adj fem gen sg   id.
σεμνότητι noun fem dat sg .... σεμνότης
σεμνοῦ adj masc and neut gen sg .... σεμνός
σεμνῶν adj gen pl   id.
σεμνῶς adverb
Σεμριμ pr noun
Σεμρων pr noun
Σεμωιθ pr noun
σεν translit (Heb. letter: ש)
Σεννα pr noun
Σεννααν pr noun
Σεννααρ pr noun
Σενναν pr noun
Σενναχηριμ pr noun
Σεπφαμ pr noun
Σεπφαμα pr noun
Σεπφαριμ pr noun
Σεπφαρουαιν pr noun
Σεπφωρ pr noun
Σεπφωρα pr noun fem nom sg
Σεπφωραν pr noun fem acc sg .... Σεπφωρα
Σεραδα pr noun
Σεραρ pr noun
σεραφιν translit
Σερεβιαν pr noun masc acc sg .... Σερεβιας
Σερεδ pr noun
Σερι pr noun
Σερουχ pr noun
Σερραν pr noun
σερσερωθ translit

Σεσαθαν pr noun
σεσάλευται vb perf m/p ind 3rd pers sg .... σαλεύω
σεσήμανται vb perf m/p ind 3rd pers pl .... σημαίνω
σεσηπότα vb perf act part masc acc sg .... σήπω
Σεσθηλ pr noun
Σεσι pr noun
σεσιωπήκαμεν vb perf act ind 1st pers pl .... σιωπάω
Σεσσι pr noun
Σεσσις pr noun
σέσωκας vb perf act ind 2nd pers sg .... σῴζω
σέσωκε vb perf act ind 3rd pers sg   id.
σεσωσμένη vb perf m/p part fem nom sg   id.
σεσωσμένοι vb perf m/p part masc nom pl   id.
σεσωσμένον vb perf m/p part masc acc sg,
            neut nom and acc sg   id.
σεσωσμένος vb perf m/p part masc nom sg   id.
σεσωσμένους vb perf m/p part masc acc pl   id.
Σετιρωθα pr noun
Σετρι pr noun
σευτλίον noun neut nom and acc sg
Σεφ pr noun
Σεφεθ pr noun
Σεφεϊ pr noun
Σεφεκ pr noun
Σεφηλα pr noun
Σεφι pr noun
Σεφινα pr noun
Σεφνι pr noun
Σεχενια pr noun
Σεχενιας pr noun
Σεχενιου pr noun
Σεχονιας pr noun
Σεωριμ pr noun
σή poss pron 2nd pers fem nom sg .... σός
σῆ poss pron 2nd pers fem dat sg   id.
Σηα pr noun
Σηγωρ pr noun
Σηδανιν pr noun
Σηθ pr noun
Σηιρ pr noun
σηκόν noun masc acc sg .... σηκός
Σηλαλεφ pr noun
Σηλι pr noun
Σηλω pr noun
Σηλωμ pr noun
Σηλων pr noun
Σηλωνι pr noun
Σηλωνιτην pr noun masc acc sg .... Σηλωνιτης
Σηλωνιτης pr noun masc nom sg   id.
Σηλωνιτου pr noun masc gen sg   id.
Σημ pr noun
σημαίαν noun fem acc sg .... σημαία

σημαίνει vb pres act ind 3rd pers sg . . . . σημαίνω
σημαίνειν vb pres act inf   id.
σημαινέτωσαν vb pres act impv 3rd pers pl   id.
σημαινομένους vb pres m/p part masc acc pl   id.
σημαινομένων vb pres m/p part gen pl   id.
σημαινούσης vb pres act part fem gen sg   id.
σημάνατε vb 1st aor act impv 2nd pers pl   id.
σημανεῖς vb fut act ind 2nd pers sg   id.
σημανεῖτε vb fut act ind 2nd pers pl   id.
σημάνῃ vb 1st aor act subj 3rd pers sg   id.
σημανῶ vb fut act ind 1st pers sg   id.
σημάνωσιν vb 2nd aor act subj 3rd pers pl   id.
σημασία noun fem nom sg
σημασίᾳ noun fem dat sg . . . . σημασία
σημασίαν noun fem acc sg   id.
σημασίας noun fem gen sg and acc pl   id.
σημασιῶν noun fem gen pl   id.
σημέας noun fem acc pl . . . . σημέα
σημεῖα noun neut nom and acc pl . . . . σημεῖον
σημείοις noun neut dat pl   id.
σημεῖον noun neut nom and acc sg   id.
σημείου noun neut gen sg   id.
σημείῳ noun neut dat sg   id.
σημείων noun neut gen pl   id.
σημειώσει noun fem dat sg . . . . σημείωσις
σημείωσιν noun fem acc sg   id.
σήμερον adverb
σήν poss pron 2nd pers fem acc sg . . . . σός
Σην pr noun
σήπη noun fem nom sg
σηπομένης vb pres m/p part fem gen sg . . . . σήπω
σηπόμενον vb pres m/p part masc acc sg,
     neut nom and acc sg   id.
Σηρων pr noun
σῆς poss pron 2nd pers fem gen sg . . . . σός
σής noun masc nom sg
σῆτες noun masc nom pl . . . . σής
σητόβρωτον adj acc sg, neut nom sg . . . . σητόβρωτος
σητός noun masc gen sg . . . . σής
σῆψιν noun fem acc sg . . . . σῆψις
σῆψον vb 1st aor act impv 2nd pers sg . . . . σήπω
Σηων pr noun
σθένει noun neut dat sg . . . . σθένος
σθένος noun neut nom and acc sg   id.
σθένους noun neut gen sg   id.
σιαγόνα noun fem acc sg . . . . σιαγών
σιαγόνας noun fem acc pl   id.
σιαγόνες noun fem nom pl   id.
σιαγόνι noun fem dat sg   id.
σιαγόνια noun neut nom and acc pl . . . . σιαγόνιον
σιαγόνος noun fem gen sg . . . . σιαγών
σιαγόνων noun fem gen pl   id.

Σιαν pr noun
Σιβα pr noun
σιβύναις noun fem dat pl . . . . σιβύνη
σίγα vb pres act impv 2nd pers sg . . . . σιγάω
σιγᾶν vb pres act inf   id.
σιγῇ noun fem dat sg . . . . σιγή
σιγηρά adj fem nom sg . . . . σιγηρός
σιγῆς noun fem gen sg . . . . σιγή
σιγήσει vb fut act ind 3rd pers sg . . . . σιγάω
σιγήσετε vb fut act ind 2nd pers pl   id.
σιγήσῃς vb 1st aor act subj 2nd pers sg   id.
σιγήσομαι vb fut mid ind 1st pers sg   id.
σιγῶντα vb pres act part masc acc sg   id.
Σιδην pr noun fem acc sg . . . . Σιδη
σιδηρᾶ adj fem nom sg, neut nom and acc pl . . . . σιδηροῦς
σιδηρᾷ adj fem dat sg   id.
σιδηραῖ adj fem nom pl   id.
σιδηραῖς adj fem dat pl   id.
σιδηρᾶς adj fem gen sg and acc pl   id.
σιδήριον noun neut nom and acc sg
σιδηροδέσμοις adj fem dat pl . . . . σιδηρόδεσμος
σιδηροῖ adj masc nom pl . . . . σιδηροῦς
σιδηροῖς adj masc and neut dat pl   id.
σίδηρον noun masc acc sg . . . . σίδηρος
σίδηρος noun masc nom sg   id.
σιδήρου noun masc gen sg   id.
σιδηροῦν adj masc acc sg, neut nom and acc sg . . σιδηροῦς
σιδηροῦς adj masc nom sg and acc pl   id.
σιδήρῳ noun masc dat sg . . . . σίδηρος
σιδηρῷ adj masc and neut dat sg . . . . σιδηροῦς
Σιδων pr noun fem nom sg
Σιδῶνα pr noun fem (and masc) acc sg . . . . Σιδών
Σιδῶνι pr noun fem dat sg   id.
Σιδωνιας pr noun fem gen sg . . . . Σιδωνια
Σιδωνιοι pr noun masc nom pl . . . . Σιδωνιος
Σιδωνιοις pr noun masc dat pl   id.
Σιδωνιον pr noun masc acc sg   id.
Σιδωνιους pr noun masc acc pl   id.
Σιδωνιων pr noun masc gen pl   id.
Σιδῶνος pr noun gen sg . . . . Σιδων
σίελα noun neut nom and acc pl . . . . σίελον
σίελος noun masc nom sg
Σικελακ pr noun
Σικελεγ pr noun
σικερα translit
Σικιμα pr noun
Σικιμίτας pr noun acc pl . . . . Σικιμῖται
Σικιμοις pr noun neut dat pl . . . . Σικιμα
Σικιμων pr noun neut gen pl   id.
σίκλοι noun masc nom pl . . . . σίκλος
σίκλον noun masc acc sg   id.
σίκλου noun masc gen sg   id.

σίκλους noun masc acc pl . . . . σίκλος
σίκλῳ noun masc dat sg   id.
σίκλων noun masc gen pl   id.
σικύας noun masc acc pl . . . . σικύς
σικυηράτῳ noun neut dat sg . . . . σικυήρατον
Σικυῶνα pr noun acc sg . . . . Σικυών
Σιλαθα pr noun
Σιλωαμ pr noun
Σιμων pr noun masc
Σιμωνα pr noun masc acc sg . . . . Σιμων
Σιμωνι pr noun masc dat sg   id.
Σιμωνος pr noun masc gen sg   id.
Σιν pr noun
Σινα pr noun
σινδόνας noun fem acc pl . . . . σινδών
Σιουαν pr noun
Σιρ pr noun
Σιρα pr noun
Σιραχ pr noun
Σιρδαθα pr noun
σιρομαστῶν noun masc gen pl . . . . σιρομάστης
σιρώνων translit
Σισαρα pr noun
Σισιννη pr noun masc dat sg . . . . Σισιννης
Σισιννης pr noun masc nom sg   id.
σισόην noun fem acc sg . . . . σισόη
σῖτα noun neut nom and acc pl . . . . σῖτος
σιτευτά adj neut nom and acc pl . . . . σιτευτός
σιτευτοί adj masc nom pl   id.
σιτευτόν adj masc acc sg, neut nom and acc sg   id.
σιτευτός adj masc nom sg   id.
σιτίων noun neut gen pl . . . . σιτίον
σιτοβολῶνας noun masc acc pl . . . . σιτοβολών
σιτοδείᾳ noun fem dat sg . . . . σιτοδεία
σιτοδείαν noun fem acc sg   id.
σιτοδοσίας noun fem gen sg . . . . σιτοδοσία
σῖτον noun masc acc sg . . . . σῖτος
σιτοποιοῦ adj gen sg . . . . σιτοποιός
σῖτος noun masc nom sg
σίτου noun masc gen sg . . . . σῖτος
σιτούμενοι vb pres dep part masc nom pl . . . . σιτέομαι
σιτοῦνται vb pres dep ind 3rd pers pl   id.
σίτῳ noun masc dat sg . . . . σῖτος
σίτων noun masc gen pl   id.
Σιφ pr noun
Σιφα pr noun
Σιων pr noun
Σιωνα pr noun
σιώπα vb pres act impv 2nd pers sg . . . . σιωπάω
σιωπᾶτε vb pres act ind 2nd pers pl,
        pres act impv 2nd pers pl   id.
σιωπήν noun fem acc sg . . . . σιωπή

σιωπῆς noun fem gen sg . . . . σιωπή
σιωπήσαιτο vb 1st aor mid opt 3rd pers sg . . . . σιωπάω
σιωπήσεται vb fut mid ind 3rd pers sg   id.
σιωπήσεως noun fem gen sg . . . . σιώπησις
σιωπήσομαι vb fut mid ind 1st pers sg . . . . σιωπάω
σιωπήσονται vb fut mid ind 3rd pers pl   id.
σιωπήσω vb fut act ind 1st pers sg   id.
σιωπῶμεν vb pres act ind 1st pers pl   id.
σιωπῶν vb pres act part masc nom sg   id.
σιωπώντων vb pres act part masc and neut gen pl   id.
Σιωρ pr noun
σκαμβή adj fem nom sg . . . . σκαμβός
σκάνδαλα noun neut nom and acc pl . . . . σκάνδαλον
σκανδαλιζούσης vb pres act part fem gen sg . σκανδαλίζω
σκανδαλισθῇς vb 1st aor pass subj 2nd pers sg   id.
σκανδαλισθήσεται vb fut pass ind 3rd pers sg   id.
σκανδαλισθήσονται vb fut pass ind 3rd pers pl   id.
σκάνδαλον noun neut nom and acc sg
σκανδάλου noun neut gen sg . . . . σκάνδαλον
σκανδάλων noun neut gen pl   id.
σκάφη noun neut nom and acc pl . . . . σκάφος
σκάφῃ noun fem dat sg . . . . σκάφη
σκαφῇ vb 2nd aor pass subj 3rd pers sg . . . . σκάπτω
σκάφην noun fem acc sg . . . . σκάφη
σκέλη noun neut nom and acc pl . . . . σκέλος
σκελίζω vb pres act ind 1st pers sg
σκέλος noun neut nom and acc sg
σκελῶν noun neut gen pl . . . . σκέλος
σκεπάζεται vb pres m/p ind 3rd pers sg . . . . σκεπάζω
σκεπαζόμενοι vb pres m/p part masc nom pl   id.
σκεπαζόμενος vb pres m/p part masc nom sg   id.
σκεπάζοντες vb pres act part masc nom pl   id.
σκεπάζων vb pres act part masc nom sg   id.
σκεπάρνοις noun neut dat pl . . . . σκέπαρνον
σκεπάρνῳ noun neut dat sg   id.
σκεπάσαι vb 1st aor act inf,
          1st aor act opt 3rd pers sg . . . . σκεπάζω
σκεπάσει vb fut act ind 3rd pers sg   id.
σκεπάσεις vb fut act ind 2nd pers sg   id.
σκεπάσῃ vb 1st aor act subj 3rd pers sg   id.
σκεπάσῃς vb 1st aor act subj 2nd pers sg   id.
σκεπασθείς vb 1st aor pass part masc nom sg   id.
σκεπασθῆναι vb 1st aor pass inf   id.
σκεπασθήσεται vb fut pass ind 3rd pers sg   id.
σκεπασθησόμεθα vb fut pass ind 1st pers pl   id.
σκεπασθῆτε vb 1st aor pass subj 2nd pers pl   id.
σκέπασις noun fem nom sg
σκεπαστό noun masc voc sg . . . . σκεπαστής
σκεπαστοί noun masc nom pl   id.
σκεπαστής noun masc nom sg   id.
σκεπάσω vb 1st aor act subj 1st pers sg,
        fut act ind 1st pers sg . . . . σκεπάζω

σκεπεινοῖς noun masc dat pl . . . . σκεπεινός
σκέπη noun fem nom sg
σκέπη noun fem dat sg . . . . σκέπη
σκέπην noun fem acc sg   id.
σκέπης noun fem gen sg   id.
σκευασίαν noun fem acc sg . . . . σκευασία
σκεύει noun neut dat sg . . . . σκεῦος
σκεύεσι noun neut dat pl   id.
σκεύη noun neut nom and acc pl   id.
σκεῦος noun neut nom and acc sg   id.
σκεύους noun neut gen sg   id.
σκευῶν noun neut gen pl   id.
σκέψαι vb 1st aor mid impv 2nd pers sg . . . . σκέπτομαι
σκηναί noun fem nom pl . . . . σκηνή
σκηναῖς noun fem dat pl   id.
σκηνάς noun fem acc pl   id.
σκηνή noun fem nom sg   id.
σκηνῇ noun fem dat sg   id.
σκηνήν noun fem acc sg   id.
σκηνῆς noun fem gen sg   id.
σκηνοπηγίας noun fem gen sg and acc pl . . . . σκηνοπηγία
σκῆνος noun neut nom and acc sg
σκηνούντων vb pres act part
　　　　masc and neut gen pl . . . . σκηνόω
σκήνωμα noun neut nom and acc sg
σκηνώμασι noun neut dat pl . . . . σκήνωμα
σκηνώματα noun neut nom and acc pl   id.
σκηνώματι noun neut dat sg   id.
σκηνώματος noun neut gen sg   id.
σκηνωμάτων noun neut gen pl   id.
σκηνῶν noun fem gen pl . . . . σκηνή
σκηνώσει vb fut act ind 3rd pers sg . . . . σκηνόω
σκηνώσεως noun fem gen sg . . . . σκήνωσις
σκῆπτρα noun neut nom and acc pl . . . . σκῆπτρον
σκήπτροις noun neut dat pl   id.
σκῆπτρον noun neut nom and acc sg   id.
σκήπτρου noun neut gen sg   id.
σκήπτρῳ noun neut dat sg   id.
σκήπτρων noun neut gen pl   id.
σκιά noun fem nom sg
σκιᾷ noun fem dat sg . . . . σκιά
σκιαγράφων noun masc gen pl . . . . σκιαγράφος
σκιαδίων noun neut gen pl . . . . σκιάδιον
σκιάζει vb pres act ind 3rd pers sg . . . . σκιάζω
σκιάζειν vb pres act inf   id.
σκιάζοντα vb pres act part masc acc sg   id.
σκιάζονται vb pres m/p ind 3rd pers pl   id.
σκιαζόντων vb pres act part masc and neut gen pl   id.
σκιάζουσα vb pres act part fem nom sg   id.
σκιάζουσαι vb pres act part fem nom pl   id.
σκιαζούσης vb pres act part fem gen sg   id.
σκιαί noun fem nom pl . . . . σκιά

σκιάν noun fem acc sg . . . . σκιά
σκιᾶς noun fem gen sg   id.
σκιάσει vb fut act ind 3rd pers sg . . . . σκιάζω
σκιρτήσετε vb fut act ind 2nd pers pl . . . . σκιρτάω
σκιρτώντων vb pres act part masc and neut gen pl   id.
σκληρά adverb
σκληρά adj fem nom sg, neut nom and acc pl . . . . . σκληρός
σκληράς adj fem acc pl   id.
σκληρᾶς adj fem gen sg   id.
σκληρίαν noun fem acc sg . . . . σκληρία
σκληροί adj masc nom pl . . . . σκληρός
σκληροῖς adj masc and neut dat pl   id.
σκληροκαρδία noun fem dat sg . . . . σκληροκαρδία
σκληροκαρδίαν noun fem acc sg   id.
σκληροκάρδιοι adj masc and fem nom pl . σκληροκάρδιος
σκληροκάρδιος adj masc and fem nom sg   id.
σκληρόν adj masc acc sg, neut nom and acc sg . . . . σκληρός
σκληρός adj masc nom sg   id.
σκληρότεροι comp adj masc nom pl   id.
σκληρότερον comp adj masc acc sg, neut nom and acc sg id.
σκληρότερον comp adverb . . . . σκληρῶς
σκληρότητα noun fem acc sg . . . . σκληρότης
σκληρότητες noun fem nom pl   id.
σκληρότητος noun fem gen sg   id.
σκληροτράχηλον adj masc acc sg,
　　　　neut nom and acc sg . . . . σκληροτράχηλος
σκληροτράχηλος adj masc nom sg   id.
σκληροτραχήλου adj masc and neut gen sg   id.
σκληροῦ adj masc and neut gen sg . . . . σκληρός
σκληρύνας vb 1st aor act part masc nom sg . . . . . σκληρύνω
σκληρυνεῖτε vb fut act ind 2nd pers pl   id.
σκληρύνητε vb 1st aor act subj 2nd pers pl   id.
σκληρυνθείη vb 1st aor pass opt 3rd pers sg   id.
σκληρυνθείς vb 1st aor pass part masc nom sg   id.
σκληρυνομένη vb pres m/p part fem nom sg   id.
σκληρυνῶ vb fut act ind 1st pers sg   id.
σκληρῷ adj masc and neut dat sg . . . . σκληρός
σκληρῶν adj gen pl   id.
σκληρῶς adverb
σκνῖπα noun masc acc sg . . . . σκνίψ
σκνῖπες noun masc nom pl   id.
σκνῖφα noun masc acc sg   id.
σκνῖφες noun masc nom pl   id.
σκολιά adj fem nom sg, neut nom and acc pl . . . . . σκολιός
σκολιάζων vb pres act part masc nom sg . . . . σκολιάζω
σκολιαί adj fem nom pl . . . . σκολιός
σκολιαῖς adj fem dat pl   id.
σκολιάς adj fem acc pl   id.
σκολιᾶς adj fem gen sg   id.
σκολιοί adj masc nom pl   id.
σκολιόν adj masc acc sg, neut nom and acc sg   id.
σκολιός adj masc nom sg

σκολιότητι noun fem dat sg . . . . σκολιότης
σκολιούς adj masc acc pl . . . . σκολιός
σκολιῶν adj gen pl   id.
σκολιῶς adverb
σκόλοπες noun masc nom pl . . . . σκόλοψ
σκολόπων noun masc gen pl   id.
σκόλοψ noun masc nom sg   id.
σκόλοψι noun masc dat pl   id.
σκοπεῖν vb pres act inf . . . . σκοπέω
σκόπελον noun neut nom and acc sg
σκοπεύει vb pres act ind 3rd pers sg . . . . σκοπεύω
σκοπεύοντες vb pres act part masc nom pl   id.
σκοπεύουσιν vb pres act ind 3rd pers pl   id.
σκόπευσον vb 1st aor act impv 2nd pers sg   id.
σκοπεύων vb pres act part masc nom sg   id.
σκοπῆς noun fem gen sg . . . . σκοπή
σκοπιᾷ noun fem dat sg . . . . σκοπιά
σκοπιάν noun fem acc sg   id.
σκοπιᾶς noun fem gen sg and acc pl   id.
σκοπιῶν noun fem gen pl   id.
σκοποί noun masc nom pl . . . . σκοπός
σκοπόν noun masc acc sg   id.
σκοπός noun masc nom sg   id.
σκοποῦ noun masc gen sg   id.
σκοπούς noun masc acc pl   id.
σκοπῶν noun masc gen pl   id.
σκορακισμοῦ noun masc gen sg . . . . σκορακισμός
σκόρδα noun neut nom and acc pl . . . . σκόρδον
σκορπίδια noun neut nom and acc pl . . . . σκορπίδιον
σκορπιεῖ vb fut act ind 3rd pers sg . . . . σκορπίζω
σκορπιεῖς vb fut act ind 2nd pers sg   id.
σκορπιζόμεθα vb pres m/p ind 1st pers pl   id.
σκορπίζων vb pres act part masc nom sg   id.
σκορπίοι noun masc nom pl . . . . σκορπίος
σκορπίοις noun masc dat pl   id.
σκορπίος noun masc nom sg   id.
σκορπίου noun masc gen sg   id.
σκορπίσαι vb 1st aor act inf . . . . σκορπίζω
σκορπισθείησαν vb 1st aor pass opt 3rd pers pl   id.
σκορπισθήσονται vb fut pass ind 3rd pers pl   id.
σκορπισθῆτε vb 1st aor pass subj 2nd pers pl   id.
σκορπισμός noun masc nom sg
σκορπιῶ vb fut act ind 1st pers sg . . . . σκορπίζω
σκορπίων noun masc gen pl . . . . σκορπίος
σκοτάσει vb fut act ind 3rd pers sg . . . . σκοτάζω
σκοτάσουσιν vb fut act ind 3rd pers pl   id.
σκότει noun neut dat sg . . . . σκότος
σκοτεινά adj neut nom and acc pl . . . . σκοτεινός
σκοτειναί adj fem nom pl   id.
σκοτεινή adj fem nom sg   id.
σκοτεινήν adj fem acc sg   id.
σκοτεινοῖς adj masc and neut dat pl   id.

σκοτεινόν adj masc acc sg, neut nom and acc sg . σκοτεινός
σκοτεινός adj masc nom sg   id.
σκοτεινούς adj masc acc pl   id.
σκοτεινῷ adj masc and neut dat sg   id.
σκοτία noun fem nom sg
σκοτίᾳ noun fem dat sg . . . . σκοτία
σκοτισθῇ vb 1st aor pass subj 3rd pers sg . . . . σκοτίζω
σκοτισθήσεται vb fut pass ind 3rd pers sg   id.
σκοτισθήτωσαν vb 1st aor pass impv 3rd pers pl   id.
σκοτοῖ vb pres act ind 3rd pers sg . . . . σκοτόω
σκοτομήνῃ noun fem dat sg . . . . σκοτομήνη
σκότος noun neut nom and acc sg
σκότους noun neut gen sg . . . . σκότος
σκοτωθείη vb 1st aor pass opt 3rd pers sg . . . . σκοτόω
σκύβαλα noun neut nom and acc pl . . . . σκύβαλον
σκυβαλισθῶσιν vb 1st aor pass subj 3rd pers pl σκυβαλίζω
Σκυθοπολῖται pr noun masc nom pl
σκυθρωπά adj neut nom and acc pl . . . . σκυθρωπός
σκυθρωπάζει vb pres act ind 3rd pers sg . . . . σκυθρωπάζω
σκυθρωπάζων vb pres act part masc nom sg   id.
σκυθρωπάσει vb fut act ind 3rd pers sg   id.
σκυθρωπόν adj acc sg, neut nom sg . . . . σκυθρωπός
σκυθρωπῶς adverb
Σκυθῶν pr noun masc gen pl . . . . Σκυθης
σκῦλα noun neut nom and acc pl . . . . σκῦλον
σκυλείαν noun fem acc sg . . . . σκυλεία
σκυλεύειν vb pres act inf . . . . σκυλεύω
σκυλευόντων vb pres act part masc and neut gen pl id.
σκυλεῦσαι vb 1st aor act inf   id.
σκυλεύσαντα vb 1st aor act part neut nom and acc pl id.
σκυλεύσαντας vb 1st aor act part masc acc pl   id.
σκυλεύσει vb fut act ind 3rd pers sg   id.
σκυλεύσετε vb fut act ind 2nd pers pl   id.
σκύλευσον vb 1st aor act impv 2nd pers sg   id.
σκυλεύσουσιν vb fut act ind 3rd pers pl   id.
σκυλμοῖς noun masc dat pl . . . . σκυλμός
σκυλμῶν noun masc gen pl   id.
σκύλοις noun neut dat pl . . . . σκῦλον
σκῦλον noun neut nom and acc sg   id.
σκύλων noun neut gen pl   id.
σκύμνοι noun masc nom pl . . . . σκύμνος
σκύμνοις noun masc dat pl   id.
σκύμνος noun masc nom sg   id.
σκύμνου noun masc gen sg   id.
σκύμνους noun masc acc pl   id.
σκύμνων noun masc gen pl   id.
σκυτάλαις noun fem dat pl . . . . σκυτάλη
σκυτάλας noun fem acc pl   id.
σκυτάλης noun fem gen sg   id.
σκῶλα noun neut nom and acc pl . . . . σκῶλον
σκώληκας noun masc acc pl . . . . σκώληξ
σκώληκες noun masc nom pl   id.

σκώληκι noun masc dat sg	σκώληξ	Σορ pr noun	
σκωλήκων noun masc gen pl	id.	Σορε pr noun	
σκώληξ noun masc nom sg		Σορος pr noun	
σκῶλον noun neut nom and acc sg		σορῷ noun fem dat sg	σορός
σκώπτει vb pres act ind 3rd pers sg	σκώπτω	σός poss pron 2nd pers masc nom sg	
σμαραγδίτου noun masc gen sg	σμαραγδίτης	Σοσομαι pr noun	
σμάραγδον noun fem acc sg	σμάραγδος	σου pers pron 2nd pers gen sg	σύ
σμάραγδος noun fem nom sg	id.	Σουα pr noun	
σμαράγδου noun fem gen sg	id.	Σουαλ pr noun	
σμαράγδῳ noun fem dat sg	id.	Σουβα pr noun	
σμῆγμα noun neut nom and acc sg		Σουβαηλ pr noun	
σμήγμασι noun neut dat pl	σμῆγμα	Σουβαλ pr noun	
σμικρύνῃς vb 1st aor act subj 2nd pers sg,		Σουβας pr noun	
pres act subj 2nd pers sg	σμικρύνω	Σουδ pr noun	
σμικρυνθήσεται vb fut pass ind 3rd pers sg	id.	Σουδι pr noun	
σμικρυνθῆτε vb 1st aor pass subj 2nd pers pl	id.	Σουδιου pr noun masc gen sg	Σουδιας
σμικρυνθῶσιν vb 1st aor pass subj 3rd pers pl	id.	Σουε pr noun	
σμίκρυνον vb 1st aor act impv 2nd pers sg	id.	Σουια pr noun	
σμίλακα noun fem acc sg	σμῖλαξ	Σουλαμῖτις pr noun	
σμῖλαξ noun fem nom sg		Σουμαν pr noun	
σμιρίτης noun masc nom sg		Σουναμ pr noun	
σμύρνα noun fem nom sg		Σουναν pr noun	
σμύρναν noun fem acc sg	σμύρνα	Σουνι pr noun	
σμύρνης noun fem gen sg	id.	Σουρ pr noun	
σμυρνίνῳ adj masc and neut dat sg	σμύρνινος	Σουρι pr noun	
Σοβακ pr noun		Σουριηλ pr noun	
Σοβαλ pr noun		Σουριν pr noun	
Σοβνια pr noun		Σουρισαδαι pr noun	
Σοβοχαι pr noun		Σουσα pr noun	
Σοδομα pr noun neut nom and acc sg		Σουσακιμ pr noun	
Σοδομῖται pr noun masc nom pl	Σοδομίτης	Σουσαν pr noun	
Σοδομιτας pr noun masc acc pl	id.	Σουσαναχαῖοι pr noun	
Σοδομοις pr noun neut dat pl	Σοδομα	Σουσαννα pr noun	
Σοδομων pr noun neut gen pl	id.	Σουσανναν pr noun fem acc sg	Σουσαννα
Σοηνην pr noun fem acc sg	Σοηνη	Σουσαννας pr noun fem gen sg	id.
σοι pers pron 2nd pers dat sg	σύ	Σουσαννης pr noun fem gen sg	Σουσαννη
σοῖς poss pron 2nd pers masc and neut dat pl	σός	Σουσι pr noun	
Σοκχωθ pr noun		Σουσιτου pr noun masc gen sg	Σουσιτης
Σοκχωθα pr noun		Σουσοις pr noun	
Σοκχωθβαινιθ pr noun		Σουσων pr noun	
Σολομῶντος pr noun masc gen sg	Σολομων	Σουταλα pr noun	
Σομα pr noun		Σουταλααμ pr noun	
Σομαρωθ pr noun		Σουταλαϊ pr noun	
Σομε pr noun		Σουτι pr noun	
Σομεα pr noun		Σουφ pr noun	
Σομεϊς pr noun		Σουφι pr noun	
Σομναν pr noun masc acc sg	Σομνας	Σουφιρ pr noun	
Σομνας pr noun masc nom sg		σοφά adj neut nom and acc pl	σοφός
Σομορων pr noun		σοφαί adj fem nom pl	id.
σόν poss pron 2nd pers masc acc sg,		σοφάς adj fem acc pl	id.
neut nom and acc sg	σός	σοφή adj fem nom sg	id.
σοομ translit		σοφήν adj fem acc sg	id.

σοφῆς adj fem gen sg . . . . σοφός
σοφία noun fem nom sg
σοφίᾳ noun fem dat sg . . . . σοφία
σοφίαν noun fem acc sg   id.
σοφίας noun fem gen sg   id.
σοφίζεται vb pres m/p ind 3rd pers sg . . . . . σοφίζω
σοφιζόμενος vb pres m/p part masc nom sg   id.
σοφίζου vb pres m/p impv 2nd pers sg   id.
σοφίζουσα vb pres act part fem nom sg   id.
σοφίσαι vb 1st aor act inf   id.
σοφισθήσεται vb fut pass ind 3rd pers sg   id.
σοφισθήσομαι vb fut pass ind 1st pers sg   id.
σοφισταῖς noun masc dat pl . . . . σοφιστής
σοφιστάς noun masc acc pl   id.
σοφιστῶν noun masc gen pl   id.
σοφοί adj masc nom pl . . . . σοφός
σοφοῖ vb pres act ind 3rd pers sg . . . . σοφόω
σοφοῖς adj masc and neut dat pl . . . . σοφός
σοφόν adj masc acc sg, neut nom and acc sg   id.
Σοφονιαν pr noun masc acc sg . . . . Σοφονιας
Σοφονιας pr noun masc nom sg   id.
Σοφονιου pr noun masc gen sg   id.
σοφός adj masc nom sg
σοφοῦ adj masc and neut gen sg . . . . σοφός
σοφούς adj masc acc pl   id.
σοφῷ adj masc and neut dat sg   id.
σοφῶν adj gen pl   id.
σοφῶς adverb
σοφώτερα comp adj neut nom and acc pl . . . . σοφός
σοφώτερον comp adj masc acc sg, neut nom and acc sg   ic.
σοφώτερος comp adj masc nom sg   ic.
σοφωτέρους comp adj masc acc pl   ic.
Σοχοχα pr noun
σπάδοντας noun masc acc pl . . . . σπάδων
σπάδοντι noun masc dat sg   ic.
σπαίροντας vb pres act part masc acc pl . . . . σπαίρω
σπάνει noun fem dat sg . . . . σπάνις
Σπανιας pr noun gen sg . . . . Σπανια
σπανίζεται vb pres m/p ind 3rd pers sg . . . . σπανίζω
σπάνιον adj masc acc sg, neut nom and acc sg . . . . σπάνιος
σπανίσαι vb 1st aor act inf . . . . σπανίζω
σπαράσσεται vb pres m/p ind 3rd pers sg . . . . . σπαράσσω
σπαργάνοις noun neut dat pl . . . . σπάργανον
σπαρήσεσθε vb fut pass ind 2nd pers pl . . . . . . σπείρω
σπαρήσεται vb fut pass ind 3rd pers sg   id.
Σπαρτης pr noun fem gen sg . . . . Σπαρτη
Σπαρτιάται pr noun masc nom pl . . . . Σπαρτιάτης
Σπαρτιαταις pr noun masc dat pl   id.
Σπαρτιατας pr noun masc acc pl   id.
Σπαρτιατῶν pr noun masc gen pl   id.
σπαρτίον noun neut nom and acc sg
σπαρτίου noun neut gen sg . . . . σπαρτίον

σπάσαι vb 1st aor act inf,
          1st aor mid impv 2nd pers sg . . . . σπάω
σπάσαι see σπάσαι
σπασάμενος vb 1st aor mid part masc nom sg . . . . σπάω
σπάσῃς vb 1st aor act subj 2nd pers sg   id.
σπασμούς noun masc acc pl . . . . σπασμός
σπάσον vb 1st aor act impv 2nd pers sg . . . . σπάω
σπατάλῃ noun fem dat sg . . . . σπατάλη
σπαταλῶν vb pres act part masc nom sg . . . . . . σπαταλάω
σπείραιμι vb 1st aor act opt 1st pers sg . . . . σπείρω
σπείραντες vb 1st aor act part masc nom pl   id.
σπείρας noun fem gen sg and acc pl . . . . σπεῖρα
σπείρατε vb 1st aor act impv 2nd pers pl . . . . σπείρω
σπεῖρε vb pres act impv 2nd pers sg   id.
σπείρει vb pres act ind 3rd pers sg   id.
σπείρεται vb pres m/p ind 3rd pers sg   id.
σπειρηδόν adverb
σπείρῃς vb 1st aor act subj 2nd pers sg,
          pres act subj 2nd pers sg . . . . σπείρω
σπείρητε vb 1st aor act subj 2nd pers pl,
          pres act subj 2nd pers pl   id.
σπειρόμενον vb pres m/p part masc acc sg,
          neut nom and acc sg   id.
σπεῖρον vb pres act part neut nom and acc sg,
          1st aor act impv 2nd pers sg   id.
σπείροντες vb pres act part masc nom pl   id.
σπείροντι vb pres act part masc and neut dat sg id.
σπείρωμεν vb 1st aor act subj 1st pers pl,
          pres act subj 1st pers pl   id.
σπείρων vb pres act part masc nom sg   id.
σπειρῶν noun fem gen pl . . . . σπεῖρα
σπείρωσι(ν) vb 1st aor act subj 3rd pers pl
          pres act subj 3rd pers pl . . . . σπείρω
σπεῖσαι vb 1st aor act inf . . . . σπένδω
σπείσει vb fut act ind 3rd pers sg   id.
σπείσεις vb fut act ind 2nd pers sg   id.
σπένδει vb pres act ind 3rd pers sg   id.
σπένδειν vb pres act inf   id.
σπερεῖ vb fut act ind 3rd pers sg . . . . σπείρω
σπερεῖς vb fut act ind 2nd pers sg   id.
σπερεῖτε vb fut act ind 2nd pers pl   id.
σπέρμα noun neut nom and acc sg
σπέρματα noun neut nom and acc pl . . . . σπέρμα
σπέρματι noun neut dat sg   id.
σπερματίζον vb pres act part
          neut nom and acc sg . . . . σπερματίζω
σπερματισθῇ 1st aor pass subj 3rd pers sg   id.
σπερματισμόν noun masc acc sg . . . . σπερματισμός
σπέρματος noun neut gen sg . . . . σπέρμα
σπερμάτων noun neut gen pl   id.
σπερῶ vb fut act ind 1st pers sg . . . . σπείρω
σπεῦδε vb pres act impv 2nd pers sg . . . . σπεύδω

σπεύδει vb pres act ind 3rd pers sg . . . . σπεύδω
σπεύδειν vb pres act inf   id.
σπεύδοντες pres act part masc nom pl   id.
σπεύδων vb pres act part masc nom sg   id.
σπεύσαντας vb 1st aor act part masc acc pl   id.
σπεύσαντες vb 1st aor act part masc nom pl   id.
σπεύσας vb 1st aor act part masc nom sg   id.
σπεύσασα vb 1st aor act part fem nom sg   id.
σπεύσατε vb 1st aor act impv 2nd pers pl   id.
σπεύσῃς vb 1st aor act subj 2nd pers sg   id.
σπεῦσον vb 1st aor act impv 2nd pers sg   id.
σπεύσουσιν vb fut act ind 3rd pers pl   id.
σπήλαια noun neut nom and acc pl . . . . σπήλαιον
σπηλαίοις noun neut dat pl   id.
σπήλαιον noun neut nom and acc sg   id.
σπηλαίου noun neut gen sg   id.
σπηλαίῳ noun neut dat sg   id.
σπιθαμή noun fem dat sg . . . . σπιθαμή
σπιθαμῆς noun fem gen sg   id.
σπιλωθέν vb 1st aor pass part neut nom and acc sg . . σπιλόω
σπινθήρ noun masc nom sg
σπινθῆρα noun masc acc sg . . . . σπινθήρ
σπινθήρας noun masc acc pl   id.
σπινθῆρες noun masc nom pl   id.
σπινθῆρος noun masc gen sg   id.
σπλάγχνα noun neut nom and acc pl . . . . σπλάγχνον
σπλαγχνίζειν vb pres act inf . . . . σπλαγχνίζω
σπλαγχνισμόν noun masc acc sg . . . . σπλαγχνισμός
σπλαγχνισμούς noun masc acc pl   id.
σπλαγχνισμῷ noun masc dat sg   id.
σπλάγχνοις noun neut dat pl . . . . σπλάγχνον
σπλαγχνοφάγον adj masc acc sg,
            neut nom and acc sg . . . . σπλαγχνοφάγος
σπλάγχνων noun neut gen pl . . . . σπλάγχνον
σποδιάν noun fem acc sg . . . . σποδιά
σποδιᾶς noun fem gen sg   id.
σποδοειδεῖς adj masc and fem nom and acc pl . . σποδοειδής
σποδοειδῆ adj neut nom and acc pl   id.
σποδόν noun fem acc sg . . . . σποδός
σποδός noun fem nom sg   id.
σποδοῦ noun fem gen sg   id.
σποδῷ noun fem dat sg   id.
σπονδαί noun fem nom pl . . . . σπονδή
σπονδάς noun fem acc pl   id.
σπονδεῖα noun neut nom and acc pl . . . . σπονδεῖον
σπονδείου noun neut gen sg   id.
σπονδείων noun neut gen pl   id.
σπονδή noun fem nom sg
σπονδήν noun fem acc sg . . . . σπονδή
σπονδύλων noun masc gen pl . . . . σπόνδυλος
σπονδῶν noun fem gen pl . . . . σπονδή
σπορά noun fem nom sg

σπορᾶς noun fem gen sg . . . . σπορά
σπόριμον adj acc sg, neut nom sg . . . . σπόριμος
σπορίμου adj gen sg   id.
σπόρον noun masc acc sg . . . . σπόρος
σπόρος noun masc nom sg   id.
σπόρου noun masc gen sg   id.
σπόρῳ noun masc dat sg   id.
σπουδαί noun fem nom pl . . . . σπουδή
σπουδαῖα adj neut nom and acc pl . . . . σπουδαῖος
σπουδαιότητι noun fem dat sg . . . . σπουδαιότης
σπουδαίως adverb
σπουδάσῃς vb 1st aor act subj 2nd pers sg . . . . . σπουδάζω
σπουδή noun fem nom sg
σπουδῇ noun fem dat sg . . . . σπουδή
σπουδήν noun fem acc sg   id.
σπουδῆς noun fem gen sg   id.
σπώμενοι vb pres m/p part masc nom pl . . . . σπάω
σπωμένων vb pres m/p part gen pl   id.
σπῶνται vb pres m/p ind 3rd pers pl   id.
σταγόνας noun fem acc pl . . . . σταγών
σταγόνες noun fem nom pl   id.
σταγόνος noun fem gen sg   id.
σταγόσιν noun fem dat pl   id.
σταγών noun fem nom sg   id.
στάδιον noun neut nom and acc sg
σταδίους noun neut nom and acc pl . . . . στάδιον
σταδίων noun neut gen pl   id.
στάξοι vb pres act opt 3rd pers sg . . . . στάζω
στάζοντα vb pres act part neut nom and acc pl   id.
στάζουσαι vb pres act part fem nom pl   id.
σταθέν vb 1st aor pass part neut nom and acc sg . . . . . ἵστημι
σταθῇ vb 1st aor pass subj 3rd pers sg   id.
σταθήσεται vb fut pass ind 3rd pers sg   id.
σταθήσονται vb fut pass ind 3rd pers pl   id.
σταθῆτε vb 1st aor pass subj 2nd pers pl   id.
στάθμια noun neut nom and acc pl . . . . στάθμιον
σταθμίοις noun neut dat pl   id.
στάθμιον noun neut nom and acc sg   id.
σταθμίων noun neut gen pl   id.
σταθμοί noun masc nom pl . . . . σταθμός
σταθμοῖς noun masc dat pl   id.
σταθμόν noun masc acc sg   id.
σταθμός noun masc nom sg   id.
σταθμοῦ noun masc gen sg   id.
σταθμούς noun masc acc pl   id.
σταθμῷ noun masc dat sg   id.
σταθμῶν noun masc gen pl   id.
σταῖς noun neut nom and acc sg
στακτή noun fem nom sg
στακτήν noun fem acc sg . . . . στακτή
στακτῆς noun fem gen sg   id.
σταλαγμοῖς noun masc dat pl . . . . σταλαγμός

στάμνον noun masc acc sg	....	στάμνος
στάντες vb 2nd aor act part masc nom pl	....	ἵστημι
στάξαι vb 1st aor act inf	....	στάζω
στάξει vb fut act ind 3rd pers sg		id.
στάξῃ vb 1st aor act subj 3rd pers sg		id.
στάς vb 2nd aor act part masc nom sg	....	ἵστημι
στᾶσα vb 2nd aor act part fem nom sg		id.
στᾶσαι vb 2nd aor act part fem nom pl		id.
στάσει noun fem dat sg	....	στάσις
στάσεως noun fem gen sg		id.
στασιάζειν vb pres act inf	....	στασιάζω
στασιάζουσιν vb pres act ind 3rd pers pl		id.
στασίμη adj fem dat sg	....	στάσιμος
στάσιν noun fem acc sg	....	στάσις
στάσις noun fem nom sg		id.
σταυρωθήτω vb 1st aor pass impv 3rd pers sg	....	σταυρόω
σταφίδα noun fem acc sg	....	σταφίς
σταφίδας noun fem acc pl		id.
σταφίδες noun fem nom pl		id.
σταφίδος noun fem gen sg		id.
σταφίδων noun fem gen pl		id.
σταφυλή noun fem nom sg		
σταφυλήν noun fem acc sg	....	σταφυλή
σταφυλῆς noun fem gen sg		id.
στάχυας noun masc acc pl	....	στάχυς
στάχυες noun masc nom pl		id.
στάχυν noun masc acc sg		id.
στάχυς noun masc nom sg		id.
στάχυσι noun masc dat pl		id.
σταχύων noun masc gen pl		id.
στέαρ noun neut nom and acc sg		
στέασι noun neut dat pl	....	στέαρ
στέατα noun neut nom and acc pl		id.
στέατι noun neut dat sg		id.
στέατος noun neut gen sg		id.
στεάτων noun neut gen pl		id.
στεγάζων vb pres act part masc nom sg	....	στεγάζω
στέγας noun fem acc pl	....	στέγη
στεγάσαι vb 1st aor act inf	....	στεγάζω
στέγη noun fem nom sg		
στέγην noun fem acc sg	....	στέγη
στεγναί adj fem nom pl	....	στεγνός
στεῖρα noun fem nom sg		
στεῖραν noun fem acc sg	....	στεῖρα
στειρωθῇ vb 1st aor pass subj 3rd pers sg	....	στειρόω
στελέχη noun neut nom and acc pl	....	στέλεχος
στέλεχος noun neut nom and acc sg		id.
στελεχῶν noun neut gen pl		id.
στέλλεσθαι vb pres m/p inf	....	στέλλω
στελλομένοις vb pres m/p part masc and neut dat pl		id.
στελλόμενος vb pres m/p part masc nom sg		id.
στεμφύλων noun neut gen pl	....	στεμφυλόν

στενά adj neut nom and acc pl	....	στενός
στεναγμοί noun masc nom pl	....	στεναγμός
στεναγμοῖς noun masc dat pl		id.
στεναγμόν noun masc acc sg		id.
στεναγμός noun masc nom sg		id.
στεναγμοῦ noun masc gen sg		id.
στεναγμῷ noun masc dat sg		id.
στεναγμῶν noun masc gen pl		id.
στενάζεις vb pres act ind 2nd pers sg	....	στενάζω
στενάζουσα vb pres act part fem nom sg		id.
στενάζω vb pres act ind 1st pers sg		id.
στενάζων vb pres act part masc nom sg		id.
στενακτή adj fem nom sg	....	στενακτός
στενάξαι vb 1st aor act inf	....	στενάζω
στενάξας vb 1st aor act part masc nom sg		id.
στενάξατε vb 1st aor act impv 2nd pers pl		id.
στενάξει vb fut act ind 3rd pers sg		id.
στενάξεις vb fut act ind 2nd pers sg		id.
στενάξῃς vb 1st aor act subj 2nd pers sg		id.
στενάξονται vb fut mid ind 3rd pers pl		id.
στενάξουσιν vb fut act ind 3rd pers pl		id.
στενάξω vb fut act ind 1st pers sg		id.
στενή adj fem nom sg	....	στενός
στενῇ adj fem dat sg		id.
στενήν adj fem acc sg		id.
στενῆς adj fem gen sg		id.
στενοῖς adj masc and neut dat pl		id.
στενόν adj masc acc sg, neut nom and acc sg		id.
στενός adj masc nom sg		id.
στενότητα noun fem acc sg	....	στενότης
στένουσι(ν) vb pres act ind 3rd pers pl	....	στένω
στενοχωρεῖ vb pres act ind 3rd pers sg	......	στενοχωρέω
στενοχωρήσει vb fut act ind 3rd pers sg		id.
στενοχωρία noun fem nom sg		
στενοχωρίᾳ noun fem dat sg	....	στενοχωρία
στενοχωρίαν noun fem acc sg		id.
στενοχωρίας noun fem gen sg		id.
στενοχωρούμενοι vb pres m/p part masc nom pl	....	στενοχωρέω
στενοχωρούμενος vb pres m/p part masc nom sg		id.
στενῷ adj masc and neut dat sg	....	στενός
στενῶν vb pres act part masc nom sg	....	στένω
στενῶς adverb		
στέξαι vb 1st aor act inf	....	στέγω
στερεά adj fem nom sg, neut nom and acc pl	.....	στερεός
στερεᾷ adj fem dat sg		id.
στερεάν adj fem acc sg		id.
στερεᾶς adj fem gen sg		id.
στερεῖσθαι vb pres m/p inf	....	στερέω
στερεόν adj masc acc sg, neut nom and acc sg	....	στερεός
στερεωθήσεται vb fut pass ind 3rd pers sg	......	στερεόω
στερέωμα noun neut nom and acc sg		

στερεώματι	noun neut dat sg	....	στερέωμα
στερεώματος	noun neut gen sg		id.
στερεῶν	adj gen pl	....	στερεός
στερεῶν	vb pres act part masc nom sg	....	στερεόω
στερεώσαντι	vb 1st aor act part		
	masc and neut dat sg		id.
στερεώσας	vb 1st aor act part masc nom sg		id.
στερεώσεις	vb fut act ind 2nd pers sg		id.
στερέωσιν	noun fem acc sg	....	στερέωσις
στερέωσον	vb 1st aor act impv 2nd pers sg	......	στερεόω
στερεωτέρων	comp adj gen pl	....	στερεός
στερηθεῖσαν	vb 1st aor pass part fem acc sg	......	στερέω
στερηθῆναι	vb 1st aor pass inf		id.
στερηθήσονται	vb fut pass ind 3rd pers pl		id.
στερῆσαι	vb 1st aor act inf		id.
στερήσει	vb fut act ind 3rd pers sg		id.
στερήσῃς	vb 1st aor act subj 2nd pers sg		id.
στερίσκω	vb pres act ind 1st pers sg		
στέρνοις	noun neut dat pl	....	στέρνον
στέρξον	vb 1st aor act impv 2nd pers sg	....	στέργω
στεφάνη	noun fem dat sg	....	στεφάνη
στεφάνην	noun fem acc sg		id.
στεφανηφοροῦσα	vb pres act part		
	fem nom sg	....	στεφανηφορέω
στεφάνοις	noun masc dat pl	....	στέφανος
στέφανον	noun masc acc sg		id.
στέφανος	noun masc nom sg		id.
στεφάνου	noun masc gen sg		id.
στεφανοῦντα	vb pres act part masc acc sg	......	στεφανόω
στεφάνους	noun masc acc pl	....	στέφανος
στεφανοῦσα	vb pres act part fem nom sg	......	στεφανόω
στεφάνῳ	noun masc dat sg	....	στέφανος
στεφανωθήσεται	vb fut pass ind 3rd pers sg	....	στεφανόω
στεφάνων	noun masc gen pl	....	στέφανος
στεφέων	noun neut gen pl	....	στέφος
στεψώμεθα	vb 1st aor mid subj 1st pers pl	....	στέφω
στῇ	vb 2nd aor act subj 3rd pers sg	....	ἵστημι
στήθει	noun neut dat sg	....	στῆθος
στηθέων	noun neut gen pl		id.
στήθη	noun neut nom and acc pl		id.
στῆθι	vb 2nd aor act impv 2nd pers sg	....	ἵστημι
στηθοδεσμίδα	noun fem acc sg	....	στηθοδεσμίς
στῆθος	noun neut nom and acc sg		
στήθους	noun neut gen sg	....	στῆθος
στηθύνια	noun neut nom and acc pl	....	στηθύνιον
στηθύνιον	noun neut nom and acc sg		id.
στηθυνίου	noun neut gen sg		id.
στήκει	vb pres act ind 3rd pers sg	....	στήκω
στῆλαι	noun fem nom pl	....	στήλη
στήλαις	noun fem dat pl		id.
στήλας	noun fem acc pl		id.
στήλη	noun fem nom sg		

στήλῃ	noun fem dat sg	....	στήλη
στήλην	noun fem acc sg		id.
στηλογραφία	noun fem nom sg		
στηλογραφίαν	noun fem acc sg	....	στηλογραφία
στηλώθητι	vb 1st aor pass impv 2nd pers sg	......	στηλόω
στήλωσον	vb 1st aor act impv 2nd pers sg		id.
στήμονα	noun masc acc sg	....	στήμων
στήμονι	noun masc dat sg		id.
στήμονος	noun masc gen sg		id.
στήμων	noun masc nom sg		id.
στῆναι	vb 2nd aor act inf	....	ἵστημι
στήρ	noun neut nom and acc sg		
στήριγμα	noun neut nom and acc sg		
στηρίγματος	noun neut gen sg	....	στήριγμα
στηριγμάτων	noun neut gen pl		id.
στηριεῖ	vb fut act ind 3rd pers sg	....	στηρίζω
στηρίζει	vb pres act ind 3rd pers sg		id.
στηρίζεται	vb pres m/p ind 3rd pers sg		id.
στηρίζουσιν	vb pres act ind 3rd pers pl		id.
στηρίζων	vb pres act part masc nom sg		id.
στηρίσαι	vb 1st aor act inf		id.
στηρίσατε	vb 1st aor act impv 2nd pers pl		id.
στηρίσει	vb fut act ind 3rd pers sg		id.
στήρισον	vb 1st aor act impv 2nd pers sg		id.
στηρίσουσιν	vb fut act ind 3rd pers pl		id.
στηριχθῇ	vb 1st aor pass subj 3rd pers sg		id.
στηριχθῆναι	vb 1st aor pass inf		id.
στηριχθήσεται	vb fut pass ind 3rd pers sg		id.
στηριῶ	vb fut act ind 1st pers sg		id.
στῇς	vb 2nd aor act subj 2nd pers sg	....	ἵστημι
στῆσαι	vb 1st aor act opt 3rd pers sg		id.
στῆσαι	vb 1st aor act inf		id.
στήσαντας	vb 1st aor act part masc acc pl		id.
στήσαντες	vb 1st aor act part masc nom pl		id.
στήσαντος	vb 1st aor act part masc and neut gen sg		id.
στήσας	vb 1st aor act part masc nom sg		id.
στήσατε	vb 1st aor act impv 2nd pers pl		id.
στήσει	vb fut act ind 3rd pers sg		id.
στήσειν	vb fut act inf		id.
στήσεις	vb fut act ind 2nd pers sg		id.
στήσεσθε	vb fut mid ind 2nd pers pl		id.
στήσεται	vb fut mid ind 3rd pers sg		id.
στήσετε	vb fut act ind 2nd pers pl		id.
στήσῃ	vb 1st aor act subj 3rd pers sg,		
	fut mid ind 2nd pers sg		id.
στήσῃς	vb 1st aor act subj 2nd pers sg		id.
στήσητε	vb 1st aor act subj 2nd pers pl		id.
στήσομαι	vb fut mid ind 1st pers sg		id.
στησόμεθα	vb fut mid ind 1st pers pl		id.
στήσομεν	vb fut act ind 1st pers pl		id.
στήσον	vb 1st aor act impv 2nd pers sg		id.
στήσονται	vb fut mid ind 3rd pers pl		id.

στήσουσιν   vb fut act ind 3rd pers pl . . . . ἵστημι

στήσω   vb 1st aor act subj 1st pers sg,

     fut act ind 1st pers sg   id.

στήσωμεν   vb 1st aor act subj 1st pers pl   id.

στῆτε   vb 2nd aor act impv 2nd pers pl,

     2nd aor act subj 2nd pers pl   id.

στήτω   vb 2nd aor act impv 3rd pers sg   id.

στήτωσαν   vb 2nd aor act impv 3rd pers pl   id.

στιβαρούς   adj masc acc pl . . . . στιβαρός

στιβαρῶς   adverb

στίβι   noun neut dat sg . . . . στίβι

στιγμάτων   noun neut gen pl . . . . στίγμα

στιγμή   noun fem nom sg

στιγμήν   noun fem acc sg . . . . στιγμή

στικτά   adj neut nom and acc pl . . . . στικτός

στίλβῃς   vb pres act subj 2nd pers sg . . . . στίλβω

στίλβοντα   vb pres act part neut nom and acc pl   id.

στίλβοντος   vb pres act part masc and neut gen sg   id.

στιλβούσης   vb pres act part fem gen sg   id.

στιλβώσει   vb fut act ind 3rd pers sg . . . . στιλβόω

στίλβωσιν   noun fem acc sg . . . . στίλβωσις

στίλψωσιν   vb 1st aor act subj 3rd pers pl . . . . στίλβω

στιππυΐνου   noun neut gen sg . . . . στιππύϊνος

στιππυΐνῳ   noun neut dat sg   id.

στιππύον   noun neut nom and acc sg

στιππύου   noun neut gen sg . . . . στιππύον

στίχοι   noun masc nom pl . . . . στίχος

στίχον   noun masc acc sg   id.

στίχος   noun masc nom sg   id.

στίχους   noun masc acc pl   id.

στίχων   noun masc gen pl   id.

στοαί   noun fem nom pl . . . . στοά

στοιβάσατε   vb 1st aor act impv 2nd pers pl . . . . . στοιβάζω

στοιβάσει   vb fut act ind 3rd pers sg   id.

στοιβῆς   noun fem gen sg . . . . στοιβή

στοιχεῖα   noun neut nom and acc pl . . . . στοιχεῖον

στοιχείων   noun neut gen pl   id.

στοιχείωσιν   noun fem acc sg . . . . στοιχείωσις

στοιχήσει   vb fut act ind 3rd pers sg . . . . στοιχέω

στολαί   noun fem nom pl . . . . στολή

στολαῖς   noun fem dat pl   id.

στολάς   noun fem acc pl   id.

στολή   noun fem nom sg   id.

στολῇ   noun fem dat sg   id.

στολήν   noun fem acc sg   id.

στολῆς   noun fem gen sg   id.

στολιεῖ   vb fut act ind 3rd pers sg . . . . στολίζω

στολίσαι   vb 1st aor act inf   id.

στολισάτω   vb 1st aor act impv 3rd pers sg   id.

στολισμόν   noun masc acc sg . . . . στολισμός

στολισμός   noun masc nom sg   id.

στολισμοῦ   noun masc gen sg   id.

στολιστής   noun masc nom sg

στολιῶ   vb fut act ind 1st pers sg . . . . στολίζω

στόλος   noun masc nom sg

στόλου   noun masc gen sg . . . . στόλος

στόλῳ   noun masc dat sg   id.

στόμα   noun neut nom and acc sg

στόμασι   noun neut dat pl . . . . στόμα

στόματα   noun neut nom and acc pl   id.

στόματι   noun neut dat sg   id.

στόματος   noun neut gen sg   id.

στόμωμα   noun neut nom and acc sg

στοργή   noun fem nom sg

στοργῇ   noun fem dat sg . . . . στοργή

στοργήν   noun fem acc sg   id.

στοχαζόμενος   vb pres dep part masc nom sg . . στοχάζομαι

στόχασαι   vb 1st aor mid impv 2nd pers sg   id.

στοχάσασθαι   vb 1st aor mid inf   id.

στοχαστήν   noun masc acc sg . . . . στοχαστής

στραγγαλιάς   noun fem acc pl   id.

στραγγαλίδων   noun fem gen pl . . . . στραγγαλίς

στραγγαλῶδες   adj neut nom and acc sg . . . . στραγγαλώδης

στραγγιεῖ   vb fut act ind 3rd pers sg . . . . στραγγίζω

στρατείαν   noun fem acc sg . . . . στρατεία

στρατεύεσθαι   vb pres m/p inf . . . . στρατεύω

στρατεύθητι   vb 1st aor pass impv 2nd pers sg   id.

στράτευμα   noun neut nom and acc sg

στρατεύμασι   noun neut dat pl . . . . στράτευμα

στρατεύματος   noun neut gen sg   id.

στρατευμάτων   noun neut gen pl   id.

στρατεύομαι   vb pres m/p ind 1st pers sg . . . . στρατεύω

στρατεύονται   vb pres m/p ind 3rd pers pl   id.

στρατευσάμενοι   vb 1st aor mid part masc nom pl   id.

στρατεύσασθε   vb 1st aor mid impv 2nd pers pl   id.

στράτευσον   vb 1st aor act impv 2nd pers sg   id.

στρατηγήματι   noun neut dat sg . . . . στρατήγημα

στρατηγίαν   noun fem acc sg . . . . στρατηγία

στρατηγοί   noun masc nom pl . . . . στρατηγός

στρατηγοῖς   noun masc dat pl   id.

στρατηγόν   noun masc acc sg   id.

στρατηγός   noun masc nom sg   id.

στρατηγοῦ   noun masc gen sg   id.

στρατηγοῦντος   vb pres act part

     masc and neut gen sg . . . . στρατηγέω

στρατηγούς   noun masc acc pl . . . . στρατηγός

στρατηγῶν   noun masc gen pl   id.

στρατιά   noun fem nom sg

στρατιᾷ   noun fem dat sg . . . . στρατιά

στρατιαί   noun fem nom pl   id.

στρατιάν   noun fem acc sg   id.

στρατιᾶς   noun fem gen sg   id.

στρατιῶται   noun masc nom pl . . . . στρατιώτης

στρατιώταις   noun masc dat pl   id.

στρατιώτας noun masc acc pl . . . . στρατιώτης
στρατιῶτι noun fem voc sg . . . . στρατιῶτις
στρατιωτῶν noun masc gen pl . . . . στρατιώτης
στρατοκῆρυξ noun masc nom sg
στρατόν noun masc acc sg . . . . στρατός
στρατοπεδείᾳ noun fem dat sg . . . . στρατοπεδεία
στρατοπεδείαν noun fem acc sg   id.
στρατοπεδευσάτωσαν vb 1st aor act impv
            3rd pers pl . . . . στρατοπεδεύω
στρατοπεδεύσεις vb fut act ind 2nd pers sg   id.
στρατοπεδεύσωσιν vb 1st aor act subj 3rd pers pl   id.
στρατόπεδον noun neut nom and acc sg
στρατοπέδου noun neut gen sg . . . . στρατόπεδον
στρατοπέδῳ noun neut dat sg   id.
στρατός noun masc nom sg
στρατοῦ noun masc gen sg . . . . στρατός
στραφεῖσαν vb 2nd aor pass part fem acc sg . . . . . . στρέφω
στραφέντος vb 2nd aor pass part masc and neut gen sg   id.
στραφῇ 2nd aor pass subj 3rd pers sg   id.
στραφῇς 2nd aor pass subj 2nd pers sg   id.
στραφήσεται vb vb fut pass ind 3rd pers sg   id.
στραφήσῃ vb fut pass ind 2nd pers sg   id.
στραφήσονται vb fut pass ind 3rd pers pl   id.
στρέβλαι noun fem nom pl . . . . στρέβλη
στρέβλαις noun fem dat pl   id.
στρέβλαν noun fem acc sg . . . . στρέβλα
στρέβλας noun fem acc pl . . . . στρέβλη
στρεβλή adj fem nom sg . . . . στρεβλός
στρέβλῃ noun fem dat sg . . . . στρέβλη
στρεβλόν adj masc acc sg, neut nom and acc sg . . στρεβλός
στρεβλοῦ adj masc and neut gen sg   id.
στρεβλούμενον vb pres m/p part masc acc sg . . . στρεβλόω
στρεβλοῦτε vb pres act impv 2nd pers pl   id.
στρεβλωθέντας vb 1st aor pass part masc acc pl   id.
στρεβλωθέντες vb 1st aor pass part masc nom pl   id.
στρεβλωθήσῃ vb fut pass ind 2nd pers sg   id.
στρεβλῶν noun fem gen pl . . . . στρέβλη
στρεβλῶσαι vb 1st aor act inf . . . . στρεβλόω
στρεβλωτήρια noun neut nom and acc pl . στρεβλωτήριον
στρέμμα noun neut nom and acc sg
στρεπτά adj neut nom and acc pl . . . . στρεπτός
στρεπτήν adj fem acc sg   id.
στρεπτόν adj masc acc sg, neut nom and acc sg   id.
στρεπτῶν adj gen pl   id.
στρέφεται vb pres m/p ind 3rd pers sg . . . . στρέφω
στρεφόμενα vb pres m/p part neut nom and acc pl   id.
στρεφομένη vb pres m/p part fem nom sg   id.
στρεφομένην vb pres m/p part fem acc sg   id.
στρεφόμενος vb pres m/p part masc nom sg   id.
στρέψαντος vb 1st aor act part masc and neut gen sg   id.
στρέψει vb fut act ind 3rd pers sg   id.
στρέψον vb 1st aor act impv 2nd pers sg   id.

στρέψω vb fut act ind 1st pers sg . . . . στρέφω
στρῆνος noun neut nom and acc sg
στρίφνος noun masc nom sg
στροβείτω vb pres act impv 3rd pers sg . . . . στροβέω
στροβήσει vb fut act ind 3rd pers sg   id.
στρογγύλην adj fem acc sg . . . . στρογγύλος
στρογγύλον adj masc acc sg, neut nom and acc sg   id.
στρουθία noun neut nom and acc pl . . . . στρουθίον
στρουθίον noun neut nom and acc sg   id.
στρουθίου noun neut gen sg   id.
στρουθοί noun masc nom pl . . . . στρουθός
στρουθόν noun masc acc sg   id.
στρουθῶν noun masc gen pl   id.
στροφαῖς noun fem dat pl . . . . στροφή
στροφάς noun fem acc pl   id.
στροφεῖς noun masc nom and acc pl . . . . στροφεύς
στροφῆς noun fem gen sg . . . . στροφή
στρόφιγγος noun masc gen sg . . . . στρόφιγξ
στρόφος noun masc nom sg
στροφωτοῖς adj masc and neut dat pl . . . . στροφωτός
στρῶμα noun neut nom and acc sg
στρωμναί noun fem nom pl . . . . στρωμνή
στρωμναῖς noun fem dat pl   id.
στρωμνή noun fem nom sg   id.
στρωμνήν noun fem acc sg   id.
στρωμνῆς noun fem gen sg   id.
στρώσουσιν vb fut act ind 3rd pers pl . . . . στρωννύω
στυγνάσουσιν vb fut act ind 3rd pers pl . . . . στυγνάζω
στυγνήν adj fem acc sg . . . . στυγνός
στυγνός adj masc nom sg   id.
στυγούμενος vb pres m/p part masc nom sg . . . . . . στυγέω
στυγοῦντες vb pres act part masc nom pl   id.
στύλοι noun masc nom pl . . . . στῦλος
στύλοις noun masc dat pl   id.
στῦλον noun masc acc sg   id.
στῦλος noun masc nom sg   id.
στύλου noun masc gen sg   id.
στύλους noun masc acc pl   id.
στύλῳ noun masc dat sg   id.
στύλων noun masc gen pl   id.
στυρακίνην adj fem acc sg . . . . στυράκινος
σύ pron of 2nd pers nom sg
Συβαΐ pr noun
συγγελάσῃς vb 1st aor act subj 2nd pers sg . . . . . συγγελάω
συγγενεῖ adj dat sg . . . . συγγενής
συγγένεια noun fem nom sg
συγγενείᾳ noun fem dat sg . . . . συγγένεια
συγγένειαν noun fem acc sg   id.
συγγενείας noun fem gen sg   id.
συγγενεῖς adj masc and fem nom and acc pl . . . . . συγγενής
συγγενειῶν noun fem gen pl . . . . συγγένεια
συγγενέσθαι vb 2nd aor mid inf . . . . συγγίνομαι

συγγενέσι adj dat pl . . . . συγγενής
συγγενής adj masc and fem nom sg . . . . id.
συγγενοῦς adj gen sg . . . . id.
συγγενώμεθα vb 2nd aor mid subj 1st pers pl . . συγγίνομαι
συγγενῶν adj gen pl . . . . συγγενής
συγγινομένους vb pres dep part masc acc pl . . συγγίνομαι
συγγνούς vb 2nd aor act part masc nom sg . . . . συγγινώσκω
συγγνώμην noun fem acc sg . . . . συγγνώμη
συγγνωμονήσειεν vb 1st aor act opt

    3rd pers sg . . . . συγγνωμονέω
συγγνώσεται vb fut mid ind 3rd pers sg . . . . συγγινώσκω
συγγνωστοί adj masc nom pl . . . . συγγνωστός
συγγνωστός adj masc nom sg . . . . id.
συγγραφαί noun fem nom pl . . . . συγγραφή
συγγραφαῖς noun fem dat pl . . . . id.
συγγραφεῖ noun masc dat sg . . . . συγγραφεύς
συγγραφήν noun fem acc sg . . . . συγγραφή
συγγράψαι vb 1st aor act inf . . . . συγγράφω
συγγυμνασία noun fem dat sg . . . . συγγυμνασία
συγκαθῆσθαι vb 1st aor act inf . . . . συγκάθημαι
συγκαθίσαι vb pres mid inf . . . . συγκαθίζω
συγκαθυφασμένα vb perf m/p part

    neut nom and acc pl . . . . συγκαθυφαίνω
συγκαίει vb pres act ind 3rd pers sg . . . . συγκαίω
συγκαιόμενος vb pres m/p part masc nom sg . . . . . id.
συγκαίοντι vb pres act part masc and neut dat sg . . . . id.
συγκαλέσας vb 1st aor act part masc nom sg . . . . συγκαλέω
συγκαλέσετε vb fut act ind 2nd pers pl . . . . id.
συγκαλοῦσα vb pres act part fem nom sg . . . . id.
συγκάλυμμα noun neut nom and acc sg
συγκαλύπτει vb pres act ind 3rd pers sg . . . . συγκαλύπτω
συγκαλύπτον vb pres act part neut nom and acc sg . . . id.
συγκαλύψαι vb 1st aor act inf . . . . id.
συγκαλύψει vb fut act ind 3rd pers sg . . . . id.
συγκαλύψεις vb fut act ind 2nd pers sg . . . . id.
συγκαλύψομαι vb fut mid ind 1st pers sg . . . . id.
συγκαλύψουσιν vb fut act ind 3rd pers pl . . . . id.
συγκαλῶ vb pres act ind 1st pers sg . . . . συγκαλέω
συγκάμψας vb 1st aor act part masc nom sg . . . συγκαμπτω
σύγκαμψον vb 1st aor act impv 2nd pers sg . . . . . . id.
συγκαταβήσεται vb fut mid ind

    3rd pers sg . . . . συγκαταβαίνω
συγκαταγηρᾶσαι vb 1st aor act inf . . . συγκαταγηράσκω
συγκαταθήσῃ vb fut mid ind 2nd pers sg . συγκατατίθημι
συγκατάθου vb 2nd aor mid impv 2nd pers sg . . . . . id.
συγκατακληρονομηθήσονται vb fut pass ind

    3rd pers pl . . . . συγκατακληρονομέομαι
συγκαταμιγῆτε vb 2nd aor pass subj

    2nd pers pl . . . . συγκαταμίγνυμι
συγκαταφάγεται vb fut mid ind 3rd pers sg . συγκατεσθίω
συγκαταφερομένη vb pres m/p part

    fem nom sg . . . . συγκαταφέρω

συγκατέβη vb 2nd aor act ind 3rd pers sg . . συγκαταβαίνω
συγκαυθήσεται vb fut pass ind 3rd pers sg . . . . . συγκαίω
συγκαύσει vb fut act ind 3rd pers sg . . . . id.
σύγκεισθε vb pres m/p ind 2nd pers pl . . . . σύγκειμαι
σύγκειται vb pres m/p ind 3rd pers sg . . . . id.
συγκεκαλυμμένος vb perf m/p part

    masc nom sg . . . . συγκαλύπτω
συγκεκαυται vb perf m/p ind 3rd pers sg . . . . . . συγκαίω
συγκεκλεικεν vb perf act ind 3rd pers sg . . . . . . συγκλείω
συγκεκλεικότας vb perf act part masc acc pl . . . . . id.
συγκεκλεῖσθαι vb perf m/p inf . . . . id.
συγκεκλεισμένα vb perf m/p part neut nom and acc pl . . id.
συγκεκλεισμένη vb perf m/p part fem nom sg . . . . . id.
συγκεκλεισμένῳ vb perf m/p part masc and neut dat sg . . id.
συγκεκυφὼς vb perf act part masc nom sg . . . . . . συγκύπτω
συγκεντῶν vb pres act part masc nom sg . . . . . . συγκεντέω
συγκερασθείς vb 1st aor pass part

    masc nom sg . . . . συγκεράννυμι
συγκερατισθήσεται vb fut pass ind

    3rd pers sg . . . . συγκερατίζομαι
συγκεχυμένος vb perf m/p part masc nom sg . . . . . συγχέω
συγκλάσει vb fut act ind 3rd pers sg . . . . συγκλάω
συγκλασμόν noun masc acc sg . . . . συγκλασμός
συγκλάσω vb fut act ind 1st pers sg . . . . συγκλάω
συγκλειομένας vb pres m/p part fem acc pl . . . . . συγκλείω
συγκλειόμενοι vb pres m/p part masc nom pl . . . . . id.
συγκλείοντα vb pres act part masc acc sg . . . . id.
συγκλείοντες vb pres act part masc nom pl . . . . . . id.
συγκλεῖσαι vb 1st aor act inf . . . . id.
συγκλείσαντες vb 1st aor act part masc nom pl . . . . id.
συγκλείσεις vb fut act ind 2nd pers sg . . . . id.
συγκλείσῃς vb 1st aor act subj 2nd pers sg . . . . . . id.
συγκλεισθεντος vb 1st aor pass part

    masc and neut gen sg . . . . id.
συγκλεισθῆναι vb 1st aor pass inf . . . . id.
συγκλεισθήσεται vb fut pass ind 3rd pers sg . . . . . id.
συγκλεισθήσονται vb fut pass ind 3rd pers pl . . . . id.
συγκλείσματα noun neut nom and acc pl . . . . σύγκλεισμα
συγκλεισμόν noun masc acc sg . . . . συγκλεισμός
συγκλεισμοῦ noun masc gen sg . . . . id.
συγκλεισμῷ noun masc dat sg . . . . id.
συγκλεισμῶν noun masc gen pl . . . . id.
σύγκλεισον vb 1st aor act impv 2nd pers sg . . . . . συγκλείω
σύγκλειστα adj neut nom and acc pl . . . . σύγκλειστος
σύγκλειστον adj neut nom and acc sg . . . . id.
συγκλείων vb pres act part masc nom sg . . . . συγκλείω
συγκληρονομήσῃς vb 1st aor act subj

    2nd pers sg . . . . συγκληρονομέω
σύγκλητοι adj masc and fem nom pl . . . . σύγκλητος
συγκλύσουσιν vb fut act ind 3rd pers pl . . . . . . συγκλύζω
συγκοίτου noun masc or fem gen sg . . . . σύγκοιτος
συγκολλῶν vb pres act part masc nom sg . . . . . συγκολλάω

συγκομισθεῖσα   vb 1st aor pass part

     fem nom sg .... συγκομίζω

συγκόπτειν   vb pres act inf .... συγκόπτω

συγκόψαι   vb 1st aor act inf   id.

συγκόψατε   vb 1st aor act impv 2nd pers pl   id.

συγκόψεις   vb fut act ind 2nd pers sg   id.

συγκόψουσιν   vb fut act ind 3rd pers pl   id.

συγκόψω   vb fut act ind 1st pers sg   id.

συγκραθῆναι   vb 1st aor pass inf .... συγκεράννυμι

σύγκρασιν   noun fem acc sg .... σύγκρασις

συγκριθῶμεν   vb 1st aor pass subj 1st pers pl .... συγκρίνω

σύγκριμα   noun neut nom and acc sg

συγκρίματα   noun neut nom and acc pl .... σύγκριμα

συγκρίματος   noun neut gen sg   id.

συγκρῖναι   vb 1st aor act inf .... συγκρίνω

συγκρινόμενα   vb pres m/p part neut nom and acc pl   id.

συγκρινομένη   vb pres m/p part fem nom sg   id.

συγκρίνων   vb pres act part masc nom sg   id.

συγκρίσει   noun fem dat sg .... σύγκρισις

σύγκρισιν   noun fem acc sg   id.

σύγκρισις   noun fem nom sg   id.

συγκρουσμοῦ   noun masc gen sg .... συγκρουσμός

συγκρύψων   vb 2nd aor act part masc nom sg ... συγκρύπτω

συγκυροῦντα   vb pres act part

     neut nom and acc pl .... συγκυρόω

συγκυρούσαις   vb pres act part fem dat pl   id.

συγκύψας   vb 1st aor act part masc nom sg ...... συγκύπτω

συγχαρεῖται   vb fut mid ind 3rd pers sg .... συγχαίρω

συγχέαι   vb 1st aor act inf .... συγχέω

συγχεῶ   vb fut act ind 1st pers sg   id.

συγχέωμεν   vb pres act subj 1st pers pl   id.

συγχρονίσας   vb 1st aor act part masc nom sg . συγχρονίζω

συγχυθέντες   vb 1st aor pass part masc nom pl ... συγχέω

συγχυθέντων   vb 1st aor pass part masc and neut gen pl   id.

συγχυθήσεται   vb fut pass ind 3rd pers sg   id.

συγχυθήσονται   vb fut pass ind 3rd pers pl   id.

συγχυθήτωσαν   vb 1st aor pass impv 3rd pers pl   id.

σύγχυσις   noun fem nom sg

συγχωρηθῆναι   vb 1st aor pass inf .... συγχωρέω

συγχωρητέον   verbal adj sg

συζυγεῖς   noun masc (or fem) nom and acc pl ..... συζυγής

Συηνη   pr noun fem nom sg

Συηνης   pr noun fem gen sg .... Συηνη

σῦκα   noun neut nom and acc pl .... σῦκον

συκαῖ   noun fem nom pl .... συκῆ

συκαῖς   noun fem dat pl   id.

συκάμινα   noun neut nom and acc pl .... συκάμινον

συκαμίνους   noun fem acc pl .... συκάμινος

συκαμίνων   noun fem gen pl   id.

συκᾶς   noun fem acc pl .... συκῆ

συκῆ   noun fem nom sg   id.

συκῇ   noun fem dat sg   id.

συκῆν   noun fem acc sg .... συκῆ

συκῆς   noun fem gen sg   id.

σύκου   noun neut gen sg .... σῦκον

συκοφαντεῖ   vb pres act ind 3rd pers sg ..... συκοφαντέω

συκοφάντην   noun masc acc sg .... συκοφάντης

συκοφάντης   noun masc nom sg   id.

συκοφαντῆσαι   vb 1st aor act inf .... συκοφαντέω

συκοφαντησάτωσαν   vb 1st aor act impv 3rd pers pl   id.

συκοφαντήσει   vb fut act ind 3rd pers sg   id.

συκοφαντία   noun fem nom sg

συκοφαντίαν   noun fem acc sg .... συκοφαντία

συκοφαντίας   noun fem gen sg and acc pl   id.

συκοφαντιῶν   noun fem gen pl   id.

συκοφαντούμενοι   vb pres m/p part

     masc nom pl .... συκοφαντέω

συκοφαντουμένων   vb pres m/p part gen pl   id.

συκοφαντούντων   vb pres act part masc and neut gen pl   id.

συκοφαντῶν   noun masc gen pl .... συκοφάντης

συκοφαντῶν   vb pres act part masc nom sg .... συκοφαντέω

σύκων   noun fem gen pl .... σῦκον

συκῶν   noun fem gen pl .... συκῆ

συκῶνας   noun masc acc pl .... συκών

συληθῶσι   vb 1st aor pass subj 3rd pers pl .... συλάω

συλλαβεῖν   vb 2nd aor act inf .... συλλαμβάνω

συλλάβετε   vb 2nd aor act impv 2nd pers pl   id.

συλλαβέτω   vb 2nd aor act impv 3rd pers sg   id.

συλλάβῃ   vb 2nd aor act subj 3rd pers sg   id.

συλλαβόντες   vb 2nd aor act part masc nom pl   id.

συλλαβοῦσα   vb 2nd aor act part fem nom sg   id.

συλλαβούσης   vb 2nd aor act part fem gen sg   id.

συλλαβών   vb 2nd aor act part masc nom sg   id.

συλλάβωσιν   vb 2nd aor act subj 3rd pers pl   id.

συλλαλεῖν   vb pres act inf .... συλλαλέω

συλλαλῇ   vb pres act subj 3rd pers sg   id.

συλλαλήσαντες   vb 1st aor act part masc nom pl   id.

συλλαμβάνεσθαι   vb pres m/p inf .... συλλαμβάνω

συλλαμβάνονται   vb pres m/p ind 3rd pers pl   id.

συλλέγειν   vb pres act inf .... συλλέγω

συλλεγέντων   vb 2nd aor pass part

     masc and neut gen pl   id.

συλλέγετε   vb pres act impv 2nd pers pl,

     pres act ind 2nd pers pl   id.

συλλεγέτω   vb pres act impv 3rd pers sg   id.

συλλέγοντα   vb pres act part masc acc sg   id.

συλλέγοντες   vb pres act part masc nom pl   id.

συλλέγουσιν   vb pres act ind 3rd pers pl   id.

συλλέγω   vb pres act ind 1st pers sg   id.

συλλέγων   vb pres act part masc nom sg   id.

συλλέξαι   vb 1st aor act inf   id.

συλλέξατε   vb 1st aor act impv 2nd pers pl   id.

συλλέξει   vb fut act ind 3rd pers sg   id.

συλλέξεις   vb fut act ind 2nd pers sg   id.

συλλέξετε vb fut act ind 2nd pers pl . . . . συλλέγω
συλλέξουσιν vb fut act ind 3rd pers pl id.
συλλέξω vb fut act ind 1st pers sg id.
Συλλημ pr noun
συλλημφθέντας vb 1st aor pass part
        masc acc pl . . . . συλλαμβάνω
συλλημφθῆναι vb 2nd aor pass inf id.
συλλημφθήσεται vb fut pass ind 3rd pers sg id.
συλλημφθήση vb fut pass ind 2nd pers sg id.
συλλημφθήσονται vb fut pass ind 3rd pers pl id.
συλλημφθήτωσαν vb 1st aor pass impv 3rd pers pl id.
σύλλημψει noun fem dat sg . . . . σύλλημψις
συλλήμψεται vb fut mid ind 3rd pers sg . . . . συλλαμβάνω
συλλήμψεων noun fem gen pl . . . . σύλλημψις
συλλήμψεως noun fem gen sg id.
συλλήμψη vb fut mid ind 2nd pers sg . . . . . . συλλαμβάνω
σύλλημψιν noun fem acc sg . . . . σύλλημψις
σύλλημψις noun fem nom sg id.
συλλημψόμεθα vb fut mid ind 1st pers pl . . . συλλαμβάνω
συλλήμψονται vb fut mid ind 3rd pers pl id.
συλλογήν noun fem acc sg . . . . συλλογή
συλλογιεῖται vb fut mid ind 3rd pers sg . . . . . . συλλογίζω
συλλογίζεσθε vb pres m/p impv 2nd pers pl id.
συλλογισθήσεται vb fut pass ind 3rd pers sg id.
συλλογισμόν noun masc acc sg . . . . συλλογισμός
συλλογισμῷ noun masc dat sg id.
συλλοχισμός noun masc nom sg
συλλύεσθαι vb pres m/p inf . . . . συλλύω
συλλυπηθήσεται vb fut pass ind 3rd pers sg . . . . συλλυπέω
συλλυπούμενον vb pres m/p part masc acc sg,
        neut nom and acc sg id.
Συμαερ pr noun
Συμαερι pr noun
Συμαριμ pr noun
συμβαίνοντα vb pres act part
        neut nom and acc pl . . . . συμβαίνω
συμβάλλει vb pres act ind 3rd pers sg . . . . συμβάλλω
συμβάλλεις vb pres act ind 2nd pers sg id.
συμβαλλόμενοι vb pres m/p part masc nom pl id.
συμβάντα vb 2nd aor act part
        neut nom and acc pl . . . . συμβαίνω
συμβασταχθήσεται vb fut pass ind
        3rd pers sg . . . . συμβαστάζω
συμβέβηκεν vb perf act ind 3rd pers sg . . . . συμβαίνω
συμβεβηκός vb perf act part neut nom and acc sg id.
συμβεβηκόσι vb perf act part masc and neut dat pl id.
συμβεβηκότα vb perf act part neut nom and acc pl id.
συμβεβηκότων vb perf act part masc and neut gen pl id.
συμβεβληκώς vb perf act part masc nom sg . . . . συμβάλλω
συμβέβληται vb perf m/p ind 3rd pers sg id.
συμβεβούλευσαι vb perf m/p ind
        2nd pers sg . . . . συμβουλεύω

συμβῇ vb 2nd aor act subj 3rd pers sg . . . . συμβαίνω
συμβῆναι vb 2nd aor act inf id.
συμβήσεται vb fut mid ind 3rd pers sg id.
συμβησόμενον vb fut mid part masc acc sg,
        neut nom and acc sg id.
συμβιβᾷ vb fut act ind 3rd pers sg . . . . συμβιβάζω
συμβιβάζω vb pres act ind 1st pers sg id.
συμβιβάσαι vb 1st aor act inf id.
συμβιβασάτω vb 1st aor act impv 3rd pers sg id.
συμβιβάσεις vb fut act ind 2nd pers sg id.
συμβιβάσω vb 1st aor act subj 1st pers sg,
        fut act ind 1st pers sg id.
συμβιβῶ vb fut act ind 1st pers sg id.
συμβιώσεται vb fut mid ind 3rd pers sg . . . . συμβιόω
συμβίωσιν noun fem acc sg . . . . συμβίωσις
συμβίωσις noun fem nom sg
συμβιωτάς noun masc acc pl . . . . συμβιωτής
συμβιωτής noun masc nom sg id.
σύμβλημα noun neut nom and acc sg
σύμβλησιν noun fem acc sg . . . . σύμβλησις
συμβοηθοί noun masc nom pl . . . . συμβοηθός
σύμβολα noun neut nom and acc pl . . . . σύμβολον
συμβολαῖς noun fem dat pl . . . . συμβολή
συμβολάς noun fem acc pl id.
συμβολῇ noun fem dat sg id.
συμβολήν noun fem acc sg id.
συμβόλοις noun neut dat pl . . . . σύμβολον
συμβολοκοπήσης vb 1st aor act subj
        2nd pers sg . . . . συμβολοκοπέω
συμβολοκοπῶν vb pres act part masc nom sg id.
σύμβολον noun neut nom and acc sg
συμβοσκηθήσεται vb fut pass ind 3rd pers sg . . συμβόσκω
σύμβουλε noun masc voc sg . . . . σύμβουλος
συμβουλεύετε vb pres act ind 2nd pers pl . . . . συμβουλεύω
συμβουλεύοντα vb pres act part masc acc sg id.
συμβουλεύοντες vb pres act part masc nom pl id.
συμβουλευόντων vb pres act part
        masc and neut gen pl id.
συμβουλεύου vb pres m/p impv 2nd pers sg id.
συμβουλεύσαιμι vb 1st aor act opt 1st pers sg id.
συμβουλεύσασι vb 1st aor act part
        masc and neut dat pl id.
συμβουλεύσομαι vb fut mid ind 1st pers sg id.
συμβουλεύσω vb fut act ind 1st pers sg id.
συμβουλευταῖς noun masc dat pl . . . . συμβουλευτής
συμβουλεύω vb pres act ind 1st pers sg
συμβουλεύων vb pres act part masc nom sg . . . συμβουλεύω
συμβουλίαι noun fem nom pl . . . . συμβουλία
συμβουλίαν noun fem acc sg id.
συμβουλίας noun fem gen sg id.
συμβούλιον noun neut nom and acc sg
σύμβουλοι noun masc nom pl . . . . σύμβουλος

σύμβουλον noun masc acc sg . . . . σύμβουλος
σύμβουλος noun masc nom sg   id.
συμβούλου noun masc gen sg   id.
συμβούλους noun masc acc pl   id.
συμβούλῳ noun masc dat sg   id.
συμβούλων noun masc gen pl   id.
Συμεων pr noun
συμμαχῆσαι vb 1st aor act inf . . . . συμμαχέω
συμμαχήσει vb fut act ind 3rd pers sg   id.
συμμαχήσετε vb fut act ind 2nd pers pl   id.
συμμαχήσουσιν vb fut act ind 3rd pers pl   id.
συμμαχία noun fem nom sg
συμμαχίᾳ noun fem dat sg . . . . συμμαχία
συμμαχίαν noun fem acc sg   id.
συμμαχίας noun fem gen sg   id.
σύμμαχοι noun masc nom pl . . . . σύμμαχος
συμμάχοις noun masc dat pl   id.
σύμμαχον noun masc acc sg   id.
συμμάχου noun masc gen sg   id.
συμμαχοῦντα vb pres m/p part masc acc sg . . . . συμμαχέω
συμμαχοῦντος pres act part masc and neut gen sg   id.
συμμάχους noun masc acc pl . . . . σύμμαχος
συμμαχοῦσιν noun masc dat pl   id.
συμμαχῶσιν vb pres act subj 3rd pers pl . . . . συμμαχέω
συμμειγεῖς see συμμιγεῖς
συμμειγήσονται vb fut pass ind 3rd pers pl . . συμμείγνυμι
συμμειγνύμενος vb pres m/p part masc nom sg   id.
συμμείξας vb 1st aor act part masc nom sg   id.
συμμείξῃ vb 1st aor act subj 3rd pers sg   id.
συμμετασχών vb 2nd aor act part masc nom sg . συμμετέχω
συμμετρίᾳ noun fem dat sg . . . . συμμετρία
σύμμετρον adj masc acc sg,
            neut nom and acc sg . . . . σύμμετρος
συμμιγεῖς adj neut nom and acc pl . . . . συμμιγής
σύμμικτοι adj masc and fem nom pl . . . . σύμμικτος
σύμμικτον adj acc sg, neut nom sg   id.
σύμμικτος adj masc and fem nom sg   id.
συμμίκτου adj gen sg   id.
συμμίκτους adj masc and fem acc pl   id.
συμμίκτῳ adj dat sg   id.
συμμίκτων adj gen pl   id.
συμμίξεων noun fem gen pl . . . . σύμμιξις
συμμίσγει vb pres act ind 3rd pers sg . . . . συμμίσγω
συμμίσγειν vb pres act inf   id.
συμμισοπονηρούντων vb pres act part
            masc and neut gen pl . . . . συμμισοπονηρέω
συμμολυνθῇ vb 1st aor pass subj
            3rd pers sg . . . . συμμολύνομαι
Συμοβορ pr noun
Συμοων pr noun
συμπαθεῖ vb pres act ind 3rd pers sg . . . . συμπαθέω
συμπάθεια noun fem nom sg

συμπαθείᾳ noun fem dat sg . . . . συμπάθεια
συμπάθειαν noun fem acc sg   id.
συμπαθεστέρας comp adj fem acc pl . . . . συμπαθής
συμπαθέστερον comp adj neut nom and acc sg   id.
συμπαθοῦς adj gen sg   id.
σύμπαιξον vb 1st aor act impv 2nd pers sg . . . . συμπαίζω
σύμπαν adj neut nom and acc sg . . . . σύμπας
σύμπαντα adj masc acc sg, neut nom and acc pl   id.
συμπαραλαβών vb 2nd aor act part
            masc nom sg . . . . συμπαραλαμβάνω
συμπαραλαμβάνοντες vb pres act part masc nom pl   id.
συμπαραλημφθῇς vb 1st aor pass subj 2nd pers sg   id.
συμπαραληφθῇ vb 1st aor pass subj 3rd pers sg   id.
συμπαραμενεῖ vb fut act ind 3rd pers sg . . . συμπαραμένω
συμπαραστήσεται vb fut mid ind
            3rd pers sg . . . . συμπαρίστημι
συμπαρεγένετο vb 2nd aor mid ind
            3rd pers sg . . . . συμπαραγίνομαι
συμπαρήμην vb impf m/p ind 1st pers sg . . . . συμπάρειμι
συμπαροῦσα vb pres act part fem nom sg   id.
σύμπασα adj fem nom sg . . . . σύμπας
σύμπασαν adj fem acc sg   id.
σύμπασι adj masc and neut dat pl   id.
συμπατηθήσεται vb fut pass ind 3rd pers sg . . . . συμπατέω
συμπατήθητι vb 1st aor pass impv 2nd pers sg   id.
συμπατήσει vb fut act ind 3rd pers sg   id.
συμπεπλεγμένον vb perf m/p part
            neut nom and acc sg . . . . συμπλέκω
συμπεπλεγμένους vb perf m/p part masc acc pl   id.
συμπέπλεκται vb perf m/p ind 3rd pers sg   id.
συμπεπορημένους vb perf m/p part
            masc acc pl . . . . συμπορπάω
συμπέπτωκα vb perf act ind 1st pers sg . . . . συμπίπτω
συμπέπτωκεν vb perf act ind 3rd pers sg   id.
συμπεριενεχθέντες vb 1st aor pass part
            masc nom pl . . . . συμπεριφέρω
συμπεριενεχθήσεσθαι vb fut pass inf   id.
συμπεριλήμψῃ vb fut mid ind
            2nd pers sg . . . . συμπεριλαμβάνω
συμπεριφερόμενοι vb pres m/p part
            masc nom pl . . . . συμπεριφέρω
συμπεριφερόμενος vb pres m/p part masc nom sg   id.
συμπεσεῖται vb fut mid ind 3rd pers sg . . . . συμπίπτω
συμπεσέτω vb 2nd aor act impv 3rd pers sg   id.
συμπεσοῦνται vb fut mid ind 3rd pers pl   id.
συμπεφυκός vb perf act part neut nom and acc sg . . . συμφύω
συμπιεῖν vb 2nd aor act inf . . . . συμπίνω
συμπλακήσεται vb fut pass ind 3rd pers sg . . . . . συμπλέκω
συμπλακήσονται fut pass ind 3rd pers pl   id.
συμπλέκεται vb pres m/p ind 3rd pers sg   id.
συμπλέκουσιν vb pres act ind 3rd pers pl   id.
συμπλεκτόν adj acc sg, neut nom sg . . . . συμπλεκτός

συμπλήρωσιν noun fem acc sg . . . . συμπλήρωσις
συμπλήρωσιν vb pres act subj 3rd pers pl . . . . συμπληρόω
συμπλοκῶν noun fem gen pl . . . . συμπλοκή
συμποδιοῦσιν vb fut act ind 3rd pers pl . . . . . . συμποδίζω
συμποδίσαντας vb 1st aor act part masc acc pl id.
συμποδίσαντες vb 1st aor act part masc nom pl id.
συμποδίσας vb 1st aor act part masc nom sg id.
συμποδισθήσεται vb fut pass ind 3rd pers sg id.
συμποιῶσιν vb pres act subj 3rd pers pl . . . . . . συμποιέω
συμπονεῖ vb pres act ind 3rd pers sg . . . . συμπονέω
συμπορεύεσθαι vb pres dep inf . . . . συμπορεύομαι
συμπορεύεται vb pres dep ind 3rd pers sg id.
συμπορευθεῖσι vb 1st aor pass part
    masc and neut dat pl id.
συμπορευθέντων vb 1st aor pass part
    masc and neut gen pl id.
συμπορεύθητι vb 1st aor pass impv 2nd pers sg id.
συμπορευθήτω vb 1st aor pass impv 3rd pers sg id.
συμπορευόμενοι vb pres dep part masc nom pl id.
συμπορευόμενος vb pres dep part masc nom sg id.
συμπορευομένου vb pres dep part
    masc and neut gen sg id.
συμπορευομένους vb pres dep part masc acc pl id.
συμπορευομένῳ vb pres dep part masc and neut dat sg id.
συμπορευομένων vb pres dep part gen pl id.
συμπορεύσεται vb fut mid ind 3rd pers sg id.
συμπορεύσῃ vb fut mid ind 2nd pers sg id.
συμπόσια noun neut nom and acc pl . . . . συμπόσιον
συμποσίαν noun fem acc sg . . . . συμποσία
συμποσίας noun fem gen sg id.
συμπόσιον noun neut nom and acc sg
συμποσίου noun neut gen sg . . . . συμπόσιον
συμποσίῳ noun neut dat sg id.
συμποτῶν noun masc gen pl . . . . συμπότης
συμπραγματευόμενοι vb pres dep part
    masc nom pl . . . . συμπραγματεύομαι
συμπροπέμπων vb pres act part masc nom sg . συμπροπέμπω
συμπροπέμψαι vb 1st aor act inf id.
συμπροσέσται vb fut mid ind 3rd pers sg . . . συμπρόσειμι
συμπροσπλακήσεται vb fut mid ind
    3rd pers sg . . . . συμπροσπλέκω
σύμπτωμα noun neut nom and acc sg
συμπτώματος noun neut gen sg . . . . σύμπτωμα
συμπτωμάτων noun neut gen pl
συμφαγεῖν vb 2nd aor act inf . . . . συνεσθίω
συμφέρει vb pres act ind 3rd pers sg . . . . συμφέρω
συμφέροντα vb pres act part neut nom and acc pl id.
συμφέροντος vb pres act part masc and neut gen sg id.
συμφερόντως adverb
συμφλέγοντες vb pres act part masc nom pl . . . . . συμφλέγω
συμφορᾷ noun fem dat sg . . . . συμφορά
συμφοραῖς noun fem dat pl id.

συμφοράν noun fem acc sg . . . . συμφορά
συμφοράς noun fem acc pl id.
συμφορᾶς noun fem gen sg id.
συμφοράσουσιν vb fut act ind 3rd pers pl . . . . συμφοράζω
σύμφορον adj acc sg, neut nom sg . . . . σύμφορος
συμφράξει vb fut act ind 3rd pers sg . . . . συμφράσσω
συμφρονοῦσι vb pres act part
    masc and neut dat pl . . . . συμφρονέω
συμφυγόντας vb 2nd aor act part masc acc pl . . . συμφεύγω
συμφυγόντων vb 2nd aor act part masc and neut gen pl id.
συμφυρόμενον vb pres m/p part masc acc sg . . . . . συμφύρω
σύμφυτοι adj masc and fem nom pl . . . . σύμφυτος
σύμφυτος adj masc and fem nom sg id.
συμφύτῳ adj dat sg id.
σύμφωνε adj masc voc sg . . . . σύμφωνος
συμφωνίας noun fem gen sg and acc pl . . . . συμφωνία
σύμφωνον adj acc sg, neut nom sg . . . . σύμφωνος
συμφώνων adj gen pl id.
συμφώνως adverb
συμψησθείς vb 1st aor pass part masc nom sg . . . . συμψάω
συμψησθῶσιν vb 1st aor pass subj 3rd pers pl id.
σύν preposition
συνάγαγε vb 2nd aor act impv 2nd pers sg . . . . συνάγω
συναγαγεῖν vb 2nd aor act inf id.
συναγάγετε vb 2nd aor act impv 2nd pers pl id.
συναγαγέτωσαν vb 2nd aor act impv 3rd pers pl id.
συναγάγῃ vb 2nd aor act subj 3rd pers sg id.
συναγάγητε vb 2nd aor act subj 2nd pers pl id.
συναγαγόντες vb 2nd aor act part masc nom pl id.
συναγαγόντι vb 2nd aor act part
    masc and neut dat sg id.
συναγάγω vb 2nd aor act subj 1st pers sg id.
συναγάγωμεν vb 2nd aor act subj 1st pers pl id.
συναγαγών vb 2nd aor act part masc nom sg id.
συναγάγωσιν vb 2nd aor act subj 3rd pers pl id.
σύναγε vb pres act impv 2nd pers sg id.
συνάγει vb pres act ind 3rd pers sg id.
συναγείοχας vb perf act ind 2nd pers sg id.
συναγελάζονται vb pres dep ind
    3rd pers pl . . . . συναγελάζομαι
συνάγεται vb pres m/p ind 3rd pers sg . . . . συνάγω
συναγμάτων noun neut gen pl . . . . σύναγμα
συναγομένης vb pres m/p part fem gen sg . . . . συνάγω
συναγόμενος vb pres m/p part masc nom sg id.
συνάγονται vb pres m/p ind 3rd pers pl id.
συνάγοντες vb pres act part masc nom pl id.
συνάγουσα vb pres act part fem nom sg id.
συνάγουσιν vb pres act ind 3rd pers pl id.
συνάγω vb pres act ind 1st pers sg id.
συναγωγαί noun fem nom pl . . . . συναγωγή
συναγωγαῖς noun fem dat pl id.
συναγωγάς noun fem acc pl id.

συναγωγή noun fem nom sg
συναγωγῇ noun fem dat sg . . . . συναγωγή
συναγωγήν noun fem acc sg   id.
συναγωγῆς noun fem gen sg   id.
συνάγων vb pres act part masc nom sg . . . . συνάγω
συνάδοντες vb pres act part masc nom pl . . . . συνάδω
συνάδωσιν vb pres act subj 3rd pers pl   id.
συναθροίζει vb pres act ind 3rd pers sg . . . . συναθροίζω
συναθροίζεσθε vb pres m/p impv 2nd pers pl   id.
συναθροιζομένων vb pres m/p part gen pl   id.
συναθροίζονται vb pres m/p ind 3rd pers pl   id.
συναθροίζουσιν vb pres act ind 3rd pers pl   id.
συναθροίσαντας vb 1st aor act part masc acc pl   id.
συναθροίσας vb 1st aor act part masc nom sg   id.
συναθροισθέντες vb 1st aor pass part masc nom pl   id.
συναθροισθῆναι vb 1st aor pass inf   id.
συναθροισθήσονται vb fut pass ind 3rd pers pl   id.
συνάθροισον vb 1st aor act impv 2nd pers sg   id.
συναθροίσω vb fut act ind 1st pers sg   id.
συναινέσαντες vb 1st aor act part masc nom pl . . συναινέω
συναινέσας vb 1st aor act part masc nom sg   id.
συνακολουθεῖν vb pres act inf . . . . συνακολουθέω
συνακολουθούντων vb pres act part
          masc and neut gen pl   id.
συναλγήσει vb fut act ind 3rd pers sg . . . . συναλγέω
συναλλάγμασι noun neut dat pl . . . . συνάλλαγμα
συναλλάγματι noun neut dat sg   id.
συναλλαγμάτων noun neut gen pl   id.
συναναβάντες vb 2nd aor act part
          masc nom pl . . . . συναναβαίνω
συναναβῆναι vb 2nd aor act inf   id.
συναναβήσεται vb fut mid ind 3rd pers sg   id.
συναναβῶ vb 2nd aor act subj 1st pers sg   id.
συνανακείμενοι vb pres m/p part
          masc nom pl . . . . συνανάκειμαι
συναναμείξεων see συναναμίξεων
συναναμίξεων noun fem gen pl . . . . συνανάμιξις
συναναμίσγεσθε vb pres m/p impv
          2nd pers pl . . . . συναναμίσγω
συναναπαύσεται vb fut mid ind 3rd pers sg . συναναπαύω
συναναστρεφόμενα vb pres m/p part
          neut nom and acc pl . . . . συναναστρέφω
συναναστροφή noun fem nom sg
συναναστροφήν noun fem acc sg . . . . . . συναναστροφή
συναναστροφῆς noun fem gen sg   id.
συναναφέρων vb pres act part masc nom sg . . συναναφέρω
συνανέβαινον vb impf act ind
          1st pers sg and 3rd pers pl . . . . συναναβαίνω
συνανέβη vb 2nd aor act ind 3rd pers sg   id.
συνανέβησαν vb 2nd aor act ind 3rd pers pl   id.
συνανεμείγνυτο vb impf m/p ind
          3rd pers sg . . . . συναναμίγνυμι

συνανεστράφη vb 2nd aor pass ind
          3rd pers sg . . . . συναναστρέφω
συνανεστράφην vb 2nd aor pass ind 1st pers sg   id.
συνανεφύροντο vb impf m/p ind 3rd pers pl . συναναφύρω
συνανοίσετε vb fut act ind 2nd pers pl . . . . . συναναφέρω
συναντᾷ vb pres act ind 3rd pers sg . . . . συναντάω
συναντᾶν vb pres act inf   id.
συναντᾶτε vb pres act impv 2nd pers pl   id.
συνάντημα noun neut nom and acc sg
συναντήματα noun neut nom and acc pl . . . . . συνάντημα
συναντήν noun fem acc sg . . . . συναντή
συναντῆσαι vb 1st aor act inf . . . . συναντάω
συναντήσας vb 1st aor act part masc nom sg   id.
συναντήσει noun fem dat sg . . . . συνάντησις
συναντήσεσθε vb fut mid ind 2nd pers pl . . . . . συναντάω
συναντήσεται vb fut mid ind 3rd pers sg   id.
συναντήσῃ vb 1st aor act subj 3rd pers sg   id.
συναντήσῃς vb 1st aor act subj 2nd pers sg   id.
συναντήσητε vb 1st aor act subj 2nd pers pl   id.
συνάντησιν noun fem acc sg . . . . συνάντησις
συνάντησον vb 1st aor act impv 2nd pers sg . . . . συναντάω
συναντήσουσιν vb fut act ind 3rd pers pl   id.
συναντήσωσιν vb 1st aor act subj 3rd pers pl   id.
συναντιλήμψεται vb fut mid ind
          3rd pers sg . . . . συναντιλαμβάνομαι
συναντιλήμψεται vb fut mid ind 3rd pers sg   id.
συναντιλήμψονται vb fut mid ind 3rd pers pl   id.
συναντῶν vb pres act part masc nom sg . . . . συναντάω
συναντῶσα vb pres act part fem nom sg   id.
συναντῶσιν vb pres act ind 3rd pers pl   id.
συνάξει vb fut act ind 3rd pers sg . . . . συνάγω
συνάξεις vb fut act ind 2nd pers sg   id.
συνάξουσιν vb fut act ind 3rd pers pl   id.
συνάξω vb fut act ind 1st pers sg   id.
συναπέστειλεν vb 1st aor act ind
          3rd pers sg . . . . συναποστέλλω
συναπήγαγεν vb 2nd aor act ind 3rd pers sg . . . . συναπάγω
συναποθανέτω vb 2nd aor act impv
          3rd pers sg . . . . συναποθνήσκω
συναποκρυβῶσι vb 2nd aor pass subj
          3rd pers pl . . . . συναποκρύπτω
συναπολέσῃ vb 1st aor act subj 3rd pers sg . . συναπόλλυμι
συναπολέσῃς vb 1st aor act subj 2nd pers sg   id.
συναπολέσθαι vb 2nd aor mid inf   id.
συναπόλῃ vb 2nd aor mid subj 2nd pers sg   id.
συναπολῇ vb fut mid ind 2nd pers sg   id.
συναπόλησθε vb 2nd aor mid subj 2nd pers pl   id.
συναποστᾶσαι vb 2nd aor act part
          fem nom pl . . . . συναφίστημι
συναποστελεῖς vb fut act ind 2nd pers sg . . συναποστέλλω
συναποστελῶ vb fut act ind 1st pers sg   id.
σύναπτε vb pres act impv 2nd pers sg . . . . συνάπτω

συνάπτειν   vb pres act inf . . . . συνάπτω
συνάπτοντες   vb pres act part masc nom pl   id.
συναπτούσης   vb pres act part fem gen sg   id.
συνάπτουσιν   vb pres act ind 3rd pers pl   id.
συναπώλετο   vb 2nd aor mid ind 3rd pers sg   . συναπόλλυμι
συναριθμήσεται   vb fut mid ind 3rd pers sg   . . συναριθμέω
συναρπάσαντες   vb 1st aor act part
     masc nom pl . . . . συναρπάζω
συναρπασθέντων   vb 1st aor pass part
     masc and neut gen pl   id.
συναρπασθῇς   vb 1st aor pass subj 2nd pers sg   id.
συναρχίαν   noun fem acc sg . . . . συναρχία
συνασπιεῖν   vb fut act inf . . . . συνασπίζω
συναυλίζου   vb pres dep impv 2nd pers sg . . συναυλίζομαι
συναύξοντα   vb pres act part masc acc sg . . . . . . συναύξω
συναυξόντων   vb pres act part masc and neut gen pl   id.
συναχθέντας   vb 1st aor pass part masc acc pl . . . . . συνάγω
συναχθέντες   vb 1st aor pass part masc nom pl   id.
συναχθέντων   vb 1st aor pass part masc and neut gen pl   id.
συναχθῇ   vb 1st aor pass subj 3rd pers sg   id.
συναχθῆναι   vb 1st aor pass inf   id.
συναχθῇς   vb 1st aor pass subj 2nd pers sg   id.
συναχθήσεσθε   vb fut pass ind 2nd pers pl   id.
συναχθήσεται   vb fut pass ind 3rd pers sg   id.
συναχθήσῃ   vb fut pass ind 2nd pers sg   id.
συναχθήσομαι   vb fut pass ind 1st pers sg   id.
συναχθήσονται   vb fut pass ind 3rd pers pl   id.
συνάχθητε   vb 1st aor pass impv 2nd pers pl   id.
συναχθήτω   vb 1st aor pass impv 3rd pers sg   id.
συναχθήτωσαν   vb 1st aor pass impv 3rd pers pl   id.
συναχθῶμεν   vb 1st aor pass subj 1st pers pl   id.
συναχθῶσιν   vb 1st aor pass subj 3rd pers pl   id.
συνάψαι   vb 1st aor act inf . . . . συνάπτω
συνάψει   vb fut act ind 3rd pers sg   id.
συνάψεις   noun fem nom and acc pl . . . . σύναψις
συνάψεις   vb fut act ind 2nd pers sg . . . . συνάπτω
συνάψητε   vb 1st aor act subj 2nd pers pl   id.
συνάψουσιν   vb fut act ind 3rd pers pl   id.
συνδεδεμένα   vb perf m/p part neut nom and acc pl   . συνδέω
συνδέθητε   vb 1st aor pass impv 2nd pers pl   id.
συνδεθήτω   vb 1st aor pass impv 3rd pers sg   id.
συνδείπνει   vb pres act impv 2nd pers sg . . . . . συνδειπνέω
σύνδειπνοι   noun masc nom pl . . . . σύνδειπνος
συνδειπνοῦσι   vb pres act part
     masc and neut dat pl . . . . συνδειπνέω
σύνδεσμοι   noun masc nom pl . . . . σύνδεσμος
σύνδεσμον   noun masc acc sg   id.
σύνδεσμος   noun masc nom sg   id.
συνδέσμους   noun masc acc pl   id.
σύνδησον   vb 1st aor act impv 2nd pers sg . . . . συνδέω
συνδήσω   vb fut act ind 1st pers sg   id.
συνδιώξαντες   vb 1st aor act part masc nom pl . . . συνδιώκω

σύνδουλοι   noun masc nom pl . . . . σύνδουλος
συνδούλοις   noun masc dat pl   id.
συνδούλους   noun masc acc pl   id.
συνδούλων   noun masc gen pl   id.
συνδραμόντες   vb 2nd aor act part masc nom pl . . συντρέχω
συνδραμοῦνται   vb fut mid ind 3rd pers pl   id.
συνδρομάς   noun fem acc pl . . . . συνδρομή
συνδρομή   noun fem nom sg   id.
συνδυάσω   vb 1st aor act subj 1st pers sg,
     fut act ind 1st pers sg . . . . συνδυάζω
συνέβαινεν   vb impf act ind 3rd pers sg . . . . συμβαίνω
συνέβαλε   vb 2nd aor act ind 3rd pers sg . . . . . . συμβάλλω
συνέβαλλον   vb impf act ind
     1st pers sg and 3rd pers pl   id.
συνέβη   vb 2nd aor act ind 3rd pers sg . . . . συμβαίνω
συνεβίβασεν   vb 1st aor act ind 3rd pers sg . . . . συμβιβάζω
συνεβλήθη   vb 1st aor pass ind 3rd pers sg . . . . . συμβάλλω
συνεβούλευσα   vb 1st aor act ind 1st pers sg . . συμβουλεύω
συνεβούλευσαν   vb 1st aor act ind 3rd pers pl   id.
συνεβουλεύσαντο   vb 1st aor mid ind 3rd pers pl   id.
συνεβουλεύσατο   vb 1st aor mid ind 3rd pers sg   id.
συνεβούλευσεν   vb 1st aor act ind 3rd pers sg   id.
συνεβράβευσαν   vb 1st aor act ind
     3rd pers pl . . . . συμβραβεύω
συνεγγίζοντος   vb pres act part
     masc and neut gen sg . . . . συνεγγίζω
συνεγγίσοντες   vb 1st aor act part masc nom pl   id.
συνεγγίσος   vb 1st aor act part masc nom sg   id.
συνεγγίσῃ   vb 1st aor act subj 3rd pers sg   id.
σύνεγγυς   adverb
συνεγείρων   vb pres act part masc nom sg . . . . . συνεγείρω
συνεγερεῖς   vb fut act ind 2nd pers sg   id.
συνέδησεν   vb 1st aor act ind 3rd pers sg . . . . συνδέω
συνεδήχθησαν   vb 1st aor pass ind 3rd pers pl . . . συνδάκνω
συνέδραμεν   vb 2nd aor act ind 3rd pers sg . . . . . συντρέχω
συνέδραμον   vb 2nd aor act ind 3rd pers pl   id.
συνέδρευε   vb pres act impv 2nd pers sg . . . . συνεδρεύω
συνεδρεύεις   vb pres act ind 2nd pers sg   id.
συνέδρια   noun neut nom and acc pl . . . . συνέδριον
συνεδρίᾳ   noun fem dat sg . . . . συνεδρία
συνεδριάζει   vb pres act ind 3rd pers sg . . . . . . συνεδριάζω
συνεδρίας   noun fem gen sg . . . . συνεδρία
συνεδρίοις   noun neut dat pl . . . . συνέδριον
συνεδρίον   noun neut nom and acc sg   id.
συνεδρίου   noun neut gen sg   id.
συνεδρίῳ   noun neut dat sg   id.
συνέδρων   noun masc gen pl . . . . σύνεδρος
συνεζευγμέναι   vb perf m/p part fem nom pl . . συζεύγνυμι
συνεζώσατο   vb 1st aor mid ind 3rd pers sg . . . . συζώννυμι
συνέζωσεν   vb 1st aor act ind 3rd pers sg   id.
συνέθεντο   vb 2nd aor mid ind 3rd pers pl . . . . . . συντίθημι
συνέθεσθε   vb 2nd aor mid ind 2nd pers pl   id.

συνέθετο vb 2nd aor mid ind 3rd pers sg ...... συντίθημι
συνέθηκαν vb 1st aor act ind 3rd pers pl   id.
συνεθιζόμενος vb pres m/p part masc nom sg ... συνεθίζω
συνεθίσῃς vb 1st aor act subj 2nd pers sg   id.
συνεθισθῇς vb 1st aor pass subj 2nd pers sg   id.
συνέθλασαν vb 1st aor act ind 3rd pers pl ...... συνθλάω
συνέθλασας vb 1st aor act ind 2nd pers sg   id.
συνέθλασεν vb 1st aor act ind 3rd pers sg   id.
συνέθου vb 2nd aor mid ind 2nd pers sg ...... συντίθημι
συνειδήσει noun fem dat sg .... συνείδησις
συνειλημμένη vb perf m/p part fem nom sg . συλλαμβάνω
συνειλημμένοι vb perf m/p part masc nom pl   id.
συνειληφυῖα vb perf act part fem nom sg   id.
συνείξαντας vb 1st aor act part masc acc sg ..... συνείκω
συνειπάμεθα vb 1st aor mid ind 1st pers pl ..... συνεῖπον
συνείπασθε vb 1st aor mid ind 2nd pers pl   id.
συνεισελεύσεται vb fut mid ind
        3rd pers sg .... συνεισέρχομαι
συνεισέλθῃ vb 2nd aor act subj 3rd pers sg   id.
συνεισελθόντας vb 2nd aor act part masc acc pl   id.
συνεισέρχεσθαι vb pres dep inf   id.
συνείχετο vb impf m/p ind 3rd pers sg .... συνέχω
συνεκάθισαν vb 1st aor act ind 3rd pers pl .... συγκαθίζω
συνεκάθισεν vb 1st aor act ind 3rd pers sg   id.
συνεκάλεσαν vb 1st aor act ind 3rd pers pl ..... συγκαλέω
συνεκάλεσεν vb 1st aor act ind 3rd pers sg   id.
συνεκάλυπτεν vb impf act ind 3rd pers sg ... συγκαλύπτω
συνεκάλυψαν vb 1st aor act ind 3rd pers pl   id.
συνεκαλύψατο vb 1st aor mid ind 3rd pers sg   id.
συνεκάλυψεν vb 1st aor act ind 3rd pers sg   id.
συνέκαμψα vb 1st aor act ind 1st pers sg ...... συγκάμπτω
συνέκαμψεν vb 1st aor act ind 3rd pers sg   id.
συνεκέντησεν vb 1st aor act ind 3rd pers sg ... συγκεντέω
συνεκεραύνωσαν vb 1st aor act ind
        3rd pers pl .... συγκεραυνόω
συνεκέχυτο vb plpf m/p ind 3rd pers sg .... συγχέω
συνέκλασας vb 1st aor act ind 2nd pers sg ..... συγκλάω
συνέκλασεν vb 1st aor act ind 3rd pers sg   id.
συνεκλάσθη vb 1st aor pass ind 3rd pers sg   id.
συνέκλεισαν vb 1st aor act ind 3rd pers pl .... συγκλείω
συνέκλεισας vb 1st aor act ind 2nd pers sg   id.
συνέκλεισεν vb 1st aor act ind 3rd pers sg   id.
συνεκλείσθησαν vb 1st aor pass ind 3rd pers pl   id.
συνέκοψα vb 1st aor act ind 1st pers sg .... συγκόπτω
συνέκοψεν vb 1st aor act ind 3rd pers sg   id.
συνεκπολεμῆσαι vb 1st aor act inf ...... συνεκπολεμέω
συνεκπολεμήσει vb fut act ind 3rd pers sg   id.
συνεκπορεύεσθαι vb pres dep inf ..... συνεκπορεύομαι
συνέκριναν vb 1st aor act ind 3rd pers pl ...... συγκρίνω
συνέκρινεν vb 1st aor act ind 3rd pers sg   id.
συνεκρότησεν vb 1st aor act ind 3rd pers sg ... συγκροτέω
συνεκροτοῦντο vb impf m/p ind 3rd pers pl   id.

συνεκρύπτετο vb impf m/p ind 3rd pers sg .... συγκρύπτω
συνεκτίσθη vb 1st aor pass ind 3rd pers sg ..... συγκτίζω
συνεκτραφέντων vb 2nd aor pass part
        masc and neut gen pl .... συνεκτρέφω
συνεκτρῖψαι vb 1st aor act inf .... συνεκτρίβω
συνεκτρόφους adj masc acc pl .... συνέκτροφος
συνέλαβε(ν) vb 2nd aor act ind 3rd pers sg .. συλλαμβάνω
συνελάβετο vb 2nd aor mid ind 3rd pers sg   id.
συνέλαβον vb 2nd aor act ind 3rd pers pl   id.
συνελάβοσαν vb 2nd aor act ind 3rd pers pl   id.
συνελάλησαν vb 1st aor act ind 3rd pers pl .... συλλαλέω
συνελαμβάνοσαν vb impf act ind
        3rd pers pl .... συλλαμβάνω
συνελασθέντων vb 1st aor pass part
        masc and neut gen pl .... συνελαύνω
συνέλεγεν vb impf act ind 3rd pers sg .... συλλέγω
συνέλεγον vb impf act ind 1st pers sg and 3rd pers pl id.
συνελέγοντο vb impf m/p ind 3rd pers pl   id.
συνελέλεκτο vb plpf m/p ind 3rd pers sg   id.
συνέλεξαν vb 1st aor act ind 3rd pers pl   id.
συνέλεξας vb 1st aor act ind 2nd pers sg   id.
συνέλεξεν vb 1st aor act ind 3rd pers sg   id.
συνελεύσεται vb fut mid ind 3rd pers sg ..... συνέρχομαι
συνέλευσιν noun fem acc sg .... συνέλευσις
συνελεύσομαι vb fut mid ind 1st pers sg ..... συνέρχομαι
συνελεύσονται vb fut mid ind 3rd pers pl   id.
συνελήμφθη vb 1st aor pass ind 3rd pers sg .. συλλαμβάνω
συνελήμφθην vb 1st aor pass ind 1st pers sg   id.
συνελήμφθης vb 1st aor pass ind 2nd pers sg   id.
συνελήμφθησαν vb 1st aor pass ind 3rd pers pl   id.
συνελθεῖν vb 2nd aor act inf .... συνέρχομαι
συνελθόν vb 2nd aor act part neut nom and acc sg   id.
συνελθόντι vb 2nd aor act part masc and neut dat sg id.
συνελθόντων vb 2nd aor act part masc and neut gen pl id.
συνελθούσης vb 2nd aor act part fem gen sg   id.
συνέλθωμεν vb 2nd aor act subj 1st pers pl   id.
συνελκύσῃς vb 1st aor act subj 2nd pers sg ...... συνέλκω
συνελοιδορήσατε vb 1st aor act ind
        3rd pers pl .... συλλοιδορέω
συνελόχησεν vb 1st aor act ind 3rd pers sg .... συλλοχάω
συνελύθη vb 1st aor pass ind 3rd pers sg .... συλλύω
συνεμάχησαν vb 1st aor act ind 3rd pers pl ..... συμμαχέω
συνεμάχουν vb impf act ind 1st pers sg and 3rd pers pl id.
συνέμειξαν vb 1st aor act ind 3rd pers pl .... συμμίγνυμι
συνέμειξεν vb 1st aor act ind 3rd pers sg   id.
συνεμιάνθης vb 1st aor pass ind 2nd pers sg ... συμμιαίνω
συνέμιξαν vb 1st aor act ind 3rd pers pl ..... συμμίγνυμι
συνέμισγον vb impf act ind
        1st pers sg and 3rd pers pl .... συμμίσγω
συνέξει vb fut act ind 3rd pers sg .... συνέχω
συνεξεκέντησεν vb 1st aor act ind
        3rd pers sg .... συνεκκεντέω

συνεξελεύσεται   vb fut mid ind 3rd pers sg . συνεξέρχομαι
συνεξεπορεύοντο   vb impf dep ind

    3rd pers pl . . . . συνεκπορεύομαι
συνεξῆλθον   vb 2nd aor act ind 3rd pers pl . . συνεξέρχομαι
συνεξορμάτωσαν   vb pres act impv

    3rd pers pl . . . . συνεξορμάω
συνέξουσιν   vb fut act ind 3rd pers pl . . . . συνέχω
συνεπάτει   vb impf act ind 3rd pers sg . . . . συμπατέω
συνεπάτησαν   vb 1st aor act ind 3rd pers pl   id.
συνεπάτησεν   vb 1st aor act ind 3rd pers sg   id.
συνεπέθεντο   vb 2nd aor mid 3rd pers pl . συνεπιτίθημι
συνέπεισαν   vb 1st aor act ind 3rd pers pl . . . . . συμπείθω
συνέπεισεν   vb 1st aor act ind 3rd pers sg   id.
συνεπέρανας   vb 1st aor act ind 2nd pers sg . . . συμπεραίνω
συνέπεσαν   vb 1st aor act ind 3rd pers pl . . . . . . συμπίπτω
συνέπεσεν   vb 2nd aor act ind 3rd pers sg   id.
συνεπεσκέπησαν   vb 2nd aor pass ind

    3rd pers pl . . . . συνεπισκέπτομαι
συνέπεσον   vb 2nd aor act ind 3rd pers pl . . . . . . συμπίπτω
συνεπηκολούθησαν   vb 1st aor act ind

    3rd pers pl . . . . συνεπακολουθέω
συνεπηκολούθησεν   vb 1st aor act ind 3rd pers sg   id.
συνεπιθῇ   vb 2nd aor act subj 3rd pers sg . . . . συνεπιτίθημι
συνεπιθῶνται   vb 2nd aor mid subj 3rd pers pl   id.
συνεπισκέψῃ   vb fut mid ind 2nd pers sg   συνεπισκέπτομαι
συνεπίσταμαι   vb pres m/p ind 1st pers sg
συνεπισχύειν   vb pres act inf . . . . συνεπισχύω
συνεπίσχυσαν   vb 1st aor act part neut nom and acc sg   id.
συνεπιτιθέμενα   vb pres m/p part

    neut nom and acc pl . . . . συνεπιτίθημι
συνεπιτιθεμένων   vb pres m/p part gen pl   id.
συνεπλάκησαν   vb 2nd aor pass ind 3rd pers pl . . συμπλέκω
συνεπλέκετο   vb impf m/p ind 3rd pers sg   id.
συνεπόδισα   vb 1st aor act ind 1st pers sg . . . . συμποδίζω
συνεπόδισας   vb 1st aor act ind 2nd pers sg   id.
συνεπόδισεν   vb 1st aor act ind 3rd pers sg   id.
συνεποδίσθησαν   vb 1st aor pass ind 3rd pers pl   id.
συνεπολέμει   vb impf act ind 3rd pers sg . . . . . συμπολεμέω
συνεπολέμησεν   vb 1st aor act ind 3rd pers sg   id.
συνεπομένας   vb pres dep part fem acc pl . . . . συνέπομαι
συνεπομένης   vb pres dep part fem gen sg   id.
συνεπομένων   vb pres dep part gen pl   id.
συνεπορεύετο   vb impf dep ind 3rd pers sg . συμπορεύομαι
συνεπορεύθησαν   vb 1st aor pass ind 3rd pers pl   id.
συνεπορεύοντο   vb impf dep ind 3rd pers pl   id.
συνεργεῖ   vb pres act ind 3rd pers sg . . . . συνεργέω
συνεργόν   adj acc sg, neut nom sg . . . . συνεργός
συνεργοῦντες   vb pres act part masc nom pl . . . . . συνεργέω
συνεργούς   adj masc and fem acc pl . . . . συνεργός
συνερίσαντες   vb 1st aor act part masc nom pl . . . συνερίζω
συνέρχεσθε   vb pres dep ind 2nd pers pl . . . . συνέρχομαι
σύνες   vb 2nd aor act impv 2nd pers sg . . . . συνίημι

συνέσει   noun fem dat sg . . . . σύνεσις
συνέσεισας   vb 1st aor act ind 2nd pers sg . . . . . . συσσείω
συνέσεισεν   vb 1st aor act ind 3rd pers sg   id.
συνέσεσι   noun fem dat pl . . . . σύνεσις
συνέσεως   noun fem gen sg   id.
συνεσθίειν   vb pres act inf . . . . συνεσθίω
σύνεσιν   noun fem acc sg . . . . σύνεσις
σύνεσις   noun fem nom sg   id.
συνεσκότασεν   vb 1st aor act ind 3rd pers sg . . . συσκοτάζω
συνεσπάσθησαν   vb 1st aor pass ind 3rd pers pl . . συσπάω
συνεστάλη   vb 2nd aor pass ind 3rd pers sg . . . . . συστέλλω
συνεστάλησαν   vb 2nd aor pass ind 3rd pers pl   id.
συνεσταλμένη   vb perf m/p part fem nom sg   id.
συνέστειλεν   vb 1st aor act ind 3rd pers sg   id.
συνέστη   vb 2nd aor act ind 3rd pers sg . . . . συνίστημι
συνέστηκεν   vb perf act ind 3rd pers sg   id.
συνεστηκός   vb perf act part neut nom and acc sg   id.
συνεστηκότων   vb perf act part masc and neut gen pl   id.
συνέστησαν   vb 1st aor act ind 3rd pers pl   id.
συνεστήσαντο   vb 1st aor mid ind 3rd pers pl   id.
συνεστήσατο   vb 1st aor mid ind 3rd pers sg   id.
συνέστησεν   vb 1st aor act ind 3rd pers sg   id.
συνεστραμμένοι   vb perf m/p part masc nom pl . . συστρέφω
συνεστράφη   vb 2nd aor pass ind 3rd pers sg   id.
συνεστράφην   vb 2nd aor pass ind 1st pers sg   id.
συνεστράφησαν   vb 2nd aor pass ind 3rd pers pl   id.
συνεστρέφετο   vb impf m/p ind 3rd pers sg   id.
συνέστρεψεν   vb 1st aor act ind 3rd pers sg   id.
συνέστω   vb pres act impv 3rd pers sg . . . . σύνειμι
συνέσφιγξεν   vb 1st aor act ind 3rd pers sg . . . . . . συσφίγγω
συνεσχέθη   vb 1st aor pass ind 3rd pers sg . . . . συνέχω
συνεσχέθησαν   vb 1st aor pass ind 3rd pers pl   id.
συνέσχεν   vb 2nd aor act ind 3rd pers sg   id.
συνετά   adj neut nom and acc pl . . . . συνετός
συνετάγη   vb 2nd aor pass ind 3rd pers sg . . . . . συντάσσω
συνεταιρίδες   noun fem nom pl . . . . συνεταιρίς
συνέταιροι   noun masc nom pl . . . . συνέταιρος
συνεταίροις   noun masc dat pl   id.
συνεταίρῳ   noun masc dat sg   id.
συνέταξα   vb 1st aor act ind 1st pers sg . . . . συντάσσω
συνέταξαν   vb 1st aor act ind 3rd pers pl   id.
συνετάξαντο   vb 1st aor mid ind 3rd pers pl   id.
συνέταξε(ν)   vb 1st aor act ind 3rd pers sg   id.
συνετάραξαν   vb 1st aor act ind 3rd pers pl . . συνταράσσω
συνετάραξας   vb 1st aor act ind 2nd pers sg   id.
συνετάραξεν   vb 1st aor act ind 3rd pers sg   id.
συνετάρασσον   vb impf act ind

    1st pers sg and 3rd pers pl   id.
συνεταράσσοντο   vb impf m/p ind 3rd pers pl   id.
συνεταράχθη   vb 1st aor pass ind 3rd pers sg   id.
συνεταράχθησαν   vb 1st aor pass ind 3rd pers pl   id.
σύνετε   vb 2nd aor act impv 2nd pers pl . . . . συνίημι

συνετέλει vb impf act ind 3rd pers sg . . . . συντελέω
συνετέλεσα vb 1st aor act ind 1st pers sg id.
συνετελέσαμεν vb 1st aor act ind 1st pers pl id.
συνετέλεσαν vb 1st aor act ind 3rd pers pl id.
συνετελέσαντο vb 1st aor mid ind 3rd pers pl id.
συνετέλεσας vb 1st aor act ind 2nd pers sg id.
συνετελέσατε vb 1st aor act ind 2nd pers pl id.
συνετελέσατο vb 1st aor mid ind 3rd pers sg id.
συνετέλεσεν vb 1st aor act ind 3rd pers sg id.
συνετελέσθη vb 1st aor pass ind 3rd pers sg id.
συνετελέσθησαν vb 1st aor pass ind 3rd pers pl id.
συνετελέσω vb 1st aor mid ind 2nd pers sg id.
συνετέλουν vb impf act ind 1st pers sg and 3rd pers pl id.
συνετή adj fem nom sg . . . . συνετός
συνετῇ adj fem dat sg id.
συνετηρήθησαν vb 1st aor pass ind 3rd pers pl . . συντηρέω
συνετήρησα vb 1st aor act ind 1st pers sg id.
συνετηρήσαμεν vb 1st aor act ind 1st pers pl id.
συνετήρησαν vb 1st aor act ind 3rd pers pl id.
συνετηρήσατε vb 1st aor act ind 2nd pers pl id.
συνετήρησε(ν) vb 1st aor act ind 3rd pers sg id.
συνετιεῖ vb fut act ind 3rd pers sg . . . . συνετίζω
συνετίζοντες vb pres act part masc nom pl id.
συνετίσαι vb 1st aor act inf id.
συνετίσαντα vb 1st aor act part masc acc sg id.
συνέτισεν vb 1st aor act ind 3rd pers sg id.
συνέτισον vb 1st aor act impv 2nd pers sg id.
συνετιῶ vb fut act ind 1st pers sg id.
συνετμήθησαν vb 1st aor pass ind 3rd pers pl . . . συντέμνω
συνετοί adj masc nom pl . . . . συνετός
συνετοῖς adj masc and neut dat pl id.
συνετόν adj masc acc sg, neut nom and acc sg id.
συνετός adj masc nom sg id.
συνετοῦ adj masc and neut gen sg id.
συνετούς adj masc acc pl id.
συνέτρεχες vb impf act ind 2nd pers sg . . . . συντρέχω
συνέτρεχον vb impf act ind 1st pers sg and 3rd pers pl id.
συνετρίβη vb 2nd aor pass ind 3rd pers sg . . . . . . συντρίβω
συνετρίβης vb 2nd aor pass ind 2nd pers sg id.
συνετρίβησαν vb 2nd aor pass ind 3rd pers pl id.
συνέτριψα vb 1st aor act ind 1st pers sg id.
συνέτριψαν vb 1st aor act ind 3rd pers pl id.
συνέτριψας vb 1st aor act ind 2nd pers sg id.
συνέτριψε(ν) vb 1st aor act ind 3rd pers sg id.
συνέτω vb 2nd aor act impv 3rd pers sg . . . . συνίημι
συνετῷ adj masc and neut dat sg . . . . συνετός
συνετῶν adj gen pl id.
συνετῶς adverb
συνετώτερος comp adj masc nom sg . . . . συνετός
συνευδόκει vb pres act impv 2nd pers sg . . . . . συνευδοκέω
συνευδοκοῦμεν vb pres act ind 1st pers pl id.
συνευδοκοῦντας vb pres act part masc acc pl id.

συνευφραίνου vb pres dep impv
  2nd pers sg . . . . συνευφραίνομαι
συνέφαγεν vb 2nd aor act ind 3rd pers sg . . . . . . συνεσθίω
συνεφλογίσθησαν vb 1st aor pass ind
  3rd pers pl . . . . συμφλογίζω
συνέφρυγεν vb impf act ind 3rd pers sg . . . . συμφρύγω
συνεφρύγησαν vb 1st aor act ind 3rd pers pl id.
συνέφυγεν vb 2nd aor act ind 3rd pers sg . . . . . . συμφεύγω
συνεφύροντο vb impf m/p ind 3rd pers pl . . . . . . συμφύρω
συνεφώνησαν vb 1st aor act ind 3rd pers pl . . . . . συμφωνέω
συνεφώνησεν vb 1st aor act ind 3rd pers sg id.
συνέχεεν vb impf act ind 3rd pers sg . . . . συγχέω
συνέχειν vb pres act inf . . . . συνέχω
συνέχομεν vb pres act ind 1st pers pl id.
συνεχόμενα vb pres m/p part neut nom and acc pl id.
συνεχόμεναι vb pres m/p part fem nom pl id.
συνεχομένη vb pres m/p part fem nom sg id.
συνεχόμενον vb pres m/p part masc acc sg id.
συνεχόμενος vb pres m/p part masc nom sg id.
συνεχομένου vb pres m/p part masc and neut gen sg id.
συνεχομένους vb pres m/p part masc acc pl id.
συνέχον vb pres act part neut nom and acc sg id.
συνέχοντα vb pres act part neut nom. and acc pl id.
συνέχονται vb pres m/p ind 3rd pers pl id.
συνέχου vb pres m/p impv 2nd pers sg id.
συνέχουσαι vb pres act part fem nom pl id.
συνεχούσας vb pres act part fem acc pl id.
συνέχουσιν vb pres act ind 3rd pers pl id.
συνεχύθη vb 1st aor pass ind 3rd pers sg . . . . συγχέω
συνεχύθησαν vb 1st aor pass ind 3rd pers pl id.
συνέχων vb pres act part masc nom sg . . . . συνέχω
συνεχώρησεν vb 1st aor act ind 3rd pers sg . . . . . συγχωρέω
συνεψήσθη vb 1st aor pass ind 3rd pers sg . . . . συμψάω
συνζυγεῖς see συζυγεῖς
συνῇ vb 2nd aor act subj 3rd pers sg . . . . συνίημι
συνήγαγεν vb 2nd aor act ind 3rd pers sg . . . . συνάγω
συνήγαγες vb 2nd aor act ind 2nd pers sg id.
συνήγαγον vb 2nd aor act ind
  1st pers sg and 3rd pers pl id.
συνηγέρθησαν vb 1st aor pass ind 3rd pers pl . . συνεγείρω
συνηγμένα vb perf m/p part neut nom and acc pl . . . συνάγω
συνηγμένη vb perf m/p part fem nom sg id.
συνηγμένοι vb perf m/p part masc nom pl id.
συνηγμένοις vb perf m/p part masc and neut dat pl id.
συνηγμένον vb perf m/p part masc acc sg,
  neut nom and acc sg id.
συνηγμένων vb perf m/p part gen pl id.
συνήγοντο vb impf m/p ind 3rd pers pl id.
συνήδρευσαν vb 1st aor act ind 3rd pers pl . . . . συνεδρεύω
συνηθείας noun fem gen sg . . . . συνήθεια
συνήθροισεν vb 1st aor act ind 3rd pers sg . . . συναθροίζω
συνηθροίσθησαν vb 1st aor pass ind 3rd pers pl id.

συνηθροισμένη vb perf m/p part fem nom sg . συναθροίζω	συνθλίβου vb pres m/p impv 2nd pers sg . . . . . . συνθλίβω
συνηθροισμένους vb perf m/p part masc acc pl id.	συνθώμεθα vb 2nd aor mid subj 1st pers pl . . . . συντίθημι
συνήθροιστο vb plpf m/p ind 3rd pers sg id.	συνιδόντες vb 2nd aor act part masc nom pl . . . . . συνοράω
συνήθων adj gen pl . . . . συνήθης	συνιδών vb 2nd aor act part masc nom sg id.
συνῆκα vb 1st aor act ind 1st pers sg . . . . συνίημι	συνίει vb pres act ind 3rd pers sg . . . . συνίημι
συνῆκαν vb 1st aor act ind 3rd pers pl id.	συνίειν vb pres act inf id.
συνῆκας vb 1st aor act ind 2nd pers sg id.	συνιεῖς vb pres act ind 2nd pers sg id.
συνῆκεν vb 1st aor act ind 3rd pers sg id.	συνίεις vb impf act ind 2nd pers sg id.
συνῆκται vb perf m/p ind 3rd pers sg . . . . συνάγω	συνιείς vb pres act part masc nom sg id.
συνήλασαν vb 1st aor act ind 3rd pers pl . . . . . συνελαύνω	συνιέναι vb pres act inf id.
συνήλαστο vb plpf m/p ind 3rd pers sg id.	συνιέντας vb pres act part masc acc pl id.
συνῆλθεν vb 2nd aor act ind 3rd pers sg . . . . συνέρχομαι	συνιέντες vb pres act part masc nom pl id.
συνῆλθον vb 2nd aor act ind 3rd pers pl id.	συνιέντων vb pres act part masc and neut gen pl id.
συνήλθοσαν vb 2nd aor act ind 3rd pers pl id.	συνίετε vb pres act ind 2nd pers pl id.
συνήλικα adj neut nom and acc pl . . . . συνήλικος	συνίῃς vb pres act subj 2nd pers sg id.
συνηλόησε vb 1st aor act ind 3rd pers sg . . . . . συναλοάω	συνίοντας vb pres act part masc acc pl id.
συνημμένος vb perf m/p part masc nom sg . . . . . συνάπτω	συνίοντος vb pres act part masc and neut gen sg id.
συνήντησαν vb 1st aor act ind 3rd pers pl . . . . . . συναντάω	συνιόντων vb pres act part masc and neut gen pl id.
συνήντησεν vb 1st aor act ind 3rd pers sg id.	συνιοῦσι vb pres act part masc and neut dat pl id.
συνήντων vb impf act ind 1st pers sg and 3rd pers pl id.	συνιστάμενοι vb pres m/p part masc nom pl . . . συνίστημι
συνῆξα vb 1st aor act ind 1st pers sg . . . . συνάγω	συνιστάμενον vb pres m/p part neut nom and acc sg id.
συνῆξεν vb 1st aor act ind 3rd pers sg id.	συνιστάμενος vb pres m/p part masc nom sg id.
συνῇς vb 2nd aor act subj 2nd pers sg . . . . συνίημι	συνίστανται vb pres m/p ind 3rd pers pl id.
συνήσει vb fut act ind 3rd pers sg id.	συνίσταντο vb impf m/p ind 3rd pers pl id.
συνήσεις vb fut act ind 2nd pers sg id.	συνίστασθαι vb pres m/p inf id.
συνήσθιον vb impf act ind	συνίστατο vb impf m/p ind 3rd pers sg id.
1st pers sg and 3rd pers pl . . . . συνεσθίω	συνίστησιν vb pres act ind 3rd pers sg id.
συνήσουσιν vb fut act ind 3rd pers pl . . . . συνίημι	συνιστῶν vb pres act part masc nom sg id.
συνήσω vb fut act ind 1st pers sg id.	συνίστωρ noun masc nom sg
συνῆτε vb 2nd aor act subj 2nd pers pl id.	συνιών vb pres act part masc nom sg . . . . συνίημι
συνηχήσαντας vb 1st aor act part masc acc pl . . . . συνηχέω	συννεφεῖν vb pres act inf . . . . συννεφέω
συνήχθη vb 1st aor pass ind 3rd pers sg . . . . συνάγω	συννεφής adj masc and fem nom sg
συνήχθημεν vb 1st aor pass ind 1st pers pl id.	συννοήσας vb 1st aor act part masc nom sg . . . . . . συννοέω
συνήχθησαν vb 1st aor pass ind 3rd pers pl id.	σύννους adj masc and fem nom sg
συνῆψα vb 1st aor act ind 1st pers sg . . . . συνάπτω	συννοῶν vb pres act part masc nom sg . . . . συννοέω
συνῆψαν vb 1st aor act ind 3rd pers pl id.	σύννυμφος noun fem nom sg
συνῆψεν vb 1st aor act ind 3rd pers sg id.	συννύμφου noun fem gen sg . . . . σύννυμφος
συνθελήσεις vb fut act ind 2nd pers sg . . . . συνθέλω	συνοδεύσαι vb 1st aor act opt 3rd pers sg . . . . . . συνοδεύω
συνθέμενοι vb 2nd aor mid part masc nom pl . . . συντίθημι	συνοδεύσω vb fut act ind 1st pers sg id.
συνθέμενον vb 2nd aor mid part masc acc sg id.	συνοδίας noun fem gen sg and acc pl . . . . συνοδία
συνθέσεις noun fem nom and acc pl . . . . σύνθεσις	σύνοδον noun fem acc sg . . . . σύνοδος
συνθέσεως noun fem gen sg id.	σύνοδος noun fem nom sg id.
συνθέσθαι vb 2nd aor mid inf . . . . συντίθημι	συνοδυνηθῆς vb 1st aor pass subj
σύνθεσιν noun fem acc sg . . . . σύνθεσις	2nd pers sg . . . . συνοδυνάομαι
σύνθετον adj acc sg, neut nom sg . . . . σύνθετος	συνόδων noun fem gen pl . . . . σύνοδος
συνθήκαις noun fem dat pl . . . . συνθήκη	σύνοιδα vb perf act ind 1st pers sg . . . . σύνοιδα
συνθήκας noun fem acc pl id.	σύνοιδεν vb perf act ind 3rd pers sg id.
συνθήκην noun fem acc sg id.	συνοικῆσαι vb 1st aor act inf . . . . συνοικέω
συνθηκῶν noun fem gen pl id.	συνοικήσει vb fut act ind 3rd pers sg id.
σύνθημα noun neut nom and acc sg	συνοικήσεως noun fem gen sg . . . . συνοίκησις
συνθλάσει vb fut act ind 3rd pers sg . . . . συνθλάω	συνοικήσῃ vb 1st aor act subj 3rd pers sg . . . . . . συνοικέω
συνθλιβῇ vb 2nd aor pass subj 3rd pers sg . . . . . . συνθλίβω	συνοικήσων vb fut act part masc nom sg id.

συνοικίσητε　vb 1st aor act subj 2nd pers pl . . . .　συνοικίζω

συνοικισθήσεται　vb fut pass ind 3rd pers sg　　　　id.

συνοικισθήσῃ　vb fut pass ind 2nd pers sg　　　　id.

συνοικοδομήσομεν　vb fut act ind

　　　　1st pers pl . . . .　συνοικοδομέω

συνοικοῦντα　vb pres act part masc acc sg . . . . . .　συνοικέω

συνοικῶν　vb pres act part masc nom sg　　　　id.

συνολκήν　noun fem acc sg . . . .　συνολκή

σύνολον　adj acc sg, neut nom sg . . . .　σύνολος

συνομολογεῖται　vb pres m/p ind

　　　　　3rd pers sg . . . .　συνομολογέω

συνόντα　vb pres act part masc acc sg . . . .　σύνειμι

συνόντων　vb pres act part masc and neut gen pl　　　　id.

συνορῶν　vb pres act part masc nom sg . . . .　συνοράω

συνορῶντες　vb pres act part masc nom pl　　　　id.

συνορώντων　vb pres act part masc and neut gen pl　　　　id.

συνορῶσα　vb pres act part fem nom sg　　　　id.

συνούλωσιν　noun fem acc sg . . . .　συνούλωσις

συνούσης　vb pres act part fem gen sg . . . .　σύνειμι

συνοῦσι　vb pres act part masc and neut dat pl　　　　id.

συνουσιασμόν　noun masc acc sg . . . .　συνουσιασμός

συνουσιασμός　noun masc nom sg　　　　id.

συνοχάς　noun fem acc pl . . . .　συνοχή

συνοχήν　noun fem acc sg　　　　id.

συνταγέντος　vb 2nd aor pass part

　　　　masc and neut gen sg . . . .　συντάσσω

συνταγή　noun fem nom sg

συνταγῇ　noun fem dat sg . . . .　συνταγή

σύνταγμα　noun neut nom and acc sg

συντάγματος　noun neut gen sg . . . .　σύνταγμα

συνταγῶν　noun fem gen pl . . . .　συνταγή

συντάξαντος　vb 1st aor act part

　　　　masc and neut gen sg . . . .　συντάσσω

συντάξει　noun fem dat sg . . . .　σύνταξις

συντάξει　vb fut act ind 3rd pers sg . . . .　συντάσσω

συντάξεις　noun fem acc pl . . . .　σύνταξις

συντάξεις　vb fut act ind 2nd pers sg . . . .　συντάσσω

συντάξεως　noun fem gen sg . . . .　σύνταξις

σύνταξιν　noun fem acc sg　　　　id.

σύνταξις　noun fem nom sg　　　　id.

σύνταξον　vb 1st aor act impv 2nd pers sg . . . . .　συντάσσω

συντάξω　vb fut act ind 1st pers sg　　　　id.

συνταράξει　vb fut act ind 3rd pers sg . . . . . .　συνταράσσω

συνταράξεις　vb fut act ind 2nd pers sg　　　　id.

συνταράσσει　vb pres act ind 3rd pers sg　　　　id.

συνταράσσεις　vb pres act ind 2nd pers sg　　　　id.

συνταράσσων　vb pres act part masc nom sg　　　　id.

συντάσσει　vb pres act ind 3rd pers sg . . . . . .　συντάσσω

συντάσσεται　vb pres m/p ind 3rd pers sg　　　　id.

συντασσόμενοι　vb pres m/p part masc nom pl　　　　id.

συντασσομένοις　vb pres m/p part masc and neut dat pl　　id.

συντάσσω　vb pres act ind 1st pers sg　　　　id.

συντάσσων　vb pres act part masc nom sg . . . . .　συντάσσω

συνταχθέν　vb 1st aor pass part neut nom and acc sg　　id.

συντέλεια　noun fem nom sg

συντελείᾳ　noun fem dat sg . . . .　συντέλεια

συντέλειαι　noun fem nom pl　　　　id.

συντέλειαν　noun fem acc sg　　　　id.

συντελείας　noun fem gen sg and acc pl　　　　id.

συντελεῖν　vb pres act inf . . . .　συντελέω

συντελεῖσθαι　vb pres m/p inf　　　　id.

συντελεῖται　vb pres m/p ind 3rd pers sg　　　　id.

συντελεῖτε　vb pres act impv 2nd pers pl　　　　id.

συντελέσαι　vb 1st aor act inf　　　　id.

συντελέσας　vb 1st aor act part masc nom sg　　　　id.

συντελέσασθαι　vb 1st aor mid inf　　　　id.

συντελέσει　vb fut act ind 3rd pers sg　　　　id.

συντελέσεις　vb fut act ind 2nd pers sg　　　　id.

συντελέσετε　vb fut act ind 2nd pers pl　　　　id.

συντελέσῃ　vb 1st aor act subj 3rd pers sg　　　　id.

συντελέσῃς　vb 1st aor act subj 2nd pers sg　　　　id.

συντελέσητε　vb 1st aor act subj 2nd pers pl　　　　id.

συντελεσθέντα　vb 1st aor pass part

　　　　neut nom and acc pl　　　　id.

συντελεσθῇ　vb 1st aor pass subj 3rd pers sg　　　　id.

συντελεσθῆναι　vb 1st aor pass inf　　　　id.

συντελεσθήσεσθε　vb fut pass ind 2nd pers pl　　　　id.

συντελεσθήσεται　vb fut pass ind 3rd pers sg　　　　id.

συντελεσθήσονται　vb fut pass ind 3rd pers pl　　　　id.

συντελεσθήτω　vb 1st aor pass impv 3rd pers sg　　　　id.

συντελεσθῶσιν　vb 1st aor pass subj 3rd pers pl　　　　id.

συντέλεσον　vb 1st aor act impv 2nd pers sg　　　　id.

συντελέσουσιν　vb fut act ind 3rd pers pl　　　　id.

συντελέσω　vb 1st aor act subj 1st pers sg,

　　　　fut act ind 1st pers sg　　　　id.

συντελούμενα　vb pres m/p part neut nom and acc pl　　id.

συντελούμενον　vb pres m/p part masc acc sg,

　　　　neut nom and acc sg　　　　id.

συντελοῦν　vb pres act part neut nom and acc sg　　　　id.

συντελοῦνται　vb pres m/p ind 3rd pers pl　　　　id.

συντελοῦντες　vb pres act part masc nom pl　　　　id.

συντελούντων　vb pres act part masc and neut gen pl　　id.

συντελοῦσι　vb pres act ind 3rd pers pl　　　　id.

συντελῶν　vb pres act part masc nom sg　　　　id.

συντέμνοντες　vb pres act part masc nom pl . . . . .　συντέμνω

συντέμνων　vb pres act part masc nom sg　　　　id.

συντέτακται　vb perf m/p ind 3rd pers sg . . . . . .　συντάσσω

συντέταχα　vb perf act ind 1st pers sg　　　　id.

συντετέλεσαι　vb perf m/p ind 2nd pers sg . . . . . .　συντελέω

συντετελέσθαι　vb perf m/p inf　　　　id.

συντετέλεσθε　vb perf m/p ind 2nd pers pl　　　　id.

συντετελεσμένα　vb perf m/p part

　　　　neut nom and acc pl　　　　id.

συντετελεσμένην　vb perf m/p part fem acc sg . .　συντελέω

συντετελεσμένον vb perf m/p part masc acc sg,
    neut nom and acc sg . . . . συντελέω
συντετελεσμένων vb perf m/p part gen pl   id.
συντετέλεσται vb perf m/p ind 3rd pers sg   id.
συντετμημένα vb perf m/p part
    neut nom and acc pl . . . . συντέμνω
συντετμημένον vb perf m/p part masc acc sg,
    neut nom and acc sg   id.
συντετμημένου vb perf m/p part
    masc and neut gen sg   id.
συντέτμηται vb perf m/p ind 3rd pers sg   id.
συντετριμμένη vb perf m/p part fem dat sg . . . . συντρίβω
συντετριμμένην vb perf m/p part fem acc sg   id.
συντετριμμένοις vb perf m/p part
    masc and neut dat pl   id.
συντετριμμένον vb perf m/p part masc acc sg.
    neut nom and acc sg   id.
συντετριμμένος vb perf m/p part masc nom sg   id.
συντετριμμένους vb perf m/p part masc acc pl   id.
συντετριμμένων vb perf m/p part gen pl   id.
συντηρεῖ vb pres act ind 3rd pers sg . . . . συντηρέω
συντηρεῖν vb pres act inf   id.
συντηρηθήσεται vb fut pass ind 3rd pers sg   id.
συντηρῆσαι vb 1st aor act inf   id.
συντηρήσατε vb 1st aor act impv 2nd pers pl   id.
συντηρήσει vb fut act ind 3rd pers sg   id.
συντηρήσεις vb fut act ind 2nd pers sg   id.
συντηρήσητε vb 1st aor act subj 2nd pers pl   id.
συντήρησον vb 1st aor act impv 2nd pers sg   id.
συντηρήσουσιν vb fut act ind 3rd pers pl   id.
συντηρήσω vb 1st aor act subj 1st pers sg   id.
συντηρουμένων vb pres m/p part gen pl   id.
συντηροῦντα vb pres act part masc acc sg   id.
συντηροῦσιν vb pres act ind 3rd pers pl   id.
συντηρῶν vb pres act part masc nom sg   id.
συντιμήσεως noun fem gen sg . . . . συντίμησις
συντίμησιν noun fem acc sg   id.
συντίμησις noun fem nom sg   id.
σύντομον adj acc sg, neut nom sg . . . . σύντομος
σύντομος adj masc and fem nom sg   id.
συντόμως adverb
συντραφέντες vb 2nd aor pass part masc nom pl . συντρέφω
συντρεφομένους vb pres m/p part masc acc pl   id.
συντρέφονται vb pres m/p ind 3rd pers pl   id.
συντρίβει vb pres act ind 3rd pers sg . . . . συντρίβω
συντριβείη vb 2nd aor pass opt 3rd pers sg   id.
συντριβείησαν vb 2nd aor pass opt 3rd pers pl   id.
συντριβέν vb 2nd aor pass part neut nom and acc sg   id.
συντριβέντα vb 2nd aor pass part neut nom and acc pl   id.
συντριβέντας vb 2nd aor pass part masc acc pl   id.
συντριβέντος vb 2nd aor pass part
    masc and neut gen sg   id.

συντρίβεται vb pres m/p ind 3rd pers sg . . . . συντρίβω
συντριβή noun fem nom sg
συντριβῇ noun fem dat sg   συντριβή
συντριβῇ vb 2nd aor pass subj 3rd pers sg . . . . . . συντρίβω
συντριβήν noun fem acc sg . . . . συντριβή
συντριβῆναι vb 2nd aor pass inf . . . . συντρίβω
συντριβῆς noun fem gen sg . . . . συντριβή
συντριβήσεται vb fut pass ind 3rd pers sg . . . . . συντρίβω
συντριβήσονται vb fut pass ind 3rd pers pl   id.
συντριβῆτε vb 2nd aor pass subj 2nd pers pl   id.
συντριβήτω vb 2nd aor pass impv 3rd pers sg   id.
συντριβόμενον vb pres m/p part masc acc sg,
    neut nom and acc sg   id.
συντρῖβον vb pres act part neut nom and acc sg   id.
συντρίβοντα vb pres act part masc acc sg   id.
συντρίβοντος vb pres act part masc and neut gen sg   id.
συντρίβω vb pres act ind 1st pers sg   id.
συντρίβων vb pres act part masc nom sg   id.
συντρίβωνται vb pres m/p subj 3rd pers pl   id.
συντριβῶσι vb 2nd aor pass subj 3rd pers pl   id.
σύντριμμα noun neut nom and acc sg
συντρίμματα noun neut nom and acc pl . . . . . . σύντριμμα
συντρίμματι noun neut dat sg   id.
συντρίμματος noun neut gen sg   id.
συντριμμοί noun masc nom pl . . . . συντριμμός
συντριμμόν noun masc acc sg   id.
συντριμμός noun masc nom sg   id.
συντρῖψαι vb 1st aor act inf . . . . συντρίβω
συντρίψας vb 1st aor act part masc nom sg
συντρίψει vb fut act ind 3rd pers sg   id.
συντρίψεις vb fut act ind 2nd pers sg   id.
συντρίψετε vb fut act ind 2nd pers pl   id.
συντρίψη vb 1st aor act subj 3rd pers sg   id.
σύντριψιν noun fem acc sg . . . . σύντριψις
σύντριψον vb 1st aor act impv 2nd pers sg . . . . . . συντρίβω
συντρίψουσιν vb fut act ind 3rd pers pl   id.
συντρίψω vb 1st aor act subj 1st pers sg,
    fut act ind 1st pers sg   id.
συντροφίας noun fem gen sg . . . . συντροφία
σύντροφοι noun masc nom pl . . . . σύντροφος
σύντροφος noun masc nom sg   id.
συντρόφους noun masc acc pl   id.
συντροχάσῃ vb 1st aor act subj 3rd pers sg . . . . συντροχάζω
συντυχεῖν vb 2nd aor act inf . . . . συντυγχάνω
συνυφᾶναι vb 1st aor act inf . . . . συνυφαίνω
συνυφάνθη vb 1st aor pass ind 3rd pers sg   id.
συνυφασμένην vb perf m/p part fem acc sg   id.
συνυφῆς noun fem gen sg . . . . συνυφή
συνῶ vb 2nd aor act subj 1st pers sg . . . . συνίημι
συνῳκηκυῖα vb perf act part fem nom sg . . . . συνοικέω
συνῴκησαν vb 1st aor act ind 3rd pers pl   id.
συνῴκησεν vb 1st aor act ind 3rd pers sg   id.

συνῳκίσαμεν vb 1st aor act ind 1st pers pl ..... συνοικίζω
συνῴκισαν vb 1st aor act ind 3rd pers pl   id.
συνῳκίσατε vb 1st aor act ind 2nd pers pl   id.
συνῳκισμένης vb perf m/p part fem gen sg   id.
συνωμόται noun masc nom pl .... συνωμότης
συνωρίδος noun fem gen sg .... συνωρίς
συνῶσιν vb 1st aor act subj 3rd pers pl .... συνίημι
Συρα pr noun fem nom sg
Συρας pr noun fem gen sg .... Συρα
Συρια pr noun fem nom sg
Συριᾳ pr noun fem dat sg .... Συρια
Συριακῇ pr noun fem dat sg .... Συριακη
Συριακῆς pr noun fem gen sg   id.
Συριαν pr noun fem acc sg .... Συρια
Συριας pr noun fem gen sg   id.
σύριγγος noun fem gen sg .... σύριγξ
σύριγμα noun neut nom and acc sg
συριγμοῖς noun masc dat pl .... συριγμός
συριγμόν noun masc acc sg   id.
συριεῖ vb fut act ind 3rd pers sg .... συρίζω
συρίζον vb pres act part neut nom and acc sg   id.
συρίζοντος vb pres act part masc and neut gen sg   id.
συριοῦσιν vb fut act ind 3rd pers pl   id.
συρισμόν noun masc acc sg .... συρισμός
συρισμοῦ noun masc gen sg   id.
συρισμούς noun masc acc pl   id.
Συριστι pr noun
Συροι pr noun masc nom pl .... Συρος
σῦρον vb pres act part neut nom and acc sg .... σύρω
Συρον pr noun masc acc sg .... Συρος
σύροντες vb pres act part masc nom pl .... σύρω
συρόντων vb pres act part masc and neut gen pl   id.
Συρος pr noun masc nom sg
Συρου pr noun masc gen sg .... Συρος
συροῦμεν vb fut act ind 1st pers pl .... σύρω
Συρους pr noun masc acc pl .... Συρος
σύρουσαι vb pres act part fem nom pl .... σύρω
συρραπτούσαις vb pres act part fem dat pl ..... συρράπτω
συρραφῇ vb 2nd aor pass subj 3rd pers sg   id.
Συρῳ pr noun masc dat sg .... Συρος
Συρων pr noun masc gen pl   id.
σῦς noun masc nom sg
συσκηνίοις noun masc dat pl .... συσκήνιος
συσκήνου noun masc gen sg .... σύσκηνος
συσκιάζον vb pres act part neut nom and acc sg .. συσκιάζω
συσκιάζοντες vb pres act part masc nom pl   id.
συσκιάζοντος vb pres act part masc and neut gen sg   id.
σύσκιος adj masc and fem nom sg
συσκίου adj gen sg .... σύσκιος
συσκοτάζων vb pres act part masc nom sg .... συσκοτάζω
συσκοτάσαι vb 1st aor act inf   id.
συσκοτασάτω vb 1st aor act impv 3rd pers sg   id.

συσκοτάσει vb fut act ind 3rd pers sg .... συσκοτάζω
συσκοτάσουσιν vb fut act ind 3rd pers pl   id.
συσκοτάσω vb fut act ind 1st pers sg   id.
συσσείονται vb pres m/p ind 3rd pers pl .... συσσείω
συσσείοντος vb pres act part masc and neut gen sg   id.
συσσείσει vb fut act ind 3rd pers sg   id.
συσσεισμόν noun masc acc sg .... συσσεισμός
συσσεισμός noun masc nom sg   id.
συσσεισμοῦ noun masc gen sg   id.
συσσεισμῷ noun masc dat sg   id.
συσσείσω vb fut act ind 1st pers sg .... συσσείω
σύσσημον noun neut nom and acc sg
συσσύρων vb pres act part masc nom sg .... συσσύρω
συσταθείς vb 1st aor pass part masc nom sg ... συνίστημι
συσταθέντες vb 1st aor pass part masc nom pl   id.
συστάς vb 2nd aor act part masc nom sg   id.
συστάσει noun fem dat sg .... σύστασις
σύστασιν noun fem acc sg   id.
συστέλλεσθαι vb pres m/p inf .... συστέλλω
σύστεμα noun neut nom and acc sg
συστέματα noun neut nom and acc pl .... σύστεμα
συστέματι noun masc dat sg   id.
σύστημα noun neut nom and acc sg
συστήματα noun neut nom and acc pl .... σύστημα
συστήματι noun neut dat sg   id.
συστῆναι vb 2nd aor act inf .... συνίστημι
συστησάμενοι vb 1st aor mid part masc nom pl   id.
συστησάμενος vb 1st aor mid part masc nom sg   id.
συστήσαντα vb 1st aor act part masc acc sg   id.
συστήσασθαι vb 1st aor mid inf   id.
συστήσασθε vb 1st aor mid impv 2nd pers pl   id.
συστραφέντας vb 2nd aor pass part masc acc pl . συστρέφω
σύστρεμμα noun neut nom and acc sg
συστρέμματος noun neut gen sg .... σύστρεμμα
συστρεμμάτων noun neut gen pl   id.
συστρέφετε vb pres act ind 2nd pers pl .... συστρέφω
συστρεφομένη vb pres m/p part fem nom sg   id.
συστρεφομένοις vb pres m/p part masc and neut dat pl   id.
συστρεφομένων vb pres m/p part gen pl   id.
συστρέφων vb pres act part masc nom sg   id.
συστρέψας vb 1st aor act part masc nom sg   id.
συστροφαί noun fem nom pl .... συστροφή
συστροφαῖς noun fem dat pl   id.
συστροφάς noun fem acc pl   id.
συστροφή noun fem nom sg   id.
συστροφήν noun fem acc sg   id.
συστροφῆς noun fem gen sg   id.
συσφίγξῃς vb 1st aor act subj 2nd pers sg ...... συσφίγγω
συσχεθῇ vb 1st aor pass subj 3rd pers sg .... συνέχω
συσχεθῆναι vb 1st aor pass inf   id.
συσχεθήσονται vb fut pass ind 3rd pers pl   id.
συσχέτω vb 2nd aor act impv 3rd pers sg   id.

συσχῇ   vb 2nd aor act subj 3rd pers sg . . . . συνέχω

συσχῶ   vb 2nd aor act subj 1st pers sg   id.

Συχεμ   pr noun

Συχεμι   pr noun

συχνούς   adj masc nom pl . . . . συχνός

σφαγαί   noun fem nom pl . . . . σφαγή

σφαγάς   noun fem acc pl   id.

σφαγέντος   vb 2nd aor pass part masc and neut gen sg . σφάζω

σφαγή   noun fem nom sg

σφαγῇ   noun fem dat sg . . . . σφαγή

σφαγήν   noun fem acc sg   id.

σφαγῆναι   vb 2nd aor pass inf . . . . σφάζω

σφαγῆς   noun fem gen sg . . . . σφαγή

σφαγήσονται   vb fut pass ind 3rd pers pl . . . . σφάζω

σφάγια   noun neut nom and acc pl . . . . σφάγιον

σφαγιάσαι   vb 1st aor act inf . . . . σφαγιάζω

σφαγιασθῆναι   vb 1st aor pass inf   id.

σφάζε   vb pres act impv 2nd pers sg . . . . σφάζω

σφάζειν   vb pres act inf   id.

σφάζετε   vb pres act ind 2nd pers pl   id.

σφαζέτω   vb pres act impv 3rd pers sg   id.

σφάζοντες   vb pres act part masc nom pl   id.

σφάζουσιν   vb pres act ind 3rd pers pl   id.

σφάζωσιν   vb pres act subj 3rd pers pl   id.

σφαιρωτήρ   noun masc nom sg

σφαιρωτῆρες   noun masc nom pl . . . . σφαιρωτήρ

σφαιρωτῆρος   noun masc gen sg   id.

σφακελίζοντας   vb pres act part masc acc pl . . . σφακελίζω

σφακελίζοντες   vb pres act part masc nom pl   id.

σφάλαι   vb 2nd aor act opt 3rd pers sg . . . . σφάλλω

σφαλέντος   vb 2nd aor pass part masc and neut gen sg   id.

σφαλεραί   adj fem nom pl . . . . σφαλερός

σφαλῇ   vb 1st aor pass subj 3rd pers sg . . . . σφάλλω

σφάλμα   noun neut nom and acc sg

σφαλοῦσιν   vb fut act ind 3rd pers pl . . . . σφάλλω

σφάξαι   vb 1st aor act inf . . . . σφάζω

σφάξει   vb fut act ind 3rd pers sg   id.

σφάξεις   vb fut act ind 2nd pers sg   id.

σφάξῃ   vb 1st aor act subj 3rd pers sg   id.

σφάξῃς   vb 1st aor act subj 2nd pers sg   id.

σφάξον   vb 1st aor act impv 2nd pers sg   id.

σφάξουσι(ν)   vb fut act ind 3rd pers pl   id.

σφάξω   vb fut act ind 1st pers sg   id.

σφενδόνας   noun fem acc pl . . . . σφενδόνη

σφενδόνῃ   noun fem dat sg   id.

σφενδόνην   noun fem acc sg   id.

σφενδόνης   noun fem gen sg   id.

σφενδονήσεις   vb fut act ind 2nd pers sg . . . . . σφενδονάω

σφενδονῆται   noun masc nom pl . . . . σφενδονήτης

σφενδονήτης   noun masc nom sg   id.

σφήκας   noun masc acc pl . . . . σφήξ

σφηκιάν   noun fem acc sg . . . . σφηκία

σφηκίας   noun fem acc pl . . . . σφηκία

σφῆνα   noun masc acc sg . . . . σφήν

σφῆνας   noun masc acc pl   id.

σφηνούσθωσαν   vb pres m/p impv 3rd pers pl . . . . . σφηνόω

σφίγγεται   vb pres m/p ind 3rd pers sg . . . . σφίγγω

σφιγγίας   noun fem gen sg . . . . σφιγγία

σφόδρα   adverb

σφοδρόν   adj masc acc sg, neut nom and acc sg . . . . σφοδρός

σφοδρότερον   comp adj masc acc sg,

     neut nom and acc sg   id.

σφοδρῷ   adj masc and neut dat sg   id.

σφοδρῶς   adverb

σφονδύλου   noun masc gen sg . . . . σφόνδυλος

σφραγῖδα   noun fem acc sg . . . . σφραγίς

σφραγῖδας   noun fem acc pl   id.

σφραγῖδες   noun fem nom pl   id.

σφραγῖδι   noun fem dat sg   id.

σφραγῖδος   noun fem gen sg   id.

σφραγίδων   noun fem gen pl   id.

σφραγιζόμενοι   vb pres m/p part masc nom pl . . . σφραγίζω

σφραγιζόντων   vb pres act part masc and neut gen pl   id.

σφραγιῇ   vb fut mid ind 2nd pers sg   id.

σφραγίς   noun fem nom sg

σφράγισαι   vb 1st aor act impv 2nd pers sg . . . . . σφραγίζω

σφραγίσαι   vb 1st aor act inf   id.

σφραγισάμενος   vb 1st aor mid part masc nom sg   id.

σφραγίσατε   vb 1st aor act impv 2nd pers pl   id.

σφραγισθῇ   vb 1st aor pass subj 3rd pers sg   id.

σφραγῖσιν   noun fem dat pl . . . . σφραγίς

σφράγισον   vb 1st aor act impv 2nd pers sg . . . . . σφραγίζω

σφῦρα   noun fem nom sg

σφῦραι   noun fem nom pl . . . . σφῦρα

σφύραις   noun fem dat pl   id.

σφύραν   noun fem acc sg   id.

σφύρῃ   noun fem dat sg   id.

σφύρης   noun fem gen sg   id.

σφυροκόπος   adj masc and fem nom sg

σχασθήσεται   vb fut pass ind 3rd pers sg . . . . σχάζω

σχεδία   noun fem dat sg . . . . σχεδία

σχεδίαις   noun fem dat pl   id.

σχεδίαν   noun fem acc sg   id.

σχεδίας   noun fem gen sg and acc pl   id.

σχεδόν   adverb

σχετλιάζοντος   vb pres act part

     masc and neut gen sg . . . . σχετλιάζω

σχετλιαζόντων   vb pres act part masc and neut gen pl   id.

σχέτλιον   adj masc acc sg, neut nom and acc sg . . . σχέτλιος

σχῇ   vb 2nd aor act subj 3rd pers sg . . . . ἔχω

σχῆμα   noun neut nom and acc sg

σχίδακας   noun fem acc pl . . . . σχίδαξ

σχίζα   noun fem nom sg

σχίζαις   noun fem dat pl . . . . σχίζα

σχίζαν	noun fem acc sg	.... σχίζα
σχίζας	noun fem acc pl	id.
σχίζῃ	noun fem dat sg	id.
σχίζης	noun fem gen sg	id.
σχιζόμενον	vb pres m/p part masc acc sg,	
	neut nom and acc sg	.... σχίζω
σχίζουσιν	vb pres act ind 3rd pers pl	id.
σχίζων	vb pres act part masc nom sg	id.
σχῖνον	noun fem acc sg	.... σχῖνος
σχίσας	vb 1st aor act part masc nom sg	.... σχίζω
σχίσει	vb fut act ind 3rd pers sg	id.
σχισθήσεται	vb fut pass ind 3rd pers sg	id.
σχισμάς	noun fem acc pl	.... σχισμή
σχιστόν	adj masc acc sg, neut nom and acc sg	.... σχιστός
σχοίη	vb 2nd aor act opt 3rd pers sg	.... ἔχω
σχοινία	noun neut nom and acc pl	.... σχοινίον
σχοινίοις	noun neut dat pl	id.
σχοινίον	noun neut nom and acc sg	id.
Σχοινισμα	pr noun neut nom and acc sg	
σχοίνισμα	noun neut nom and acc sg	
σχοινίσματα	noun neut nom and acc pl	...... σχοίνισμα
σχοινίσματος	noun neut gen sg	id.
σχοινισμός	noun masc nom sg	
σχοινίῳ	noun neut dat sg	.... σχοινίον
σχοινίων	noun neut gen pl	id.
σχοῖνον	noun fem acc sg	.... σχοῖνος
σχοῖνος	noun masc (and fem) nom sg	id.
σχοίνους	noun masc acc pl	id.
σχοίνων	noun masc gen pl	id.
σχολάζετε	vb pres act ind 2nd pers pl	.... σχολάζω
σχολάζουσιν	vb pres act ind 3rd pers pl	id.
σχολάσατε	vb 1st aor act impv 2nd pers pl	id.
σχολασταί	noun masc nom pl	.... σχολαστής
σχολήν	noun fem acc sg	.... σχολή
σχολῆς	noun fem gen sg	id.
σῷ	poss pron 2nd pers masc and neut dat sg	.... σός
σῶα	adj neut nom and acc pl	.... σῶος
Σωβ	pr noun	
Σωβα	pr noun	
Σωβαβ	pr noun	
Σωβαι	pr noun	
Σωβακ	pr noun	
Σωβαλ	pr noun	
Σωβηκ	pr noun	
Σωγαλ	pr noun	
Σωγαρ	pr noun	
Σωε	pr noun	
σῷζε	vb pres act impv 2nd pers sg	.... σῴζω
σῴζει	vb pres act ind 3rd pers sg	id.
σῴζειν	vb pres act inf	id.
σῴζεις	vb pres act ind 2nd pers sg	id.
σῴζεσθαι	vb pres m/p inf	id.

σῴζεται	vb pres m/p ind 3rd pers sg	.... σῴζω
σῴζετε	vb pres act ind 2nd pers pl	id.
σῴζῃ	vb pres m/p subj 2nd pers sg	id.
σῴζοιο	vb pres m/p opt 2nd pers sg	id.
σῴζοιτο	vb pres m/p opt 3rd pers sg	id.
σωζόμενοι	vb pres m/p part masc nom pl	id.
σωζόμενον	vb pres m/p part masc acc sg,	
	neut nom and acc sg	id.
σωζόμενος	vb pres m/p part masc nom sg	id.
σῷζον	vb pres act part neut nom and acc sg	id.
σῴζοντα	vb pres act part masc acc sg	id.
σῴζοντι	vb pres act part masc and neut dat sg	id.
σῴζοντος	vb pres act part masc and neut gen sg	id.
σῴζου	vb pres m/p impv 2nd pers sg	id.
σῴζουσαν	vb pres act part fem acc sg	id.
σῴζουσιν	vb pres act ind 3rd pers pl	id.
σῴζωμεν	vb pres act subj 1st pers pl	id.
σῴζων	vb pres act part masc nom sg	id.
Σωηα	pr noun	
Σωθαλα	pr noun	
σωθείς	vb 1st aor pass part masc nom sg	.... σῴζω
Σωθελε	pr noun	
σωθέντες	vb 1st aor pass part masc nom pl	.... σῴζω
σωθέντος	vb 1st aor pass part masc and neut gen sg	id.
σωθέντων	vb 1st aor pass part masc and neut gen pl	id.
σωθῇ	vb 1st aor pass subj 3rd pers sg	id.
Σωθηβα	pr noun	
σωθῆναι	vb 1st aor pass inf	.... σῴζω
σωθῇς	vb 1st aor pass subj 2nd pers sg	id.
σωθήσεσθε	vb fut pass ind 2nd pers pl	id.
σωθήσεται	vb fut pass ind 3rd pers sg	id.
σωθήσῃ	vb fut pass ind 2nd pers sg	id.
σωθήσομαι	vb fut pass ind 1st pers sg	id.
σωθησόμεθα	vb fut pass ind 1st pers pl	id.
σωθήσονται	vb fut pass ind 3rd pers pl	id.
σωθῆτε	vb 1st aor pass subj 2nd pers pl	id.
σώθητι	vb 1st aor pass impv 2nd pers sg	id.
σωθήτω	vb 1st aor pass impv 3rd pers sg	id.
σωθῶ	vb 1st aor pass subj 1st pers sg	id.
σωθῶσι	vb 1st aor pass subj 3rd pers pl	id.
Σωκαθιιμ	pr noun	
Σωκλαγ	pr noun	
Σωλα	pr noun	
σῶμα	noun neut nom and acc sg	
Σωμαν	pr noun	
Σωμανῖτιν	pr noun fem acc sg	.... Σωμανῖτις
Σωμανῖτις	pr noun fem nom sg	id.
σώμασι	noun neut dat pl	.... σῶμα
σώματα	noun neut nom and acc pl	id.
σώματι	noun neut dat sg	id.
σωματικαί	adj fem nom pl	.... σωματικός
σωματικῶν	adj gen pl	id.

σώματος	noun neut gen sg	σῶμα
σωματοφύλακες	noun masc nom pl	σωματοφύλαξ
σωματοφύλαξι	noun masc dat pl	id.
σωμάτων	noun neut gen pl	σῶμα
Σωμηρ	pr noun	
σῶν	poss pron 2nd pers gen pl	σός
σῷοι	adj masc nom pl	σῶος
σῶον	adj masc acc sg, neut nom and acc sg	id.
σώους	adj masc acc pl	id.
σωρεύσεις	vb fut act ind 2nd pers sg	σωρεύω
σωρηδόν	adverb	
σωρηκ	translit	
Σωρης	pr noun	
σωρηχ	translit	
Σωρηχ	pr noun	
Σωρθ	pr noun	
Σωριν	pr noun	
σωροί	noun masc nom pl	σωρός
σωρόν	noun masc acc sg	id.
σωρός	noun masc nom sg	id.
σωρούς	noun masc acc pl	id.
σωρῶν	noun masc gen pl	id.
σώσαι	vb 1st aor act opt	σῴζω
σῶσαι	vb 1st aor act inf	id.
Σωσαν	pr noun	
σώσας	vb 1st aor act part masc nom sg	σῴζω
σώσατε	vb 1st aor act impv 2nd pers pl	id.
σωσάτω	vb 1st aor act impv 3rd pers sg	id.
σωσάτωσαν	vb 1st aor act impv 3rd pers pl	id.
σώσει	vb fut act ind 3rd pers sg	id.
σώσεις	vb fut act ind 2nd pers sg	id.
σώσετε	vb fut act ind 2nd pers pl	id.
σώσῃ	vb 1st aor act subj 3rd pers sg	id.
Σωσηκ	pr noun	
σώσῃς	vb 1st aor act subj 2nd pers sg	σῴζω
Σωσιμ	pr noun	
Σωσιπατρον	pr noun masc acc sg	Σωσιπατρος
Σωσιπατρος	pr noun masc nom sg	id.
σῶσον	vb 1st aor act impv 2nd pers sg,	
	fut act part neut nom and acc sg	σῴζω
Σῶσον	pr noun	
σώσουσιν	vb fut act ind 3rd pers pl	σῴζω
Σωστρατος	pr noun masc nom sg	
Σωστρατου	pr noun masc gen sg	Σωστρατος
σώσω	vb fut act ind 1st pers sg	σῴζω
σωτήρ	noun masc nom sg	
σωτήρα	noun masc acc sg	σωτήρ
σωτήρας	noun masc acc pl	id.
σωτήρι	noun masc dat sg	id.
σωτήρια	noun neut nom and acc pl	σωτήριον
σωτηρία	noun fem nom sg	
σωτηρίᾳ	noun fem dat sg	σωτηρία
σωτηρίαν	noun fem acc sg	id.
σωτηρίας	noun fem gen sg	id.
σωτήριοι	adj masc and fem nom pl	σωτήριος
σωτήριον	adj acc sg, neut nom sg	id.
σωτήριον	noun neut nom and acc sg	
σωτηρίου	noun neut gen sg	σωτήριον
σωτηρίῳ	noun neut dat sg	id.
σωτηρίων	noun neut gen pl	id.
σωτῆρος	noun masc gen sg	σωτήρ
Σωυε	pr noun	
Σωφ	pr noun	
Σωφα	pr noun	
Σωφαν	pr noun	
Σωφανι	pr noun	
Σωφαρ	pr noun	
Σωφαρφακ	pr noun	
Σωφατ	pr noun	
Σωφαχ	pr noun	
σωφερ	translit	
Σωφηρα	pr noun	
Σωφιρ	pr noun	
Σωφιρα	pr noun	
σώφρονα	adj masc and fem acc sg	σώφρων
σώφρονες	adj masc and fem nom pl	id.
σώφρονος	adj gen sg	id.
σωφρόνως	adverb	
σωφροσύνη	noun fem nom sg	
σωφροσύνῃ	noun fem dat sg	σωφροσύνη
σωφροσύνην	noun fem acc sg	id.
σωφροσύνης	noun fem gen sg	id.
σώφρων	adj masc and fem nom sg	
Σωχα	pr noun	
Σωχαρ	pr noun	
Σωχω	pr noun	
Σωχων	pr noun	

T τ

τά art neut nom and acc pl . . . . ὁ

Τααμ pr noun

Ταβαθ pr noun

Ταβαωθ pr noun

Ταβεηλ pr noun

Ταβεκ pr noun

Ταβελλιος pr noun

Ταβερεμμαν pr noun

Ταβλαι pr noun

Ταβληθ pr noun

τάγμα noun neut nom and acc sg

ταγμάτων noun neut gen pl . . . . τάγμα

τάδε dem pron neut nom and acc pl . . . . ὅδε

ταινίαι noun fem nom pl . . . . ταινία

ταῖς art fem dat pl . . . . ὁ

τακείς vb 2nd aor pass part masc nom sg . . . . τήκω

τακεῖσα vb 2nd aor pass part fem nom sg   id.

τακῇ vb 2nd aor pass subj 3rd pers sg   id.

τακήσεται vb fut pass ind 3rd pers sg   id.

τακήσονται vb fut pass ind 3rd pers pl   id.

τακτικοί noun masc nom pl . . . . τακτικός

τακτικούς noun masc acc pl   id.

τακτόν adj masc acc sg, neut nom and acc sg . . . . . . τακτός

ταλαιπωρησάντων vb 1st aor act part

masc and neut gen pl . . . . ταλαιπωρέω

ταλαιπωρήσουσιν vb fut act ind 3rd pers pl   id.

ταλαιπωρία noun fem nom sg

ταλαιπωρίᾳ noun fem dat sg . . . . ταλαιπωρία

ταλαιπωρίαι noun fem nom pl   id.

ταλαιπωρίαις noun fem dat pl   id.

ταλαιπωρίαν noun fem acc sg   id.

ταλαιπωρίας noun fem gen sg and acc pl   id.

ταλαίπωροι adj masc and fem nom pl . . . . ταλαίπωρος

ταλαιπώροις adj dat pl   id.

ταλαίπωρον adj acc sg, neut nom sg   id.

ταλαίπωρος adj masc and fem nom sg   id.

ταλαιπωροῦμεν vb pres act ind 1st pers pl . . . ταλαιπωρέω

ταλαιπωροῦντες vb pres act part masc nom pl   id.

ταλαιπωρούντων vb pres act part

masc and neut gen pl   id.

ταλαιπώρους adj masc and fem acc pl . . . . . . ταλαίπωρος

ταλαιπωροῦσιν vb pres act ind 3rd pers pl . . . ταλαιπωρέω

ταλαιπώρων adj gen pl . . . . ταλαίπωρος

τάλανες adj masc nom pl . . . . τάλας

τάλανες adj masc nom pl   id.

τάλαντα noun neut nom and acc pl . . . . τάλαντον

ταλάντοις noun neut dat pl   id.

τάλαντον noun neut nom and acc sg

ταλάντου noun neut gen sg . . . . τάλαντον

ταλάντῳ noun neut dat sg   id.

ταλάντων noun neut gen pl   id.

τάλας adj masc nom sg

τἀληθές = τό + ἀληθές

τἆλλα = τά + ἄλλα

Ταλμαν pr noun

ταμίαν noun masc acc sg . . . . ταμίας

ταμίεια see ταμιεῖα

ταμιεῖα noun neut nom and acc pl . . . . ταμιεῖον

ταμιείοις noun neut dat pl   id.

ταμιεῖον see ταμιεῖον

ταμιεῖον noun neut nom and acc sg   id.

ταμιείου noun neut gen sg   id.

ταμιείῳ noun neut dat sg   id.

ταμιείων noun neut gen pl   id.

ταμιεύεται vb pres dep ind 3rd pers sg . . . . . . ταμιεύομαι

ταμιεύσεται vb fut mid ind 3rd pers sg   id.

Ταναθαν pr noun

Ταναχ pr noun

Ταναχι pr noun

τἀνδρός = τοῦ + ἀνδρός

Τανει pr noun fem dat sg . . . . Τανις

Τανεως pr noun fem gen sg   id.

Τανιν pr noun

Τανιν pr noun fem acc sg . . . . Τανις

Τανυ pr noun

τανύσας vb 1st aor act part masc nom sg . . . . τανύω

Τανω pr noun

τάξαι vb 1st aor act inf . . . . τάσσω

τάξαι vb 1st aor mid impv 2nd pers sg   id.

ταξάμενος vb 1st aor mid part masc nom sg   id.

τάξαντα vb 1st aor act part masc acc sg   id.

τάξαντος vb 1st aor act part masc and neut gen sg   id.

τάξας vb 1st aor act part masc nom sg   id.

τάξατε vb 1st aor act impv 2nd pers pl   id.

τάξει noun fem dat sg . . . . τάξις

τάξει vb fut act ind 3rd pers sg . . . . τάσσω

τάξεις vb fut act ind 2nd pers sg   id.

τάξεως noun fem gen sg . . . . τάξις

τάξῃ vb 1st aor act subj 3rd pers sg . . . . τάσσω

τάξιν noun fem acc sg . . . . τάξις

τάξις noun fem nom sg   id.

τάξομαι vb fut mid ind 1st pers sg . . . . τάσσω

τάξον vb 1st aor act impv 2nd pers sg   id.

τάξουσιν vb fut act ind 3rd pers pl   id.

τάξω vb fut act ind 1st pers sg   id.

ταπεινά adj neut nom and acc pl . . . . ταπεινός

ταπεινή adj fem nom sg	. . . .	ταπεινός
ταπεινῆ adj fem dat sg		id.
ταπεινοί adj masc nom pl		id.
ταπεινοῖ vb pres act ind 3rd pers sg,		
pres act subj 3rd pers sg	. . . .	ταπεινόω
ταπεινοῖς adj masc and neut dat pl	. . . .	ταπεινός
ταπεινόν adj masc acc sg, neut nom and acc sg		id.
ταπεινός adj masc nom sg		id.
ταπεινοτέρα comp adj fem nom sg		id.
ταπεινότης noun fem nom sg		
ταπείνου vb pres act impv 2nd pers sg	. . . .	ταπεινόω
ταπεινοῦ adj masc and neut gen sg	. . . .	ταπεινός
ταπεινουμένην vb pres m/p part fem acc sg	. . .	ταπεινόω
ταπεινοῦν vb pres act inf		id.
ταπεινοῦντες vb pres act part masc nom pl		id.
ταπεινούς adj masc acc pl	. . . .	ταπεινός
ταπεινοῦσθαι vb pres m/p inf	. . . .	ταπεινόω
ταπεινοῦται vb pres m/p ind 3rd pers sg		id.
ταπεινόφρονας noun masc acc pl	. . . .	ταπεινόφρων
ταπεινῷ adj masc and neut dat sg	. . . .	ταπεινός
ταπεινωθείη vb 1st aor pass opt 3rd pers sg	. . . .	ταπεινόω
ταπεινωθείς vb 1st aor pass part masc nom sg		id.
ταπεινωθῆ vb 1st aor pass subj 3rd pers sg		id.
ταπεινωθῆναι vb 1st aor pass inf		id.
ταπεινωθῆς vb 1st aor pass subj 2nd pers sg		id.
ταπεινωθήσεται vb fut pass ind 3rd pers sg		id.
ταπεινωθήσονται vb fut pass ind 3rd pers pl		id.
ταπεινώθητε vb 1st aor pass impv 2nd pers pl		id.
ταπεινώθητι vb 1st aor pass impv 2nd pers sg		id.
ταπεινῶν adj gen pl	. . . .	ταπεινός
ταπεινῶν vb pres act part masc nom sg	. . . .	ταπεινόω
ταπεινῶσαι vb 1st aor act inf		id.
ταπεινωσάντων vb 1st aor act part masc and neut gen pl	id.
ταπεινώσας vb 1st aor act part masc nom sg		id.
ταπεινώσατε vb 1st aor act impv 2nd pers pl		id.
ταπεινώσει noun fem dat sg	. . . .	ταπείνωσις
ταπεινώσει vb fut act ind 3rd pers sg	. . . .	ταπεινόω
ταπεινώσεις vb fut act ind 2nd pers sg		id.
ταπεινώσετε vb fut act ind 2nd pers pl		id.
ταπεινώσεως noun fem gen sg	. . . .	ταπείνωσις
ταπεινώσῃς vb 1st aor act subj 2nd pers sg	. . . . .	ταπεινόω
ταπείνωσιν noun fem acc sg	. . . .	ταπείνωσις
ταπείνωσις noun fem nom sg		id.
ταπεινώσον vb 1st aor act impv 2nd pers sg	. . . .	ταπεινόω
ταπεινώσουσιν vb fut act ind 3rd pers pl		id.
ταπεινώσω vb fut act ind 1st pers sg		id.
Ταραθ pr noun		
ταράξαι vb 1st aor act inf	. . . .	ταράσσω
ταράξας vb 1st aor act part masc nom sg		id.
ταράξει vb fut act ind 3rd pers sg		id.
ταράξεις vb fut act ind 2nd pers sg		id.
ταράξῃ vb 1st aor act subj 3rd pers sg		id.

ταράξουσιν vb fut act ind 3rd pers pl	. . . .	ταράσσω
ταράσσει vb pres act ind 3rd pers sg		id.
ταράσσεσθαι vb pres m/p inf		id.
ταράσσεται vb pres m/p ind 3rd pers sg		id.
ταρασσέτωσαν vb pres act impv 3rd pers pl		id.
ταρασσομένοις vb pres m/p part masc and neut dat pl	id.
ταρασσομένους vb pres m/p part masc acc pl		id.
ταράσσονται vb pres m/p ind 3rd pers pl		id.
ταράσσοντας vb pres act part masc acc pl		id.
ταράσσοντες vb pres act part masc nom pl		id.
ταράσσουσα vb pres act part fem nom sg		id.
ταράσσουσιν vb pres act ind 3rd pers pl		id.
ταράσσων vb pres act part masc nom sg		id.
ταραχαῖς noun fem dat pl	. . . .	ταραχή
ταραχάς noun fem acc pl		id.
ταραχή noun fem nom sg		id.
ταραχῇ noun fem dat sg		id.
ταραχήν noun fem acc sg		id.
ταραχῆς noun fem gen sg		id.
ταραχθείησαν vb 1st aor pass opt 3rd pers pl	. . .	ταράσσω
ταραχθέντες vb 1st aor pass part masc nom pl		id.
ταραχθέντος vb 1st aor pass part masc and neut gen sg	id.
ταραχθῆναι vb 1st aor pass inf		id.
ταραχθήσεσθε vb fut pass ind 2nd pers pl		id.
ταραχθήσεται vb fut pass ind 3rd pers sg		id.
ταραχθήσονται vb fut pass ind 3rd pers pl		id.
ταραχθῆτε vb 1st aor pass subj 2nd pers pl		id.
ταραχθητωσαν vb 1st aor pass impv 3rd pers pl		id.
τάραχος noun masc nom sg		
ταράχῳ noun masc dat sg	. . . .	τάραχος
ταραχῶδες adj neut nom and acc sg	. . . .	ταραχώδης
ταραχώδους adj gen sg		id.
ταριχεύουσαι vb pres act part fem nom pl	. . . . .	ταριχεύω
Ταρσεῖς pr noun		
ταρσῶν noun masc gen pl	. . . .	ταρσός
τάρταρον noun masc acc sg	. . . .	τάρταρος
τάρταρος noun masc nom sg		id.
ταρτάρῳ noun masc dat sg		id.
Ταρφαλλαῖοι pr noun		
τάς art fem acc pl	. . . .	ὁ
τάσδε dem pron fem acc pl	. . . .	ὅδε
τάσσονται vb pres m/p ind 3rd pers pl	. . . .	τάσσω
Ταταμ pr noun		
Ταταμι pr noun		
ταττόμενοι vb pres m/p part masc nom pl	. . . .	τάττω
ταῦθ' see ταῦτα		
ταυρηδόν adverb		
ταῦροι noun masc nom pl	. . . .	ταῦρος
ταῦρον noun masc acc sg		id.
ταῦρος noun masc nom sg		id.
ταύρου noun masc gen sg		id.
ταύρους noun masc acc pl		id.

ταύρων noun masc gen pl . . . . ταῦρος

ταῦτ᾽ *see* ταῦτα

ταῦτα dem pron neut nom and acc pl   id.

ταὐτά = τά + ταῦτα

ταύταις dem pron fem dat pl . . . . οὗτος

ταύτας dem pron fem acc pl   id.

ταύτῃ dem pron fem dat sg   id.

ταύτην dem pron fem acc sg   id.

ταύτης dem pron fem gen sg   id.

Ταφεθ pr noun

ταφείς vb 1st aor pass part masc nom sg . . . . θάπτω

ταφή noun fem nom sg

ταφῇ noun fem dat sg . . . . ταφή

ταφήν noun fem acc sg   id.

ταφῆς noun fem gen sg   id.

ταφήσεται vb fut pass ind 3rd pers sg   θάπτω

ταφήσῃ vb fut pass ind 2nd pers sg   id.

ταφήσομαι vb fut pass ind 1st pers sg   id.

ταφήσονται vb fut pass ind 3rd pers pl   id.

Ταφνας pr noun

τάφοι noun masc nom pl . . . . τάφος

τάφοις noun masc dat pl   id.

τάφον noun masc acc sg   id.

τάφος noun masc nom sg   id.

τάφου noun masc gen sg   id.

Ταφου pr noun

Ταφουγ pr noun

τάφους noun masc acc pl . . . . τάφος

τάφρῳ noun fem dat sg . . . . τάφρος

τάφῳ noun masc dat sg . . . . τάφος

τάφων noun masc gen pl   id.

τάχα adverb

τάχει noun neut dat sg . . . . τάχος

ταχεῖα adj fem nom sg . . . . ταχύς

ταχεῖς adj neut nom and acc pl   id.

ταχέως adverb

ταχθέν vb 1st aor pass part neut nom and acc sg . . . . . τάσσω

ταχινά adj neut nom and acc pl . . . . ταχινός

ταχινῇ adj fem dat sg   id.

ταχινοί adj masc nom pl   id.

ταχινόν adj masc acc sg, neut nom and acc sg   id.

τάχιον comp adverb

τάχιστα superl adj masc acc sg . . . . ταχύς

ταχίστην superl adj fem acc sg   id.

τάχος adverb

τάχος noun neut nom and acc sg

τάχους noun neut gen sg . . . . τάχος

ταχύ adj neut nom and acc sg . . . . ταχύς

ταχύ adverb   id.

ταχύν adj masc acc sg   id.

ταχύναι vb 1st aor act opt 3rd pers sg . . . . ταχύνω

ταχύναντες vb 1st aor act part masc nom pl   id.

ταχύνας vb 1st aor act part masc nom sg . . . . ταχύνω

ταχύνατε vb 1st aor act impv 2nd pers pl   id.

ταχυνάτω vb 1st aor act impv 3rd pers sg   id.

ταχύνει vb pres act ind 3rd pers sg   id.

ταχυνεῖ vb fut act ind 3rd pers sg   id.

ταχύνῃ vb pres act subj 3rd pers sg

       1st aor act subj 3rd pers sg   id.

τάχυνον vb 1st aor act impv 2nd pers sg   id.

ταχύς adj masc nom sg

τε enclitic copulative particle

τέγους noun neut gen sg . . . . τέγος

τεθανατωμένων vb perf m/p part gen pl . . . . θανατόω

τεθανάτωνται vb perf m/p ind 3rd pers pl   id.

τέθαπται vb perf m/p ind 3rd pers sg . . . . θάπτω

τεθαύμακας vb perf act ind 2nd pers sg . . . . θαυμάζω

τεθαυμασμένος vb perf m/p part masc nom sg   id.

τεθεαμένος vb perf dep part masc nom sg . . . . θεάομαι

τέθεικα vb perf act ind 1st pers sg . . . . τίθημι

τέθειμαι vb perf m/p ind 1st pers sg   id.

τέθειται vb perf m/p ind 3rd pers sg   id.

τεθέληκας vb perf act ind 2nd pers sg . . . . θέλω

τεθεμελιωμένην vb perf m/p part fem acc sg . . . . θεμελιόω

τεθεμελιωμένοι vb perf m/p part masc nom pl   id.

τεθεμελιωμένον vb perf m/p part masc acc sg,

       neut nom and acc sg   id.

τεθεμελίωται vb perf m/p ind 3rd pers sg   id.

τεθερισμένα vb perf m/p part neut nom and acc pl . . θερίζω

τεθῇ vb 1st aor pass subj 3rd pers sg . . . . τίθημι

τεθῆναι vb 1st aor pass inf   id.

τεθηριωμένος vb perf dep part masc nom sg . . . θηριόομαι

τεθησαυρίσθαι vb perf m/p inf . . . . θησαυρίζω

τεθήσονται vb fut pass ind 3rd pers pl . . . . τίθημι

τεθήτω vb 1st aor pass impv 3rd pers sg   id.

τεθλασμένην vb perf m/p part fem acc sg . . . . θλάω

τεθλιμμένοι vb perf m/p part masc nom pl . . . . θλίβω

τεθλιμμένου vb perf m/p part masc and neut gen sg   id.

τεθνάναι vb perf act inf . . . . θνήσκω

τεθνᾶσιν vb perf act ind 3rd pers pl   id.

τεθνεῶτες vb perf act part masc nom pl   id.

τεθνήκασιν vb perf act ind 3rd pers pl   id.

τεθνήκει vb plpf act ind 3rd pers sg   id.

τέθνηκεν vb perf act ind 3rd pers sg   id.

τεθνηκέναι vb perf act inf   id.

τεθνηκός vb perf act part neut nom and acc sg   id.

τεθνηκότα vb perf act part masc acc sg   id.

τεθνηκότας vb perf act part masc acc pl   id.

τεθνηκότες vb perf act part masc nom pl   id.

τεθνηκότι vb perf act part masc and neut dat sg   id.

τεθνηκότος vb perf act part masc and neut gen sg   id.

τεθνηκότων vb perf act part masc and neut gen pl   id.

τεθνηκώς vb perf act part masc nom sg   id.

τεθνήξῃ vb fut perf mid ind 2nd pers sg   id.

τεθνήξομαι vb fut perf mid ind 1st pers sg	θνήσκω
τεθνηξόμεθα vb fut perf mid ind 1st pers pl	id.
τεθορυβημένος vb perf m/p part masc nom sg	θορυβέω
τεθραυσμένος vb perf m/p part masc nom sg	θραύω
τεθραυσμένους vb perf m/p part masc acc pl	id.
τέθυκα vb perf act ind 1st pers sg	θύω
τεθύκασιν vb perf act ind 3rd pers pl	id.
τεθυμιαμένη vb perf m/p part fem nom sg	θυμιάω
τεθωρακισμένην vb perf m/p part fem acc sg	θωρακίζω
τεθωρακισμένον vb perf m/p part masc acc sg,	
neut nom and acc sg	id.
τεθωρακισμένους vb perf m/p part masc acc pl	id.
τεινέτω vb pres act impv 3rd pers sg	τείνω
τείνοντες vb pres act part masc nom pl	id.
τείνων vb pres act part masc nom sg	id.
τείσομαι vb fut mid ind 1st pers sg	τίνω
τείσονται vb fut mid ind 3rd pers pl	id.
τείσουσιν vb fut act ind 3rd pers pl	id.
τείχα noun neut nom and acc pl	τεῖχος
τείχει noun neut dat sg	id.
τείχεσι noun neut dat pl	id.
τειχέων noun neut gen pl	id.
τείχη noun neut nom and acc pl	id.
τειχήρεις adj masc and fem nom and acc pl	τειχήρης
τειχήρεσι adj dat pl	id.
τειχισταῖς noun masc dat pl	τειχιστής
τεῖχος noun neut nom and acc sg	
τείχους noun neut gen sg	τεῖχος
τειχῶν noun neut gen pl	id.
τεκεῖν vb 2nd aor act inf	τίκτω
τέκη vb 2nd aor act subj 3rd pers sg	id.
τεκμηρίοις noun neut dat pl	τεκμήριον
τεκμήριον noun neut nom and acc sg	id.
τεκμηρίων noun neut gen pl	id.
τέκνα noun neut nom and acc pl	τέκνον
τέκνοις noun neut dat pl	id.
τέκνον noun neut nom and acc sg	id.
τεκνοποιήσατε vb 1st aor act impv 2nd pers pl	τεκνοποιέω
τεκνοποιήσῃ vb fut mid ind 2nd pers sg	id.
τεκνοποιήσῃς vb 1st aor act subj 2nd pers sg	id.
τεκνοποιήσομαι vb fut mid ind 1st pers sg	id.
τεκνοποιήσουσιν vb fut act ind 3rd pers pl	id.
τέκνου noun neut gen sg	τέκνον
τεκνοφόνους adj masc and fem acc pl	τεκνοφόνος
τέκνων noun neut gen pl	τέκνον
τεκοῦσα vb 2nd aor act part fem nom sg	τίκτω
τεκούσαις vb 2nd aor act part fem dat pl	id.
τεκοῦσαν vb 2nd aor act part fem acc sg	id.
τεκούσῃ vb 2nd aor act part fem dat sg	id.
τεκούσης vb 2nd aor act part fem gen sg	id.
τεκταίνει vb pres act ind 3rd pers sg	τεκταίνω
τεκταίνεται vb pres m/p ind 3rd pers sg	id.

τεκταινομένη vb pres m/p part fem nom sg	τεκταίνω
τεκταινόμενος vb perf m/p part masc nom sg	id.
τεκταινομένου vb pres m/p part masc and neut gen sg	id.
τεκταίνοντες vb pres act part masc nom pl	id.
τεκταινόντων vb pres act part masc and neut gen pl	id.
τεκταίνουσι(ν) vb pres act ind 3rd pers pl	id.
τεκτήνῃ vb 2nd aor mid subj 2nd pers sg	id.
τέκτονα noun masc acc sg	τέκτων
τέκτονας noun masc acc pl	id.
τέκτονες noun masc nom pl	id.
τεκτονικά adj neut nom and acc pl	τεκτονικός
τέκτονος noun masc gen sg	τέκτων
τεκτόνων noun masc gen pl	id.
τέκτοσι noun masc dat pl	id.
τέκτων noun masc nom sg	id.
τέκωσιν vb 2nd aor act subj 3rd pers pl	τίκτω
Τελαμιν pr noun	
τελαμῶνα noun masc acc sg	τελαμών
τελαμῶνι noun masc dat sg	id.
τέλει noun neut dat sg	τέλος
τελεία adj neut nom and acc pl	τέλειος
τελεία adj fem nom sg	id.
τελείᾳ adj fem dat sg	id.
τέλειαι adj fem nom pl	id.
τελείαν adj fem acc sg	id.
τελείας adj fem gen sg and acc pl	id.
τελείοις adj masc and neut dat pl	id.
τέλειον adj masc acc sg, neut nom and acc sg	id.
τέλειος adj masc nom sg	id.
τελειότης noun fem nom sg	
τελειότητι noun fem dat sg	τελειότης
τελείου adj masc and neut gen sg	τέλειος
τελειωθείς vb 1st aor pass part masc nom sg	τελειόω
τελειωθῇ vb 1st aor pass subj 3rd pers sg	id.
τελειωθῆναι vb 1st aor pass inf	id.
τελειωθήσῃ vb fut pass ind 2nd pers sg	id.
τελείων adj gen pl	τέλειος
τελείως adverb	
τελειώσαι vb 1st aor act opt 3rd pers sg	τελειόω
τελειῶσαι vb 1st aor act inf	id.
τελειώσει vb fut act ind 3rd pers sg	id.
τελειώσεις vb fut act ind 2nd pers sg	id.
τελειώσεως noun fem gen sg	τελείωσις
τελείωσιν noun fem acc sg	id.
τελείωσις noun fem nom sg	id.
τελειώσουσιν vb fut act ind 3rd pers pl	τελειόω
τελειώσω vb fut act ind 1st pers sg	id.
Τελεμ pr noun	
τέλεον adj masc acc sg, neut nom and acc sg	τέλεος
τελέσαι vb 1st aor act inf	τελέω
τελέσῃ vb 1st aor act subj 3rd pers sg	id.
τελεσθεῖσα vb 1st aor pass part fem nom sg	id.

τελεσθέντων vb 1st aor pass part

    masc and neut gen pl . . . . τελέω

τελεσθῆναι vb 1st aor pass inf   id.

τελεσθήσεται vb fut pass ind 3rd pers sg   id.

τελεσθήτω vb 1st aor pass impv 3rd pers sg   id.

τελεσιουργεῖ vb pres act ind 3rd pers sg . . . . τελεσιουργέω

τελέσοντα vb fut act part masc acc sg . . . . τελέω

τελεσφορηθέντες vb 1st aor pass part

    masc nom pl . . . . τελεσφορέω

τελεσφόρος adj masc and fem nom sg

τελέσωσιν vb 1st aor act subj 3rd pers pl . . . . τελέω

τελεταί noun fem nom pl . . . . τελετή

τελετάς noun fem acc pl   id.

τελεύτα vb pres act impv 2nd pers sg . . . . τελευτάω

τελευτᾷ vb pres act ind 3rd pers sg   id.

τελευταία adj fem nom sg . . . . τελευταῖος

τελευταῖα adj neut nom and acc pl   id.

τελευταίοις adj masc and neut dat pl   id.

τελευταῖον adj masc acc sg, neut nom and acc sg   id.

τελευτᾶν vb pres act inf . . . . τελευτάω

τελευτᾶτε vb pres act impv 2nd pers pl   id.

τελευτάτω vb pres act impv 3rd pers sg   id.

τελευτή noun fem nom sg

τελευτῇ noun fem dat sg . . . . τελευτή

τελευτήν noun fem acc sg   id.

τελευτῆς noun fem gen sg   id.

τελευτῆσαι vb 1st aor act inf . . . . τελευτάω

τελευτήσαντος vb 1st aor act part masc and neut gen sg   id.

τελευτήσας vb 1st aor act part masc nom sg   id.

τελευτήσει vb fut act ind 3rd pers sg   id.

τελευτήσεις vb fut act ind 2nd pers sg   id.

τελευτήσῃ vb 1st aor act subj 3rd pers sg   id.

τελευτήσουσι(ν) vb fut act ind 3rd pers pl   id.

τελευτήσω vb fut act ind 1st pers sg   id.

τελευτήσωσιν vb 1st aor act subj 3rd pers pl   id.

τελευτῶμεν vb pres act ind 1st pers pl   id.

τελευτῶσιν vb pres act ind 3rd pers pl   id.

τέλη noun neut nom and acc pl . . . . τέλος

Τελημ pr noun

τελισκόμενος vb pres dep part masc nom sg . . . τελίσκομαι

Τελμων pr noun

τέλος noun neut nom and acc sg

τέλους noun neut gen sg . . . . τέλος

τελῶν noun neut gen pl   id.

τελωνείσθω vb pres dep impv 3rd pers sg . . . . τελωνέομαι

Τεμα pr noun

τεμεῖς vb fut act ind 2nd pers sg . . . . τέμνω

τεμένεσι noun neut dat pl . . . . τέμενος

τεμένη noun neut nom and acc pl   id.

τέμενος noun neut nom and acc sg   id.

τεμένους noun neut gen sg   id.

τέμνε vb pres act impv 2nd pers sg . . . . τέμνω

τέμνετε vb pres act impv 2nd pers pl . . . . τέμνω

τενόντων noun masc gen pl . . . . τένων

τέξεται vb fut mid ind 3rd pers sg . . . . τίκτω

τέξῃ vb fut mid ind 2nd pers sg   id.

τέξομαι vb fut mid ind 1st pers sg   id.

τέρας noun neut nom and acc sg

τέρασι noun neut dat pl . . . . τέρας

τέρατα noun neut nom and acc pl   id.

τερατεύεσθαι vb pres dep inf . . . . τερατεύομαι

τερατοποιόν adj acc sg, neut nom sg . . . . . . τερατοποιός

τερατοσκόποι noun masc nom pl . . . . . . τερατοσκόπος

τερατοσκόπος noun masc nom sg   id.

τεράτων noun neut gen pl . . . . τέρας

τερέβινθος noun fem nom sg

τερέμινθον noun fem acc sg . . . . τερέμινθος

τερέμινθος noun masc nom sg   id.

τερεμίνθου noun fem gen sg   id.

τερέτρῳ noun neut dat sg . . . . τέρετρον

τέρμα noun neut nom and acc sg

τέρπει vb pres act ind 3rd pers sg . . . . τέρπω

τέρπεται vb pres m/p ind 3rd pers sg   id.

τερπνόν adj masc acc sg, neut nom and acc sg . . . . τερπνός

τερπνότητα noun fem acc sg . . . . τερπνότης

τερπνότητες noun fem nom pl   id.

τερπόμενοι vb pres m/p part masc nom pl . . . . τέρπω

τερπομένων vb pres m/p part gen pl   id.

τέρπου vb pres m/p impv 2nd pers sg   id.

τερφθήσεται vb fut pass ind 3rd pers sg   id.

τερφθήτωσαν vb 1st aor pass impv 3rd pers pl   id.

τέρψει noun fem dat sg . . . . τέρψις

τέρψει vb fut act ind 3rd pers sg . . . . τέρπω

τέρψεις vb fut act ind 2nd pers sg   id.

τέρψεως noun fem gen sg . . . . τέρψις

τέρψις noun fem nom sg   id.

τέσσαρα adj masc and fem acc sg,

         neut nom and acc pl . . . . τέσσαρες

τεσσαράκοντα indecl number

τεσσαρακοστόν adj masc acc sg,

         neut nom and acc sg . . . . τεσσαρακοστός

τεσσαρακοστοῦ adj masc and neut gen sg   id.

τεσσαρακοστῷ adj masc and neut dat sg   id.

τέσσαρας adj masc and fem acc pl . . . . τέσσαρες

τέσσαρες adj masc and fem nom pl   id.

τεσσαρεσκαιδεκάτη adj fem

         dat sg . . . . τεσσαρεσκαιδέκατος

τεσσαρεσκαιδεκάτην adj fem acc sg   id.

τεσσαρεσκαιδεκάτης adj fem gen sg   id.

τεσσαρεσκαιδέκατος adj masc nom sg   id.

τεσσαρεσκαιδεκάτου adj masc and neut gen sg   id.

τεσσαρεσκαιδεκάτῳ adj masc and neut dat sg   id.

τέσσαρσι adj dat pl . . . . τέσσαρες

τεσσάρων adj gen pl   id.

τεταγμένα vb perf m/p part neut nom and acc pl	.... τάσσω	
τεταγμέναι vb perf m/p part fem nom pl	id.	
τεταγμένη vb perf m/p part fem nom sg	id.	
τεταγμένης vb perf m/p part fem gen sg	id.	
τεταγμένοι vb perf m/p part masc nom pl	id.	
τεταγμένοις vb perf m/p part masc and neut dat pl	id.	
τεταγμένος vb perf m/p part masc nom sg	id.	
τεταγμένου vb perf m/p part masc and neut gen sg	id.	
τεταγμένων vb perf m/p part gen pl	id.	
τεταγμένως adverb		
τέτακα vb perf act ind 1st pers sg	.... τείνω	
τέτακται vb perf m/p ind 3rd pers sg	.... τάσσω	
τεταλαιπώρηκεν vb perf act ind 3rd pers sg	.. ταλαιπωρέω	
τεταμένοις vb perf m/p part masc and neut dat pl	..... τείνω	
τεταμένους vb perf m/p part masc acc pl	id.	
τεταπεινωμένα vb perf m/p part		
neut nom and acc pl	.... ταπεινόω	
τεταπεινωμένη vb perf m/p part fem nom sg	id.	
τεταπεινωμένην vb perf m/p part fem acc sg	id.	
τεταπεινωμένος vb perf m/p part masc nom sg	id.	
τεταπεινωμένου vb perf m/p part masc and neut gen sg	id.	
τεταπεινωμένῳ vb perf m/p part masc and neut dat sg	id.	
τεταραγμέναι vb perf m/p part fem nom pl	..... ταράσσω	
τεταραγμένη vb perf m/p part fem nom sg	id.	
τεταραγμένοι vb perf m/p part masc nom pl	id.	
τεταραγμένον vb perf m/p part masc acc sg,		
neut nom and acc sg	id.	
τεταραγμένος vb perf m/p part masc nom sg	id.	
τετάρακται vb perf m/p ind 3rd pers sg	id.	
τετάρτη adj fem nom sg	.... τέταρτος	
τετάρτῃ adj fem dat sg	id.	
τετάρτην adj fem acc sg	id.	
τετάρτης adj fem gen sg	id.	
τέταρτοι adj masc nom pl	id.	
τέταρτον adj masc acc sg, neut nom and acc sg	id.	
τέταρτος adj masc nom sg	id.	
τετάρτου adj masc and neut gen sg	id.	
τετάρτῳ adj masc and neut dat sg	id.	
τέταχα vb perf act ind 1st pers sg	.... τάσσω	
τέταχας vb perf act ind 2nd pers sg	id.	
τετειχισμέναι vb perf m/p part fem nom pl	...... τειχίζω	
τετειχισμέναις vb perf m/p part fem dat pl	id.	
τετειχισμένας vb perf m/p part fem acc pl	id.	
τετειχισμένῃ vb perf m/p part fem dat sg	id.	
τετειχισμένην vb perf m/p part fem acc sg	id.	
τετειχισμένων vb perf m/p part gen pl	id.	
τετελειωμένος vb perf m/p part masc nom sg	..... τελειόω	
τετελειωμένου vb perf m/p part masc and neut gen sg	id.	
τετελεκώς vb perf act part masc nom sg	.... τελέω	
τετελεσμένον vb perf m/p part masc acc sg,		
neut nom and acc sg	id.	
τετελεσμένων vb perf m/p part gen pl	id.	

τετέλεσται vb perf m/p ind 3rd pers sg	.... τελέω	
τετελεύτηκεν vb perf act ind 3rd pers sg	...... τελευτάω	
τετελευτηκός vb perf act part neut nom and acc sg	id.	
τετελευτηκότος vb perf act part masc and neut gen sg	id.	
τετελευτηκυίᾳ vb perf act part fem dat sg	id.	
τετελευτηκώς vb perf act part masc nom sg	id.	
τετευχότες vb perf act part masc nom pl	.... τυγχάνω	
τετευχώς vb perf act part masc nom sg	id.	
τετηκότι vb perf act part masc and neut dat sg	...... τήκω	
τετιλμένου vb perf m/p part masc and neut gen sg	... τίλλω	
τετιμημένου vb perf m/p part masc and neut gen sg	.. τιμάω	
τετίμηνται vb perf m/p ind 3rd pers pl	id.	
τετιμώρηται vb perf m/p ind 3rd pers sg	.... τιμωρέω	
τέτοκας vb perf act ind 2nd pers sg	.... τίκτω	
τέτοκεν vb perf act ind 3rd pers sg	id.	
τετοκυιῶν vb perf act part fem gen pl	id.	
τετοκώς vb perf act part masc nom sg	id.	
τετράγωνα adj neut nom and acc pl	.... τετράγωνος	
τετράγωνοι adj masc and fem nom pl	id.	
τετράγωνον adj acc sg, neut nom sg	id.	
τετραγώνων adj gen pl	id.	
τετράδι noun fem dat sg	.... τετράς	
τετράδος noun fem gen sg	id.	
τετράδραχμον noun neut nom and acc sg		
τετρακισμύριοι adj masc nom pl		
τετρακισχίλια adj neut nom and acc pl	.. τετρακισχίλιοι	
τετρακισχίλιοι adj masc nom pl		
τετρακισχιλίοις adj masc and neut dat pl	. τετρακισχίλιοι	
τετρακισχιλίους adj masc acc pl	id.	
τετρακόσια adj neut nom and acc pl	.... τετρακόσιοι	
τετρακόσιαι adj fem nom pl	id.	
τετρακοσίαις adj fem dat pl	id.	
τετρακοσίας adj fem acc pl	id.	
τετρακόσιοι adj masc nom pl	id.	
τετρακοσίοις adj masc and neut dat pl	id.	
τετρακοσιοστῷ adj masc and neut dat sg	τετρακοσιοστός	
τετρακοσίους adj masc acc pl	.... τετρακόσιοι	
τετρακοσίων adj gen pl	id.	
τετραμερές adj neut nom and acc pl	.... τετραμερής	
τετράμηνον adj acc sg, neut nom sg	.... τετράμηνος	
τετραπέδοις adj dat pl	.... τετράπεδος	
τετραπέδους adj masc and fem acc pl	id.	
τετραπλῶς adverb		
τετράποδα adj neut nom and acc pl	.... τετράπους	
τετράποδι adj dat sg	id.	
τετραπόδων adj gen pl	id.	
τετράποσι adj dat pl	id.	
τετράπουν adj acc sg, neut nom sg	id.	
τετράς noun fem nom sg		
τέτρασι adj fem dat pl	.... τέσσαρες	
τετράστιχον adj acc sg, neut nom sg	...... τετράστιχος	
τετραστίχου adj gen sg	id.	

τετραυματισμένοι vb perf m/p part

    masc nom pl . . . . τραυματίζω

τετραυματισμένους vb perf m/p part masc acc pl   id.

τετραυματισμένων vb perf m/p part gen pl   id.

τετρημένος vb perf m/p part masc nom sg . . . . . . τετραίνω

τετριμμέναι vb perf m/p part fem nom pl . . . . τρίβω

τετροπωμένους vb perf m/p part masc acc pl . . . . . . τροπόω

τετρόπωνται vb perf m/p ind 3rd pers pl   id.

τετρόπωται vb perf m/p ind 3rd pers sg   id.

τετρυπημένον vb perf m/p part masc acc sg,

    neut nom and acc sg . . . . τρυπάω

τέτρωμαι vb perf m/p ind 1st pers sg . . . . τιτρώσκω

τετρωμένη vb perf m/p part fem nom sg   id.

τετρωμένου vb perf m/p part masc and neut gen sg   id.

τετυρωμένα vb perf m/p part neut nom and acc pl . . . τυρόω

τετυρωμένον vb perf m/p part masc acc sg,

    neut nom and acc sg   id.

τεύξασθαι vb 1st aor mid inf . . . . τυγχάνω

τευξόμενος vb fut mid part masc nom sg   id.

τέφρα noun fem nom sg

τέφραν noun fem acc sg . . . . τέφρα

Τεφων pr noun

τεχθείς vb 1st aor pass part masc nom sg . . . . τίκτω

τεχθεῖσα vb 1st aor pass part fem nom sg   id.

τεχθέντες vb 1st aor pass part masc nom pl   id.

τεχθέντων vb 1st aor pass part masc and neut gen pl   id.

τεχθῇ vb 1st aor pass subj 3rd pers sg   id.

τεχθησόμενοι vb fut pass part masc nom pl   id.

τεχθησομένῳ vb fut pass part masc and neut dat sg   id.

τεχνάσασθε vb 1st aor mid impv 2nd pers pl . . τεχνάζομαι

τέχνη noun fem dat sg . . . . τέχνη

τέχνην noun fem acc sg   id.

τέχνης noun fem gen sg   id.

τεχνησάμενος vb 1st aor mid part masc nom sg . τεχνάομαι

τεχνῖται noun masc nom pl . . . . τεχνίτης

τεχνίτας noun masc acc pl   id.

τεχνίτην noun masc acc sg   id.

τεχνῖτις noun fem nom sg

τεχνίτου noun masc gen sg . . . . τεχνίτης

τεχνιτῶν noun masc gen pl   id.

τῇ art fem dat sg . . . . ὁ

τήγανα noun neut nom and acc pl . . . . τήγανον

τηγανίζειν vb pres act inf . . . . τηγανίζω

τήγανον noun neut nom and acc sg

τηγάνου noun neut gen sg . . . . τήγανον

τηγάνων noun neut gen pl   id.

τῆδε dem pron fem dat sg . . . . ὅδε

τηθ translit (Heb. letter: ‪ט‬)

τήκει vb pres act ind 3rd pers sg . . . . τήκω

τήκεται vb pres m/p ind 3rd pers sg   id.

τηκόμεθα vb pres m/p ind 1st pers pl   id.

τηκομένας vb pres m/p part fem acc pl   id.

τηκομένη vb pres m/p part fem nom sg . . . . τήκω

τηκομένην vb pres m/p part fem acc sg   id.

τηκόμενοι vb pres m/p part masc nom pl   id.

τηκόμενον vb pres m/p part masc acc sg,

    neut nom and acc sg   id.

τηκόμενος vb pres m/p part masc nom sg   id.

τηκτόν adj masc acc sg, neut nom and acc sg . . . . . . τηκτός

τήκω vb pres act ind 1st pers sg

τηλαυγές adj neut nom and acc sg . . . . τηλαυγής

τηλαύγημα noun neut nom and acc sg

τηλαυγής adj masc and fem nom sg

τηλαυγήσεως noun fem gen sg . . . . τηλαύγησις

τηλικαῦτα dem pron neut nom and acc pl . . . . τηλικοῦτος

τηλικοῦτο dem pron neut nom and acc sg   id.

τήν art fem acc sg . . . . ὁ

τήνδε dem pron fem acc sg . . . . ὅδε

τήξει vb fut act ind 3rd pers sg . . . . τήκω

τήξειας vb 1st aor act opt 2nd pers sg   id.

τῆξον vb 1st aor act impv 2nd pers sg   id.

τήρει vb pres act impv 2nd pers sg . . . . τηρέω

τηρεῖ vb pres act ind 3rd pers sg   id.

τηρεῖν vb pres act inf   id.

τηρεῖτε vb pres act impv 2nd pers pl   id.

τηρείτω vb pres act impv 3rd pers sg   id.

τηρείτωσαν vb pres act impv 3rd pers pl   id.

τηρήσατε vb 1st aor act impv 2nd pers pl   id.

τηρήσει vb fut act ind 3rd pers sg   id.

τηρήσεις vb fut act ind 2nd pers sg   id.

τηρήσῃ vb 1st aor act subj 3rd pers sg   id.

τηρήσῃς vb 1st aor act subj 2nd pers sg   id.

τήρησιν noun fem acc sg . . . . τήρησις

τήρησις noun fem nom sg   id.

τήρησον vb 1st aor act impv 2nd pers sg . . . . τηρέω

τηροῦντες vb pres act part masc nom pl   id.

τηροῦσι(ν) vb pres act ind 3rd pers pl,

    pres act part masc and neut dat pl   id.

τηρῶν vb pres act part masc nom sg   id.

τῆς art fem gen sg . . . . ὁ

τῆσδε dem pron fem gen sg . . . . ὅδε

τι indef pron neut nom and acc sg . . . . τις

τί interr pron neut nom and acc sg . . . . τίς

τιάραι noun fem nom pl . . . . τιάρα

τιάραις noun fem dat pl   id.

τιάρας noun fem acc pl   id.

Τιγρης pr noun

Τιγριδος pr noun masc gen sg . . . . Τιγρις

Τιγριν pr noun masc acc sg

Τιγρις pr noun masc acc sg   id.

τιθείς vb pres act part masc nom sg . . . . τίθημι

τιθέμενοι vb pres m/p part masc nom pl   id.

τιθέμενος vb pres m/p part masc nom sg   id.

τιθεμένων vb pres m/p part gen pl   id.

τιθέναι vb pres act inf	τίθημι	τιμίου adj masc and neut gen sg	τίμιος
τιθέντες vb pres act part masc nom pl	id.	τιμίους adj masc acc pl	id.
τίθεσθαι vb pres m/p inf	id.	τιμίῳ adj masc and neut dat sg	id.
τίθεσθε vb pres m/p ind 2nd pers pl	id.	τιμίων adj gen pl	id.
τίθημι vb pres act ind 1st pers sg	id.	τιμιωτάτη superl adj fem nom sg	id.
τιθηνήσασθαι vb 1st aor mid inf	τιθηνέω	τιμιωτέρα comp adj fem nom sg, neut nom and acc pl	id.
τιθήνησον vb 1st aor act impv 2nd pers sg	id.	Τιμοθεον pr noun masc acc sg	Τιμοθεος
τιθηνίαι noun fem nom pl	τιθηνία	Τιμοθεος pr noun masc nom sg	id.
τιθηνοί adj masc and fem nom pl	τιθηνός	Τιμοθεου pr noun masc gen sg	id.
τιθηνόν adj acc sg, neut nom sg	id.	τιμώμενοι vb pres m/p part masc nom pl	τιμάω
τιθηνός adj masc and fem nom sg	id.	τιμωμένου vb pres m/p part masc and neut gen sg	id.
τιθηνούμενοι vb pres m/p part masc nom pl	τιθηνέω	τιμῶν noun fem gen pl	τιμή
τιθηνούς adj masc and fem acc pl	τιθηνός	τιμῶν vb pres act part masc nom sg	τιμάω
τίκτει vb pres act ind 3rd pers sg	τίκτω	τιμῶντες vb pres act part masc nom pl	id.
τίκτειν vb pres act inf	id.	τιμωρηθῆναι vb 1st aor pass inf	τιμωρέω
τίκτεται vb pres m/p ind 3rd pers sg	id.	τιμωρήσειεν vb 1st aor act opt 3rd pers sg	id.
τικτομένῳ vb pres m/p part masc and neut dat sg	id.	τιμωρήσεται vb fut mid ind 3rd pers sg	id.
τίκτουσα vb pres act part fem nom sg	id.	τιμωρήσομαι vb fut mid ind 1st pers sg	id.
τίκτουσαι vb pres act part fem nom pl	id.	τιμωρητας noun masc acc pl	τιμωρητής
τίκτουσαν vb pres act part fem acc sg	id.	τιμωρία noun fem dat sg	τιμωρία
τικτούσῃ vb pres act part fem dat sg	id.	τιμωρίαι noun fem nom pl	id.
τικτούσης vb pres act part fem gen sg	id.	τιμωρίαις noun fem dat pl	id.
τίκτουσιν vb pres act ind 3rd pers pl	id.	τιμωρίαν noun fem acc sg	id.
τίμα vb pres act impv 2nd pers sg	τιμάω	τιμωρίας noun fem gen sg and acc pl	id.
τιμᾷ vb pres act ind 3rd pers sg	id.	τιμωρούμενον vb pres m/p part masc acc sg,	
τιμαῖς noun fem dat pl	τιμή	neut nom and acc sg	τιμωρέω
τιμᾶν vb pres act inf	τιμάω	τιμῶσιν vb pres act ind 3rd pers pl	τιμάω
τιμάς noun fem acc pl	τιμή	τινα indef pron masc and fem acc sg, neut nom and acc pl	τις
τιμᾶσθε vb pres m/p ind 2nd pers pl	τιμάω	τίνα inter pron masc and fem acc sg, neut nom and acc pl	τίς
τιμή noun fem nom sg		τινά see τινα	
τιμῇ noun fem dat sg	τιμή	τινάγματι noun neut dat sg	τιναγμα
τιμηθέντα vb 1st aor pass part masc acc sg	τιμάω	τινας indef pron masc and fem acc pl	τις
τιμηθήσεται vb fut pass ind 3rd pers sg	id.	τίνας interr pron masc and fem acc pl	τίς
τίμημα noun neut nom and acc sg		τινάς see τινας	
τιμήν noun fem acc sg	τιμή	τινες indef pron masc and fem nom pl	τις
τιμῆς noun fem gen sg	id.	τίνες interr pron masc and fem nom pl	τίς
τιμῆσαι vb 1st aor act inf	τιμάω	τινές see τινες	
τιμήσασα vb 1st aor act part fem nom sg	id.	τινι indef pron dat sg	τις
τιμήσατε vb 1st aor act impv 2nd pers pl	id.	τίνι inter pron dat sg	τίς
τιμήσει vb fut act ind 3rd pers sg	id.	τινί see τινι	
τιμήσεις vb fut act ind 2nd pers sg	id.	τινος indef pron gen sg	τις
τιμήσεται vb fut mid ind 3rd pers sg	id.	τίνος interr pron gen sg	τίς
τίμησον vb 1st aor act impv 2nd pers sg	id.	τινός see τινος	
τιμήσω vb 1st aor act subj 1st pers sg,		τινων indef pron gen pl	τις
fut act ind 1st pers sg	id.	τίνων interr pron gen pl	τίς
τίμια adj neut nom and acc pl	τίμιος	τινῶν see τινων	
τιμία adj fem nom sg	id.	τις indef pron masc and fem nom sg	
τιμίας adj fem gen sg	id.	τίς interr pron masc and fem nom sg	
τίμιοι adj masc nom pl	id.	τισι indef pron dat pl	τις
τιμίοις adj masc and neut dat pl	id.	τισί see τισι	
τίμιον adj masc acc sg, neut nom and acc sg	id.	τιτάνων noun masc gen pl	τιτάν
τίμιος adj masc nom sg		Τιτος pr noun masc nom sg	

τιτρώσκειν vb pres act inf	τιτρώσκω
τιτρώσκεσθαι vb pres m/p inf	id.
τιτρωσκομένη vb pres m/p part fem nom sg	id.
τιτρωσκόμενοι vb pres m/p part masc nom pl	id.
τιτρώσκουσα vb pres act part fem nom sg	id.
τιτρώσκουσιν vb pres act ind 3rd pers pl	id.
τμηθείς vb 1st aor pass part masc nom sg	τέμνω
τμηθῇ vb 1st aor pass subj 3rd pers sg	id.
τμηθῆναι vb 1st aor pass inf	id.
τμητούς adj masc acc pl	τμητός
τό art neut nom and acc sg	ὁ
τόδε dem pron neut nom and acc sg	ὅδε
τοι particle	
τοῖα adj neut nom and acc pl	τοῖος
τοιάδε dem pron neut nom and acc pl	τοιόσδε
τοιαῦτα adj neut nom and acc pl	τοιοῦτος
τοιαῦται adj fem nom pl	id.
τοιαύτας adj fem acc pl	id.
τοιαύτη adj fem nom sg	id.
τοιαύτην adj fem acc sg	id.
τοιγαροῦν particle	
τοίνυν particle	
τοιοῦτο adj neut nom and acc sg	τοιοῦτος
τοιοῦτοι adj masc nom pl	id.
τοιούτοις adj masc and neut dat pl	id.
τοιοῦτον adj masc acc sg	id.
τοιοῦτος adj masc nom sg	id.
τοιούτους adj masc acc pl	id.
τοιούτῳ adj masc and neut dat sg	id.
τοιούτων adj gen pl	id.
τοῖς art masc and neut dat pl	ὁ
τοῖχοι noun masc nom pl	τοῖχος
τοίχοις noun masc dat pl	id.
τοῖχον noun masc acc sg	id.
τοῖχος noun masc nom sg	id.
τοίχου noun masc gen sg	id.
τοίχους noun masc acc pl	id.
τοίχῳ noun masc dat sg	id.
τοίχων noun masc gen pl	id.
τοκάδες noun fem nom pl	τοκάς
τοκετοῦ noun masc gen sg	τοκετός
τοκετῷ noun masc dat sg	id.
τόκον noun masc acc sg	τόκος
τόκος noun masc nom sg	id.
τόκου noun masc gen sg	id.
τόκους noun masc acc pl	id.
τόκῳ noun masc dat sg	id.
τόκων noun masc gen pl	id.
Τολβανης pr noun	
τόλμαις noun fem dat pl	τόλμα
τόλμαν noun fem acc sg	id.
Τολμαν pr noun	

τόλμῃ noun fem dat sg	τόλμα
τολμηρά adj fem nom sg	τολμηρός
τολμηρότερος comp adj masc nom sg	id.
τολμηροῦ adj masc and neut gen sg	id.
τολμήσαντες vb 1st aor act part masc nom pl	τολμάω
τολμήσουσιν vb fut act ind 3rd pers pl	id.
τολμῶμεν vb pres act ind 1st pers pl	id.
τολύπην noun fem acc sg	τολύπη
τομή noun fem nom sg	
τομῆς noun fem gen sg	τομή
τομίδας noun fem acc pl	τομίς
Τομμαν pr noun	
τόμον noun masc acc sg	τόμος
τόμος noun masc nom sg	id.
τόν art masc acc sg	ὁ
τόνδε dem pron masc acc sg	ὅδε
τόνων noun masc gen pl	τόνος
τόξα noun neut nom and acc pl	τόξον
τόξευμα noun neut nom and acc sg	
τοξεύμασι noun neut dat pl	τόξευμα
τοξεύματα noun neut nom and acc pl	id.
τοξεύματι noun neut dat sg	id.
τοξεύματος noun neut gen sg	id.
τοξευμάτων noun neut gen pl	id.
τοξεύοντες vb pres act part masc nom pl	τοξεύω
τοξεύσατε vb 1st aor act impv 2nd pers pl	id.
τοξεύσει vb fut act ind 3rd pers sg	id.
τόξευσον vb 1st aor act impv 2nd pers sg	id.
τοξεύσουσιν vb fut act ind 3rd pers pl	id.
τοξικοῦ adj masc and neut gen sg	τοξικός
τόξοις noun neut dat pl	τόξον
τόξον noun neut nom and acc sg	id.
τοξόται noun masc nom pl	τοξότης
τοξότας noun masc acc pl	id.
τοξότης noun masc nom sg	id.
τόξου noun neut gen sg	τόξον
τόξῳ noun neut dat sg	id.
τόξων noun neut gen pl	id.
τοπάζιον noun neut nom and acc sg	
τοπάρχαι noun masc nom pl	τοπάρχης
τοπάρχαις noun masc dat pl	id.
τοπάρχας noun masc acc pl	id.
τοπάρχην noun masc acc sg	id.
τοπαρχίας noun fem acc pl	τοπαρχία
τοπάρχου noun masc gen sg	τοπάρχης
τόποι noun masc nom pl	τόπος
τόποις noun masc dat pl	id.
τόπον noun masc acc sg	id.
τόπος noun masc nom sg	id.
τόπου noun masc gen sg	id.
τόπους noun masc acc pl	id.
τόπῳ noun masc dat sg	id.

τόπων	noun masc gen pl	τόπος
τορευτά	adj neut nom and acc pl	τορευτός
τορευταί	adj fem nom pl	id.
τορευτή	adj fem nom sg	id.
τορευτήν	adj fem acc sg	id.
τορευτόν	adj masc acc sg, neut nom and acc sg	id.
τορευτός	adj masc nom sg	id.
τορευτῶν	adj gen pl	id.
τοσαῦτα	adj neut nom and acc pl	τοσοῦτος
τοσαύτη	adj fem nom sg	id.
τοσαύτης	adj fem gen sg	id.
τοσοῦτο	adj neut nom and acc sg	id.
τοσοῦτοι	adj masc nom pl	id.
τοσοῦτον	adj masc acc sg	id.
τοσούτῳ	adj masc and neut dat sg	id.
τοσούτων	adj gen pl	id.
τόσῳ	adj masc and neut dat sg	τόσος
τότε	adverb	
τοῦ	art masc and neut gen sg	ὁ
Τουβαν	pr noun	
Τουβιανους	pr noun masc acc pl	Τουβινοι
Τουβιου	pr noun masc gen sg	Τουβιας
τοῦδε	dem pron masc and neut gen sg	ὅδε
τοὐναντίον	= τοῦ + ἐναντίον	
τούς	art masc acc pl	ὁ
τούσδε	dem pron masc acc pl	ὅδε
τοῦτ'	see τοῦτο	
τοῦτο	dem pron neut nom and acc sg	οὗτος
τούτοις	dem pron masc and neut dat pl	id.
τοῦτον	dem pron masc acc sg	id.
τούτου	dem pron masc and neut gen sg	id.
τούτους	dem pron masc acc pl	id.
τούτῳ	dem pron masc and neut dat sg	id.
τούτων	dem pron gen pl	id.
Τοφολ	pr noun	
Τοχος	pr noun	
τραγέλαφον	noun masc acc sg	τραγέλαφος
τραγελάφων	noun masc gen pl	id.
τράγοι	noun masc nom pl	τράγος
τράγος	noun masc nom sg	id.
τράγου	noun masc gen sg	id.
τράγους	noun masc acc pl	id.
τράγῳ	noun masc dat sg	id.
τράγων	noun masc gen pl	id.
τρανάς	adj fem acc pl	τρανός
τρανή	adj fem nom sg	id.
τρανόν	adj masc acc sg, neut nom and acc sg	id.
τράπεζα	noun fem nom sg	
τράπεζαι	noun fem nom pl	τράπεζα
τράπεζαν	noun fem acc sg	id.
τραπέζας	noun fem acc pl	id.
τραπέζῃ	noun fem dat sg	id.

τραπέζης	noun fem gen sg	τράπεζα
τραπεζῶν	noun fem gen pl	id.
τραπεις	vb 2nd aor pass part masc nom sg	τρέπω
τραπείσης	vb 2nd aor pass part fem gen sg	id.
τραπέντες	vb 2nd aor pass part masc nom pl	id.
τραπῆναι	vb 2nd aor pass inf	id.
τραπήσεται	vb fut pass ind 3rd pers sg	id.
τραῦμα	noun neut nom and acc sg	
τραύματα	noun neut nom and acc pl	τραῦμα
τραυματίᾳ	noun masc dat sg	τραυματίας
τραυματίαι	noun masc nom pl	id.
τραυματίαις	noun masc dat pl	id.
τραυματίαν	noun masc acc sg	id.
τραυματίας	noun masc nom sg and acc pl	id.
τραυματίου	noun masc gen sg	id.
τραυματιῶν	noun masc gen pl	id.
τραύματος	noun neut gen sg	τραῦμα
τραυμάτον	noun neut gen pl	id.
τραφῶσιν	vb 2nd aor pass subj 3rd pers pl	τρέφω
τραχεῖα	adj fem nom sg	τραχύς
τραχεῖαν	adj fem acc sg	id.
τραχείας	adj fem gen sg and acc pl	id.
τραχήλοις	noun masc dat pl	τράχηλος
τράχηλον	noun masc acc sg	id.
τράχηλος	noun masc nom sg	id.
τραχήλου	noun masc gen sg	id.
τραχήλους	noun masc acc pl	id.
τραχήλῳ	noun masc dat sg	id.
τραχήλων	noun masc gen pl	id.
τραχύτητα	noun fem acc sg	τραχύτης
τρεῖς	adj masc and fem nom and acc pl	
τρέμει	vb pres act ind 3rd pers sg	τρέμω
τρέμειν	vb pres act inf	id.
τρέμοντα	vb pres act part masc acc sg, neut nom and acc pl	id.
τρέμοντος	vb pres act part masc acc pl	id.
τρέμοντες	vb pres act part masc nom pl	id.
τρέμων	vb pres act part masc nom sg	id.
τρεπόμενος	vb pres m/p part masc nom sg	τρέπω
τρέφε	vb pres act impv 2nd pers sg	τρέφω
τρέφειν	vb pres act inf	id.
τρέφεις	vb pres act ind 2nd pers sg	id.
τρέφεσθαι	vb pres m/p inf	id.
τρέφῃς	vb pres act subj 2nd pers sg	id.
τρεφόμενοι	vb pres m/p part masc nom pl	id.
τρεφομένους	vb pres m/p part masc acc pl	id.
τρέφοντος	vb pres act part masc and neut gen sg	id.
τρέφουσιν	vb pres act ind 3rd pers pl	id.
τρέφων	vb pres act part masc nom sg	id.
τρέχει	vb pres act ind 3rd pers sg	τρέχω
τρέχεις	vb pres act ind 2nd pers sg	id.
τρέχῃς	vb pres act subj 2nd pers sg	id.

τρέχοντα vb pres act part masc acc sg	. . . .	τρέχω
τρέχοντας vb pres act part masc acc pl		id.
τρέχοντες vb pres act part masc nom pl		id.
τρεχόντων vb pres act part masc and neut gen pl		id.
τρέχουσιν vb pres act ind 3rd pers pl		id.
τρέχων vb pres act part masc nom sg		id.
τρέψομαι vb fut mid ind 1st pers sg	. . . .	τρέπω
τρήσει vb fut act ind 3rd pers sg	. . . .	τετραίνω
τρία adj neut nom and acc pl	. . . .	τρεῖς
τριακάδος noun fem gen sg	. . . .	τριακάς
τριάκοντα indecl number		
τριακονταετούς noun neut gen sg	. . . . . .	τριακονταετής
τριακόσια adj neut nom and acc pl	. . . .	τριακόσιοι
τριακόσιαι adj fem nom pl		id.
τριακοσίαις adj fem dat pl		id.
τριακοσίας adj fem gen sg and acc pl		id.
τριακόσιοι adj masc nom pl		id.
τριακοσίοις adj masc and neut dat pl		id.
τριακοσίους adj masc acc pl		id.
τριακοσίων adj gen pl		id.
τριακοστοῦ adj masc and neut gen sg	. . . .	τριακοστός
τριακοστῷ adj masc and neut dat sg		id.
τρίβοι noun masc or fem nom pl	. . . .	τρίβος
τρίβοι vb pres act opt 3rd pers sg	. . . .	τρίβω
τρίβοις noun fem dat pl	. . . .	τρίβος
τρίβολοι noun masc nom pl	. . . .	τρίβολος
τριβόλοις noun masc dat pl		id.
τριβόλους noun masc acc pl		id.
τρίβον noun masc or fem acc sg	. . . .	τρίβος
τρίβος noun masc or fem nom sg		id.
τρίβου noun masc or fem gen sg		id.
τρίβους noun masc or fem acc pl		id.
τρίβουσιν vb pres act ind 3rd pers pl	. . . .	τρίβω
τρίβῳ noun masc or fem dat sg	. . . .	τρίβος
τρίβων noun masc or fem gen pl		id.
τριετῆ adj masc and fem acc sg	. . . .	τριετής
τριετής adj masc and fem nom sg		id.
τριετίζοντα vb pres act part masc acc sg	. . . .	τριετίζω
τριετίζοντι vb pres act part masc and neut dat sg		id.
τριετίζουσαν vb pres act part fem acc sg		id.
τριετοῦς adj gen sg	. . . .	τριετής
τριημερίαν noun fem acc sg	. . . .	τριημερία
τριηρέων noun fem gen pl	. . . .	τριήρης
τρικυμίαις noun fem dat pl	. . . .	τρικυμία
τριμερεῖς vb fut act ind 2nd pers sg	. . . .	τριμερίζω
τρίμηνον adj acc sg, neut nom sg	. . . .	τρίμηνος
τριόδους adj masc and fem nom sg		
τριπλαῖ adj fem nom pl	. . . .	τριπλοῦς
τριπλασίως adverb		
Τριπολιν pr noun fem acc sg	. . . .	Τριπολις
τρίς adverb		
τρισαθλία adj fem nom sg	. . . .	τρισάθλιος
τρισαλιτήριος adj masc and fem nom sg		
τρισαλιτηρίου adj masc and fem gen sg	. . .	τρισαλιτήριος
τρισί adj dat pl	. . . .	τρεῖς
τρισκαίδεκα indecl number		
τρισκαιδεκάτῃ adj fem dat sg	. . . .	τρισκαιδέκατος
τρισκαιδεκάτην adj fem acc sg		id.
τρισκαιδέκατος adj masc nom sg		id.
τρισκαιδεκάτου adj masc and neut gen sg		id.
τρισκαιδεκάτῳ adj masc and neut dat sg		id.
τρισμυρίων adj gen pl	. . . .	τρισμύριοι
τρισσαί adj fem nom pl	. . . .	τρισσός
τρισσεύσεις vb fut act ind 2nd pers sg	. . . .	τρισσεύω
τρισσεύσω vb fut act ind 1st pers sg		id.
τρισσή adj fem nom sg	. . . .	τρισσός
τρισσούς adj masc acc pl		id.
τρισσῶς adverb		
τρισσώσατε vb 1st aor act impv 2nd pers pl	. . . . . .	τρισσόω
τριστάται noun masc nom pl	. . . .	τριστάτης
τριστάταις noun masc dat pl		id.
τριστάτας noun masc acc pl		id.
τριστάτην noun masc acc sg		id.
τριστάτης noun masc nom sg		id.
τρισχίλια adj neut nom and acc pl	. . . .	τρισχίλιοι
τρισχίλιαι adj fem nom pl		id.
τρισχιλίαν adj fem acc sg	. . . .	τρισχίλιος
τρισχιλίας adj fem acc pl	. . . .	τρισχίλιοι
τρισχίλιοι adj masc nom pl		id.
τρισχιλίοις adj masc and neut dat pl		id.
τρισχιλίους adj masc acc pl		id.
τρισχιλίων adj gen pl		id.
τριταῖος adj masc nom sg		
τριταίων adj gen pl	. . . .	τριταῖος
τρίτη adj fem nom sg	. . . .	τρίτος
τρίτῃ adj fem dat sg		id.
τρίτην adj fem acc sg		id.
τρίτης adj fem gen sg		id.
τρίτοι adj masc nom pl		id.
τρίτον adj masc acc sg, neut nom and acc sg		id.
τρίτος adj masc nom sg		id.
τρίτου adj masc and neut gen sg		id.
τρίτους adj masc acc pl		id.
τρίτῳ adj masc and neut dat sg		id.
τρίχα noun fem acc sg	. . . .	θρίξ
τρίχαπτα adj neut nom and acc pl	. . . .	τρίχαπτος
τριχάπτῳ adj dat sg		id.
τρίχας noun fem acc pl	. . . .	θρίξ
τρίχες noun fem nom pl		id.
τριχίνας adj fem acc pl	. . . .	τρίχινος
τριχίνην adj fem acc sg		id.
τριχός noun fem gen sg	. . . .	θρίξ
τρίχωμα noun neut nom and acc sg		
τριχώματος noun neut gen sg	. . . .	τρίχωμα

τριχῶν noun fem gen pl . . . . θρίξ

τρῖψον vb 1st aor act impv 2nd pers sg . . . . τρίβω

τριῶν adj gen pl . . . . τρεῖς

τριώροφα adj neut nom and acc pl . . . . τριώροφος

τρόμον noun masc acc sg . . . . τρόμος

τρόμος noun masc nom sg   id.

τρόμου noun masc gen sg   id.

τρόμῳ noun masc dat sg   id.

τρόπαια noun neut nom and acc pl . . . . τρόπαιον

τρόπαιον noun neut nom and acc sg   id.

τροπάς noun fem acc pl . . . . τροπή

τροπή noun fem nom sg   id.

τροπῇ noun fem dat sg   id.

τροπήν noun fem acc sg   id.

τροπῆς noun fem gen sg   id.

τρόπιος noun fem gen sg . . . . τρόπις

τρόπον noun masc acc sg . . . . τρόπος

τρόπος noun masc nom sg   id.

τροπούμενον vb pres act part masc acc sg,

        neut nom and acc sg . . . . τροπόω

τροπούμενος vb pres m/p part masc nom sg   id.

τροποῦται vb pres m/p ind 3rd pers sg   id.

τρόπῳ noun masc dat sg . . . . τρόπος

τροπωθέντα vb 1st aor pass part

        neut nom and acc pl . . . . τροπόω

τρόπων noun masc gen pl . . . . τρόπος

τροπῶν noun fem gen pl . . . . τροπή

τροπώσασθαι vb 1st aor mid inf . . . . τροπόω

τροπώσεται vb fut mid ind 3rd pers sg   id.

τροπώσομαι vb fut mid ind 1st pers sg   id.

τροφάς noun fem acc pl . . . . τροφή

τροφεία noun fem nom sg

τροφεύουσαν vb pres act part fem acc sg . . . . τροφεύω

τροφεύσαντα vb 1st aor act part masc acc sg   id.

τροφή noun fem nom sg

τροφήν noun fem acc sg . . . . τροφή

τροφῆς noun fem gen sg   id.

τροφοί noun fem nom pl . . . . τροφός

τροφόν noun fem acc sg   id.

τροφός noun fem nom sg   id.

τροφοφορήσασαν vb 1st aor act part

        fem acc sg . . . . τροφοφορέω

τροφοφορήσει vb fut act ind 3rd pers sg   id.

τροφῶν noun fem gen pl . . . . τροφός

τροχαντήρας noun masc acc pl . . . . τροχαντήρ

τροχιαί noun fem nom pl . . . . τροχιά

τροχιαῖον adj masc acc sg, neut nom and acc sg . τροχιαῖος

τροχιαῖς noun fem dat pl . . . . τροχιά

τροχιάς noun fem acc pl   id.

τροχισθέντας vb 1st aor pass part masc acc pl . . . . τροχίζω

τροχίσκους noun masc acc pl . . . . τροχίσκος

τροχοί noun masc nom pl . . . . τροχός

τροχοῖς noun masc dat pl . . . . τροχός

τροχόν noun masc acc sg   id.

τροχός noun masc nom sg   id.

τροχοῦ noun masc gen sg   id.

τροχούς noun masc acc pl   id.

τροχῷ noun masc dat sg   id.

τροχῶν noun masc gen pl   id.

τρύβλια see τρυβλία

τρυβλία noun neut nom and acc pl . . . . τρυβλίον

τρυβλίον noun neut nom and acc sg   id.

τρυβλίῳ noun neut dat sg   id.

τρυγᾶν vb pres act inf . . . . τρυγάω

τρυγηθείη vb 1st aor pass opt 3rd pers sg   id.

τρυγήσατε vb 1st aor act impv 2nd pers pl   id.

τρυγήσεις vb fut act ind 2nd pers sg   id.

τρυγήσετε vb fut act ind 2nd pers pl   id.

τρυγήσῃς vb 1st aor act subj 2nd pers sg   id.

τρυγηταί noun masc nom pl . . . . τρυγητής

τρυγηταῖς noun masc dat pl

τρύγητον noun masc acc sg . . . . τρύγητος

τρυγητόν noun masc acc sg   τρύγητος

τρύγητος noun masc nom sg   τρύγητος

τρυγητός noun masc nom sg   τρυγητός

τρυγήτου noun masc gen sg   τρύγητος

τρυγήτῳ noun masc dat sg   id.

τρυγητῶν noun masc gen pl   τρυγητός

τρυγίας noun masc nom sg

τρυγόνα noun fem acc sg . . . . τρυγών

τρυγόνας noun fem acc pl   id.

τρυγόνες noun fem nom pl   id.

τρυγόνος noun fem gen sg   id.

τρυγόνων noun fem gen pl   id.

τρυγών noun fem nom sg   id.

τρυγῶν vb pres act part masc nom sg . . . . τρυγαω

τρυγῶντες vb pres act part masc nom pl   id.

τρυγῶσιν vb pres act ind 3rd pers pl   id.

τρυμαλιᾷ noun fem dat sg . . . . τρυμαλιά

τρυμαλιάν noun fem acc sg   id.

τρυμαλιάς noun fem acc pl   id.

τρυμαλιῶν noun fem gen pl   id.

τρυπήσει vb fut act ind 3rd pers sg . . . . τρυπάω

τρυπήσεις vb fut act ind 2nd pers sg   id.

τρυφαῖς noun fem dat pl . . . . τρυφή

τρυφάς noun fem acc pl   id.

τρυφερά adj fem nom sg, neut nom and acc pl . . . τρυφερός

τρυφερευομένη vb pres dep part

        fem nom sg . . . . τρυφερεύομαι

τρυφεροί adj masc nom pl . . . . τρυφερός

τρυφερός adj masc nom sg   id.

τρυφερότητα noun fem acc sg . . . . τρυφερότης

τρυφή noun fem nom sg

τρυφῇ noun fem dat sg . . . . τρυφή

τρυφημάτων	noun neut gen pl	τρύφημα	
τρυφήν	noun fem acc sg	τρυφή	
τρυφῆς	noun fem gen sg	id.	
τρυφήσητε	vb 1st aor act subj 2nd pers pl	τρυφάω	
τρυφήσουσιν	vb fut act ind 3rd pers sg	id.	
Τρυφων	pr noun masc nom sg		
Τρυφωνα	pr noun masc acc sg	Τρυφων	
Τρυφωνι	pr noun masc dat sg	id.	
Τρυφωνος	pr noun masc gen sg	id.	
τρυχόμενος	vb pres m/p part masc nom sg	τρύχω	
τρώγλαι	noun fem nom pl	τρώγλη	
τρώγλαις	noun fem dat pl	id.	
τρώγλας	noun fem acc pl	id.	
τρώγλην	noun fem acc sg	id.	
Τρωγλοδυται	pr noun		
τρωγλῶν	noun fem gen pl	τρώγλη	
τρωθήσῃ	vb fut pass ind 2nd pers sg	τιτρώσκω	
τρωθήσομαι	vb fut pass ind 1st pers sg	id.	
τρώσαι	vb 1st aor act opt 3rd pers sg	id.	
τρώσασα	vb 1st aor act part fem nom sg	id.	
τρωσάτω	vb 1st aor act impv 3rd pers sg	id.	
τρώσῃ	vb 1st aor act subj 3rd pers sg	id.	
τυγχάνει	vb pres act ind 3rd pers sg	τυγχάνω	
τυγχάνειν	vb pres act inf	id.	
τυγχάνεις	vb pres act ind 2nd pers sg	id.	
τυγχάνουσιν	vb pres act ind 3rd pers pl	id.	
τυγχάνω	vb pres act ind 1st pers sg	id.	
τυθῇ	vb 1st aor pass subj 3rd pers sg	θύω	
τυμπανιστριῶν	noun fem gen pl	τυμπανίστρια	
τυμπάνοις	noun neut dat pl	τύμπανον	
τύμπανον	noun neut nom and acc sg	id.	
τυμπάνῳ	noun neut dat sg	id.	
τυμπάνων	noun neut gen pl	id.	
τύπον	noun masc acc sg	τύπος	
τύπος	noun masc nom sg	id.	
τύπους	noun masc acc pl	id.	
τύπτε	vb pres act impv 2nd pers sg	τύπτω	
τύπτει	vb pres act ind 3rd pers sg	id.	
τύπτειν	vb pres act inf	id.	
τύπτεις	vb pres act ind 2nd pers sg	id.	
τύπτετε	vb pres act ind 2nd pers pl	id.	
τυπτόμενος	vb pres m/p part masc nom sg	id.	
τύπτοντα	vb pres act part masc acc sg	id.	
τύπτοντας	vb pres act part masc acc pl	id.	
τύπτοντες	vb pres act part masc nom pl	id.	
τύπτοντος	vb pres act part masc and neut gen sg	id.	
τύπτουσιν	vb pres act ind 3rd pers pl	id.	
τύπτω	vb pres act ind 1st pers sg	id.	
τύπτων	vb pres act part masc nom sg	id.	
τυπώσει	vb fut act ind 3rd pers sg	τυπόω	
τύραννε	noun masc voc sg	τύραννος	
τυραννεῖ	vb pres act ind 3rd pers sg	τυραννέω	
τυραννήσεις	vb fut act ind 2nd pers sg	τυραννέω	
τυραννίδα	noun fem acc sg	τυραννίς	
τυραννίδες	noun fem nom pl	id.	
τυραννίδι	noun fem dat sg	id.	
τυραννίδος	noun fem gen sg	id.	
τυραννική	adj fem nom sg	τυραννικός	
τυραννικόν	adj masc acc sg, neut nom and acc sg	id.	
τύραννοι	noun masc nom pl	τύραννος	
τύραννον	noun masc acc sg	id.	
τύραννος	noun masc nom sg	id.	
τυράννου	noun masc gen sg	id.	
τυραννούντων	vb pres act part masc and neut gen pl	τυραννέω	
τυράννους	noun masc acc pl	τύραννος	
τυραννοῦσι	vb pres act part masc and neut dat pl	τυραννέω	
τυράννῳ	noun masc dat sg	τύραννος	
τυράννων	noun masc gen pl	id.	
Τυριοι	pr noun masc nom pl	Τυριος	
Τυριοις	pr noun masc dat pl	id.	
Τυριος	pr noun masc nom sg	id.	
Τυριων	pr noun masc gen pl	id.	
Τυρον	pr noun fem acc sg	Τυρος	
Τυρος	pr noun fem nom sg	id.	
Τυρου	pr noun fem gen sg	id.	
Τυρῳ	pr noun fem dat sg	id.	
τυρῷ	noun masc dat sg	τυρός	
τυφλοί	adj masc nom pl	τυφλός	
τυφλοῖς	adj masc and neut dat pl	id.	
τυφλόν	adj masc acc sg, neut nom and acc sg	id.	
τυφλός	adj masc nom sg	id.	
τυφλοῦ	adj masc and neut gen sg	id.	
τυφλούς	adj masc acc pl	id.	
τυφλῶν	adj gen pl	id.	
τύφοις	noun masc dat pl	τῦφος	
τυχεῖν	vb 2nd aor act inf	τυγχάνω	
τύχῃ	noun fem dat sg	τύχη	
τύχῃ	vb 2nd aor act subj 3rd pers sg	τυγχάνω	
τυχόντα	vb 2nd aor act part masc acc sg	id.	
τυχόντι	vb 2nd aor act part masc and neut dat sg	id.	
τύχω	vb 2nd aor act subj 1st pers sg	id.	
τῷ	art masc and neut gen sg	ὁ	
Τωβ	pr noun		
Τωβει	pr noun		
Τωβια	pr noun		
Τωβιαν	pr noun masc acc sg	Τωβιας	
Τωβιας	pr noun masc nom sg		
Τωβιηλ	pr noun		
Τωβιθ	pr noun		
Τωβιν	pr noun	Τωβιθ	
Τωβιου	pr noun masc gen sg	Τωβιας	
Τωβις	pr noun		
Τωβιτ	pr noun		

τῶν art gen pl .... ὁ | τῶνδε dem pron gen pl .... ὅδε

Υ υ

ὑαίνη noun fem dat sg .... ὕαινα	ὑγιασθέν vb 1st aor pass part neut nom and acc sg .. ὑγιάζω
ὑαίνης noun fem gen sg	id.	ὑγιασθῇ vb 1st aor pass subj 3rd pers sg	id.
ὑακίνθινα adj neut nom and acc pl .... ὑακίνθινος	ὑγιασθῆναι vb 1st aor pass inf	id.
ὑακίνθινας adj fem acc pl	id.	ὑγιάσθησαν vb 1st aor pass ind 3rd pers pl	id.
ὑακίνθινον adj masc acc sg, neut nom and acc sg	id.	ὑγιάσωσιν vb 1st aor act subj 3rd pers pl	id.
ὑακινθίνῳ adj masc and neut dat sg	id.	ὑγίεια noun fem nom sg
ὑάκινθον noun fem acc sg .... ὑάκινθος	ὑγιείᾳ noun fem dat sg .... ὑγίεια
ὑακίνθου noun fem gen sg	id.	ὑγίειαν noun fem acc sg	id.
ὑακίνθῳ noun fem dat sg	id.	ὑγιείας noun fem gen sg	id.
ὕαλος noun fem nom sg	ὑγιεῖς adj masc and fem nom and acc pl .... ὑγιής
ὕβρει noun fem dat sg .... ὕβρις	ὑγιῆ adj masc and fem acc sg, neut nom and acc pl	id.
ὕβρεις noun fem nom and acc pl	id.	ὑγιής adj masc and fem nom sg	id.
ὕβρεων noun fem gen pl	id.	ὑγιοῦς adj gen sg	id.
ὕβρεως noun fem gen sg	id.	ὑγιῶς adverb
ὑβρίζειν vb pres act inf .... ὑβρίζω	ὑγραίνονται vb pres m/p ind 3rd pers pl .... ὑγραίνω
ὑβριζομένοις vb pres m/p part masc and neut dat pl	id.	ὑγραῖς adj fem dat pl .... ὑγρός
ὑβρίζοντες vb pres act part masc nom pl	id.	ὑγράς adj fem acc pl	id.
ὕβριν noun fem acc sg .... ὕβρις	ὑγρασίᾳ noun fem dat sg .... ὑγρασία
ὕβρις noun fem nom sg	id.	ὑγρός adj masc nom sg
ὑβρίσας vb 1st aor act part masc nom sg .... ὑβρίζω	ὑγροῦ adj masc and neut gen sg .... ὑγρός
ὕβρισεν vb 1st aor act ind 3rd pers sg	id.	ὕδασι noun neut dat pl .... ὕδωρ
ὑβρισθῆναι vb 1st aor pass inf	id.	Ὑδάσπην pr noun masc acc sg .... Ὑδάσπης
ὑβριστάς noun masc acc pl .... ὑβριστής	ὕδατα noun neut nom and acc pl .... ὕδωρ
ὑβριστήν noun masc acc sg	id.	ὕδατι noun neut dat sg	id.
ὑβριστής noun masc nom sg	id.	ὕδατος noun neut gen sg	id.
ὑβριστικόν adj masc acc sg,		ὑδάτων noun neut gen pl	id.
neut nom and acc sg .... ὑβριστικός	ὑδραγωγοῖς noun masc dat pl .... ὑδραγωγός
ὑβριστοῦ noun masc gen sg .... ὑβριστής	ὑδραγωγόν noun masc acc sg	id.
ὑβρίστριαν noun fem acc sg .... ὑβρίστρια	ὑδραγωγός noun masc nom sg	id.
ὑβριστῶν noun masc gen pl .... ὑβριστής	ὑδραγωγῷ noun masc dat sg	id.
ὑγίαινε vb pres act impv 2nd pers sg .... ὑγιαίνω	ὑδρευόμεναι vb pres dep part fem nom pl ..... ὑδρεύομαι
ὑγιαίνει vb pres act ind 3rd pers sg	id.	ὑδρευομένων vb pres dep part gen pl	id.
ὑγιαίνειν vb pres act inf	id.	ὑδρεύονται vb pres dep ind 3rd pers pl	id.
ὑγιαίνεις vb pres act ind 2nd pers sg	id.	ὑδρεύσαντο vb 1st aor mid ind 3rd pers pl	id.
ὑγιαίνετε vb pres act impv 2nd pers pl	id.	ὑδρεύσασθαι vb 1st aor mid inf	id.
ὑγιαίνομεν vb pres act ind 1st pers pl	id.	ὑδρεύσατο vb 1st aor mid ind 3rd pers sg	id.
ὑγιαίνοντα vb pres act part masc acc sg,		ὑδρεύσομαι vb fut mid ind 1st pers sg	id.
neut nom and acc pl	id.	ὑδρεύωνται vb pres dep subj 3rd pers pl	id.
ὑγιαίνοντας vb pres act part masc acc pl	id.	ὑδρία noun fem nom sg
ὑγιαίνοντες vb pres act part masc nom pl	id.	ὑδρίᾳ noun fem dat sg .... ὑδρία
ὑγιαίνουσα vb pres act part fem nom sg	id.	ὑδρίαις noun fem dat pl	id.
ὑγιαίνουσιν vb pres act ind 3rd pers pl	id.	ὑδρίαν noun fem acc sg	id.
ὑγιαίνων vb pres act part masc nom sg	id.	ὑδρίας noun fem gen sg and acc pl	id.
ὑγίακεν vb perf act ind 3rd pers sg .... ὑγιάζω	ὑδρίσκην noun fem acc sg .... ὑδρίσκη
ὑγιάσει vb fut act ind 3rd pers sg	id.	ὑδριῶν noun fem gen pl .... ὑδρία

ὑδροποτεῖν vb pres act inf	....	ὑδροποτέω
ὑδροφόροι noun masc nom pl	....	ὑδροφόρος
ὑδροφόρου noun masc gen sg		id.
ὑδροφόρους noun masc acc pl		id.
ὕδωρ noun neut nom and acc sg		
ὕεια adj neut nom and acc pl	....	ὕειος
ὕειον adj masc acc sg, neut nom and acc sg		id.
ὑείων adj gen pl		id.
ὕες noun fem nom pl	....	ὗς
ὑετίζων vb pres act part masc nom sg	....	ὑετίζω
ὑετίσαι vb 1st aor act inf		id.
ὑετοί noun masc nom pl	....	ὑετός
ὑετοῖς noun masc dat pl		id.
ὑετόν noun masc acc sg		id.
ὑετός noun masc nom sg		id.
ὑετοῦ noun masc gen sg		id.
ὑετῷ noun masc dat sg		id.
ὑετῶν noun masc gen pl		id.
υἱέ noun masc voc sg	....	υἱός
υἱοί noun masc nom pl		id.
υἱοῖς noun masc dat pl		id.
υἱόν noun masc acc sg		id.
Υἱος pr noun masc nom sg		id.
υἱός noun masc nom sg		id.
υἱοῦ noun masc gen sg		id.
υἱούς noun masc acc pl		id.
υἱῷ noun masc dat sg		id.
υἱῶν noun masc gen pl		id.
ὕλαις noun fem dat pl	....	ὕλη
ὑλακτεῖν vb pres act inf	....	ὑλακτέω
ὕλας noun fem acc pl	....	ὕλη
ὕλη noun fem nom sg		id.
ὕλην noun fem acc sg		id.
ὕλης noun fem gen sg		id.
ὑλοτόμος adj masc and fem nom sg		
ὑλώδης adj masc and fem nom sg		
ὑμᾶς pron of 2nd pers acc pl	....	σύ
ὑμεῖς pron of 2nd pers nom pl		id.
ὑμεναίων noun masc gen pl	....	ὑμέναιος
ὑμετέρᾳ adj fem dat sg	....	ὑμέτερος
ὑμετέραν adj fem acc sg		id.
ὑμέτερον adj masc acc sg, neut nom and acc sg		id.
ὑμετέρων adj gen pl		id.
ὑμῖν pron of the 2nd pers dat pl	....	σύ
ὑμνεῖ vb pres act ind 3rd pers sg	....	ὑμνέω
ὑμνεῖν vb pres act inf		id.
ὑμνεῖται vb pres m/p ind 3rd pers sg		id.
ὑμνεῖτε vb pres act impv 2nd pers pl, pres act ind 2nd pers pl		id.
ὑμνείτω vb pres act impv 3rd pers sg		id.
ὕμνησαν vb 1st aor act ind 3rd pers pl		id.
ὑμνήσατε vb 1st aor act impv 2nd pers pl		id.

ὑμνήσειν vb fut act inf	....	ὑμνέω
ὕμνησεν vb 1st aor act ind 3rd pers sg		id.
ὕμνησις noun fem nom sg		
ὑμνήσουσιν vb fut act ind 3rd pers pl	....	ὑμνέω
ὑμνήσω vb 1st aor act subj 1st pers sg, fut act ind 1st pers sg		id.
ὑμνητός adj masc nom sg		
ὑμνογράφον noun masc acc sg	....	ὑμνογράφος
ὕμνοι noun masc nom pl	....	ὕμνος
ὕμνοις noun masc dat pl		id.
ὕμνον noun masc acc sg		id.
ὕμνος noun masc nom sg		id.
ὕμνουν vb impf act ind 3rd pers pl	....	ὑμνέω
ὑμνοῦντες vb pres act part masc nom pl		id.
ὑμνούντων vb pres act part masc and neut gen pl		id.
ὕμνους noun masc acc pl	....	ὕμνος
ὑμνῳδοῦντες vb pres act part masc nom pl	.....	ὑμνῳδέω
ὑμνῶμεν vb pres act subj 1st pers pl	....	ὑμνέω
ὕμνων noun masc gen pl	....	ὕμνος
ὑμνῶν vb pres act part masc nom sg	....	ὑμνέω
ὑμῶν pron of the 2nd pers gen pl	....	σύ
ὗν noun masc acc sg	....	ὗς
ὑός noun masc gen sg		id.
ὑπ' see ὑπό		
ὕπαγε vb pres act impv 2nd pers sg	....	ὑπάγω
ὑπαγορεύσωσιν vb 1st aor act subj 3rd pers pl	.	ὑπαγορεύω
ὑπαίθρου adj masc and fem gen sg	....	ὕπαιθρος
ὑπαίθρῳ noun dat sg		id.
ὑπακοή noun fem nom sg		
ὑπακούει vb pres act ind 3rd pers sg	....	ὑπακούω
ὑπακούειν vb pres act inf		id.
ὑπακούοντος vb pres act part masc and neut gen sg		id.
ὑπακοῦσαι vb 1st aor act inf		id.
ὑπακούσεται vb fut mid ind 3rd pers sg		id.
ὑπακούσῃ vb 1st aor act subj 3rd pers sg, fut mid ind 2nd pers sg		id.
ὑπακούσῃς vb 1st aor act subj 2nd pers sg		id.
ὑπακούσηται vb 1st aor mid subj 3rd pers sg		id.
ὑπακούσητε vb 1st aor act subj 2nd pers pl		id.
ὑπακούσομαι vb fut mid ind 1st pers sg		id.
ὑπάκουσον vb 1st aor act impv 2nd pers sg		id.
ὑπακούσονται vb fut mid ind 3rd pers pl		id.
ὑπακούσωσιν vb 1st aor act subj 3rd pers pl		id.
ὑπακούω vb pres act ind 1st pers sg		id.
ὑπακούων vb pres act part masc nom sg		id.
ὕπανδρον adj fem acc sg	....	ὕπανδρος
ὑπάνδρου adj fem gen sg		id.
ὑπάντα vb pres act impv 2nd pers sg	....	ὑπαντάω
ὑπαντᾷ vb pres act ind 3rd pers sg		id.
ὑπαντήσεται vb fut mid ind 3rd pers sg		id.
ὑπαντήσῃ vb 1st aor act subj 3rd pers sg		id.
ὑπάντησιν noun fem acc sg	....	ὑπάντησις

ὕπαρ   noun neut nom and acc sg

ὑπάρξαντες   vb 1st aor act part masc nom pl ..... ὑπάρχω

ὑπαρξάτω   vb 1st aor act impv 3rd pers sg   id.

ὑπάρξει   noun fem dat sg .... ὕπαρξις

ὑπάρξει   vb fut act ind 3rd pers sg .... ὑπάρχω

ὑπάρξεις   vb fut act ind 2nd pers sg   id.

ὑπάρξεως   noun fem gen sg .... ὕπαρξις

ὑπάρξῃ   vb 1st aor act subj 3rd pers sg .... ὑπάρχω

ὕπαρξιν   noun fem acc sg .... ὕπαρξις

ὕπαρξις   noun fem nom sg

ὑπάρξουσιν   vb fut act ind 3rd pers pl .... ὑπάρχω

ὑπάρξω   vb 1st aor act subj 1st pers sg   id.

ὑπάρξωσιν   vb 1st aor act subj 3rd pers pl   id.

ὑπάρχει   vb pres act ind 3rd pers sg   id.

ὑπάρχειν   vb pres act inf   id.

ὑπαρχέτω   vb pres act impv 3rd pers sg   id.

ὑπάρχῃ   vb pres act subj 3rd pers sg   id.

ὑπάρχον   vb pres act part neut nom and acc sg   id.

ὑπάρχοντα   vb pres act part masc acc sg,

        neut nom and acc pl   d.

ὑπάρχοντες   vb pres act part masc nom pl   d.

ὑπάρχοντος   vb pres act part masc and neut gen sg   d.

ὑπαρχόντων   vb pres act part masc and neut gen pl   d.

ὑπάρχουσα   vb pres act part fem nom sg   id.

ὑπάρχουσι(ν)   vb pres act ind 3rd pers pl

        pres act part masc and neut dat pl   id.

ὑπάρχουσι   adj masc and neut dat pl .... ὕπαρχος

ὑπάρχω   vb pres act ind 1st pers sg

ὑπάρχων   vb pres act part masc nom sg .... ὑπάρχω

ὑπάρχωσιν   vb pres act subj 3rd pers pl   id.

ὑπασπισταί   noun masc nom pl .... ὑπασπιστής

ὑπασπιστῶν   adj gen pl   id.

ὕπατοι   adj masc nom pl .... ὕπατος

ὕπατος   adj masc nom sg   id.

ὑπάτους   adj masc acc pl   id.

ὑπαχθείς   vb 2nd aor pass part masc nom sg .... ὑπάγω

ὑπέγραψεν   vb 1st aor act ind 3rd pers sg ...... ὑπογράφω

ὑπεδείκνυεν   vb impf act ind 3rd pers sg ..... ὑποδεικνύω

ὑπέδειξα   vb 1st aor act ind 1st pers sg   id.

ὑπέδειξαν   vb 1st aor act ind 3rd pers pl   id.

ὑπέδειξε(ν)   vb 1st aor act ind 3rd pers sg   id.

ὑπεδείχθη   vb 1st aor pass ind 3rd pers sg   id.

ὑπεδέξαντο   vb 1st aor mid ind 3rd pers pl .... ὑποδέχομαι

ὑπεδέξατο   vb 1st aor mid ind 3rd pers sg   id.

ὑπέδησα   vb 1st aor act ind 1st pers sg .... ὑποδέω

ὑπέδησαν   vb 1st aor act ind 3rd pers pl   id.

ὑπεζωσμέναι   vb 1st aor mid part fem nom pl .. ὑποζώννυμι

ὑπέθεντο   vb 2nd aor mid ind 3rd pers pl .... ὑποτίθημι

ὑπέθηκαν   vb 1st aor act ind 3rd pers pl   id.

ὑπέθηκεν   vb 1st aor act ind 3rd pers sg   id.

ὑπείκειν   vb pres act inf .... ὑπείκω

ὑπειληφότες   vb perf act part masc nom pl ... ὑπολαμβάνω

ὑπεκαίετο   vb impf m/p ind 3rd pers sg .... ὑποκαίω

ὑπέκαιον   vb impf act ind 3rd pers pl   id.

ὑπέκειτο   vb impf m/p ind 3rd pers sg .... ὑπόκειμαι

ὑπεκρέων   vb pres act part masc nom sg .... ὑπεκρέω

ὑπεκρίνοντο   vb impf dep ind 3rd pers pl .... ὑποκρίνομαι

ὑπέλαβεν   vb 2nd aor act ind 3rd pers sg .... ὑπολαμβάνω

ὑπέλαβες   vb 2nd aor act ind 2nd pers sg   id.

ὑπελάβομεν   vb 2nd aor act ind 1st pers pl   id.

ὑπέλαβον   vb 2nd aor act ind 1st pers sg and 3rd pers pl   id.

ὑπελάμβανον   vb impf act ind 1st pers sg and 3rd pers pl   id.

ὑπελείποντο   vb impf m/p ind 3rd pers pl .... ὑπολείπω

ὑπελείφθη   vb 1st aor pass ind 3rd pers sg   id.

ὑπελείφθην   vb 1st aor pass ind 1st pers sg   id.

ὑπελείφθησαν   vb 1st aor pass ind 3rd pers pl   id.

ὑπεληλυθυῖαι   vb perf act part fem nom pl .... ὑπέρχομαι

ὑπέλιπεν   vb 2nd aor act ind 3rd pers sg .... ὑπολείπω

ὑπελίπετο   vb 2nd aor mid ind 3rd pers sg   id.

ὑπελίποντο   vb 2nd aor mid ind 3rd pers pl   id.

ὑπελίπω   vb 2nd aor mid ind 2nd pers sg   id.

ὑπελύετο   vb impf m/p ind 3rd pers sg .... ὑπολύω

ὑπελύσατο   vb 1st aor mid ind 3rd pers sg   id.

ὑπέμεινα   vb 1st aor act ind 1st pers sg .... ὑπομένω

ὑπεμείναμεν   vb 1st aor act ind 1st pers pl   id.

ὑπέμειναν   vb 1st aor act ind 3rd pers pl   id.

ὑπέμεινας   vb 1st aor act ind 2nd pers sg   id.

ὑπέμεινε(ν)   vb 1st aor act ind 3rd pers sg   id.

ὑπέμενε   vb impf act ind 3rd pers sg   id.

ὑπέμενον   vb impf act ind 3rd pers pl   id.

ὑπεμίμνῃσκεν   vb impf act ind 3rd pers sg ... ὑπομιμνήσκω

ὑπεμνημάτιστο   vb plpf dep ind

        3rd pers sg .... ὑπομνηματίζομαι

ὑπεναντίοι   adj masc nom pl .... ὑπεναντίος

ὑπεναντίοις   adj masc and neut dat pl   id.

ὑπεναντίον   adj masc acc sg, neut nom and acc sg   id.

ὑπεναντίος   adj masc nom sg   id.

ὑπεναντίους   adj masc acc pl   id.

ὑπεναντίων   adj gen pl   id.

ὑπενέγκαντες   vb 1st aor act part masc nom pl .... ὑποφέρω

ὑπενεγκεῖν   vb 2nd aor act inf   id.

ὑπενόει   vb impf act ind 3rd pers sg .... ὑπονοέω

ὑπενόησεν   vb 1st aor act ind 3rd pers sg   id.

ὑπενόθευσεν   vb 1st aor act ind 3rd pers sg .... ὑπονοθεύω

ὑπενόουν   vb impf act ind 1st pers sg .... ὑπονοέω

ὑπεξῄρηται   vb perf m/p ind 3rd pers sg ...... ὑπεξαιρέω

ὑπέπεσεν   vb 1st aor act ind 3rd pers sg .... ὑποπίπτω

ὑπέρ   preposition

ὑπεράγαν   adverb

ὑπεράγει   vb pres act ind 3rd pers sg .... ὑπεράγω

ὑπεράγον   vb pres act part neut nom and acc sg   id.

ὑπεραγόντως   adverb

ὑπεράγων   vb pres act part masc nom sg .... ὑπεράγω

ὑπεραινετόν   adj acc sg, neut nom sg .... ὑπεραινετός

ὑπεραινετός adj masc and fem nom sg

ὑπεραλοῦνται vb fut mid ind 3rd pers pl ... ὑπεράλλομαι

ὑπεράνω adverb and preposition

ὑπεράνωθεν adverb

ὑπεραρθήσεται vb fut pass ind 3rd pers sg ..... ὑπεραίρω

ὑπεράρσει noun fem dat sg .... ὑπέραρσις

ὑπερασπιεῖ vb fut act ind 3rd pers sg ...... ὑπερασπίζω

ὑπερασπίζει vb pres act ind 3rd pers sg   id.

ὑπερασπίζοντα vb pres act part masc acc sg   id.

ὑπερασπίζοντας vb pres act part masc acc pl   id.

ὑπερασπίζω vb pres act ind 1st pers sg   id.

ὑπερασπίζων vb pres act part masc nom sg   id.

ὑπερασπίσαι vb 1st aor act inf,

          1st aor act opt 3rd pers sg   id.

ὑπερασπίσῃ vb 1st aor act subj 3rd pers sg   id.

ὑπερασπισμόν noun masc acc sg .... ὑπερασπισμός

ὑπερασπισμός noun masc nom sg   id.

ὑπερασπιστά noun masc voc sg .... ὑπερασπιστής

ὑπερασπιστήν noun masc acc sg   id.

ὑπερασπιστής noun masc nom sg   id.

ὑπερασπίστρια noun fem nom sg

ὑπερασπιῶ vb fut act ind 1st pers sg .... ὑπερασπίζω

ὑπερβαίνοντες vb pres act part masc nom pl ... ὑπερβαίνω

ὑπερβαίνουσιν vb pres act ind 3rd pers pl   id.

ὑπερβαίνων vb pres act part masc nom sg   id.

ὑπερβάλλοντι vb pres act part

        masc and neut dat sg .... ὑπερβάλλω

ὑπερβαλλόντως adverb

ὑπερβάλλου vb pres m/p impv 2nd pers sg .... ὑπερβάλλω

ὑπερβάλλουσαν vb pres act part fem acc sg   id.

ὑπερβαλλούσας vb pres act part fem acc pl   id.

ὑπερβαλών vb 2nd aor act part masc nom sg   id.

ὑπερβεβήκατε vb perf act ind 2nd pers pl .... ὑπερβαίνω

ὑπερβῇ vb 2nd aor act subj 3rd pers sg   id.

ὑπερβήσεται vb fut mid ind 3rd pers sg   id.

ὑπερβήσῃ vb fut mid ind 2nd pers sg   id.

ὑπερβήσομαι vb fut mid ind 1st pers sg   id.

ὑπερβολήν noun fem acc sg .... ὑπερβολή

ὑπερέβαλεν vb 2nd aor act ind 3rd pers sg ..... ὑπερβάλλω

ὑπερέβη vb 2nd aor act ind 3rd pers sg .... ὑπερβαίνω

ὑπερέβην vb 2nd aor act ind 1st pers sg   id.

ὑπερέβησαν vb 2nd aor act ind 3rd pers pl   id.

ὑπερεδυνάμωσαν vb 1st aor act ind

        3rd pers pl .... ὑπερδυναμόω

ὑπερεῖδεν vb 2nd aor act ind 3rd pers sg .... ὑπεροράω

ὑπερεῖδες vb 2nd aor act ind 2nd pers sg   id.

ὑπερείδομεν vb 2nd aor act ind 1st pers pl   id.

ὑπερεῖδον vb 2nd aor act ind 1st pers sg and 3rd pers pl   id.

ὑπερείσῃ vb 1st aor act subj 3rd pers sg .... ὑπερείδω

ὑπερεῖχον vb impf act ind 3rd pers pl .... ὑπερέχω

ὑπερεκέρασαν vb 1st aor act ind 3rd pers pl ... ὑπερκεράω

ὑπερεκέρων vb impf act ind 3rd pers pl   id.

ὑπερεκράτησεν vb 1st aor act ind 3rd pers sg . ὑπερκρατέω

ὑπερεκχείσθω vb pres m/p impv 3rd pers sg ... ὑπερεκχέω

ὑπερεκχεῖται vb pres m/p ind 3rd pers sg   id.

ὑπερεκχυθήσονται vb fut pass ind 3rd pers pl   id.

ὑπερένδοξος adj masc and fem nom sg

ὑπερέξει vb fut act ind 3rd pers sg .... ὑπερέχω

ὑπερέξω vb fut act ind 1st pers sg   id.

ὑπερέφερε vb impf act ind 3rd pers sg .... ὑπερφέρω

ὑπερεφρόνησαν vb 1st aor act ind 3rd pers pl . ὑπερφρονέω

ὑπερεφρόνησεν vb 1st aor act ind 3rd pers sg   id.

ὑπερεφώνει vb impf act ind 3rd pers sg ...... ὑπερφωνέω

ὑπερέχει vb pres act ind 3rd pers sg .... ὑπερέχω

ὑπερέχοντος vb pres act part masc and neut gen sg   id.

ὑπερεχόντων vb pres act part masc and neut gen pl   id.

ὑπερέχουσι vb pres act part masc and neut dat pl   id.

ὑπερεχύθη vb 1st aor act pass ind 3rd pers sg ...... ὑπερχέω

ὑπερέχων vb pres act part masc nom sg .... ὑπερέχω

ὑπερεωραμένη vb perf m/p part fem nom sg ... ὑπεροράω

ὑπερήνεγκαν vb 1st aor act ind 3rd pers pl ..... ὑπερφέρω

ὑπερῆραν vb 1st aor act ind 3rd pers pl .... ὑπεραίρω

ὑπερῆρας vb 1st aor act ind 2nd pers sg   id.

ὑπερῆρεν vb 1st aor act ind 3rd pers sg   id.

ὑπερήρετο vb impf m/p ind 3rd pers sg   id.

ὑπερήρθη vb 1st aor pass ind 3rd pers sg   id.

ὑπερησπικότα vb perf act part masc acc sg ... ὑπερασπίζω

ὑπερηφανεῖται vb pres m/p ind 3rd pers sg ... ὑπερηφανέω

ὑπερηφανεύεσθαι vb pres dep inf ..... ὑπερηφανεύομαι

ὑπερηφανεύεται vb pres dep ind 3rd pers sg   id.

ὑπερηφανεύου vb 2nd aor mid impv 2nd pers sg   id.

ὑπερηφανεύσαντο vb 1st aor mid ind 3rd pers pl   id.

ὑπερηφανεύσασθαι vb 1st aor mid inf   id.

ὑπερηφανεύσατο vb 1st aor mid ind 3rd pers sg   id.

ὑπερηφάνησαν vb 2nd aor pass ind

        3rd pers pl .... ὑπερηφανέω

ὑπερηφανία noun fem nom sg

ὑπερηφανίᾳ noun fem dat sg .... ὑπερηφανία

ὑπερηφανίαν noun fem acc sg   id.

ὑπερηφανίας noun fem gen sg and acc pl   id.

ὑπερηφανιῶν noun fem gen pl   id.

ὑπερήφανοι adj masc and fem nom pl ...... ὑπερήφανος

ὑπερηφάνοις adj dat pl   id.

ὑπερήφανον adj acc sg, neut nom sg   id.

ὑπερήφανος adj masc and fem nom sg   id.

ὑπερηφάνου adj gen sg   id.

ὑπερηφάνους adj masc and fem acc pl   id.

ὑπερηφάνῳ adj dat sg   id.

ὑπερηφάνων adj gen pl   id.

ὑπερηφάνως adverb

ὑπέρθυρον noun neut nom and acc sg

ὑπεριδεῖν vb 2nd aor act inf .... ὑπεροράω

ὑπερίδῃ vb 2nd aor act subj 3rd pers sg   id.

ὑπερίδῃς vb 2nd aor act subj 2nd pers sg   id.

ὑπεριδόντες	vb 2nd aor act part masc nom pl	.... ὑπεροράω
ὑπεριδοῦσα	vb 2nd aor act part fem nom sg	id.
ὑπεριδών	vb 2nd aor act part masc nom sg	id.
ὑπερίδωσιν	vb 2nd aor act subj 3rd pers pl	id.
ὑπερισχύει	vb pres act ind 3rd pers sg	.... ὑπερισχύω
ὑπερισχύεις	vb pres act ind 2nd pers sg	id.
ὑπερίσχυεν	vb impf act ind 3rd pers sg	id.
ὑπερισχύουσιν	vb pres act ind 3rd pers pl	id.
ὑπερισχύσει	vb fut act ind 3rd pers sg	id.
ὑπερίσχυσεν	vb 1st aor act ind 3rd pers sg	id.
ὑπέρκεισαι	vb pres m/p ind 2nd pers sg	..... ὑπέρκειμαι
ὑπερμαχεῖτε	vb pres act impv 2nd pers pl	..... ὑπερμαχέω
ὑπέρμαχον	noun masc acc sg	..... ὑπέρμαχος
ὑπέρμαχος	noun masc nom sg	id.
ὑπερμεγέθη	adj neut nom and acc pl	.... ὑπερμεγέθης
ὑπερμεγέθης	adj masc and fem nom sg	id.
ὑπερμήκεις	noun masc nom and acc pl	...... ὑπερμήκης
ὑπέρογκα	adj neut nom and acc pl	.... ὑπέρογκος
ὑπέρογκον	adj acc sg, neut nom sg	id.
ὑπέρογκος	adj masc and fem nom sg	id.
ὑπεροίσει	vb fut act ind 3rd pers sg	.... ὑπερφέρω
ὑπερορᾷς	vb pres act ind 2nd pers sg	.... ὑπεροράω
ὑπερόρασει	noun fem dat sg	.... ὑπερόρασις
ὑπερορᾶτε	vb pres act ind 2nd pers pl	.... ὑπεροράω
ὑπερορῶ	vb pres act ind 1st pers sg	id.
ὑπερορῶν	vb pres act part masc nom sg	id.
ὑπέρου	noun neut gen sg	.... ὕπερον
ὑπεροφθήσεται	vb fut pass ind 3rd pers sg	... ὑπεροράω
ὑπεροχή	noun fem nom sg	
ὑπεροχῇ	noun fem dat sg	.... ὑπεροχή
ὑπεροχήν	noun fem acc sg	id.
ὑπεροχῆς	noun fem gen sg	id.
ὑπερόψει	noun fem dat sg	.... ὑπερόψις
ὑπερόψεται	vb fut mid ind 3rd pers sg	.... ὑπεροράω
ὑπερόψῃ	vb fut mid ind 2nd pers sg	id.
ὑπερόψομαι	vb fut mid ind 1st pers sg	id.
ὑπερπλεονάσῃ	vb 1st aor act subj	
3rd pers sg	.... ὑπερπλεονάζω	
ὑπέρραψεν	vb 1st aor act ind 3rd pers sg	..... ὑπορράπτω
ὑπερρίπτοσαν	vb impf act ind 3rd pers pl	..... ὑπερρίπτω
ὑπερτηκόμενος	vb pres m/p part masc nom sg	... ὑπερτήκω
ὑπερτίθενται	vb pres m/p ind 3rd pers pl	..... ὑπερτίθημι
ὑπερτιμῶν	vb pres act part masc nom sg	...... ὑπερτιμάω
ὑπερυμνητός	adj masc and fem nom sg	
ὑπερυψούμενον	vb pres m/p part masc acc sg,	
neut nom and acc sg	.... ὑπερυψόω	
ὑπερυψούμενος	vb pres m/p part masc nom sg	id.
ὑπερυψοῦτε	vb pres act impv 2nd pers pl	id.
ὑπερυψοῦτω	vb pres act impv 3rd pers sg	id.
ὑπερυψῶ	vb pres act ind 1st pers sg	id.
ὑπερυψώθης	vb 1st aor pass ind 2nd pers sg	id.

ὑπερυψωμένον	vb pres m/p part masc acc sg,	
neut nom and acc sg	.... ὑπερυψόω	
ὑπερυψωμένος	vb pres m/p part masc nom sg	id.
ὑπερφερής	adj masc and fem nom sg	
ὑπερφέρων	vb pres act part masc nom sg	...... ὑπερφέρω
ὑπερφόβου	adj gen sg	.... ὑπερφόβος
ὑπερχαρεῖς	adj masc and fem nom and acc pl	.. ὑπερχαρής
ὑπερχαρῆς	adj masc and fem nom sg	id.
ὑπερῷα	noun neut nom and acc pl	.... ὑπερῷον
ὑπερῷοι	adj masc nom pl	.... ὑπερῷος
ὑπερῴοις	noun neut dat pl	.... ὑπερῷον
ὑπερῷον	noun neut nom and acc sg	id.
ὑπερῴου	noun neut gen sg	id.
ὑπερῴῳ	noun neut dat sg	id.
ὑπερῴων	noun neut gen pl	id.
ὑπεσκελίσθησαν	vb 1st aor pass ind	
3rd pers pl	.... ὑποσκελίζω	
ὑπέστη	vb 2nd aor act ind 3rd pers sg	.... ὑφίστημι
ὑπέστησαν	vb 2nd aor act ind 3rd pers pl	id.
ὑπεστρέψαμεν	vb 1st aor act ind 1st pers pl	... ὑποστρέφω
ὑπέστρεψαν	vb 1st aor act ind 3rd pers pl	id.
ὑπέστρεψεν	vb 1st aor act ind 3rd pers sg	id.
ὑπέστρωσαν	vb 1st aor act ind 3rd pers pl	... ὑποστρωννύω
ὑπέσχομεν	vb 2nd aor act ind 1st pers pl	.... ὑπέχω
ὑπέσχον	vb 2nd aor act ind 3rd pers pl	id.
ὑπετάγη	vb 2nd aor pass ind 3rd pers sg	...... ὑποτάσσω
ὑπετάγημεν	vb 2nd aor pass ind 1st pers pl	id.
ὑπετάγησαν	vb 2nd aor pass ind 3rd pers pl	id.
ὑπέταξας	vb 1st aor act ind 2nd pers sg	id.
ὑπέταξεν	vb 1st aor act ind 3rd pers sg	id.
ὑπεύθυνοι	noun masc nom pl	.... ὑπεύθυνος
ὑπευλαβεῖτο	vb impf act ind 3rd pers pl	... ὑπευλαβέομαι
ὑπήγαγεν	vb 2nd aor act ind 3rd pers sg	.... ὑπάγω
ὑπήκοοι	adj masc nom pl	.... ὑπήκοος
ὑπήκοος	noun masc nom sg	id.
ὑπηκόους	noun masc acc pl	id.
ὑπήκουεν	vb impf act ind 3rd pers sg	.... ὑπακούω
ὑπήκουσα	vb 1st aor act ind 1st pers sg	id.
ὑπηκούσαμεν	vb 1st aor act ind 1st pers pl	id.
ὑπήκουσαν	vb 1st aor act ind 3rd pers pl	id.
ὑπήκουσας	vb 1st aor act ind 2nd pers sg	id.
ὑπηκούσατε	vb 1st aor act ind 2nd pers pl	id.
ὑπήκουσεν	vb 1st aor act ind 3rd pers sg	id.
ὑπήνεγκα	vb 1st aor act ind 1st pers sg	.... ὑποφέρω
ὑπήνεγκας	vb 1st aor act ind 2nd pers sg	id.
ὑπήνεγκεν	vb 1st aor act ind 3rd pers sg	id.
ὑπήντησεν	vb 1st aor act ind 3rd pers sg	.... ὑπαντάω
ὑπήρεισεν	vb 1st aor act ind 3rd pers sg	.... ὑπερείδω
ὑπηρεσία	noun fem nom sg	
ὑπηρεσίαν	noun fem acc sg	.... ὑπηρεσία
ὑπηρέται	noun masc nom pl	.... ὑπηρέτης
ὑπηρέτει	vb impf act ind 3rd pers sg	.... ὑπηρετέω

ὑπηρέτης noun masc nom sg

ὑπηρετήσει vb fut act ind 3rd pers sg .... ὑπηρετέω

ὑπηρετοῦσα vb pres act part fem nom sg   id.

ὑπηρετῶν vb pres act part masc nom sg   id.

ὑπῆρξεν vb 1st aor act ind 3rd pers sg .... ὑπάρχω

ὑπῆρχεν vb impf act ind 3rd pers sg   id.

ὑπῆρχον vb impf act ind 3rd pers pl   id.

ὑπισχνεῖτο vb impf dep ind 3rd pers sg ..... ὑπισχνέομαι

ὑπισχνούμενοι vb pres dep part masc nom pl   id.

ὑπισχνούμενος vb pres dep part masc nom sg   id.

ὕπνοις noun masc dat pl .... ὕπνος

ὑπνοῖς vb pres act ind 2nd pers sg .... ὑπνόω

ὕπνον noun masc acc sg .... ὕπνος

ὕπνος noun masc nom sg

ὕπνου noun masc gen sg   id.

ὑπνοῦντας vb pres act part masc acc pl .... ὑπνόω

ὑπνοῦντες vb pres act part masc nom pl   id.

ὑπνούντων vb pres act part masc and neut gen pl   id.

ὕπνους noun masc acc pl .... ὕπνος

ὕπνῳ noun masc dat sg   id.

ὑπνώδης adj masc and fem nom sg

ὕπνων noun masc gen pl .... ὕπνος

ὑπνῶν vb pres act part masc nom sg .... ὑπνόω

ὕπνωσα vb 1st aor act ind 1st pers sg   id.

ὑπνῶσαι vb 1st aor act inf   id.

ὕπνωσαν vb 1st aor act ind 3rd pers pl   id.

ὑπνώσας vb 1st aor act part masc nom sg   id.

ὑπνώσατε vb 1st aor act impv 2nd pers pl   id.

ὑπνώσει vb fut act ind 3rd pers sg   id.

ὑπνώσεις vb fut act ind 2nd pers sg   id.

ὕπνωσεν vb 1st aor act ind 3rd pers sg   id.

ὑπνώσουσιν vb fut act ind 3rd pers pl   id.

ὑπνώσω vb 1st aor act subj 1st pers sg,

     fut act ind 1st pers sg   id.

ὑπνώσωσιν vb 1st aor act subj 3rd pers pl   id.

ὑπό preposition

ὑποβάλλονται vb pres m/p ind 3rd pers pl ..... ὑποβάλλω

ὑποβλεπόμενος vb pres m/p part masc nom sg .. ὑποβλέπω

ὑποβλεπομένου vb pres m/p part

     masc and neut gen sg   id.

ὑπογεγραμμένα vb perf m/p part

     neut nom and acc pl .... ὑπογράφω

ὑπογεγραμμένην vb perf m/p part fem acc sg   id.

ὑπογεγραμμένον vb perf m/p part masc acc sg,

     neut nom and acc sg   id.

ὑπόγειον adj masc and fem acc sg .... ὑπόγειος

ὑπογραμμοῖς noun masc dat pl .... ὑπογραμμός

ὑπογράφῃ vb 2nd aor act subj 3rd pers sg ...... ὑπογράφω

ὑπογραφῇ vb 2nd aor pass subj 3rd pers sg   id.

ὑπογύου adj gen sg .... ὑπόγυος

ὑπόδειγμα noun neut nom and acc sg

ὑποδείκνυμεν vb pres act ind 1st pers pl ..... ὑποδεικνύω

ὑποδεικνύοντες vb pres act part masc nom pl   id.

ὑποδεικνύοντος vb pres act part masc and neut gen sg   id.

ὑποδείκνυτε vb pres act impv 2nd pers pl   id.

ὑποδεικνύω vb pres act ind 1st pers sg   id.

ὑποδεικνύων vb pres act part masc nom sg   id.

ὑποδεῖξαι vb 1st aor act inf   id.

ὑποδείξαντος vb 1st aor act part masc and neut gen sg   id.

ὑποδείξατε vb 1st aor act impv 2nd pers pl   id.

ὑποδείξῃ vb 1st aor act subj 3rd pers sg   id.

ὑπόδειξον vb 1st aor act impv 2nd pers sg   id.

ὑποδείξουσιν vb fut act ind 3rd pers pl   id.

ὑποδείξω vb 1st aor act subj 1st pers sg,

     fut act ind 1st pers sg   id.

ὑποδέξονται vb fut mid ind 3rd pers pl ...... ὑποδέχομαι

ὑπόδημα noun neut nom and acc sg

ὑποδήμασι noun neut dat pl .... ὑπόδημα

ὑποδήματα noun neut nom and acc pl   id.

ὑποδήματι noun neut dat sg   id.

ὑποδήματος noun neut gen sg   id.

ὑποδημάτων noun neut gen pl   id.

ὑποδύσαντες vb 1st aor act part masc nom pl ..... ὑποδύω

ὑποδύτην noun masc acc sg .... ὑποδύτης

ὑποδύτου noun masc gen sg   id.

ὑποζύγια noun neut nom and acc pl .... ὑποζύγιον

ὑποζυγίοις noun neut dat pl   id.

ὑποζύγιον noun neut nom and acc sg   id.

ὑποζυγίου noun neut gen sg   id.

ὑποζυγίῳ noun neut dat sg   id.

ὑποζυγίων noun neut gen pl   id.

ὑπόζωσον vb 1st aor act impv 2nd pers sg .... ὑποζώννυμι

ὑποθέματα noun neut nom and acc pl .... ὑπόθεμα

ὑποθεμένου vb 2nd aor mid part

     masc and neut gen sg .... ὑποτίθημι

ὑπόθες vb 2nd aor act impv 2nd pers sg   id.

ὑποθέσεως noun fem gen sg .... ὑπόθεσις

ὑπόθετε vb 2nd aor act impv 2nd pers pl ...... ὑποτίθημι

ὑποθήσεις vb fut act ind 2nd pers sg   id.

ὑποίσει vb fut act ind 3rd pers sg .... ὑποφέρω

ὑποίσομεν vb fut act ind 1st pers pl   id.

ὑποίσω vb fut act ind 1st pers sg   id.

ὑπόκαιε vb pres act impv 2nd pers sg .... ὑποκαίω

ὑποκαιομένης vb pres m/p part fem gen sg   id.

ὑποκαιόμενον vb pres m/p part masc acc sg,

     neut nom and acc sg   id.

ὑποκαιομένους vb pres m/p part masc acc pl   id.

ὑποκαλύψεις vb fut act ind 2nd pers sg ...... ὑποκαλύπτω

ὑποκάτω adverb and preposition

ὑποκάτωθεν adverb and preposition

ὑποκείμενον vb pres m/p part masc acc sg,

     neut nom and acc sg .... ὑπόκειμαι

ὑποκειμένου vb pres m/p part masc and neut gen sg   id.

ὑπόκειται vb pres m/p ind 3rd pers sg . . . . ὑπόκειμαι

ὑποκριθείς vb 1st aor pass part masc nom sg ὑποκρίνομαι

ὑποκριθῆναι vb 1st aor pass inf id.

ὑποκριθῇς vb 1st aor pass subj 2nd pers sg id.

ὑποκρίνασθαι vb 1st aor mid inf id.

ὑποκρινόμενος vb pres dep part masc nom sg id.

ὑποκρινομένων vb pres dep part gen pl id.

ὑποκρίσει noun fem dat sg . . . . ὑπόκρισις

ὑπόκρισιν noun fem acc sg id.

ὑποκριταί noun masc nom sg . . . . ὑποκριτής

ὑποκριτήν noun masc acc sg id.

ὑπολάβῃς vb 2nd aor act subj 2nd pers sg . . . ὑπολαμβάνω

ὑπολάβητε vb 2nd aor act subj 2nd pers pl id.

ὑπολάβοι vb 2nd aor act opt 3rd pers sg id.

ὑπολαβόντες vb 2nd aor act part masc nom pl id.

ὑπολαβών vb 2nd aor act part masc nom sg id.

ὑπολαμβάνεις vb pres act ind 2nd pers sg id.

ὑπολαμβάνετε vb pres act ind 2nd pers pl id.

ὑπολαμβάνομεν vb pres act ind 1st pers pl id.

ὑπολαμβάνοντες vb pres act part masc nom pl id.

ὑπολαμβάνουσιν vb pres act ind 3rd pers pl id.

ὑπολαμβάνω vb pres act ind 1st pers sg id.

ὑπολαμβάνων vb pres act part masc nom sg id.

ὑπόλειμμα noun neut nom and acc sg

ὑπολείπεσθαι vb pres m/p inf . . . . ὑπολείπω

ὑπολείπεται vb pres m/p ind 3rd pers sg id.

ὑπολειπόμενα vb pres m/p part neut nom and acc pl id.

ὑπολειπόμενοι vb pres m/p part masc nom pl id.

ὑπολειφθεῖσι vb 1st aor pass part masc and neut dat pl id.

ὑπολειφθέν vb 1st aor pass part neut nom and acc sg id.

ὑπολειφθέντα vb 1st aor pass part neut nom and acc pl id.

ὑπολειφθῇ vb 1st aor pass subj 3rd pers sg id.

ὑπολειφθήσεται vb fut pass ind 3rd pers sg id.

ὑπολειφθήσονται vb fut pass ind 3rd pers pl id.

ὑπολειφθῶσιν vb 1st aor pass subj 3rd pers pl id.

ὑπολείψεται vb fut mid ind 3rd pers sg id.

ὑπολείψῃ vb fut mid ind 2nd pers sg id.

ὑπολείψομαι vb fut mid ind 1st pers sg id.

ὑπολειψόμεθα vb fut mid ind 1st pers pl id.

ὑπολέλειμμαι vb perf m/p ind 1st pers sg id.

ὑπολελειμμένα vb perf m/p part neut nom and acc pl id.

ὑπολελειμμέναι vb perf m/p part fem nom pl id.

ὑπολελειμμένοι vb perf m/p part masc nom pl id.

ὑπολελειμμένοις vb perf m/p part masc and neut dat pl id.

ὑπολελειμμένον vb perf m/p part masc acc sg,

      neut nom and acc sg id.

ὑπολελειμμένος vb perf m/p part masc nom sg id.

ὑπολελειμμένους vb perf m/p part masc acc pl id.

ὑπολελειμμένων vb perf m/p part gen pl id.

ὑπολέλειπται vb perf m/p ind 3rd pers sg id.

ὑπόλημψις noun fem nom sg

ὑπολήνια noun neut nom and acc pl . . . . ὑπολήνιον

ὑπολήνιον noun neut nom and acc sg

ὑπολήνίων noun neut gen pl . . . . ὑπολήνιον

ὑπολίπεσθε vb 2nd aor mid impv 2nd pers pl . . . . ὑπολείπω

ὑπολίποιτο vb 2nd aor mid opt 3rd pers sg id.

ὑπολίπωμεν vb 2nd aor act subj 1st pers pl id.

ὑπόλοιπον adj acc sg, neut nom sg . . . . ὑπόλοιπος

ὑπολυθέντος vb 1st aor pass part

      masc and neut gen sg . . . . ὑπολύω

ὑπόλυσαι vb 1st aor mid impv 2nd pers sg id.

ὑπολύσει vb fut act ind 3rd pers sg id.

ὑπόλυσις noun fem nom sg

ὑπομαστιδίων adj gen pl . . . . ὑπομάσθιος

ὑπομεῖναι vb 1st aor act opt 3rd pers sg . . . . ὑπομένω

ὑπομεῖναι vb 1st aor act inf id.

ὑπομείναντες vb 1st aor act part masc nom pl id.

ὑπομεινάντων vb 1st aor act part masc and neut gen pl id.

ὑπομείνασαν vb 1st aor act part fem acc sg id.

ὑπομείνατε vb 1st aor act impv 2nd pers pl id.

ὑπομείνῃ vb 1st aor act subj 3rd pers sg id.

ὑπομείνῃς vb 1st aor act subj 2nd pers sg id.

ὑπόμεινον vb 1st aor act impv 2nd pers sg id.

ὑπομείνω vb 1st aor act subj 1st pers sg id.

ὑπομείνωσιν vb 1st aor act subj 3rd pers pl id.

ὑπομένει vb pres act ind 3rd pers sg id.

ὑπομενεῖ vb fut act ind 3rd pers sg id.

ὑπομένειν vb pres act inf id.

ὑπομένοντας vb pres act part masc acc pl id.

ὑπομένοντες vb pres act part masc nom pl id.

ὑπομενοῦμεν vb fut act ind 1st pers pl id.

ὑπομένουσι(ν) vb pres act ind 3rd pers pl,

      pres act part masc and neut dat pl id.

ὑπομενοῦσιν vb fut act ind 3rd pers pl id.

ὑπομένω vb pres act ind 1st pers sg id.

ὑπομενῶ vb fut act ind 1st pers sg id.

ὑπομένων vb pres act part masc nom sg id.

ὑπομιμνῃσκων vb pres act part

      masc nom sg . . . . ὑπομιμνήσκω

ὑπόμνημα noun neut nom and acc sg

ὑπομνηματισμοῖς noun masc dat pl . . . . ὑπομνηματισμός

ὑπομνηματισμοῦ noun masc gen sg id.

ὑπομνηματισμούς noun masc acc pl id.

ὑπομνηματογράφον noun masc

      acc sg . . . . ὑπομνηματογράφος

ὑπομνηματογράφος noun masc nom sg id.

ὑπομνημάτων noun neut gen pl . . . . ὑπόμνημα

ὑπομνήσας vb 1st aor act part masc nom sg . . ὑπομιμνήσκω

ὑπομνήσεως noun fem gen sg . . . . ὑπόμνησις

ὑπόμνησιν noun fem acc sg id.

ὑπομονή noun fem nom sg

ὑπομονῇ noun fem dat sg . . . . ὑπομονή

ὑπομονήν noun fem acc sg id.

ὑπομονῆς noun fem gen sg id.

ὑπομονῶν noun fem gen pl . . . . ὑπομονή

ὑπονοήματα noun neut nom and acc pl . . . . ὑπονόημα

ὑπονοήσει vb fut act ind 3rd pers sg . . . . ὑπονοέω

ὑπονοθευθείς vb 1st aor pass part masc nom sg . ὑπονοθεύω

ὑπονοθεύσας vb 1st aor act part masc nom sg   id.

ὑπόνοια noun fem nom sg

ὑπόνοιαι noun fem nom pl . . . . ὑπόνοια

ὑπονύσσετε vb pres act ind 2nd pers pl . . . . ὑπονύσσω

ὑποπίπτῃ vb pres act subj 3rd pers sg . . . . ὑποπίπτω

ὑποπίπτοντα vb pres act part neut nom and acc pl   id.

ὑποπίπτουσα vb pres act part fem nom sg   id.

ὑποπόδιον noun neut nom and acc sg

ὑποποδίου noun neut gen sg . . . . ὑποπόδιον

ὑποποδίῳ noun neut dat sg   id.

ὑποπτεύσῃς vb 1st aor act subj 2nd pers sg . . . . . ὑποπτεύω

ὕποπτον adj acc sg, neut nom sg . . . . ὕποπτος

ὕποπτος adj masc and fem nom sg   id.

ὑποπυρρίζον vb pres act part

          neut nom and acc sg . . . . ὑποπυρρίζω

ὑποσημανθῆναι vb 1st aor pass inf . . . . ὑποσημαίνω

ὑποσκελίσαι vb 1st aor act inf . . . . ὑποσκελίζω

ὑποσκελισθήσεται vb fut pass ind 3rd pers sg   id.

ὑποσκελισθήσονται vb fut pass ind 3rd pers pl   id.

ὑποσκελίσματι noun masc dat sg . . . . ὑποσκέλισμα

ὑποσκέλισον vb 1st aor act impv 2nd pers sg . ὑποσκελίζω

ὑποστάσει noun fem dat sg . . . . ὑπόστασις

ὑποστάσεως noun fem gen sg   id.

ὑπόστασιν noun fem acc sg   id.

ὑπόστασις noun fem nom sg   id.

ὑποστείλῃ vb 1st aor mid subj 2nd pers sg . . . . . ὑποστέλλω

ὑποστείληται vb 1st aor mid subj 3rd pers sg   id.

ὑποστελεῖσθε vb fut mid ind 2nd pers pl   id.

ὑποστελεῖται vb fut mid ind 3rd pers sg   id.

ὑποστῇ vb 2nd aor act subj 3rd pers sg . . . . ὑφίστημι

ὑπόστημα noun neut nom and acc sg

ὑποστήματι noun neut dat sg . . . . ὑπόστημα

ὑποστῆναι vb 2nd aor act inf . . . . ὑφίστημι

ὑποστηρίγματα noun neut nom and acc pl . . ὑποστήριγμα

ὑποστηρίζει vb pres act ind 3rd pers sg . . . . . ὑποστηρίζω

ὑποστήσεται vb fut mid ind 3rd pers sg . . . . ὑφίστημι

ὑποστήσομαι vb fut mid ind 1st pers sg   id.

ὑποστήσονται vb fut mid ind 3rd pers pl   id.

ὑπόστητε vb 2nd aor act impv 2nd pers pl   id.

ὑποστρέφει vb pres act ind 3rd pers sg . . . . ὑποστρέφω

ὑποστρέψει vb fut act ind 3rd pers sg   id.

ὑποστρέψωμεν vb 1st aor act subj 1st pers pl   id.

ὑποστρώσῃ vb 1st aor act subj 3rd pers sg . . . ὑποστρωννύω

ὑποστρώσῃς vb 1st aor act subj 2nd pers sg   id.

ὑποστρώσονται vb fut mid ind 3rd pers pl   id.

ὑποστῶσιν vb 2nd aor act subj 3rd pers pl . . . . . . ὑφίστημι

ὑποσχάσει vb fut act ind 3rd pers sg . . . . ὑποσχάζω

ὑποσχέσεων noun fem gen pl . . . . ὑπόσχεσις

ὑπόσχεσιν noun fem acc sg . . . . ὑπόσχεσις

ὑποτάγηθι vb 2nd aor pass impv 2nd pers sg . . . ὑποτάσσω

ὑποταγήσεται vb fut pass ind 3rd pers sg   id.

ὑποταγήσονται vb fut pass ind 3rd pers pl   id.

ὑποτάξας vb 1st aor act part masc nom sg   id.

ὑποτάξατε vb 1st aor act impv 2nd pers pl   id.

ὑποτάξει vb fut act ind 3rd pers sg   id.

ὑποτάσσεσθαι vb pres m/p inf   id.

ὑποτάσσων vb pres act part masc nom sg   id.

ὑποτεταγμένοις vb perf m/p part masc and neut dat pl   id.

ὑποτεταγμένους vb perf m/p part masc acc pl   id.

ὑποτεταγμένων vb perf m/p part gen pl   id.

ὑποτίτθια noun neut nom and acc pl . . . . ὑποτίτθιον

ὑπουργῷ adj dat sg . . . . ὑπουργός

ὑποφαινούσης vb pres act part fem gen sg . . . . . ὑποφαίνω

ὑποφαύσεις noun fem nom and acc pl . . . . ὑπόφαυσις

ὑποφέρει vb pres act ind 3rd pers sg . . . . ὑποφέρω

ὑποφέρω vb pres act ind 1st pers sg

ὑπόφρικον adj acc sg, neut nom sg . . . . ὑπόφρικος

ὑποχείριοι adj masc and fem nom pl . . . . ὑποχείριος

ὑποχειρίοις adj dat pl   id.

ὑποχείριον adj acc sg, neut nom sg   id.

ὑποχείριος adj masc and fem nom sg   id.

ὑποχειρίους adj masc and fem acc pl   id.

ὑποχόνδρια noun neut nom and acc pl . . . . . ὑποχόνδριον

ὑπόχρεῳ adj dat sg . . . . ὑπόχρεως

ὑπόχρεως adj masc and fem nom sg

ὑποχυτῆρας noun masc acc pl . . . . ὑποχύτηρ

ὑποχωρῆσαι vb 1st aor act inf . . . . ὑποχωρέω

ὑποχωρῶν vb pres act part masc nom sg   id.

ὑποψίᾳ noun fem dat sg . . . . ὑποψία

ὕπτια adj neut nom and acc pl . . . . ὕπτιος

ὑπτιάζεις vb pres act ind 2nd pers sg . . . . ὑπτιάζω

ὑπώπια noun neut nom and acc pl . . . . ὑπώπιον

ὑπώπτευσα vb 1st aor act ind 1st pers sg . . . . . . ὑποπτεύω

Ὑρκανοῦ pr noun masc gen sg . . . . Ὑρκανος

ὗς noun fem nom sg

ὕσσωπον noun masc or fem acc sg . . . . ὕσσωπος

ὑσσώπου noun masc or fem gen sg   id.

ὑσσώπῳ noun masc or fem dat sg   id.

ὑστάτην superl adj fem acc sg . . . . ὕστερος

ὑστέρει vb pres act impv 2nd pers sg . . . . ὑστερέω

ὑστερεῖσθαι vb pres m/p inf   id.

ὑστερεῖται vb pres m/p ind 3rd pers sg   id.

ὑστέρημα noun neut nom and acc sg

ὑστέρησαν vb 1st aor act ind 3rd pers pl . . . . ὑστερέω

ὑστερησάτω vb 1st aor act impv 3rd pers sg   id.

ὑστερήσει vb fut act ind 3rd pers sg   id.

ὑστερήσῃ vb 1st aor act subj 3rd pers sg   id.

ὑστερήσῃς vb 1st aor act subj 2nd pers sg   id.

ὑστερήσωμεν vb 1st aor act subj 1st pers pl   id.

ὑστεροβουλίαν noun fem acc sg . . . . ὑστεροβουλία ὕστεροι comp adj masc nom pl . . . . ὕστερος

ὕστερον adverb

ὕστερον comp adj neut nom and acc sg . . . . ὕστερος

ὑστέρου comp adj masc and neut gen sg . . . . d.

ὑστερούμενος vb pres m/p part masc nom sg . . . . ὑστερέω

ὑστεροῦσα vb pres act part fem nom sg . . . . d.

ὑστερῶ vb pres act ind 1st pers sg . . . . d.

ὑστέρῳ comp adj masc and neut dat sg . . . . ὕστερος

ὑστερῶν vb pres act part masc nom sg . . . . ὑστερέω

ὑφ᾽ see ὑπό

ὑφαίνειν vb pres act inf . . . . ὑφαίνω

ὕφαινον vb pres act part neut nom and acc sg . . . . d.

ὑφαινόντων vb pres act part masc and neut gen pl . . . . . . id.

ὑφαίνουσιν vb pres act ind 3rd pers pl . . . . id.

ὑφαιρούμενοι vb pres m/p part masc nom pl . . . . . ὑφαιρέω

ὑφᾶναι vb 1st aor act inf . . . . ὑφαίνω

ὕφανεν vb 1st aor act ind 3rd pers sg . . . . id.

ὑφάνῃς vb 1st aor act subj 2nd pers sg . . . . id.

ὑφαντά adj neut nom and acc pl . . . . ὑφάντης

ὑφαντόν adj masc acc sg, neut nom and acc sg . . . . id.

ὑφάντου noun masc gen sg . . . . ὑφάντης

ὑφάπτειν vb pres act inf . . . . ὑφάπτω

ὕφασμα noun neut nom and acc sg

ὑφάσματι noun neut dat sg . . . . ὕφασμα

ὑφάσματος noun neut gen sg . . . . id.

ὑφασμένον vb perf m/p part masc acc sg,
         neut nom and acc sg . . . . ὑφαίνω

ὑφείλατο vb 2nd aor mid ind 3rd pers sg . . . . ὑφαιρέω

ὑφεῖλον vb 2nd aor act ind 3rd pers pl . . . . id.

ὑφέξεται vb fut mid ind 3rd pers sg . . . . ὑπέχω

ὑφῆψαν vb 1st aor act ind 3rd pers pl . . . . ὑφάπτω

ὑφῆψεν vb 1st aor act ind 3rd pers sg . . . . id.

ὑφίστασο vb pres m/p impv 2nd pers sg . . . . ὑφίστημι

ὑφίσταται vb pres m/p ind 3rd pers sg . . . . id.

ὑφίστατο vb impf m/p ind 3rd pers sg . . . . id.

ὑφορώμενοι vb pres m/p part masc nom pl . . . . ὑφοράω

ὑφορώμενος vb pres m/p part masc nom sg . . . . id.

ὑψαυχενοῦντες vb pres act part masc nom pl . . ὑψαυχενέω

ὑψαυχενῶν vb pres act part masc nom sg . . . . id.

ὕψει noun neut dat sg . . . . ὕψος

ὕψεσι noun neut dat pl . . . . id.

ὕψεων noun neut gen pl . . . . id.

ὕψη noun neut nom and acc pl . . . . id.

ὑψηλά adj neut nom and acc pl . . . . ὑψηλός

ὑψηλαί adj fem nom pl . . . . id.

ὑψηλάς adj fem acc pl . . . . id.

ὑψηλή adj fem nom sg . . . . id.

ὑψηλῇ adj fem dat sg . . . . id.

ὑψηλήν adj fem acc sg . . . . id.

ὑψηλῆς adj fem gen sg . . . . id.

ὑψηλοί adj masc nom pl . . . . id.

ὑψηλοῖς adj masc and neut dat pl . . . . id.

ὑψηλοκάρδιος adj masc and fem nom sg

ὑψηλόν adj masc acc sg, neut nom and acc sg . . . . . . ὑψηλός

ὑψηλός adj masc nom sg . . . . id.

ὑψηλοτάτη superl adj fem nom sg . . . . id.

ὑψηλότερον comp adj masc acc sg, neut nom and acc sg . . id.

ὑψηλοῦ adj masc and neut gen sg . . . . id.

ὑψηλούς adj masc acc pl . . . . id.

ὑψηλῷ adj masc and neut dat sg . . . . id.

ὑψηλῶν adj gen pl . . . . id.

ὕψιστε superl adj masc voc sg . . . . ὕψιστος

ὑψίστοις superl adj masc and neut dat pl . . . . id.

ὕψιστον superl adj masc acc sg, neut nom and acc sg . . . . . id.

ὕψιστος superl adj masc nom sg . . . . id.

ὑψίστου superl adj masc and neut gen sg . . . . id.

ὑψίστῳ superl adj masc and neut dat sg . . . . id.

ὑψίστων superl adj gen pl . . . . id.

ὑψοῖ vb pres act ind 3rd pers sg . . . . ὑψόω

ὕψος noun neut nom and acc sg

ὕψου vb impf act ind 3rd pers sg . . . . ὑψόω

ὑψουμένη vb pres m/p part fem nom sg . . . . id.

ὑψοῦν vb pres act inf . . . . id.

ὑψοῦντα vb pres act part masc acc sg . . . . id.

ὑψοῦνται vb pres m/p ind 3rd pers pl . . . . id.

ὑψοῦντες vb pres act part masc nom pl . . . . id.

ὕψους noun neut gen sg . . . . ὕψος

ὑψούσθωσαν vb pres m/p impv 3rd pers pl . . . . ὑψόω

ὑψοῦται vb pres m/p ind 3rd pers sg . . . . id.

ὑψοῦτε vb pres act impv 2nd pers pl . . . . id.

ὑψῶ vb pres act ind 1st pers sg . . . . id.

ὑψωθείς vb 1st aor pass part masc nom sg . . . . id.

ὑψώθη vb 1st aor pass ind 3rd pers sg . . . . id.

ὑψωθῇ vb 1st aor pass subj 3rd pers sg . . . . id.

ὑψωθῆναι vb 1st aor pass inf . . . . id.

ὑψώθης vb 1st aor pass ind 2nd pers sg . . . . id.

ὑψωθῇς vb 1st aor pass subj 2nd pers sg . . . . id.

ὑψώθησαν vb 1st aor pass ind 3rd pers pl . . . . id.

ὑψωθήσεται vb fut pass ind 3rd pers sg . . . . id.

ὑψωθήσομαι vb fut pass ind 1st pers sg . . . . id.

ὑψωθήσονται vb fut pass ind 3rd pers pl . . . . id.

ὑψώθητι vb 1st aor pass impv 2nd pers sg . . . . id.

ὑψωθήτω vb 1st aor pass impv 3rd pers sg . . . . id.

ὑψωθῶσιν vb 1st aor pass subj 3rd pers pl . . . . id.

ὕψωμα noun neut nom and acc sg

ὑψωμένος vb pres m/p part masc nom sg . . . . ὑψόω

ὑψῶν vb pres act part masc nom sg . . . . id.

ὕψωσα vb 1st aor act ind 1st pers sg . . . . id.

ὑψῶσαι vb 1st aor act inf . . . . id.

ὕψωσαν vb 1st aor act ind 3rd pers pl . . . . id.

ὕψωσας vb 1st aor act ind 2nd pers sg . . . . id.

ὑψώσατε vb 1st aor act impv 2nd pers pl . . . . id.

ὑψωσάτωσαν vb 1st aor act impv 3rd pers pl . . . . id.

ὕψωσε(ν) vb 1st aor act ind 3rd pers sg . . . . id.

ὑψώσει vb fut act ind 3rd pers sg . . . . ὑψόω
ὑψώσεις noun fem nom and acc pl . . . . ὕψωσις
ὑψώσεις vb fut act ind 2nd pers sg . . . . ὑψόω
ὑψώσῃ vb 1st aor act subj 3rd pers sg   id.
ὑψώσῃς vb 1st aor act subj 2nd pers sg   id.

ὕψωσον vb 1st aor act impv 2nd pers sg . . . . ὑψόω
ὑψώσουσιν vb fut act ind 3rd pers pl   id.
ὑψώσω vb fut act ind 1st pers sg   id.
ὑψώσωμεν vb 1st aor act subj 1st pers pl   id.
ὕω vb pres act ind 1st pers sg

Φ φ

Φααθμωαβ pr noun
Φαγαιηλ pr noun
Φαγγαι pr noun
φάγε vb 2nd aor act impv 2nd pers sg . . . . ἐσθίω
φαγεῖν vb 2nd aor act inf   id.
φάγεσαι vb fut mid ind 2nd pers sg   id.
φάγεσθε vb 2nd aor mid impv 2nd pers pl,
          fut mid ind 2nd pers pl   id.
φάγεται vb fut mid ind 3rd pers sg   id.
φάγετε vb 2nd aor act impv 2nd pers pl   id.
φαγέτω vb 2nd aor act impv 3rd pers sg   id.
φαγέτωσαν vb 2nd aor act impv 3rd pers pl   id.
φάγῃ vb 2nd aor act subj 3rd pers sg,
        fut mid ind 2nd pers sg   id.
φάγῃς vb 2nd aor act subj 2nd pers sg   id.
φάγητε vb 2nd aor act subj 2nd pers pl   id.
φάγοι vb 2nd aor act opt 3rd pers sg   id.
φάγοισαν vb 2nd aor act opt 3rd pers pl   id.
φάγομαι vb fut mid ind 1st pers sg   id.
φαγόμεθα vb fut mid ind 1st pers pl   id.
φάγονται vb fut mid ind 3rd pers pl   id.
φαγόντας vb 2nd aor act part masc acc pl   id.
φαγόντες vb 2nd aor act part masc nom pl   id.
φαγόντος vb 2nd aor act part masc and neut gen sg   id.
φάγω vb 2nd aor act subj 1st pers sg   id.
φάγωμεν vb 2nd aor act subj 1st pers pl   id.
φαγών vb 2nd aor act part masc nom sg   id.
Φαγωρ pr noun
φάγωσιν vb 2nd aor act subj 3rd pers pl . . . . ἐσθίω
Φαδαηλ pr noun
Φαδαια pr noun
Φαδαιας pr noun
Φαδαιος pr noun masc nom sg
Φαδαιου pr noun masc gen sg . . . . Φαδαιος
Φαδασσουρ pr noun
Φαδουρα pr noun
Φαδων pr noun
φαζ translit
Φαθαια pr noun
Φαθουρα pr noun

φαιδροί adj masc nom pl . . . . φαιδρός
Φαιθων pr noun
φαίνειν vb pres act inf . . . . φαίνω
φαίνεσθαι vb pres m/p inf   id.
φαίνεται vb pres m/p ind 3rd pers sg   id.
φαίνηται vb pres m/p subj 3rd pers sg   id.
φαίνοντα vb pres act part neut nom and acc pl   id.
φαιόν adj masc acc sg, neut nom and acc sg . . . . φαιός
Φαισουρ pr noun
Φακαρεθ-σαβιη pr noun
Φακεε pr noun
Φακεϊας pr noun masc nom sg
Φακεϊου pr noun masc gen sg . . . . Φακεϊας
φακόν noun masc acc sg . . . . φακός
φακός noun masc nom sg   id.
φακοῦ noun masc gen sg   id.
Φακουα pr noun
Φακουδ pr noun
φάλαγγα noun fem acc sg . . . . φάλαγξ
φάλαγγας noun fem acc pl   id.
φάλαγγος noun fem gen sg   id.
φάλαγξ noun fem nom sg   id.
φάλαγξιν noun fem dat pl   id.
Φαλαϊ pr noun
Φαλαια pr noun
φαλακρά adj fem nom sg . . . . φαλακρός
φαλακρέ adj masc voc sg   id.
φαλακρός adj masc nom sg   id.
φαλάκρωμα noun neut nom and acc sg
φαλακρώματι noun neut dat sg . . . . φαλάκρωμα
Φαλαλ pr noun
Φαλαριδος pr noun fem gen sg . . . . Φαλαρις
Φαλαρις pr noun
Φαλδας pr noun
Φαλεθ pr noun
Φαλεκ pr noun
Φαλετ pr noun
Φαλεττια pr noun
Φαλιας pr noun masc nom sg
Φαλλετια pr noun
Φαλλου pr noun

Φαλλουι pr noun

Φαλλους pr noun

Φαλτι pr noun

Φαλτια pr noun

Φαλτιαν pr noun masc acc sg . . . . Φαλτιας

Φαλτιας pr noun masc nom sg   id.

Φαλτιηλ pr noun

Φαλωχ pr noun

φάμενος vb pres m/p part masc nom sg . . . . φημί

φανείσης vb 2nd aor pass part fem gen sg . . . . φαίνω

φανεῖσθε vb fut mid ind 2nd pers pl   id.

φανεῖται vb fut mid ind 3rd pers sg   id.

φανερά adj neut nom and acc pl . . . . φανερός

φανερά adj fem nom sg   id.

φανεράν adj fem acc sg   id.

φανεροί adj masc nom pl   id.

φανερόν adj masc acc sg, neut nom and acc sg   id.

φανερῶς adverb

φανερώσω vb fut act ind 1st pers sg . . . . φανερόω

φάνῃ vb 1st aor act subj 3rd pers sg . . . . φαίνω

φανῇ vb 2nd aor pass subj 3rd pers sg   id.

φανῆναι vb 2nd aor pass inf   id.

φανήσεται vb fut pass ind 3rd pers sg   id.

φανήσομαι vb fut pass ind 1st pers sg   id.

φανήσονται vb fut pass ind 3rd pers pl   id.

φανήτω vb 2nd aor pass impv 3rd pers sg   id.

φάνοιεν vb fut act opt 3rd pers pl   id.

Φανουηλ pr noun

φανοῦμαι vb fut mid ind 1st pers sg . . . . φαίνω

φανοῦνται vb fut mid ind 3rd pers pl   id.

φανοῦσιν vb fut act ind 3rd pers pl   id.

φαντάζεται vb pres dep ind 3rd pers sg . . . . . . φαντάζομαι

φαντασία noun fem nom sg

φαντασίαι noun fem nom pl . . . . φαντασία

φαντασίαν noun fem acc sg   id.

φαντασίας noun fem gen sg and acc pl   id.

φαντασιοκοπῶν vb pres act part

         masc nom sg . . . . φαντασιοκοπέω

φαντασμάτων noun neut gen pl . . . . φάντασμα

Φαρα pr noun

Φαραγγα pr noun fem acc sg . . . . φάραγξ

φάραγγα noun fem acc sg . . . . φάραγξ

φάραγγας noun fem acc pl   id.

φάραγγες noun fem nom pl   id.

φάραγγι noun fem dat sg   id.

Φαραγγος pr noun fem gen sg . . . . φάραγξ

φάραγγος noun fem gen sg   id.

φαράγγων noun fem gen pl   id.

φάραγξ noun fem nom sg   id.

φάραγξι(ν) noun fem dat pl   id.

Φαραθωμ pr noun

Φαραθων pr noun

Φαραθωνι pr noun

Φαραθωνιτης pr noun masc nom sg

Φαραϊ pr noun

Φαρακιμ pr noun

Φαραν pr noun

φαρασιν translit

Φαραω pr noun

Φαραω pr noun

Φαρδαθα pr noun

φαρες translit

Φαρες pr noun

φαρέτρᾳ noun fem dat sg . . . . φαρέτρα

φαρέτραν noun fem acc sg   id.

φαρέτρας noun fem gen sg and acc pl   id.

Φαρζελλαιου pr noun masc gen sg . . . . Φαρζελλαιας

Φαριδα pr noun

φάρμακα noun neut nom and acc pl . . . . φάρμακον

φαρμακείᾳ noun fem dat sg . . . . φαρμακεία

φαρμακείαις noun fem dat pl   id.

φαρμακείας noun fem gen sg and acc pl   id.

φαρμακειῶν noun fem gen pl   id.

φαρμακευομένου vb pres m/p part

         masc and neut gen sg . . . . φαρμακεύω

φαρμακεύσας vb 1st aor act part masc nom sg   id.

φαρμακοί noun masc nom pl . . . . φαρμακός

φαρμάκοις noun neut dat pl . . . . φάρμακον

φαρμακοῖς noun masc dat pl . . . . φαρμακός

φάρμακον noun neut nom and acc sg

φαρμακός noun masc nom sg

φαρμάκου noun neut gen sg . . . . φάρμακον

φαρμακούς noun masc or fem acc pl . . . . φαρμακός

φαρμάκων noun neut gen pl . . . . φάρμακον

φαρμακῶν noun masc gen pl . . . . φαρμακός

Φαρναχ pr noun

Φαρουαιμ pr noun

φαρουριμ translit

Φαρσαννεσταιν pr noun

φάρυγγα noun masc or fem acc sg . . . . φάρυγξ

φάρυγγος noun masc or fem gen sg   id.

φάρυγξ noun masc or fem nom sg   id.

Φαρφαρ pr noun

Φασγα pr noun

φασεκ translit

Φασεκ pr noun

φασεχ translit

Φαση pr noun

Φασηλίδα pr noun fem acc sg . . . . Φασηλίς

φασιν vb pres act ind 3rd pers pl . . . . φημί

φάσιν noun fem acc sg . . . . φάσις

Φασιρων pr noun

φάσκοντες vb pres act part masc nom pl . . . . φάσκω

φασκόντων vb pres act part masc and neut gen pl   id.

φάσκων vb pres act part masc nom sg . . . . φάσκω

φάσμα noun neut nom and acc sg

φάσματα noun neut nom and acc pl . . . . φάσμα

φάσματι noun neut dat sg   id.

Φασοδομιν pr noun

Φασουρ pr noun

Φασσουρ pr noun

Φασσουρου pr noun masc gen sg . . . . Φασσουρος

Φασφα pr noun

φάτναι noun fem nom pl . . . . φάτνη

φάτναις noun fem dat pl   id.

φάτνας noun fem acc pl   id.

φάτνην noun fem acc sg   id.

φάτνης noun fem gen sg   id.

φατνώμασι noun neut dat pl . . . . φάτνωμα

φατνώματα noun neut nom and acc pl   id.

φατνώματος noun neut gen sg   id.

φαῦλα adj neut nom and acc pl . . . . φαῦλος

φαύλη adj fem dat sg   id.

φαυλίζει vb pres act ind 3rd pers sg . . . . φαυλίζω

φαυλίζοντα vb pres act part masc acc sg   id.

φαυλίζοντες vb pres act part masc nom pl   id.

φαυλίσασι vb 1st aor act part masc and neut dat pl   id.

φαυλίσματα noun neut nom and acc pl . . . . φαύλισμα

φαυλισμόν noun masc acc sg . . . . φαυλισμός

φαυλισμός noun masc nom sg   id.

φαυλισμῷ noun masc dat sg   id.

φαυλίστρια noun fem nom sg

φαῦλοι adj masc nom pl . . . . φαῦλος

φαῦλον adj masc acc sg, neut nom and acc sg   id.

φαῦλος adj masc nom sg   id.

φαυλότητος noun fem gen sg . . . . φαυλότης

φαύλους adj masc acc pl . . . . φαῦλος

φαῦσιν noun fem acc sg . . . . φαῦσις

Φαχαραθ pr noun

Φαχεραθ-ασεβωιν pr noun

Φεγγιθ pr noun

φέγγος noun neut nom and acc sg

φέγγους noun neut gen sg . . . . φέγγος

Φεδεϊα pr noun

φείδεσθαι vb pres dep inf . . . . φείδομαι

φείδεσθε vb pres dep ind 2nd pers pl   id.

φείδεται vb pres dep ind 3rd pers sg   id.

φείδῃ vb pres dep ind 2nd pers sg   id.

φειδοῖ noun fem dat sg . . . . φειδώ

φειδόμενοι vb pres dep part masc nom pl . . . . φείδομαι

φειδόμενος vb pres dep part masc nom sg   id.

φείδονται vb pres dep ind 3rd pers pl   id.

φειδοῦς noun fem gen sg . . . . φειδώ

φειδωλός adj masc nom sg

φεῖσαι vb 1st aor mid impv 2nd pers sg . . . . φείδομαι

φεισάμενος vb 1st aor mid part masc nom sg   id.

φείσασθαι vb 1st aor mid inf . . . . φείδομαι

φείσασθε vb 1st aor mid impv 2nd pers pl   id.

φείσεται vb fut mid ind 3rd pers sg   id.

φείσῃ vb 1st aor mid subj 2nd pers sg,
        fut mid ind 2nd pers sg   id.

φείσησθε vb 1st aor mid subj 2nd pers pl   id.

φείσηται vb 1st aor mid subj 3rd pers sg   id.

φείσομαι vb fut mid ind 1st pers sg   id.

φείσονται vb fut mid ind 3rd pers pl   id.

φείσωμαι vb 1st aor mid subj 1st pers sg   id.

φεισώμεθα vb 1st aor mid subj 1st pers pl   id.

φείσωνται vb 1st aor mid subj 3rd pers pl   id.

φελεθθι translit

Φελεθθι pr noun

Φελεϊα pr noun

Φελεθι pr noun

Φελεττι pr noun

Φελητι pr noun

Φελιηλ pr noun

Φελλανι pr noun

φελμουνι translit

Φελωθι pr noun

Φελωνι pr noun

Φεννανα pr noun

φέρε vb pres act impv 2nd pers sg . . . . φέρω

Φερεζαῖοι pr noun masc nom pl . . . . Φερεζαῖος

Φερεζαιοις pr noun masc dat pl   id.

Φερεζαῖον pr noun masc acc sg   id.

Φερεζαῖος pr noun masc nom sg   id.

Φερεζαιου pr noun masc gen sg   id.

Φερεζαιους pr noun masc acc pl   id.

Φερεζαιων pr noun masc gen pl   id.

Φερεζι pr noun

φέρει vb pres act ind 3rd pers sg . . . . φέρω

φέρειν vb pres act inf   id.

φέρεσθαι vb pres m/p inf   id.

φέρετε vb pres act impv 2nd pers pl,
        pres act ind 2nd pers pl   id.

φέρητε vb pres act subj 2nd pers pl   id.

Φεριδα pr noun

φερνή noun fem nom sg

φερνῇ noun fem dat sg . . . . φερνή

φερνήν noun fem acc sg   id.

φερνῆς noun fem gen sg   id.

φερνιεῖ vb fut act ind 3rd pers sg . . . . φερνίζω

φερόμενα vb pres m/p part neut nom and acc pl . . . . . . φέρω

φερομένη vb pres m/p part fem nom sg   id.

φερόμενοι vb pres m/p part masc nom pl   id.

φερόμενον vb pres m/p part masc acc sg,
        neut nom and acc sg   id.

φερόμενος vb pres m/p part masc nom sg   id.

φερομένου vb pres m/p part masc and neut gen sg   id.

φερομένους   vb pres m/p part masc acc pl . . . . οἴσω

φερομένῳ   vb pres m/p part masc and neut dat sg   d.

φερομένων   vb pres m/p part gen pl   d.

φέροντα   vb pres act part neut nom and acc pl   d.

φέρονται   vb pres m/p ind 3rd pers pl   d.

φέροντας   vb pres act part masc acc pl   id.

φέροντες   vb pres act part masc nom pl   id.

φέροντος   vb pres act part masc and neut gen sg   id.

φερόντων   vb pres act part masc and neut gen pl   id.

φέρουσα   vb pres act part fem nom sg   id.

φερούσης   vb pres act part fem gen sg   id.

φέρουσιν   vb pres act ind 3rd pers pl   id.

φέρω   vb pres act ind 1st pers sg   id.

φέρων   vb pres act part masc nom sg   id.

Φεση   pr noun

Φεσηχι   pr noun

Φεσσηε   pr noun

Φεταια   pr noun

φεῦγε   vb pres act impv 2nd pers sg . . . . φεύγω

φεύγει   vb pres act ind 3rd pers sg   id.

φεύγειν   vb pres act inf   id.

φεύγεις   vb pres act ind 2nd pers sg   id.

φεύγετε   vb pres act impv 2nd pers pl   id.

φεύγετε   vb pres act ind 2nd pers pl   id.

φευγέτω   vb pres act impv 3rd pers sg   id.

φεῦγον   vb pres act part neut nom and acc sg   id.

φεύγοντα   vb pres act part masc acc sg   id.

φεύγοντας   vb pres act part masc acc pl   id.

φεύγοντες   vb pres act part masc nom pl   id.

φευγόντων   vb pres act part masc and neut gen pl   id.

φεύγουσιν   vb pres act ind 3rd pers pl   id.

φεύγω   vb pres act ind 1st pers sg   id.

φεύγων   vb pres act part masc nom sg   id.

φευκτόν   adj masc acc sg, neut nom and acc sg . . . . φευκτός

φεύξεσθε   vb fut mid ind 2nd pers pl . . . . φεύγω

φεύξεται   vb fut mid ind 3rd pers sg   id.

φεύξῃ   vb fut mid ind 2nd pers sg   id.

φευξόμεθα   vb fut mid ind 1st pers pl   id.

φεύξονται   vb fut mid ind 3rd pers pl   id.

φη   translit (Heb. letter: פ)

φήμη   noun fem nom sg

φήμης   noun fem gen sg . . . . φήμη

φησίν   vb pres act ind 3rd pers sg . . . . φημί

Φθαιηλ   pr noun

φθάνει   vb pres act ind 3rd pers sg . . . . φθάνω

φθάνειν   vb pres act inf   id.

φθάνοντα   vb pres act part masc acc sg   id.

φθαρῇ   vb 2nd aor pass subj 3rd pers sg . . . . φθείρω

φθαρήσεται   vb fut pass ind 3rd pers sg   id.

φθάρματα   noun neut nom and acc pl . . . . φθάρμα

φθαρτόν   adj masc acc sg, neut nom and acc sg . . . . φθαρτός

φθαρτός   adj masc nom sg

φθάσαι   vb 1st aor mid impv 2nd pers sg . . . . φθάνω

φθάσας   vb 1st aor act part masc nom sg   id.

φθάσῃ   vb 1st aor act subj 3rd pers sg   id.

φθάσωσιν   vb 1st aor act subj 3rd pers pl   id.

φθέγγεσθε   vb pres dep ind 2nd pers pl . . . . φθέγγομαι

φθεγγόμεναι   vb pres dep part fem nom pl   id.

φθεγγόμενος   vb pres dep part masc nom sg   id.

φθεγγομένῳ   vb pres dep part masc and neut dat sg   id.

φθέγγου   vb pres dep impv 2nd pers sg   id.

φθέγμα   noun neut nom and acc sg

φθέγξαιτο   vb 1st aor mid opt 3rd pers sg . . . . φθέγγομαι

φθεγξάμενος   vb 1st aor mid part masc nom sg   id.

φθέγξασθε   vb 1st aor mid impv 2nd pers pl   id.

φθεγξάσθωσαν   vb 1st aor mid impv 3rd pers pl   id.

φθέγξεται   vb fut mid ind 3rd pers sg   id.

φθέγξομαι   vb fut mid ind 1st pers sg   id.

φθέγξονται   vb fut mid ind 3rd pers pl   id.

φθεῖραι   vb 1st aor act inf . . . . φθείρω

φθεριεῖ   vb fut act ind 3rd pers sg . . . . φθειρίζω

φθειρίζει   vb pres act ind 3rd pers sg   id.

φθειρόμενον   vb pres m/p part neut nom and acc sg . . φθείρω

φθερεῖ   vb fut act ind 3rd pers sg   id.

φθερεῖτε   vb fut act ind 2nd pers pl   id.

φθερῶ   vb fut act ind 1st pers sg   id.

φθίνουσαν   vb pres act part fem acc sg . . . . φθίνω

φθόγγοι   noun masc nom pl . . . . φθόγγος

φθόγγος   noun masc nom sg   id.

φθονερός   adj masc nom sg

φθονεσάτω   vb 1st aor act impv 3rd pers sg . . . . φθονέω

φθόνος   noun masc nom sg

φθόνου   noun masc gen sg . . . . φθόνος

φθόνῳ   noun masc dat sg   id.

φθορά   noun fem nom sg

φθορᾷ   noun fem dat sg . . . . φθορά

φθοράν   noun fem acc sg   id.

φθορᾶς   noun fem gen sg   id.

φθορεύς   noun masc nom sg

φιάλαι   noun fem nom pl . . . . φιάλη

φιάλας   noun fem acc pl   id.

φιάλη   noun fem nom sg   id.

φιάλην   noun fem acc sg   id.

φιαλῶν   noun fem gen pl   id.

Φιδων   pr noun

Φιθων   pr noun

Φικολ   pr noun

φιλάγαθον   adj masc acc sg,
       neut nom and acc sg . . . . φιλάγαθος

φιλαδελφίαν   noun fem acc sg . . . . φιλαδελφία

φιλαδελφίας   noun fem gen sg   id.

φιλάδελφοι   adj masc and fem nom pl . . . . φιλάδελφος

φιλάδελφος   adj masc and fem nom sg   id.

φιλαμαρτήμων   adj masc and fem nom sg

φιλάνθρωπα adj neut nom and acc pl . . . . . . φιλάνθρωπος
φιλανθρωπίᾳ noun fem dat sg . . . . φιλανθρωπία
φιλανθρωπίαν noun fem acc sg   id.
φιλανθρωπίας noun fem gen sg   id.
φιλάνθρωπον adj acc sg, neut nom sg . . . . . . φιλάνθρωπος
φιλανθρώπως adverb
φιλαργυρήσαντες vb 1st aor act part
        masc nom pl . . . . φιλαργυρέω
φιλαργυρία noun fem nom sg
φιλάργυρος adj masc and fem nom sg
φιλαρχίας noun fem gen sg . . . . φιλαρχία
φιλεῖ vb pres act ind 3rd pers sg . . . . φιλέω
φιλεῖν vb pres act inf   id.
φιλελεήμων adj masc and fem nom sg
φιλεχθρήσῃς vb 1st aor act subj 2nd pers sg . . . φιλεχθρέω
φίλη adj fem nom sg . . . . φίλος
φιληκοΐαν noun fem acc sg . . . . φιληκοΐα
φιλήματα noun neut nom and acc pl . . . . φίλημα
φιλημάτων noun neut gen pl   id.
φιλῆσαι vb 1st aor act inf . . . . φιλέω
φιλησάτω vb 1st aor act impv 3rd pers sg   id.
φίλησον vb 1st aor act impv 2nd pers sg   id.
φιλήσουσιν vb fut act ind 3rd pers pl   id.
φιλήσω vb 1st aor act subj 1st pers sg   id.
φιλία noun fem nom sg
φιλίᾳ noun fem dat sg . . . . φιλία
φιλιάζειν vb pres act inf . . . . φιλιάζω
φιλιάζεις vb pres act ind 2nd pers sg   id.
φιλιάζων vb pres act part masc nom sg   id.
φιλίαν noun fem acc sg . . . . φιλία
φιλίας noun fem gen sg   id.
Φίλιππον pr noun masc acc sg . . . . Φίλιππος
Φίλιππος pr noun masc nom sg   id.
Φιλίππου pr noun masc gen sg   id.
Φιλίππῳ pr noun masc dat sg   id.
φιλογέωργος noun masc nom sg
φιλογύναιος adj masc nom and fem sg
φιλοδοξία noun fem nom sg
φιλοδοξίᾳ noun fem dat sg . . . . φιλοδοξία
φίλοι adj masc nom pl . . . . φίλος
φίλοις adj masc and neut dat pl   id.
φιλοκόσμῳ adj dat sg . . . . φιλόκοσμος
φιλομαθεῖν vb pres act inf . . . . φιλομαθέω
φιλομαθεῖς adj masc and fem nom and acc pl . . . φιλομαθής
φιλομαθοῦντας vb pres act part masc acc pl . . . φιλομαθέω
Φιλομήτορα pr noun masc acc sg . . . . Φιλομήτωρ
φιλομήτορες noun masc nom pl . . . . φιλομήτωρ
Φιλομήτορος pr noun masc gen sg . . . . Φιλομήτωρ
φίλον adj masc acc sg, neut nom and acc sg . . . . φίλος
φιλονεικία noun fem nom sg
φιλονεικίας noun fem gen sg . . . . φιλονεικία
φιλόνεικοι adj masc and fem nom pl . . . . φιλόνεικος

φιλονεικοῦντας vb pres act part masc acc pl . . . φιλονεικέω
Φιλοπάτωρ pr noun masc nom sg
Φιλοπάτωρ pr noun masc nom sg
φιλοπολίτης noun masc nom sg
φιλοπονίαν noun fem acc sg . . . . φιλοπονία
φίλος adj masc nom sg
φιλόσοφε noun masc voc sg . . . . φιλόσοφος
φιλοσοφεῖν vb pres act inf . . . . φιλοσοφέω
φιλοσοφήσεις vb fut act ind 2nd pers sg   id.
φιλοσοφίᾳ noun fem dat sg . . . . φιλοσοφία
φιλοσοφίαν noun fem acc sg   id.
φιλοσοφίας noun fem gen sg   id.
φιλοσοφοῦντες vb pres act part masc nom pl . . . φιλοσοφέω
φιλοσόφους noun masc acc pl . . . . φιλόσοφος
φιλοσοφῶν noun masc gen pl   id.
φιλοσοφώτατον superl adj masc acc sg,
        neut nom and acc sg   id.
φιλόστοργε adj masc and fem voc sg . . . . φιλόστοργος
φιλοστοργίαν noun fem acc sg . . . . φιλοστοργία
φιλοστόργως adverb
φιλότεκνα adj neut nom and acc pl . . . . φιλότεκνος
φιλοτεκνίαν noun fem acc sg . . . . φιλοτεκνία
φιλοτεκνίας noun fem gen sg   id.
φιλοτεκνοτέρα comp adj fem nom sg . . . . φιλότεκνος
φιλοτεκνότεραι comp adj fem nom pl   id.
φιλοτιμία noun fem nom sg
φιλοτίμου adj masc and fem gen sg . . . . φιλότιμος
φιλοτίμως adverb
φίλου adj masc and neut gen sg . . . . φίλος
φιλούμενος vb pres m/p part masc nom sg . . . . φιλέω
φιλοῦντας vb pres act part masc acc pl   id.
φιλοῦντες vb pres act part masc nom pl   id.
φιλοῦντος vb pres act part masc and neut gen sg   id.
φιλούντων vb pres act part masc and neut gen pl   id.
φίλους adj masc acc pl . . . . φίλος
φιλοῦσιν vb pres act ind 3rd pers pl . . . . φιλέω
φιλοφρονοῦσιν vb pres act ind 3rd pers pl . . . φιλοφρονέω
φιλοφρόνως adverb
φιλόψυχε adj masc and fem voc sg . . . . φιλόψυχος
φίλτρα noun neut nom and acc pl . . . . φίλτρον
φιλῶ vb pres act ind 1st pers sg . . . . φιλέω
φίλῳ adj masc and neut dat sg . . . . φίλος
φίλων adj gen pl   id.
φιλῶν vb pres act part masc nom sg . . . . φιλέω
φιμόν noun masc acc sg . . . . φιμός
φιμός noun masc nom sg   id.
φιμοῦ noun masc gen sg   id.
φιμοῦται vb pres m/p ind 3rd pers sg . . . . φιμόω
φιμώσεις vb fut act ind 2nd pers sg   id.
Φινεές pr noun
Φινοε pr noun
Φινω pr noun

Φινων	pr noun	
Φιρα	pr noun	
Φισων	pr noun	
φλέβας	noun fem acc pl	φλέψ
φλέγει	vb pres act ind 3rd pers sg	φλέγω
φλεγμαίνουσα	vb pres act part fem nom sg	φλεγμαίνω
φλεγμονάς	noun fem acc pl	φλεγμονή
φλεγόμενον	vb pres m/p part masc acc sg	φλέγω
φλεγομένου	vb pres m/p part masc and neut gen sg	id.
φλέγον	vb pres act part neut nom and acc sg	id.
φλέξει	vb fut act ind 3rd pers sg	id.
φλιαί	noun fem nom pl	φλιά
φλιάν	noun fem acc sg	id.
φλιάς	noun fem gen sg	id.
φλιᾶς	noun fem acc pl	id.
φλιῶν	noun fem gen pl	id.
φλόγα	noun fem acc sg	φλόξ
φλόγες	noun fem nom pl	id.
φλογί	noun fem dat sg	id.
φλογιεῖ	vb fut act ind 3rd pers sg	φλογίζω
φλογιζόμενον	vb pres m/p part masc acc sg,	
	neut nom and acc sg	id.
φλογίζον	vb pres act part neut nom and acc sg	id.
φλογιζούσης	vb pres act part fem gen sg	id.
φλογίνην	adj fem acc sg	φλόγινος
φλογός	noun fem gen sg	φλόξ
φλοιόν	noun masc acc sg	φλοιός
φλόξ	noun fem nom sg	
φλυάρου	noun masc gen sg	φλύαρος
φλυκτίδες	noun fem nom pl	φλυκτίς
φοβεῖσθαι	vb pres m/p inf	φοβέω
φοβεῖσθε	vb pres m/p impv 2nd pers pl,	
	pres m/p ind 2nd pers pl	id.
φοβείσθω	vb pres m/p impv 3rd pers sg	id.
φοβεῖται	vb pres m/p ind 3rd pers sg	id.
φοβερά	adj fem nom sg, neut nom and acc pl	φοβερός
φοβεράν	adj fem acc sg	id.
φοβερᾶς	adj fem gen sg	id.
φοβερίζοντες	vb pres act part masc nom pl	φοβερίζω
φοβερίζουσιν	vb pres act ind 3rd pers pl	id.
φοβερίσαι	vb 1st aor act inf	id.
φοβερισμοί	noun masc nom pl	φοβερισμός
φοβέρισον	vb 1st aor act impv 2nd pers sg	φοβερίζω
φοβεροειδεῖς	noun masc nom and acc pl	φοβεροειδής
φοβεροῖς	adj masc and neut dat pl	φοβερός
φοβερόν	adj masc acc sg, neut nom and acc sg	id.
φοβερός	adj masc nom sg	id.
φοβεροῦ	adj masc and neut gen sg	id.
φοβερῷ	adj masc and neut dat sg	id.
φοβερῶν	adj gen pl	id.
φοβερῶς	adverb	
φοβῇ	vb pres act subj 3rd pers sg,	
	pres m/p ind 2nd pers sg,	
	pres m/p subj 2nd pers sg	φοβέω
φοβηθείς	vb 1st aor pass part masc nom sg	id.
φοβηθεῖσι	vb 1st aor pass part masc and neut dat pl	id.
φοβηθέντα	vb 1st aor pass part masc acc sg	id.
φοβηθέντας	vb 1st aor pass part masc acc pl	id.
φοβηθέντες	vb 1st aor pass part masc nom pl	id.
φοβηθῇ	vb 1st aor pass subj 3rd pers sg	id.
φοβηθῆναι	vb 1st aor pass inf	id.
φοβηθῇς	vb 1st aor pass subj 2nd pers sg	id.
φοβηθήσεσθε	vb fut pass ind 2nd pers pl	id.
φοβηθήσεται	vb fut pass ind 3rd pers sg	id.
φοβηθήσῃ	vb fut pass ind 2nd pers sg	id.
φοβηθήσομαι	vb fut pass ind 1st pers sg	id.
φοβηθησόμεθα	vb fut pass ind 1st pers pl	id.
φοβηθήσονται	vb fut pass ind 3rd pers pl	id.
φοβήθητε	vb 1st aor pass impv 2nd pers pl	id.
φοβήθητε	vb 1st aor pass subj 2nd pers pl	id.
φοβηθῆτε	vb 1st aor pass impv 2nd pers pl	id.
φοβηθῆτε	vb 1st aor pass subj 2nd pers pl	id.
φοβήθητι	vb 1st aor pass impv 2nd pers sg	id.
φοβηθήτω	vb 1st aor pass impv 3rd pers sg	id.
φοβηθήτωσαν	vb 1st aor pass impv 3rd pers pl	id.
φοβηθῶ	vb 1st aor pass subj 1st pers sg	id.
φοβηθῶμεν	vb 1st aor pass subj 1st pers pl	id.
φοβηθῶσιν	vb 1st aor pass subj 3rd pers pl	id.
φοβῆσαι	vb 1st aor act inf	id.
φοβῆσθε	vb pres m/p subj 2nd pers pl	id.
φόβητρον	noun neut nom and acc sg	
φόβοι	noun masc nom pl	φόβος
φόβοις	noun masc dat pl	id.
φόβον	noun masc acc sg	id.
φόβος	noun masc nom sg	id.
φόβου	noun masc gen sg	id.
φοβοῦ	vb pres m/p impv 2nd pers sg	φοβέω
φοβοῦμαι	vb pres m/p ind 1st pers sg	id.
φοβούμεθα	vb pres m/p ind 1st pers pl	id.
φοβούμεναι	vb pres m/p part fem nom pl	id.
φοβουμένη	vb pres m/p part fem nom sg	id.
φοβούμενοι	vb pres m/p part masc nom pl	id.
φοβουμένοις	vb pres m/p part masc and neut dat pl	id.
φοβούμενον	vb pres m/p part masc acc sg,	
	neut nom and acc sg	id.
φοβούμενος	vb pres m/p part masc nom sg	id.
φοβουμένου	vb pres m/p part masc and neut gen sg	id.
φοβουμένους	vb pres m/p part masc acc pl	id.
φοβουμένῳ	vb pres m/p part masc and neut dat sg	id.
φοβουμένων	vb pres m/p part gen pl	id.
φοβοῦνται	vb pres m/p ind 3rd pers pl	id.
φόβῳ	noun masc dat sg	φόβος
φοβῶνται	vb pres m/p subj 3rd pers pl	φοβέω

Φογωρ pr noun

φοιβήσετε vb fut act ind 2nd pers pl . . . . φοιβάω

φοίνικα noun masc acc sg . . . . φοῖνιξ

φοίνικας noun masc acc pl   id.

φοίνικες noun masc nom pl   id.

Φοινικες pr noun

Φοινικη pr noun fem dat sg . . . . Φοινικη

Φοινικην pr noun fem acc sg   id.

Φοινικης pr noun fem gen sg   id.

φοίνικι noun masc dat sg . . . . φοῖνιξ

φοίνικος noun masc gen sg   id.

φοινικοῦν adj masc acc sg, neut nom and acc sg . . φοινικοῦς

φοινίκων noun masc gen pl . . . . φοῖνιξ

Φοινικων pr noun fem gen pl . . . . Φοινικη

Φοινικῶνος pr noun masc gen sg . . . . Φοινικων

φοῖνιξ noun masc nom sg

Φοινισσης pr noun fem gen sg . . . . Φοινισσα

Φολλαθι pr noun

φονάς noun masc acc pl . . . . φονεύς

φονεύειν vb pres act inf . . . . φονεύω

φονεύετε vb pres act ind 2nd pers pl   id.

φονευθείσης vb 1st aor pass part fem nom sg   id.

φονευθῆναι vb 1st aor pass inf   id.

φονευθήσονται vb fut pass ind 3rd pers pl   id.

φονεύονται vb pres m/p ind 3rd pers pl   id.

φονεύουσιν vb pres act ind 3rd pers pl   id.

φονεῦσαι vb 1st aor act inf   id.

φονεύσαντα vb 1st aor act part masc acc sg   id.

φονεύσαντας vb 1st aor act part masc acc pl   id.

φονεύσαντι vb 1st aor act part masc and neut dat sg   id.

φονεύσαντος vb 1st aor act part masc and neut gen sg   id.

φονεύσας vb 1st aor act part masc nom sg   id.

φονεύσασι vb 1st aor act part masc and neut dat pl   id.

φονεύσεις vb fut act ind 2nd pers sg   id.

φονεύσῃ vb 1st aor act subj 3rd pers sg   id.

φονεύσωμεν vb 1st aor act subj 1st pers pl   id.

φονευταί noun masc nom pl . . . . φονευτής

φονευτῇ noun masc dat sg   id.

φονευτήν noun masc acc sg   id.

φονευτής noun masc nom sg   id.

φονευτοῦ noun masc gen sg   id.

φονεύων vb pres act part masc nom sg . . . . φονεύω

φόνοις noun masc dat pl . . . . φόνος

φονοκτονεῖ vb pres act ind 3rd pers sg . . . . . . φονοκτονέω

φονοκτονήσητε vb 1st aor act subj 2nd pers pl   id.

φονοκτονίαν noun fem acc sg . . . . φονοκτονία

φόνον noun masc acc sg . . . . φόνος

φόνος noun masc nom sg   id.

φόνου noun masc gen sg   id.

φόνους noun masc acc pl   id.

φόνῳ noun masc dat sg   id.

φονώδης adj masc and fem nom sg

φορβεάν noun fem acc sg . . . . φορβεά

φορεῖ vb pres act ind 3rd pers sg . . . . φορέω

φορεῖον noun neut nom and acc sg

φορεῖς vb pres act ind 2nd pers sg . . . . φορέω

φορείῳ noun neut dat sg . . . . φορεῖον

φορέσει vb fut act ind 3rd pers sg . . . . φορέω

φορθομμιν translit

φόροι noun masc nom pl . . . . φόρος

φορολογεῖσθαι vb 1st aor act inf . . . . φορολογέω

φορολόγητοι adj masc and fem nom pl . . . . . φορολόγητος

φορολογία noun fem nom sg

φορολογίαν noun fem acc sg . . . . φορολογία

φορολογίας noun fem gen sg   id.

φορολόγος noun masc nom sg

φορολόγου noun masc gen sg . . . . φορολόγος

φορολογοῦντες vb pres act part masc nom pl . . φορολογέω

φορολόγῳ noun masc dat sg . . . . φορολόγος

φόρον noun masc acc sg . . . . φόρος

φόρος noun masc nom sg   id.

Φορος pr noun

φόρου noun masc gen sg . . . . φόρος

φοροῦντος vb pres act part masc and neut gen sg . . . . φορέω

φόρους noun masc acc pl . . . . φόρος

φορτία noun neut nom and acc pl . . . . φορτίον

φορτίον noun neut nom and acc sg   id.

φορῶ vb pres act ind 1st pers sg . . . . φορέω

φόρων noun masc gen pl . . . . φόρος

Φουα pr noun

Φουαϊ pr noun

Φουασουδ pr noun

Φουδ pr noun

Φουλ pr noun

Φουτιηλ pr noun

Φρααθων pr noun

Φρααθωνιτης pr noun masc nom sg

φραγμοί noun masc nom pl . . . . φραγμός

φραγμόν noun masc acc sg   id.

φραγμός noun masc nom sg   id.

φραγμοῦ noun masc gen sg   id.

φραγμούς noun masc acc pl   id.

φραγμῷ noun masc dat sg   id.

φραγμῶν noun masc gen pl   id.

φραζων translit

φράσατε vb 1st aor act impv 2nd pers pl . . . . φράζω

φράσῃ vb 1st aor act subj 3rd pers sg   id.

φράσομεν vb fut act ind 1st pers pl   id.

φράσσει vb pres act ind 3rd pers sg . . . . φράσσω

φράσσοι vb pres act opt 3rd pers sg   id.

φράσσω vb pres act ind 1st pers sg   id.

φρέαρ noun neut nom and acc sg

Φρεαρ pr noun neut nom and acc sg

φρέατα noun neut nom and acc pl . . . . φρέαρ

φρέατι noun neut dat sg	...... φρέαρ		φροντιστέον verbal adj sg	
φρέατος noun neut gen sg	id.		φρονῶν vb pres act part masc nom sg ...... φρονέω	
φρεάτων noun neut gen pl	id.		φρουρά noun fem nom sg	
φρένα noun fem acc sg	...... φρήν		Φρουραι pr noun	
φρένες noun fem nom pl	id.		φρουράν noun fem acc sg ...... φρουρά	
φρενί noun fem dat sg	id.		φρουράς noun fem acc pl	id.
φρενῶν noun fem gen pl	id.		φρούριον noun neut nom and acc sg	
φρικασμός noun masc nom sg			φρουροῦσι vb pres act part masc and neut dat pl .. φρουρέω	
φρίκη noun fem nom sg			φρύαγμα noun neut nom and acc sg	
φρίκην noun fem acc sg	...... φρίκη		φρυάγματι noun neut dat sg ...... φρύαγμα	
φρικτά adj neut nom and acc pl	...... φρικτός		φρυάγματος noun neut gen sg	id.
φρικτοί adj masc nom pl	id.		φρυαττόμενος vb pres dep part masc nom sg .. φρυάττομαι	
φρικτῶς adverb			Φρύγα pr noun masc acc sg ...... Φρύξ	
φρικώδη adj masc and fem acc sg ...... φρικώδης			φρύγανα noun neut nom and acc pl ...... φρύγανον	
φρίττει vb pres act ind 3rd pers sg ...... φρίττω			φρύγανον noun neut nom and acc sg	id.
φρίττομεν vb pres act ind 1st pers pl	id.		φρύγιον noun neut nom and acc sg	
φρονεῖν vb pres act inf	...... φρονέω		φυγάδα noun masc acc sg ...... φυγάς	
φρονήμασι noun neut dat pl	...... φρόνημα		φυγάδας noun masc acc pl	id.
φρονήματι noun neut dat sg	id.		φυγάδες noun masc nom pl	id.
φρονῆσαι vb 1st aor act inf	...... φρονέω		φυγαδεύοντες vb pres act part masc nom pl ...... φυγαδεύω	
φρονήσαιμεν vb 1st aor act opt 1st pers pl	id.		φυγαδεύσαντας vb 1st aor act part masc acc pl	id.
φρονήσατε vb 1st aor act impv 2nd pers pl	id.		φυγαδευτήρια noun neut nom and acc pl .. φυγαδευτήριον	
φρονήσει noun fem dat sg	...... φρόνησις		φυγαδευτήριον noun neut nom and acc sg	id.
φρονήσεως noun fem gen sg	id.		φυγαδευτηρίου noun neut gen sg	id.
φρόνησιν noun fem acc sg	id.		φυγαδευτηρίῳ noun neut dat sg	id.
φρόνησις noun fem nom sg	id.		φυγαδευτηρίων noun neut gen pl	id.
φρονίμη adj fem nom sg	...... φρόνιμος		φυγαδεύων vb pres act part masc nom sg ...... φυγαδεύω	
φρονίμην adj fem acc sg	id.		φυγάδια noun neut nom and acc pl ...... φυγάδιον	
φρονίμοις adj masc and neut dat pl	id.		φυγάδιον noun neut nom and acc sg	id.
φρόνιμον adj masc acc sg, neut nom and acc sg	id.		φυγάς noun fem acc pl ...... φυγή	
φρόνιμος adj masc nom sg	id.		φυγάς noun masc nom sg	
φρονίμου adj masc and neut gen sg	id.		φύγε vb 2nd aor act impv 2nd pers sg ...... φεύγω	
φρονίμους adj masc acc pl	id.		φυγεῖν vb 2nd aor act inf	id.
φρονίμῳ adj masc and neut dat sg	id.		φυγέτωσαν vb 2nd aor act impv 3rd pers pl	id.
φρονίμων adj gen pl	id.		φυγή noun fem nom sg	
φρονιμώτατος superl adj masc nom sg	id.		φύγῃ vb 2nd aor act subj 3rd pers sg ...... φεύγω	
φρονιμώτερος comp adj masc nom sg	id.		φυγῇ noun fem dat sg ...... φυγή	
φρονοῦσι vb pres act part masc and neut dat pl ...... φρονέω			φυγήν noun fem acc sg	id.
φροντίδας noun fem acc pl ...... φροντίς			φυγῆς noun fem gen sg	id.
φροντίδι noun fem dat sg	id.		φύγῃς vb 2nd aor act subj 2nd pers sg ...... φεύγω	
φροντίδος noun fem gen sg	id.		φυγόντα vb 2nd aor act part masc acc sg	id.
φροντίδων noun fem gen pl	id.		φύγω vb 2nd aor act subj 1st pers sg	id.
φροντιεῖ vb fut act ind 3rd pers sg ...... φροντίζω			φύγωμεν vb 2nd aor act subj 1st pers pl	id.
φρόντιζε vb pres act impv 2nd pers sg	id.		φύγωσιν vb 2nd aor act subj 3rd pers pl	id.
φροντίζει vb pres act ind 3rd pers sg	id.		φύει vb pres act ind 3rd pers sg ...... φύω	
φροντίζῃ vb pres act subj 3rd pers sg	id.		φύεται vb pres m/p ind 3rd pers sg	id.
φροντίζων vb pres act part masc nom sg	id.		φυή noun fem nom sg	
φροντίς noun fem nom sg			φυήν noun fem acc sg ...... φυή	
φροντίσαι vb 1st aor act inf ...... φροντίζω			φυήσουσιν vb fut act ind 3rd pers pl ...... φύω	
φροντίσας vb 1st aor act part masc nom sg	id.		φύκει noun neut dat sg ...... φῦκος	
φροντίσιν noun fem dat pl ...... φροντίς			φυλάγματα noun neut nom and acc pl ...... φύλαγμα	
φρόντισον vb 1st aor act impv 2nd pers sg ...... φροντίζω			φυλαί noun fem nom pl ...... φυλή	

φυλαῖς noun fem dat pl . . . . φυλή

φύλακα noun masc acc sg . . . . φύλαξ

φυλακαῖς noun fem dat pl . . . . φυλακή

φύλακας noun masc acc pl . . . . φύλαξ

φύλακάς noun fem acc pl . . . . φυλακή

φύλακες noun masc nom pl . . . . φύλαξ

φυλακή noun fem nom sg

φυλακῇ noun fem dat sg . . . . φυλακή

φυλακήν noun fem acc sg   id.

φυλακῆς noun fem gen sg   id.

φύλακι noun masc dat sg . . . . φύλαξ

φυλακισθῆναι vb 1st aor pass inf . . . . φυλακίζομαι

φυλάκισσαν noun fem acc sg . . . . φυλάκισσα

φύλαξ noun masc nom sg

φύλαξαι vb 1st aor mid impv 2nd pers sg . . . . φυλάσσω

φυλάξαι vb 1st aor act inf,

       1st aor act opt 3rd pers sg   id.

φυλάξαντες vb 1st aor act part masc nom pl   id.

φυλάξασθαι vb 1st aor mid inf   id.

φυλάξασθε vb 1st aor mid impv 2nd pers pl   id.

φυλαξάσθω vb 1st aor mid impv 3rd pers sg   id.

φυλάξατε vb 1st aor act impv 2nd pers pl   id.

φυλάξει vb fut act ind 3rd pers sg   id.

φυλάξεις vb fut act ind 2nd pers sg   id.

φυλάξεσθε vb fut mid ind 2nd pers pl   id.

φυλάξεται vb fut mid ind 3rd pers sg   id.

φυλάξετε vb fut act ind 2nd pers pl   id.

φυλάξῃ vb 1st aor act subj 3rd pers sg,

       fut mid ind 2nd pers sg   id.

φυλάξῃς vb 1st aor act subj 2nd pers sg   id.

φυλάξησθε vb 1st aor mid subj 2nd pers pl   id.

φυλάξηται vb 1st aor mid subj 3rd pers sg   id.

φυλάξητε vb 1st aor act subj 2nd pers pl   id.

φυλάξομαι vb fut mid ind 1st pers sg   id.

φύλαξον vb 1st aor act impv 2nd pers sg   id.

φυλάξονται vb fut mid ind 3rd pers pl   id.

φυλάξουσιν vb fut act ind 3rd pers pl   id.

φυλάξω vb fut act ind 1st pers sg   id.

φυλάξωνται vb 1st aor mid subj 3rd pers pl   id.

φυλάξωσιν vb 1st aor act subj 3rd pers pl   id.

φυλάρχην noun masc acc sg . . . . φυλάρχης

φυλάρχοις noun masc dat pl . . . . φύλαρχος

φυλάρχους noun masc acc pl   id.

φυλάρχων noun masc gen pl   id.

φυλάς noun fem acc pl . . . . φυλή

φύλασσε vb pres act impv 2nd pers sg . . . . φυλάσσω

φυλάσσει vb pres act ind 3rd pers sg   id.

φυλάσσειν vb pres act inf   id.

φυλάσσεις vb pres act ind 2nd pers sg   id.

φυλάσσεσθαι vb pres m/p inf   id.

φυλάσσεσθε vb pres m/p impv 2nd pers pl,

       pres m/p ind 2nd pers pl   id.

φυλάσσεται vb pres m/p ind 3rd pers sg . . . . φυλάσσω

φυλάσσετε vb pres act impv 2nd pers pl,

       pres act ind 2nd pers pl   id.

φυλασσέτω vb pres act impv 3rd pers sg   id.

φυλάσσησθε vb pres m/p subj 2nd pers pl   id.

φυλάσσομαι vb pres m/p ind 1st pers sg   id.

φυλάσσομεν vb pres act ind 1st pers pl   id.

φυλασσόμενα vb pres m/p part neut nom and acc pl   id.

φυλασσόμενοι vb pres m/p part masc nom pl   id.

φυλασσόμενον vb pres m/p part masc acc sg,

       neut nom and acc sg   id.

φυλασσόμενος vb pres m/p part masc nom sg   id.

φυλασσομένους vb pres m/p part masc acc pl   id.

φυλάσσον vb pres act part neut nom and acc sg   id.

φυλάσσοντα vb pres act part masc acc sg   id.

φυλάσσονται vb pres m/p ind 3rd pers pl   id.

φυλάσσοντας vb pres act part masc acc pl   id.

φυλάσσοντες vb pres act part masc nom pl   id.

φυλάσσοντος vb pres act part masc and neut gen sg   id.

φυλασσόντων vb pres act part masc and neut gen pl   id.

φυλάσσου vb pres m/p impv 2nd pers sg   id.

φυλάσσουσαν vb pres act part fem acc sg   id.

φυλάσσουσι(ν) vb pres act ind 3rd pers pl,

       pres act part masc and neut dat pl   id.

φυλάσσω vb pres act ind 1st pers sg   id.

φυλασσώμεθα vb pres m/p subj 1st pers pl   id.

φυλάσσων vb pres act part masc nom sg   id.

φυλάσσωνται vb pres m/p subj 3rd pers pl   id.

φυλάσσωσιν vb pres act subj 3rd pers pl   id.

φυλάττοντας vb pres act part masc acc pl . . . . φυλάττω

φυλαχθῆναι vb 1st aor pass inf . . . . φυλάσσω

φυλαχθήσονται vb fut pass ind 3rd pers pl   id.

φυλαχθήτω vb 1st aor pass impv 3rd pers sg   id.

φυλαχθῶσιν vb 1st aor pass subj 3rd pers pl   id.

φυλή noun fem nom sg

φυλῇ noun fem dat sg . . . . φυλή

φυλήν noun fem acc sg   id.

φυλῆς noun fem gen sg   id.

Φυλιστιιμ pr noun

φύλλα noun neut nom and acc pl . . . . φύλλον

φύλλον noun neut nom and acc sg   id.

φύλλου noun neut gen sg   id.

φῦλον noun neut nom and acc sg

φυλῶν noun fem gen pl . . . . φυλή

φυόμενα vb pres m/p part neut nom and acc pl . . . . φύω

φυόμενον vb pres m/p part neut nom and acc sg   id.

φύονται vb pres m/p ind 3rd pers pl   id.

φύουσα vb pres act part fem nom sg   id.

φύουσαι vb pres act part fem nom pl   id.

φυράμασι noun neut dat pl . . . . φύραμα

φυράματα noun neut nom and acc pl   id.

φυράματος noun neut gen sg   id.

φυράσεως noun fem gen sg .... φύρασις

φύρασον vb 1st aor act impv 2nd pers sg .... φυράω

φύρδην adverb

φύρεται vb pres dep ind 3rd pers sg .... φύρομαι

φυρμόν noun masc acc sg .... φυρμός

φυρμῷ noun masc dat sg   id.

φύρονται vb pres dep ind 3rd pers pl .... φύρομαι

φύσει noun fem dat sg .... φύσις

φύσεις noun fem nom and acc pl   id.

φύσεως noun fem gen sg   id.

φυσήσῃς vb 1st aor act subj 2nd pers sg .... φυσάω

φυσητήρ noun masc nom sg

φύσιν noun fem acc sg .... φύσις

φύσις noun fem nom sg   id.

φυσῶν vb pres act part masc nom sg .... φυσάω

φυσῶντας vb pres act part masc acc pl   id.

φυτά noun neut nom and acc pl .... φυτόν

φυτεία noun fem nom sg

φυτείαν noun fem acc sg .... φυτεία

φυτείας noun fem gen sg   id.

φυτεύει vb pres act ind 3rd pers sg .... φυτεύω

φύτευμα noun neut nom and acc sg

φυτεύοντας vb pres act part masc acc pl .... φυτεύω

φυτεύουσιν vb pres act ind 3rd pers pl   id.

φυτεῦσαι vb 1st aor act inf   id.

φυτεύσας vb 1st aor act part masc nom sg   id.

φυτεύσασα vb 1st aor act part fem nom sg   id.

φυτεύσατε vb 1st aor act impv 2nd pers pl   id.

φυτεύσεις vb fut act ind 2nd pers sg   id.

φυτεύσῃς vb 1st aor act subj 2nd pers sg   id.

φυτεύσουσιν vb fut act ind 3rd pers pl   id.

φυτεύσω vb fut act ind 1st pers sg   id.

φυτεύσωσιν vb 1st aor act subj 3rd pers pl   id.

φυτόν noun neut nom and acc sg

φυτῷ noun neut dat sg .... φυτόν

φυτῶν noun neut gen pl   id.

φωναί noun fem nom pl .... φωνή

φωναῖς noun fem dat pl   id.

φωνάς noun fem gen sg and acc pl   id.

φωνή noun fem nom sg   id.

φωνῇ noun fem dat sg   id.

φωνήν noun fem acc sg   id.

φωνῆς noun fem gen sg   id.

φωνῆσαι vb 1st aor act inf .... φωνέω

φωνήσαντες vb 1st aor act part masc nom pl   id.

φωνήσας vb 1st aor act part masc nom sg   id.

φωνήσει vb fut act ind 3rd pers sg   id.

φώνησον vb 1st aor act impv 2nd pers sg   id.

φωνήσουσιν vb fut act ind 3rd pers pl   id.

φωνήσω vb 1st aor act subj 1st pers sg,

　　　fut act ind 1st pers sg .... φωνέω

φωνοῦντας vb pres act part masc acc pl   id.

φωνοῦντες vb pres act part masc nom pl   id.

φωνούντων vb pres act part masc and neut gen pl id.

φωνοῦσιν vb pres act ind 3rd pers pl   id.

φωνῶν noun fem gen pl .... φωνή

φωραθῇ vb 1st aor pass subj 3rd pers sg .... φωράομαι

φωραθῶσιν vb 1st aor pass subj 3rd pers pl   id.

φῶς noun neut nom and acc sg

φωστήρ noun masc nom sg

φωστῆρα noun masc acc sg .... φωστήρ

φωστῆρας noun masc acc pl   id.

φωστῆρες noun masc nom pl   id.

φῶτα noun neut nom and acc pl .... φῶς

φωταγωγήσασα vb 1st aor act part fem nom sg . φωταγωγέω

φωτεινότεροι comp adj masc nom pl .... φωτεινός

φωτεινότερον comp adj masc acc sg,

　　　neut nom and acc sg   id.

φωτί noun neut dat sg .... φῶς

φωτιεῖ vb fut act ind 3rd pers sg .... φωτίζω

φωτιεῖ vb fut act ind 3rd pers sg   id.

φωτιεῖς vb fut act ind 2nd pers sg   id.

φωτίζει vb pres act ind 3rd pers sg   id.

φωτίζειν vb pres act inf   id.

φωτίζεις vb pres act ind 2nd pers sg   id.

φωτίζον vb pres act part neut nom and acc sg   id.

φωτίζου vb pres m/p impv 2nd pers sg   id.

φωτίζουσα vb pres act part fem nom sg   id.

φωτίζουσαν vb pres act part fem acc sg   id.

φωτίζουσιν vb pres act ind 3rd pers pl   id.

φωτίζων vb pres act part masc nom sg   id.

φωτιοῦσιν vb fut act ind 3rd pers pl   id.

φωτιοῦσιν vb fut act ind 3rd pers pl   id.

φωτίσαι vb 1st aor act inf   id.

φωτίσατε vb 1st aor act impv 2nd pers pl   id.

φωτισάτω vb 1st aor act impv 3rd pers sg   id.

φωτίσει vb fut act ind 3rd pers sg   id.

φωτισθήσεται vb fut pass ind 3rd pers sg   id.

φωτίσθητε vb 1st aor pass impv 2nd pers pl   id.

φωτισμόν noun masc acc sg .... φωτισμός

φωτισμός noun masc nom sg   id.

φωτισμῷ noun masc dat sg   id.

φώτισον vb 1st aor act impv 2nd pers sg .... φωτίζω

φωτίσουσιν vb fut act ind 3rd pers pl   id.

φωτίσων vb fut act part masc nom sg   id.

φωτιῶ vb fut act ind 1st pers sg   id.

φωτός noun neut gen sg .... φῶς

Χ χ

Χαβασιν pr noun
Χαββα pr noun
Χαβερ pr noun
Χαβια pr noun
Χαβρα pr noun
χαβραθα translit
Χαβραθα pr noun
Χαβριν pr noun
Χαβρις pr noun
Χαβωλ pr noun
Χαβωρ pr noun
Χαδιασαι pr noun
Χαθλως pr noun
Χαιλων pr noun
χαῖρε vb pres act impv 2nd pers sg . . . . χαίρω
Χαιρεαν pr noun masc acc sg . . . . Χαιρεας
χαίρει vb pres act ind 3rd pers sg . . . . χαίρω
χαίρειν vb pres act inf   id.
Χαιρεου pr noun masc gen sg . . . . Χαιρεας
χαίρετε vb pres act ind 2nd pers pl,
         pres act impv 2nd pers pl . . . . χαίρω
χαιρέτω vb pres act impv 3rd pers sg   id.
χαίροιεν vb pres act opt 3rd pers pl   id.
χαίροντας vb pres act part masc acc pl   id.
χαίροντες vb pres act part masc nom pl   id.
χαιρόντων vb pres act part masc and neut gen pl   id.
χαίρων vb pres act part masc nom sg   id.
χάλαζα noun fem nom sg
Χαλαζα pr noun
χάλαζαι noun fem nom pl . . . . χάλαζα
χαλάζαις noun fem dat pl   id.
χάλαζαν noun fem acc sg   id.
χαλάζῃ noun fem dat sg   id.
χαλάζης noun fem gen sg   id.
Χαλαμακ pr noun
Χαλαννη pr noun
χαλάσει vb fut act ind 3rd pers sg . . . . χαλάω
χαλαστά noun neut nom and acc pl . . . . χαλαστόν
χαλαστῶν noun neut gen pl   id.
χαλᾶται vb pres m/p subj 3rd pers sg . . . . χαλάω
Χαλαχ pr noun
χαλβάνη noun fem nom sg
χαλβάνην noun fem acc sg . . . . χαλβάνη
Χαλδαια pr noun fem nom sg
Χαλδαϊκην adj fem acc sg . . . . Χαλδαϊκος
Χαλδαῖοι pr noun masc nom pl . . . . Χαλδαῖος
Χαλδαιοις pr noun masc dat pl   id.
Χαλδαιου pr noun masc gen sg   id.

Χαλδαιους pr noun masc acc pl . . . . Χαλδαῖος
Χαλδαϊστι adverb
Χαλδαιων pr noun masc gen pl . . . . Χαλδαῖος
Χαλεβ pr noun
χαλεπά adj neut nom and acc pl . . . . χαλεπός
χαλεπαίνετε vb pres act ind 2nd pers pl,
             pres act impv 2nd pers pl . . . . χαλεπαίνω
χαλεπή adj fem nom sg . . . . χαλεπός
χαλεπόν adj masc acc sg, neut nom and acc sg   id.
χαλεπώτερα comp adj neut nom and acc pl   id.
χαλεπωτέραν comp adj fem acc sg   id.
χαλεπωτέρας comp adj fem acc pl   id.
χαλεπώτερον comp adj masc acc sg,
             neut nom and acc sg   id.
χαλεπωτέρων comp adj gen pl   id.
Χαληλ pr noun
Χαλια pr noun
χάλικες noun masc nom pl . . . . χάλιξ
χαλίκων noun masc gen pl   id.
χαλινόν noun masc acc sg . . . . χαλινός
χαλινούς noun masc acc pl   id.
χαλινῷ noun masc dat sg   id.
χαλκᾶ adj neut nom and acc pl . . . . χαλκοῦς
χαλκαῖ adj fem nom pl   id.
χαλκαῖς adj fem dat pl   id.
Χαλκαλ pr noun
χαλκᾶς adj fem acc pl . . . . χαλκοῦς
χάλκειαι adj fem nom pl . . . . χάλκειος
χαλκείαις adj fem dat pl   id.
χάλκειοι adj masc nom pl   id.
χαλκείοις noun neut dat pl . . . . χαλκεῖον
χάλκειον noun neut nom and acc sg . . . . χάλκειος
χαλκεῖον noun neut nom and acc sg
χαλκεῖς noun masc nom pl . . . . χαλκεύς
χαλκείῳ adj masc and neut dat sg . . . . χάλκειος
χαλκεύειν vb pres act inf . . . . χαλκεύω
χαλκεύς noun masc nom sg
χαλκέως noun masc gen sg . . . . χαλκεύς
χαλκῆ adj fem nom sg . . . . χαλκοῦς
χαλκῆν adj fem acc sg   id.
χαλκίον noun neut nom and acc sg
χαλκοῖ adj masc nom pl . . . . χαλκοῦς
χαλκοῖς adj masc and neut dat pl   id.
χαλκόν noun masc acc sg . . . . χαλκός
χαλκοπλάστας noun masc acc pl . . . . χαλκοπλάστης
χαλκός noun masc nom sg
χαλκοῦ adj masc and neut gen sg . . . . χαλκοῦς
χαλκοῦ noun masc gen sg . . . . χαλκός

χαλκοῦν adj masc acc sg, neut nom and acc sg . . . . χαλκοῦς

χαλκοῦς adj masc nom sg and acc pl   id.

χαλκοῦς noun masc acc pl . . . . χαλκός

χαλκῷ adj masc and neut dat sg . . . . χαλκοῦς

χαλκῷ noun neut dat sg . . . . χαλκός

χαλκῶν adj gen pl . . . . χαλκοῦς

Χαλου pr noun

Χαλφι pr noun

Χαλχαλ pr noun

Χαμ pr noun

Χαμααμ pr noun

χαμαί adverb

χαμαιλέοντες noun masc nom pl . . . . χαμαιλέων

χαμαιλέων noun masc nom sg   id.

χαμαιπετής adj masc nom sg

χαμανιμ noun neut nom and acc pl

Χαμματα pr noun

Χαμωθ pr noun

Χαμως pr noun

Χανααν pr noun

Χαναανίτιδος pr noun fem gen sg . . . . Χαναανῖτις

Χαναανῖτιν pr noun fem acc sg   id.

Χανανα pr noun

Χαναναιοι pr noun masc nom pl . . . . Χαναναῖος

Χαναναιοις pr noun masc dat pl   id.

Χαναναιον pr noun masc acc sg   id.

Χαναναιος pr noun masc nom sg   id.

Χαναναιου pr noun masc gen sg   id.

Χαναναιους pr noun masc acc pl   id.

Χαναναιω pr noun masc dat sg   id.

Χαναναιων pr noun masc gen pl   id.

Χανανι pr noun

Χανανιν pr noun masc acc sg . . . . Χανανις

Χανανις pr noun masc nom sg

Χανανιτην pr noun masc acc sg . . . . Χανανιτης

Χανανιτιδι pr noun fem dat sg . . . . Χανανιτις

Χανανιτιδος pr noun fem gen sg   id.

χάνε vb 2nd aor act impv 2nd pers sg . . . . χαίνω

Χαννα pr noun

Χανουναιου pr noun masc gen sg . . . . Χανουναῖος

χάος noun neut nom and acc sg

χαρα translit

χαρά noun fem nom sg

χαρᾷ noun fem dat sg . . . . χαρά

Χαρααθ pr noun

Χαραδαθ pr noun

χαραδριόν noun masc acc sg . . . . χαραδριός

Χαραιφι pr noun

χάρακα noun masc acc sg . . . . χάραξ

Χαρακα pr noun masc acc sg . . . . Χαραξ

χάρακας noun masc acc pl . . . . χάραξ

χάρακες noun masc nom pl   id.

χάρακι noun masc dat sg . . . . χάραξ

χαρακοβολία noun fem dat sg . . . . χαρακοβολία

χαρακτήρ noun masc nom sg

χαρακτῆρα noun masc acc sg . . . . χαρακτήρ

χαράκωσιν noun fem acc sg . . . . χαράκωσις

χαράν noun fem acc sg . . . . χαρά

χαρᾶς noun fem gen sg   id.

χαράσσεσθαι vb pres m/p inf . . . . χαράσσω

Χαρεα pr noun

χαρεῖται vb fut mid ind 3rd pers sg . . . . χαίρω

χάρηθι vb 2nd aor pass impv 2nd pers sg   id.

Χαρημ pr noun

χαρήσεται vb fut mid ind 3rd pers sg . . . . χαίρω

χαρήσομαι vb fut mid ind 1st pers sg   id.

χαρήσονται vb fut mid ind 3rd pers pl   id.

χάρητε vb 2nd aor pass impv 2nd pers pl   id.

χαρίεντες adj masc nom pl . . . . χαρίεις

χαρίζῃ vb pres dep ind 2nd pers sg . . . . χαρίζομαι

χαριζομένου vb pres dep part masc and neut gen sg   id.

χαριζομένῳ vb pres dep part masc and neut dat sg   id.

χάριν noun fem acc sg . . . . χάρις

χάρις noun fem nom sg   id.

χαρισάμενοι vb 1st aor mid part masc nom pl . . χαρίζομαι

χαρίσασθαι vb 1st aor mid inf   id.

χαρισομένους vb fut mid part masc acc pl   id.

χαριστήριον adj masc acc sg,

         neut nom and acc sg . . . . χαριστήριος

χάριτα noun fem acc sg . . . . χάρις

χάριτας noun fem acc pl   id.

χάριτες noun fem nom pl   id.

χάριτι noun fem dat sg   id.

χάριτος noun fem gen sg   id.

χαρίτων noun fem gen pl   id.

Χαρκαμυς pr noun

Χαρμαλι pr noun

Χαρμαν pr noun

Χαρμη pr noun

Χαρμι pr noun

Χαρμιν pr noun

Χαρμις pr noun

χαρμονή noun fem nom sg

χαρμονήν noun fem acc sg . . . . χαρμονή

χαρμονῆς noun fem gen sg   id.

χαρμοσύνη noun fem nom sg

χαρμοσύνῃ noun fem dat sg . . . . χαρμοσύνη

χαρμοσύνης noun fem gen sg   id.

χαρμοσυνῶν noun masc gen pl   id.

χαροποί adj masc nom pl . . . . χαροπός

Χαρουβ pr noun

χαροῦνται vb fut mid ind 3rd pers pl . . . . χαίρω

Χαρραν pr noun

Χαρρι pr noun

χαρσιθ   translit

χαρτηρίαν   noun fem acc sg . . . . χαρτηρία

χάρτης   noun masc nom sg

χαρτίον   noun neut nom and acc sg

χαρτίου   noun neut gen sg . . . . χαρτίον

χαρτίῳ   noun neut dat sg   id.

Χαρχαμις   pr noun

Χασαδ   pr noun

Χασαλωθ   pr noun

Χασβι   pr noun

Χασεβα   pr noun

Χασεηλου   pr noun

Χασελευ   pr noun

Χασελωθαιθ   pr noun

Χασιλ   pr noun

χάσκοντες   vb pres act part masc nom pl . . . . χάσκω

χάσκων   vb pres act part masc nom sg   id.

Χασλων   pr noun

Χασλωνιιμ   pr noun

χάσμα   noun neut nom and acc sg

Χασφω   pr noun

Χαταρωθι   pr noun

Χαττους   pr noun

χαῦνος   adj masc nom sg

χαυῶνας   noun masc acc pl . . . . χαυών

χαφ   translit (Heb. letter: כ)

Χαφαρσαλαμα   pr noun

Χαφεναθα   pr noun

Χεβρων   pr noun

Χεβρωνι   pr noun

Χεβρωνις   pr noun

χέει   vb pres act ind 3rd pers sg . . . . χέω

χεεῖ   vb fut act ind 3rd pers sg   id.

Χεζραθ   pr noun

χείλεσι   noun neut dat pl . . . . χεῖλος

χειλέων   noun neut gen pl   id.

χείλη   noun neut nom and acc pl   id.

χείλος   noun neut nom and acc sg   id.

χείλους   noun neut gen sg   id.

χειμάζεται   vb pres m/p ind 3rd pers sg . . . . χειμάζω

χείμαρροι   noun masc nom pl . . . . χειμάρρους

χειμάρροις   noun masc dat pl   id.

χείμαρρον   noun masc acc sg   id.

χειμάρρου   noun masc gen sg   id.

χειμάρρουν   noun masc acc sg   id.

χειμάρρους   noun masc nom sg and acc pl   id.

χειμάρρῳ   noun masc dat sg   id.

χειμάρρων   noun masc gen pl   id.

χειμερινή   adj fem nom sg . . . . χειμερινός

χειμερινῇ   adj fem dat sg   id.

χειμερινόν   adj masc acc sg, neut nom and acc sg   id.

χειμερινός   adj masc nom sg

χειμερινῷ   adj masc and neut dat sg . . . . χειμερινός

χειμέριος   adj masc and fem nom sg

χειμών   noun masc nom sg

χειμῶνα   noun masc acc sg . . . . χειμών

χειμῶνας   noun masc acc pl   id.

χειμῶνος   noun masc gen sg   id.

Χειρ   pr noun fem nom sg . . . . Χειρ

χείρ   noun fem nom sg

χεῖρα   noun fem acc sg . . . . χείρ

χειραγωγούμενον   vb pres m/p part

              masc acc sg . . . . χειραγωγέω

χειραγωγοῦντα   vb pres act part masc acc sg   id.

χείρας   noun fem acc pl . . . . χείρ

χεῖρες   noun fem nom pl   id.

χειρί   noun fem dat sg   id.

χειρίζειν   vb pres act inf . . . . χειρίζω

χείριστα   superl adj neut nom and acc pl . . . . χείριστος

χειρίστους   superl adj masc acc pl   id.

χειρίστῳ   superl adj masc and neut dat sg   id.

χειρίστως   adverb

χειρόγραφον   noun neut nom and acc sg

χείρονα   comp adj fem acc sg, neut nom and acc pl . . χείρων

χειρονομίαις   noun fem dat pl . . . . χειρονομία

χειροπέδαι   noun fem nom pl . . . . χειροπέδη

χειροπέδαις   noun fem dat pl   id.

χειροπέδων   noun fem gen pl   id.

χειροποίητα   adj neut nom and acc pl . . . . . . χειροποίητος

χειροποιήτοις   adj dat pl   id.

χειροποίητον   adj acc sg, neut nom sg   id.

χειρός   noun fem gen sg . . . . χείρ

χειροτονίαν   noun fem acc sg . . . . χειροτονία

χείρω   comp adj neut nom and acc sg . . . . χείρων

χειρῶν   noun fem gen pl . . . . χείρ

χειρωσάμενοι   vb 1st aor mid part masc nom pl . . χειρόομαι

χειρώσασθαι   vb 1st aor mid inf   id.

χειρώσηται   vb 1st aor mid subj 3rd pers sg . . . . id.

χεῖται   vb pres m/p ind 3rd pers sg . . . . χέω

Χελαιων   pr noun

Χελβα   pr noun

Χελβων   pr noun

Χελεγ   pr noun

Χελεγι   pr noun

Χελεθθι   pr noun

Χελεουδ   pr noun

Χελεων   pr noun

Χελια   pr noun

χελιδόνες   noun fem nom pl . . . . χελιδών

χελιδών   noun fem nom sg   id.

Χελκαθ   pr noun

Χελκανα   pr noun

Χελκατ   pr noun

Χελκια   pr noun

Χελκια	pr noun masc dat sg	Χελκιας
Χελκιαν	pr noun masc acc sg	id.
Χελκιας	pr noun masc nom sg	id.
Χελκιου	pr noun masc gen sg	id.
Χελλης	pr noun masc nom sg	
Χελουβ	pr noun	
Χελους	pr noun	
χελύνια	noun neut nom and acc pl	χελύνιον
Χελχα	pr noun	
χελῶναι	noun fem nom pl	χελώνη
χελωνίδος	noun fem gen sg	χελωνίς
Χεναρα	pr noun	
Χενερεθ	pr noun	
χερεθ	translit	
χερεθθι	translit	
Χερεθθι	pr noun	
Χερμελ	pr noun	
χερουβ	translit	
χερουβιμ	translit	
χερουβιν	translit	
Χερουβιν	pr noun	
χερσαῖα	adj neut nom and acc pl	χερσαῖος
χερσαῖος	adj masc nom sg	id.
χερσί(ν)	noun fem dat pl	χείρ
χέρσον	noun fem acc sg	χέρσος
χέρσος	noun fem nom sg	id.
χέρσου	noun fem gen sg	id.
χερσωθήσεται	vb fut pass ind 3rd pers sg	χερσόομαι
χερσωθήσονται	vb fut pass ind 3rd pers pl	id.
Χετ	pr noun	
Χετταια	pr noun	
Χετταιας	pr noun fem acc pl	Χετταια
Χετταιοι	pr noun masc nom pl	Χετταῖος
Χετταῖον	pr noun masc acc sg	id.
Χετταῖος	pr noun masc nom sg	id.
Χετταιου	pr noun masc gen sg	id.
Χετταιους	pr noun masc acc pl	id.
Χετταιων	pr noun masc gen pl	id.
Χεττι	pr noun	
Χεττιιμ	pr noun	
χεττιιν	translit	
Χεττιιν	pr noun	
Χεττουρα	pr noun	
Χεττουρας	pr noun fem gen sg	Χεττουρα
Χεφιρα	pr noun	
Χηζιρ	pr noun	
χηλῶν	noun fem gen pl	χηλή
χήρα	noun fem nom sg	
χήρᾳ	noun fem dat sg	χήρα
χῆραι	noun fem nom pl	id.
χήραις	noun fem dat pl	id.
χήραν	noun fem acc sg	id.

χήρας	noun fem gen sg and acc pl	χήρα
χηρεία	noun fem nom sg	
χηρείαν	noun fem acc sg	χηρεία
χηρείας	noun fem gen sg	id.
χηρεύουσα	vb pres act part fem nom sg	χηρεύω
χηρεύσεως	noun fem gen sg	χήρευσις
χηρῶν	noun fem gen pl	χήρα
χθιζοί	adj masc nom pl	χθιζός
χίδρα	noun neut nom and acc pl	χίδρον
χίδρων	noun neut gen pl	id.
χίλια	adj neut nom and acc pl	χίλιοι
χιλιαδας	noun fem acc pl	χιλιάς
χιλιαδες	noun fem nom pl	id.
χιλιαδων	noun fem gen pl	id.
χίλιαι	adj fem nom pl	χίλιοι
χιλίαις	adj fem dat pl	id.
χιλίαν	adj fem acc sg	id.
χιλιαρχίαν	noun fem acc sg	χιλιαρχία
χιλιαρχίας	noun fem gen sg and acc pl	id.
χιλίαρχοι	noun masc nom pl	χιλίαρχος
χιλιάρχοις	noun masc dat pl	id.
χιλίαρχον	noun masc acc sg	id.
χιλίαρχος	noun masc nom sg	id.
χιλιάρχους	noun masc acc pl	id.
χιλιάρχων	noun masc gen pl	id.
χιλίας	adj fem acc pl	χίλιοι
χιλιάς	noun fem nom sg	
χιλιάσιν	noun fem dat pl	χιλιάς
χίλιοι	adj masc nom pl	
χιλίοις	adj masc and neut dat pl	χίλιοι
χιλιοπλασίως	adverb	
χιλίους	adj masc acc pl	χίλιοι
Χιλουων	pr noun	
χίμαιραν	noun fem acc sg	χίμαιρα
χίμαροι	noun masc nom pl	χίμαρος
χίμαρον	noun masc acc sg	id.
χίμαρος	noun masc nom sg	id.
χιμάρου	noun masc gen sg	id.
χιμάρους	noun masc acc pl	id.
χιμάρων	noun masc gen pl	id.
Χιναναδοβ	pr noun	
χιόνα	noun fem acc sg	χιών
χιόνες	noun fem nom pl	id.
χιόνι	noun fem dat sg	id.
χιόνος	noun fem gen sg	id.
χιονωθήσονται	vb fut pass ind 3rd pers pl	χιονόομαι
Χιραμ	pr noun	
χιτών	noun masc nom sg	
χιτῶνα	noun masc acc sg	χιτών
χιτῶνας	noun masc acc pl	id.
χιτῶνος	noun masc gen sg	id.

χιτώνων noun masc gen pl . . . . χιτών

χιτῶσι noun masc dat pl   id.

χιών noun fem nom sg

χλαίνας noun fem acc pl . . . . χλαῖνα

χλαμύδος noun fem gen sg . . . . χλαμύς

χλευάζεις vb pres act ind 2nd pers sg . . . . χλευάζω

χλευάζοντες vb pres act part masc nom pl   id.

χλευάσασα vb 1st aor act part fem nom sg   id.

χλεύασμα noun neut nom and acc sg

χλευασμόν noun masc acc sg . . . . χλευασμός

χλευασμός noun masc nom sg   id.

χλιδών noun masc nom sg

χλιδῶνα noun masc acc sg . . . . χλιδών

χλιδῶνας noun masc acc pl   id.

χλόη noun fem nom sg

χλόη noun fem dat sg . . . . χλόη

χλόην noun fem acc sg   id.

χλόης noun fem gen sg   id.

χλοηφόρον adj acc sg, neut nom sg . . . . χλοηφόρος

χλωρά adj fem nom sg, neut nom and acc pl . . . . χλωρός

χλωράν adj fem acc sg   id.

χλωρίζουσα vb pres act part fem nom sg . . . . χλωρίζω

χλωριζουσάς vb pres act part fem acc pl   id.

χλωρόν adj masc acc sg, neut nom and acc sg . . . . . . χλωρός

χλωρός adj masc nom sg   id.

χλωρότητι noun fem dat sg . . . . χλωρότης

χλωροῦ adj masc and neut gen sg . . . . χλωρός

χλωρῶν adj gen pl   id.

χνοῦν noun masc acc sg . . . . χνοῦς

χνοῦς noun masc nom sg

Χοβαρ pr noun

Χοβερ pr noun

Χοβερι pr noun

Χοβορ pr noun

Χοβωρ pr noun

Χοδδαδ pr noun

Χοδλι pr noun

Χοδολλογομορ pr noun

χοεῖς noun masc nom and acc pl . . . . χοεύς

χοθωνωθ translit

χοΐ noun masc dat sg . . . . χοῦς

χοῖνιξ noun fem nom sg

χοιρογρύλλιοι noun masc nom pl . . . . χοιρογρύλλιος

χοιρογρυλλίοις noun masc dat pl   id.

χοιρογρύλλιον noun masc acc sg   id.

Χολασεωλα pr noun

Χολδαι pr noun

χολέραν noun fem acc sg . . . . χολέρα

χολέρας noun fem gen sg   id.

χολή noun fem nom sg

χολῇ noun fem dat sg . . . . χολή

χολήν noun fem acc sg   id.

χολῆς noun fem gen sg . . . . χολή

Χολθι pr noun

Χολοδ pr noun

χόλον noun masc acc sg . . . . χόλος

Χολουβ pr noun

χόλῳ noun masc dat sg . . . . χόλος

χονδριτῶν noun masc gen pl . . . . χονδρίτης

χοός noun masc gen sg . . . . χοῦς

Χορβε pr noun

χορδαῖς noun fem dat pl . . . . χορδή

χορδήν noun fem acc sg   id.

χορεία noun fem dat sg . . . . χορεία

χορεύειν vb pres act inf . . . . χορεύω

χορεύοντες vb pres act part masc nom pl   id.

χορεύουσαι vb pres act part fem nom pl   id.

χορευουσῶν vb pres act part fem gen pl   id.

χορεῦσαι vb 1st aor act inf   id.

χορηγεῖν vb pres act inf . . . . χορηγέω

χορηγηθήσεται vb fut pass ind 3rd pers sg   id.

χορηγήσαντος vb 1st aor act part masc and neut gen sg   id.

χορηγήσει vb fut act ind 3rd pers sg   id.

χορηγήσειν vb fut act inf   id.

χορηγήσῃς vb 1st aor act subj 2nd pers sg   id.

χορηγία noun fem dat sg . . . . χορηγία

χορηγίαν noun fem acc sg   id.

χορηγίας noun fem gen sg   id.

χορηγός noun masc nom sg

χορηγούμενοι vb pres m/p part masc nom pl . . . . . χορηγέω

χόριον noun neut nom and acc sg

χοροί noun masc nom pl . . . . χορός

χοροῖς noun masc dat pl   id.

χορόν noun masc acc sg   id.

χορός noun masc nom sg   id.

χορούς noun masc acc pl   id.

Χορραθ pr noun

Χορραιον pr noun masc acc sg . . . . Χορραῖος

Χορραιος pr noun masc nom sg   id.

Χορραιου pr noun masc gen sg   id.

Χορραιους pr noun masc acc pl   id.

Χορρι pr noun

χορτάσαι vb 1st aor act inf . . . . χορτάζω

χορτασθήσεται vb fut pass ind 3rd pers sg   id.

χορτασθήσομαι vb fut pass ind 1st pers sg   id.

χορτασθήσονται vb fut pass ind 3rd pers pl   id.

χορτασθῶσιν vb 1st aor pass subj 3rd pers pl   id.

χορτασία noun fem dat sg . . . . χορτασία

χορτάσματα noun neut nom and acc pl . . . . χόρτασμα

χορτάσω vb fut act ind 1st pers sg . . . . χορτάζω

χορτομανήσει vb fut act ind 3rd pers sg . . . . . χορτομανέω

χόρτον noun masc acc sg . . . . χόρτος

χόρτος noun masc nom sg   id.

χόρτου noun masc gen sg   id.

χόρτῳ noun masc dat sg . . . . χόρτος
χορτώδη adj masc and fem acc sg . . . . χορτώδης
Χορχορ pr noun
χορῷ noun masc dat sg . . . . χορός
χορῶν noun masc gen pl   id.
Χοσαμαιος pr noun
Χουθ pr noun
χοῦν noun masc acc sg . . . . χοῦς
Χουνθα pr noun
χοῦς noun masc nom sg
Χους pr noun
Χουσαρσαθαιμ pr noun
Χουσαρσαθωμ pr noun
Χουσι pr noun
Χουχι pr noun
χρᾶσθαι vb pres dep inf . . . . χράομαι
χρεία noun fem nom sg
χρείαις noun fem dat pl . . . . χρεία
χρείαν noun fem acc sg   id.
χρείας noun fem gen sg and acc pl   id.
χρειῶν noun fem gen pl   id.
χρεμετίζει vb pres act ind 3rd pers sg . . . . χρεμετίζω
χρεμετίσατε vb 1st aor act impv 2nd pers pl   id.
χρεμετισμός noun masc nom sg
χρεμετισμοῦ noun masc gen sg . . . . χρεμετισμός
χρεμετισμῷ noun masc dat sg   id.
χρεοκοπούμενος vb pres dep part
          masc nom sg . . . . χρεοκοπέομαι
χρέος noun neut nom and acc sg
χρέους noun neut gen sg . . . . χρέος
χρεοφειλέτου noun masc gen sg . . . . χρεοφειλέτης
χρή vb pres act ind 3rd pers sg
χρήζετε vb pres act ind 2nd pers pl . . . . χρήζω
χρήμασι noun neut dat pl . . . . χρῆμα
χρήματα noun neut nom and acc pl   id.
χρηματιεῖ vb fut act ind 3rd pers sg . . . . χρηματίζω
χρηματιεῖς vb fut act ind 2nd pers sg   id.
χρηματίζει vb pres act ind 3rd pers sg   id.
χρηματίσαι vb 1st aor act inf   id.
χρηματισμόν noun masc acc sg . . . . χρηματισμός
χρηματισμός noun masc nom sg   id.
χρηματισμοῦ noun masc gen sg   id.
χρηματιστηρίῳ noun neut dat sg . . . . . . χρηματιστήριον
χρημάτων noun neut gen pl . . . . χρῆμα
χρῆσαι vb 1st aor act inf . . . . χράω
χρησαίμεθα vb 1st aor mid opt 1st pers pl . . . . . . χράομαι
χρησάμενος vb 1st aor mid part masc nom sg   id.
χρησαμένων vb 1st aor mid part gen pl   id.
χρήσασθε vb 1st aor mid impv 2nd pers pl   id.
χρησάσθω vb 1st aor mid impv 3rd pers sg   id.
χρήσεται vb fut mid ind 3rd pers sg   id.

χρήσῃ vb 1st aor mid subj 2nd pers sg,
          fut mid ind 2nd pers sg . . . . χράομαι
χρήσηται vb 1st aor mid subj 3rd pers sg   id.
χρῆσθαι vb pres dep inf   id.
χρησθῇ vb 1st aor pass subj 3rd pers sg . . . . χράω
χρησθήσεται vb fut pass ind 3rd pers sg   id.
χρήσιμα adj neut nom and acc pl . . . . χρήσιμος
χρησιμεύσει vb fut act ind 3rd pers sg . . . . . . χρησιμεύω
χρησιμεύσῃς vb 1st aor act subj 2nd pers sg   id.
χρησίμης adj fem gen sg . . . . χρήσιμος
χρήσιμοι adj masc nom pl   id.
χρησίμοις adj masc and neut dat pl   id.
χρήσιμον adj masc acc sg, neut nom and acc sg   id.
χρησίμους adj masc acc pl   id.
χρησίμων adj gen pl . . . . χρήσιμος
χρησιμώτερον comp adj masc acc sg,
          neut nom and acc sg   id.
χρῆσιν noun fem acc sg . . . . χρῆσις
χρῆσις noun fem nom sg   id.
χρησμολογεῖ vb pres act ind 2nd pers sg . . . . χρησμολογέω
χρήσομαι vb fut mid ind 1st pers sg . . . . χράομαι
χρήσονται vb fut mid ind 3rd pers pl   id.
χρηστά adj neut nom and acc pl . . . . χρηστός
χρηστεύῃ vb fut mid ind 2nd pers sg . . . . . . χρηστεύομαι
χρηστοηθείας noun fem gen sg . . . . χρηστοήθεια
χρηστοί adj masc nom pl . . . . χρηστός
χρηστοῖς adj masc and neut dat pl   id.
χρηστόν adj masc acc sg, neut nom and acc sg   id.
χρηστός adj masc nom sg   id.
χρηστότης noun fem nom sg
χρηστότητα noun fem acc sg . . . . χρηστότης
χρηστότητι noun fem dat sg   id.
χρηστότητος noun fem gen sg   id.
χρηστοῦ adj masc and neut gen sg . . . . χρηστός
χρηστῶν adj gen pl   id.
χρηστῶς adverb
χρησώμεθα vb 1st aor mid subj 1st pers pl . . . . . . χράομαι
χρήσωμεν vb 1st aor act subj 1st pers pl . . . . χράω
χρήσωνται vb 1st aor mid subj 3rd pers pl . . . . . . χράομαι
χρίειν vb pres act inf . . . . χρίω
χρίετε vb pres act ind 2nd pers pl   id.
χριόμενοι vb pres m/p part masc nom pl   id.
χρίουσιν vb pres act ind 3rd pers pl   id.
χρῖσαι vb 1st aor act inf   id.
χρισάτω vb 1st aor act impv 3rd pers sg   id.
χρίσεις vb fut act ind 2nd pers sg   id.
χρίσεως noun fem gen sg . . . . χρῖσις
χρίσῃ vb fut mid ind 2nd pers sg . . . . χρίω
χρίσῃς vb 1st aor act subj 2nd pers sg   id.
χρισθῆναι vb 1st aor pass inf   id.
χρισθήσεται vb fut pass ind 3rd pers sg   id.
χρῖσις noun fem nom sg

χρῖσμα noun neut nom and acc sg

χρίσματος noun neut gen sg . . . . χρῖσμα

χρῖσον vb 1st aor act impv 2nd pers sg . . . . χρίω

χρίσονται vb fut mid ind 3rd pers pl   id.

Χριστε pr noun masc voc sg . . . . Χριστος

χριστόν adj masc acc sg, neut nom and acc sg . . . . χριστός

χριστός adj masc nom sg

Χριστος pr noun masc nom sg

χριστοῦ adj masc and neut gen sg . . . . χριστός

χριστούς adj masc acc pl   id.

χριστῷ adj masc and neut dat sg   id.

χριστῶν adj gen pl   id.

χρίσωσιν vb 1st aor act subj 3rd pers pl . . . . χρίω

χρίων vb pres act part masc nom sg   id.

χρόαν noun fem acc sg . . . . χρόα

χρόας noun fem gen sg   id.

χρονιεῖ vb fut act ind 3rd pers sg . . . . χρονίζω

χρονιεῖς vb fut act ind 2nd pers sg   id.

χρονίζῃ vb pres act subj 3rd pers sg   id.

χρονίσῃ vb 1st aor act subj 3rd pers sg   id.

χρονίσῃς vb 1st aor act subj 2nd pers sg   id.

χρονίσητε vb 1st aor act subj 2nd pers pl   id.

χρονίσκον noun masc acc sg . . . . χρονίσκος

χρονίσω vb 1st aor act subj 1st pers sg . . . . χρονίζω

χρόνοις noun masc dat pl . . . . χρόνος

χρόνον noun masc acc sg   id.

χρόνος noun masc nom sg   id.

χρόνου noun masc gen sg   id.

χρόνους noun masc acc pl   id.

χρόνῳ noun masc dat sg   id.

χρόνων noun masc gen pl   id.

χρυσᾶ adj neut nom and acc pl . . . . χρυσοῦς

χρυσαῖ adj fem nom pl   id.

χρυσᾶς adj fem gen sg and acc pl   id.

χρυσαυγοῦντα vb pres act part

　　　　　neut nom and acc pl . . . . χρυσαυγέω

χρύσεοι adj masc nom pl . . . . χρύσεος

χρύσεον adj masc acc sg, neut nom and acc sg   id.

χρύσεος adj masc nom sg   id.

χρυσέων adj gen pl   id.

χρυσῆ adj fem nom sg . . . . χρυσοῦς

χρυσῇ adj fem dat sg   id.

χρυσῆν adj fem acc sg   id.

χρυσῆς adj fem gen sg   id.

χρυσία noun neut nom and acc pl . . . . χρυσίον

χρυσίον noun neut nom and acc sg   id.

χρυσίου noun neut gen sg   id.

χρυσίῳ noun neut dat sg   id.

χρυσοειδῆ adj neut nom and acc pl . . . . χρυσοειδής

χρυσοῖ adj masc nom pl . . . . χρυσοῦς

χρυσοῖς adj masc and neut dat pl   id.

χρυσόλιθον noun masc acc sg . . . . χρυσόλιθος

χρυσόλιθος noun masc nom sg

χρυσόν noun masc acc sg . . . . χρυσός

χρυσός noun masc nom sg   id.

χρυσοῦ noun masc gen sg   id.

χρυσοῦν adj masc acc sg, neut nom and acc sg . . . . χρυσοῦς

χρυσουργοῖς noun masc dat pl . . . . χρυσουργός

χρυσοῦς adj masc acc pl . . . . χρυσοῦς

χρυσοῦς adj masc nom sg

χρυσοφορῇ vb pres act subj 3rd pers sg . . . . . . χρυσοφορέω

χρυσοχάλινον adj acc sg, neut nom sg . . . . χρυσοχάλινος

χρυσοχαλίνων adj gen pl   id.

χρυσοχόον noun masc acc sg . . . . χρυσοχόος

χρυσοχόος noun masc nom sg   id.

χρυσοχόων noun masc gen pl   id.

χρυσῷ noun masc dat sg . . . . χρυσός

χρυσώμασι noun neut dat pl . . . . χρύσωμα

χρυσώματα noun neut nom and acc pl   id.

χρυσωμάτων noun neut gen pl   id.

χρυσῶν adj gen pl . . . . χρυσοῦς

χρυσώσεις vb fut act ind 2nd pers sg . . . . χρυσόω

χρῶ vb pres dep impv 2nd pers sg . . . . χράομαι

χρῶμα noun neut nom and acc sg

χρώμασι noun neut dat pl . . . . χρῶμα

χρώματος noun neut gen sg   id.

χρώμενοι vb pres dep part masc nom pl . . . . χράομαι

χρωμένοις vb pres dep part masc and neut dat pl   id.

χρώμενον vb pres dep part masc acc sg,

　　　　　neut nom and acc sg   id.

χρώμενος vb pres dep part masc nom sg   id.

χρωμένους vb pres dep part masc acc pl   id.

χρωμένων vb pres dep part gen pl   id.

χρώς noun masc nom sg

χρῶτα noun masc acc sg . . . . χρώς

χρωτός noun masc gen sg   id.

χυδαῖοι adj masc and fem nom pl . . . . χυδαῖος

χυθήσεται vb fut pass ind 3rd pers sg . . . . χέω

χυλούς noun masc acc pl . . . . χυλός

χύμα noun neut nom and acc sg

χυτήν adj fem acc sg . . . . χυτός

χυτός adj masc nom sg

χύτρα noun fem nom sg

χύτρᾳ noun fem dat sg . . . . χύτρα

χύτραν noun fem acc sg   id.

χύτρας noun fem gen sg   id.

χυτρόκαυλον noun masc acc sg . . . . χυτρόκαυλος

χυτρόκαυλος noun masc nom sg   id.

χυτροκαύλους noun masc acc pl   id.

Χωβα pr noun

Χωβαι pr noun

Χωζηβα pr noun

Χωθαμ pr noun

Χωθαν pr noun

χωθαρ	translit	
χωθαρεθ	translit	
χωλά	adj neut nom and acc pl	χωλός
χωλανεῖτε	vb fut act ind 2nd pers pl	χωλαίνω
χωλοί	adj masc nom pl	χωλός
χωλόν	adj masc acc sg, neut nom and acc sg	id.
χωλός	adj masc nom sg	id.
χωλούς	adj masc acc pl	id.
χωλῶν	adj gen pl	id.
χῶμα	noun neut nom and acc sg	
χωμαριμ	translit	
χώματι	noun neut dat sg	χῶμα
χώματος	noun neut gen sg	id.
Χωνενια	pr noun masc nom sg	
Χωνενιας	pr noun masc nom sg	
Χωνενιου	pr noun masc gen sg	Χωνενια
χωνεύεται	vb pres m/p ind 3rd pers sg	χωνεύω
χωνευθῆναι	vb 1st aor pass inf	id.
χωνευθήσεσθε	vb fut pass ind 2nd pers pl	id.
χώνευμα	noun neut nom and acc sg	
χωνεύσας	vb 1st aor act part masc nom sg	χωνεύω
χωνεύσει	noun fem dat sg	χώνευσις
χωνεύσεις	vb fut act ind 2nd pers sg	χωνεύω
χώνευσιν	noun fem acc sg	χώνευσις
χωνεύσω	vb fut act ind 1st pers sg	χωνεύω
χωνευτά	adj neut nom and acc pl	χωνευτός
χωνευτῇ	noun masc dat sg	χωνευτής
χωνευτήριον	noun neut nom and acc sg	
χωνευτηρίου	noun neut gen sg	χωνευτήριον
χωνευτηρίῳ	noun neut dat sg	id.
χωνευτοῖς	adj masc and neut dat pl	χωνευτός
χωνευτόν	adj masc acc sg, neut nom and acc sg	id.
χωνευτούς	adj masc acc pl	id.
χωνευτῶν	adj gen pl	id.

χωνεύων	vb pres act part masc nom sg	χωνεύω
χώρα	noun fem nom sg	
χώρᾳ	noun fem dat sg	χώρα
χῶραι	noun fem nom pl	id.
χώραις	noun fem dat pl	id.
χώραν	noun fem acc sg	id.
χώρας	noun fem gen sg and acc pl	id.
χωρεῖ	vb pres act ind 3rd pers sg	χωρέω
Χωρηβ	pr noun	
χωρησάντων	vb 1st aor act part masc and neut gen pl	χωρέω
χωρήσασαν	vb 1st aor act part fem acc sg	id.
χωρίζεσθαι	vb pres m/p inf	χωρίζω
χωριζόμενος	vb pres m/p part masc nom sg	id.
χωρίζουσιν	vb pres act ind 3rd pers pl	id.
χωρίοις	noun neut dat pl	χωρίον
χωρίον	noun neut nom and acc sg	id.
χωρίου	noun neut gen sg	id.
χωρίς	adverb and preposition	
χωρίσαντες	vb 1st aor act part masc nom pl	χωρίζω
χωρισθέντες	vb 1st aor pass part masc nom pl	id.
χωρισθῇς	vb 1st aor pass subj 2nd pers sg	id.
χωρίσθητε	vb 1st aor pass impv 2nd pers pl	id.
χωρισμόν	noun masc acc sg	χωρισμός
χωρισμοῦ	noun masc gen sg	id.
χωρισμῷ	noun masc dat sg	id.
χωρίῳ	noun neut dat sg	χωρίον
χωρίων	noun neut gen pl	id.
χωροβατῆσαι	vb 1st aor act inf	χωροβατέω
χωροβατήσατε	vb 1st aor act impv 2nd pers pl	id.
χωροῦν	vb pres act part neut nom and acc sg	χωρέω
χωροῦντα	vb pres act part masc acc sg	id.
χωροῦσαν	vb pres act part fem acc sg	id.
χωρῶν	noun fem gen pl	χώρα
χῶσαι	vb 1st aor act inf	χόω

Ψ ψ

ψάλατε	vb 1st aor act impv 2nd pers pl	ψάλλω
ψαλάτωσαν	vb 1st aor act impv 3rd pers pl	id.
ψαλεῖ	vb fut act ind 3rd pers sg	id.
ψάλῃ	vb 1st aor act subj 3rd pers sg	id.
ψαλίδας	noun fem acc pl	ψαλίς
ψαλίδες	noun fem nom pl	id.
ψάλλε	vb pres act impv 2nd pers sg	ψάλλω
ψάλλειν	vb pres act inf	id.
ψάλλοντα	vb pres act part masc acc sg	id.
ψαλλόντων	vb pres act part masc and neut gen pl	id.
ψαλλούσης	vb pres act part fem gen sg	id.
ψάλλων	vb pres act part masc nom sg	id.

ψαλμοί	noun masc nom pl	ψαλμός
ψαλμοῖς	noun masc dat pl	id.
ψαλμόν	noun masc acc sg	id.
ψαλμός	noun masc nom sg	id.
ψαλμοῦ	noun masc gen sg	id.
ψαλμῶν	noun masc gen pl	id.
ψαλοῦμεν	vb fut act ind 1st pers pl	ψάλλω
ψαλτά	adj neut nom and acc pl	ψαλτός
ψάλται	noun masc nom pl	ψάλτης
ψαλτήρια	noun neut nom and acc pl	ψαλτήριον
ψαλτήριον	noun neut nom and acc sg	id.
ψαλτηρίου	noun neut gen sg	id.

ψαλτηρίῳ noun neut dat sg	. . . .	ψαλτήριον
ψαλτηρίων noun neut gen pl		id.
ψαλτῳδεῖν vb pres act inf	. . . .	ψαλτῳδέω
ψαλτῳδοί noun masc nom pl	. . . .	ψαλτῳδός
ψαλτῳδοῖς noun masc dat pl		id.
ψαλτῳδός noun masc nom sg		id.
ψαλτῳδούς noun masc acc pl		id.
ψάλω vb 1st aor act subj 1st pers sg	. . . .	ψάλλω
ψαλῶ vb fut act ind 1st pers sg		id.
ψάμμος noun masc or fem nom sg		
ψάμμου noun masc gen sg	. . . .	ψάμμος
ψαμμωτός adj masc nom sg		
ψαροί adj masc nom pl	. . . .	ψαρός
ψαύσειεν vb 1st aor act opt 3rd pers sg	. . . .	ψαύω
ψεκάδων noun fem gen pl	. . . .	ψεκάς
ψέλια noun neut nom and acc pl	. . . .	ψέλιον
ψέλιον noun neut nom and acc sg		id.
ψελίῳ noun neut dat sg		id.
ψελλίζουσαι vb pres act part fem nom pl	. . . .	ψελλίζω
ψεύδει noun neut dat sg	. . . .	ψεῦδος
ψευδεῖ adj dat sg	. . . .	ψευδής
ψευδεῖς adj masc and fem nom and acc pl		id.
ψευδές adj neut nom and acc sg		id.
ψεύδεσθαι vb pres dep inf	. . . .	ψεύδομαι
ψεύδεσι noun neut dat pl	. . . .	ψεῦδος
ψευδέσι adj dat pl	. . . .	ψευδής
ψεύδεται vb pres dep ind 3rd pers sg	. . . .	ψεύδομαι
ψεύδη noun neut nom and acc pl	. . . .	ψεῦδος
ψευδῆ adj masc and fem acc sg,		
neut nom and acc pl	. . . .	ψευδής
ψεύδη vb pres dep ind 2nd pers sg	. . . .	ψεύδομαι
ψευδής adj masc and fem nom sg		
ψευδοθύρια noun neut nom and acc pl	. . . . .	ψευδοθύριον
ψευδοθυρίδων noun fem gen pl	. . . .	ψευδοθυρίς
ψευδολογήσουσι vb fut act ind 3rd pers pl	. . .	ψευδολογέω
ψευδομάρτυρας noun masc acc pl	. . . .	ψευδομάρτυς
ψευδομαρτυρήσαντας vb 1st aor act part		
masc acc pl	. . . .	ψευδομαρτυρέω
ψευδομαρτυρήσεις vb fut act ind 2nd pers sg		id.
ψευδόμενος vb pres dep part masc nom sg	. . . . . .	ψεύδομαι
ψευδοπροφῆται noun masc nom pl	. . . . .	ψευδοπροφήτης
ψευδοπροφήτας noun masc acc pl		id.
ψευδοπροφήτης noun masc nom sg		id.
ψευδοπροφήτου noun masc gen sg		id.
ψευδοπροφητῶν noun masc gen pl		id.
ψεῦδος noun neut nom and acc sg		
ψεύδους see ψευδοῦς		
ψευδοῦς adj gen sg	. . . .	ψευδής
ψευδῶν adj gen pl		id.
ψεύσεσθε vb fut mid ind 2nd pers pl	. . . .	ψεύδομαι
ψεύσεται vb fut mid ind 3rd pers sg		id.
ψεύσῃ vb 1st aor mid subj 2nd pers sg		id.

ψεύσησθε vb 1st aor mid subj 2nd pers pl	. . . . .	ψεύδομαι
ψεύσηται vb 1st aor mid subj 3rd pers sg		id.
ψευσθέντες vb 1st aor pass part masc nom pl		id.
ψεύσομαι vb fut mid ind 1st pers sg		id.
ψεύσονται vb fut mid ind 3rd pers pl		id.
ψεῦσται noun masc nom pl	. . . .	ψεύστης
ψεύστην noun masc acc sg		id.
ψεύστης noun masc nom sg		id.
ψεύσωνται vb 1st aor mid subj 3rd pers pl		id.
ψηλαφηθήσεται vb fut pass ind 3rd pers sg	. . . .	ψηλαφάω
ψηλαφῆσαι vb 1st aor act opt 3rd pers sg		id.
ψηλαφῆσαι vb 1st aor act inf		id.
ψηλαφήσαισαν vb 1st aor act opt 3rd pers pl		id.
ψηλαφήσῃ vb 1st aor act subj 3rd pers sg		id.
ψηλάφησιν noun fem acc sg	. . . .	ψηλάφησις
ψηλαφήσουσιν vb fut act ind 3rd pers pl	. . . . . .	ψηλαφάω
ψηλαφήσω vb 1st aor act subj 1st pers sg,		
fut act ind 1st pers sg		id.
ψηλαφητόν adj masc acc sg,		
neut nom and acc sg	. . . .	ψηλαφητός
ψηλαφῶν vb pres act part masc nom sg,		
neut nom and acc sg	. . . .	ψηλαφάω
ψήφισμα noun neut nom and acc sg		
ψηφίσματος noun neut gen sg	. . . .	ψήφισμα
ψηφολογηθήσονται vb fut pass ind 3rd pers pl	.	ψηφολογέω
ψῆφον noun fem acc sg	. . . .	ψῆφος
ψῆφος noun fem nom sg		id.
ψήφους noun fem acc pl		id.
ψήφῳ noun fem dat sg		id.
ψιθυρίζουσιν vb pres act ind 3rd pers pl	. . . .	ψιθυρίζω
ψιθυρίζων vb pres act part masc nom sg		id.
ψιθυρισμῷ noun masc dat sg	. . . .	ψιθυρισμός
ψιθύροις adj dat pl	. . . .	ψίθυρος
ψίθυρον adj acc sg, neut nom sg		id.
ψίθυρος adj masc and fem nom sg		id.
ψιθύρου adj gen sg		id.
ψιθύρων adj gen pl		id.
ψιλήν adj fem acc sg	. . . .	ψιλός
ψιλώσουσιν vb fut act ind 3rd pers pl	. . . .	ψιλόω
ψόαις noun fem dat pl	. . . .	ψόα
ψόαν noun fem acc sg		id.
ψογίσαι vb 1st aor act inf	. . . .	ψογίζω
ψόγον noun masc acc sg	. . . .	ψόγος
ψόγῳ noun masc dat sg		id.
Ψονθομφανηχ pr noun		
ψόφησον vb 1st aor act impv 2nd pers sg	. . . .	ψοφέω
ψόφος noun masc nom sg		
ψύαι noun fem nom pl	. . . .	ψύα
ψυγμός noun masc nom sg		
ψυγμούς noun masc acc pl	. . . .	ψυγμός
ψυκτῆρες noun masc nom pl	. . . .	ψυκτήρ
ψύλλου noun masc gen sg	. . . .	ψύλλος

ψύξουσιν vb fut act ind 3rd pers pl . . . . ψύχω
ψυχαγωγίαν noun fem acc sg . . . . ψυχαγωγία
ψυχαί noun fem nom pl . . . . ψυχή
ψυχαῖς noun fem dat pl   id.
ψυχάς noun fem acc pl   id.
ψύχει vb pres act ind 3rd pers sg . . . . ψύχω
ψυχή noun fem nom sg
ψυχῇ noun fem dat sg . . . . ψυχή
ψυχήν noun fem acc sg   id.
ψυχῆς noun fem gen sg   id.
ψυχικαί adj fem nom pl . . . . ψυχικός
ψυχικῶς adverb
ψῦχος noun neut nom and acc sg
ψυχουλκούμενοι vb pres dep part
       masc nom pl . . . . ψυχουλκέομαι
ψύχους noun neut gen sg . . . . ψῦχος
ψυχρόν adj masc acc sg, neut nom and acc sg . . . . . . ψυχρός
ψυχρός adj masc nom sg   id.
ψυχῶν noun fem gen pl . . . . ψυχή

ψωμιεῖ vb fut act ind 3rd pers sg . . . . ψωμίζω
ψωμιεῖς vb fut act ind 2nd pers sg   id.
ψωμιοῦσιν vb fut act ind 3rd pers pl   id.
ψωμίσαντος vb 1st aor act part masc and neut gen sg   id.
ψωμισάτω vb 1st aor act impv 3rd pers sg   id.
ψώμισον vb 1st aor act impv 2nd pers sg   id.
ψωμίσουσι vb fut act ind 3rd pers pl   id.
ψωμιῶ vb fut act ind 1st pers sg   id.
ψωμόν noun masc acc sg . . . . ψωμός
ψωμός noun masc nom sg   id.
ψωμοῦ noun masc gen sg   id.
ψωμούς noun masc acc pl   id.
ψωμῷ noun masc dat sg   id.
ψώρα noun fem nom sg
ψώρᾳ noun fem dat sg . . . . ψώρα
ψωραγριῶντα vb pres act part
       neut nom and acc pl . . . . ψωραγριάω
ψώραν noun fem acc sg . . . . ψώρα

Ω ω

ὦ interjection
ὦ vb pres act subj 1st pers sg . . . . εἰμί
ᾧ rel pron masc and neut dat sg . . . . ὅς
ᾠά noun neut nom and acc pl . . . . ᾠόν
ᾠάν noun fem acc sg . . . . ᾠα
Ωβαδιος pr noun
Ωβηδ pr noun
Ωβηθ pr noun
Ωβιλ pr noun
Ωβωθ pr noun
Ωγ pr noun
Ωδ pr noun
ᾠδαί noun fem nom pl . . . . ᾠδή
ᾠδαῖς noun fem dat pl   id.
ᾠδάς noun fem acc pl   id.
ᾧδε adverb
ὤδευον vb impf act ind 3rd pers pl . . . . ὁδεύω
ᾠδή noun fem nom sg
ᾠδῇ noun fem dat sg . . . . ᾠδή
ὡδήγησα vb 1st aor act ind 1st pers sg . . . . ὁδηγέω
ὡδήγησαν vb 1st aor act ind 3rd pers pl   id.
ὡδήγησας vb 1st aor act ind 2nd pers sg   id.
ὡδήγησεν vb 1st aor act ind 3rd pers sg   id.
Ωζηδ pr noun
ᾠδήν noun fem acc sg . . . . ᾠδή
ᾠδῆς noun fem gen sg   id.

Ωδιηλ pr noun
ὠδίν noun fem nom sg
ὠδῖνας noun fem acc pl . . . . ὠδίν
ὤδινε vb pres act impv 2nd pers sg,
       1st aor act ind 3rd pers sg . . . . ὠδίνω
ὠδῖνες noun fem nom pl . . . . ὠδίν
ὠδινήσαμεν vb 1st aor act ind 1st pers pl . . . . ὠδίνω
ὠδίνησαν vb 1st aor act ind 3rd pers pl   id.
ὠδινήσει vb fut act ind 3rd pers sg   id.
ὠδινήσεις vb fut act ind 2nd pers sg   id.
ὠδίνησεν vb 1st aor act ind 3rd pers sg   id.
ὠδινήσουσιν vb fut act ind 3rd pers pl   id.
ὠδῖνι noun fem dat sg . . . . ὠδίν
ὤδινον vb impf act ind 1st pers sg . . . . ὠδίνω
ὠδίνουσα vb pres act part fem nom sg   id.
ὠδίνουσαν vb pres act part fem acc sg   id.
ὠδινούσης vb pres act part fem gen sg   id.
ὠδίνων noun fem gen pl . . . . ὠδίν
ᾠδοί noun masc nom pl . . . . ᾠδός
ᾠδοῖς noun masc dat pl   id.
ὡδοποίησαν vb 1st aor act ind 3rd pers pl . . . . . . ὁδοποιέω
ὡδοποίησας vb 1st aor act ind 2nd pers sg   id.
ὡδοποίησεν vb 1st aor act ind 3rd pers sg   id.
Ωδουε pr noun
Ωδουια pr noun
ὠδυνήθη vb 1st aor pass ind 3rd pers sg . . . . ὀδυνάω

ᾠδῶν noun fem gen pl	....	ᾠδή
ὥδωρ *see* ὕδωρ		
ᾤετο vb impf dep ind 3rd pers sg	....	οἴομαι
ὤζεσεν vb 1st aor act ind 3rd pers sg	....	ὄζω
ᾠήθη vb 1st aor pass ind 3rd pers sg	....	οἴομαι
Ωθηρι pr noun		
Ωιμ pr noun		
ᾤκει vb impf act ind 3rd pers sg	....	οἰκέω
ᾠκήσαμεν vb 1st aor act ind 1st pers pl		id.
ᾤκησαν vb 1st aor act ind 3rd pers pl		id.
ᾤκησεν vb 1st aor act ind 3rd pers sg		id.
Ωκιδηλος pr noun		
ᾤκισας vb 1st aor act ind 2nd pers sg	....	οἰκίζω
ὤκλασαν vb 1st aor act ind 3rd pers pl	....	ὀκλάζω
ὤκλασεν vb 1st aor act ind 3rd pers sg		id.
ὤκνησας vb 1st aor act ind 2nd pers sg	....	ὀκνέω
ὤκνησεν vb 1st aor act ind 3rd pers sg		id.
ᾠκοδομεῖτο vb impf m/p ind 3rd pers sg	......	οἰκοδομέω
ᾠκοδόμεσεν vb 1st aor act ind 3rd pers sg		id.
ᾠκοδομήθη vb 1st aor pass ind 3rd pers sg		id.
ᾠκοδόμηκα vb perf act ind 1st pers sg		id.
ᾠκοδομήκατε vb perf act ind 2nd pers pl		id.
ᾠκοδομημέναι vb perf m/p part fem nom pl		id.
ᾠκοδομημένην vb perf m/p part fem acc sg		id.
ᾠκοδομημένον vb perf m/p part masc acc sg, neut nom and acc sg		id.
ᾠκοδομημένος vb perf m/p part masc nom sg		id.
ᾠκοδόμηνται vb perf m/p ind 3rd pers pl		id.
ᾠκοδόμησα vb 1st aor act ind 1st pers sg		id.
ᾠκοδομήσαμεν vb 1st aor act ind 1st pers pl		id.
ᾠκοδόμησαν vb 1st aor act ind 3rd pers pl		id.
ᾠκοδόμησας vb 1st aor act ind 2nd pers sg		id.
ᾠκοδομήσατε vb 1st aor act ind 2nd pers pl		id.
ᾠκοδόμησε(ν) vb 1st aor act ind 3rd pers sg		id.
ᾠκοδόμηται vb perf m/p ind 3rd pers sg		id.
ᾠκοδόμητο vb plpf m/p ind 3rd pers sg		id.
ᾠκοδομοῦσαν vb impf act ind 3rd pers pl		id.
ᾠκοῦμεν vb impf act ind 1st pers pl	....	οἰκέω
ᾤκουν vb impf act ind 3rd pers pl		id.
Ωλα pr noun		
Ωλαμ pr noun		
Ωλαμος pr noun masc nom sg		
Ωλαμου pr noun masc gen sg	....	Ωλαμος
ὠλέθρευον vb impf act ind 3rd pers pl	....	ὀλεθρεύω
ὠλέθρευσας vb 1st aor act ind 2nd pers sg		id.
ὠλέθρευσεν vb 1st aor act ind 3rd pers sg		id.
ὠλέθρευτο vb plpf m/p ind 3rd pers sg		id.
ὤλετο vb 2nd aor mid ind 3rd pers sg	....	ὄλλυμι
ὠλιγοποίησεν vb 1st aor act ind 3rd pers sg	...	ὀλιγοποιέω
ὠλιγοψύχησαν vb 1st aor act ind 3rd pers pl	..	ὀλιγοψυχέω
ὠλιγοψύχησεν vb 1st aor act ind 3rd pers sg		id.
ὠλιγώθη vb 1st aor pass ind 3rd pers sg	....	ὀλιγόω
ὠλιγώθησαν vb 1st aor pass ind 3rd pers pl	....	ὀλιγόω
ὠλίσθησα vb 1st aor act ind 1st pers sg	......	ὀλισθαίνω
ὠλίσθησεν vb 1st aor act ind 3rd pers sg		id.
ὠλόλυζον vb impf act ind 3rd pers pl	....	ὀλολύζω
ὠλόλυξεν vb 1st aor act ind 3rd pers sg		id.
ὤλοντο vb 2nd aor mid ind 3rd pers pl	....	ὄλλυμι
ὠλοφύρετο vb impf dep ind 3rd pers sg	......	ὀλοφύρομαι
Ωμαθα pr noun		
ὡμάλισαν vb 1st aor act ind 3rd pers pl	....	ὁμαλίζω
ὡμαλισμένη vb perf m/p part fem nom sg		id.
Ωμαν pr noun		
Ωμαρ pr noun		
ᾤμην vb impf dep ind 1st pers sg	....	οἴομαι
ὠμίαι noun fem nom pl	....	ὠμία
ὠμίαν noun fem acc sg		id.
ὠμίας noun fem gen sg		id.
ὡμίλησεν vb 1st aor act ind 3rd pers sg	....	ὁμιλέω
ὡμίλουν vb impf act ind 3rd pers pl		id.
ὡμιλοῦσαν vb impf act ind 3rd pers pl		id.
ὤμνυον vb impf act ind 3rd pers pl	....	ὄμνυμι
ὦμοι noun masc nom pl	....	ὦμος
ὤμοις noun masc dat pl		id.
ὤμοῖς noun masc dat pl	....	ὠμός
ὡμοιώθη vb 1st aor pass ind 3rd pers sg	....	ὁμοιόω
ὡμοιώθημεν vb 1st aor pass ind 1st pers pl		id.
ὡμοιώθην vb 1st aor pass ind 1st pers sg		id.
ὡμοιώθης vb 1st aor pass ind 2nd pers sg		id.
ὡμοιωμένοι vb perf m/p part masc nom pl		id.
ὡμοίωσα vb 1st aor act ind 1st pers sg		id.
ὡμοίωσας vb 1st aor act ind 2nd pers sg		id.
ὡμοιώσατε vb 1st aor act ind 2nd pers pl		id.
ὡμοίωσεν vb 1st aor act ind 3rd pers sg		id.
ὠμόλινον noun neut nom and acc sg		
ὡμολογήσαμεν vb 1st aor act ind 1st pers pl	....	ὁμολογέω
ὡμολόγησαν vb 1st aor act ind 3rd pers pl		id.
ὦμον noun masc acc sg	....	ὦμος
ὠμόν noun masc acc sg	....	ὠμός
ὦμος noun masc nom sg		
ὤμοσα vb 1st aor act ind 1st pers sg	....	ὄμνυμι
ὠμόσαμεν vb 1st aor act ind 1st pers pl		id.
ὤμοσαν vb 1st aor act ind 3rd pers pl		id.
ὤμοσας vb 1st aor act ind 2nd pers sg		id.
ὤμοσε(ν) vb 1st aor act ind 3rd pers sg		id.
ὠμότατε superl adj masc voc sg	....	ὠμός
ὠμότητα noun fem acc sg	....	ὠμότης
ὠμότητι noun fem dat sg		id.
ὠμοτόκησεν vb 1st aor act ind 3rd pers sg	......	ὠμοτοκέω
ὤμου noun masc gen sg	....	ὦμος
ὠμοῦ noun masc gen sg	....	ὠμός
ὤμους noun masc acc pl	....	ὦμος
ὠμόφρων adj masc and fem nom sg		
ὤμῳ noun masc dat sg	....	ὦμος

ὤμων noun masc gen pl	ὦμος
Ων pr noun	
ὧν rel pron gen pl	ὅς
ὤν vb pres act part masc nom sg	εἰμί
Ωναμ pr noun	
Ωναν pr noun	
Ωνας pr noun	
ὠνάσθης vb 1st aor pass ind 2nd pers sg	ὀνίνημι
ὠνείδιζον vb impf act ind 3rd pers pl	ὀνειδίζω
ὠνείδισα vb 1st aor act ind 1st pers sg	id.
ὠνείδισαν vb 1st aor act ind 3rd pers pl	id.
ὠνείδισας vb 1st aor act ind 2nd pers sg	id.
ὠνειδίσατε vb 1st aor act ind 2nd pers pl	id.
ὠνείδισεν vb 1st aor act ind 3rd pers sg	id.
ὠνειδίσθη vb 1st aor pass ind 3rd pers sg	id.
ὠνειδίσθης vb 1st aor pass ind 2nd pers sg	id.
Ωνι pr noun	
ὠνομάσθη vb 1st aor pass ind 3rd pers sg	ὀνομαζω
ὠνομάσθης vb 1st aor pass ind 2nd pers sg	id.
ὠνομάσθησαν vb 1st aor pass ind 3rd pers pl	id.
Ωνους pr noun	
ὠνυχίσατο vb 1st aor mid ind 3rd pers sg	ὀνυχίζω
Ωνω pr noun	
Ωξ pr noun	
ὤξυνεν vb impf act ind 3rd pers sg,	
1st aor act ind 3rd pers sg	ὀξύνω
ᾠοῖς noun neut dat pl	ᾠόν
ᾤου vb impf dep ind 2nd pers sg	οἴομαι
Ωουδας pr noun	
ὦπται vb perf m/p ind 3rd pers sg	ὁράω
ὠπτανόμην vb impf m/p ind 1st pers sg	ὀπτάνω
ὠπτάνοντο vb impf m/p ind 3rd pers pl	id.
ὤπτησαν vb 1st aor act ind 3rd pers pl	ὀπτάω
ὤπτησεν vb 1st aor act ind 3rd pers sg	id.
Ωρ pr noun	
ὥρα noun fem nom sg	
ὥρᾳ noun fem dat sg	ὥρα
ὡράθησαν vb 1st aor pass ind 3rd pers pl	ὁράω
Ωραι pr noun	
ὧραι noun fem nom pl	ὥρα
ὡραία adj fem nom sg	ὡραῖος
ὡραῖα adj neut nom and acc pl	id.
ὡραίαν adj fem acc sg	id.
ὡραῖοι adj masc nom pl	id.
ὡραῖον adj masc acc sg, neut nom and acc sg	id.
ὡραῖος adj masc nom sg	id.
ὡραιότης noun fem nom sg	
ὡραιότητα noun fem acc sg	ὡραιότης
ὡραιότητι noun fem dat sg	id.
ὡραιότητος noun fem gen sg	id.
ὡραίους adj masc acc pl	ὡραῖος
ὥραις noun fem dat pl	ὥρα
ὡραΐσθην vb 1st aor pass ind 1st pers sg	ὡραΐζομαι
ὡραϊσμός noun masc nom sg	
ὡραιώθης vb 1st aor pass ind 2nd pers sg	ὡραιόομαι
ὡραιώθησαν vb 1st aor pass ind 3rd pers pl	id.
Ωραμ pr noun	
ὥραν noun fem acc sg	ὥρα
ὥρας noun fem gen sg and acc pl	id.
ὀργίσθη vb 1st aor pass ind 3rd pers sg	ὀργίζω
ὀργίσθην vb 1st aor pass ind 1st pers sg	id.
ὀργίσθης vb 1st aor pass ind 2nd pers sg	id.
ὀργίσθησαν vb 1st aor pass ind 3rd pers pl	id.
Ωρηβ pr noun	
Ωρηρ pr noun	
ὤρθρευσαν vb 1st aor act ind 3rd pers pl	ὀρθρεύω
ὤρθριζον vb impf act ind 3rd pers pl	ὀρθρίζω
ὤρθρισαν vb 1st aor act ind 3rd pers pl	id.
ὤρθρισε(ν) vb 1st aor act ind 3rd pers sg	id.
ὠρθώθη vb 1st aor pass ind 3rd pers sg	ὀρθόω
ὠρθωμένος vb perf m/p part masc nom sg	id.
ὤρθωται vb perf m/p ind 3rd pers sg	id.
ὥριμος adj masc and fem nom sg	
ὡρίσατο vb 1st aor mid ind 3rd pers sg	ὁρίζω
ὡρίσω vb 1st aor mid ind 2nd pers sg	id.
Ὡριων pr noun masc nom sg	
Ὡριωνος pr noun masc gen sg	Ὡριων
ὥρκισα vb 1st aor act ind 1st pers sg	ὁρκίζω
ὥρκισας vb 1st aor act ind 2nd pers sg	id.
ὥρκισεν vb 1st aor act ind 3rd pers sg	id.
ὥρμησα vb 1st aor act ind 1st pers sg	ὁρμάω
ὥρμησαν vb 1st aor act ind 3rd pers pl	id.
ὥρμησας vb 1st aor act ind 2nd pers sg	id.
ὥρμησεν vb 1st aor act ind 3rd pers sg	id.
ὀρύματος noun neut gen sg	ὤρυμα
ὤρυξα vb 1st aor act ind 1st pers sg	ὀρύσσω
ὤρυξαν vb 1st aor act ind 3rd pers pl	id.
ὠρύξατε vb 1st aor act ind 2nd pers pl	id.
ὤρυξεν vb 1st aor act ind 3rd pers sg	id.
ὠρυόμενοι vb pres dep part masc nom pl	ὠρύομαι
ὠρυόμενος vb pres dep part masc nom sg	id.
ὠρυομένων vb pres dep part gen pl	id.
ὠρυόμην vb impf dep ind 1st pers sg	id.
ὠρύονται vb pres dep ind 3rd pers pl	id.
ὠρύοντο vb impf dep ind 3rd pers pl	id.
ὠρύσεται vb fut mid ind 3rd pers sg	id.
ὠρῶν noun fem gen pl	ὥρα
Ωρωναιμ pr noun	
Ωρωνην pr noun	
Ωρωνιν pr noun	
Ωρωνιτου pr noun masc gen sg	Ωρωνιτης
ὡς adverb, conjunction, preposition	

Ως pr noun	ὤτων noun neut gen pl . . . . οὖς
ὥς see ὡς	Ωφαζ pr noun
ὧς see ὡς	Ωφαλ pr noun
Ωσα pr noun	Ωφε pr noun
Ωσαια pr noun masc nom sg	ὤφειλεν vb impf act ind 3rd pers sg . . . . ὀφείλω
Ωσαιαν pr noun masc acc sg . . . . Ωσαια	ὠφείλετε vb impf act ind 2nd pers pl id.
Ωσαιαν pr noun masc acc sg . . . . Ωσαιας	ὠφελεῖ vb pres act ind 3rd pers sg . . . . ὠφελέω
Ωσαμ pr noun	ὠφέλεια noun fem nom sg
Ωσαμω pr noun	ὠφέλειαν noun fem acc sg . . . . ὠφέλεια
Ωσαν pr noun	ὠφεληθῆναι vb 1st aor pass inf . . . . ὠφελέω
ὡσανεί adverb	ὠφεληθήσεσθε vb fut pass ind 2nd pers pl id.
Ωσαρ pr noun	ὠφεληθήσονται vb fut pass ind 3rd pers pl id.
ὤσας vb 1st aor act ind 2nd pers sg . . . . ὠθέω	ὠφέλημα noun neut nom and acc sg
ὡσαύτως adverb	ὠφέλησα vb 1st aor act ind 1st pers sg . . . . ὠφελέω
ὡσεί adverb	ὠφελῆσαι vb 1st aor act inf id.
ὤσεις vb fut act ind 2nd pers sg . . . . ὠθέω	ὠφέλησαν vb 1st aor act ind 3rd pers pl id.
Ωση pr noun	ὠφελήσει vb fut act ind 3rd pers sg id.
ὤση vb 1st aor act subj 3rd pers sg . . . . ὠθέω	ὠφελήσειν vb fut act inf id.
Ωσηε pr noun	ὠφελήσεις vb fut act ind 2nd pers sg id.
ὠσθείς vb 1st aor pass part masc nom sg . . . . ὠθέω	ὠφέλησεν vb 1st aor act ind 3rd pers sg id.
ὦσι(ν) vb pres act subj 3rd pers pl . . . . εἰμί	ὠφελήσουσιν vb fut act ind 3rd pers pl id.
ὠσί noun neut dat pl . . . . οὖς	ὤφθη vb 1st aor pass ind 3rd pers sg . . . . ὁράω
Ωσιμ pr noun	ὤφθην vb 1st aor pass ind 1st pers sg
ὠσμένῳ vb perf m/p part masc and neut dat sg . . . . ὠθέω	ὤφθησαν vb 1st aor pass ind 3rd pers pl id.
ὥσπερ adverb	Ωφιρ pr noun
ὥστε adverb, conjunction, particle	Ωχαζαμ pr noun
ὠσφράνθη vb 1st aor pass ind 3rd pers sg . . . . ὀσφραίνομαι	ᾤχετο vb impf dep ind 3rd pers sg . . . . οἴχομαι
ὦτα noun neut nom and acc pl . . . . οὖς	ᾠχόμεθα vb impf dep ind 1st pers pl id.
ὠτία noun neut nom and acc pl . . . . ὠτίον	ᾠχόμην vb impf dep ind 1st pers sg id.
ὠτίοις noun neut dat pl id.	ᾤχοντο vb impf dep ind 3rd pers pl id.
ὠτίον noun neut nom and acc sg id.	ᾤχου vb impf dep ind 2nd pers sg id.
ὠτίου noun neut gen sg id.	ὤχρα noun fem dat sg . . . . ὤχρα
ὠτίων noun neut gen pl id.	ὠχυρώθησαν vb 1st aor pass ind 3rd pers pl . . . . . . ὀχυρόω
ὠτός noun neut gen sg . . . . οὖς	ὠχυρωμένη vb perf m/p part fem nom sg id.
ὠτότμητον adj acc sg, neut nom sg . . . . ὠτότμητος	ὠχύρωσαν vb 1st aor act ind 3rd pers pl id.
ὠτότμητος adj masc and fem nom sg id.	ὠχύρωσεν vb 1st aor act ind 3rd pers sg id.
ὤτρυνε vb impf act ind 3rd pers sg . . . . ὀτρύνω	ᾠῶν noun neut gen pl . . . . ᾠόν